SERVICESMARKETING
PEOPLE, TECHNOLOGY, STRATEGY   CANADIAN EDITION

Christopher Lovelock
YALE UNIVERSITY

Jochen Wirtz
NATIONAL UNIVERSITY OF SINGAPORE

Harvir Singh Bansal
WILFRID LAURIER UNIVERSITY

PEARSON
Prentice
Hall

Toronto

Library and Archives Canada Cataloguing in Publication

Lovelock, Christopher H.
    Services marketing : people, technology, strategy / Christopher Lovelock,
Jochen Wirtz, Harvir Singh Bansal.—Canadian ed.

Includes index.

ISBN-13: 978-0-13-187928-7
ISBN-10:   0-13-187928-6

1. Marketing—Management—Textbooks. 2. Professions—Marketing—Textbooks.
3. Service industries—Marketing—Textbooks. 4. Customer services—Marketing—
Textbooks. I. Wirtz, Jochen II. Bansal, Harvir S. (Harvir Singh) III. Title.

HD9980.5.L69 2008   658.8   C2006-905988-8

ISBN-13: 978-0-13-187928-7
ISBN-10:   0-13-187928-6

Editor-in-Chief: Gary Bennett
Acquisitions Editor: Don Thompson
Marketing Manager: Eileen Lasswell
Senior Developmental Editor: Paul Donnelly
Production Editor: Jen Handel
Copy Editor: Jonathan Dore
Proofreader: Audrey Dorsch
Production Coordinator: Patricia Ciardullo
Composition: Christine Velakis
Photo and Permissions Research: Natalie Barrington
Art Director: Julia Hall
Cover Design: Miguel Acevedo
Interior Design: Geoff Agnew
Cover Image: Getty Images/Peter Dazeley

1 2 3 4 5   11 10 09 08 07

Printed and bound in the United States of America.

To my brothers, Roger and Jeremy, and my sister, Rachel, with love
−CHL

To Jeannette, the light of my life and wonderful mother of our three children,
Lorraine, Stefanie, and Alexander, with love

−JW

Dedicated with all my love to Riya
−HSB

About the Authors

Christopher Lovelock is one of the pioneers of services marketing. Based in Massachusetts, he consults and gives seminars and workshops for managers around the world, with a particular focus on strategic planning in services and managing the customer experience. Since 2001, he has been an adjunct professor at the Yale School of Management, where he teaches MBA and EMBA services marketing courses.

After obtaining a BCom and an MA in economics from the University of Edinburgh, he worked in advertising with the London office of J. Walter Thompson Co. and then in corporate planning with Canadian Industries Ltd. in Montreal. Later, he obtained an MBA from Harvard and a Ph.D. from Stanford, where he was also a postdoctoral fellow.

Professor Lovelock's distinguished academic career has included 11 years on the faculty of the Harvard Business School and two years as a visiting professor at IMD in Switzerland. He has also held faculty appointments at Berkeley, Stanford, and the Sloan School at MIT, as well as visiting professorships at INSEAD in France and The University of Queensland in Australia. He is fluent in French and conversant in Spanish.

Author or co-author of over 60 articles, more than 100 teaching cases, and some two dozen books, Dr. Lovelock has also seen his work translated into 11 languages. He serves on the editorial review boards of the *International Journal of Service Industry Management, Journal of Service Research, Service Industries Journal, Cornell Hotel and Restaurant Administration Quarterly, Managing Service Quality,* and *Marketing Management,* and is also an ad-hoc reviewer for the *Journal of Marketing.*

Widely acknowledged as a thought leader in services, Christopher Lovelock has been honored by the American Marketing Association's prestigious Award for Career Contributions in the Services Discipline. In 2005 his article with Evert Gummesson, "Whither Services Marketing? In Search of a New Paradigm and Fresh Perspectives," won the AMA's Best Services Article Award and was a finalist for the IBM award for the best article in the *Journal of Service Research.* Earlier, he received a best article award from the *Journal of Marketing.* Recognized many times for excellence in case writing, he has twice won top honors in the *BusinessWeek* "European Case of the Year" Award.

Christopher has many connections to Canada and has traveled widely across the country. Early in his career, he lived in Montreal for two years. He has worked with several respected Canadian scholars, most notably Charles Weinberg at UBC, with whom he has coauthored many books, articles, and cases, primarily on public and nonprofit marketing. He has given presentations at the University of Victoria, UBC, University of Western Ontario, Humber College, UQAM, and HEC Montreal.

Jochen Wirtz has worked in the field of services for more than 18 years, and holds a Ph.D. in services marketing from the London Business School. He is an associate professor at the National University of Singapore (NUS), where he teaches services marketing in executive, MBA, and undergraduate programs and is co-director of the dual-degree UCLA–NUS Executive MBA Program.

Professor Wirtz's research focuses on service management topics, including customer satisfaction, service guarantees, and revenue management. He has published over 60 academic articles, 80 conference papers, and some 50 book chapters, and is co-author of 10 books, including his latest book, *Flying High in a Competitive Industry—Cost-Effective Service Excellence at Singapore Airlines* (Singapore: McGraw-Hill, 2006).

Professor Wirtz has received seven awards for outstanding teaching at the NUS Business School and in 2003 was honored by the prestigious, university-wide "Outstanding Educator Award." His six research awards include the Emerald Literati Club 2003 Award for Excellence for the year's most outstanding article in the *International Journal of Service Industry Management*. He serves on the editorial review boards of seven academic journals, including the *International Journal of Service Industry Management*, *Journal of Service Research*, and *Cornell Hotel and Restaurant Administration Quarterly*, and is also an ad-hoc reviewer for the *Journal of Consumer Research* and *Journal of Marketing*. Professor Wirtz chaired the American Marketing Association's biennial Service Research Conference in 2005, and in 2006 he was the chair for the Services Marketing Track at the Academy of Marketing Science Annual Conference.

Dr. Wirtz has been an active management consultant, working with international consulting firms, including Accenture, Arthur D. Little, and KPMG, and major service firms in the areas of strategy, business development, and customer feedback systems. Originally from Germany, Jochen Wirtz spent seven years in London before moving to Asia.

Harvir S. Bansal is an associate professor of marketing at Wilfrid Laurier University, where he teaches courses in services marketing in the undergraduate, executive, and MBA programs. He obtained a BSc (Pure Sciences) and an MBA (Marketing) from India and later earned his Ph.D. from Queen's University in Kingston, Ontario. His research interests are focused in the area of services marketing with emphasis on customer switching behaviour, word-of-mouth processes in services, structural equation modeling, and tourism. His research has been published in *Journal of the Academy of Marketing Science, Journal of Services Marketing, Journal of Service Research, Marketing Theory, Psychology and Marketing, Tourism Management*, and *Journal of Quality Management*, and he has also pre-

sented at and published articles in the proceedings of various national and international conferences. He has been actively involved in management consulting activities with various companies over the last eight years and is the principal of Friya Consulting, focusing primarily on management of customer relationship initiatives at various service organizations. He also currently serves as an external Senior Research Consultant for comScore Networks Inc., a Honomichl global top-25 marketing research firm, where he has worked with clients such as Microsoft, Intel, Scotia Bank, AOL, and Yahoo! among others.

About the Contributors of the Readings and Cases

Leonard L. Berry is Distinguished Professor of Marketing and M.B. Zale Chair in Retailing and Marketing Leadership at Mays Business School, Texas A&M University.

Diane Brady writes for *BusinessWeek.*

Susan Cadwallader is an assistant professor at the Mays Business School, Texas A&M University.

Lisa Callaghan is a graduate of the MBA program at Wilfied Laurier University's School of Business and Economics.

Lewis P. Carbone is founder, president, and CEO of Experience Engineering.

T. F. Cawsey recently retired and was a Professor at the School of Business & Economics, Wilfrid Laurier University.

Richard B. Chase is Justin B. Dart Professor of Operations Management and director of the center for Service Excellence, University of Southern California.

Prosenjit Datta writes for *Businessworld*, India.

John Deighton is Harold M. Brierley Professor of Business Administration at Harvard Business School.

Thomas Dotzel is a doctoral candidate at the Mays Business School, Texas A&M University.

Robert J. Fisher is Nabisco Professor in Marketing at the Richard Ivey School of Business, The University of Western Ontario.

Raymond P. Fisk is a professor at the College of Business Administration, University of New Orleans.

Lorelle Frazer is an associate professor at Griffith University, Australia.

Stephen J. Grove is a professor at the College of Business and Behavioural Science, Clemson University.

Stephan H. Haeckel is founder of Adaptive Business Systems and past chairman of the Marketing Science Institute.

Kenneth G. Hardy is a professor at the Richard Ivey School of Business, The University of Western Ontario.

Loizos Heracleous is a fellow in strategy and organization, Templeton College, Oxford University, UK.

Robert Johnston is a professor at Warwick Business School, University of Warwick, UK.

Sheryl E. Kimes is a professor at the School of Hotel Administration, Cornell University.

Gina S. Krishnan writes for *Businessworld*, India.

John J. Lawrence is a professor at the College of Business & Economics, University of Idaho.

Ken Mark is a full-time case writer at the Richard Ivey School of Business, University of Western Ontario. He graduated in 1998 from the HBA program at Ivey.

Gordon H. G. McDougall is a professor at the School of Business & Economics, Wilfrid Laurier University.

Alan Middleton is an Assistant Professor of Marketing and Executive Director of Executive Development at the Schulich School of Business, York University.

Youngme Moon is an associate professor at Harvard Business School.

Linda J. Morris is Vice Provost for Academic Affairs at University of Idaho

Janet Turner Parish is an assistant professor at the Mays Business School, Texas A&M University.

John A. Quelch is Senior Associate Dean and Lincoln Filene Professor of Business Administration at Harvard Business School.

Douglas A. Ready is Founder and President of the International Consortium for Executive Development Research and contributes to executive education programs at London Business School.

Venkatesh Shankar holds the Coleman Chair in marketing at the Mays Business School, Texas A&M University.

Stowe Shoemaker is Donald Hubbs Distinguished Professor at the Conrad N. Hilton College, University of Houston.

Nick Wingfield is a staff reporter at *The Wall Street Journal.*

Brief Contents

Contents

Preface

Services dominate the expanding world economy as never before and nothing stands still. Technology continues to evolve in dramatic ways. Established industries must adapt or sink into decline. Famous old companies merge or disappear as new industries emerge and rising stars seize the business headlines. Competitive activity is fierce, with firms often employing new strategies and tactics in response to customers' ever-changing needs, expectations, and behaviour. Customers themselves are being forced to confront change, which some see as presenting opportunities and others as being an inconvenience or even a threat. If one thing is clear, it's that skills needed in marketing and managing services have never been more important, and even more so in an economy like ours, where the services sector accounts for over two-thirds of the GDP and nearly three-quarters of the employment.

It is our hope that the Canadian edition of this book provides the information needed to achieve that aim within a uniquely Canadian perspective on services marketing. Readers can be confident that this book reflects the reality of today's world, incorporates recent academic and managerial thinking, and illustrates cutting-edge service concepts.

Preparing the Canadian edition has been an exciting challenge. You'll find that this text takes a strongly managerial perspective, yet is rooted in solid academic research, complemented by memorable frameworks. Our goal is to bridge the all-too-frequent gap between theory and the real world. Practical management applications are reinforced by numerous examples within the 15 chapters. Complementing the text are 11 interesting, up-to-date readings and 18 outstanding cases.

Services marketing, once a tiny academic niche championed by just a handful of pioneering professors, has become a thriving area of activity for both research and teaching. There's growing student interest in taking courses in this field, which makes good sense from a career standpoint because most business school graduates will be going to work in service industries, and managers report that manufacturing-based models of business practice are not always useful to them.

Highlights of this Edition

The contents of this book reflect ongoing developments in the service economy, new research findings, and elaboration on issues uniquely related to services marketing in Canada.

Topics and Structure

- The text is organized around a new framework for developing effective service marketing strategies that emphasizes the value exchange between suppliers and their customers. This framework, which allows for a flexible approach to teaching, is depicted in Figure 1.12 (see Chapter 1, p. 27), and forms the structure of the book, enabling students to see how different chapter topics relate to one another.

- Each of the 15 chapters incorporates examples and references to recent research, and the chapters are sequenced in a logical, streamlined fashion. Figure A on the next page displays the four-part structure of the book, showing how chapter topics are sequenced.

- New applications of technology—from Internet-based strategies to biometrics—and the opportunities and challenges they pose for customers and service marketers alike are woven into the text at relevant points in virtually all chapters.

- Among the significant discussion of contemporary issues related to services marketing, you will find an innovative treatment of service pricing, including coverage of revenue management and thought-provoking coverage of abusive and confusing pricing practices; recent developments in electronic communications such as iTV,

Figure A   Four-Part Structure of the Book

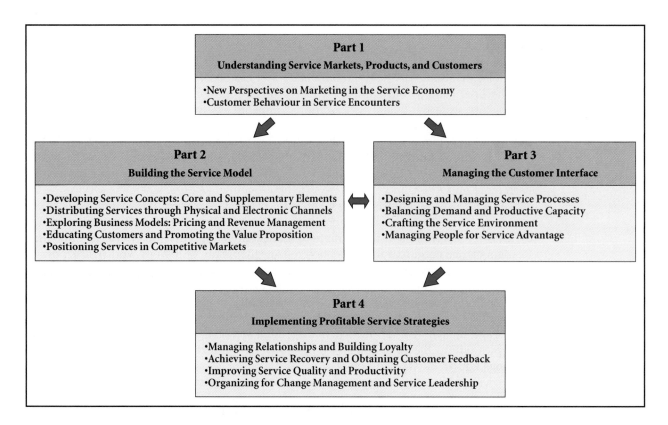

blogs, and Internet advertising; the latest thinking on cost-effective service excellence; an in-depth section on the Wheel of Loyalty and CRM; and discussion of current thinking on change management and service leadership.

- In preparing this book, we worked hard to create a text that is clear, readable, and focused. Boxed inserts within the chapters are designed to capture student interest and provide opportunities for in-class discussion. They describe significant research findings, illustrate practical applications of important service marketing concepts, and explain best practices by innovative service organizations from Canada and other countries.

Readings

- Readings are short, well written, and appealing to both undergraduates and MBAs.
- Drawn from such respected publications as *The Wall Street Journal, Harvard Business Review, Journal of Service Research, MIT Sloan Management Review, Marketing Magazine,* and *Business Week,* the readings complement the text and offer students a chance to explore key issues in greater depth, as well as to examine interesting and provocative market trends.
- Among the authors of the readings are leading professors and management consultants from around the world, as well as journalists writing for noted business publications.

Cases

- This book features an exceptional selection of 18 up-to-date, classroom-tested cases of varying lengths and levels of difficulty. More than half are set in a Canadian context.
- The selection provides a broad coverage of service marketing issues and application areas, with cases featuring a wide array of industries and organizations, ranging in size from multinational giants to small entrepreneurial start-ups.

What Aids Are Available for Instructors?

We've developed the following pedagogical aids to help instructors develop and teach courses built around this book and to create stimulating learning experiences for their students both in and out of the classroom.

Teaching Aids within the Text

- An introduction to each chapter highlights the key issues and questions addressed.
- Three types of boxed inserts appear throughout the chapters and lend themselves well to in-class discussions:
  - *Best Practice in Action* demonstrates the application of best practices.
  - *Research Insights* summarizes relevant and often provocative academic research.
  - *Service Perspectives* provides in-depth examples that illustrate key concepts.
- Interesting graphics, photographs, and reproductions of advertisements enhance student learning, provide opportunities for discussion, and add visual appeal.
- Review Questions and Application Exercises are located at the end of each chapter.

Pedagogical Materials Available from the Publisher

Accompanying the textbook is a broad range of instructor support resources. The full suite is available on one convenient Instructor's Resource CD-ROM (ISBN-13: 978-0-13-238087-4); you may also download individual components from our online catalogue. These resources include the following:

- **Instructor's Manual** that includes chapter-by-chapter teaching suggestions, sample course outlines, detailed teaching notes on readings and cases, and much more.
- **TestGen**, an electronic test bank of over 650 questions in a variety of formats.
- **PowerPoint** slides, keyed to each chapter and featuring word slides and graphics. All slides have been designed to be clear, comprehensible, and easy to read.
- **Image Library** containing charts, graphs, and tables from the book (available on IRCD only).

For students, we also offer the following:

- **Companion Website (www.pearsoned.ca/lovelock),** containing self-test quizzes and other text review resources, organized by chapter.
- **CBC/Pearson Education Canada Video Library,** featuring segments from popular CBC programs selected by the author to complement themes discussed in the book; available to instructors in VHS or DVD format and accessible to students online in streaming form. (VHS ISBN-13: 978-0-13-238084-3; DVD ISBN-13: 978-0-13-206508-5)

For What Types of Courses Can this Book Be Used?

This text is equally suitable for courses directed at advanced undergraduates or MBA and EMBA students as it places marketing issues within a broader general management context. The book will appeal both to full-time students headed for a career in management and to EMBAs and executive program participants who are combining their studies with ongoing work in managerial positions.

Whatever a manager's specific job may be, he or she has to understand and acknowledge the close ties that link the marketing, operations, and human resource functions. With that perspective in mind, we've designed this book so that instructors can make selective use of chapters, readings, and cases to teach courses of different lengths and formats in either services marketing or service management.

What Are the Book's Distinguishing Features?

Key features of this highly readable book include the following:

- A strong managerial orientation and strategic focus that address the need for service marketers to understand not only customer needs and behaviour but also how to use these insights to develop strategies for competing effectively in the marketplace
- Use of memorable conceptual frameworks that have been classroom tested for relevance among both undergraduates and MBA students
- Incorporation of key academic research findings
- Use of interesting examples to link theory to practice
- Inclusion of carefully selected readings and cases to accompany the text chapters
- Extensive and up-to-date references at the end of each chapter

We've designed this book to complement the materials found in traditional marketing principles texts. Recognizing that the service sector of the economy can best be characterized by its diversity, we believe that no single conceptual model suffices to cover marketing-relevant issues among organizations ranging from huge international corporations (in fields such as airlines, banking, insurance, telecommunications, freight transportation, and professional services) to locally owned and operated small businesses (such as restaurants, laundries, taxis, optometrists, and many business-to-business services). In response, we offer a carefully-designed "toolbox" for service managers, teaching students how different concepts, frameworks, and analytical procedures can best be used to examine and resolve the varied challenges faced by managers in different situations.

Acknowledgments

Over the years, many colleagues in both the academic and business worlds have provided us with valued insights into the management and marketing of services through their publications, in conference or seminar discussions, and during stimulating individual conversations. We have benefited enormously from in-class and after-class discussions with our students and executive program participants. We're also much indebted to those researchers and teachers who helped to pioneer the study of services marketing and management, and from whose work we continue to draw inspiration.

It's a pleasure to acknowledge the insightful and helpful comments of reviewers of the Canadian edition who challenged our thinking and provided numerous thoughtful suggestions for improvement:

Richard Appleby, Okanagan College
Mark Colgate, University of Victoria
Simon Hudson, University of Calgary
Steve Letovsky, McGill University
Richard J. Lindsey, British Columbia Institute of Technology
Paul Nyhof, University of Manitoba
Christine W. Oldfield, Centennial College of Applied Arts and Technology
Michael Pearl, Humber College
Patricia Peel, University of Guelph – Humber
Donna Sears, University of New Brunswick – Saint John
Diana Serafini, Dawson College
Brian Wrightson, The Northern Alberta Institute of Technology

It takes more than authors to create a book and its supplements. We are very appreciative of all the hard work put in by staff at Pearson Education Canada who helped to transform our manuscript into a handsome published text. They include Laura Forbes, former Acquisitions Editor; Don Thompson, Acquisitions Editor; Paul Donnelly, Developmental Editor; Jennifer Handel, Production Editor; Christine Kwan and Patricia Ciardullo, Production Coordinators; Jonathan Dore, Copyeditor; and Audrey Dorsch, Proofreader.

Christopher Lovelock

Jochen Wirtz

Harvir Bansal

A Great Way to Learn and Instruct Online

The Pearson Education Canada Companion Website is easy to navigate and is organized to correspond to the chapters in this textbook. Whether you are a student in the classroom or a distance learner you will discover helpful resources for in-depth study and research that empower you in your quest for greater knowledge and maximize your potential for success in the course.

[www.pearsoned.ca/lovelock]

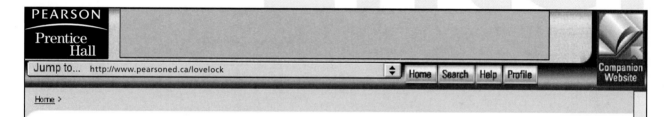

PEARSON
Prentice
Hall

Jump to... http://www.pearsoned.ca/lovelock   ◆ | Home | Search | Help | Profile   Companion Website

Home >

Companion Website

Services Marketing: People, Technology, Strategy, Canadian Edition, by Lovelock, Wirtz, and Bansal

Student Resources

This online study guide provides students with tools for learning course material. Modules may include:
- Chapter Objectives
- Chapter Overview
- Quizzes
- Internet Exercises
- Weblinks

In the quiz modules students can send answers to the grader and receive instant feedback on their progress through the Results Reporter. Coaching comments and references to the textbook may be available to ensure that students take advantage of all available resources to enhance their learning experience.

Instructor Resources

A link to this book on the Pearson Education Canada online catalogue (www.pearsoned.ca) provides instructors with additional teaching tools. Downloadable PowerPoint Presentations and an Instructor's Manual are just some of the materials that may be available. The catalogue is password protected. To get a password, simply contact your Pearson Education Canada Representative or call Faculty Sales and Services at 1-800-850-5813.

PART I

Understanding Service Markets, Products, and Customers

Part 1 lays out the building blocks for studying services and learning how you can become an effective service marketer. In Chapter 1, we define the nature of services and how they create value for customers without transfer of ownership. Highlighting some of the distinctive challenges involved in marketing services, we present a framework for developing a services marketing strategy that forms the basis for each of the chapters in Parts 2, 3, and 4 of the book.

Chapter 2 provides a foundation for understanding consumer needs and behaviour in both high-contact and low-contact service environments. We employ practical concepts to help you analyze and interpret the roles that customers play in the creation and delivery of different types of services, including those involving self-service technologies. In particular, we present a three-stage model of service consumption that explores how customers make decisions, respond to service encounters, and evaluate service performance

---

UNDERSTANDING CUSTOMER NEEDS, DECISION-MAKING AND BEHAVIOUR IN SERVICE ENCOUNTERS

Differences among Services Affect Customer Behaviour

Three-Stage Model of Service Consumption
- Pre-purchase stage: search, evaluation of alternatives, decision
- Service encounter stage: role in high-contact vs. low-contact delivery
- Post-encounter stage: evaluation against expectations, future intentions

(Chapter 2)

Building the Service Model
- Develop service concept: core and supplementary elements
- Select physical and electronic channels for service delivery
- Set prices with reference to costs, competition, and value
- Educate customers and promote the value proposition
- Position the value proposition against competing alternatives

---

Managing the Customer Interface
- Design and manage service processes
- Balance demand against productive capacity
- Plan the service environment
- Manage service employees for competitive advantage

Implementing Profitable Service Strategies
- Create customer relationships and build loyalty
- Plan for service recovery and create customer feedback systems
- Continuously improve service quality and productivity
- Organize for change management and service leadership

CHAPTER 1

New Perspectives on Marketing in the Service Economy

Canada's reputation today as a resource-based economy is largely undeserved. Indeed, its economy is well diversified, with the services sector accounting for over two-thirds of the country's output and providing employment for nearly three-quarters of the working population.

—*The Economist*

Like every reader of this book, you're an experienced service consumer. You use an array of services every day—although some, such as talking on the phone, using a credit card, riding a bus, or withdrawing money from an ATM, may be so routine that you hardly notice them unless something goes wrong. Other service purchases may involve more thought or be more memorable—for instance, getting your hair cut or styled, booking a cruise vacation, getting financial advice, or undergoing a dental procedure. Enrolling in college or graduate school may be one of the biggest service purchases you will ever make. The typical university is a complex service organization that offers not only educational services, but also libraries, student accommodation, athletic facilities, museums, security, counselling, and career services. On campus you may find a bookstore, post office, photocopying services, internet access, bank, mail, food, entertainment, and more. Your uses of these services are examples of service consumption at the individual, or business-to-consumer (B2C), level.

Companies and not-for-profit organizations use a wide array of business-to-business (B2B) services, varying to some degree according to the nature of their industry, but usually involving purchases on a much larger scale than those made by individuals or households. Nowadays, business customers are outsourcing more and more tasks to external service suppliers in order to focus on their core business, or at least the essential co-ordinating tasks that can only be done in-house. Without these needed services, offering them good value at a price they can afford, their companies can't hope to succeed.

Unfortunately, customers are not always happy with the quality and value of the services they receive. Sometimes, you may be delighted with your service experience, but there have probably been times when you were very disappointed. Both individual and corporate purchasers complain about broken promises, poor value for money, lack of understanding of their needs, rude or incompetent personnel, inconvenient service hours, bureaucratic procedures, wasted time, malfunctioning self-service machines, complicated websites, and a host of other problems.

Suppliers of services, who often face stiff competition, sometimes appear to have a very different set of concerns. Many owners and managers of such services complain about how difficult it is to keep costs down and make a profit, to find skilled and motivated employees, or to satisfy customers who, they sometimes grumble, have become unreasonably demanding. Fortunately, there are service companies that know how to please their customers while also running a productive, profitable operation, staffed by pleasant and competent employees, and accessible through user-friendly, self-service technology.

You probably have some favourite services that you like to patronize. Have you ever stopped to think about how these organizations succeed in delivering service that meets your needs and even exceeds your expectations? This book will teach you how service businesses should be managed to achieve customer satisfaction and profitable performance. In addition to studying the key concepts, organizing frameworks, and tools of services marketing, you'll also be introduced to a wide array of examples from across Canada and around the world. From their experiences you can draw important lessons on how to succeed in service markets that are becoming increasingly competitive.

In this opening chapter, we present an overview of today's dynamic service economy and invite you to explore the following questions:

1. Why study services?
2. How important is the service sector in our economy, and what are its principal industries?
3. What exactly *is* a service, and how should it be conceptualized and defined?
4. What distinctive marketing challenges do services present relative to goods?
5. Why do services need an expanded marketing mix, comprising 8Ps rather than 4Ps?

We conclude the chapter by presenting a framework for developing and implementing service-marketing strategies. This framework provides the structure for the book.

WHY STUDY SERVICES?

Figure 1.1

Contribution of Service Industries to Canadian Gross Domestic Product, 2005

Here's a paradox: we live in a service economy, but the academic study and teaching of marketing is still dominated by a manufacturing perspective in most business schools. If you have previously taken a marketing course, you most likely learned more about marketing manufactured products, especially consumer goods, than services. Fortunately, a growing and enthusiastic group of scholars, consultants, and teachers, including the authors of this text, have chosen to focus on services marketing, and to build on the extensive research conducted in this field over the past three decades. You can be confident that this book will provide you with information and skills that are highly relevant in today's business climate.

Services Dominate the Economy in Most Developed Nations

The size of the service sector is increasing around the world in countries with both developed and emerging economies. Figure 1.1 displays the composition of the Canadian economy in 2005, where private service industries account for more than half the value of the gross domestic product (GDP). When we add the output of federal, provincial, and local governments—which are primarily involved in service delivery, the total for services reaches almost 71 percent of the value of GDP.

For-profit and not-for-profit services differ in their underlying goals,

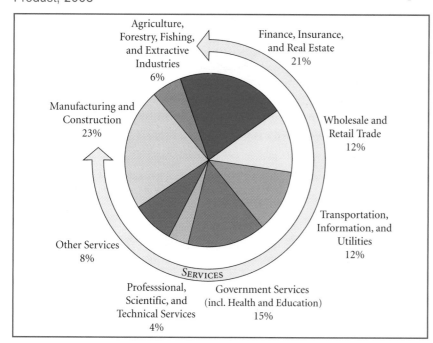

Note: Percentages do not add to 100 due to rounding.

Source: Data is adapted from the Statistics Canada CANSIM database http://cansim2.statcan.ca, Tables 379-0017 and 379-0020, January 2007.

although both want to create value for themselves and their stakeholders. For-profit businesses seek to achieve financial profits subject to social constraints, whereas not-for-profit service suppliers seek to achieve social profits subject to financial constraints.[1] Many public agencies and non-profit organizations charge a price for their services that partially covers their costs, but they often depend on donations, grants, or tax-based subsidies to cover the rest. (For simplicity, we will use the terms *business, company, corporation, firm,* and *organization* in this book to apply generically to all types of service providers.)

Like Canada, most emerging and developed economies have seen their service sectors grow rapidly. Figure 1.2 shows the relative size of the service sector in an array of economies from the very small to the large. In most of the more highly developed economies, services typically account for between two-thirds and three-fourths of GDP, although manufacturing-oriented South Korea (only 56 percent services) is an exception. Which is the world's most service-dominated economy? It's probably the Cayman Islands (95 percent), a group of small, British-administered islands in the western Caribbean, known for both tourism and offshore financial and insurance services. Jersey, the Bahamas, and Bermuda, all small islands with a similar economic mix, are not far behind. Luxembourg (86 percent) has the most service-dominated economy in the European Union. Panama's strong showing (76 percent), reflects not only the operation of the Panama Canal—widely used by cruise ships as well as freight vessels (Figure 1.3)—but also such related services as container ports, flagship registry, and a free port zone, as well as financial services, insurance, and tourism.

Figure 1.2 Estimated Size of Service Sector in Selected Countries as a Percentage of Gross Domestic Product

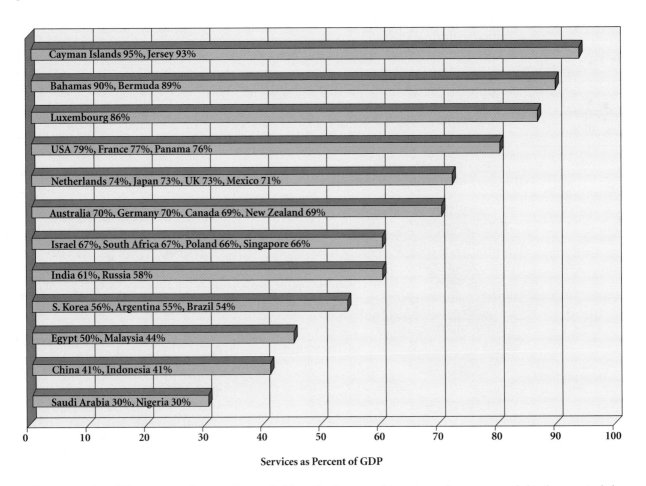

Services as Percent of GDP

Note: Estimates are from different years and may not be compiled from directly comparable measures; figures are rounded to the nearest whole percentage.

Source: The World Factbook 2007, Central Intelligence Agency, www.odci.gov/cia/publications/factbook.

Figure 1.3

The Panama Canal forms the backbone of this country's service economy.

Near the opposite end of the scale are China and Indonesia (41 percent services). China's emerging economy is dominated by a substantial agricultural sector and booming manufacturing and construction industries. However, China's economic growth is now leading to increased demand for business and consumer services. China's government is investing heavily in service infrastructure, including shipping facilities and new airport terminals. Shanghai, the country's major commercial centre, even boasts the world's fastest city-to-airport train service, featuring German-designed vehicles powered by magnetic levitation and capable of speeds of up to 420 kilometres per hour. Last among the countries in this table are Saudi Arabia and Nigeria, with their oil-dominated economies to which services contribute only 30 percent of GDP.

Classifying Service Industries   What industries make up the service sector, and which are the biggest? The latter may not be the ones you first imagine, because this diverse sector includes many services targeted at business customers, some of which are not highly visible to the general public, unless you happen to work in that industry. National economic statistics are a useful starting point. To provide a better understanding of today's service-dominated economy, government statistical agencies have developed new ways to classify industries. The manufacturing-oriented Standard Industrial Classification (SIC) system, developed in the 1930s, is being replaced in the United States, Canada and Mexico by the new North American Industry Classification System (NAICS)[2]. (For details, see Research Insights 1.1.)

Contribution to Gross Domestic Product   To see how much value each of the major service-industry groups contributes to the Canadian gross domestic product, take a look at Fig. 1.4. Would you have guessed that the largest portion of contribution to the GDP, roughly $199 billion (all dollar figures in this book are Canadian dollars unless otherwise specified), is accounted for by the government services sector, which includes the subsectors of public administration, educational services, health and social assistance services? Not surprisingly, health and social assistance services account for over 36 percent of this figure. Real estate and rental/leasing is the second-largest service-industry sector in Canada, accounting for $167 billion in 2005, almost 13 percent of the GDP. Another large cluster of services provides for distribution of physical products. Wholesale and retail trade, plus freight transportation and warehousing, collectively account for about 17 percent of GDP.

Research Insights 1.1

NAICS: A New Way to Classify the Economies of North America

The North American Industry Classification System (NAICS)—developed jointly by the statistical agencies of Canada, Mexico, and the United States—offers a new approach to classifying industries in the economic statistics of the three North American Free Trade Agreement (NAFTA) countries. It replaces previous national systems, such as the SIC codes formerly used in the United States.

NAICS (pronounced "nakes") includes many new service industries that have emerged in recent decades, and also reclassifies "auxiliary" establishments that provide support to manufacturing industries (examples include accounting, catering, and transportation) as services. Every sector of the economy has been restructured and redefined. NAICS includes 358 new industries that the SIC did not identify, 390 that are revised from their SIC counterparts, and 422 that continue substantially unchanged. These industries are grouped into sectors and further subdivided into subsectors, industry groups, and establishments.

Among the new sectors and subsectors devoted to services are: *Information,* which recognizes the emergence and uniqueness of businesses in the "information economy"; *Health Care and Social Assistance; Professional, Scientific and Business Services; Educational Services; Accommodation and Food Services;* and *Arts, Entertainment and Recreation* (which includes most businesses engaged in meeting consumers' cultural, leisure, or entertainment interests).

NAICS uses a consistent principle for classification, grouping together businesses that use similar production processes. Its goal is to make economic statistics more useful and to capture developments that encompass applications of high technology (e.g., cellular telecommunications), new businesses that previously did not exist (e.g., environmental consulting), and changes in the way business is done (e.g., warehouse clubs).

The NAICS codes are set up in such a way that researchers can "drill down" within broad industry sectors to obtain information on tightly defined types of service establishments. For instance, at the top level of classification, NAICS code 71 designates arts, entertainment, and recreation. At the next level, code 7112 designates spectator sports, and at a third level code 711211 designates sports teams and clubs. By looking at changes over time in current dollars (adjusted for inflation), it's possible to determine which industries have been growing and which have not. The NAICS codes are also being used to categorize employment statistics and numbers of firms within a particular industry. Meanwhile, a new North American Product Classification System (NAPCS) defines thousands of service products. If you want to research service industries and service products, NAICS data is a great place to start.

Sources: Economic Classification Policy Committee, "NAICS—North American Industry Classification System: New Data for a New Economy," Washington, DC: Bureau of the Census, October 1998; *North American Industry Classification System, United States 2002* [Official NAICS manual], Washington, DC: National Technical Information Service, PB 2002-101430*SS, 2002. See also www.census.gov/epcd/www/naics.html.

Figure 1.4 Value Added by Service Industries to Canadian Gross Domestic Product, 2005 (billions of current dollars)

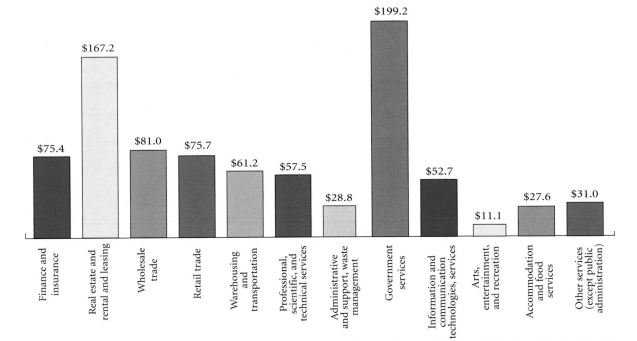

Note: Original data available in 1997 constant dollars. Conversion to current dollars by the inflation calculator available through Bank of Canada (www.bankofcanada.ca/en/rates/inflation_calc.html).

Source: Data is adapted from the Statistics Canada CANSIM database http://cansim2.statcan.ca, Tables 379-0017 and 379-0020; and from Statistics Canada websites www40.statcan.ca/l01/cst01/fin06.htm and www.statcan.ca/english/freepub/15-001-XIE/01106/tables_html/Table3_en.htm.

Other substantial industry sectors or subsectors are finance and insurance (6.0 percent), information and communication technologies and services (4.6 percent), and professional, scientific and technical services (4.4 percent). Accommodation and food services constitute only 2.2 percent, while the arts, entertainment, and recreation subsector—which includes such high-profile consumer services as spectator sports, fitness centres, skiing facilities, museums and zoos, performing arts, casinos, golf courses, marinas, and theme parks—collectively represents a mere 0.9 percent of GDP. Nevertheless, in an economy with an output of over $1 trillion, this last group of services was still valued at roughly $11 billion in 2005.

Most New Jobs Are Generated by Services

Employment is predicted to continue shrinking in manufacturing, mining, and agriculture in Canada, although since 2001 the economy has shown some strength in construction jobs. Like most developed economies, Canada will look to service industries for new job creation. And contrary to popular impressions, many new service jobs are likely to be well-paid positions that require a good educational foundation. Some of the fastest growth is expected in knowledge-based industries—such as professional and business services, education, and health services. Many jobs in these industries demand significant training and educational qualifications, and employees are often highly compensated.[3] In fact, researchers at IBM document that the so-called "information" or "knowledge" economy has been the principal engine of new job creation since as long ago as the 1950s, and will continue to be so for decades to come (Fig. 1.5).

Will service jobs be lost to countries with lower employment costs? New communications technology means that some service work can be carried out far from where customers are located. A study by the international consulting firm McKinsey & Co. in 2005 estimated that 11 percent of service jobs around the world could be carried out remotely.

Figure 1.5 Widening Gap between Employment in the Goods-Producing and the Services-Producing Sectors of Canada, 1976–2006

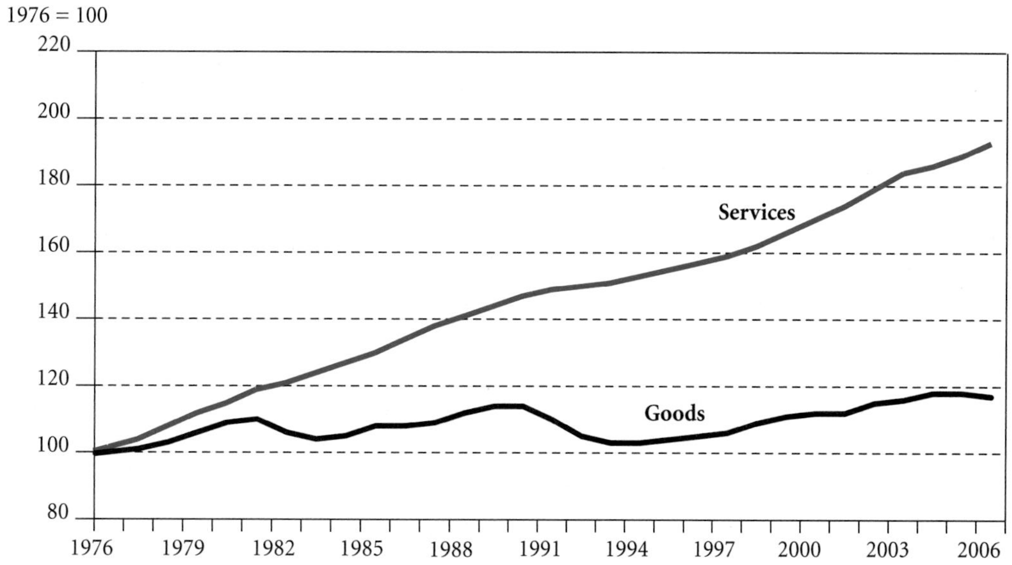

Note: For a definition of an index, please refer to the glossary.

Source: Data is adapted from the Statistics Canada CANSIM database http://cansim2.statcan.ca, Table 282-0008, January 2007.

But in practice, McKinsey predicts that the percentage of service jobs actually "offshored" will prove much more limited, reaching only 1 percent of all service employment in developed countries by 2008.[4] Of course, loss of even that small percentage will still affect a large number of workers, including some well-paid professionals whose work can be performed much less expensively by, say, highly qualified engineers working in India.

Powerful Forces Are Transforming Service Markets

Service markets are shaped by government policies, social changes, business trends, advances in information technology, and internationalization (Figure 1.6). Collectively, these forces are reshaping demand, supply, the competitive landscape, and even customers' styles of decision-making. *The Economist* argues that the internet is transferring power from suppliers to customers, especially in consumer markets.[5] Deregulation and advances in technology have broken the rigid structure of the financial services industry.[6] The travel industry will never be the same again. Electronic distribution is changing

Figure 1.6

Factors Stimulating the Transformation of the Service Economy

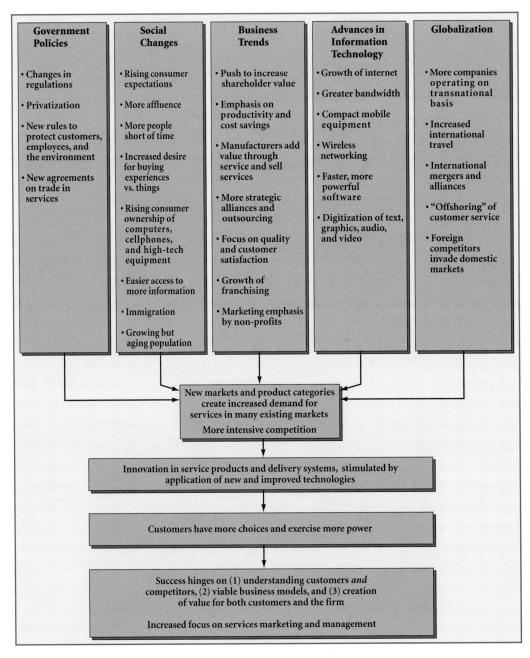

relationships and roles between suppliers, intermediaries, and customers as traditional channel members (such as local travel agencies) are replaced by innovative newcomers such as Orbitz, Travelocity, and Priceline.[7]

From one industry to another, competition is stimulating innovation, especially through application of new and improved technologies. Competition occurs not only among firms within the same industry, but also among firms from other industries that can offer customers new solutions to their needs through alternative approaches.[8] Think for a moment about person-to-person communications. Voice telephone has long competed with first-class letter mail, then internet-based email emerged to compete with both voice telephone and letter mail, and more recently, text messaging (primarily on mobile phones) has emerged to compete with all of them. Which of these options are you currently using more, and which less, than you did a few years ago? In the past few years, you've been able to watch how the internet and mobile telephony have evolved, adding new services and features. Consider what you can download to your cellphone (mobile handset) today that you couldn't have done a few years ago!

Customer needs and behaviour are evolving in response to changing demographics and lifestyles. The implications? Managers of service organizations need to focus more sharply on marketing strategy if they hope to meet, or even anticipate, these needs with services that customers see as offering value.

Customers are a vital source of ideas, not only for new products but also improvements to existing ones.[9] Even established, traditional services, such as hotels, need enhancement. By working with experts in research and development, and with operations and human resource managers, marketers may be able to create new service features that customers will value. Research into customer needs and priorities can provide vital insights into what specific features to emphasize and how much they might be worth to customers. The hotel chain Courtyard by Marriott boasts that its hotels were "designed by business travellers for business travellers," with rooms containing all the services and amenities they require to be comfortable and productive.

Understanding Services Offers Personal Competitive Advantage

Learning about the distinctive characteristics of services, and how they affect both customer behaviour and marketing strategy, will give you important insights—and perhaps create a competitive advantage for your own career. Unless you work in a family manufacturing or agricultural business, the probability is high that you'll spend most of your working life in service organizations. You may also find yourself serving as a volunteer or board member for a non-profit organization. Maybe the knowledge gained from studying this book will even stimulate you to think about starting your own service business!

WHAT ARE SERVICES?

Thus far, our discussion of services has focused on different types of service industries. But now it's time to ask the question: what exactly is a *service*?

The Historical View

Attempts to describe and define services in economic terms go back more than two centuries. In the late-18th and early-19th centuries, classical economists focused on the creation and possession of wealth. They contended that goods (initially referred to as "commodities") were objects of value over which ownership rights could be established and exchanged. Ownership implied tangible possession of an object that had been acquired through purchase, barter, or gift from the producer or a previous owner, and was legally identifiable as the property of the current owner.

Adam Smith's famous book *The Wealth of Nations*, published in Great Britain in 1776, distinguished between the outputs of what he termed "productive" and "unproductive" labour.[10] The former, he stated, produced goods that could be stored after production and subsequently exchanged for money or other items of value. But unproductive labour, however "honourable . . . useful, or . . . necessary" created services that "perished" at the time of production and therefore didn't contribute to wealth. Building on this theme, the French economist Jean-Baptiste Say argued that production and consumption were inseparable in services, coining the term "immaterial products" to describe them. [11]

Today, we know that production and consumption are indeed *separable* for many services (think of dry cleaning, lawn mowing, and weather forecasting) and technical developments have meant that services are no longer all perishable (consider audio or video recordings of concert performances and sports events). Indeed, many services are designed specifically to create *durable value* for their recipients (your own education being a case in point!). But the distinction between ownership and non-ownership remains a valid one, emphasized by several leading service-marketing scholars.[12]

A Fresh Perspective: Benefits without Ownership

Consider this: you didn't acquire ownership of the hotel room in which you stayed last weekend, nor of the physical therapist who worked on your injured knee, nor of the concert you just attended. But if you and other customers didn't receive a transfer of ownership the last time you purchased a service, then what did you buy? What have you got to show for your money, as well as the time and effort involved? What are, or were, the benefits? What problems did the service help you solve? In short: where's the value?

Christopher Lovelock and Evert Gummesson contend that services involve a form of *rental*. Service customers obtain benefits by renting the right to use a physical object, to hire the labour and expertise of personnel, or to pay for access to facilities and networks.[13] (Many services involve all three elements.) Value is created when customers benefit from obtaining desired experiences and solutions. We use the word *rent* here as a generic term to denote the payment made for using or accessing something—typically for a defined period of time—instead of buying it outright. You can't own people—slavery has been outlawed—but you can rent their labour and expertise.

Paying for temporary use of an object or for access to a physical facility is a way for customers to enjoy use of things that they cannot afford to buy, cannot justify purchasing, or prefer not to retain and store after use. In addition, renting—in the form of access and usage fees—offers customers a means to participate in network systems that individuals and most organizations couldn't possibly afford to own and operate themselves.

We can identify five broad categories within the non-ownership framework:

- *Rented-goods services.* These services enable customers to obtain the temporary right to exclusive use of a physical good that they prefer not to own. Examples include boats, power tools, combine harvesters, and formal clothing worn only for weddings and proms.

- *Defined space and place rentals.* Here, customers obtain use of a defined portion of a larger space in a building, vehicle, or other area, sharing its use with other customers under varying levels of privacy. A space ("my place") is the most individual unit of rental for an individual. Examples of this type of rental include a hotel room, a seat in an aircraft, a suite in an office building, a table and chairs in a restaurant, or a storage container in a warehouse. The space is typically designated by location, but the purpose to which it's put may vary widely, ranging from a place in which to perform business activities to one where a meal may be enjoyed. In other words, renting the space may be either an end in itself, or simply a means to an end. Some spaces may be physically identical but carry varying value because of location, such as a room with or without a view, or a seat closer to or further from the theatre stage.

- *Labour and expertise rentals.* Customers hire other people to perform work that they either choose not to do for themselves (for instance, cleaning a house) or are unable to do because they lack the necessary expertise, tools, or skills. In many instances, customers may effectively rent the services of an entire team, as in car repair, home renovation, and management consultancy.

- *Access to shared physical environments.* These environments may be located indoors or outdoors—or a combination of both. Examples include museums (at least, those with entrance fees), theme parks, trade shows, gyms, zoos, ski resorts, and golf courses. In return for a fee, customers rent the right to share use of the environment with other customers. Which of these have you used or visited lately?

- *Systems and networks: access and usage.* Here, customers rent the right to participate in a specified network such as telecommunications, utilities, banking, insurance, or specialized information services. Service providers often create a veritable menu of terms for access and use in response to varying customer needs and differing abilities to pay.

In many instances, two or more of these categories may be combined. When you take a taxi, you're hiring both a driver and a vehicle. If you take ski lessons, you are paying for instruction by a skilled ski instructor as well as the use of the ski slopes. If you undergo cosmetic surgery, you are, in essence, hiring a skilled team of medical personnel, led by the surgeon, as well as renting temporary (but exclusive) use of specialized equipment in a dedicated operating theatre at a hospital or clinic.

How does the distinction between ownership and non-ownership affect the nature of marketing tasks and strategy? Service Perspectives 1.1 highlights six important implications.

Defining Services

Already it will be clear that services cover a vast array of different and often very complex activities. The word *service* was originally associated with the work that servants did for their masters. In time, a broader association emerged, captured in the dictionary definition of "the action of serving, helping, or benefiting; conduct tending to the welfare or advantage of another."[14] Early marketing definitions of services contrasted them with goods. John Rathmell defined services in broad terms as "acts, deeds, performances, or efforts" and argued that they had different characteristics from goods—which he defined as "articles, devices, materials, objects, or things."[15]

But we believe that services need to be defined in their own right, not in relation to goods. A short and snappy definition, like the oft-repeated "something which can be bought and sold but which cannot be dropped on your foot"[16] may be amusing and memorable, but unfortunately it's not particularly helpful as a guide to marketing strategy. Instead, we offer the comprehensive definition shown below:

DEFINITION OF SERVICES

Services are economic activities offered by one party to another, most commonly employing time-based performances to bring about desired results in recipients themselves or in objects or other assets for which purchasers have responsibility.

In exchange for their money, time, and effort, service customers expect to obtain value from access to goods, labour, professional skills, facilities, networks, and systems; but they do not normally take ownership of any of the physical elements involved.[17]

Note that we define services as *economic activities* between two parties, implying an exchange of value between seller and buyer in the marketplace. We describe services as *performances* that are most commonly *time based*. We emphasize that purchasers buy services because they are looking for *desired results*. In fact, many firms explicitly market their services as "solutions" to prospective customers' needs. And finally, our definition emphasizes that while customers *expect to obtain value* from their service purchases *in exchange for their money, time, and effort*, this value comes from *access to a variety of value-creating elements rather than transfer of ownership*. (Spare parts installed during car repairs and restaurant-prepared food and beverages are among the few exceptions, but the value added by these items is usually less than that of the accompanying service elements.)

Service Perspectives 1.1

Six Marketing Implications of Renting vs. Owning

1. **There's a market for renting durable goods instead of selling them.** Solutions to temporary needs can often be better met by renting than owning. Among the most widely rented products are vehicles, construction and excavation equipment, generators, tents, party supplies, power tools, furniture, formal wear, and sporting goods such as skis. For longer-term usage, there may be financial advantages to making rental or lease payments instead of the capital investment of purchasing something. Marketers can add further value through such services as delivery and pickup, cleaning, insurance, and maintenance. They can even supply trained personnel to operate rented equipment.

2. **Renting portions of a larger physical entity can form the basis for services.** You can think of some types of service facility as "sausages" from which customers rent "slices"—such as seats in a movie theatre or aircraft, rooms in a hotel, or suites in an office building—for defined periods of time. Renting "my apartment" or "our office suite" conveys the right to exclusive but temporary use of a unit within a larger building. Customers benefit from economies of scale by sharing a large facility with many users, while enjoying varying degrees of separation and even privacy.

3. **Customers need to be more closely engaged with service suppliers.** When buyers acquire ownership of a product, they are free to use it where, when, and as they wish (within reason). But in services, suppliers need to exercise some control over how customers use equipment and facilities, interact with service personnel, and interface with systems and networks. Many services involve a division of labour between suppliers and customers, with the latter expected to know and obey the "rules." And most rented goods also require formalized return procedures at designated times and locations.

4. **Time plays a central role in most services.** Ownership is for as long as the object lasts or until the owner chooses to dispose of it. Rental or access is most typically defined in terms of specified time periods, with pricing often related to units of time. A key marketing challenge for service suppliers is to make sure that the objects,

facilities, and labour they offer are "rented out" over time as fully as possible at the most favourable rates—that's the route to creating value through higher revenues and profits. Achieving this objective places a premium on developing strategies to bring supply and demand into balance. Customers, too, are concerned with time. In order to improve the convenience and appeal of their service offerings, marketers must understand the role that time plays in customers' lifestyles, and how different people perceive, value, and budget time.

5. **Customer choice criteria may differ between rentals and outright purchases.** Marketing a rental car for a few days to a couple vacationing in Hawaii is a very different task from a local dealer's attempts to sell a car to these same people back in their hometown. Renters usually reserve a particular class or category of vehicle rather than a specific brand and model. Instead of worrying about physical characteristics like colour, upholstery, and number of cup holders, customers will focus on the location and hours of the rental office, insurance coverage, cleanliness and maintenance of vehicles, ease of using reservation systems, the quality of service provided by customer-contact personnel, and loyalty rewards such as miles for airline travel.

6. **Services offer opportunities for resource sharing.** In developing countries, improving the quality of life among poor consumers requires finding creative ways of sharing access to goods, physical facilities, systems, and expertise to bring prices down to affordable levels. And in a world where many resources are believed to be finite, replacing ownership by rental may be the best way in both emerging and developed economies to avoid waste by sharing use of the products that incorporate these scarce resources. An example is Grameen Telecom's scheme in Bangladesh, in which one person leases a cellphone and then rents it to fellow villagers for the use of individual calls (both incoming and outgoing).

Source: Adapted from Christopher Lovelock and Evert Gummesson, "Whither Services Marketing? In Search of a New Paradigm and Fresh Perspectives," *Journal of Service Research* 7 (August 2004): 20–41.

Service Products versus Customer Service and After-Sales Service

With the growth of the service economy, and emphasis on adding value-enhancing services to manufactured goods, the line between services and manufacturing sometimes becomes blurred. Many manufacturing firms—such as car makers Ford and Fiat, aerospace engine producers GE and Rolls Royce, and high-tech equipment manufacturers IBM and Xerox, are moving aggressively into service businesses.[18] Theodore Levitt, respected as one of the world's leading marketing experts, long ago observed that: "There are no such things as service industries. There are only industries whose service components are greater or less than those of other industries. Everybody is in service."[19] More recently, Roland Rust suggested that manufacturing firms had got this message when he noted that "most goods businesses now view themselves primarily as services."[20] Nevertheless, it's important to clarify the distinction between *service products* and what is often termed *customer service* (or customer support). Every business should have a customer-service orientation, but not every business markets what NAICS data categorizes as a service product.

In this book, we describe a firm's market offerings as being divided into *core product* elements and *supplementary service* elements—those activities or amenities that facilitate and enhance use of the core offering. We draw a clear distinction between *marketing of services*—where a service itself is the core product—and *marketing through service.* Certainly, good service often helps to sell a physical good and even make it more useful—and thereby valuable—to the buyer. Many firms in manufacturing, agricultural, natural resource, or construction industries now base their marketing strategies on a philosophy of serving customers well and adding supplementary service elements to the core product. But that core product still remains a physical good (a term we use here to include structures and commodities) if marketing's goal is to sell the item and transfer ownership. Supplementary services may include consultation, finance, shipping, installation, maintenance, upgrades and, finally, removal and environmentally responsible disposal. These services may be offered "free" (meaning effectively that their cost is bundled with the price of the initial product purchase) or charged for separately.

Many manufacturing firms have made a transition from simply bundling supplementary services with their physical products to reformulating and enhancing certain elements so that they can be marketed as stand-alone services. Having done so, the firm may target new customers who haven't previously purchased its manufactured products—and may even have no interest in doing so. As the organization's expertise builds, it may add new service products that it never offered before. IBM, once known only as a manufacturer of computers and business machines, offers four main groups of services: strategic outsourcing, business consulting, integrated technology services, and maintenance. Collectively, they generated US$46.2 billion in service revenues in 2004—almost half of IBM's total revenues—and contributed a gross profit of US$11.6 billion.[21]

You'll find that the same distinction between customer service and service products exists for consumer goods, especially durables. Purchasers of a luxury car, such as one marketed under Toyota's Lexus brand, receive not only excellent warranty coverage but also an exceptional level of service from the Lexus-trained dealer, a franchisee who is running a service business. However, these cars are still manufactured products and we must distinguish between marketing that product at the time of sale and marketing services that customers will pay for to maintain their car in good working order for several years after the sale. Lexus dealers don't compete with Jaguar or BMW for service sales; instead they compete with the best independent repair garages, which not only offer excellent repair and maintenance service, but may also be more conveniently located relative to many Lexus owners' homes or offices.

SERVICES POSE DISTINCTIVE MARKETING CHALLENGES

Are the marketing concepts and practices developed in manufacturing companies directly transferable to service organizations where no transfer of ownership takes place? The answer is often "no." In particular, when customers rent goods rather than buying them, their expectations and decision criteria will be different—and so will the nature of their experiences, including how they interact with the service firm that rents them the physical product. As a result, marketing-management tasks in the service sector tend to differ from those in the manufacturing sector in several important respects.

Table 1.1 lists eight common differences between services and goods, and highlights key managerial implications that will form the basis for analysis and discussion in this and later chapters. It's important to recognize that these differences, while useful generalizations, *do not apply equally to all services.*

Most Service Products Cannot Be Inventoried

Because services involve actions or performances, they are *ephemeral*—transitory and perishable—and so can't usually be stocked as inventory following production. (Exceptions are found among those service activities that can be recorded for later use in electronic or printed form.) Although facilities, equipment, and labour can be held in readiness to create the service, each represents productive capacity, not the product itself. If there's no

Table 1.1 Marketing Implications of Eight Common Differences between Services and Goods

DIFFERENCE	IMPLICATIONS	MARKETING-RELATED TASKS
Most service products cannot be inventoried	• Customers may be turned away or have to wait	• Smooth demand through promotions, dynamic pricing, and reservations • Work with operations to adjust capacity
Intangible elements usually dominate value creation	• Customers can't taste, smell, or touch these elements and may not be able to see or hear them • Harder to evaluate service and distinguish from competitors	• Make services tangible through emphasis on physical clues • Employ concrete metaphors and vivid images in advertising, branding
Services are often difficult to visualize and understand	• Customers perceive greater risk and uncertainty	• Educate customers to make good choices, explain what to look for, document performance, offer guarantees
Customers may be involved in co-production	• Customers interact with provider's equipment, facilities, and systems • Poor task execution by customers may hurt productivity, spoil service experience, curtail benefits	• Develop user-friendly equipment, facilities, and systems • Train customers to perform effectively; provide customer support
People may be part of the service experience	• Appearance, attitude, and behaviour of service personnel and other customers can shape the experience and affect satisfaction	• Recruit, train, and reward employees to reinforce the planned service concept • Target the right customers at the right times, shape their behaviour
Operational inputs and outputs tend to vary more widely	• Harder to maintain consistency, reliability, and service quality or to lower costs through higher productivity • Difficult to shield customers from results of service failures	• Set quality standards based on customer expectations; redesign product elements for simplicity and failure-proofing • Institute good service recovery procedures • Automate customer–provider interactions; perform work while customers are absent
The time factor often assumes great importance	• Customers see time as a scarce resource to be spent wisely; dislike wasting time waiting, want service at times that are convenient	• Find ways to compete on speed of delivery, minimize burden of waiting, offer extended service hours
Distribution may take place through nonphysical channels	• Information-based services can be delivered through electronic channels such as the internet or voice telecommunications, but core products involving physical activities or products cannot	• Seek to create user-friendly, secure websites and free access by telephone • Ensure that all information-based service elements can be downloaded from site

demand, unused capacity is wasted and the firm loses the chance to create value from these assets. During periods when demand exceeds capacity, customers may be sent away disappointed or asked to wait until later. A key task for service marketers, therefore, is to find ways of smoothing demand levels to match available capacity through promotions, reservations, and dynamic pricing strategies.

Intangible Elements Usually Dominate Value Creation

Many services include important physical elements, such as hotel beds, theatre interiors, spare parts installed during repairs, and bank cards and chequebooks. But it's often the intangible elements—such as processes, internet-based transactions, and the expertise and attitudes of service personnel—that create the most value in service performances. Customers can't taste, smell, or touch these elements and may not be able to see or hear them, either. That situation makes it more difficult for them to assess important service features before use, or evaluate the quality of the performance itself. Similarly, the lack of easy reference points can make it hard for customers to distinguish between competing suppliers.

A useful way to distinguish between goods and services, first suggested by Lynn Shostack, is to place them on a spectrum from tangible-dominant to intangible-dominant (see Figure 1.7 for a hypothesized scale presenting an array of examples).[22] Clearly, there are some potentially ambiguous products in the middle. Are custom tailors, plumbers, and fast-food restaurants delivering goods or services? One suggested economic test of whether a product should be regarded as a good or a service is whether more than half the value comes from intangible service elements.[23] At full-service restaurants, for example, the cost of the food ingredients may account for as little as 20–30 percent of the price of the meal. Most of the value added comes from the quality of food preparation and cooking, table service, the restaurant environment, and facilities such as parking, toilets, and coat-room.

When there are few physical elements, marketers often employ physical images and metaphors to highlight service benefits and demonstrate the firm's competencies. Creating physical clues and strong brand associations helps to "tangibilize" services.[24]

Figure 1.7

Relative Value Added by Physical vs. Intangible Elements in Goods and Services

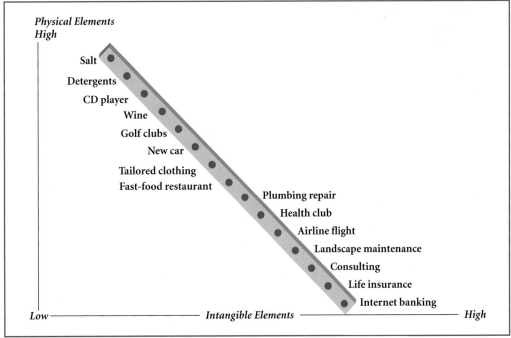

Source: Adapted from an earlier schematic by G. Lynn Shostack.

Services Are Often Difficult to Visualize and Understand

Many services can be described as "mentally intangible," meaning that it's difficult for customers to visualize the experience in advance of purchase and to understand what they will be getting. This situation can make service purchases seem risky. Many goods are relatively high in *search properties*—tangible characteristics that customers can evaluate prior to purchase—such as colour, shape, texture, style, fit, and feel. More complex goods and most services, by contrast, emphasize *experience properties* such as reliability, ease of use, and customer support that inexperienced purchasers can only discern during delivery and consumption. Finally, there are *credence properties*, characteristics that customers find hard to evaluate even after consumption—often relating to the benefits actually delivered.[25] Let's consider the purchase of professional services. People seek assistance from a professional precisely because they lack the necessary training and expertise themselves—think about counselling, surgery, consulting services, and many technical repairs. How can you really be sure after the fact that the best possible job was done? Sometimes it comes down to a matter of simply trusting the provider.

Mental intangibility is most likely to present a problem (and thus a perceived risk) for first-time customers who lack prior exposure to a particular type of service. Based on a study of a British police department, Paul Flanagan, Robert Johnston, and Derek Talbot argue that infrequently used service organizations, especially those in the public sector, need to build *confidence* in their abilities in advance of usage and then justify that confidence by actions that create lasting trust.[26] Frequent users have the advantage of past experiences that can serve as benchmarks, so they know what clues to look for. A point for you to remember is that any memorable experience can build trust—or destroy it.

Service marketers can reduce perceived risk for customers by helping them to make good choices—such as selecting the specific service features they need—and by educating them on what to expect both during and after service delivery. Documenting performance, explaining what was done and why, and offering guarantees are additional ways to reassure them and reduce anxiety. Confidence can be created in advance by emphasizing credentials and experience.

Customers May Be Involved in Co-production

Some services require customers to participate actively in creating the service product—a scenario often described as *co-production*. You're expected to co-operate with service personnel in settings such as hair salons, hotels, quick-service restaurants, libraries, even doing some of the work yourself rather than being waited on. In fact, service scholars argue that customers often function as *partial employees*.[27] (How do you feel about being described that way?) Increasingly, your involvement takes the form of self-service, often using the technology of smart machines, telecommunications, and the internet.[28] Simple examples include withdrawing money from an ATM, using an automated kiosk to check yourself in for a flight at the airport, and reserving seats for the big game via a website. Access to self-service technologies (SSTs) is important, too, for customers using B2B and professional services.[29] A key issue for marketers is: How satisfied are customers with the quality of service delivered by SSTs? Do customers see electronic channels that require them to do more work as better or worse than face-to-face alternatives? What needs do SSTs meet that traditional alternatives can't? What are their strong and weak attributes? Good research can help us to learn the answers and we'll be examining the impact of technology-driven services on customers—and how to manage them well—throughout this book.[30]

In many industries customers now have a choice. They can do their banking through multiple channels, shop at a store or order goods online, attend classes in a lecture hall, or watch a cable or satellite-based transmission of that same class.[31] They'll even find choices within the same physical site. For instance, at a hair salon they can choose between getting the benefits they want by asking the stylist to give them a particular hairstyle picked from a fashion magazine or obtaining knowledgeable advice from the stylist about a hairstyle that best complements their facial profile (Figure 1.8).

Figure 1.8

Co-producing the Service: Customer and Stylist Working Together for a Perfect Hairstyle

Service firms have much to gain from helping customers to become more competent and productive.[32] And so do customers. After all, if you as a customer do a poor job of performing the tasks for which you're responsible, that may spoil your service experience and curtail the benefits you hope to receive. By contrast, if things are made easy for you, you'll not only have a better experience and outcome, but your greater efficiency may boost the firm's productivity, lower its costs, and even enable it to reduce the price you pay. This means that service marketers should work with specialists from different departments to develop websites, equipment, facilities, and systems that are user-friendly. They should ensure that customers get the training they need to use these options well, and they should ensure that operations personnel can offer real-time support.

People May Be Part of the Service Experience

You must have remarked many times on how the difference between one service supplier and another lies in the attitude and skills of their employees. Well-managed firms devote special care to selecting, training, and motivating those people who will be responsible for serving customers directly. In addition to possessing the technical skills required by the job, these individuals also need to possess good interpersonal skills and display positive attitudes.

When you encounter other customers at a service facility, you know that they, too, can affect your satisfaction. How they're dressed, how many are present, who they are, and how they behave might all serve to reinforce or negate the image that a firm is trying to project and the experience it's trying to create. Were you annoyed by the customer at the next table talking loudly on her phone about problems at work, or angered by the fellow seated beside you in the theatre who spilled his sticky drink on your clothes? Alternatively, were you grateful to the friendly traveller who showed you how to operate the complicated ticketing machine? At a play or circus or sporting event, the enthusiasm of the audience can add to the excitement. However, if some members become too rowdy and abusive, it may detract from your enjoyment. Customer *misbehaviour* presents a marketing problem.

Figure 1.9
Two Types of Websites

A website can deliver Athabasca University's services directly, but . . .

The marketing implications are clear: in addition to managing their own employees effectively to ensure good service delivery, firms must also manage and shape their customers. In a shared service setting, other customers should enhance the experience of each user, not detract from its value. In some instances, service marketers need to think carefully about whether it's a good idea to mix several segments together in the same service facility at the same time. One of the authors has never forgotten staying at a hotel where half the guests were attending an academic conference and the rest were football fans from out of town who had come for the weekend to support their team. The two groups differed in their expectations of what constituted a good experience!

Operational Inputs and Outputs Tend to Vary More Widely

Unlike many services, manufactured goods can be produced at a distant factory, under controlled conditions, and checked for conformity with quality standards long before they reach the customer. But when a service is delivered face to face, and consumed as it's produced, final "assembly" must take place in real time. You've probably noticed that service execution often differs among employees, between the same employee and different customers, and even from one time of day to another. Attitudes, transactional speed, and quality of performance can vary widely, and it's harder, even impossible, to shield customers from the results of service failures. These factors can make it difficult for service organizations to improve productivity, control quality, and ensure reliable delivery. As a former packaged-goods marketer once observed after moving to a new position at Holiday Inn:

> We can't control the quality of our product as well as a Procter and Gamble control engineer on a production line can . . . When you buy a box of Tide, you can reasonably be 99 and 44/100ths percent sure that this stuff will work to get your clothes clean. When you buy a Holiday Inn room, you're sure at some lesser percentage that it will work to give you a good night's sleep without any hassle, or people banging on the walls and all the bad things that can happen in a hotel.[33]

Nevertheless, the best service firms have made significant progress in reducing variability by adopting standardized procedures, implementing rigorous management of service quality, training employees more carefully, and automating tasks previously performed by human beings. They also make sure that employees are well trained in service recovery procedures in case things do go wrong.

. . . HBC's products can only be delivered through physical channels.

The Time Factor Frequently Assumes Great Importance

Many services are delivered in real time while customers are physically present. Today's customers are the most time-sensitive in history, are in more of a hurry, and see wasted time as a cost to avoid.[34] You probably do too. They may be willing to pay extra to save time, such as taking a taxi even though a city bus serves the same route, or to get a needed task performed faster. Increasingly, busy customers expect service to be available when it suits them, rather than when it suits the supplier. If one firm responds by offering extended hours, its competitors often feel obliged to follow suit. Nowadays, a growing number of services are available 24/7.

Another concern of customers is how much time elapses between making a request for service and receiving the finished output. If you've used a particular type of service previously, you're likely to have expectations of how long a certain task—whether it involves repairing a car, cleaning a suit, or ordering a book online—should take to complete. Successful service marketers understand customers' time constraints and priorities. They collaborate with operations managers to find new ways to compete on speed. They strive to minimize customer waiting times and they seek to make waiting itself less burdensome.

Distribution May Take Place through Non-physical Channels

Manufacturers require physical distribution channels to move their products from the factory to customers, either directly or through wholesale and retail intermediaries. Some service businesses are able to use electronic channels to deliver all (or at least some) of their service elements. Today's banks offer customers a choice of distribution channels, including visiting a branch, using a network of ATMs, doing business by telephone, or conducting banking transactions on the internet. Many information-based services can be delivered almost instantaneously to any location in the world that has internet access.

The internet, and its key component, the World Wide Web (www), is reshaping distribution strategy for a broad array of industries.[35] But we need to distinguish between its potential for delivering information-based *core products* (those that respond to customers' primary requirements) and simply providing *supplementary services* that facilitate purchase and use of physical goods. Examples of the former include the online educational programs offered by Athabasca University (www.athabascau.ca) and investment services from RBC Action Direct Inc. (www.rbcdirectinvesting.com).

Contrast these two web-enabled services with the website of the Hudson's Bay Company (HBC), Canada's largest diversified general merchandise retailer, with over department store, mass merchandise, and specialty store outlets across Canada. While it remains the country's oldest corporation (it was founded in 1670), it was bought in early 2006 by U.S. billionaire Jerry Zucker, who now serves as governor and chief executive officer (CEO) of HBC. You can browse the company's website (www.hbc.com) and find an exhaustive list of products, obtain pricing information, place an order for specific products, and pay for them online. Similarly, without leaving your home, let alone the country, you can review British Airways' worldwide schedules at www.ba.com, check out how fares vary according to time of day and day of week (you'll find huge variations in economy fares on some routes within Europe), make a reservation, indicate any special needs, and pay for the electronic ticket. But in both cases, delivery of the core product itself must take place through physical channels. The Olympic-themed hockey jersey and parka that you bought from HBC will be delivered to your home by regular or expedited postal services, or you might wish to pick them up from a store near you. You'll have to go to the airport in person to board your BA flight. Much electronic-commerce (ecommerce) activity concerns supplementary services that are based on *transfer of information and payments relating to the product*, as opposed to downloading the core product itself. Figure 1.9 (pp. 20–21) displays examples of both types of website.

SERVICES REQUIRE AN EXPANDED MARKETING MIX

Marketing can be viewed in several ways. You can look at it as a strategic and competitive thrust pursued by top management, as a set of functional activities performed by line managers, or as a customer-driven orientation for the entire organization. In this book, we seek to integrate all three perspectives. In our teaching and consulting, we like to emphasize to senior managers that *marketing is the only function that acts to bring operating revenues into a business.* All other functions, however important they may be, are effectively cost centres. Sometimes that news comes as a shock!

The 8Ps of Services Marketing

When developing strategies to market manufactured goods, marketers usually address four basic strategic elements: product, price, place (or distribution), and promotion (or communication). As a group, these are often referred to as the "4Ps" of the marketing mix.[36] This concept is one of the staples of almost any introductory marketing course. But to capture the distinctive nature of service performances, we need to refine the original terminology and speak instead of *product elements, place and time, price and other user outlays*, and *promotion and education*. We then extend the mix by adding four elements associated with service delivery—*physical environment, processes, people,* and *productivity and quality*.[37] Collectively, these eight elements, which we refer to as the "8Ps" of services marketing, represent the ingredients required to create viable strategies for meeting customer needs profitably in a competitive marketplace. You can think of these elements as the eight strategic levers of services marketing.

Our visual metaphor for the 8Ps is the racing "eight," a lightweight boat or "shell" powered by eight rowers, made famous by the Oxford and Cambridge boat race that has taken place annually on the River Thames in London for over 150 years. Today, similar races involving multiple teams are a staple of rowing competitions around the world and a featured sport in the Summer Olympics. Speed comes not only from the rowers' physical strength but also from their harmony and cohesion as a team. To achieve full effectiveness, each of the eight rowers must pull on his or her oar in unison with the others, following the direction of the coxswain, who sits in the stern. A similar synergy and integration between each of the 8Ps is required for success in any competitive service business. The "cox"—who steers the boat, sets the pace, motivates the crew, and keeps a close eye on competing boats in the race—is a metaphor for management (Figure 1.10, page 23)

Now, let's look briefly at each of the 8Ps in turn. We'll be covering each one in depth later in the book, as indicated by the chapter numbers following each subheading below.

Figure 1.10
Working in Unison:
The 8Ps of Services
Marketing

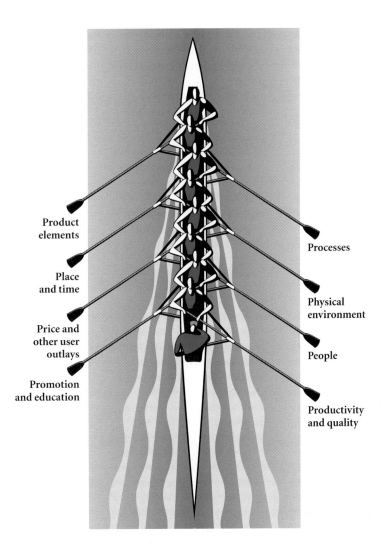

Product
elements

Place
and time

Price and
other user
outlays

Promotion
and education

Processes

Physical
environment

People

Productivity
and quality

Product Elements (Chapter 3)   Service products lie at the heart of a firm's marketing strategy. If a product is poorly designed, it won't create meaningful value for customers, even if the rest of the 8Ps are well executed. Planning the marketing mix begins with creating a service concept that will offer value to target customers and satisfy their needs better than competing alternatives. Working to transform this concept into reality involves design of a cluster of different, but mutually reinforcing elements. Service products consist of a core product that responds to the customers' primary need and an array of supplementary service elements that help customers to use the core product effectively, as well as adding value through significant enhancements.

Place and Time (Chapter 4)   Delivering product elements to customers involves decisions on where and when the former are delivered to the latter, as well as the methods and channels employed. Delivery may involve use of physical or electronic channels (or both), depending on the nature of the service. Use of messaging services and the internet allows information-based services to be delivered in cyberspace for retrieval, wherever and whenever it suits customers. Firms may deliver service directly to end-users or through intermediary organizations, such as retail outlets, which receive a fee or commission and which perform certain tasks associated with sales, service, and customer-contact. Speed and convenience of place and time have become important determinants of effective service delivery today.

Price and Other User Outlays (Chapter 5)   This component must address the twin perspectives of the service firm and its customers. Like product value, the value inherent in payments is central to marketing's role in facilitating a value exchange between the firm and its customers. For suppliers, pricing strategy is the financial mechanism though which income is generated to offset the costs of providing service, and to create a surplus for profits. Pricing strategy is often highly dynamic, with price levels being adjusted over time according to such factors as type of customer, time and place of delivery, level of demand, and available capacity. Customers, by contrast, see price as a key part of the costs they must incur to obtain wanted benefits. To calculate whether a particular service is "worth it," they may go beyond just the price and also assess the outlays of their time and effort. Service marketers, therefore, must not only set prices that the targeted customers are willing and able to pay, but also understand—and seek to minimize, where possible—other burdensome outlays that customers incur in using the service. These outlays may include additional monetary costs (such as travel expenses to a service location), time expenditure, unwanted mental and physical effort, and exposure to negative sensory experiences.

Promotion and Education (Chapter 6)
What should we tell existing and prospective customers about our services? No marketing program can succeed without effective communications. This component plays three vital roles: providing needed information and advice, persuading target customers of the merits of a specific brand or service product, and encouraging them to take action at specific times. In services marketing, much communication is educational in nature, especially for new customers unfamiliar with the type of service being offered. Suppliers need to inform these customers about the benefits of the service, where and when to obtain it, and how their participation in the process can achieve the best results. Communication may be delivered by individuals, such as salespeople and front-line staff; on websites; on display screens in self-service equipment; and through a wide array of advertising media. Promotional activities—which may include a monetary incentive—are often designed to stimulate immediate trial purchases or to encourage consumption when demand is low.

Process (Chapter 8)
Smart managers know that where services are concerned, *how* a firm does things—the underlying processes—are often as important as *what* it does, particularly if the product is a common one offered by many competitors. So creating and delivering product elements requires design and implementation of effective processes. Customers are often actively involved in these processes, especially when acting as co-producers. Badly designed processes lead to slow, bureaucratic, and ineffective service delivery, wasted time, and a disappointing experience. They also make it difficult for front-line staff to do their jobs well, resulting in low productivity and increased likelihood of service failure.

Physical Environment (Chapter 10)
The appearance of buildings, landscaping, vehicles, interior furnishing, equipment, staff uniforms, signs, printed materials, and other visible cues all provide tangible evidence of a firm's service quality. Service firms need to manage physical evidence carefully, since it can have a profound impact on customers' impressions.

People (Chapter 11)
Despite technological advances, many services will always require direct interaction between customers and customer-contact personnel. The nature of these interactions strongly influences how customers perceive service quality.[38] Knowing that (dis)satisfaction with service quality often reflects customers' assessments of front-line staff, successful service firms devote significant effort to recruiting, training, and motivating employees. And recognizing that customers may themselves contribute (positively or negatively) to how others experience service performances, proactive marketers try to shape customers' roles and manage their behaviour.

Productivity and Quality (Chapter 14)
Often treated separately, productivity and quality should be seen as two sides of the same coin. No service organization can afford to address one in isolation from the other. Improving *productivity* is essential to any strategy for reducing costs. But managers must beware of making inappropriate cuts in service that are resented by customers (and perhaps by employees too). Improving *quality*, which should be defined from a customer perspective, is essential for product differ-

entiation and for building customer satisfaction and loyalty. But it's unwise to invest in service-quality improvements without understanding the trade-off between the incremental costs involved and the incremental revenues anticipated from offering better quality on specific dimensions. If customers aren't willing to pay extra for more quality, then the firm will lose money! The strategies with the biggest potential payoffs may be those that seek to improve productivity and quality simultaneously. Advances in technology sometimes offer promising opportunities, but innovations must be user-friendly and deliver benefits that customers will value.

Marketing Must Be Integrated with Other Management Functions

Earlier, we described the 8Ps as the strategic levers of services marketing. As you think about these different elements, it should quickly become clear that marketers working in a service business can't expect to operate successfully in isolation from managers in other functions. In fact, three management functions play central and interrelated roles in meeting the needs of service customers: marketing, operations, and human resources (HR). Figure 1.11 illustrates this interdependency. One of the responsibilities of top management is to ensure that managers and other employees in each of these three functions don't isolate themselves in departmental silos.

Operations is the primary line function in a service business, responsible for managing service delivery through equipment, facilities, systems, and many tasks performed by customer-contact employees. In most service organizations, you can also expect to see operations managers actively involved in product and process design, many aspects of the physical environment, and implementation of productivity and quality-improvement programs. HR is often seen as a staff function, responsible for job definition, recruitment, training, reward systems, and quality of the working environment—all of which are, of course, central to the concerns of the firm's employees. But in a well-managed service business, HR managers view these activities from a strategic perspective: they are engaged in the design and monitoring of all service-delivery processes that involve employees; they work with marketers to ensure that employees have the skills and training to deliver promotional messages and educate customers; and they design those aspects of the physical environment that directly involve employees—including uniforms, personal appearance, and stage-managed behaviour.

For these reasons, we don't limit our coverage in this book exclusively to marketing. In many of the chapters you'll also find us referring to service operations and human resource management. Some firms deliberately rotate their managers among different job functions, especially between marketing and operations positions, precisely so that they will be able to appreciate different perspectives. Your own career in services might follow a similar path.

Figure 1.11

Marketing, operations, and human resources functions must collaborate to serve the customer.

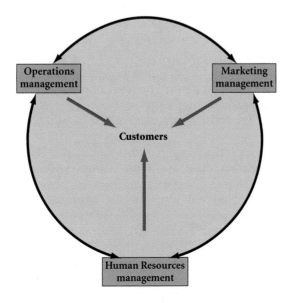

Imagine yourself as the manager of a small hotel. Or, if you like, think big and picture yourself as the CEO of a major bank. In both instances, you need to be concerned about satisfying your customers on a daily basis, about ensuring that operational systems run smoothly and efficiently, and about making sure that your employees are not only working productively, but are also delivering good service. In short, integration of activities between functions is the name of the game in services. Problems in any one of these three areas can negatively affect execution of tasks in the other functions, resulting in dissatisfied customers. Only a minority of people who work in a service firm are employed in formal marketing positions. But, argues Evert Gummesson, all those whose work affects the customer in some way—either through direct contact or through the design of processes and policies that shape customers' experiences—need to think of themselves as *part-time marketers*.[39]

A Framework for Developing Effective Service Marketing Strategies

To help you understand what is involved in developing marketing strategies that will be appropriate for different types of services, Figure 1.12 presents a framework that outlines the key steps. It shows how each of the chapters in this book fits together with the others as they address related topics and issues. Note the arrows linking the different boxes in the diagram: they make it clear that the process of creating a strategy is not like stopping at a series of points along a one-way street. Instead, it's an iterative process—that is, one whose components may have to be revisited more than once, because they are interdependent. Decisions in one area must be consistent with those taken in another, so that each strategic element will mutually reinforce the remainder. A good services-marketing strategy is based on a solid knowledge of the market, customers, and the competition. It is *actionable*—that is to say, the firm possesses the necessary resources. And it sets realistic goals toward which progress can readily be measured.

Understanding the Customer   Now it's time to put you in the driver's seat, thinking like a manager rather than a student, as you negotiate the different steps. Our framework begins with—and will continually involve—your ability to understand customers' needs and how they behave in service environments (this will be dealt with further in Chapter 2). Important concerns for you and your colleagues will include how people search for information, how they establish expectations, and how they choose between alternative suppliers. You should also be monitoring how customers respond to *service encounters*, those moments of truth when they interact with the firm and the proverbial rubber meets the road. Are their expectations being met or missed? As a result, are they satisfied or disappointed? And do they plan to use your firm's services again, or switch to a competitor?

Building the Service Model   This task (addressed in Part 2 of the book) requires you and other members of the management team to create a meaningful *value proposition*—a package that specifies what benefits and solutions your firm intends to offer, and how it proposes to deliver them to target customers. You'll do better if this emerges from a distinctive underlying *service concept* that responds to specific customer needs and market opportunities, as opposed to a generic, "me-too" offering. Transforming this concept into a service product means developing a specific package of core and supplementary product elements, and then distributing each element of this package to customers at appropriate places and times. Depending on the nature of the product, you may be selecting from among a variety of both physical and electronic channels. More and more, "place" is no longer a geographic location, open during only limited hours, but somewhere in cyberspace that the customer can access at will, 24/7.

To ensure that your strategy will be financially viable, you must create a *business model* that will allow the costs of creating and delivering the service (plus a margin for profits) to be recovered through realistic pricing strategies. But you know that customers won't buy unless they perceive that the benefits obtained from this *value exchange* exceed the financial and other costs *they* incur, including their time and effort. So, your value proposition must be actively promoted through effective communication, and there must be a

Figure 1.12   Framework for Developing a Services Marketing Strategy

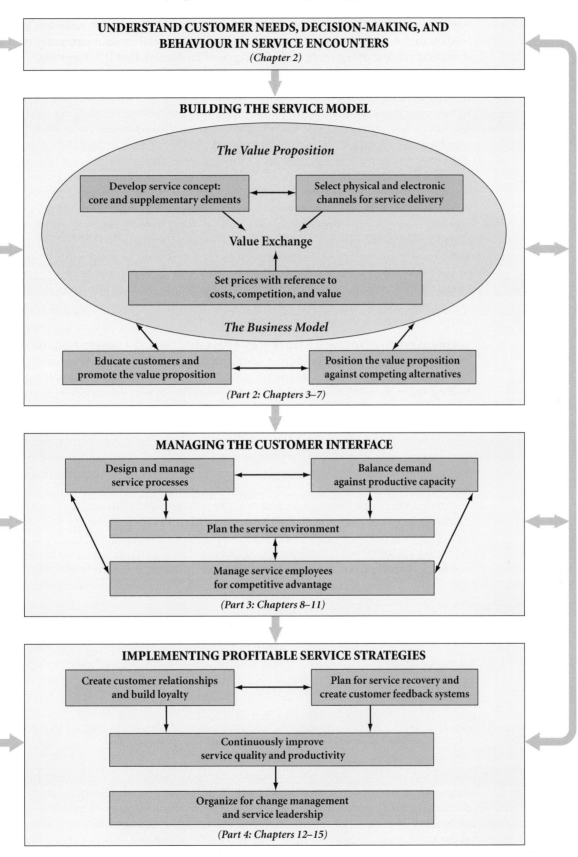

strategy for educating customers—especially first-time users—about how to make good choices and how to use the service to their best advantage. And finally, to ensure that this value proposition will be commercially viable, your strategy must stake out a defensible *position* in the market against competing alternatives, so that your company can attract a sufficient volume of business from the types of customers that it is targeting.

Managing the Customer Interface (Part 3)   Your task continues with the development of strategies for managing the customer interface—that is, embracing all points at which customers interact with your company. It will involve working with your colleagues in operations and HR to design effective service processes, with your own particular focus as a marketer being on the role played by customers, and the experiences you wish to engineer for them as they move through each step of the process toward a desired outcome. Closely related to the task is the question of how best to balance demand for the service (which in some markets may fluctuate widely over time) against the organization's productive capacity. If your job is in a service business that requires customers to enter the "service factory"—the firm's place of business—you'll also have to spend time thinking about design of the physical environment or *servicescape*.[40] And if the service involves contact between customers and service personnel, you'll need to work with your colleagues in HR to develop strategies for managing employees in ways that enable them to deliver outstanding performances. HR managers who think strategically recognize that loyal, skilled, motivated, employees who work well—whether independently, or together in teams—represent a key competitive advantage.

Implementing Service Strategies (Part 4)   Next, it's time to focus on some of the activities involved in implementing service-marketing strategies. Achieving profitability will require creating relationships with customers from the right market segments and finding ways to build on and reinforce their loyalty. When things go wrong (as they do from time to time in even the best-run service businesses), your goal must be to achieve service recovery and retain customers; an important task will be to obtain customer feedback to help the firm avoid repeating failures and to better meet customers' future needs and expectations. Developing strategies for improving service quality and productivity will provide the necessary leverage for financial success: unless your customers are satisfied with the quality of service they receive, the company's revenues will decline as those customers take their business to competitors. Unless your firm can continually improve productivity, it may lose control of its costs and fail to create value for its owners. Long-term planning requires you to consider how the organization should evolve in response to emerging customer needs, market trends, competitive dynamics, and technologies. What needs to change if your firm is to achieve and maintain service leadership? And how should the process of change be led and managed? Consider this: eventually, you may be in charge of such an initiative yourself!

Conclusion

Why study services? Because modern economies are driven by individual service businesses operating within a remarkable array of industries. Collectively, they're responsible for the creation of a substantial majority of all new jobs, both skilled and unskilled, around the world. Many of these industries are undergoing dramatic transformations, driven by advances in technology, globalization, changes in government policies, and evolving consumer needs and lifestyles.

Important business trends include outsourcing and strategic alliances. In such an environment, effective marketing plays a vital role in determining whether an individual organization survives and thrives or declines and fails.

In this chapter, we've demonstrated that services require a distinctive approach to marketing, because the context and the tasks often differ in important respects from those in the manufacturing sector. To succeed as a marketing manager in a service business requires that you not only understand key marketing concepts and tools, but also know how to use them effectively. Each of the 8Ps—the strategic levers of services marketing—potentially has a role to play, but it's how well you tie them together that will make the difference. As you study this book, attend classes, and undertake projects, remember that the winners in today's highly competitive service markets progress by continually rethinking the way they do business, by looking for innovative ways to serve their customers better, by taking advantage of new developments in technology, and by embracing a disciplined and well-organized approach to developing and implementing marketing strategy.

Review Questions

1. Is it possible for an economy to be based entirely on services? Is it a sign of weakness when a national economy manufactures few of the goods that it consumes?

2. What are the main reasons for the growing share of the service sector in all major economies of the world?

3. What is so distinctive about services marketing that it requires a special approach, set of concepts, and body of knowledge? "The 4Ps are all a marketing manager needs to create a marketing strategy for a service business!" Prepare a response that argues the contrary, and back up your conclusions.

4. What types of services do you think are (a) most affected and (b) least affected by the problem of variable inputs and outputs. Why?

5. Why is time so important in services?

6. Explain each of the following terms, provide examples, and explain their importance for services marketing: (a) partial employee; (b) part-time marketer; (c) value proposition.

7. How has the development of self-service technologies affected services marketing strategy? What factors determine whether customers make use of them or not?

8. Why do marketing, operations, and human resources have to be more closely linked in services than in manufacturing? Give examples.

9. The term "marketing mix" could suggest that marketing managers are mixers of ingredients. Is that perspective a recipe for success when employing the 8Ps to develop a services marketing strategy?

Application Exercises

1. Visit the websites of the following national statistical bureaus: United States Bureau of Economic Analysis (ww.bea.gov); Statistics Canada (www.statcan.ca); British Office of National Statistics (www.statistics.gov.uk): and Statistics Singapore (www.singstat.gov.sg). In each instance, obtain data on the latest trends in services as (a) a percentage of gross domestic product; (b) the percentage of employment accounted for by services; (c) breakdowns of these two statistics by type of industry; and (d) service exports and imports.

2. Visit Statistics Canada's website (www.statcan.ca) and see the contribution of the government services sector to Canada's GDP over the past decade. How have the subsectors of educational services, health care and social assistance, and public administration fared relative to each other?

3. Visit Bell Canada Enterprises (BCE) website (www.bce.ca/en/), which describes its different businesses and other information. Review BCE's annual report and recent quarterly reports at www.bce.ca/en/investors/financialperformance/corporatefinancial/bce/. What con-

clusions do you draw about future opportunities in different markets? What do you see as competitive threats?

4. Give examples of how internet and telecommunications technologies, such as interactive voice response systems (IVRs) and mobile commerce (m-commerce) have changed some of the services that you use.

5. Choose two service companies you're familiar with that operate in the same industry (e.g., Tim Hortons and The Second Cup Coffee Company) and compare how the two companies manage each of the eight elements (8 Ps) of integrated service management for effective service delivery.

6. Identify two applications in each of the following categories of SST: (a) web-based; (b) free-standing equipment (part of network); (c) free-standing equipment with only credit/debit card connections for payment; (d) free-standing equipment, no connections except to power supply. How long have these SSTs been around in their present form? Can you determine when a less sophisticated predecessor was first introduced? What is their significance for both customers and the firm?

Endnotes

1. Christopher H. Lovelock and Charles B. Weinberg, *Public and Nonprofit Marketing*, 2nd ed., Redwood City, CA: Scientific Press, 1989; Paul Flanagan, Robert Johnston, and Derek Talbot, "Customer Confidence: The Development of 'Pre-Experience' Concept, *International Journal of Service Industry Management*16/4 (2005): 373–84.

2. U.S. Department of Commerce, *North American Industry Classification System: United States.* Washington, DC: National Technical Information Service, # PB 2002-101430, 2002

3. "The Great Jobs Switch," *The Economist*, October 1, 2005: 11, 14.

4. Diana Farrell, Martha A. Laboissière, and Jaeson Rosenfeld, "Sizing the Emerging Global Labor Market," *McKinsey Quarterly* 3 (2005): 93–103.

5. "Crowned at Last," *The Economist*, April 2, 2005: 3–6.

6. Barry Howcroft, Paul Hewer, and Robert Hamilton, "Consumer Decision-Making Styles and the Purchase of Financial Services," *Service Industries Journal* 23/2 (May 2003): 63–81.

7. Bill Carroll and Judy Siguaw, "The Evolution of Electronic Distribution: Effects on Hotels and Intermediaries," *Cornell Hotel and Restaurant Administration Quarterly* 44 (August 2003): 38–51.

8. Michael D. Johnson and Anders Gustafsson, *Competing in a Service Economy*, San Francisco: Jossey-Bass, 2003.

9. Jonas Mathing, Bodil Sandén, and Bo Edvardsson, "New Service Development: Learning from and with Customers," *International Journal of Service Industry Management* 15/5 (2004): 479–98.

10. Adam Smith, *The Wealth of Nations*, 3 vols., with an introduction by A. Skinner. London: Penguin, 1969 (originally published 1776).

11. Jean Baptiste Say, *A Treatise on Political Economy*, New York: Augustus M. Kelly, 1964 (originally published 1803).

12. Robert C. Judd, "The Case for Redefining Services," *Journal of Marketing* 28 (January 1964): 59; John M. Rathmell, *Marketing in the Service Sector*, Cambridge, MA: Winthrop, 1974; Christopher H. Lovelock and Evert Gummesson, "Whither Services Marketing? In Search of a New Paradigm and Fresh Perspectives," *Journal of Service Research* 7 (August 2004): 20–41.

13. Lovelock and Gummesson, op. cit.

14. "Service," *Shorter Oxford English Dictionary*, 5th edition, Oxford and New York: Oxford University Press, 2002.

15. Rathmell, John M., "What is Meant by Services?" *Journal of Marketing* 30 (October 1966): 32–36.

16. Evert Gummesson (citing an unknown source) "Lip Service: A Neglected Area in Services Marketing," *Journal of Consumer Services* 1 (Summer 1987): 19–22.

17. Adapted from a definition by Christopher Lovelock (identified anonymously as Expert 6, Table II, p. 112) in Bo Edvardsson, Anders Gustafsson, and Inger Roos, "Service Portraits in Service Research: A Critical Review," *International Journal of Service Industry Management* 16/1 (2005): 107–21.

18. Rogelio Oliva and Robert L. Kallenberg, "Managing the Transition from Products to Services," *International Journal of Service Industry Management* 14/2 (2003): 160–72; Jeremy Howells, "Innovation, Consumption and Services: Encapsulation and the Combinatorial Role of Services," *The Service Industries Journal* 24 (January 2004): 19–36; Mohanbir Sawhney, Sridhar Balasubramanian, and Vish V. Krishnan, "Creating Growth with Services," *MIT Sloan Management Review* 45 (Winter 2004): 34–43.; Sara Brax, "A Manufacturer Becoming Service Provider— Challenges and a Paradox," *Managing Service Quality* 15/2 (2005): 142–55; Wayne A. Neu and Stephen A. Brown, "Forming Successful Business-to-Business Services in Goods-Dominant Firms," *Journal of Service Research* 8 (August 2005): 3–17.

19. Theodore Levitt, *Marketing for Business Growth*, New York: McGraw-Hill, 1974: 5.

20. Roland Rust, "What is the Domain of Service Research?", (editorial), *Journal of Service Research* 1 (November 1998): 107.

21. *IBM Annual Report 2004*, Armonk, NY: International Business Machines Corporation, 2005 (available online at ftp://ftp.software.ibm.com/annualreport/2004/2004_ibm _annual.pdf).

22. G. Lynn Shostack, "Breaking Free from Product Marketing," *Journal of Marketing* 41 (April 1977):73–80.

23. W. Earl Sasser, R. Paul Olsen, and D. Daryl Wyckoff, *Management of Service Operations: Text, Cases, and Readings*, Boston: Allyn & Bacon, 1978.

24. William R. George and Leonard L. Berry, "Guidelines for the Advertising of Services," *Business Horizons* (July–August 1981): 52–56; Banwari Mittal, "The Advertising of Services: Meeting the Challenge of Intangibility," *Journal of Service Research* 2 (August 1999): 98–116; Banwari Mittal and Julie Baker, "Advertising Strategies for Hospitality Services," *Cornell Hotel and Restaurant Administration Quarterly* 43 (April 2002): 51–63.

25. Valarie A. Zeithaml, "How Consumer Evaluation Processes Differ between Goods and Services," in J.A. Donnelly and W.R. George, *Marketing of Services*, Chicago: American Marketing Association, 1981: 186–90.

26. Flanagan, Johnston, and Talbot, op. cit.

27. The term "partial employee" was coined by P.K. Mills and D.J. Moberg, "Perspectives on the Technology of Service Operations," *Academy of Management Review* 7/3 (1982): 467–78. For recent research on this topic, see: Karthik Namasivayam, "The Consumer as Transient Employee: Consumer Satisfaction through the Lens of Job-performance Models," *International Journal of Service Industry Management* 14/4 (2004): 420–35; An-Tien Hsieh, Chang-Hua Yen, and Ko-Chien Chin, "Participative

Customers as Partial Employees and Service Provider Workload," *International Journal of Service Industry Management* 15/2 (2004): 187–200.

28. Matthew L. Meuter, Mary Jo Bitner, Amy L. Ostrom, and Stephen W. Brown, "Choosing Among Alternative Delivery Modes: An Investigation of Customer Trial of Self Service Technologies," *Journal of Marketing* 69 (April 2005): 61–84.

29. Devashish Pujari, "Self-service with a Smile: Self-service Technology (SST) Encounters among Canadian Business-to-business," *International Journal of Service Industry Management* 15/2 (2004): 200–219; Angus Laing, Gillian Hogg, and Dan Winkelman, "The Impact of the Internet on Professional Relationships: The Case of Health Care," *Service Industries Journal* 25 (July 2005): 675–88.

30. Matthew L. Meuter, Amy Ostrom, Robert Roundtree, and Mary Jo Bitner, "Self-Service Technologies: Understanding Customer Satisfaction with Technology-Based Service Encounters," *Journal of Marketing* 64 (July 2000): 50–64; A. Parasuraman, Valarie Zeithaml, and Arvind Malhotra, "E-S-QUAL: A Multiple Item Scale for Assessing Electronic Service Quality," *Journal of Service Research* 7 (February 2005): 213–33.

31. Philip J. Coelho and Chris Easingwood, "Multiple Channel Systems in Services: Pros, Cons, and Issues," *Service Industries Journal* 24 (September 2004): 1–30.

32. Bonnie Farber Canziani, "Leveraging Customer Competency in Service Firms," *International Journal of Service Industry Management* 8/1 (1997): 5–25.

33. Gary Knisely, "Greater Marketing Emphasis by Holiday Inns Breaks Mold," *Advertising Age* (January 15, 1979), 47–51.

34. Gary Stix, "Real Time," *Scientific American* (September 2002): 36–39.

35. Coelho and Easingwood, op. cit.

36. The 4Ps classification of marketing decision variables was created by E. Jerome McCarthy, *Basic Marketing: A Managerial Approach,* Homewood, IL: Richard D. Irwin, 1960. It was a refinement of a longer list of marketing ingredients created by Professor Neil Borden at Harvard University in the 1950s. Borden got the idea from a colleague who described a marketing manager's job as being a "mixer of ingredients."

37. An expanded 7Ps marketing mix was first proposed by Bernard H. Booms and Mary J. Bitner, "Marketing Strategies and Organization Structures for Service Firms," in J.H. Donnelly and W.R. George, *Marketing of Services,* Chicago: American Marketing Association, 1981: 47–51. The eighth P, productivity and quality, was added by Christopher Lovelock and Lauren Wright, *Principles of Service Marketing and Management,* Upper Saddle River, NJ: Prentice Hall, 1999.

38. For a review of the literature on this topic, see Michael D. Hartline and O.C. Ferrell, "The Management of Customer Contact Service Employees," *Journal of Marketing* 60/4 (October 1996): 52–70.

39. The term "part-time marketer" was coined by Evert Gummesson in "The New Marketing: Developing Long-Term Interactive Relationships," *Long Range Planning* 20/4 (1987): 10–20. See also Christian Grönroos, *Service Management and Marketing,* 2nd ed., Chichester, UK: John Wiley, 2001; and Evert Gummesson, *Total Relationship Marketing,* 2nd ed., Oxford: Butterworth Heinemann, 2002.

40. The term "servicescape" was coined by Mary Jo Bitner in "Servicescapes: The Impact of Physical Surroundings on Customers and Employees," *Journal of Marketing* 56 (April 1992): 57–71.

CHAPTER 2

Customer Behaviour in Service Encounters

The single most important thing to remember about any enterprise is that there are no results inside its walls. The result of a business is a satisfied customer.

—Peter Drucker

All the world's a stage and all the men and women merely players; they have their exits and their entrances and one man in his time plays many parts.

—William Shakespeare
As You Like It

Understanding customer behaviour lies at the heart of marketing. Without this understanding, no organization can hope to create and deliver services that will result in satisfied customers.

In order to develop effective marketing strategies, we first need to understand why customers use services, and how they choose between competing service suppliers. Our interest then shifts to examining the nature of the encounters that customers have with their chosen service provider during service delivery and consumption. How are customers interacting with service facilities, service personnel, and even other customers? What are their expectations at each step in service delivery? Finally, we should determine whether or not the experience of using the service and receiving its benefits has met customers' expectations and left them satisfied and ready to repurchase in the future.

An important theme in this chapter is that not all services are alike and that differences among services have important implications for customer behaviour. In particular, "high-contact" encounters between customers and service organizations differ sharply from "low-contact" encounters. The nature of some services, such as restaurants, hair stylists, dental services, and airlines, requires customers to visit their facilities and engage in face-to-face interactions with employees. By contrast, customers of service industries such as credit card and cable TV rarely, if ever, visit the supplier's offices; even if something goes wrong or they wish to make changes, they will generally speak to a representative by phone, mail a letter, or send an email.

In this chapter, we analyze the nature of service consumption and consider how firms should manage encounters to create satisfied customers and desirable outcomes for the business itself. We introduce four categories of services, and show how the extent of customer contact—and the nature of the underlying delivery processes—affect both the nature of the service encounter and customer behaviour.

We explore the following questions:

1. What are the four broad categories of services? And why does each pose such distinctive service-management challenges?

2. What is the Three-Stage Model of service consumption? And which perspectives help us to understand and better manage consumer behaviour at each stage?

3. What perceived risks do customers face in selecting, purchasing, and using services? And how can firms reduce consumer risk perceptions?

4. How do customers form expectations of service?

5. How do role theory and script theory help to understand consumer behaviour during the service encounter?

6. What insights can be gained from viewing service delivery as a form of theatre?

DIFFERENCES BETWEEN SERVICES AFFECT CUSTOMER BEHAVIOUR

Important marketing-relevant differences exist between services. These differences include whether service is targeted at customers in person or at their possessions, whether service actions and output are tangible or intangible in nature, whether customers need to be involved in service production; and how much contact (if any) they need to have with service facilities, employees, and other customers.

We turn to the most fundamental of the 8Ps (see Chapter 1)—the *processes* by which service products are created and delivered—to categorize services in ways that help us understand how these and other relevant differences arise, and what they mean for customer behaviour.

Four Broad Categories of Services

Marketers don't usually need to know the specifics of how physical goods are manufactured—that responsibility belongs to the people who run the factory. However, the situation is different in services. Because their customers are often involved in service production, and may have preferences for certain methods of service delivery, marketers must understand the nature of the processes through which services are created and delivered.

As you learned in Chapter 1, a *process* is a particular method of operation or a series of actions, typically involving multiple steps that often need to take place in a defined sequence. Think about the steps that a customer goes through at a dentist for a regular cleaning and check-up: phoning in advance to make an appointment, arriving at the dentist's office, waiting for the dental hygienist, undergoing a check-up and cleaning with the dental hygienist, waiting for a final check-up by the dentist, paying after the final check-up, setting up the next appointment, and finally leaving the dentist's office. Service processes range from relatively simple procedures involving only a few steps—such as filling a car's tank with fuel at a local gas station—to highly complex activities like transporting passengers on a non-stop flight from Toronto to New Delhi.

From an operational perspective, a process involves taking inputs and transforming them into output. But what is each service organization actually processing, and how does it perform this task? Three broad categories of things are processed in services: people, physical objects, and data. In many cases, ranging from health clubs to education, customers themselves are the principal input to the service process. In other instances, the key input is an object (whether material or abstract) like a defective machine or a piece of financial data. In some services, as in all manufacturing, the process is physical, and something tangible takes place. But where data is concerned, as in services such as insurance or research, the process can be almost entirely intangible.

Viewing services from this perspective, we can categorize them into four broad groups (Figure 2.1), based on tangible actions to either people's bodies or to customer's physical possessions, and intangible actions to either people's minds or to their intangible assets.[1]

We refer to these categories as *people processing, possession processing, mental-stimulus processing,* and *information processing.* Although the industries within each category may appear at first sight to be very different, analysis will show that they do, in fact, share important process-related characteristics. As a result, managers from different industries within the same category may obtain useful insights by studying another, related industry,

Figure 2.1

Four Categories
of Services

	Who or What Is the Direct Recipient of the Service?	
What Is the Nature of the Service Act?	**People**	**Possessions**
Tangible Actions	**People processing** (services directed at people's bodies): Passenger transportation Health care Lodging Beauty salons Physical therapy Fitness centres Restaurants/bars Barbers Funeral services	**Possession processing** (services directed at physical possessions): Freight transportation Repair and maintenance Warehousing/storage Office cleaning services Retail distribution Laundry and dry cleaning Refuelling Landscaping/gardening Disposal/recycling
Intangible Actions	**Mental-stimulus processing** (services directed at people's minds): Advertising/PR Arts and entertainment Broadcasting/cable Management consulting Education Information services Music concerts Psychotherapy Religion Voice telephone	**Information processing** (services directed at intangible assets): Accounting Banking Data processing Data transmission Insurance Legal services Programming Research Securities investment Software consulting

and then create useful innovations for their own organization. We now examine why these four different types of processes often have distinctive implications for marketing, operations, and human resource strategies.

People Processing

From ancient times, people have sought out services directed at themselves—being transported, fed, lodged, restored to health, or made more beautiful. To receive these types of services, customers must physically enter the service system. Why? Because they are an integral part of the process and cannot obtain the desired benefits by dealing at arm's length with service suppliers. In short, they must enter the *service factory*, a physical location where people or machines (or both) create and deliver service benefits to customers. Sometimes, of course, service providers are willing to come to customers, bringing the necessary tools of their trade to create the desired benefits at the customers' preferred location.

If you, as a customer, want the benefits that a people-processing service has to offer, you must also be prepared to co-operate actively with the service operation. For example, if you wanted to have a haircut, you would have to co-operate with the hairstylist by either specifying what you want or seeking the stylist's advice, and sitting still or moving your head as requested by the stylist until the haircut is complete. If you needed an eye exam, the optometrist would ask you to submit to a number of tests and, for those that checked the acuity of your vision, to report what you saw on the chart or other display.

The amount of time required of customers in people-processing services varies widely, ranging from boarding a city bus for a short ride to undergoing a lengthy course of treatments at a hospital. In between these extremes are such activities as ordering and eating a meal; having hair washed, cut, and styled; and spending several nights in a hotel room. The output from these services (after a period of time that can vary from minutes to months) is a customer who has reached her destination or satisfied his hunger, is now sporting clean and stylishly cut hair or has had a good night's sleep away from home, or is now in physically better health.

Managers need to pay attention not only to the service output but also to the service process from the standpoint of what happens to the customer (or the physical object being processed). Reflecting on the service process helps to identify not only what benefits are being created at each point in the process, but also the non-financial costs incurred by the customer in terms of time, mental and physical effort, and even (in such cases as a visit to the dentist) fear and pain.

Possession Processing

Often, customers ask a service organization to provide tangible treatment for some physical possession—a house that has been invaded by insects, a hedge that has grown too high, a malfunctioning snow blower, a parcel that needs to be sent to another city, dirty clothes, or a sick pet.

Many such activities are quasi-manufacturing operations and do not involve simultaneous production and consumption. Examples include cleaning, maintaining, storing, improving, or repairing physical objects—both living and inanimate—that belong to the customer in order to extend their usefulness. Additional possession-processing services include transport and storage of goods; wholesale and retail distribution; and installation, removal, and disposal of equipment—in short, the entire value-adding chain of activities that may take place during the lifetime of the object in question. The actual service process could involve applying insecticide to a house to get rid of ants, trimming a hedge at an office park, repairing the snow blower, sending a box of chocolates on Valentine's Day via expedited postal services, cleaning a jacket, or giving an injection to the family dog. In each instance, the output should be a satisfactory solution to the customer's problem.

Customers are less physically involved with this type of service than with people-processing services. Consider the difference between a passenger being transported from Calgary to Atlanta and a parcel making the same trip. In the former, the passenger has to physically board a plane at Calgary's airport to obtain the benefit of travelling to Atlanta. But with parcels, one can drop the package off at a mailbox or post office counter (or request a courier to collect it from the home or office) and wait for it to be delivered to the recipient in Atlanta.

In most possession-processing services, the customer's involvement is usually limited to dropping off the item that needs processing, requesting the service, explaining the service requirements, and later returning to pick up the item and pay the bill. In such instances, production and consumption can be described as *separable*. However, in some instances, the customer may prefer to be present during service delivery, perhaps wishing to supervise cutting of the hedge, or to comfort the family dog while it receives an injection at the veterinary clinic.

Mental-Stimulus Processing

Services directed at people's minds include education, news and information, professional advice, psychotherapy, entertainment, and certain religious activities. Anything affecting people's minds has the power to shape attitudes and influence behaviour. So, when customers are in a position of dependency or there is potential for manipulation, strong ethical standards and careful oversight are required. Obtaining the full benefit of such services requires an investment of time and a degree of mental effort on the customer's part. However, recipients don't necessarily have to be physically present in a service factory—thanks to writing and telecommunications, they need only be mentally in communication with the information being presented. There's an interesting contrast here with people-processing services. You can sleep through a flight and still arrive at your desired destination. But if you fall asleep in class or during an educational teleconference session, you won't be any wiser at the end than at the beginning!

Services such as entertainment and education are often created in one place and transmitted by television, radio or the internet to individual customers in distant locations.

Figure 2.2

A Live Performance by the Toronto Symphony Orchestra

However, they can also be delivered to groups of customers at the originating location in a facility such as a theatre or lecture hall. As you know, watching a live concert on television does not give the same experience as watching it in person in the company of hundreds or even thousands of other people. Managers of concert halls face many of the same challenges as their colleagues in people-processing services. Similarly, the experience of participating in a discussion-based class through teleconferencing lacks the intimacy of people debating one another in the same room.

Because the core content of services in this category is information based (whether that information be in the form of music, voice, or visual images), it can be converted to digital bits or analog signals; recorded for posterity; and transformed into a manufactured product, such as a CD or DVD, which may then be packaged and marketed much like any other physical good. For instance, the Toronto Symphony Orchestra's concerts can be attended live, viewed or heard live or pre-recorded on TV, or sold as digital recordings (Figure 2.2). Once in this form, services in this category can thus be "inventoried" for consumption at a later date than their production. In fact, the same performance can be consumed repeatedly. For some customers, purchasing an educational video to play at home may be a better solution than taking a class. Increasingly, customers can download electronic content such as music and video through their computers from a supplier such as Apple's iTunes Music Store, or TV through their cellphones via wireless service providers such as Bell Mobility.

Information Processing

Information processing has been revolutionized by computers. But not all information is processed by machines. Professionals in a wide variety of fields also use their brains to perform information processing and packaging. Information is the most intangible form of service output, but it may be transformed into more enduring, tangible forms such as letters, reports, books, CDs, or DVDs. Among the services that are highly dependent on the effective collection and processing of information are financial services and professional services such as accounting, law, marketing research, management consulting, and medical diagnosis.

At times, the line between information processing and mental-stimulus processing becomes blurred. For instance, a stockbroker may use an analysis of your brokerage transactions to recommend the most appropriate type of investment strategy for the future. A lawyer in a corporate law firm may spot patterns that pose legal risks for clients and advise them accordingly. And market researchers may see opportunities to publish useful insights that they have gained from reviewing trends over time. For simplicity, we will periodically combine our coverage of mental-stimulus processing services and information processing services under the umbrella term of *information-based services*.

Insights and Implications

The preceding discussion has a clear implication for managers of service industries. While the differences between the four categories suggest that it might be unwise to overgeneralize, at the same time, managers in a particular service industry shouldn't fall into the trap of believing that their situation is unique and they have nothing to learn from any other service industry.

As customers, the nature of our involvement in service production varies widely and is also changing rapidly. We have to visit the service factory for people processing, but not for the other types of services—although tradition or personal preferences may still lead us to do so. For example, it is widely known that older bank customers use ATMs less frequently than younger customers. Our choices may reflect such factors as whether we like to be served by employees face to face or prefer to engage in self-service, whether we're willing to travel to a service facility or prefer to obtain service from a remote location such as our home or office, how sociable we are, and how tightly we budget our time for conducting service transactions. The consumption activities associated with some types of services are inherently tangible in nature, others are intangible. Information-based service output can be recorded and stored for later use, thus offering customers greater convenience and more control over how they use their time.

The extent of customer involvement in both information and mental-stimulus processing is often determined more by tradition and a personal desire to meet the supplier face to face than by the needs of the operational process. Strictly speaking, personal contact is usually quite unnecessary in industries like banking or insurance (providing all systems are functioning properly). As a customer, why go to the service factory when there's no compelling need to do so? In practice, habit and tradition often lie at the root of existing service-delivery systems and consumption patterns. Professionals and their clients may say they prefer to meet face to face because they feel they thus learn more about each other's needs, capabilities, and personalities. However, experience shows that successful personal relationships, built on trust, can be created and maintained through arm's-length contact via telephone and email.

CUSTOMER DECISION MAKING: THE THREE-STAGE MODEL OF SERVICE CONSUMPTION

Consumption of a service involves all consumer activities linked to its purchase and use. To develop effective marketing strategies, we must understand how people make decisions about buying and using a service, what the experience of service delivery and consumption is like for customers, and how they evaluate that experience.

Service consumption can be divided into three principal stages: pre-purchase, service encounter, and post-encounter. As shown in Figure 2.3, each stage in the Three-Stage Model of Service Consumption contains two or more steps. However, as noted on the left-hand side of the diagram, the nature of these steps often varies between high- and low-contact services. Furthermore, at each stage, different concepts offer insights that can help us to understand, analyze, and manage what is taking place. On the right-hand side of the diagram, you will find the key concepts discussed in this chapter.

Pre-purchase Stage   A person's decision to buy and use a service reflects an unmet need or want. Are there dirt marks on the suit that you're planning to wear for that important interview next week? Does your car need an oil and filter change? Are you feeling hungry? Do you need help in preparing your tax return? Are you looking to fly some-

Figure 2.3 The Three-Stage Model of Service Consumption

High-Contact Services	Low-Contact Services		Key Concepts
		1. PRE-PURCHASE STAGE	
		Awareness of Need	*Need arousal*
Can visit physical sites, observe	Surf web, phone calls, visit library	**Information search**	
		• Clarify needs	
(+ low-contact options)		• Explore solutions	*Evoked set*
		• Identify alternative service products and suppliers	*Search, experience, and credence attributes*
		Evaluation of alternatives (solutions and suppliers)	*Perceived risk*
		• Review supplier information (e.g., advertising, brochures, websites, etc.)	
		• Review information from third parties (e.g., published reviews, ratings, comments on web, blogs, complaints to public agencies, satisfaction ratings, awards)	*Formation of expectations* - *desired service level* - *predicted service level* - *adequate service level* - *zone of tolerance*
Can visit in person and observe (possibly test) facilities, equipment, operation in action; meet personnel, see customers (+ remote options)	Primarily remote contact (websites, blogs, phone, email, publications, etc.)	• Discuss options with service personnel • Get advice and feedback from third party advisers, other customers	
		Make decision on service purchase	
		2. SERVICE ENCOUNTER STAGE	
At physical site (or remote reservation)	Remote	**Request service from chosen supplier or initiate self-service** (payment may be upfront or billed later)	*Moments of truth* *Service encounters* *Servuction system*
At physical site *only*	Remote	**Service delivery by personnel or self-service**	*Role and script theories* *Theatre as metaphor*
		3. POST-ENCOUNTER STAGE	
		Evaluation of service performance	*Confirmation/disconfirmation of expectations* *Dissatisfaction, satisfaction, and delight*
		Future intentions	

where warm and tropical during the winter? Once you recognize a need, you start to look for a solution, and that requires searching for information and sometimes advice. While these scenarios apply to a consumer context, the concept of unmet needs applies equally to organizations. Organizations also have needs, and corporate-purchasing decisions, while often more complex than those of individuals and households, also seek to find appropriate solutions.

If your purchase is routine and relatively low risk, you may move quickly to selecting and using a specific service provider. Indeed, many of your decisions involve simply repeating your previous usage behaviour. But in situations where more is at stake, or you're using a service for the first time, you may be willing to invest time and effort to figure out your requirements more precisely, learning about the pros and cons of possible courses of action, and identifying and evaluating alternative suppliers (contrast, for instance, how you approached the process of choosing a university or a college versus deciding where to go for an inexpensive meal.) The next step is to identify potential service providers and then weigh the benefits and risks of each option before making a final decision. By this point, you have developed some expectations about the nature of your forthcoming service experience and the benefits that you anticipate.

Service Encounter Stage After making a purchase decision, customers move on to the core of the service experience: the service encounter stage. It includes a series of contacts with the chosen service provider (or its designated agents). This stage often begins with placing an order, requesting a reservation, or even submitting an application (consider the process of obtaining a loan, seeking insurance coverage, or getting into college or university). Contacts may take the form of personal exchanges between customers and service employees, or arm's-length interactions with the service provider through machines or computers. In high-contact services such as restaurants, hair styling, hotels, and passenger transportation, customers may become actively involved in one or more stages of the service-delivery process, each of which may provide clues to service quality. During service delivery, many customers start evaluating the quality of service they are receiving and deciding whether it meets their expectations.

Post-Encounter Stage During this stage, customers continue the ongoing evaluation of service quality that they began earlier. Depending on whether or not their expectations were met, this evaluation may lead them to feel satisfaction or dissatisfaction with the service experience, an outcome that will affect their future intentions, such as whether or not to remain loyal to the provider that delivered service and whether to pass on positive or negative recommendations to family members and other associates.

THE PRE-PURCHASE STAGE

The pre-purchase stage begins with *need arousal*—the prospective customer's awareness of a need—and continues through information search and evaluation of alternatives to a decision on whether or not to make a service purchase.

Customers Seek Solutions to Aroused Needs

People buy goods and services to meet some specific needs or wants. Some needs are often deeply rooted in people's unconscious minds and may concern issues relating to personal identity and aspirations. Other needs, such as alleviating hunger (a short-term issue but one that arises several times daily) or dealing with, say, chronic back pain (a long-term problem), are more overt because they're based on the customer's physical condition. External sources, including marketing activities, may also stimulate awareness of a need. Although we are used to seeing these marketing activities originate from private-sector companies, they are also used effectively by public-sector organizations in creating awareness about social issues. As shown in Figure 2.4, the Government of Ontario uses advertising to urge people to think about being tested for Hepatitis C, encouraging them to visit

Figure 2.4

The Government of Ontario's advertising aims to stimulate thinking about a need to get tested for Hepatitis C.

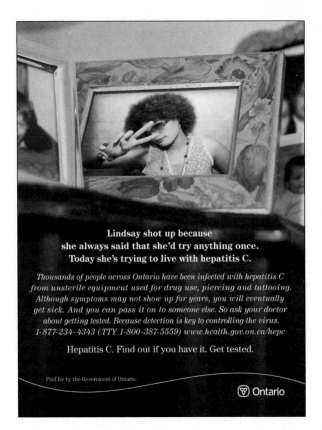

Lindsay shot up because she always said that she'd try anything once. Today she's trying to live with hepatitis C.

Thousands of people across Ontario have been infected with hepatitis C from unsterile equipment used for drug use, piercing and tattooing. Although symptoms may not show up for years, you will eventually get sick. And you can pass it on to someone else. So ask your doctor about getting tested. Because detection is key to controlling the virus.
1-877-234-4343 (TTY 1-800-387-5559) www.health.gov.on.ca/hepc

Hepatitis C. Find out if you have it. Get tested.

Paid for by the Government of Ontario.

Ontario

a website or call a toll-free number where they can learn more about their options. When people recognize a need, they are more likely to be motivated to take action to resolve it.

In developed economies, increased spending on more elaborate vacations, sports, entertainment, restaurant meals, and other service experiences is assuming greater priority for consumers, even at the expense of spending slightly less on physical goods. This shift in consumer behaviour and attitudes provides opportunities for those service companies that understand and meet changing needs. Some astute service providers have capitalized on the increased interest in extreme sports by offering such services as guided mountain climbs, paragliding, whitewater rafting trips and heliskiing (Figure 2.5). The notion of the service experience also extends to business and industrial situations; consider the example of modern trade shows, where exhibitors, including manufacturers, set out to engage the customer's interest through interactive presentations and even entertainment.[2]

As they review and clarify their needs, consumers can start to explore potential solutions and suppliers. Alternative solutions might involve deciding between different approaches to addressing the same basic problem, such as hiring a landscaping firm to cut down a dying tree in your yard as opposed to buying a chainsaw and doing it yourself. Or choosing between going out to a movie theatre, renting a DVD to play at home, or downloading an on-demand movie from your cable service company. And, of course, there's always the alternative of doing nothing—at least for the time being. The alternatives that consumers consider actively are known as the *evoked set*, which is derived from options that consumers remember from past experience and exposure, plus new options that are highlighted by external sources, including advertising, retail displays, news stories, and recommendations from both service personnel and other customers.

Evaluating a Service May Be Difficult

Many services—especially those that contain few tangible clues—can be difficult to evaluate before purchase. As a result, customers may worry about the risk of making a purchase that subsequently proves to be disappointing. If you buy a physical good that proves unsatisfactory, you can usually return or replace it—although it may take extra

Figure 2.5

TLH Heliskiing offers customers access to skiing in the pristine Chilcotin Mountains of British Columbia.

effort on your part to do so. These options are not as readily available with services. Although some services can be repeated, such as re-cleaning clothes that have not been satisfactorily laundered, this is not a practical solution in the case of a poorly performed play or a badly taught course (do you really want to take "principles of cost accounting" again next semester?).

Ease or difficulty of evaluation in advance of purchase is a function of product attributes. Many goods and some services are relatively high in *search attributes*—tangible characteristics that customers can evaluate prior to purchase. More complex goods and most services, by contrast, emphasize *experience attributes* such as reliability, ease of use, and customer support, that inexperienced purchasers can only discern during delivery and consumption. Finally, there are *credence attributes*, characteristics that customers find hard to evaluate even after consumption—often relating to the benefits actually delivered.[3] When discussing these three dimensions, we should be careful not to over-generalize. In particular, there may be a big difference between an experienced customer's ability to evaluate a service and a first-time user's.

Search Attributes   These characteristics help customers to evaluate a product before purchasing it. Style, colour, texture, taste, and sound are features that allow prospective consumers to try out, taste test, or "test drive" the product prior to purchase. These tangible attributes help customers understand and evaluate what they will get in exchange for their money, and reduce the sense of uncertainty or risk associated with the purchase occasion. Clothing, furniture, cars, electronic equipment, and foods are among the manufactured products that are high in search attributes. Search attributes are found in many service environments, too. For example, you can assess many attributes before visiting a particular restaurant, including the type of food, location and availability of parking, the positioning of the restaurant (e.g., fine dining, casual, family-type restaurant, etc.), and the price level. Other examples might include asking a hotel clerk to let you look at alternate rooms, checking out a golf course without actually playing a round, or taking a tour of a fitness facility and sampling one or two pieces of equipment.

Experience Attributes   Attributes that can't be evaluated prior to purchase must be "experienced" by the customer for them to know what they are getting. In our restaurant example, it is only by consuming the service that you will know how much you actually like the food, or the service provided by your waiter, or the atmosphere in the restaurant on that particular evening.

Holidays, live entertainment performances, sporting events, and many medical procedures fall into this category. Although people can examine brochures, scroll through websites describing a specific holiday destination, view travel films, or read reviews by travel experts, they can't really evaluate or feel the dramatic beauty associated with, say, hiking in the Canadian Rockies or scuba diving in the Caribbean until they experience these activities. Nor can customers always rely on information from friends, family, or other personal sources when evaluating these and similar services, because different people may interpret or respond to the same stimuli in different ways. Consider your own experiences in following up on recommendations from friends to see a particular movie. Perhaps you can recall an occasion when you walked into the theatre with high expectations, but felt disappointed afterward because you simply didn't like the movie as much as your friends did.

Credence Attributes   Product characteristics that customers find impossible to evaluate confidently even after purchase and consumption are known as credence attributes, because the customer is forced to trust that certain tasks have been performed from which benefits will result. In our restaurant example, credence attributes include the hygiene conditions of the kitchen and the healthiness of the cooking ingredients.

It's often not easy for a customer to determine the quality of repair and maintenance work performed on a car, household appliance, or piece of industrial machinery. Patients usually can't immediately evaluate how well their dentists have performed complex dental procedures. And consider the purchase of professional services. People seek such assistance precisely because they lack the necessary training and expertise themselves—think about counselling, surgery, legal advice, and consulting services. How can you really be sure after the fact that the best possible job was done? Sometimes it comes down to a matter of having confidence in the provider's skills (Figure 2.6).

Uncertainty about the Outcomes Increases Perceived Risk

Perceived risk is especially relevant for services that are difficult to evaluate prior to purchase and consumption. First-time users are likely to face greater uncertainty. Think about how you felt the first time you had to make decisions about choosing and using an unfamiliar service, especially one with important consequences. It's likely that you worried about the probability of a negative outcome. The worse the possible outcome, and the more likely it is to occur, the higher the perception of risk. Table 2.1 outlines seven categories of perceived risks.

Figure 2.6

Eye surgeons need to create confidence about their expertise.

Table 2.1 Perceived Risks in Purchasing and Using Services

Type of Risk	Examples of Customer Concerns
Functional (unsatisfactory performance outcomes)	• Will this training course give me the skills I need to get a better job? • Will this credit card be accepted wherever and whenever I want to make a purchase? • Will the dry cleaner be able to remove the stains from this jacket?
Financial (monetary loss, unexpected costs)	• Will I lose money if I make the investment recommended by my stockbroker? • Could my identity be stolen if I make this purchase on the internet? • Will I incur a lot of unanticipated expenses if I go on this vacation? • Will repairing my car cost more than the original estimate?
Temporal (wasting time, consequences of delays)	• Will I have to wait in line before entering the exhibition? • Will service at this restaurant be so slow that I will be late for my afternoon meeting? • Will the renovations to our bathroom be completed before our friends come to stay with us?
Physical (personal injury or damage to possessions)	• Will I get hurt if I go skiing at this resort? • Will the contents of this package get damaged in the mail? • Will I fall sick if I travel abroad on vacation?
Psychological (personal fears and emotions)	• How can I be sure that this aircraft won't crash? • Will the consultant make me feel stupid? • Will the doctor's diagnosis upset me?
Social (how others think and react)	• What will my friends think of me if they learn that I stayed at this cheap motel? • Will my relatives approve of the restaurant I have chosen for the family reunion dinner? • Will my business colleagues disapprove of my selection of an unknown law firm?
Sensory (unwanted effects on any of the five senses)	• Will I get a view of the parking lot rather than the beach from my restaurant table? • Will the hotel bed be uncomfortable? • Will I be kept awake by noise from the guests in the room next door? • Will my room smell of stale cigarette smoke? • Will the coffee at breakfast taste disgusting?

How Might Consumers Handle Perceived Risk? Individuals who feel uncomfortable with perceived risks during the pre-purchase stage can use a variety of methods to reduce them. In fact, you've probably tried some of the following risk-reduction strategies yourself before deciding to purchase a service:

- seeking information from respected personal sources (family, friends, peers)
- relying on a firm that has a good reputation
- looking for guarantees and warranties
- visiting service facilities or trying aspects of the service before purchasing
- asking knowledgeable employees about competing services
- examining tangible cues or other physical evidence
- using the web to compare service offerings and search for independent reviews and ratings

What Risk Reduction Strategies Can Service Suppliers Develop? Well-managed firms work hard to reduce the perceived risk of purchasing their services, especially when these are expensive and have durable outcomes. Strategies vary according to the nature of the service. They may include all or some of the following:

- offering performance warranties
- money-back (or service-repeat) guarantees
- enabling prospective customers to preview the service through brochures, websites, and videos
- encouraging prospective customers to visit the service facilities in advance of purchase
- instituting visible safety procedures

- training staff members to be respectful and empathetic in their dealings with customers
- providing 24/7 access by a toll-free telephone call to a customer service centre or informative website
- delivering automated messages about anticipated problems to a designated cellphone (e.g., airline will update customer on flight delays)
- giving customers access to online information about the status of an order or procedure.

Perhaps you've had the experience of tracking the progress of an important package sent by Canada Post, FedEx, DHL, UPS or another logistics firm. Knowing that you will be able to follow your package moving through the system can be very reassuring. So is dealing with a service representative who takes time to put you at your ease and answer all your questions in a helpful and straightforward manner. It gives you confidence that you'll make the right decisions, get solutions that are relevant for your situation, and feel afterwards that you obtained fair value in exchange for your money, time, and effort.

Strategic Responses to Managing Customer Perceptions of Risk Among the factors that cause services to be high in experience and credence attributes are that performances are transitory, many intangible elements are involved, and the variability of inputs and outputs often leads to quality-control problems. These characteristics present special challenges for service marketers, requiring them to find ways to reassure customers and reduce the perceived risks associated with buying and using services the performance and value of which can't easily be predicted, and may even be difficult to ascertain after consumption.

Marketers whose products are high in experience characteristics often try to create more search attributes to assist prospective customers. One approach is to offer a free trial. Some providers of online computer services have adopted this strategy. For example, in the past AOL Canada has offered potential users free software and the chance to try its services without charge for up to 1000 hours in a period of 45 days. This strategy reduces customers' concerns about entering into a paid contract without first being able to test the service. AOL hopes that consumers will be "hooked" on its web services by the end of the free trial period (Figure 2.7).

Advertising is another way to help customers visualize service benefits. For instance, the only tangible thing credit card customers get directly from the company is a small plastic card, followed at monthly intervals by an account statement. But that's hardly the essence of the benefits provided by this low-contact service. Think about the credit card

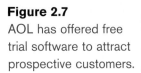

Figure 2.7
AOL has offered free trial software to attract prospective customers.

advertisements you've seen recently. Did they promote the card itself or did they feature exciting products you could purchase and exotic places to which you could travel by using your card? Such advertisements stimulate consumer interest by showing physical evidence of the benefits of credit card use. Insurance companies often use metaphors in their advertising. To demonstrate its fundamental strengths in helping protect Canadians from risks as well as providing guidance for management of their finances, The Equitable Life Insurance Company of Canada has used the symbol of the lighthouse (Figure 2.8). The company states: "Representing strength, stability and reliability, the lighthouse reinforces Equitable Life's continuing commitment to provide its customers with protection and guidance toward financial security."

Providers of services that are high in credence characteristics have an even greater challenge. Their benefits may be so intangible that customers can't evaluate the quality of what they've received even after the service has been purchased and consumed. In this case, marketers often try to provide tangible cues to customers about their services.

Professionals like doctors, architects, and lawyers often display their degrees and other certificates for the same reason—they want customers to "see" the credentials that qualify them to provide expert service. Many professional firms have developed websites to inform prospective clients about their services, highlight their expertise, and even showcase successful past engagements.

Evaluations of such services may be affected by customers' interactions with the physical setting of the business, with employees, and even with other customers. For example, your experience of a haircut may combine your impression of the hair salon, how well you can describe what you want to the stylist, the stylist's ability to understand and do what you've requested, and the appearance of the other customers and employees in the salon. Savvy organizations that have multiple points of contact with customers engage in *evidence management,* an organized and explicit approach to presenting customers with coherent evidence of their abilities in the form of clues emitted by their employees' dress and behaviour, and the appearance of furnishings, equipment, and facilities.[4]

Many credence services have few tangible characteristics and rely on the expertise of a professional service provider to provide a high-quality offering. In this case, providers must be able to interact with customers effectively to produce a satisfactory product. Problems can occur when this interaction doesn't produce an outcome that meets customers' expectations, even though the service provider may not be at fault.

Figure 2.8
Equitable Life® promotes its strengths in providing protection and guidance.

Understanding Customers' Service Expectations

Customers evaluate service quality by comparing what they expected with what they perceive they received from a particular supplier. If their expectations are met or exceeded, customers believe they have received high-quality service. Provided that the price/quality relationship is acceptable, and other situational and personal factors are positive, customers are likely to be satisfied and are therefore more likely to make repeat purchases and remain loyal to that supplier. However, if the service experience does not meet their expectations, customers may complain about poor service quality, suffer in silence, or switch providers in the future.[5] In highly competitive service markets, customers expect service providers to anticipate their needs and deliver on them more than ever.[6]

Customers' expectations about what constitutes good service vary from one business to another. For example, although accounting and veterinary surgery are both professional services, the experience of meeting an accountant to talk about your tax return is very different from visiting a vet to get treatment for your sick pet. Expectations are also likely to vary in relation to differently positioned service providers in the same industry. While travellers expect no-frills service for a short domestic flight on a discount carrier, they would undoubtedly be very dissatisfied with the same level of service if they encountered it on a full-service airline on a long-haul international route, even in economy class. When individual or corporate purchasers evaluate the quality of a service, they may be judging it against an internal standard that existed prior to the service experience.[7] Perceived service quality results from comparing the service that you perceived you obtained against what you expected to receive. People's expectations about services are influenced by prior experiences with a particular service provider, competing services in the same industry, or related services in different industries. If you have no relevant prior experience, you may base your pre-purchase expectations on word-of-mouth comments, news stories, or the firm's own marketing efforts. Smart firms manage customers' expectations at each step in the service encounter so that they do not expect more than the firm can deliver.[8]

Expectations change over time, too, being influenced by both supplier-controlled factors such as advertising, pricing, new technologies, and service innovation, as well as social trends, advocacy by consumer organizations, and increased access to information through the media and the internet. For instance, healthcare consumers are now better informed and often seek a more participatory role in decisions relating to medical treatment. Service Perspectives 2.1 describes a new assertiveness among Canadians with respect to their involvement in decision-making regarding health care accessibility.

Service Perspectives 2.1

Canadian Patients and Consumers Ready to be Involved in Health Decision-Making

According to the results of a new study, consumers and patients in Canada are keen to become involved in health technology assessment (HTA)—a process that helps determine what new treatments, procedures, and technologies should be covered by health plans. The study reports the results of interviews with Canadian voluntary health association leaders. Respondents were asked about the type of involvement they would be willing to have with regard to the assessment of treatments or therapies. The results indicate an enthusiastic response, with a vast majority expressing their willingness to be involved in health decision- making via participation in primary research (82 percent willing to fill out surveys, 80 percent willing to participate in focus groups, and 74 percent willing to participate in key informant interviews),

community involvement (71 percent willing to participate in community forums), and decision-making (88 percent willing to be part of a decision-making committee at the national level, 71 percent willing to be part of a decision-making committee at the provincial level). Decisions regarding the coverage of new treatments have a critical impact on the provision of health care to Canadians. The study shows that those Canadians most affected by health care decision-making want to participate actively in the decision-making process, even if it requires a significant commitment of time and effort. These findings highlight the importance that Canadians place on consumer and patient participation in HTA.

Source: www.consumeradvocare.org, accessed February 2006. Reprinted with permission of Consumer Advocare.

The Components of Customer Expectations Expectations embrace several elements, including desired service, adequate service, predicted service, and a zone of tolerance that falls between the desired and adequate service levels. The model shown in Figure 2.9, originated by Professors A. Parasuraman, Leonard Berry, and Valarie Zeithaml, shows how expectations for desired service and adequate service are formed.[9]

Desired and Adequate Service Levels The type of service customers hope to receive is termed *desired service*. It's a "wished for" level—a combination of what customers believe can and should be delivered in the context of their personal needs. However, most customers are realistic. Recognizing that a firm can't always deliver their preferred level of service, they also have a threshold level of expectations, termed *adequate service*, defined as the minimum level of service customers will accept without being dissatisfied. Among the factors that set this expectation are situational factors affecting service performance and the service level that might be anticipated from alternative suppliers. The levels of both desired and adequate service expectations may reflect explicit and implicit promises by the provider, word-of-mouth comments, and the customer's past experience (if any) with this organization.[10]

Predicted Service Level The level of service that customers actually anticipate receiving is known as *predicted service*, which directly affects how they define "adequate service" on that occasion. If good service is predicted, the level deemed "adequate" will be higher than if poorer service is predicted. Customer predictions of service may be situation-specific. From past experience, for example, customers visiting a museum on a summer day may expect to see larger crowds if the weather is poor than if the sun is shining. So a 10-minute wait to buy tickets on a cool, rainy day in summer might not fall below their adequate service level.

Zone of Tolerance It can be hard too for firms to achieve consistent delivery across all employees in the same company and even by the same employee from hour to hour or from one day to another. The extent to which customers are willing to accept this variation is called the *zone of tolerance* (see Figure 2.9) Performing too low causes frustration and dissatisfaction, whereas exceeding the desired service level should please and surprise customers. Another way of looking at the zone of tolerance is to think of it as the range of service within which customers don't pay explicit attention to service performance.[11] It is when service falls outside this range, above or below, that customers will react either positively or negatively.

Figure 2.9

Factors Influencing Customer Expectations of Service

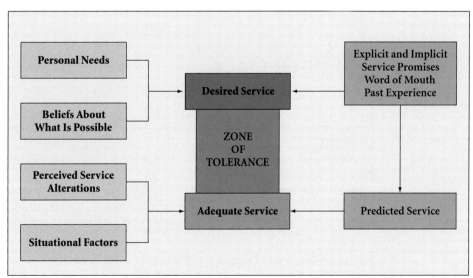

Source: Adapted from Valarie A. Zeithaml, Leonard L. Berry, and A. Parasuraman, "The Nature and Determinants of Customer Expectations of Service," *Journal of the Academy of Marketing Science* 21/1 (1993): 1–12.

The size of the zone of tolerance can increase or decrease for individual customers, depending on such factors as competition, price, or importance of specific service attributes, each of which can influence the level of adequate service levels. By contrast, desired service levels tend to move up very slowly in response to accumulated customer experiences. Consider a small-business owner who needs some advice from her accountant. Her ideal level of professional service may be a thoughtful response by the following day. But if she makes the request at the time of year when all accountants are busy preparing corporate and individual tax returns, she will probably know from experience not to expect a fast response. Although her ideal service level probably won't change, her zone of tolerance for response time may be broader because she has a lower adequate service threshold at busy times of year. On the other hand, a customer who's about to undergo a critical surgical procedure would have an almost negligible zone of tolerance in terms of service performance by the surgeon; his adequate and desired service levels would overlap almost completely.

It's important for firms to understand exactly how wide customers' zone of tolerance is. In a study of guests at four-star, five-star, and resort hotels in Northern Cyprus (in the eastern Mediterranean), Halil Nadiri and Kashif Hussain found a relatively narrow zone of tolerance between desired and adequate service levels.[12] Examination of individual attributes showed that customers were more sensitive about intangibles such as prompt service, employee courtesy, and convenience of operating hours than about tangibles such as physical facilities and modern-looking equipment.

Making a Service Purchase Decision

Having evaluated possible alternatives, the consumer may now be ready to make a decision, selecting one option in preference to the others. Many purchase decisions are quite simple and can be made fast, without too much thought—the perceived risks are low, the alternatives are clear and, because they have been used before, their characteristics are easily understood. If the consumer already has a favourite supplier, he or she will probably choose it again in the absence of a compelling reason to do otherwise.

But in many instances, decisions involve trade-offs. Price is often the key variable. Is it worth paying more for faster service, as in choosing between a taxi and a bus? Or for a better seat in a theatre so that you can be closer to the performers? Or for a larger rental car that will give family members more room on a long vacation drive? For more complex decisions, trade-offs can involve multiple attributes: in choosing an airline, convenience of schedules, reliability, seat comfort, attentiveness of cabin crew, and availability of meals may well vary between different carriers, even at the same fares. Once the decision has been made, the consumer is ready to move to the service encounter stage. This next step may take place immediately, as in deciding to hail a taxi or enter a quick-service food store, or may first involve an advance reservation, as usually happens when taking a flight or attending a live theatre performance.

THE SERVICE ENCOUNTER STAGE

Your experience of purchasing and consuming a service typically takes the form of a series of encounters. A *service encounter* is a period of time during which you, as a customer, interact directly with a service provider.[13] Although some of these encounters are very brief and consist of just a few steps—consider what is involved in a taxi ride or a phone call—others may extend over a longer time frame and involve multiple actions of varying degrees of complexity. A leisurely restaurant meal might stretch over a couple of hours, while a visit to a theme park might last all day. If you use a service that requires advance reservation, that first step might have taken place days or even weeks before arriving at the service facility.

Service Encounters as "Moments of Truth"

Richard Normann borrowed the metaphor of the "moment of truth" from bullfighting to show the importance of contact points with customers:

[W]e could say that the perceived quality is realized at the moment of truth, when the service provider and the service customer confront one another in the arena. At that moment they are very much on their own. . . . It is the skill, the motivation, and the tools employed by the firm's representative and the expectations and behavior of the client which together will create the service delivery process.[14]

In bullfighting, what is at stake is the life of either the bull or the matador (or possibly both). The moment of truth is the instant at which the matador is either gored by the bull, or deftly slays the bull with his sword—hardly a very comfortable analogy for a service organization intent on building long-term relationships with its customers! Normann's point, of course, is that it's the life of the relationship that is at stake. Contrary to bullfighting, the goal of relationship marketing—which we explore in depth in Chapter 12—is to prevent one unfortunate (mis)encounter from destroying what is already, or has the potential to become, a mutually valued, long-term relationship.

Jan Carlzon, the former chief executive of Scandinavian Airlines System, used the "moment-of-truth" metaphor as a reference point for transforming SAS from an operations-driven business into a customer-driven airline. Carlzon made the following comments about his airline:

Last year, each of our 10 million customers came into contact with approximately five SAS employees, and this contact lasted an average of 15 seconds each time. Thus, SAS is "created" 50 million times a year, 15 seconds at a time. These 50 million "moments of truth" are the moments that ultimately determine whether SAS will succeed or fail as a company. They are the moments when we must prove to our customers that SAS is their best alternative.[15]

Each service business faces similar challenges in defining and managing the moments of truth that its customers will encounter in that particular industry.

Service Encounters Range from High Contact to Low Contact

Each of the four categories of services described at the beginning of the chapter involves different levels of contact with the service operation. In Figure 2.10, we've grouped

Figure 2.10

Levels of Customer Contact with Service Organizations

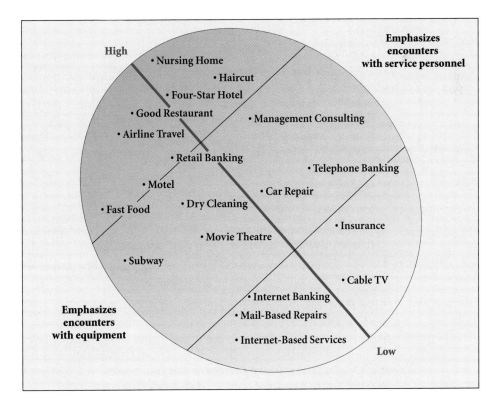

services into three levels of customer contact, representing the extent of interaction with service personnel, physical service elements, or both. You'll notice that traditional retail banking, person-to-person telephone banking, and internet banking are each located in very different parts of that chart. While recognizing that the level of customer contact covers a spectrum rather than being fixed, it's nevertheless useful to examine the differences between organizations at the high and low ends, respectively.

High-Contact Services   Using this type of service entails interaction throughout service delivery between customers and the organization. The customer's exposure to the service provider takes on a physical and tangible nature. When customers visit the facility where service is delivered, they enter a service "factory"—something that rarely happens in a manufacturing environment. Viewed from this perspective, a motel is a lodging factory, a hospital is a health-treatment factory, an airliner is a flying transportation factory, and a restaurant is a food-service factory. But because each of these industries focuses on "processing" people rather than inanimate objects, the marketing challenge is to make the experience an appealing one for customers in terms of both the physical environment and their interactions with service personnel. During the course of service delivery, customers are usually exposed to many physical clues about the organization—the exterior and interior of its buildings, equipment and furnishings, appearance and behaviour of service personnel, and even other customers.

Low-Contact Services   At the opposite end of the spectrum, low-contact services involve little, if any, physical contact between customers and service providers. Instead, contact takes place at arm's length through the medium of electronic or physical distribution channels—a fast-growing trend in today's convenience-oriented society. Many high-contact and medium-contact services are being transformed into low-contact services as customers undertake more self-service, conduct their insurance and banking transactions by mail, telephone, and internet, or research and purchase a host of information-based services by visiting websites rather than bricks-and-mortar facilities. As highlighted earlier in Figure 2.10, some service industries offer customers a choice of delivery systems featuring different levels of contact.

If you're like many people, you may alternate between high-contact and low-contact delivery channels in your use of retail banking services. The nature of your encounters with the bank varies accordingly.

The Servuction System

The French researchers Pierre Eiglier and Eric Langeard were the first to conceptualize the service business as a system that integrated marketing, operations, and customers themselves. They coined the term *servuction system* (combining the terms *service* and *production*) to describe that part of the service organization's physical environment that is visible to customers, contact personnel, other customers and—very importantly, the customer in person.[16] Christopher Lovelock subsequently expanded this conceptual framework to embrace three overlapping elements:

- *Service operations*, where inputs are processed and the elements of the service product are created

- *Service delivery*, where final "assembly" of these elements takes place and the product is delivered to the customer, often in the presence of other customers

- *Other contact points*, which embraces all points of contact with customers, including advertising, billing, and market research.

Parts of this system are visible (or otherwise apparent) to customers; other parts are hidden and, as Richard Chase points out, the customer may not even know of their existence.[17] Some writers use the terms "front office" and "back office" in referring to the visible and invisible parts of the operation. Others talk about "front stage" and "backstage," using the analogy of theatre to dramatize the notion that service is a performance.[18] We discuss this analogy in more detail later in the chapter.

Service Operations Like a theatrical play, the visible components of service operations can be divided into those relating to the actors (or service personnel) and those relating to the stage set (or physical facilities, equipment, and other tangibles). Like any audience, customers evaluate the production on those elements they actually experience during their encounters, and on the perceived service outcome. What goes on backstage is of little interest. Of course, if backstage personnel and systems (e.g., billing, ordering, and account keeping) fail to perform their support tasks properly, in ways that affect the quality of front-stage activities, customers will notice. For instance, a customer waiting to get his steeped tea and toasted bagel at the drive-thru window of a Tim Hortons will be disappointed if he is told that the steeped tea is temporarily unavailable or find that the bagel is burnt. The proportion of the overall service operation that is visible to customers varies according to the level of customer contact. Because high-contact services directly involve the physical person of the customer, the visible component of the service-operations element tends to be substantial.

Low-contact services usually strive to minimize customer contact with the service provider, so most of the service-operations element is confined to a remotely located backstage (sometimes referred to as a *technical core*); front-stage elements are often limited to mail and telecommunications contacts. Think for a moment about the telephone company that you use. Do you have any idea where its exchange is located? If you have a credit card, it's likely that your transactions are processed far from where you live.

Service Delivery Service delivery is concerned with where, when, and how the service product is delivered to the customer. This subsystem embraces not only the visible elements of the service-operating system—buildings, equipment, and personnel—but may also involve exposure to other customers. Continuing the theatrical analogy, the distinction between high-contact and low-contact services can be likened to the differences between live theatre on a stage and a drama created for television. That's because customers of low-contact services normally never see the "factory" where the work is performed; at most, they will talk with a service provider (or problem solver) by telephone. Without buildings and furnishings or even the appearance of employees to provide tangible clues, customers must make judgments about service quality based on ease of telephone access, followed by the voice and responsiveness of a telephone-based customer-service representative.

When service is delivered through impersonal electronic channels, such as self-service machines, interactive voice response (IVR) systems, or via the customer's own computer, there is very little traditional "theatre" left to the performance. Some firms compensate for this by giving their machines names, playing recorded music, installing moving colour graphics on video screens, adding sounds, and creating computer-based interactive capabilities to give the experience a more human feeling. Responsibility for designing and managing service delivery systems has traditionally fallen to operations managers. But marketing needs to be involved, too, to research how consumers behave during service delivery and ensure that the system is designed with their needs and concerns in mind.

Other Contact Points In addition to the service-delivery system, other elements that contribute to the customer's overall view of a service business include communication efforts by the advertising and sales departments, telephone calls and letters from service personnel, billings from the accounting department, random exposure to service personnel and facilities, news stories and editorials in the mass media, word-of-mouth comments from current or former customers, and even participation in market-research studies.

Service-Marketing Systems for High- and Low-Contact Services

Collectively, the visible part of service operations, service delivery, and other contact points add up to what we call the *service-marketing system*. This represents all the many different ways the customer may learn about and encounter the organization in question. Since services are experiential, each of these many elements offers clues about the nature and quality of the service product. Inconsistency between various elements may weaken the organization's credibility in the customer's eyes. Figure 2.11 depicts the service-marketing system for a high-contact service like a hotel, health club, or full-service restaurant.

Figure 2.11

The Service-Marketing System for a High-Contact Service

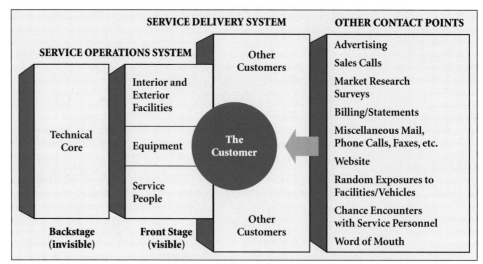

Source: Adapted and expanded from an original concept by Eric Langeard and Pierre Eiglier.

Figure 2.12 shows how things change when customers deal with a low-contact service, such as a credit card account or internet-based insurance firm, where, by definition, service encounters are unlikely to involve visits to company sites or meetings with service personnel. Instead, access to the service will be made through self-service equipment, either a card reader in a store, a kiosk at a remote location, or perhaps the customer's own computer. Additional contact will come through mailings or emailings from the company. The list of other contact points is also shorter. As a result, customers will have fewer encounters in each service transaction, and a failing at one "moment of truth" may therefore take on greater significance than in a high-contact environment.

An individual's behaviour often reflects personal attitudes and beliefs. Research published in 2000 by A. Parasuraman shows that customer readiness to accept new self-service technologies (SSTs) is associated with certain personal characteristics, which are factors of critical importance for companies seeking to persuade customers to use low-contact forms of service delivery. These attributes include innovativeness, a positive view of technology, and a belief that technology offers increased control, flexibility, and efficiency to people's lives.[19] Factors that are negatively associated with the adoption of technology include distrust, a perceived lack of control, feelings of being overwhelmed by technology, and skepticism about whether the technology will perform satisfactorily. Service providers must consider these factors before implementing new technologies that may negatively affect customers' evaluations of the service experience.

Figure 2.12

The Service-Marketing System for a Low-Contact Service

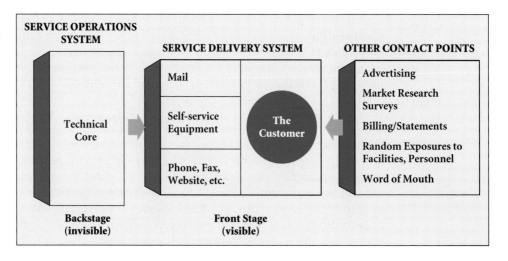

Role and Script Theories

The servuction model is static and describes a single service encounter or moment of truth. Service processes, however, usually consist of a series of encounters, such as your experience on a flight, from making the reservation, to checking in, taking the flight, and retrieving your bags on arrival. A knowledge of role and script theories can help us to understand, design, and manage both customer behaviour and employee behaviour during such encounters.

Roles   If we view service delivery from a theatrical perspective, then both employees and customers act out their parts in the performance according to predetermined *roles*. Stephen Grove and Ray Fisk define a role as "a set of behaviour patterns learned through experience and communication, to be performed by an individual in a certain social interaction in order to attain maximum effectiveness in goal accomplishment."[20] Roles have also been defined as combinations of social cues, or expectations of society, that guide behaviour in a specific setting or context.[21] In service encounters, employees and customers each have roles to play. The satisfaction and productivity of both parties depends on role congruence, or the extent to which each person acts out his or her prescribed role during a service encounter. Employees must perform their roles with reference to customer expectations, or risk dissatisfying or losing customers altogether. And customers too must "play by the rules," or risk causing problems for the firm, its employees and even other customers.

Scripts   Much like a movie script, a service script specifies the actions that customers and employees are expected to perform. Scripts are sequences of behaviour that both employees and customers are expected to learn and follow during service delivery. Customers learn scripts through experience, education, and communication with others.[22] The more experience a customer has with a service company, the more familiar that particular script becomes. Unwillingness to learn a new script may be a reason for a customer not to switch to a competing organization. Any deviations from this known script may frustrate both customers and employees, and can lead to high levels of dissatisfaction. If a company decides to change a service script (for example, grocery stores using self-checkout machines to transform a high-contact service into a low-contact one), service personnel and customers need to be educated about the new approach and the benefits it provides.

Some scripts are highly structured and allow service employees to move through their duties quickly and efficiently (like flight attendants' scripts for economy class). This approach helps to overcome two of the inherent challenges facing service firms—how to reduce variability and ensure uniform quality. The risk is that frequent repetition may lead to mindless service delivery that ignores customers' needs.

Not all services involve tightly scripted performances. Scripts tend to be more flexible for providers of highly customized services—such as designers, educators, hair stylists, or consultants—and may vary by situation and by customer. When customers are new to a service, they may not know what to expect and may be fearful of behaving incorrectly. Organizations should be ready to educate them about their roles in service delivery, since inappropriate behaviours can disrupt service delivery and make new customers feel embarrassed and uncomfortable.

A well-planned script prescribes what should take place during a service encounter, including the roles played by customers and service personnel at different points in the process. Figure 2.13 shows a script for teeth cleaning and a simple dental examination, involving three players—the patient, the receptionist, and the dental hygienist. Each has a specific role to play, reflecting what they bring to the encounter. The role of the customer (who is probably not looking forward to this encounter!) is different from that of the two service providers, and the receptionist's role differs from the hygienist's, reflecting their distinctive jobs. This script is driven partly by the need to run an efficient dental office, but even more importantly by the need to perform a technical task proficiently and safely (note the mask and gloves). The core service of examining and cleaning teeth can only be accomplished satisfactorily if the patient co-operates in delivery of a service that is at best neutral and at worst uncomfortable or even painful.

Figure 2.13

Script for Teeth Cleaning and Simple Dental Exam

Patient	Receptionist	Dental Hygienist
1. Phone for appointment	2. Confirm needs and set date	
3. Arrive at dental office	4. Greet patient; verify purpose; direct to waiting room; notify hygienist of arrival	5. Review notes on patient
6. Sit in waiting room		7. Greet patient and lead way to treatment room
8. Enter room; sit in dental chair		9. Verify medical and dental history; ask about any issues since previous visit
10. Respond to hygienist's questions		11. Place protective covers over patient's clothes
		12. Lower dental chair; put on own protective face mask, gloves, and glasses
		13. Inspect patient's teeth (option to ask questions)
		14. Place suction device in patient's mouth
		15. Use high-speed equipment and hand tools to clean teeth in sequence
		16. Remove suction device; complete cleaning process
		17. Raise chair to sitting position; ask patient to rinse
18. Rinse mouth		19. Remove and dispose of mask and gloves; remove glasses
		20. Complete notes on treatment; return patient file to receptionist
		21. Remove covers from patient
		22. Give patient free toothbrush; offer advice on personal dental care for future
23. Rise from chair		24. Thank patient and say good-bye
25. Leave treatment room	26. Greet patient; confirm treatment received; present bill	
27. Pay bill	28. Give receipt; agree on date for next appointment; document agreed-on date	
29. Take appointment card	30. Thank patient and say good-bye	
31. Leave dental office		

Several elements in this script relate to information flows. Confirming and honouring appointments avoids delays for customers and ensures effective use of dental professionals' time. Obtaining patient histories and documenting analysis and treatment is vital for maintaining complete dental records and also for accurate billing. Payment on receipt of treatment improves cash flow and avoids the problem of bad debts. And finally, adding greetings, statements of thanks, and farewells displays friendly good manners and helps to humanize what most people see as a slightly unpleasant experience.

Role theory and script theory govern both consumer and employee behaviour during an encounter. Think, for example, of professor and student *roles* in the lecture classes that you've attended. What is the role of the professor? Typically, it's to deliver a well-structured lecture, focusing on the key topics assigned for that day, making them interesting, and moderating the discussion with students. And what about the role of a student? Basically, it's to come to class prepared and on time, listen attentively, take notes, participate in discussions, and not disrupt the class. By contrast, the opening portion of the *script* for a lecture describes the actions to be taken by each party (for instance, students should arrive at the lecture hall before class starts, select a seat, sit down, and open their notebooks; the professor enters, puts notes on the table, turns on the projector, greets the class, makes any preliminary announcements that are needed, and starts the class on time). As you can see, the frameworks offered by the two theories are complementary, describing behaviour during the encounter from two different perspectives. Excellent service marketers understand perspectives, designing and managing service encounters accordingly.

Theatre as a Metaphor for Service Delivery: An Integrative Perspective

The theatre is a good metaphor for services, because service delivery consists of a series of events that customers experience as a *performance*.[23] It's a particularly useful approach for high-contact service providers, such as physicians, educators, restaurants, and hotels, and for businesses that serve many people simultaneously, such as professional sports, hospitals, and entertainment.

Imagine service facilities as containing the stage on which the drama unfolds. Sometimes the setting changes from one act to another (for example, when airline passengers move from the terminal entrance to the check-in stations and then on to the boarding lounge before finally stepping inside the aircraft). Some stages have minimal "props," as in a typical Canada Post outlet (those in other countries are often more attractively outfitted), or elaborate scenery (architecture, interior design, and landscaping), as in some modern resort hotels in places like Las Vegas. Many service dramas are tightly scripted (consider the formal style of service in the Passport Canada offices), while others are improvisational in nature (such as teaching a university seminar). In highly structured environments like dental services, "blocking" may define how the actors (in this case, receptionists, dental hygienists, technicians, and dentists) should move relative to the stage (the dentist's office), items of scenery (equipment and furnishings), and other actors.

Not all service providers require customers to attend performances at the company's "theatre," especially in a business-to-business context. In many instances, the customer's own facilities provide the stage where the service employees perform with their props. For example, outside accountants are often hired to provide specialized services at a client's site. (While this may be convenient for customers, it isn't always very appealing for the visiting accountants, who have sometimes found themselves housed in rat-infested basements or inventorying frozen food for hours in a cold storage locker![24]) Telecommunication linkages offer an alternative performance environment, allowing customers to be involved in the drama from a remote location—a delivery option long awaited by those travelling accountants, who would probably much prefer to work from the comfort of their own offices via the internet!

Front-stage personnel are members of a cast, playing roles as *actors* in a drama, and supported by a backstage production team. In some instances, they are expected to wear special costumes when on stage (such as the protective clothing—traditionally white but now increasingly coloured and patterned—worn by dental professionals, the fanciful uniforms often worn by hotel doormen, or the more basic brown ones worn by UPS drivers). When service employees wear distinctive apparel, they stand out from personnel at other firms, providing physical evidence of brand identity. In many service companies, the choice of uniform design and colours is carefully integrated with other corporate design elements. Front-stage employees are often required to conform to both a dress code and grooming standards (for instance, Tim Hortons hygiene standards require that employees wear hairnets in the bakery and use gloves when preparing food for customers).

Depending on the nature of their work, employees may have to learn and repeat specific lines, such as announcements in several languages in a location attracting a diverse audience, singsong sales spiels (just think of the last telemarketer who called you!) or a parting salutation of "Have a nice day!" And just like the theatre, companies often use scripting to define actors' behaviour as well as their lines. Eye contact, smiles, and handshakes may be required in addition to a spoken greeting. Other rules of conduct may include bans on smoking, eating, drinking, or gum chewing while on duty.

Implications of Customer Participation in Service Creation and Delivery

The more work that customers are expected to do in their role as co-producers, the greater their need for information about how to perform for best results. The necessary information

Figure 2.14

Tourists appreciate easy-to-understand instructions when checking in or out of Fairmont hotels.

can be provided in many different ways. Advertising for new services often contains significant educational content. Brochures, posted instructions, and websites are also widely used approaches. During a service encounter, customers are more likely to engage in self-service when automated machines provide user-friendly operating instructions (Figure 2.14). Thoughtful banks place a telephone beside their ATMs so that customers can call a "real person" for help and advice at any time if the machine malfunctions or they are confused about the on-screen instructions. Increasingly, machines are programmed to provide information and instructions in several languages—a marketing advantage when serving a multilingual population.

In many businesses, customers look to employees for advice and assistance and are frustrated if they can't obtain it. Service providers, ranging from sales assistants and customer service representatives to flight attendants and nurses, must be trained to help them improve their teaching skills. As a last resort, people may turn to other customers for help. Think about your own experiences in unfamiliar surroundings when you were grateful for the friendly advice or assistance provided by a fellow customer. And you've probably reached out yourself to assist someone who seemed to be having difficulties in a service setting where you already knew the ropes.

Benjamin Schneider and David Bowen recommend giving customers a realistic service preview in advance of service delivery, so that they have a clear picture of the role they're expected to play in co-production.[25] For example, a company might show a video presentation to help customers understand their role in the service encounter. This technique is used by some dentists to help patients understand the surgical processes they are about to experience and to indicate how they should co-operate to help make things go as smoothly as possible. Bo Edvardsson, Bo Enquist, and Robert Johnson propose creation of what they term a "hyperreal prepurchase service experience," involving active customer participation in a physical setting.[26] This approach involves active customer development of an "experience room" in which prospective customers are exposed in groups to both physical and intangible artifacts.

During the post-encounter stage, customers evaluate the service performance they have received and contrast it with their prior expectations. Let's explore how expectations relate to customer satisfaction and future intentions.

How Confirmation or Disconfirmation of Expectations Relates to Satisfaction and Delight

The terms "quality" and "satisfaction" are sometimes used interchangeably. But some researchers believe that perceived service quality is just one component of customer satisfaction, which also reflects price/quality trade-offs and personal and situational factors.[27]

Satisfaction can be defined as an attitude-like judgment following a purchase act or a series of consumer product interactions.[28] Most studies are based on the theory that the confirmation/disconfirmation of pre-consumption expectations is the essential determinant of satisfaction.[29] This means that customers have certain service standards in mind prior to consumption (their expectations), observe service performance and compare it to their standards, and then form satisfaction judgments based upon this comparison. The resulting judgment is labelled *negative disconfirmation* if the service is worse than expected, *positive disconfirmation* if better than expected, and simple *confirmation* if *as* expected.[30] When there is substantial positive disconfirmation, plus pleasure and an element of surprise, then customers are likely to be delighted.

Customer Delight   Findings from a research project by Richard Oliver, Roland Rust, and Sajeev Varki suggest that delight is a function of three components: (1) unexpectedly high levels of performance, arousal (e.g., surprise, excitement), and positive affect (e.g., pleasure, joy, or happiness).[31] By contrast, satisfaction alone is a function of positively disconfirmed expectations (better than expected) and positive affect. The researchers asked: "If delight is a function of surprisingly unexpected pleasure, is it possible for delight to be manifest in truly mundane services and products, such as newspaper delivery or trash collecting?" It certainly seems to be possible in seemingly mundane businesses like selling mattresses (see Best Practice in Action 2.1). However, once customers have been delighted, their expectations are raised. They will be dissatisfied if the service then returns to previous levels, and it may take more effort to "delight" them in the future.[32] So achieving delight requires focusing on what is currently unknown or unexpected by the customer. It's more than just avoiding problems—the "zero defects" strategy.

Based on analysis of ten years of data from the American Customer Satisfaction Index (ACSI), Claes Fornell and his colleagues caution against trying to exceed customer expectations on a continual basis, arguing that reaching for unobtainable objectives may backfire. They note that such efforts often come close to the point of diminishing returns.[33]

Strategic Links between Customer Satisfaction and Corporate Performance

Why is satisfaction important to service managers? There's convincing evidence of strategic links between the level of customer satisfaction achieved by a company's services and the firm's overall performance. Researchers from the University of Michigan found that on average, every 1 percent increase in customer satisfaction is associated with a 2.37 percent increase in a firm's return on investment (ROI).[34] And analysis of companies' scores on the American Customer Satisfaction Index (ACSI) shows that, on average among publicly traded firms, a 5 percent change in ACSI score is associated with a 19 percent change in the market value of common equity.[35] In other words, by creating more value for the customer, as measured by increased satisfaction, the firm creates more value for its owners.

Susan Fournier and David Mick state:

> Customer satisfaction is central to the marketing concept. . . . [I]t is now common to find mission statements designed around the satisfaction notion, marketing plans and incentive programs that target satisfaction as a goal, and consumer communications that trumpet awards for satisfaction achievements in the marketplace.[36]

Best Practice in Action 2.1

Sleep Country Canada: Why Buy a Mattress Anywhere Else?

Could one delight and build a loyal base of customers via exceptional customer service around such an unexciting product as a mattress? The answer appears to be a resounding yes! Sleep Country Canada is a Canadian success story built by founders Christine Magee, Stephen Gunn, and Gord Lownds, which has grown from four stores and one warehouse in British Columbia in 1994 to over 110 stores and nine distribution centres with more than 600 staff operating in BC, Alberta, Manitoba, and Ontario. Today they are the number one mattress specialist in the country.

Sleep Country Canada has transformed the way Canadian consumers buy mattresses. What used to be a boring, mundane exercise in shopping for mattresses in big box stores has been completely replaced by an extensive customer experience that focuses on making each part of the experience—before, during and after the sale—an enjoyable one. The stores are clean, bright, and airy and offer a wide variety of bed displays for easy demonstration and testing. The sales associates are knowledgeable, friendly, and have been extensively trained in helping customers choose the right mattress by listening to their needs (such as unusual sleep patterns), providing them with expert product knowledge, and not engaging in any pressure sales tactics. The experience concludes by provision of extensive guarantees such as a sixty-night comfort guarantee, a variety of payment options to suit individual needs, and a quick and easy delivery of the product to the customer. A customer

testimonial at the company's website succinctly captures this experience:

> "Actually, I told a friend on Monday and he went out Wednesday and bought a bed at your store. Amazing service! Jay was excellent to volunteer information at will. Product was delivered on time. Guys were great, polite and skilful! Service was the main reason for purchase—couldn't resist. Payment plan was exactly what I wanted."

Sleep Country Canada prides itself in being customer-focused and actively seeks feedback from each customer via response cards about their "experience" at the store. There is even a section in these cards labelled "Tell the President!" which allows consumers to provide feedback about their shopping experience directly to Christine Magee, president of Sleep Country Canada. This customer-focused, service-oriented approach is what makes mattresses offered by Sleep Country "superior" to identical products offered by the competition. Success has brought about domestic growth as well as ambitions of expansion into international markets. In February 2006, the company signed a letter of intent to acquire the Arizona-based retail chain Sleep America Inc., giving them entry into the markets of Phoenix and Tucson.

Source: Information adapted from www.sleepcountry.ca, accessed February 2006. "Sleep Country Canada Plans Expansion into the U.S. with Sleep America Inc.," www.globeinvestor.com, February 9, 2006, accessed September 29, 2006.

Most service providers wait until after service delivery has been completed before asking customers to complete satisfaction surveys (if they even bother to do this). But in extended, high-contact encounters this approach inevitably misses opportunities to address problems while the customer is still engaged in the process—or before they have even made a decision to purchase. If customers are uneasy with the prospect of using a particular service, they may decide against purchasing it. And if they feel uncomfortable with some aspect of a service encounter, they may decide to quit before completing a transaction, especially if they haven't yet had to pay for it.

Getting Feedback during Service Delivery Although it's not always practical to administer formal surveys in mid-encounter, managers can train service personnel to be more observant, so that they can identify customers who appear to be having difficulties, look frustrated, or seem otherwise ill at ease, and then ask if they need assistance. If experience shows that customers are continually discomforted by a particular aspect of the service encounter, this would indicate a need for redesign and improvement.

Deborah Spake and her colleagues have developed a methodology for measuring a consumer's comfort level, which can be applied at every stage from pre-purchase to post-purchase and is particularly applicable to high-contact services.[37] In surveying consumers, they found that respondents associated an increased comfort level with a reduction in perceived risk. Words and phrases such as "safety," "security," being "worry-free" and having "assurance" of the "quality" of the service provided were mentioned, as were having "peace of mind," being "at ease" with the service provider, and "trusting" them.

The importance of getting feedback during service delivery is that when things are going badly for the customer, there may still be an opportunity to practise service recovery so that the customer leaves feeling satisfied. Such an outcome improves the likelihood that the customer will remain loyal. The importance of customer loyalty is discussed in depth in Chapter 12.

Conclusion

Customer behaviour in a service environment is affected by the nature of the service being used. Services vary widely and can be categorized according to the nature of the underlying process: is the service directed at customers in person or their possessions? And are service actions tangible or intangible in nature? Each of the resulting four categories of services tends to involve different types of encounters between customers and the organization.

The three-stage model of service consumption helps us to understand how individuals recognize their needs, search for alternative solutions, choose and use services, and then evaluate their experiences against their prior expectations. Service consumption places the customer in the servuction system, which in a high-contact environment combines the visible, physical aspects of the service operation—facilities, equipment, and service personnel—plus other customers. The higher the level of contact, the greater the number of touch points between the customer and the service business. In a low-contact environment, by contrast, the customer may never see the company's facilities nor deal face-to-face with its employees. A knowledge of role and script theories can help us to understand and manage both customer behaviour and employee behaviour in these encounters.

During the post-encounter stage, customers evaluate the service performance they have received, contrast it with their prior expectations, and start to make decisions about future intentions. In all types of services, managing service encounters effectively is central to creating satisfied customers who will be willing to enter into long-term relationships with the service provider. Whether or not a customer is satisfied will depend on how well (if at all) these expectations were met. Gaining a better understanding of how customers evaluate, select, and use services should lie at the heart of strategies for designing and delivering the service product, which we discuss in the following chapter.

Review Questions

1. Clarify the differences between the four broad categories of services, provide typical examples of each, and explain the service-management challenges related to each category.

2. Explain the Three-Stage Model of service consumption.

3. Describe search, experience, and credence attributes, and give examples of each.

4. Explain why services tend to be harder for customers to evaluate than goods.

5. Why is consumer perception of risk an important aspect in selecting, purchasing, and using services? How can firms reduce consumer risk perceptions?

6. How are customers' expectations formed? Explain the difference between desired service and adequate service, with reference to a service experience you've had recently.

7. Choose a service that you are familiar with and create a diagram that represents the servuction system. Define the "front-stage" and "backstage" activities.

8. Describe the difference between high-contact and low-contact servuction systems, and explain how the nature of the customer's experience may differ between the two.

9. What are "moments of truth"?

10. How do the concepts of role theory, script theory, and theatrical perspective help to gain insights into consumer behaviour during the service encounter?

11. Describe the relationship between customer expectations and customer satisfaction.

Application Exercises

1. Develop two different customer scripts, one for a standardized service and one for a customized service. Map all key customer steps of this script across all three stages of service consumption. What are the key differences between the standardized and customized service?

2. Select three services, one high in search attributes, one high in experience attributes, and one high in credence attributes. Specify what product characteristics make them easy or difficult for consumers to evaluate, and suggest specific strategies that marketers can adopt in each case to facilitate evaluation and reduce perceived risk.

3. Maintain a diary of service encounters over a period of three days. After each service encounter, reflect upon it and record your perceptions of the key components of customer expectations (desired, adequate, and predicted levels of service). Relate these to the evaluation of the zone of tolerance, and how that impacted on your evaluation of the service encounter in terms of satisfaction. What are the backstage elements of (a) a car repair facility, (b) an airline, (c) a university, and (d) a consulting firm? Under what circumstances would it be appropriate to allow customers to see some of these backstage elements, and how would you do it?

4. What roles are played by front-stage service personnel in low-contact organizations? Are these roles more or less important to customer satisfaction than in high-contact services?

5. Apply the script theory and role theory concepts to a fitness facility such as a local gym. What insights can you give that would be useful for management?

6. Describe a low-contact service encounter via email or mail, a low-contact encounter via phone, and a high-contact, face-to-face encounter that you have had recently. How satisfied were you with each of the encounters? What were the key drivers of your overall level of satisfaction with this encounter? In each instance, what could the service provider have done to improve the situation?

Endnotes

1. These classifications are derived from Christopher H. Lovelock, "Classifying Services to Gain Strategic Marketing Insights," *Journal of Marketing* 47 (Summer 1983): 9–20.

2. B. Joseph Pine and James H. Gilmore, "Welcome to the Experience Economy," *Harvard Business Review* 76 (July–August 1998): 97–108.

3. Valarie A. Zeithaml, "How Consumer Evaluation Processes Differ between Goods and Services," in J.A. Donnelly and W.R. George, *Marketing of Services,* Chicago: American Marketing Association, 1981: 186–90.

4. Leonard L. Berry and Neeli Bendapudi, "Clueing in Customers," *Harvard Business Review* 81 (February 2003): 100–107.

5. Jaishankar Ganesh, Mark J. Arnold, and Kristy E. Reynolds, "Understanding the Customer Base of Service Providers: An Examination of the Differences Between Switchers and Stayers," *Journal of Marketing* 64/3 (2000): 65–87.

6. Uday Karmarkar, "Will You Survive the Service Revolution?" *Harvard Business Review* 82 (June 2004): 101–108.

7. See Benjamin Schneider and David E. Bowen, *Winning the Service Game,* Boston, MA: Harvard Business School Press, 1995; and Valarie A. Zeithaml, Leonard L. Berry, and A. Parasuraman, "The Nature and Determinants of Customer Expectations of Services," *Journal of the Academy of Marketing Science,* Vol. 21, 1993: 1–12).

8. Ray W. Coye, "Managing Customer Expectations in the Service Encounter," *International Journal of Service Industry Management* 15, No. 4, 2004: 54-71.

9. Valarie A. Zeithaml, Leonard L. Berry, and A. Parasuraman, "The Behavioral Consequences of Service Quality," *Journal of Marketing* 60 (April 1996): 31–46; R. Kenneth Teas and Thomas E. DeCarlo, "An Examination and Extension of the Zone-of-Tolerance Model: A Comparison to Performance-Based Models on Perceived Quality," *Journal of Service Research* 6/3 (2004): 272–86.

10. Cathy Johnson and Brian P. Mathews, "The Influence of Experience on Service Expectations," *International Journal of Service Industry Management* 8/4 (1997): 46–61.

11. Robert Johnston, "The Zone of Tolerance: Exploring the Relationship between Service Transactions and Satisfaction with the Overall Service," *International Journal of Service Industry Management* 6/5 (1995): 46–61.

12. Halil Nadiri and Kashif Hussain, "Diagnosing the Zone of Tolerance for Hotel Services," *Managing Service Quality* 15/5 (2005): 259–77.

13. Lynn Shostack, "Planning the Service Encounter," in J.A. Czepiel, M.R. Solomon, and C.F. Surprenant (eds.), *The Service Encounter,* Lexington, MA: Lexington Books, 1985: 243–54.

14. Normann first used the term "moments of truth" in a Swedish study in 1978; subsequently it appeared in English in his *Service Management: Strategy and Leadership in Service Businesses,* Chichester, UK: John Wiley, 2nd edition, 1991: 16–17.

15. Jan Carlzon, *Moments of Truth,* Cambridge, MA: Ballinger, 1987: 3.

16. Pierre Eiglier and Eric Langeard, "Services as Systems: Marketing Implications," in Pierre Eiglier, Eric Langeard, et al., *Marketing Consumer Services: New Insights.* Cambridge, MA: Marketing Science Institute, Report # 77-115 (November 1977): 83–103 (An earlier version was published in French in *Révue Française de Gestion* [March–April 1977]: 72–84); Eric Langeard, John E. Bateson, et al., *Services Marketing: New Insights from Consumers and Managers.* Marketing Science Institute, Report # 81-104 (August 1981).

17. Richard B. Chase, "Where Does the Customer Fit in a Service Organization?" *Harvard Business Review* 56 (November–December 1978): 137–42.

18. Stephen J. Grove, Raymond P. Fisk, and Joby John, "Services as Theater: Guidelines and Implications," in Teresa A. Schwartz and Dawn Iacobucci, eds., *Handbook of Services Marketing and Management,* Thousand Oaks, CA: Sage Publications, Inc., 2000: 21–36.

19. A. Parasuraman, "Technology Readiness Index (TRI): A Multiple-item Scale to Measure Readiness to Embrace New Technologies," *Journal of Service Research* 2 (2000): 307–20.

20. Stephen J. Grove and Raymond P. Fisk, "The Dramaturgy of Services Exchange: An Analytical Framework for Services Marketing," in L.L. Berry, G.L. Shostack, and G.D. Upah, eds., *Emerging Perspectives on Services Marketing,* Chicago: American Marketing Association, 1983: 45–49.

21. Michael R. Solomon, Carol Surprenant, John A. Czepiel and Evelyn G. Gutman, "A Role Theory Perspective on Dyadic Interactions: The Service Encounter," *Journal of Marketing* 49 (Winter 1985): 99–111.

22. See R.P. Abelson, "Script Processing in Attitude Formation and Decision-Making," in J.S. Carrol and J.W. Payne, eds., *Cognitive and Social Behavior,* Hillsdale, NJ: Erlbaum, 1976: 33–45; Ronald H. Humphrey and Blake E. Ashforth, "Cognitive Scripts and Prototypes in Service Encounters," in *Advances in Service Marketing and Management,* Greenwich, CT: JAI Press, 1994: 175–99; and Richard Harris, Kim Harris, and Steve Baron, "Theatrical Service Experiences: Dramatic Script Development with Employees," *International Journal of Service Industry Management* 14/2 (2003): 184–99.

23. Grove, Fisk, and John, 2000, op. cit.; Steve Baron, Kim Harris, and Richard Harris, "Retail Theater: The 'Intended Effect' of the Performance," *Journal of Service Research* 4 (May 2003): 316–32; Harris, Harris, and Baron, 2003, op. cit.

24. Elizabeth MacDonald, "Oh, the Horrors of Being a Visiting Accountant," *Wall Street Journal* (March 10, 1997): B1.

25. Benjamin Schneider and David E. Bowen, *Winning the Service Game,* Boston: Harvard Business School Press, 1995: 92.

26. Bo Edvardsson, Bo Enquist, and Robert Johnson, "Cocreating Customer Value in the Prepurchase Service Experience," *Journal of Service Research* 8 (November 2005): 149–61.

27. Valarie A. Zeithaml, Mary Jo Bitner, and Dwayne D. Gremler, *Services Marketing: Integrating Customer Focus Across the Firm,* fourth edition, Boston: McGraw-Hill/Irwin, 2006.

28. Youjae Yi, "A Critical Review of Customer Satisfaction," in V.A. Zeithaml (ed.), *Review of Marketing 1990,* Chicago: American Marketing Association, 1990.

29. Richard L. Oliver, "Customer Satisfaction with Service," in Schwartz and Iacobucci, 2000, op. cit.: 247–54; Jochen Wirtz and Anna S. Mattila, "Exploring the Role of Alternative Perceived Performance Measures and Needs-Congruency in the Consumer Satisfaction Process," *Journal of Consumer Psychology* 11/3 (2001): 181–92.

30. Richard L. Oliver, *Satisfaction: A Behavioral Perspective on the Consumer,* New York: McGraw-Hill, 1997.

31. Richard L. Oliver, Roland T. Rust, and Sajeev Varki, "Customer Delight: Foundations, Findings, and Managerial Insight," *Journal of Retailing* 73 (Fall 1997): 311–36.

32. Roland T. Rust and Richard L. Oliver, "Should We Delight the Customer?," *Journal of the Academy of Marketing Science* 28/1 (2000): 86–94.

33. Claes Fornell, David VanAmburg, Forrest Morgeson et al., *The American Customer Satisfaction Index at Ten Years – A Summary of Findings: Implications for the Economy, Stock Returns and Management.* Ann Arbor, MI: National Quality Research Center, University of Michigan, 2005: 54.

34. Eugene W. Anderson and Vikas Mittal, "Strengthening the Satisfaction–Profit Chain," *Journal of Service Research* 3 (November 2000): 107–20.

35. Fornell VanAmburg, and Morgeson, et al., 2005, op. cit. 40.

36. Susan Fournier and David Glen Mick, "Rediscovering Satisfaction," *Journal of Marketing* 63 (October 1999): 5–23.

37. Deborah F. Spake, Sharon E. Beatty, Beverly K. Brockman, and Tammy Neal Crutchfield, "Development of the Consumer Comfort Scale: A Multi-Study Investigation of Service Relationships," *Journal of Service Research* 5/4 (May 2003): 316–32.

In a Dizzying World, One Way to Keep Up: Renting Possessions

DVDS, MUSIC AND HANDBAGS LOSE THRILL OF OWNERSHIP; "BUY IT, LOVE IT, SELL IT"

NICK WINGFIELD

Developing trends in consumer behavior offer opportunities for service entrepreneurs. In a search for new benefits, some consumers are moving away from extended ownership of durable goods. Instead they are choosing to rent products, to resell goods on eBay after brief use, or to quickly trade in relatively new goods for the latest model. The products involved range from consumer electronics and music to handbags and sporting goods.

Karl Marx thought private property needed to be abolished before society could perfect itself. Then again, he never saw Mark Rosa flip golf clubs.

The 45-year-old high-school teacher from Antlers, Okla., used to buy new clubs every 10 years or so. Thanks to a program set up by Callaway Golf Co., he now upgrades virtually every year. Mr. Rosa buys his new gear online, which Callaway ships by mail. He sends back the old clubs in the same box, typically getting a trade-in price of about $300 for a set that originally cost $500.

"I play with a guy at a local club—he's 70 years old, and he's still playing on a 1950s set" of golf clubs, says Mr. Rosa. "There are people like me, the newer generation, who trade up technology, looking for an edge."

All over the consumer marketplace, people who used to buy things for keeps are renting, flipping, or instantly upgrading. These shoppers care less about whether things are truly theirs and more about whether they can get the latest and best. Whereas once they could only shop this way in niche areas such as car leases, now they can also try handbags, consumer electronics, movies and music.

The best-known model is Netflix Inc. Since it started in 1999, the Los Gatos, Calif., company has signed up more than 3.5 million subscribers who typically pay $18 a month to rent DVD movies that are sent to them in the mail. Users send them back in pre-paid envelopes.

In recent years, companies like Jiggerbug and GameFly have taken the Netflix approach to audio books and videogames. RealNetworks Inc. rents access to music online. Encyclopaedia Britannica Inc.'s fastest-growing business isn't books or CD-ROMs, but selling access to its encyclopedia online, for a fee. Customers "don't think about owning that kind of product in perpetuity anymore," says Patti Ginnis, a Britannica marketing executive.

Technology both creates and satisfies this desire. Hot products are now rendered obsolete or unfashionable at a dizzying rate. At the same time, the Internet has created a huge and efficient market for ordering new goods and selling them fast on sites such as eBay.

Paul Archambault, a Waterford, N.Y., computer programmer, buys and sells on eBay the way some people check out books from the library. At 3 a.m. one recent morning, on his way to the Albany airport, Mr. Archambault popped into a Wal-Mart and paid nearly $200 for a Nintendo DS videogame console and two games to keep him busy on a trip to Des Moines, Iowa.

While waiting to board his flight, Mr. Archambault photographed the device, which was still in its box, and sent the images to an eBay auction from his laptop through the terminal's wireless connection. His ad mentioned that he planned to use the game for just the weekend. The auction closed the day after Mr. Archambault returned and fetched slightly more than the $200 he paid.

"I love to have the latest and greatest," he explains.

Several years ago, eBay Inc. of San Jose, Calif., began sending emails to users suggesting a price at which the item they just acquired might be resold. The response was strong from people wanting to flip cellphones, iPods, PCs and sporting equipment, says Michael Dearing, senior vice president and general merchandise manager at eBay, "The duration for which [those items are] considered good or leading or appealing is getting shorter and shorter over time," he says. To encourage these new virtual renters, eBay has begun using the slogan; "Buy It, Love It, Sell It."

David Wasmund, an office manager in Sterling Heights, Mich., recently sold one type of iPod on eBay so he could buy another, newer model. He's used the same tactic to flip cellphones. He says the resale price is typically 25% to 30% below what he paid if he unloads the product within a year. "I know even if I buy something and I don't like it, I can turn around and put it on" eBay, he says.

Matt Morgan has stopped buying music altogether. A 29-year-old recruiter in San Francisco, he rents music through RealNetwork's Rhapsody service for $10 a month, which gives him unlimited access to more than a million music tracks. The catch: If he stops paying, he won't be able to listen to the music. Mr. Morgan says he "can't remember the last time I went into a store and bought a CD."

Nicole Mazzola Ferrer, a 30-year-old project manager for a Kirkland, Wash., technology company, pays $50 a month to rent handbags from a Web service called Bag Borrow or Steal.

One at a time, she checks out bags that sell for up to $500 in retail stores. Ms. Mazzola Ferrer uses a bag anywhere from a few days to a month, before mailing it back in exchange for a fresh one when novelty fades or a special occasion arises.

One hitch: Some women might be reluctant to borrow used bags. Adam Dell, a venture capitalist in New York, who invested in Bag Borrow or Steal, says all the company's bags are delivered in excellent condition, after being inspected and cleaned. Mr. Dell compares the process to certified pre-owned vehicle programs.

Carrying a used bag doesn't bother Ms. Mazzola Ferrer, who figures she used to spend more than $100 a month buying handbags she would "get sick" of quickly. By renting, she can carry around nicer bags than she could afford at retail. And, she says, "my husband appreciates that half the closet isn't consumed by handbags."

Reading 1-2

Service Theater: An Analytical Framework for Services Marketing

STEPHEN J. GROVE AND RAYMOND P. FISK

The theater metaphor is a useful framework for describing and analyzing service performances. Employees serving customers may be thought of as actors and customers as the audience that experiences the performance. The marketing implications of this metaphor are discussed for airline travel and electronic performances in cyberspace.

INTRODUCTION

The significant differences between services and physical goods have spawned numerous prescriptions for the successful design and delivery of service products. A keen understanding of the nature of services is an important first step toward achieving service excellence. Various models have been developed to help practitioners and scholars comprehend the complex character of the service experience. One early model suggests expanding the traditional marketing-mix elements of product, price, promotion, and place to include three additional Ps (i.e., participants, physical evidence, and process of service assembly) among a services marketing mix (Booms and Bitner 1981). A second model depicts the service experience as an elaborate production system of technology, management, resources, and personnel that is driven by a business mission and is responsive to customer expectations (Grönroos 1991). In a third model, services are described as a "servuction system" (a hybrid of service and production) that includes physical areas that are visible and invisible to the service customer, an inanimate environment, contact personnel, and customer interaction. (Langeard et al. 1981)

Although these models generate valuable insights regarding service experiences, none describes the complex nature of services, demonstrates their common characteristics, captures their interactive essence, and facilitates communication about their enactment in a lucid and simple fashion. Based on observations derived from the sociology and theater literatures, we propose a simple yet comprehensive framework for understanding service experiences. We contend that service experiences are theater and encompass many of the same features and principles as theatrical performances. This article explores service theater as a comprehensive framework for understanding, analyzing, and discussing service experiences. First, we examine the social and physical context of service experiences. Second, the theatrical nature of service experiences is explained. Third, airlines services are described as an example of service theater. Fourth, the service metaphor is extended to the realm of cyberspace.

THE SOCIAL AND PHYSICAL CONTEXT OF SERVICE EXPERIENCES

At any moment of any day, you may be involved in a service experience. A *service experience* occurs whenever a customer and a service organization interact. A visit to the dentist's office, a night's stay in a hotel, a session surfing the World Wide Web, or a meal in a restaurant are all examples of service experiences. Listening to a rock concert, mailing a letter, or

Portions of this article are based on our earlier publication, "The Dramaturgy of Services Exchange: An Analytical Framework for Services Marketing," published by the American Marketing Association in 1983.

purchasing a pair of shoes are service experiences as well. While not always the case, a service experience frequently occurs in an organization's physical environment and involves the presence of other customers. The service provided by an ocean liner, for example, encompasses the vessel and the passengers. The layout of the ship, its decor and comfort, its features and furnishings, and other environmental aspects affect the cruise experience. In addition, the people sharing space on the ocean liner affect one another by their number, character, and actions.

Most services are the result of one or more workers performing various tasks. To illustrate, consider the number of employees involved in making a hospital stay a success. Physicians and orderlies, nurses and their aides, porters and desk clerks, and a host of others all play a part in fashioning the patient's experience. Overall, the physical setting, the service workers and their tasks, and the other customers combine to influence the nature of the service experience.

Due to intangibility and the simultaneity of production and consumption of services, customers often have difficulty assessing the quality of the services they receive (Zeithaml 1981). Hence, the social milieu (i.e., the interaction with the workers and other customers) and the service's physical environment (i.e., the nature of the facilities and equipment) provide important cues to the excellence of the service rendered. Based on this observation, astute service organizations are wise to "tangibilize" their service offering by managing these aspects of the customers' experience (Berry 1981; Lovelock 1994; Shostack 1977). Because the staging of a theatrical performance involves many of the same considerations that are important for fashioning a successful service experience (i.e., expressive physical cues, performers and their actions, and audience participation), we suggest that it is plausible to approach services as theater.

THE THEATRICAL NATURE OF SERVICE EXPERIENCES[1]

Describing human behavior as theater is not new, but systematically applying a theater metaphor to service experiences is unique. Much of the basis for applying theater to services can be linked to observations anchored in the sociological school of thought known as *dramaturgy* as well as to an appreciation of theater as a performing art. Dramaturgy depicts social interaction in the terms and concepts of a theatrical production. The contemporary dramaturgical perspective is significantly based on the work of Erving Goffman and his book *The Presentation of Self in Everyday Life* (1959). Goffman examined the structure of social interaction when people are in the presence of others and how a definition of the behavioral situation is created and maintained, even in the face of potential disruptions. Although Goffman contends that people use theatrical devices and insights to accomplish these goals, we propose

that service organizations can use similar tools to create successful service experiences for their customers. After all, just as theater is described as "an experience—a shared indivisible event that includes both those who perform and those who observe" (Wilson 1991, 3), services can be characterized in the same way. Several of the concepts that Goffman offers and others have found in the theater literature are relevant for framing services as theater. Among these are performance, performance teams, regions and region behavior, and impression management.

Performance

Performance describes an *actor's* activity when there is continuous contact with an *audience*. By their nature, performances are designed to have some impact on an audience. Performances can be characterized as sincere or cynical. Sincere performances occur when an actor essentially becomes the role that he is playing. Cynical performances occur when an actor views a performance only as a means to an end. To create and communicate a believable performance, actors often employ various expressive devices, such as aspects of the setting, their personal appearance, and their behavioral manner.

The *setting* is comprised of the decor, furnishings, and physical layout at the performance's location, while the actor's *personal appearance* and *manner* are reflected in their dress, facial expression, gestures, demographic profile, and personality. When consistent with each other, the setting and the actor's personal profile create an important set of cues for the audience. With this in mind, it's not surprising that actors may conceal or underplay aspects of the expressive devices that may be incompatible with the desired performance. The reality portrayed in a service performance is fragile and is easily upset by even minor contradictions.

Service experiences are performances They reflect the efforts of a service organization and its workers (actors) to satisfy customer (audience) needs. Those needs might be a stylish haircut, transportation from Chicago to Toronto, care for a pet poodle, or safe storage of a person's life savings. In each of these cases, to create and sustain customer perceptions of excellence, service personnel must adhere to the principles of a successful performance. They must (1) believe in the importance of customer satisfaction (i.e., be sincere), (2) consider the communicative capability of the service setting and workers' personal profiles (i.e., attend to the expressive devices), and (3) work hard to avoid contradicting the image of excellence they seek (i.e., present a consistent front). Consider the example of Ritz Carlton, where each of these performance-related directives is fastidiously followed. The result is a well-designed service delivery system that has garnered the esteemed Malcolm Baldrige Award and is a widely recognized image of excellence.

---

[1]Much of this discussion relies on the insight of Erving Gofman and his book, *The Presentation of Self in Everyday Life*, published by Doubleday and Company in 1959.

Performance Teams

Most theatrical productions require the coordinated effort of several actors to create an audience's experience. *Performance teams* are sets of actors who cooperate to create a single impression to which the audience responds. Although each member contributes in her own way, it is the combined effort of the entire team that fashions an audience's experience. In a sense, the importance of the performance is the common bond that holds a team together. Those participating in any theatrical production must respect each other's role if the performance is to be perceived as credible. When actors criticize their teammates, fail to cooperate, or neglect the effort to portray a unified front, a performance may be shattered.

Service organizations face similar consideration in the process of service delivery. Most service experiences are the result of several workers cooperating as a team. These workers may operate in full view of the customer, that is, the *cast,* or be among those who are instrumental to the service delivery yet are seldom seen. Even providing simple services such as changing automobile oil or laundering clothes requires that all employees recognize the importance of the performance promised to the customer.

A single employee can ruin the service experience for the customer by failing to enact his tasks correctly, ridiculing others' efforts, or failing to project the desired image. When the service process goes well, it is usually the result of a team effort that is unnoticed by the customer. When service fails, it is frequently because a team member did not play her assigned part. This issue takes on greater complexity as the size of the cast and support personnel increases. For instance, compare the difficulty of ensuring a successful team effort for a hotel versus a full-service car wash. The complex nature of a hotel service requires more workers, which makes creating and sustaining teamwork more difficult.

The Setting: Regions and Region Behavior

The setting where a performance occurs is an important source of information for the audience and a critical component of any theatrical production. The setting is comprised of front and back regions. The front region, or *frontstage,* is in full view of the audience and is the part of the setting that carries significant communicative capability. The frontstage and the cast members who perform there must meet the audience's approval. Attention to detail, careful planning of the physical cues, well-rehearsed scripts, and choreographed movements by the actors are all important. The back region, or *backstage,* is hidden from the audience's view and is where the preparation and support for the frontstage performance occurs. Here, actors drop their front and step out of character. In the backstage, actors may rehearse their parts, memorize their scripts, perfect their teamwork, or work through flaws in their parts. Also found backstage are various workers and equipment that contribute to the frontstage performance, but they are usually unnoticed by the audience. In a theatrical production, these include wardrobe personnel, stage crews, lighting, and sound equipment.

Normally, the two regions are kept separate owing to the risk of the audience discovering behavior and physical cues contradictory to a credible performance. Beyond observing imperfection in performances, the audience could be exposed to improper behavior and unappealing physical evidence. Cursing, slovenly demeanor, complaining, unkempt equipment, and dirty conditions might be seen. To protect against such mishaps, careful attention is often given to keeping the passageway between the two regions closed.

The typical service experience occurs in a setting marked by distinct front- and backstage areas, too. The service setting, sometimes referred to as the *servicescape* (Bitner 1992), is comprised of a front region designed to appeal to customers and to facilitate service delivery and a back region housing the operational support system of the service. The frontstage involves various props, decor, and furnishings that define the service for the customer and frame the performance. Lighting, music, air temperature, and aroma play a role here, too. For example, a restaurant can present itself as an Italian eatery, a Chinese take-out, or a French bistro by the selection of frontstage devices. However, if the backstage equipment, support staff, and management in the kitchen area go awry, all may be lost. If a diner stumbles into a food preparation area on his way to the restroom, the appearance of the chef, the backstage work conditions, the behavior of the staff, or other disruptive cues may shatter the perception of excellence. For that reason, most restaurants do not allow patrons to enter their back regions.

Actors and Impression Management

At the heart of any theatrical performance are the actors whose presence and behavior fashion the show for the audience. Some performances are better than others due to the casting and the abilities of the actors involved. The actors' task is to present or contribute to a believable performance. In general, it is the actors that the audience views as the key determinant of a show's quality. Hence, actors in a theatrical production engage in *impression management,* or the creation and maintenance of a credible show. Impression management relies on actors' abilities to convey their roles effectively. Beyond learning their parts, actors' interpretations of their roles through such things as facial expressions, gestures, and vocal inflections have much to do with a play's effect on the audience (Wilson 1991). Impression management also involves the various performers (and backstage personnel, too) adhering to defensive practices that are designed to guard against mistakes. Specifically, the actors must demonstrate loyalty, discipline, and circumspection regarding the performance.

Loyalty means that the actors must accept the importance of the performance and avoid disclosing secrets regarding its enactment to the audience or others not directly involved in the production. *Discipline* means that they are obliged to learn their parts and guard against unwittingly committing gestures or mistakes that might destroy a performance.

Finally, *circumspection* means that the actors need to plan in advance how best to stage the show. If an actor reveals inside information, he is being disloyal. If he allows his personal problems to interfere with his stage responsibilities, he lacks discipline. If he fails to consider what it takes to be credible in his role, he is not circumspect. For a successful performance to occur, none of these can happen, or the impression will be damaged.

Service experiences rely on the impression-management expertise of the workers in much the same way that stage performances do. From the customers' point of view, the employees *are* the service (Schneider and Bowen 1995; Surprenant and Solomon 1987; Tansik 1990), and their attitudes and behavior have a significant impact (Hartline and Ferrell 1996). What the workers do (their technical skills) and how they do it (their functional skills) are critical to customers' evaluations of service excellence (Grönroos 1990). The dentist, hotel clerk, and educator are assessed on how well they perform regarding the outcome of their effort (e.g., a filled cavity, properly assigned room, and information learned, respectively) and the manner in which it was done (e.g., the concern shown, the courtesy displayed, the responsiveness demonstrated).

In each service, the workers must strive to manage an impression of excellence through their adherence to defensive practices. They must (1) keep potentially destructive information undisclosed (e.g., the risk of abnormal pain from the dental drill), (2) guard against the intrusion of personal strife (e.g., resist the urge to share financial problems with the hotel guest), and (3) ensure a well-devised service delivery through forethought (e.g., anticipate students' questions regarding lecture material). These considerations can be addressed by service organizations in the hiring, training, and monitoring of their workers. The significance of impression management and the various ways an impression might be destroyed are important issues to stress in service organizations and in theatrical productions. It is not surprising that some have advocated that service training should include an acting class (Billingsley 1998; Grove, Fisk, and Knowles 1996).

Audience

Every theatrical performance is designed to appeal to a particular audience. Stated differently, if any performance is to be fully appreciated, it must conform to the audience's desires and expectations. Great performances are sometimes lost on the wrong audience. Individuals expecting to see a comedy are often disappointed with a drama. Even with the right audience, adaptations or adjustments by the actors are sometimes needed to keep the audience entertained. Hence, a successful performance requires attracting and reaching the appropriate audience. The right audience has a vested interest in seeing the show unfold smoothly. Specifically, the audience can be expected to engage in so-called protective practices which allow the show to go on when minor mishaps occur. After all, the audience attends a performance to see the entire show. If an actor misses a line or is out of place on stage or if a stage prop is missing, the audience will typically allow such miscues in the interest of enjoying the entire production. At the same time, those responsible for a stage production must ensure that some audience members do not disrupt others through their verbal or physical actions. Someone talking too loudly or crowding another's personal space can ruin the performance for other audience members.

Many services are delivered to multiple customers sharing the same servicescape, such as hotels, hospitals, schools, airlines, and restaurants. For a service experience to be successful, "recruiting the right customers is as important as recruiting the right personnel" (Gummesson 1993). Similar to the case of a stage production, the wrong customers (audience) for a service designed for others are likely to be dissatisfied (Lovelock 1994). The young couple who enter a restaurant expecting full-service, romantic dining only to find buffet-style, family dining will be disappointed. Most services are not likely to exclude paying customers simply because they do not fit the desired target audience profile. Also, antidiscrimination laws often prohibit attempts to exclude customer groups. Consequently, efforts at maintaining customer compatibility (Martin and Pranter 1989), policing the customers (Lovelock 1981), and recognizing how customers affect each other (Grove and Fisk 1997) ensure that everyone's service experience is positive.

Like theatrical productions, service providers can expect that the customers will overlook small flaws or minor problems during the process of service delivery in the interest of enjoying the service in its entirety. For that reason the dirty utensil, the hotel room that is missing a towel, or the taxi that's five minutes late are usually overlooked. Although any of these may be a failed "moment of truth" (Carlzon 1987), each is seldom significant enough by itself to destroy the overall quality of the service experience.

As a final note, successful service strategy begins with knowing the customers. Disney stresses the critical role of "guestology" (the study of the customers it services) as a key reason for its success. Disney conducts over two hundred external surveys a year; tracks demographic profiles, price sensitivity, and evaluation of attractions by guests; monitors the tens of thousands of letters and comment cards it receives; and practices management by walking around. By doing so, Disney gathers critical information that enables the design of a service experience that delights its guests (Johnson 1991).

AIRLINE SERVICE: AN APPLICATION OF SERVICE THEATER

This section develops a theatrical explanation of airline services as an illustration of the service theater concepts we have developed. Throughout the example, the service actors (airport and airline employees), service setting (airport facilities and airplane cabin), service audience (passengers), and service performance (enactment of the airline service) are interwoven to create a successful service experience. The example is developed around the theatrical device of the three-act play. Act 1 is the airport departure. Act 2 is the airline flight. Act 3 is the destination arrival.

Act 1: Airport Departure

Act 1 begins as airline passengers arrive at the front door of the airport. A porter might approach a passenger at the curb and offer to check her bags, or the passenger may decide to proceed inside the airport to the ticket counter. The ticket counter is the first frontstage area controlled by the airline. The passengers may note the cleanliness of the area and the state of the computer terminals and information displays. A performance team of ticket counter staff must work together to check in each passenger and the passenger's baggage. Every passenger's identity must be verified, his or her ticket and seating assignment must be confirmed, security questions must be asked, and any baggage must be tagged for its destination. The counter personnel are likely to exhibit efficiency, courtesy, and composure as they deal with one passenger after another. The uniforms they wear and the scripts they follow enhance their professionalism.

Once the baggage is checked, it disappears into the backstage region of the airport. The passenger is then instructed to proceed to a second frontstage area, the departure gate, where a smaller performance team of two or three airline staff prepares passengers for departure. The decor and comfort of the waiting area, the size and mix of passengers waiting to board the plane, and the efficiency with which the process unfolds will all impact passenger experiences. The staff is expected to display the same professionalism as their ticket-counter peers as they process passengers, handle ticket or seating problems, and announce airline boarding procedures and times. Like the waiting area, the staff's actions and demeanor are aspects of the unfolding service performance.

Every airline develops its own version of boarding procedures, which must be clearly conveyed to passengers to ensure efficiency. As an example, when a recent British Airways flight to London was called to board, the U.S. passengers formed a rather haphazard line of people two to three people across. One of the British Airways uniformed staff looked at the line in dismay and announced over the loudspeaker that "no one is going to go to London until you form a *proper* line." The Americans looked at each other in puzzlement and then realized that a "proper line" must be a single-file line. By contrast, Southwest Airlines has developed a nearly legendary reputation for the speed and efficiency of its boarding procedures by issuing a numbered plastic tag at check-in but no seat assignment. Based on these numbers, passengers on Southwest are boarded in groups, and they are expected to take the first seat available.

Act 2: The Airline Flight

Act 2 is the main act of the airline service and begins as passengers enter the airplane cabin. New performance teams of airline pilots and cabin personnel are the key players in act 2. The frontstage area is the cabin itself, and the backstage areas are the cockpit and the baggage compartment. A crew member, smartly attired and neatly groomed, greets the passengers as they board the plane and directs them to their

seats. Once passengers have taken their seats and buckled their seat belts, the airplane will begin to pull away from the gate and taxi toward the runway. Already the passengers will be forming impressions of act 2 based on many different cues. The comfort of the seats, the amount of leg room, the air quality, the clarity of the public address system, and the colors and patterns of the cabin furnishings and carpet are consciously and unconsciously scanned. Even the number and mix of other passengers are noticed. Along the way, passengers are instructed about safety procedures. Most airlines follow a standard script to recite the safety procedures, yet others improvise. For example, it is common for a crew member on Southwest Airlines to sing the safety instructions to the passengers.

After the plane takes off, the cabin crew begins food and beverage service, and in-flight entertainment may commence. Each of these provides further cues to help passengers form impressions of the service. Meanwhile, the captain will greet the passengers over the loudspeaker and comment on flying conditions, flight time, visible landmarks along the flight, and weather at the destination. The pilot usually closes with a comment that the crew will do everything they can to make the flight pleasant and comfortable. It is noteworthy that the cabin crew usually introduce themselves to passengers, whereas the land-based crews almost never introduce themselves. The gestures and expressions of the flight attendants, the affability ascribed to the pilot by virtue of his voice, and the helpfulness of the crew in general furnish additional information that fashions the flight experience for the service's audience. Other passengers in the service audience can also strongly influence each passenger's evaluation of the flight. Babies crying, children kicking the back of seats, or drunks trying to start a conversation can play a very negative role in the evaluation of the service despite the best efforts of the airline crew.

Although standard flight procedures or scripts must be followed, flight crews must sometimes go to extra lengths to make passengers comfortable. Several years ago, one of the authors boarded a Delta Air Lines flight the morning after a major airline crash. Safety anxieties were on the minds of passengers that morning as they nervously buckled their seat belts while the plane prepared to depart. Fortunately, the pilot and crew were well aware that the passengers might be unusually tense. As the plane made its last turn onto the runway and began its acceleration for liftoff, the sounds of the *William Tell* Overture burst from the loudspeakers. The unexpected but well-known music broke the anxiety among the travelers, and the plane hurtled into the air with a cabin full of passengers laughing uproariously.

Act 3: Destination Arrival

Act 3 begins as passengers line up to exit the airplane cabin and enter the airport facilities at their destination. The airplane crew and the workers at the destination must cooperate to move the passengers out of the cabin and on their way. Attempts are made to open the cabin doors quickly and speed travelers into the terminal. The cabin crew will often take advantage of one last opportunity to demonstrate efficiency through the manner by which they dispatch this task. They also attempt to convey a personal touch by bidding the passengers farewell and thanking them for flying their airline. However, most of the activity in this act of the service performance is self-service or occurs backstage as the airline's baggage crew unloads the plane and delivers the baggage to the baggage claim area. Occasionally, passengers may catch a glimpse of baggage handlers tossing luggage onto trams to be whisked away to the terminal as they wait to deplane. This normally backstage activity then becomes a frontstage spectacle that may have significant consequences for impressions of service excellence. The horror of observing a carefully packed suitcase containing breakable souvenirs haphazardly hurled into a heap of bags has caused many travelers considerable distress.

Most airlines have at least one person directing passengers to their connecting flights, to airport exits, or to the baggage claim area once they surge into the terminal. Aided by computer devices, experience with exasperated voyagers, and a personality that can withstand the pressure akin to that faced by a traffic officer, this service performer is likely to be the final face that the passenger puts on the service personnel. The clarity of his directions, the urgency he conveys, and the courtesy he displays can confirm the excellence of the service experience. If the passenger must find her way to the baggage claim, one last scene of the airline's service performance remains to be played: the speed of baggage delivery. It is an aspect of the airline's service that often goes unappreciated when the backstage personnel and systems operate efficiently, but it is a significant source of dissatisfaction if bags are slow to arrive or are lost in transit. Once the airline passengers locate their baggage and exit the airport, the airline service experience is completed.

Throughout the three-act service experience depicted here, various actors and their roles, setting conditions and regions, audience participation and circumstances, and performance attributes play significant parts in the passengers' impression of service excellence. Conceiving the entire service as theater provides a common framework that links and organizes the many factors that contribute to a service experience. Regardless of the service considered, the metaphor of theater can be applied.

SERVICE THEATER IN CYBERSPACE

As the twentieth century drew to a close, a remarkable phenomenon occurred: the emergence and widespread adoption of electronic commerce (e-commerce). *Cyberspace* is a term used to describe the artificial reality created by computers and the Internet that makes e-commerce possible. Today, a vast array of products are bought and sold through the medium of cyberspace. Whether purchasing an automobile, financial advice, a tanning bed, or tax preparation, cyberspace brings the seller and buyer together in a manner far removed from typical retailing. Cyberspace also makes it possible for organizations to disseminate all sorts of information pertaining to their operations. Business location, availability of merchandise, hours of operation, prices, installation instructions, and more can be communicated quickly and efficiently through cyberspace. In essence, cyberspace provides a means for organizations to provide a service (whether it is the retailing of a product or provision of information). All of the service theater concepts discussed in the previous sections pertain to cyberspace just as they do for marketing services in physical space. Although the boundaries between the various components of service theater may become blurred in the seamless world of cyberspace, they are nevertheless present and pliable.

In cyberspace the service performance is electronic. Unlike most services that are delivered in physical space, a cyberspace performance can be carefully automated and tightly scripted. Like its physical-space counterpart, much of what transpires during a cyberspace performance is dictated by the stage on which it occurs. However, the setting and the service stage in cyberspace are inherently more limited in terms of physical size than those found in physical space. The user's computer screen and the narrow bandwidth feeding it constitute a cyberspace service's frontstage. These frontstage dimensions combine to create a special challenge for cyberspace service marketers, forcing them to work hard to grab their audience's attention and to provide their audience with provocative reasons to "remain seated" during the performance's enactment. After all, cyberspace customers can switch performances with the mere click of a button! Yet what a cyberspace service may lack in frontstage dimensions, it *can* compensate for greatly with its backstage operation. Because of the interconnected nature of the Internet, the backstage in cyberspace may be much larger than is typical in physical space. The cyberspace backstage can range from one computer server and the support staff who operate it to a large network of servers and support staff across a multisite organization that collectively sustain the service performance 24 hours a day, 7 days a week. Delivering an excellent cyberspace service experience to its audience requires an organization to choreograph and direct a performance that takes advantage of the backstage domain. Failure to do so may result in the audience's quick exit, perhaps to another service's performance. In cyberspace, there is no distance or travel time between service theaters. Further, because there are so many free services in cyberspace, there are virtually no switching costs to barricade the exit doors. Only a riveting performance will prevent switching. Obviously, the design of the frontstage, the ease of its navigation, and the story it tells must be compelling.

In cyberspace, the service actors are often masked by the performance itself. In one sense, the Web site that provides the service portrays the actors as well as the performance. Essentially, the automated nature of the Web site makes it difficult to distinguish the cyberspace performance from the actors' roles. The two are frequently seamless. Across most cyberspace services, the actions of the service actor—the behaviors that create and deliver the service—are captured by and hidden in the text and texture of the Web site itself. Although they are impossible to discern separately from the Web site, they are there nonetheless. As the technology for delivering services in cyberspace improves, it may be feasible to simulate the appearance of human actors on the Web site and produce an anthropomorphic presence that more closely reflects service interaction in physical space. For those few cyberspace services that currently provide access to a live human being via their electronic link, that is, someone who can respond to questions or inquiries, the service actor is simply a participant in a remote servicescape (Bitner 1992). In such cases, his or her performance must exhibit all of the same considerations as any service actor that is invisible yet interactive with the customer (e.g., telephone receptionists or catalogue sales personnel).

Finally, the audience that participates in cyberspace's service theater is in control of most of the action. The audience can choose the time that the "curtain will go up" and the location of the service performance itself. Hence, cyberspace organizations must design their performances so that their audience can begin the service at its convenience and depart when it wishes. The backstage support and the frontstage design must facilitate the audience's entrance into, movement about, and exit from the cyberspace setting. A further, interesting aspect is that once the audience has gained access to the service organization, it commonly chooses the story line of a service performance in cyberspace. Due to the interactive nature of an Internet Web site such as Amazon.com or Yahoo!, each customer may select a set of pages uniquely suited to his or her interests. Amazon.com tries to encourage this behavior by greeting each repeat visitor with a customized page that includes suggested books and other items based on the pattern of previous purchases. This self-directed component of the service performance ostensibly provides a greater opportunity for a satisfying outcome to the service performance, but only if care is taken to design the various theatrical dimensions of the cyberspace service with the audience in mind. The performance must be simple but provocative; the staging must be inviting yet beguiling; and the actors must be caring and creative in meeting the audience's needs. Otherwise, the cyberspace service experience bytes.

SUMMARY AND CONCLUSION

The preceding passages demonstrate the correspondence between theatrical concepts rooted in dramaturgy or stage productions and those that are important for managing the service experience. From our perspective, both theater and services are involved in a large-scale effort to manage impressions. If service organizations explore the theatrical nature of services in their industry, they are likely to discover that the concepts discussed here (and other theatrical elements) may have profound significance.

To some, viewing and framing services as theater may hint at artificiality and manipulation. In reality, when a theatrical approach to services is successfully developed, the opposite is

probable. Organizations and their personnel begin to see that they are in the business of creating experiences and recognize that this effort involves all of the trappings that are commonly found in theatrical productions. Hence, there is no room for insincerity. Poor performances—ones that are not credible—are not tolerated. No one can slouch in his or her responsibility, whether it is frontstage or backstage, because everyone plays a part in the overall production. The ultimate goal is a performance that engages the customer in an experience that suspends beliefs of organizational disinterest, commercialism, impersonality, and disregard. A theatrical approach attempts this through a unified and well-executed portrayal designed to create and sustain impressions that reflect the audience's desires. This cannot happen unless the service organization accepts the premise that services are theater in their own right and works hard to ensure an excellent performance.

If customers discover that a service organization has presented a false front, they are likely to take their patronage elsewhere. Hence, service marketers must convey the significance of service theater and stress authenticity throughout the service organization. In most cases, service organizations must guard against the temptation to display canned performances. Many performances are rigidly scripted with little room for actors to improvise. Managers should learn the importance of adapting to customer needs and wants and pursuing flexible strategies in fashioning the service experience. Rather than follow a fixed script, the service worker should be empowered to tailor the performance to the audience. Service managers should also appreciate the need for appropriateness. Absurd, ludicrous, or uncaring performances are likely to yield very negative customer reviews and may result in a service performance that closes early, whereas pertinent, seemly, and caring performances are likely to be held over by popular demand. In short, service performances must respond to the desires of the service audience.

In summary, service theater provides a unifying framework for describing and communicating the service experience. To that end, we have identified the many ways service organizations share characteristics and practices that are similar to theater or a dramaturgical depiction of human behavior. Whether it is a vendor selling Lucky Dogs on Bourbon Street in New Orleans, the combined efforts of the cast members at Disney World, the telephone receptionist taking customers' orders at L.L. Bean, or the cyberspace service offered by Amazon.com, a theatrical performance is occurring. Different service experiences are likely to reflect theatrical elements to varying degrees, yet from the customer's perspective, a show is always unfolding. For example, although the appearance of L.L. Bean's setting or actors is unlikely to carry much importance for its audience's experience, the actors' demeanor and defensive practices and the service's backstage operations are sure to have a significant impact. In contrast, the Lucky Dog vendor has a different set of theatrical elements to address. The frontstage, that is, the vending cart, and the merchant's appearance are quite important to the audience's enjoyment of the service. Organizations must determine which theatrical elements are of greatest significance for forming the customers' impressions and experience.

As a conceptual tool, therefore, service theater demonstrates the implicit and explicit relationships among the service organization, its customers, its employees, and its physical or cyberspace properties. As with any metaphor, the description of services in theatrical terms facilitates communication and analysis of the phenomenon and can be used to generate researchable propositions. It is our contention that applying the theater metaphor to services provides a holistic framework and vocabulary for understanding and managing service experiences.

References

Berry, Leonard L. 1981. "Perspectives on the Retailing of Services," In *Theory in Retailing: Traditional and Nontraditional Sources*, edited by Ronald W. Stampfl and Elizabeth C. Hirschman, Chicago: American Marketing Association.

Billingsley, Kevin. 1998. "Service Providers Can Learn A Lot in Acting 101." *Marketing News* 32 (23): 13A4.

Bitner, Mary Jo. 1992. "Servicescapes: The Impact of Physical Surroundings on Customers and Employees." *Journal of Marketing* 56 (April): 57–71.

Booms, Bernard H., and Mary Jo Bitner. 1981. "Marketing Strategies and Organizational Structures for Service Firms." In *Marketing of Services*, edited by James H. Donnelly and William R. George. Chicago: American Marketing Association.

Carlzon, Jan. 1987. *Moments of Truth*, New York: Ballinger.

Goffman, Erving. 1959. *The Presentation of Self in Everyday Life*. Garden City, NY: Doubleday.

Grönroos, Christian. 1990. *Services Marketing and Management*. Lexington, MA: Lexington Books.

Grove, Stephen J., and Raymond P. Fisk. 1983. "The Dramaturgy of Services Exchange: An Analytical Framework for Services Marketing." In *Emerging Perspectives on Services Marketing*, edited by Leonard L. Berry, C. Lynn Shostack, and Gregory D. Upah. Chicago: American Marketing Association.

———. 1997. "The Impact of Other Customers on Service Experiences: A Critical Incident Examination of 'Getting Along.'" *Journal of Retailing* 73(1): 63–85.

Grove, Stephen J., Raymond P. Fisk, and Patricia A. Knowles. 1996. "Developing the Impression Management Skills of the Service Actor." Paper presented at the Frontiers in Services Marketing Conference, Nashville, Tennessee.

Gummesson, Evert. 1993. *Quality Management in Service Organizations*. St. Johns University. NY: International Service Quality Association.

Hartline, Michael D., and O.C. Ferrell. 1996. "The Management of Customer-Contact Service Employees: An Empirical Investigation." *Journal of Marketing* 60 (October): 52–70.

Johnson, Rick. 1991. "A Strategy for Service—Disney Style." *Journal of Business Strategy* (September/October): 38–43.

Langeard, Eric, John F.C. Bateson, Christopher H. Lovelock, and Pierre Eiglier. eds. 1981. *Marketing of Services: New Insights from Consumers and Managers.* Cambridge, MA: Marketing Science Institute.

Lovelock, Christopher H. 1981. "Why Marketing Management Needs to be Different for Services." In *Marketing of Services*, edited by James H. Donnelly and William R. George. Chicago: American Marketing Association.

———. 1994. *Product Plus: How Product + Service = Competitive Advantage*. New York: McGraw-Hill.

Martin, Charles L., and Charles A. Pranter. 1989. "Compatibility Management: Customer-to-Customer Relationships in Service Environments." *Journal of Services Marketing* 3 (summer): 6–15.

Schneider, Benjamin, and David E. Bowen. 1995. *Winning the Service Game*. Boston: Harvard Business School Press.

Shostack, G. Lynn. 1977. "Breaking Free from Product Marketing." *Journal of Marketing* 41 (April): 73–80.

Surprenant, Carol F., and Michael R. Solomon. 1987. "Predictability and Personalization in Service Encounter." *Journal of Marketing* 51 (April): 86–96.

Tansik, David A. 1990. "Managing Human Resource Issues for High-Contact Service Personnel." In *Service Management Effectiveness: Balancing Strategy Organization and Human Resources, Operations, and Marketing*, edited by David Bowen, Richard B. Chase, Thomas C. Cummings, and associates. San Francisco: Jossey-Bass.

Wilson, Edwin. 1991. *The Theater Experience*. 5th ed. New York: McGraw-Hill.

Zeithaml, Valarie A. 1981. "How Consumer Evaluation Processes Differ between Goods and Services." In *Marketing of Services*, edited by James H. Donnelly and William R. George. Chicago: American Marketing Association.

PART 2

Building the Service Model

Part 2 of the book shows how to build a service model, a central aspect of our strategic marketing framework. We stress the importance of creating a meaningful *value proposition*—a specified package of benefits and solutions that highlights key points of difference relative to competing alternatives. This value proposition must address and integrate two components: creation of a *service concept* and delivery of its different elements through physical and electronic channels.

The next step involves developing a *business model* for recovering all costs (plus a margin for profits) through realistic pricing strategies. To ensure that target customers perceive the benefits from this *value exchange* as exceeding the financial costs, time, and effort that they incur, the value proposition must be communicated in ways that help customers to make good choices and use the service to best advantage. Finally, the strategy must stake out a distinctive and defensible *position* in the market against competing alternatives.

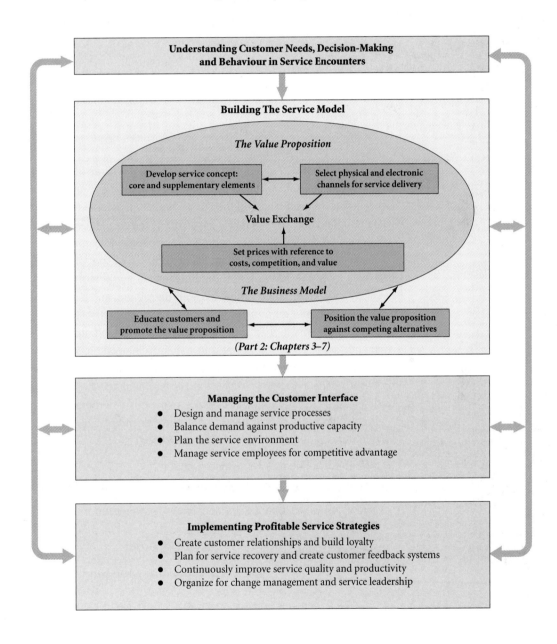

CHAPTER 3

Developing Service Concepts: Core and Supplementary Elements

Consumers build an image [of a brand] as birds build nests. From the scraps and straws they chance upon.

—Jeremy Bullmore

Each and every one of you will make or break the promise that our brand makes to customers.

—An American Express manager speaking to his employees

All service organizations face choices concerning the types of products to offer and how to deliver them to customers. To better understand the nature of service products, it is useful to distinguish between the core product and the supplementary elements that facilitate its use and enhance its value for customers. By making a flowchart of the sequence of encounters that customers have with a service organization, we can gain valuable insights into the nature of an existing service.

Recognizing that a value proposition consists of the whole cluster of benefits that a firm promises to deliver to the target market, service marketers need to create a coherent offering in which each element is compatible with the others, and all are mutually reinforcing.

Many firms offer an array of different service products. Giving each a distinctive brand name serves to differentiate them from each other, and from competing offerings. In competitive environments, service marketers need to focus on innovation, seeking to develop new services or enhance existing ones. New service development may involve either the product itself or the processes used to create it. In fact, the availability of new delivery processes for existing services often changes the nature of the service experience, and may even create new benefits.

In this chapter, we consider the nature of service products, how to add value to them, and how to design them. We explore such questions as:

1. What do we mean by a service product?
2. What insights can we obtain from flowcharting service usage?
3. How can we categorize the supplementary services that surround core products, and how do they add value for customers?
4. Why should service firms create separate brand names for their different products?
5. What are the main approaches to designing new services?

PLANNING AND CREATING SERVICES

What do we mean by a service "product"? When customers purchase a manufactured good such as a camera, a commodity such as diesel fuel, or an agricultural product such as a bag of potatoes, they take title to physical objects. But service performances are experienced rather than owned. Even when there are physical elements to which the customer does take title—such as a cooked meal (which is promptly consumed), a surgically implanted pacemaker, or a replacement part for a car—a significant portion of the price paid by customers is for the value added by the service elements, including expert labour and the use of specialized equipment. A service product comprises all the elements of the service performance, both physical and intangible, that create value for customers.

Augmenting the Core Product

Services are usually defined with reference to a particular industry—for instance, health care or transportation—based on the core set of benefits and solutions delivered to customers. But delivery of this *core product* is usually accompanied by a variety of other service-related activities that we refer to collectively as *supplementary services*, which facilitate use of the core product and add value and differentiation to the customer's overall experience. Core products tend to become commodities as an industry matures and competition increases, so the search for competitive advantage often emphasizes performance on supplementary services.

The core and supplementary combination represents the *service concept* (sometimes referred to in a manufacturing context as the *augmented product*). Lynn Shostack developed a molecular model (Figure 3.1), which uses a chemical analogy to help marketers visualize and manage what she termed a "total market entity."[1] Her model can be applied to either goods or services. At the centre is the core benefit, addressing the basic customer need, linked to a series of other service characteristics. She argues that, as in chemical formulations, a change in one element may completely alter the nature of the entity. Surrounding the molecules are a series of bands representing price, distribution, and market positioning (communication messages).

The molecular model helps us to identify the tangible and intangible elements involved in service delivery. In an expedited parcel delivery service, for example, the intangible elements include transportation of the package itself, service frequency, package tracking, and service guarantees. But the outlet (if the customer chooses to go to the service factory),

Figure 3.1

Shostack's Molecular Model: Passenger Airline Service

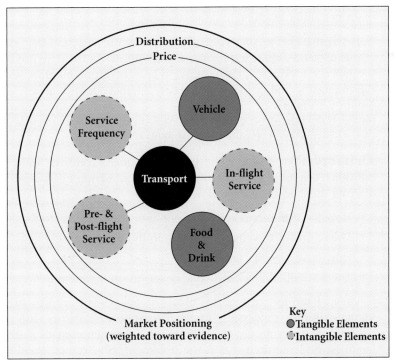

Source: G. Lynn Shostack, "Breaking Free from Product Marketing," *Journal of Marketing* 44 (April 1977): 73–80, published by the American Marketing Association. Reprinted with permission.

the packaging provided by the company, the service personnel, and the trucks and/or aircraft used for transportation of the package are all tangible. The greater the proportion of intangible elements, the more necessary it is to provide tangible clues about the features and quality of the service.[2]

Pierre Eiglier and Eric Langeard proposed a model in which the core service is surrounded by a circle containing a series of supplementary services that are specific to that particular product.[3] Their approach, like Shostack's, emphasizes the interdependence of the various components. They distinguish between those elements needed to facilitate use of the core service (such as the reception desk at a hotel) and those that enhance the appeal of the core service (such as a hotel's fitness centre or business services).

Both models offer useful insights. Shostack wants us to determine which service elements are tangible and which are intangible in order to help formulate product policy and communication programs. Eiglier and Langeard ask us to think about two issues: first, whether supplementary services are needed to facilitate use of the core service, or simply add extra appeal; and second, whether customers should be charged separately for each service element or whether all elements should be bundled under a single price tag. Further insight is provided by Christian Grönroos, who clarifies the different roles ascribed to supplementary services by describing them as either facilitating services (or goods), which enable use of the core product, and supporting services (or goods), which increase the value of the service and/or help to differentiate it.[4] (For greater clarity, we will refer to the latter as enhancing services.)

Designing a Service Concept

When designing a service concept, marketing planners need to take a holistic view of the entire performance that they want customers to experience, highlighting the specific dimensions on which the firm plans to compete. The value proposition must address and integrate three components: core product, supplementary services, and delivery processes.

Core Product This component supplies the central, problem-solving benefits that customers seek. Thus, transport solves the need to move a person or a physical object from one location to another; fitness training should yield expert advice on what actions a client should take to achieve their fitness goals; and repair services should restore a damaged or malfunctioning machine to good working order.

Supplementary Services These elements augment the core product, both facilitating its use and enhancing its value and appeal. As the core product in a particular industry gets commoditized, the extent and level of supplementary services often play a role in differentiating and positioning the core against competing services. Adding more supplementary elements or increasing the level of performance should be done in ways that enhance the perceived value of the core product for prospective customers and enable the service provider to charge a higher price.

Delivery Processes The third component concerns the processes used to deliver both the core product and each of the supplementary services. The design of the service offering must address the following issues:

- How the different service components are delivered to the customer
- The nature of the customer's role in those processes
- How long delivery lasts
- The prescribed level and style of service to be offered.

Each of the four categories of processes—people processing, possession processing, mental-stimulus processing, and information processing—has different implications for operational procedures, the degree of customer contact with service personnel and facilities, and requirements for supplementary services. Possession processing services typically involve more supplementary elements, because the customer must come to the service factory and spend time there during service delivery.

The integration of the core product, supplementary services, and delivery processes is captured in Figure 3.2, which illustrates the components of the service offering for an overnight stay at a luxury hotel—one that not only offers more services than the motel discussed earlier, but also a higher level of performance on those tangible and intangible elements that are common to both types of accommodation.

The core product—overnight rental of a bedroom—contains the following elements: service level, scheduling (how long the room may be used before another payment becomes due), the nature of the process (in this instance, people processing), and the role of customers in terms of what they are expected to do for themselves and what the hotel will do for them, such as making the bed, supplying bathroom towels, and cleaning the room.

Surrounding the core is an array of supplementary services, ranging from reservations to meals and in-room service elements. As with the core product, delivery processes must be specified for each of these elements. The more expensive the hotel, the higher the level of service in each element (for example, covered parking with valet assistance, better food, broadband internet access, and a broader array of movies on Pay TV). Additional services might also be offered, such as a business centre, a bar, a pool, and a health club. One of the characteristics of a top-of-the line hotel is doing things for customers that they might otherwise have to do for themselves, and providing an extended schedule for service delivery, including 24-hour room service.

Documenting the Delivery Sequence over Time

Next, product planners must address the sequence in which customers will use each of the core and supplementary services, and the approximate length of time required in each instance. This information, which should reflect a good understanding of customer needs, habits, and expectations, is necessary not only for marketing purposes but also for facilities

Figure 3.2

The Service Offering for an Overnight Hotel Stay

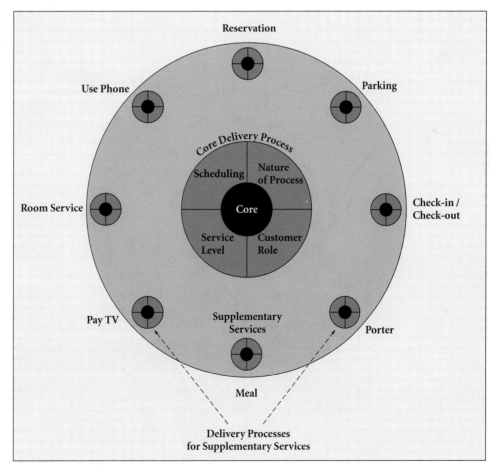

planning, operations management, and allocation of personnel. In some instances, as in the script for teeth-cleaning services at the dentist, discussed earlier in Chapter 2 (see Figure 2.13, page 54), certain service elements must be delivered in a prescribed sequence. In other instances, there may be some flexibility.

Time plays a key role in services, not only from an operational standpoint as it relates to allocating and scheduling purposes, but also from the perspective of customers themselves. For example, in the case of dental services, time plays a crucial role, since it relates to scheduling of an appointment, waiting time before dental services are provided, time spent during service delivery, and finally the time the patient spends after the dental procedure paying for the service and setting up additional appointments. Similarly, in the hotel industry, neither the core service nor its supplementary elements are all delivered continuously throughout the duration of the service performance. Certain services must necessarily be used before others. In this industry, as in many services, consumption of the core product is sandwiched between use of supplementary services that are needed earlier or later in the delivery sequence. Figure 3.3 adds a temporal dimension to the different elements of the luxury hotel service concept (as depicted in Figure 3.2), identifying when and for how long they are likely to be consumed by a typical guest from a given segment. Not every guest uses every service, of course, and schedules may vary.

An important aspect of service planning is determining the amount of time that customers may spend on different service elements. In some instances, research may show that customers from a given segment expect to budget a specific amount of time for a given activity that has value for them and they would not wish to rush (for instance, 8 hours for sleeping, an hour and a half for a business dinner, 20 minutes for breakfast). In other instances, such as making a reservation, checking in, payment, or waiting for a car to be retrieved from valet parking, customers may wish to minimize or even eliminate time spent on what they perceive as non-productive activities.

Do customers' expectations change during the course of service delivery in light of the perceived quality of sequential encounters? In many cases, the answer is yes. Ideally, service firms should try to provide consistently high performance at each step; but, in reality, many service performances are inconsistent. Research Insights 3.1 provides some additional food for thought.

While the scenarios presented above refer to physical encounters, the principle of enhancing experience at every step of a service encounter applies equally well in an internet environment. Arguing that it's more important to end on a strong note than to begin on one, Richard Chase and Sriram Dasu note that many commercial websites are designed with attractive home pages that create high expectations, but become progressively less appealing and even problematic to use as customers move toward conclusion of a purchase.[5] This situation can lead customers to abandon their electronic shopping carts in mid-transaction. Kim Guenther provides ten practical ways of increasing the "stickiness" of the website, with the aim of enhancing the overall experience of customers on a website, which in turn impacts on customer behaviour and loyalty toward a website. For

Figure 3.3

Temporal Dimension of Augmented Hotel Product

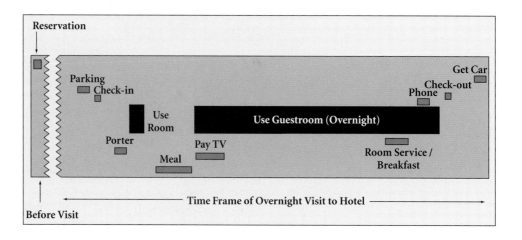

Research Insights 3.1

Learning from Studies of Sequential Service Encounters

A laboratory study is one that simulates real-world events in a controlled setting. One such study explored how respondents judged hypothetical service encounters in three different service categories: a weekend car rental, an international flight, and a retail purchase (Hansen and Danaher, 1999). Within each category, one of three scenarios was presented to participants. In the first, the initial service events were performed well, the core service adequately, and the concluding steps poorly, thus creating a deteriorating trend; in the second, the situation was reversed, to create an improving trend; and in the third, a consistently adequate service was delivered from start to finish. The findings showed that a weak start that built towards a strong finish received more favourable judgments than did the other scenarios. A conclusion to be drawn from this research is that managers who are not immediately able to raise all elements of the service encounter should begin by focusing on improving the concluding events in the process rather than the opening steps.

Another laboratory study simulated a visit to a restaurant (Hamer et al., 1999). Respondents were presented with two scenarios in which they were going out to eat with a group of friends and were given information at certain key steps during the service encounter. The findings showed that respondents continuously updated their expectations during service delivery, and that these evolving expectations had a larger effect on their perceptions of service quality than did perceived service performance. A key managerial insight from this study is that it's very important for managers to shape and control customers' expectations as service delivery proceeds.

An exploratory study of sequential service encounters in a real-world setting was conducted by Verhoef et al. (2004). It examined inbound telephone calls by customers to the call centre of a large financial service provider. The findings suggested that customer satisfaction was not created solely by the average quality of the events in the service process but could be enhanced by a positive peak experience at some point in the process.

In a study of customers of a club-resort holiday service, Strauss and Weinlich (1997) used the sequential incident technique (SIT) to show how the overall evaluation of service quality could be understood in terms of customer experiences with distinct incidents in a sequential manner. They argue that looking at perceived service quality as a sequence of episodes provides management with valuable insights not only into managing service-delivery system failures but also service personnel training programs.

Sources: David E. Hansen and Peter J. Danaher, "Inconsistent Performance During the Service Encounter," *Journal of Service Research* 1 (February 1999): 227–35; Lawrence O. Hamer, Ben Shaw-Ching Liu, and D. Sudharshan, "The Effects of Intraencounter Changes in Expectations on Perceived Service Quality Models," *Journal of Service Research* 1 (February 1999): 275–89; Peter C. Verhoef, Gerrit Antonides, and Arnoud N. de Hoog, "Service Encounters as a Sequence of Events: The Importance of Peak Experiences," *Journal of Service Research* 7 (August 2004): 53–64; and Bernd Strauss, and Bernhard Weinlich, "Process-Oriented Measurement of Service Quality: Applying the Sequential Incident Technique," *European Journal of Marketing* 31/1 (1997): 33–55.

increasing stickiness, she suggests keeping the website simple, delivering value at each click, creating fresh content, tailoring the experience, engaging users, seeking feedback from users, creating trust, making online shopping better than the bricks-and-mortar equivalent, putting information and services before extolling company virtues, and providing tools such as charts and calculators that users can take advantage of while browsing the website.[6]

Flowcharting Service Delivery Helps to Clarify Product Elements

Flowcharting, a technique for displaying the nature and sequence of the different steps involved in delivering service to customers, offers a way to understand the totality of the customer's service experience. Marketers find that creating a flowchart for a specific service is particularly useful for distinguishing between those steps where customers use the core service and those involving service elements that supplement the core product. For instance, for restaurants, food and beverages constitute the core product, but supplementary services may include reservations, valet parking, coatroom, being escorted to a table, ordering from the menu, billing, payment, and use of restrooms. If you prepare flowcharts for a variety of services, you will soon notice that although the core products may differ widely, common supplementary elements—from information to billing and from reservations or order-taking to problem resolution—keep recurring.

Using this approach enables us to see the different nature of the customer's involvement with the service organization for each of the four categories of services introduced in Chapter 2—people processing, possession processing, mental-stimulus processing, and information processing. Let's take one example of each category—staying in a motel, getting a DVD player repaired, obtaining a weather forecast, and purchasing health insurance. Figure 3.4 displays a simple flowchart that demonstrates what's involved in each of four scenarios. Imagine that you are the customer in each instance and think about the extent and nature of your involvement in the service-delivery process and the types of encounters with the organization that take place.

- *Stay at a motel (people processing).* It's late evening. You're driving on a long trip and are getting tired. Spotting a motel displaying a vacancy sign you decide it's time to stop for the night, but on closer inspection, the building exterior looks rundown, there are weeds growing through cracks in the asphalt parking lot, and the grass needs cutting. You decide to continue and soon come to another motel which, in addition to a vacancy sign, also displays a price that seems very reasonable. You park your car, noting that the grounds are clean and that the buildings seem freshly painted. On entering the

Figure 3.4 Simple Flowcharts for Delivery of Various Types of Services

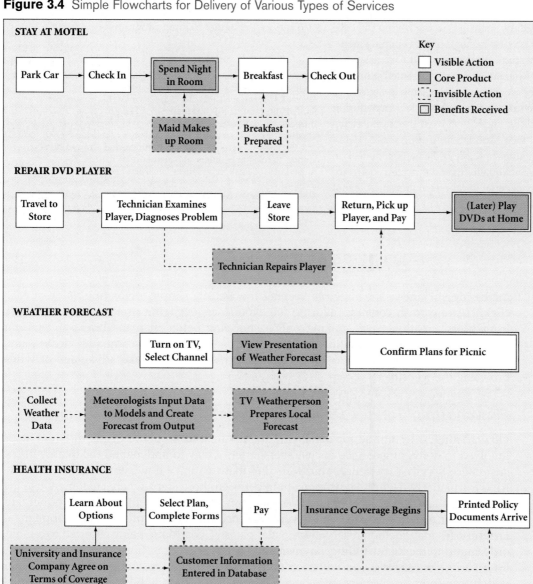

reception area, you're greeted by a friendly clerk who checks you in and gives you the key to a room. You move your car to the space in front of your assigned unit and let yourself in. After undressing and using the bathroom, you go to bed. Following a good night's sleep, you rise the next morning, shower, dress, and pack. Then you walk to reception, where you take advantage of the free coffee, juice, and doughnuts, return your key to a different clerk, pay, and drive away.

- *Repair a DVD player (possession processing).* When you use your DVD player, the picture quality on the TV screen is poor. Fed up with the situation, you search the Yellow Pages to find an appliance repair store in your area. At the store, the neatly dressed technician checks your machine carefully but quickly and declares that it needs to be adjusted and cleaned. His professional manner inspires confidence. The estimated price seems realistic and you're reassured to learn that repairs are guaranteed for three months, so you agree to the work and are told that the player will be ready in three days' time. The technician disappears into the back office with your machine and you leave the store. On the appointed day, you return to pick up the product, the technician explains the work that he did and demonstrates that the machine is now working well. You pay the agreed price and leave the store with your machine. Back home, you plug in the player, insert a DVD, and find that the picture is now much improved.

- *Weather forecast (mental-stimulus processing).* You're planning a picnic trip to the lake, but one of your friends says she's heard that it's going to be really cold this weekend. Back home that evening, you check the weather forecast on TV. The meteorologist shows animated charts indicating the probable path of a cold front over the next 72 hours and states that the latest Environment Canada computer projections suggest the front will remain well to the north of your area (Figure 3.5). Armed with this information, you call your friends to tell them that the picnic is on.

- *Health insurance (information processing).* Your university mails you a package of information before the beginning of the new semester. This package includes a student health service brochure describing the extended health and dental insurance option available to students. You can also get further information from a website or by telephoning. You consider opting out of the plan, but you remember the experience of a friend who recently incurred heavy dentist bills for treatment after an unfortunate fall. Uninsured, he was forced to liquidate his modest savings to pay the bills. Not wish-

Figure 3.5
Weather forecasting is a service directed at customers' minds.

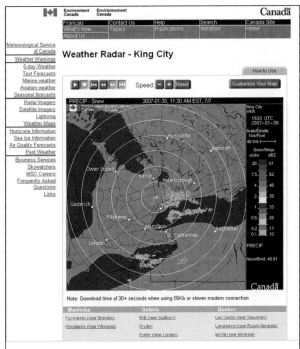

Source: Accessed from Environment Canada website (http://www.weatheroffice.ec.gc.ca/radar/index_e.html?id=WKR), January 23, 2007.

ing to pay for more coverage than you need, you telephone and ask for information and advice from a counsellor. At the time of registration, you fill in a printed form that includes some standard questions about your medical history and then sign it. The cost of the insurance is added to your term bill. Subsequently, you receive printed confirmation of your coverage in the mail. Now you no longer have to worry about the risk of unexpected medical expenses.

Insights from Flowcharting   As you can see from these flowcharts, your role as a customer for each of these service products varies sharply from one category to another. The first two examples involve physical processes and the latter two are information-based. At the two motels, you made advance judgments on service quality based on the physical appearance of the buildings and grounds, deciding not to stay at the first one because of negative clues to service quality. At the second one, you rent use of a bedroom, bathroom, and other physical facilities for the night. Parking is included, too. The management has added value by offering a simple breakfast as part of the package.

Your role at the appliance repair store, however, is limited to briefly explaining the symptoms, leaving the machine, and returning several days later to pick it up. You have to trust the technician's competence and honesty in executing the service in your absence. However, inclusion of a guarantee lowers the risk. You enjoy the benefits later when using the repaired machine.

The other two services, weather forecasting and health insurance, involve intangible actions and a less active role for you as consumer. The TV station you watch competes with other stations (and with radio stations, newspapers, and the internet) for an audience, so must appeal on the design of its graphics, personality and presentation skills of its meteorologist, convenience of its schedule, and reputation for accuracy. You incur no financial cost to obtain the forecast, but may have to watch some ads first, since advertising revenues constitute the business model that funds the station's operations. Delivery of the information you need takes only a couple of minutes and you can act on it immediately. By contrast, obtaining extended health and dental insurance takes more time and mental effort, because you have to evaluate the option and complete a detailed application. Then you may have to wait for the policy to be issued, and coverage to begin. Your choice of opting in for the health and dental plan will reflect the cost relative to the benefits offered. How clearly these benefits are explained may influence your decision.

Each of the flowcharts in Figure 3.4 features a core product, of course, and three of the four (motel, repair, and insurance) include several supplementary services. We now take an in-depth look at the role played by different types of supplementary services, demonstrating the importance of designing a service concept in which both core and supplementary service elements meet consistent standards and mutually reinforce each other.

THE FLOWER OF SERVICE[7]

Supplementary services play one of two roles. *Facilitating supplementary services* are either required for service delivery, or aid in the use of the core product. *Enhancing supplementary services* add extra value for customers. There are potentially dozens of different supplementary services, but almost all of them can be classified into one of the following eight clusters. We've listed them according to whether they are categorized as facilitating or enhancing.

Facilitating Services	Enhancing Services
• Information	• Consultation
• Order-taking	• Hospitality
• Billing	• Safekeeping
• Payment	• Exceptions

In Figure 3.6 these eight clusters are displayed as petals surrounding the centre of a flower—which we call the *Flower of Service*. We've shown them clockwise in the sequence

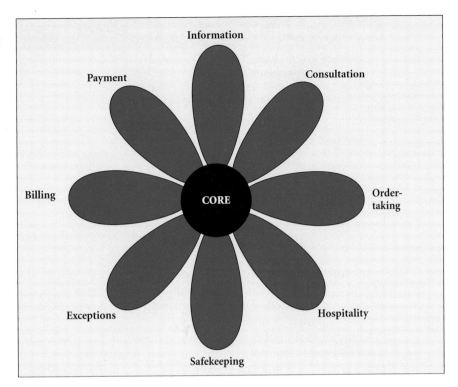

in which they are often likely to be encountered by customers (although this sequence may vary—for instance, in the case of an amusement park, payment has to be made before the service is delivered rather than afterwards). In a well-designed and well-managed service organization, the petals and core are fresh and well-formed. A badly designed or poorly executed service is a like a flower with missing, wilted or discoloured petals. In such a case, the overall impression of the flower is unattractive even if the core itself is perfect. Think about your own experiences as a customer (or when purchasing on behalf of an organization). When you were dissatisfied with a particular purchase, was it the core that was at fault, or a problem with one or more of the petals?

Not every core product is surrounded by supplementary elements from all eight clusters. As we'll see, the nature of the product helps to determine which supplementary services must be offered, and which might usefully be added to enhance value and make the organization easy to do business with. In general, people-processing services tend to be accompanied by more supplementary services than do the other three categories; similarly, high-contact services will have more supplementary aspects than low-contact services.

A company's market-positioning strategy helps to determine which supplementary services should be included (see Chapter 7). A strategy of adding benefits to increase customers' perceptions of quality will probably require more supplementary services (and also a higher level of performance on all such elements) than a strategy of competing on low prices. Firms that offer different grades of service—such as an airline's first class, business class, and economy class—often differentiate them by adding extra supplementary services for each upgrade in service.

Information

To obtain full value from any good or service, customers need relevant information (Table 3.1). New customers and prospects are especially information-hungry. Customers' needs may include directions to the site where the product is sold (or details of how to order it), service hours, prices, and usage instructions. Further information, sometimes required by law, could include conditions of sale and use, warnings, reminders, and notification of changes.

Table 3.1 Examples of Information Elements

Directions to service site
Schedules/service hours
Prices
Instructions on using core product/supplementary services
Reminders
Warnings
Conditions of sale/service
Notification of changes
Documentation
Confirmation of reservations
Summaries of account activity
Receipts and tickets

Customers also appreciate advice on how to get the most value from a service and how to avoid problems (Figure 3.7). Finally, customers may want documentation of what has already taken place, such as confirmation of reservations, receipts and tickets, and monthly summaries of account activity.

Companies should make sure the information they provide is both timely and accurate, since incorrect information can annoy or inconvenience customers. Traditional ways of providing information to customers include using front-line employees (who are not always as well-informed as customers might like), printed notices, brochures, and instruction books. Other information media include videotapes/DVDs or software-driven tutorials, touch-screen video displays, and menu-driven recorded telephone messages. The most significant recent innovation has been corporate use of websites. Examples of useful applications include train and airline schedules, hotel details, assistance in locating specific retail outlets such as restaurants and stores, and information on the services of professional firms. Many business logistics companies offer shippers the opportunity to track the movements of their packages—each of which has been assigned a unique identification number (Figure 3.8).

Figure 3.7
Credit card companies join forces to educate consumers.

Order-Taking

Once customers are ready to buy, a key supplementary element comes into play—accepting applications, orders, and reservations (Table 3.2). The process of order-taking should be polite, fast, and accurate so that customers do not waste time and endure unnecessary mental or physical effort. Technology can be used to make order-taking easier and faster for both customers and suppliers. The key lies in minimizing the time and effort required of both parties, while also ensuring completeness and accuracy.

Banks, insurance companies, and utilities require prospective customers to go through an application process designed to gather relevant information and to screen out those who do not meet basic enrolment criteria (like a bad credit record or serious existing health problems). Universities also require prospective students to apply for admission. Reservations (including appointments and check-in) represent a special type of order-taking that entitles customers to a specified unit of service—for example, an airline seat, a restaurant table, a hotel room, time with a qualified professional, or admission to a facility such as a theatre or sports arena with designated seating. Accuracy in scheduling is vital—reserving seats for the wrong day is likely to be unpopular with customers.

Ticketless systems, based upon telephone or website reservations, provide enormous cost savings for airlines, since there is no travel agent commission—customers book directly—and the administrative effort is drastically reduced. A paper ticket at an airline

---

Table 3.2 Examples of Order-Taking Elements

Applications
- Membership in clubs or programs
- Subscription services (e.g., utilities)
- Prerequisite-based services (e.g., financial credit, college enrolment)

Order Entry
- On-site order fulfillment
- Mail/telephone order placement
- Email/website order placement

Reservations and Check-in
- Seats/tables/rooms
- Vehicle or equipment rental
- Professional appointments
- Admission to restricted facilities (e.g., museums, aquariums)

may be handled 15 times, while an electronic ticket requires just one step. Customers receive a confirmation number when they make the reservations and need only show identification at the airport to claim their seats and receive a boarding pass. It is no surprise that the International Air Transport Association (IATA) working group on electronic ticketing has worked with world's airlines to set a deadline of December 31, 2007 for complete migration to electronic ticketing. As of January 1, 2008 only electronic tickets will be issued—no more paper tickets![8]

Billing

Billing is common to almost all services (unless the service is provided free of charge). Inaccurate, illegible, or incomplete bills risk disappointing customers who may, up to that point, have been quite satisfied with their experience, while such failures are perceived as adding insult to injury if the customer is already dissatisfied. Billing should also be timely, because it serves to stimulate faster payment. Procedures range from verbal statements to a machine-displayed price, and from handwritten invoices to elaborate monthly statements of account activity and fees (Table 3.3). Perhaps the simplest approach is self-billing, when the customer tallies up the amount of an order and authorizes a card payment or writes a cheque. In such instances, billing and payment are combined into a single act, although the seller may still need to check for accuracy.

Customers usually expect bills to be clear and informative, and itemized in ways that make it clear how the total was computed. Unexplained, arcane symbols that have all the meaning of hieroglyphics on an Egyptian monument (and are decipherable only by the high priests of accounting and data processing) do not create a favourable impression of the supplier. Nor does fuzzy printing or illegible handwriting. Laser printers, with their ability to switch fonts and typefaces, to box and to highlight, can produce statements that are not only more legible but also organize information in more useful ways. Marketing research can help here, by asking customers what information they want and how they would like it to be organized.

Busy customers hate to be kept waiting for a bill to be prepared in a hotel, restaurant, or rental car lot. Many hotels and rental car firms have now created express check-out options, taking customers' credit card details in advance and documenting charges later by mail. But accuracy is essential—since customers use the express check-outs to *save* time, they certainly don't want to *waste* time later seeking corrections and refunds. An alternative express check-out procedure is used by some car rental companies. An agent meets customers as they return their cars, checks the kilometrage and fuel gauge readings, and then prints a bill on the spot using a portable wireless terminal. Many hotels push bills under guestroom doors on the morning of departure showing charges to date; others offer customers the option of previewing their bills before checkout on the TV monitors in their rooms.

Payment

In most cases, a bill requires the customer to take action on payment (and such action may be very slow in coming!). One exception is bank statements detailing charges that have already been deducted from the customer's account. Increasingly, customers expect ease and convenience of payment, including credit, when they make purchases in their own countries and while travelling abroad.

Table 3.3 Examples of Billing Elements

- Periodic statements of account activity
- Invoices for individual transactions
- Verbal statements of amount due
- Machine display of amount due
- Self-billing (computed by customer)

Table 3.4 Examples of Payment Elements

Self-Service
- Insert card, cash, or token in machine
- Electronic funds transfer
- Mail a cheque
- Enter credit card number online

Direct to Payee or Intermediary
- Cash handling and change giving
- Cheque handling
- Credit/charge/debit card handling
- Coupon redemption
- Tokens, vouchers, etc.

Automatic Deduction from Financial Deposits (e.g., bank charges) Control and Verification
- Automated systems (e.g., machine-readable tickets that operate entry gates)
- Human systems (e.g., toll collectors, ticket inspectors)

A variety of options exist for customers to make payment (Table 3.4). Self-service payment systems, for instance, require insertion of coins, banknotes, tokens, or cards in machines. But equipment breakdowns destroy the whole purpose of such a system, so good maintenance and rapid-response troubleshooting are essential. Much payment still takes place through hand-to-hand transfers of cash and cheques, but credit and debit cards are growing in importance as more and more establishments accept them. Other alternatives include vouchers, coupons, or prepaid tickets. Firms benefit from prompt payment, since it reduces the amount of accounts receivable. While it is not a popular practice in the B2C environment, offering discounts for prompt payment of invoices is standard procedure in B2B contexts.

Consultation

Now we move to enhancing supplementary services, led by consultation. In contrast to information, which suggests a simple response to customers' questions (or printed information that anticipates their needs), consultation involves a dialogue to probe customer requirements and then develop a tailored solution. Table 3.5 provides examples of several supplementary services in the consultation category. At its simplest, consultation consists of immediate advice from a knowledgeable service person in response to the request: "What do you suggest?" (For example, as we saw in Chapter 1, you might seek advice from the hairstylist on styles that best complement your facial profile.) Effective consultation requires an understanding of each customer's current situation, before suggesting a suitable course of action. Good customer records can be a great help in this respect, particularly if relevant data can be retrieved easily from a remote terminal.

Counselling represents a more subtle approach to consultation because it involves helping customers better understand their situation so that they can come up with solutions and action programs that they can think of as their own. This approach can be a particularly valuable supplement to services such as health treatment, when part of the challenge is to get customers to take a long-term view of their personal situation and to adopt more

Table 3.5 Examples of Consultation Elements

- Customized advice
- Personal counselling
- Tutoring/training in product use
- Management or technical consulting

healthy behaviour, often involving significant lifestyle changes. For example, fitness centres like Goodlife Fitness offer personal training services where personal trainers work closely with customers so that they can achieve their long-term fitness goals. This is done through a variety of services and motivational techniques that go beyond a general fitness program. The hope is that with proper counselling and training the customers change their fitness lifestyle so that the impact of the program can be sustained over time.

More formalized efforts to provide management and technical consulting for corporate customers include the "solution selling" associated with expensive industrial equipment and services. The sales engineer researches the customer's situation and then offers objective advice about what particular package of equipment and systems will yield the best results for the customer. Some consulting services are offered free of charge in the hope of making a sale. However, in other instances the service is "unbundled" and customers are expected to pay for it. Advice can also be offered through tutorials, group training programs, and public demonstrations.

Hospitality

Hospitality-related services should, ideally, reflect pleasure at meeting new customers and greeting old ones when they return. Well-managed businesses try, at least in small ways, to ensure that their employees treat customers as guests. Courtesy and consideration for customers' needs apply to both face-to-face encounters and telephone interactions (Table 3.6). Hospitality finds its full expression in face-to-face encounters. In some cases, it starts (and ends) with an offer of transport to and from the service site, as with courtesy shuttle buses. If customers must wait outdoors before the service can be delivered, then a thoughtful service provider will offer weather protection; if indoors, then a waiting area with seating and even entertainment (TV, newspapers, or magazines) to pass the time. Recruiting employees who are naturally warm, welcoming, and considerate for customer-contact jobs helps to create a hospitable atmosphere.

The quality of the hospitality services offered by a firm can increase or decrease satisfaction with the core product. This is especially true for people-processing services where customers cannot easily leave the service facility. Hotel chains such as Ritz Carlton are examples of organizations where management of customer satisfaction through hospitality elements has been very carefully codified so that it can be reproduced in all their hotels. Some airlines seek to differentiate themselves from their competitors with better meals and more attentive cabin crew; Singapore Airlines is well-recognized on both counts.[9]

Although pre-flight and in-flight hospitality is important, an airline journey doesn't really end until passengers reach their final destination. Air travellers have come to expect departure lounges, but British Airways (BA) came up with the novel idea of an arrivals lounge for its terminals at London's Heathrow and Gatwick airports, to serve passengers arriving early in the morning after a long, overnight flight from the Americas, Asia, Africa, or Australia. It offers holders of first and business class tickets, or a BA Executive Club gold card (awarded to the airline's most frequent flyers), the opportunity to use a special lounge where they can take a shower, change, use a spa, have breakfast, and make phone calls and check their email before continuing to their final destination feeling a lot fresher.

Table 3.6 Examples of Hospitality Elements

Greeting
Food and beverages
Toilets and washrooms
Waiting facilities and amenities
• Lounges, waiting areas, seating
• Weather protection
• Magazines, entertainment, newspapers
Transport
Security

Cosmetic Surgeons' Offices Turn Off Patients

It appears that plastic surgeons could use some service-marketing training along with their other courses in medical school. That's the diagnosis of two experts, Kate Altork and Douglas Dedo, who did a study of patients' reactions to doctors' offices. They found that many patients will cancel a surgery, change doctors, or refuse to consider future elective surgery if they feel uneasy in the doctor's office. The study results suggested that patients don't usually "doctor-jump" because they don't like the doctor but because they don't like the context of the service experience. The list of common patient dislikes includes: graphic posters of moles and skin cancers decorating office walls; uncomfortable plastic identification bracelets for patients; claustrophobic examining rooms with no windows or current reading material; bathrooms that aren't clearly marked; and not enough wastebaskets and water coolers in the waiting room.

What do patients want? Most requests are surprisingly simple and involve creature comforts like tissues, water coolers, telephones, plants, and bowls of candy in the waiting room, or live flower arrangements in the lobby. Patients also want windows in the examining rooms and gowns that wrap around the entire body. They would like to sit on a real chair when they talk to a doctor instead of perching on a stool or examining table. Finally, pre-operative patients prefer to be separated from post-operative ones, since they are disturbed by sitting next to someone in the waiting room whose head is enclosed in bandages.

These results suggest that cosmetic surgery patients would rather visit an office that looks like a health spa than a hospital ward. By thinking like service marketers, savvy surgeons could use this information to create patient-friendly environments that will complement, rather than counteract, their technical expertise.

Source: Adapted from Lisa Bannon, "Plastic Surgeons Are Told to Pay More Attention to Appearances," *Wall Street Journal* (March 15, 1997): B1.

It's a nice competitive advantage, which BA actively promotes. Other airlines have since felt obliged to copy this innovation, although few can match the array of services offered by BA.

Failures in hospitality extend to the physical design of the areas where customers wait prior to receiving service. A survey found that unappealing offices and lack of creature comforts can drive away patients of cosmetic surgeons (Research Insights 3.2).

Safekeeping

While visiting a service site, customers often want assistance with their personal possessions. In fact, unless certain safekeeping services are provided (like safe and convenient parking for their cars), some customers may not come at all. On-site safekeeping services include coatrooms; baggage transport, handling and storage; safekeeping of valuables; and even child care and pet care (Table 3.7). Additional safekeeping services involve physical products that customers buy or rent. They may include packaging, pickup and delivery, assembly, installation, cleaning, and inspection. These services may be offered free or for an additional fee.

Table 3.7 Examples of Safekeeping Elements

Caring for Possessions Customers Bring with Them	Caring for Goods Purchased (or Rented) by Customers
• Child care	• Packaging
• Pet care	• Pickup
• Parking facilities for vehicles	• Transportation and delivery
• Valet parking	• Installation
• Coat rooms	• Inspection and diagnosis
• Baggage handling	• Cleaning
• Storage space	• Refuelling
• Safe deposit boxes	• Preventive maintenance
• Security personnel	• Repairs and renovation
	• Upgrade

Figure 3.9

Wilfrid Laurier University's community safety and security department monitors safety and security issues, and provides relevant educational information.

Responsible businesses pay close attention to safety and security issues for customers who are visiting the firm's premises. Almost all universities have a campus safety and security department that caters to the security needs of the on-campus (and sometimes even off-campus) students, faculty, and staff, as well as their possessions. For example, Wilfrid Laurier University's community safety and security department not only actively monitors for safety and security issues around campus but also provides relevant information to educate students, faculty, and staff so that they can be proactive in protecting themselves and their possessions (Figure 3.9).

Exceptions

Exceptions involve supplementary services that fall outside the routine of normal service delivery (Table 3.8). Astute businesses anticipate exceptions and develop contingency plans and guidelines in advance. That way, employees will not appear helpless and surprised when customers ask for special assistance. Well-defined procedures make it easier for employees to respond promptly and effectively.

There are several types of exceptions:

1. *Special requests.* There are many circumstances when a customer may request a service that requires a departure from normal operating procedures. Advance requests often

Table 3.8 Examples of Exception Elements

Special Requests in Advance of Service Delivery	Problem Solving
• Children's needs • Dietary requirements • Medical or disability needs • Religious observances • Deviations from standard operating procedures	• Warranties and guarantees against product malfunction • Resolving difficulties that arise from using the product • Resolving difficulties caused by accidents, service failures, and problems with staff or other customers • Assisting customers who have suffered an accident or medical emergency
Handling Special Communications	**Restitution**
• Complaints • Compliments • Suggestions	• Refunds • Compensation in kind for unsatisfactory goods and services • Free repair of defective goods

relate to personal needs, including care of children, dietary requirements, medical needs, religious observance, and personal disabilities. Such special requests are common in the travel and hospitality industries.

2. *Problem-solving.* Situations arise when normal service delivery (or product performance) fails to run smoothly as a result of accidents, delays, equipment failures, or customers experiencing difficulty in using the product.

3. *Handling of complaints/suggestions/compliments.* This activity requires well-defined procedures. It should be easy for customers to express dissatisfaction, offer suggestions for improvement, or pass on compliments, and service providers should be able to make an appropriate response quickly.

4. *Restitution.* Many customers expect to be compensated for serious performance failures. Compensation may take the form of repairs under warranty, legal settlements, refunds, an offer of free service, or other forms of payment in kind.

Managers need to keep an eye on the level of exception requests. Too many requests may indicate that standard procedures need revamping. For instance, if a fitness facility constantly receives requests for yoga classes since none are offered, this may indicate that it's time to revise the offerings and perhaps hire a yoga instructor to cater to customer needs. A flexible approach to exceptions is generally a good idea, because it reflects responsiveness to customer needs. On the other hand, too many exceptions may compromise safety, negatively impact other customers, and overburden employees.

Managerial Implications

The eight categories of supplementary services forming the Flower of Service collectively provide many options for enhancing core products, both goods and services. Most supplementary services do (or should) represent responses to customer needs. As noted earlier, some are facilitating services—like information and reservations—that enable customers to use the core product more effectively. Others are "extras" that enhance the core or even reduce its non-financial costs (for example, meals, magazines, and entertainment are hospitality elements that help pass the time). Some elements—notably billing and payment—are, in effect, imposed by the service provider. But even if not actively desired by the customer, they still form part of the overall service experience. Any badly handled element may negatively affect customers' perceptions of service quality. The "information" and "consultation" petals illustrate the emphasis in this book on the need for education as well as promotion in communicating with service customers.

Not every core product is surrounded by supplementary services from all eight petals. People-processing services tend to be the most demanding in terms of supplementary elements—especially hospitality—since they involve close (and often extended) interactions with customers. When customers don't visit the service factory, the need for hospitality may be limited to simple courtesies in letters and telecommunications. Possession-processing services sometimes place heavy demands on safekeeping elements, but there may be no need for this particular petal when providing information-processing services in which customers and suppliers deal entirely at arm's length. Financial services that are provided electronically are an exception to this, however—companies must ensure that their customers' intangible financial assets and their privacy are carefully safeguarded in transactions that occur via phone or the web. Most good financial institutions, for example RBC Royal Bank, will provide detailed instructions on security issues—such as safe computing practices, protection of identity, and avoidance of email fraud—to customers conducting electronic transactions.[10]

A study of Japanese, American and European firms serving business-to-business markets found that most companies simply added layer upon layer of services to their core offerings without knowing what customers really valued.[11] Managers surveyed in the study indicated that they had no clear basis for deciding which services should be offered as a standard package accompanying the core, and which could be offered as options for an extra charge. Without this knowledge, developing effective pricing policies can be tricky. There are no simple rules governing pricing decisions for core products and supplementary services. But managers should continually review their own policies and those of competitors to make sure they are in line with both market practice and customer needs. We'll discuss these and other pricing issues in more detail in Chapter 5.

In summary, Tables 3.1 to 3.8 can serve as a checklist in the continuing search for new ways to augment existing core products and to design new offerings. The lists provided in these eight tables are not all encompassing, since some products may require specialized supplementary elements. In general, a firm that competes on a low-cost, no-frills basis will require fewer supplementary elements than would one marketing an expensive, high-value-added product. Alternative levels of supplementary services around a common core may offer the basis for a product line of differentiated offerings, similar to the various classes of travel offered by airlines. Regardless of which supplementary services a firm decides to offer, all of the elements in each petal should receive the care and attention needed to meet defined service standards consistently. That way the resulting "flower" will always have a fresh and appealing appearance—rather than looking wilted or disfigured by neglect.

PLANNING AND BRANDING SERVICE PRODUCTS

In recent years, more and more service businesses have started talking about their *products*—a term previously associated with manufactured goods. Some will even speak of their "products and services," an expression also used by service-driven manufacturing firms. What is the distinction between these two terms in today's business environment?

A *product* implies a defined and consistent "bundle of output," and also the ability to differentiate one bundle of output from another. In a manufacturing context, the concept is easy to understand and visualize. Service firms can also differentiate their products in similar fashion to the various "models" offered by manufacturers. Quick-service restaurants are sometimes described as "quasi-manufacturing" operations since they produce a physical output combined with value-added service. At each site, they display a menu of their products, which are of course highly tangible—burger connoisseurs in Ontario can easily distinguish Lick's Homeburger from a Hulk Homeburger, or a Hulk Homeburger from a Big Mac. The service comes from the show-biz attitude of the employees (taking and passing on orders for food in a sing-song fashion), quick delivery of a freshly prepared food item, the option (in some instances) to order and pick up freshly cooked food from a drive-in location without leaving one's car, the availability within the restaurant of self-service drinks, condiments, and napkins, and the opportunity to sit down and eat one's meal at a table.

Providers of more intangible services also offer a "menu" of products, representing an assembly of carefully prescribed elements built around the core product, and may bundle in certain value-added supplementary services. For instance, banks offer a variety of accounts, insurance providers offer different types of policies, and universities offer different degree programs, each composed of a mix of required and elective courses. Let's look in more detail at some examples from hotels, a computer-support service, and an international airline.

Product Lines and Brands

Most service organizations offer a line of products rather than just a single product. As a result, they must choose among three broad alternatives: using a single brand identity to cover all products and services, a separate, stand-alone brand for each offering, or some combination of these two extremes.[12] These alternatives are represented as a spectrum in Figure 3.10. David Aaker and E. Joachimsthaler use the term *branded house* to describe a company, such as the Virgin Group, that applies its brand name to multiple offerings in often unrelated fields.[13] Next on this spectrum are what they term *sub-brands*, where the master brand is the primary frame of reference but the product itself has a distinctive name too (Singapore Airlines' Raffles Class, denoting the company's business class

Figure 3.10

The Spectrum of Branding Alternatives

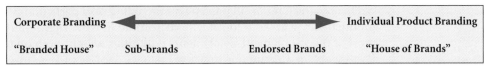

Source: Adapted from James Devlin, "Brand Architecture in Services: The Example of Retail Financial Services," *Journal of Marketing Management* 19 (2003): 1046.

service, is an example), followed by *endorsed brands*, where the product brand dominates but the corporate name is still featured (many hotel corporations adopt this approach). At the far end of the spectrum is the *house of brands* strategy, exemplified by Procter and Gamble, with some 80 packaged goods products, each actively promoted under its own brand name.

Hotel Branding   North America has over 200 hotel brands competing for business, more than any other product category. Many hotel chains offer a family of sub-brands/ endorsed brands. For instance, Hilton Hotels Corporation, Intercontinental, and Starwood each has 7 sub-brands, while Marriott International has 12 (plus the wholly owned Ritz-Carlton chain which, to protect its exclusive image, is not normally identified for marketing purposes as part of the Marriott Group).

For a multi-brand strategy to succeed, each brand must promise a distinctive value proposition, targeted at a different customer segment. Because accommodations vary by service level (and thus price), room configurations and amenities will vary. Certain brands are targeted at guests who are making an extended stay, and finally, there are resort brands, which primarily target vacationers. In some instances, segmentation is situation-based: the same individual may have different needs (and willingness to pay) under differing circumstances, such as when travelling with family or travelling on business. A strategy of brand extension is aimed at encouraging customers to continue patronizing units within the brand family, and may be reinforced by loyalty programs. A study of the brand-switching behaviour of some 5400 hotel customers found that brand extensions do seem to encourage customer retention, but that the strategy may be less effective in discouraging switching when the number of brands reaches four or more.[14]

Sun Microsystems Hardware and Software Support   As an example of branding a high-tech, business-to-business product line, consider Sun Microsystems. The company offers a comprehensive hardware and software support program branded as "SunSpectrum Support."[15] Four different levels of support are available, sub-branded from platinum to bronze. The objective is to give buyers the flexibility to choose a level of support consistent with their own organization's needs (and willingness to pay), ranging from expensive, mission-critical support at the enterprise level (Platinum Service Plan) to relatively inexpensive assistance with self-service maintenance support (Bronze Service Plan). Service availability ranges from 24/7, with onsite hardware service coverage delivered within two hours (Platinum), to telephone and online support on weekdays from 8 a.m.–5 p.m. and replacement parts delivered the second business day.

Air Canada Sub-brands   A comprehensive example of strong sub-branding in the Canadian airline industry comes from Air Canada, which offers three distinct air-travel products for passengers: Air Canada mainline, which provides jet service to 20 Canadian cities, 35 destinations in the United States, and 59 cities in Europe, the Middle East, Asia, Australia, the Caribbean, Mexico, and South America; Air Canada Jazz, which provides services to an additional 40 Canadian cities and 16 cities in United States; and Air Canada Jetz, which provides private air travel to professional sports teams and corporate travellers. For international travel within the main brand, Air Canada offers five distinct offerings—Executive First, Premium Economy, Latitude Plus, Leisure, and Tourist. For travel within North America, Air Canada again offers five classes—Executive Class, Latitude Plus, Latitude, Tango Plus, and Tango. Each Air Canada sub-brand, and the offerings within each, represent a specific service concept and a set of clearly stated product specifications for pre-flight, in-flight, and on-arrival service elements.

On any given route, all passengers travelling on a particular flight receive the same core product—say a 17-hour journey from Toronto to New Delhi—but the nature and extent of most of the supplementary elements will differ widely, both on the ground and in the air. Passengers in Executive First, for instance, not only benefit from better tangible elements—such as more comfortable seats that fold into beds, noise reduction headsets, audio and video on demand, better food, and the use of a Maple Leaf Lounge at the airport before the flight, but also receive more personalized service from airline employees, and benefit from faster service on the ground (priority handling) at check-in and baggage retrieval. The higher the service level, of course, the higher the price!

Offering a Branded Experience

Branding can be employed at both the corporate and product level by almost any service business. In a well-managed firm the corporate brand is not only easily recognized but also has meaning for customers, standing for a particular way of doing business. Applying distinctive brand names to individual products enables the firm to communicate to the target market the distinctive experiences and benefits associated with a specific service concept. In short, it helps marketers to establish a mental picture of the service in customers' minds and to clarify the nature of the value proposition.

The Forum Corporation, a consulting firm, differentiates between (1) a random customer experience with high variability, (2) a generic branded experience by suppliers who offer a consistently similar experience, differentiated only by the presence of the brand name (ATMs are a good example), and (3) a "Branded Customer Experience" in which the customer's experience is shaped in specific and meaningful ways.[16] (See Service Perspectives 3.1 for Forum's recommendations on how to achieve this.)

Around the world, many financial service firms continue to create and register brand names to distinguish the different accounts and service packages that they offer. Their objective is to transform a series of service elements and processes into a consistent and recognizable service experience, offering a definable and predictable output at a specified price. Unfortunately, there is often little discernible difference—other than name—between, say, one bank's branded offering and another's, and the value proposition is unclear. Not surprisingly, in a study done with 28 leading-edge consultants, de Chernatony and Segal-Horn found that the two critical criteria for succeeding with service brands were to have a focused position and to be consistent.[17] And these factors are much more than the visual elements that the customer is exposed to. Don Shultz emphasizes that "The brand promise or value proposition is not a tag line, an icon, or a color or a graphic element, although all of these may contribute. It is, instead, the heart and soul of the brand . . . "[18]

Service Perspectives 3.1

Moving Toward the Branded Customer Experience

Forum Corporation identifies eight basic steps to develop and deliver the Branded Customer Experience:

1. Target profitable customers, employing behaviour segmentation rather than demographics.

2. Achieve a superior understanding of what your targeted customers value.

3. Create a brand promise—an articulation of what target your customers can expect from their experience with your organization—that is of value to customers, addresses a need, is actionable, can be incorporated into standards, and provides focus for the organization and its employees.

4. Apply that understanding to shape a truly differentiated customer experience.

5. Give employees the skills, tools, and supporting processes needed to deliver the defined customer experience.

6. Make everyone a brand manager.

7. Make promises that your processes can exceed.

8. Measure and monitor. Consistency of delivery is paramount.

Sources: "Forum Issues #17," Boston: The Forum Corporation, 1997; Forum Corporation Customer Experience Team, "Loyalty by Design," Forum Corporation, 2003, www.forum.com/library/white_papers-85.aspx (requires free registration), accessed October 26, 2006.

An important role for service marketers is to become brand champions, familiar with and responsible for shaping every aspect of the customer's experience. We can relate the notion of a branded service experience to the Flower of Service metaphor by emphasizing the need for consistency in the colour and texture of each petal. Unfortunately, many service experiences remain very haphazard and create the impression of a flower stitched together with petals drawn from many different plants!

We return to a discussion of branding in the context of marketing-communications strategy in Chapter 6.

NEW SERVICE DEVELOPMENT

Competitive intensity and customer expectations are increasing in nearly all service industries. Thus, success lies not only in providing existing services well, but also in creating new approaches to service. Because the outcome and process aspects of a service often combine to create the experience and benefits obtained by customers, both aspects must be addressed in new service development.

A Hierarchy of New Service Categories

Below we identify seven categories of new services, ranging from major innovations to simple style changes.

1. *Major service innovations* are new core products for markets that have not been previously defined. They usually include both new service characteristics and radical new processes. Examples include FedEx's introduction of overnight, nationwide, express package delivery in 1971, the advent of a global news service from CNN, eBay's launch of online auction services, and the launch of reverse auctions by Priceline.com in travel services in 1998.

2. *Major process innovations* consist of using new processes to deliver existing core products in new ways, with additional benefits. For example, Athabasca University competes with other Canadian universities by delivering undergraduate and graduate degree programs in a non-traditional way. It has a physical facility, but offers courses either online or at classrooms of one of the collaborative institutions. Similarly, in the United States, the University of Phoenix offers programs either online or at night in rented facilities. Its students get most of the benefits of a college degree in half the time and at a much lower price than other universities.[19] In recent years, the growth of the internet has led to the creation of many new start-up businesses employing new retailing models that exclude use of traditional stores but save customers time and travel. Often, these models add new, information-based benefits, such as greater customization, the opportunity to visit chat rooms with fellow customers, and suggestions for additional products that match well with what has already been purchased.

3. *Product-line extensions* are additions to current product lines by existing firms. The first company in a market to offer such a product may be seen as an innovator, the others are merely followers, often acting defensively. These new services may be targeted at existing customers to serve a broader array of needs, or designed to attract new customers with different needs (or both). Air Canada launched a separate low-cost operation called "Zip" in 2002, based in Calgary, Alberta, as a direct competition to discount carrier WestJet, but the venture folded in 2004. Telephone companies have introduced numerous value-added services, such as call-waiting, call-forwarding, call-screening, and integrated message centres.

4. *Process-line extensions* are less innovative than process innovations, but often represent distinctive new ways of delivering existing products, either with the intent of offering more convenience and a different experience for existing customers, or of attracting new customers who find the traditional approach unappealing. Most commonly, they involve adding a lower-contact distribution channel to an existing high-contact

channel, such as creating a telephone-based or internet-based banking service. Canadian Tire, Canada's most shopped retailer (i.e., the one with the most customers over a given time frame) with over 1000 stores and gas bars across Canada, launched the Canadiantire.ca website in 2001 to help further expand the business generated in its bricks-and-mortar stores. Now it is counted as one of the three busiest ecommerce sites in Canada.[20] Such dual-track approaches are sometimes referred to as "clicks and mortar." Creating self-service options to complement delivery by service employees is another form of process-line extension.

5. *Supplementary-service innovations* take the form of adding new facilitating or enhancing service elements to an existing core service, or of significantly improving an existing supplementary service. FedEx Kinkos now offers customers high-speed internet access around the clock, seven days a week at most of its locations in the United States and Canada. Low-tech innovations for an existing service can be as simple as adding parking at a retail site or agreeing to accept credit cards for payment. Multiple improvements may have the effect of creating what customers perceive as an altogether new experience, even though it is built around the same core. Theme restaurants such as the Rainforest Café enhance the core food service with new experiences. The cafés are designed to keep customers entertained, with aquariums, live parrots, waterfalls, fibreglass monkeys, talking trees that spout environmentally related information, and regularly timed thunderstorms, complete with lightning.[21]

6. *Service improvements* are the most common type of innovation. They involve modest changes in the performance of current products, including improvements to either the core product or to existing supplementary services. The decision by TD Canada Trust to have many of its branches open on Saturdays from 10 a.m.–3 p.m. is an example of a supplementary service improvement.

7. *Style changes* represent the simplest type of innovation, typically involving no changes in either processes or performance. However, they are often highly visible, create excitement, and may serve to motivate employees. Examples include repainting retail branches and vehicles in new colour schemes, outfitting service employees in new uniforms, introducing a new bank cheque design, or minor changes in service scripts for employees. One Canadian company that has gone through numerous style changes through the transformation of its logo is the Canadian Pacific Railway (CPR). In a period spanning more than a century (it was founded in 1881), CPR's corporate logo has gone through 14 incarnations; some discreet, others striking.[22]

As the above typology suggests, service innovation can occur at many different levels; not every type of innovation has an impact on the characteristics of the service product or is experienced by the customer.

Re-engineering Service Processes

The design of service processes has implications not only for customers but also for the cost, speed, and productivity with which the desired outcome is achieved. Improving productivity in services often requires speeding up the overall process (or cycle time), since the cost of creating a service is usually related to how long it takes to deliver each step in the process, plus any dead time between each step. Re-engineering involves analyzing and redesigning processes to achieve faster and better performance.[23] To reduce overall process time, analysts must identify each step, measure how long it takes, look for opportunities to speed it up (or even eliminate it altogether), and cut out dead time. Running tasks in parallel rather than in sequence is a well-established approach to speeding up processes (a simple household example would be to cook the vegetables for a meal while the main dish was in the oven, rather than waiting to cook them until after the main dish was removed). Service companies can use flowcharts to visualize these aspects of service operations in a systematic way.

Examination of processes may also lead to the creation of alternative delivery methods that are so radically different as to constitute entirely new service concepts. Options may

Figure 3.11 Alternative Service Concepts for Meal Delivery

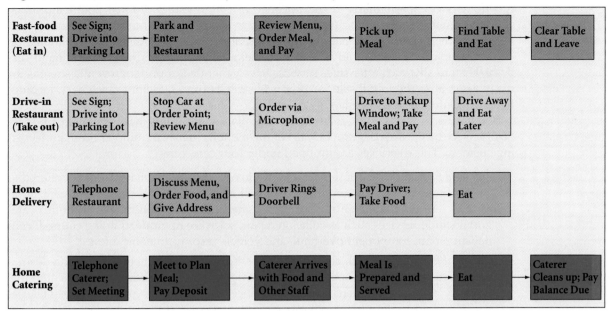

include eliminating certain supplementary services, addition of new ones, instituting self-service procedures, and rethinking where and when service is delivered.

Figure 3.11 illustrates this principle with simple flowcharts of four ways to deliver meal service that are alternatives to a full-service restaurant. Take a look and contrast what happens front-stage at a fast-food restaurant, a drive-in restaurant, home delivery, and home catering. From the customer's perspective, what has been added to or deleted from the service level represented by a full-service restaurant? And in each instance, how do these changes affect backstage activities?

Physical Goods as a Source of New Service Ideas

Goods and services may be competitive substitutes when they offer the same key benefits. For example, if your lawn needs mowing, you could buy a lawn mower and do it yourself, or you could retain a lawn maintenance service to take care of the chore, effectively avoiding ownership of a lawn mower and renting both labour and machines. Such decisions may be shaped by the customer's skills, physical capabilities, and time budget, as well as such factors as cost comparisons between purchase price (plus operating costs) and service fees, storage space for purchased products, and anticipated frequency of need.

Many services can be built around providing an alternative to owning a physical good and doing the work oneself. Figure 3.12 shows four possible delivery alternatives each for car travel and word processing. Three of these alternatives present service opportunities. Each alternative is based on choosing between ownership and rental of the necessary physical goods, and between performing self-service or hiring another person to perform the necessary tasks. Additional services can be added to enhance the value proposition.

Figure 3.12

Services as Substitutes for Goods Ownership and Task Performance

	OWN A PHYSICAL GOOD	RENT THE USE OF A PHYSICAL GOOD
PERFORM THE WORK ONESELF	• Drive Own Car • Type on Own Computer	• Rent a Car and Drive It • Rent a Computer and Type on It
HIRE SOMEONE TO DO THE WORK	• Hire a Chauffeur to Drive Car • Hire a Typist to Use Computer	• Hire a Taxi or Limousine • Send Work Out to a Secretarial Service

Any new physical product has the potential to create a need for related possession-processing services (particularly if the product is a high-value, durable item.) Industrial equipment may require servicing throughout its lifespan, beginning with financing and insurance, then shipping (and possibly installation), and continuing with maintenance, cleaning, repair, consulting advice and problem-solving, upgrading, and ultimate disposal. Historically, such after-sales services have generated important revenue streams for many years after the initial sale for products such as trucks, factory machinery, locomotives, computers, and jet engines.

Bombardier, a well-known manufacturer of planes and trains, has developed a portfolio of service businesses (Figure 3.13) to complement its high-variability train-manufacturing business. These services are grouped under four categories:[24]

- *Standard Services*, which comprise a portfolio of eighteen distinct "products" offered to clients. Standard services use the expertise of Bombardier Transportation organization to offer services that keep trains running safely. Particular offerings within this category include services such as collision repair, software upgrade, training courses, vandalism repair, component overhaul, and vehicle respray, to name a few.

- *Tailored Fleet Solutions*, which offers five distinct products aimed at achieving desired results, customized for a specific fleet of vehicles. The five services offered within this category are fleet maintenance (maintenance and technical support), fleet material (supplies and parts), fleet modernization (vehicle and system upgrades), fleet overhaul (scheduled heavy overhaul activities), and fleet support (customized package where customer retains control over fleet maintenance performance).

- *Total Management Solutions*, which constitutes the most comprehensive offering of services whereby Bombardier's participation is fully integrated into the customer's transportation business. Service offerings in this category include total maintenance (comprehensive program of overall servicing and maintenance within a business segment), total material (complete material and logistics management for a designated business segment), and total overhaul (full management of all major maintenance, including heavy overhaul and modernization projects).

- *Operations and Maintenance*, which is aimed at planning and implementation of complete operations and maintenance organizations for their customers, for any of the transit technologies (rapid transit, light rail, monorail, people mover system) that Bombardier offers.

Figure 3.13

Bombardier promotes its service businesses.

Using Research to Design New Services

If a company is designing a new service from scratch, how can it figure out what features and price will create the best value for target customers? It's hard to know without asking these customers—hence the need for research. Research Insights 3.3 presents a classic example of how the Marriott Corporation used market research experts to help with new service development in the hotel industry.

Marriott was sufficiently encouraged by the findings to build three "Courtyard by Marriott" prototype hotels. After testing the concept under real-world conditions and making some refinements, the company subsequently developed a large chain whose

Research Insights 3.3

Designing the "Courtyard by Marriott" Concept

In 1982, when Marriott was designing a new chain of hotels for business travellers (which eventually became known as Courtyard by Marriott), it hired marketing research experts to help establish an optimal design concept. Since there are limits to how much service and how many amenities can be offered at any given price, Marriott needed to know what trade-offs customers would be willing to make to arrive at the most satisfactory compromise in terms of value for money. The intent of the research was to get respondents to trade off different hotel service features to see which they valued most. Marriott's goal was to determine if a niche existed between full-service hotels and inexpensive motels, especially in locations where demand was not high enough to justify a large full-service hotel. If such a niche existed, Marriott wanted to develop a product to fill that gap.

A sample of 601 consumers from four metropolitan areas participated in the study. Researchers used a sophisticated technique known as conjoint analysis, which asks survey respondents to make trade-offs between different groupings of attributes. The objective was to determine which mix of attributes at specific prices offers them the highest degree of utility. The 50 attributes in the Marriott study were divided into the following seven factors (or sets of attributes), each containing a variety of different features based on detailed studies of competing offerings:

1. *External factors:* building shape, landscaping, pool type and location, hotel size.

2. *Room features:* room size and decor, climate control, location and type of bathroom, entertainment systems, other amenities.

3. *Food-related services:* type and location of restaurants, menus, room service, vending machines, guest shop, in-room kitchen.

4. *Lounge facilities:* location, atmosphere, type of guests.

5. *Services:* reservations, registration, check-out, airport limousine, bell desk (baggage service), message centre, secretarial services, car rental, laundry, valet.

6. *Leisure facilities:* sauna, whirlpool, exercise room, racquetball and tennis courts, game room, children's playground.

7. *Security:* guards, smoke detectors, 24-hour video camera.

For each of these seven factors, respondents were presented with a series of stimulus cards displaying different levels of performance for each attribute. For instance, the "Rooms" stimulus card displayed nine attributes, each of which had three to five different levels. Thus, the *amenities* attribute, for instance, ranged from "small bar of soap" to "large soap, shampoo packet, shoeshine mitt" to "large soap, bath gel, shower cap, sewing kit, shampoo, special soap" and then to the highest level, "large soap, bath gel, shower cap, sewing kit, special soap, toothpaste," and so on.

In the second phase of the analysis, respondents were shown a number of alternative hotel profiles, each featuring different levels of performance on the various attributes. They were asked to indicate on a five-point scale how likely they would be to stay at a hotel with these features, given a specific room-price per night. Fifty different profiles were developed for this research, with each respondent being asked to evaluate five of them.

The research yielded detailed guidelines for the selection of almost 200 features and service elements, representing those attributes that provided the highest utility for the customers in the target segments, at prices they were willing to pay. An important aspect of the study was that it focused not only on what business travellers wanted, but also identified what they liked but weren't prepared to pay for. (There's a difference, after all, between wanting something ideally and being willing to pay for it!) Using these inputs, the design team was able to meet the specified price, when they launched the first Courtyard hotels in 1983, while retaining the features most desired by the target market.

Sources: Jerry Wind et al., "Courtyard by Marriott: Designing a Hotel Facility with Customer Based Marketing Models," *Interfaces* 19 (January–February 1989): 25–47; Paul E. Green, Abba M. Krieger, and Yoram (Jerry) Wind, "Thirty Years of Conjoint Analysis: Reflections and Prospects," *Interfaces* 31 (May–June 2001): S56–S73.

advertising slogan became "Courtyard by Marriott—the hotel designed by business travellers." Marriott continues to use this theme, with recent advertisements for Courtyard promoting free high-speed internet access and 24-hour business services.

The new service concept filled a gap in the market with a product that represented the best balance between the price customers were prepared to pay and the physical and service features they most desired. The success of the Courtyard concept led Marriott to use the same research methodology to develop additional customer-driven products. They include Fairfield Inn, a moderately priced chain whose rooms are supported by only limited hotel services, and SpringHill Suites, a moderately priced all-suites hotel targeted at both business and pleasure travellers and offering separate working, sleeping and eating areas in each suite, including a pantry with sink, microwave, and coffee maker.

Achieving Success in New Service Development

Consumer goods are notorious for their high failure rates, with more than 90 percent of the 30 000 new products introduced each year ending in failure.[25] Services are not immune to the high failure rates plaguing new manufactured products. The advent of the internet stimulated entrepreneurs to create numerous "dot com" companies to deliver internet-based services, but the vast majority failed within just a few years. The reasons ranged widely, including failure to meet a demonstrable consumer need, inability to cover costs from revenues, and poor execution. One just needs to pay a visit to the "Museum of E-Failures" to get a glimpse of how many online businesses have collapsed over the years.[26] In the restaurant business, H.T. Parsa and his colleagues found a failure rate of about 26 percent during the first year rising to close to 60 percent within three years. But the rate varied widely by type of food served, ranging from 33 percent failure (in three years) for seafood and burger restaurants to 76 percent for subs and bakeries and 86 percent for restaurants serving Mexican food.[27]

Chris Storey and Christopher Easingwood argue that in developing new services, the core product is of only secondary importance. It is the quality of the total service offering, and also of the marketing support that goes with this, that are vital. Underlying success in these areas, they emphasize, is market knowledge: "Without an understanding of the marketplace, knowledge about customers, and knowledge about competitors, it is very unlikely that a new product will be a success."[28] Stephen Tax and Ian Stuart contend that new services should be defined in terms of the extent of change required to the existing service system, relative to the interactions between participants (people), processes, and physical elements (e.g., facilities and equipment).[29] They propose a seven-step planning cycle to evaluate the feasibility and associated risks of integrating a new service development into a firm's existing service system.

To what extent can rigorously conducted and controlled development processes for new services enhance their success rate? A study by Scott Edgett and Steven Parkinson focused on discriminating between successful and unsuccessful new financial services.[30] They found that the three factors contributing most to success were, in order of importance:

1. *Market synergy:* the new product fit well with the existing image of the firm, provided an advantage over competing products in terms of meeting customers' known needs, and received strong support during and after the launch from the firm and its branches; further, the firm had a good understanding of its customers' purchasing-decision behaviour.

2. *Organizational factors:* there was strong interfunctional co-operation and co-ordination; development personnel were fully aware of why they were involved and of the importance of new products to the company.

3. *Market-research factors:* detailed and scientifically designed market research studies were conducted early in the development process with a clear idea of the type of information to be obtained; a good definition of the product concept was developed before undertaking field surveys.

Another survey of financial service firms, to determine what distinguished successful from unsuccessful products, yielded similar findings.[31] In this instance, the key factors underlying success were determined to be *synergy* (the fit between the product and the firm in terms of the presence of needed expertise and resources) and *internal marketing* (the support given to staff prior to launch, to help them understand the new product and its underlying systems, plus details about direct competitors, and support).

Courtyard by Marriott's success in a very different industry—a people-processing service with many tangible components—supports the notion that a highly structured development process will increase the chances of success for a complex service innovation. However, it's worth noting that there may be limits to the degree of structure that can and should be imposed. The Swedish researchers Bo Edvardsson, Lars Haglund, and Jan Mattson reviewed new service development in telecommunications, transport, and financial services. They concluded that

> [C]omplex processes like the development of new services cannot be formally planned altogether. Creativity and innovation cannot only rely on planning and control. There must be some elements of improvisation, anarchy, and internal competition in the development of new services. . . . We believe that a contingency approach is needed and that creativity on the one hand and formal planning and control on the other can be balanced, with successful new services as the outcome.[32]

An important conclusion from subsequent research in Sweden concerns the role of customers in service innovation. Researchers found that in the idea-generation stage, the quality of submitted ideas differed significantly depending on whether they were created by professional service developers or by the users themselves. Users' ideas were judged to be more original, and holding a higher perceived value for customers. However, on average, these ideas were harder to convert into commercial services.[33]

Conclusion

A service concept consists of a core product bundled with a variety of supplementary service elements. The core product responds to the customer's need for a basic benefit, such as transportation to a specific location, resolution of a specific health problem, or repair of malfunctioning equipment. Supplementary services are those elements that facilitate and enhance use of the core service. They range from provision of needed information and advice to taking a reservation, offering hospitality to customers, and billing.

Designing a service concept is a complex task that requires an understanding of how the core and supplementary services should be combined, sequenced, delivered, and scheduled to create a value proposition that meets the needs of target market segments. Flowcharting, a technique for displaying the nature and sequence of the different steps involved in delivering service to customers, offers a way to understand the totality of the customer's service experience.

Different types of core products often share use of similar supplementary elements. The Flower of Service concept categorizes supplementary services into eight groups (each represented as a petal surrounding the core). The eight groups are information, consultation, order-taking, hospitality, safekeeping, exceptions, billing, and payment. Use of the flower analogy helps us to understand the need for consistent performance on all supplementary elements, so that a weakness in one element doesn't spoil the overall impression. Because supplementary elements are often common to several industries, managers should be studying businesses outside their own industries in a search for "best-in-class" performers on specific supplementary services.

Many firms create several service concepts with different performance attributes, and brand each package with a distinctive name. But unless each of these sub-brands offers and fulfills a meaningful value proposition, this strategy is likely to be ineffective from a competitive standpoint.

Although innovation is central to effective marketing, major service innovations are relatively rare. More common is the use of new technologies, such as the internet, to deliver existing services in new ways. In mature industries, where the core service can become a commodity, the search for competitive advantage often centres on creating new supplementary services or significantly improving performance on existing ones. The chances of success for a new service concept increase when it fits well with the firm's expertise, resources, and existing image, provides an advantage over competing services in terms of meeting customers' needs, and is well supported by co-ordinated efforts between the different functional areas.

Review Questions

1. Explain the role of supplementary services. Can they be applied to goods as well as services? If so, how might they relate to marketing strategy?

2. How do flowcharts help us to understand:
   (a) the differences between people-processing services, possession-processing services, mental-stimulus processing services, and information-processing services?
   (b) the nature and role of the supplementary services accompanying a core product?

3. Explain the distinction between enhancing and facilitating supplementary services. Give several examples of each, based on services that you have used recently.

4. How is branding used in services marketing? What is the distinction between an overall corporate brand such as Marriott and the names of its different inn and hotel chains?

5. What does Air Canada gain from using such sub-brand names as Executive, Latitude, Tango, Leisure or Tourist? Explain the Flower of Service concept and identify each of the petals. What insights does this concept provide for service marketers?

6. Visit Bombardier's website, www.bombardier.com, which describes its various businesses. Look through the pages relating to its aerospace business and identify the service offerings it has developed to complement its manufacturing of aircraft.

7. Why do new services often fail? What factors are associated with successful development of new services?

Application Exercises

1. Think of an experience at a restaurant where you ate recently. Evaluate the restaurant using the Flower of Service metaphor, identifying how each enhancing and facilitating supplementary service has been managed by the restaurant. Further, evaluate the relative influence that the core, enhancing, and facilitating services had on the level of satisfaction experienced by you during that visit.

2. Identify some real-world examples of branding from financial services, such as specific types of retail bank accounts or insurance policies, and define their characteristics. How meaningful are these brands likely to be to customers?

3. Choose a service that you are familiar with and create a simple flowchart for it. Define the "front-stage" and "back-stage" activities.

4. Identify two key opportunities to develop new services. What kind of service innovations do these opportunities represent? If you were able to develop one of these services, describe what issues you would need to address to make it a success in the marketplace.

Endnotes

1. Lynn Shostack, "Breaking Free from Product Marketing," *Journal of Marketing* 44 (April 1977): 73–80.
2. Ibid.
3. Pierre Eiglier and Eric Langeard, "Services as Systems: Marketing Implications," in Pierre Eiglier, Eric Langeard, et al., *Marketing Consumer Services: New Insights*, Cambridge, MA: Marketing Science Institute, Report # 77-115 (November 1977): 83–103. An earlier version of this article was published in French in *Révue Française de Gestion* (March–April 1977): 72–84.
4. Christian Grönroos, *Service Management and Marketing*, Lexington, MA: Lexington Books, 1990: 74.
5. Richard B. Chase and Sriram Dasu, "Want to Perfect Your Company's Service? Use Behavioral Science," *Harvard Business Review* 79 (June 2001): 79–84.
6. Kim Guenther, "Pull Up a Chair and Stay Awhile: Strategies to Maximize Site Stickiness," *Online* (November/December 2004): 55–57.
7. The "Flower of Service" concept presented in this section was first introduced in Christopher H. Lovelock, "Cultivating the Flower of Service: New Ways of Looking at Core and Supplementary Services," in P. Eiglier and E. Langeard (eds.), *Marketing, Operations, and Human Resources: Insights into Services*, Aix-en-Provence: IAE, Université d'Aix-Marseille III, 1992: 296–316.
8. www.iata.org/workgroups/etwg.htm, accessed March 16, 2006.
9. Loizos Heracleous, Jochen Wirtz and Nitin Pangarkar, *Flying High in a Competitive Industry: Cost Effective Service Excellence at Singapore Airlines*. Singapore: McGraw Hill, 2006.

10. www.rbc.com/security/online.html, accessed March 16, 2006.

11. James C. Anderson and James A. Narus, "Capturing the Value of Supplementary Services," *Harvard Business Review* 73 (January–February 1995): 75–83.

12. James Devlin, "Brand Architecture in Services: The Example of Retail Financial Services," *Journal of Marketing Management* 19 (2003): 1043–65.

13. David Aaker and E. Joachimsthaler, "The Brand Relationship Spectrum: The Key to the Brand Challenge," *California Management Review* 42/4 (2000): 8–23.

14. Weizhong Jiang, Chekitan S. Dev, and Vithala R. Rao, "Brand Extension and Customer Loyalty: Evidence from the Lodging Industry," *Cornell Hotel and Restaurant Administration Quarterly* (August 2002): 5–16.

15. www.sun.com/service/support/sunspectrum, accessed January 2, 2006.

16. Joe Wheeler and Shaun Smith, *Managing the Experience,* Upper Saddle River, NJ: Prentice Hall, 2003.

17. Leslie de Chernatony and Susan Segal-Horn, "The Criteria for Successful Services Brands," *European Journal of Marketing* 37/7–8 (2003): 1095–1118.

18. Don E. Shultz, "Getting to the Heart of the Brand," *Marketing Management* (September–October 2001): 8–9.

19. See James Traub, "Drive-Thru U.," *New Yorker* (October 20 and 27, 1997); and Joshua Macht, "Virtual You," *Inc. Magazine* (January 1998): 84–87.

20. www2.canadiantire.ca/CTenglish/busoverview.html, accessed March 16, 2006.

21. Chad Rubel, "New Menu for Restaurants: Talking Trees and Blackjack," *Marketing News* (July 29, 1996): 1.

22. www.cprheritage.com/logo/index.htm, accessed March 16, 2006

23. See, for example, Michael Hammer and James Champy, *Reengineering the Corporation,* New York: HarperBusiness, 1993.

24. www.bombardier.com/index.jsp, accessed March 16, 2006.

25. Clayton M. Christenson, Scott Cook, and Taddy Hall, "Marketing Malpractice: The Cause and the Cure," *Harvard Business Review* 83/12 (December 2005): 74–83.

26. www.disobey.com/ghostsites/mef.shtml, accessed March 16, 2006.

27. H.T. Parsa, John T. Self, David Njite, and Tiffany King, "Why Restaurants Fail," *Cornell Hotel and Restaurant Administration Quarterly* 46 (August 2005): 304–22.

28. Chris D. Storey and Christopher J. Easingwood, "The Augmented Service Offering: A Conceptualization and Study of Its Impact on New Service Success," *Journal of Product Innovation Management* 15 (1998): 335–51.

29. Stephen S. Tax and Ian Stuart, "Designing and Implementing New Services: The Challenges of Integrating Service Systems," *Journal of Retailing* 73/1 (1997): 105–34.

30. Scott Edgett and Steven Parkinson, "The Development of New Financial Services: Identifying Determinants of Success and Failure," *International Journal of Service Industry Management* 5/4 (1994): 24–38.

31. Christopher Storey and Christopher Easingwood, "The Impact of the New Product Development Project on the Success of Financial Services," *Service Industries Journal* 13/3 (July 1993): 40–54.

32. Bo Edvardsson, Lars Haglund, and Jan Mattsson, "Analysis, Planning, Improvisation and Control in the Development of New Services," *International Journal of Service Industry Management* 6/2 (1995): 24–35 (at page 34). See also Bo Edvardsson and Jan Olsson, "Key Concepts for New Service Development," *Service Industries Journal* 16 (April 1996): 140–164.

33. Peter R. Magnusson, Jonas Matthing, and Per Kristensson, "Managing User Involvement in Service Innovation: Experiments with Innovating End Users," *Journal of Service Research* 6 (November 2003): 111–24; Jonas Matthing, Bodil Sandén, and Bo Edvardsson, "New Service Development: Learning from and with Customers," *International Journal of Service Industry Management* 15/5 (2004): 479–98.

CHAPTER 4

Distributing Services through Physical and Electronic Channels

Companies best equipped for the twenty-first century will consider investment in real time systems as essential to maintaining their competitive edge and keeping their customers.

—Regis McKenna

No theatre could sanely flourish until there was an umbilical connection between what was happening on the stage and what was happening in the world.

—Kenneth Tynan

Think globally, act locally.

—John Naisbitt

An important part of the service model is the distribution of core and supplementary service elements through selected physical and electronic channels. Delivering a service to customers involves decisions about where, when, and how. The rapid growth of the internet and broadband mobile communications means that service-marketing strategy must address issues of place, cyberspace, and time, paying at least as much attention to speed, scheduling, and electronic access as to the more traditional notion of physical location. Furthermore, with increasing globalization, important questions are being raised concerning the design and implementation of international service-marketing strategies.

In this chapter, we discuss the role that delivery plays in service-marketing strategy locally and globally, and explore the following questions:

1. How can services be distributed? What are the main modes of distribution?
2. What are the distinctive challenges of distributing people-processing, possession-processing, and information-based services?
3. What are the implications for a firm of delivering through both physical and electronic channels?
4. What roles should intermediaries play in distributing services?
5. What are the drivers of globalization of services, and their distribution?

DISTRIBUTION IN A SERVICES CONTEXT

Mention distribution, and many people think of moving boxes to retailers and other channels for sale to end-users. In a services context, we often have nothing to move. Experiences, performances, and solutions are not being physically shipped and stored. Meantime, informational transactions are increasingly conducted via electronic rather than physical channels. How, then, does distribution work in a services context? In a typical sales cycle, distribution embraces three interrelated elements:

- **Information and promotion flow:** distribution of information and promotion materials relating to the service offer. The objective is to get the customer interested in buying the service.
- **Negotiation flow:** reaching an agreement on the service features and configuration, and the terms of the offer so that a purchase contract can be closed. The objective is to sell the *right* to use a service (e.g., sell a reservation or a ticket).
- **Product flow:** Many services, especially those involving people or physical-possession processing, require physical facilities for delivery. Here, distribution strategy requires development of a network of local sites. For information-processing services, such as internet banking, distance learning, broadcast news and entertainment, the product flow can be undertaken via electronic channels, employing one or more centralized sites.

Distinguishing between Distribution of Supplementary and Core Services

Distribution can relate to the core service as well as to supplementary services. That is an important distinction, as many core services require a physical location, which severely restricts distribution. For instance, an overnight stay at the four-star Delta Hotel and Resorts chain can only be consumed at one of their 35 city-centre, airport, or resort properties spread across the ten provinces, and a live performance of a Mirvish Productions show must take place at the Princess of Wales or Royal Alexandra theatres, both situated in Toronto. However, many of the supplementary services are informational in nature and can be distributed widely and cost-effectively via other means. Prospective Delta Hotel and Resort customers can get information by consulting a travel agent, either face-to-face, online, by phone, or even by mail, and then make a booking through one of these same channels. In similar fashion, tickets to the Mirvish shows can be purchased through their agent, TicketKing, online, by telephone, or through their several outlets across southern Ontario, without the need for an advance trip to one of the theatres.

As we look at the eight petals of the Flower of Service, we can see that no fewer than five supplementary services are information-based (Figure 4.1). Information, consultation, order-taking, billing, and payment can all be transmitted using the digital language of computers. Even service businesses that involve physical core products, such as retailing and repair, are shifting delivery of many supplementary services to the internet, closing

Figure 4.1

Information and Physical Processes of the Augmented Service Product

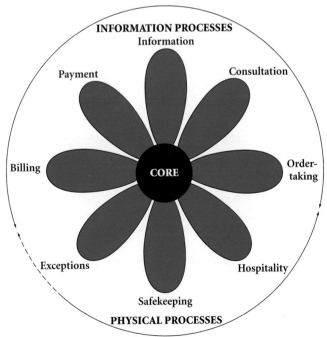

physical branches, and relying on speedy business logistics to enable a new strategy of arm's-length transactions with their customers.

The distribution of information, consultation, and order-taking (or reservations and ticket sales) has reached extremely sophisticated levels in some global service industries, requiring a number of carefully integrated channels targeted at key customer segments. For instance, Starwood Hotels & Resorts Worldwide—whose 725 hotels include such brands as Sheraton, Westin, and St. Regis—has more than 30 global sales offices (GSOs) around the world to manage customer relationships with key global accounts, offering a one-stop solution to corporate travel planners, wholesalers, meeting planners, incentive houses, and major travel organizations.[1] The company has also set up 12 customer servicing centres (CSCs) around the world to provide one-stop customer service for its guests, covering worldwide hotel reservations, enrolment and redemption of Starwood's loyalty program, and general customer service. You only need to call one toll-free number to book any Starwood hotel. Alternatively, you can reserve through electronic channels, including the Westin and Sheraton websites.

DETERMINING THE TYPE OF CONTACT: OPTIONS FOR SERVICE DELIVERY

Decisions on where, when, and how to deliver service have an important impact on the nature of customers' service experiences. They determine the types of encounters (if any) with service personnel, and the price and other costs incurred to obtain the service.

Several factors serve to shape distribution and delivery strategies. A key question is: does the nature of the service, or the firm's positioning strategy, require customers to be in direct physical contact with its personnel, equipment, and facilities? (As we saw in Chapter 2, this is unavoidable for people-processing services, but optional for other categories.) If so, do customers have to visit the facilities of the service organization, or will the latter send personnel and equipment to customers' own sites? Alternatively, can transactions between provider and customer be completed at arm's length through the use of either telecommunications or physical channels of distribution?

Distribution Options for Serving Customers

Another issue concerns the firm's strategy in terms of distribution sites. As shown in Table 4.1, there are six possible options. Should the firm expect customers to come to a company site? Or should service personnel go to visit customers at their own locations? Alternatively, can service be delivered at arm's length, without either side having to meet? And for each of these three options, should the firm maintain just a single outlet, or offer to serve customers through multiple outlets at different locations?

Customers Visit the Service Site The convenience to the customer of service-factory locations and operational schedules assumes great importance when a customer

Table 4.1 Six Options for Service Delivery

NATURE OF INTERACTION BETWEEN CUSTOMER AND SERVICE ORGANIZATION	AVAILABILITY OF SERVICE OUTLETS	
	SINGLE SITE	MULTIPLE SITES
Customer goes to service organization	Theatre Barbershop	Bus service Fast-food chain
Service organization comes to customer	House painting Mobile car wash	Mail delivery Auto club road service
Customer and service organization transact remotely (mail or electronic communications)	Credit card company Local TV station	Broadcast network Telephone company

has to be physically present—either throughout service delivery or just to initiate or terminate the transaction. Elaborate statistical analysis, in the form of *retail gravity models* (which predict the probability of customers shopping at a given store in terms of its distance from their home), is sometimes used to aid decisions on where to locate supermarkets and similar large stores relative to prospective customers' homes and workplaces. Traffic counts and pedestrian counts help to establish how many prospective customers pass by certain locations in a day. For example, Tim Hortons goes through an elaborate analysis of real estate and market research data when deciding where to locate a new Tim Hortons outlet. Similarly, construction of an expressway, or the introduction of a new bus or rail service, may have a significant effect on travel patterns and, in turn, determine which sites have become more desirable as a result, and which less so.

The tradition of having customers visit the service site for services that don't involve people processing is now being challenged by advances in telecommunications and business logistics. The result is a shift to services delivered at arm's length.

Service Providers Go to Their Customers
For some types of services, the supplier visits the customer. Weed Man, which provides a variety of lawn care and maintenance services to a wide array of customers across Canada, must necessarily bring its tools and personnel to the customer's site, because the need is location-specific. Going to the customer's site is unavoidable whenever the object of the service is some immovable physical item, such as a tree to be pruned, installed machinery to be repaired, or a house that requires pest-control treatment.

In other instances, going to the customer is optional. Because it's more expensive and time-consuming for service personnel and their equipment to travel to the customer than vice-versa, the trend has been toward requiring customers to come to the service provider instead. (Fewer doctors make house calls nowadays!) In remote areas such as Alaska or Canada's Northwest Territories, service providers often fly to visit their customers, because the latter find it so difficult to travel. Australia is famous for its Royal Flying Doctor Service, in which physicians fly to make house calls at farms and sheep stations in the Outback.

In general, service providers are more likely to visit corporate customers at their premises than to visit individuals in their homes, reflecting the larger volume and financial value associated with business-to-business transactions. However, there may be a profitable niche in serving individuals who are willing to pay a premium for the convenience of receiving personal visits. With increasing pressure to manage successful careers, double-income families are finding it progressively harder to spend mealtimes together in the evenings. To cater to the demands of families in this situation who prefer not to order food or eat out on a regular basis, the concept of a personal chef is becoming increasingly popular. In fact, associations such as the Canadian Personal Chef Alliance (www.canadianpersonalchefalliance.ca) provide potential customers with detailed information on this service, ranging from searching for a certified chef to providing information on resources devoted to healthy eating. Other consumer services of this nature include mobile car-washing, at-home veterinary services, and made-to-measure tailoring services for business people.

A growing service activity involves the rental of both equipment and labour for special occasions or in response to customers wishing to increase their productive capacity during busy periods. Service Perspectives 4.1 describes the business-to-business services of Aggreko, an international company that rents generating and cooling equipment around the world.

Service Transaction is Conducted at Arm's Length
Dealing with a service firm through arm's-length transactions may mean that a customer never sees the service facilities and never meets the service personnel face to face. An important consequence is that the number of service encounters tends to be fewer, and those encounters that do take place with service personnel are more likely to be made via a call centre or, even more remotely, by mail or email.

Repair services for small pieces of equipment sometimes require customers to ship the product to a maintenance facility, where it will be serviced and then returned by mail

Service Perspectives 4.1

Power and Temperature Control for Rent

You probably think of electricity as coming from a distant power station, and of air conditioning and heating as fixed installations. So how would you deal with the following challenges?

- Luciano Pavarotti, the famous tenor, is giving an open-air concert in Münster, Germany, and the organizers require an uninterruptible source of electrical power for the duration of the concert, independent of the local electricity supply.

- A tropical cyclone has devastated the small mining town of Pannawonica in Western Australia, destroying everything in its path, including power lines, and electrical power must be restored as soon as possible so that the town and its infrastructure can be rebuilt.

- In Amsterdam, organizers of the World Championship Indoor Windsurfing competition need to power 27 wind turbines that will be installed along the length of a huge indoor pool to create winds of 32–48 kilometres per hour.

- A U.S. Navy submarine needs a shore-based source of power for use when located in a remote Norwegian port.

- Sri Lanka faces an acute shortage of electricity-generating capability after water levels fall dangerously low at major hydroelectric dams due to insufficient monsoon rains two years in a row.

- Hotels in Florida need to be dried out following water damage in a hurricane.

- A large power-generating plant in Oklahoma urgently seeks temporary capacity to replace one of its cooling towers, destroyed the previous day in a tornado.

These are all challenges faced and met by a company called Aggreko, which describes itself as "the world leader in temporary utility rental solutions." Aggreko operates from more than 100 depots in 28 countries worldwide. It rents a "fleet" of mobile electricity generators, oil-free air compressors, and temperature-control devices ranging from water chillers and industrial air-conditioners to giant heaters and dehumidifiers. In 2005, it served customers in 80 countries, using equipment with a replacement value of more than US$1 billion.

Aggreko's customer base is dominated by large companies and government agencies. Although much of its business comes from predicted needs, such as backup operations during planned factory maintenance or the filming of a James Bond movie, the firm is also poised to resolve problems arising unexpectedly from emergencies.

Much of the firm's rental equipment is contained in soundproofed, boxlike structures that can be shipped anywhere in the world to create the specific type and level of electrical power output or climate-control capability required by the client. Consultation, installation, and ongoing technical support add value to the core service. Emphasis is placed on solving customer problems rather than just renting equipment. Some customers have a clear idea of their needs in advance, while others require advice on how to develop innovative and cost-effective solutions to what may be unique problems, and still others are desperate to restore power that has been lost due to an emergency. In the last-mentioned instance, speed is of the essence, since downtime can be extremely expensive, and lives may even depend on the promptness of Aggreko's response.

The company's website declares: "Our customers are our focus—

- We listen to them
- We learn about them
- We embrace their challenges as our own
- We know their issues
- We anticipate their concerns, and
- We inspire them with exceptional service."

Delivering service requires Aggreko to ship its equipment to the customer's site. Following the Pannawonica cyclone, Aggreko's West Australian team swung into action, rapidly dispatching some 30 generators ranging from 60 to 750 kVA, plus cabling, refuelling tankers, and other equipment. The generators were transported by means of four "road trains," each comprising a giant tractor unit hauling three 13-metre trailers. Technicians and additional equipment were flown in on two Hercules aircraft. The Aggreko technicians remained on site for six weeks, providing 24/7 service while the town was being rebuilt.

Sources: Adapted from Aggreko's *International Magazine*, 1997; www.aggreko.com, accessed May 2006.

(with the option of paying extra for express shipment). Many service providers offer solutions with the help of integrated logistics firms such as DHL, FedEx or UPS. These solutions range from storage and express delivery of spare parts for aircraft (B2B delivery) to pickup of defective cellphones from customers' homes and subsequent return of the repaired phone to the customer (B2C pickup and delivery).

Any information-based product can be delivered almost instantaneously through the internet to almost any point in the globe. As a result, physical logistics services now find themselves competing with telecommunications services.

Channel Preferences Vary among Consumers

The use of different channels to deliver the same service not only has different cost implications for the bank, but also drastically affects the nature of the service experience for the customer—banking services, for instance, can be delivered remotely via internet, cellphone, voice response system, call centre, and automatic teller machines; or face to face in a branch, or in person at a wealthy customer's home, in the case of private banking. Recent research has explored how customers choose between personal, impersonal and self-service channels and has identified the following key drivers:[2]

- For complex and high-perceived-risk services, people tend to rely on personal channels. For example, customers are happy to apply for credit cards using remote channels, but prefer a face-to-face transaction when obtaining a mortgage.
- Individuals with higher confidence and knowledge about a service and/or the channel are more likely to use impersonal and self-service channels.
- Consumers with a high need for personal interaction are less likely to be motivated to try out self-service channels.
- Customers who look for the instrumental aspects of a transaction prefer more convenience, and this often means the use of impersonal and self-service channels.
- Customer demographics can also play a key role in their choice of self-service versus personal channels of service delivery. Factors such as higher income and younger age may increase the motivation to use self-service channels.
- Convenience is a key driver of channel choice for the majority of consumers. Service convenience means saving time and effort rather than saving money. A customer's search for convenience is not just confined to the purchase of core products but also extends to convenient times and places. People want easy access to supplementary services, too—especially information, reservations, and problem solving.

Service providers have to be careful when channels are priced differently—increasingly, sophisticated customers will *arbitrage*.[3] For example, customers can ask an expensive full-service broker for advice (and perhaps place a small order) and then conduct the bulk of their trades via a much lower-priced discount broker. Service providers need to develop effective strategies that will enable them to deliver value and capture it through the appropriate channel.

PLACE AND TIME DECISIONS

How should service managers make decisions on the places where service is delivered and the times when it is available? The answer is to start by understanding customer needs and expectations, competitive activity, and the nature of the service operation. As we noted earlier, the distribution strategies employed for some of the supplementary service elements may differ from those used to deliver the core product itself. For instance, as a customer, you're probably willing to go to a particular location at a specific time to attend a sporting or entertainment event. But you probably want greater flexibility and convenience when reserving a seat in advance, so may expect the reservations service to be open for extended hours, to offer booking and credit card payment by phone or web, and to deliver tickets through postal or electronic channels.

Where Should Service Be Delivered in a Bricks-and-Mortar Context?

Deciding where to locate a service facility for customers involves very different considerations from locating the backstage elements (in which cost, productivity and access to

Reprinted from Christopher Lovelock, *Product Plus: How Product + Service = Competitive Advantage,* New York: McGraw-Hill, 1994: 283. Copyright © Christopher H. Lovelock 1994.

labour are often key determinants). In the first instance, customer convenience and preference are key. Firms should make it easy for people to access frequently purchased services facing active competition.[4] Examples include retail banks and quick service restaurants. However, customers may be willing to travel further from their homes or workplaces to reach specialty services.

Locational constraints   Although customer convenience is important, operational requirements set tight constraints for some services. Airports, for instance, are often inconveniently located relative to travellers' homes, offices, or destinations. Because of noise and environmental factors, finding suitable sites for construction of new airports or expansion of existing ones is a very difficult task. (The only way to make airport access more convenient is to offer dedicated shuttle services such as L'Aérobus, which links the Pierre Elliott Trudeau International Airport to the Montréal Central Bus Station, or install fast rail links such as the futuristic 420 kilometres-per-hour service to Shanghai's new airport, the first in the world to use magnetic levitation technology.) A different type of location constraint is imposed by other geographic factors, such as terrain and climate. By definition, ski resorts have to be in the mountains and ocean beach resorts on the coast, although some companies find resources as well as customers to offer a service that would not be a natural choice given the geographic constraints (Figure 4.2).

The need for economies of scale is another operational issue that may restrict choice of locations. Major hospitals offer many different health-care services—even a medical school—at a single location, requiring a very large facility. Customers requiring complex, in-patient treatment must go to the service factory, rather than be treated at home. However, an ambulance—or even a helicopter—can be sent to pick them up. Consolidation of activities in a single location is particularly necessary in cases where specialized medical and nursing care is limited to a few hospitals that possess the necessary equipment and skills.

Ministores   An interesting innovation among multi-site service businesses involves creating numerous small service factories to maximize geographic coverage. Automated

Figure 4.2

Ski Dubai offers a year-round snow setting for skiing, snowboarding, and tobogganing.

kiosks represent one approach. ATMs offer many of the functions of a bank branch within a small, self-service machine that can be located within stores, hospitals, colleges, airports, and office buildings. Another approach results from separating the front and back stages of the operation. Taco Bell's innovative K-Minus strategy involves restaurants without kitchens.[5] Food preparation takes place in a central commissary from which meals are shipped to restaurants (which can now devote more of their expensive floor-area to customer use) and to other "points of access" (such as mobile food-carts), where they can be reheated prior to serving.

Increasingly, firms offering one type of service business are purchasing space from another provider in a complementary field. Examples include mini-bank branches within supermarkets, such as Western Union money transfer facilities within A&P, Dominion and Ultra Food & Drug stores across Canada, and food outlets such as Tim Hortons sharing space with a convenience store at a local Esso gas station.

Locating in Multi-purpose Facilities The most obvious locations for consumer services are close to where customers live or work. Modern buildings are often designed to be multi-purpose, featuring not only office or production space, but also such services as a bank (or at least an ATM), a restaurant, a hair salon, several stores, and maybe a health club. Some companies even include a children's daycare facility to make life easier for busy working parents.

Interest is growing in siting retail and other services on transportation routes and in bus, rail, and air terminals. With many domestic airlines in Canada and the United States either abandoning on-board food service on short flights or charging for meals on longer flights, entrepreneurs now staff small retail stands on airport concourses, selling passengers packaged salads, sandwiches, and beverages before they board their flights. Most major oil companies have developed chains of small retail stores to complement the fuel pumps at their service stations, thus offering customers the convenience of one-stop shopping for fuel, car supplies, food, and household products. Truckstops on major highways often include laundromats, toilets, ATMs, internet access, restaurants, and inexpensive hotels, in addition to a variety of vehicle maintenance and repair services for both trucks and cars. In one of the most interesting new retailing developments, airport terminals, which were designed as part of the infrastructure for air transportation services, are being transformed into vibrant shopping malls—a big change from the nondescript areas where passengers and their bags were processed (see Service Perspectives 4.2 on page 112).

When Should Service Be Delivered?

In the past, most retail and professional services in industrialized countries followed a traditional schedule of about 40–50 hours a week. In large measure, this routine reflected

Service Perspectives 4.2

From Airports to Air Malls

Large airports used to be places where thousands of people spent time waiting with little to keep them occupied. Airports were often bound by contract to a single food operator, which translated into low-quality food at high prices. Other than visiting stores selling newspapers, magazines, and paperback books, there wasn't much opportunity for travellers to shop unless they wanted to spend money on expensive (and often tawdry) souvenirs. The one exception was the duty- and tax-free shop at international airports, where opportunities to save money created a brisk trade in alcohol, perfumes, tobacco, and consumer products such as cameras. Today, however, some airports have terminals that have been transformed into shopping malls. London's Heathrow Airport even has a branch of Harrods, the famous department store.

Three factors make investments in airport retailing very appealing. One is the upscale demographics of airline passengers, whose numbers continue to grow rapidly. A second is that many passengers have time to spare while waiting for their flights, and more so now than ever as tighter security requirements mean they have to check in even earlier in advance of their flights. Finally, many existing terminal interiors have free space that can be put to profitable use. As terminals are expanded, new retail sites can be included as an integral part of the design.

Vancouver International Airport is ranked as the #1 mid-sized airport in North America by the International Air Transport Association (IATA). This ranking is based on traveller perceptions on a variety of factors such as ground transportation, parking facilities, signage, courtesy of airport staff, shopping, and restaurants, to name a few. Catering to the needs of over 16 million passengers in 2005, it is the second-busiest airport in Canada. Passengers at Vancouver can shop at a variety of brand outlets, from apparel stores such as Roots to personal-care product stores such as Crabtree & Evelyn, or shop for golfing accessories and paraphernalia at the PGA Tour Store. The airport also offers a wide variety of dining choices to the passengers from casual dining at the Hanami Japanese Restaurant to the upscale fine dining at Globe@YVR. In addition, passengers can shop at one of the twelve tax- and duty-free shops and specialty boutiques such as Burberry and Hermès. As a statement on their website (www.yvr.ca) says, "You can never arrive too early for your departure from Vancouver International Airport. Everything you need to do, you can do here."

In United States, the first (and still the most successful) custom-built airport retail complex is the Pittsburgh Air Mall, created as part of a new airport terminal and operated under a 15-year contract by BAA International (the former British Airports Authority, now privatized), the largest global airport operator. Pittsburgh is an important hub airport serving 26 million passengers a year, most of whom are domestic travellers. Goods and services available in the Air Mall's more than 100 stores and restaurants range from tasty take-out sandwiches for passengers who don't expect a meal on their discount-priced flight, to $15 massages for tired travellers with aching backs. Perhaps the most striking statistic is that value of sales per square metre is four to five times those of typical U.S. regional shopping centres.

BAA also operates long-term retail contracts at Baltimore-Washington and Boston Logan in the United States, as well as at seven airports in the U.K. It has equity investments in six Australian airports and one in Naples, Italy.

Source: BAA International (www.baa.com), accessed November 2005; Vancouver International Airport (www.yvr.ca), accessed March 2006.

social norms (and even legal requirements or union agreements) as to what were appropriate hours for people to work and for enterprises to sell things. The situation inconvenienced working people who either had to shop during their lunch break or on Saturdays. Historically, Sunday opening was strongly discouraged in most Christian cultures, and was often prohibited or restricted by law, reflecting a long tradition based on religious practice.

Today, the situation has changed. For some highly responsive service operations, the standard has become "24/7" service—24 hours a day, 7 days a week, around the world. (For an overview of the factors behind the move to more extended hours, see Service Perspective 4.3.) But there has been some resistance to the trend of seven-day operations. Until recently, Nova Scotia remained the only province in Canada that had a year-round ban on Sunday shopping. Interestingly, the impetus for this had come from the customer base. In a plebiscite held in October 2004, Nova Scotians decided to stick with the tradition and opted to keep the ban on Sunday shopping in place. However, in October 2006, the province's Supreme Court made it possible for businesses to be open seven days a week by ruling in favour of two grocery chains that had been restricted from opening on Sundays under earlier regulations. While there was a positive reaction from the chambers of commerce, critics saw it as a violation of the spirit of the 2004 plebiscite, where a majority, albeit slight, had voted against Sunday shopping.[6]

Service Perspective 4.3

Factors that Encourage Extended Operating Hours

At least five factors are driving the move toward extended operating hours and seven-day operations. The trend has been most noticeable in Canada and the United States, but is now spreading to many other countries around the world.

- *Economic pressure from consumers.* The growing number of two-income families and single wage-earners who live alone need time outside normal working hours to shop and use other services. Companies that initiate longer opening hours often benefit from being the first to do so, in terms of increased revenue sufficient to cover their increased costs. Besides these direct financial consequences, a company may also benefit indirectly from the use of longer operating hours as a mean of differentiating itself from its competitors. For instance, Tim Hortons has been extremely successful with its 24-hour outlets by appealing to customer-convenience needs. However, once one store or firm in any given area extends its hours to meet the needs of these market segments, competitors often feel obliged to follow. Chain stores have often led the way. Nevertheless, the value of a particular market (the total amount that consumers will spend) does not necessarily grow because of longer hours, meaning that there is only positional advantage to be gained, and in such cases successful businesses' gains are necessarily at the cost of their competitors' losses.

- *Changes in legislation.* Support has declined for the traditional religious view that a specific day (Sunday in predominantly Christian cultures) should be legislated as a day of rest for one and all, regardless of religious affiliation. In a multicultural society, of course, it's a moot point which day should be designated as special for observant Jews and Seventh Day Adventists, Saturday is the Sabbath; for Muslims, Friday is the holy day; and agnostics or atheists are presumably indifferent to the choice of day. There has been a gradual erosion of such legislation in western nations in recent years.

- *Economic incentives to improve asset utilization.* A great deal of capital is often tied up in service facilities. The incremental cost of extending hours is often relatively modest, and if it reduces crowding and increases revenues, then it is economically attractive. There are costs involved in shutting down and reopening a facility like a supermarket, yet climate control and some lighting must be left running all night, and security personnel must be paid 24/7. So, even if the number of extra customers served is minimal, there are both operational and marketing advantages to remaining open 24 hours.

- *Availability of employees to work during "unsocial" hours.* Changing lifestyles and a desire for part-time employment have created a growing labour pool of people who are willing to work evenings and nights. They include students looking for part-time work outside classroom hours, people working a second job, parents juggling child-care responsibilities, and others who simply prefer to work by night and relax or sleep by day.

- *Automated self-service facilities.* Self-service equipment has become increasingly reliable and user friendly. Many machines now accept card-based payments in addition to coins and banknotes. Installing unattended machines may be an economically feasible alternative for locations that cannot support a staffed facility. Unless a machine requires frequent servicing or is particularly vulnerable to vandalism, the incremental cost of going from limited hours to 24-hour operation is minimal. In fact, it may be simpler to leave machines running continuously than to turn them on and off.

DELIVERING SERVICES IN CYBERSPACE

Developments in telecommunications and computer technology have spurred many new approaches to service delivery. In the hospitality industry, reservations are increasingly channelled via firms' websites. For example, Swissôtel Hotels & Resorts devoted an entire campaign to increasing online bookings, especially among the important business-traveller segment. Within seven months of launch in early 2005, its revamped website (www.swissotel.com) more than doubled online revenues.[7] Apart from the enhanced express reservation functions (with fewer clicks), user-friendly navigation, and online promotions and incentives, the chain's "best rate guarantee" was a key driver of its success. Guests booking via its website were guaranteed the best rate for their booking. If they found another website with a lower rate (which is technically possible since they book a certain

Figure 4.3
Swissôtel's logo
incorporates its website
address.

proportion of their rooms through third-party brokers), Swissôtel would not only match this rate, but would also give an additional 50 percent discount for the first night of the guest's stay. The guarantee gave customers peace of mind. Swissôtel's logo (see Figure 4.3) now contains its website address to direct its guests towards online reservations and services.

However, not all customers like to use self-service equipment, so migration of customers to new electronic channels, for businesses that started out serving customers another way, may require different strategies for different segments,[8] as well as recognition that some proportion of customers will never voluntarily shift from their preferred high-contact delivery environments. An alternative that appeals to many people, perhaps because it uses a familiar technology, is banking by voice telephone.

Service Delivery Innovations Facilitated by Technology

More recently, entrepreneurs have taken advantage of the internet to create new services. Four innovations of particular interest are:

- Development of "smart" cellphones and PDAs, and Wi-Fi high-speed internet technology that can link users to the internet wirelessly.
- Use of voice recognition technology that allows customers to give information and request service simply by speaking into a phone or microphone.
- Creation of websites that provide information, take orders, and even serve as a delivery channel for information-based services.
- Commercialization of smart cards containing a microchip that can store detailed information about the customer and act as an electronic purse containing digital money. The ultimate in self-service banking will be when you can not only use a smart card as an electronic wallet for a wide array of transactions, but also refill it from a special card reader connected to your PC.

Singly or in combination, electronic channels offer a complement or alternative to traditional physical channels for delivering information-based services. Best Practice in Action 4.1 describes a multi-channel application for electronic banking.

Ecommerce: The Move to Cyberspace

As a distribution channel, the internet facilitates five categories of "flow": *information, negotiation, service, transactions,* and *promotion.* Compared to traditional channels, it's better able to help researchers collect data on consumer information-seeking and search behaviours, obtain feedback quickly from consumers, and create online communities to help market goods and services.[9]

Amazon.com has become the most successful of virtual stores, but now there are thousands of them all over the world. Among the factors luring customers into virtual stores are convenience, ease of search (obtaining information and searching for desired items or services), a broader selection, and the potential for better prices. Enjoying 24-hour service

Best Practice in Action 4.1

Multi-channel Banking without Branches at First Direct

First Direct, a division of HSBC, has become famous as the originator of the concept of a bank without branches. By late 2005, it was serving more than 1.2 million customers throughout the United Kingdom (and abroad) through call centres located far from the financial powerhouses of London, a website, text messaging on mobile phones, and access to HSBC's large network of ATMs. Some 750 000 customers use internet banking and 460 000 use SMS text messaging.

In January 2000 First Direct—by then describing itself as "the largest virtual bank in the world"—announced that it would transform itself into an e-bank and set the standard for e-banking. At the heart of the strategy is a multi-channel approach to banking that combines First Direct's telephone-banking experience with the strengths of the internet and the versatility of cellphone technologies to deliver a superior service at fiercely competitive prices. As noted by chief executive Alan Hughes: "We are the first bank in the world to re-engineer our entire business for the e-age. The scale of the initiative creates a new category of e-banking and sets a

benchmark for the industry around the globe. More than a bank, firstdirect.com will be the first internet banking store."

A central element in this strategy is to offer Britain's most comprehensive cellphone banking service, recognizing that almost all adults in the UK either own or use a mobile phone. Through SMS text messages, First Direct customers have access to mini-statements on up to three accounts and can be advised when credits or debits enter or leave the account. In addition, they are alerted automatically if their accounts go into the red.

Although person-to-person voice telephone still remains the backbone of the bank's relationship with its customers, in August 2005 the bank launched a new webchat service, enabling customers to "talk" with banking reps through a keyboard and mouse rather than by phone. It promotes this service as offering the immediacy of a phone conversation with the convenience of email.

Source: Press releases distributed on www.firstdirect.com, accessed 2001 and November 2005.

with prompt delivery is particularly appealing to customers whose busy lives leave them short of time (see Service Perspectives 4.4). What products have you purchased lately through the internet?

Many retailers, such as the Chapters-Indigo chain of bookstores, have developed a strong internet presence to complement their physical stores in an effort to counter competition in books and music from "cyberspace retailers" such as Amazon.com, which has no stores. However, adding an internet channel to an already established physical channel is a double-edged strategy. It carries high set-up costs, and no one can be sure if the investment will lead to long-term profits and high growth.[10]

Service Perspectives 4.4

Online vs. Bricks-and-Mortar: The Great Shopping Race

In a test of comparative shopping speed, in 2005 the *Wall Street Journal* sent two reporters on a mission on one of America's busiest shopping days of the year, the day after Thanksgiving (retailers call it Black Friday because it puts them back in the black!). Each had a budget of US$2000 and an identical list of 12 gifts to purchase—ranging from a variety of unbranded items (cashmere sweater for sister, sport watch for husband) to a Barbie Magic Pegasus for a 4-year-old girl and the hard-to-find new Microsoft Xbox 360 videogame system for an 11-year-old boy). Their goal was to see how quickly they could complete the assignment, and who could get the best gifts for the least money.

One reporter went to the huge Mall at Short Hills in New Jersey, which includes five anchor stores; the second stayed at home and shopped online, ordering items for overnight delivery. In a parallel race, a professional shopper at the

same mall and a web expert were given the same assignment. The results? The web expert completed the task in just under three hours and $800 under budget (though a couple of the items he purchased were deemed inferior in quality to those obtained at the mall). The personal shopper came in second, with a total bill $500 under budget but having taken seven hours, 15 minutes. Third was the reporter shopping online, who spent $1906 (including shipping costs) and took seven hours, 40 minutes, but admitted he had become distracted and wasted time surfing the web. Meantime, the reporter shopping at the mall took eight hours and spent $1836. However, neither reporter succeeded in buying the Xbox 360.

Source: Ellen Gamermann and Reed Albergotti, "The Great Holiday Shopping Race," *Wall Street Journal* (December 3–4, 2005): P6–P7.

Websites are becoming increasingly sophisticated, but also more user-friendly. They often simulate the services of a well-informed sales assistant in steering customers toward items that are likely to be of interest (based on a database of items that customer has previously purchased or browsed at the same site). Some even provide the opportunity for "live" email dialogue with helpful customer-service personnel. Facilitating searches is another useful service on many sites, ranging from looking at what books are available by a particular author to finding schedules of flights between two cities on a specific date.

Particularly exciting are recent developments that link websites, customer relationship management (CRM) systems, and mobile telephony. Integrating mobile devices into the service delivery infrastructure can be used as a means to (1) *access* services, (2) *alert* customers to opportunities or problems by delivering the right information or interaction at the right time, and (3) *update* information in real time to ensure that it is continuously accurate and relevant.[11] For example, if you were a customer of brokerage services offered by Scotiabank, through a subsidiary such as ScotiaMcLeod Direct Investing or ScotiaMcLeod *i*:PARTNER, you would have wireless access to all of the following services: placing orders to buy and sell Canadian and U.S. equities; obtaining real-time quotes on equities and market indices; accessing your personal library list; checking the status of your order; transferring funds in real time between your brokerage and banking accounts; and receiving real-time stock alerts and order notifications.[12]

THE ROLE OF INTERMEDIARIES

Many service organizations find it cost-effective to outsource certain tasks. Most frequently, this delegation concerns supplementary service elements. For instance, despite their greater use of telephone call centres and the internet to take bookings, cruise lines and resort hotels still rely on travel agents to handle a significant portion of their customer interactions, such as giving out information, taking reservations, accepting payment, and ticketing. Of course, many manufacturers rely on the services of distributors or retailers to stock and sell their physical products to end users, and also take on responsibility for supplementary services like information, advice, order-taking, delivery, installation, billing, payment, and certain types of problem-solving. In some cases, they may also handle certain types of repairs and upgrades.

How should a service provider work in partnership with one or more intermediaries to deliver a complete service package to customers? In Figure 4.4 we use the Flower of Service framework to depict an example in which the core product is delivered by the originating supplier (together with certain supplementary elements in the information, consultation, and exceptions categories), but delivery of the remaining supplementary services packaged with this offering has been delegated to an intermediary, who must complete the offering as experienced by the customer. In other instances, several specialist outsourcers might be involved as intermediaries for specific elements. The challenge for the original supplier is to act as guardian of the overall process, ensuring that each element offered by intermediaries fits the overall service concept to create a consistent and seamless branded service experience.

Figure 4.4

Splitting Responsibilities for Supplementary Service Elements

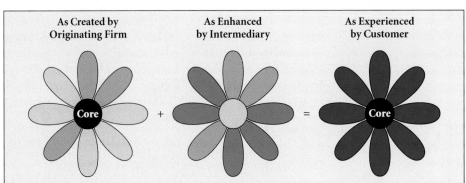

As Created by Originating Firm + As Enhanced by Intermediary = As Experienced by Customer

Franchising

Even delivery of the core product can be outsourced to an intermediary. Franchising has become a popular way to expand delivery of an effective service concept—embracing all of the 8 Ps—to multiple sites without the level of investment capital that would be needed for rapid expansion of company-owned and -managed sites.[13] It's an appealing strategy for growth-oriented service firms because franchisees are highly motivated to ensure customer orientation and high-quality service operations.[14] Although most commonly associated with fast-food outlets (for an example, see Figure 4.5), franchising has been applied to a very wide array of both consumer and business-to-business services, and now spans some 75 different product categories. New concepts are being created and commercialized all the time in countries around the world.[15]

According to the International Franchise Association, some 760 000 franchise businesses in the United States generate jobs for more than 18 million people and create over $1.5 trillion in economic activity—about 9.5 percent of the private sector's total output.[16] Among the cases featured in this book is that of "Aussie Pooch Mobile," which describes a successful Australian-based franchised dog washing service (see page 502).

Nevertheless, there is a significant attrition rate among franchisors in the early years of a new franchise system, with one-third of all systems failing within the first 4 years and no less than three-quarters of all franchisors ceasing to exist after 12 years.[17] Success factors for franchisors include being able to achieve a larger size with a more recognizable brand name, offering franchisees fewer supporting services but longer-term contracts, and having fewer headquarters staff per outlet. Since growth is very important to achieve an efficient scale, some franchisors adopt a strategy known as master franchising, which involves delegating the responsibility for recruiting, training, and supporting franchisees within a given geographic area. Master franchisees are often individuals who have already succeeded as operators of an individual franchise outlet.

A franchisor recruits entrepreneurs who are willing to invest their own time and equity in managing a previously developed service concept. In return, the franchisor provides training in how to operate and market the business, sells necessary supplies, and provides promotional support at a national or regional level to augment local marketing activities (which are paid for by the franchisee, but must adhere to copy and media guidelines prescribed by the franchisor).

Figure 4.5
Cara Food Corporation uses franchising to distribute its branded service concept for Harvey's, a fast-food grill restaurant.

A disadvantage of delegating activities to franchisees is that it entails some loss of control over the delivery system and, thereby, over how customers experience the actual service. Ensuring that an intermediary adopts exactly the same priorities and procedures as prescribed by the franchisor is difficult, yet vital to effective quality control. Franchisors usually seek to exercise control over all aspects of the service performance through a contract that specifies adherence to tightly defined service standards, procedures, scripts, and physical presentation. Franchisors control not only output specifications, but also the appearance of the servicescape, employee performance, and such elements as service timetables.

An ongoing problem is that as franchisees gain experience, they may start to resent the various fees they pay the franchisor and believe that they can operate the business better without the constraints imposed by the agreement. The resulting disputes often lead to legal fights between the two parties.

An alternative to franchising is licensing another supplier to act on the original supplier's behalf to deliver the core product. Trucking companies regularly make use of independent agents, instead of locating company-owned branches in each of the different cities they serve. They may also choose to contract with independent "owner-operators," who drive their own trucks, rather than buy trucks for the company and employ full-time drivers themselves.[18]

Other service distribution agreements include financial services. Banks seeking to move into investment services will often act as the distributor for mutual fund products created by an investment firm that lacks extensive distribution channels of its own.

THE CHALLENGE OF DISTRIBUTION IN LARGE AND DIVERSE DOMESTIC MARKETS

There are important differences between marketing services in a unitary nation covering a compact geographic area, such as France or Japan, and those in a federal nation covering a large area, such as Canada, Australia, or the United States.

In such countries, a challenge faced by many types of services is the issue of physical logistics because of the distances involved and the existence of multiple time zones. Serving customers across Canada requires covering distances as large as the 4634 kilometres between Cape Columbia on Ellesmere Island, Nunavut and Middle Island in Lake Erie, Ontario (north to south), and the 5514 kilometres between Cape Spear on Newfoundland and the Yukon–Alaska boundary (east to west). While it is a complex logistical undertaking, organizations operating across Canada benefit from an exceptionally well developed communications, transportation, and distribution infrastructure. Also, the federal political structure of Canada means there are differences between the laws and tax rates of the various provinces. For example, if companies engaged in any research and development (R&D) can see a wide variation in tax credits between the provinces, it is likely to affect their decision on where to conduct those activities. Provincial incentives can range from 0 percent in Alberta to a high of 37.5 percent in Quebec, with multiple variations in between for other provinces.

In addition, firms marketing across Canada have to work in two official languages, English and French. This certainly has a significant impact on all aspects of the functioning of an organization, both internal and external, from their hiring policies and procedures to their marketing efforts. Another issue increasingly faced by service organizations in Canada is the growth in the proportion of immigrants who speak neither official language as a mother tongue. As the Canadian population becomes increasingly multicultural, market segmentation issues have become more complex for Canadian service marketers operating on a national scale as they encounter growing populations of immigrants who speak many languages. Some companies have faced this challenge head-on in order to tap into the long-term potential offered by this segment of the population (see Service Perspectives 4.5).

Faced with an enormous and diverse domestic marketplace, most large Canadian service companies simplify their marketing and management tasks by targeting specific

Service Perspectives 4.5

"TD Taps Canada's Mosaic for Growth," by Sinclair Stewart (*Globe and Mail*, February 28, 2006)

When Toronto-Dominion Bank scooped up Canadian auto finance company VFC Inc. recently, it raised more than a few eyebrows among investors. Why was TD, with its new-found aversion to risky lending, suddenly courting car buyers with weak credit profiles [VFC's specialty market]? TD provided a number of answers, ranging from the potential size of the market to the strength and experience of VFC's management team. But there was another, equally compelling reason for the purchase that didn't receive much attention: this was a way for TD to grab a larger share of the immigrant market, one of the most lucrative sources of domestic growth available to Canada's big banks.

No one needs to explain this to TD. The bank has quietly forged a commanding share of the business among the country's ethnic[-minority] groups, according to a study to be released today by Toronto-based Solutions Research Group Consultants Inc. The firm conducted telephone interviews in nine languages with 3000 Canadians last summer, and found that TD's retail bank ranked No. 1 for primary relationships among all six of the country's major ethnic [-minority] populations: Chinese, South Asian, Italian, Black, West Asian/Arab, and Hispanic.

"TD has done a little bit more, a little bit more aggressively, particularly with the South Asian community," said Kaan Yigit, who directed the diversity study for SRG. "If you have a leadership position with the fastest-growing segments,

you're going to get disproportionate rewards if you can maintain these relationships." These rewards, especially for banks scrounging for growth on their home turf, could be huge. Immigration accounts for nearly 70 percent of Canada's population expansion; one in five Canadians is expected to belong to a visible minority by 2017. New Canadians are also much younger, and many tend to be highly educated.

TD has seen the demographics, and plans to almost triple its ethnic[-minority] marketing budget this year, said chief marketing officer, Dom Mercuri. "It is the future: You just have to go to the Statscan Web site," said Mr. Mercuri, who chairs a diversity committee within the bank. "It is a huge opportunity. But it's one of those opportunities that if you don't capture the growth segment now, organizations will see their customer base erode." The challenge is that these immigrants often arrive with no brand preference, no banking relationships, and no credit profile—one of the reasons that companies such as VFC, which services people with little or no credit profile, can help TD make another point of contact with new Canadians.

Article source: Sinclair Stewart, "TD taps Canada's Mosaic for Growth: Bank Leads Charge in Carving a Share of Lucrative Market," *Globe and Mail,* February 28, 2006. Available online at www.theglobeandmail.com/servlet/story/LAC.20060228.RTD28/ TPStory/Business, accessed April 2006. Reprinted with permission from *The Globe and Mail.*

New Canada Rates the Old Banks
What is the name of your primary financial institution or bank?

RANK	CHINESE	SOUTH ASIAN	WEST ASIAN / ARAB	BLACK	HISPANIC	ITALIAN
1	TD	TD	TD	TD	TD	TD
2	CIBC	CIBC	RBC	CIBC	RBC	CIBC
3	RBC	RBC	CIBC	RBC	CIBC	RBC
4	HSBC	Scotiabank	BMO	Scotiabank	Dejardins	BMO
5	BMO	BMO	National Bank	BMO	Scotiabank	Scotiabank

Source: Solutions Research Group.

market segments. Some firms segment the market on a geographic basis. Others target certain groups based on demographics, lifestyle, needs, or—in B2B services—on industry type and company size. Smaller firms wishing to operate nationally usually choose to seek out narrow market niches, a task made easier today by the growing use of websites and email. Yet, the largest national service operations face tremendous challenges as they seek to serve multiple segments across a huge geographic area. They must strike a balance between standardization of strategies across all the elements embraced by the 8 Ps (see Chapter 1) and adaptation to different segments and local market conditions—decisions that are especially challenging when they concern high-contact services where customers visit the delivery site in person.

What are the alternative ways for a service company to tap the potential of international markets? It depends in part on the nature of the underlying processes and delivery system. People-, possession-, and information-based services have vastly different requirements in an international distribution strategy.

How Service Processes Affect International Market Entry

People-Processing Services   These services require direct contact with the customer. Three options present themselves:

- *Export the service concept.* Acting alone or in partnership with local suppliers, the firm establishes a service factory in another country. The objective may be to reach out to new customers, or to follow existing corporate or individual customers to new locations (or both). This approach is commonly used by chain restaurants, hotels, car-rental firms, and weight-reduction clinics, where a local presence is essential in order to be able to compete. For example, Tim Hortons has successfully rolled its service concept across the border and now operates over 291 stores across 10 American states.[19] For corporate customers, the industries are likely to be in fields such as banking, professional services, and business logistics (among others).

- *Import customers.*[20] Customers from other countries are invited to come to a service factory with distinctive appeal or competences in the firm's home country. People will travel from abroad to ski at outstanding resorts, such as Whistler-Blackcomb in British Columbia or Vail in Colorado.

- *Transport customers to new locations.* In the case of passenger transportation, embarking on international service takes the form of opening new routes to desired destinations. This strategy is generally used to attract new customers, in addition to expanding the choices for existing customers.

Best Practice in Action 4.2 describes some of the ways in which Groupe Accor, a major international hotel chain, has developed a global presence.

Possession-Processing Services   This category involves services to the customer's physical possessions and includes repair and maintenance, freight transport, cleaning, and warehousing. Most services in this category require an ongoing local presence, regardless of whether customers drop off items at a service facility or personnel visit the customer's site. Sometimes, however, expert personnel may be flown in from a base in another country. In a few instances, a transportable item of equipment may be shipped to a foreign service centre for repair, maintenance, or upgrade. Like passenger carriers, operators of freight transport services enter new markets by opening new routes.

Information-Based Services   This group includes two categories, *mental-processing services* (services to the customer's mind, such as news and entertainment) and *information-processing services* (services to customers' intangible assets, such as banking and insurance). Information-based services can be distributed internationally in one of three ways:

- *Export the service to a local service factory.* The service can be made available in a local facility that customers visit. For instance, a film made in Hollywood can be shown in movie theatres around the world, or a college course can be designed in one country and then be taught by approved teachers elsewhere.

- *Import customers.* Customers may travel abroad to visit a specialist facility, in which case the service takes on the characteristics of a people-processing service. For instance, large numbers of foreign students study in Canadian and U.S. universities.

- *Export the information via telecommunications and transform it locally.* Rather than ship object-based services from their country of origin, the data can be downloaded from that country for physical production in local markets (even by customers themselves).

Best Practice in Action 4.2

Groupe Accor: Hotel Innovation in a Global Setting

Paris-based Groupe Accor is one of the world's leaders in several complementary and integrated services: hotels, travel agencies, and car rentals. According to industry experts, Accor is one of a few truly global hotel companies, with some 4000 hotels and 168 000 associates in 140 countries. Over the years, the group has proved itself to be a highly innovative service provider, as reflected by its in-depth market-opportunity analysis, integrated offerings, and international growth strategies.

Accor has gone from being the first truly pan-European hotel chain to one of the largest hotel chains in the world. It operates several distinct categories of hotels, such as the four/five-star Sofitel brand, the three/four-star Novotel, the three/four star Mercure, and the two/three-star Ibis. Accor has also pioneered an easily prefabricated, replicable budget hotel concept known as the Formula 1 chain. In the United States, Accor operates the Motel 6 chain of budget motels and the Red Roof Inns, and has plans for other acquisitions. Care is given to maintaining the distinctive identities of each of its hotel brands.

Accor's chairman, Jean-Marc Espalioux, seeks to give the company the integrated structure it needs to operate and compete on a global basis. Hotel activities have been restructured into three strategic segments, reflecting their market positioning. There are also two functional divisions. The first, a global services division, is being created to spearhead the major functions common to all hotel activities: information systems, reservation systems, maintenance and technical assistance, purchasing, key accounts, and partnerships and synergy between hotel and other activities. The second, the hotel development division, is structured by brand and by region, and is responsible for working with the management of each hotel to develop marketing, service development, and growth strategies. Says Espalioux: "In view of the revolution in the service sector which is now taking place, I do not see any future for purely national hotel chains—except for very specific niche markets with special architecture and locations, such as Raffles in Singapore or the Ritz in Paris. National chains can't invest enough money."

The group is continuing its internationalization drive, focusing on further consolidating and integrating its network, as well as building a presence in such emerging markets as Poland, Hungary, and other ex-Soviet-bloc countries. Mr. Espalioux is also very aware that the underlying obstacle to successful globalization in services is people: "Globalization brings considerable challenges which are often underestimated. The principal difficulty is getting our local management to adhere to the values of the group. [They] must understand our market and culture, for example, and we have to learn about theirs."

Because international co-operation, communication, and teamwork are integral to achieving global consistency, Accor has eliminated—as far as possible—hierarchies, rigid job descriptions and titles, and even organizational charts. Employees are encouraged to interact as much as possible both with their colleagues and with guests. They define the limits of their jobs within the context of the overall "customer experience," and are recognized and rewarded on how well they meet these definitions. In addition to these structural and organizational initiatives, video conferencing and other technologies are used extensively to create and reinforce a common, global culture among Accor employees around the world. All of the group's European hotels are linked together through a sophisticated IT network, which may eventually be expanded worldwide.

Sources: Andrew Jack, "The Global Company: Why There is No Future for National Hotel Chains," *Financial Times* (October 10, 1997); W. Chan Kim and Renée Mauborgne, "Value Innovation: The Strategic Logic of High Growth," *Harvard Business Review* 75/1 (January–February 1997): 102–12; and the firm's website, www.accor.com, accessed May 2006.

In theory, none of these information-based services require face-to-face contact with customers, since all can potentially be delivered at arm's length through telecommunications or mail. Banking and insurance are good examples of services that can be delivered from other countries, with cash delivery available through global ATM networks. In practice, however, a local presence may be necessary to build personal relationships, conduct on-site research (as in consulting or auditing), or even to fulfill legal requirements.

Barriers to International Trade in Services

The marketing of services internationally has been the fastest growth segment of international trade.[21] Transnational strategy involves the integration of strategy formulation and its implementation across all the countries in which the company elects to do business. Barriers to entry, historically a serious problem for foreign firms wishing to do business abroad, are slowly diminishing. The passage of free trade legislation in recent years has been an important facilitator of transnational operations. Notable developments include NAFTA (linking Canada, Mexico, and the United States), Latin American economic blocs like Mercosur and Pacto Andino, and the European Union, which is expected to expand its membership in the coming years (see Service Perspectives 4.6).

However, operating successfully in international markets remains difficult for some services. Despite the efforts of the World Trade Organization (WTO) and its predecessor, GATT (General Agreement on Tariffs and Trade) there are many hurdles to overcome. Airline access is a sore point. Many countries require bilateral (two-country) agreements on establishing new routes. If one country is willing to allow entry by a new carrier, but the other is not, then access will be blocked. Compounding government restrictions of this nature are capacity limits at certain major airports, which lead to denial of new or additional landing rights for foreign airlines. Both passenger and freight transport are affected by such restrictions.

Other constraints may include administrative delays, refusals by immigration offices to provide work-permit applications for foreign managers and workers, heavy taxes on foreign firms, domestic-preference policies designed to protect local suppliers, legal restrictions on operational and marketing procedures (including international data flows), and the lack of broadly agreed accounting standards for services. Different languages and cultural norms may require expensive changes in the nature of a service and how it is delivered and promoted. The cultural issue has been particularly significant for the entertainment industry. Many nations are wary of seeing their own culture swamped by American imports.

Factors Favouring Adoption of Transnational Strategies

Several forces or *industry drivers* influence the trend toward globalization and the creation of transnationally integrated strategy.[22] As applied to services, these forces are market drivers, competition drivers, technology drivers, cost drivers, and government drivers. Their relative significance may vary by type of service.

Service Perspectives 4.6

The European Union: Moving to Borderless Trade

The 25-country European Union (EU) has a large population (460 million), is culturally and politically diverse, with distinct variations in tastes and lifestyles, and has the added complication of 20 official national languages and a variety of regional tongues, from Catalan to Welsh. As new countries join the EU, the "single market" will become even larger. The anticipated admission of several more Eastern European countries in the next few years and the possibility of a formal link with (and eventual membership for) Turkey (whose land area straddles Europe and Asia) will add further cultural diversity and bring the EU market closer to Russia and the countries of Central Asia.

Within the EU, the European Commission has made huge progress in harmonizing standards and regulations to level the competitive playing field and discourage efforts by individual member countries to protect their own service and manufacturing industries. The results are already evident, with many service firms operating across Europe (as well as overseas).

Another important economic step facilitating transnational marketing on a pan-European basis is monetary union. In January 1999, the exchange values of 11 national European currencies was linked to a new currency, the Euro, which completely replaced those currencies in 2002. Today, services are priced in Euros from Finland to Portugal. Other European countries, including Britain and Sweden, may well decide to switch to Euros in due course.

However, although the potential for freer trade in services within the EU continues to increase, we need to recognize that "Greater Europe"—ranging from Iceland to Russia west of the Ural Mountains—includes many countries that are likely to remain outside the Union for some years to come. Some of these countries, such as Switzerland and Norway (which have both rejected membership in referenda), tend to enjoy much closer trading relations with the EU than others. Whether there will ever be full political union—a "United States of Europe"—remains a hotly debated and contested issue. However, from a services-marketing standpoint, the EU is certainly moving towards the U.S. model in terms of both scale and freedom of movement. See http://europa.eu.int for more information on the EU.

Market Drivers   Market factors that stimulate the move toward transnational strategies include common customer needs across many countries, global customers who demand consistent service from suppliers around the world, and the availability of international channels in the form of efficient physical supply chains or electronic networks. As large corporate customers become global, they often seek to standardize and simplify the suppliers they use in different countries for a wide array of B2B services. For instance, companies that operate globally often seek to minimize the number of auditors they use around the world, expressing a preference for using one of the "Big Four" multinational accounting firms that can apply a consistent approach (within the context of the national rules prevailing within each country of operation). Corporate banking, insurance, and management consulting are further examples. In each instance, there are real advantages in consistency, ease of access, consolidation of information, and accountability. Similarly, international business travellers and tourists often feel more comfortable with predictable international standards of performance for such travel-related services as airlines and hotels. Also, the development of global logistics and supply chain management capabilities among such firms as DHL, FedEx, and UPS has encouraged many manufacturers to outsource responsibility for their logistics function to a single firm (Figure 4.6).

Competition Drivers   The presence of competitors from different countries, interdependence of countries, and the transnational policies of competitors themselves are among the key competition drivers that exercise a powerful force in many service industries. Firms may be obliged to follow their competitors into new markets in order to protect their positions elsewhere. Similarly, once a major player moves into a new foreign market, a scramble for territory among competing firms may ensue.

Technology Drivers   These factors tend to centre around advances in information technology—such as enhanced performance and capabilities in telecommunications, computerization, and software, miniaturization of equipment, and the digitization of voice, video, and text so that all can be stored and transmitted in the digital language of computers. For information-based services, the growing availability of broadband telecommunications channels, capable of moving vast amounts of data at great speed, is playing a major role in opening up new markets.[23] Access to the internet is accelerating around the world. Significant economies may be gained by centralizing "information hubs" on a continent-wide or even global basis. Firms can take advantage of favourable labour costs and exchange rates by consolidating operations of supplementary services (such as reservations) or back office functions (such as accounting) in just one or a few selected countries.

Figure 4.6
DHL combines multiple transport modes to create integrated logistics solutions for its global customer base.

Cost Drivers   Big is sometimes beautiful from a cost standpoint. There may be economies of scale to be gained from operating on an international or even global basis, plus sourcing efficiencies as a result of favourable logistics and lower costs in certain countries. Lower operating costs for telecommunications and transportation, accompanied by improved performance, facilitate entry into international markets. The effect of these drivers varies according to the level of fixed costs required to enter an industry, and the potential for cost savings. Barriers to entry caused by the upfront cost of equipment and facilities may be reduced by such strategies as equipment leasing (as in airlines), seeking investor-owned facilities such as hotels and then obtaining management contracts, or awarding franchises to local entrepreneurs. However, cost drivers may be less applicable for services that are primarily people-based. For services in which most elements of the service factory must be replicated in multiple locations, scale economies tend to be lower, and experience curves flatter.

Government Drivers   Government policies can serve to encourage or discourage development of a transnationally integrated strategy. Among these drivers are favourable trade policies, compatible technical standards, and common marketing regulations. For instance, the actions taken by the European Commission to create a single market throughout the EU are a stimulus to the creation of pan-European service strategies in numerous industries.

Furthermore, the World Trade Organization (WTO) and its focus on the internationalization of services has pressured governments around the world to create more favourable regulatory environments for transnational service strategies. The power of the drivers for internationalization can be seen in the case of the Qantas airliner arriving in Hong Kong described in Service Perspectives 4.7 on page 126.

Many of the factors driving internationalization and the adoption of transnational strategies also promote the trend toward nationwide operations. The market, cost, and technological and competitive forces that encourage creation of nationwide service businesses or franchise chains are often the same as those that subsequently drive some of the same firms to operate transnationally.

How the Nature of Service Processes Affects Opportunities for Internationalization

Are some types of services easier to internationalize than others? Our analysis suggests that this is indeed the case. Table 4.2 summarizes important variations in the impact of each of the five groups of drivers on three broad categories of services: people-processing services, possession-processing services, and information-based services

People-Processing Services   The service provider needs to maintain a local geographic presence, stationing the necessary personnel, buildings, equipment, vehicles, and supplies within reasonably easy reach of target customers. If the customers are themselves mobile, as in the case of business travellers and tourists, then the same customers may patronize a company's offerings in many different locations and make comparisons between them.

Possession-Processing Services   These may also be geographically constrained in many instances. A local presence is still required when the supplier must come to repair or maintain objects in a fixed location. However, smaller, transportable items can be shipped to distant service centres, although transportation costs, customs duties, and government regulations may constrain shipment across large distances or national frontiers. On the other hand, modern technology now allows certain types of service processes to be administered from a distance through electronic diagnostics and transmission of so-called "remote fixes."

Information-Based Services   These are, perhaps, the most interesting category of services from the standpoint of global strategy development, because they depend on the transmission or manipulation of data in order to create value. The advent of modern global telecommunications, linking powerful machines to large databases, makes it

Table 4.2 Impact of Globalization Drivers on Various Service Categories

GLOBALIZATION DRIVERS	PEOPLE PROCESSING	POSSESSION PROCESSING	INFORMATION BASED
Competition	Simultaneity of production and consumption limits leverage of foreign-based competitive advantage in front stage of service factory, but advantage in management systems can be basis for globalization.	Lead role of technology creates driver for globalization of competitors with technical edge (e.g., Singapore Airlines' technical servicing for other carriers' aircraft).	Highly vulnerable to global dominance by competitors with monopoly or competitive advantage in information (e.g., BBC, Hollywood, CNN), unless restricted by governments.
Market	People differ economically and culturally, so need for service and ability to pay may vary. Culture and education may affect willingness to do self-service.	Less variation for service to corporate possessions, but level of economic development affects demand for services to individually owned goods.	Demand for many services is derived to a significant degree from economic and educational levels. Cultural issues may affect demand for entertainment.
Technology	Use of IT for delivery of supplementary services may be a function of ownership and familiarity with technology, including telecommunications and intelligent terminals.	Need for technology-based service delivery systems is a function of the types of possessions requiring service and the cost trade-offs in labour substitution.	Ability to deliver core services through remote terminals may be a function of investments in computerization, quality of telecommunications infrastructure, and education levels.
Cost	Variable labour rates may affect pricing in labour-intensive services (consider self-service in high-cost locations).	Variable labour rates may favour low-cost locations if not offset by shipment costs. Consider substituting equipment for labour.	Major cost elements can be centralized and minor cost elements localized.
Government	Social policies (e.g., health care) vary widely and may affect labour costs, role of women in front-stage jobs, and hours/days on which work can be performed.	Tax laws, environmental regulations, and technical standards may decrease/increase costs and encourage/discourage certain types of activity.	Policies on education, censorship, public ownership of communications, and infrastructure standards may affect demand and supply, and distort pricing.

increasingly easy to deliver information-based services around the world. Local presence requirements may be limited to a terminal, ranging from a simple telephone or fax machine to a computer or more specialized equipment like a bank ATM, connected to a reliable telecommunications infrastructure. If the local infrastructure is not of sufficiently high quality, then the use of mobile or satellite communications may solve the problem in some instances.

Service Perspectives 4.7

Flight to Hong Kong: A Snapshot of Globalization

A white and red Boeing 747, sporting the flying kangaroo of Qantas, banks low over Hong Kong's dramatic harbour, crowded with merchant vessels, as it nears the end of its 10-hour flight from Australia. Once landed, the aircraft taxis past a kaleidoscope of tail fins, representing airlines from more than a dozen different countries on several continents—just a sample of all the carriers that offer service to this remarkable city.

The passengers include business travellers and tourists, as well as returning residents. After passing through immigration and customs, most visitors will be heading first for their hotels, many of which belong to global chains (some of them Hong Kong based). Some travellers will be picking up cars, reserved earlier from Hertz or one of the other well-known rental car companies with facilities at the airport. Others will take the fast train into the city. Tourists on package vacations are looking forward to enjoying Hong Kong's renowned Cantonese cuisine. Parents, however, are resigned to having their children demand to eat at the same fast-food chains that can be found back home. Many of the more affluent tourists are planning to go shopping, not only in the distinctive Chinese jewellery and antiques stores, but also in the internationally branded luxury stores that can be found in most world-class cities.

What brings the business travellers to this SAR ("special administrative region") of China? Many are negotiating supply contracts for manufactured goods ranging from clothing to toys to computer components, whereas others have come to market their own goods and services. Some are in the shipping or construction businesses, others in an array of service industries ranging from telecommunications to entertainment and international law. The owner of a large Australian tourism operation has come to negotiate a deal for package vacations on Queensland's famous Gold Coast. The Brussels-based, Canadian senior partner of a Big Four accounting firm is half way through a gruelling round-the-world trip to persuade the offices of an international

conglomerate to consolidate all its auditing business on a global basis with his firm alone. An American executive and her British colleague, both working for a large Euro-American telecom partnership, are hoping to achieve similar goals by interesting a multinational corporation in the concept of employing their firm to manage all of its telecommunications activities worldwide. And more than a few of the passengers either work for international banking and financial service firms or have come to Hong Kong, one of the world's most dynamic financial centres, to seek financing for their own ventures.

In the Boeing's freight hold can be found not only passengers' bags, but also cargo for delivery to Hong Kong and other Chinese destinations. The freight includes mail, Australian wine, some vital spare parts for an Australian-built high-speed ferry operating out of Hong Kong, a container full of brochures and display materials about the Australian tourism industry for an upcoming trade promotion, and a variety of other high-value merchandise. Waiting at the airport for the aircraft's arrival are local Qantas personnel, baggage handlers, cleaners, mechanics and other technical staff, customs and immigration officials, and, of course, people who have come to greet individual passengers. A few are Australians, but the great majority are local Hong Kong Chinese, many of whom have never travelled very far afield. Yet in their daily lives, they patronize banks, fast-food outlets, retail stores, and insurance companies whose brand names—promoted by global advertising campaigns—may be equally familiar to their expatriate relatives living in countries such as Australia, Britain, Canada, Singapore, and the United States. They can watch CNN on cable TV, listen to the BBC World Service on the radio, make phone calls through Hong Kong Telecom (itself part of a worldwide operation), and watch movies from Hollywood either in English or dubbed into the Cantonese dialect of Chinese. Welcome to the world of global services marketing!

Conclusion

"Where? When? and How?" Responses to these three questions form the foundation of service-delivery strategy. The customer's service experience is a function of both service performance and delivery characteristics.

"Where?" relates, of course, to the places where customers can obtain delivery of the core product, one or more supplementary services, or a complete package. In this chapter, we presented a categorization scheme for thinking about alternative place-related strategies, ranging from customers coming to the service site, to service personnel visiting the customer,

and finally a variety of options for arm's-length transactions, including delivery through both physical and electronic channels.

"When?" involves decisions on scheduling of service delivery. Customer demands for greater convenience are leading many firms to extend their hours and days of service, with the ultimate flexibility being offered by 24/7 service every day of the year.

"How?" concerns channels and procedures for delivering the core and supplementary service elements to customers.

Advances in technology are having a major impact on the alternatives available and on the economics of those alternatives. Responding to customer needs for flexibility, many firms now offer several alternative choices of delivery channels.

Although service firms are much more likely than a manufacturer to control their own delivery systems, there is also a role for intermediaries to deliver either the core services—as is the case for franchisees—or supplementary services, such as travel agents.

More and more service firms are marketing across national borders. Stimulating (or constraining) the move to transnational strategies are five key industry drivers: market factors, costs, technology, government policies, and competitive forces. However, significant differences exist in the extent to which the various drivers apply to people-processing, possession-processing, and information-based services.

Review Questions

1. What is meant by "distributing services?" How can an experience or something intangible be distributed?

2. Why is it important to consider the distribution of core and supplementary services separately?

3. What risks and opportunities are entailed for a retail-service firm in adding electronic channels of delivery (a) paralleling a channel involving physical stores, or (b) replacing the physical stores with an internet-cum-call-centre channel? Give examples.

4. Why should service marketers be concerned with new developments in mobile communications?

5. What marketing and management challenges are raised by the use of intermediaries in a service setting?

6. What are the key drivers for increasing globalization of services?

7. How does the nature of the service affect the opportunities for globalization?

Application Exercises

1. Visit the websites of Vancouver International Airport (www.yvr.ca) and Toronto Pearson International Airport (www.gtaa.com). What similarities and differences do you see in the operation of these "air malls"? Do you think one is doing a better job than the other?

2. Using the same service organization, or another of your choice, examine their use of technology in facilitating service delivery. Might there be other opportunities for technology to be employed beneficially? What are these?

3. Identify three situations in which you use self-service delivery. What is your motivation for using this approach to delivery, rather than having service personnel do it for you?

4. Think of three services that you mostly or exclusively buy or use via the internet. What is the value proposition of this channel to you over alternative channels (e.g., phone, mail, or a physical location)?

5. Go to the Canadian Franchise Association's website (www.cfa.ca). Select two Canadian franchises from two different business formats (other than food service), choosing one targeted primarily at consumer markets and the other primarily at B2B markets. Develop a profile of each, examining their strategy across each of the 8Ps and evaluating their competitive positioning.

6. Besides financial services, identify other service industries that have been targeting, or have begun to target, immigrant communities as distinct customer segments. Evaluate the strategies of three leading competitors within one of these industries, and discuss which of the competitors are likely to fail or succeed in the long run, and why.

7. Obtain recent statistics for international trade in services for Canada and another country of your choice. What are the dominant categories of service exports and imports? What factors do you think are driving trade in specific service categories? What differences do you see between the countries?

Endnotes

1. Jochen Wirtz and Jeannette P.T. Ho, "Westin in Asia: Distributing Hotel Rooms Globally," in Jochen Wirtz and Christopher H. Lovelock (eds.), *Services Marketing in Asia: A Case Book,* Singapore: Prentice Hall, 2005: 253–59.

2. The section was based on the following research: Nancy Jo Black, Andy Lockett, Christine Ennew et al., "Modelling Consumer Choice of Distribution Channels: An Illustration from Financial Services," *International Journal of Bank Marketing* 20/4 (2002): 161–73; Jinkook Lee, "A Key to Marketing Financial Services: The Right Mix of Products, Services, Channels and Customers," *Journal of Services Marketing* 16/3 (2002): 238–58; Leonard L. Berry, Kathleen Seiders, and Dhruv Grewal, "Understanding Service Convenience," *Journal of Marketing* 66/3 (July 2002): 1–17; and Matthew L. Meuter, Mary Jo Bitner, Amy L. Ostrom, and Stephen W. Brown, "Choosing among Alternative Service Delivery Modes: An Investigation of Customer Trial of Self-Service Technologies," *Journal of Marketing* 69/2 (April 2005): 61–83.

3. Paul F. Nunes and Frank V. Cespedes, "The Customer has Escaped," *Harvard Business Review* 81/11 (2003): 96–105.

4. Michael A. Jones, David L. Mothersbaugh, and Sharon E. Beatty, "The Effects of Locational Convenience on Customer Repurchase Intentions across Service Types," *Journal of Services Marketing* 17/7 (2004): 701–12.

5. James L. Heskett, W. Earl Sasser Jr., and Leonard A. Schlesinger, *The Service Profit Chain,* New York: Free Press, 1997: 218–20.

6. www.cbc.ca/ns/story/ns_sunshopresults20041016.html, accessed March 2006, and www.cbc.ca/canada/nova-scotia/story/2006/10/04/ns-sunday-shopping.html, accessed January 2007.

7. www.swisshotel.com and www.eyefortravel.com, accessed November 2005.

8. Recent research on the adoption of self-service technologies includes: L. Michelle Bobbitt and Pratibha A. Dabholkar, "Integrating Attitudinal Theories to Understand and Predict Use of Technology-based Self-service: The Internet as an Illustration," *International Journal of Service Industry Management* 12/5 (December 2001): 423–50; Meuter, Bitner, Ostrom, and Brown, op. cit.; and James M. Curran and Matthew L. Meuter, "Self-Service Technology Adoption: Comparing Three Technologies," *Journal of Services Marketing* 19/2 (2005): 103–13.

9. P.K. Kannan, "Introduction to the Special Issue: Marketing in the E-Channel," *International Journal of Electronic Commerce* 5/3 (2001): 3–6; Customer satisfaction and loyalty can be built with electronic channels that build "digital proximity"; see Sonja M. Salmen and Andrew Muir, "Electronic Customer Care: The Innovative Path to E-Loyalty," *Journal of Financial Services Marketing* 8/2 (2003): 133–44.

10. Inge Geyskens, Katrijn Gielens, and Marnik G Dekimpe, "The Market Valuation of Internet Channel Additions," *Journal of Marketing* 66/2 (April 2002): 102–19. For a study showing that customer perception of greater integration of physical and online channels is important in a multi-channel strategy, and is associated with higher loyalty, see Elliot Bendoly, James D. Blocher, Kurt M. Bretthauer, et al., "Online/In-Store Integration and Customer Retention," *Journal of Service Research* 7/4 (2005): 313–27.

11. Katherine N. Lemon, Frederick B. Newell, and Loren J. Lemon, "The Wireless Rules for e-Service," in Roland T. Rust and P.K. Kannan (eds.), *New Directions in Theory and Practice,* New York: Armonk, M.E. Sharpe, 2002: 200–32.

12. www.scotiabank.com/cda/content/0,1608,CID407_LIDen,00.html, accessed April 2006

13. Richard C. Hoffman and John F. Preble, "Global Franchising: Current Status and Future Challenges," *Journal of Services Marketing* 18/2 (2004): 101–13.

14. James Cross and Bruce J. Walker, "Addressing Service Marketing Challenges Through Franchising," in Teresa A. Swartz and Dawn Iacobucci (eds.), *Handbook of Services Marketing and Management,* Thousand Oaks, CA: Sage Publications, 2000: 473–84; Lavent Altinay, "Implementing International Franchising: The Role of Intrapreneurship," *International Journal of Service Industry Management* 15/5 (2004): 426–43.

15. Hoffman and Preble, op.cit.

16. Stacy Perman, "Extending the Front Lines of Franchising," *Business Week* (12 April 2005); available online at www.businessweek.com/smallbiz/content/apr2005/sb20050412_7035.htm (accessed 28 October 2006).

17. Scott Shane and Chester Spell, "Factors for New Franchise Success," *Sloan Management Review* (Spring 1998): 43–50.

18. For a discussion of what to watch for when parts of the service are outsourced, see Lauren Keller Johnson, "Outsourcing Postsale Service: Is Your Brand Protected? Before You Spin Off Repairs, or Parts Distribution, or Customer Call Centers, Consider the Cons as well as the Pros," *Harvard Business Review Supply Chain Strategy* (July 2005): 3–5.

19. www.timhortons.com/en/about/faq.html, accessed April 2006.

20. This term was coined by Curtis P. McLauglin and James A. Fitzsimmons, "e-Service: Strategies for Globalizing Service Operations," *International Journal of Service Industry Management* 7/4 (1996): 43–57.

21. Rajshekhar G. Javalgi, and D. Steven White, "Strategic Challenges for the Marketing of Services Internationally," *International Marketing Review* 19/6 (2002): 563–81.

22. John K. Johansson and George S. Yip, "Exploiting Globalization Potential: US and Japanese Strategies," *Strategic Management Journal* 15 (October 1994): 579–601; Christopher H. Lovelock and George S. Yip, "Developing Global Strategies for Service Businesses," *California Management Review* 38 (Winter 1996): 64–86; May Aung and Roger Heeler, "Core Competencies of Service Firms: A Framework for Strategic Decisions in International Markets," *Journal of Marketing Management* 17 (2001): 619–43; Javalgi and White (2002), op. cit.; Rajshekhar G. Javalgi, David A. Griffith, and D. Steven White, "An Empirical Examination of Factors Influencing the Internationalization of Service Firms," *Journal of Services Marketing* 17/2–3 (2003): 185–201.

23. Rajshekhar G. Javalgi, Charles L. Martin, and Patricia R. Todd, "The Export of E-Services in the Age of Technology Transformation: Challenges and Implications for International Service Providers," *Journal of Services Marketing* 18/7 (2004): 560–73.

CHAPTER 5

Exploring Business Models: Pricing and Revenue Management

There are two fools in any market. One does not charge enough. The other charges too much.

—Russian Proverb

The price is what you pay; the value is what you receive.

—Author Unknown

Viable service products are based on business models that allow the costs of creating and delivering the service, plus a margin for profits, to be recovered through realistic pricing and revenue-management strategies.

However, pricing of services is complicated. Consider the bewildering fee schedules of many consumer banks or cellphone service providers, or try to understand the fluctuating fare structure of a full-service airline! Service organizations even use different terms to describe the *prices* they set. Universities talk about "tuition," professional firms collect "fees," banks impose interest and service "charges," brokers take "commissions," some expressways impose "tolls," utilities set "tariffs," and insurance companies determine "premiums"—the list goes on.

A key goal of an effective pricing strategy is to manage revenues in ways that support the firm's profitability objectives. Doing so requires a good understanding of costs, competitors' pricing, and the value created for customers. This sounds straightforward, but is a real challenge for services firms, where unit costs may be difficult to determine, and fixed costs difficult to allocate appropriately across multiple service offerings. No firm can compare its own pricing dollar-for-dollar with a competitor's, as services are often location- and time-specific, and switching costs can be significant. Finally, value to customers usually varies widely between segments, and even within the same segment across time. And customers won't buy unless they perceive that the benefits they are obtaining in this value exchange exceed the financial and other costs they incur. Increasingly, customers complain of pricing schedules that they perceive as confusing and unfair.

In this chapter, we review the role of pricing in services marketing and provide some guidelines on how to develop an effective pricing strategy. Specifically, we address the following questions:

1. What are the three main foundations to pricing a service?
2. Why is cost-based pricing so challenging for many service firms, and how can activity-based costing improve costing of services?
3. How do customers perceive the non-monetary costs of obtaining service, and what might service providers do to reduce them?
4. How does revenue management improve profitability?
5. What are some key ethical concerns today about service pricing strategies?
6. What are the seven questions marketers need to answer before designing an effective pricing schedule?

Marketing is the only function that brings operating revenues into a service organization. All other management functions incur costs. A *business model* is the mechanism whereby, through effective pricing, sales are transformed into revenues, costs are covered, and value is created for the owners of the business. In many service industries, pricing was traditionally driven by a financial and accounting perspective, which often used cost-plus pricing. Price schedules were often tightly constrained by government regulatory agencies—and some still are. Today, however, most service businesses enjoy significant freedom in setting prices, and have a good understanding of value-based and competitive pricing. These developments have led to creative pricing schedules and sophisticated revenue-management systems.

In this chapter we focus on business models that require end-users to pay the price of receiving service. However, there are many instances where all or part of the cost is covered by third parties. Thus, advertising revenues pay the cost of supplying most broadcast radio and TV services in North America, health insurers pay much of the cost of supplementary medical care services for patients who carry such insurance, donations enable museums to set admission prices lower than they would otherwise be, and tax revenues allow public schools to offer free education.

Pricing is typically more complex in services than it is in manufacturing. Because there is no ownership of services, it is usually harder for managers to determine the financial costs of creating a process or performance for a customer, compared to identifying the costs associated with creating and distributing a physical good. The inability to inventory services places a premium on bringing demand and supply into balance, a task in which pricing has a key role to play. The importance of the time factor in service delivery means that speed of delivery and avoidance of waiting time often increase value. With the increase in value, customers are prepared to pay a higher price for the service.

What does a marketing perspective bring to pricing? Effective pricing strategies seek to enhance (or even maximize) the level of revenues, often by discriminating between different market segments based on their value-perceptions and ability to pay, and between different time periods based on variations in demand levels over time.

Consumers often find service pricing difficult to understand (e.g., insurance products or automobile repair bills), risky (when you make a hotel reservation on three different days, you might be offered three different prices!), and sometimes even unethical (e.g., many bank customers complain about an array of fees and charges they perceive as unfair). Examine your own purchasing behaviour—how did you feel the last time you had to decide on booking a holiday, a rental car, or getting a new bank account? In this chapter, we will learn how to set an effective pricing and revenue-management strategy that fulfills the promise of the value proposition so that a value exchange takes place (in other words, so that the consumer decides to buy your service).

Objectives for Establishing Prices

Any pricing strategy must be based on a clear understanding of a company's pricing objectives. The most common objectives are related to revenue and profits, building demand, and to developing a user base (Table 5.1).

Generating Revenues and Profits
Within certain limits, profit-seeking firms aim to maximize long-term revenue, contribution, and profits. Perhaps top management is eager to reach a particular landmark financial target, or seeks a specific percentage return on investment. Revenue targets may be broken down by division, geographic unit, type of service, and even by key customer segments. This practice requires prices to be set based on a good knowledge of costing, competition, and price elasticity of the market and value perceptions, all of which we will discuss later in this chapter.

In capacity-constrained organizations, financial success is often a function of ensuring optimal use of productive capacity at any given time. Hotels, for instance, seek to fill their

Table 5.1 Alternative Objectives for Pricing

Revenue and Profit Objectives

Seek Profit
- Make the largest possible contribution or profit.
- Achieve a specific target level, but do not seek to maximize profits.
- Maximize revenue from a fixed capacity by varying prices and target segments over time, typically using a yield or revenue management system.

Cover Costs
- Cover fully allocated costs, including institutional overhead.
- Cover costs of providing one particular service, excluding overhead.
- Cover incremental costs of selling one extra unit or to one extra customer.

Patronage and User-Base Objectives

Build Demand
- Maximize demand (when capacity is not a constraint), subject to achieving a certain minimum level of revenues.
- Achieve full capacity utilization, especially when high capacity utilization adds to the value created for all customers (e.g., a "full house" adds excitement to a play or a basketball game).

Build a User Base
- Stimulate trial and adoption of a service. This is especially important for new services with high infrastructure costs and for membership-type services that generate significant revenues from their continued use after adoption (e.g., cellphone service subscriptions, life insurance plans).
- Build market share and/or a large user base, especially if there are significant economies of scale that can lead to a competitive cost advantage (e.g., if development or fixed costs are high).

rooms, since an empty room is an unproductive asset. Similarly, professional firms want to keep their staff members occupied. Thus, when demand is low, such organizations may offer special discounts to attract additional business. Conversely, when demand exceeds capacity, these types of businesses may increase their prices, and focus on segments that are willing to pay higher amounts. We will discuss these practices in detail in the section on revenue management.

Building Demand In some instances, maximizing patronage, subject to achieving a certain minimum level of profits, may be more important than profit maximization. Getting a full house in a theatre, sports stadium, or race track usually creates excitement that enhances the customer's experience. It also creates an image of success that serves to attract new patrons.

Developing a User Base New services, in particular, often have trouble attracting customers. Yet in order to create the impression of a successful launch, and to enhance the image of the firm, it is important that the firm is seen to be attracting a good volume of business from the right types of customers. Introductory price discounts are often used to stimulate trial and sign up customers, sometimes in combination with promotional activities such as contests and giveaways. In order to compete in the fitness club market in the Greater Vancouver Area, Just Ladies Fitness offers a free 14-day trial period to stimulate demand for its services (Figure 5.1).

In industries with membership relationships and/or where heavy infrastructure investments have to be made (e.g., cellphone or broadband services), it is often important to get a critical mass of users fast. Market leadership often means low cost per user, and it generates sufficient revenue for future investments, such as upgrading technology and infrastructure. As a result, penetration pricing is often used in such industries.

PRICING STRATEGY STANDS ON THREE FOUNDATIONS

The foundations underlying pricing strategy can be described as a tripod, with costs to the provider, competition, and value to the customer as the three legs (Figure 5.2). The costs that a firm needs to recover usually impose a minimum price, or floor, for a specific service offering, while the customer's perceived value of the offering sets a maximum price, or ceiling. The price charged by competitors for similar or substitute services typically determine

Figure 5.1

Just Ladies Fitness offers a free trial period to stimulate demand for its services.

where, within the floor-to-ceiling range, the price can be set. The pricing objectives of the organization then determine where actual prices should be set, within the feasible range provided by the pricing tripod analysis. Let's look at each leg of the pricing tripod in more detail in the next three sections.

Cost-Based Pricing

It's usually harder to establish the costs involved in producing an intangible performance than it is to identify the labour, materials, machine time, storage, and shipping costs associated with producing a physical good. Yet without a good understanding of costs, how can managers price at levels sufficient to yield a desired profit margin? Because of the labour and infrastructure needed to create performances, many service organizations have a much higher ratio of fixed costs to variable costs than is found in manufacturing firms.

Figure 5.2

The Pricing Tripod

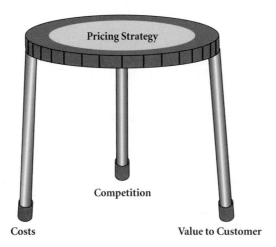

Establishing the Costs of Providing Service   Even if you have already taken a marketing course, you may find it helpful to review how service costs can be estimated, using fixed, semi-variable, and variable costs, as well as how the notions of contribution and break-even analysis can help in pricing decisions (see Marketing Review box on the following page). These traditional cost-accounting approaches work well for service firms with significant variable costs and/or semi-variable costs (e.g., many professional services). For complex product lines with shared infrastructure (e.g., retail banking products), it may be worthwhile considering the more complex activity-based costing (ABC) approach.

Activity-Based Costing   A growing number of organizations have reduced their dependence on traditional cost accounting systems and developed activity-based cost (ABC) management systems, which recognize that virtually all activities taking place within a firm directly or indirectly support the production, marketing, and delivery of goods and services. Moreover, ABC systems link resource expenses to the variety and complexity of goods and services produced, not just to their physical volume. A set of activities is combined that compose the processes needed to create and deliver the service. Each step in a flowchart constitutes an activity with which costs can be associated. This approach makes ABC ideally suited to a service organization.

If implemented well, the ABC approach yields reasonably accurate cost information about service-business activities and processes—and about the costs of creating specific types of services, performing activities in different locations (even different countries), or serving specific customers.[1] The net result is a management tool that can help companies to pinpoint the profitability of different services, channels, market segments, and individual customers.[2]

It's essential to distinguish between those activities that are essential for operation within a particular service business and those that are discretionary. The traditional approach to cost control often results in a reduction of the value generated for customers, because the activity that is being pruned back is, in fact, essential for providing a certain level and quality of service. For instance, many firms have created marketing problems for themselves when they try to save money by firing large numbers of customer-service employees. This strategy has boomeranged where it resulted in a rapid decline in service levels that then spurred discontented customers to take their business elsewhere. For more details on ABC, see Service Perspectives 5.1, "Activity-Based Costing in Services." on page 136.

Pricing Implications of Cost Analysis   To make a profit, a firm must set its price sufficiently high to recover the full costs of producing and marketing the service, and add a sufficient margin to yield the desired profit at the predicted sales volume. Service businesses with high fixed costs include those with expensive fixed facilities (such as a university or an airport), or a fleet of vehicles (such as an airline or a trucking company), or a network (such as a telecommunications company, a railway, or a gas pipeline). For such services, the variable costs of serving each individual customer may be minimal.

Under these conditions, managers may feel that they have tremendous pricing flexibility, and so be tempted to set a very low price to boost sales. Some firms promote *loss leaders*, which are services sold at less than full cost to attract customers, who will then be tempted to buy profitable service offerings from the same organization in the future. However, there will be no profit at the end of the year unless all relevant costs have been recovered. Many service businesses have gone bankrupt because they ignored this fact. The failure of the discount airline Jetsgo is a case in point. Launched as a discount airline based in Montreal in June 2002, the airline survived a little less than three years, entering bankruptcy protection and ending its service abruptly on March 11, 2005, with thousands of passengers stranded right at the start of the busy March break season. Although the airline announced that it would come back as a charter-only airline, it officially declared bankruptcy on March 13, 2005. Hence, firms that compete on the basis of low prices need to have a very good understanding of their cost structure and of the sales volume needed to break even at a given price.

One advantage of outsourcing is that the cost of service provision becomes more explicit, with outsourced services such as customer contact centres and ownership and

Fixed costs—sometimes referred to as overheads—are those economic costs that a supplier would continue to incur (at least in the short run) even if no services were sold. These costs are likely to include rent, depreciation, utilities, taxes, insurance, salaries and wages for managers and long-term employees, security, and interest payments.

Variable costs refer to the economic costs associated with serving each individual customer—such as making a bank transaction—or selling each individual seat on a flight. In many services, such costs are very low. For instance, very little labour or fuel cost is involved in transporting each individual passenger on a flight. In a theatre, the cost of seating one patron is close to zero. More significant variable costs are associated with such activities as serving food and beverages, or installing new parts when undertaking repairs, since they include provision of often costly physical products in addition to labour. Just because a firm has sold a service at a price that exceeds its variable cost doesn't mean that the firm is now profitable, for there are still fixed and semi-variable costs to be recouped.

Semi-variable costs fall in between fixed and variable costs. They represent expenses that rise or fall in a stepwise fashion as the volume of business increases or decreases. Examples include adding an extra flight to meet increased demand on a specific air route, or hiring a part-time employee to work in a restaurant on busy weekends.

Contribution is the difference between the variable cost of selling each individual unit of service and the money received from the buyer of that service. It goes to cover fixed and semi-variable costs before creating profits.

Determining and allocating economic costs can be a challenging task in some service operations because of the difficulty of deciding how to assign fixed costs in a multi-service facility, such as a physical rehabilitation clinic, which in its simplest form might offer, say, two distinct services: physiotherapy and massage therapy. There are certain fixed costs associated with running the physiotherapy part of the business. But beyond that there are fixed costs for running the overall clinic, of which the physiotherapy is a part. How much of the clinic's fixed costs should be allocated to running the physiotherapy business? A clinic manager might use one of several approaches to calculate physiotherapy's share of overheads. These could include (1) the percentage of total floor space that it occupies, (2) the percentage of employee hours or payroll that it accounts for; or (3) the percentage of total patient contact hours involved. Each method is likely to yield a totally different fixed-cost allocation: one method might show the physiotherapy operation of the clinic to be very profitable, while the other might make it seem loss-making.

Break-even analysis. Managers need to know at what sales volume a service will become profitable. This is called the break-even point. The necessary analysis involves dividing the total fixed and semi-variable costs by the contribution obtained on each unit of service. For instance, if a 100-room hotel needs to cover fixed and semi-variable costs of $2 million a year, and the average contribution per room-night is $100, then the hotel will need to sell 20 000 room-nights per year out of a total annual capacity of 36 500. If prices are cut by an average of $20 per room night (*or* variable costs rise by $20), then the contribution will drop to $80 and the hotel's break-even volume will rise to 25 000 room nights. The required sales volume needs to be related to *price sensitivity* (will customers be willing to pay this much?), *market size* (is the market large enough to support this level of patronage, taking competition into account?), and *maximum capacity* (the hotel in our example has a capacity of 36 500 room-nights per year, assuming no rooms are taken out of service for maintenance or renovation).

operation of equipment or software often being priced on a per-usage, transaction, per-call, or per-minute basis, thereby avoiding the misperception that variable costs are negligible.

Managers need to move beyond seeing costs from just an accounting perspective. Rather, they should view them as an integral part of the company's efforts to create value for its customers. Carù and Cugini clarify the limitations of traditional cost measurement systems, and recommend relating the costs of any given activity to its value generated:

> Costs have nothing to do with value, which is established by the market and, in the final analysis, by the degree of customer acceptance. The customer is not interested a priori in the cost of a product . . . but in its value and price . . .
>
> Management control which limits itself to cost monitoring without interesting itself in value is completely one-sided . . . The problem of businesses is not so much that of cost control as it is the separation of value activities from other activities. The market only pays for the former. Businesses which carry out unnecessary activities are destined to find themselves being overtaken by competitors which have already eliminated these.[3]

Competition-based Pricing

Firms with relatively undifferentiated services need to monitor what competitors are charging and should to try to price accordingly. When customers see little or no difference between competing offerings, they may just choose what they perceive as the cheapest. In such a situation, the firm with the lowest cost per unit of service enjoys an enviable market advantage, and often assumes *price leadership*. Here, one firm acts as the price leader, with others taking their cue from this company. You can sometimes see this phenomenon at the local level when several gas stations compete within a short distance of one another. As soon as one station raises or lowers its prices, the others follow promptly. When a lower price advantage may not be sufficient to sway potential customers, firms may augment the value of their offering by promoting high quality and service as compared to the competition (Figure 5.3).

Price competition intensifies with (1) increasing number of competitors, (2) increasing number of substituting offers, (3) wider distribution of competitor and/or substitution offers, and (4) increasing surplus capacity in the industry. Although some service industries can be fiercely competitive (e.g., online banking or telecommunications services), not all are, especially when one or more of the following circumstances reduce price competition:

- **Non-price-related costs of using competing alternatives are high.** When saving time and effort are of equal or greater importance to customers than price in selecting a supplier, the intensity of price competition is reduced.

- **Personal relationships matter.** In services that are highly personalized and customized, such as hair styling or dental services, relationships with individual providers are often very important to customers, thus discouraging them from responding to price-competitive offers.

- **Switching costs are high.** When it takes time, money, and effort to switch providers, customers are less able to take advantage of competing offers. Cellphone providers often require their subscribers to sign one- or two-year contracts, specifying significant financial penalties for early cancellation of service.

- **Time and location specificity reduce choice.** When people want to use a service at a specific location or at a particular time (or perhaps both, simultaneously), they usually find they have fewer options.[4]

Figure 5.3

Tom's Place competes with other business fashion retailers by promoting lower prices, high-quality products, and personalized services.

Firms that are always reacting to competitors' price changes run the risk of pricing *lower* than might really be necessary. Managers should beware of falling into the trap of comparing competitors' prices dollar for dollar, and then seeking to match them. A better strategy is to take into account the entire cost to customers of each competitive offering, including all related financial and non-monetary costs, plus potential switching costs, and then compare this total with that of the provider's own service. Managers should also assess the impact of distribution, time and location factors, as well as estimating competitors' available capacity before deciding on what response is appropriate.

Value-Based Pricing

Unless their options are limited for some reason, no customer will pay more for a service than he or she thinks it is worth. (Of course, as an experienced customer, you already knew that!) So marketers need to understand how customers perceive service value in order to set an appropriate price. Gerald Smith and Thomas Nagle emphasize the importance of understanding the monetary worth of the incremental value created by a service, a task that often requires extensive marketing research, especially in business-to-business markets.[5]

Service Perspectives 5.1

Activity-Based Costing in Services

Traditional cost systems provide useful data for pricing purposes when a single operation creates one homogeneous product for customers who behave in broadly similar ways. However, when service businesses experience considerable variability in both inputs and outputs, it is unrealistic to assign the same proportion of indirect and support costs to each unit of output. Customers, too, often vary in the demands they place upon the firm.

Costs are not intrinsically fixed or variable, argue Cooper and Kaplan:

> Different products, brands, customers, and distribution channels make tremendously different demands on a company's resources.
> ... ABC analysis enables managers to slice into the business many different ways—by product or group of similar products, by individual customer or client group, or by distribution channel—and gives them a close-up view of whatever slice they are considering. ABC analysis also illuminates exactly what activities are associated with that part of the business and how those activities are linked to the generation of revenues and the consumption of resources.

Instead of focusing on expense categories, ABC analysis begins with the identification of the different activities being performed and then determines the cost of each activity as it relates to each expense category. When managers segregate activities in this way, a cost hierarchy emerges, reflecting the level at which the cost is incurred. For instance, unit-level activities need to be performed for every unit of service produced (e.g., rotating the tires on a customer's car at a service garage), whereas batch-level activities are those that have to be done for each batch or setup of work performed (e.g., periodically maintaining the equipment needed for tire rotation).

Other activities provide the overall capability that enables the company to produce a given type of service (e.g., establishing performance standards for tire rotation), or to support customers (e.g. account management), and product lines (e.g., advertising), or to sustain facilities (e.g., building maintenance, insurance). Expenses are attached to each activity based on estimates by employees of how they divide up their time between different tasks and what percentage of other resources (e.g., electricity consumption) is being consumed by each activity.

In short, the ABC hierarchy provides a structured way of thinking about the relationship between activities and the resources that they consume. A key question is whether each enumerated activity actually adds customer value to the services that the firm is selling.

Table A: Cost per Service Transaction Using Traditional Activity-Based Costing

CUSTOMER SERVICE PROCESS	PROPORTION OF TIME SPENT	ALLOCATED COSTS	NUMBER OF TRANSACTIONS	COST PER TRANSACTION
Billing Inquiries	30%	$189 000	15 800	$11.96
Activation of Value-added Services	50%	$315 000	43 500	$7.25
Cancellation of Value-added Services	20%	$126 000	19 700	$6.40
Total	**100%**	**$630 000**	**79 000**	**$7.97**

Table A (p. 136) shows a simple example of ABC cost analysis for a section within a call centre, whereby the proportion of time spent on each type of customer service activity (or process) is determined by an employee survey. Next, the total department costs, including staff costs, systems, rental, etc. ($630 000 in this example), are allocated based on the time spent on each activity. The cost per transaction for each activity is then simply computed by dividing the costs by the number of transactions. In our example, each billing inquiry incurs costs of $11.96 for each transaction.

ABC cost analysis works well for simple processes with a small number of activities (as shown in the example above) and with stable capacity utilization, but becomes rather complex when many activities or processes are involved, or when capacity utilization varies a lot—note that the complete costs are allocated across activities. A time-based ABC analysis, proposed in 2004, addresses the shortcoming of the traditional ABC and works better for more complex service operations. Here, managers directly estimate the time and costs involved in each transaction (rather than estimating the resource costs to be allocated to activities first and then computing the cost per transaction). Then, the cost per minute per employee is computed (total costs as for the first

example, divided by total minutes available, based on the number of available staff and systems capacity). In Table B, we recomputed the cost per transaction, but this time explicitly account for capacity utilization of the call centre. Here, we can see that each billing inquiry costs the firm $15, with the costs for unutilized capacity being shown directly rather than being allocated across transactions. These costs per transaction can then be allocated to individual customer accounts or segments based on their transaction record, and a more detailed profitability analysis can be conducted.

Determining customer profitability is a key issue for many businesses. Traditional cost analysis tends to result in loading the same overhead costs on all customers, leading to the assumption that larger purchasers are more profitable. By contrast, ABC analysis can pinpoint differences in the costs of serving different customers, not only by identifying the types of activity associated with each customer but also by determining the amount of resources (measured in employee-minutes) consumed for each activity demanded. For instance, a customer who buys in large volumes, but who is extremely demanding in terms of the amount and level of support required may, in fact, prove to be less profitable than a small customer who requires little support.

Table B Cost per Service Transaction Using Time-Based Activity-Based Costing

Customer Service Process	Number of Transactions	Minutes Needed per Transaction	Cost per Transaction	Total Time Used	Cost Allocated to Customer Service Process
Billing Inquiries	15 800	6 min	$15	94 800 min	$237 000
Activation of Value-Added Services	43 500	1.5 min	$3.75	65 250 min	$163 125
Cancellation of Value-Added Services	19 700	2 min	$5.00	39 400 min	$98 500
Total Utilization	**79 000**		**$2.50 per min**	**199 450 min**	**$498 625**
Unused Capacity			$2.50 per min	52 550 min	$131 375
Total Costs			**$2.50 per min**	**252 000 min**	**$630 000**

Sources: Robin Cooper and Robert S. Kaplan, "Profit Priorities from Activity-Based Costing," *Harvard Business Review* 69/3 (May–June 1991): 130–35; Craig A. Latshaw and Teresa M. Cortese-Danile, "Activity-Based Costing: Usage and Pitfalls," *Review of Business* 23/1 (Winter 2002): 30–32; Robert S. Kaplan and Steven R. Anderson, "Time-Driven Activity Based Costing," *Harvard Business Review* 82/11 (November 2004): 131–40.

Understanding Net Value When customers purchase a service, they are weighing the perceived benefits obtained from the service against the perceived costs they will incur. As we saw in Chapter 3, companies sometimes create several tiers of service, recognizing the different trade-offs that customers are willing to make between these various costs. Customer definitions of value may be highly personal and idiosyncratic. Valarie Zeithaml proposes four broad expressions of value:

- value is low price
- value is whatever I want in a product
- value is the quality I get for the price I pay
- value is what I get for what I give.[6]

In this book, we focus on the fourth category; to clarify it we use the term *net value*, which is defined as the sum of all the perceived benefits (gross value) minus the sum of all the perceived costs of service. The greater the positive difference between the two, the greater the net value. Economists use the term *consumer surplus* to define the difference between the price customers pay and the amount they would actually have been willing to pay to obtain the desired benefits (or "utility") offered by a specific product.

If the perceived costs of a service are greater than the perceived benefits, then the service in question will possess negative net value, and the consumer will not buy. You can think of calculations that customers make in their minds as being similar to weighing materials on a pair of old-fashioned scales, with product benefits in one tray and the costs associated with obtaining those benefits in the other tray (Figure 5.4). When customers evaluate competing services, they are basically comparing the relative net values.

Enhancing Gross Value   Hermann Simon, an international consultant, argues that service-pricing strategies are often unsuccessful because they lack a clear association between price and value.[7] As we discussed in Chapter 3, a marketer can increase the gross value of a service by adding benefits to the core product and by enhancing supplementary services. There are four distinct but related strategies for capturing and communicating the value of a service: uncertainty reduction, relationship enhancement, low-cost leadership, and value perception management.[8]

Reducing Uncertainty   If customers are unsure about how much value they will receive from a particular service, they may remain with a supplier they already know or not purchase at all. Possible ways, individually or in combination, to reduce this uncertainty, include benefit-driven pricing and flat-rate pricing.

Figure 5.4
Net Value Equals
Benefits Minus Costs

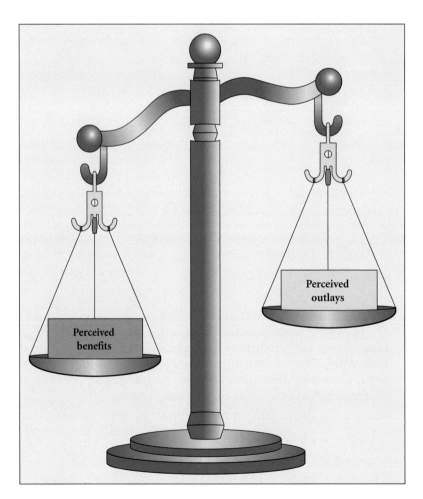

- *Benefit-driven pricing* involves pricing the aspect of the service that directly benefits customers (requiring marketers to research which aspects of the service their customers value most and which least.) For instance, prices for online information services are often based on the length of time users are logged on, but what customers really value is the information that is browsed and retrieved. Poorly designed websites often waste customers' time because they are difficult to navigate and make it hard for users to find what they are looking for. The result is that pricing and value creation are out of sync.

- *Flat-rate pricing* involves quoting a fixed price in advance of service delivery so as to avoid surprises for users. In essence, the risk is transferred from the customer to the supplier in the event that the service takes longer to deliver, or that costs were underestimated. Flat-rate pricing can be effective in situations where service prices are unpredictable, suppliers are poor at cost control, or competitors make low estimates to win business but subsequently claim that they were not making a firm pricing commitment.

Relationship Pricing
Discounting to win new business is not the best approach if a firm is seeking to attract customers who will remain loyal. Research indicates that those who are attracted by cut-price offers are easily enticed away by another offer from a competitor.[9] More creative strategies focus on giving customers both price and non-price incentives to consolidate their business with a single supplier. A strategy of discounting prices for large purchases can often be profitable for both parties, because the customer benefits from lower prices while the supplier may enjoy lower variable costs resulting from economies of scale. An alternative to volume discounting on a single service is to offer discounts when two or more services are purchased together. The greater the number of different services a customer purchases from a single supplier, the closer the relationship is likely to be.

Cost Leadership
Low-priced services appeal to customers on tight financial budgets and may also stimulate larger purchases. One challenge when pricing low is to convince customers that instead of equating price with quality, they should feel they're getting good value. A second challenge is to ensure that economic costs are kept low enough to enable profits. Some service businesses have built their entire strategy around being the cost leader. A classic example of a cost leader in the airline business comes from the U.S. firm of Southwest Airlines, whose low fares often compete with the price of bus, train, or car travel. Southwest's low-cost operations strategy has been studied by airlines all over the world (e.g., by Ryanair and easyJet in Europe) and has led to the development of a Canadian success story in WestJet.

Managing the Perception of Value
Value is subjective, and not all customers have the expertise to assess the quality and value they receive. This is true in particular for credence services (discussed in Chapter 2) where customers have difficulty assessing the quality of a service even after consumption.[10] Marketers of services such as strategy consulting must find ways to communicate the time, research, professional expertise, and attention to detail that go into, for example, completing a best-practice consulting project. Why? Because the invisibility of backstage facilities and labour makes it hard for customers to see what they're getting for their money. For example, it is not surprising for customers to find that on a $100 repair bill for their car, the cost of the replacement part was only $15–$20.

Consider a homeowner who calls an electrician to repair a defective circuit. The electrician arrives, carrying a small bag of tools. He disappears into the closet where the circuit board is located, soon locates the problem, replaces a defective circuit breaker, and presto! Everything works. A mere 20 minutes has elapsed. A few days later, the homeowner is horrified to receive a bill for $90, most of it for labour charges. Just think what the couple could have bought for that amount of money—new clothes, several compact discs, a nice dinner. Not surprisingly, customers are often left feeling that they have been exploited—Take a look at Blondie's reaction to the plumber in Figure 5.5!

Effective communications and even personal explanations are needed to help customers understand the value they receive. What they often fail to recognize are the fixed

Figure 5.5 Blondie seeks her money's worth from the plumber.

costs that business owners need to recoup: the office, telephone, insurance, vehicles, tools, fuel, and office support staff. The variable costs of a home visit are also higher than they appear. To the 20 minutes spent at the house might be added 15 minutes of driving each way, plus five minutes each to unload and reload needed tools and supplies from the van, thus effectively tripling the labour time to a total of 60 minutes devoted to this call. And the firm still has to add a margin in order to make a profit.

More recently, auctions and dynamic pricing have become increasingly popular as a way to price according to value perceptions of customers (see Service Perspectives 5.2).

Reducing Related Monetary and Non-monetary Costs

From a customer's standpoint, the price charged by a supplier is only part of the costs involved in purchasing and using a service. There are other *costs of service*, which comprise both the *incremental financial outlays* and *non-monetary* costs incurred by customers.

Incremental Financial Outlays Customers often incur significant financial costs in searching for, purchasing, and using the service, above and beyond the purchase price paid to the supplier. For instance, the cost of an evening at the theatre for a couple with young children usually far exceeds the price of the two tickets, because it can include such expenses as hiring a babysitter, travel, parking, food and beverages.

Non-monetary Costs These costs reflect the time, effort, and discomfort associated with the search, purchase, and use of a service. Customers sometimes refer to them collectively as "effort" or "hassle." Non-monetary costs tend to be higher when customers are involved in production (which is particularly important in people-processing services and in self-service) or must travel to the service site. Services that are high on experience and credence attributes may also create psychological costs, such as anxiety. There are four distinct categories of such costs: time, physical, psychological, and sensory.

- *Time costs* are inherent in service delivery. Today's customers are often time-constrained and may use similar terms to define time usage as they do for money, speaking of budgeting, spending, investing, wasting, losing, and saving time. Time spent on one activity represents an opportunity cost because it might have been spent more profitably in other ways. Internet users are often frustrated by the amount of time spent to find information on a website. Many people loathe visiting government offices to obtain passports, driving licences, or permits not because of the fees involved, but because of the time "wasted."

- *Physical costs* (fatigue, discomfort etc.) may be incurred in obtaining services, especially if customers must go to the service factory, if queuing is involved, or if delivery entails self-service.

- *Psychological costs* such as mental effort, perceived risk, cognitive dissonance, feelings of inadequacy, or fear are sometimes attached to buying and using a particular service.

Service Perspectives 5.2

Dynamic Pricing on the Internet

Dynamic pricing—also known as customized or personalized pricing—is a new version of the age-old practice of price discrimination, and is popular with service suppliers because of its potential to increase profits. Etailing, or retailing over the internet, lends itself well to this strategy because changing prices electronically is a simple procedure. Dynamic pricing enables etailers to charge different customers different prices for the same products based on information collected about their purchase history, preferences, price sensitivity, and so on. Tickets.com gained up to 45 percent more revenue per event when pricing of concerts and events was adjusted to meet demand and supply.

Etailers are often uncomfortable about admitting to the use of dynamic pricing, due to the ethical and legal issues associated with price discrimination. Customers of Amazon.com were upset when they learned that the online megastore was not charging everyone the same price for the same movie DVDs. Price varied depending on factors, such as time when the DVD was purchased, whether the customer was a first-time buyer or a repeat buyer, which browser was being used, and what internet service provider address a customer was using. A study of online consumers by the University of Pennsylvania's Annenberg Public Policy Center found that 87 percent of respondents did not think dynamic pricing was acceptable.

Reverse Auctions. Travel etailers such as Priceline.com, Hotwire.com, and Lowestfare.com follow a customer-driven pricing strategy known as a reverse auction. Each firm acts as an intermediary between prospective buyers, who request quotations for a product or service, and multiple suppliers who quote the best price they're willing to offer. Buyers can then review the offers and select the supplier that best meets their needs. Although the offer usually describes product attributes, it often doesn't provide brand information. Priceline has moved to correct this deficiency. Says a spokesperson: "Customers can now choose the exact brand name and product from a published list price, whereas before they could only use our name-your-own-price [service]. As a result, people were never sure what

hotel they would get until they make their purchase, so if you were travelling with friends, you wouldn't know if you'd get the same hotel."

Different business models underlie these services. While some are provided free to end-users, most etailers either receive a commission from the supplier or do not pass on the whole savings. Others charge customers either a fixed fee or one based on a percentage of the savings.

Traditional Auctions. Other Etailers like eBay and Yahoo! Auctions follow the traditional online auction model in which bidders place bids for an item and compete with each other to determine who buys it. Marketers of both consumer and industrial products use such auctions to sell obsolete or overstock items, collectibles, rare items and second-hand merchandise. This form of retailing has become immensely successful since eBay first launched it in 1995.

Shopbots Help Consumers to Benefit from Dynamic Pricing. Consumers now have tools of their own to combat the potentially exploitative practices of dynamic pricing. One approach involves using shopbots to track competitive prices. *Shopbots*, or shopping robots, are basically intelligent agents that automatically collect price and product information from multiple online vendors. A customer has only to visit a shopbot site, such as Dealtime.com, and run a search for the desired item. The shopbot instantly queries all the associated retailers to check availability, features and price, then presents the results in a comparison table.

There's little doubt that dynamic pricing is here to stay. With further advances in technology and wider applications, it is extending its reach to more and more service categories.

Sources: Stephan Biller, Lap Mui Ann Chan, David Simchi-Levi, and Julie Swann, "Dynamic Pricing and Direct-to-Customer Model in the Automotive Industry," *Electronic Commerce Research* 5/2 (April 2005): 309–34; Melissa Campanelli, "Getting Personal: Will Engaging in Dynamic Pricing Help or Hurt Your Business?" *Entrepreneur* 33/10 (October 2005): 44–46; Mikhail I. Melnik and James Alm, "Seller Reputation, Information Signals, and Prices for Heterogeneous Coins on eBay," *Southern Economic Journal* 72/2 (2005): 305–28.

- *Sensory costs* relate to unpleasant sensations affecting any of the five senses. In a service environment, these costs may include putting up with noise, unpleasant smells, drafts, excessive heat or cold, uncomfortable seating, visually unappealing environments, and even nasty tastes.

As shown in Figure 5.6, service users can incur costs during any of the three stages of the service consumption model introduced in Chapter 2. Consequently, firms have to consider (1) *search costs*, (2) *purchase and service encounter costs*, and (3) *post-consumption* or *after-costs*. When you were looking at universities, how much money, time, and effort did you spend before deciding where to apply? How much time and effort would you put into selecting a new cellphone service provider or a bank, or planning a vacation?

Figure 5.6
Defining Total User
Costs

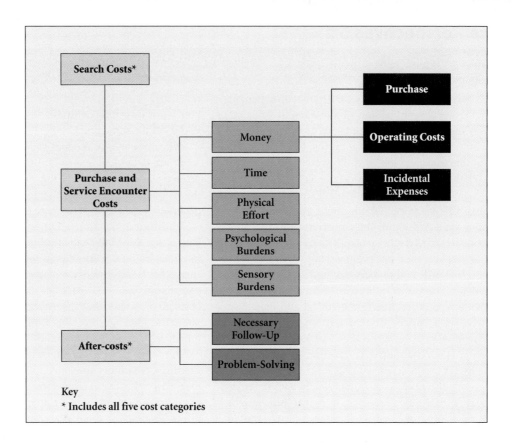

A strategy of minimizing non-monetary and related monetary costs, in order to increase consumer value, can create competitive advantage for a firm. Possible approaches include:

- Working with operations experts to reduce the time required to complete service purchase, delivery, and consumption

- Minimizing unwanted psychological costs of service at each stage by eliminating or redesigning unpleasant or inconvenient procedures, educating customers on what to expect, and retraining staff to be friendlier and more helpful

- Eliminating or minimizing unwanted physical effort, notably during search and delivery processes

- Decreasing unpleasant sensory costs of service by creating more attractive visual environments, reducing noise, installing more comfortable furniture and equipment, curtailing offensive smells, and the like

- Suggesting ways in which customers can reduce associated monetary costs, including discounts with partner suppliers (for instance, parking) or offering mail or online delivery of activities that previously required a personal visit

Perceptions of net value may vary widely between customers and from one situation to another for the same customer. Service markets can often be segmented by sensitivity to time savings and convenience versus sensitivity to price savings.[11] Consider Figure 5.7, which identifies a choice of three options available to a student who needs to get ten copies of her group project copied and bound. In addition to varying dollar prices for the service, there are different time and effort costs associated with using each service. Depending on the student's priorities, non-monetary costs may be as important, or even more important, than the price charged by the service providers.

Figure 5.7
Trading Off Monetary
and Non-monetary
Costs

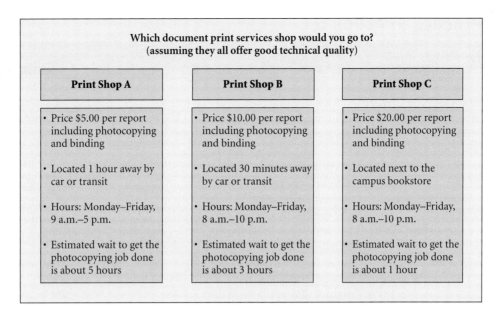

REVENUE MANAGEMENT: WHAT IT IS AND HOW IT WORKS

Many service businesses now focus on strategies to maximize the revenue (or contribution) that can be derived from available capacity at any given point in time. Revenue management is important in value creation, as it ensures better utilization of capacity while reserving capacity for higher-paying segments. It is a sophisticated approach to managing supply and demand under varying degrees of constraint. Airlines, hotels, and car rental firms, in particular, have become adept at varying their prices in response to the price sensitivity and needs of different market segments at different times of the day, week, or season.

Reserving Capacity for High-Yield Customers

In practice, revenue management (also known as yield management) involves setting prices according to predicted demand levels among different market segments. The least price-sensitive segment is the first to be allocated capacity, paying the highest price; other segments follow at progressively lower prices. As higher-paying segments often book closer to the time of actual consumption, firms need a disciplined approach to save capacity for them instead of simply using up all their capacity on a first-come-first-served basis. For example, business travellers often reserve airline seats, hotel rooms, and rental cars at short notice, but vacationers may book leisure travel months in advance, and convention organizers often book hotel space years in advance of a big event.

A well-designed revenue management system can predict with reasonable accuracy how many customers will use a given service at a specific time at each of several different price levels, and then allocate the relevant amount of capacity to each level, or *price bucket*. Sophisticated firms use complex mathematical models for this purpose, and employ revenue managers to make decisions about inventory allocation.

In the case of airlines, these models integrate massive historical databases on past passenger travel and can forecast demand up to a year in advance for each individual departure. At fixed intervals, the revenue manager—who may be assigned specific routes at a large airline—will check the actual pace of bookings (i.e., sales at a given time before departure) and compare it with the forecasted pace. If there are significant deviations between actual and forecasted demand, the manager will adjust the size of the inventory buckets. For example, if the booking pace for a higher-paying segment is stronger than expected, additional capacity will be allocated to this segment and taken away from the lowest-paying segment. The objective is to maximize the revenues from the flight. Best Practice in Action 5.1 shows how revenue management has been implemented at American Airlines, long an industry leader in this field.

Best Practice in Action 5.1

Pricing Seats on Flight AA 2015

Revenue management departments use sophisticated yield-management software and powerful computers to forecast, track, and manage the bookings for each flight on each separate date. Let's look at American Airlines 2015, a popular flight from Chicago to Phoenix, Arizona, which departs daily at 5:30 p.m. on the 2200 kilometre journey.

The 125 seats in coach (economy class) are divided into seven fare categories, referred to by yield-management specialists as "buckets." There is an enormous variation in ticket prices among these seats: round-trip fares range from US$238 for a bargain excursion ticket (with various restrictions and a cancellation penalty attached) all the way up to an unrestricted fare of $1404. Seats are also available at an even higher price in the small first-class section. Scott McCartney tells how ongoing analysis by the computer program changes the allocation of seats between each of the seven buckets in economy class:

> In the weeks before each Chicago–Phoenix flight, American's yield management computers constantly adjust the number of seats in each bucket, taking into account tickets sold, historical ridership patterns, and connecting passengers likely to use the route as one leg of a longer trip.

If advance bookings are slim, American adds seats to low-fare buckets. If business customers buy unrestricted fares earlier than expected, the yield management computer takes seats out of the discount buckets and preserves them for last-minute bookings that the database predicts will still show up.

With 69 of 125 coach seats already sold four weeks before one recent departure of Flight 2015, American's computer began to limit the number of seats in lower-priced buckets. A week later, it totally shut off sales for the bottom three buckets, priced $300 or less. To a Chicago customer looking for a cheap seat, the flight was 'sold out'. . . .

One day before departure, with 130 passengers booked for the 125-seat flight, American still offered five seats at full fare because its computer database indicated 10 passengers were likely not to show up or take other flights. Flight 2015 departed full and no one was bumped.

Although AA 2015 for that date is now history, it has not been forgotten. The booking experience for this flight was saved in the memory of the yield-management program to help the airline do an even better job of forecasting in the future.

Source: Adapted from Scott McCartney, "Ticket Shock: Business Fares Increase Even as Leisure Travel Keeps Getting Cheaper," *Wall Street Journal* (3 November, 1997): A1, A10.

How Does Competitors' Pricing Affect Revenue Management? Revenue management systems monitor booking pace, so they indirectly pick up the impact of competitors' pricing. If a firm prices too low, it will experience a higher booking pace, and its cheaper seats fill up quickly. That is generally not good, as it means a higher share of late-booking but high-fare-paying customers will not be able to get their seats confirmed, and will therefore fly on competing airlines. If the initial pricing is too high, the firm will get too low a share of early booking segments (which still tend to offer a reasonable yield), and may later have to offer deeply discounted "last-minute" prices to sell excess capacity and thus obtain *some* contribution toward fixed costs from those seats, rather than none at all. Some of these sales may take place through reverse auctions, using intermediaries such as Priceline.com.

Revenue management has been most effective when applied to operations characterized by one or more of the following: relatively fixed capacity, a high fixed-cost structure, perishable inventory, variable and uncertain demand, or varying customer price sensitivity. Industries that have successfully implemented revenue management include airlines, car rentals, hotels, and more recently hospitals, restaurants, golf courses, on-demand IT services, data-processing centres, and even non-profit organizations.[12] Service Perspectives 5.3 gives an insight into the work and thinking of a revenue manager.

Price Elasticity

Revenue management requires two or more segments that attach different value to the service and have different price elasticities. To allocate and price capacity effectively, the revenue manager needs to determine how sensitive demand is to price, and what net revenues will be generated at different prices for each target segment. The concept of elasticity describes how sensitive demand is to changes in price, and is computed (over any given time period) as follows:

Service Perspectives 5.3

(Q) What is your role as a revenue manager?

(A) When I started in 1993, the primary focus was on forecasting, inventory control, pricing, market segment and geographic mix, and allotment control. The internet changed the scene significantly and several global giants, like Expedia and Travelocity, emerged after 9/11 when travel bookings plummeted and the industry realized the power of the internet to help them sell distressed inventory. But airlines and hotels want to control their own inventory and pricing to cut costs and reduce reliance on intermediaries, so there's increasing focus on driving bookings via direct channels such as their own branded websites, building online brands, and implementing CRM programs. My role has also broadened to include revenue management of secondary income sources such as restaurants, golf courses, and spas, as well as mainstream hotel rooms.

(Q) What differences do you see between revenue management for airlines and hotels?

(A) Fundamentally, the techniques of forecasting and optimizing pricing and inventory controls are the same. However, some key differences exist. Airlines have a larger ability to use pricing to expand travel demand from the home market. By contrast, pricing practices in hotels can shift market share within a location but, as a rule, not overall market size. Although consumers see many pricing practices—such as advance purchase restrictions and discounts—as fair practice for the airline industry, they see them as less fair when applied by the hotel industry.

Organizational structure also tends to be different. The airlines adopt central revenue management control for all flights, and revenue managers have little interaction with the reservations and sales teams in the field. A more precise and statistical application of pricing and inventory control is thus the focus. In the hotel industry, revenue management is decentralized to every hotel, requiring daily interaction with reservations and sales. The human element is key for successful implementation in hotels, requiring acceptance of pricing and inventory decisions not only by consumers but also by internal departments, such as reservations, sales, and even front office.

(Q) What skills do you need to succeed as a revenue manager?

(A) Strong statistical and analytical skills are essential, but to be really successful, revenue managers need to have equally strong interpersonal and influencing skills in order for their decisions to be accepted by other departments. Traditional ways of segmenting customers via their transactional characteristics, such as booking lead time, channel of reservation, and type of promotion are insufficient. Both behavioural characteristics (such as motive for travel, products sought, spending pattern, and degree of autonomy) and emotional characteristics (such as self-image, conspicuous consumer or reluctant traveller, impulse or planned) need to be incorporated into revenue management considerations.

(Q) How are revenue management practices perceived by customers?

(A) The art of implementation is not to let the customers feel that your pricing and inventory control practices are unfair and meant primarily to increase the top and bottom line of the company. Intelligent and meaningful rate fences have to be used to allow customers to self-segment so that they retain a feeling of choice.

(Q) What is the day-to-day nature of the job?

(A) The market presents a lot of demand changes and you need to monitor your competitors' price as it fluctuates daily across the various distribution changes. It's definitely a prerequisite to be quick in analysis, and decisive. One needs to feel comfortable taking calculated risks and choose from a plethora of revenue management and pricing tools to decide on the best fit for the situation.

Source: We thank Jeannette Ho, Vice President, Distribution Marketing & Revenue Management at Raffles International Limited, for this interview, conducted on January 6, 2006. Jeannette has been responsible for spearheading and implementing the revenue management initiatives for the Group since February 2005. Her team drives the company's global distribution strategy and oversees its ecommerce channels and central reservations system. Over the past 12 years, Jeannette has been working in revenue management with various international companies such as Singapore Airlines, Banyan Tree, and The Westin Stamford & Westin Plaza Hotels.

$$\text{Price elasticity} = \frac{\text{Percentage change in demand}}{\text{Percentage change in price}}$$

When price elasticity is at "unity," sales of a service rise (or fall) by the same percentage that the price falls (or rises). If a small change in price has a big impact on sales, demand for that product is said to be *price elastic*. But if a change in price has little effect on sales, demand is described as *price inelastic*. The concept is illustrated in the simple chart presented in Figure 5.8, which shows the price elasticity for two segments, one with a highly

Figure 5.8

Illustrations of
Price Elasticity

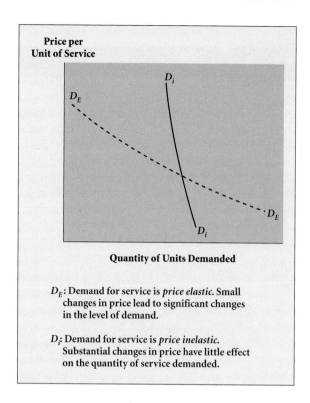

D_E: Demand for service is *price elastic*. Small
changes in price lead to significant changes
in the level of demand.

D_i: Demand for service is *price inelastic*.
Substantial changes in price have little effect
on the quantity of service demanded.

elastic demand (where a small change in price results in a big change in the amount demanded), and the other with a highly inelastic demand (where even big changes in price have little impact on the amount demanded).

Designing Rate Fences   Inherent in revenue management is the concept of *price customization*—that is, charging different customers different prices for what is, in effect, the same product. As noted by Hermann Simon and Robert Dolan,

> The basic idea of price customization is simple: Have people pay prices based on the value they put on the product. Obviously you can't just hang out a sign saying "Pay me what it's worth to you" or "It's $80 if you value it that much but only $40 if you don't." You have to find a way to segment customers by their valuations. In a sense, you have to "build a fence" between high-value customers and low-value customers so the "high" buyers can't take advantage of the low price.[13]

How can a firm ensure that customers for whom the service offers high value are unable to take advantage of lower price buckets? Properly designed rate fences allow customers to self-segment on the basis of service characteristics and willingness to pay, and help companies to restrict lower prices to customers who are willing to accept certain restrictions on their purchase and consumption experiences.

Fences can be either *physical* or *non-physical*. Physical fences refer to tangible product differences related to the different prices, such as the seat location in a theatre, or the size and furnishing of a hotel room. Non-physical fences refer to consumption, transaction, or buyer characteristics. For example, they include staying a certain length of time in a hotel, playing golf on a weekday afternoon, cancellation or change penalties, or booking a certain length of time ahead. Examples of common rate fences are shown in Table 5.2.

Physical fences reflect tangible differences in the actual service (e.g., first class is better than economy class), whereas non-physical services actually refer to the same basic service (e.g., there is no difference in economy class service whether a person bought a ticket really cheaply or paid full fare for it). In summary, using a detailed understanding of customer needs, preferences, and willingness to pay, product and revenue managers can jointly design effective products comprising the core service, physical product features (physical fences), and non-physical product features (non-physical fences). A good understanding of the demand curve is needed so that "buckets" of inventory can be assigned to

Table 5.2 Key Categories of Rate Fences

RATE FENCES	EXAMPLES
Physical (product-related) Fences	
Basic product	• Class of travel (business/economy class) • Size and furnishing of a hotel room • Seat location in a theatre
Amenities	• Free breakfast at a hotel, airport pick up, etc. • Free golf cart at a golf course
Service level	• Priority wait listing, separate check-in counters with no or only short lines • Increase in baggage allowance • Dedicated service hotlines • Dedicated account management team
Nonphysical Fences	
Transaction Characteristics	
Time of booking or reservation	• Requirements for advance purchase • Must pay full fare two weeks before departure
Location of booking or reservation	• Passengers booking air tickets for same route in different countries charged different prices
Flexibility of ticket use	• Fees/penalties for cancelling or changing a reservation (up to loss of entire ticket price) • Nonrefundable reservations fees
Consumption Characteristics	
Time or duration of use	• Early-bird special in a restaurant before 6:00 p.m. • Must stay over a Saturday night for an airline, hotel, or car rental booking. • Must stay at least for five nights
Location of consumption	• Price based on departure location, especially in international travel • Prices vary by location (between cities, city centre versus edges of the city)
Buyer Characteristics	
Frequency or volume of consumption	• Member of certain loyalty tier with the firm (e.g., Platinum member) gets priority pricing, discounts, or loyalty benefits
Group membership	• Child, student, senior citizen discounts • Affiliation with certain groups (e.g., alumni)
Size of customer group	• Group discounts based on size of group

the various products and price categories. An example from the airline industry is shown in Figure 5.9 (p. 148). And lastly, the design of revenue management systems needs to incorporate safeguards for consumers. For additional insights into revenue management strategies, see the reading by Sheryl E. Kimes and Richard B. Chase, "The Strategic Levers of Yield Management," on page 215.

ETHICAL CONCERNS IN SERVICE PRICING

Do you sometimes have difficulty understanding how much it's going to cost you to use a service? Do you believe that many prices are unfair? If so, you're not alone.[14] The fact is, service users can't always be sure in advance what they will receive in return for their payments. There's an implicit assumption among many customers that a higher-priced service should offer more benefits and greater quality than a lower-priced one. For example, a professional—say a lawyer—who charges very high fees is assumed to be more skilled than one who is relatively inexpensive. Although price can serve as a surrogate for quality, it is sometimes hard to be sure if the extra value is really there.

Figure 5.9

Relating Price Buckets to the Demand Curve

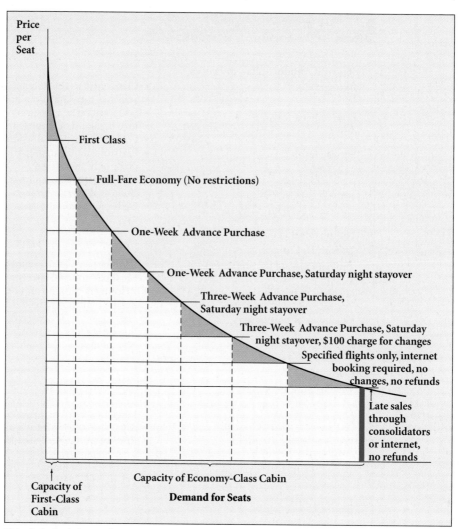

Note: dark-shaded areas denote amount of consumer surplus. (Goal of segmented pricing is to minimize this.)

Are Service Pricing Schedules Too Complex?

Pricing schedules for services tend to be complex and hard to understand. Comparison across providers may even require complex spreadsheets or even mathematical formulas. Consumer advocates sometimes charge that this complexity represents a deliberate choice on the part of service suppliers who don't want customers to be able to determine who offers the best value for money. Indeed, complexity makes it easy (and perhaps more tempting) for firms to engage in unethical behaviour. The quoted prices typically used by consumers for price comparisons may be only the first of several charges they can be billed. As described in Service Perspectives 5.4, cellphone service is particularly problematic in this respect.

Many people find it difficult to forecast their own usage, which makes it hard to compute comparative prices when evaluating competing suppliers whose fees are based on a variety of usage-related factors. It's no coincidence that the humorist Scott Adams (creator of the Dilbert cartoon strip) used exclusively service examples when he "branded" the future of pricing as "confusiology." Noting that firms, such as telecommunications companies, banks, insurance firms, and other financial service providers offer nearly identical services, Adams remarks:

> You would think this would create a price war and drive prices down to the cost of providing it (that's what I learned between naps in my economic classes), but it isn't happening. The companies are forming efficient confusopolies so customers can't tell

Service Perspectives 5.4

Since the mid 1990s there has been a rapid expansion in the availability of cellphone services. Significant technological improvements have expanded the capability of these services, including the ability to transmit photos and download music. Not surprisingly, demand has exploded and competition has become intense.

In tailoring their services to the widely varying needs and calling patterns of different market segments, cellphone companies have developed a bewildering array of plans that defy easy comparison across suppliers. Plans can be national, regional, or purely local in scope. Monthly fees vary according to the number of minutes selected in advance, which typically include separate allowances for peak and off-peak minutes. Overtime minutes and "roaming minutes" on other carriers are charged at higher rates. Some plans allow unlimited off-peak calling, while others allow free incoming calls. Some providers charge calls per second, per six-second blocks, or even per minute blocks, resulting in vastly different costs per call. Family plans let parents and children pool their monthly minutes for use on several phones as long as the total for everyone's calling doesn't exceed the monthly quota. In addition, fees such as the "system access fees" and charges applied to the bill if the customer requests a paper invoice rather than an electronic one, baffle the customer further. Bundled plans that include mobile, fixed line, and internet services compound the confusion further, whereby the various surcharges can increase the total bill by 20 to 25 percent. Phone bills of course include real taxes (e.g., sales tax), but on many bills the majority of surcharges, which users often misread as taxes, go directly to the phone company. For instance, separating the "system access fees" from the overall charges is supposed to give an illusion that it's a fee that's going to someone other than the carrier. This also allows the carriers to advertise a lower price point for their services, with the system access fees being added to the bill once the consumer signs on. In a CBC *Marketplace* documentary titled "Cellphone Secrets," broadcast on January 23, 2005, it was found that some of the carriers still couch the system access fees in terms such as "it's like a government fee" or "it's like taxes." This happened despite the fact that in 2004 Industry

Canada gave clear instructions to the carriers to stop suggesting that the fees are somehow attributable to the government. In fact, a condition of their operating licence is that they are not allowed to say that the fees go to the government.

In the United States, research by the Consumers Union (CU) found high levels of customer dissatisfaction with cellphone service. In addition to poor-quality reception, dropped calls, and inaccessible service, many concerns related to billing and pricing, with complaints about overcharging, billing mistakes, and bills padded with extra charges. Compounding the problem was the fact that companies made it hard to switch. Typically, subscribers sign a one- or two-year contract that imposes significant penalties, often in the range $100–200, for early termination. In an editorial entitled "Cell Hell," Jim Guest, CU's president, observed:

> In the 10 years since *Consumer Reports* started rating cellphones and calling plans, we've never found an easy way to compare actual costs. From what our readers tell us, they haven't either. Each carrier presents its rates, extra charges, and calling areas differently. Deciphering one company's plan is hard enough, but comparing plans from various carriers is nearly impossible.

CU advocates stronger regulation of the industry to protect consumers from confusing and abusive practices, including a government-mandated standard format for presenting calling plan features and charges. According to David Bergmann from the Office of the Ohio Consumers' Council and chairman of the telecommunications committee at the National Association of State Utility Consumer Advocates, all these extra and confusing charges should be included in the advertised prices of calling plans. He said, "I don't pay a health and safety fee to restaurants. If they want to raise the price of a meal, that's fine. But customers shouldn't order something and not know what is going into the bill."

Sources: Jim Guest, "Cell Hell" (p. 3) and "Complete Cell-Phone Guide," *Consumer Reports* (February 2003): 11–27; and Ken Belson, "A Monthly Mystery," *New York Times* (August 27, 2005); CBC *Marketplace* website: www.cbc.ca/consumers/market/files/services/cellphones/accessfee.html, accessed April 03, 2006.

---

who has the lowest prices. Companies have learned to use the complexities of life as an economic tool.[15]

One of the roles of effective government regulation, says Adams, should be to discourage this tendency for certain service industries to evolve into "confusopolies."

Piling on the Fees

Not all business models are based on generating income from sales. There is a growing trend today to impose fees that sometimes have little to do with usage. The car rental industry has attracted some notoriety for advertising bargain rental prices and then tacking on fees such as collision insurance and personal insurance on customers' arrival. Also, staff sometimes fails to clarify certain "small print" contract terms such as, say, a high-kilometrage charge that is added once the car exceeds a (very low) threshold of free kilometres. A not-uncommon practice when the car is returned is to charge fees for refuelling a partially empty tank that far exceed what the driver would pay at the pump.[16]

There has also been a trend toward adding (or increasing) fines and penalties. Banks have been heavily criticized for using penalties as an important revenue-generating tool as opposed to using them merely to educate customers and achieve compliance with payment deadlines. In Quebec, there have been five separate class-action lawsuits involving one or more of eleven Canadian financial institutions in violation of the Quebec Consumer Protection Act, mostly concerned with the grace period for payments of credit card charges. One case that is proceeding at the time of writing is that of Sheri Aberback-Ptack, who is suing American Express on behalf of those who have been charged a penalty even after paying their account (whether by telephone, internet, or ABM) on or before the due date. Her lawyer, Arthur Wechsler, clarifies the reason behind the penalty charges: "Amex charges consumers a finance charge or interest penalty under the pretext that it was not able to process the payment for three to five days after the reception of the payment."[17] Such practices by service organizations do little to alleviate the perception that financial institutions use unfair practices to increase their bottom line.

It's possible to design penalties that do not seem unfair to customers. Research Insights 5.1 describes what drives customers' fairness perceptions on service fees and penalties.

Designing Fairness into Revenue Management

A well-implemented revenue-management strategy does not mean blind pursuit of short-term yield maximization. The following specific approaches can help to reconcile yield management practices with customer satisfaction, trust, and good will:[18]

- *Design Price Schedules and Fences that are Clear, Logical, and Fair.* Firms should proactively spell out all fees and expenses (e.g., no-show or cancellation charges) clearly in advance, so that there are no surprises. A related approach is to develop a simple fee structure so that customers can more easily understand the financial implications of a specific usage situation. For rate fences to be perceived as fair, customers must be able to easily understand them (i.e., fences have to be transparent and upfront), see the logic in them, and be convinced that they are difficult to circumvent and therefore fair.

- *Use High Published Prices and Frame Fences as Discounts.* Rate fences framed as customer gains (i.e., discounts) are generally perceived as fairer than those framed as customer losses (i.e., surcharges) even if the situations are economically equivalent. For example, a customer who has no option but to patronize her hair salon on Saturdays may perceive the salon as profiteering if she finds herself facing a weekend surcharge. However, she is likely to find the higher weekend price more acceptable if the hair salon advertises its peak weekend price as the published price while offering a $5 discount for weekday haircuts. Furthermore, having a high published price also helps to increase the reference price and, potentially, perceptions of quality, in addition to the feeling of being rewarded for the weekday patronage.

- *Communicate Consumer Benefits of Revenue Management.* Marketing communications should position revenue management as a win–win practice. Providing different price and value balances allows a broader spectrum of customers to self-segment and enjoy the service. It allows each customer to find the balance between price and benefits (value) that best satisfies his or her needs. For example, charging a higher price for the best seats in the theatre recognizes that some people are willing and able to pay more for a better location, making it possible to sell other seats at a lower price.

- *Use Bundling to "Hide" Discounts.* Bundling a service into a package effectively obscures the discounted price. When a cruise line includes the price of air travel or ground transportation in the cruise package, the customer only knows the total price, not the cost of the individual components. Bundling usually makes price comparisons between the bundles and its components impossible, and thereby side-steps potential unfairness perceptions and reductions in reference prices.

Research Insights 5.1

Crime and Punishment: How Customers Respond to Fines and Penalties

Various types of "penalties" are part and parcel of many pricing schedules, and range from late fees for DVD rentals and cancellation charges for hotel bookings, to charges for late payments. Customer responses to penalties can be highly negative and can lead to switching of provider and negative word of mouth. Young Kim and Amy Smith conducted an online survey using the Critical Incident Technique (CIT), in which the 201 respondents were asked to recall a recent penalty incident, describe the situation, and then complete a set of structured questions based on how the respondents felt and responded to that incident. Their findings showed that negative consumer responses can be reduced significantly by following these three guidelines:

1. *Make Penalties Relative to the "Crime" Committed.* The results found that customers' negative emotions to a penalty increased drastically when they found that the penalty was out of line with the "crime" committed. Customers' negative feelings were further aggravated if they were "surprised" by the penalty being suddenly charged to them without being previously aware of the fee or its magnitude. These findings suggest that firms can reduce negative customer responses significantly by exploring which amounts are seen as reasonable or fair for a given "customer lapse," and clearly communicating the fines/fees before an incident happens that leads to a charge (e.g., in a banking context, through a clearly explained fee schedule and through front-line staff that explain at the point of opening an account or selling of additional services the potential fines or fees that are associated with various violations, such as overdrawing beyond the authorized limits, bounced cheques, or late payments).

2. *Consider Causal Factors and Customize Penalties.* The study showed that customers' perceptions of fairness were lower, and negative responses higher, when they perceived the causes that led to the penalty as being out of their control (e.g., "I mailed the cheque on time—there must have been a delay in the postal system"), rather than when they felt it was within their control and really their fault (e.g., "I forgot to mail the cheque"). To increase the perception of fairness, firms may want to identify common violations that are typically out of the control of the customer, and allow front-line staff the discretion to waive or reduce such fees.

In addition, it was found that customers who generally observe all the rules, and therefore have not paid fines in the past, react particularly negatively should they be fined. One respondent said, "I have always made timely payments and have never been late with a payment—they should have considered this fact and waived the fee." Service firms should take customers' penalties history into account and offer them differential treatments based on their past behaviour. Fairness perception could be improved by, for instance, waiving the first fine for an incident, while at the same time communicating that the next time the fee will be charged.

3. *Focus on Fairness, and Manage Emotions During Penalty Situations.* Consumers' responses are heavily driven by fairness perceptions. Customers are likely to perceive penalties as excessive and respond negatively if they find that a penalty is out of proportion to the damage or extra work caused to the firm by the incident. One consumer complained, "I thought this particular penalty [credit card late payment] was excessive. You are already paying high interest; the penalty should have been more in line with the payment. The penalty was more than the payment!" Considering fairness perceptions would mean, for example, that the late fee for keeping a DVD should not exceed the potentially lost rental fee for the same period.

Service companies can also make penalties seem fairer by providing adequate explanations and justifications for the penalty. Ideally, penalties should be imposed for the good of other customers (e.g., we kept the room for you, which we could have given to another guest on our waiting list) or community, but not as a means of generating a significant proportion of overall profit. Finally, front-line staff should be trained in how to handle customers who have become angry and distressed in complaining about their penalties (see Chapter 13 on how we recommend that you deal with such situations).

Source: Adapted from Young "Sally" K. Kim and Amy K. Smith, "Crime and Punishment: Examining Customers' Responses to Service Organizations' Penalties," *Journal of Service Research* 8/2 (2005): 162–80.

- *Take Care of Loyal Customers.* Firms should build in strategies for retaining valued customers, even to the extent of not charging the maximum feasible amount on a given transaction. After all, customer perceptions of price gouging do not build trust. Yield management systems can be programmed to incorporate "loyalty multipliers" for regular customers, so that reservations systems can give them "special treatment" status at peak times, even when they are not paying premium rates.

- *Use Service Recovery to Compensate for Overbooking.* Many service firms overbook to compensate for anticipated cancellations and no-shows—the legal justification for the practice arising from service terms that allow such customers to change their dates or obtain a refund, which would otherwise lead the service provider to lose revenue altogether from the unused capacity. Profits increase—at least in the short term—but so too does the incidence of being unable to honour reservations. Being "bumped" by an airline, or "walked" by a hotel, can lead to a loss of customer loyalty and adversely affect a firm's reputation. So it's important to back up overbooking programs with well-designed service recovery procedures, such as the following:

1. Give customers a choice between retaining their reservation and receiving compensation.
2. Provide sufficient advance notice so that customers are able to make alternative arrangements.
3. If possible, offer a substitute service that delights customers.

A Westin beach resort has found that it can free up capacity by offering guests who are departing the next day the option of spending their last night in a luxury hotel near the airport or in the city at no extra cost. Guest feedback on the free room, upgraded service, and a night in the city after a beach holiday has been very positive. From the hotel's perspective, this practice trades the cost of securing a one-night stay in another hotel against that of turning away a multiple-night guest arriving the same day.

PUTTING SERVICE PRICING INTO PRACTICE

Although the main decision in pricing is usually seen as how much to charge, there are other decisions to be made. Table 5.3 summarizes the questions that service marketers need to ask themselves as they prepare to create and implement a well-thought-out pricing strategy. Let's look at each in turn.

How Much to Charge?

Realistic decisions on pricing are critical for financial solvency. The pricing tripod model, discussed earlier (see Figure 5.2), provides a useful departure point. The three elements involve determining the relevant economic costs to be recovered at different sales volumes and setting the relevant floor price; assessing the elasticity of demand of the service from both the providers' and customers' perspectives, as it helps to set a "ceiling" price for any given market segment; and analyzing the intensity of price competition among the providers.

A specific figure must be set for the price itself. This task involves several considerations, including the need to consider the pros and cons of setting a rounded price and the ethical issues involved in setting a price exclusive of taxes, service charges, and other extras.

What Should Be the Specified Basis for Pricing?

It's not always easy to define a unit of service as the specified basis for pricing. There may be many options. For instance, should price be based on completing a promised service task, such as repairing a piece of equipment, or cleaning a jacket? Should it be based on admission to a service performance, such as an educational program, concert, or sports event? Should it be time-based, such as using an hour of a lawyer's time, or occupying a hotel room for a night? Alternatively, should it be related to a monetary value associated with service delivery, as when an insurance company scales its premiums to reflect the amount of coverage provided or a realtor takes a commission that is a percentage of the selling price of a house?

Some service prices are tied to the consumption of physical resources, such as food, drinks, water, or natural gas. In the hospitality industry, rather than charging customers an hourly rate for occupying a table and chairs, restaurants put a sizable markup on the food and drink items consumed. Recognizing the fixed cost of table service—such as a

Table 5.3 Some Pricing Issues

1. How much should be charged for this service?
- What costs is the organization attempting to recover? Is the organization trying to achieve a specific profit margin or return on investment by selling this service?
- How sensitive are customers to various prices?
- What prices are charged by competitors?
- What discount(s) should be offered from basic prices?
- Are psychological pricing points (e.g., $4.95 versus $5.00) customarily used?

2. What should be the basis of pricing?
- Execution of a specific task
- Admission to a service facility
- Units of time (hour, week, month, year)
- Percentage commission on the value of the transaction
- Physical resources consumed
- Geographic distance covered
- Weight or size of object serviced
- Should each service element be billed independently?
- Should a single price be charged for a bundled package?

3. Who should collect payment?
- The organization that provides the service
- A specialist intermediary (travel or ticket agent, bank, retailer, etc.)
- How should the intermediary be compensated for this work—flat fee or percentage commission?

4. Where should payment be made?
- The location at which the service is delivered
- A convenient retail outlet or financial intermediary (e.g., bank)
- The purchaser's home (by mail or phone)

5. When should payment be made?
- Before or after delivery of the service
- At which times of day
- On which days of the week

6. How should payment be made?
- Cash (exact change or not?)
- Token (where can these be purchased?)
- Stored value card
- Cheque (how to verify?)
- Electronic funds transfer
- Charge card (credit or debit)
- Credit account with service provider
- Vouchers
- Third-party payment (e.g., insurance company or government agency)?

7. How should prices be communicated to the target market?
- Through what communication medium? (advertising, signage, electronic display, salespeople, customer service personnel)
- What message content (how much emphasis should be placed on price?)

clean tablecloth for each party—restaurants in some countries impose a fixed cover charge, which is added to the cost of the meal. Others may establish a minimum meal charge per person. Transport firms have traditionally charged by distance, with freight companies using a combination of weight or volume plus distance to set their rates. Such a policy has the virtue of consistency and reflects calculation of an average cost per kilometre. However, it ignores relative market strength on different routes, which should be included when a yield-management system is used. Simplicity may suggest a flat rate, as with postal charges for domestic letters below a certain weight, or a rate for packages that groups geographic distances into broad zones.

For some services, prices may include separate charges for access and for usage. Recent research suggests that access or subscription fees are an important driver of adoption and customer retention, whereas usage fees are much more important drivers of actual usage.[19]

Price Bundling   As we emphasize throughout this book, many services unite a core product with a variety of supplementary services. Meals and bar service on a cruise ship offer one example; baggage service on a train or aircraft is another. Should such service packages be priced as a whole (referred to as a "bundle"), or should each element be priced separately? To the extent that people prefer to avoid making many small payments, bundled pricing may be preferable, and is certainly simpler to administer. But if customers dislike feeling that they have been charged for product elements they did not use, and perhaps had no interest in using, itemized pricing may be preferable.

Bundled prices offer firms certain guaranteed revenue from each customer while giving the latter a clear idea in advance how much the bill will be. Unbundled pricing provides customers with flexibility in what they choose to acquire and pay for.[20] However, they may be angered if they discover that the actual price of what they consume, inflated by all the "extras," is substantially higher than the advertised base price that attracted them in the first place.

Discounting   As discussed in the context of yield management, selective price discounting targeted at specific market segments can offer important opportunities to attract new customers and fill capacity that would otherwise go unused. However, unless used with effective rate fences that allow a clean targeting of specific segments, a strategy of discounting should be approached cautiously. It reduces the average price and contribution received, and may attract customers whose only loyalty is to the firm that can offer the lowest price on the next transaction. Volume discounts are sometimes used to cement the loyalty of large corporate customers who might otherwise spread their purchases among several different suppliers.

Who Should Collect Payment?

As discussed in Chapter 3, supplementary services include information, order-taking, billing, and payment. Customers appreciate it when a firm makes it easy to obtain price information and make reservations. They also expect well-presented billing and convenient procedures for making payment. Sometimes, firms delegate these tasks to intermediaries, such as travel agents who make hotel and transport bookings and collect payment from customers, and ticket agents who sell seats for theatres, concert halls, and sports stadiums. Although the original supplier pays a commission, the intermediary is usually able to offer customers greater convenience in terms of where, when, and how payment can be paid. Using intermediaries may also result in a net savings in administrative costs, though at the risk of putting off customers by the increased cost from the intermediary's surcharge. Nowadays, however, many service firms are promoting their websites as direct channels for customer self-service, thus bypassing traditional intermediaries and avoiding payment of commissions.

Where Should Payment Be Made?

Service delivery sites are not always conveniently located. Airports, theatres, and stadiums, for instance, are often situated some distance from where potential patrons live or work. When consumers have to purchase a service before using it, there are obvious benefits to using intermediaries that are more conveniently located, or allowing payment by mail or bank transfer. A growing number of organizations now accept internet, telephone and fax bookings with payment by credit card.

When Should Payment Be Made?

Two basic options are to ask customers to pay in advance (as with an admission charge, airline ticket, or postage stamps), or to bill them once service delivery has been completed, as with restaurant bills and repair charges. Occasionally, a service provider may ask for an initial payment in advance of service delivery, with the balance due on completion. This approach is quite common with expensive repair and maintenance jobs, when the firm—often a small business with limited working capital—must buy materials up front.

Asking customers to pay in advance means that the buyer is paying before the benefits are received. However, prepayments may be advantageous to the customer as well as to the provider. Sometimes it is inconvenient to pay each time a regularly patronized service—such as the post or public transport—is used. To save time and effort, customers may prefer the convenience of buying a book of stamps or a monthly travel pass. Performing arts organizations with heavy up-front financing requirements offer discounted subscription tickets in order to bring in money before the season begins.

Finally, the timing of payment can determine usage pattern. From an analysis of the payment and attendance records of a health club, John Gourville and Dilip Soman found that members' usage patterns were closely related to their payment schedules. When members made payments annually, their use of the club was highest during the months immediately following payment, and then declined steadily until the next payment. Members with monthly payment plans, on the other hand, attended the health club much more consistently and were more likely to renew, perhaps because each month's payment encouraged them to use what they were paying for.

Gourville and Soman conclude that the timing of payment can be used more strategically to manage capacity utilization. For instance, if a golf club wants to reduce the demand during its busiest time, it can bill its fees long before the season begins (e.g., in January rather than in May or June), as the member's pain of payment will have faded by the time the peak summer months come, and thereby reduces the perceived need to get his/her "money's worth" by using the service heavily. The resulting reduction in demand during the peak period would then allow the club to increase its membership.[21]

How Should Payment Be Made?

As shown earlier in Table 5.3, there are many different forms of payment. Cash may appear to be the simplest method, but it raises security problems and is inconvenient when exact change is required to operate machines. Accepting payment by cheque for all but the smallest purchases is now fairly widespread and offers customer benefits, although it may require controls to discourage bad cheques, such as a hefty charge for returned cheques ($15–$20 on top of any bank charges is not uncommon at retail stores).

Credit and debit cards can be used around the world. As their acceptance has become more universal, businesses that refuse to accept them increasingly find themselves at a competitive disadvantage. Many companies also offer customers the convenience of a credit account, which generates a membership relationship between the customer and the firm. Other payment procedures include tokens or vouchers as supplements to (or instead of) cash. Tokens with a predefined value can simplify the process of paying road and bridge tolls or bus and metro fares. Vouchers are sometimes provided by social service agencies to elderly or low-income people. Such a policy achieves the same benefits as discounting but avoids the need to publicize different prices and to require cashiers to check eligibility.

Now coming into broader usage are prepayment systems based on cards that store value on a magnetic strip or in a microchip embedded in the card. Service firms that want to accept payment in this form, however, must first install card readers. Service marketers should remember that the simplicity and speed with which payment is made may influence the customer's perception of overall service quality. To cater to consumers' and merchants' need for speed, convenience, and security, VISA began commercial implementation of a contactless smart card, named "Wave," in Malaysia in February 2005. The card communicates with the card reader via radio waves, when the two are held within five centimetres of each other (Figure 5.10).

Interestingly, a 2003 study found that the choice of payment mechanism has an impact on the total spending of customers, especially for discretionary consumption items such as spending in cafés.[22] The less tangible or immediate the payment mechanism, the more

Figure 5.10

VISA's contactless smart card "Wave" caters to the needs of speed, convenience, and security.

consumers tend to spend. Cash is the most tangible (i.e., consumers tend to spend less when using it), followed by credit cards, prepayment cards, and finally more sophisticated and even less tangible and immediate mechanisms such as payment via one's cellphone bill.

How Should Prices Be Communicated to the Target Markets?

The final task, once the other issues have been addressed, is to decide how the organization's pricing policies can best be communicated to its target market(s). People need to know the price for some product offerings well in advance of purchase. They may also need to know how, where, and when that price is payable. This information must be presented in ways that are intelligible and unambiguous, so that customers will not be misled and question the ethical standards of the firm.

Managers must decide whether or not to include information on pricing in advertising for the service. It may be appropriate to relate the price to the costs of competing products. Certainly, salespeople and customer service representatives should be able to give prompt, accurate responses to customer queries about pricing, payment, and credit. Good signage at retail points of sale will save staff members from having to answer basic questions on prices.

Finally, when the price is presented in the form of an itemized bill, marketers should ensure that it is both accurate and intelligible. Hotel bills, despite containing fewer entries, are also notoriously inaccurate. One study estimated that business travellers in the United States may be overpaying for their hotel rooms by US$500 million dollars a year, with 11.6 percent of all bills incorrect, resulting in an average overpayment of US$11.36.[23]

Conclusion

To determine an effective pricing strategy, a firm has to have a good understanding of its costs, the value created for customers, and competitor pricing. Defining costs tends to be more difficult in a service business than in a manufacturing operation. Without a good understanding of costs, managers cannot be sure that the prices set are, in fact, sufficient to recover all costs.

Another challenge is to relate the value that customers perceive in a service to the price they are willing to pay for it. This step requires an understanding of other costs that the customer may be incurring in purchase and use, including costs of a non-financial nature, such as time and effort. Managers also need to recognize that the same service may not be valued in the same way by all customers, offering the potential to set different prices for different market segments.

Competitor pricing cannot be compared dollar for dollar. Services tend to be location- and time-specific, and competitor services have their own set of related monetary and non-monetary costs, sometimes to the extent that the actual prices charged become secondary for competitive comparisons. Competitive pricing needs to take all those factors into account.

Revenue management is a powerful tool that helps to manage demand by pricing different segments closer to their reservation prices. Well-designed physical and non-physical rate fences help to define "products" for each target segment. However, great care has to be taken in the way revenue management is implemented, so that customer satisfaction and perceived fairness are not compromised.

A pricing strategy must address the central issue of what price to charge for selling a given unit of service at a particular point in time (however that unit may be defined). Because services often combine multiple elements, pricing strategies need to be highly creative.

Finally, firms need to be careful not to let pricing schedules become so complex and difficult to compare that they simply confuse customers. A policy of deliberately creating confusing price schedules, including hiding certain costs that only become apparent to customers after usage, is likely to lead to accusations of unethical behaviour and to loss of trust and customer dissatisfaction.

Review Questions

1. What is the role of service pricing and revenue management in a business model?

2. How can the three main approaches to service pricing be integrated to arrive at a good pricing point for a particular service?

3. This chapter talks about using activity-based costing (ABC) in order to establish costs for providing a particular service. Explain what is meant by the following statement: "ABC hierarchy provides a structured way of thinking about the relationship between activities and the resources that they consume."

4. Why is the price charged by the firm only one, and often not the most important, component of the total cost to the consumer? When should we cut non-price-related costs to the bone, even if that incurs higher costs and a higher price to be charged?

5. What is the role of non-monetary costs in a business model, and how do they relate to the consumer's perception of the offered value exchange?

6. What is revenue management, and how does it work? What type of service operations benefit most from good revenue-management systems, and why?

7. Why are ethical concerns and fairness perception important issues when designing service-fee schedules and revenue-management strategies? What are potential consumer responses to service-pricing schedules or policies that are seen as unfair?

8. How can we improve the perceived fairness of pricing schedules, and what are the implications of these recommendations? How can perceptions of unfairness be mitigated, and fairness perceptions created?

9. How can we charge different prices to different market segments without customers feeling cheated? How can we even charge the same customer different prices at different times, contexts and/or occasions, and still be seen as fair?

10. What are the seven key decisions that managers need to make when designing an effective pricing schedule?

Application Exercises

1. Select a service organization of your choice and find out what their pricing policies and methods are. In what respects are they similar to or different from what has been discussed in this chapter?

2. From a customer perspective, what serves to define value in the following services: (a) a hairdressing salon, (b) a legal firm specializing in business and taxation law, and (c) a nightclub.

3. Think about the example of a physical rehabilitation clinic that we discussed early on in the chapter. The clinic runs two separate businesses: 1) physiotherapy and 2) massage therapy. Identify the key elements of the service process and the type of information that would be needed for each of these elements in order to come up with an activity-based costing approach to allocating costs across the two businesses. How is that different from the information that you would have needed for traditional costing?

4. Explore two highly successful business models that are based on innovative service pricing and/or revenue-management strategies, and identify two business models that failed because of major issues in their pricing or revenue-management strategy. What lessons can you learn from your analysis of these successful and unsuccessful examples?

5. Visit the website of a successful Canadian yield-management solution provider, Northwind, at www.maestropms.com/northwind.aspx. Explore the success stories of various hotels and resorts across Canada that have used the "Maestro" yield-management solution that is profiled on the website. Has the implementation of "Maestro" resulted

in better revenues for the firms, or in increased customer satisfaction, or both? Why?

6. How might revenue management be applied to (a) a professional firm (e.g., consulting), (b) a restaurant, and (c) a golf course? What rate fences would you use, and why?

7. Review recent bills that you have received from service businesses, such as those for telephone, car repair, cable TV, credit card, etc. Evaluate each one against the following criteria: (a) general appearance and clarity of presentation, (b) easily understood terms of payment, (c) avoidance of confusing terms and definitions, (d) appropriate level of detail, (e) unanticipated ("hidden") charges, (f) accuracy, and (g) ease of access to customer service in case of problems or disputes.

8. Take a service of your choice and develop a comprehensive pricing schedule. Apply the seven questions marketers need to answer for designing an effective pricing schedule.

Endnotes

1. Daniel J. Goebel, Greg W. Marshall, and William B. Locander, "Activity Based Costing: Accounting for a Marketing Orientation," *Industrial Marketing Management* 27/6 (1998): 497–510; Thomas H. Stevenson and David W.E. Cabell, "Integrating Transfer Pricing Policy and Activity-Based Costing," *Journal of International Marketing* 10/4 (2002): 77–88.

2. Robin Cooper and Robert S. Kaplan, "Profit Priorities from Activity-Based Costing," *Harvard Business Review* 69/3 (May–June 1991): 130–35.

3. Antonella Carù and Antonella Cugini, "Profitability and Customer Satisfaction in Services: An Integrated Perspective between Marketing and Cost Management Analysis," *International Journal of Service Industry Management* 10/2 (1999): 132–56.

4. Kristina Heinonen, "Reconceptualizing Customer Perceived Value: The Value of Time and Place," *Managing Service Quality* 14/3 (2004): 205–15.

5. Gerald E. Smith and Thomas T. Nagle, "How Much Are Customers Willing to Pay?" *Marketing Research* (Winter 2002): 20–25.

6. Valarie A. Zeithaml, "Consumer Perceptions of Price, Quality, and Value: A Means-End Model and Synthesis of Evidence," *Journal of Marketing* 52 (July 1988): 2–21. A recent paper exploring alternative conceptualizations of value is Chien-Hsin Lin, Peter J. Sher, and Hsin-Yu Shih, "Past Progress and Future Directions in Conceptualizing Customer Perceived Value," *International Journal of Service Industry Management* 16/4 (2005): 318–36.

7. Hermann Simon, "Pricing Opportunities and How to Exploit Them," *Sloan Management Review* 33 (Winter 1992): 71–84.

8. This discussion is based primarily on Leonard L. Berry and Manjit S. Yadav, "Capture and Communicate Value in the Pricing of Services," *Sloan Management Review* 37 (Summer 1996): 41–51.

9. Frederick F. Reichheld, *The Loyalty Effect,* Boston: Harvard Business School Press, 1996: 82–84.

10. Anna S. Mattila and Jochen Wirtz, "The Impact of Knowledge Types on the Consumer Search Process: An Investigation in the Context of Credence Services," *International Journal of Service Industry Management* 13/3 (2002): 214–30.

11. Leonard L. Berry, Kathleen Seiders, and Dhruv Grewal, "Understanding Service Convenience," *Journal of Marketing* 66/3 (July 2002): 1–17.

12. For application of yield management to industries beyond the traditional airline, hotel, and car rental contexts, see: Anthony Ingold, Una McMahon-Beattie, and Ian Yeoman (eds.),*Yield Management Strategies for the Service Industries.* 2nd ed., London: Continuum, 2000; Sheryl E. Kimes and Jochen Wirtz, "Perceived Fairness of Revenue Management in the US Golf Industry," *Journal of Revenue and Pricing Management* 1/4 (2003): 332–44; Sheryl E. Kimes and Jochen Wirtz, "Has Revenue Management Become Acceptable? Findings from an International Study and the Perceived Fairness of Rate Fences," *Journal of Service Research* 6 (November 2003): 125–35; Richard Metters and Vicente Vargas, "Yield Management for the Nonprofit Sector," *Journal of Service Research* 1 (February 1999): 215–26; Sunmee Choi and Anna S. Mattila, "Hotel Revenue Management and Its Impact on Customers' Perception of Fairness," *Journal of Revenue and Pricing Management* 2/4 (2004): 303–14; Alex M. Susskind, Dennis Reynolds, and Eriko Tsuchiya, "An Evaluation of Guests' Preferred Incentives to Shift Time-Variable Demand in Restaurants," *Cornell Hotel and Restaurant Administration Quarterly* 44/1 (2004): 68–84; and Parijat Dube, Yezekael Hayel, and Laura Wynter, "Yield Management for IT Resources on Demand: Analysis and Validation of a New Paradigm for Managing Computing Centres," *Journal of Revenue and Pricing Management* 4/1 (2005): 24–38.

13. Hermann Simon and Robert J. Dolan, "Price Customization," *Marketing Management* (Fall 1998): 11–17.

14. Lisa E. Bolton, Luk Warlop, and Joseph W. Alba, "Consumer Perceptions of Price (Un)Fairness," *Journal of Consumer Research* 29/4 (2003): 474–91; Lan Xia, Kent B. Monroe, and Jennifer L. Cox, "The Price is Unfair! A Conceptual Framework of Price Fairness Perceptions," *Journal of Marketing* 68 (October 2004): 1–15; Christian Homburg, Wayne D. Hoyer, and Nicole Koschate, "Customer's Reactions to Price Increases: Do Customer Satisfaction and Perceived Motive Fairness Matter?" *Journal of the Academy of Marketing Science* 33/1 (2005): 36–49.

15. Scott Adams, *The Dilbert™ Future: Thriving on Business Stupidities in the 21st Century,* New York: HarperBusiness, 1997: 160.

16. Ian Ayres and Barry Nalebuff, "In Praise of Honest Pricing," *Sloan Management Review* (Fall 2003): 24–28.

17. Mike King, "Credit Card Penalties for Bills Paid on Time Challenged," *The Gazette* (March 23, 2006): www.canada.com/montrealgazette/news/business/story.html?id=0d800562-b03b-4f24-bda3-0b4af9542345&k=61767, accessed April 4, 2006.

18. Parts of this section are based on Jochen Wirtz, Sheryl E. Kimes, Jeannette P.T. Ho, and Paul Patterson, "Revenue Management: Resolving Potential Customer Conflicts," *Journal of Revenue and Pricing Management* 2/3 (2003): 216–28.

19. Peter J. Danaher, "Optimal Pricing of New Subscription Services: An Analysis of a Market Experiment," *Marketing Science* 21 (Spring 2002): 119–29; and Gilia E. Fruchter and Ram C. Rao, "Optimal Membership Fee and Usage Price Over Time for a Network Service," *Journal of Services Research* 4 (2001): 3–15.

20. Avery Johnson, "Northwest to Charge Passengers in Coach for Meals," *Wall Street Journal* (February 16, 2005).

21. John Gourville and Dilip Soman, "Pricing and the Psychology of Consumption," *Harvard Business Review* 80/9 (September 2002): 90–96.

22. Dilip Soman, "The Effect of Payment Transparency on Consumption: Quasi-Experiments from the Field," *Marketing Letters* 14/3 (2003): 173–83.

23. See, for example, Anita Sharpe, "The Operation Was a Success; The Bill Was Quite a Mess," *Wall Street Journal* (September 17, 1997): 1; Gary Stoller, "Hotel Bill Mistakes Mean Many Pay Too Much," *USA Today* (July 12, 2005; accessed at www.usatoday.com/travel/news/2005-07-11-overcharge-usat_x.htm).

CHAPTER 6

Educating Customers and Promoting the Value Proposition

Life is for one generation; a good name is forever.

—Japanese Proverb

Education costs money, but then so does ignorance.

—Sir Claus Moser

I don't know the rules of grammar. If you're trying to persuade people to do something, or buy something, it seems to me you should use their language.

—David Ogilvy

Communication is the most visible, or audible—some would say intrusive—of marketing activities, but its value is limited unless it is used intelligently in conjunction with other marketing efforts. An old marketing axiom says that the fastest way to kill a poor product is to advertise it heavily. By the same token, an otherwise well-researched and well-planned marketing strategy, designed to deliver, say, new web-based services at a reasonable price, is likely to fail if people lack knowledge of the service and how to access it.

Through communication, marketers explain and promote the value proposition that their firm is offering. They inform existing or prospective customers in the target segments about service features and benefits, price and other costs, the channels through which service is delivered, and when and where it is available. Where appropriate, they marshal persuasive arguments for using a particular service and seek to create preference for selecting their firm's brand. And through both personal instructions from customer contact employees and use of educational tools, marketers seek to help customers make well-informed choices, and become effective participants in service-delivery processes.

Much confusion surrounds the scope of marketing communication. Some people still define this element of the services-marketing mix too narrowly. Communications must be viewed more broadly than as just the use of paid media advertising, public relations, and professional salespeople. Today, there are many other ways for a service business to communicate with current and prospective customers. The location and atmosphere of a service-delivery facility, the use of corporate design features such as a consistent use of colours and graphic elements, the appearance and behaviour of employees, the design of a website—all these contribute to an impression in the customer's mind that reinforces or contradicts the specific content of formal communication messages. The past few years have seen the emergence of new and exciting opportunities for reaching prospects through the internet, with degrees of targeting and message specificity that were previously unimaginable, especially in consumer markets.

In this chapter, we explore the following questions:

1. What is distinctive about the nature of marketing communications for services?

2. What are the elements of the marketing communications mix, and what are the strengths and weaknesses of each major element in a services context?

3. How does the level of customer contact affect communication strategy?

4. How should marketing communication objectives be defined?

5. What is the potential value of the internet, cellular, and other new electronic media as communication channels?

THE ROLE OF MARKETING COMMUNICATION

In a service setting, marketing-communications tools are especially important because they help create powerful images and a sense of credibility, confidence, and reassurance. Marketing communications, in one form or another, are essential to a company's success. Without effective communications, prospects may never learn of a service firm's existence, let alone details of what it has to offer them, the value proposition of each of its products, or how to use them to best advantage. Existing customers might be more easily lured away by competitors and competitive offerings. And there would be no proactive management and control of the firm's identity.

Let's look at some specific tasks that can be performed by marketing communication.

Adding Value through Communication Content

Information and consultation represent important ways to add value to a product. Prospective customers may need information and advice about what service options are available to them, where and when these services are available, how much they cost, and what specific features, functions, and service benefits there are. Companies also use marketing communications to persuade target customers that their service product offers the best solution to those customers' needs, relative to the offerings of competing firms. See Figure 6.1 for an advertisement showing how AIC conveys these ideas, focusing on its message of "Buy. Hold. And Prosper" by stressing the value of rewards gained through a long-term commitment.

Figure 6.1
AIC promotes the value of rewards gained through long-term commitment.

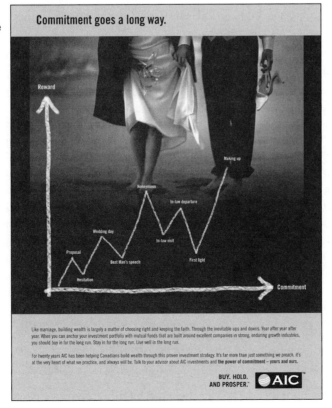

Communication efforts serve not only to attract new users but also to maintain contact with an organization's existing customers, and build relationships with them. Nurturing customer relationships depends on a comprehensive and up-to-date customer database, and the ability to make use of this in a personalized way.

Techniques for keeping in touch with customers and building their loyalty include direct mail and contacts by telephone or other forms of telecommunication, including email, websites and cellphone text messages. Firms such as auto service shops, dentists, and household maintenance services often post periodical reminders to their customers. Some businesses even send birthday and anniversary cards to valued customers. Banks and utility companies often include a brief newsletter with their account statements or print customized information on each statement in an effort to cross-sell additional services.

COMMUNICATING SERVICES PRESENTS BOTH CHALLENGES AND OPPORTUNITIES

Traditional marketing communication strategies were largely shaped by the needs and practices associated with marketing manufactured goods. But several of the differences distinguishing services from goods have a significant impact on the ways we approach the design of marketing communication programs in service businesses.[1] In particular, we need to consider the implications of intangibility in service performances, customer involvement in production, the role of customer-contact personnel, the difficulty of evaluating many services, and the need to bring demand and supply into balance.

Overcome the Problems of Intangibility

Since services are performances rather than objects, their benefits can be difficult to communicate to customers.[2] Banwari Mittal suggests that intangibility creates four problems for marketers seeking to promote its attributes or benefits: abstractness, generality, non-searchability, and mental impalpability.[3] Emphasizing that service marketers need to create messages that clearly communicate intangible service attributes and benefits to potential consumers, he and Julie Baker discuss the implications of each of these problems[4] and propose specific communications strategies for dealing with them (see Table 6.1).

- *Abstractness.* Because abstract concepts such as financial security, expert advice, or safe transportation do not have a one-to-one correspondence with physical objects, it can be challenging for marketers to connect their services to those concepts.

- *Generality* refers to items that comprise a class of objects, persons, or events—for instance, airline seats, flight attendants, and cabin service. These general classes do have physical analogues, and most consumers of the service know what they are, but a key task for marketers is to communicate what makes a specific offering distinctly different from (and superior to) competing offerings.

- *Non-searchability* refers to the fact that intangibles cannot be searched or inspected before they are purchased. Physical service attributes, such as the appearance of a health club and the type of equipment installed, can be checked in advance, but the experience of working with the trainers can only be determined through experience. And as noted in Chapter 2, credence attributes are those that must be taken on faith, such as a surgeon's expertise.

- *Mental impalpability.* Many services are sufficiently complex, multi-dimensional, or novel that it is difficult for consumers—especially new prospects—to understand what the experience of using them will be like and what benefits will result.

Commonly used strategies in advertising include the use of tangible cues whenever possible, especially for low-contact services that involve few tangible elements. It's also helpful to include "vivid information" that catches the audience's attention and will produce a strong, clear impression on the senses, especially for services that are complex and highly intangible.[5] Consider the advertising campaign created by Accenture, the inter-

Table 6.1 Advertising Strategies for Overcoming Intangibility

INTANGIBILITY PROBLEM	ADVERTISING STRATEGY	DESCRIPTION
INCORPOREAL EXISTENCE	PHYSICAL REPRESENTATION	SHOW PHYSICAL COMPONENTS OF SERVICE
Generality:		
• For objective claims	System documentation	Objectively document physical system capacity
	Performance documentation	Document and cite past performance statistics
• For subjective claims	Service performance episode	Present an actual service delivery incident
Nonsearchability	Consumption documentation	Obtain and present customer testimonials
	Reputation documentation	Cite independently audited performance
Abstractness	Service consumption episode	Capture and display typical customers benefiting from the service
Impalpability	Service process episode	Present a vivid documentary on the step-by-step service process
	Case history episode	Present an actual case history of what the firm did for a specific client
	Service consumption episode	An articulate narration or depiction of a customer's subjective experience

Source: Banwari Mittal and Julie Baker, "Advertising Strategies for Hospitality Services," *Cornell Hotel and Restaurant Administration Quarterly* 43 (April 2002): 53.Copyright Cornell University. All rights reserved. Used by permission.

national consulting firm, to dramatize the abstract notion of helping clients capitalize on innovative ideas in a fast-moving world. It features the champion golfer Tiger Woods in eye-catching situations to highlight the firm's ability to help clients "develop the reflexes of a high-performance business" (Figure 6.2).

A successful campaign right from the time it was launched in October 1997, MasterCard television and print advertisements emphasize the tangible things that can be purchased with its credit card—complete with a listing of the price of each item. In each ad, the final item on the list is the "priceless" experience resulting from all of the purchased items (a clever and memorable reference to the concept of intangibility.) Research Insights 6.1 on page 165 shows how visualization and comparative advertising affect consumer perceptions of both utilitarian and hedonic (pleasurable) services.

Using Metaphors to Communicate the Value Proposition

Some companies have created metaphors that are tangible in nature to help communicate the benefits of their service offerings. Insurance companies often use this approach to market their highly intangible products. Thus Allstate advertises that "You're in Good Hands"; Prudential uses the Rock of Gibraltar as a symbol of corporate strength; and—as we saw in Chapter 2—Equitable Life of Canada uses a lighthouse as a symbol reflecting strength, stability, and reliability. Professional service firms sometimes use metaphors to communicate their value propositions more dramatically. Where possible, advertising metaphors should highlight *how* service benefits are actually provided.[6] Cisco Canada uses the metaphor of an empty meeting room to convey a key benefit of its Unified Communications Solution offering—making business a priority and location irrelevant. (Figure 6.3).

The challenge facing DHL, the international logistics and delivery firm, was to promote the efficiency of its import express service. Its advertising agency's clever solution was to use the easily grasped metaphor of a heavily knotted string to represent how complex importing can be, and a straight, unknotted string to show how easy it would be using DHL's service (Figure 6.4 on page 166).

Figure 6.2
Accenture promotes its ability to turn innovative ideas into results.

Courtesy of Accenture.

Figure 6.3
CISCO uses metaphors to communicate its value proposition.

Visualization and Comparative Advertising for Services

Experts often recommend using visual stimuli and documentation to communicate the value proposition of a service, as a way of overcoming service intangibility and to better communicate a firm's value proposition. To test the effectiveness of visualization and documentations strategies for hedonic services (those that bring pleasure and enjoyment) and utilitarian services (those that are consumed for practical or functional purposes), four academic researchers conducted a laboratory experiment.

They showed the 160 participating student subjects one print advertisement each, and then measured their responses. A spring break travel service was used as the hedonic service in the study, and a bank with specific student offers for the utilitarian service. In the visualization condition, one picture of the hotel and one of young adults in an ocean-side pool were added to the text for the hedonic service. For the bank, photos of the exterior of the bank building and an ATM were shown. The study then compared the text-only condition with the ad that contained the pictures. Documentation was operationalized using an indirect comparative advertising copy stating the high performance of the service provider in the three most important categories of attributes for the two services.

The findings showed that for both types of services, ads based on a visualization strategy were perceived as more informative than text-only ads. Participants who viewed the visualization ads perceived the services to be of higher quality, and were more likely to say they intended to use these services. By contrast, documentation worked well for the hedonic service but not the utilitarian one (further research is needed to explain why).

The study has two important managerial implications:

1. Use pictures to tangibilize the value proposition. Whether you market a hedonic or a utilitarian service, use pictures and photos to communicate the potential benefits of your service. For example, Hilton Hotels Corp. started using photos to market its Chef's Signature Catering Collection, replacing its more traditional method of sending text-only menu information to clients who wanted to plan a dinner at the hotel. One Hilton executive noted, "people eat with their eyes, and when they see something they can relate to, something they can recognize, it develops a level of confidence and comfort level for the customer."

2. Documentation helps readers to visualize, especially hedonic services. The study indicated that hedonic services can benefit from adding comparative information into their ads. For example, if Six Flags Great America advertises that its Déjà Vu roller coaster is 60 metres tall, compared to the 36 metres of other top roller coasters, and that its speed is up to 104 kilometres per hour compared to only 80 to 96 kilometres per hour for other roller coasters, then one should expect readers to better visualize the Déjà Vu as one of the tallest and fastest roller coasters in the world. Simply listing its height and speed alone, without comparators, wouldn't be as effective. Readers need the benchmark provided by the comparative information.

Source: Adapted from Donna J. Hill, Jeff Blodgett, Robert Baer, and Kirk Wakefield, "An Investigation of Visualization and Documentation Strategies in Service Advertising," *Journal of Service Research* 7/2 (November 2004): 155–66.

Facilitate Customer Involvement in Production

When customers are actively involved in service production, they need training to help them perform well—just as employees do. Improving productivity often involves innovations in service delivery. But the desired benefits won't be achieved if customers resist new, technologically based systems or avoid self-service alternatives.

One approach to training customers, recommended by advertising experts, is to show service delivery in action. Television is a good medium because of its ability to engage the viewer as it displays a seamless sequence of events in visual form. Herzig Eye Institute, a laser vision-correction service provider with four locations in the greater Toronto area, routinely advertises on television, focusing on various aspects of the service process. In addition, potential customers can visit the company website (www.herzigeye.com) and access videos describing the procedure, as well as video answers, by all four surgeons affiliated with the institute, to frequently asked questions (FAQs). Another example, also located in Toronto, is the Shouldice Hospital, featured in Case 15 on page 566, which specializes exclusively in hernia repair. It offers prospective patients an opportunity to

Figure 6.4

DHL uses a clever metaphor to communicate its value proposition.

view an online simulation of hernia repair, and explains the hospital experience on their website (www.shouldice.com). This educational technique helps patients prepare mentally for the experience and shows them what role they need to play in service delivery to ensure a successful surgery and satisfying experience.

Advertising and publicity can make customers aware of changes in service features and delivery systems. Marketers often use sales promotions to motivate customers, offering them incentives to make the necessary changes in their behaviour. Publicizing price discounts is one way to encourage self-service on an ongoing basis. At self-service gas pumps, for instance, the price difference from full-service is often substantial. EastLink, a telecommunications company based in Halifax, offers a one-time discount if customers switch from the regular monthly invoicing to either a pre-authorized chequing (PAC) or a pre-authorized credit card (PACC) option. Besides using sales promotions, discounts, and incentives,[7] other inducements to change include promotions that offer a chance to win a reward. And if necessary, well-trained customer-contact personnel can also provide one-to-one tutoring to help customers adapt to new procedures.

Help Customers to Evaluate Service Offerings

Even if customers understand what a service is supposed to do, they may have difficulty distinguishing one firm from another and knowing what level of performance to expect from a particular supplier. Possible solutions include providing tangible clues related to service performance; highlighting the quality of equipment and facilities; and emphasizing employee characteristics, such as their qualifications, experience, commitment, and professionalism.

Some performance attributes lend themselves better to advertising than others. When an airline wants to boast about its punctuality, reporting favourable statistics collected by a government agency offers credible support for this claim. However, airlines don't like to talk overtly about safety, because even the admission that things *might* go wrong makes many passengers nervous. Instead, they approach this ongoing customer concern indirectly, advertising the expertise of their pilots, the newness of their aircraft, and the skills and training of their mechanics. To communicate the concept of customer care, WestJet launched a campaign in September 2005 where the advertisements featured various WestJet employees, from a call-centre customer service representative to a pilot, talking about actions taken by WestJet to enhance customer care (Figure 6.5). The reason employees were featured in these advertisements was to drive home the message that these people care because they are also WestJet owners (more than 80 percent of WestJet employees own company shares).

In low-contact services, where much of the firm's expertise is hidden, firms may need to illustrate equipment, procedures, and employee activities that are taking place backstage. For instance, how do credit card users know if their card information is secure and is not being used fraudulently by someone else? One approach is to show how the firm is trying to reduce such occurrences. VISA Canada has run ads using attention-getting headlines like "It's not a perfect copy if it doesn't work," which shows a fake pencil impression of a credit card. Also mentioned in the advertisement is how, along with various other security measures, the company uses neural networks to monitor unusual spending patterns so as to "stop possible fraud before it can even start."

Stimulate or Dampen Demand to Match Capacity

Many live service performances—like a seat at the theatre for Friday evening's performance, or a haircut at Supercuts on Tuesday morning—are time-specific and can't be stored for resale at a later date. Advertising and sales promotions can help to change the timing of customer use, and thus help to match demand with the capacity available at a given time.

Demand-management strategies include reducing usage during peak demand periods and stimulating it during off-peak periods. Low demand outside peak periods poses a serious problem for service industries with high fixed costs, such as hotels. One strategy is to run promotions that offer extra value—such as a room upgrade and a free breakfast, in an attempt to stimulate demand without decreasing price. When demand increases, the

Figure 6.5

WestJet uses employees to promote the message of customer care.

number of promotions can be reduced or eliminated. For example, resorts in the Ontario cottage country area of Muskoka routinely run promotions in the off-peak seasons of fall and winter that are not available during the peak times of spring and summer.

Promote the Contribution of Service Personnel

In high-contact services, frontline personnel are central to service delivery. Their presence makes the service more tangible and, in many cases, more personalized. An ad that shows employees at work helps prospective customers understand the nature of the service encounter and implies a promise of the personalized attention that they can expect to receive. The promotional strategy of Singapore Airlines is a case in point; a consistent feature of all their communications efforts is the image of the "Singapore Girl" portraying the culture of hospitality for its passengers.

Advertising, brochures, and websites can also show customers the work that goes on behind the scenes to ensure good service delivery. Highlighting the expertise and commitment of employees whom customers normally never encounter may enhance trust in the organization's competence and commitment to service quality.

Advertisers must be reasonably realistic in their depictions of service personnel, since their messages help set customers' expectations. If a firm's communications show friendly, smiling workers when, in reality, most employees turn out to be glum, frazzled, or rude, customers will most certainly be disappointed. At a minimum, service personnel should be informed about the content of new advertising campaigns or brochures.

SETTING COMMUNICATION OBJECTIVES

What role should communication play in helping a service firm achieve its marketing goals? A useful checklist for marketing-communications planning is provided by the "5 Ws" model:

- <u>W</u>ho is our target audience?
- <u>W</u>hat do we need to communicate and achieve?
- *Ho<u>w</u>* should we communicate this?
- <u>W</u>here should we communicate this?
- <u>W</u>hen do the communications need to take place?

Let's consider the issues of defining the target audience and specifying communication objectives. Then we'll review the wide array of communication tools available to service marketers. Issues relating to the location and scheduling of communication activities tend to be situation-specific, and so we will not address them here.

Target Audience Prospects, users, and employees represent three broad target audiences, each of which can be further divided. Because marketers of consumer services do not usually know prospects in advance, they usually need to employ a traditional communications mix, comprising such elements as media advertising, public relations, and use of purchased lists for direct mail or telemarketing. By contrast, more cost-effective channels may be available to reach existing users, including selling efforts by customer contact personnel, point-of-sale promotions, and other information distributed during service encounters. If the firm has a membership relationship with its customers and has a database containing contact information, it can distribute highly targeted information through direct mail, email, or telephone. These channels may serve to complement and reinforce the broader, less targeted communications channels, or simply replace them.

Employees serve as a secondary audience for communication campaigns through public media. A well-designed campaign targeted at users, non-users, or both can also be motivating for employees, especially those who play front-stage roles. In particular, it may help to shape employees' behaviour if the advertising content shows them what is being promised to customers. However, there's a risk of generating cynicism among employees

Table 6.2 Common Educational and Promotional Objectives in Service Settings

- Create memorable images of specific companies and their brands.
- Build awareness of and interest in an unfamiliar service or brand.
- Build preference by communicating the strengths and benefits of a specific brand.
- Compare a service with competitors' offerings and counter competitive claims.
- Reposition a service relative to competing offerings.
- Stimulate demand in low-demand periods and discourage demand during peak periods.
- Encourage trial by offering promotional incentives.
- Reduce uncertainty and perceived risk by providing useful information and advice.
- Provide reassurance, such as by promoting service guarantees.
- Familiarize customers with service processes in advance of use.
- Teach customers how to use a service to their own best advantage.
- Recognize and reward valued customers and employees.

and actively demotivating them if the communication in question promotes levels of performance that employees regard as unrealistic or even impossible to achieve (particularly if they are considered unrealistic because of a perceived lack of support or training from management). Communications directed specifically at staff are normally part of an internal marketing campaign, using company-specific channels, and so are not accessible to customers. We will discuss internal communications in Chapter 11.

Specifying Communication Objectives   Marketers need to be clear about their goals, otherwise it will be difficult to formulate specific communications objectives and select the most appropriate messages and communication tools to achieve them. Table 6.2 presents a list of common educational and promotional objectives for service businesses. Objectives may include shaping and managing customer behaviour in any of the three stages of the purchase and consumption process that we discussed in Chapter 2: the pre-purchase, service encounter, and post-consumption stages.

Key Planning Considerations   Planning a marketing communications campaign should reflect a good understanding of the service product and how well prospective buyers can evaluate its characteristics in advance of purchase. It's essential to understand target market segments and their exposure to different media, as well as consumers' awareness of the product and their attitudes toward it. Decisions include determining the content, structure, and style of the message to be communicated, its manner of presentation, and the media most suited to reaching the intended audience. Additional considerations include: the budget available for execution; time frames (as defined by such factors as seasonality, market opportunities, and anticipated competitive activities), and methods of measuring and evaluating performance.

THE MARKETING COMMUNICATIONS MIX

Most service marketers have access to numerous forms of communication, referred to collectively as the *marketing communications mix*. Different communication elements have distinctive capabilities relative to the types of messages that they can convey and the market segments most likely to be exposed to them. As shown in Figure 6.6, the mix includes personal contact, advertising, publicity and public relations, sales promotion, instructional materials, and corporate design.

Communication experts draw a broad division between *personal* communications (those in the left-hand column of boxes in Figure 6.6), which involve personalized messages that move in both directions between the two parties—such as personal selling, telemarketing, customer training, customer service, and word of mouth—and *impersonal* communications (a much larger group of possibilities depicted in the other five columns), in which messages move in only one direction and are generally targeted at a large group of customers and prospects rather than at a single individual.

Figure 6.6 The Marketing Communications Mix for Services

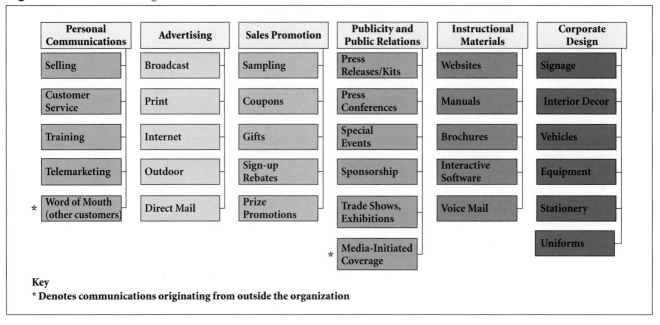

Personal Communications	Advertising	Sales Promotion	Publicity and Public Relations	Instructional Materials	Corporate Design
Selling	Broadcast	Sampling	Press Releases/Kits	Websites	Signage
Customer Service	Print	Coupons	Press Conferences	Manuals	Interior Decor
Training	Internet	Gifts	Special Events	Brochures	Vehicles
Telemarketing	Outdoor	Sign-up Rebates	Sponsorship	Interactive Software	Equipment
* Word of Mouth (other customers)	Direct Mail	Prize Promotions	Trade Shows, Exhibitions	Voice Mail	Stationery
			* Media-Initiated Coverage		Uniforms

Key
* Denotes communications originating from outside the organization

However, technology has created a grey area between personal and impersonal communications. For instance, firms often combine word-processing technology with information from a database to create an impression of personalization. This includes communication efforts in the form of direct mail and email messages containing a personal salutation and perhaps some reference to your specific situation or past use of a particular service. A personalized letter or email from the automobile service provider that serviced your car two days ago, seeking feedback on the quality of service, is an example. Similarly, interactive software, voice recognition technology, and computer-generated voice prompts and responses can simulate a two-way conversation. A few firms are beginning to experiment with web-based agents, on-screen simulations that move, speak, and even change expression.

New Opportunities for Highly Targeted Communications

With the advance of on-demand technologies, consumers are increasingly empowered to decide how and when they like to be reached. This development is transforming marketing communications on television, radio and the internet (see Service Perspectives 6.1 on page 172).

Communications Originate from Different Sources

As shown in Figure 6.7 on page 171, not all communications messages received by the target audience originate from the service provider. Specifically, word-of-mouth and media stories or editorials originate from outside the organization and are not under its direct control. Messages from an internal source can be divided into those received through production channels and those transmitted through marketing channels. Let's look at the options within each of these three originating sources.

Messages Transmitted through Production Channels

This category comprises communications developed within the organization and transmitted through the production channels that deliver the service itself—primarily service outlets and front-line staff. A further subdivision exists when the originating service firm employs intermediaries to deliver service.

Customer Service from Front-Line Staff Employees in front-line positions may serve customers face to face or by telephone. Customers' perceptions of the firm are

Figure 6.7 Sources of Messages Received by a Target Audience

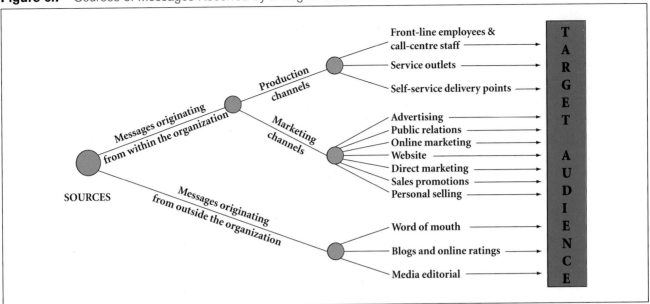

Source: Adapted from a diagram by Adrian Palmer, *Principles of Services Marketing*, 4th ed., London: McGraw-Hill, 2005: 397

shaped by how they view these individuals.[8] For example, customers of Enterprise Rent-A-Car are pleasantly surprised by the professional appearance of its customer-contact personnel. In contrast to other rental car firms, male employees wear suits and females wear dresses or smart skirts. In short, they dress in such a way as to differentiate themselves from the competition.[9] Those responsible for delivering the core service may also be responsible for delivery of a variety of supplementary services, such as providing information, taking reservations, receiving payments, and solving problems. New customers, in particular, often rely on customer service personnel for assistance in learning how to use a service effectively and how to resolve problems.

When several different products are available from the same supplier, firms encourage their customer-service staff to cross-sell additional services. However, this approach is likely to fail if strategies are not properly planned and executed.[10] In the banking industry, for example, a highly competitive marketplace and new technologies have forced banks to add more services in an attempt to increase their profitability. In many banks, tellers who traditionally provided customer service are now expected to promote new services to their customers as well. Despite training, many employees feel uncomfortable in this role and don't perform as effectively as salespeople.

Customer Training   Some companies, especially those selling complex B2B services, offer formal training courses to familiarize their customers with the service product and teach them how to use it to their best advantage. Alternatively (or additionally), this task may be assigned to the same front-line personnel who handle service delivery.

Many firms offer customer-education training programs and resources to their clients to promote increased and effective usage of their services. Customers learn how to use and benefit from the full potential of service offerings. In January 2006, Microsoft Canada launched Microsoft Small Business +, a free online resource for their small business customers that gives them access to business and software training, market research, and customized technical support and content. The aim of this training resource is to allow their customers to better plan their technology investments, improve their technology skills, and also enhance productivity. Commenting on the value of this training resource, Beth Stefaniuk, VP of Group Client Services at Blevins Insurance Group, said, "I have never seen anything like Small Business + before and am excited that Microsoft is taking initiative and really helping small business get a handle on how they are using technology and providing business training

Service Perspectives 6.1

New Media: Their Implications for Marketing Communications

Technology has created some exciting new communications channels, offering important opportunities for targeting. Among the key developments are on-demand television technologies (TiVos/VODs/PVRs), Podcasting, and Pop-ups.

TiVo (also known as Digital Video Recorder (DVR)) can record programs digitally on its hard disk, very much like a VCR. However, unlike a VCR, TiVo is "always on" and continuously recording. While the recording capacity can vary from 35 hours to over 300 hours—depending on size of the hard-disk drive, the signal quality, and the type of programming recorded—one can only pause the TV for 30 minutes. After 30 minutes, programming resumes, albeit 30 minutes behind real time. That allows users to watch a TV program after the broadcast has started so that they can fast-forward and skip the commercials. (While the TiVo service has recently become available in Canada, TiVo boxes are not, at the time of writing, sold in Canada, and Canadian residents have to purchase and import boxes from the United States. Moreover, if the TiVo unit is defective, a replacement unit sent under warranty can only be delivered to a U.S. address.) In Canada, the more popular technologies are **VOD** (Video on Demand) as well as the **PVR** (Personal Video Recorders).

According to a Solutions Research Group study, in 2005 more than a million Canadians were experiencing on-demand television either through VOD or their PVRs. Further, approximately 36 percent of all digital cable households in Canada had used VOD, and roughly 10 percent had a PVR. While not yet impressive, these percentages are likely to be just a prelude to what's to come. According to Kaan Yigit, the study director, "We are on the early part of the growth curve for on-demand television in Canada . . . and there is every indication of strong growth ahead based on very positive consumer response to technologies that offer greater flexibility and control." With the extremely high advertisement-avoidance rates that these technologies typically lead to, marketers will have to respond quickly by experimenting with options beyond their traditional 30- or 60-second spots. Creative strategies such as "telescopic" advertising may be an option, whereby advertisements featuring multiple stored layers of video are created, giving viewers control over the amount of advertising content they want to access.

Podcasting. This term comes from the words "iPod" and "broadcasting." It refers to a group of technologies for distributing audio or video programs over the internet using a publisher/subscriber model. Podcasting enables independent producers to create self-published, syndicated "shows," and gives broadcast radio or television programs a new distribution method. Subscribing to podcasts allows users to collect individual programs from a variety of sources for replay at the user's convenience. Initially, podcasting spread rapidly through word-of-mouth via the already popular weblogs of early podcasters and podcast listeners. Blogger and technology columnist Doc Searls kept track of how many "hits" Google found for the word "podcasts." There were 24 hits on 28 September 2004, 526 hits on September 30, and 2750 hits three days later. The number doubled every few days, passing 100 000 by October 18, 2004; a year later, Google recorded over 100 million hits.

While podcasters took advantage of the sound-file synchronization feature of Apple Computer's iPod and iTunes software, the technology had always been compatible with other players and programs.

Traditional broadcasters have been quick to adopt the podcasting format. National broadcasters such as CBC Radio and TSN now offer a variety of their programs in the podcast format, such as the Quirks and Quarks Show (CBC) and The NHL Insider (TSN).

Pop-ups. Pop-ups refer to a form of web ad that launches automatically in a new browser window when a web page is loaded. The problem with pop-ups is that they are often regarded as annoying and intrusive, distracting web users with unrequested commercial messages. Recent research findings by Chan, Dodd, and Stevens suggest that many people have a strong and intense dislike for pop-up ads, resulting in a negative attitude toward the advertiser and even the website from which the pop-up is launched. Pop-ups cause damage if they create a poor online experience (which they tend to do since they slow down the loading of the page the user actually wants to see), and viewers have learned to ignore pop-up ads in their various forms, often closing the pop-up window before the message can even be seen or read, or blocking them from opening altogether through pop-up blockers. With so many disadvantages to pop-ups, service companies need to think carefully before employing this tool.

Sources: TiVo website: www.tivo.com, accessed April 5, 2006; Kaan Yigit and Stacey Atkin, "On-Demand TV Use Surges In Canada" (news release, August 23, 2005), available online at www.srgnet.com, accessed on April 5, 2006; W. Friedman "PVR Users Skip Most Ads," *Advertising Age* (July 1, 2002): 4, 45; N. Reading, "Next Level Please: An Investigation into the Effectiveness of Telescopic Advertising Facilitated Through PVRs," unpublished thesis, Perth: Murdoch University, 2002; Kenneth C. Wilbur, "Modeling the Effects of Advertisement-avoidance Technology on Advertisement-supported Media: The Case of Digital Video Recorders," Mimeo Working Paper, University of Virginia, 2004; Sean Silverthorne, "TiVo Ready to Fast Forward?" *HBS Working Knowledge,* 15 November 2004; Doc Searls, "DIY Radio with PODcasting," Doc Searls' IT Garage, September 28, 2004, available online at www.itgarage.com/node/462, accessed December 20, 2005; Anne Chan, Jon Dodd, and Robert Stevens, "The Efficacy of Pop-ups and the Resulting Effect on Brands: A White Paper by Bunnyfoot Universality," 2004, available online at www.bunnyfoot.com/bunnyfoot_popup.pdf, accessed December 20, 2005.

too." She added, "We have just started to use this resource but found the training modules helped us do more with the technology, and Canadian market research will help us make more informed business decisions and technology decisions in the future."[11]

Service Outlets   Both planned and unintended messages reach customers through the medium of the service delivery environment itself. Impersonal messages can be distributed in the form of banners, posters, signage, brochures, video screens, and audio. As noted in other chapters, the physical design of the service outlet—what we call the *servicescape*—also sends a message to customers.[12] Corporate design consultants are sometimes asked to advise on servicescape design, to co-ordinate the visual elements of both interiors and exteriors so that they may complement and reinforce the positioning of the firm and shape the nature of the customers' service experiences in desired ways.

Messages Transmitted through Marketing Channels

As shown earlier in Figure 6.6 (p. 170), service marketers have a wide array of communication tools at their disposal. We will now briefly review the principal elements.

Personal Selling   Interpersonal encounters in which efforts are made to educate customers and promote preference for a particular brand or product are referred to as personal selling. Many firms, especially those marketing business-to-business services, maintain dedicated salesforces or employ agents and distributors to undertake personal selling efforts on their behalf. For infrequently purchased services like property, insurance, and funeral services, the firm's representative may act as a consultant to help buyers make their selections.

Relationship-marketing strategies are often based on account-management programs, where customers are assigned a designated account manager who acts as an interface between the customer and the supplier. Account management is commonly practised in industrial and professional firms that sell relatively complex services, resulting in an ongoing need for advice, education, and consultation. Examples of account management for individual consumers can be found in insurance, investment management, and medical services.

However, face-to-face selling to new prospects is expensive. A lower-cost alternative is *telemarketing*, involving use of the telephone to reach prospective customers. At the

Research Insights 6.2

Making Electronic Recommendation Agents More Effective

Consumers often face a bewildering array of choices when purchasing goods and services from online vendors. One way in which etailers try to assist consumers is to offer electronic recommendation agents as part of their service. Recommendation agents are relatively low-cost "virtual salespeople" designed to help consumers make their selections among large numbers of competing offerings by generating rank-ordered alternative lists based on consumer preferences. However, research by Lerzan Aksoy for her doctoral dissertation showed that many existing online agents rank options in different ways from the consumers they are designed to help. First, they weight product attributes differently from consumers; second, they may use alternative decision strategies that do not match the simple rules of thumb used by consumers themselves. The research simulated selection of a cellphone from among 32 alternatives, described on a website as each having differing features relating to price, weight, talk time, and standby time. The study results demonstrated that it helps consumers to use a recommendation agent, but only if it thinks like them, either in terms of attribute weights or decision strategies. When the ways in which agents work are completely dissimilar, then consumers may be no better off—and are sometimes worse served—than if they simply used a randomly ordered list of options. Even though the subjects in this research tended to defer to the agent's recommendations, those who felt it had a dissimilar decision strategy and dissimilar attribute weights from their own were less likely to come back to the website, recommend it to friends, or believe that the site had met their expectations well.

Source: Lerzan Aksoy, Paul N. Bloom, Nicholas H. Lurie, and Bruce Cooil, "Should Recommendation Agents Think Like People?" *Journal of Service Research* 8 (May 2006): 297–315.

consumer level, there is growing frustration with the intrusive nature of telemarketing, which is often timed to reach people when they are at home in the evening or at weekends.

Trade Shows   In the B2B marketplace, trade shows are a popular form of publicity that also combine important personal selling opportunities.[13] In many industries, trade shows stimulate extensive media coverage and offer business customers an opportunity to find out about the latest offerings from a wide array of suppliers in the field. Service vendors provide physical evidence in the form of exhibits, samples, and demonstrations, and brochures to educate and impress these potential customers. Trade shows can be very productive promotional tools, since it is one of the few situations in which large numbers of prospective buyers come to the marketer, rather than the other way around. A sales representative who usually reaches four to five prospective clients per day may be able to generate five qualified leads per *hour* at a show.

Advertising   As the most dominant form of communication in consumer marketing, advertising is often the first point of contact between service marketers and their customers, serving to build awareness, inform, persuade, and remind. It plays a vital role in providing factual information about services and educating customers about product features and capabilities. To demonstrate this role, Grove, Pickett, and Laband carried out a study comparing newspaper and television advertising for goods and services.[14] Based on a review of 11 543 television advertisements over a 10-month period, and of 30 940 newspaper display advertisements that appeared over a 12-month period, they found that ads for services were significantly more likely than those for goods to contain: factual information on prices, guarantees/warranties, documentation of performance, and availability (where, when, and how to acquire products).

One of the challenges facing advertisers is how to get their messages noticed. In general, people are tiring of ads in all their forms. A recent study by Yankelovich Partners, a marketing-services consultancy firm that aims to provide innovative, solutions-oriented consulting and research across a broad range of industries, says that consumer resistance to the growing intrusiveness of advertising has been pushed to an all-time high. The study found that 65 percent of people feel "constantly bombarded" by ad messages, and that

Figure 6.8

TELUS uses imagery inspired by nature to make its advertising for wireless high-speed networks stand out.

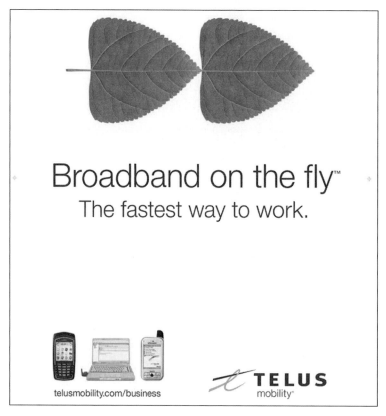

59 percent feel that ads have very little relevance to them.[15] Television and radio broadcasts are cluttered with commercials, while newspapers and magazines sometimes seem to contain more ads than news and features. How can a firm hope to stand out from the crowd? Longer, louder commercials and larger-format ads are not necessarily the answer. Some advertisers stand out by employing striking designs or a distinctively different format. Others, like TELUS, seek to catch the audience's attention by using a creative platform involving imagery inspired by nature, as it seeks to promote the benefits of its wireless network technology in a simple, clear, and unintimidating fashion (Figure 6.8).

Meantime, Royal Bank of Canada attempts to catch viewers' curiosity by using contrast, portraying the handful of seats that would be available on a Boeing 767 if booked with the loyalty reward points using another credit card, compared to all the seats available when booking with an RBC Avion card, which has no seating restrictions and no blackout periods (Figure 6.9).

A broad array of paid advertising media is available, including broadcast (TV and radio), print (magazines and newspapers), movie theatres, and many types of outdoor media (posters, billboards, electronic message boards, and the exteriors of buses or bicycles). Some media are more focused than others, targeting specific geographic areas or audiences with a particular interest. Advertising messages delivered through mass media are often reinforced by direct marketing tools like mailings, telemarketing, or email.

Despite being the most dominant form of communication in consumer marketing, the effectiveness of advertising remains hugely controversial. Conventional wisdom in the industry is that sales may well increase for a certain period even after the end of the advertising campaign. However, there comes a point when sales start to decline, and it becomes extremely expensive to rebuild the brand. Robert Shaw of Cranfield School of Management runs a forum in which large companies try to monitor the "marketing payback" from advertising. According to Shaw, the results were "never terribly good," with less than half of the ads generating a positive return on their investment.[16]

Direct Marketing This category embraces such tools as mailings, recorded telephone messages, faxes, and email. This channel offers the potential to send personalized messages to highly targeted micro-segments. Direct strategies are most likely to be

Figure 6.9
Royal Bank of Canada compares rewards offered by its Avion card with those available from other cards.

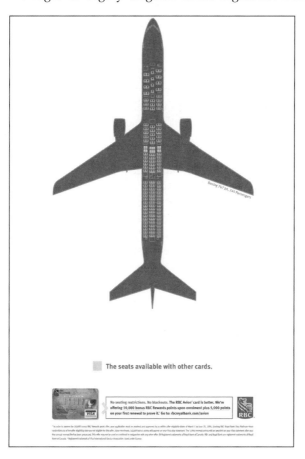

successful when marketers possess a detailed database of information about customers and prospects. Advances in on-demand technologies such as email spam filters, TiVo, VOD, PVRs, podcasting, and pop-up blockers empower consumers to decide how and when they prefer to be reached, and by whom. Because a 30-second television spot interrupts a viewer's favourite program, and a telemarketing call interrupts a meal, customers increasingly use such technologies to protect their time from such intrusions, thereby reducing the marketing effectiveness of the mass media. These developments give rise to *permission marketing*, where customers are encouraged to "raise their hands" and agree to learn more about a company and its products in anticipation of receiving useful marketing information or something else of value. Instead of annoying prospects by interrupting their personal time, permission marketing allows customers to self-select into the target segments.

In the permission-marketing model, the goal is to persuade consumers to volunteer their attention. By reaching out only to individuals who have expressed prior interest in receiving a certain type of message, permission marketing enables service firms to build stronger relationships with their customers. Email in combination with websites can, in particular, be integrated into a one-to-one permission-based medium.[17] For instance, people can be invited to register at the firm's website and can specify what type of information they would like to receive via email. These emails can be designed as the start of a more interactive, multi-layered communication process, where customers can request regular information about topics of their interest, and if they are particularly excited about a new service or piece of information, they can click on an URL embedded in the email to access a website with more in-depth information, video materials and so on, and to finally subscribe online to additional services, or recommend their friends, and the like.

The higher effectiveness of permission-based communications, combined with the falling prices and improving quality of customer-relationship management (CRM) and online technology (which together power permission-based marketing), has led many service firms to increase their focus on permission-based marketing strategies. To see how some firms have implemented excellent permission-based marketing strategies, go to Amazon.com or Hallmark.com and register at these websites.

Sales Promotion   A useful way of looking at sales promotions is as a communication attached to an incentive. Sales promotions are usually specific to a time period, price, or customer group—sometimes all three. Typically, the objective is to accelerate the purchasing decision, or motivate customers to use a specific service sooner, or in greater volume with each purchase, or more frequently.[18] Sales promotions for service firms may take such forms as samples, coupons, and other discounts, gifts, and competitions with prizes. Used in these forms, sales promotions add value, provide a "competitive edge," boost sales during periods when demand would otherwise be weak, speed the introduction and acceptance of new services, and generally get customers to act faster than they would in the absence of any promotional incentive.[19]

Some years ago, SAS International Hotels devised an interesting sales promotion targeted at older customers. If a hotel had vacant rooms, guests over 65 years of age could get a discount equivalent to their years (e.g., a 75-year-old could save 75 percent of the normal room price). All went well until a Swedish guest checked into one of the SAS chain's hotels in Vienna, announced his age as 102, and asked to be paid 2 percent of the room rate in return for staying the night. This request was granted, whereupon the spry centenarian challenged the general manager to a game of tennis—and got that, too. (The results of the game, however, were not disclosed!) Events like these are the stuff of dreams for PR people. In this case, a clever promotion led to a humorous, widely reported story that placed the hotel chain in a favourable light.

The ad shown in Figure 6.10 is a simple example of a sales promotion designed to encourage customers to buy a membership at a new Gold's Gym in Regina.

Public Relations   Public Relations (PR) involves efforts to stimulate positive interest in an organization and its products by sending out news releases, holding press conferences, staging special events, and sponsoring newsworthy activities put on by third parties. A basic element in public relations strategy is the preparation and distribution of press releases (including photos and/or videos) that feature stories about the company, its

Figure 6.10

A new Gold's Gym uses sales promotions to get customers.

products, and its employees. PR executives also arrange press conferences and distribute press kits when they feel a story is especially newsworthy. A key task performed by corporate PR specialists at many service organizations involves teaching senior managers how to present themselves well at news conferences or in radio and television interviews, especially at times of crisis for their company, or when faced with hostile questioning.

Other widely used PR techniques include recognition and reward programs, obtaining testimonials from public figures, community involvement and support, fundraising, and obtaining favourable publicity for the organization through special events and *pro bono* work. These tools can help a service organization build its reputation and credibility, form strong relationships with its employees, customers, and the community, and secure an image conducive to business success.

Firms can also win wide exposure through sponsorship of sporting events and other high-profile activities, where banners, decals, and other visual displays provide continuing repetition of the corporate name and symbol. For instance, the RBC has been the longest-running supporter of Canadian Olympic teams, since 1947. One way it supports the athletes is through the RBC Olympians program, where it hires a number of Canadian Olympic and Paralympic athletes who, acting as community ambassadors, participate in a number of events across the country. These activities, and the use of RBC logos by these athletes while competing in the Olympics and Paralympics, provide significant media exposure for the RBC. The winning athletes generate prestige for the bank, which can then incorporate this success in subsequent advertising campaigns for an extended period after the games. As a reward for its longstanding support of Canadian Olympic athletes, the Vancouver Organizing Committee for the 2010 Olympic and Paralympic Winter Games (VANOC) has chosen RBC as the premier national partner in the banking category.[20]

Unusual activities can present an opportunity to promote a company's expertise. FedEx gained significant favourable publicity when it safely transported two giant pandas from Chengdu, China, to the National Zoo in Washington, DC. The pandas flew in specially designed containers aboard a FedEx aircraft renamed "FedEx PandaOne." In addition to press releases, the company also featured information about the unusual shipment on a special page in its website.

Messages Originating from Outside the Organization   Some of the most powerful messages about a company and its products come from outside the organization and are not controlled by the marketer.

Word of Mouth (WOM)   Recommendations from other customers are generally viewed by potential customers as more credible than promotional activities initiated by the company itself, and can have a powerful influence on people's decisions to use (or avoid using) a service. In fact, the greater the risk that customers perceive in purchasing a service, the more actively they will seek, and rely on, WOM to guide their decision-making.[21] Customers who are less knowledgeable about a service rely more on WOM than expert consumers.[22] WOM even takes place during service encounters. When customers talk with each other about some aspect of service, this information can influence both their behaviour and their satisfaction with the service.[23] Frederick Reichheld argues that whether or not customers are willing to give positive WOM for a firm is the single most important predictor of top-line growth.[24]

Because WOM can act as such a powerful and highly credible selling agent, some marketers employ a variety of strategies to stimulate positive and persuasive comments from existing customers.[25] These include:

- Referencing other purchasers and knowledgeable individuals; for instance: "We have done a great job for ABC Corp., and if you wish, feel free to talk to Mr. Cabral, their MIS manager, who oversaw the implementation of our project."
- Creating exciting promotions that get people talking about the great service that the firm provides.
- Developing referral incentive schemes, such as offering an existing customer some units of free or discounted service in return for introducing new customers to the firm.
- Offering promotions that encourage customers to persuade others to join them in using the service, such as "Bring two friends, and the third eats for free" or "Subscribe to two mobile service plans, and we'll waive the monthly subscription fee for all subsequent family members."
- Presenting and publicizing testimonials that simulate WOM. Advertising and brochures sometimes feature comments from satisfied customers.

Research shows that the extent and content of WOM is related to satisfaction levels. Customers holding strong views, good or bad, are likely to tell more people about their experiences than those with milder views. And extremely dissatisfied customers tell more people than those who are highly satisfied.[26] Noting the important role that service employees play in customer satisfaction, Dwayne Gremler and his colleagues suggest that measures to improve the quality of customer–employee interactions may be an appropriate strategy for stimulating positive WOM.[27] Interestingly, even customers who were initially dissatisfied with a service can end up spreading positive WOM, if they are delighted with the way the firm handled service recovery.[28]

The ubiquity of the internet has accelerated the spread of personal influence, causing it to evolve into a "viral marketing" phenomena that businesses can ill afford to ignore.[29] Research Insights 6.3 details some research from 2004 on why and how people pass on emails. In fact, viral marketing, which takes advantage of networks among customers and prospects to influence attitudes and behaviours, has now become an industry in itself. One of the early success stories of viral marketing was the Hotmail free email service, which grew from zero to 12 million users in 18 months on a minuscule advertising budget, thanks mostly to the inclusion of a promotional message with Hotmail's URL in every email sent by its users.[30] EBay, and other firms engaged in electronic auctions, rely on users to rate sellers and buyers in order to build trust in the items offered on their websites and thereby facilitate transactions between strangers who, without access to such peer ratings, might be reluctant to transact on these sites.

Blogs: A New Type of Online WOM[31]   Web logs, commonly referred to a blogs, are becoming increasingly popular. Blogs are frequently modified web pages in which entries are listed in reverse chronological sequence, the newest appearing at the top. They

Research Insights 6.3

Pass Along Emails: Consumers' Motivations, Attitudes, and Behaviours

How can firms make better use of viral marketing and the habit of passing along (forwarding) emails? First, managers need to understand how consumers respond when they receive pass-along emails, what senders write in such messages, and what motivates recipients to forward them. The following three studies sought answers to these questions.

Study 1 explored how recipients responded to pass-along emails and how these communications differed from undesirable spam. Eight focus groups were conducted, involving a total of 66 individuals. Respondents considered emails as spam when the sender wasn't known. By contrast, the recipient typically knew who had sent them a pass-along email. When questioned about the types of viral messages they receive, there was consistent mention of jokes, followed by virus alerts, inspirational stories, religious messages, requests to vote on certain issues, lost children, chain letters, poems, animated clips, links to specific websites, and urban legends.

The positive emotions that recipients experienced when receiving what they viewed as meaningful messages ranged from simply *good* (e.g., "someone is thinking about me") and *brightens my day* ("when it's someone I haven't heard from in a while") to *excited* ("it's like seeing a letter in the mail . . . ") and *rewarded* ("when I get something from the church"). Negative emotions included *irritation* (e.g., when the message seemed irrelevant, felt like wasting time, or when an individual kept sending too many messages), *anger* (e.g., when an individual had asked to be taken off a list), *disappointment* (e.g., when a person wanted a more personal note from someone), to *skeptical* (if an offer looked too good to be true), *burdened* (e.g., when the recipient had too much work or felt overwhelmed or obliged to answer).

In *study 2*, the researchers conducted a content analysis of 1259 pass-along messages sent by 34 focus-group participants in order to better understand what type of messages were forwarded. The analysis revealed that 40 percent of messages were actually forwarded to others. The main reasons for not doing so involved messages that were perceived to be out of date, uninteresting, or inappropriate. Alternatively, respondents were in a rush and did not have time to forward messages. About one-third of the forwarded emails were sent with a personalized note, mostly to motivate the recipient to read the message. When recipients forwarded pass-along emails, the great majority did not change the subject line. Only a few of the forwarded emails concerned products, services, or companies, suggesting either that firms are not making much use of pass-along emails or that they are not using them effectively.

Study 3 focused on the reasons why people forward pass-along emails. The six top-rated reasons centred on enjoyment and entertainment (e.g., "it's fun," "I enjoy it," and "it's entertaining"), and social motivations (e.g., "to help others," and "to let others know I care about their feelings"). The findings also showed that for a message to be forwarded it must either be important or contain something the sender believes the recipient will like.

This research demonstrates untapped potential that exists for service marketers to use pass-along emails in their communications efforts. However, the findings also suggest that (1) firms need to be careful in crafting messages their target segments will find relevant enough to forward, and (2) the message content should spark emotions (e.g., humour, concern, or inspiration) and appeal to desires for fun, entertainment, and social connection, and finally, (3) firms should think carefully about the wording of the subject line as it is likely to be forwarded in unchanged format.

Source: Adapted from Joseph E. Phelps, Regina Lewis, Lynne Mobilio, et al., "Viral Marketing or Electronic Word-of-Mouth Advertising: Examining Consumer Responses and Motivations to Pass Along Emails," *Journal of Advertising Research* (December 2004): 333–48.

can be best described as online journals, diaries, or news listings, where people can post anything, about whatever they like. Their authors, known as bloggers, usually focus on narrowly focused topics, and quite a few have become de facto watchdogs and self-proclaimed experts in certain fields. Blogs can be about anything, ranging from baseball and sex to karate, financial engineering, and politics. There are a growing number of travel-oriented sites, ranging from Hotelchatter.com (focused on boutique hotels), CruiseDiva.com (reporting on the cruise industry), and pestiside.hu ("the daily dish of cosmopolitan Budapest"). Some sites, such as the travel-focused Tripadvisor.com, allow users to post their own reviews or ask questions that more experienced travellers may be able to answer.[32]

Marketers are interested in the way that blogs have evolved into a new form of social interaction on the web: a massively distributed but completely connected conversation covering every imaginable topic, including consumers' experiences with service firms and their recommendations on avoiding or patronizing certain firms. A byproduct of this online communication is the set of hyperlinks made between blogs in the exchange of dialogue. These links allow customers to share information with others and influence opinions of a brand or product—just google for the terms "Air Canada" or "Bell Canada" together with "blog" and you will see an entire list of blogs or blog entries relating to these service firms. A few savvy service firms have started monitoring blogs, viewing them as a form of immediate market research and feedback. Some service companies have even started their own blogs, see for example Auto Trader Canada's blog at http://canadaauto trader.blogspot.com/ or that for Vancouver's NHL hockey team, the Canucks, at http://blog.canucks.com/

Editorial Coverage   Although some media coverage of firms and their services is stimulated by public relations activity, broadcasters and publishers often initiate their own coverage. In addition to news stories about a company and its services, editorial coverage can take several other forms. Some columnists specialize in helping customers who have been unable to get complaints resolved. Investigative reporters may conduct an in-depth study of a company, especially if they believe it is putting customers at risk, cheating them, employing deceptive advertising, or otherwise exploiting them.

Such reports can end up having a significant impact on not only the marketing practices of the organization but also result in public policy changes. An investigation carried on by business reporter Grant Robertson of the *Calgary Herald* over the course of one year looked at the deceptive marketing practices of Direct Energy. In 2004 this UK-based energy company, which offers residential services in Alberta and Ontario, was in a position to be the leading energy supplier to Alberta families even though concerns about the marketing practices of this company in Ontario, and in some American states, had been brought before the Alberta government. After publication of this investigative report, the provincial government launched a consumer education program, and Direct Energy promised to bring about a number of changes in its sales tactics in addition to establishing independent monitoring. Robertson's report, titled "The Direct Sell," was awarded a 2004 Citation of Merit by the prestigious Michener Awards Foundation.[33]

Ethical Issues in Communication

Few aspects of marketing lend themselves so easily to misuse (and even abuse) as advertising, selling, and sales promotion. The fact that customers often find it hard to evaluate services makes them more dependent on marketing communication for information and advice. Communication messages often include promises about the benefits that customers will receive, and the quality of service delivery. When promises are made and then broken, customers are disappointed because their expectations have not been met.[34] Their disappointment and even anger will be even greater if they have wasted money, time, and effort, and have no benefits to show in return or have actually suffered a negative impact. Employees, too, may feel disappointed and frustrated as they listen to customers' complaints about unfulfilled expectations.

Some unrealistic service promises result from poor internal communications between operations and marketing personnel concerning the level of service performance that customers can reasonably expect. In other instances, unethical advertisers and salespeople deliberately make exaggerated promises to secure sales. Finally, there are deceptive promotions that lead people to think they have a much higher chance of winning prizes or awards than is really the case. Fortunately, there are many consumer watchdogs on the lookout for these deceptive marketing practices (seen earlier in the "Direct Sell" story). They include consumer protection agencies, trade associations within specific industries, and journalists who investigate customer complaints and seek to expose fraud and misrepresentation.

A different type of ethical issue concerns unwanted intrusion by aggressive marketers into people's personal lives. The increase in telemarketing, direct mail, and email is frustrating for those who receive unwanted sales communications. How do you feel if your evening meal at home is interrupted by a telephone call from a stranger trying to interest you in buying services in which you have no interest? And even if you are interested, you may feel, as many do, that your privacy has been violated. The Canadian Marketing

Association (CMA) offers a way for the consumers to remove their names from tele-marketing lists via its "Do Not Contact Service" (www.the-cma.org/consumer/donotcontact.cfm) in an attempt to address the growing hostility towards these types of direct-marketing techniques. This service is effective only to the extent that it applies to companies who are members of the CMA, so the interruption of your dinnertime by telemarketers is, sadly, by no means over!

THE ROLE OF CORPORATE DESIGN

Many service firms employ a unified and distinctive visual appearance for all tangible elements to facilitate recognition and reinforce a desired brand image. Corporate design strategies are usually created by external consulting firms and include such features as stationery and promotional literature, retail signage, uniforms, and colour schemes for painting vehicles, equipment, and building interiors. The objective is to provide a unifying and recognizable theme linking all the firm's operations in a branded service experience through the strategic use of physical evidence.

Corporate design is particularly important for companies operating in competitive markets where it's necessary to stand out from the crowd and to be instantly recognizable in different locations. For example, gasoline retailing provides striking contrasts in corporate designs, from Petro Canada's red and white service stations to Canadian Tire's use of red, white and green, and Sunoco's blue, maroon, and yellow.

Companies in the highly competitive express delivery industry tend to use their names as a central element in their corporate designs. When Federal Express changed its trading name to the more "modern" FedEx, it also changed its logo to feature the new name in a distinctive logo. Consistent applications of this design were developed for use in settings ranging from business cards to boxes and from employee caps to aircraft exteriors. When FedEx Corporation decided to rebrand a ground delivery service it had acquired, it chose the name FedEx Ground and developed an alternative colour treatment of the standard logo. Its goal was to transfer the positive image of the reliable, on-time service associated with its air cargo deliveries to its less expensive small-package ground service. The well-known air service was then rebranded as FedEx Express. Other sub-brands in what the firm refers to as "the FedEx family of companies" include FedEx Home Delivery (delivers to residential addresses), FedEx Freight (regional, less-than-truckload transportation for heavyweight freight), FedEx Custom Critical (non-stop, door-to-door delivery of time-critical shipments), FedEx Trade Networks (customs brokerage, international freight forwarding, and trade facilitation), FedEx Supply Chain Services (comprehensive suite of solutions that synchronize the movement of goods), and FedEx Kinko's (office and printing services located in retail stores).

Many companies use a trademarked symbol, rather than a name, as their primary logo.[35] The RBC has used its lion and globe design (with minor variations) for over four decades, making it one of the most recognizable symbols of corporate Canada. At a global level, McDonald's "Golden Arches" is said to be the most widely recognized corporate symbol, and is featured not only at its restaurants and on employee uniforms, but also in the company's advertising. However, international companies operating in many countries need to select their designs carefully to avoid conveying a culturally inappropriate message through unfortunate choices of names, colours, or images.

At a basic level, some companies have succeeded in creating tangible, recognizable symbols to associate with their corporate brand names. Animal motifs are common physical symbols for services across the globe. Examples include the stylized crane of the German airline Lufthansa, the lions of the Dutch bank ING as well as that of Canadian RBC Financial Group, the ram of the U.S. investment firm T. Rowe Price, and the Chinese dragon of Hong Kong's Dragonair. Easily recognizable corporate symbols are especially important when services are offered in markets where the local language is not written in roman script or where a significant proportion of the population is functionally illiterate.

The internet is now an integral part of marketing communications strategy. Perhaps its most remarkable aspect is its ubiquity: A website hosted in one country can be accessed from almost anywhere in the world, offering the simplest form of international market entry available—in fact, as Christian Grönroos points out, "the firm cannot avoid creating interest in its offerings outside its local or national market."[36] However, creating international access and developing an international strategy are two very different things.

Internet Marketing Offers Powerful Opportunities for Interactivity

Marketers use the internet for a variety of communications tasks. These tasks include promoting consumer awareness and interest, providing information and consultation, facilitating two-way communications with customers through email and chat rooms, stimulating product trial, enabling customers to place orders, and measuring the effectiveness of specific advertising or promotional campaigns. Firms can not only market through their own websites but can also place advertising on a variety of other sites. Advertising on the web allows companies to supplement conventional communications channels at a reasonable cost. But like any of the elements of the marketing communications mix, internet advertising should be part of an integrated, well-designed communications strategy.[37]

Enabling marketers to communicate and establish a rapport with individual customers is one of the web's greatest strengths. The interactive nature of the internet has the potential to increase customer involvement dramatically. In addition to facilitating email-based permission marketing, as discussed earlier in this chapter, the internet enables "self-service" marketing, in which individual customers control the nature and extent of their contact with those websites that they choose to visit. Many banks allow customers to pay bills electronically, apply for loans over the internet, and check their account balances online. Whistler/Blackcomb ski resort in British Columbia uses its website (www.whistlerblackcomb.com) to promote advance online purchase of lift tickets at a discount. This site also offers instructions on how the online ticket window works, describes where to pick up the tickets, and provides responses to frequently asked questions (FAQ).

Web Site Design Considerations

From a communication standpoint, a website should contain information that a company's target customers will find useful and interesting. Internet users expect speedy access, easy navigation, and content that is both relevant and up to date.

Service firms should set explicit communication goals for their websites. Is the site to be a promotional channel, a self-service option that diverts customers away from contact with service personnel, an automated newsroom that disseminates information about the company and its products, as well as offering an archive of past press releases? Or even all of these? Some firms choose to emphasize promotional content, seeking to present the firm and its products in a favourable light and to stimulate purchase; others view their sites as educational, and encourage visitors to search for needed information, even providing links to related sites.

Innovative companies are continually looking for ways to improve the appeal and usefulness of their sites. The appropriate communication content varies widely from one type of service to another. A B2B site may offer visitors access to a library of technical information (e.g., Siebel and SAP both provide substantial information on their customer-relationship management solutions at their respective websites, www.oracle.com/siebel/index. html and www.sap.com). By contrast, an MBA program website may include attractive photographs featuring the location, the facilities, past students, and short videos showing the university, its professors and facilities, student testimonials, and even the graduation ceremony. For example, see the website of the UCLA/National University of Singapore Executive MBA Program (of which one of us is currently academic co-director) at www. ucla.nus.edu.

Marketers must also address other attributes, such as downloading speed, that affect website "stickiness" (that is, its ability to make visitors willing to spend time on the site, and revisit it in the future). A sticky site has:

- *High quality content.* Relevant and useful content is king. A site needs to contain what visitors are looking for on the site.

- *Ease of use.* Easy to use means clear navigation between pages on the site, and a site structure that is well signposted, is not over-complicated, nor too big. Customers do not get lost on well-designed sites!

- *Quick download speed.* Viewers don't want to wait, and will often give up if it takes too long for pages to download from a site. Good sites download quickly, and bad sites are slow. That means all graphic elements, both static and dynamic, need to be compressed to the smallest feasible file size, and should be sparingly used, especially on the home page, which users generally arrive at first.

- *Frequent updates.* Good sites look fresh and up to date. They include recently posted information that visitors find relevant and timely.[38]

A memorable web address helps to attract visitors to a site. Ideally, it is based on the company's name (e.g., www.canadiantire.ca or www.westjet.com), although sometimes an alternative must be found if the simple form of the name has already been taken by a similarly named company in another industry. Ensuring that people are aware of the address requires displaying it prominently on business cards, letterhead stationery, email templates, brochures, advertising, promotional materials and even vehicles. EasyJet, one of the largest of the European discount airlines, has painted its address in huge orange letters on each of its aircraft (Figure 6.11).

Effective Advertising on the Internet

Internet advertising, also called "webvertising," has become an important part of the communications mix for most service firms. There are two main options: banner advertising and search-engine advertising. In each instance, advertisers can include moving images and create links to more extended video presentations.

Banner Advertising   Many firms pay to place advertising banners and buttons on portals like Yahoo or Netscape, as well as on other firms' websites. The usual goal is to draw online traffic to the advertiser's own site by providing links that users can "click through" to reach the advertised site. In many instances, websites include advertising

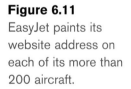

Figure 6.11

EasyJet paints its website address on each of its more than 200 aircraft.

Source: www.easyjet.com/EN/About/photogallery.html.
© easyJet airline company limited.

messages from other marketers with related but non-competing services. Yahoo's stock quotes page, for example, features a sequence of advertisements for various financial service providers. Similarly, many web pages devoted to a specific topic feature a small message from Amazon.com, inviting the reader to identify books on these same topics by clicking the accompanying hyperlink button to the internet retailer's site. In such instances, it's easy for the advertiser to measure how many visits to its own site are generated by click-throughs, and from which other site they came.

Simply obtaining a large number of exposures ("eyeballs") to a banner (a thin horizontal ad running across the top or bottom of all or part of a webpage), a skyscraper (a long skinny ad running vertically down one side of a website), or a button doesn't necessarily lead to increases in awareness, preference, or sales for the advertiser. One consequence is that the practice of paying a flat monthly rate for banner advertising is falling out of favour. Even when visitors click through to the advertiser's site, this action doesn't necessarily result in sales. Consequently, there's now more emphasis on advertising contracts that tie fees to marketing-relevant behaviour by these visitors, such as providing the advertiser with some information about themselves or making a purchase. Today, internet advertisers usually pay only if a visitor to the host site clicks through on the link to the advertiser's site. This is the equivalent of paying for the delivery of junk mail only to households that read it.[39]

Search-Engine Advertising   Search engines are a form of a reverse broadcast network. Instead of advertisers broadcasting their messages to consumers, search engines let advertisers know exactly what consumers want through their key word search, and advertisers can then target relevant marketing communications directly at these consumers.[40] One of the phenomenal success stories of internet advertising has been Google (see Service Perspectives 6.2), with firms like Yahoo!, AOL, and MSN also seeking to become major players in this field.

Advertisers have several options. They can pay for the placement of ads that are targeted by keyword searches relevant to the advertising firm; they can sponsor a short text message with a click-through link, located parallel to the search results; or they can buy top rankings in the display of search results through a "pay-for-placement" option. This last approach is somewhat controversial because it conflicts with users' expectations that the rankings will reflect the best fit with the keywords employed in the search, and the most visited sites among those fitting the keywords. Google's policy is to shade paid listings that appear at the top of the rankings column and identify them as "sponsored links." Pricing for these ads and placements can be based on either the number of impressions (i.e., the number of times a page has been viewed) or click-throughs, high scores for both of which are achieved by placing sponsored links at the top of search results.

Developing an Integrated Marketing Communications Strategy

Many service firms initially organized their website and online marketing activities into separate groups that were mostly isolated from other marketing activities. But when isolated, the firm's online communications—or for that matter any other market communications channel—can deliver messages with those from other channels, resulting in confused consumers who will not have a clear picture of a firm's positioning and value proposition.

Have you ever seen a new, exciting service promotion being touted at a firm's website only to find, when you then visited a branch office, that the counter staff were not aware of the promotion and couldn't sell it to you? What went wrong? In many service firms different departments look after different aspects of a firm's market communications. For example, the marketing department is in charge of advertising, the PR department of public relations, functional specialists look after a company's website and its direct marketing and promotions activities, operations deals with customer service, and HR with training.

Service Perspectives 6.2

Google: The Online Marketing Powerhouse

Graduate students Larry Page and Sergey Brin, who were both fascinated by mathematics, computers, and programming from an early age, founded Google in 1998. Seven years later, following Google's successful public offering, they had become billionaires, and Google itself had become one of the world's most valuable companies.

The company has the grand vision "to organize the world's information and make it universally accessible and useful." The utility and ease of its search engine has made it immensely successful, almost entirely through word of mouth from satisfied users. Few company names ever become verbs, but to "google" has already come to mean "to run a search on the internet's most popular search engine."

This popularity has enabled Google to become a new and highly targeted advertising medium, selling advertisements that appear next to its search results. Branded as Google AdWords, this service allows businesses to connect with potential customers at the precise moment when the latter are looking at related topics or even specific product categories. Specifically, firms buy the opportunity to be associated with particular search categories or terms. To explore Google's advertising business model, just "google" a few words and observe what appears on your screen in addition to the search results.

Google prices its "sponsored links" service as "cost per click." This price depends on the popularity of the search terms with which the advertiser wants to be associated. Heavily used terms such as "MBA" are more expensive than less popular terms such as "MSc in Business." Advertisers can easily keep track of their ad performance using the reports in Google's online account control centre.

Advertisers can also display their ads at websites that are part of the Google content network. Google calls them "site targeted ads." Advertisers can specify either individual websites or website content (e.g., about travel or baseball). Site targeting allows advertisers to handpick their target audiences, which can be really large (e.g., all hockey fans in Canada, or even in the world) or small and focused (e.g., people interested in fine dining in the greater Vancouver area). When an advertiser designs a site-targeted campaign, it can either name the sites where it would like to advertise or simply give Google a list of keywords that describes the site. The Google AdWords matching system then analyzes the terms and creates a list of available content network sites.

Google has also created a separate service called Google AdSense. It's a fast and convenient service targeted at website publishers of all sizes. In return for displaying relevant Google text and image ads on their website's content pages, publishers receive a share of the advertising revenue generated. It cites a number of success stories such as those of ScienceDaily (www.sciencedaily.com), an online publisher of contemporary stories and headlines on topics related to science and technology. To increase the revenue stream from online advertising (all company revenues come through this channel), ScienceDaily used Google's AdSense to deliver contextual ads. The result was that online advertising effectiveness increased, and by the end of 2005 AdSense accounted for 66 percent of total revenue generated through online advertising.

Google's ability to deliver an advertising medium that is highly targeted, contextual, and results-based has been extremely attractive to advertisers, and has led to rapid revenue growth and profits. It's no surprise that Google's success is frightening other advertising media.

Sources: Roben Farzad and Ben Elgin, "Googling for Gold," *BusinessWeek* (December 5, 2005): 60–70; www.google.com, accessed April 6, 2006.

The service failure described above is a consequence of these various departments not communicating with each other, and thus not co-ordinating their efforts effectively.

With so many channels delivering messages to customers and prospects, it becomes more and more important for firms to adopt the concept of integrated marketing communications (IMC). IMC ties together and reinforces all communications to deliver a strong brand identity. It means that a firm's various media deliver the same messages and have the same "look and feel," and messages from the different media and communications approaches all become part of a single, overall message about the service firm and its products. Firms can achieve this by giving ownership of IMC to a single department (e.g., marketing), or by appointing a marketing communications director who has overall responsibility for all of the firm's market communications.

Conclusion

The marketing communication strategy for services requires a somewhat different emphasis from that used to market goods. The communication tasks facing service marketers include emphasizing tangible clues for services that are difficult to evaluate, clarifying the nature and sequence of the service performance, highlighting the performance of customer-contact personnel, and educating the customer about how to participate in service delivery effectively.

Many different communication elements are available to help companies create a distinctive position in the market and reach prospective customers. The options in the marketing communication mix include personal communications, such as personal selling and customer service, as well as impersonal communications such as advertising, sales promotions, public relations, corporate design, and the physical evidence offered by the servicescape of the service delivery site. Instructional materials, from brochures to websites, often play an important role in educating customers on how to make good choices and obtain the best use from the services they have purchased. Developments in technology, especially the internet, are changing the face of marketing communications, driving innovations such as permission marketing, leading to exciting possibilities of highly targeted online advertising.

Review Questions

1. In what ways do the objectives of services communications differ substantially from those of goods marketing?

2. Which elements of the marketing communications mix would you use for each of the following scenarios? Explain your answers.

   - A newly established hair salon in a suburban shopping centre
   - An established restaurant facing declining patronage because of new competitors
   - A large, single-office accounting firm in a major city that serves primarily business clients

3. Discuss the relative effectiveness of brochures and websites for promoting (a) a ski resort, (b) a business school, (c) a fitness centre, and (d) an online broker.

4. Why is word of mouth considered to be so important for the marketing of services? How can a service firm that is the quality leader in its industry induce and manage good word of mouth?

5. Why is permission-based marketing gaining so much focus in service firms' communications strategies?

6. What do you see as the important opportunities and threats of viral marketing? How can service firms use viral marketing effectively, and how can they overcome its potential challenges?

7. Explain why weblogs are potentially powerful influencers in market spaces, particularly those with a high proportion of technologically savvy consumers.

8. What are the different forms of online marketing? Which do you think would be the most effective online marketing strategies for (a) an online broker, (b) a new discotheque in Montréal, and (c) a fine-dining restaurant in Halifax?

Application Exercises

1. Describe four common educational and promotional objectives in service settings, and provide a specific example for each of the objectives you list.

2. Identify one advertisement (or other means of communication) that aims mainly at managing consumer behaviour in each of the following: (a) choice, (b) consumption, and (c) post-consumption. Explain how they try to achieve their objectives, and discuss how effective they may be.

3. Use of telescopic advertisements is one way of addressing challenges faced by traditional advertisers because of the success of on-demand television technologies such as TiVo, VOD, and PVRs. Research and suggest other ways that television commercials may be designed to overcome the problem of high advertisement avoidance rates brought about by the use of these technologies.

4. Identify two cases of deceptive marketing practices used by service companies that have generated significant discussion in the media within the last five years. Has this coverage had any subsequent impact on the marketing practices of these firms? Also, have there been any public policy implications as a result of the coverage?

5. If you were to select now the university where you are currently studying, what could you learn from blogs and any other online WOM you can find? How would that information influence the decision of a prospective new applicant to your university? Given that you are an expert about the school and degree you are taking, how accurate do you think is the information you managed to find online?

6. Analyze public relations efforts being made by Canadian service firms in preparation for the Winter Olympics to be held in 2010 in Vancouver. Do you think that all firms would benefit from these efforts? Why? Why not?

7. What tangible cues could a diving school or a dentist use to position these services as appealing to upscale customers?

8. Track on a weekly basis over one month the websites of (a) a management consulting firm, (b) an internet retailer, and (c) an insurance company. Critique them based on the four factors that contribute to the stickiness of a site. What, if anything, would you change about each site?

9. Subscribe to www.chapters.indigo.ca and www.sears.ca, and analyze their permission-based communications strategy. What are their marketing objectives? Evaluate their permission-based marketing for a specific customer segment of your choice. What is excellent, what is good, and what could be further improved in terms of reaching this segment?

10. Conduct a Google search for (a) MBA programs in Canada, and (b) resort holidays in the Caribbean. Examine two or three contextual adverts that are triggered by your searches. Critique these ads: what are they doing right, and what can be improved?

Endnotes

1. For a useful review, see Kathleen Mortimer and Brian P. Mathews, "The Advertising of Services: Consumer Views v. Normative Dimensions," *Service Industries Journal* 18 (July 1998): 14–19.

2. James F. Devlin and Sarwar Azhar, "Life Would be a Lot Easier if We Were a Kit Kat: Practitioners' Views on the Challenges of Branding Financial Services Successfully," *Brand Management* 12/1, 2004: 12–30.

3. Banwari Mittal, "The Advertising of Services: Meeting the Challenge of Intangibility," *Journal of Service Research* 2 (August 1999): 98–116.

4. Banwari Mittal and Julie Baker, "Advertising Strategies for Hospitality Services," *Cornell Hotel and Restaurant Administration Quarterly* 43 (April 2002): 51–63.

5. Donna Legg and Julie Baker, "Advertising Strategies for Service Firms," in C. Surprenant (ed.), *Add Value to Your Service,* Chicago: American Marketing Association, 1987: 163–68. See also Donna J. Hill, Jeff Blodgett, Robert Baer, and Kirk Wakefield, "An Investigation of Visualization and Documentation Strategies in Service Advertising," *Journal of Service Research* 7/2 (November 2004): 155–66; and Debra Grace and Aron O'Cass, "Service Branding: Consumer Verdicts on Service Brands," *Journal of Retailing and Consumer Services* 12 (2005): 125–39.

6. Mittal (1999), op. cit.

7. EastLink website: www.eastlink.ca/ accessed April 2006.

8. For a framework and checklist to identify and sustain service brand values, see Leslie de Chernatony and Susan Drury, "Identifying and Sustaining Service Brands' Values," *Journal of Marketing Communications* 10 (June 2004): 73–93.

9. Leonard L. Berry, "Cultivating Service Brand Equity," *Journal of the Academy of Marketing Science* 28/1 (2000): 128–37.

10. David H. Maister, "Why Cross-Selling Hasn't Worked," from his *True Professionalism*, New York: Free Press, 1997: 178–84.

11. www.microsoft.com/canada/smallbiz/pressrelease/200 60131.mspx, accessed April 05, 2006.

12. Mary Jo Bitner, "Servicescapes: The Impact of Physical Surroundings on Customers and Employees," *Journal of Marketing* 56 (April 1992): 57–71.

13. Dana James, "Move Cautiously in Trade Show Launch," *Marketing News* (November 20, 2000): 4, 6; Elizabeth Light, "Tradeshows and Expos: Putting Your Business on Show," *Her Business* (March–April 1998): 14–18; and Susan Greco, "Trade Shows versus Face-to-Face Selling," *Inc.* (May 1992): 142.

14. Stephen J. Grove, Gregory M. Pickett, and David N. Laband, "An Empirical Examination of Factual Information Content among Service Advertisements," *Service Industries Journal* 15 (April 1995): 216–33.

15. "The Future of Advertising: The Harder Hard Sell," *The Economist* (June 24, 2004).

16. Ibid.

17. Seth Godin and Don Peppers, *Permission Marketing: Turning Strangers into Friends and Friends into Customers,* New York: Simon & Schuster, 1999; Ray Kent and Hege Brandal, "Improving Email Response in a Permission Marketing Context," *International Journal of Market Research* 45/4 (2003): 489–503.

18. Gila E. Fruchter and Z. John Zhang, "Dynamic Targeted Promotions: A Customer Retention and Acquisition Perspective," *Journal of Service Research* 7 (August 2004): 3–19.

19. Ken Peattie and Sue Peattie, "Sales Promotion: A Missed Opportunity for Service Marketers," *International Journal of Service Industry Management* 5/1 (1995): 6–21.

20. Information from various pages on www.rbc.com, accessed April 5, 2006.

21. Harvir S. Bansal and Peter A. Voyer, "Word-of-Mouth Processes Within a Services Purchase Decision Context," *Journal of Service Research* 3/2 (November 2000): 166–77.

22. Anna S. Mattila and Jochen Wirtz, "The Impact of Knowledge Types on the Consumer Search Process: An Investigation in the Context of Credence Services," *International Journal of Service Industry Management* 13/3 (2002): 214–30.

23. Kim Harris and Steve Baron, "Consumer-to-Consumer Conversations in Service Settings," *Journal of Service Research* 6/3 (2004): 287–303.

24. Frederick F. Reichheld, "The One Number You Need to Grow," *Harvard Business Review* 81/12 (2003): 46–55. Malcolm Gladwell explains how different types of epidemics, including word-of-mouth epidemics, develop. Malcolm Gladwell, *The Tipping Point*, New York: Little, Brown, 2000: 32.

25. Jochen Wirtz and Patricia Chew, "The Effects of Incentives, Deal Proneness, Satisfaction and Tie Strength on Word-of-Mouth Behaviour," *International Journal of Service Industry Management* 13/2 (2002): 141–62; Tom J. Brown, Thomas E. Barry, Peter A. Dacin, and Richard F. Gunst, "Spreading the Word: Investigating Antecedents of Consumers' Positive Word-of-Mouth Intentions and Behaviors in a Retailing Context," *Journal of the Academy of Marketing Science* 33/2 (2005): 123–38; and John E. Hogan, Katherine N. Lemon, and Barak Libai, "Quantifying the Ripple: Word-of-Mouth and Advertising Effectiveness," *Journal of Advertising Research* (September 2004): 271–80.

26. Eugene W. Anderson, "Customer Satisfaction and Word of Mouth," *Journal of Service Research* 1 (August 1998): 5–17; Magnus Söderlund, "Customer Satisfaction and Its Consequences on Customer Behaviour Revisited: The Impact of Different Levels of Satisfaction on Word of Mouth, Feedback to the Supplier, and Loyalty," *International Journal of Service Industry Management* 9/2 (1998): 169–88; Srini S. Srinivasan, Rolph Anderson, and Kishore Ponnavolu, "Customer Loyalty in e-Commerce: An Exploration of its Antecedents and Consequences," *Journal of Retailing* 78/1 (2002): 41–50.

27. Dwayne D. Gremler, Kevin P. Gwinner, and Stephen W. Brown, "Generating Positive Word-of-Mouth Communication through Customer–Employee Relationships," *International Journal of Service Industry Management* 12/1 (2000): 44–59.

28. Jeffrey G. Blodgett, Kirk L. Wakefield, and James H. Barnes, "The Effects of Customer Service on Consumers Complaining Behavior," *Journal of Services Marketing* 9/4 (1995): 31–42; Jeffrey G. Blodgett and Ronald D. Anderson, "A Bayesian Network Model of the Consumer Complaint Process," *Journal of Service Research* 2/4 (May 2000): 321–38; "Analyzing Service Failures and Recoveries: A Process Approach," *International Journal of Service Industry Management* 12/1 (2001): 20–33; and, "A Longitudinal Study of Complaining Customers' Evaluations of Multiple Service Failures and Recovery Efforts," *Journal of Marketing* 66/4 (2002): 57–72.

29. Renee Dye, "The Buzz on Buzz," *Harvard Business Review* (November–December 2000): 139–46; Sandeep Krishnarmurthy, "Viral Marketing: What Is It and Why Should Every Service Marketer Care?" *Journal of Services Marketing* 15 (2001): 422–24; Joseph E. Phelps, Regina Lewis, Lynne Mobilio, et al., "Viral Marketing or Electronic Word-of-Mouth Advertising: Examining Consumer Responses and Motivations to Pass Along Emails," *Journal of Advertising Research* (December 2004): 333–48.

30. Steve Jurvetson, "What Exactly is Viral Marketing?" *Red Herring* 78 (May 2000): 110–12.

31. This section draws from Lev Grossman, "Meet Joe Blog," *Time* (June 21, 2004): 65; S.C. Herring, L.A. Scheidt, E. Wright, and S. Bonus, "Weblogs as a Bridging Genre," *Information, Technology & People* 18/2 (2005): 142–71; C. Marlow, "Audience, Structure and Authority in the Weblog Community," paper presented at the International Communication Association Conference, New Orleans, 2004, available online at http://alumni.media.mit.edu/~cameron/cv/pubs/04-01.pdf, accessed December 19, 2005; Ericka Menchen Trevino, "Blogger Motivations: Power, Pull, and Positive Feedback," paper presented at AoIR 6.0, October 9, 2005, available online at http://blog.erickamenchen.net/MenchenBlogMotivations.pdf, accessed December 19, 2005.

32. Steven Kurutz, "For Travelers, Blogs Level the Playing Field," *New York Times* (August 7, 2005): TR-3.

33. Michener Awards Foundation website, www.michenerawards.ca/, accessed April 05, 2006; Calgary Herald Website, www.canada.com/calgaryherald/features/ directenergy/, accessed April 05, 2006.

34. Louis Fabien, "Making Promises: The Power of Engagement," *Journal of Services Marketing* 11/3 (1997): 206–14.

35. Abbie Griffith, "Product Decisions and Marketing's Role in New Product Development," in *Marketing Best Practices*, Orlando, FL: Dryden Press, 2000: 253.

36. Christian Grönroos, "Internationalization Strategies for Services," *Journal of Services Marketing* 13/4–5 (1999): 290–97.

37. Stefan Lagrosen, "Effects of the Internet on the Marketing Communication of Service Companies," *Journal of Services Marketing* 19/2 (2005): 63–69.

38. Paul Smith and Dave Chaffey, *eMarketing Excellence*. Oxford: Elsevier Butterworth-Heinemann, 2005: 173.

39. "The Future of Advertising", op. cit.

40. Catherine Seda, *Search Engine Advertising: Buying Your Way to the Top to Increase Sales*, Indianapolis, IN: New Riders Press, 2004: 4–5.

CHAPTER 7

Positioning Services in Competitive Markets

To succeed in our overcommunicated society, a company must create a position in the prospect's mind, a position that takes into consideration not only a company's own strengths and weaknesses, but those of its competitors as well.

—Al Reis and Jack Trout

The essence of strategy is choosing to perform activities differently than rivals do.

—Michael Porter

If you're trying to persuade people to do something, or buy something, it seems to me you should use their language, the language in which they think.

—David Ogilvy

Ask a group of managers from different service businesses how they compete, and the chances are high that many will say simply, "on service." Press them a little further, and they may add words and phrases like "value for money," "service quality," "our people", or "convenience."

None of this is very helpful to a marketing specialist who is trying to develop a value proposition and business model for a service product to enable it to compete profitably in the marketplace. At issue is what makes consumers or institutional buyers select—and remain loyal to—one supplier over another. Terms such as "service" typically subsume a variety of specific characteristics, ranging from the speed with which a service is delivered to the quality of interactions between customers and service personnel, and from avoiding errors to providing desirable "extras" to supplement the core service. Likewise, "convenience" could refer to a service that's delivered at a convenient location, available at convenient times, or easy to use. Without knowing which product features are of specific interest to customers, it's hard for managers to develop an appropriate strategy. In a highly competitive environment, there's a risk that customers will perceive little real difference between competing alternatives, and so make their choices based only on who offers the lowest price.

Positioning strategy is concerned with creating, communicating, and maintaining distinctive differences that will be noticed and valued by those customers with whom the firm would most like to develop a long-term relationship. Successful positioning requires managers to understand both their target customers' preferences, their conception of value, and the characteristics of their competitors' offerings. Pricing and product attributes are the two types of marketing variables most commonly associated with positioning strategy, but delivery systems, service schedules, and locations also play a role for many services.

In this chapter, we examine the need for focus in a competitive environment and review the issues involved in developing a positioning strategy. Specifically, we explore the following questions:

1. Why is it so important for service firms to adopt focused strategies in their choice of markets and products?

2. What is the distinction between important and determinant attributes in consumer decision making?

3. What are the key concepts underlying competitive positioning strategy for services?

4. When is it appropriate to reposition an existing service offering?

5. How can positioning maps help you to better understand and respond to competitive dynamics?

FOCUS UNDERLIES THE SEARCH FOR COMPETITIVE ADVANTAGE

As competition intensifies in the service sector, it's becoming ever more important for service organizations to differentiate their offerings in ways that are meaningful to customers. In highly developed economies, growth is slowing in mature consumer service industries such as banking, insurance, hospitality, and education. So for a firm to grow in these industries, it has to take share from domestic competitors or expand into international markets. In each instance, firms should be selective in targeting customers and seeking to be distinctive in the way they present themselves. A market niche that may seem too narrow to offer sufficient sales within one country may represent a substantial market when viewed from an international or even global perspective.

Competitive strategy can take many different routes. George Day observes:

> The diversity of ways a business can achieve a competitive advantage quickly defeats any generalizations or facile prescriptions. . . . First and foremost, a business must set itself apart from its competition. To be successful, it must identify and promote itself as the best provider of attributes that are important to target customers.[1]

What this means is that managers need to think systematically about all facets of the service package and to emphasize competitive advantage on those attributes that will be valued by customers in the target segment(s).

Four Focus Strategies

It's usually not realistic for a firm to try to appeal to *all* potential buyers in a market, because customers are varied in their needs, purchasing behaviour, and consumption patterns, and often also too numerous and geographically widespread. Different service firms also vary widely in their abilities to serve different types of customers. So, rather than attempting to compete in an entire market, each company needs to focus its efforts on those customers it can serve best. In marketing terms, *focus* means providing a relatively narrow product mix for a particular market segment—a group of buyers who share common characteristics, needs, purchasing behaviour, or consumption patterns. This concept is at the heart of virtually all successful service firms, who have identified the strategically important elements in their service operations and have concentrated their resources on them.

The extent of a company's focus can be described along two dimensions: market focus and service focus.[2] *Market focus* is the extent to which a firm serves few or many markets, while *service focus* describes the extent to which a firm offers few or many services. These two dimensions define the four basic focus strategies shown in Figure 7.1.

A *fully focused* organization provides a limited range of services (perhaps just a single core product) to a narrow and specific market segment. A *market-focused* company concentrates on a narrow market segment but has a wide range of services. *Service-focused* firms offer a narrow range of services to a fairly broad market. Finally, many service providers fall into the *unfocused* category, because they try to serve broad markets and provide a wide range of services.

Figure 7.1

Basic Focus Strategies
for Services

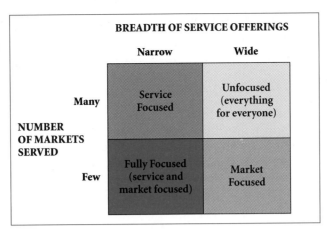

Source: Robert Johnston, "Achieving Focus in Service Organizations,"
Service Industries Journal 16 (January 1996): 10–20.

How should a firm select which of the three alternative "focused" strategies to pursue? Adopting a fully focused strategy presents both risks and opportunities. Developing recognized expertise in a well-defined niche may provide protection against would-be competitors and allows a firm to charge premium prices. The biggest risk is that the market may be too small to generate the volume of business needed for financial success. The story of Grocery Gateway, a Mississauga-based company, is a case in point. Launched in 1999, the company hoped to cash in on the needs of time-starved consumers who would be willing to pay for the convenience of shopping for groceries online. It learned very quickly that consumer habits die hard! Claiming cumulative losses of $105 million, the firm filed for voluntary receivership in August 2004 (examples from the UK and the United States suggest that such a service could probably only be sustained by an already-established supermarket chain).[3] Other risks include the danger that demand for the service may be displaced by generic competition from alternative products, or that purchasers in the chosen segment may be very susceptible to an economic downturn. One reason that firms with a narrow product line elect to serve multiple segments (a service-focused strategy) is to create a wide portfolio of customers, thereby hedging against such a risk. However, as new segments are added, the firm needs to develop expertise in serving each segment, which may require a broader sales effort and greater investment in marketing communication—particularly in B2B markets.

Offering a broad product line to a narrowly defined target segment often looks attractive because it offers the potential of selling multiple services to a single purchaser. But before adopting a market-focused strategy, managers need to be sure that their firms have the operational capability to do an excellent job of delivering each of the different services selected. They also need to understand customer purchasing practices and preferences. In a business-to-business context, when trying to cross-sell additional services to the same client many firms have been disappointed to find that decisions on purchasing the new service are made by an entirely different group within the client company. An online market research company may find that selling services related to online panels, online survey administration, and analytics requires them to approach three distinct groups within a particular client organization.

MARKET SEGMENTATION FORMS THE BASIS FOR FOCUSED STRATEGIES

Different service firms vary widely in their abilities to serve different types of customers. Hence, rather than trying to compete in an entire market, perhaps against superior competitors, each firm should adopt a strategy of market segmentation and targeting, identifying those parts, or segments, of the market that it can serve best. Firms that are in tune with customer requirements may choose to employ a needs-based segmentation approach, focusing on those customers whom research shows to value specific attributes that the firm can provide.[4]

Market and Micro Segmentation

Because each person or corporate purchaser has distinctive (even unique) characteristics and needs, any prospective buyer is potentially a separate target segment. Traditionally, firms have sought to achieve economies of scale by marketing to all customers within a specific market segment and serving each in a similar fashion. A strategy of *mass customization*—offering a large number of customers a service with some individualized product elements at a relatively low price—may be achieved by offering a standardized core product but tailoring supplementary service elements to fit the requirements of individual buyers.

The creation of customer databases and sophisticated analytical software makes it now possible for firms to adopt *micro-segmentation* strategies targeted at small groups of customers that share certain relevant characteristics at a specific point in time (note the strategy employed by the Royal Bank of Canada as described in Best Practice in Action 7.1).

Identifying and Selecting Target Segments

A *market segment* is composed of a group of buyers who share common characteristics, needs, purchasing behaviour, or consumption patterns. Effective segmentation should group buyers into segments in ways that result in as much similarity as possible on the relevant characteristics within each segment, but dissimilarity on those same characteristics between segments.

Best Practice in Action 7.1

Continuous Segmentation at the Royal Bank of Canada

At least once a month, Toronto-based analysts at the Royal Bank of Canada (the country's largest bank) use data modelling to segment its base of 10 million customers. The segmentation variables include credit-risk profile, current and projected profitability, life stage, likelihood of leaving the bank, channel preference (i.e., whether customers like to use a branch, self-service machines, the call centre, or online banking), product activation (how quickly customers actually use a product they have bought), and propensity to purchase another product (i.e., cross-selling potential). Says a senior vice president, "Gone are the days when we had mass buckets of customers that would receive the same treatment or same offer on a monthly basis. Our marketing strategy is [now] much more personalized. Of course, it's the technology that allows us to do that."

The main source of data is the marketing information file, which records what products customers hold with the bank, the channels they use, their responses to past campaigns, transactional data, and details of any restrictions on soliciting customers. Another source is the enterprise data warehouse, which stores billing records and information from every document that a new or existing customer fills out.

Royal Bank analysts run models based on complex algorithms that can slice the bank's massive customer database into tightly profiled micro-segments that are based on simultaneous use of several variables, including the probability that target customers will respond positively to a particular offer. Customized marketing programs can then be developed for each of these micro-segments, giving the appearance of a highly personalized offer. The data can also be used to improve the bank's performance on unprofitable accounts by identifying these customers and offering them incentives to use lower-cost channels.

An important goal of Royal Bank's segmentation analysis is to maintain and enhance profitable relationships. The bank has found that customers who hold packages of several services are more profitable than those who don't. These customers also stay with the bank an average of three years longer. As a result of the sophisticated segmentation practices at Royal Bank, the response rates to its direct marketing programs have jumped from an industry average of only 3 percent to as high as 30 percent.

Source: Adapted from Meredith Levinson, "Slices of Lives," *CIO Magazine* (August 15, 2000).

A *target segment* is one that a firm has selected from among those in the broader market; it may be defined on the basis of several variables. For instance, a department store in a particular city might target residents of the metropolitan area (geographic segmentation), who have incomes within a certain range (demographic segmentation), value personal service from knowledgeable staff, and are not highly price sensitive (both reflecting segmentation according to expressed attitudes and behavioural intentions). Because at least some competing retailers in the city would be targeting the same customers, the department store would have to create a distinctive appeal (highlighting such characteristics as their wide array of merchandise categories, breadth of selection within each product category, and the availability of supplementary services such as advice and home delivery). Service firms that are developing strategies based on use of technology recognize that customers can also be segmented according to their degree of competence and comfort in using technology-based delivery systems.

An important marketing issue for any business is to accept that some market segments offer better opportunities than others. Target segments should be selected not only on the basis of their sales and profit potential, but also with reference to the firm's ability to match or exceed competing offerings directed at the same segment. Sometimes research will show that certain market segments are "underserved," meaning that their needs are not well met by existing suppliers. Such markets are often surprisingly large.

In many emerging-market economies, there are huge numbers of consumers whose incomes are too small to attract the interest of service businesses accustomed to focusing on the needs of more affluent customers. Collectively, however, small-wage earners represent a very big market, and may offer even greater potential for the future as many of them move upward towards middle-class status. ICICI, the largest private bank in India, has demonstrated that serving low-income customers through micro-finance can not only improve the lives of poor people but also gives the firm exposure to a profitable niche that mainstream financial institutions were wary of serving. From roughly 10 000 micro-finance customers in 2001, the bank was serving about 1.2 million clients in 2005. Within this time frame, its outstanding portfolio size increased from US$4.5 million to an impressive US$227 million. With such successes, the notion of micro-finance being a charitable activity conducted by non-profit organizations is being increasingly challenged. As Nachiket Mor, executive director of ICICI Bank, suggests, "We need to stop sending government and funding agencies the signal that micro-finance is not a commercially viable system."[5]

In a different part of the world, a similar notion is at play. Service Perspectives 7.1 describes an innovative approach to providing financial services to lower-income households in Mexico.

SERVICE ATTRIBUTES AND LEVELS

How can a firm develop the right service concept for a particular target segment? Formal research is often needed to identify which attributes of a given service are important to specific market segments, and how well prospective customers perceive competing organizations as performing against these attributes. But it's dangerous to overgeneralize. Strategists should recognize that the same individuals may set different priorities for attributes according to

- The purpose of using the service
- Who makes the decision
- The timing of use (time of day/week/season)
- Whether the individual is using the service alone or with a group
- The composition of that group

Consider the criteria that you might use when choosing a restaurant for lunch when (a) on vacation with friends or family, (b) meeting with a prospective business client, (c) going for a quick meal with a co-worker. Given a reasonable selection of alternatives, it's

Service Perspectives 7.1

Banco Azteca Caters to the Little Guy

Banco Azteca, which opened in 2002, is Mexico's first new bank in nearly a decade. It targets the 16 million households in the nation that earn US$250–$1300 a month—people such as taxi drivers, factory hands, and teachers. Despite their combined annual income of $120 billion, these individuals are of little interest to most banks, which consider small accounts a nuisance. Not surprisingly, only one in twelve has a savings account.

Banco Azteca was the brainchild of Ricardo Salinas Pliego, head of a retail-media-telecommunications empire that includes Grupo Elektra, Mexico's largest appliance retailer. Its branches, located within the more than 900 Elektra stores, are decorated in the green, white, and red colours of the Mexican flag. They seek to create a welcoming atmosphere and feature posters with the Azteca slogan, which translates as "A bank that's friendly and treats you well."

Azteca's relationship with Elektra seeks to take advantage of the retailer's 50-year track record in consumer finance, and the fact that some 70 percent of its merchandise is sold on credit. Elektra has an excellent record in credit sales, with a 97 percent repayment rate, and a rich database of customers' credit histories. So top management felt it made sense to convert Elektra credit departments in each store into Azteca branches, with an expanded line of services. The new bank has invested heavily in information technology, including high-tech fingerprint readers that eliminate the need for customers to present printed identification or passbooks. It also takes its services out to the people through a 3000-strong force of loan agents on motorcycles. The bank offers personal loans and time deposits, and is rolling out used-car loans, low-income mortgages, and debit cards. Loans may often use customers' previously purchased possessions as collateral.

In 2003, Grupo Elektra received authorization from the Ministry of Finance to purchase a private insurance company, renaming it Seguros Azteca. It offers basic insurance products at very low prices to a population segment that has historically been ignored by the Mexican insurance industry. Policies are distributed through Banco Azteca's branch network.

Sources: Geri Smith, "Buy a Toaster, Open a Banking Account," *Business Week* (January 13, 2003): 54; www.gruposalinas.com/companies/banco.shtml, accessed May 2006.

---

unlikely that you would choose even the same type of restaurant in each instance, let alone the same one. It's possible, too, that if you left the decision to another person in the party, he or she would make a different choice.

Important versus Determinant Attributes

Consumers usually make their choices between alternative service offerings on the basis of perceived differences between them. But the attributes that distinguish competing services from one another are not always the most important ones. For instance, in choosing a dentist, patients might rank "reputation" of the dentist as a prime consideration in their decision. They may avoid considering dentists who are relatively unknown or have a poor reputation, but after eliminating such alternatives from consideration, a patient is still likely to have several choices available who are perceived as equally reputable. Hence, reputation may not be an attribute that influences the patient's choice at this point.

Determinant attributes (i.e., those that actually determine buyers' choices between competing alternatives) are often some way down the list of service characteristics that are important to purchasers, but they are the attributes on which customers see significant differences between competing alternatives. For example, hours of operation, location, no requirement for appointments, and parking facilities, might be examples of determinant attributes for frequent users of dental services. For infrequent users of dental services, on the other hand, attributes such as personality and attitude of dentist and support personnel, availability of emergency services, methods of pain control, and ease of making appointments might assume primary importance.[6]

The marketing researchers' task, of course, is to survey customers in the target segment, identify the relative importance of different attributes and then ask which ones have been determinant during recent decisions involving a choice of service suppliers. Researchers also need to be aware how well each competing service is perceived by customers as performing on these attributes. Findings from such research form the necessary basis for developing a positioning (or repositioning) campaign.[7]

Establishing Service Levels

Creating a positioning strategy requires more than just identifying those attributes that are important to customers in the target segment. Decisions must also be made on what level of performance to offer on each attribute. Some service attributes are easily quantified, whereas others are qualitative and highly dependent on the judgment of the individual. Price, for instance, is a straightforward quantitative measure. Punctuality of transport services can be expressed in terms of the percentage of trains, buses, or flights arriving within a specified number of minutes of the scheduled time. Both of these measures are easy to understand and therefore generalizable. But characteristics such as the quality of personal service, or a hotel's degree of luxury, are more qualitative, and therefore subject to individual interpretation. To clarify the situation and facilitate both service design and performance measurement, each attribute needs to be operationalized, and standards established. For instance, if customers say they value physical comfort, what does that mean for a hotel versus an airline? In a hotel context, does it refer to ambient conditions, such as temperature and absence of noise? Or to visible, tangible elements such as the bed? In practice, both ambient conditions and tangible elements must be addressed.

Customers can often be segmented according to their willingness to trade off price versus service level across a broad array of attributes within the service concept. Price-insensitive customers are willing to pay a relatively high price to obtain high levels of service on each of the attributes that are important to them. By contrast, price-sensitive customers will look for an inexpensive service that offers relatively low levels of performance on many key attributes—although there may be others, such as safety, on which they are unwilling to compromise.

In a number of service industries, the most explicit form of positioning strategy is based upon offering several price-based classes of service concept, each based on packaging a distinctive level of service performance across many attributes. This phenomenon, known as *service tiering*, is particularly evident in industries such as hotels, airlines, car rentals, hardware and software support. Table 7.1 displays examples of the key tiers within each of these industries. Other examples of tiering include healthcare insurance, cable television, and credit/charge cards.

In the hotel industry, the tiers are created by external rating agencies. For instance, hotels and motels are rated by independent organizations, such as Canada Select or Yahoo, automobile associations (such as the CAA), or (in some countries) government agencies. Hotels and motels are inspected by the agency at periodic intervals and evaluated against an array of specific criteria. An existing lodging establishment may be upgraded or downgraded, based upon whether the inspectors find that service levels have improved or deteriorated. For instance, under the Canada Select ratings program, a full rating evaluation is conducted every second year. However, if there is a change of ownership, renovations and upgrades are undertaken, or complaints are received against a specific property, the evaluation might be conducted annually.[8]

In the car rental industry, the size and type of car forms the primary basis of tiering. Obtaining higher levels of performance on service attributes requires participation in membership programs. In the airline industry, individual carriers decide what levels of performance should be included with each class of service. Pressures to save money often result in a financially troubled airline reducing its service level standards. However, innovative carriers, such as British Airways, Singapore Airlines, and Virgin Atlantic, are continually trying to add new service features—particularly in business class—that will create a competitive advantage and enable them to sell more seats at full fare. These three carriers each offer business-class seats that fold flat into beds for overnight travel, but many competing airlines have not yet matched this feature. As a result, there is inconsistency within tiers among competing airlines. In other industries, tiering often reflects an individual firm's strategy of bundling service elements into a limited number of packages, rather than offering a broad à la carte menu of options, each priced separately.

Table 7.1 Examples of Service Tiering

INDUSTRY	TIERS	KEY SERVICE ATTRIBUTES AND PHYSICAL ELEMENTS USED IN TIERING
Lodging	Star or diamond ratings (5 to 1)	Architecture; landscaping; room size, furnishings, and decor; restaurant facilities and menus; room-service hours; array of services and physical amenities; staffing levels; calibre and attitudes of employees
Airline	Classes (intercontinental): first, business, premium economy, economy[a]	Seat pitch (distance between rows), seat width, and reclining capability; meal and beverage service; staffing ratios; check-in speed; departure and arrival lounges; baggage retrieval speed
Car rental	Class of vehicle[b]	Based on vehicle size (from subcompact to full size), degree of luxury, plus special vehicle types (minivan, SUV, convertible)
Hardware and software support	Support levels[c]	Hours and days of service; speed of response; speed of delivering replacement parts; technician-delivered service versus advice on self-service; availability of additional services

[a]Only a few airlines offer as many as four classes of intercontinental service; domestic services usually feature one or two classes.

[b]Avis and Hertz offer seven classes based on size and luxury, plus several special vehicle types.

[c]Sun Microsystems offers four support levels.

Not every player in an industry chooses to compete within each tier. Discount airlines, for instance, offer only a stripped-down version of economy class. Similarly, luxury hotel chains choose not to offer options below the four-star level. New entrants to an industry often do best to seek a niche position within a single tier, rather than trying to serve customers with a me-too product in every tier, which is a very expensive proposition. In the airline industry, 2005 saw the launch of two business-class-only airlines catering to the lucrative transatlantic business travellers' market: MAXjet and Eos. While Eos is "unashamedly upmarket," MAXjet offers business travel at a more basic level, with airfares less than half of what Eos charges.[9] MAXjet's value proposition is based on "providing business-class-only travel at startlingly low prices."[10] Competition in this segment is expected to heat up even more. In April 2006, a new British airline, Silverjet, announced its plans to start operating a business-class-only service in early 2007. It is positioning itself as offering service levels comparable to that of Eos while maintaining a price point close to that of MAXjet.[11]

POSITIONING DISTINGUISHES A BRAND FROM ITS COMPETITORS

Competitive positioning strategy is based on establishing and maintaining a distinctive place in the market for an organization and/or its individual product offerings. Jack Trout has distilled the essence of positioning into the following four principles:[12]

- A company must establish a position in the minds of its targeted customers.
- The position should be singular, providing one simple and consistent message.
- The position must set a company apart from its competitors.
- A company cannot be all things to all people—it must focus its efforts.

These principles apply to any type of organization that competes for customers. Understanding the principles of positioning is key to developing an effective competitive posture. The concept of positioning is certainly not limited to services—indeed it had its origins in packaged goods marketing—but it offers valuable insights by forcing service managers to analyze their firm's existing offerings and to provide specific answers to the following questions:

- What does our firm currently stand for in the minds of current and prospective customers?
- What customers do we serve now, and which ones would we like to target for the future?
- What is the value proposition for each of our current service offerings (core products and their accompanying supplementary service elements), and what market segments is each one targeted at?
- In each instance, how do our service offerings differ from those of our competitors?
- How well do customers in the chosen target segments perceive our service offerings as meeting their needs?
- What changes do we need to make to our offerings in order to strengthen our competitive position within our target segment(s)?

One of the challenges in developing a viable positioning strategy is to avoid the trap of investing too heavily in points of difference that can easily be copied. As researchers Kevin Keller, Brian Sternthal, and Alice Tybout note: "Positioning needs to keep competitors out, not draw them in."[13] When Roger Brown and Linda Mason, founders of the Bright Horizons chain of child care centres, were developing their service concept and business model, they took a long, hard look at the industry.[14] Discovering that for-profit child-care companies had adopted low-cost strategies and were running their centres as a commodity business, the Browns selected a different approach that competitors would find very difficult to copy (Best Practice in Action 7.2).

Product Positioning versus Copy Positioning

Customers' brand choices reflect, first, which brands they know and remember, and then, how they perceive each of these brands to be positioned. These positions are perceptual. We need to remember that people make their decisions based upon their perceptions of reality, rather than on an expert's definition of that reality.

Many marketers associate positioning primarily with the communication elements of the marketing mix—notably advertising, promotions, and public relations. This view reflects the widespread use of advertising in packaged-goods marketing to create images and associations for broadly similar branded products so as to give them a special distinction in the customer's mind—an approach sometimes known as *copy positioning*. A classic example is the rugged Western cowboy—the "Marlboro man"—created for the major cigarette brand. Note, however, that this imagery has nothing to do with the physical qualities of the tobacco; it is just a means of differentiating and adding glamour to what is essentially a commodity. Mahajan and Wind maintain that consumers who derive emotional satisfaction from a brand are likely to be less price sensitive.[15]

Examples of how imagery may be used for positioning purposes in services are found in McDonald's efforts to appear child friendly (including its emphasis on Ronald McDonald, the clown), humorous advertisements by cellphone service provider Fido, featuring dogs, or the gracious service offered by Singapore Airlines' distinctively uniformed female flight attendants. (The company's advertising never features their male cabin staff!)

But markets are constantly changing, creating both threats and opportunities among competing firms. For instance, it used to be that when large companies were looking for auditing services, they typically turned to one of the Big Four accounting firms, prestigious players offering global coverage. But a growing number of clients are now switching to so-called "Tier Two" accounting firms in a search for better service, a lower bill, or both.[16] Grant Thornton, currently the fifth-largest firm in the industry, has successfully positioned itself as offering easy access to partners and having "a passion for the business of accounting." Its advertising promotes an award from J.D. Powers ranking it as achieving

Best Practice in Action 7.2

Positioning a Chain of Childcare Centres away from the Competition

Roger Brown and Linda Mason met at business school, following prior experience as management consultants. After graduation, they operated programs for refugee children in Cambodia and then ran a Save the Children relief program in East Africa. Returning to the United States in 1986, they saw a need for child care centres that would provide caring, educational environments and give parents confidence in their children's wellbeing. So they set out to create a profitable chain of childcare centres that would be differentiated from the commoditized services offered by existing chains and many independent centres.

Their analysis showed an industry with many unappealing characteristics: no barriers to entry, chronically low margins, high labour intensity, no proprietary technology, low economies of scale, weak brand distinctions, and heavy regulatory oversight. So Brown and Mason developed and evolved a service concept that would allow them to turn these industry weaknesses into strengths for their own company, Bright Horizons (BH). Instead of marketing their services directly to parents—a one-customer-at-a-time sale—BH formed partnerships with companies seeking to offer an on-site day care centre for employees with small children. The advantages included

- a powerful, low-cost marketing channel

- a partner/customer who supplied the capital to build and outfit the centre and would have a vested interest in helping BH achieve its goal of delivering high-quality care

- benefits for parents, who would be attracted to a BH centre (rather than competing alternatives) because of its proximity to their own workplace, thus lowering commute times and offering greater peace of mind

To achieve differentiation based on higher quality, Bright Horizons offered a premium pay and benefits package to attract the best staff. Determining that traditional approaches to child care either lacked curricular guidance or mandated strict, cookie-cutter lesson plans, BH developed a flexible curriculum, "World at Their Fingertips,"

which outlined a course of study but gave teachers control over daily lesson plans.

Going beyond variable state and local licensing requirements, the company sought accreditation for its centres from the National Association for the Education of Young Children (NAEYC) and actively promoted this credential. BH's emphasis on quality meant that it could meet or exceed the highest local or state government licensing standards. As a result, heavy regulatory oversight represents an opportunity, not a threat, for BH, and gives it a source of competitive advantage.

With the support and expertise of its clients, which include many hi-tech firms, BH has developed innovative technologies such as streaming video of its classrooms to the parents' desktops; digitally scanned or photographed artwork; electronic posting of menus, calendars, and student assessments; and online student assessment capabilities. All serve to differentiate BH and help it to stay ahead of the competition.

BH sees labour as a competitive advantage, not a commodity, seeks to recruit and retain the best people, and has achieved "employer of choice" status in the child-care industry. Clients want to hire BH as a partner because they know they can trust the staff.

Brown believes that traditional child care chains get little value from their brands, despite expensive brand-building advertising campaigns directed at parents. Parents don't look for a national brand, he says; they want a great local program, and are indifferent to whether or not it's part of a national network. By contrast, employers are aware of and value BH's strong brand reputation.

By late 2005, Bright Horizons was operating more than 550 centres in the United States, Canada, and Europe for over 400 of the world's leading employers, including corporations, hospitals, universities, and government offices.

Sources: Roger Brown, "How We Built a Strong Company in a Weak Industry," *Harvard Business Review* 79 (February 2001): 51–57; www.brighthorizons.com, accessed May 2006.

"Highest Performance Among Audit Firms Serving Companies with up to [US]$12 billion in Annual Revenue" (Figure 7.2).

Some slogans promise a specific benefit, designed to make the company stand out from its competitors, such as Telus's "The future is friendly," or Air Canada's 2006 slogan "It's a revolution. Get on board," FedEx Ground's "Relax, It's FedEx," CIBC's "For what matters," Harry Rosen's "Make a statement," or Workopolis.com's "Your life awaits." However, as Dibb and Simkin point out:

Figure 7.2

Grant Thornton links its passion for accounting to high client satisfaction with its auditing services.

Evidence of strong branding in the service sector does not end with such catch phrases. [The leading organizations in different fields] already have a strong brand image in the sense that customers generally know exactly what they stand for. They are, already, clearly positioned in the customers' minds.[17]

Positioning strategy is becoming more sophisticated as growing numbers of firms engage in co-branding.[18] This endeavour can take several forms, including shared facilities, joint promotions, and even co-branded products. RBC Royal Bank, which has large numbers of ATMs in Esso gas stations across Canada, introduced a VISA card with Esso in 2000 to further enhance the co-branding relationship. Yogen Früz, a Canadian franchise success story, has grown from a single outlet in Toronto in 1986 to the "the largest franchisor and licenser of stores and other locations serving primarily frozen yogurt, through company owned, franchised, and non-traditional partnership locations."[19] Part of its success is attributable to co-branding activities with companies such as Cineplex Entertainment, Subway, and the Pickle Barrel. It actively seeks co-branding partners in non-traditional locations such as hospitals, airports, theme parks, and art galleries, to name a few. In each instance, the imagery associated with one brand has the potential to influence consumer perceptions of the other(s).

Our primary concern in this chapter is the role of positioning in guiding marketing-strategy development for services that compete on more than just imagery or vague promises. This entails decisions on substantive attributes that are important to customers, relating to product performance, price, and service availability. To improve a product's appeal to a specific target segment, it may be necessary to change its performance on certain attributes, to reduce its price, to alter the times and locations when it is available, or the forms of delivery that are offered. In such instances, the primary task of communication—advertising, personal selling, and public relations—is to ensure that prospective customers accurately perceive the position of the service on dimensions that are important to them in making choice decisions (Figure 7.3). Additional excitement and interest may be created by evoking certain images and associations in the advertising, but these are likely to play only a secondary role in customer choice decisions unless competing services are perceived as virtually identical on performance, price, and availability.

The Role of Positioning in Marketing Strategy

Positioning plays a pivotal role in marketing strategy because it links market analysis and competitive analysis to internal corporate analysis. From these three, a position statement can be developed that enables the service organization to answer the questions, "What is our product (or service concept), what do we want it to become, and what actions must we take to get there?" Table 7.2 summarizes the principal uses of positioning analysis as a diagnostic tool, providing input to decisions relating to product development, service delivery, pricing, and communication strategy.

Developing a positioning strategy can take place at several different levels, depending on the nature of the business in question. Among multi-site, multi-product service

Figure 7.3

Disnat Direct, an online brokerage service from Desjardins Bank, focuses on the attribute of low price per trade as a way to attract customers.

Table 7.2 Principal Uses of Positioning Analysis as a Diagnostic Tool

1. Provide a useful diagnostic tool for defining and understanding the relationships between products and markets:
   - How does the product compare with competitive offerings on specific attributes?
   - How well does product performance meet consumer needs and expectations on specific performance criteria?
   - What is the predicted consumption level for a product with a given set of performance characteristics offered at a given price?

2. Identify market opportunities for
   a. Introducing new products
      - What segments to target?
      - What attributes to offer relative to the competition?
   b. Redesigning (repositioning) existing products
      - Appeal to the same segments or to new ones?
      - What attributes to add, drop, or change?
      - What attributes to emphasize in advertising?
   c. Eliminating products that
      - Do not satisfy consumer needs
      - Face excessive competition

3. Make other marketing mix decisions to pre-empt or respond to competitive moves:
   a. Distribution strategies
      - Where to offer the product (locations, types of outlet)?
      - When to make the product available?
   b. Pricing strategies
      - How much to charge?
      - What billing and payment procedures to use?
   c. Communication strategies
      - What target audience(s) are most easily convinced that the product offers a competitive advantage on attributes that are important to them?
      - What message(s)? Which attributes should be emphasized and which competitors, if any, should be mentioned as the basis for comparison on those attributes?
      - Which communication channels: personal selling versus different advertising media? (Selected for their ability not only to convey the chosen message(s) to the target audience(s) but also to reinforce the desired image of the product.)

businesses, a position might be established for the entire organization, for a given service outlet, or for a specific service offered at that outlet. There must be consistency between the positioning of different services offered at the same location, because the image of one may spill over onto the others, especially if they are perceived to be related. For instance, if an airline has an excellent reputation for warm and hospitable in-flight customer service, that may enhance perceptions of its online- and telephone-contact customer services. By contrast, it would be detrimental to all three services if their positioning was conflicting.

Because of the intangible, experiential nature of many services, an explicit positioning strategy is valuable in helping prospective customers to get a mental "fix" on what to expect. Failure to select a desired position in the marketplace—and to develop a marketing action plan designed to achieve and hold this position—may result in one of several possible outcomes, all undesirable:

1. The organization (or one of its products) is pushed into a position where it faces head-on competition from a stronger competitor.

2. The organization (product) is pushed into a position that nobody else wants, because there is little customer demand.

3. The organization's (product's) position is so blurred that nobody knows what its distinctive competence really is.

The research and analysis that underlie development of an effective positioning strategy are designed to highlight both opportunities and threats to the firm in the competitive marketplace, including the presence of generic competition and competition from substitute products. Figure 7.4 identifies the basic steps involved in identifying a suitable market position and developing a strategy to reach it.

Market Analysis   This analysis addresses such factors as the overall level and trend of demand, and the geographic location of this demand. Is demand increasing or decreasing for the benefits offered by this type of service? Are there regional or international variations in the level of demand? Alternative ways of segmenting the market should be considered, and an appraisal made of the size and potential of different market segments. Research may be needed to gain a better understanding not only of customer needs and preferences within each of the different segments, but also of how each perceives the competition.

Internal Corporate Analysis   Here the objective is to identify the organization's resources (financial, human labour and know-how, and physical assets), any limitations or constraints, its goals (profitability, growth, professional preferences and so on), and how its values shape the way it does business. Using insights from this analysis, management should be able to select a limited number of target market segments that can be served with either new or existing services.

Competitor Analysis   Identification and analysis of competitors can provide a marketing strategist with a sense of their strengths and weaknesses, which, in turn, may suggest opportunities for differentiation. Relating these insights back to the internal corporate analysis should suggest what might be viable opportunities for differentiation and competitive advantage, and thereby enable managers to decide which benefits should be emphasized to which target segments. This analysis should consider both direct and indirect competition.

Position Statement   The outcome of integrating these three forms of analysis is a statement that articulates the desired position of the organization in the marketplace (and,

Figure 7.4

Developing a Market Positioning Strategy

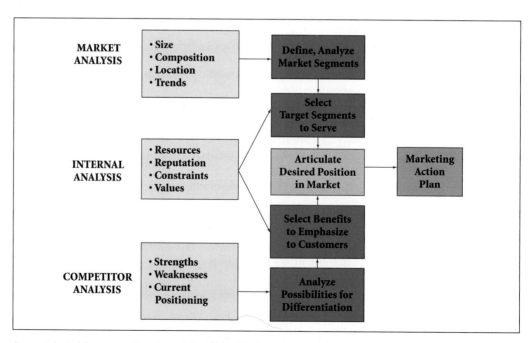

Source: Adapted from an earlier schematic by Michael R. Pearce.

if desired, that of each of the component services that it offers). Armed with this understanding, marketers should be able to develop a specific plan of action. The cost of implementing this plan must, of course, be related to the expected payoff.

Anticipating Competitive Response

Before embarking on a specific plan of action, however, management should consider the possibility that one or more competitors might pursue the same market position. Perhaps another service organization has independently conducted the same positioning analysis and arrived at similar conclusions? Or an existing competitor may feel threatened by the new strategy and take steps to reposition its own service so as to compete more effectively. Alternatively, a new entrant to the market may decide to play "follow the leader," yet be able to offer customers a higher service level on one or more attributes and/or a lower price.

The best way to anticipate possible competitive responses is to identify all current or potential competitors and to put oneself in their own management's shoes by conducting an internal corporate analysis for each of these competitors.[20] Coupling the insights from this analysis with data from existing market and competitive analysis (with one's own firm cast in the role of competitor) should provide a good sense of how competitors might be likely to act. If chances seem high that a stronger competitor will move to occupy the same niche with a superior service concept, then it would be wise to reconsider the situation.

Some firms develop sophisticated simulation models to analyze the impact of alternative competitive moves. How would a price cut affect demand, market share, and profits? Based upon past experience, how might customers in different segments respond to increases or decreases in the level of quality on specific service attributes? How long would it take before customers responded to a new advertising campaign designed to change perceptions?

Evolutionary Positioning

Positions are rarely static: they need to evolve over time in response to changing market structures, technology, competitive activity, and the evolution of the firm itself. Many types of businesses lend themselves to evolutionary repositioning by adding or deleting services and target segments. Some companies have shrunk their offerings and divested certain lines of business in order to be more focused. Others have expanded their offerings in the expectation of increasing sales to existing customers and attracting new ones. Thus service stations have added small convenience stores offering extended hours of service, while supermarkets and other retailers have added banking services. New developments in technology provide many opportunities for introducing not only new services but also new delivery systems for existing products.

When a company has a trusted and successful brand, it may be possible to extend a position based on perceived quality in one type of service to a variety of related services under the same umbrella brand. Best Practice in Action 7.3 features the example of Rentokil Initial, a provider of B2B services, which has profited from the growing trend toward outsourcing of services related to facilities maintenance.

USING POSITIONING MAPS TO PLOT COMPETITIVE STRATEGY

Developing a positioning "map"—a task sometimes referred to as perceptual mapping— is a useful way of representing consumers' perceptions of alternative products graphically. A map is usually confined to two attributes (although three-dimensional models can be used to portray three of these attributes). When more than three dimensions are needed to describe product performance in a given market, then a series of separate charts need to be drawn for visual presentation purposes. A computer model, of course, can handle as many attributes as are relevant.[21]

Best Practice in Action 7.3

Positioning a Brand Across Multiple Services at Rentokil Initial

With sales of $2 billion in 2005, Rentokil Initial is one of the world's largest business services companies. The UK-based firm operates in 43 countries, including the United States and Canada, where it employs the Initial brand name. It has evolved substantially from its origins as a manufacturer of rat poison and a pesticide for killing wood-destroying beetles. When the firm determined that it could make more money by providing a service to kill rodents than by selling products that customers would use themselves to target these pests, it shifted to pest control and extermination services.

Through organic growth and acquisition, Rentokil Initial has developed an extensive product range that includes testing and safety services; security; parcels delivery; interior plants landscaping (including sale or rental of tropical plants); specialized cleaning services; pest control; rental and laundering of uniforms; clinical waste collection and disposal; personnel services; and a washroom solutions service that supplies and maintains a full array of equipment, dispensers, and consumables.

The firm sees its core competence as "the ability to carry out high quality services on other people's premises through well-recruited, well-trained, and motivated staff." In the United States and Canada, Chicago-headquartered Initial Tropical Plants serves 25 000 customers coast to coast. Its 1400 co-workers manage 1.6 million plants, producing revenues of $112 million. It is the only national supplier of such services in a highly fragmented industry where competition tends to be local in character.

Promoting use of additional services to existing customers is an important aspect of the firm's strategy. Initial Integrated Services offers clients the opportunity to move beyond the established concept of "bundling" services—bringing together several free-standing support services contracts from one provider—to full integration of services. Clients purchase sector-specific solutions delivering multiple services but featuring just "one invoice, one account manager, one helpdesk, one contract and one motivated service team."

According to former chief executive, Sir Clive Thompson:

Our objective has been to create a virtuous circle. We provide a quality service in industrial and commercial activities under the same brand-name, so that a customer satisfied with one Rentokil Initial Service is potentially a satisfied customer for another. . . . Although it was considered somewhat odd at the time, one of the reasons we moved into [providing and maintaining] tropical plants [for building interiors] was in fact to put the brand in front of decision makers. Our service people maintaining the plants go in through the front door and are visible to the customer. This contrasts with pest control where no one really notices unless we fail. . . . The brand stands for honesty, reliability, consistency, integrity and technical leadership.

Rentokil Initial's success lies in its ability to position each of its many business and commercial services in terms of the company's core brand values, which include providing superior standards of customer care and utilizing the most technically advanced services and products. The brand image is reinforced through physical evidence in terms of distinctive uniforms, vehicle colour schemes, and use of the corporate logo.

Investment in R&D ensures constant improvement. In December 2005 the company announced its latest achievement, the RADAR intelligent rodent trap. RADAR attracts rats and mice into a sealable chamber and kills them humanely by injecting carbon dioxide. Using Rentokil's unique "pestconnect" technology, the trap causes emails to be sent to the customer and the local branch when a rodent is caught; a Rentokil technician receives a text message identifying which unit has been activated at which customer's premises, and its precise location. Now technicians can promptly remove dead animals and better control future infestation.

Sources: Clive Thompson, "Rentokil Initial: Building a Strong Corporate Brand for Growth and Diversity," in F. Gilmore (ed.) *Brand Warriors,* London: HarperCollinsBusiness, 1997: 123–24; TXT Technology 4 Pest Control, press release, December 6, 2005, www.rentokil-initial.com, accessed May 2006.

Information about a product (or a company's position relative to any one attribute) can be inferred from market data, derived from ratings by representative consumers, or both. If consumer perceptions of service characteristics differ sharply from "reality" as defined by management, then marketing efforts may be needed to change these perceptions.

An Example of Applying Positioning Maps to the Hotel Industry

The hotel business is highly competitive, especially during seasons when the supply of rooms exceeds demand. Within each class of hotels, customers visiting a large city may find that they have several alternatives from which to select a place to stay. The degree of luxury and comfort in physical amenities will be one choice criterion; research shows that business travellers are concerned not only with the comfort and facilities offered by their rooms (where they may wish to work as well as sleep), but also with other physical spaces, ranging from the reception area, meeting rooms, and a business centre to restaurants, swimming pool, and exercise facilities.

The quality and range of services offered by hotel staff is another key criterion: can a guest get 24-hour room service? Can clothes be laundered and pressed? Is there a knowledgeable concierge on duty? Are staff available to offer professional business services? There are other choice criteria, too, perhaps relating to the ambience of the hotel (modern architecture and decor are favoured by some customers, others may prefer old-world charm and antique furniture). Additional attributes include factors such as quietness, safety, cleanliness, and special rewards programs for frequent guests.

Let's look at an example, based on a real-world situation, of how developing a positioning map of their own and competing hotels helped managers of the Palace, a successful four-star hotel, develop a better understanding of future threats to their established market position in a large city that we will call Belleville.

Located on the edge of the booming financial district, the Palace was an elegant old hotel that had been extensively renovated and modernized a few years earlier. Its competitors included eight four-star establishments, and the Grand, one of the city's oldest hotels, which had a five-star rating. The Palace had been very profitable for its owners in recent years and boasted an above-average occupancy rate. For many months of the year, it was sold out on weekdays, reflecting its strong appeal to business travellers, who were very attractive to the hotel because of their willingness to pay a higher room rate than tourists or congress delegates. But the general manager and his staff saw problems on the horizon. Planning permission had recently been granted for four large new hotels in the city, and the Grand had just started a major renovation and expansion project, which included construction of a new wing. There was a risk that customers might believe the Palace to be falling behind.

To understand better the nature of the competitive threat, the hotel's management team worked with a consultant to prepare charts that displayed the Palace's position in the business-traveller market both before and after the advent of new competition. Four attributes were selected for study: room price, level of physical luxury, level of personal service, and location. In this instance, management did not conduct new consumer research; instead they inferred customer perceptions based on published information, data from past surveys, and reports from travel agents and knowledgeable hotel staff members who interacted frequently with customers. Information on competing hotels was not difficult to obtain, since the locations were known, the physical structures were relatively easy to visit and evaluate, and the sales staff kept themselves informed on pricing policies and discounts. A convenient surrogate measure for service level was the ratio of rooms per employee, easily calculated from the published number of rooms and employment data provided to the city authorities. Data from surveys of travel agents conducted by the Palace provided additional insights on the quality of personal service at each competitor.

Scales were then created for each attribute. Price was simple, since the average price charged to business travellers for a standard single room at each hotel was already quantified. The rooms per employee ratio formed the basis for a service level scale, with low ratios being equated with high service. This scale was then modified slightly in the light of what was known about the quality of service actually delivered by each major competitor. Level of physical luxury was more subjective. The management team identified the hotel that members agreed was the most luxurious (the Grand) and then the four-star hotel that they viewed as having the least luxurious physical facilities (the Airport Plaza). All other four-star hotels were then rated on this attribute relative to these two benchmarks.

Location was defined with reference to the stock exchange building in the heart of the financial district, because past research had shown that a majority of the Palace's business guests were visiting destinations in this area. The location scale plotted each hotel in terms of its distance from the stock exchange. The competitive set of ten hotels lay within a 6.5-kilometre, fan-shaped radius, extending from the exchange through the city's principal retail area (where the convention centre was also located) to the inner suburbs and the nearby airport. Two positioning maps were created to portray the existing competitive situation. The first (Figure 7.5) showed the ten hotels on the dimensions of price and service level; the second (Figure 7.6) displayed them on location and degree of physical luxury.

A quick glance at Figure 7.5 shows a clear correlation between the attributes of price and service: hotels offering higher levels of service are relatively more expensive. The shaded bar running from upper left to lower right highlights this relationship, which is not a surprising one (and can be expected to continue diagonally downwards for three-star and lesser-rated establishments). Further analysis shows that there appear to be three clusters of hotels within what is already an upscale market category. At the top end, the four-star Regency is close to the five-star Grand; in the middle, the Palace is clustered with four other hotels, and at the lower end, there is another cluster of three hotels. One surprising insight from this map is that the Palace appears to be charging significantly more (on a relative basis) than its service level would seem to justify. Since its occupancy rate is very high, guests are evidently willing to pay the going rate.

In Figure 7.6 we see how the Palace is positioned relative to the competition on location and degree of luxury. We would not expect these two variables to be related, and they do

Figure 7.5

Positioning Map of Belleville's Principal Business Hotels: Service Level versus Price Level (Before New Competition)

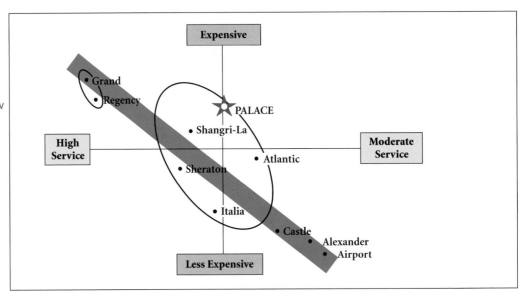

Figure 7.6

Positioning Map of Belleville's Principal Business Hotels: Location versus Physical Luxury (Before New Competition)

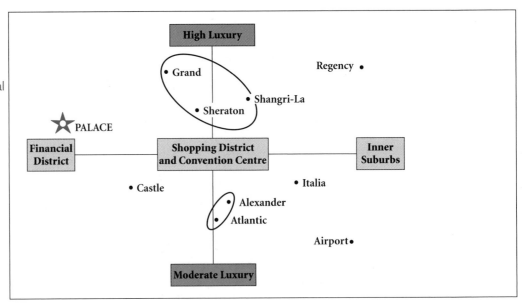

not appear to be so. A key insight here is that the Palace occupies a relatively empty portion of the map. It is the only hotel in the financial district—a fact that probably explains its ability to charge more than its service level (or degree of physical luxury) would seem to justify. There are two clusters of hotels in the vicinity of the shopping district and convention centre: a relatively luxurious group of three, led by the Grand, and a second group of two offering a moderate level of luxury.

Mapping Future Scenarios to Identify Potential Competitive Responses

What of the future? The Palace's management team next sought to anticipate the positions of the four new hotels being constructed in Belleville, as well as the probable repositioning of the Grand (see Figures 7.7 and 7.8). The construction sites were already known; two would be in the financial district and two in the vicinity of the convention centre, itself under expansion. Press releases distributed by the Grand had already declared its management's intentions: The "New Grand" would not only be larger, but the renovations would also be designed to make it even more luxurious, and there were plans to add new service features.

Figure 7.7

Future Positioning Map of Belleville's Business Hotels: Service Level versus Price Level

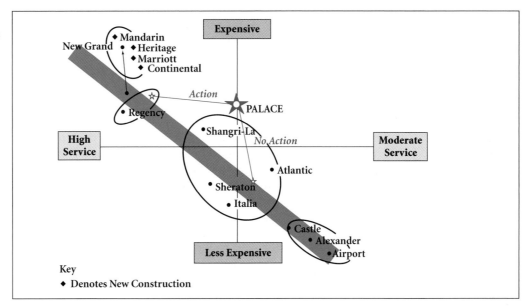

Figure 7.8

Future Positioning Map of Belleville's Business Hotels: Location versus Physical Luxury

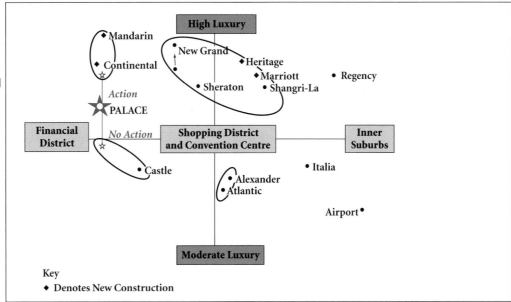

Predicting the positions of the four new hotels was not difficult for experts in the field; however, they recognized that customers might initially have more difficulty in predicting each hotel's level of performance on different attributes, especially if they were unfamiliar with the chain that would be operating the hotel in question. Preliminary details of the new hotels had already been released to city planners and the business community. The owners of two of the hotels had declared their intentions to seek five-star status, although this might take a few years to achieve. Three of the newcomers would be affiliated with international chains, and their strategies could be guessed by examining recent hotels opened in other cities by these same chains.

Pricing was also easy to project. New hotels use a formula for setting posted room prices (the prices typically charged to individuals staying on a week-night in high season). This price is linked to the average construction cost per room at the rate of one dollar per night for every thousand dollars of construction costs. Thus, a 200-room hotel that costs $40 million to build (including land costs) would have an average room cost of $200 000 and would need to set a price of $200 per room night. Using this formula, Palace managers concluded that the four new hotels would have to charge significantly more than the Grand or Regency, in effect establishing what marketers call a *price umbrella* above existing price levels and thereby giving competitors the option of raising their own prices. To justify their high prices, the new hotels would have to offer customers very high standards of service and luxury. At the same time, the New Grand would need to raise its own prices to recover the costs of renovation, new construction, and enhanced service offerings (see Figure 7.7).

Assuming no changes by either the Palace or other existing hotels, the impact of the new competition in the market clearly posed a significant threat to the Palace, which would lose its unique locational advantage and in future be one of three hotels in the immediate vicinity of the financial district (Figure 7.8). The sales staff believed that many of the Palace's existing business customers would be attracted to the Continental and the Mandarin, and would be willing to pay their higher rates in order to obtain the superior benefits offered. The other two newcomers, on the other hand, were seen as being more of a threat to the Shangri-La, Sheraton, and New Grand in the shopping district/convention centre cluster. Meanwhile, the New Grand and the newcomers would create a high price/high service (and high luxury) cluster at the top end of the market, leaving the Regency in what might prove to be a distinctive—and therefore defensible—space of its own.

Positioning Charts Help Executives Visualize Strategy

The Palace Hotel example demonstrates the insights that come from visualizing competitive situations. One of the challenges that strategic planners face is to ensure that all executives have a clear understanding of the firm's current situation before moving to discuss changes in strategy. Chan Kim and Renée Mauborgne argue that graphic representations of a firm's strategic profile and product positions are much easier to grasp than tables of quantitative data or paragraphs of prose. Charts and maps can facilitate what they call a "visual awakening." By enabling senior managers to compare their business with that of competitors, and understand the nature of competitive threats and opportunities, visual presentations can highlight gaps between how customers (or prospects) see the organization and how management sees it, and thus help confirm or dispel beliefs that a service or a firm occupies a unique niche in the marketplace.[22] Such analysis has proven successful for modern-day camera manufacturers who have been able to ward off competition from computer manufacturers such as Apple and Dell by moving away from a product-focused positioning (the celluloid film business) to a service-focused positioning (image-capturing).[23]

In the case of the Palace Hotel, examining anticipated changes in the competitive environment would literally redraw the current positioning map; the management team could see that the hotel could not hope to remain in its current market position once it lost its locational advantage. Unless they moved proactively to enhance its level of service and physical luxury, while raising its prices to pay for such improvements, the hotel was likely to find itself being pushed into a lower price bracket that might even make it difficult to maintain current standards of service and physical upkeep.

Sometimes firms have to make a significant change in an existing position. Such a strategy, known as *repositioning*, could mean revising service characteristics or redefining target market segments. At the firm level, repositioning may entail abandoning certain products and withdrawing completely from some market segments.

Changing Perceptions through Advertising

Improving negative brand perceptions may require extensive redesign of the core product and/or supplementary services. However, weaknesses are sometimes perceptual rather than real. Ries and Trout describe the case of Long Island Trust, historically the leading bank serving this large suburban area to the east of New York City.[24]

After laws were passed to permit unrestricted branch banking throughout New York state, many of the big banks from Manhattan began invading neighbouring Long Island. Research showed that Long Island Trust had come to be rated below banks like Chase Manhattan and Citibank on such key selection criteria as branch availability, full range of services offerings, service quality, and capital resources. However, Long Island Trust ranked first on helping Long Island residents and the Long Island economy.

The bank's advertising agency developed a campaign promoting the "Long Island position," playing to its perceived strengths rather than seeking to improve perceptions on attributes where it was perceived less favourably. The tenor of the campaign can be gauged from the following extract from a print ad:

> Why send your money to the city if you live on the Island? It makes sense to keep your money close to home. Not at a city bank but at Long Island Trust. Where it can work for Long Island. After all, we concentrate on developing Long Island. Not Manhattan Island or some island off Kuwait. . . .

Other advertisements in the campaign promoted similar themes, such as, "The city is a great place to visit, but would you want to bank there?"

When identical research was repeated 15 months later, Long Island Trust's position had improved on every attribute. The campaign had succeeded in reframing its brand image by changing its customers' frame of reference from a global to a local perspective. Although the firm had not changed any of its core or supplementary services, the perceived strength of being a Long Island bank for Long Islanders now had a strongly positive "halo effect" on all other attributes.

Innovation in Positioning

Most companies focus on matching and beating their rivals, with the result that their strategies tend to emphasize the same basic dimensions of competition. However, one way to compete is to introduce new dimensions into the positioning equation that other firms cannot immediately match.

James Heskett frames the issue nicely:

> The most successful service firms separate themselves from "the pack" to achieve a distinctive position in relation to their competition. They differentiate themselves ... by altering typical characteristics of their respective industries to their competitive advantage.[25]

Conclusion

Most service businesses face active competition, so marketers need to find ways of creating meaningful competitive advantages for their products. Ideally, a firm should target segments that it can serve better than other providers, offering a higher level of performance than competitors on those attributes that are particularly valued by the target segment. The nature of services introduces a number of distinctive possibilities for competitive differentiation, including location, scheduling, and speed of service delivery; the calibre of service personnel; and a range of options for customer involvement in the production process.

The concept of positioning is valuable because it forces explicit recognition of the different attributes comprising the overall service concept and emphasizes the need for marketers to understand which attributes determine customer-choice behaviour. Positioning maps provide a visual way of summarizing research data, and display how different firms are perceived as performing relative to each other on key attributes. When combined with information on the preferences of different segments, including the level of demand that might be anticipated from such segments, positioning maps may suggest opportunities for creating new services or repositioning existing ones to take advantage of unserved market needs.

Review Questions

1. Why should service firms focus their efforts? Describe the four basic focus strategies, and illustrate them with examples.

2. What is the distinction between important and determinant attributes in consumer choice decisions? How can research help you to understand which is which?

3. Describe what is meant by positioning strategy, and explain the marketing concepts that underlie it.

4. How can positioning maps help managers better understand and respond to competitive dynamics?

Application Exercises

1. Find examples of companies that illustrate each of the four focus strategies discussed in this chapter.

2. Consider the online brokerage industry in Canada and create a perceptual map showing the competitive positions of different competitors in the industry (such as Disnat Direct from Desjardin Bank and Action Direct from Royal Bank), using attributes that you consider to represent key consumer choice criteria.

3. The travel agency business is losing business to online bookings offered to passengers by airline websites. Identify some possible focus options open to travel agencies wishing to develop new lines of business that would compensate for this loss of airline ticket sales.

4. Find examples of companies that have been successful—and others that have been unsuccessful—at extending a position in one type of service to a variety of related services under the same umbrella brand. What are the factors responsible for the two different outcomes?

5. Imagine that you are a consultant to the Palace Hotel. Consider the options facing the hotel based upon the four attributes appearing in the positioning charts (Figures 7.5 and 7.6). What actions do you recommend that the Palace should take in these circumstances? Justify your recommendations.

Endnotes

1. George S. Day, *Market Driven Strategy*, New York: Free Press, 1990: 164.

2. Robert Johnston, "Achieving Focus in Service Organizations," *Service Industries Journal* 16 (January 1996): 10–20.

3. Michael Snider, "Too Good to be True," *Profit* 23/5 (2004): 18–19.

4. A best-practice example in a B2B context is discussed in Ernest Waaser, Marshall Dahneke, Michael Pekkarinen, and Michael Weissel, "How You Slice It: Smarter Segmentation for Your Sales Force," *Harvard Business Review* 82/3 (2004): 105–11.

5. Annie Duflo, "ICICI Banks the Poor in India: Demonstrates that Serving Low-Income Segments is Profitable," *Microfinance Matters* 17 (2005): 13–16.

6. Zhengyuan Wang, Swinder Janda, and C.P. Rao, "Dental Services Marketing: Do Market Segments Based on Usage Rate Differ in Terms of Determinant Attributes?" *Journal of Services Marketing* 10/4 (1996): 41–55.

7. For further insights into multi-attribute modelling, see William D. Wells and David Prensky, *Consumer Behavior*, New York: John Wiley, 1996: 321–25.

8. www.canadaselect.com, accessed April 27, 2006.

9. "Silverjet Joins Three-way Race for Business Class," http://business.timesonline.co.uk, April 16, 2006, accessed April 28, 2006.

10. www.maxjet.net, accessed December 28, 2005.

11. "Silverjet joins three-way race for business class," http://business.timesonline.co.uk, April 16, 2006, accessed April 28, 2006.

12. Jack Trout, *The New Positioning: The Latest on the World's #1 Business Strategy*, New York, NY: McGraw-Hill, 1997.

13. Kevin Lane Keller, Brian Sternthal, and Alice Tybout, "Three Questions You Need to Ask about Your Brand," *Harvard Business Review* 80 (September 2002): 84.

14. Roger Brown, "How We Built a Strong Company in a Weak Industry," *Harvard Business Review* 79 (February 2001): 51–57.

15. Vijay Mahajan and Yoram (Jerry) Wind, "Got Emotional Product Positioning?" *Marketing Management* (May–June, 2002): 36–41.

16. Nanette Byrnes, "The Little Guys Doing Large Audits," *BusinessWeek* (August 22/29, 2005): 39.

17. Sally Dibb and Lyndon Simkin, "The Strength of Branding and Positioning in Services," *International Journal of Service Industry Management* 4/1 (1993): 25–35.

18. Chris Lederer and Sam Hill, "See Your Brands through Your Customers' Eyes," *Harvard Business Review* 79 (June 2001): 125–33.

19. www.yogenfruz.com, accessed May 03, 2006.

20. For a detailed approach, see Michael E. Porter, *Competitive Strategy*, Chapter 3, "A Framework for Competitor Analysis," New York: Free Press, 1980: 47–74.

21. For examples of developing research data for perceptual mapping purposes, see Glen L. Urban and John M. Hauser, *Design and Marketing of New Products*, 2nd ed., Englewood Cliffs, NJ: Prentice Hall, 1993.

22. W. Chan Kim and Renée Mauborgne, "Charting Your Company's Future," *Harvard Business Review* 80 (June 2002): 77–83.

23. Lon Zimmerman, "Product Positioning Maps Secure Future," *Marketing News* 39/17 (October 2005): 47.

24. Al Ries and Jack Trout, *Positioning: The Battle for Your Mind*, rev. 1st ed, New York: Warner Books, 1986.

25. James L. Heskett, *Managing in the Service Economy*, Boston: Harvard Business School Press, 1984: 45.

Reading 2-1

The Health Travellers

PROSENJIT DATTA AND GINA S. KRISHNAN

As international trade builds, one alternative to exporting services is to import customers. Cross-border travel for medical services is a growing market in health care delivery, stimulated by demand from aging consumers in affluent nations. Countries that can offer inexpensive but high-quality treatment in modern hospitals are creating a boom in health care tourism. Patients seeking joint replacements, cardiac care, organ transplants, dental care, facelifts, and laser eye surgery find they can get needed treatments faster and more cheaply by travelling to Asia, South Africa, or Eastern Europe. They can even combine treatment and recuperation with a vacation.

Cyril Parry waited for a very long time for his turn to come. The 59-year-old retiree from Birmingham, UK, was suffering from rheumatoid-arthritis. He needed a hip replacement operation urgently. He waited patiently though his pain was getting worse and his movements increasingly restricted. Unfortunately, Parry was stuck at the end of a very long queue. The overburdened National Health Service orthopaedic surgeons in the UK were booked solid—for several years. Finally, Parry was told that his turn would come four years and nine months down the line.

That was when Parry started surfing the Net to see if he could get his hip surgery done elsewhere in the world. After a full year of research, he shortlisted two destinations: a hospital in Thailand and Apollo Speciality Hospital, Chennai. In November this year, Parry opted for the latter because, at £4,000 (excluding airfare but inclusive of a 10-day stay, post-operative care and a full health check-up), it was almost £5,000 cheaper than the Thai option.

It was ironic that Parry needed to travel abroad for his treatment. He was, after all, undergoing a procedure called the 'Birmingham Hip Resurfacing'—a new technique considered as a superior alternative to the full-hip replacement surgery, and named after the city it was pioneered in. It was perfected at the Royal Orthopedic Hospital in Birmingham as recently as 1998.

Cyril Parry needed to travel because of the healthcare system followed in the UK which is creating long waiting lists of patients in that country. More on that later. But long waiting lists are not the only reason that there's been a huge surge in medical travel globally in recent years. Patients from rich countries in the Middle East travel to the US when they need top notch medical care. Residents of poor developing nations such as Nigeria or Bangladesh travel to their more developed neighbours for medical treatment because there aren't enough good facilities available in their own countries. Thousands of Japanese citizens seeking medical treatment fly abroad because of the prohibitive costs of treatment in their home country. Americans seeking cosmetic surgery often fly to South Africa for face tucks and breast augmentation because their insurance coverage doesn't pay for those—and it is cheaper to get them done in South Africa than back home.

Table 1   An Overview of Health Tourism

Country	No of Foreigners Treated Last Year	From	Money Earned	Strengths
Thailand	60 000	US, UK	$470 m	Cosmetic surgery, organ transplants, dental treatment, joint replacements
Jordan	126 000	Middle East	$600 m	Organ transplants, fertility treatment, cardiac care
India	100 000	Middle East Bangladesh, UK, developing countries	N.A.	Cardiac care, joint replacements, Lasik
Malaysia	85 000	US, Japan, developing countries	$40 m	Cosmetic surgery
South Africa	50 000	US, UK	N.A.	Cosmetic surgery, Lasik, dental treatment
Cuba	N.A.	Latin America, US	$25 m–$50 m	Specialist niche treatment: Vitiligo [skin], night blindness; cosmetic surgery

"The Health Travellers," by Prosenjit Datta and Gina S. Krishnan from *Businessworld,* www.businessworldindia.com/Dec2203/coverstory01.asp. Reprinted by permission.

Nobody has collated the complete worldwide statistics about how many people travel abroad for health and medical care-related reasons every year or how much they spend. But a Saudi Arabian report pointed out that in 2000, medical travellers from the Gulf region alone spent over $27 billion seeking treatment in various nations around the world. If the medical travellers from around the world spent even half as much that year, the total business in 2000 alone would have been in excess of $40 billion. And even that could be an underestimate.

"The estimate is that the healthcare market in the Organisation of Economic Cooperation and Development countries alone is worth about $3 trillion, and expected to go up to $4 trillion in 2005," says Rupa Chanda, professor at the Indian Institute of Management—Bangalore, and who was part of a working group led by Isher Ahiuwalia of ICRIER which prepared a report for the World Trade Organization on the potential for trade in health services. Chanda refuses to hazard a guess on how much of this is actually cross-border medical traffic, just saying that the opportunity is huge.

More importantly, it is growing rapidly and turning out to be an immense business opportunity for nations that are positioning themselves correctly. Last year, just five countries in Asia—Thailand, Malaysia, Jordan, Singapore and India—pulled in over 1.3 million medical travellers and earned over $1 billion (in treatment costs alone). In each of these nations, medical travel spends are growing at 20%-plus year-on-year.

Elsewhere around the world, Hong Kong, Lithuania and South Africa are emerging as big medical/healthcare destinations. And a dozen other nations including Croatia and Greece plan to make themselves attractive healthcare destinations.

By itself, travelling abroad for health is not a new phenomenon—even in ancient times, there were examples of people travelling abroad to spas or famous medical centres for health treatment. But in the past five years or so, the movement has accelerated sharply. It has developed a massive momentum for two critical reasons.

The first is, of course, the demographics of the developed nations and also the problems that are cropping up in their healthcare systems. In the US, the UK, Japan and many European nations, the proportion of the elderly (60 years and above) vis-à-vis the total population is increasing rapidly. In the US, the baby boomers—the biggest chunk of the population—have either hit retirement age or are heading towards it. The number of people aged 65 years and above is expected to double in the next 15 years. In the UK, the people aged 60 years and above will form 25% of the population in the next

30 years—up from 16% now. Similar trends are being seen in almost all nations in Western Europe. Meanwhile, life expectancy here has risen steadily over the years. Add the two up and you get a big surge in demand for healthcare.

The big problem is that as their health needs increase exponentially, the healthcare systems in these countries are beginning to creak under the pressure. The number of doctors and nurses joining the workforce in both the UK and the US is not keeping pace with all the demands of the ageing population. This is creating the push factor.

Meanwhile, there is a pull factor being created by a handful of developing countries like Thailand and Malaysia that have good doctors and excellent facilities, and which are positioning themselves as medical destinations in order to boost their economies. Both Thailand and Malaysia see this developing into a multi-billion dollars-a-year business. There is also the other factor—people from the least developed countries who find affordable sophisticated medical care facilities in developing countries like India and Malaysia. "The competence and skills of Indian doctors is accepted internationally and people are coming from all over the world to our hospital to get treatment," says Prathap C. Reddy, chairman, Apollo hospital group. Curt Schroeder, CEO of Thailand's Bumrungrad Hospital, echoes that sentiment about his country's healthcare facilities.

Cross-border travel for healthcare reasons is still a highly disorganised movement, but nations are slowly waking up to its potential. In some places the governments have taken a lead. In others, like South Africa and Lithuania, travel agents specialising in medical tourism are driving the trend. In India, private hospitals like Apollo and Escorts Heart Institute and Research Centre are trying to attract patients on their own.

Though the movement can still be considered to be in its infancy, medical travel has come under the radar of both the World Health Organisation (WHO) and the World Trade Organization (WTO). As far back as the early 1990s, the WHO commissioned the Social Sector Development Strategies, Inc. (SSDS, Inc.), a Boston-based non-profit organisation specialising in global healthcare systems, to see whether the English-speaking Caribbean islands could become a significant healthcare destination for travellers from the US, the UK and Canada. The study took a hard look at both the advantages and the disadvantages of these nations before reluctantly coming to the conclusion that they would be uncompetitive in most of the areas. The WHO's interest is simple—it realises that medical travel can help boost the medical facilities (and the medical economy) in developing countries while also

Table 2 Treatment Costs (US$)

Procedure	US	India	South Africa	Thailand
Facelift	6 000–20 000	10 000–20 000	1 252	2 882
Hip replacement	17 000	2 500	9 671	N.A
Open heart Surgery	150 000	5 000–10 000	13 333	7 500
Eye (Lasik)	3 100	7 000	2 166	730

taking care of some of the problems of rich nations. The WTO sees medical travel as one of the four modes . . . that will help boost trade in healthcare services worldwide. Both WHO and WTO understand that medical travel could ameliorate much of the demand–supply imbalance in global healthcare. Developed nations benefit as costs or waiting time—or both—come down for a significant chunk of their population. Developing countries benefit as it brings in revenues—and provides the right spur to improve their overall healthcare sector, apart from reducing brain drain in their medical fraternities. Least developed countries, too, benefit as they lack facilities for cutting-edge treatment.

THE TRAVELLERS

You could divide the world's medical travellers into four distinct geographical groups who travel for distinctly different reasons. The first is made up of the Americans. Indeed, countries like Thailand, Malaysia and South Africa, which were the first to try and tap "medical tourists", all geared their systems to attract the growing American clientele.

Why would the Americans travel abroad when their own country boasts of the best medical facilities in the world? And especially as they don't have to wait in queue like the British? The two Es: ego and economy. The US healthcare system is predominantly insurance-driven. But health insurance covers critical care—not cosmetic care. And there are vast numbers of Americans today who are looking for cosmetic surgery—whether it involves a facelift, a liposuction or dental treatment for a brighter smile.

According to the American Society of Aesthetic Plastic Surgery, in 2002, 6.6 million Americans went in for cosmetic surgery in the US itself. They were also the biggest chunk of foreign customers for cosmetic surgeons in Thailand, Malaysia and South Africa. These three countries, between them, pulled in over 100 000 Americans seeking cosmetic surgery.

As the baby boomers—those 76 million Americans born between 1946 and 1964—age, they are increasingly going in for facelifts, botox treatments, tummy tucks, et al. And since cosmetic surgery is mostly not covered by medical insurance, many Americans prefer to travel abroad. A full facelift costs $8000–20 000 in the US and only $1252 in South Africa. Thailand is slightly more expensive at $2682. Best of all, going abroad means a vacation as well after the surgery is over.

Vanity isn't the only reason why Americans seek treatment abroad though. Lack of insurance cover is another. Last year, 15.2% of the US population—some 43.6 million people—had no health insurance coverage. And a significant proportion of even the 84% with insurance were under-insured.

Many of these people weren't poor—at least according to developing country standards. Some of them were people between jobs who didn't have insurance simply because they were earlier covered by their employers. Given the increasing cost of medical treatment in the US, it made sound economic sense to seek treatment abroad.

If cosmetic surgery and costs were the factors driving the Americans to travel abroad, the second major group—the British—were being forced to seek medical treatment in other countries by the sheer waiting lists caused by the National Health Service (NHS). Unlike in the US, the British healthcare system ensures free treatment to all its citizens. The only problem is that the NHS, which was set up in 1948, is struggling to cope because of a shortage of both doctors and hospital beds. (Private medical facilities are available in the UK, but they are prohibitively expensive and also relatively fewer in number.) In 2001, more than 1 million British citizens were waiting for inpatient treatment and half-a-million for outpatient treatment according to a study by the Vienna University of Economics and Business Administration. At least 40% of the people requiring inpatient care needed to wait over three months for their turn to come. Hip replacement and eyecare had the longest waiting periods.

The situation is so bad that in 2002, the NHS started a pilot scheme "overseas treatment" to see if surgery services abroad could be bought to shorten the waiting lists. The project focussed mainly on facilities available in the European Union—in countries like Austria and Germany. Meanwhile, many thousands of British patients take the initiative to seek their own treatment abroad without waiting for the NHS to sort out its problems.

The third big group of medical travellers comes from the Middle East. These are citizens of the oil rich nations flying abroad to seek medical facilities that are either unavailable or in short supply in their own countries. An agency in Saudi Arabia estimated that every year, more than 500 000 people from the Middle East travel seeking medical treatment for everything from open heart surgery to infertility treatments. They travel everywhere—to Jordan, Saudi Arabia and Bahrain; to the US; to India, Thailand and Malaysia. By some estimates, India itself attracted 70 000-plus medical travellers from the Middle East last year.

Finally, the last group of medical travellers form a motley lot. They are from the least developed countries and countries with generally poor medical infrastructure, who usually seek treatment facilities at some neighbouring country with better infrastructure. Last year, it was estimated that at least 50 000 people from Bangladesh and Nepal came for medical treatment to India. A significant majority of the 126 000 medical travellers to Jordan came from neighbours with poor medical infrastructure facilities.

TAPPING THE BIG MARKET

A $40-billion-plus market growing at over 20% a year throws up huge opportunities for anyone smart enough to tap into it. The SSDS, Inc. study for the WHO pointed out that business opportunities covered a big spectrum—from retirement homes and spas, to cosmetic and dental surgery, to critical but non-emergency surgery needs like hip replacements, organ transplants, angioplasty and vision correction. Other studies show even alternative healthcare could be a significant niche opportunity.

In the initial years, most countries that tapped into the medical destination opportunity essentially focussed either on spas or on the "vanity" and the "exotic" surgery requirements. In South Africa a number of outfits (travel agents with hospital connections) sprang up to tap into the market for facelifts, tummy tucks and cosmetic dental surgery. Thailand initially had a somewhat dubious reputation as an excellent country to go to for sex change operations. India's primary claim to fame was its ayurvedic treatment centres. "Beauty, youth and wellness is a huge area for growth and we need to promote it aggressively," says Apollo's Reddy.

Over the past few years, though, many countries have realised that an equally big opportunity lies in promoting the more conventional treatments. Some of this, of course, was always happening in the background—like people from Mauritius, Bangladesh and the Gulf coming to India for conventional surgeries and people from Japan flying to Singapore, Malaysia or Thailand for similar reasons. Only now, the nations have started pitching themselves as world-class but inexpensive destinations for almost all health requirements.

They might be getting some unexpected help soon—from insurance giants. Healthcare insurers in the developed countries are not blind to the fact that the option of medical treatment in countries like Thailand and Malaysia could help them reduce premiums and offer options to people who are currently uninsured. Over the next few years, insurance firms are expected to provide a fillip to the medical travel business.

Most insurance companies in the US and the UK have already accredited hospitals worldover where Western visitors can seek emergency medical treatment. Now a few hospitals in Thailand are going a step further—they are getting themselves accredited by the Joint Commission Accreditation of Healthcare Organizations (JCAHO). A full accreditation from this organisation allows a hospital to pitch for the insurance traffic too. Travelling has never been so healthy before.

Reading 2-2

The Strategic Levers of Yield Management

SHERYL E. KIMES AND RICHARD B. CHASE

Yield management, controlling customer demand through the use of variable pricing and capacity management to enhance profitability, has been examined extensively in the services literature. Most of this work has been tactical and mathematical rather than managerial. In this article, the authors suggest that a broader view of yield management is valuable to both traditional and nontraditional users of the approach. Central to this broader view is the recognition of how different combinations of pricing and duration can be used as strategic levers to position service firms in their markets and the identification of tactics by which management can deploy these strategic levers. The authors also propose that further development of yield management requires that when the service is delivered it should be treated as a design variable that should be as carefully managed as the service process itself.

Although commonly associated with marketing as a revenue management tool, yield management has significant impacts on other service business functions. It affects operations in capacity planning, human resource management in worker selection and training, and business strategy through the way the service firm positions itself in the market. Despite this widespread impact and the considerable attention it has received, formal yield management is still viewed primarily as a pricing/inventory management tool. What is lacking is a broader theory of yield management that would permit other service industries to gain the benefits of yield management-type thinking and provide insights into new areas in which experienced companies might further apply the concept. Our objective in this article is to develop the groundwork for such a theory. Our focus will be on the strategic levers available for yield management, how they have been applied in traditional yield management settings, and how they, along with some tactical tools, can be applied to other service settings.

A MODIFIED DEFINITION OF YIELD MANAGEMENT

A common definition of yield management is the application of information systems and pricing strategies to "sell the right capacity to the right customers at the right prices" (Smith, Leimkuhler, and Darrow 1992). Implicit in this definition is the notion of time-perishable capacity and, by extension, the notion of segmentation of capacity according to when it is booked, when and how long it is to be used, and according to the customer who uses it. In other words, "an hour is not an hour is not an hour" when it comes to customer preferences or capacity management. In light of this subtle point, we offer a slightly modified definition of the term. That is, yield management may be defined as managing the four Cs of perishable service: calendar (how far in advance reservations are made), clock (the time of day service is offered), capacity (the inventory of service resources), and cost (the price of the service) to manage a fifth C, customer demand, in such a way as to maximize profitability.

The Strategic Levers of Yield Management," by Sheryl E. Kimes and Richard B. Chase from *Journal of Service Research*, 1, no. 2 (November 1998): 156–166. Sponsored by Center for Service Marketing, Owen Graduate School of Management, Vanderbilt University. Copyright © 1998 by Sage Publications, Inc. Reprinted by permission of Sage Publications, Inc.

Strategic Levers

A successful yield management strategy is predicated on effective control of customer demand. Businesses have two interrelated strategic levers with which to accomplish this: pricing and duration of customer use. Prices can be fixed (one price for the same service for all customers for all times) or variable (different prices for different times or for different customer segments), and duration can be predictable or unpredictable.

Variable pricing to control demand is conceptually a straightforward process. It can take the form of discount prices at off-peak hours for all customers, such as low weekday rates for movies, or it can be in the form of price discounts for certain classes of customers, such as senior discounts at restaurants.

Duration control presents a more complicated decision problem but at the same time represents an area that would improve the effectiveness of yield management. By implementing duration controls, companies maximize overall revenue across all time periods rather than just during high-demand periods. If managers want to increase control over duration, they can refine their definition of duration, reduce the uncertainty of arrival, reduce the uncertainty of the duration, or reduce the amount of time between customers. We will discuss each of these tactics later.

Different industries use different combinations of variable pricing and duration control (Figure 1). Industries traditionally associated with yield management (hotel, airline, rental car, and cruise line) tend to use variable pricing and a specified or predictable duration (Quadrant 2). Movie theaters, performing arts centers, arenas, and convention centers use a fixed price for a predictable duration (Quadrant 1), whereas restaurants, golf courses, and Internet service providers use a fixed price with unpredictable customer duration (Quadrant 3).

Many health care industries charge variable prices (Medicare or private pay) but do not know the duration of patient use (Quadrant 4). There is no fixed demarcation point between quadrants, so an industry may lie partially in one quadrant and partially in another. The intent of this classification method is to help industries not currently using yield management develop a strategic framework for developing yield management. More specifically, what we are trying to show is which quadrant industries are in and what they can do to move to Quadrant 2. For example, restaurant management does not have control of duration; they need to pursue some duration management approach. Or, if hotel management does not adequately control length of stay, they may want to modify their forecasting system from room nights to arrivals to enhance their reservation system.

As indicated above, successful yield management applications are generally found in Quadrant 2 industries. The reason is that a predictable duration enables clear delineation of the service portfolio, and variable pricing enables generating maximum revenue from each service offering within the portfolio. We hasten to point out that even those industries that are listed in this quadrant have structural features that inhibit them from achieving their full profit potential. A brief review of the development of yield management in the airline and hotel industries will help illustrate these points.

Airline Industry

Deregulation of the American airline industry was the major impetus for the development of yield management. Before deregulation in 1978, major carriers offered one-price service between cities. Essentially, most airlines were operating in Quadrant 1: Their flight durations were extremely predictable, and their price was fixed (Figure 2).

Figure 1 Typical Pricing and Duration Positioning of Selected Service Industries

		Price	
		Fixed	**Variable**
Duration	**Predictable**	**Quadrant 1:** Movies Stadiums/Arenas Convention Centers	**Quadrant 2:** Hotels Airlines Rental Cars Cruise Lines
	Unpredictable	**Quadrant 3:** Restaurants Golf Courses Internet Service Providers	**Quadrant 4:** Continuing Care Hospitals

Figure 2 The Airline Industry

		Price	
		Fixed	**Variable**
Duration	**Predictable**	Quadrant 1: Before De-regulation	Quadrant 2: Immediately after De-regulation
	Unpredictable	Quadrant 3: None Identified	Quadrant 4: Hub-and-Spoke System

Immediately after deregulation, many new airlines emerged, and one airline, People's Express, developed an aggressive low-cost strategy. The People's Express story is well known: Their airfares were considerably lower than those of the major carriers, and customers were attracted to the limited service that People's Express flights offered. The major carriers such as American Airlines, United Airlines, and Delta Airlines, aided by new computerized reservation systems, employed variable pricing on a flight-by-flight basis to match or undercut fares offered by People's Express. Cost-conscious passengers then switched to the major carriers, and People's Express was eventually forced out of business. Donald Burr, the former CEO of People's Express, attributes his airline's failure to the lack of good information technology and the subsequent inability to practice yield management (Anonymous 1992; Cross 1997).

Seeing the benefits of differential pricing, most major North American carriers instituted yield management and moved into Quadrant 2. Yield management allowed airlines to determine the minimum fare (of a set mix of fares) that should be available for a specific flight. Differential pricing, in combination with the predictability of flight duration, gave them the enviable position of variable pricing with predictable duration.

Another trend that emerged after deregulation was the hub-and-spoke system. Previously, airlines operated on an origin–destination basis, and although connecting flights existed, the concept of a hub city did not. Most major airlines now operate with a hub-and-spoke system, and their forecasting and yield management systems are based around the associated flight legs (Skwarek 1996). Leg-based solutions have inherent problems and may lead to suboptimal solutions. Although the revenue on each flight leg may be optimized, revenue over the entire airline network may not. In an attempt to circumvent this problem, some airlines (notably American Airlines) developed virtual nesting systems (Smith, Leimkuhler, and Darrow 1992), in which different origin–destination pairs were classified by revenue generated. Unfortunately, current origin–destination forecasting and yield management systems have a high forecast error that results in an unreliable solution.

The lack of origin–destination forecasting may seem like a minor point, but it prevents airlines from truly managing the predictability of their duration. In a sense, the hub-and-spoke system has caused the airline industry to move into the bottom half of Quadrant 2 or the top half of Quadrant 4. The hub-and-spoke system, in combination with airline pricing systems, has created problems such as passengers attempting to obtain a lower fare by completing only one leg of their multileg flight (a "hidden city"). The empty seat on the remaining flight leg represents lost revenue to the airlines so safeguards have been instituted to avoid this problem. Only one major carrier, Southwest Airlines, has resisted the temptation of the hub-and-spoke system. This represents a competitive advantage for their yield management system because they are better able to manage the predictability of their flight durations (Anonymous 1994b).

Hotel Industry

Unlike the airline industry, traditional hotels are usually located in Quadrant 3. Although group and tour operators have multiple negotiated rates (Hoyle, Dorf, and Jones 1991; Vallen and Vallen 1991), most traditional hotels charge essentially one room rate (or perhaps a low-season and high-season rate) for transient guests. Length of stay is not explicitly considered, and forecasts are designed to predict nightly occupancy (Figure 3). Typically, the goal of the traditional hotel is to maximize occupancy for a given night, and managers seldom look at long-term revenue generation.

After the airlines started using yield management, many hotel managers were impressed with the increased revenue claimed by the airlines and applied the concept of variable pricing to the hotel industry. When hotels started using variable pricing, they did not apply the concept of qualified rates, in which customers had to meet certain requirements to obtain a lower room rate. They instead relied on top-down pricing, in which reservation agents quoted the highest rate first and, if faced with resistance, offered the next of several lower rates until the customers acquiesced or they reached a minimum

Figure 3 The Hotel Industry

		Price	
		Fixed	**Variable**
Duration	**Predictable**	Quadrant 1: Forte	Quadrant 2: Marriott Sheraton Holiday Inn
	Unpredictable	Quadrant 3: Traditional Hotels	Quadrant 4: Initial Yield Management Attempts

level previously established by management. Many major hotel chains still use this pricing method. Although short-term revenue gains may result from top-down pricing, customers view this practice unfavorably (Kimes 1994). Most hotels using this approach forecast room nights and use the forecasted nightly occupancy rate to develop pricing recommendations (Kimes 1989). Length-of-stay issues are not considered, and occupancy and rates are managed for one night at a time.

Some hotel chains, notably Marriott and Forte Hotels, saw the benefits associated with predictable durations (Anonymous 1994a). To reap the benefits associated with duration controls, they switched from forecasting room nights to forecasting arrivals by length of stay and/or room rate. Forte charged only one rate and concentrated solely on length of stay. Guests requesting a 2-night stay might be accepted, whereas those requesting a 1-night stay might be rejected depending on the projected demand. Marriott forecasted by arrival day, length of stay, and room rate and was able to determine the best set of reservation requests to accept. Still other hotel chains tried to implement length-of-stay controls without changing their forecasting system from room nights to arrivals. Without arrival information, they had no way of knowing if their restrictions made sense or if they were unnecessarily turning away potential customers.

The focus on length of stay not only changed the forecasting systems in place at leading hotels but also changed the mathematical methods used to develop yield management recommendations. Many hotel chains (e.g., Holiday Inn, Hilton, Sheraton, and Hyatt) have instituted linear-programming-based systems in which length of stay and room rate are explicitly considered (Hensdill 1998; Vinod 1995).

USING THE STRATEGIC LEVERS

Industries in Quadrants 1, 3, and 4 can move into Quadrant 2 to achieve some of the revenue gains associated with yield management by manipulating duration and price. Although there are still problems facing the hotel and airline industries,

their experience provides a rich context from which to understand the tactical tools needed to improve revenue generation. Specific tools associated with each strategic yield management lever can allow managers to move their company into a better revenue-generating position.

Duration Methods

If managers want to increase control over duration, they can refine their definition of duration, reduce the uncertainty of arrival, reduce the uncertainty of the duration, or reduce the amount of time between customers (Figure 4).

Refining the Definition of Duration Duration is how long customers use a service and is measured either in terms of time (i.e., the number of nights or number of hours) or by event (i.e., a meal or a round of golf). When duration is defined as an event rather than time, forecasting the length of duration generally becomes more difficult. Thus, if duration for an industry could be defined in time rather than events, better forecasting, and hence control of duration, would likely result.

Even industries that use time-based duration definitions can refine this definition and thereby enhance their operations. Most hotels sell rooms by the day, or more specifically, they sell rooms from 3 p.m. (check-in) to noon (check-out). Sheraton Hotels and The Peninsula Hotel in Beverly Hills allow customers to check in at any time of the day and check out at any time without penalty (Anonymous 1997; Barker 1998). By refining their definition of duration, they have improved customer satisfaction, made better use of capacity, and increased revenue.

Uncertainty of Arrival Because many capacity-constrained firms have perishable inventory, they must protect themselves from no-shows or late arrivals. Firms can use both internal (not involving customers) and external (involving customers) approaches to decrease uncertainty of arrival.

Figure 4 Methods of Managing Duration

	Possible Approaches
Refine Definition	Time Event
Uncertainty of Arrival: Internal Measures	Forecasting Overbooking
Uncertainty of Arrival: External Measures	Penalties Deposits
Uncertainty of Duration: Internal Measures	Forecasting by Time of Arrival, Length of Stay, and Customer Characteristics
Uncertainty of Duration External Measures	Penalties Restrictions Process Analysis
Reduce Time Between Customers	Process Analysis

Internal Approaches. Most capacity-constrained service firms use overbooking to protect themselves against no-shows. Published overbooking models often use Markovian decision processes or simulation approaches (for example, Lieberman and Yechialli 1978; Rothstein 1971, 1985; Schlifer and Vardi 1975), but in practice many companies use service-level approaches (Anonymous 1993; Smith, Leimkuhler, and Darrow 1992) or the critical fractile method (as suggested by Sasser, Olsen, and Wyckoff 1978). The key to a successful overbooking policy is to obtain accurate no-show and cancellation information and to develop overbooking levels that will maintain an acceptable level of customer service.

Once an overbooking policy is implemented, companies must develop good internal methods for handling displaced customers. The frontline personnel who must assist displaced customers should receive appropriate training and compensation for dealing with potentially angry consumers. Companies can choose to select which customers to displace on either a voluntary or involuntary manner. The airline industry, with its voluntary displacement system, has increased customer goodwill while increasing long-term profit (Anonymous 1993; Rothstein 1985). Other industries base their displacement decision on time of arrival (if customers are late, their reservation is no longer honored), frequency of use (regular customers are never displaced), or perceived importance (important customers are never displaced).

External Approaches. External approaches to reduce arrival uncertainty shift the responsibility of arriving to the customer. The deposit policies used at many capacity-constrained service firms such as cruise lines and resorts are excellent examples of external approaches. In addition, the cancellation penalties imposed by these companies represent an attempt to make customers more responsible for arriving. Restaurants are experimenting with cancellation penalties and ask customers for their credit card numbers when taking

reservations (Brehaus 1998). If patrons do not arrive within 15 minutes of the reservation time, a penalty fee is charged to their credit cards. Interestingly, the car rental industry, which has considerable yield management experience, makes very limited use of external approaches. With the exception of specialty cars and vans, customers are not asked to guarantee their rental and have no responsibility for showing up. With no incentives for customers to arrive, it is not surprising that in busy tourist markets such as Florida, no-shows can account for as much as 70 percent of the reservations (Stern and Miller 1995). Besides these negative incentives, some companies use service guarantees to encourage people to show up on time. American Golf, for example, offers discounted or free play to golfers whose actual tee-off time is delayed by more than 10 minutes of their reservation time.

Uncertainty of Duration Reducing duration uncertainty enables management to better gauge capacity requirements and hence make better decisions as to which reservation requests to accept. As in the case of arrival uncertainty, both internal and external approaches can be used for this purpose.

Internal Approaches. Internal approaches include accurate forecasting of the length of use and the number of early and late arrivals and departures and improving the consistency of service delivery. By knowing how long customers plan to use the service, managers can make better decisions as to which reservation requests to accept. If a restaurant manager knows that parties of two take approximately 45 minutes to dine and parties of four take about 75 minutes, he or she can make better allocation decisions. Likewise, knowing how many customers will change their planned duration of use enhances capacity decisions. For example, in a hotel, accurately forecasting how many customers book for 4 nights but leave after 3, or request additional nights, facilitates room and staff allocations. Similarly, if a rental car company knows that 20 percent of its week-long rentals are returned after 5 days, the fleet supply requirement can be adjusted accordingly.

Early research and practice in yield management focused on single flight legs or room nights and did not consider duration. Expected marginal seat revenue (EMSR) based models (Belobaba 1987; Littlewood 1972) are widely used in the airline industry (Williamson 1992) and result in allocation decisions for flight legs at various days before departure. Early hotel yield management systems based minimum rate decisions on forecasted occupancy but did not consider the impact of length of stay (Kimes 1989). Some airlines have tried to compensate for the lack of duration control by using actual nesting (Smith, Leimkuhler, and Darrow 1992; Vinod 1995; Williamson 1992) but still have not achieved the goal of full origin–destination control (Vinod 1995).

Linear programming has been used to help make better duration and pricing allocation decisions (Kimes 1989; Weatherford 1995; Williamson 1992). The bid price, defined as the shadow price of the capacity constraint, can be used to determine the marginal value of an additional seat, room, or other inventory unit (Phillips 1994; Vinod 1995; Williamson 1992). This value can then be used to determine the minimum price available for different durations. Dynamic programming (Bitran and Mondschein 1995) has also been suggested as a possible method for considering hotel length of stay.

The accuracy of the forecast affects the effectiveness of the yield management system. Lee (1990), in his study of airline forecasting, found that a 10 percent improvement in forecast accuracy resulted in a 3 percent to 5 percent increase in revenue on high-demand flights.

If duration is to be explicitly addressed, forecasts of customer duration must be developed. Airlines typically forecast demand by flight leg (Lee 1990; Vinod 1995), but to truly practice duration control, airlines must forecast demand by all possible origin–destination pairs. As previously mentioned, the hub-and-spoke system has increased the number of forecasts required and the subsequent accuracy of those forecasts. Some airlines have tried to reduce the number of forecasts needed by using virtual nesting (Smith, Leimkuhler, and Darrow 1992; Vinod 1995). Preliminary research on airline-forecasting accuracy (Weatherford 1998) shows that an increase in the number of daily forecasts required increases the forecast error.

When hotels forecast customer duration, they must forecast by day of arrival, length of stay, and possible rate class (Kimes, O'Sullivan, and Scott 1998). Hotels using linear programming and bid-price approaches forecast at this level of detail, and some have developed even more detailed forecasts. The magnitude of this problem becomes apparent when you consider that for each day of arrival, a hotel might consider 10 different lengths of stay and 10 different rate classes. If room type is included, a hotel may have 200 to 300 different forecasts per day.

Consistency of duration (i.e., most customers using the service for about the same length of time) is typically achieved through internal process changes. For example, TGI Fridays redesigned their restaurant menus and service delivery systems to make dining time more consistent as well as faster. Some restaurants in the theater district of New York City have placed an hourglass on the table of each party. When the sand in the hourglass is gone, patrons have a visual cue to finish dinner and leave so they will not be late to the theater. Or, in a much different context, if a prison warden knows that 25 percent of prisoners sentenced to 10 years serve only 4, additional prisoners may be incarcerated.

External Approaches. External approaches for handling uncertainty of duration generally reach the customer in the form of deposits or penalties. Some hotels have instituted early and late departure fees (Miller 1995), and airlines have penalized passengers who purchase tickets through hidden cities. Although penalties may work in the short term, they risk incurring customer wrath and hurting the company in the long run. For this reason, internal approaches are generally preferable.

Reduce Time Between Customers Reducing the amount of time between customers (changeover time reduction), by definition, means that more customers can be served in the same or a shorter period of time. Although changeover time reduction is not normally considered a tool of yield management, it is a tactic that can be used to increase revenue per available inventory unit. Such tactics play an important role in the yield management strategy. Changeover time reduction has become a common strategy for airlines. Southwest Airlines and Shuttle by United both boast of 20-minute ground turnarounds of their aircraft (compared to the average of 45 minutes at most airlines) and have been able to increase the utilization of their planes (Kimes and Young 1997). Many restaurants have instituted computerized table management systems that track tables in use, the progress of the meal, and when the bill is paid. When customers leave, the table management system notifies bussers, and the table is cleared and reset (Liddle 1996). The result is an increase in table utilization and, hence, revenue per table.

Price

Industries actively practicing yield management use differential pricing—charging customers using the same service at the same time different prices, depending on customer and demand characteristics. Passengers in the economy section of a flight from New York City to Los Angeles may pay from nothing (for those using frequent-flyer vouchers) to more than $1,500. The fares vary according to the time of reservation, the restrictions imposed, or the group or company affiliation. In contrast to such Quadrant 2 pricing, Quadrant 1 and 3 industries use relatively fixed pricing and charge customers using the same service at the same time the same price.

Customers tend to develop reference prices for various transactions. If companies change price, they must do so carefully to avoid upsetting their customers (Kahneman, Knetsch, and Thaler 1986). Although it is possible to charge more solely based on high demand, customers may resent being charged different prices for essentially the same service. Two mechanisms—proper price mix and rate fences—provide opportunities to alter price while maintaining goodwill (Figure 5).

Proper Price Mix Companies must be sure that they offer a logical mix of prices from which to choose. If customers do not see much distinction between the different prices being quoted, a differential-pricing strategy may not work. Determining the best mix of prices is difficult because management often has little information on price elasticities. This, in turn, often results in pricing decisions based solely on competitive pressures. It should be noted, however, that airlines such as American Airlines have been working hard on the issues of elasticity and of multiple legs and have made some progress.

Optimal pricing policies, in which customers are asked to name the prices that they would consider to be cheap, expensive, too cheap to be of reasonable quality, and too expensive to be considered, have been developed by Taco Bell and have been tested for use with meeting planners (Lewis and Shoemaker 1997). Optimal pricing policies represent a relatively simple way of determining price sensitivity and acceptable price ranges.

Although not widely publicized, some restaurant companies are experimenting with menu pricing based on price elasticities. Large chain restaurant companies analyze the price elasticities of various menu items and make appropriate pricing changes (Kelly, Kiefer, and Burdett 1994).

Rate Fences The possession of a good pricing structure does not ensure the success of a variable pricing strategy. Companies must also have a logical rationale or, in industry terms, rate fences that can be used to justify price discrimination. (Or, as one somewhat cynical hotel executive states, "We want something we can say out loud without laughing.")

Quadrant 2 industries often use rate fences such as when the reservation is booked or when the service is consumed, to determine the price a customer will pay. Rate fences refer to qualifications that must be met to receive a discount (Hanks, Cross, and Noland 1992). Rate fences can be physical or nonphysical in nature and represent a rationale for why some customers pay different prices for the same service.

Physical rate fences include tangible features such as room type or view for hotels, seat type or location for airlines, or table location for restaurants. Other physical rate fences are the presence or absence of certain amenities (free golf cart use with a higher price, free breakfast with a higher price, or free soft drinks at a movie theater).

Nonphysical rate fences can be developed that can help shift demand to slower periods, reward regular customers, or reward reliable customers. Nonphysical rate fences include cancellation or change penalties and benefits based on when the reservation was booked, desired service duration, group membership or affiliation, and time of use.

Even today, it is common practice for companies to adopt differential pricing schemes without rate fences. Hotels use top-down pricing in which reservation agents quote the rack rate (generally the highest rate) and only quote lower rates if customers ask for them. Knowledgeable customers may know to ask for the lower rate, but inexperienced customers may not. Customers view this practice highly unfavorably (Kimes 1994).

MOVING TO A MORE PROFITABLE QUADRANT

The strategic levers described above can be used to help companies move into more profitable quadrants by making duration more predictable and/or by varying prices. Generally, companies try to manipulate one strategic lever at a time, but it is possible, although difficult, for a company to try to simultaneously adjust price and duration. The following examples of potential moves show the possibilities for various industries.

Differential Pricing: Quadrant 1 to Quadrant 2

Movie Theaters Although reservation systems and differential pricing have been used in Europe for many years, American movie theaters usually charge the same price for all seats and offer discounted seats only for matinees or for sen-

Figure 5 Methods of Managing Price

	Possible Approaches
Proper Price Mix	Price Elasticities Competitive Pricing Optimal Pricing Policies
Rate Fences: Physical	Type of Inventory Amenities
Rate Fences: Nonphysical	Restrictions Time of Usage Time of Reservation Group Membership

ior citizens. However, things are changing rapidly, and some new movie houses are now offering differential pricing based on seat location, time of show, and access to amenities. For example, the 70-seat Premium Cinema in Lombard, Illinois, has been booked solid since its opening April 3, 1998. Guests willing to pay $15 for access to a separate entrance with valet parking are admitted to a private lounge, where they can purchase champagne at $12 per glass and buy prime-rib sandwiches at the same price. They offer free popcorn (all you can eat) and have a full-time concierge to get it for the customers. As of yet, they have not gone to the next step of developing an overbooking strategy.

Control Duration: Quadrant 3 to Quadrant 1

Golf Courses   Golf courses seem to be in the worst possible position—they charge a fixed price for an event of unknown duration. Much of the problem stems from the definition of duration as an event, typically 18 holes of golf played during daylight hours. Alternative definitions of duration abound. The golf course could sell 9-hole rounds; it could institute shotgun golf, in which different groups start simultaneously at multiple holes; or it could use express golf, in which golfers run between holes and receive two scores, elapsed time and stroke count, at the end of each round. (The latter perhaps becoming a new Olympic event.) None of these modifications reduce variability in and of themselves; however, they do provide ways of redefining duration for more creative applications of yield management.

Arrival uncertainty could be reduced by instituting deposit policies or by developing good overbooking policies. Duration uncertainty could be reduced by adding marshals to help move golfers along on the course, by provision of free golf carts to speed the time between holes, and by more accurately forecasting play length based on time of day, week, and party size. More golfers could be accommodated if tee-time intervals were reduced or if party size were better regulated.

Control Duration: Quadrant 4 to Quadrant 2

Health Care   Health care organizations use differential pricing (often government mandated) but have difficulties managing duration. If hospital or nursing home managers do not know how long patients will be using beds or rooms, it is difficult to effectively plan and manage capacity. In a nursing home, the health of potential patients could be evaluated and actuarial tables used to estimate the duration of patient stay. In private and nonprofit facilities, attempts could be made to select the best mix of private-pay and Medicare patients with a bias toward private-pay patients with a long duration.

The issue of duration control of health care has caused political controversy. During the mid-1990s, insurance companies in New York reduced the maximum length of insurable hospital stay for childbirth to 1 day. After intensive lobbying pressure from hospitals and medical associations, the state legislature outlawed this practice and guaranteed all new mothers a minimum length of stay of 48 hours.

Differential Pricing: Quadrant 3 to Quadrant 4

Internet Service Providers (ISPs)   ISPs offer Internet bandwidth to customers. Because not all customers use their full allotment of bandwidth at the same time, the ISP overbooks the bandwidth. If too many customers try to access the Internet at once, service deteriorates.

ISPs operate at 100 percent capacity during certain times of the day and at other times have available bandwidth. Currently, most ISPs charge a flat monthly rate for Internet access, and there is no off-peak discount. Some customers are heavy users during the day, whereas others are heavy nighttime users. ISPs must maintain a mix of these customers to operate effectively. By identifying common demographic characteristics within each segment, ISPs could target specific types of users to add to the mix (M. Freimer, personal communication, 1998).

CONCLUSION

Effective use of the strategic levers of pricing and duration control can help capacity-constrained firms make more profitable use of their resources. Real potential exists for novel use of these tools in industries not typically associated with yield management. Even companies with yield management experience can improve performance by refining their deployment of these levers. The research challenge is to help managers identify yield management opportunities and to develop appropriate pricing and duration control approaches.

Beyond where to apply yield management, there are the questions of how to develop a yield management strategy, how to train people in the tools to implement it, and how to maintain and improve customer satisfaction while applying yield management practices. In the long run, achieving the full potential from yield management lies in management's ability to market and manage every available moment as a unique product. This, in turn, requires that we treat when the service is provided as a design variable that should be as carefully managed as the service process itself. Such a reformulation presents an exciting conceptual challenge to the emerging field of service research.

References

"Adding to Forte's Fortune," (1994a), *Scorecard*, Second Quarter, 4–5.

Barker, J. (1998), "Flexible Check-in Expands," *Successful Meetings* 47 (January): 32.

Belobaba, P.P. (1987), "Air Travel Demand and Airline Seat Inventory Management," Ph.D. thesis, Massachusetts Institute of Technology.

Bitran, G.R., and S.V. Mondschein (1995), "An Application of Yield Management to the Hotel Industry Considering

Multiple Day Stays," *Operations Research*, 43, 427–43.

Brehaus, B. (1998), "Handling No-Shows: Operators React to Reservation Plan," *Restaurant Business Magazine* 1 (16): 13.

"A Conversation with Don Burr," (1992), *Scorecard*, Fourth Quarter, 6–7.

Cross, R.G. (1997), *Revenue Management: Hard-Core Tactics for Market Domination.* New York: Broadway Books.

"Flying High with Herb Kelleher," (1994b), *Scorecard*, Third Quarter, 1–3.

Freimer, M. (1998), personal communication.

Hanks, R.D., R.G. Cross, and R.P. Noland. (1992), "Discounting in the Hotel Industry: A New Approach," *Cornell Hotel and Restaurant Administration Quarterly* 33 (3): 40–45.

Hensdill, C. (1998), "The Culture of Revenue Management," *Hotels* (March): 83–86.

"Hotel Adopts 24-Hour Check-in Policy," (1997), *Hospitality Law* 12 (1): 7.

Hoyle, L.H., D.C. Dorf, and T.J.A. Jones. (1991), *Managing Conventions and Group Business,* Washington, DC: The Educational Institute of the American Hotel and Motel Association.

Kahneman, D., J. Knetsch, and R. Thaler. (1986), "Fairness as a Constraint on Profit Seeking: Entitlements in the Market," *American Economic Review* 76 (4): 728–41.

Kelly, T.J., N.M. Kiefer, and K. Burdett. (1994), "A Demand-Based Approach to Menu Pricing," *Cornell Hotel and Restaurant Administration Quarterly* 34 (3): 40–45.

Kimes, S.E. (1989), "Yield Management: A Tool for Capacity-Constrained Service Firms," *Journal of Operations Management* 8 (4): 348–63.

———. (1994), "Perceived Fairness of Yield Management," *Cornell Hotel and Restaurant Administration Quarterly* 34 (1): 22–29.

Kimes, S.E., and Franklin Young. (1997), "Shuttle by United," *Interfaces* 27 (3): 1–13.

Kimes, S.E., M. O'Sullivan, and D. Scott. (1998), "Hotel Forecasting Methods," working paper. Cornell University School of Hotel Administration.

Lee, A.O. (1990), "Airline Reservations Forecasting: Probabilistic and Statistical Models of the Booking Process," Ph.D. thesis, Massachusetts Institute of Technology.

Lewis, R.C., and S. Shoemaker (1997), "Price Sensitivity Measurement: A Tool for the Hospitality Industry," *Cornell Hotel and Restaurant Administration Quarterly* 38 (2): 44–54.

Liddle, A. (1996), "New Computerized Table Management Reduces Guests' Waits, Empty Seats," *Nation's Restaurant News* (August 5): 22.

Lieberman, V., and U. Yechialli (1978), "On the Hotel Overbooking Problem: An Inventory Problem with Stochastic Cancellations," *Management Science* 24, 1117–26.

Littlewood, K. (1972), "Forecasting and Control of Passenger Bookings," *AGIFORS Symposium Proceedings* 12, 95–117.

Miller, L. (1995), "Check-Out Made Pricier," *Wall Street Journal*, October 20, B6.

Phillips, R.L. (1994), "A Marginal Value Approach to Airline Origin and Destination Revenue Management," in *Proceedings of the 16th Conference on System Modeling and Optimization*, J. Henry and P. Yvon, eds. New York: Springer-Verlag, 907–17.

Rothstein, M. (1971), "An Airline Overbooking Model," *Transportation Science* 5, 180–92.

———. (1985), "OR and the Airline Overbooking Problem," *Operations Research* 33 (2): 237–48.

Sasser, W.E., R.P. Olsen, and D.D. Wyckoff (1978), *Management of Service Operations.* Boston: Allyn and Bacon.

Schlifer, E., and Y. Vardi. (1975), "An Airline Overbooking Policy," *Transportation Sciences* 9, 101–14.

"Simon Says," (1993), *Scorecard*, First Quarter, 10–12.

Skwarek, D.K. (1996), "Competitive Impacts of Yield Management System Components: Forecasting and Sell-Up Models," MIT Flight Transportation Lab Report No. R96–6. Cambridge, MA: Massachusetts Institute of Technology.

Smith, B.C., J.F. Leimkuhler, and R.M. Darrow. (1992), "Yield Management at American Airlines," *Interfaces* 22 (1): 8–31.

Stern, G., and L. Miller (1995), "Rental Car Companies Set to Impose Cancellation Penalties for No-Shows," *The Wall Street Journal,* December 26, A3.

Vallen, J.J. and G.K. Vallen (1991), *Check-in, Check-Out,* Dubuque, IA: William C. Brown.

Vinod, B. (1995), "Origin-and-Destination Yield Management," in *Handbook of Airline Economics*, D. Jenkins, ed. New York: McGraw-Hill, 459–68.

Weatherford, L.R. (1995), "Length of Stay Heuristics: Do They Really Make a Difference?" *Cornell Hotel and Restaurant Administration Quarterly* 36 (6): 47–56.

———. (1998), "Forecasting Issues in Revenue Management," INFORMS conference presentation, Montreal, Canada, May.

Williamson, E.L. (1992), "Airline Network Seat Control," Ph.D. thesis, Massachusetts Institute of Technology.

Death by Acronym

The powerful potential of IMC is being lost by those who can't comprehend or act on its real meaning

ALAN MIDDLETON

Unfortunately for both business and the health of the English language, we live in a world of acronyms. Business is full of them: BPM, CEO, CFO, CMO, HR, IPO, P/E, R&D, ROI. Marketing too: CI, CPM, CRP, CRM, DM, IMC, PBR, POP, PR, ROMI and so on.

The problem is that because the meanings are not clear, many groups claim to be adept at whatever the acronym stands for without really understanding what it means.

IMC (integrated marketing communications) is one that causes as much discussion about what it is, as how to achieve it. Many, if not most, communications agencies claim to offer IMC. Most have a very limited understanding and capability in delivering the promise. IMC is important but extremely tough to deliver and marketers need to beware of accepting the overpromise of such groups on such an important issue.

In their textbook, *Advertising Principles and Practice* (Prentice Hall), Wells, Burnett and Moriarty supply a useful and complete definition. In part, it reads: "IMC is the practice of unifying all marketing communication tools and corporate and brand messages to communicate in a consistent way to and with stakeholder audiences. IMC programs arc designed to co-ordinate all the various communications messages and sources. These messages can he grouped as:

(a) planned, or controlled, messages by the company [everything from advertising to packaging and internal marketing];

(b) unplanned, or uncontrolled, messages such as employee gossip and behaviour, media/government investigations, chat groups, etc.;

(c) often unconsidered messages delivered by other aspects of the marketing mix (product/service, price and distribution) and other contact points (the appearance of the parking lot outside of the store): facilities, after-sales support, and distributors appearance and behaviour."

Both academic research and my experience suggest that both (a) and (c) are essential to integrate to build strong brands. Marketing communications, however integrated, are irresponsible if they suggest experiences substantially different from those delivered by the product/service, distribution and price-based experiences. That is why advertising from certain large retailers and certain financial institutions, while much lauded by the creative community, have been disastrous for the business.

The essence of IMC is that all target group touchpoints need to deliver a co-ordinated and appropriate message. Merely slapping a theme line, logo or graphic on the differing vehicles is not IMC.

Many users of the IMC acronym fail to understand three important things about it:

1. Internal communications are as important, if not often more important, than the external ones. In a service economy, employee understanding of the brand is a crucial first step to customer understanding.

2. The use of differing forms of marketing communication should be planned and executed around a deep understanding of the target group and its brand choice and buying system. Only then can the choice of vehicles be made and the message designed appropriately.

3. Co-ordination of the differing communications vehicles means a common strategy and personality, but not necessarily the same message.

Without understanding these elements, IMC is only an acronym and not a planned series of activities necessary to build a strong brand reputation.

A real IMC approach requires detailed knowledge of the target group. Not only who they are, how they relate to the brand, and where the strengths and weaknesses are versus competition and their ideal, but also what this indicates about their involvement level and their buying system and on what stages in it to focus. The marketer then uses this knowledge to develop a brand communications strategy.

Alan Middleton is assistant professor of marketing and executive director, executive education centre at the Schulich School of Business, York University, Toronto.

This strategy should have two components: latitudinal and longitudinal. The latitudinal component uses the target group's buying system to determine media choice in the short term (roughly one year). The longitudinal component determines what aspects of the brand's reputation are the focus in each of the short, medium and long terms.

In the short term, the latitudinal component, media and creative are selected to carry the central concept across all media used, be adapted to the specific task in the buying system and provide a seamless connection across media.

In an increasingly networked world, IMC must also focus on two critically important additional groups: any opinion leaders and employees. These must be included in any IMC plan for it to be truly effective.

The benefit of this approach lies in a more systematic development of the brand's value to its target group, and therefore to its owner. IMC in this way becomes an important marketing strategy and not just a confusing and imprecise acronym.

PART 3

Managing the Customer Interface

Part 3 of the book focuses on managing the interface between customers and the service organization. It begins with design of an effective service delivery **Process**, specifying how operating and delivery systems link together to create the promised value proposition. Customers are often actively involved in service creation, especially if they are acting as co-producers, and the process becomes their experience. A related task in markets with widely fluctuating demand levels is to balance the level and timing of customer demand against available productive capacity.

The next steps involve two elements of the 8Ps that are particularly important in high-contact services. **Physical service environments** help to engineer customers' service experiences and provide clues to positioning strategy and service quality. **People** are a defining element of many services. Effective management of frontline employees is key to delivering customer satisfaction, productivity, and competitive advantage.

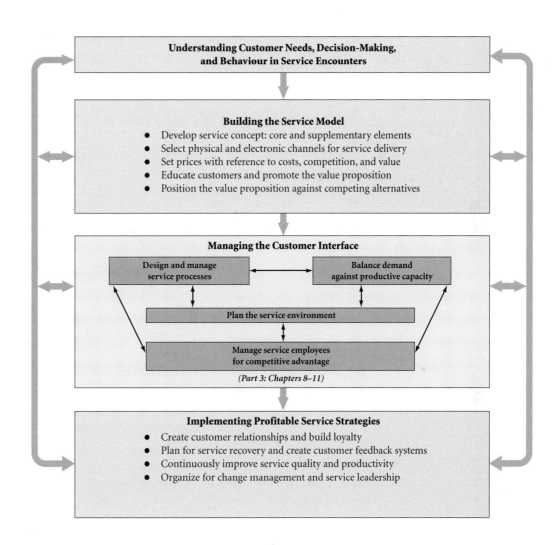

CHAPTER 8

Designing and Managing Service Processes

The new frontier of competitive advantage is the customer interface. Making yours a winner will require the right people and, increasingly, the right machines—on the front lines.

—Jeffrey Rayport and Bernard Jaworski

Ultimately, only one thing really matters in service encounters—the customer's perceptions of what occurred.

—Richard B. Chase and Sriram Dasu

The customer's story about you is crafted by your words and deeds.

—Jeffery Gitomer

Processes are the architecture of services. They describe the method and sequence in which service operating systems work, specifying how they link together to create the value proposition that has been promised to customers. In high-contact services, customers themselves are an integral part of the operation, and the process becomes their experience. Badly designed processes are likely to annoy customers because they often result in slow, frustrating, and poor-quality service delivery. Similarly, poor processes make it difficult for front-line staff to do their jobs well, result in low productivity, and increase the risk of service failures.

One of the distinctive characteristics of many services is the way in which the customer is involved in their creation and delivery. But all too often, service design and operational execution seems to ignore the customer perspective, with each step in the process being handled as a discrete event rather than being integrated into a seamless process.

In this chapter, we emphasize the importance for service marketers of understanding how service processes work and where customers fit within the operation. Specifically, we address the following questions:

1. How can service blueprinting be used to design a service and create a satisfying experience for customers?

2. What can be done to reduce the likelihood of failures during service delivery?

3. How can redesigning services improve both quality and productivity?

4. Under what circumstances should customers be viewed as co-producers of service, and what are the implications?

5. What factors lead customers to embrace or reject new self-service technologies?

6. What should managers do to control unco-operative or abusive customers?

BLUEPRINTING SERVICES TO CREATE VALUED EXPERIENCES AND PRODUCTIVE OPERATIONS

It's no easy task to create a service, especially one that must be delivered in real time with customers present in the service factory. To design services that are both satisfying for customers and operationally efficient, marketers and operations specialists need to work together. In high-contact services, where employees interact directly with customers, it may also be appropriate to involve human-resource experts too.

A key tool that we use to design new services (or redesign existing ones) is known as *blueprinting*. It's a more sophisticated version of *flowcharting*, which we introduced in Chapter 3. As we distinguish between these terms in a service context, a flowchart describes an existing process, often in fairly simple form, while a blueprint specifies in some detail how a service process should be constructed from scratch.

Perhaps you're wondering where the term blueprinting comes from, and why we're using it here? The design for a new building or a ship is usually captured on architectural drawings called blueprints, so called because reproductions have traditionally been printed by a special process using blue ink. These blueprints show what the product should look like and detail the specifications to which it should conform. In contrast to the physical architecture of a building or piece of equipment, service processes have a largely intangible structure. That makes them all the more difficult to visualize. As Lynn Shostack has pointed out, the same is true of processes such as logistics, industrial engineering, decision theory, and computer systems analysis, each of which employs blueprint-like techniques to describe processes involving flows, sequences, relationships, and dependencies.[1]

DEVELOPING A BLUEPRINT

How should you get started on developing a service blueprint? First, you need to identify all the key activities involved in creating and delivering the service in question, and then specify the linkages between these activities.[2] Initially, it's best to keep activities relatively aggregated in order to define the "big picture." You can later refine any given activity by "drilling down" to obtain a higher level of detail. In an airline context, for instance, the passenger activity of "security check" at Toronto's Pearson International Airport actually represents a series of actions, and can be decomposed into such steps as "wait in line; give security officer boarding pass for verification; empty contents of pockets; remove shoes and belts; walk through the metal detector; get electronic equipment (such as a laptop) physically examined; gather all belongings and leave the security checkpoint."

A key characteristic of service blueprinting is that it distinguishes between what customers experience "front-stage" and the activities of employees and support processes "backstage," where customers can't see them. Between the two lies what is called the line of visibility. Operationally oriented businesses are sometimes so focused on managing backstage activities that they neglect the customer's purely front-stage perspective. Auto-repair firms, for instance, often have elaborately documented procedures on how to assess and repair faults, but may lack clear standards for how staff members should greet customers or answer the telephone.

Service blueprints clarify the interactions between customers and employees, and how these are supported by backstage activities and systems. By clarifying interrelationships between employee roles, operational processes, information technology, and customer interactions, blueprints can facilitate the integration of marketing, operations and human resource management within a firm. Although there's no single, required way to prepare a service blueprint, we recommended that a consistent approach be used within any one organization. To illustrate blueprinting later in this chapter, we adapt and simplify an approach proposed by Jane Kingman-Brundage.[3]

Blueprinting also gives managers the opportunity to identify potential *fail points* in the process—points where there is a significant risk of things going wrong and service quality being diminished. When managers are aware of these fail points, they are better able to take preventive measures, prepare contingency plans, or both. They can also pinpoint stages in the process where customers commonly have to wait. Armed with this knowledge, marketing and operations specialists can then develop standards for the execution of each activity, including times for completion of a task, maximum wait times in between tasks, and scripts to guide interactions between staff members and customers.

Creating a Script for Employees and Customers

A well-planned script should provide a full description of the service encounter and can, in itself, help to identify potential or existing problems in a specific service process. Recall from Chapter 2 the script for teeth cleaning and a simple dental examination involving three players—the patient, the receptionist, and the dental hygienist. Each of these players may be invited to review the script and to identify either missing or superfluous steps, to suggest changes in sequence, or to highlight ways in which developments in either information technology or dental equipment and treatment might require changes in the procedures.

By examining existing scripts, service managers may discover ways to modify the nature of customer and employee roles in order to improve service delivery, increase productivity, and enhance the nature of the customer's experience. As service delivery procedures evolve in response to new technology or other factors, revised scripts may need to be developed.

Blueprinting the Restaurant Experience: A Three-Act Performance

To illustrate blueprinting of a high-contact, people-processing service, we examine the experience of dinner for two at Chez Jean, an upscale restaurant that enhances its core food service with a variety of other supplementary services (Figure 8.1, pp. 232–235) A typical rule of thumb in full-service restaurants is that the cost of purchasing the food ingredients represents between 20 and 30 percent of the price of the meal. The balance can be seen as the "fees" that the customer is willing to pay for renting a table and chairs in a pleasant setting, hiring the services of food preparation experts and their kitchen equipment, and providing serving staff to wait on them both inside and outside the dining room.

The key components of the blueprint, reading from top to bottom, are:

- Definition of standards for each front-stage activity (only a few examples are actually specified in the figure).
- Physical and other evidence for front-stage activities (specified for all steps).
- Principal customer actions (illustrated by pictures).
- Line of interaction.
- Front-stage actions by customer contact personnel.
- Line of visibility.
- Backstage actions by customer-contact personnel.
- Support processes involving other service personnel.
- Support processes involving information technology.

Reading from left to right, the blueprint prescribes the sequence of actions over time. In Chapter 2, we likened service performances to theatre. To emphasize the involvement of human actors in service delivery, we've followed the practice adopted by some service organizations of using pictures to illustrate each of the 14 principal steps involving our two customers (there are other steps not shown), beginning with making a reservation and concluding with departure from the restaurant after the meal. Like many high-contact services involving discrete transactions—as opposed to the continuous delivery found in, say, utility or insurance services—the "restaurant drama" can be divided into three "acts," representing activities that take place before the core product is encountered, delivery of the core product (in this case, the meal), and subsequent activities while still involved with the service provider.

The "stage" or servicescape includes both the exterior and interior of the restaurant. Front-stage actions take place in a very visual environment; restaurants are often quite theatrical in their use of physical evidence (such as furnishings, decor, uniforms, lighting, and table settings) and may also employ background music in their efforts to create a themed environment that matches their market positioning.

Act I: Prologue and Introductory Scenes   In this particular drama, Act I begins with a customer making a reservation by telephone with an unseen employee. This action could take place hours or even days in advance of visiting the restaurant. In theatrical terms, the telephone conversation can be likened to a radio drama, with impressions being created by the nature of the respondent's voice, speed of response, and style of conversation. When our customers arrive at the restaurant, a valet parks their car, they leave their coats in the coatroom and enjoy a drink in the bar area while waiting for their table. The act concludes with their being escorted to a table and seated.

These five steps constitute the couple's initial experience of the restaurant performance, with each involving an interaction with an employee—either by phone or face to face. By the time the two of them reach their table in the dining room, they've been exposed to several supplementary services, and have also encountered a sizeable cast of characters, including five or more contact personnel, as well as many other customers.

Standards can be set for each service activity, but should be based on a good understanding of guest expectations. (Remember our discussion in Chapter 2 about how expectations are formed.) Below the line of visibility, the blueprint identifies key actions to ensure that each front-stage step is performed in a manner that meets or exceeds those expectations. These actions include recording reservations, handling customers' coats, delivery and preparation of food, maintenance of facilities and equipment, training and assignment of staff for each task, and use of information technology to access, input, store and transfer relevant data.

Act II: Delivery of the Core Product   As the curtain rises on Act II, our customers are finally about to experience the core service they came for. For simplicity, we've condensed the meal into just four scenes. In practice, reviewing the menu and placing the order are two separate activities; meantime, meal service proceeds on a course-by-course basis. If you were actually running a restaurant yourself, your blueprint would need to go into greater detail at this point to identify each of the many steps involved in what is often a tightly scripted drama. Assuming all goes well, the two guests will have an excellent meal, nicely served in a pleasant atmosphere, with perhaps a fine wine to enhance it. But if the restaurant fails to satisfy their expectations (and those of its many other guests) during Act II, it's going to be in serious trouble. There are numerous potential fail points. Is the menu information complete? Is it intelligible? Is everything listed on the menu actually available this evening? Will explanations and advice be given in a friendly and uncondescending manner for guests who have questions about specific menu items or are unsure about which wine to order?

After our customers decide on their meals, they place their orders with the server, who must then pass on the details to personnel in the kitchen, bar, and billing desk. Mistakes in transmitting information are a frequent cause of quality failures in many organizations. Bad handwriting or unclear verbal requests can lead to delivery of the wrong items altogether—or of the right items incorrectly prepared.

In subsequent scenes of Act II, our customers may evaluate not only the quality of food and drink—the most important dimensions of all—but also how promptly it is served (not late, but not too promptly either, for that might suggest frozen foods cooked by microwave!), and the style of service. A technically correct performance by the server can still be spoiled by such human failures as an uninterested, cold, grating, or overly casual manner.

Act III: The Drama Concludes   The meal may be over, but much is still taking place both front stage and backstage as the drama moves to its close. The core service has now been delivered, and we'll assume that our customers are happily digesting it. Act III should be short. The action in each of the remaining scenes should move smoothly,

Figure 8.1

Blueprinting a Full-
Service Restaurant
Experience

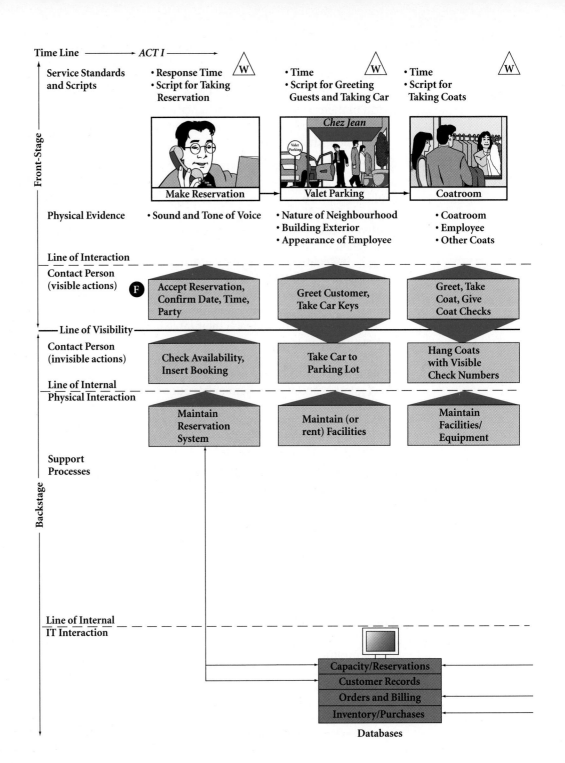

Figure 8.1 (Continued)

| • Time
 • Order Accuracy
 • Script for Serving Drinks $\boxed{W}$ | • Punctuality vs. Reservation
 • Script for Seating $\boxed{W}$ | *ACT II* ⟶
 • Time
 • Script for Greeting Guests, Taking Order $\boxed{W}$ | • Time
 • Script for Wine Service $\boxed{W}$ |

| Cocktails | → | Seating | → | Order Food and Wine | → | Wine Service |

| • Cocktail Lounge Decor
 • Furnishings
 • Table Setting
 • Staff, Other Customers | • Dining Room Decor
 • Appearance / Demeanour of Staff
 • Table Setting
 • Other Guests | | • Wine Quality |

Greet, Take Orders, Deliver Drinks **F** Escort Guests to Table, Help Seat, Offer Menus **F** Greet, Take Orders **F** Deliver Wine, Open, Pour

Give Orders to Bar, Collect Drinks | Verify Reservation, Pick Up Menus | Place Order with Kitchen/ Cellarer | Retrieve Wine

Cocktail Preparation | Prepare Menu Copies | Maintain Order/ Billing Records | Maintain Cellars

Maintain Bar Supplies | Maintain Seating Plan | | Wine Storage

Beverage Storage | | | Wine Purchase/ Delivery

Beverage Purchase/ Delivery

Key

F Points Fail

$\boxed{W}$ Risk of Excessive Wait (Standard times should specify limits.)

Figure 8.1 (Continued)

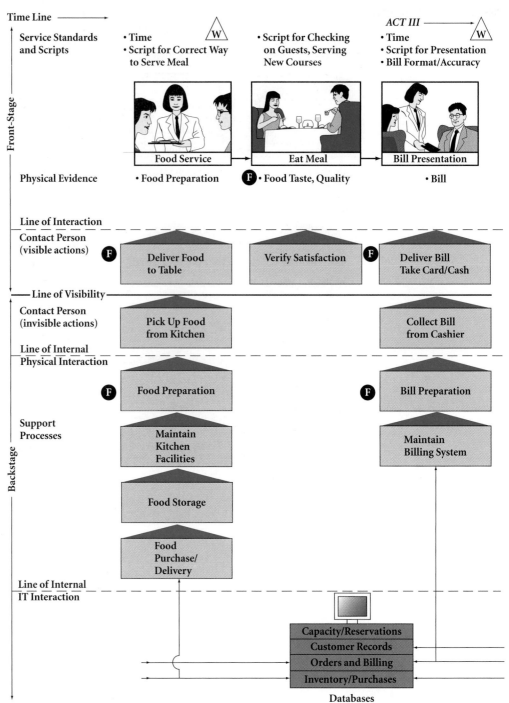

Figure 8.1 (Continued)

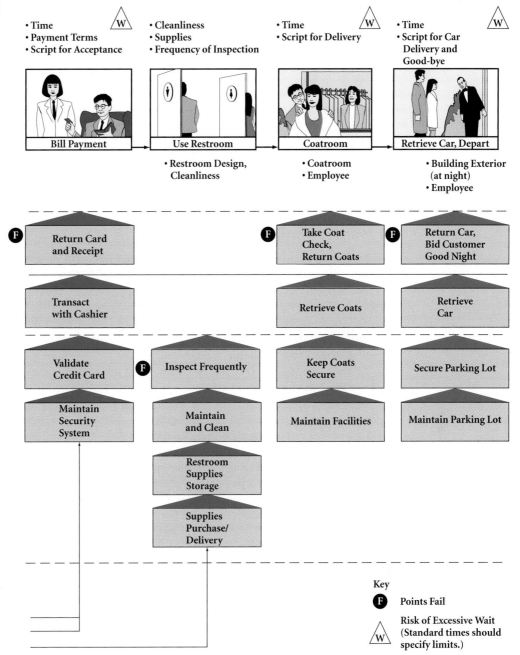

quickly, and pleasantly, with no shocking surprises at the end. We can hypothesize that in a North American environment, most customers' expectations would probably include the following:

- An accurate, intelligible bill is presented promptly as soon as the customer requests it.
- Payment is handled politely and expeditiously (with all major credit cards accepted).
- The guests are thanked for their patronage and invited to come again.
- Customers visiting the restrooms find them clean and properly supplied.
- The right coats are promptly retrieved from the coatroom.
- The customer's car is brought promptly to the door in the same condition as when it was left; the attendant thanks them again and bids them a good evening.

Identifying Fail Points

Running a good restaurant is a complex business, and much can go wrong. A good blueprint should draw attention to points in service delivery where things are particularly at risk of going wrong. From a customer perspective, the most serious fail points, marked in our blueprint by **F** , are those that will result in failure to access or enjoy the core product. They involve the reservation (Could the customer get through by phone? Was a table available at the desired time and date? Was the reservation recorded accurately?) and seating. (Was a table available when promised?)

Since service delivery takes place over time, there is also the possibility of delays between specific actions, requiring the customers to wait. Common locations for such waits are identified by ⚠. Customers might experience different wait times for a specific action across different service contexts. For example, the wait time to see a doctor with a pre-booked appointment will be likely different (and most probably longer) than the wait time to see a hairstylist with a pre-booked appointment. Customers form notions of reasonable wait times in these contexts; in a full-service restaurant setting a certain amount of waiting, allowing time for conversation, is considered a positive part of the experience, but in any service encounter excessive waits annoy customers. In practice, every step in the process—both front stage and backstage—has some potential for failures and delays. In fact, failures often lead directly to delays, reflecting orders that were never passed on, or time spent correcting mistakes.

David Maister coined the term OTSU ("opportunity to screw up") to highlight the importance of thinking about all the things that might go wrong in delivering a particular type of service.[4] OTSUs are funny when you talk about them. John Cleese made millions laugh with his portrayal of an inept hotel manager in the television series *Fawlty Towers*. Chevy Chase entertained movie audiences for years by playing a customer tortured by inept, rude, or downright cruel service employees. And few would forget *Seinfeld's* remarks on car rental agencies, "See, you know how to take the reservation, you just don't know how to *hold* the reservation, and that's really the most important part of the reservation, the holding. Anybody can just take them." But customers don't always see the funny side when the joke is on them. It's only by identifying all the possible OTSUs associated with a particular task that service managers can put together a delivery system that's explicitly designed to avoid such problems.

Setting Service Standards

Through both formal research and on-the-job experience, service managers can learn the nature of customer expectations at each step in the process. As outlined in Chapter 2, customers' expectations range across a spectrum—referred to as the zone of tolerance—from desired service (an ideal) to a threshold level of merely adequate service (see Figure 2.9 on p. 47). Service providers should design standards for each step sufficiently high to satisfy customers; if that's not possible, then they will need to modify customer expectations. These standards may include time parameters, the script for a technically correct performance, and prescriptions for appropriate style and demeanour. Standards must be expressed in ways that permit objective measurement.

The opening scenes of a service drama are particularly important, since customers' first impressions can affect their evaluations of quality during later stages of service delivery. Perceptions of their service experiences tend to be cumulative.[5] If a couple of things go badly wrong at the outset, customers may simply walk out. Even if they stay, they may now be looking for other things that aren't quite right. On the other hand, if the first steps go really well, their zones of tolerance may increase so that they are more willing to over-look minor mistakes later in the service performance. Recent research suggests that, when a consumer has little experience with a service, positive initial impressions about a single service provider can lead to positive inferences about other service providers to a far greater extent than a similar impact for negative initial impressions.[6] Research by Marriott Hotels indicates that four of the five top factors contributing to customer loyalty come into play during the first ten minutes of service delivery.[7] Research into the design of plastic surgeons' offices and procedures suggests that unfavourable initial impressions can lead patients to cancel surgery or even change doctors.[8] However, performance standards should not be allowed to fall off toward the end of service delivery. Other research findings point to the importance of a strong finish, and suggest that a service encounter that is perceived to start poorly but then builds in quality will be better rated than one that starts well but declines and ends poorly.[9]

Our restaurant example was deliberately chosen to illustrate a high-contact, people-processing service with which you and other readers are likely to be familiar. But many possession-processing services (like repair or maintenance) and information-processing services (like insurance or accounting) involve far less contact with customers, since much of the action takes place backstage. In these situations, a failure committed front stage is likely to represent a higher proportion of the customer's service encounters with a company and may therefore be viewed even more seriously, because there are fewer subsequent opportunities to create a favourable impression.

Failure Proofing Can Improve Reliability of Service Processes[10]

Careful analysis of the reasons for failure in service processes often reveals opportunities for "failure proofing" certain activities in order to reduce or even eliminate the risk of errors. Fail-safe methods need to be designed not only for employees but also for customers, especially in services where the latter participate actively in creation and delivery processes. Service Perspectives 8.1 describes the Poka Yoke technique, which is widely used to fail-safe service processes.

SERVICE PROCESS REDESIGN

Service process redesign revitalizes processes that have become outdated. But that doesn't necessarily mean that the processes were poorly designed in the first place. Rather, changes in technology, customer needs, added service features and new offerings have made existing processes crack and creak.[11] Mitchell T. Rabkin MD, formerly president of Boston's Beth Israel Hospital (now Beth Israel-Deaconess Medical Center), characterized the problem as "institutional rust," and declared: "Institutions are like steel beams—they tend to rust. What was once smooth and shiny and nice tends to become rusty."[12] He suggested that there were two main reasons for this situation. The first involves changes in the external environment that make existing practices obsolete and require redesign of the underlying processes—or even creation of brand-new processes—in order for the organization to remain relevant and responsive. In health care, such changes may reflect new forms of competition, legislation, technology, health insurance policies, and evolving customer needs.

The second reason for institutional rusting occurs internally. Often, it reflects a natural deterioration of internal processes, creeping bureaucracy, or the evolution of spurious,

Service Perspectives 8.1

Poka Yokes: An Effective Tool to Design Fail Points Out of Service Processes

One of the most useful Total Quality Management (TQM: an approach centred on quality and customer satisfaction) methods in manufacturing is the application of poka-yoke, or fail-safe methods to prevent errors in manufacturing processes. Richard Chase and Douglas Steward introduced this concept to fail-safe service processes.

Part of the challenge of implementing poka-yokes (which is simply "fail-safing" in Japanese, where the concept was pioneered by Toyota) in a service context is the need to address not only server errors, but also customer errors. Server poka-yokes ensure that service staff do things correctly, as requested, in the right order, and at the right speed. Examples include surgeons whose surgical instrument trays have indentations for each instrument. For a given operation, all of the instruments are nested in the tray, so it is clear if the surgeon has not removed all instruments from the patient before closing the incision.

Some service firms use poka-yokes to ensure that certain steps or standards in the customer-staff interaction are adhered to. A bank ensures eye contact by requiring tellers to record the customer's eye colour on a checklist at the start of a transaction. Some firms place mirrors at the exits of staff areas to foster a neat appearance. Front-line staff can then automatically check their appearance before greeting a customer. At one restaurant, servers place round coasters in front of those diners who have ordered a decaffeinated coffee and square coasters in front of the others.

Customer poka-yokes usually focus on preparing the customer for the encounter (including getting them to bring the right materials for the transaction and to arrive on time, if applicable), understanding and anticipating their role in the service transaction, and selecting the correct service or transaction. Examples that prepare the customer for the encounter include printing dress-code requests on invitations, sending reminders of dental appointments, and printing guidelines on customer cards (e.g., "please have your account and pin number ready before calling our service reps"). Poka-yokes that address customer errors during the encounter include beepers at automated teller machines (ATMs) so that customers do not forget to take their card, and locks on aircraft lavatory doors that must be closed to switch on the lights.

Designing poka-yokes is part art and part science. Most of the procedures seem trivial, but this is actually a key advantage of the method. It can be used to design frequently occurring service failures out of service processes, and to ensure adherence to certain service standards or service steps.

Source: Adapted from Richard B. Chase and Douglas M. Stewart, "Make Your Service Fail-Safe," *Sloan Management Review* (Spring 1994): 35–44.

---

unofficial standards (see Best Practice in Action 8.1). Symptoms such as extensive information exchange, data redundancy, a high ratio of checking or control activities to value-adding activities, increased exception processing, and growing numbers of customer complaints about inconvenient and unnecessary procedures often indicate that a process is not working well and requires redesign.

Examining blueprints of existing services may suggest opportunities for product improvement that might be achieved by reconfiguring delivery systems, adding or deleting specific elements, or repositioning the service to appeal to other segments. Each year, Avis determines a set of factors that car renters care about the most. The company breaks down the car rental process into more than 100 incremental steps, including making reservations, finding the pickup counter, getting to the car, driving it, returning it, paying the bill, and so forth.[13] Because Avis knows customers' key concerns, it claims it can quickly identify ways to improve their satisfaction. What travellers most desire is to get their rental car quickly and drive away, so the firm has designed its processes to achieve that goal. "We're constantly making little enhancements around the edges," says Scott Deaver, the company's executive vice president for marketing. He sees this as Avis's ongoing attempt to live up to its tagline, "We Try Harder," which the company has employed for some 40 years. "It's not a slogan," says Deaver, "It's in the DNA of the place."

Managers in charge of service-process redesign projects should look for opportunities to achieve a quantum leap in both productivity and service quality at the same time. Restructuring or re-engineering the ways in which tasks are performed has significant potential to increase output, especially in many backstage jobs.[14] Redesign efforts typically focus on achieving the following key performance measures: (1) reduced number of service

Best Practice in Action 8.1

Rooting Out Unofficial Standards in a Hospital

One of the distinctive characteristics of Mitchell T. Rabkin's 30-year tenure as president of Boston's Beth Israel Hospital was his policy of routinely visiting all areas of the hospital. He usually did so unannounced and in a low-key fashion. No one working at the hospital was surprised to see Dr. Rabkin drop by at almost any time of day or night. His natural curiosity gave him unparalleled insight into how effectively service procedures were working, and the subtle ways in which things could go wrong. As the following story reveals, he discovered that there is often a natural deterioration of messages over time.

> One day, I was in the EU [emergency unit], chatting with a house officer [physician] who was treating a patient with asthma. He was giving her medication through an intravenous drip. I looked at the formula for the medication and asked him, "Why are you using this particular cocktail?" "Oh," he replied, "that's hospital policy." Since I was certain that there was no such policy, I decided to investigate.

What had happened went something like this. A few months earlier, Resident [physician] A says to Intern B, who is observing her treat a patient: "This is what I use for asthma." On the next month's rotation, Intern B says to new Resident C: "This is what Dr. A uses for asthma." The following month, Resident C says to Intern D, "This is what we use for asthma." And finally, within another month, Intern D is telling Resident E, "It's hospital policy to use this medication."

As a result of conversations like these, well-intentioned but unofficial standards keep cropping up. It's a particular problem in a place like this, which isn't burdened by an inhuman policy manual where you must look up the policy for everything you do. We prefer to rely on people's intelligence and judgment and limit written policies to overall, more general issues. One always has to be aware of the growth of institutional rust and to be clear about what is being done and why it is being done.

Source: Christopher Lovelock, *Product Plus*. New York: McGraw-Hill, 1994: 355.

---

failures, (2) reduced cycle time from customer initiation of a service process to its completion, (3) enhanced productivity, and (4) increased customer satisfaction. Ideally, redesign efforts should achieve all of the four measures simultaneously.

Service process redesign encompasses reconstitution, rearrangement, or substitution of service processes.[15] These efforts can be categorized into a number of types, including

- *Eliminating non-value-adding steps.* Often, activities at the front-end and back-end processes of services can be streamlined with the goal of focusing on the benefit-producing part of the service encounter. The outcomes are typically increased productivity and customer satisfaction. For example, customers checking out of a hotel in the morning may not be interested in going to the front desk, lining up for the bill to be processed, and then paying the balance. For such customers, most hotel chains have eliminated these non-value-adding steps by means of offering express check-outs, which essentially involves all charges being posted to a credit card provided by the customer at the time of check-in and a summary statement left under the door of the customer's room on the last night of stay. If the bill is correct, the customer can just leave the hotel next morning without having to visit the front desk.

- *Shifting to self-service.* Significant gains in productivity, and sometimes even service quality, can be achieved by increasing self-service when redesigning services. For example, FedEx succeeded in shifting more than 50 percent of its transactions from its call centres to its website, thus reducing the number of employees in its call centres by about 20 000.

- *Delivering direct service.* This type of redesign involves bringing the service to the customer instead of bringing the customer to the service firm. This is often done to improve convenience for the customer, but can also result in productivity gains if companies can do away with expensive high-street locations. For example, Auto Glass Canada (www.autoglasscanada.com) operates a successful business offering mobile services for automobile windshield repair across various locations in Ontario.

- *Bundling services.* Bundling services involves bundling, or grouping, multiple services into one offering, focusing on a well-defined customer group. Bundling can help increase productivity (the bundle is already tailored for a particular segment, making the transaction faster, and the marketing costs of each service are often reduced), while at the same time adding value to the customer through lower transaction costs. It often has a better fit to the needs of the target segment. For example, most telecommunication service providers (such as Look Communications—www.look.ca—which offers high-speed internet access and digital TV programming) offer bundled pricing that provides substantial savings over the typical cost of stand-alone digital TV programming and/or high-speed internet access.

- *Redesigning the physical aspects of service processes.* Physical service redesign focuses on the tangible elements of a service process and includes improvements to the service facilities and equipment. This increases convenience and productivity of the service experience and often also enhances the satisfaction and productivity of front-line staff. For example, the Art Gallery of Hamilton (www.artgalleryofhamilton.com) invested $18 million over the span of two years before it reopened in 2005 with improvements such as exterior recladding, a more welcoming entrance, an increase in exhibition space, new rental and customer service facilities, and a new gallery shop.[16]

Table 8.1 summarizes five types of service redesign, provides an overview of their potential benefits for the firm and its customers, and highlights potential challenges or limitations. You should note that these redesigns are often used in combination. For example, central to chapter.indigo.ca's success is the combined appeal of self-service, direct service, and minimization of non-value-added steps through the effective capture of customer preferences, plus shipping and payment data.

Another dimension of service redesign concerns decisions on who should be responsible for delivery of each of the component elements in the blueprint. Increasingly, companies

Table 8.1 Five Types of Service Redesign

Approach and Concept	Potential Company Benefits	Potential Customer Benefits	Challenges/Limitations
Elimination of non–value-added steps (streamlines process)	• Improves efficiency • Increases productivity • Increases ability to customize service • Differentiates company	• Improves efficiency, speed • Shifts tasks from customer to service firm • Separates service activation from delivery • Customizes service	• Requires customer education and employee training to implement smoothly and effectively
Self-service (customer assumes role of producer)	• Lowers cost • Improves productivity • Enhances technology reputation • Differentiates company	• Increases speed of service • Improves access • Saves money • Increases perception of control	• Must prepare customers for the role • Limits face-to-face interaction and opportunities to build relationships • Harder to get customer feedback
Direct service (service delivered to the customer's location)	• Eliminates store location limitations • Expands customer base • Differentiates company	• Increases convenience • Improves access	• Imposes logistical burdens • May be costly • Needs credibility and trust
Bundled service (combines multiple services into a package)	• Differentiates company • Aids customer retention • Increases per-capita service use	• Increases convenience • Customizes service	• Requires extensive knowledge of targeted customers • May be perceived as wasteful
Physical service (manipulation of tangibles associated with the service)	• Improves employee satisfaction • Increases productivity • Differentiates company	• Increases convenience • Enhances function • Generates interest	• Easily imitated • Requires expense to effect and maintain • Raises customer expectations for the industry

Source: Adapted from Leonard L. Berry and Sandra K. Lampo, "Teaching an Old Service New Tricks: The Promise of Service Redesign," *Journal of Service Research* 2, no. 3 (2000): 265–75.

are outsourcing non-core activities to specialist suppliers. IBM employs the term *componentization* to describe the deconstruction (or unbundling) of a company's activities and subsequent reconstruction into *value nets* (as opposed to a *value chain*) in which value is created by businesses and their suppliers, buyers, and partners by combining and enhancing the component services collectively provided by participants.[17] "Businesses," argue Luba Cherbakov and her colleagues at IBM, "should view themselves as a federation of capabilities that collaborate with other enterprises within a business "ecosystem.'"[18]

THE CUSTOMER AS CO-PRODUCER

Blueprinting helps to specify the role of customers in service delivery, and to identify the extent of contact between them and service providers. Blueprinting also clarifies whether the customer's role in a given service process is primarily that of passive recipient, or entails active involvement in creating and producing the service.

Levels of Customer Participation

Customer participation refers to the actions and resources supplied by customers during service production and/or delivery, including mental, physical, and even emotional inputs.[19] Some degree of customer participation in service delivery is inevitable in people-processing services and in many other services involving real-time contact between customers and providers. However, as Mary Jo Bitner and her colleagues show, the extent of such participation varies widely and can be divided into three broad levels, which they characterize as follows.[20]

Low Participation Level Employees and systems do all the work. Products tend to be standardized. Payment may be the only required customer input. In situations where customers come to the service factory, all that is required is the customers' physical presence. Visiting a movie theatre or taking a bus are examples. In possession-processing services such as routine cleaning or maintenance, customers can remain entirely uninvolved with the process other than providing access to service providers and making payment.

Moderate Participation Level Customer inputs are required to assist the firm in creating and delivering service, and in providing a degree of customization. These inputs may include provision of information, personal effort, or even physical possessions. When getting their hair washed and cut, customers must let the cutter know what they want, and co-operate during the different steps in the process. If a client wants an accountant to prepare a tax return, she must first pull together information and physical documentation that the accountant can use to prepare the return correctly, and then be prepared to respond to any questions that the latter may have.

High Participation Level In these instances, customers work actively with the provider to co-produce the service. Service cannot be created apart from the customer's purchase and active participation. In fact, if customers fail to assume this role effectively and don't perform certain mandatory production tasks, they will jeopardize the quality of the service outcome. Marriage counselling and some health-related services fall into this category, especially those related to improvement of the patient's physical condition, such as rehabilitation or weight loss, where customers work under professional supervision. Successful delivery of many B2B services requires customers and providers to work closely together as members of a team, such as for management consulting and supply-chain management services.

Self-Service Technologies

The ultimate form of involvement in service production is for customers to undertake a specific activity themselves, using facilities or systems provided by the service supplier. In effect, the customer's time and effort replaces that of a service employee. In the case of telephone- and internet-based service, customers even provide their own terminals.

Figure 8.2

Self-Service Check-In
Kiosk at the Airport in
Kelowna, BC

Consumers are faced with an array of self-service technologies (SSTs) that allow them to produce a service independent of direct service employee involvement.[21] SSTs include automated banking terminals, self-service scanning at supermarket checkouts and self-service gasoline pumps, self-service check-ins at airports (see Figure 8.2), automated telephone systems such as phone banking, automated hotel check-out, and numerous internet-based services.

Information-based services lend themselves particularly well to the use of SSTs, and include not only such supplementary services as getting information, placing orders and reservations, and making payment, but also delivery of core products in fields such as banking, research, entertainment, and self-paced education. One of the most significant innovations of the internet era has been the development of on-line auctions, led by eBay. No human auctioneer is needed as an intermediary between buyers and sellers. While eBay remains the global leader in online auctions, some Canadian players such as Ezead Canada Auction (www.u-1.ca) are actively trying to carve a local niche for themselves in the online auction space.

Many companies have developed strategies designed to encourage customers to undertake self-service through the World Wide Web. They hope to divert customers from using more expensive alternatives such as direct contact with employees, use of intermediaries such as brokers and travel agents, or voice-to-voice telephone. Nevertheless, not all customers take advantage of SSTs. Matthew Meuter and his colleagues observe: "For many firms, often the challenge is not managing the technology but rather getting consumers to try the technology."[22]

Psychological Factors in Customer Co-production

The logic of self-service historically relied on an economic rationale, emphasizing the productivity gains and cost savings that result when customers take over work previously performed by employees. In many instances, a portion of the resulting savings is shared with customers in the form of lower prices, as an inducement for them to change their behaviour.

Given the significant investment in time and money required for firms to design, implement, and manage SSTs, it's critical for service marketers to understand how consumers decide between using an SST option and relying on a human provider. We need to recognize that SSTs present both advantages and disadvantages. In addition to benefiting from time and cost savings, flexibility, convenience of location, greater control over service delivery, and a higher perceived level of customization, customers may also derive fun, enjoyment, and even spontaneous delight from SST usage.[23] However, there's evidence that some consumers see the introduction of SSTs into the service encounter as something of a threat, causing anxiety and stress among those who are uncomfortable with using them.[24] Some consumers view service encounters as social experiences and prefer to deal with people, while others purposely try to avoid such contact—especially if they have a poor perception of a firm's employees. Another possible reason for customer disquiet is the perception that SSTs shift tasks onto them that were formerly performed by an employee, to lower the company's costs, though there has so far been no empirical research to test the extent of this perception.

Research by James Curran, Matthew Meuter, and Carol Surprenant found that multiple attitudes drive customer intentions to use a specific SST, including global attitudes toward related service technologies, global attitudes toward the specific service firm, and attitudes toward its employees.[25]

What Aspects of SSTs Please or Annoy Customers?

Research suggests that customers both love and hate SSTs.[26] They love SSTs when they bail them out of difficult situations, often because SST machines are conveniently located and accessible 24/7. And of course, as Figure 8.3 shows, a website is as close as the nearest computer, making this option much more accessible than the company's physical sites. Customers also love SSTs when they perform better than the alternative of being served by a service employee, enabling users to get detailed information and complete transactions faster than they could through face-to-face or telephone contact. Experienced travellers rely on SSTs to save time and effort at airports, rental car facilities, and hotels. As a *Wall Street Journal* article summarized the trend, "Have A Pleasant Trip: Eliminate All

Figure 8.3
HSBC, "The World's Local Bank," brings its global site to your local computer.

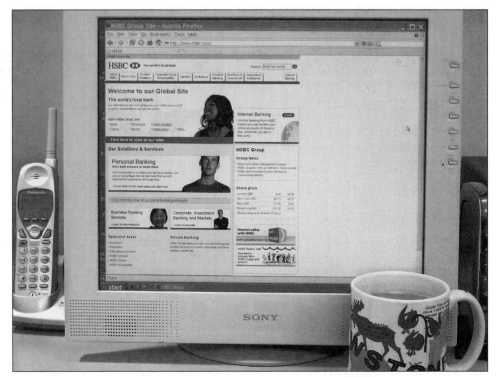

Courtesy HSBC.

Human Contact."[27] Consultants Jeffrey Rayport and Bernard Jaworski argue that success at the customer interface requires an understanding of what target customers want from an interaction. Sometimes a well-designed SST can deliver better service than a human being. Said one customer about the experience of purchasing convenience store items from a new model of automated vending machine, "A guy in the store can make a mistake or give you a hard time, but not the machine. I definitely prefer the machine."[28] In short, many customers are still in awe of technology and what it can do for them—when it works well.

However, customers hate SSTs when they fail. Users get angry when they find that machines are out of service, their pin numbers are not accepted, websites are down, or tracking numbers do not work. Even when SSTs do work, customers are frustrated by poorly designed technologies that make service processes difficult to understand and use. A common complaint is difficulty in navigating one's way around a website. Users also get frustrated when they themselves mess up, due to such errors as forgetting their passwords, failing to provide information as requested, or simply hitting the wrong buttons. Self-service logically implies that customers can cause their own dissatisfaction. But Neeli Bendapudi and Robert Leone note that even when it is the customers' own fault, they may still blame the service provider for not providing a simpler and more user-friendly system, and then, on the next occasion, revert to the traditional human-based system.[29]

Designing a website to be virtually failure-proof is no easy task and can be very expensive, but it is through such investments that companies create loyal users and achieve impressive growth. Best Practice in Action 8.2 describes the emphasis on the payoffs of investments in SPUD's (Small Potatoes Urban Delivery) website.

A key problem with SSTs is that so few of them incorporate service recovery systems. In too many instances, when the process fails, there is no simple way to recover on the spot. Typically, customers are forced to telephone or make a personal visit to resolve the problem, which may be exactly what they were trying to avoid in the first place! Mary Jo Bitner suggests that managers should put their firms' SSTs to the test by asking the following basic questions:[30]

Best Practice in Action 8.2

Investments in Website Secret to Success of spud.ca

Starting out with a mere nine customers when David Van Peters went online with his Vancouver-based organic produce delivery service, he has managed to create a loyal base of over 5000 customers with revenues exceeding $7.5 million. And what has been the primary driver behind the success? A detailed website that features over 1300 products and provides additional services such as recipes and meal planning. Although the customers can still buy their groceries over the phone, the vast majority of the sales, 94 percent, are through its web business.

Van Peters, who was an environmental management consultant for ten years before he launched the business in 1998, started the website with a goal of reducing the paper consumption at his three-month-old company. That modest goal, however, has led to substantial payoffs for his business. In addition to creating an accessible, self-service, virtual storefront where consumers can do research on organic produce, look up recipes, and create personalized shopping lists, the website also serves as an invaluable tool for gaining insights about customers' preferences and purchasing patterns. Tracking customer preferences based on budget,

product assortment, and seasonality has helped Van Peters adapt his ordering schedules and quantities, hence reducing waste resulting from overstocking perishable items. According to Van Peters, this customized information system is the single biggest competitive advantage for spud.ca.

The success, though impressive, comes with a substantial price tag. Spud.ca invests over $250 000 annually for maintenance and improvements to its website that allows for improved customer experience as well as detailed customer research. Van Peters sees this as a valuable investment. "To offer a good quality service, we needed an excellent website and information system, and we're amortizing those costs over more and more deliveries." Not surprisingly, spud.ca has managed to operate as a profitable business over the last five years. This success has helped spud.ca expand its customer base by merging with or absorbing five other organic grocers in the Vancouver area, and also by expanding its business to Calgary and also [in 2005] to Seattle [where it trades as spud.com]. It's certainly not small potatoes anymore!

Source: Will Gibson, "Do the Bright Thing," *Financial Post Business* (October 2005): 74–77; www.spud.ca, accessed August 21, 2006. © Will Gibson.

- *Does the SST work reliably?* Firms must ensure that SSTs work as dependably as promised and that the design is user-friendly for customers. The U.S.-based Southwest Airlines' online ticketing services have set a high standard for simplicity and reliability. It boasts the highest percentage of online ticket sales of any airline—clear evidence of customer acceptance.

- *Is the SST better than the interpersonal alternative?* If it doesn't save time or provide ease of access, cost savings, or some other benefit, then customers will continue to use familiar conventional processes. Spud.ca's success reflects its efforts to create a highly personalized, efficient alternative to visiting a grocery store.

- *If it fails, what systems are in place to recover?* It's critical for firms to provide systems, structures, and recovery technologies that will enable prompt service recovery when things go wrong. Some banks have a phone beside each ATM, giving customers direct access to a 24-hour customer service centre if they have questions or run into difficulties. Supermarkets that have installed self-service checkout lanes usually assign one employee to monitor the lanes; this practice combines security with customer assistance. In telephone-based service systems, well-designed voicemail menus include an option for customers to reach a customer service rep.

Customers as Partial Employees

Some researchers argue that firms should view customers as "partial employees," who can influence the productivity and quality of service processes and outputs.[31] This perspective requires a change in management mindset, as Schneider and Bowen make clear:

> If you think of customers as partial employees, you begin to think very differently about what you hope customers will bring to the service encounter. Now they must bring not only expectations and needs but also relevant service production competencies that will enable them to fill the role of partial employees. The service management challenge deepens accordingly.[32]

They suggest that customers who are offered an opportunity to participate at an active level are more likely to be satisfied—regardless of whether or not they actually choose the more active role—because they like to be offered a choice.

Managing customers as partial employees requires using the same human resource strategy as managing a firm's paid employees, and should follow these four steps:

1. Conduct a "job analysis" of customers' present roles in the business, and compare it with the roles the firm would like them to play.

2. Determine if customers are aware of how they are expected to perform and have the skills needed to perform as required. The more work that customers are expected to do, the greater their need for education on how to perform their roles for best results. The necessary education can be provided in many different ways. Brochures and posted instructions are two widely used approaches. Automated machines often contain detailed operating instructions and diagrams. Many websites include an FAQ (frequently asked questions) section. EBay Canada's website (www.ebay.ca) provides detailed instructions for getting started, including how to submit an item for auction and how to bid for items you might want to buy. See also Chapter 14, p. 426, on how to manage customer reluctance to adopt new service processes.

3. Motivate customers by ensuring that they will be rewarded for contributing and performing well (e.g., satisfaction from better quality and more customized output, enjoyment of participating in the actual process, or a belief that their own productivity speeds the process and keeps costs down).

4. Regularly appraise customers' performance. If it is unsatisfactory, seek to change their roles and the procedures in which they are involved. Alternatively, consider "terminating" your business with these customers (nicely, of course!) and look for new ones.

Effective human-resource management starts with recruitment and selection. The same approach should hold true for "partial employees." So if co-production requires specific skills, firms should target their marketing efforts to recruit new customers who have the competency to perform the necessary tasks.[33] After all, many universities do just this in their student selection process! When the relationship is not working out, termination remains an option of last resort. Lawyers, for instance, have a legal duty to help their clients, but the relationship will only succeed if it is mutually co-operative. Sooner or later most lawyers encounter a client who treats them inappropriately, abuses the office staff, or is non-compliant in fee payments; then the lawyer simply has to ask that individual to seek care elsewhere.[34]

DYSFUNCTIONAL CUSTOMER BEHAVIOUR DISRUPTS SERVICE PROCESSES

Other customers often form an important element in service encounters. In many people-processing services we expect to find other customers present and to share service facilities with them. Their behaviour can contribute positively or negatively to the functioning of specific service delivery processes, and may even affect the outcome.

Customers who act in unco-operative or abusive ways are a problem for any organization. But they have more potential for mischief in service businesses, particularly those in which many other customers are present in the service factory. As you know from your own experience, other people's behaviour can affect your enjoyment of a service. If you like classical music and attend symphony concerts, you expect audience members to keep quiet during the performance, rather than spoiling the experience by talking or coughing loudly. By contrast, a silent audience would be deadly during a rock concert or a team sports event, where active audience participation adds to the excitement. There's a fine line, however, between spectator enthusiasm and abusive behaviour by supporters of rival sports teams. Firms that fail to deal effectively with customer misbehaviour risk damaging their relationships with all the other customers they'd like to keep.

Addressing the Challenge of Jaycustomers[35]

Visitors to North America from other English-speaking countries are often puzzled by the term "jaywalker," that distinctively American word used to describe people who cross streets at unauthorized places or in a dangerous manner. The prefix "jay" comes from a nineteenth-century slang term for a stupid person. We can create a whole vocabulary of derogatory terms by adding the prefix "jay" to existing nouns and verbs. How about *jaycustomer*, for example, to denote someone who "jayuses" a service or "jayconsumes" a physical product (and then "jaydisposes" of it afterwards)? We define a jaycustomer as one who acts in a thoughtless or abusive way, causing problems for the firm, its employees, and other customers.

Every service has its share of jaycustomers. But opinions on this topic seem to polarize around two opposing views of the situation. One is denial: "The customer is king and can do no wrong." The other view sees the marketplace of customers as positively overpopulated with nasty people who cannot be trusted to behave in ways that self-respecting service providers should expect and require. The first viewpoint has received wide publicity in gung-ho management books and in motivational presentations to captive groups of employees. But the second view often appears to be dominant among cynical managers and employees who have been burned at some point by customer misbehaviour. As with so many opposing viewpoints in life, there are important grains of truth in both perspectives. What is clear, however, is that no self-respecting firm would want to have an ongoing relationship with an abusive customer.

Six Types of Jaycustomers

Jaycustomers are undesirable. At worst, a firm needs to control or prevent their abusive behaviour. At best, it would like to avoid attracting them in the first place. Since defining the problem is the first step in resolving it, let's start by considering the different segments of jaycustomers who prey upon providers of both goods and services. We've identified six broad categories and given them generic names, but many customer contact personnel have come up with their own special terms. As you reflect on these categories, you may be temped to add a few more of your own.

The Thief This jaycustomer has no intention of paying and sets out to steal goods and services (or to pay less than full price by switching price tickets or contesting bills on baseless grounds). Shoplifting is a major problem in retail stores. What retailers euphemistically call "shrinkage" is estimated to cost them huge sums of money in annual revenues. According to the Retail Council of Canada's 2003 Canadian Retail Security Report, as much as $3 billion annually, or $8 million per day, were lost due to shrinkage at retailers across Canada.[36] Many services lend themselves to clever schemes for avoiding payment. For those with technical skills, it's sometimes possible to bypass electricity meters, access telephone lines free of charge, or circumvent normal cable TV feeds. Riding free on public transportation, sneaking into movie theatres, or not paying for restaurant meals are also popular. And we mustn't forget the use of fraudulent forms of payment such as stolen credit cards or cheques drawn on empty accounts. Finding out how people steal a service is the first step in preventing theft or catching thieves and, where appropriate, prosecuting them. But managers should try not to alienate honest customers by degrading their service experiences. And provision must be made for honest but absent-minded customers who forget to pay.

The Rule-Breaker Just as highways need safety regulations (including "Don't Jaywalk"), many service businesses need to establish rules of behaviour for employees and customers to guide them safely through the various steps of the service encounter. Some of these rules are imposed by government agencies for health and safety reasons. The sign found in many restaurants that states "No shirt, no shoes—no service" demonstrates a health-related regulation. And air travel provides one of the best of examples of rules designed to ensure safety—there are few other environments outside prison where healthy, mentally competent adult customers are quite so constrained (albeit with good reason).

In addition to enforcing government regulations, suppliers often impose their own rules to facilitate smooth operations, avoid unreasonable demands on employees, prevent misuse of products and facilities, protect themselves legally, and discourage individual customers from misbehaving. Ski resorts, for instance, are getting tough on careless skiers who pose risks to both themselves and others. Collisions can cause serious injury and even kill. So ski patrol members must be safety oriented and sometimes take on a policing role. Just as dangerous drivers can lose their licences, so dangerous skiers can lose their lift tickets.

At Vail and Beaver Creek in Colorado, ski patrollers once revoked nearly 400 lift tickets in a single weekend. At BC's Whistler Blackcomb resort, reckless behaviour results in a verbal warning followed by suspension of skiing privileges if such behaviour is not corrected. Ski patrollers at Vermont's Okemo Mountain may issue warnings to reckless skiers by attaching a bright orange sticker to their lift tickets. If pulled over again for inappropriate behaviour, such skiers may be escorted off the mountain and banned for a day or more. "We're not trying to be Gestapos on the slopes," says the resort's marketing director, "just trying to educate people."

How should a firm deal with rule-breakers? Much depends on which rules have been broken. In the case of legally enforceable ones—theft, bad debts, trying to take guns onto an aircraft—the courses of action need to be laid down explicitly to protect employees and to punish or discourage wrongdoing by customers. Company rules are a little more ambiguous. Are they really necessary in the first place? If not, the firm should get rid of them. Do they deal with health and safety? If so, educating customers about the rules should reduce the need for taking corrective action. The same is true for rules designed to protect the comfort and enjoyment of all customers. There are also unwritten social norms such as "thou shalt not jump the queue" (although this is a much stronger cultural expectation in Canada or the United States than in many countries, as any visitor to Disneyland Paris can attest). Other customers can often be relied upon to help service personnel enforce rules that affect everybody else; they may even take the initiative in doing so.

There are risks attached to making lots of rules. They can make an organization appear bureaucratic and overbearing. And they can transform employees, whose orientation should be service to customers, into police officers who see (or are told to see) their most important task as enforcing all the rules. The fewer the rules, the more explicit the important ones can be.

The Belligerent   You've probably seen him (or her) in a store, at the airport, in a hotel or restaurant—red in the face and shouting angrily, or perhaps icily calm and mouthing off insults, threats, and obscenities. Things don't always work as they should: machines break down, service is clumsy, customers are ignored, a flight is delayed, an order is delivered incorrectly, staff are unhelpful, a promise is broken. Or perhaps the customer in question is expressing resentment at being told to abide by the rules. Service personnel are often abused, even when they are not to blame. If an employee lacks authority to resolve the problem, the belligerent may become madder still, even to the point of physical attack. Unfortunately, when angry customers rant at service personnel, the latter sometimes respond in kind, thus escalating the confrontation and reducing the likelihood of resolution (Figure 8.4).

Drunkenness and drug abuse add extra layers of complication. Organizations that care about their employees go to great efforts to develop skills in dealing with these difficult situations. Training exercises that involve role-playing help employees develop the self-confidence and assertiveness that they need to deal with upset, belligerent customers (sometimes referred to as "irates"). Employees also need to learn how to defuse anger, calm anxiety, and comfort distress (particularly when there is good reason for the customer to be upset with the organization's performance).

Figure 8.4
Confrontations between customers and service employees can easily escalate.

"We seem to live in an age of rage," declare Stephen Grove, Raymond Fisk, and Joby John, noting a general decline in civility.[37] They suggest that rage behaviours are learned, via socialization, as appropriate responses to certain situations. Research by Roger Bougie and his colleagues determined that anger and dissatisfaction are qualitatively different emotions. Whereas dissatisfied customers had a feeling of unfulfillment or "missing out," and wanted to find out who or what was responsible for the event, angry customers were thinking how unfair the situation was, sought to get back at the organization, and wanted to hurt someone.[38]

The problem of "Air Rage" has attracted particular attention in recent years because of the risks that it poses to innocent people (see Service Perspectives 8.2). Blair Berkley and Mohammad Ala note that even before the events of September 11, 2001, violent passengers were considered to be the number-one security concern in the airline industry.[39]

What should an employee do when an aggressive customer brushes off attempts to defuse the situation? In a public environment, one priority should be to move the person away from other customers. Sometimes supervisors may have to arbitrate disputes between customers and staff members; at other times, they need to stand behind the employee's actions. If a customer has physically assaulted an employee, then it may be necessary to summon security officers or the police. Some firms try to conceal such events, fearing bad publicity. But others feel obliged to make a public stand on behalf of their employees, like the Body Shop manager who ordered an ill-tempered customer out of the store, telling her: "I won't stand for your rudeness to my staff."

Telephone rudeness poses a different challenge. Service personnel have been known to hang up on angry customers, but that action doesn't resolve the problem. Bank customers, for instance, tend to get upset when learning that cheques have been returned because they are overdrawn (which means they've broken the rules) or that a request for a loan has been denied. One approach for handling customers who continue to berate a telephone-based employee is for the latter to say firmly: "This conversation isn't getting us anywhere. Why don't I call you back in a few minutes when you've had time to digest the information?" In many cases, a break for reflection is exactly what's needed.

The Family Feuders People who get into arguments (or worse) with other customers—often members of their own family—make up a category of belligerents we call family feuders. Employee intervention may calm the situation, or it may actually make it worse. Some situations require detailed analysis and a carefully measured response. Others, like customers starting a food fight in a nice restaurant (yes, such things do happen!), require almost instantaneous response. Service managers in these situations need to be prepared to think on their feet and act fast.

The Vandal The level of physical abuse to which service facilities and equipment can be subjected is truly astonishing. Soft drinks are poured into bank cash machines; graffiti are scrawled on both interior and exterior surfaces; burn holes from cigarettes scar carpets, tablecloths, and bedcovers; bus seats are slashed and hotel furniture broken; telephone handsets are torn off; customers' cars are vandalized; glass is smashed and fabrics are torn. The list is endless. Customers don't cause all of the damage, of course. Bored or drunk young passers-by are the source of much exterior vandalism. And disgruntled employees have been known to commit sabotage. But much of the problem does originate with paying customers who choose to misbehave. Alcohol and drugs are sometimes the cause; psychological problems may contribute; and carelessness can play a role. There are also occasions when unhappy customers, feeling mistreated by the service provider, try to take revenge in some way.

The best cure for vandalism is prevention. Improved security discourages some vandals. Good lighting helps, as does open design of public areas. Companies can choose pleasing yet vandal-resistant surfaces, protective coverings for equipment, and rugged furnishings. Educating customers on how to use equipment properly (rather than fighting with it) and providing warnings about fragile objects can reduce the likelihood of abuse or careless handling. And there are economic sanctions: security deposits or signed agreements in which customers agree to pay for any damage that they cause.

Air Rage: Unruly Passengers Pose a Continuing Problem

Joining the term "road rage"—coined in 1988 to describe angry, aggressive drivers who threaten other road users—is "air rage," describing the behaviour of violent, unruly passengers who endanger flight attendants, pilots, and other passengers. Incidents of air rage are perpetrated by only a tiny fraction of all airline passengers—reportedly about 5000 times a year—but each incident in the air may affect the comfort and safety of hundreds of other people.

Although terrorism is an ongoing concern, out-of-control passengers pose a serious threat to safety, too. On a flight from Orlando, Florida to London, a drunken passenger smashed a video screen and began ramming a window, telling fellow passengers they were about to "get sucked out and die." The crew strapped him down and the aircraft made an unscheduled landing in Bangor, Maine, where U.S. marshals arrested him. Another unscheduled stop in Bangor involved a drug smuggler flying from Jamaica to the Netherlands. When a balloon filled with cocaine ruptured in his stomach, he went berserk, pounding a bathroom door to pieces and grabbing a female passenger by the throat.

In a bizarre incident in 2002, a drunken Toronto police officer had to be dragged off the plane by other officers after he sexually assaulted a female flight attendant and threatened to kill passengers on an Edmonton to Hamilton WestJet flight; the 14-year veteran of the police force was subsequently convicted. Other dangerous incidents have included throwing hot coffee at flight attendants, head-butting a co-pilot, trying to break into the cockpit, throwing a flight attendant across three rows of seats, and attempting to open an emergency door in flight. On a U.S. domestic flight with a tragic outcome, a violent passenger was restrained and ultimately suffocated by other passengers after he kicked through the cockpit door of an airliner 20 minutes before it was scheduled to land in Salt Lake City.

A growing number of carriers are taking air rage perpetrators to court. Northwest Airlines permanently blacklisted three violent travellers from flying on its aircraft. British Airways gives out "warning cards" to any passenger getting dangerously out of control. Celebrities are not immune to air rage. Rock star Courtney Love blamed her "potty mouth" after being arrested on arrival in London for disruptive behaviour on board a flight from Los Angeles. Marzena Kamizela, a Swedish supermodel who has worked for Versace, Lamborghini, and Martini, was ordered to pay more than $28 000 in fines and restitution following an air rage incident aboard a British Airways flight that had to make an emergency landing at Happy Valley-Goose Bay in central Labrador.

In Canada, passengers convicted of disruptive behaviour on aircraft could receive a monetary penalty of up to $100 000, a jail sentence of up to five years, or both. In the United States, the civil penalty for air rage has been increased to US$25 000 and criminal penalties range from a US$10 000 fine and up to 20 years in jail for the most serious incidents. Some airlines have been reluctant to publicize this information for fear of appearing confrontational or intimidating. However, the visible implementation of anti-terrorist security precautions have made it more acceptable to tighten enforcement of procedures designed to control and punish air rage.

What causes air rage? Psychological feelings of a loss of control, or problems with authority figures, may be causal factors for angry behaviour in many service settings. Researchers suggest that air travel, in particular, has become increasingly stressful as a result of crowding and longer flights; the airlines themselves may have contributed to the problem by squeezing rows of seats more tightly together and failing to explain delays. Findings suggest that risk factors for air travel stress include anxiety and an anger-prone personality; they also show that travelling on unfamiliar routes is more stressful than on a familiar one. Another factor may be restrictions on smoking. But alcohol abuse underlies a majority of incidents.

Airlines are training their employees to handle violent individuals and to spot problem passengers before they start causing serious problems. Some carriers offer travellers specific suggestions on how to relax during long flights. And some airlines have considered offering nicotine patches to passengers who are desperate for a smoke but are no longer allowed to light up. Increased security in the air may be curtailing rage behaviour on board flights, but concern continues to grow about passenger rage on the ground. An Australian survey of airport employees found that 96 percent of airport staff had experienced air rage at work: 31 percent of agents experienced some form of air rage daily and another 35 percent witnessed it weekly, 70 percent had witnessed a passenger threaten an agent or fellow passenger, 32 percent had seen a passenger physically assault a fellow agent or passenger, and 15 percent of agents reported that they had been physically touched or assaulted by a passenger.

Sources: Daniel Eisenberg, "Acting Up in the Air," *Time* (December 21, 1998); "Air Rage Capital: Bangor Becomes Nation's Flight Problem Drop Point," *Baltimore Sun,* syndicated article, September, 1999; Melanie Trottman and Chip Cummins, "Passenger's Death Prompts Calls for Improved 'Air Rage' Procedures," *Wall Street Journal* (September 26, 2000); Blair J. Berkley and Mohammad Ala, "Identifying and Controlling Threatening Airline Passengers," *Cornell Hotel and Restaurant Administration Quarterly* 42 (August–September 2001): 6–24; "Police Officer Terrorized WestJet flight", *Toronto Star* (16 April, 2004); www.airsafe.com/issues/rage.htm, accessed January 16, 2006; Australian Services Union, www.asu.asn.au/media/airlines_general/20031021_airrage.html, accessed January 16, 2006; "Model Pleads Guilty in Air Rage Fracas", May 15, 2005, www.cbc.ca/story/canada/national/2006/05/15/model-plane060515.html, accessed August 22, 2006.

What should managers do if prevention fails and damage is done? If the perpetrator is caught, they should first clarify whether there are any extenuating circumstances (because accidents do happen). Sanctions for deliberate damage can range from a warning to prosecution. As far as the physical damage itself is concerned, it's best to fix it fast (within any constraints imposed by legal or insurance considerations). The general manager of a bus company had the right idea when he said: "If one of our buses is vandalized, whether it's a broken window, a slashed seat, or graffiti on the ceiling, we take it out of service immediately, so nobody sees it. Otherwise you just give the same idea to five other characters who were too dumb to think of it in the first place!"

The Deadbeat   Leaving aside those individuals who never intended to pay in the first place (see "the thief" above), there are many reasons why customers fail to pay for services they have received. Once again, preventive action is better than a cure. A growing number of firms insist on prepayment. Any form of ticket sale is a good example of this. Direct marketing organizations ask for your credit card number as they take your order, as do most hotels when you make a reservation. The next best thing is to present the customer with a bill immediately on completion of service. If the bill is to be sent by mail, the firm should send it fast, while the service is still fresh in the customer's mind.

Not every apparent delinquent is a hopeless deadbeat. Perhaps there's good reason for the delay, and acceptable payment arrangements can be worked out. A key question is whether such a personalized approach can be cost-justified, relative to the results obtained by purchasing the services of a collection agency. There may be other considerations, too. If the client's problems are only temporary, what is the long-term value of maintaining the relationship? Will it create positive goodwill and word-of-mouth to help the customer work things out? These decisions are judgment calls, but if creating and maintaining long-term relationships is the firm's ultimate goal, they bear exploration.

Consequences of Dysfunctional Customer Behaviour

Lloyd Harris and Kate Reynolds emphasize that dysfunctional customer behaviour has consequences for staff working front stage, for other customers, and for the organization itself.[40] Employees who are abused may not only find their mood or temper negatively affected in the short run, but may eventually suffer long-term psychological damage. Their own behaviour, too, may take on negative dimensions, such as taking revenge on abusive customers. Staff morale can be hurt, with implications for both productivity and quality.

The consequences for customers can take both positive and negative forms. Other customers may rally to the support of an employee whom they perceive as having been abused; however, bad behaviour can also be contagious, causing a bad situation to escalate as others join in. More broadly, being exposed to negative incidents can spoil the consumption experience for many customers, even leading them to terminate their use of the service in question. Companies suffer financially when demotivated employees no longer work as efficiently and effectively as before, or when employees are forced to take medical leave. There may also be direct financial losses from restoring stolen or damaged property, legal costs, and paying fraudulent claims.

As suggested by the earlier discussion of air rage, the nature of jaycustomer behaviour is likely to be shaped by the characteristics of the service industry in which it occurs. Research Insights 8.1 reports on a study of jaycustomers in the hospitality industry.

Implications for Service Design and Management

When customers come to the service factory and interact with service personnel and facilities, how they behave may have crucial implications for the effectiveness and profitability of the organization. The stakes are raised further in a high-contact environment in which many other customers are present simultaneously. Some jaycustomer behaviour is premeditated, but some is situational. Designing a process that minimizes the risk of failure, eliminates steps that add no value for customers, avoids undesired waits, and maintains a comfortable physical environment may help reduce some of the factors that generate customer anger and frustration.

Research Insights 8.1

Categorizing Jaycustomers in Hotels, Restaurants, and Bars

To learn more about dysfunctional customer behaviour in the hospitality industry, Lloyd Harris and Kate Reynolds of Cardiff University developed a research project to identify and categorize different types of misconduct. Open-ended interviews, typically lasting an hour (but sometimes longer) were conducted with 31 managers, 46 front-line employees, and 29 customers. These interviews took place in 19 hotels (all of which had restaurants and bars), 13 restaurants, and 16 bars. A purposive sampling plan was employed, with the goal of selecting informants with extensive participation in, and insights into, service encounters. All informants had encountered—or had perpetrated—what could be considered as jaycustomer behaviour, and were invited to give details of specific incidents. In total, the 106 respondents generated 417 critical incidents.

Based on analysis of these incidents, Harris and Reynolds codified eight types of behaviour:

1. *Compensation letter writers* who deliberately and fraudulently write to centralized customer service departments with largely unjustified complaints in anticipation of receiving a cheque or gift voucher.

2. *Undesirable customers* whose behaviour falls into three subgroups: (a) irritating behaviour by "jaykids" and "jayfamilies"; (b) criminal behaviour, typically involving drug sales or prostitution; and (c) homeless individuals who use an organization's facilities and steal other customers' refreshments.

3. *Property abusers* who vandalize facilities and steal items—most often to keep as souvenirs.

4. *[Off-duty] service workers* who know how to work the system to their own advantage as customers and deliberately disrupt service encounters, either for financial gain or simply to cause problems for front-line staff.

5. *Vindictive customers* who are violent toward people or property, possibly because of some perceived injustice.

6. *Oral abusers* include professional complainers seeking compensation and "ego hunters" who take pleasure in offending front-line staff and other customers.

7. *Physical abusers* who physically harm frontline staff.

8. *Sexual predators*—often acting in groups—who engage in sexual harassment of front-line personnel either verbally or behaviourally.

Some of these behaviours, such as letter-writing and property abuse, are covert in nature (that is, not evident to others at the time they are committed). Certain underlying causes assert themselves across multiple categories, including desire for personal gain, drunkenness, personal psychological problems, and negative group dynamics.

Table A shows the percentage of employees and customers reporting incidents within each category. Rather remarkably, with the exception of the "undesirable customers" and "sexual predators" categories, the incidents in the customer column are all self-reports of the respondents' own misbehaviour.

The verbatim reports of jaycustomer behaviour recorded in this study make sombre—even scary—reading. In particular, they demonstrate especially the challenges posed to management and staff by manipulative customers seeking personal financial gain, and by the abusive behaviour of individuals, sometimes acting in groups and fuelled by alcohol, who appear unconstrained by traditional societal norms.

Table A: **Percentage of Respondents Reporting Incidents by Category**

CATEGORY	PERCENTAGE OF EMPLOYEES	PERCENTAGE OF CUSTOMERS
Compensation letter writers	30	20
Undesirable customers	39	47
Property abusers	51	20
[Off-duty] service workers	11	11
Vindictive customers	30	22
Oral abusers	92	70
Physical abusers	49	20
Sexual predators	38	0

Source: Adapted from Lloyd C. Harris and Kate L. Reynolds, "Jaycustomer Behaviour: An Exploration of Types and Motives in the Hospitality Industry," *Journal of Services Marketing 18/5* (2004): 339–57.

Conclusion

In this chapter, we emphasized the importance of designing and managing service processes, which are central in creating the service product and significantly shape the customer experience. We covered in-depth blueprinting as a powerful tool to understand, document, analyze, and improve service processes. Blueprinting helps to identify and reduce service fail points, and provides important insights for redesigning service processes.

An important part of process design is to define the roles customers should play in the production of services. Their level of desired participation needs to be determined, and customers need to be motivated and taught to play their part in the service delivery.

Review Questions

1. What is the role of blueprinting in designing, managing, and redesigning service processes?

2. How can fail-safe procedures be used to reduce service failures?

3. Describe how blueprinting helps to identify the relationship between core and supplementary services.

4. Why is periodic process redesign necessary, and what are the main types of service process redesign? Highlight their benefits for the firm and its customers, and also the potential challenges involved in the service redesign process.

5. Why does the customer's role as a co-producer need to be designed into service processes? What are the implications of considering customers as partial employees?

6. Explain what factors make customers like or dislike self-service technologies (SSTs). Additionally, what three factors should management consider internally for successful implementations of SSTs?

7. What are the different types of jaycustomers, and how can a service firm deal with the behaviour of such customers?

Application Exercises

1. Review the blueprint of the restaurant visit in Figure 8.1. Identify several possible "OTSUs" for each step in the front-stage process. Consider possible causes underlying each potential failure, and suggest ways to eliminate or minimize these problems.

2. Prepare a blueprint for a service with which you are familiar. On completion, consider (a) what the tangible cues or indicators of quality are from the customer's perspective considering the line of visibility, (b) whether all steps in the process are necessary, (c) the extent to which standardization is possible, and advisable, throughout the process, (d) the location of potential fail points, and how they could be designed out of the process, or what service recovery procedures could be introduced, and (e) what are potential measures of process performance.

3. Observe customers at businesses that have self-service lanes as well as service personnel (supermarkets, home improvement centres, cinemas). What differences do you observe in customers using the two options? How many of those conducting self-service appear to run into difficulties, and how do they resolve their problems? Do these differences vary by the type of service business (e.g., supermarkets versus cinemas)?

4. Identify one website that is exceptionally user friendly, and another that is not. What are the factors that make for a satisfying user experience in the first instance and a frustrating one in the second? Specify recommendations for improvements in the second website.

5. Refer to the case study in Best Practice in Action 8.2 (spud.ca). Visit their website and pay attention to the information provided under "About SPUD" and "SPUD in the news." Based on this information, and your independent research on the online grocery business, what are the chances that Spud will continue on the path to growth and profitability in the next five years? Do you foresee any challenges that need to be addressed?

6. Identify the potential behaviour of jaycustomers for a service of your choice. How can the service process be designed to minimize or control the behaviour of jay customers?

Endnotes

1. See G. Lynn Shostack, "Understanding Services through Blueprinting" in T. Schwartz et al., *Advances in Services Marketing and Management, 1992.* Greenwich, CT: JAI Press, 1992: 75–90.

2. G. Lynn Shostack, "Designing Services That Deliver," *Harvard Business Review* 62/1 (January–February 1984) 133–39.

3. Jane Kingman-Brundage, "The ABCs of Service System Blueprinting," in M.J. Bitner and L.A. Crosby (eds.), *Designing a Winning Service Strategy,* Chicago: American Marketing Association, 1989.

4. David Maister, now president of Maister Associates, coined the term OTSU while teaching at Harvard Business School in the 1980s.

5. See for example, Eric J. Arnould and Linda L. Price, "River Magic: Extraordinary Experience and the Extended Service Encounter," *Journal of Consumer Research* 20 (June 1993): 24–25; Eric J. Arnould and Linda L. Price, "Collaring the Cheshire Cat: Studying Customers' Services Experience Through Metaphors," *Service Industries Journal* 16 (October 1996): 421–42; and Nick Johns and Phil Tyas, "Customer Perceptions of Service Operations: Gestalt, Incident or Mythology?" *Service Industries Journal* 17 (July 1997): 474–88.

6. Valerie S. Folkes and Vanessa M. Patrick, "The Positivity Effect in Perceptions of Services: Seen One, Seen Them All?," *Journal of Consumer Research* 30/1 (2003): 125–37.

7. "How Marriott Makes a Great First Impression," *Service Edge* 6/5 (May 1993): 5.

8. Lisa Bannon, "Plastic Surgeons Are Told to Pay More Attention to Appearances," *Wall Street Journal* (15 March, 1997): B1.

9. David E. Hansen and Peter J. Danaher, "Inconsistent Performance during the Service Encounter: What's a Good Start Worth?" *Journal of Service Research,* Vol. 1 (February 1999), pp. 227-235; Richard B. Chase and Sriram Dasu OP. COIT., 2001

10. This section is based in part on Richard B. Chase and Douglas M. Stewart, "Make Your Service Fail-Safe," *Sloan Management Review* (Spring 1994): 35–44.

11. Jochen Wirtz and Monica Tomlin, "Institutionalizing Customer-driven Learning through Fully Integrated Customer Feedback Systems," *Managing Service Quality* 10/4 (2000): 205–15.

12. Mitchell T. Rabkin, cited in Christopher H. Lovelock, *Product Plus,* New York: McGraw-Hill, 1994: 354–55.

13. Thomas Mucha, "The Payoff for Trying Harder," *Business 2.0* (July 2002): 84–86.

14. See, for example, Michael Hammer and James Champy, *Reeingineering the Corporation,* New York: HarperBusiness, 1993.

15. This section is partially based on Leonard L. Berry and Sandra K. Lampo, "Teaching an Old Service New Tricks: The Promise of Service Redesign," *Journal of Service Research* 2/3 (February 2000): 265–75. Berry and Lampo identified the following five service redesign concepts: self-service, direct service, pre-service, bundled service, and physical service. We have expanded some of these concepts in this section to embrace more of the productivity-enhancing aspects of process redesign, such as eliminating non-value-adding work steps in all stages of service delivery.

16. Art Gallery of Hamilton Press Release, May 4, 2005; available online at www.artgalleryofhamilton.ca, accessed August 22, 2006.

17. D. Bovet and J. Martha, *Breaking the Supply Chain to Unlock Hidden Profits,* New York: John Wiley, 2000.

18. L. Cherbakov, G. Galambos, R. Harishankar, et al., "Impact of Service Orientation at the Business Level," *IBM Systems Journal* 44/4 (2005): 653–68.

19. Amy Risch Rodie and Susan Schultz Klein, "Customer Participation in Services Production and Delivery," in Teresa A. Schwartz and Dawn Iacobucci, (eds.), *Handbook of Service Marketing and Management,* Thousand Oaks, CA: Sage, 2000: 111–25.

20. Mary Jo Bitner, William T. Faranda, Amy R. Hubbert, and Valarie A. Zeithaml, "Customer Contributions and Roles in Service Delivery," *International Journal of Service Industry Management* 8/3 (1997): 193–205.

21. Matthew L. Meuter, Amy L. Ostrom, Robert I. Roundtree, and Mary Jo Bitner, "Self-service Technologies: Understanding Customer Satisfaction with Technology-based Service Encounters," *Journal of Marketing* 64 (July 2000): 50–64.

22. Matthew L. Meuter, Mary Jo Bitner, Amy L. Ostrom, and Stephen W. Brown, "Choosing Among Alternative Service Delivery Modes: An Investigation of Customer Trial of Self-service Technologies," *Journal of Marketing* 69/2 (April 2005): 61–83.

23. Pratibha A. Dabholkar, "Consumer Evaluations of New Technology-Based Self-Service Options: An Investigation of Alternative Models of Service Quality," *International Journal of Research in Marketing* 13 (1996): 29–51; Mary Jo Bitner, Stephen W. Brown, and Matthew L. Meuter, "Technology Infusion in Service Encounters," *Journal of the Academy of Marketing Science* 28/1 (2000): 138–49; Pratibha A. Dabholkar, L. Michelle Bobbitt, and Eun-Ju Lee, "Understanding Consumer Motivation and Behavior Related to Self-Scanning in Retailing," *International Journal of Service Industry Management* 14/1 (2003): 59–95.

24. David G. Mick and Susan Fournier, "Paradoxes of Technology: Consumer Cognizance, Emotions, and Coping Strategies," *Journal of Consumer Research* 25 (September 1998): 123–43.

25. James M. Curran, Matthew L. Meuter, and Carol G. Surprenant, "Intentions to Use Self-Service Technologies: A Confluence of Multiple Attitudes," *Journal of Service Research* 5 (February 2003): 209–24.

26. Meuter, Ostrom, Roundtree, and Bitner (2000), op. cit.; Mary Jo Bitner, "Self-Service Technologies: What Do Customers Expect?" *Marketing Management* (Spring 2001): 10–11.

27. Kortney Stringer, "Have a Pleasant Trip: Eliminate All Human Contact," *Wall Street Journal* (October 31, 2002).

28. Jeffrey F. Rayport and Bernard J. Jaworski, "Big Picture: Best Face Forward," *Harvard Business Review* 82/12 (December 2004): 47–59.

29. Neeli Bendapudi and Robert P. Leone, "Psychological Implications of Customer Participation in Co-Production," *Journal of Marketing* 67 (January 2003): 14–28.

30. Bitner (2001), op. cit.

31. David E. Bowen, "Managing Customers as Human Resources in Service Organizations," *Human Resources Management* 25/3 (1986): 371–83.

32. Benjamin Schneider and David E. Bowen, *Winning the Service Game,* Boston: Harvard Business School Press, 1995: 85.

33. Bonnie Farber Canziani, "Leveraging Customer Competency in Service Firms," *International Journal of Service Industry Management* 8/1 (1997): 5–25.

34. Norm Brodsky "Street Smarts: Firing Customers," *Inc. Magazine* (July 2002): www.inc.com, accessed August 30, 2006.

35. This section is adapted from Lovelock, *Product Plus,* op. cit., Chapter 15.

36. Retail Council of Canada 2003 *Canadian Retail Security Report,* Executive Summary, released at RCC's resources protection conference, September 23, 2003, Toronto.

37. Stephen J. Grove, Raymond P. Fisk, and Joby John, "Surviving in the Age of Rage," *Marketing Management* (March/April 2004): 41–46.

38. Roger Bougie, Rik Pieters, and Marcel Zeelenberg, "Angry Customers Don't Come Back, They Get Back: The Experience and Behavioral Implications of Anger and Dissatisfaction in Services," *Journal of the Academy of Marketing Science* 31/4 (2003): 377–93.

39. Blair J. Berkley and Mohammad Ala, "Identifying and Controlling Threatening Airline Passengers," *Cornell Hotel and Restaurant Administration Quarterly* 42 (August–September 2001): 6–24.

40. Lloyd C. Harris and Kate L. Reynolds, "The Consequences of Dysfunctional Customer Behavior," *Journal of Service Research* 6 (November 2003): 144–61; Lloyd C. Harris and Kate L. Reynolds, "Jaycustomer Behavior: An Exploration of Types and Motives in the Hospitality Industry," *Journal of Services Marketing* 18/5 (2004): 339–57.

CHAPTER 9

Balancing Demand and Productive Capacity

Balancing the supply and demand sides of a service industry is not easy, and whether a manager does it well or not makes all the difference.

—Earl Sasser

They also serve who only stand and wait.

—John Milton

Fluctuating demand is a major challenge for many types of service organizations, including airlines, restaurants, vacation resorts, courier services, consulting firms, theatres, and call centres. These demand fluctuations, which may range in frequency from as long as a season of the year to as short as an hour, play havoc with efficient use of productive assets, thus eroding profitability. By working collaboratively with managers in operations and human resources, service marketers may be able to develop strategies to bring demand and capacity into balance in ways that create benefits for customers as well as generating more financial value for business owners.

In this chapter, we consider the nature of demand and supply in services and explore the following questions:

1. What is meant by "capacity" in a service context, and how is it measured?
2. Can variations in demand be predicted, and their causes identified?
3. How can capacity management techniques be employed to match variations in demand?
4. What marketing strategies are available to service firms to smooth out fluctuations in demand?
5. If customers must wait for service, how can this activity be made less burdensome for them?
6. What is involved in designing an effective reservations system?

FLUCTUATIONS IN DEMAND THREATEN SERVICE PRODUCTIVITY

Unlike manufactured goods, services are perishable and normally cannot be stockpiled for sale at a later date. This is a problem for any capacity-constrained service that faces wide swings in demand. The problem is most commonly found among services that process people or physical possessions—such as transportation, lodging, food service, repair and maintenance, entertainment, and health care. It also affects labour-intensive, information-processing services that face cyclical shifts in demand. Accounting and tax preparation are cases in point.

Effective use of expensive productive capacity is one of the secrets of success in such businesses. The goal should not be to utilize staff, labour, equipment, and facilities as much as possible, but rather to use them as *productively* as possible. At the same time, the search for productivity must not be allowed to undermine service quality and degrade the customer experience.

From Excess Demand to Excess Capacity

The problem is a familiar one. "It's either feast or famine for us!" sighs the manager. "In peak periods, we're disappointing prospective customers by turning them away. And in low periods, our facilities are idle, our employees are standing around looking bored, and we're losing money."

At any given moment, a fixed-capacity service may face one of four conditions (see Figure 9.1):

- *Excess demand.* The level of demand exceeds maximum available capacity, with the result that some potential customers are denied service and business is lost.

- *Demand exceeds optimum capacity.* No one is actually turned away, but conditions are crowded and customers are likely to perceive a deterioration in quality of service and feel dissatisfied.

- *Demand and supply are well balanced.* This is the level of optimum capacity. Staff and facilities are busy without being overworked, and customers receive good service without delays.

- *Excess capacity.* Demand is below optimum capacity and productive resources are underutilized, resulting in low productivity. Low usage also poses a risk that customers may find the experience disappointing or have doubts about the viability of the service.

Sometimes optimum and maximum capacities are one and the same. At a live theatre or sports performance, a full house is grand, since it stimulates the players and creates a sense of excitement and audience participation. The net result? A more satisfying experience for all. But with most other services, you probably feel that you get better service if the facility is not operating at full capacity. For instance, universities try hard to maintain a reasonable student-to-teacher ratio in order to mitigate the negative impacts of large class sizes on student learning and experience. And if you are travelling alone in an aircraft with high density seating, you tend to feel more comfortable if the seat next to you is empty. When repair and maintenance shops are fully scheduled, delays may result if there is no slack in the system to allow for unexpected problems in completing particular jobs.

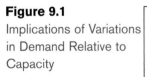

Figure 9.1

Implications of Variations in Demand Relative to Capacity

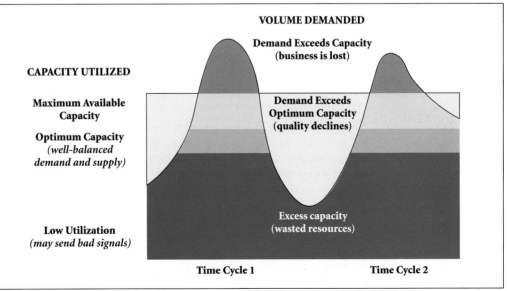

There are two basic approaches to the problem of fluctuating demand. One is to adjust the level of capacity to meet variations in demand. This approach requires an understanding of what constitutes productive capacity and how it may be increased or decreased on an incremental basis. The second approach is to manage the level of demand, using marketing strategies to smooth out the peaks and fill in the valleys so as to generate a more consistent flow of demand for the service firm. Many firms use a mix of both approaches.[1]

MANY SERVICE ORGANIZATIONS ARE CAPACITY CONSTRAINED

There are often limits to a firm's capacity to serve additional customers at a particular point in time. Service firms may also be constrained in terms of being unable to reduce their productive capacity during periods of low demand. In general, organizations that engage in physical processes such as people or possession processing are more likely to face capacity constraints than those that engage in information-based processes. A radio station, for instance, may be constrained in its geographic reach by the strength of its signal, but within that radius, any number of listeners can tune in to a broadcast. The advent of satellite radio has made even that constraint wane!

Defining Productive Capacity

What do we mean by productive capacity? The term refers to the resources or assets that a firm can employ to create goods and services. In a service context, productive capacity can take on several forms:

1. *Physical facilities designed to contain customers* and used for delivering people-processing services or mental-stimulus processing services. Examples include medical clinics, hotels, passenger aircraft, and university classrooms. The primary capacity constraint is likely to be defined in terms of such furnishings as beds, rooms, or seats. In some cases, safety regulations, such as those required by the fire department for student capacity in classrooms of varying sizes, may set an upper limit on the physical capacity of a service facility.

2. *Physical facilities designed for storing or processing goods* that either belong to customers or are being offered to them for sale. Examples include pipelines, warehouses, parking lots, or railway freight wagons.

3. *Physical equipment used to process people, possessions, or information* may embrace a huge range of items and be very situation-specific; diagnostic equipment, airport security detectors, toll gates, bank ATMs, and "seats" in a call centre are among the many items whose absence in sufficient numbers for a given level of demand can bring service to a crawl (or a complete stop).

4. *Labour* is a key element of productive capacity in all high-contact services and many low-contact ones. Staffing levels for restaurant servers, nurses, or call-centre staff need to be sufficient to meet anticipated demand—otherwise customers are kept waiting or service is rushed. Professional services are especially dependent on highly skilled staff to create high-value-added, information-based output.

5. *Infrastructure.* Many organizations are dependent on access to sufficient capacity in the public or private infrastructure to be able to deliver high-quality service to their own customers. Capacity problems of this nature may include congested airways that lead to air traffic restrictions on flights, traffic jams on major highways, and power failures such as the one witnessed on August 14, 2003, when Ontario and most of the northeastern United States was hit by the largest blackout in North America's history as 50 million customers were cut from the power grid.[2]

Measures of capacity utilization include the number of hours (or percentage of total available time) that facilities, labour, and equipment are productively employed in revenue operation, and the units or percentage of available space (e.g., seats, cubic freight

Best Practice in Action 9.1

Improving Check-In Service at Logan Airport

To streamline its check-in service at Boston's Logan International Airport, in 1992 a major airline turned to MIT Professor Richard Larson, who heads a consulting firm called QED. Technicians from QED installed pressure-sensitive rubber mats on the floor in front of the ticket counters. Pressure from each customer's foot on approaching or leaving the counter recorded the exact time on an electronic device embedded in the mats. From these data, Larson was able to profile the waiting situation at the airline's counters, including average waiting times, how long each transaction took, how many customers waited longer than a given length of time (and at what hours on what days), and even how many bailed out of a long line before reaching the desk. Analysis of these data, collected over a long time period, yielded information that helped the airline to plan its staffing levels to match more closely the demand levels projected at different times.

Source: Richard Saltus, "Lines, Lines, Lines, Lines . . . The Experts Are Trying to Ease the Wait," *Boston Globe* (October 5, 1992): 39, 42.

---

capacity, telecommunications bandwidth) that is utilized in revenue operations. Human beings tend to be far more variable than equipment in their ability to sustain consistent levels of output over time. One tired or poorly trained employee staffing a single station in an assembly-line service operation, such as a cafeteria or a provincial Driver and Vehicle Licensing Centre, can slow the entire service to a crawl.

Many services, such as health care or repair and maintenance, involve multiple actions delivered sequentially. What this means is that a service organization's capacity to satisfy demand is constrained by one or more of its physical facilities, equipment, personnel, and the number and sequence of services provided. In a well-planned, well-managed service operation, the capacity of the facility, supporting equipment, and service personnel will be in balance. Similarly, sequential operations will be designed to minimize the likelihood of bottlenecks at any point in the process. Best Practice in Action 9.1 describes how one airline sought to improve its capacity to serve at the check-in stage.

Financial success in capacity-constrained businesses is, in large measure, a function of management's ability to use productive capacity—staff, labour, equipment, and facilities—as efficiently and as profitably as possible. In practice, however, it is difficult to achieve this ideal all the time. Not only does the level of demand vary over time, often randomly, but the time and effort required to process each person or thing may vary widely at any point in the process. In general, processing times for people are more variable than for objects or things, reflecting varying levels of preparedness ("I need clarification on some of my credit card transactions"), argumentative versus co-operative personalities ("If you cannot give me break on my cable package, I'll have to ask for your supervisor"), and so forth. But service tasks are not necessarily homogeneous. In both professional services and repair jobs, diagnosis and treatment times vary according to the nature of the customers' problems. A routine oil and filter change of your automobile takes substantially less time than overhauling a faulty transmission.

Capacity Levels Can Sometimes Be Stretched or Shrunk

Some capacity is elastic in its ability to absorb extra demand. A Calgary Transit LRT car, for instance, has seating for 64 passengers plus room for a further 98 standing, based upon an allocation of 0.25 square metres per passenger, making a total desirable capacity of 162 passengers. Yet at rush hours as many as 256 passengers can be accommodated under sardine-like conditions.[3] Similarly, the capacity of service personnel can be stretched, and may be able to work at high levels of efficiency for short periods of time. However, staff would quickly tire and begin providing inferior service if they had to work that fast all day long.

Even where capacity appears fixed, as when it is based on the number of seats, there may still be opportunities to accept extra business at busy times. Some airlines, for instance, increase the capacity of a given flight by switching a larger aircraft to its route on a busy day. Similarly, a restaurant may have a certain amount of room in which to add extra tables and chairs. Upper limits to such practices are often set by safety standards or by the capacity of supporting services, such as the kitchen.

Another strategy for stretching capacity within a given time frame is to utilize the facilities for longer periods. Examples of this include restaurants that open for early dinners and late suppers, extended shopping hours during the holiday season, and universities that offer evening classes and summer semester programs. Alternatively, the average amount of time that customers (or their possessions) spend in the service process may be reduced. Sometimes this is achieved by minimizing slack time, as when the bill is presented promptly to a group of diners relaxing at the table after a meal. In other instances, it may be achieved by cutting back the level of service—say, by offering a simpler menu at busy times of day.

Adjusting Capacity to Match Demand

Another set of options involves tailoring the overall level of capacity to match variations in demand—a strategy also known as *chasing demand.* There are several actions that managers can take to adjust capacity as needed:

- *Schedule downtime during periods of low demand.* To ensure that 100 percent of capacity is available during peak periods, repairs and renovations should be conducted when demand is expected to be low. Employee holidays should also be taken during such periods.

- *Use temporary employees.* Many organizations hire extra workers during their busiest periods. Examples include retail shop assistants at Christmastime, extra staff within tax preparation service firms at the end of the financial year, and additional hotel employees during holiday periods and major conventions.

- *Rent or share extra facilities and equipment.* To limit investment in fixed assets, a service business may be able to rent extra space or machines at peak times. Firms with complementary demand patterns may enter into formal sharing agreements.

- *Cross-train employees.* Even when the service-delivery system appears to be operating at full capacity, certain physical elements—and their attendant employees—may be under-utilized. If employees can be cross-trained to perform a variety of tasks, they can be shifted to bottleneck points as needed, thereby increasing total system capacity. Delta Hotels and Resorts, named as one of the "50 Best Employers in Canada" in 2005 by the *Globe and Mail*'s *Report on Business* magazine, even offers employees a "training guarantee" that entitles full-time employees to a total of 12 hours of cross training each calendar year.[4]

- *Let customers perform self-service.* If the number of employees is limited, capacity can be increased by involving customers in co-production of certain tasks. One way to do this is by adding self-service technologies, such as electronic kiosks at the airport for airline ticketing and check-in (see Figure 9.2) or automated check-out stations at supermarkets.

Creating Flexible Capacity   Sometimes, the problem lies not in the overall capacity but in the mix that's available to serve the needs of different market segments. For instance, on a given flight, an airline may have too few seats in economy even though there are empty places in the business class cabin; or a hotel may find itself short of suites one day when there are standard rooms still available. One solution lies in designing physical facilities to be flexible. Some hotels build rooms with connecting doors. With the door between two rooms locked, the hotel can sell two bedrooms; with the door unlocked and one of the bedrooms converted into a sitting room, the hotel can now offer a suite.

Facing stiff competition from Airbus, Boeing received what were described, tongue-in-cheek, as "outrageous demands" from prospective customers when it was designing its

777 airliner. The airlines wanted an aircraft in which galleys and lavatories could be relocated, plumbing and all, almost anywhere in the cabin within a matter of hours. Boeing gulped but solved this challenging problem. As a result, airlines can rearrange the passenger cabin of the "Triple Seven" within hours, reconfiguring it with varying numbers of seats allocated among one, two, or three classes.

The Air Canada Centre in Toronto, a 61 780-square-metre sports and entertainment complex that is home to the NBA franchise of Toronto Raptors and the NHL franchise of Toronto Maple Leafs, can go from basketball mode to a full professional-standard ice rink within four to six hours.[5]

Not all unsold productive capacity is wasted. Many firms take a strategic approach to disposition of anticipated surplus capacity, allocating it in advance to build relationships with customers, suppliers, employees, and intermediaries.[6] Possible applications include free trials for prospective customers and for intermediaries who sell to end customers, employee rewards, and bartering with the firm's own suppliers. Among the most widely bartered services are advertising space or airtime, airline seats, and hotel rooms.

PATTERNS AND DETERMINANTS OF DEMAND

Now let's look at the other side of the equation. To control variations in demand for a particular service, managers need to determine what factors govern that demand.

Understanding Patterns of Demand

Research should begin by getting some answers to a series of important questions about the patterns of demand and their underlying causes (see Table 9.1).[7]

As you think about some of the seemingly "random" causes, consider how rain and cold affect the use of indoor and outdoor recreational or entertainment services. Then reflect on how heart attacks and births affect the demand for hospital services. Imagine what it is like to be a police officer, firefighter, or ambulance driver—you never know exactly where your next call will come from nor what the nature of the emergency will be.

Table 9.1 Questions about Demand Patterns and Their Underlying Causes

1. *Do demand levels follow a predictable cycle?*
   If so, is the duration of the **demand cycle**
   - One *day* (varies by hour)
   - One *week* (varies by day)
   - One *month* (varies by day or by week)
   - One *year* (varies by month or by season or reflects annual public holidays)
   - Another period

2. *What are the underlying causes of these cyclical variations?*
   - Employment schedules
   - Billing and tax payment/refund cycles
   - Wage and salary payment dates
   - School hours and vacations
   - Seasonal changes in climate
   - Occurrence of public or religious holidays
   - Natural cycles, such as coastal tides

3. *Do demand levels seem to change randomly?*
   If so, could the underlying causes be
   - Day-to-day changes in the weather
   - Health events whose occurrence cannot be pinpointed exactly
   - Accidents, fires, and certain criminal activities
   - Natural disasters (e.g., earthquakes, storms, mudslides, and volcanic eruptions)

4. *Can demand for a particular service over time be disaggregated by market segment to reflect such components as*
   - Use patterns by a particular type of customer or for a particular purpose
   - Variations in the net profitability of each completed transaction

Finally, consider the impact of natural disasters such as earthquakes, tornadoes, and hurricanes, not only on emergency services but also for disaster recovery specialists and insurance firms.

Most periodic cycles influencing demand for a particular service vary in length from one day to twelve months. The impact of seasonal cycles is well known, and affects demand for a broad array of services. Low demand in the off-season poses significant problems for tourism businesses. For instance, tourism in Prince Edward Island (PEI) is primarily concentrated in the summer months, and that has a significant impact on the occupancy rates of various tourist accommodations. For the year 2005, the occupancy of the tourist inns peaked at around 79 percent in July–August, but was less than 20 percent in the months of December and January.[8] This poses significant challenges for operators in managing these inns in a profitable manner during the off-season.

In many instances, multiple cycles may operate simultaneously. For example, demand levels for public transport may vary by time of day (highest during commute hours), day of week (less travel to work on weekends but more leisure travel), and season of year (more travel by tourists in summer). The demand for service during the peak period on a Monday in summer is likely to be very different from the level during the peak period on a Saturday in winter, reflecting both day-of-week and seasonal variations.

Analyzing Drivers of Demand

No strategy for smoothing demand is likely to succeed unless it is based on an understanding of why customers from a specific market segment choose to use the service when they do. It's difficult for hotels to convince business travellers to remain on Saturday nights since few executives do business over the weekend. Instead, hotel managers may do better to promote weekend use of their facilities for conferences or pleasure travel. Attempts to get commuters to shift their travel to off-peak periods will probably fail, since such travel is determined by people's employment hours. Instead, efforts should be directed at employers to persuade them to adopt flextime or staggered working hours. As discussed earlier, tourism businesses face significant challenges in the off-peak season. These firms recognize that no amount of price discounting is likely to develop business out of season. However, summer resort areas like Muskoka may have good opportunities to build business during the "shoulder seasons" of spring and fall by promoting different attractions—such as hiking to see the spectacular fall colours of the trees, visiting the studios and galleries of famous local artists, watching the wildlife—and altering the mix and focus of services to target a different type of clientele.

Keeping good records of each transaction helps enormously when it comes to analyzing demand patterns based on past experience. Best-practice queuing systems supported by sophisticated software can automatically track customer consumption patterns by date and by time of day. Where relevant, it's also useful to record weather conditions and other special factors (e.g., a strike, an accident, a big convention in town, a price change, or launch of a competing service) that might have influenced demand.

Dividing Up Demand by Market Segment

Random fluctuations are usually caused by factors beyond management's control. But analysis will sometimes reveal that a predictable demand cycle for one segment is concealed within a broader, seemingly random pattern. This fact illustrates the importance of breaking down demand on a segment-by-segment basis. For instance, a repair and maintenance shop that services industrial electrical equipment may already know that a certain proportion of its work consists of regularly scheduled contracts to perform preventive maintenance. The balance may come from "walk-in" business and emergency repairs.

While it might seem hard to predict or control the timing and volume of such work, further analysis could show that walk-in business was more prevalent on some days of the week than others, and that emergency repairs were frequently requested following damage sustained during thunderstorms (which tend to be seasonal in nature and can often be forecast a day or two in advance). Not all demand is desirable. In fact, some requests for service are inappropriate and make it difficult for the organization to respond to the legitimate needs of its target customers. As discussed in Best Practice in Action 9.2, many calls to 911 are not real emergencies, nor even problems that fire, police, or ambulance services are the relevant agencies to solve. Discouraging undesirable demand such as this through marketing campaigns or screening procedures will not, of course, eliminate random fluctuations in the remaining demand. But it may help to keep peak demand levels within the service capacity of the organization.

Can marketing efforts smooth out random fluctuations in demand? The answer is generally no, since these fluctuations are usually caused by factors beyond the organization's control. But detailed market analysis may sometimes reveal that a predictable demand cycle for one segment is concealed within a broader, seemingly random pattern. For example, a coffee shop might experience wide swings in daily patronage, but note that a core group of customers visit every morning to buy their cup of coffee and a muffin.

The ease with which total demand can be broken down into smaller components depends on the nature of the records kept by management. If each customer transaction is recorded separately, and backed up by detailed notes (as in a medical or dental visit or an accountant's audit) then the task of understanding demand is greatly simplified. In subscription and charge account services, when each customer's identity is known and itemized monthly bills are sent, managers can gain some immediate insights into usage patterns. Some services, such as telephone and electricity, even have the ability to track subscriber consumption patterns by time of day. Although these data may not always yield specific information on the purpose for which the service is being used, it is often possible to make informed judgments about the volume of sales generated by different user groups.

Best Practice in Action 9.2

Have you ever wondered what it's like to be a dispatcher for an emergency telephone service such as 911? People differ widely in what they consider to be an emergency.

Imagine yourself in the huge communications room at police headquarters in New York. A grey-haired sergeant is talking patiently by phone to a woman who has dialled 911 because her cat has run up a tree and she's afraid it's stuck there. "Ma'am, have you ever seen a cat skeleton in a tree?" the sergeant asks her. "All those cats get down somehow, don't they?" After the woman has hung up, the sergeant turns to a visitor and shrugs. "These kinds of calls keep pouring in," he says. "What can you do?" The trouble is, when people call the emergency number with complaints about noisy parties next door, pleas to rescue cats, or requests to turn off leaking fire hydrants, they may be slowing response times to real emergencies such as fires, heart attacks, or violent crimes.

At one point, the situation in New York City got so bad that officials were forced to develop a marketing campaign to discourage people from making inappropriate requests for emergency assistance through the 911 number. The problem was that what might seem like an emergency to the caller—a beloved cat stuck up a tree, a noisy party that was preventing a tired person from getting needed sleep—was not a life (or property) threatening situation of the type that the city's emergency services were poised to resolve. So a communications campaign, using a variety of media, was developed to urge people not to call 911 unless they were reporting a *dangerous emergency*. For help in resolving other problems, they were asked to call their local police station or other city agencies. The ad shown below appeared on New York buses and subways (Figure 9.A).

Police services across Canada also face problems with the misuse of the 911 services. While they have not undertaken a promotional campaign to counter such abuses of the system, they focus their efforts on educating people through detailed information on their websites as to what constitutes an emergency under which a 911 call can legitimately be made, and the underlying dangers in making a trivial or prank call. For instance, the Ontario Provincial Police's website (www.opp.ca/Community/911/index.htm) clearly states that a 911 call should be made only in situations where " . . . there are people or property at risk. Examples include fires, crimes in progress or medical emergencies," and should not be used for: seeking information about school closings, road conditions, or directions; asking for directory assistance; seeking information about paying parking tickets; and when you're bored and just want to talk.

Figure 9.A Ad Discouraging Non-emergency Calls to 911

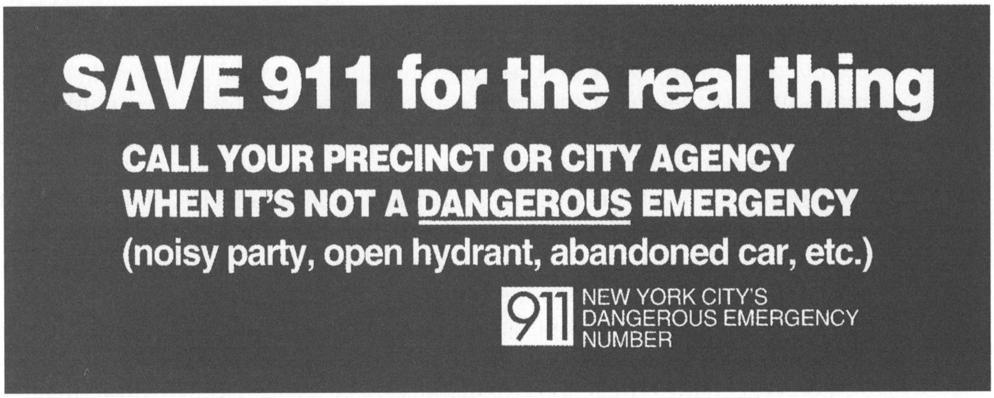

DEMAND LEVELS CAN BE MANAGED

There are five basic approaches to managing demand. The first, which has the virtue of simplicity but little else, involves *taking no action and leaving demand to find its own level.* Eventually customers learn from experience or word-of-mouth when they can expect to stand in line to use the service and when it will be available without delay. The morning drive-through line-ups experienced by people all across Canada at Tim Hortons coffee shops is almost legendary. While Tim Hortons has a very loyal following, the trouble for most firms in these situations is that the customers may also learn to find a competitor

Table 9.2 Alternative Demand-Management Strategies for Different Capacity Situations

| | CAPACITY SITUATION RELATIVE TO DEMAND | |
APPROACH USED TO MANAGE DEMAND	INSUFFICIENT CAPACITY (EXCESS DEMAND)	EXCESS CAPACITY (INSUFFICIENT DEMAND)
Take no action	Unorganized queuing results (may irritate customers and discourage future use)	Capacity is wasted (customers may have a disappointing experience for services such as theatre)
Reduce demand	Higher prices will increase profits; communication can encourage use in other time slots (can this effort be focused on less profitable and desirable segments?)	Take no action (but see preceding)
Increase demand	Take no action unless opportunities exist to stimulate (and give priority to) more profitable segments	Lower prices selectively (try to avoid cannibalizing existing business; ensure that all relevant costs are covered); use communications and variation in products and distribution (but recognize extra costs, if any, and make sure that appropriate trade-offs are made between profitability and use levels)
Inventory demand by reservation system	Consider priority system for most desirable segments; make other customers shift to off-peak period or to future peak	Clarify that space is available and that no reservations are needed
Inventory demand by formalized queuing	Consider override for most desirable segments; try to keep waiting customers occupied and comfortable; try to predict wait period accurately	Not applicable

who is more responsive, and will switch to avoid delays. Further, the low off-peak utilization cannot be improved unless action is taken. More interventionist approaches involve influencing the level of demand at any given time, by taking active steps to *reduce demand in peak periods* and to *increase demand when there is excess capacity*.

Two more approaches both involve *inventorying demand until capacity becomes available*. A firm can accomplish this either by introducing a booking or *reservations system* that promises customers access to capacity at specified times, or by *creating formalized queuing systems* (or by a combination of the two).

Table 9.2 links these five approaches to the two problem situations of excess demand and excess capacity, and provides a brief strategic commentary on each. Many service businesses face both situations at different points in the cycle of demand, and should consider use of the interventionist strategies described.

Marketing Strategies Can Reshape Some Demand Patterns

Several marketing mix variables have roles to play in stimulating demand during periods of excess capacity, and in decreasing or shifting demand during periods of insufficient capacity. Price is often the first variable to be proposed for bringing demand and supply into balance, but changes in product, distribution strategy, and communication efforts can also play an important role. Although each element is discussed separately, effective demand management efforts often require changes in two or more elements jointly.

Use Price and Other Costs to Manage Demand   One of the most direct ways of reducing excess demand at peak periods is to charge customers more money to use the service during those periods. Other costs, too, may have a similar effect. For instance, if customers learn that they are likely to face costs of increased time and effort during peak periods, this information may lead those who dislike spending time waiting in crowded and unpleasant conditions to try later. Similarly, the lure of cheaper prices and an expectation of no waiting may encourage at least some people to change the timing of their behaviour, whether it be shopping, travel, or visiting a museum.

Some firms use pricing strategy in sophisticated ways in order to balance supply and demand. For the monetary price of a service to be effective as a demand management tool, managers must have some sense of the shape and slope of a product's demand curve—that is, how the quantity of service demanded responds to increases or decreases in the price per unit at a particular point in time. (Figure 9.3 shows a sample demand curve.) It's important to determine whether the demand curve for a specific service varies sharply from one time period to another. For instance, will the same person be willing to pay more for a weekend stay in a hotel on Nova Scotia's Cape Breton Island in summer than in winter (when the weather can be freezing)? The answer is probably "yes." If so, significantly different pricing schemes may be needed to fill capacity in each time period. To complicate matters further, there may be separate demand curves for different segments within each time period (business travellers are usually less price sensitive than vacationers).

One of the most difficult tasks facing service marketers is to determine the nature of all these different demand curves. Research, trial and error, and analysis of parallel situations in other locations or in comparable services, are all ways of obtaining an understanding of the situation. Many service businesses explicitly recognize the existence of different demand curves by establishing distinct classes of service, each priced at levels appropriate to the demand curve of a particular segment. In essence, each segment receives a variation of the basic product, with value being added to the core service through supplementary services that appeal to higher-paying segments. For instance, in marketing research firms, service enhancement takes the form of faster turnaround times and more specialized services such as advanced analytics; while in hotels, a distinction is made between rooms of different size and amenities and with different views.

In each case, the objective is to maximize the revenues received from each segment. When capacity is constrained, however, the goal in a profit-seeking business should be to ensure that as much capacity as possible is utilized by the most profitable segments available at any given time. Airlines, for instance, hold a certain number of seats for business passengers paying full fare, and place restrictive conditions on excursion fares for tourists (such as requiring advance purchase and a Saturday night stay) in order to prevent business travellers from taking advantage of cheap fares designed to attract tourists who can help fill the aircraft. Pricing strategies of this nature are known as *revenue management,* and are discussed in Chapter 5.

Figure 9.3

Hotel Demand Curves by Segment and by Season

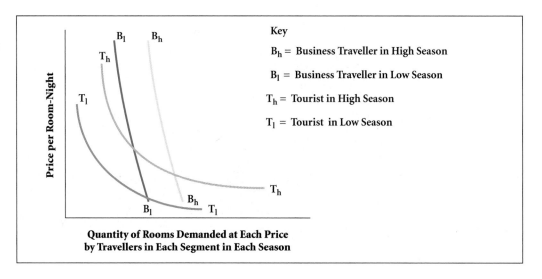

Key

B_h = Business Traveller in High Season

B_l = Business Traveller in Low Season

T_h = Tourist in High Season

T_l = Tourist in Low Season

Price per Room-Night

**Quantity of Rooms Demanded at Each Price
by Travellers in Each Segment in Each Season**

Change Product Elements Although pricing is often a commonly advocated method of balancing supply and demand, it is not quite as universally feasible for services as for goods. A rather obvious example is provided by the respective problems of a ski

Best Practice in Action 9.3

Summer on the Ski Slopes

It used to be that ski resorts shut down once the snow melted and the slopes became unskiable. The chairlifts stopped operating, the restaurants closed, and the lodges were locked and shuttered until winter approached and the snows fell again. In time, however, some ski operators recognized that a mountain offers summer pleasures, too, and kept lodging and restaurants open for hikers and picnickers. Some even built Alpine Slides—curving tracks in which wheeled toboggans could run from the summit to the base—and thus created demand for tickets on the ski lifts. With the construction of condominiums for sale, demand increased for warm-weather activities as the owners flocked to the mountains in summer and early fall.

The arrival of the mountain biking craze created opportunities for equipment rentals as well as chairlift rides. Blue Mountain Resort in Collingwood, Ontario, has long encouraged summer visitors to ride to the top of the escarpment to see the view. But now it also enjoys a booking business in renting Norco downhill and cross country bikes and related equipment (such as helmets and arm guards) and offering lessons ranging from private instruction to downhill biking performance clinics. Beside the base, where in winter skiers would find rack after rack of skis for rent, the summer visi-

tor can now choose from rows of mountain bikes. Bikers transport their vehicles up to the summit on lifts, and then ride them down designated trails. Once in a while, a biker will actually choose to ride up the mountain, but such gluttons for punishment are few and far between.

Most large ski resorts look for a variety of additional ways to attract guests to their hotels and rental homes during the summer. Mont Tremblant, Quebec, for instance, is located beside an attractive lake. In addition to swimming and other water sports on the lake, the resort offers visitors such activities as a championship golf course, tennis, rollerblading, and a children's daycamp. And hikers and mountain bikers come to ride the lifts up the mountain.

Similar thinking prevails at a variety of other seasonal businesses. Thus, tax preparation firms offer bookkeeping and consulting services to small businesses in slack months, educational institutions offer weekend and summer programs for adults and senior citizens, and small pleasure boats offer cruises in the summer and a dockside venue for private functions in winter months. These firms recognize that no amount of price discounting is likely to develop their core business out of season, and so new value propositions are needed, targeted at different segments.

Figure 9B Riding the Chairlift up Mont Tremblant to Hike and Bike Rather than Ski

manufacturer and a ski-slope operator during the summer. The former can either produce for inventory or try to sell skis in the summer at a discount. If the skis are sufficiently discounted, some customers will buy before the ski season in order to save money. However, in the absence of skiing opportunities, no skiers would buy lift tickets for use on a mid-summer day at any price. So, to encourage summer use of the lifts, the operator has to change the service product offering.

Many service offerings remain unchanged throughout the year, but others undergo significant modifications according to the season. Dentists, for example, offer the same array of services throughout the year. By contrast, resort hotels sharply alter the mix and focus of their peripheral services, such as dining, entertainment, and sports, to reflect customer preferences in different seasons.

There can be variations in the product offering even during the course of a 24-hour period. Some restaurants provide a good example of this, marking the passage of the hours with changing menus and levels of service, variations in lighting and decor, opening and closing of the bar, and the presence or absence of entertainment. The goal is to appeal to different needs within the same group of customers, to reach out to different customer segments, or to do both, according to the time of day.

Modify the Place and Time of Delivery
Rather than seeking to modify demand for a service that continues to be offered at the same time in the same place, some firms respond to market needs by modifying the time and place of delivery. Three basic options are available.

The first represents a strategy of *no change*: regardless of the level of demand, the service continues to be offered in the same location at the same times. By contrast, a second strategy involves *varying the times when the service is available*, to reflect changes in customer preference by day of week, by season, and so forth. Theatres and cinema complexes often offer matinees at weekends when people have more leisure time throughout the day; during the summer, cafés and restaurants may stay open later because of the general inclination of people to enjoy the longer, balmier evenings outdoors; and shops extend their hours in the lead-up to Christmas season.

A third strategy involves *offering the service to customers at a new location*. One approach is to operate mobile units that take the service to customers, rather than requiring them to visit fixed-site service locations. Mobile document shredding services, travelling libraries, mobile car-wash services, and home-delivered meals and catering services are examples of this. A cleaning and repair firm that wishes to generate business during low demand periods might offer free pickup and delivery of portable items that need servicing. Alternatively, service firms whose productive assets are mobile may choose to follow the market when that, too, is mobile. For instance, some car rental firms establish seasonal branch offices in resort communities. In these new locations, they often change the schedule of service hours (as well as certain product features) to conform to local needs and preferences.

Promotion and Education
Even if the other variables of the marketing mix remain unchanged, communication efforts alone may be able to help smooth demand. Signage, advertising, publicity, and sales messages can be used to educate customers about the timing of peak periods and encourage them to avail themselves of the service at off-peak times when there will be fewer delays. Examples include the Canada Revenue Agency's reminders to file tax returns early for faster refunds, public transport messages urging non-commuters—such as shoppers or tourists—to avoid the crush conditions of the commute hours, and communications from sales reps for industrial maintenance firms advising customers of periods when preventive maintenance work can be done quickly. In addition, management can ask service personnel (or intermediaries such as travel agents) to encourage customers with discretionary schedules to favour off-peak periods.

Changes in pricing, product characteristics, and distribution must be communicated clearly. If a firm wants to obtain a specific response to variations in marketing mix elements it must, of course, inform customers fully about their options. As discussed in Chapter 6, short-term promotions, combining both pricing and communication elements as well as other incentives, may provide customers with attractive incentives to shift the timing of service usage.

One of the challenges of services is that, being performances, they cannot normally be stored for later use. A haircutter cannot pre-package a haircut for the following day: it must be done in real time. In an ideal world, nobody would ever have to wait to conduct a service transaction. But firms cannot afford to provide extensive extra capacity that would go unutilized most of the time. As we have seen, there are a variety of procedures for bringing demand and supply into balance. But what's a manager to do when the possibilities for shaping demand and adjusting capacity have been exhausted, yet supply and demand are still out of balance? Not taking any action and leaving customers to sort things out is no recipe for customer satisfaction. Rather than allowing matters to degenerate into a random free-for-all, customer-oriented firms try to develop strategies for ensuring order, predictability, and fairness.

In businesses where demand regularly exceeds supply, managers can often take steps to inventory demand. This task can be achieved in one of two ways: (1) by asking customers to wait in line (queuing), usually on a first-come, first-served basis, or (2) by offering them the opportunity of reserving or booking space in advance.

Best Practice in Action 9.4

Cutting the Wait for Retail Banking Customers

How should a big retail bank respond to increased competition from new financial service providers? A large bank decided that enhancing service to its customers would be an important element in its strategy. One opportunity for improvement was to reduce the amount of time that customers spent waiting in line for service in the bank's retail branches—a frequent source of complaints. Recognizing that no single action could resolve the problem satisfactorily, the bank adopted a three-pronged approach.

First, technological improvements were made to the service operation, starting with introduction of an electronic queuing system that not only routed customers to the next available teller station but also provided supervisors with online information to help match staffing to customer demand. Meanwhile, computer enhancements provided tellers with more information about their customers, enabling them to handle more requests without leaving their stations. And new cash machines for tellers saved them from having to select bills and count them twice (yielding an average time saving of 30 seconds for each cash withdrawal transaction).

Second, changes were made to human resource strategies. The bank adopted a new job description for teller managers that made them responsible for customer queuing times and for expediting transactions. It created an officer-of-the-day program, under which a designated officer was equipped with a beeper and assigned to help staff with complicated transactions that might otherwise slow them

down. A new job category of peak-time teller was introduced, paying premium wages for 12–18 hours of work a week. Existing full-time tellers were given cash incentives and recognition to reward improved productivity on predicted high-volume days. Lastly, management reorganized meal arrangements. On busy days, lunch breaks were reduced to half-hour periods and staff received catered meals; meantime, the bank cafeteria was opened earlier to serve peak-time tellers.

A third set of changes centred on customer-oriented improvements to the delivery system. Quick-drop desks were established on busy days to handle deposits and simple requests, while newly created express teller stations were reserved for deposits and cheque cashing. Lobby hours were expanded from 38 to 56 hours a week, including Sundays. A customer brochure, *How to Lose Wait*, alerted customers to busy periods and suggested ways of avoiding delays.

Subsequently, internal measures and customer surveys showed that the improvements had not only reduced customer wait times but also increased customer perceptions that this bank was "the best" bank in the region for minimal waits in teller lines. The bank also found that adoption of extended hours had deflected some of the "noon rush" to before-work and after-work periods.

Source: Adapted from Leonard L. Berry and Linda R. Cooper, "Competing with Time-Saving Service," *Business* 40/2 (1990): 3–7.

Waiting Is a Universal Phenomenon

Nobody likes to be kept waiting (Figure 9.4). It's boring, time-wasting, and sometimes physically uncomfortable, especially if there is nowhere to sit or you are outdoors. And yet waiting for a service process is an almost universal phenomenon: almost every organization faces the problem of waiting lines somewhere in its operation. People are kept waiting on the phone, they line up with their supermarket carts to check out their grocery purchases, and they wait for their bills after a restaurant meal. They sit in their cars waiting to enter drive-in car washes and to pay at toll-booths. And in Canada, nothing strikes a chord closer to heart than the long waiting times for access to health care services. Richard Larson suggests that, when everything is added up, the average person may spend the equivalent of half an hour per day waiting in line, or 20 months over an 80-year lifetime![9]

Physical and inanimate objects wait for processing, too. Customers' emails sit in customer service staff's inboxes, appliances wait to be repaired, cheques wait to be cleared at a bank, an incoming phone call waits to be switched to a customer service rep. In each instance, a customer may be waiting for the outcome of that work—an answer to an email, an appliance that is working again, a cheque credited to the customer's balance, or useful contact with the service rep (instead of being kept on hold listening to a recorded message that keeps repeating, "Your call is important to us").

Why Waiting Lines Occur

Waiting lines—known to operations researchers as "queues"—occur whenever the number of arrivals at a facility exceeds the capacity of the system to process them. In a very real sense, queues are basically a symptom of unresolved capacity-management problems. Analysis and modelling of queues is a well-established branch of operations management. Queuing theory has been traced back to 1917, when a Danish telephone engineer was charged with determining how large the switching unit in a telephone system had to be to keep the number of busy signals within reason.[10]

Figure 9.4

TELUS makes a promise of fast customer service and an account credit if the wait is too long.

Get fast client service.

Nobody likes a slowpoke. That's why our fast client service promise means we'll credit your account if you wait too long.* So get where the going's good and get all our future friendly* promises.

TELUS
the future is friendly*

As the telephone example suggests, not all queues take the form of a physical waiting line in a single location. When customers deal with a service supplier at arm's length, as in information-processing services, they call from home, office, or college using telecommunication channels such as the telephone or the internet. Typically, calls are answered in the order received, often requiring customers to wait their turn in a virtual line. Some physical queues are geographically dispersed. Travellers wait at many different locations for the taxis they have ordered by phone to arrive and pick them up.

Many websites now allow people to do things for themselves, like obtaining information or making reservations, which formerly required making telephone calls or visiting a service facility in person. Companies often promote the time savings that can be obtained. Although accessing the web can be slow sometimes, at least the wait is conducted while the customer is comfortably seated and able to attend to other matters.

Increasing capacity by adding more tellers was only one of several actions taken to reduce wait times in our earlier example of the large bank. But adding extra servers is not always the optimal solution in situations where customer satisfaction must be balanced against cost considerations. Like that bank, managers should consider a variety of alternatives, such as:

- Rethinking the design of the queuing system.
- Redesigning processes to shorten the time of each transaction.
- Managing customers' behaviour and their perceptions of the wait.
- Installing a reservations system.

Different Queue Configurations

There are a variety of different types of queues, and the challenge for managers is to select the procedure most appropriate to the service in question. Figure 9.5 shows diagrams of several types that you have probably experienced yourself. In *single line, sequential stages*, customers proceed through several serving operations, as in a cafeteria. Bottlenecks may occur at any stage where the process takes longer to execute than at previous stages. Many cafeterias have lines at the cash register because the cashier takes longer to calculate how much you owe and to make change than the servers take to slap food on your plate.

Parallel lines to multiple servers offer more than one serving station, allowing customers to select one of several lines in which to wait. Banks and ticket windows are common examples. Fast-food restaurants usually have several serving lines in operation at busy times of day, with each offering the full menu. A parallel system can have either a single stage or multiple stages. The disadvantage of this design is that lines may not move at equal speed. How many times have you chosen what looked like the shortest line only to watch in frustration as the lines either side of you move at twice the speed because someone in your line has a complicated transaction? A common solution here is to create a *single line to multiple servers* (commonly known as a "snake"). This approach is encountered frequently at post offices and airport check-ins.

Designated lines involve assigning different lines to specific categories of customer. Examples include express lines (for instance, 12 items or less) and regular lines at supermarket checkouts, and different check-in stations for first class, business class, and economy class airline passengers.

Take a number saves customers the need to stand in a queue, because they know they will be called in their order of arrival. This procedure allows them to sit down and relax (if seating is available) or to guess how long the wait will be and do something else in the meantime—but at the risk of losing their place if earlier customers are served faster than expected. Users of this approach include large travel agents and supermarket departments, such as the butcher or baker.

Hybrid approaches to queue configuration also exist. For instance, a cafeteria with a single serving line might offer two cash register stations at the final stage. Similarly, patients at a dental clinic might visit a single receptionist for registration, proceed sequentially through multiple channels for dental and medical history update, examination, treatment and/or cleaning and conclude by returning to a single line for payment at the

Figure 9.5

Alternative Queue
Configurations

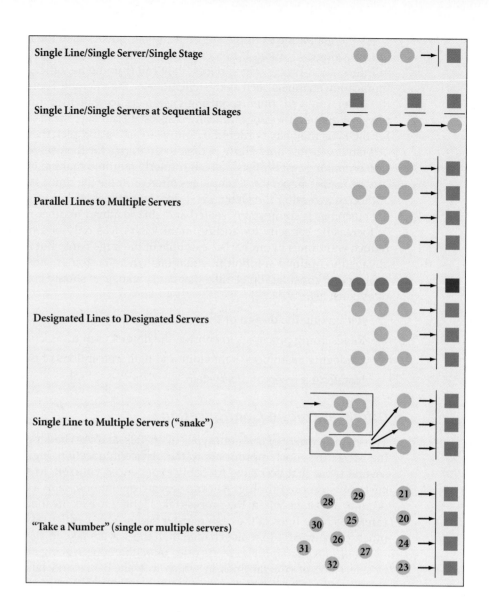

cashier's desk. Research suggests that selecting the most appropriate type of queue for the service is important to customer satisfaction. Rafaeli, Barron, and Haber found that the way a waiting area is structured can produce feelings of injustice and unfairness in customers. Customers who waited in parallel lines to multiple servers reported significantly higher agitation and greater dissatisfaction with the fairness of the service-delivery process than customers who waited in a single line ("snake") to access multiple servers, even when both groups of customers waited an identical amount of time and were involved in completely fair service processes.[11]

Virtual Waits

One of the problems associated with waiting in line is the waste of time this involves for customers. When two or more people are waiting together, it's sometimes possible for one to remain and the others to go off and do something else for a while. The "virtual queue" strategy is an innovative way to take the physical waiting out of the wait altogether. Instead, customers register their place in line on a computer, which estimates the time at which they will reach the front of the virtual line and should return to claim their place. Best Practice in Action 9.5 describes the virtual queuing systems used at Disney and Six Flags theme parks, practices yet to be adopted at Canadian theme parks.

Best Practice in Action 9.5

Waiting in a Virtual Queue for Theme Park Attractions

Disney is well known for its efforts to give visitors to its theme parks information on how long they may have to wait to ride a particular attraction, and for entertaining guests while they are waiting in line. However, the company found that the long waits at its most popular attractions still represented a major source of dissatisfaction, and so they created an innovative solution.

The concept of the virtual queue was first tested at Disney World. At the most popular attractions there, guests were able to register their place in line with a computer and were then free to use the wait time visiting other places in the park. Surveys showed that guests who used the new system spent more money, saw more attractions, and had significantly higher satisfaction. After further refinement, the system—now named FASTPASS—was introduced at the five most popular attractions at Disney World, and subsequently extended to all Disney parks worldwide. It is now used by more than 50 million guests a year. The system is easy to use. When guests approach a FASTPASS attraction, they are given two clear choices: obtain a FASTPASS ticket there and return at a designated time, or wait in a standby line. Signs indicate how long the wait is in each instance. The wait time for each line tends to be self-regulating, because a large difference between the two will lead to increasing numbers of people choosing the shorter line. In practice, the virtual wait tends to be slightly longer than the physical one. To use the FASTPASS option, guests insert their park admission ticket into a special turnstile and receive a FASTPASS ticket specifying a return time. Guests have some flexibility because the system allows them a 60-minute window beyond the printed return time.

The Six Flags chain of theme parks has developed its own approach, originally called FastLane (later renamed Flash Pass), which involves an extra fee. At five of the parks, you can rent a palm-sized device called a Q-bot. At the Texas and St. Louis parks, the fee is $10 for the Q-bot plus an additional $10 for each person in the group who wishes to use Flash Pass. At the other three parks, guests can choose between standard and gold service, which costs $25 per Q-bot and per guest at the New England and Georgia parks; at the Great America park near Philadelphia, standard service costs $15 and gold costs $33.

At each ride you wish to use, you insert the Q-bot into a slot at the Flash Pass sign. The device calculates how long the current wait is, then schedules a reservation that allows a 10-minute window, after which you lose your place. For purchasers of standard service, the Flash Pass virtual wait is the same as the physical wait; for gold service purchasers, however, the wait is reduced by up to 75 percent. A few minutes before your scheduled time, the Q-bot will vibrate, beep, and display a message saying, "Next Ride Soon," reminding you to go to the ride, where you enter through a special Flash Pass channel. The Q-bot will also display messages notifying you in the event that a ride malfunction has caused delays and giving you a new return time.

Sources: Duncan Dickson, Robert C. Ford, and Bruce Laval, "Managing Real and Virtual Waits in Hospitality and Service Organizations," *Cornell Hotel and Restaurant Administration Quarterly* 46 (February 2005): 52–68; Arthur Levine, "Six Flags Guests Get Out of Line," About.com Travel, http://themeparks.about.com/cs/sixflagsparks/a/blfastlanea.htm, accessed December 20, 2005; Lo-Q Virtual Queuing Inc., www.lo-qusa.com/flashpass.html, accessed November 7, 2006.

Queuing Systems Can Be Tailored to Market Segments

Although the basic rule in most queuing systems is "first come, first served," not all queuing systems are organized on this basis. Market segmentation is sometimes used to design queuing strategies that set different priorities for different types of customers. Allocation to separate queuing areas may be based on

- *Urgency of the job.* At many hospital emergency units, a triage nurse is assigned to greet incoming patients and decide which ones require priority medical treatment and which can safely be asked to register and then sit down while they wait their turn.

- *Duration of service transaction.* Banks, supermarkets, and other retail services often institute "express lanes" for shorter, less complicated tasks.

- *Payment of a premium price.* Airlines usually offer separate check-in lines for first class and economy-class passengers, with a higher ratio of personnel to passengers in the first-class line, resulting in reduced waits for those who have paid more for their tickets.

- *Importance of the customer.* A special area may be reserved for members of frequent-user clubs. Airlines often provide lounges, offering newspapers and free refreshments, where frequent flyers can wait for their flights in greater comfort. Similarly, most banks have special wickets for business customers so that they can avoid delays by standing in lines to see a customer service representative.

MINIMIZE PERCEPTIONS OF WAITING TIME

Research shows that people often think they have waited longer for a service than they actually have. Studies of public transportation use, for instance, have shown that travellers perceive time spent waiting for a bus or train as passing between one-and-a-half and seven times more slowly than the time actually spent travelling in the vehicle.[12] People don't like wasting their time on unproductive activities, any more than they like wasting money. Customer dissatisfaction with delays in receiving service can often stimulate strong emotions, even anger.[13]

The Psychology of Waiting Time

The noted philosopher William James observed: "Boredom results from being attentive to the passage of time itself." Savvy service marketers recognize that customers experience waiting time in differing ways, depending on the circumstances. Table 9.3 highlights ten propositions by David Maister and other researchers on the psychology of waiting lines.

When increasing capacity is simply not feasible, service providers should try to be creative and look for ways to make waiting more palatable for customers. Doctors and dentists stock their waiting rooms with piles of magazines for people to read while waiting. Car repair facilities may have a television for customers to watch. One tire dealer goes even further, providing customers with free popcorn, soft drinks, coffee, and ice cream while they wait for their cars to be returned.

Jiffy Lube, a leading North American fast oil-change provider, with over 2200 service centres in Canada and the United States, recently announced that it would deploy what is labelled as the J-TV network on high-definition televisions in Jiffy Lube waiting rooms. J-TV's internet-transmitted content will include car-care tips, additional service options and specials, and third-party programming. "Our customers wait an average of 20 minutes or less for their Jiffy Lube Signature Service® Oil Change," said Lisa Carlson, global director of marketing for Jiffy Lube International. "This network will enhance the customer experience with entertaining content and useful information they can employ to best protect their vehicles." Initial deployment is scheduled for approximately 280 company-owned service centres, with up to 1000 franchised locations expected to join by year-end 2007.[14]

An experiment at a large bank in Boston found that installing an electronic news display in the lobby led to greater customer satisfaction, but it didn't reduce the perceived time spent waiting for teller service.[15] Restaurants solve the waiting problem by inviting dinner guests to have a drink in the bar until their table is ready (an approach that makes money for the house as well as keeping the customer occupied). In similar fashion, guests waiting in line for a show at a casino may find themselves queuing in a corridor lined with slot-machines.

The doorman at one Marriott Hotel has taken it upon himself to bring a combination barometer/thermometer to work each day, hanging it on a pillar at the hotel entrance where guests waiting can spend a moment or two examining it while they wait for a taxi or for their car to be delivered from the valet parking.[16] Theme park operators cleverly design their waiting areas to make the wait look shorter than it really is, finding ways to give customers in line the impression of constant progress, and make time seem to pass more quickly by keeping customers amused or diverted while they wait. Recognizing that customers don't want to waste time on either pre-process or post-process waits, rental car firms try to minimize customer waiting when the car is returned, employing agents with wireless, hand-held terminals to meet customers in the parking area, enter fuel and mileage, and then compute and print bills on the spot.

Table 9.3 Ten Propositions on the Psychology of Waiting Lines

1. *Unoccupied time feels longer than occupied time.* When you're sitting around with nothing to do, time seems to crawl. The challenge for service organizations is to give customers something to do or to distract them while waiting.

2. *Pre- and post-process waits feel longer than in-process waits.* Waiting to buy a ticket to enter a theme park is different from waiting to ride on a roller coaster once you're in the park. There's also a difference between waiting for coffee to arrive near the end of a restaurant meal and waiting for the server to bring you the check once you're ready to leave.

3. *Anxiety makes waits seem longer.* Can you remember waiting for someone to show at a rendezvous and worrying about whether you had got the time or the location correct? While waiting in unfamiliar locations, especially outdoors and after dark, people often worry about their personal safety.

4. *Uncertain waits are longer than known, finite waits.* Although any wait may be frustrating, we can usually adjust mentally to a wait of known length. It's the unknown that keeps us on edge. Imagine waiting for a delayed flight and not being told how long the delay is going to be. You don't know whether you have the time to get up and walk around the terminal or whether to stay at the gate in case the flight is called any minute.

5. *Unexplained waits are longer than explained waits.* Have you ever been in a subway or an elevator that has stopped for no apparent reason, without anyone telling you why? In addition to uncertainty about the length of the wait, there's added worry about what is going to happen. Has there been an accident on the line? Will you have to leave the train in the tunnel? Is the elevator broken? Will you be stuck for hours in close proximity with strangers?

6. *Unfair waits are longer than equitable waits.* Expectations about what is fair or unfair sometimes vary from one culture or country to another. In the United States, Canada, or Britain, for example, people expect everybody to wait their turn in line and are likely to get irritated if they see others jumping ahead or being given priority for no apparently good reason.

7. *The more valuable the service, the longer people will wait.* People will queue overnight under uncomfortable conditions to get good seats at a major concert or sports event that is expected to sell out.

8. *Solo waits feel longer than group waits.* Waiting with one or more people you know is reassuring. Conversation with friends can help to pass the time, but not everyone is comfortable talking to a stranger.

9. *Physically uncomfortable waits feel longer than comfortable waits.* "My feet are killing me!" is one of the most frequently heard comments when people are forced to stand in line for a long time. And whether seated or unseated, waiting seems more burdensome if the temperature is too hot or too cold, if it's drafty or windy, and if there is no protection from rain or snow.

10. *Unfamiliar waits seem longer than familiar ones.* Frequent users of a service know what to expect and are less likely to worry while waiting. New or occasional users of a service, by contrast, are often nervous, wondering not only about the probable length of the wait but also about what happens next.

Source: (items 1–8) David H. Maister, "The Psychology of Waiting Lines," in J.A. Czepiel, M. R. Solomon, and C.F. Surprenant (eds.), *The Service Encounter,* Lexington, MA: Lexington Books/D.C. Heath, 1986: 113–23; (item 9) M.M. Davis and J. Heineke, "Understanding the Roles of the Customer and the Operation for Better Queue Management," *International Journal of Service Industry Management* 7/5 (1994): 21–34; and (item 10) Peter Jones and Emma Peppiat, "Managing Perceptions of Waiting Times in Service Queues," *International Journal of Service Industry Management* 7/5 (1996): 47–61.

Give Customers Information on Waits

Does it help to tell people how long they are likely to have to wait for service? Common sense would suggest that this is useful information for customers, since it allows them to make decisions as to whether they can afford to take the time to wait now or should come back later. It also enables them to plan the use of their time while waiting.

An experimental study in Canada looked at how students responded to waits while conducting transactions by computer—a situation similar to waiting on the telephone in that there are no visual clues as to the probable wait time.[17] The study examined dissatisfaction with waits of 5, 10, or 15 minutes under three conditions: (1) the student subjects were told nothing, (2) they were told how long the wait was likely to be, or (3) they were told what their place in line was. The results suggested that for 5-minute waits, it was not necessary to provide information to improve satisfaction. For waits of 10 or 15 minutes, offering information appeared to improve customers' evaluations of service. However, for longer waits, the researchers suggest that it may be more positive to let people know how their place in line is changing than to let them know how much time remains before they will be served. One conclusion we might draw is that people prefer to see (or sense) that the line is moving, rather than to watch the clock.

CREATE AN EFFECTIVE RESERVATIONS SYSTEM

Ask someone what services come to mind when you talk about reservations and most likely they will cite airlines, hotels, restaurants, car rentals, and theatre seats. Suggest synonyms like "bookings" or "appointments" and they may add haircuts, visits to professionals such as doctors and consultants, vacation rentals, and service calls to fix anything from a broken refrigerator to a neurotic computer.

Reservations are intended to guarantee that service will be available when the customer wants it. They are commonly used by many people-processing services including restaurants, hotels, airlines, dentists, and hairdressing salons (Figure 9.6). The presence of such systems enables demand to be controlled and smoothed out in a more manageable way. By capturing data, reservation systems also help organizations to prepare operational and financial projections for future periods. Systems vary from handwritten entries in a simple appointments book for a dentist's office to a central, computerized data bank for an airline's worldwide operations.

When goods require servicing, their owners may not wish to be parted from them for long, so it's important to be able to promise a particular time when the item should be dropped off, and to guarantee prompt completion of the needed work. Households with only one car, for example, or factories with a vital piece of equipment, often cannot afford to be without such items for more than a day or two. Reservations systems serve the interests of both customers and the business. By requiring reservations for routine repair and maintenance, management can ensure that some time will be kept free for handling emergency jobs which, because they are unpredictable and carry a premium price, generate a much higher margin.

Taking bookings also serves to pre-sell a service, to inform customers, and to educate them about what to expect. Customers who hold reservations should be able to count on avoiding a queue, since they have been guaranteed service at a specific time. A well-organized reservations system allows the organization to deflect demand for service from a first-choice time to earlier or later times, from one class of service to another ("upgrades" and "downgrades"), and even from first-choice locations to alternative ones. However, problems arise when customers fail to show up, or when service firms over-book. Marketing strategies for dealing with these operational problems include requiring a deposit, cancelling unpaid bookings after a certain time, and providing compensation to victims of over-booking.

The challenge in designing reservation systems is to make them fast and user-friendly for both staff and customers. Many firms now allow customers to make their own reservations on a website—a trend that seems certain to grow. Most hotels will even offer discounted rates if the reservations are made online. Whether customers talk with a reservations agent or make their own bookings, they want quick answers to queries about service availability at a preferred time. They also appreciate it if the system can provide further information about the type of service they are reserving. For instance, can a hotel assign a specific room on request? Or at least, can it assign a room with a view of the lake rather than one with a view of the parking lot and the nearby power station?

Reservations Strategies Should Focus on Yield

Service organizations often use percentage of capacity sold as a measure of operational efficiency. Transport services talk of the "load factor" achieved, hotels of their "occupancy rate," and hospitals of their "census." Similarly, professional firms can calculate what proportion of a partner's or an employee's time is classified as billable hours, and repair shops can look at utilization of both equipment and labour. By themselves, however, these percentage figures tell us little of the relative profitability of the business attracted, since high utilization rates may be obtained at the expense of heavy discounting—or even outright giveaways.

More and more, service firms are looking at their "yield"—that is, the average revenue received per unit of capacity. The aim is to maximize this yield in order to improve profitability. As noted in Chapter 5, pricing strategies designed to achieve this goal are widely used as an element in the revenue management programs employed in such capacity-constrained industries as passenger airlines, hotels, and car rentals. Formalized revenue management systems, based upon mathematical modelling, are of greatest value for service firms that find it expensive to modify their capacity but incur relatively low costs for the sale of each unit of available capacity.[18] Other characteristics encouraging use of such programs include fluctuating demand levels, ability to segment markets by extent of price sensitivity, and sale of services well in advance of usage.

Yield analysis forces managers to recognize the opportunity cost of allocating capacity to one customer or market segment when another might subsequently yield a higher rate. Consider the following problems facing sales managers for different types of capacity-constrained service organizations:

- Should a hotel accept an advance booking from a tour group of 200 room nights at $80 each when these same room nights might possible be sold later at short notice to business travellers at the full posted rate of $140?

- Should a railroad with 30 empty freight cars at its disposal accept an immediate request for a shipment worth $900 per car, or hold the cars idle for a few more days in the hope of getting a priority shipment that would be twice as valuable?

- How many seats on a particular flight should an airline sell in advance to tour groups and passengers travelling at special excursion rates?

- Should an industrial repair and maintenance shop reserve a certain proportion of productive capacity each day for emergency repair jobs that offer a high contribution margin and the potential to build long-term customer loyalty, or should it simply follow a strategy of making sure that there are sufficient jobs, mostly involving routine maintenance, to keep its employees fully occupied?

Figure 9.6

Reservations are required at busy restaurants.

- Should a print-shop process all jobs on a first-come, first-served basis, with a guaranteed delivery time for each job, or should it charge a premium rate for "rush" work, and tell customers with "standard" jobs to expect some variability in completion dates?

Decisions on such problems deserve to be handled with a little more sophistication than just resorting to the "bird in the hand is worth two in the bush" formula. So managers need a way of figuring out what the chances actually are of getting more profitable business if they wait. Good information, based upon detailed record-keeping of past usage and supported by current market intelligence and good marketing sense, is the key. The decision to accept or reject business should be based on a realistic estimate of the probabilities of obtaining higher-rated business instead, and awareness of the need to maintain established (and desirable) customer relationships. Managers who decide on the basis of guesswork and "gut feel" are little better than gamblers who bet on rolls of the dice.

There has to be a clear plan, based on analysis of past performance and current market data, that indicates how much capacity should be allocated on specific dates to different types of customers at certain prices. Based on this plan, "selective sell" targets can be assigned to advertising and sales personnel, reflecting allocation of available capacity among different market segments on specific future dates. The last thing a firm wants its sales force to do is to encourage price-sensitive market segments to buy capacity on dates when sales projections predict that there will be strong demand from customers willing to pay full price. In some industries, however, the lowest-rated business often books the furthest ahead: tour groups, which pay much lower room rates than individual travellers, often ask airlines and hotels to block space more than a year in advance.

Figure 9.7 illustrates capacity allocation in a hotel setting, where demand from different types of customers varies not only by day of the week but also by season. These allocation decisions by segment, captured in reservation databases that are accessible worldwide, tell reservations personnel when to stop accepting reservations at certain prices, even though many rooms may still remain unbooked. Loyalty-program members, who are primarily business travellers, are obviously a particularly desirable segment.

Similar charts can be constructed for most capacity-constrained businesses. In some instances, capacity is measured in terms of seats for a given performance, seat miles, or room nights; in others it may be in terms of machine time, labour time, billable professional hours, vehicle miles, or storage volume whichever is the scarce resource. Unless it's easy to divert business from one facility to a similar alternative, allocation planning decisions will have to be made at the level of geographic operating units. So each hotel, repair

Figure 9.7

Setting Capacity Allocation Targets by Segment for a Hotel

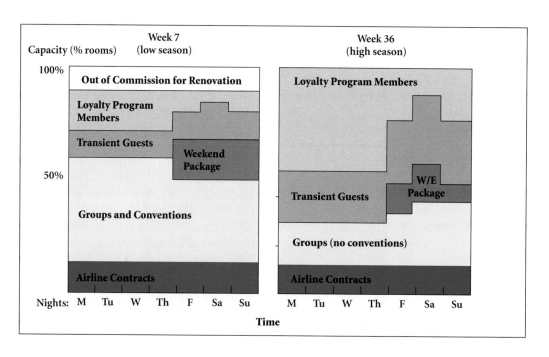

and maintenance centre, or computer service bureau may need its own plan. On the other hand, transport vehicles represent a mobile capacity that can be allocated across any geographic area the vehicles are able to serve.

In large organizations, such as major airlines or hotel chains, the market is very dynamic, since the situation is changing all the time. For instance, the demand for both business and pleasure travel reflects current or anticipated economic conditions. While business travellers tend to be less price sensitive than leisure travellers, pressures on the bottom line are forcing many companies to revisit their policies regarding employee travel. Now companies insist that employees shop for the best travel bargains they can find within the constraints of their business travel needs, and some even encourage employees to stay over Saturday night if the resulting reduction in airfare exceeds the additional lodging and meals expense. Pleasure travellers are often very price sensitive; a special promotion, involving discounted fares and room rates, may encourage people to undertake a trip that they would not otherwise have made.

Viewed from the perspective of the individual hotel or airline, competitive activity has the potential to play havoc with patronage forecasts. Imagine that you are a hotel owner, and a new hotel opens across the street with a special discount offer. How will it affect you? Alternatively, consider the impact if an existing competitor burns down! The airline business is notoriously changeable. Fares can be slashed overnight. A competitor may introduce a new non-stop service between two cities or cut back its existing schedule on another route. Travel agents and savvy customers watch these movements like hawks and may be quick to cancel one reservation (even if it involves paying a penalty) in order to take advantage of a better price or a more convenient schedule that can be obtained elsewhere.

Effective Demand and Capacity Management Requires Information

Managers require substantial information to help them develop effective strategies to manage demand and capacity and then monitor subsequent performance in the marketplace. Following are some important categories of information for this purpose.

- *Historical data* on the level and composition of demand over time, including responses to changes in price or other marketing variables.
- *Forecasts* of the level of demand for each major segment under specified conditions.
- *Segment-by-segment data* to help management evaluate the impact of periodic cycles and random demand fluctuations.
- *Cost data* to enable the organization to distinguish between fixed and variable costs, and to determine the relative profitability of incremental unit sales to different segments and at different prices.
- *Meaningful variations in demand levels and composition* on a location-by-location basis (in multi-site organizations).
- *Customer attitudes* toward queuing under varying conditions.
- *Customer opinions* on whether the quality of service delivered varies with different levels of capacity utilization.

Where might all this information come from? Many large organizations with expensive fixed capacity have implemented revenue management systems (discussed in Chapter 5). For organizations without such systems, much of the needed data are probably already being collected within the organization—not necessarily by marketers—and new studies can be conducted to obtain additional data. A stream of information comes into most service businesses, notably concerning individual customer transactions. Sales receipts alone often contain vast detail. Service businesses need to collect detailed information for operational and accounting purposes, and can frequently associate specific customers with specific transactions.

Unfortunately, the marketing value of such data is often overlooked, and they are not always stored in ways that permit easy retrieval and analysis by marketers. Nevertheless, collection and storage of customer transaction data can often be reformatted to provide at least some of the desired information, including how existing segments have responded to past changes in marketing variables.

Other information may have to be collected through special studies, such as customer surveys, or reviews of analogous situations. It may also be necessary to collect information on competitive performance, because changes in the capacity or strategy of competitors may require corrective action.

When new strategies are under consideration, operations researchers can often contribute useful insights by developing simulation models of the impact of changes on different variables. Such an approach is particularly useful in service "network" environments, such as theme parks and ski resorts, where customers can choose between multiple activities at the same site. Madeleine Pullman and Gary Thompson modelled customer behaviour at a ski resort, where skiers can choose between different lifts and ski runs of varying lengths and levels of difficulty. Through analysis, they were able to determine the potential future impact of lift capacity upgrades (bigger or faster chair lifts), capacity expansion in the form of extended skiing terrain, industry growth, day-to-day price variations, customer response to information about wait times at different lifts, and changes in the customer mix.[19]

Conclusion

Because many capacity-constrained service organizations have heavy fixed costs, even modest improvements in capacity utilization can have a significant effect on the bottom line. In this chapter we have also shown how managers can transform fixed costs into variable costs through such strategies as using rented facilities or part-time labour. Creating a more flexible approach to productive capacity allows a firm to adopt strategy to match capacity to demand (also called the "chase demand" strategy), thereby improving productivity.

Decisions on *place and time* are closely associated with balancing demand and capacity. Demand is often a function of where the service is located and when it is offered. As we saw with the example of the mountain resorts, the appeal of many destinations varies with the seasons. Marketing strategies involving use of *product elements, price,* and *promotion and education* are often useful in managing the level of demand for a service at a particular place and time.

The time-bound nature of services is a critical management issue today, especially with customers becoming more time-sensitive and more conscious of their personal time constraints and availability. People-processing services are particularly likely to impose the burden of unwanted waiting on their customers, since the latter cannot avoid coming to the "factory" for service. Reservations can shape the timing of arrivals, but sometimes queuing is inevitable. Managers who can act to save customers more time (or at least make time pass more pleasantly) than the competition are often able to create a competitive advantage for their organizations.

Review Questions

1. Why is capacity management particularly significant for service firms?

2. What is meant by "chasing demand"?

3. How does optimum capacity utilization differ from maximum capacity utilization? Give examples of situations where the two may be the same, and of situations where they differ.

4. Select a service organization of your choice and identify its particular patterns of demand with reference to Figure 9.1.

   (a) What is the nature of this service organization's approach to capacity and demand management?

   (b) What changes would you recommend in relation to its management of capacity and demand, and why?

5. Why should service marketers be concerned about the amount of time that customers spend in (a) pre-process waits, (b) in-process waits, and (c) post-process waits?

6. What do you see as the advantages and disadvantages of the different types of queues for an organization serving large numbers of customers?

7. What are the important inputs required for the successful implementation and monitoring of capacity- and demand-management strategies?

Application Exercises

1. What are the factors that come into play in determining the productive capacity of a service organization? Examine these factors in the context of a department at a university, and discuss how they might reduce or increase the productive capacity in terms of number of students who could be taught at this department. In your opinion, would maximum capacity differ from optimum capacity in this situation?

2. Identify some specific examples of companies in your region that significantly change their product and/or marketing mix variables in order to encourage patronage during periods of low demand.

3. Review the ten propositions on the psychology of waiting lines. Which are the most relevant in (a) a city bus stop on a cold, dark evening, (b) check-in for a flight at the airport, (c) a dentist's office where patients are seated, and (d) a ticket line for a hockey game that is expected to be a sell-out.

4. Give examples, based on your own experience, of a reservation system that worked really well, and of one that worked really badly. Identify and evaluate the reasons for the success and failure of these two systems. What recommendations would you make to both firms to improve (or further improve in the case of the good example) their reservation systems?

Endnotes

1. Kenneth J. Klassen and Thomas R. Rohleder, "Combining Operations and Marketing to Manage Capacity and Demand in Services," *Service Industries Journal* 21 (April 2001): 1–30.

2. www.cbc.ca/news/background/poweroutage, accessed August 26, 2006.

3. Data from www.calgarytransit.com/html/technical_information.html, accessed August 26, 2006.

4. "The Delta Whistler Village Suites Goes 'To The Top'," http://www.go2hr.ca/ForbrEmployers/EmployerAwards/DeltaWhistlerVillageSuitesGoesToTheTop/tabid/622/Default.aspx, accessed January 29, 2007.

5. www.theaircanadacentre.com, accessed August 26, 2006.

6. Irene C.L. Ng, Jochen Wirtz, and Khai Sheang Lee, "The Strategic Role of Unused Service Capacity," *International Journal of Service Industry Management* 10/2 (1999): 211–38.

7. Christopher H. Lovelock, "Strategies for Managing Capacity-Constrained Service Organisations," *Service Industries Journal* 3 (November 1984): 12–30.

8. "Tourism Performance 2005," Tourism Advisory Council Prince Edward Island, www.tiapei.pe.ca/documents/files/tourism_05final.pdf, accessed August 27, 2006.

9. Dave Wielenga, "Not So Fine Lines," *Los Angeles Times*, November 28, 1997, p. E1.

10. Richard Saltus, "Lines, Lines, Lines, Lines . . . The Experts Are Trying to Ease the Wait," *Boston Globe* (October 5, 1992): 39, 42.

11. Anat Rafaeli, G. Barron, and K. Haber, "The Effects of Queue Structure on Attitudes," *Journal of Service Research* 5, November, 2002, 125-139.

12. Jay R. Chernow, "Measuring the Values of Travel Time Savings," *Journal of Consumer Research* 7 (March 1981): 360–71. This entire issue of the journal was in fact devoted to the consumption of time.

13. Ana B. Casado Diaz and Francisco J. Más Ruiz, "The Consumer's Reaction to Delays in Service," *International Journal of Service Industry Management* 13/2 (2002): 118–40.

14. "Jiffy Lube® Enhances Customers' Wait-Time AlivePromo to Deploy New J-TV Media Network in Waiting Rooms across North America" Company Press Release. www.jiffylube.com/Company/cpy_PressRoom.aspx, accessed September 7, 2006.

15. Karen L. Katz, Blaire M. Larson, and Richard C. Larson, "Prescription for the Waiting-in-Line Blues: Entertain, Enlighten, and Engage," *Sloan Management Review* (Winter 1991): 44–53.

16. Bill Fromm and Len Schlesinger, *The Real Heroes of Business and Not a CEO Among Them*, New York: Currency Doubleday, 1994: 7.

17. Michael K. Hui and David K. Tse, "What to Tell Customers in Waits of Different Lengths: An Integrative Model of Service Evaluation," *Journal of Marketing* 80/2 (April 1996): 81–90.

18. Sheryl E. Kimes and Richard B. Chase, "The Strategic Levers of Yield Management," *Journal of Service Research* 1 (November 1998): 156–66; Anthony Ingold, Una McMahon-Beattie, and Ian Yeoman (eds.), *Yield Management Strategies for the Service Industries*. 2nd ed., London: Continuum, 2000.

19. Madeleine E. Pullman and Gary M. Thompson, "Evaluating Capacity- and Demand-Management Decisions at a Ski Resort," *Cornell Hotel and Restaurant Administration Quarterly* 43 (December 2002): 25–36; Madeleine E. Pullman and Gary M. Thompson, "Strategies for Integrating Capacity with Demand in Service Networks," *Journal of Service Research* 5 (February 2003): 169–83.

CHAPTER 10

Crafting the Service Environment

Managers ... need to develop a better understanding of the interface between the resources they manipulate in atmospherics and the experience they want to create for the customer.

—Jean-Charles Chebat and Laurette Dubé

Restaurant design has become as compelling an element as menu, food and wine ... in determining a restaurant's success.

—Danny Meyer

The physical service environment plays an important role in shaping the service experience and delivering customer satisfaction. Theme parks, such as Paramount Canada's Wonderland in Vaughan, Ontario, are often cited as vivid examples of service environments that make every customer feel comfortable and highly satisfied, and leave a long-lasting impression. But in fact organizations from hospitals to hotels and from restaurants to the offices of professional firms have come to recognize that the service environment is an important component of their marketing mix and overall value proposition.

Service environments communicate as well as determine the positioning of the service, are a key part of the delivery system, and as such significantly shape employee as well as customer productivity. They also play a role in guiding customers through the delivery system, and can be a core component of a firm's value proposition.

In this chapter, we look at the importance of carefully designing service environments that help to engineer customer experiences, convey the target image of the firm, solicit the desired responses from customers and employees, and support service operations and productivity. Specifically, we explore the following questions:

1. What is the purpose of the service environment?
2. What are the various effects that the service environment can have on people?
3. What are the theories behind people's responses?
4. What are the dimensions of the service environment?
5. How can we design a servicescape to achieve the desired effects?

WHAT IS THE PURPOSE OF SERVICE ENVIRONMENTS?

Service environments, also called *servicescapes,* relate to the style and appearance of the physical surroundings and other experiential elements encountered by customers at service-delivery sites ("service factories").[1] Designing the service environment is an art that takes considerable time and effort, and can be expensive to implement. Once designed and built, service environments are not easy to change. Let's examine why many service firms take so much trouble to shape the environment in which their customers and service personnel will interact.

Shaping Customers' Experiences and Behaviour

For organizations delivering high-contact services, the design of the physical environment and the way in which tasks are performed by customer-contact personnel jointly play a vital role in creating a particular corporate identity and shaping the nature of customers' experiences. This environment and its accompanying atmosphere affect buyer behaviour in three important ways:

1. *As a message-creating medium,* using symbolic cues to communicate to the intended audience about the distinctive nature and quality of the service experience

2. *As an attention-creating medium,* to make the servicescape stand out from that of competing establishments, and to attract customers from target segments

3. *As an effect-creating medium,* employing colours, textures, sounds, scents, and spatial design to enhance the desired service experience, and/or to heighten an appetite for certain goods, services or experiences

Image, Positioning, and Differentiation   Services are often intangible, and since customers cannot therefore assess their quality easily, they use the service environment as an important quality proxy. Firms thus take great pains to signal quality and portray the desired image. Think about the reception area of successful professional firms such as investment banks or management consulting firms, where the decor and furnishings tend to be elegant and designed to impress. In retailing, the store environment affects how customers perceive the quality of the merchandise. Like other people, you probably infer higher merchandise quality if the goods are displayed in an environment with a prestige image than in one that creates a discount image.[2] Similarly, hotel servicescapes clearly communicate and reinforce a hotel's positioning, and are particularly important in setting service expectations as guests arrive. Consider Figure 10.1, which shows the lobbies of (A) a Howard Johnson hotel and (B) the Fairmont Banff Springs Hotel in Banff, Alberta, which cater to two very different target segments. One caters to overnight guests on vacation who have low budgets, and the other to a more affluent, prestigious clientele that includes upscale business and international travellers.

Many servicescapes are purely functional. Firms that are trying to convey the impression of low-price service do so by locating in inexpensive neighbourhoods, occupying buildings with a simple appearance, minimizing wasteful use of space, and dressing their employees in practical, inexpensive uniforms. However, servicescapes do not always shape customer perceptions and behaviour in ways intended by their creators. Véronique Aubert-Gamet notes that customers often make creative use of physical spaces and objects for different purposes. For instance, business people may set aside a restaurant table for use as a temporary office desk, with papers spread around and a laptop computer and mobile phone positioned on its surface, competing for space with the food and beverages.[3] Students meeting for a study date in a restaurant or coffee shop often do the same with their textbooks and notepads. Smart designers keep an eye open for such trends—they may even lead to the creation of a new service concept!

The Servicescape as Part of the Value Proposition   Physical surroundings help to shape appropriate feelings and reactions in customers and employees.[4] Consider how effectively many amusement parks use the servicescape concept to enhance their service offerings. The clean environment of Disneyland Resort in California or Denmark's Legoland, plus employees in colourful costumes, all contribute to the sense of fun and excitement that visitors encounter on arrival and throughout their visit.

An illustration of servicescapes being a core part of the value proposition through engineering service experiences are resort hotels. Club Med's villages, designed to create a totally carefree atmosphere, may have provided the original inspiration for "get-away" holiday environments. New destination resorts are not only far more luxurious than Club Med, but also draw inspiration from theme parks to create fantasy environments, both inside and outside. Perhaps the most extreme examples come from Las Vegas. Facing competition from numerous casinos in other locations, Las Vegas has successfully repositioned

Figure 10.1

Comparison of Hotel Lobbies

A Lobby of a Howard Johnson hotel.

B Lobby of Fairmont Banff Springs Hotel, inviting its guests to indulge in luxury.

itself away from its original image as an adult destination—once described in a London newspaper as "the electric Sodom and Gomorrah"—to a somewhat more wholesome resort where families, too, can have fun. The gambling is still there, of course, but many of the huge hotels recently built (or rebuilt) have been transformed into visually striking entertainment centres that feature such attractions as erupting "volcanoes," mock sea battles, and striking reproductions of the Pyramids and of buildings in Paris and Venice. More recently it's been trying to reinvent itself yet again, as a place of sophistication where baby boomers and their echo-boomer offspring can experience "the taste of the good life." As lines from one article in the *New York Times* suggest, "With the recent confluence of star chefs, designer boutiques, glamorous nightclubs, and acclaimed multimillion-dollar shows, Las Vegas's deluxe appeal has reached critical mass. A recent Monet exhibition with record attendance was extended twice. In March, *Interior Design* magazine devoted 32 pages to design in Las Vegas."[5]

Even movie theatres are discovering the power of servicescapes. Attendance has been falling in the United States as more people view DVDs on sophisticated, large-screen TV home entertainment centres, and some of the big chains are hurting. But a few upstart boutique chains are trying a different approach. By building extravagant theatres and offering plush amenities, including lavishly decorated bars and restaurants and super-vised playrooms for children, chains like Florida-based Muvico are successfully enticing moviegoers to abandon their home entertainment centres—despite sharply higher admission prices. Says Muvico's CEO, Hamid Hashemi, of his competitors, "At the end of the day, you all get the same 35-mm tape. . . . What sets you apart is how you package it."[6] At one Egyptian-themed Muvico cinema, moviegoers follow a purple-tiled pattern represent-ing the Nile into the lobby, passing between hieroglyph-covered pillars. Inside the audito-rium, they find wide aisles and seats upholstered in red velvet. It's a very different experience from the megaplex at the local mall.

Facilitate the Service Encounter and Enhance Productivity

Service environments are often designed to facilitate the service encounter and to increase productivity. Richard Chase and Douglas Stewart highlighted ways in which fail-safe methods embodied in the service environment can help reduce service failures and sup-port a fast and smooth service-delivery process.[7] For example, colour-coded keys on cash registers allow cashiers to identify the numerical figures and product codes that each but-ton stands for. To foster a neat appearance among front-line staff, mirrors can be placed where staff can easily check their appearance just before going "on stage" to meet cus-tomers. Childcare centres use toy outlines on walls and floors to show where toys should be placed after use. In fast-food restaurants and school canteens, strategically located tray-return stands and notices on walls remind customers to return their trays. Golf courses routinely hand out free divot-repair tools so that a player can fix the damage made by a ball to the putting green and leave it in proper condition for fellow golfers on the course.

UNDERSTANDING CONSUMER RESPONSES TO SERVICE ENVIRONMENTS

The field of environmental psychology studies how people respond to specific environ-ments. By applying theories from this field, service marketers can better understand and manage customer responses in different service settings.

Feelings Are a Key Driver of Customer Responses to Service Environments

Two important models help us better understand consumer responses to service environ-ments. The first, the Mehrabian-Russell stimulus-response model, shows that it is in fact feelings, or affect, that are central to how we respond to the many environmental stimuli we are exposed to. The second, Russell's model of affect, focuses on how we can better understand those feelings and their implications on response behaviours.

The Mehrabian-Russell Stimulus-Response Model Figure 10.2 displays a simple yet fundamental model of how people respond to environments. The model holds that the conscious and unconscious perception and interpretation of an environment influ-ence how people feel when they are in it.[8] People's feelings in turn drive their responses to that environment. Feelings are central to the model, which posits that feelings, rather

Figure 10.2

Model of Environmental Responses

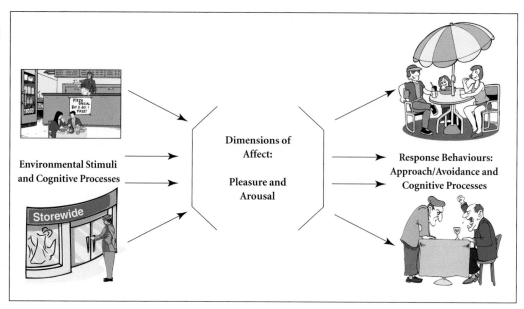

Environmental Stimuli and Cognitive Processes

Storewide

Dimensions of Affect:

Pleasure and Arousal

Response Behaviours: Approach/Avoidance and Cognitive Processes

than perceptions or thoughts, drive behaviour. For example, we don't avoid an environment simply because there are a lot of people around us; rather, we are deterred by the unpleasant feeling of crowding, of people being in our way, of lacking perceived control, and of not being able to get what we want as fast as we wish to. In another context, however—if we had all the time in the world, or felt excited about being part of a crowd during seasonal festivities, say, then exposure to the same number of people might lead to feelings of pleasure and excitement, which would lead us to want to stay and explore that environment further.

In environmental psychology, the typical outcome variable is "approach" or "avoidance" of an environment. Of course, in services marketing, we can add a long list of additional outcomes that a firm might want to manage, including how much money people spend and how satisfied they are with the service experience after they have left the firm's premises.

The Russell Model of Affect Given that affect, or feelings, are central to how people respond to an environment, we need to understand those feelings better. Russell's model of affect (Figure 10.3) is widely used to help understand feelings in service environments, and suggests that emotional responses to those environments can be described along two main dimensions, pleasure and arousal.[9] Pleasure is a direct, subjective response that depends on how much the individual likes or dislikes the environment. Arousal refers to how stimulated the individual feels, ranging from deep sleep (lowest level of internal activity) to the levels of adrenalin in the bloodstream that one gets, for example, when bungee-jumping (highest level of internal activity). The arousal quality, which depends largely on the information rate or load of an environment, is much less subjective than its pleasure quality. For example, environments are stimulating (i.e., have a high information rate) when they are complex, have motion or change, and have novel and surprising elements. A low-stimulus, relaxing environment has the opposite characteristics.

You may ask how all our feelings and emotions can be explained by only two dimensions? Russell separated the cognitive or thinking part of emotions from these two basic underlying emotional dimensions. Thus, the emotion of anger about a service failure could be modelled simply as high arousal and high displeasure, which would locate it in the distressing region in our model, combined with a cognitive attribution process. When a customer attributes a service failure to the firm (i.e., he thinks it is the firm's fault that this has happened, that it is under the firm's control, and that the firm is not doing much to avoid it happening again), then this powerful cognitive attribution process feeds directly into high arousal and displeasure. Similarly, most other emotions can be dissected into their cognitive and affective components.

Figure 10.3

The Russell Model
of Affect

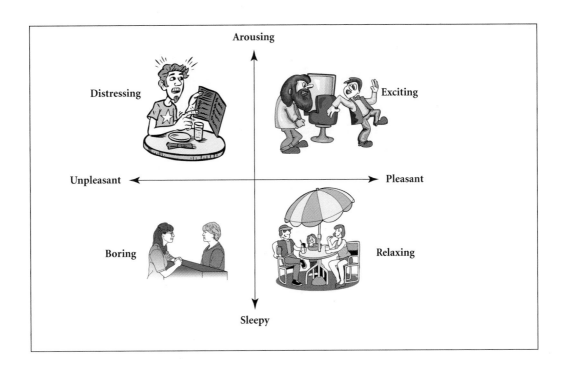

The advantage of Russell's model of affect is its simplicity, as it allows a direct assessment of how customers feel while they are in the service environment. Firms can set targets for affective states. For example, a ride operator such as Marineland Canada, which has the world's highest triple tower ride, the Sky Screamer™ (Figure 10.4), might want its customers to feel aroused (assuming that there is little pleasure when having to gather all one's courage before the ride). A nightclub operator may want customers to feel excited (which is a relatively high arousal environment combined with pleasure); a bank may want its customers to feel confident. A spa may want customers to feel relaxed, and so on. Later in this chapter we discuss how service environments can be designed to deliver the types of service experiences desired by customers.

Drivers of Affect   Affect can be caused by perceptions and cognitive processes of any degree of complexity. However, the more complex a cognitive process becomes, the more powerful is its potential impact on affect. For example, a customer's disappointment with service level and food quality in a restaurant (a complex cognitive process, where perceived quality is compared to previously held service expectations) cannot be compensated for by a simple cognitive process such as the subconscious perception of pleasant background music. Yet this does not mean that such simple processes are unimportant.

In practice, the large majority of service encounters are routine, with little high-level cognitive processing. We tend to be on "autopilot" and follow our service scripts when doing routine transactions such as using public transit, ordering at a fast-food restaurant, or entering a bank. Here, it is the simple cognitive processes that determine how people feel in the service setting. Those include the conscious and even unconscious perceptions of space, colours, scents, etc. However, should higher levels of cognitive processes be triggered, for instance through something surprising in the service environment, then it is the interpretation of this surprise that determines people's feelings.[10]

Behavioural Consequences of Affect   At the most basic level, pleasant environments encourage potential customers to approach, while unpleasant ones result in avoidance behaviours. Arousal acts as an amplifier of the basic effect of pleasure on behaviour. If the environment is pleasant, increasing arousal can lead to excitement, leading to a stronger positive consumer response. Conversely, if a service environment is inherently unpleasant, one should avoid increasing arousal levels, as this would move customers into the "distressed" region. For example, loud fast-beat music would increase the stress levels

Figure 10.4A
A Thrill Ride on the
Sky Screamer™

of shoppers trying to make their way through crowded aisles on a pre-Christmas Friday evening. In such situations, the information load of the environment should be lowered. However, as will be discussed in the next section, it is important to note that there is not universal agreement on defining the pleasantness or unpleasantness of an environment or the stimulus used in it: some customers might enjoy loud, fast-beat music in almost any environment, while others will dislike it to the same extent.

For some services, customers have strong affective expectations. Think of a romantic candle-lit dinner in a restaurant, a relaxing spa visit, or an exciting time at the stadium or the nightclub. When customers have strong affective expectations, it is important to design the environment to match those expectations.[11]

Finally, how people feel during the service encounter is an important driver of customer loyalty. For example, positive affect has been shown to drive hedonic shopping value, which in turn increased repeat purchasing behaviour, while negative affect mostly reduced utilitarian shopping value and thereby lowered customer share.[12]

The Servicescapes Model: An Integrative Framework of Consumer Responses to Service Environments

Building on the basic models in environmental psychology, Mary Jo Bitner has developed a comprehensive model that she named the servicescape.[13] Figure 10.5 shows the main dimensions that she identified in service environments, which include ambient conditions, space/functionality, and signs, symbols and artifacts. Because individuals tend to perceive these dimensions holistically, the key to effective design is how well each individual dimension fits together with everything else.

Next, the model shows that there are customer- and employee-response moderators. This means that the same service environment can have different effects on different customers, depending on who that customer is and what s/he likes. (Beauty lies in the eyes of the beholder, and is subjective.) A concert of heavy metal music may be sheer pleasure to some customer segments and sheer torture to others.

One important contribution of Bitner's model is the inclusion of employee responses to the service environment. After all, employees spend much more time there than do customers, and it's crucially important that designers become aware of how a particular environment enhances (or at least does not reduce) the productivity of front-line personnel, and thus the quality of service that they deliver.

Internal customer and employee responses can be categorized into cognitive responses (e.g., quality perceptions and beliefs), emotional responses (e.g., feelings and moods), and psychological responses (e.g., pain and comfort). These internal responses lead to overt behavioural responses, such as avoiding a crowded department store or responding positively to a relaxing environment by remaining there longer and spending extra money on impulse purchases. It's important to understand that the behavioural responses of customers and employees must be shaped in ways that facilitate production and purchase of

Figure 10.5 The Servicescapes Model

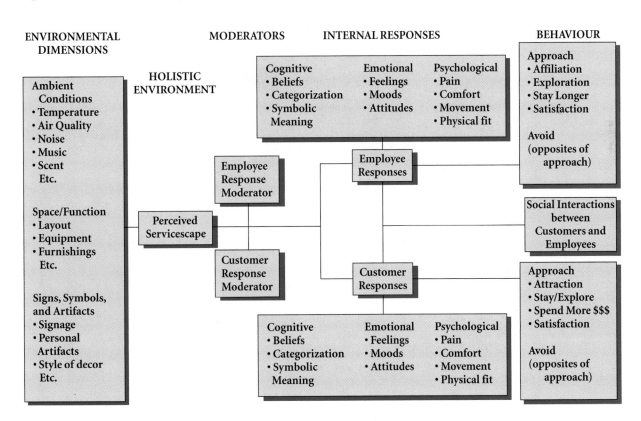

Source: Mary Jo Bitner, "Servicescapes: The Impact of Physical Surroundings on Customers and Employees," *Journal of Marketing* 56 (April 1992): 57–71. American Marketing Association.

high quality services. Consider how the outcomes of service transactions may differ in situations where both customers and front-line staff feel agitated and stressed rather than relaxed and happy.

DIMENSIONS OF THE SERVICE ENVIRONMENT

Service environments are complex and have many design elements. In Table 10.1, for example, we can see an overview of all the design elements that might be encountered in a retail outlet. We will focus, in this section, on the main dimensions of the service environment in the servicescape model, which are the ambient conditions, space and functionality, and signs, symbols and artifacts.[14]

The Impact of Ambient Conditions

Ambient conditions refer to those characteristics of the environment pertaining to our five senses. Even when not consciously noted, they may still affect people's emotional wellbeing,

Table 10.1 Design Elements of a Retail Store Environment

Dimensions	Design Elements	
Exterior facilities	• Architectural style • Height of building • Size of building • Colour of building • Exterior walls and exterior signs • Storefront • Marquee • Lawns and gardens	• Window displays • Entrances • Visibility • Uniqueness • Surrounding stores • Surrounding areas • Parking and accessibility • Congestion
General interior	• Flooring and carpeting • Colour schemes • Lighting • Scents • Odours (e.g., tobacco smoke) • Sounds and music • Fixtures • Wall composition • Wall textures (paint, wallpaper) • Ceiling composition	• Temperature • Cleanliness • Width of aisles • Dressing facilities • Vertical transportation • Dead areas • Merchandise layout and displays • Price levels and displays • Cash register placement • Technology/modernization
Store layout	• Allocation of floor space for selling, merchandise, personnel, and customers • Placement of merchandise • Grouping of merchandise • Workstation placement • Placement of equipment • Placement of cash register	• Waiting areas • Traffic flow • Waiting queues • Furniture • Dead areas • Department locations • Arrangements within departments
Interior displays	• Point-of-purchase displays • Posters, signs, and cards • Pictures and artwork • Wall decorations • Themesetting • Ensemble	• Racks and cases • Product display • Price display • Cut cases and dump bins • Mobiles
Social dimensions	• Personnel characteristics • Employee uniforms • Crowding	• Customer characteristics • Privacy • Self-service

Sources: Adapted from Barry Berman and Joel R. Evans, *Retail Management: A Strategic Approach,* 8th ed., Upper Saddler River, NJ: Prentice-Hall, 2001: 604; L.W. Turley and Ronald E. Milliman, "Atmospheric Effects on Shopping Behavior: A Review of the Experimental Literature," *Journal of Business Research* 49 (2000): 193–211.

perceptions, and even attitudes and behaviours. The ambient environment or atmosphere is a gestalt concept (one in which the whole is more than the sum of its parts), composed of literally hundreds of design elements and details in the service environment that have to work together to create the desired service environment.[15] The resulting atmosphere creates a mood that is perceived and interpreted by the customer.[16] Ambient conditions are perceived both separately and holistically, and include lighting and colour schemes, size and shape perceptions, sounds (including noise and music), temperature, and scents or smells. Clever design of these conditions can elicit desired behavioural responses among consumers. Consider the innovative thinking underlying the new trend to transform dental clinics into relaxing dental spas, as described in Best Practice in Action 10.1.

Music In service settings, music can have a powerful effect on perceptions and behaviours, even if played at barely audible volumes. As shown in the servicescape model in Figure 10.5, the various structural characteristics of music such as tempo, volume, and harmony are perceived holistically, and their effect on internal and behavioural responses is moderated by respondent characteristics (e.g., younger people tend to like different music and therefore respond differently from older people to the same piece of music).[17] Numerous research studies have found that fast-tempo music and high-volume music increases arousal levels,[18] which can then lead customers to increase their pace of various

Best Practice in Action 10.1

Cutting the Fear Factor at the Dentist

Dentistry is not a service that most people look forward to. Some patients simply find it uncomfortable, especially if they have to remain in a dental chair for an extended period. Many are afraid of the pain associated with certain procedures. And others risk their health by avoiding going to the dentist altogether. But now some practitioners are embracing "spa dentistry," where juice bars, neck rubs, foot massages, and even scented candles and the sound of wind chimes are used to pamper patients and distract them from necessarily invasive treatments inside their mouths.

"It's not about gimmicks," says Timothy Dotson, owner of the Perfect Teeth Dental Spa in Chicago, as a patient breathed strawberry-scented nitrous oxide. "It's treating people the way they want to be treated. It helps a lot of people overcome fear." His patients seem to agree. "Nobody likes coming to the dentist, but this makes it so much easier," remarked one woman as she waited for a crown while a heated massage pad was kneading her back.

Amenities such as hot towels, massages, aromatherapy, coffee, fresh cranberry-orange bread, and white wine spritzers reflect dentists' efforts to meet changing consumer expectations, especially at a time when there is growing consumer demand for aesthetic care to whiten and reshape teeth to create a perfect smile. The goal is to entice patients who might otherwise find visiting the dentist a stressful situation. Many dentists who offer spa services do not charge extra for them, arguing that their cost is more than covered by repeat business and increased patient referrals.

In Victoria, British Columbia, Babin Dentistry (www.babindentistry.com) offers a spa experience to its cus-

tomers via an environment that ranges from the "soothing decor" of their office to the provision of "special touches" such as the use of warm towels, lotions, tooth products, and hair products, to make the patient look and feel their best; a refreshment centre that offers a range of beverages and fresh baked cookies; the use of I-Glasses—portable DVD glasses allowing patients to watch a movie during a dental procedure; the use of wireless, noise reducing headsets that allow access to over 40 channels of crystal-clear music; the viewing of HD programmes (or their digital X-Rays) on large screen HDTVs, and finally the use of luxury custom-designed Comfort Craft Heat and Massage Chairs—currently the only dental clinic in Canada to offer this amenity.

In Houston, Texas, Max Greenfield has embellished his Image Max Dental Spa with fountains and modern art. Patients can change into a robe, sample eight different aromas of oxygen, and meditate in a relaxation room decorated like a Japanese garden. The actual dental area features lambskin leather chairs, hot aromatherapy towels, and a procedure known as "bubble gum jet massage" that uses air and water to clean teeth.

Although dental offices from across North America are adopting spa techniques, some question whether this touchy-feely approach is good dentistry or just a passing fad. "I just can't see mingling the two businesses together," remarked the dean of one university dental school.

Source: Adapted from "Dentists Offer New Services to Cut the Fear Factor," *Chicago Tribune* syndicated article, February 2003; www.babindentistry.com/spa.html, accessed September 6, 2006.

behaviours. People tend to adjust their pace, either voluntarily or involuntarily, to match the tempo of music. This means that restaurants can speed up table turnover by increasing the tempo and volume of the music and serve more diners (though this must be carefully judged if the music is not to become merely irritating) or slow diners down with slow beat music and softer volume to keep them longer in the restaurant and increase beverage revenues, as shown in Research Insights 10.1.

Would it surprise you to learn that music can also be used to *deter* the "wrong" type of customers? Many service environments, including subway systems, supermarkets, and other publicly accessible locations, attract individuals who are not bona fide customers. Some are jaycustomers (see Chapter 8) whose behaviour causes problems for management and customers alike. In the United Kingdom an increasingly popular strategy for driving such individuals away is to play classical music, which is apparently painful to vandals' and loiterers' ears! Co-op, a UK grocery chain, has been experimenting with playing music outside its outlets to stop teenagers from hanging around and intimidating customers. Its staff have a remote control and, as reported by Steve Broughton of Co-op, "can turn the music on if there's a situation developing and they need to disperse people."

In Alberta, Steve Parkin from the City of Red Deer Transit Department knows that some commuters aren't enamoured of the classical music played at all hours over a public address system at the main bus terminal. "Well, the younger ones don't like it," he clarified. This was, of course, precisely the outcome that transit administrators had hoped for when they decided to play classical music. They were hoping to deter loitering at the terminal, and thus the vandalism and violence that loitering can lead to. "It's stopped a lot of the loitering because many don't enjoy that music," he says.[19]

The London Underground (subway) system has made the most extensive use of classical music as a deterrent. Thirty stations pump out Mozart and Haydn to discourage loitering and vandalism. A London Underground spokesperson reports that the most effective deterrents are anything written by Mozart or sung by Pavarotti. According to Adrian North, a psychologist researching music–behaviour links at Leicester University, unfamiliarity is a key factor in driving people away. When the target individuals are unused to strings and woodwind, Mozart will do (Figure 10.6). However, for the more musically literate loiterer, an atonal barrage is likely to work better. For instance, North tormented Leicester's students in the union bar with what he describes as "computer-game music." It cleared the place!

Scent   An ambient smell is one that pervades an environment, may or may not be consciously perceived by customers, and is not related to any particular product. We are experiencing the power of smell when we are hungry and get a whiff of freshly baked bread

Research Insights 10.1

Music as a Tool to Shape Customer Behaviour in Service Settings

A number of field experiments have shown the dramatic effects music can have on customers. For example, a restaurant study conducted over eight weeks showed that beverage revenue increased substantially when slow-beat rather than fast-beat music was played. Customers who dined in a slow-music environment spent longer in the restaurant than individuals in a fast-music condition. Likewise, shoppers walked less rapidly when slow music was played and increased their level of impulse purchases. Playing familiar music in a store was shown to stimulate shoppers, and thereby reduce their browsing time, whereas playing unfamiliar music induced shoppers to spend more time there.

In situations that require waiting for service, effective use of music may shorten perceived waiting time, influence consumer's mood, and increase customer satisfaction. Relaxing music proved effective in lowering stress levels in a hospital's surgery waiting room. And pleasant music has even been shown to enhance customers' perceptions of, and attitude toward, service personnel.

Source: Laurette Dubé and Sylvie Morin, "Background Music Pleasure and Store Evaluation Intensity Effects and Psychological Mechanisms," *Journal of Business Research* 54 (2001): 107–13; Clare Caldwell and Sally A. Hibbert, "The Influence of Music Tempo and Musical Preference on Restaurant Patrons' Behaviour," *Psychology and Marketing* 19/11 (2002): 895–917; Michaelle Ann Cameron, Julie Baker, Mark Peterson, and Karin Braunsberger, "The Effects of Music, Wait-Length Evaluation, and Mood on a Low-Cost Wait Experience," *Journal of Business Research* 56/6 (2003): 421–30.

Figure 10.6

Classical music can be used to deter vandals and loiterers.

long before we pass a neighbourhood bakery. This smell makes us aware of our hunger and points us to the solution (i.e., walk into bakery and get some food). The same works for cafés, pizzerias, and the like. Other examples include the smell of freshly baked cookies on Main Street in Disney's Magic Kingdom—used to relax customers and provide a feeling of warmth—or the smell of potpourri in Victoria's Secret stores to create the ambience of a lingerie closet.[20] The presence of scent can have a strong impact on mood, affective and evaluative responses, and even purchase intentions and in-store behaviours.[21]

Olfaction researcher Alan R. Hirsch of the Smell and Taste Treatment and Research Foundation, based in Chicago, is convinced that in a few years we will understand scents so well that we will be able to use them to effectively manage people's behaviours.[22] Service marketers will be interested in how to make you hungry and thirsty in the restaurant, relax you in a dentist's waiting room, and energize you to work out harder in a gym. For instance, aromatherapists believe that scents have distinct characteristics and can be used to solicit certain emotional, physiological, and behavioural responses, although what scientific research has been carried out does not support such detailed equivalences. Table 10.2 shows the generally assumed effects of specific scents on people as prescribed by aromatherapists. In service settings, research has shown that scents might have a significant impact on customer perceptions, attitudes, and behaviours. For example,

- In an experiment conducted at a shopping mall in the Montreal metropolitan area, it was found that the use of ambient scent (citrus was used in this experiment) seemed to contribute to favourable perceptions of the mall environment, and indirectly of product quality, which further influenced the amount of spending by the shoppers at the mall.[23]

- Gamblers plunked 45 percent more quarters into slot machines when a Las Vegas casino was scented with a pleasant artificial smell. When the intensity of the scent was increased, spending jumped by 53 percent.[24]

- People were more willing to buy Nike sneakers—and to pay more for them (an average of US$10.33 more per pair)—when they tried on the shoes in a floral-scented room. The same effect was found even when the scent was so faint that people could not consciously detect it.[25]

Colour Colour "is stimulating, calming, expressive, disturbing, impressional, cultural, exuberant, symbolic. It pervades every aspect of our lives, embellishes the ordinary, and gives beauty and drama to everyday objects."[26] Researchers have found that colours have

Table 10.2 Aromatherapy: The Claimed Effects of Selected Fragrances

Fragrance	Aroma Type	Aromatherapy Class	Traditional Use	Psychological Effect Claimed
Eucalyptus	Camphoraceous	Toning, stimulating	Deodorant, antiseptic, soothing agent; helps remove odour and can be used to cleanse skin	Stimulating and energizing; helps to create balance and the feeling of cleanliness and hygiene
Lavender	Herbaceous	Calming, balancing, soothing	Muscle relaxant, soothing agent, astringent, skin conditioner	Relaxing and calming; helps to create a homey and comfortable feel
Lemon	Citrus	Energizing, uplifting	Antiseptic, soothing agent	Boosts energy levels and helps to make people feel happy and rejuvenated
Black pepper	Spicy	Balancing, soothing	Muscle relaxant, aphrodisiac	Helps to balance emotions and enables sexual arousal

Sources: www.fragrant.demon.co.uk and www.naha.org/what_is_aromatherapy.htm; Dana Butcher, "Aromatherapy: Its Past and Future," *Drug and Cosmetic Industry* 16/3 (1998): 22–24; Shirley Price and Len Price, *Aromatherapy for Health Professionals,* 2nd ed., New York: Churchill Livingstone, 1999: 145–60; Anna S. Mattila and Jochen Wirtz, "Congruency of Scent and Music as a Driver of In-store Evaluations and Behavior," *Journal of Retailing* 77 (2001): 273–89.

a strong impact on people's feelings.[27] The de facto system used in psychological research is the Munsell System, which defines colours in the three dimensions of hue, value, and chroma.[28] Hue is the pigment of the color (i.e., the name of the colour, such as red, orange, yellow, green, blue, or violet). Value (which in painting terminology is called "tone") is the degree of lightness or darkness of the colour, relative to a scale that extends from pure black to pure white. Chroma refers to hue-intensity, saturation, or brilliance; high-chroma colours have a high intensity of pigmentation in them and are perceived as rich and vivid, whereas low-chroma colours are perceived as dull.

Hues are classified into warm colours (red, orange, and yellow hues) and cold colours (blue and green), with orange (a mix of red and yellow) being the warmest, and blue being the coldest. These colours can be used to manage the warmth of an environment. For example, if a violet is too warm, you can cool it off by reducing the red in the mix. Or if a yellow is too cold, warm it up by giving it a shot of red.[29] Warm colours are associated with elated mood states and arousal, but also heightened anxiety, while cool colours reduce arousal levels and can elicit emotions such as peacefulness, calmness, love, and happiness.[30] Table 10.3 summarizes common associations and responses to colours. Research in a service environment context has shown that despite differing colour preferences, people are generally drawn to warm-colour environments. However, paradoxically, findings show that red-hued retail environments are seen as negative, tense, and less attractive than cool-colour environments.[31] Warm colours encourage fast decision-making, and in service situations are best suited for low-involvement decisions or impulse purchases. Cool colours are favoured when consumers need time to make high-involvement purchases.[32]

Although we have an understanding of the general impact of colours, their use in any specific context needs to be approached with caution. For example, a transportation company in Israel decided to paint its buses green as part of an environmentalist public-relations campaign. Reactions to this seemingly simple act from multiple groups of people were unexpectedly negative. Some customers found the green colour as hamper-

Table 10.3 Common Associations and Human Responses to Colours

Colour	Degree of Warmth	Nature Symbol	Common Associations and Human Responses to Colours
Red	Warm	Earth	High energy and passion; can excite, stimulate, and increase arousal levels and blood pressure
Orange	Warmest	Sunset	Emotions, expression, and warmth; noted for its ability to encourage verbal expression of emotions
Yellow	Warm	Sun	Optimism, clarity, and intellect; bright yellow often noted for its mood-enhancing ability
Green	Cool	Growth, grass, and trees	Nurturing, healing, and unconditional love
Blue	Coolest	Sky and ocean	Relaxation, serenity, and loyalty; lowers blood pressure; is a healing colour for nervous disorders and for relieving headaches, because of its cooling and calming nature
Indigo	Cool	Sunset	Meditation and spirituality
Violet	Cool	Violet flower	Spirituality; reduces stress and can create an inner feeling of calm

Sources: Sara O. Marberry and Laurie Zagon, *The Power of Color: Creating Healthy Interior Spaces,* New York: John Wiley, 1995: 18; Saray Lynch, *Bold Colors for Modern Rooms: Bright Ideas for People Who Love Color,* Gloucester, MA: Rockport, 2001: 24–29.

ing service performance (because the green buses blended in with the environment and were more difficult to see), or as representing undesirable notions such as terrorism or enemy sports teams (green is often a colour favoured by militant Islamic groups), and as aesthetically unappealing and inappropriate.[33]

Similarly, a few years back, a Canadian bank discovered that Chinese-Canadians represented a largely untapped market in retail banking. In addition to adapting its services by opening 60 branches across the country in which all business was conducted in Chinese, translating banking forms into Chinese, and hiring employees at other branches who could speak Chinese and understand cultural nuances, it also repainted those bank branches by adopting a colour scheme different from the "corporate standards" in order to attract this new clientele. The result was a 400 percent increase in business from the Chinese community over a five year period.[34]

Another good example of using colour schemes to enhance the service experience is provided by the HealthPark Medical Center in Fort Meyers, Florida, which has combined full-spectrum colour in its lobby with unusual lighting to achieve a dreamlike setting. The lobby walls are washed with rainbow colours by an arrangement of high intensity blue, green, violet, red, orange, and yellow lamps. Craig Roeder, the lighting designer for the hospital, explained: "It's a hospital. People walk into it worried and sick. I tried to design an entrance space that provides them with light and energy – to 'beam them up' a little bit before they get to the patient rooms."[35]

Spatial Layout and Functionality

As service environments generally have to fulfill specific purposes and customer needs, spatial layout and functionality are particularly important. "Spatial layout" refers to the floor plan, size and shape of furnishings and counters, and arrangement of the machinery and equipment. Functionality refers to the ability of those items to facilitate the performance of service transactions. Spatial layout and functionality create the visual as well as functional servicescape for delivery and consumption of the service. They determine the user-friendliness and the ability of the facility to service customers well, and they not only affect the efficiency of the service operation, but also have direct impact on the customer experience (Figure 10.7). Tables that are too close in a café, counters in a bank that lack privacy, uncomfortable chairs in a lecture theatre, and lack of car parking space can all leave negative impressions on customers, affect their buying behaviour, customer satisfaction, and consequently the business performance of the service facility.

The spatial layout has to deliver its part of the value proposition. For example, in a community centre that aims to bring people together who would like to learn subjects such as a language or astronomy, a U-shaped classroom, or a space in which chairs are grouped around tables, can help to enhance the learning experience.

Signs, Symbols, and Artifacts

Many things in the service environment act as explicit or implicit signals to communicate the firm's image, help customers find their way (e.g., to certain service counters, departments, or the exit), and to convey the service script (e.g., queuing systems). In particular, first-time customers will automatically try to draw meaning from these signs, symbols, and artifacts, and will want to draw cues from the environment to guide them through the service environment and service processes.

Examples of explicit signals include signs, which can be used as labels (e.g., to indicate the name of the department or counter), for giving directions (e.g., entrance, exit, way to elevators or toilets), for communicating the service script (e.g., take a number and watch for it to be called, or clear the tray after your meal) and behavioural rules (e.g., switch off your mobile devices, or turn them to silent mode during the performance, smoking/no-smoking areas, no outside drinks or food allowed in theatres). Signs are frequently used to teach and reinforce behavioural rules in service settings. Singapore, which strictly enforces rules in many service settings, especially in public buildings and on public transportation, is sometimes referred to ironically as a "fine" city for the number of fines that are imposed there for infractions of these behavioural rules (see Figure 10.8).

The challenge for servicescape designers is to use signs, symbols, and artifacts to guide customers clearly through the process of service delivery, so as to teach the service process in as intuitive a manner as possible. This task assumes particular importance in situations where there is a high proportion of new or infrequent customers, and/or a high degree of self-service, especially when there are few service staff available to help guide customers through the process.

Customers become disoriented when they cannot derive clear signals from a servicescape, resulting in anxiety and uncertainty about how to proceed and how to obtain

Figure 10.7
Signs around Vancouver International Airport are designed to help travellers find their way.

Figure 10.8

Signs are frequently used to teach and reinforce behavioural rules in service settings.

Note: Fines are in Singapore dollars ($500 equivalent to roughly CDN$350).

the desired service. Customers can easily feel lost in a confusing environment, and experience anger and frustration as a result. Think about the last time you were in a hurry and tried to find your way through an unfamiliar hospital, shopping centre or airport, where the signs and other directional cues were not intuitive to you. At many service facilities, customers' first point of contact is likely to be the location where they park their cars. As emphasized in Best Practice in Action 10.2, the principles of effective environment design apply even in this most mundane environment.

Winner of the 2003 Award of Merit from the International Parking Institute (www. parking.org), the Arboretum Lane parking structure at York University is a five-level multi-purpose structure that accommodates 787 parking spaces along with a 5060-square-metre office space. The landscaping around the structure is done in such a way that it appears "green" while eliminating places where someone could hide. Safety is further enhanced by well-lit, glass-backed stairwells that serve as "beacons of light" at four corners of the structure, and by placing emergency phones on each floor with direct links to security, which is located on the second floor of the structure itself. Parking is regulated by a fully automated transponder system working symbiotically with a fully automated pay-on-the-foot system. Besides well-marked parking spaces on each floor, ease of access

Best Practice in Action 10.2

Guidelines for Parking Design

Parking lots play an important role at many service facilities. Effective use of signs, symbols, and artifacts in a parking lot or garage helps customers find their way, manages their behaviour, and portrays a positive image for the sponsoring organization.

- *Friendly warnings:* All warning signs should communicate a customer benefit. For instance, "Fire lane—for everyone's safety we ask you not to park in the fire lane."

- *Fresh paint:* Curbs, crosswalks, and lot lines should be repainted regularly before any cracking, peeling, or disrepair become evident. Proactive and frequent repainting give positive cleanliness cues, and project a positive image.

- *Safety lighting:* Good lighting that penetrates all areas makes life easier for customers and enhances safety. Firms may want to draw attention to this feature with notices stating, "The parking lot has been specially lit for your safety."

- *Maternity parking:* Handicapped spaces are often required by law but require special stickers on the vehicle. A few thoughtful organizations have designated expectant mother parking spaces, painted with a blue/pink stork. This strategy demonstrates a sense of caring and understanding of customer needs.[36]

- *Help customers remember where they left their vehicle:* Forgetting where one left the car in a huge lot or parkade can be a nightmare. Many parking garages have adopted colour-coded floors to help customers remember which level they parked on.

and exit is configured in the form of three lanes (inbound, outbound, and middle reversible), which meets the demand for a stress-free entry and exit at key times of the day.[37]

People are Part of the Service Environment Too

The appearance and behaviour of both service personnel and customers can reinforce or detract from the impression created by a service environment. Within the constraints imposed by legal obligations and skill requirements, service firms may seek to recruit staff to fill specific roles, costume them in uniforms that are consistent with the servicescape in which they will be working, and script their speech and movements. Dennis Nickson and his colleagues use the term "aesthetic labour" to capture the importance of the physical imagery conveyed by customer-facing staff.[38] Likewise, marketing communications may seek to attract customers who will not only appreciate the ambience created by the service provider but actively enhance it by their appearance and behaviour. In hospitality and retail settings, newcomers often survey the array of existing customers before deciding whether to patronize the establishment.

Consider Figure 10.9, which shows the interior of two restaurants. Imagine that you have just entered each of these two dining rooms. How is each positioning itself within the restaurant industry? What sort of meal experience can you expect? And what are the clues that you employ to make your judgments? In particular, what inferences do you draw from looking at the customers who are already seated in each restaurant?

PUTTING IT ALL TOGETHER

Although individuals often perceive particular aspects or individual design features of an environment, it is the total configuration of all those design features that determines consumer responses. Consumers perceive service environments holistically, and consumer responses to a physical environment depend on ensemble effects or configurations.[39]

Design with a Holistic View

Whether a dark, glossy wooden floor is the perfect flooring for a given service environment depends on everything else in that environment, including the type, colour scheme, and materials of the furniture, the lighting, the promotional materials, and the overall brand perception and positioning of the firm. Servicescapes have to be seen holistically, which means no dimension of the design can be optimized in isolation, because everything depends on everything else. Research Insights 10.2 shows that even the arousal elements of scent and music interact and need to be considered in conjunction to elicit the desired consumer responses.

The holistic characteristic of environments makes designing service environments an art—so much so that professional designers tend to focus on specific types of servicescapes. For example, a handful of famous interior designers do nothing but create hotel lobbies around the world. Similarly, there are design experts who focus exclusively on restaurants, bars, clubs, cafés, and bistros, or retail outlets, or healthcare facilities, and so forth.[40]

Design from a Customer's Perspective

Many service environments are built with an emphasis on aesthetic values, and designers sometimes forget the most important factor to consider when designing service environments: the customers who will be using them. Ron Kaufman, a consultant and trainer on service excellence, experienced the following design flaws in two new high-profile service environments:

"A new Sheraton Hotel just had opened in Jordan without clear signage that would guide guests from the ballrooms to the restrooms. The signs that did exist were etched in

Figure 10.9

Distinctive restaurant servicescapes—from table settings to furniture and room design—create different customer expectations of these two restaurants.

muted gold on dark marble pillars. More 'obvious' signs were apparently inappropriate amidst such elegant decor. Very swish, very chic, but who were they designing it for?"

"At the Dragon Air lounge in Hong Kong's new airport, a partition of colourful glass hung from the ceiling. My luggage lightly brushed against it as I walked inside. The entire partition shook and several panels came undone. A staff member hurried over and began carefully reassembling the panels (thank goodness nothing broke). I apologized profusely. 'Don't worry,' she replied, 'This happens all the time.'" An airport lounge is a heavy traffic area. People are always moving in and out. Ron Kaufman keeps asking "What were the interior designers thinking? Who were they designing it for?"

"I am regularly amazed," declared Kaufman, "by brand new facilities that are obviously user 'unfriendly'! Huge investments of time and money . . . but who are they designing it for? What were the architects thinking about? Size? Grandeur? Physical exercise? Who were they designing it for?" He draws the following key learning point: "It's easy to get caught up in designing new things that are 'cool' or 'elegant' or 'hot.' But if you don't keep your customer in mind throughout, you could end up with an investment that's not."[41]

Match and Mismatch of Scent and Music in the Servicescape

Whether a certain type of background enhances consumer responses depends on the ambient scent of the service environment. Using a field experiment, Anna Mattila and Jochen Wirtz manipulated two types of pleasant music and pleasant scent, which differed in their arousing qualities, in a gift store. Consumer impulse purchasing and satisfaction were measured for the various music and scent conditions.

The experiment used two compact discs from the Tune Your Brain™ series by Elizabeth Miles, an ethnomusicologist. The low arousal music was the *Relaxing Collection* featuring slow-tempo music, while the high arousal music consisted of the *Energizing Collection*, featuring fast-tempo music. Similarly, scent was manipulated to have high or low arousal quality. Lavender was used for the low arousal scent because of its relaxing and calming properties. Grapefruit was used for the high arousal scent because of its stimulating properties, which can refresh, revive and improve alertness.

The results of this experiment show that when the arousal qualities of music and ambient scent were matched, consumers responded more favourably. The figures below show these effects clearly. For instance, using low-arousal scent (lavender) combined with slow-tempo music led to higher satisfaction and more impulse purchases than using that scent with high-arousal music. Similarly, playing fast-tempo music had a more positive effect when the store was scented with grapefruit (high-arousal scent) than with lavender. This study showed that when environmental stimuli act together to provide a coherent atmosphere, consumers in that environment will respond more positively.

These findings suggest that bookstores might induce people to linger longer and buy more by playing slow-tempo music combined with a relaxing scent, or event managers might consider using arousing scents to enhance excitement.

Figure 10.A The Effect of Scent and Music on Satisfaction

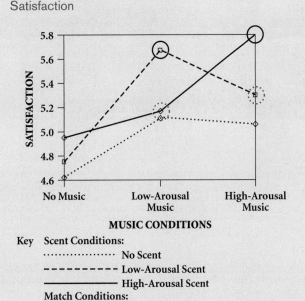

Figure 10.B The Effect of Scent and Music on Impulse Purchases

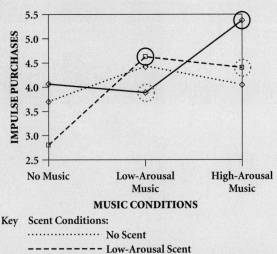

Note: Both charts are on a scale from 1 to 7, with 7 being the extreme positive response. The solid-line circles show the match conditions, where both music and scent are either stimulating or relaxing, and the broken-line circles show the mismatch conditions, where one stimulus is relaxing and the other stimulating (i.e., relaxing music with stimulating scent, or stimulating music with relaxing scent).

Source: Adapted from Anna S. Mattila and Jochen Wirtz, "Congruency of Scent and Music as a Driver of In-store Evaluations and Behavior," *Journal of Retailing* 77 (2001): 273–89.

Alain d'Astous explored environmental aspects that irritate shoppers. His findings highlighted the following problems:

Ambient Conditions (ordered by severity of irritation):

- Store is not clean
- Too hot inside the store or the shopping centre
- Music inside the store is too loud
- Bad smell in the store

Environmental Design Variables:

- No mirror in the dressing room
- Unable to find what one needs
- Directions within the store are inadequate
- Arrangement of store items has been changed
- Store is too small
- Hard to find way in a large shopping centre.[42]

Now, contrast Kaufman's experiences and d'Astou's findings with the Disney example in Best Practice in Action 10.3. What conclusions do you draw?

Use Tools That Can Guide Servicescape Design

As a manager, how might you determine which aspects of the servicescape irritate customers and which they like? Among the tools that you can use are

- *Keen observation* of customers' behaviour and responses to the service environment by management, supervisors, branch managers, and front-line staff.
- *Feedback and ideas from front-line staff and customers,* using a broad array of research tools ranging from suggestion boxes to focus groups and surveys. (The latter are often called environmental surveys if they focus on the design of the service environment.)
- *Field experiments* can be used to manipulate specific dimensions in an environment and the effects observed. For instance, one can experiment with the use of various types of music and scents, and then measure the time and money customers spend in the environment, and their level of satisfaction. Laboratory experiments, using slides or videos or other ways to simulate real-world service environments (such as computer simulated virtual tours), can be used effectively to examine the impact of changes in

Best Practice in Action 10.3

Design of Disney's Magic Kingdom

Walt Disney was one of the undisputed champions of designing service environments. His tradition of amazingly careful and detailed planning has become one of his company's hallmarks, and is visible everywhere in its theme parks. For example, Main Street is angled to make it seem longer upon entry into the Magic Kingdom than it actually is. With myriad facilities and attractions strategically inclined and located on each side of the street, this makes people look forward to the relatively long journey to the castle. However, looking down the slope from the castle back toward the entrance makes Main Street appear shorter than it really is, relieving exhaustion and rejuvenating guests. It encourages strolling, which minimizes the number of people who take buses and so eliminates the threatening problem of traffic congestion.

Meandering sidewalks with multiple attractions keep guests feeling entertained by both the planned activities and also by watching other guests; rubbish bins are plentiful and always in sight to convey the message that littering is prohibited; and repainting of facilities is a routine procedure that signals a high level of maintenance and cleanliness.

Disney's servicescape design and upkeep help to script customer experiences and create pleasure and satisfaction for guests, not only in its theme parks but also in its cruise ships and hotels.

Sources: Lewis P. Carbone and Stephen H. Haeckel, "Engineering Customer Experiences," *Marketing Management* 3/3 (Winter 1994): 10–11; Kathy Merlock Jackson, *Walt Disney: A Bio-Bibliography,* Westport, CT: Greenwood Press (1993): 36–39; Andrew Lainsbury, *Once Upon An American Dream: The Story of Euro Disneyland,* Lawrence, KS: University Press of Kansas (2000): 64–72.

design elements that cannot easily be manipulated in a field experiment. Examples include testing of alternative colour schemes, spatial layouts, or styles of furnishing.

- *Blueprinting* or service mapping (described in Chapter 8) can be extended to include the physical evidence in the environment. Design elements and tangible cues can be documented as the customer moves through each step of the service delivery process. Photos and videos can supplement the map to make it more vivid.

Table 10.4 shows an analysis of a customer's visit to a movie theatre, identifying how different environmental elements at each step met, exceeded, or failed to meet expectations. The service process was broken up into increments, steps, decisions, duties, and activities, all designed to take the customer through the entire service encounter. The more a service company can see, understand, and experience the same things as its customers, the better equipped it will be to realize errors in the design of its environment, and to further improve upon what is already functioning well.

Table 10.4 A Visit to the Movies: The Service Environment as Perceived by the Customer

STEPS IN THE SERVICE ENCOUNTER	DESIGN OF THE SERVICE ENVIRONMENT	
	EXCEEDS EXPECTATIONS	FAILS EXPECTATIONS
Locate a parking lot	Ample room in a bright place near the entrance, with a security officer protecting your valuables	Insufficient parking spaces, so patrons have to park in another lot
Queuing up to obtain tickets	Strategic placement of mirrors, posters of upcoming movies, and entertainment news to ease perception of long wait, if any; movies and time slots easily seen; ticket availability clearly communicated	A long queue and having to wait for a long while; difficult to see quickly what movies are being shown at what time slots and whether tickets are still available
Checking of tickets to enter the theatre	A very well maintained lobby with clear directions to the theatre and posters of the movie to enhance patrons' experience	A dirty lobby with rubbish strewn and unclear or misleading directions to the movie theater
Go to the restroom before the movie starts	Sparkling clean, spacious, brightly lit, dry floors, well stocked, nice decor, clear mirrors wiped regularly	Dirty, with an unbearable odor; broken toilets; no hand towels, soap, or toilet paper; overcrowded; dusty and dirty mirrors
Enter the theater and locate your seat	Spotless theatre; well designed with no bad seats; sufficient lighting to locate your seat; spacious, comfortable chairs, with drink and popcorn holders on each seat; and a suitable temperature	Rubbish on the floor, broken seats, sticky floors, gloomy and insufficient lighting, burned-out exit signs
Watch the movie	Excellent sound system and film quality, nice audience, an enjoyable and memorable entertainment experience overall	Substandard sound and movie equipment, uncooperative audience that talks and smokes because of lack of "No Smoking" and other signs; a disturbing and unenjoyable entertainment experience overall
Leave the theater and return to the car	Friendly service staff greet patrons as they leave; an easy exit through a brightly lit and safe parking area back to the car with the help of clear lot signs	A difficult trip, as patrons squeeze through a narrow exit, unable to find the car because of no or insufficient lighting

Source: Adapted from Steven Albrecht, "See Things from the Customer's Point of View: How to Use the 'Cycle of Service' to Understand What the Customer Goes Through to Do Business with You," *World's Executive Digest* (December 1996): 53–58.

Conclusion

The service environment plays a major part in shaping customers' perception of a firm's image and positioning. As service quality is often difficult to assess objectively, customers frequently use the service environment as an important quality signal. Finally, a well-designed service environment makes customers feel good and boosts their satisfaction, while enhancing the productivity of the service operation at the same time.

The theoretical underpinning for understanding the effects of service environments on customers comes from the environmental psychology literature. The Mehrabian-Russell Stimulus-Response model holds that environments influence peoples' affective state (or feelings), which in turn drives their behaviour in that environment. Affect can be modelled with the two key dimensions of pleasure and arousal, which together determine whether people approach and spend time and money in an environment, or whether they avoid it. The servicescape model is built on these theories and has developed a comprehensive framework to explain how customers and service staff respond to service environments.

The main dimensions of service environments are ambient conditions (including music, scents and colours), spatial layout and functionality, and signs, symbols, and artifacts. Each dimension can have important effects on customer responses. For example, the type of music and its structural characteristics, including its tempo and volume, can make significant differences in customer satisfaction, quality perceptions, and even behaviours such as time and money spent in the environment. The other design variables can have similar effects.

Putting it all together is difficult, as environments are perceived holistically. That means no individual aspect of the environment can be optimized without considering everything else in that environment. This makes designing service environments an art, and professional designers focus on the design of specific service environments such as hotel lobbies, restaurants, clubs, cafés, bistros, retail outlets, healthcare facilities, and so on. Furthermore, apart from an aesthetic perspective, the best service environments are designed with the customer's perspective in mind. The environment needs to facilitate smooth movement through the service process.

Review Questions

1. Compare and contrast the strategic and functional roles of service environments within a service organization.

2. What is the relationship or link between the Russell model of affect and Bitner's servicescape model?

3. Why is it likely that different customers and service staff respond differently to the same service environment?

4. Explain the dimensions of ambient conditions and how each can influence customer responses to the service environment.

5. What are the roles of signs, symbols, and artifacts in customer perceptions of service environments?

6. What are the implications of the fact that environments are perceived holistically?

7. What tools are available for aiding our understanding of customer responses, and for guiding the design and improvement of service environments?

Application Exercises

1. Identify firms from three different service sectors where the service environment is a crucial part of the overall value proposition. Analyze and explain in detail the value that is being delivered by the service environment.

2. Think of a bad and a good waiting experience that you had recently, and contrast the situations with respect to the aesthetics of the surroundings, diversions, people waiting, and attitude of servers.

3. Visit a service environment and have a detailed look around. Experience the environment and try to feel how the various design parameters shape what you feel and how you behave in that setting.

4. Visit a self-service environment and analyze how the design dimensions guide you through the service process. What do you find works most effectively for you, and what seems least effective? How could that environment be improved to further ease the "way-finding" of self-service customers?

5. Servicescapes in electronic commerce settings, known as e-servicescapes or e-scapes (the looks and aesthetics of websites), have become a significant source of interest lately in terms of their impact on consumer attitudes, and ultimately behaviours. Identify the similarities and differences between servicescapes and e-servicescapes in relation to the role of various environment characteristics in shaping attitudes and behaviours.

Endnotes

1. The term *servicescape* was coined by Mary Jo Bitner in her paper "Servicescapes: The Impact of Physical Surroundings on Customers and Employees," *Journal of Marketing* 56 (April 1992): 57–71.

2. Julie Baker, Dhruv Grewal, and A. Parasuraman, "The Influence of Store Environment on Quality Inferences and Store Image," *Journal of the Academy of Marketing Science* 22/4 (1994): 328–39.

3. Véronique Aubert-Gamet, "Twisting Servicescapes: Diversion of the Physical Environment in a Reappropriation Process," *International Journal of Service Industry Management* 8/1 (1997): 26–41.

4. Madeleine E. Pullman and Michael A. Gross, "Ability of Experience Design Elements to Elicit Emotions and Loyalty Behaviors," *Decision Sciences* 35/1 (2004): 551–78.

5. Sally Horchow, "There's a New Kind of Action on the Strip," *New York Times* (April 17, 2005).

6. Lisa Takeuchi Cullen, "Is Luxury the Ticket?" *Time* (August 22, 2005): 38–39.

7. Richard B. Chase and Douglas M. Stewart, "Making Your Service Fail-Safe," *Sloan Management Review* 35 (1994): 35–44.

8. Robert J. Donovan and John R. Rossiter, "Store Atmosphere: An Environmental Psychology Approach," *Journal of Retailing* 58/1 (1982): 34–57.

9. James A. Russell, "A Circumplex Model of Affect," *Journal of Personality and Social Psychology* 39/6 (1980): 1161–78.

10. Jochen Wirtz and John E.G. Bateson, "Consumer Satisfaction with Services: Integrating the Environmental Perspective in Services Marketing into the Traditional Disconfirmation Paradigm," *Journal of Business Research* 44/1 (1999): 55–66.

11. Jochen Wirtz, Anna S. Mattila, and Rachel L. P. Tan, "The Moderating Role of Target-Arousal on the Impact of Affect on Satisfaction: An Examination in the Context of Service Experiences," *Journal of Retailing* 76/3 (2000): 347–65.

12. Barry J. Babin and Jill S. Attaway, "Atmospheric Affect as a Tool for Creating Value and Gaining Share of Customer," *Journal of Business Research* 49 (2000): 91–99.

13. Bitner (April 1992), op. cit.

14. For a comprehensive review of experimental studies on atmospheric effects, refer to L.W. Turley and Ronald E. Milliman, "Atmospheric Effects on Shopping Behavior: A Review of the Experimental Literature," *Journal of Business Research* 49 (2000): 193–211.

15. Patrick M. Dunne, Robert F. Lusch, and David A. Griffith, *Retailing*, 4th ed., Orlando, FL: Hartcourt (2002): 518.

16. Barry Davies and Philippa Ward, *Managing Retail Consumption*, Chichester, UK: John Wiley (2002): 179.

17. Steve Oakes, "The Influence of the Musicscape Within Service Environments," *Journal of Services Marketing* 14/7 (2000): 539–56 .

18. Morris B. Holbrook and Punam Anand, "Effects of Tempo and Situational Arousal on the Listener's Perceptual and Affective Responses to Music," *Psychology of Music* 18 (1990): 150–62; and S.J. Rohner and R. Miller, "Degrees of Familiar and Affective Music and Their Effects on State Anxiety," *Journal of Music Therapy* 17/1 (1980): 2–15.

19. Alexandra Lopez-Pacheco "Music in the Metro," Society of Composers, Authors and Music Publishers of Canada (SOCAN) Customer Newsletter, Spring 2006. www.socan.ca/pdf/en/Spring2006.pdf, accessed September 8, 2006.

20. Dunne, Lusch, and Griffith (2002), op. cit.: 520.

21. Eric R. Spangenberg, Ayn E. Crowley, and Pamela W. Henderson, "Improving the Store Environment: Do Olfactory Cues Affect Evaluations and Behaviors?" *Journal of Marketing* 60 (April 1996): 67–80; Paula Fitzgerald Bone and Pam Scholder Ellen, "Scents in the Marketplace: Explaining a Fraction of Olfaction," *Journal of Retailing* 75/2 (1999): 243–62.

22. Alan R. Hirsch, *Dr. Hirsch's Guide to Scentsational Weight Loss,* London: Element Books (1997): 12–15.

23. Jean-Charles Chebat and Richard Michon, "Impact of Ambient Odors on Mall Shoppers' Emotions, Cognition, And Spending: A Test of Competitive Causal Theories," *Journal of Business Research* 56 (2003): 529–39.

24. Alan R. Hirsch, "Effects of Ambient Odors on Slot Machine Usage in a Las Vegas Casino," *Psychology and Marketing* 12/7 (1995): 585–94.

25. Alan R. Hirsch and S.E. Gay, "Effect on Ambient Olfactory Stimuli on the Evaluation of a Common Consumer Product," *Chemical Senses* 16 (1991): 535.

26. Linda Holtzschuhe, *Understanding Color: An Introduction for Designers,* 2nd ed., New York: John Wiley (2002): 1.

27. Gerald J. Gorn, Amitava Chattopadhyay, Tracey Yi, and Darren Dahl, "Effects of Color as an Executional Cue in Advertising: They're in the Shade", *Management Science* 43/10 (1997): 1387–1400; Ayn E. Crowley, "The Two-Dimensional Impact of Color on Shopping," *Marketing Letters* 4/1 (1993): 59–69; Gerald J. Gorn, Amitava Chattopadhyay, Jaideep Sengupta, and Shashank Tripathi, "Waiting for the Web: How Screen Color Affects Time Perception," *Journal of Marketing Research* 41 (May 2004): 215–25; Iris Vilnai-Yavetz and Anat Rafaeli, "Aesthetics and Professionalism of Virtual Servicescapes," *Journal of Service Research* 8/3 (2006): 245–59.

28. Albert Henry Munsell, *A Munsell Color Product,* New York: Kollmorgen Corporation, 1996.

29. Holtzschuhe (2002) op. cit.: 51.

30. Heinrich Zollinger, *Color: A Multidisciplinary Approach,* Zurich: Verlag Helvetica Chimica Acta (VHCA) and Chichester: Wiley (1999): 71–79.

31. Joseph A. Bellizzi, Ayn E. Crowley, and Ronald W. Hasty, "The Effects of Color in Store Design," *Journal of Retailing* 59/1 (1983): 21–45.

32. John E.G. Bateson and K. Douglas Hoffman, *Managing Services Marketing*, 4th ed., Orlando, FL: Dryden Press (1999): 143.

33. Anat Rafaeli and Iris Vilnai-Yavetz, "Discerning Organizational Boundaries through Physical Artifacts," in N. Paulsen and T. Hernes, (eds.), *Managing Boundaries in Organizations: Multiple Perspectives*, Basingstoke, Hampshire: Macmillan, 2003; Anat Rafaeli and Iris Vilnai-Yavetz, "Emotion as a Connection of Physical Artifacts and Organizations," *Organization Science* 15/6 (2004): 671–86; and Anat Rafaeli and Iris Vilnai-Yavetz, "Managing Organizational Artifacts to Avoid Artifact Myopia," in A. Rafaeli and M. Pratt (eds.), *Artifacts and Organization: Beyond Mere Symbolism*, Mahwah, NJ: Lawrence Erlbaum Associates (2005): 9–21.

34. P.J. Poole, *Diversity: A Business Imperative*, Ajax, ON: Poole, 1997.

35. Sara O. Marberry and Laurie Zagon, *The Power of Color: Creating Healthy Interior Spaces*, New York: John Wiley (1995): 38.

36. Lewis P. Carbone and Stephen H. Haeckel, "Engineering Customer Experiences," *Marketing Management* 3, no. 3, Winter 1994: 9-18.

37. 2003 Awards of Excellence, International Parking Institute, www.parking.org/pdf/2003awards.pdf, accessed September 10, 2006.

38. Dennis Nickson, Chris Warhurst, and Eli Dutton, "The Importance of Attitude and Appearance in the Service Encounter in Retail and Hospitality," *Managing Service Quality* 2 (2005): 195–208.

39. Anna S. Mattila and Jochen Wirtz, "Congruency of Scent and Music as a Driver of In-store Evaluations and Behavior," *Journal of Retailing* 77 (2001): 273–89.

40. Christine M. Piotrowski and Elizabeth A. Rogers, *Designing Commercial Interiors*, New York: John Wiley, 1999; Martin M. Pegler, *Cafes & Bistros*, New York: Retail Reporting Corporation, 1998; Paco Asensio, *Bars & Restaurants*, New York: HarperCollins International, 2002; Bethan Ryder, *Bar and Club Design*, London: Laurence King, 2002.

41. Ron Kaufman, "Service Power: Who Were They Designing it For?" Ron Kaufman Newsletter (May 2001), www.ronkaufman.com.

42. Alan d'Astous, "Irritating Aspects of the Shopping Environment," *Journal of Business Research* 49, 2000: 149-156. See also: K. Douglas Hoffman, Scott W. Kelly, and Beth C. Chung, "A CIT Investigation of Servicscape Failures and Associated Recovery Strategies," *Journal of Services*.

CHAPTER 11

Managing People For Service Advantage

*The old adage "People are your most important asset" is wrong. The **right** people are your most important asset.*

— Jim Collins

Without great employees you can never have great customer service.

— Ricard F. Gerson

Among the most demanding jobs in service businesses are the so-called front-line jobs. Employees are expected to be fast and efficient at executing operational tasks, as well as courteous and helpful in dealing with customers. In fact, front-line employees are a key input for delivering service excellence and competitive advantage. Behind most of today's successful service organizations stands a firm commitment to effective management of human resources (HR), including recruitment, selection, training, motivation and retention of employees. Organizations that display this commitment are also characterized by a distinctive culture of service leadership and role modelling by top management. It is probably harder for competitors to duplicate high-performance human assets than any other corporate resource.

In this chapter, we focus on the people side of service management, and explore the following questions:

1. Why is the front line so crucially important to the success of a service firm?
2. Why is the work of service employees so demanding, challenging, and often difficult?
3. What are the cycles of failure, mediocrity, and success in HR for service firms?
4. How do we get it right? How are we to attract, select, train, motivate, and retain outstanding front-line employees?
5. What is the role of a service culture and service leadership in sustainable service excellence?

SERVICE EMPLOYEES ARE CRUCIALLY IMPORTANT

Almost everybody can recount some horror story of a dreadful experience they have had with a service business. If pressed, many of these same people can also recount a really good service experience. Service personnel usually feature prominently in such dramas. They are either in roles as uncaring, incompetent, mean-spirited villains, or in roles as heroes who went out of their way to help customers by anticipating their needs or resolving problems in a helpful and empathetic manner. From the firm's perspective, service staff are crucially important, as they can be a key determinant of customer loyalty (or defection) and therefore play an important role in creating long-term profits for the firm.

Service Personnel as a Source of Customer Loyalty and Competitive Advantage

From a customer's perspective, the encounter with service staff is probably the most important aspect of a service. From the firm's perspective, the service levels and the way service is delivered by the front line can be an important source of differentiation as well as competitive advantage. In addition, the strength of the customer–front-line-employee relationship is often an important driver of customer loyalty.[1] Among the reasons why service employees are so important to customers and the firm's competitive positioning are that the front line

- *Is a core part of the product:* often, the service employee is the most visible element of the service, delivers the service, and significantly determines service quality.
- *Is the service firm:* front-line employees represent the service firm, and from a customer's perspective, are the firm.
- *Is the brand:* front-line employees and service are often a core part of the brand. It is the employees who determine whether the brand promise gets delivered or not.

Furthermore, front-line employees play a key role in anticipating customers' needs, customizing the service delivery, and building personalized relationships with customers, which ultimately lead to customer loyalty. How attentive employees can be in anticipating customers' needs is shown in the following example. Steve Posner, a veteran room-service waiter at Ritz-Carlton, says that he constantly tries to anticipate what guests might want. He puts extra silverware on the table: "This may be for a child, so I also bring a small spoon for the soup." He includes Al steak sauce with hamburger orders: "They may not even have thought they wanted it, but they're happy to find it there." He puts a plate of lemon wedges next to a Coke: "Always bring more than you think people need." The aim isn't to lay out a table in some fussily proper way, but to make sure that guests' "unexpressed wishes and needs" are met. "As a waiter, you're the pre-guest. You have to try to think the way a guest would."[2]

This and many other success stories of employees showing discretionary effort that made a difference have reinforced the truism that highly motivated people are at the core of service excellence.[3] They are increasingly a key variable for creating and maintaining competitive positioning and advantage.

The intuitive importance of the impact of service employees on customer loyalty was integrated and formalized by James Heskett and his colleagues in their research on the service–profit chain, in which they demonstrate the chain of relationships between (1) employee satisfaction, retention, and productivity; (2) service value; (3) customer satisfaction and loyalty; and (4) revenue growth and profitability for the firm.[4] These issues are further explored in their book, *The Value–Profit Chain: Treat Employees Like Customers and Customers Like Employees.*[5] Unlike manufacturing, the service equivalent of "shop-floor workers" (i.e., front-line staff) are in constant contact with customers, and there is strong solid evidence to show that employee satisfaction and customer satisfaction are highly correlated.[6] This present chapter focuses on how to get satisfied, loyal, and productive service employees.

The Front Line in Low-Contact Services

Most research in service management, and many of the best-practice examples featured in this chapter, relate to high-contact services. This is not entirely surprising, since the people in these jobs are so visible. They are the actors who appear front-stage in the service drama when they serve the customer. Here, it is obvious why the front line is crucially important to customers, and therefore also to the competitive positioning and profitability of the firm. However, there is an increasing trend across virtually all types of services toward low-contact delivery channels such as call centres. Many routine transactions are now being conducted without even involving front-line staff at all. Some examples include the many types of services that are provided via websites, automatic teller machines (ATMs)

Figure 11.1

A friendly technical employee of MDG Computers Canada delivers a "moment of truth."

and interactive voice response (IVR) systems. In the light of these trends, is the front line really that important, especially when more and more routine transactions are being shifted to low- or no-contact channels?

Although the quality of the technology and self-service interface (e.g., the website, the ATM network, and the IVRs) is becoming the core engine for service delivery, and its importance has been elevated drastically, the quality of front-line employees still remains crucially important. Most people would not have called the service hotline or visited a service centre of their cellphone operator or their credit card company more than once or twice in the last 12 months and interacted with front-line staff there. However, it is these one or two service encounters that are absolutely critical. These are the "moments of truth" that drive a customer's perceptions of the service firm. Also, it is likely that these interactions will not be about routine transactions, but about service problems and special requests. These very few contacts determine whether a customer thinks, "Customer service is excellent! When I need help, I can call you, and this is one important reason why I bank with you," or instead, "Your service stinks. I don't like interacting with you, and I am going to spread the word about how bad your service is!"

A service firm's differentiation rests on these few moments of truth, given that technology is relatively commoditized. Therefore, the service delivered by the front line, whether it is "ear to ear" or via email rather than face to face, is still highly visible and important to the customer, and therefore a critical component of the services strategy and marketing mix of service firms.

FRONT-LINE WORK IS DIFFICULT AND STRESSFUL

The service–profit chain has high-performing, satisfied employees as key requirements for achieving service excellence and customer loyalty. However, these employees work in some of the most demanding jobs in service firms. We will next discuss the main reasons why these jobs are so demanding.

Boundary Spanning

The organizational behaviour literature refers to service employees as boundary spanners. Boundary spanners link the inside of an organization to the outside world, operating at the boundary of the company and transferring information between the inside and the outside world. Because of the position they occupy, boundary spanners often have conflicting roles. Customer-contact personnel must attend to both operational and marketing goals. To illustrate, service staff are expected to delight customers, and at the same time be fast and efficient at executing operational tasks. On top of that, they are often expected to do selling, cross-selling and up-selling as well. For instance, "Now would be a good time to open a separate account to save for your children's education," or "For only 25 dollars more per night, you can upgrade to the executive floor." Finally, sometimes they are even responsible for enforcing rate integrity and pricing schedules, which might be in direct conflict with customer satisfaction (e.g., "I am sorry, but we don't serve ice water in this restaurant, but we have an excellent selection of still and carbonated mineral waters," or "I am sorry, but we cannot waive the fee for the bounced cheque for the third time this quarter").

In short, front-line staff may perform triple roles, producing service quality, productivity, and sales. The multiplicity of roles in service jobs often leads to role conflict and role stress among employees, which are discussed next.[7]

Sources of Conflict

There are three main causes of role stress in front-line positions: Person/Role, Organization/Client, and Inter-client conflicts.

Person/Role Conflict Service staff feel conflicts between what their job requires and their own personalities, self-perception, and beliefs. For example, the job may require staff to smile and be friendly even to rude customers. Providing quality service requires an independent, warm, and friendly personality. These traits are more likely to be found in people with higher self-esteem. However, many front-line jobs are often perceived as low-level jobs, which require little education, offer low pay, and often lack future prospects. If an organization is not able to "professionalize" their front-line jobs and move away from such an image, these jobs may be inconsistent with staff's self-perception and lead to person/role conflicts.

Organization/Client Conflict Service employees frequently face the dilemma of whether they should follow the company's rules or satisfy customer demands. This conflict is also called the two-bosses dilemma, and arises when customers request services, extras, or exceptions that violate the organizational rules. This conflict is especially acute in organizations that are not customer oriented. Here, staff frequently have to deal with conflicting customer needs and requests, as well as organizational rules, procedures, and productivity requirements.

Inter-client Conflict Conflicts between customers are not uncommon (e.g., smoking in non-smoking sections, jumping queues, speaking on a cellphone in a cinema, and noisy guests in a restaurant), and it is usually the service staff who are summoned to call the miscreant customer to order. This is a stressful and unpleasant task, as it is difficult and often impossible to satisfy both sides.

Emotional Labour

The term *emotional labour* was coined by Arlie Hochschild in her book *The Managed Heart*.[8] Emotional labour arises when there is a discrepancy between the way front-line staff feel and the emotions that management requires them to portray in front of customers. Front-line staff are expected to have a cheerful disposition, be genial, compassionate, sincere, or even self-effacing—emotions that can be conveyed through facial expressions, gestures, tone of voice, and words. Although some service firms make an effort to recruit employees with such characteristics, there will inevitably be situations when employees do not feel such positive emotions, yet are required to quell their true feelings in order to conform to customer expectations. As Panikkos Constanti and Paul Gibbs point out, "the power axis for emotional labor tends to favor both the management and the customer, with the front line employee . . . being subordinate," thus creating a potentially exploitative situation.[9]

The stress of emotional labour is nicely illustrated in the following, probably apocryphal story. A flight attendant was approached by a passenger with "Let's have a smile." She replied with "Okay. I'll tell you what, first you smile and then I'll smile, okay?" He smiled. "Good," she said. "Now hold that for 15 hours," and walked away.[10]

Emotional labour is a very real problem faced by front-line staff, and companies are now taking steps to help staff deal with the problem. For example, because of Singapore Airlines' reputation for service excellence, its customers tend to have very high expectations and can be very demanding. This puts considerable pressure on its front line. The commercial training manager of Singapore Airlines (SIA) explained:

> We have recently undertaken an external survey and it appears that more of the "demanding customers" choose to fly with SIA. So the staff are really under a lot of pressure. We have a motto: "If SIA can't do it for you, no other airline can." So we encourage staff to try to sort things out, and to do as much as they can for the customer. Although they are very proud, and indeed protective of the company, we need to help them deal with the emotional turmoil of having to handle their customers well, and at the same time, feel they're not being taking advantage of. The challenge is to help our staff deal with difficult situations and take the brickbats. This will be the next thrust of our training programs.[11]

Figure 11.2 captures emotional labour with humour.

Firms need to be aware of ongoing emotional stress among their employees, and need to devise ways of alleviating it, which includes training on how to deal with stress and how to cope with pressure from customers. Solutions include efforts by the management in 1) aligning the requirements for emotional expression with customer expectations—for instance, customers in a busy convenience store may not require pleasant conversation from the employee. In such a context, it's better to focus on helping customers quickly purchase their items rather than train employees in increasing eye contact, smiling, and holding pleasant conversation during these encounters; 2) encouraging and training employees to "deep act"—"lifting" the mood of employees by encouraging them to bring a part of their personal lives to work, such as decorating workstations with family photos or having them socialize briefly with co-workers; and 3) avoiding "overscripting"—by letting employees express required behaviours and emotions in their own way rather than following a detailed script.[12]

Service Sweat Shops?

Rapid developments in information technology are permitting service businesses to make radical improvements in business processes, and even to completely re-engineer their operations. These developments sometimes result in wrenching changes in the nature of

Figure 11.2

Dilbert encounters emotional labour at the bank.

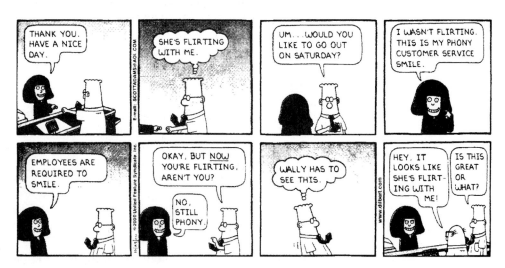

DILBERT: © Scott Adams/Dist. by permission of United Syndicate, Inc.

Figure 11.3

Work in customer contact centres is intense, but how customer service representatives perform often determines how a firm's service quality is perceived by customers.

work for existing employees. In instances where face-to-face contact has been replaced by use of the internet or call-centre services, firms have redefined and relocated jobs, created new employee profiles for recruiting purposes, and sought to hire employees with a different set of qualifications.

As a result of the growing shift from high-contact to low-contact services, a large and increasing number of customer-contact employees work by telephone or email, never meeting customers face to face.[13] For example, the call-centre industry now employs over three percent of the Canadian population holding jobs, offering direct employment (full and part time) to over half a million Canadians.[14]

At best, when well designed, such jobs can be rewarding, and often offer parents and students flexible working hours and part-time jobs (some 50 percent of call-centre workers are single mothers or students). In fact, it has been shown that part-time workers are more satisfied with their work as Customer Service Representatives (CSRs) than full-time staff, and performed just as well.[15] At worst, they place employees in an electronic equivalent of the old-fashioned sweatshop. Even in the best-managed call centres (also often called "customer contact centres") the work is intense, with CSRs expected to deal with up to two calls a minute under a high level of monitoring (including timing of trips to the toilet and breaks). As we will discuss in this chapter, some of the keys to success in this area involve screening applicants to make sure they already know how to present themselves well on the telephone and have the potential to learn additional skills, training them carefully, and giving them a well-designed working environment.[16]

CYCLES OF FAILURE, MEDIOCRITY, AND SUCCESS

All too often, bad working environments translate into dreadful service, with employees treating customers the way their managers treat them. Businesses with high employee turnover are frequently stuck in what has been termed the *cycle of failure*. Others, which offer job security but little scope for personal initiative, may suffer from an equally undesirable *cycle of mediocrity*. However, if managed well, there is potential for a virtuous cycle in service employment, termed the *cycle of success*.[17]

The Cycle of Failure

In many service industries, the search for productivity is on with a vengeance. One solution takes the form of simplifying work routines and hiring workers as cheaply as

Figure 11.4

The Cycle of Failure

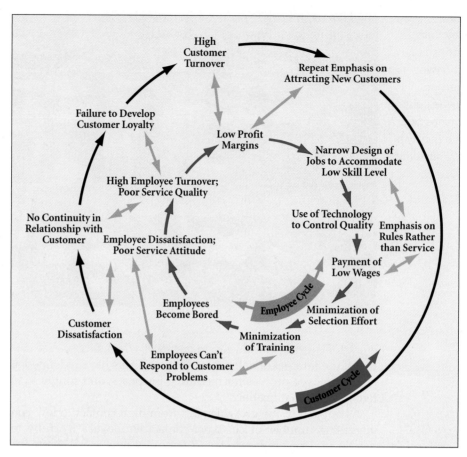

possible to perform repetitive work tasks that require little or no training. Among consumer services, departmental stores, fast food restaurants and call-centre operations are often cited as examples where this problem abounds (although there are notable exceptions). The cycle of failure captures the implications of such a strategy, with its two concentric but interactive cycles: one involving failures with employees, the second with customers (Figure 11.4).

The *employee cycle of failure* begins with a narrow design of jobs to accommodate low skill levels, an emphasis on rules rather than service, and the use of technology to control quality. A strategy of low wages is accompanied by minimal effort on selection or training. Consequences include bored employees who lack the ability to respond to customer problems, who become dissatisfied, and who develop a poor service attitude. Outcomes for the firm are low service quality and high employee turnover. Because of weak profit margins, the cycle repeats itself with the hiring of more low-paid employees to work in this unrewarding atmosphere. Some service firms can reach such low levels of employee morale that front-line staff become hostile toward customers and may even engage in "service sabotage," as featured in Research Insights 11.1, rather than deliver service excellence.[18]

The *customer cycle of failure* begins with repeated emphasis on attracting new customers, who become dissatisfied with employee performance and the lack of continuity implicit in continually changing faces. These customers fail to develop any loyalty to the supplier, and turn over as rapidly as the staff. This involves the firm in an ongoing search for new customers to maintain sales volume. The departure of discontented customers is especially worrying in the light of what we now know about the greater profitability of a loyal customer base.

Managers have offered excuses and justifications for perpetuating this cycle:

- "You just can't get good people nowadays."
- "People just don't want to work today."
- "To get good people would cost too much and you can't pass on these cost increases to customers."

Research Insights 11.1

Service Sabotage by the Front Line

The next time we are dissatisfied with the service provided by service employees—in a restaurant, for example—it's worth pausing for a moment to think about the consequences of complaining about the service. One might just become the unknowing victim of a malicious case of service sabotage, such as having something unhygienic added to one's food.

Interestingly, there is a relatively high incidence of service sabotage by front-line employees. Lloyd Harris and Emmanuel Ogbonna found in their study of 182 front-line staff that 90 percent of them admitted to front-line behaviour

with malicious intent to reduce or spoil the service. Service sabotage is an everyday occurrence in their organizations.

They classify service sabotage along two dimensions: covert–overt and routinized–intermittent behaviour. Covert actions are concealed from customers, whereas overt ones are purposefully displayed—often to co-workers, and sometimes also to customers. Routinized actions are ingrained into the culture of the firm's employees, whereas intermittent actions are sporadic and less common. Some true examples of service sabotage classified along these two dimensions appear in Figure 11.A.

Figure 11.A Examples of Service Sabotage

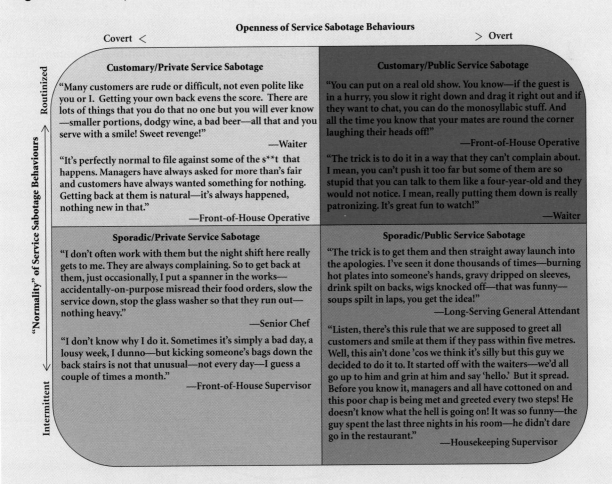

Source: Adapted from Lloyd C. Harris and Emmanuel Ogbonna, "Exploring Service Sabotage: The Antecedents, Types, and Consequences of Frontline, Deviant, Antiservice Behaviors," *Journal of Service Research* 4/3 (2002): 163–83. Copyright © 2002 by Sage Publications, Inc. Reprinted by permission of Sage Publications, Inc.

- "It's not worth training our front-line people when they leave you so quickly."
- "High turnover is simply an inevitable part of our business. You've got to learn to live with it."[19]

Too many managers make short-sighted assumptions about the financial implications of low-pay/high-turnover human resource strategies. Part of the problem is the failure to measure all relevant costs. Often omitted are three key cost variables: (1) the cost of constant recruiting, hiring, and training (which is as much a time cost for managers as a financial cost); (2) the lower productivity of inexperienced new workers; and (3) the costs of constantly attracting new customers (requiring extensive advertising and promotional discounts). Also ignored are two revenue variables: future revenue streams that might have continued for years, but are lost when unhappy customers take their business elsewhere; and potential income from prospective customers who are turned off by negative word of mouth. Finally, there are less easily quantifiable costs such as disruptions to service while a job remains unfilled, and loss of the departing employee's knowledge of the business (and its customers).

The Cycle of Mediocrity Another vicious employment cycle is the cycle of mediocrity (Figure 11.5). It is most likely to be found in large, bureaucratic organizations. These are often typified by state monopolies, industrial cartels, or regulated oligopolies, where there is little incentive to improve performance, and where fear of entrenched unions may discourage management from adopting more innovative labour practices.

In such environments, service delivery standards tend to be prescribed by rigid rule-books, oriented toward standardized service, operational efficiencies, and prevention of both employee fraud and favouritism toward specific customers. Job responsibilities tend to be narrowly and unimaginatively defined, tightly categorized by grade and scope of responsibilities, and further rigidified by union work rules. Salary increases and promotions are largely based on longevity. Successful performance in a job is often measured by absence of mistakes, rather than by high productivity or outstanding customer service.

Figure 11.5

The Cycle of Mediocrity

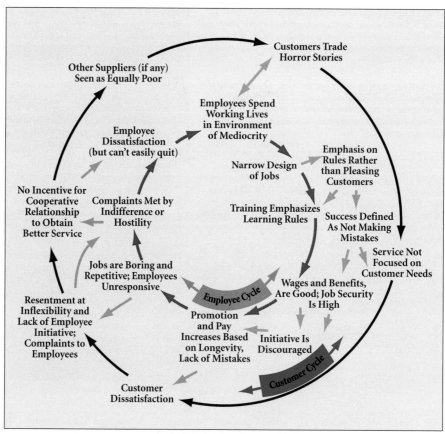

Source: Christopher Lovelock, "Managing Services: The Human Factor," in W.J. Glynn and J.G. Barnes (eds.), *Understanding Service Management*, Chichester, UK: John Wiley, 1995: 228.

Training focuses on learning the rules and the technical aspects of the job, not on improving human interactions with customers and co-workers. Since there are minimal allowances for flexibility or employee initiative, jobs tend to be boring and repetitive. However, in contrast to the cycle of failure, most positions provide adequate pay and often good benefits, combined with high security. Thus, employees are reluctant to leave. This lack of mobility is compounded by an absence of marketable skills that would be valued by organizations in other fields of endeavour.

Customers find such organizations frustrating to deal with. Faced with bureaucratic hassles, lack of service flexibility, and unwillingness of employees to make an effort to serve them well, users of the service can become resentful. However, customers often remain "held hostage" by the organization as there is nowhere else for them to go, either because the service provider holds a monopoly, or because all other available players are perceived as being equally bad or worse.

We shouldn't be surprised if dissatisfied customers display hostility toward service employees who feel trapped in their jobs and are powerless to improve the situation. Employees may then protect themselves through such mechanisms as withdrawal into indifference, playing overtly by the rulebook, or countering rudeness with rudeness. The net result is a vicious cycle of mediocrity in which unhappy customers continually complain to sullen employees (and also to other customers) about poor service and bad attitudes, generating greater defensiveness and lack of caring on the part of the staff. Under such circumstances, there's little incentive for customers to co-operate with the organization to achieve better service.

The Cycle of Success   Some firms reject the assumptions underlying the cycles of failure or mediocrity. Instead, they take a longer-term view of financial performance, seeking to prosper by investing in their people in order to create a cycle of success (Figure 11.6).

Figure 11.6

The Cycle of Success

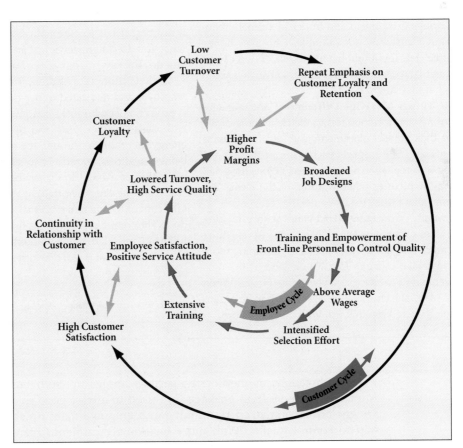

Best Practice in Action 11.1

Cora Griffith: The Outstanding Waitress

Cora Griffith, a waitress for the Orchard Café at the Paper Valley Hotel in Appleton, Wisconsin, is superb in her role, appreciated by first-time customers, famous with her regular customers, and revered by her co-workers. Cora loves her work and it shows. Comfortable in a role that she believes is the right one for her, she implements the following nine rules of success:

1. Treat Customers Like Family. First-time customers are not allowed to feel like strangers. Cheerful and proactive, Cora smiles, chats, and includes everyone at the table in the conversation. She is as respectful to children as she is to adults and makes it a point to learn and use everyone's name. "I want people to feel like they're sitting down to dinner right at my house. I want them to feel they're welcome, that they can get comfortable, that they can relax. I don't just serve people, I pamper them."

2. Listen First. Cora has developed her listening skills to the point that she rarely writes down customers' orders. She listens carefully and provides a customized service: "Are they in a hurry? Or do they have a special diet, or like their selection cooked in a certain way?"

3. Anticipate Customers' Wants. She replenishes beverages and brings extra bread and butter in a timely manner. One regular customer, for example, who likes honey with her coffee, gets it without having to ask. "I don't want my customers to have to ask for anything, so I always try to anticipate what they might need."

4. Simple Things Make the Difference. She manages the details of her service, monitoring the cleanliness of the utensils and their correct placement. The fold for napkins must be just right. She inspects each plate in the kitchen before taking it to the table. She provides crayons for small children to draw pictures while waiting for the meal. "It's the little things that please the customer."

5. Work Smart. Cora scans all her tables at once, looking for opportunities to combine tasks. "Never do just one thing at a time. And never go from the kitchen to the dining room empty-handed. Take coffee or iced tea or water with you." When she refills one water glass, she refills others. When clearing one plate, she clears others. "You have to be organized, and you have to keep in touch with the big picture."

6. Keep Learning. Cora makes it an ongoing effort to improve existing skills and learn new ones.

7. Success Is Where You Find It. Cora is contented with her work. She finds satisfaction in pleasing her customers, and she enjoys helping other people enjoy. Her positive attitude is a positive force in the restaurant. She is hard to ignore. "If customers come to the restaurant in a bad mood, I'll try to cheer them up before they leave." Her definition of success: "To be happy in life."

8. All for One, One for All. She has been working with many of the same co-workers for more than eight years. The team supports one another on the crazy days when 300 conventioneers come to the restaurant for breakfast at the same time. Everyone pitches in and helps. The wait staff cover for one another, the managers bus the tables, the chefs garnish the plates. "We are like a little family. We know each other very well and we help each other out. If we have a crazy day, I'll go in the kitchen towards the end of the shift and say, 'Man, I'm just proud of us. We really worked hard today.'"

9. Take Pride in Your Work. Cora believes in the importance of her work and in the need to do it well. "I don't think of myself as 'just a waitress'. . . . I've chosen to be a waitress. I'm doing this to my full potential, and I give it my best. I tell anyone who's starting out: take pride in what you do. You're never just an anything, no matter what you do. You give it your all . . . and you do it with pride."

Cora Griffith is a success story. She is loyal to her employer and dedicated to her customers and co-workers. A perfectionist who seeks continuous improvement, Cora's enthusiasm for her work and unflagging spirit creates an energy that radiates through the restaurant. She is proud of being a waitress, proud of "touching lives." Says Cora, "I have always wanted to do my best. However, the owners really are the ones who taught me how important it is to take care of the customer and who gave me the freedom to do it. The company always has listened to my concerns and followed up. Had I not worked for the Orchard Café, I would have been a good waitress, but I would not have been the same waitress."

Source: Leonard L. Berry, *Discovering the Soul of Service: The Nine Drivers of Sustainable Business Success,* New York: Free Press (1999): 156–59.

As with failure or mediocrity, success applies to both employees and customers. Attractive compensation packages are used to attract good-quality staff. Broadened job designs are accompanied by training and empowerment practices that allow front-line staff to control quality. With more focused recruitment, intensive training, and better wages, employees are likely to be happier in their work and to provide higher-quality, customer-pleasing service. Regular customers also appreciate the continuity in service relationships resulting from lower staff turnover, and so are more likely to remain loyal.

Profit margins tend to be higher, and the organization is free to focus its marketing efforts on reinforcing customer loyalty through customer retention strategies. These strategies are usually much more profitable than strategies for attracting new customers. Public service organizations in many countries are increasingly working towards cycles of success, too, and offer their users good quality service at a lower cost to the public.[20] In 2005 the Institute for Citizen-Centred Service (www.iccs-isac.org) was established in Canada with an explicit mandate to "promote high levels of citizen satisfaction with public-sector service delivery." This co-operative venture among the federal, provincial, and territorial governments aims to achieve its mission by "undertaking research to identify citizens' service needs and expectations and by assisting the public sector in identifying and applying innovative, best-practice service solutions which support quality service across all channels and respond effectively to citizens' service needs."[21]

A powerful demonstration of a front-line employee working in the cycle of success is waitress Cora Griffin (featured in Best Practice in Action 11.1). Many of the themes in her nine rules of success are the result of good HR strategies for service firms, which we will discuss next.

HUMAN RESOURCES MANAGEMENT: HOW TO GET IT RIGHT?

Any rational manager would like to operate in the cycle of success. We will next discuss HR strategies that will help service firms to move in that direction. Specifically, we will discuss how firms will be able to hire, motivate, and retain engaged service employees who are willing and able to perform along the three common dimensions of their jobs: delivering service excellence/customer satisfaction, productivity, and (often) sales. Figure 11.7 summarizes our main recommendations for successful HR strategies in service firms, and we will discuss each strategy in turn in this section.

It is naive to think that once employees are sufficiently satisfied, they will perform. Employee satisfaction should be seen as necessary but not sufficient for having high-performing staff. For instance, a recent study showed that employee effort was a strong driver of customer satisfaction over and above employee satisfaction.[22] As Jim Collins said, "The old adage 'People are the most important asset' is wrong. The *right* people are your most important asset." We would like to add to this: " . . . and the wrong people are a liability that is often difficult to get rid of." Getting it right starts with hiring the right people.

Hiring the Right People

Hiring the right people includes competing for applications from the best employees in the labour market, then selecting from this pool the best candidates for the specific jobs to be filled.

Be the Preferred Employer　To be able to select and hire the best people, they first have to apply for a job with you, and then accept your job offer over other potential offers (the best people tend to be selected by several firms). That means a firm has to first compete for market share in the available talent,[23] or as McKinsey & Company called it, "the war for talent."[24] This issue is particularly salient for employers in Canada, where, according to the Conference Board of Canada, the shortage of skilled workers is going to be more than 1 million by 2020. Competing in this type of labour market means having an attractive value proposition for prospective employees, and includes factors such as building and using internally and externally consistent employment messages, leveraging the talent pool by effective "Talent Pool Management," having "Great Start" programs for new employees,[25] and delivering high-quality products and services that make employees feel proud to be part of the team.

Furthermore, for a company wishing to attract the top talent, the compensation package cannot be below average: top people expect above-average packages. In our experience, it takes a salary in the range of the 65th to 80th percentile of the market to attract top performers to top companies. However, one does not necessarily have to be a top paymaster

Figure 11.7

Wheel of Successful HR in Service Firms

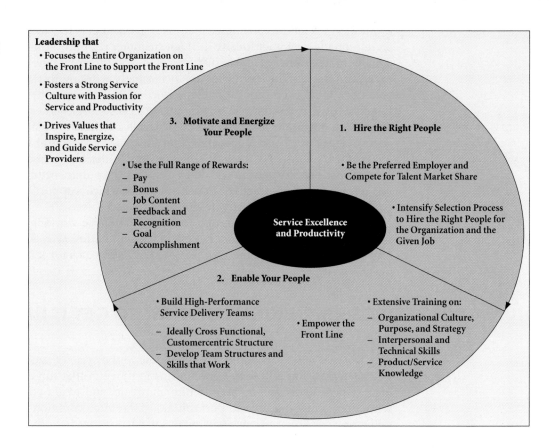

Leadership that
- Focuses the Entire Organization on the Front Line to Support the Front Line
- Fosters a Strong Service Culture with Passion for Service and Productivity
- Drives Values that Inspire, Energize, and Guide Service Providers

3. Motivate and Energize Your People
- Use the Full Range of Rewards:
  - Pay
  - Bonus
  - Job Content
  - Feedback and Recognition
  - Goal Accomplishment

1. Hire the Right People
- Be the Preferred Employer and Compete for Talent Market Share
- Intensify Selection Process to Hire the Right People for the Organization and the Given Job

Service Excellence and Productivity

2. Enable Your People
- Build High-Performance Service Delivery Teams:
  - Ideally Cross Functional, Customercentric Structure
  - Develop Team Structures and Skills that Work
- Empower the Front Line
- Extensive Training on:
  - Organizational Culture, Purpose, and Strategy
  - Interpersonal and Technical Skills
  - Product/Service Knowledge

if other important aspects of the value proposition are attractive. In short, understand the needs of your target employees and get your value proposition right.

Select the Right People   There's no such thing as the perfect employee. Different positions are often best filled by people with different skill sets, styles, and personalities. Service firms are increasingly engaged in examining the "fit" of potential candidates to the job profile to select the right candidates for a job. And companies such as the Edmonton-based Psychometrics Canada Ltd. (www.psychometrics.com) help firms make such decisions. For instance, their Customer Service Aptitude Profile (Customer Service AP) test measures aspects such as diplomacy, co-operativeness, self-confidence, patience, achievement motivation, and assertiveness—factors important for assessing the suitability of a potential candidate for a customer service job.

What makes outstanding service performers so special? Often it is things that *cannot* be taught. It is the qualities that are intrinsic to the people, and qualities they would bring with them to any employer. As one study of high performers observed:

> Energy . . . cannot be taught, it has to be hired. The same is true for charm, for detail orientation, for work ethic, for neatness. Some of these things can be enhanced with on-the-job training . . . or incentives. . . . But by and large, such qualities are instilled early on.[26]

Also, HR managers have discovered that while good manners and the need to smile and make eye contact can be taught, warmth itself cannot. The only realistic solution is to change the organization's recruitment criteria to favour candidates with naturally warm personalities. Jim Collins emphasizes that "The right people are those who would exhibit the desired behaviours anyway, as a natural extension of their character and attitude, regardless of any control and incentive system."[27]

The logical conclusion is that service firms should devote great care to attracting and hiring the right candidates. Best Practice in Action 11.2 shows how WestJet Airlines goes about hiring staff with the right attitude and a personality that fits the WestJet culture.

Best Practice in Action 11.2

Hiring at WestJet Airlines

There aren't many companies where some employees' duties include writing comedy. But that's what nine flight attendants do at WestJet Airlines. Those cornball jokes you hear at the end of a flight as the plane pulls up to the gate? They're the work of a group called the Westjesters, one of several committees of flight attendants that meet regularly to discuss everything from customer service to language and culture. A pillar of the Calgary-based carrier's culture is that employees ("people" in WestJetspeak) in direct contact with customers ("guests") not only have a stake in the success of the company through profit-sharing, but also openly contribute ideas about how the airline runs.

As famous as WestJet is for its fun and informal in-flight atmosphere, its corporate culture is no laughing matter. In fact, it has been critical to its success in a cut-throat industry during the company's nine years of flying, distinguishing it in striking fashion from incumbent Air Canada. "Everybody's unique," says Don Bell, a WestJet founder and the airline's executive vice-president, "and if you embrace people's personalities rather than turn them into robots, and give them the guidelines and the working environment to blossom, it creates something that's very hard to reckon with."

Bell often mentions "the right people" when talking about WestJet's employees, which might leave other execs wondering how you build such a staff. As Bell sees it, it's pretty simple. "We hire for attitude and we train for skills," he says, with pilots being an exception. If it turns out that someone isn't quite fitting in, management will try to coach that person to coax him or her back into the fold. And if that doesn't work, the airline isn't afraid to let people go. Bell says employees can be "dehired" for not being in sync with corporate culture, although such individuals usually end up leaving on their own first.

To help select people with the right attitude, WestJet invites supervisors and peers (with whom future candidates will be working) to participate in the in-depth interviewing and selection process, and uses non-traditional interview formats when hiring new fun-loving members to the WestJet family. A typical interview at Westjet might involve having a potential candidate go through the steps of: 1) a group interview—a "fun session where WestJet can discover whether you and the other applicants have what it takes to make a great WestJetter"; and 2) a panel interview—"a behavioural interview with more than one recruiter in attendance." Westjet describes the painstaking interview process as a way "to better understand why you would make a great addition to the team" and promises an "interview experience that is relaxed and meaningful" to the potential candidates. And what is their top advice to prospective "WestJetters" on their preparation for the interview process? Not surprisingly, it says "Above all, smile and have fun—this is your chance to shine!"

By hiring people with the right attitude, the company is able to foster the so-called WestJettitude—an intangible mix of positive, customer-focused, entrepreneurial, honest, friendly, caring, and hard-working qualities in people that causes them to want to do whatever it takes and to want to go that extra mile whenever they need to. It's little wonder then that, in a recent study by Waterstone Human Capital Ltd. and *Canadian Business*, WestJet stood out as having the most admired Canadian corporate culture, noted for its "entrepreneurial spirit," "delivering what they promise," and its "winning attitude."

Sources: Andrew Wahl, "Culture Shock," *Canadian Business* 78/20 (October 10–23, 2005): 115–16; Michelle Magnan, "People Power," *Canadian Business* 78/20 (October 10–23, 2005): 125–26; www.westjet.com, accessed September 16, 2006. Reprinted with permission of *Canadian Business*.

How to Identify the Best Candidates

Excellent service firms use a number of approaches to identifying the best candidates in their applicant pool. These include observing behaviour, conducting personality tests, interviewing applicants, and providing applicants with a realistic job preview.[28]

Observe Behaviour   The hiring decision should be based on the behaviour that recruiters observe, not the words they hear. As John Wooden said: "Show me what you can do, don't tell me what you can do. Too often, the big talkers are the little doers."[29] Behaviour can be directly or indirectly observed by using behavioural simulations or assessment centre tests that use standardized situations where applicants can be observed to see whether they display the kind of behaviours the firms' clients would expect. WestJet Airlines observes applicants closely during a day of interviews. Also, past behaviour is the best predictor of future behaviour: hire the person who has won service excellence awards, received many complimentary letters, and has great references from past employers.

Conduct Personality Tests   Use personality tests that are relevant for a particular job. For example, willingness to treat customers and colleagues with courtesy, consideration, and tact, perceptiveness of customer needs, and ability to communicate accurately and pleasantly are traits that can be measured. Hiring decisions based on such tests tend to be accurate.

For example, the Ritz-Carlton Hotels Group uses personality profiles on all job applicants. Staff are selected for their natural predisposition for working in a service context. Inherent traits such as a ready smile, a willingness to help others, and an affinity for multi-tasking enable them to go beyond learned skills. An applicant to Ritz-Carlton described her experience of going through the personality test for a job as a junior-level concierge at the Ritz-Carlton Millenia Singapore. Her best advice: tell the truth. These are experts; they will know if you are lying. "On the big day, they asked if I liked helping people, if I was an organized person and if I liked to smile a lot. Yes, yes, and yes, I said. But I had to support it with real life examples. This, at times, felt rather intrusive. To answer the first question for instance, I had to say a bit about the person I had helped—why she needed help, for example. The test forced me to recall even insignificant things I had done, like learning how to say hello in different languages, which helped to get a fix on my character."[30] It's better to hire upbeat and happy people, because customers report higher satisfaction when being served by more satisfied staff.[31]

Apart from intensive interview-based psychological tests, cost-effective internet-based testing kits are available. Here, applicants enter their test responses to a web-based questionnaire, and the prospective employer receives the analysis, the suitability of the candidate for the post, and a hiring recommendation. Developing and administering such tests has become a significant service industry in its own right. As profiled earlier, Psychometrics Canada Ltd. has been a key player in the Canadian marketplace for over 30 years, providing these services in both official languages. The leading global supplier of assessment products, SHL Group, serves some 5500 clients in 30 languages in over 40 countries.

Employ Multiple, Structured Interviews   To improve hiring decisions, successful recruiters like to employ structured interviews built around job requirements, and to use more than one interviewer. People tend to be more careful in their judgments when they know that another individual is also evaluating the same applicant. Another advantage of using two or more interviewers is that it reduces the risk of "similar to me" biases—we all like people who are similar to ourselves.

Give Applicants a Realistic Preview of the Job[32]   During the recruitment process, service companies should let candidates know the reality of the job, thereby giving them a chance to "try on the job" and assess whether it's a good fit or not. At the same time, recruiters can observe how candidates respond to the job's realities. This approach allows some candidates to withdraw if they determine that the job is not suitable for them. At the same time, the company can manage new employees' expectations of their job. Many service companies adopt this approach. For example, Au Bon Pain, a chain of French bakery cafés, lets applicants work for two paid days in a café prior to the final selection interview. Here, managers can observe candidates in action, and candidates can assess whether they like the job and the work environment.[33]

Train Service Employees Actively

When a firm has good people, investments in training can yield outstanding results. Service champions show a strong commitment in words, dollars, and action to training. As Benjamin Schneider and David Bowen put it: "The combination of attracting a diverse and competent applicant pool, utilizing effective techniques for hiring the most appropriate people from that pool, and then training the heck out of them would be gangbusters in any market."[34] Service employees need to learn:

- *The Organizational Culture, Purpose and Strategy.* Start strong with new hires, focus on getting emotional commitment to the firm's core strategy, and promote core values such as commitment to service excellence, responsiveness, team spirit, mutual respect, honesty, and integrity. Use managers to teach, and focus on "what," "why," and "how" rather than on the specifics of the job.[35] For example, new recruits at Disneyland attend the "Disney University Orientation." It starts with a detailed discussion of the company history and philosophy, the service standards expected of cast members, and a comprehensive tour of Disneyland's operations.[36] At VanCity, the credit union based in Vancouver that ranked No. 1 in the 2006 Best Workplaces in Canada list (published by *Canadian Business*), orientation begins even before their first day at the job. How so? Because 60 percent of new hires arrive through referrals by current staff, and its existing employees are extremely proud of their organization and protective of its culture.[37]

- *Interpersonal and Technical Skills.* Interpersonal skills tend to be generic across service jobs, and include visual communications skills such as making eye contact, attentive listening, body language, and even facial expressions. Technical skills encompass all the required knowledge related to processes (e.g., how to handle a merchandized return), machines (e.g., how to operate the terminal, or cash machine), and rules and regulations related to customer service processes. Both technical and interpersonal skills are *necessary*, but neither alone is *sufficient* for optimal job performance.[38]

- *Product/Service Knowledge.* Knowledgeable staff are a key aspect of service quality. They must be able to explain product features effectively and also position the product correctly. For instance, in Best Practice in Action 11.3, Jennifer Grassano of U.S.-based Dial-A-Mattress coaches individual staff members on how to paint pictures in the customer's mind.

Of course, training has to result in tangible changes in behaviour. If staff do not apply what they have learned, the investment is wasted. Learning is not only about becoming smarter, but about changing behaviour and improving decision-making. To achieve this, practice and reinforcement are needed. Supervisors can play a crucial role by following up regularly on learning objectives, for instance meeting with staff to reinforce key lessons from recent complaints and compliments (see Figure 11.8). Training and learning professionalizes the front line, moving these individuals away from the common (self)-image of being in low-end jobs that have no significance. Well-trained employees are, and feel like, professionals. A waiter who knows about food, cooking, wines, dining etiquette, and how to effectively interact with customers (even complaining ones), feels professional, has a higher self-esteem, and is respected by his customers. Training is therefore extremely effective in reducing person/role stress.

Figure 11.8

Morning briefings by a supervisor offer effective training opportunities.

Best Practice in Action 11.3

Coaching is a common method employed by services leaders to train and develop staff. Dial-A-Mattress's Jennifer Grassano is a bedding consultant (BC) for three days a week, and a coach to other BCs for one day a week. She focuses on staff whose productivity and sales performance are slumping.

Her first step is to listen in on the BC's telephone calls with customers. She will listen for about an hour and take detailed notes on each call. The BCs understand that their calls may be monitored, but they receive no advance notice, as that would defeat the purpose.

Next, she conducts a coaching session with that staff member, where strengths and areas for improvements are reviewed. Grassano knows how difficult it is to maintain a high energy level and convey enthusiasm when handling some 60 calls per shift. She likes to suggest new tactics and phrasings "to spark up their presentation." One BC was not responding effectively when customers asked why one mattress was more expensive than another. Here, she stressed the need to paint a picture in the customer's mind:

"Customers are at our mercy when buying bedding. They don't know the difference between one coil system and another. It is just like buying a carburetor for my car. I don't even know what a carburetor looks like. We have to use very descriptive words to help bedding customers make the decision that is right for them. Tell the customer that the more costly mattress has richer, finer padding with a blend of silk and wool. Don't just say the mattress has more layers of padding."

About two months after the initial coaching session, Grassano conducts a follow-up monitoring session with the BC. She then compares the BC's performance before and after the coaching session to assess the effectiveness of the training.

Grassano's experience and productivity as a BC give her credibility as a coach. "If I am not doing well as a BC, then who am I to be a coach? I have to lead by example. I would be much less effective if I was a full-time trainer." She clearly relishes the opportunity to share her knowledge and pass on her craft.

Source: Leonard L. Berry, *Discovering the Soul of Service: The Nine Drivers of Sustainable Business Success*, New York: Free Press, 1999: 171–72.

Empower the Frontline[39]

Virtually all breakthrough service firms have legendary stories of employees who recovered failed service transactions, or walked the extra mile to make a customer's day or avoid some kind of disaster for a client (as an example, see Best Practice in Action 11.4: Empowerment at FedEx). To allow this to happen, employees have to be empowered. FedEx trains and trusts its employees to do the right thing. Employee self-direction has become increasingly important, especially in service firms, because front-line staff frequently operate on their own, face-to-face with their customers, and it tends to be difficult for managers to closely monitor their behaviour.[40] Research also linked high empowerment to higher customer satisfaction.[41]

For many services, providing employees with greater discretion (and training in how to use their judgment) enables them to provide superior service on the spot, rather than taking time to get permission from supervisors. Empowerment looks to front-line staff to find solutions to service problems and to make appropriate decisions about customizing service delivery.

Is Empowerment Always Appropriate?   Advocates claim that the empowerment approach is more likely to yield motivated employees and satisfied customers than the "production-line" alternative, where management designs a relatively standardized system and expects workers to execute tasks within narrow guidelines.

However, David Bowen and Edward Lawler suggest that different situations may require different solutions, declaring that "both the empowerment and production-line approaches have their advantages . . . and . . . each fits certain situations. The key is to choose the management approach that best meets the needs of both employees and customers." Not all employees are necessarily eager to be empowered, and many employees do not seek personal growth within their jobs, and would prefer to work to specific directions rather than

Best Practice in Action 11.4

Empowerment at FedEx

Brenda McWilliams (managing director of marketing) and Gary Burkett (managing director of human resources) at FedEx's Mississauga office stress the importance of empowered employees in business success. According to them, delivering outstanding customer experiences is the key, and that requires understanding customer needs and delivering specialized solutions to them. And the resource most critical to making this happen is a "motivated and focused workforce." FedEx's "people first" philosophy comprises various initiatives such as "open-door" and "guaranteed fair treatment" policies that creates an atmosphere where employees feel secure enough to be innovative in responding to customer needs—even in the most unusual circumstances.

A case in point is that of a customer who was busy preparing a package from her home and did not realize that her cat had accidentally made its way into the package. When she became aware of what had happened, she frantically called FedEx. A representative quickly tracked down the package and notified local management. An employee took care of the cat over the weekend and then safely returned it to the owner on Monday.

Another instance is that of a medical patient who was waiting for a package containing life-saving heart medication from France. Due to unanticipated problems, the package did not leave France as planned. To make sure that the patient received the medication on time, one of the FedEx managers personally flew to Ottawa with the precious cargo in hand.

Employee empowerment is integral to FedEx's way of doing things; it is "not a part-time commitment," and its "credibility relies on an unwavering promise to employees." The basic tenet is that a satisfied employee is a productive employee, and is the one that is more likely to deliver on FedEx's brand promise to make every experience outstanding.

Source: Adapted from Brenda McWilliams and Gary Burkett, "Empowered Employees," *Marketing* 111/22 (June 19, 2006): 40.

to use their own initiative. Research has shown that a strategy of empowerment is most likely to be appropriate when most of the following factors are present within the organization and its environment:

- The firm's business strategy is based on competitive differentiation, and on offering personalized, customized service.
- The approach to customers is based on extended relationships rather than on short-term transactions.
- The organization uses technologies that are complex and non-routine in nature.
- The business environment is unpredictable and surprises are to be expected.
- Existing managers are comfortable with letting employees work independently for the benefit of both the organization and its customers.
- Employees have a strong need to grow and deepen their skills in the work environment, are interested in working with others, and have good interpersonal and group process skills.[42]

Control versus Involvement The production-line approach to managing people is based on the well-established "control" model of organization design and management. There are clearly defined roles, top-down control systems, hierarchical pyramid structures, and an assumption that the management knows best. Empowerment, by contrast, is based upon the "involvement" (or "commitment") model, which assumes that employees can make good decisions, and produce good ideas for operating the business, if they are properly socialized, trained, and informed. This model also assumes that employees can be internally motivated to perform effectively, and that they are capable of self-control and self-direction.

Schneider and Bowen emphasize that "empowerment isn't just 'setting the front line free' or 'throwing away the policy manuals.' It requires systematically redistributing four key ingredients throughout the organization, from the top downwards."[43] The four features are outlined on the next page.

- *Power* to make decisions that influence work procedures and organizational direction (e.g., through quality circles and self-managing teams)
- *Information* about organizational performance (e.g., operating results and measures of competitive performance)
- *Rewards* based on organizational performance, such as bonuses, profit sharing and stock options
- *Knowledge* that enables employees to understand and contribute to organizational performance (e.g., problem-solving skills)

In the control model, the four features are concentrated at the top of the organization, while in the involvement model, these features are pushed down through the organization.

Levels of Employee Involvement   The empowerment and production-line approaches are at opposite ends of a spectrum that reflects increasing levels of employee involvement as additional knowledge, information, power, and rewards are pushed down to the front line. Empowerment can take place at several levels:

- *Suggestion involvement* empowers employees to make recommendations through formalized programs. McDonald's, often portrayed as an archetype of the production-line approach, listens closely to its front line. Innovations, ranging from the Egg McMuffin to methods of wrapping burgers without leaving a thumbprint on the bun, were invented by employees.
- *Job involvement* represents a dramatic opening up of job content. Jobs are redesigned to allow employees to use a wider array of skills. In complex service organizations such as airlines and hospitals, where individual employees cannot offer all facets of a service, job involvement is often accomplished through use of teams. To cope with the added demands accompanying this form of empowerment, employees require training, and supervisors need to be reoriented from directing the group to facilitating its performance in supportive ways.
- *High involvement* gives even the lowest-level employees a sense of involvement in the company's overall performance. Information is shared. Employees develop skills in teamwork, problem-solving, and business operations, and they participate in work-unit management decisions. There is profit sharing, often in the form of bonuses.

WestJet Airlines illustrates a high-involvement company, promoting common sense and flexibility. It trusts its employees and gives them the latitude, discretion, and authority they need to do their jobs. This gives employees the flexibility to help each other when needed. "Pitching in to make it work" and "equality" are key themes at the airline. Those themes percolate deeply through the organization, irrespective of rank. Senior management helps out on flights, though they do not receive pay perks over and above anyone else in the organization. Even the CEO, Clive Beddoe, is known to help pick up garbage at the end of a flight!

There is also a strong belief within that organization that aligning employee interests with business interests fosters a great culture—and to that end, employees receive profit-sharing cheques twice a year and can choose to receive up to 20 percent of their salaries in shares, which WestJet then matches with a bonus of shares in the same amount. As Lisa Puchala, director of in-flight training and standards, says "All of us are owners here, and we're all very passionate about what we do." She adds, "When you have a stake in the company, you want to do whatever it takes to make it work."[44]

Build High-Performance Service-Delivery Teams

The nature of many services requires people to work in teams, often across functions, if they want to offer seamless customer service processes. Traditionally, many firms were organized by functional structures, where, for example, one department is in charge of consulting and selling (e.g., selling a cellphone with a subscription contract), another is in charge of customer service (e.g., activation of value-added services, changes of subscription plans), and the last, of billing. This structure prevents internal service teams from viewing end-customers as their own, and this structure can also mean poorer teamwork across functions, slower service, and more errors between functions. When customers have service problems, they easily fall through the cracks.

Empirical research has confirmed that front-line staff themselves regard lack of interdepartmental support as an important factor in hindering them from satisfying their customers.[45] Because of these problems, service organizations in many industries need to create cross-functional teams with the authority and responsibility to serve customers from end to end of the service process. Such teams are also called self-managed teams.[46]

The Power of Teamwork in Services

Jon Katzenbach and Douglas Smith define a team as "a small number of people with complementary skills who are committed to a common purpose, set of performance goals, and approach for which they hold themselves mutually accountable."[47] Teams, training, and empowerment go hand in hand. Teams facilitate communication between members and the sharing of knowledge. By operating like a small, independent unit, service teams take on more responsibility and require less supervision than more traditional functionally organized customer-service units. Furthermore, teams often set higher performance targets for themselves than supervisors would. Pressure to perform is high within a good team.[48] Best Practice in Action 11.5 shows how Singapore Airlines not only uses teams to provide emotional support and to mentor its cabin crew, but also how the company effectively assesses, rewards and promotes staff.

Some academics even feel that there is often too much emphasis on hiring "individual stars" and too little attention paid to team ability and the motivation of potential hires. Stanford professors Charles O'Reilly and Jeffrey Pfeffer emphasize that how well people work in teams is often as important as how good people are individually, and that stars can be outperformed by others through superior team work.[49]

At Customer Research Inc. (CRI), a progressive and successful marketing research firm, team members' feelings of pride are illustrated in the following quotes:

- "I like being on the team. You feel like you belong. Everyone knows what's going on."
- "We take ownership. Everyone accepts responsibility and jumps in to help."
- "When a client needs something in an hour, we work together to solve the problem."
- "There are no slugs. Everyone pulls their weight."[50]

Team ability and motivation are crucial for effective delivery of many types of services, especially those involving individuals who are each playing specialist roles. Emergency services depend heavily on effective teamwork (Figure 11.9).

Figure 11.9
Emergency rescue teams work under particularly demanding conditions.

Best Practice in Action 11.5

SIA understands the importance of teamwork in the delivery of service excellence, and has always worked hard to create esprit de corps among its cabin crew. This is made more difficult by the fact that crew members are scattered around the world. SIA's answer is the "team concept."

Choo Poh Leong, senior manager of cabin crew performance, explained: "In order to effectively manage our 6600 crew, we divide them into teams, small units, with a team leader in charge of about 13 people. We will roster them to fly together as much as we can. Flying together, as a unit, allows them to build up camaraderie, and crew members feel like they are part of a team, not just a member. The team leader will get to know them well, their strengths and weaknesses, and will become their mentor and their counsel, and someone to whom they can turn if they need help or advice. The 'check trainers' oversee 12 or 13 teams and fly with them whenever possible, not only to inspect their performance, but also to help their team develop.

"The interaction within each of the teams is very strong. As a result, when a team leader does a staff appraisal they really know the staff. You would be amazed how meticulous and detailed each staff record is. So, in this way, we have good control, and through the control, we can ensure that the crew delivers the promise. They know that they're being constantly monitored and so they deliver. If there are problems, we will know about them and we can send them for retraining. Those who are good will be selected for promotion."

According to Toh Giam Ming, senior manager of crew performance, "What is good about the team concept is that despite the huge number of crew, people can relate to a team and have a sense of belonging. 'This is my team.' And they are put together for 1–2 years and they are rostered together for about 60–70 percent of the time, so they do fly together quite a fair bit. . . . So especially for the new people, I think they find that they have less problems adjusting to the flying career, no matter what their background is. Because once you get familiar with the team, there is support and guidance on how to do things." Choo Poh Leong adds: "The individual, you see, is not a digit or a staff number, because if you don't have team-flying, you have 6000 odd people, it can be difficult for you to really know a particular person."

SIA also has a lot of seemingly unrelated activities in the cabin crew division. For example, there is a committee called the "Performing Arts Circle" made up of talented employees with an interest in the arts. During a recent biennial cabin crew gala dinner, members of SIA raised over half a million dollars for charity. In addition, SIA has a gourmet circle, language circles (such as a German- and French-speaking group), and even sports circles (such as football and tennis teams). As mentioned by Sim Kay Wee, "SIA believes that all these things really encourage camaraderie and teamwork."

Sources: Jochen Wirtz and Robert Johnston, "Singapore Airlines: What It Takes to Sustain Service Excellence—A Senior Management Perspective," *Managing Service Quarterly* 13/1 (2003): 10–19; and Loizos Heracleous, Jochen Wirtz, and Nitin Pangarkar, *Flying High in a Competitive Industry: Cost-Effective Service Excellence at Singapore Airlines*, Singapore: McGraw-Hill, 2006: 145–73.

Creating Successful Service-Delivery Teams   It's not easy to make teams function well. If people are not prepared for teamwork, and the team structure is not set up right, a firm risks having initially enthusiastic volunteers who lack the competencies that teamwork requires. The skills needed include not only co-operation, listening to others, coaching, and encouraging one another, but also an understanding of how to air differences, tell one another hard truths, and ask tough questions. All these require training.[51] Management also needs to set up a structure that will steer the teams towards success. A good example is American Express Latin America, which developed the following rules for making its teams work:

- Each team has an "owner"—a person who "owns" (takes responsibility for) the team's problems.

- Each team has a leader who monitors team progress and team process. Team leaders are selected for their strong business knowledge and people skills.

- Each team has a quality facilitator—someone who knows how to make teams work and who can remove barriers to progress and train others to work together effectively.[52]

Motivate and Energize People[53]

Once a firm has hired the right people, trained them well, empowered them, and organized them into effective service-delivery teams, how can it ensure that they will deliver service excellence? Staff performance is a function of ability and motivation. Hiring, training, empowerment, and teams give you able people, and reward systems are the key to motivation. Service staff must get the message that providing quality service holds the key for them being rewarded. Motivating and rewarding strong service performers are some of the most effective ways of retaining them. Staff pick up quickly if those who get promoted are the truly outstanding service providers, and if those who get fired are those that do not deliver at the customer level.

A major way service businesses fail is that they do not utilize the full range of available rewards effectively. Many firms think in terms of salary as reward, but it does not pass the test of effectiveness for this purpose. Receiving a fair salary is a "hygiene" factor (when present it is taken for granted, but when absent it causes dissatisfaction) rather than a motivating factor (whose absense would be taken for granted, but presence causes satisfaction). Paying more than what is seen as fair only has short-term motivating effects, and wears off quickly. On the other hand, bonuses that are contingent on performance have to be earned again and again, and therefore tend to be more lasting in their effectiveness. Other lasting rewards are the job content itself, recognition and feedback, and goal accomplishment.

Job Content
People are motivated and satisfied simply by knowing that they are doing a good job. They feel good about themselves and like to reinforce that feeling. This is true especially if the job also offers a variety of different activities, requires the completion of "whole" and identifiable pieces of work, is seen as significant in the sense that it has an impact on the lives of others, comes with autonomy, and if performing the job itself has a source of direct and clear feedback about how well employees did their work (e.g., sales and grateful customers).

Feedback and Recognition
Humans are social beings, and they derive a sense of identity and belonging to an organization from the recognition and feedback they receive from the people around them, such as their customers, colleagues, and bosses. If employees are being recognized and thanked for service excellence, they will desire to deliver it. We will discuss how to measure and use customer feedback in detail in Chapter 13.

Goal Accomplishment
Goals focus people's energy. Goals that are specific, difficult but attainable, and accepted by the staff are strong motivators and yield higher performance than no goals, or vague goals (e.g., "do your best"), or goals that are impossible to achieve.[54] In short, goals are effective motivators.

The following are important points to note for effective goal setting:[55]

- Achieving goals is a reward in itself when those goals are seen as important.
- Goal accomplishment can be used as a basis for giving rewards, including pay, feedback, and recognition. Feedback and recognition from peers can be given faster, more cheaply and effectively than pay, and have the additional benefit of gratifying an employee's self-esteem.
- Service-employee goals that are specific and difficult must be set publicly to be accepted. Although goals must be specific, they can be something intangible like improved employee courtesy ratings.
- Progress reports about goal accomplishment (feedback), and goal accomplishment itself must be public events (recognition), if they are to gratify employees' esteem need.
- It is mostly unnecessary to specify the means to achieve goals. Feedback on progress while pursuing the goal serves as a corrective function. As long as the goal is specific, difficult, but achievable, and is accepted, goal pursuit will result in goal accomplishment, even in the absence of other rewards.

Successful firms recognize that people issues are complex. Hewitt Associates, a professional firm delivering human capital management services in over 35 countries, captures the challenge of employee complexity in its advertising (Figure 11.10). Charles O'Reilly and Jeffrey Pfeffer conducted in-depth research on why some companies can succeed over long periods of time in highly competitive industries without having the usual sources of competitive advantage such as barriers of entry or proprietary technology. They concluded that these firms did not succeed by winning the war for talent (although they were hiring extremely carefully for fit), "but by fully using the talent and unlocking the motivation of the people" they already had in their organizations.[56]

For InSystems, a business-automation software company based in Markham, Ontario, the key to enhancing employee motivation has been the transformation of its traditional employee compensation system to the adoption of a "total reward" system. Precipitated by an employee satisfaction survey in 2002, the revamped total reward system now goes beyond the strictly financial (or "hard") elements and places substantial emphasis on the "soft" factors as well. The total rewards program has these elements grouped into five categories: 1) direct financial, which includes base salary, bonuses, and incentives; 2) indirect

Figure 11.10

"People issues are complex. Managing them doesn't have to be," declares Hewitt Associates.

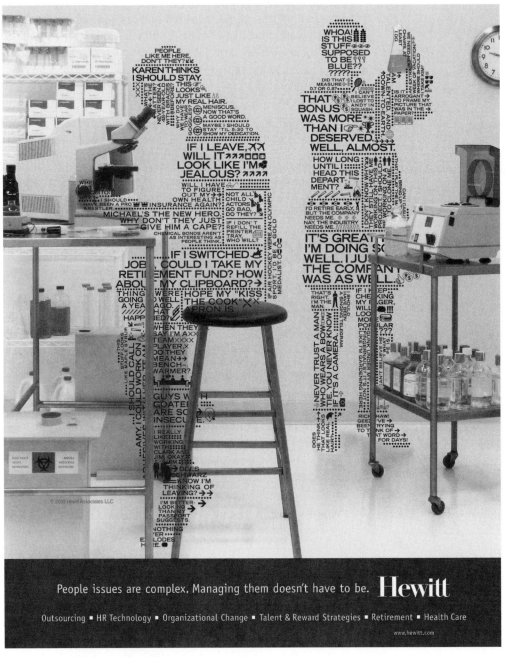

financial, such as group health benefits, retirement savings, and service recognition; 3) role, which takes into account the challenge, complexity, and variety of a position; 4) career development; and 5) affiliation, which includes the corporate culture, opportunity to work in teams and the social environment. According to Laurie McRae, vice president of HR and organizational development, the "guiding philosophy" behind the total reward system is that any factor that employees take into account when considering the value of working at InSystems should be a part of the total rewards package. Improvements in any of those elements means increased employee satisfaction, which in turn should deliver improved customer satisfaction and better business numbers.[57]

The Role of Unions

Unions and service excellence are sometimes seen as incompatible. The power of organized labour is widely cited as an excuse for not adopting new approaches in both service and manufacturing businesses. "We'd never get it past the unions," managers say, wringing their hands and muttering darkly about restrictive work practices. Unions are often portrayed as villains in the press, especially when high-profile strikes inconvenience millions. Many managers seem to be strongly antagonistic toward unions.

Jeffrey Pfeffer has observed wryly that "the subject of unions and collective bargaining is . . . one that causes otherwise sensible people to lose their objectivity."[58] He urges a pragmatic approach to this issue, emphasizing that "the effects of unions depend very much on what *management* does." The higher wages, lower turnover, clearly established grievance procedures, and improved working conditions often found in highly unionized organizations are all characteristics that, as this chapter has shown, can be associated with the cycle of success; they will yield positive benefits in a well-managed service organization.

Contrary to the negative view of some managers, many of the world's most successful service businesses are, in fact, highly unionized—the US based Southwest Airlines is one example. The presence of unions in a service company is not an automatic barrier to high performance and innovation, unless there is a long history of mistrust, acrimonious relationships, and confrontation. However, management consultation and negotiation with union representatives are essential if employees are to accept new ideas (this is equally true of non-unionized firms). The challenge is to work with unions jointly, to reduce conflict, and to create a climate for service.[59]

SERVICE LEADERSHIP AND CULTURE

So far, we have discussed the key strategies that help to move an organization toward service excellence. However, to truly get there, we need a strong service culture that is continuously reinforced and developed by management to achieve alignment with the firm's strategy.[60] A "charismatic leadership," also called transformational leadership, fundamentally changes the values, goals, and aspirations of the front line to be consistent with the firm's. Here, staff are more likely to perform their best and show performance "above and beyond the call of duty," because it is consistent with their own values, beliefs, and attitudes.[61]

Leonard Berry advocates a value-driven leadership that inspires and guides service providers. Leadership should bring out the passion for serving. It should also tap the creativity of service providers, nourish their energy and commitment, and give them a fulfilled working life. Some of the core values Berry found in excellent service firms included excellence, innovation, joy, teamwork, respect, integrity, and social profit.[62] These values are part of the firm's culture. A service culture can be defined as

- Shared perceptions of *what* is important in an organization, and
- Shared values and beliefs of *why* those things are important.[63]

To form an opinion of what is important in a company, employees rely heavily on their perceptions of what the company and their leaders do, rather than what they say.

Employees gain their understanding of what is important through the daily experiences they have with the firm's human resource, operations, and marketing practices and procedures.

A strong service culture is one where the entire organization focuses on the front line, and understands that it is the lifeline of the business. The organization understands that today's as well as tomorrow's revenues are largely driven by what happens at the service encounter. Figure 11.11 shows the inverted pyramid model of organization, which highlights the importance of the front line and shows that the role of top management and middle management is to support the front line in their task of delivering service excellence to their customers.

In firms with a passion for service, top management show by their actions that what happens at the front line is crucially important to them, by being informed and actively involved. They achieve this by regularly talking to and working with front-line staff and customers. Many actually spend significant amounts of time at the front line serving customers. For example, Disney World's management spends two weeks every year in front-line staff jobs such as sweeping streets, selling ice-cream, or being the ride attendant, to gain a better appreciation and understanding of what really happens on the ground.[64]

Service leaders are not only interested in the big picture, but focus on the details of service. They see opportunities in nuances that competitors might consider trivial, and they believe that the way the firm handles little things sets the tone for how it handles everything else.

Internal Marketing

Apart from a strong leadership that focuses on the front line, it takes a strong communications effort to shape the culture and get the message to the troops. Service leaders use multiple tools to build their service culture, ranging from internal marketing and training to core principles and company events and celebrations.

Internal communications from senior managers to their employees play a vital role in maintaining and nurturing a corporate culture founded on specific service values. Well-planned internal marketing efforts are especially necessary in large service businesses that operate in widely dispersed sites, sometimes around the world. Even when employees are working far from the head office in the home country, they still need to be kept informed of new policies, changes in service features, and new quality initiatives. Communications may also be needed to nurture team spirit and support common corporate goals. Consider the challenge of maintaining a unified sense of purpose at the overseas offices of Canadian companies such as Air Canada, Four Seasons Hotels and Resorts, Scotiabank, or Sun Life Financial, where people from different cultures who speak different languages must work together to create consistent levels of service.

Figure 11.11

The Inverted Organizational Pyramid versus the Inverted Pyramid with a Customer and Front-Line Focus.

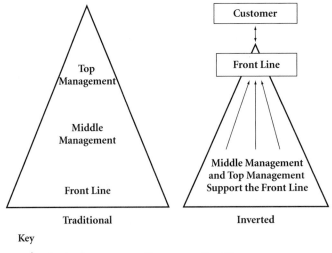

Effective internal communications can help ensure efficient and satisfactory service delivery, achieve productive and harmonious working relationships, and build employee trust, respect, and loyalty. Commonly used media include internal newsletters and magazines, DVDs, private corporate television networks like those owned by FedEx, intranets (private networks of websites and email that are only accessible within the company), face-to-face briefings, and promotional campaigns using displays, prizes, and recognition programs.

For example, Ritz-Carlton translated the key product and service requirements of its customers into the Ritz-Carlton Gold Standards, which include a credo, motto, three steps of service, 20 "Ritz-Carlton Basics" and the employee promise (see Best Practice in Action 11.6). Tim Kirkpatrick, director of training and development of Ritz-Carlton's Boston Common Hotel, said, "The Gold Standards are part of our uniform, just like your name tag. But remember, it's just a laminated card until you put it into action."[65] To reinforce these standards, every morning briefing includes a discussion of one of the standards. The aim of rotating these discussions is to keep the Ritz-Carlton philosophy at the centre of its employees' minds, which entails providing the "finest personal service and facilities" to its guest while fostering a great working environment for its own "ladies and gentlemen."

Best Practice in Action 11.6

Ritz-Carlton's Gold Standards

THREE STEPS OF SERVICE

1
A warm and sincere greeting. Use the guest name, if and when possible.

2
Anticipation and compliance with guest needs.

3
Fond farewell. Give them a warm good-bye and use their names, if and when possible.

"We Are Ladies and Gentlemen Serving Ladies and Gentlemen"

©1999, The Ritz-Carlton Hotel Company, L.L.C. All rights reserved

THE EMPLOYEE PROMISE

At The Ritz-Carlton, our Ladies and Gentlemen are the most important resource in our service commitment to our guests.

By applying the principles of trust, honesty, respect, integrity and commitment, we nurture and maximize talent to the benefit of each individual and the company.

The Ritz-Carlton fosters a work environment where diversity is valued, quality of life is enhanced, individual aspirations are fulfilled, and The Ritz-Carlton mystique is strengthened.

THE RITZ-CARLTON®

CREDO

The Ritz-Carlton Hotel is a place where the genuine care and comfort of our guests is our highest mission.

We pledge to provide the finest personal service and facilities for our guests who will always enjoy a warm, relaxed yet refined ambience.

The Ritz-Carlton experience enlivens the senses, instills well-being, and fulfills even the unexpressed wishes and needs of our guests.

THE RITZ-CARLTON® BASICS

1. The Credo is the principal belief of our Company. It must be known, owned and energized by all.

2. Our Motto is: "We Are Ladies and Gentlemen serving Ladies and Gentlemen." As service professionals, we treat our guests and each other with respect and dignity.

3. The Three Steps of Service are the foundation of Ritz-Carlton hospitality. These steps must be used in every interaction to ensure satisfaction, retention and loyalty.

4. The Employee Promise is the basis for our Ritz-Carlton work environment. It will be honored by all employees.

5. All employees will successfully complete annual Training Certification for their position.

6. Company objectives are communicated to all employees. It is everyone's responsibility to support them.

7. To create pride and joy in the workplace, all employees have the right to be involved in the planning of the work that affects them.

8. Each employee will continuously identify defects (M.R. B.I.V.) throughout the Hotel.

9. It is the responsibility of each employee to create a work environment of teamwork and lateral service so that the needs of our guests and each other are met.

10. Each employee is empowered. For example, when a guest has a problem or needs something special, you should break away from your regular duties to address and resolve the issue.

11. Uncompromising levels of cleanliness are the responsibility of every employee.

12. To provide the finest personal service for our guests, each employee is responsible for identifying and recording individual guest preferences.

13. Never lose a guest. Instant guest pacification is the responsibility of each employee. Whoever receives a complaint will own it, resolve it to the guest's satisfaction and record it.

14. "Smile – We are on stage." Always maintain positive eye contact. Use the proper vocabulary with our guests and each other. (Use words like – "Good Morning," "Certainly," "I'll be happy to" and "My pleasure.")

15. Be an ambassador of your Hotel in and outside of the workplace. Always speak positively. Communicate any concerns to the appropriate person.

16. Escort guests rather than pointing out directions to another area of the Hotel.

17. Use Ritz-Carlton telephone etiquette. Answer within three rings with a "smile." Use the guest's name when possible. When necessary, ask the caller "May I place you on hold?"

Do not screen calls. Eliminate call transfers whenever possible. Adhere to voice mail standards.

18. Take pride in and care of your personal appearance. Everyone is responsible for conveying a professional image by adhering to Ritz-Carlton clothing and grooming standards.

19. Think safety first. Each employee is responsible for creating a safe, secure and accident free environment for all guests and each other. Be aware of all fire and safety emergency procedures and report any security risks immediately.

20. Protecting the assets of a Ritz-Carlton hotel is the responsibility of every employee. Conserve energy, properly maintain our Hotels and protect the environment.

Source: The Ritz-Carlton Hotel Company, LLC. Reprinted with permission.

Empirical research in the hotel industry shows why it is so important for the management to "walk the talk." Judi McLean Park and Tony Simons conducted a study on 6500 employees at 76 Holiday Inn hotels. They measured whether the hotel managers showed behavioural integrity using measures such as "My manager delivers on promises," and "My manager practises what he preached." These statements were correlated with employee responses to questions such as "I am proud to tell others I am part of this hotel," and "My co-workers go out of their way to accommodate guests' special requests," and then to revenues and profitability. The results were stunning. They showed that behavioural integrity of a hotel's manager was highly correlated to employees' trust, commitment, and willingness to go the extra mile. Furthermore, of all manager behaviours measured, it was the single most important factor driving profitability. In fact, a mere one-eighth point increase in a hotel's overall behavioural integrity score on a five-point scale was associated with a 2.5 percent increase in revenue, and a US$250,000 increase in profits per year per hotel.[66]

Conclusion

Successful service organizations are committed to effective management of human resources (HR). Best-practice HR strategies start with competing for talent by being the preferred employer, followed by careful hiring, painstaking training, and empowering staff, who then have the authority and self-confidence to use their own initiative in delivering service excellence. It also involves effective use of service-delivery teams, and energizing and motivating the front line with a full set of rewards, ranging from pay, satisfying job content, recognition, and feedback to goal accomplishment. Top and middle management continuously reinforce a strong culture that emphasizes service excellence and productivity. Employees understand and support the goals of an organization, and a value-driven leadership inspires and guides service providers, bringing their passion for serving to the full and giving them a fulfilled working life.

The market and financial impact of this approach can be phenomenal, and often leads to a sustainable competitive advantage. It is probably harder to duplicate high-performance human assets than any other corporate resource.

Review Questions

1. Discuss the role service personnel play in creating or destroying customer loyalty.

2. What is emotional labour? Explain the ways in which it may cause stress for employees in specific jobs. Illustrate with suitable examples.

3. What are the key barriers for firms seeking to break the cycle of failure and move into the cycle of success?

4. List five ways in which investment in hiring and selection, training, and ongoing motivation of employees will pay dividends in customer satisfaction for such organizations as (a) a restaurant, (b) an airline, (c) a hospital, and (d) a consulting firm.

5. Identify the factors favouring a strategy of employee empowerment.

6. Define what is meant by the control and involvement models of management.

7. Identify the factors needed to make service teams successful in (a) an airline, (b) a restaurant.

8. How can a service firm build a strong service culture that emphasizes service excellence and productivity?

Application Exercises

1. An airline runs a recruiting advertisement for cabin crew that shows a picture of a small boy sitting in an airline seat and clutching a teddy bear. The headline reads: "His mom told him not to talk to strangers. So what's he having for lunch?" Describe the types of personalities that you think would be (a) attracted to apply for the job by that ad and (b) discouraged from applying.

2. Consider the following jobs: emergency ward nurse, bill collector, computer repair technician, supermarket cashier, dentist, kindergarten teacher, prosecuting attorney, server in a family restaurant, server in an expensive French restaurant, stockbroker, and undertaker. What type of emotions would you expect each of them to display to customers in the course of doing their job? What drives your expectations?

3. As a human resources manager, which issues do you see as most likely to create boundary-spanning problems for customer-contact employees in a customer call centre at a major internet service provider? Select four issues and indicate how you would mediate between operations and marketing to create a satisfactory outcome for all three groups.

Endnotes

1. Liliana L. Bove and Lester W. Johnson, "Customer Relationships with Service Personnel: Do We Measure Closeness, Quality or Strength?" *Journal of Business Research* 54 (2001): 189–97.

2. Paul Hemp, "My Week as a Room-Service Waiter at the Ritz," *Harvard Business Review* 80/6 (June 2002): 8–11.

3. Recent research established the link between extra-role effort and customer satisfaction, e.g., Carmen Barroso Castro, Enrique Martín Armario, and David Martín Ruiz, "The Influence of Employee Organizational Citizenship Behavior on Customer Loyalty," *International Journal of Service Industry Management* 15/1 (2004): 27–53.

4. James L. Heskett, Thomas O. Jones, Gary W. Loveman, et al., "Putting the Service–Profit Chain to Work," *Harvard Business Review* 72/3 (March–April 1994), 164–74.

5. James L. Heskett, W. Earl Sasser, Jr., and Leonard A. Schlesinger, *The Value–Profit Chain: Treat Employees Like Customers and Customers Like Employees,* New York: Free Press, 2003.

6. Benjamin Schneider and David E. Bowen, "The Service Organization: Human Resources Management is Crucial," *Organizational Dynamics* 21/4 (Spring 1993): 3 –52.

7. David E. Bowen and Benjamin Schneider, "Boundary-Spanning Role Employees and the Service Encounter: Some Guidelines for Management and Research," in J.A. Czepiel, M. R. Solomon, and C.F. Surprenant, *The Service Encounter*, Lexington MA: Lexington Books, 1985: 127–48.

8. Arlie R. Hochschild, *The Managed Heart: Commercialization of Human Feeling,* Berkeley: University of California Press, 1983.

9. Panikkos Constanti and Paul Gibbs, "Emotional Labor and Surplus Value: The Case of Holiday 'Reps'," *Service Industries Journal* 25 (January 2005): 103–16.

10. Arlie Hochschild, "Emotional Labor in the Friendly Skies," *Psychology Today* (June 1982): 13–15, cited in Valarie A. Zeithaml, Mary Jo Bitner, and Dwayne D. Gremler, *Services Marketing: Integrating Customer Focus Across the Firm*, 4th ed., New York: McGraw-Hill (2006): 359. See also: Aviad E. Raz, "The Slanted Smile Factory: Emotion Management in Tokyo Disneyland," *Studies in Symbolic Interaction* 21 (1997): 201–17.

11. Jochen Wirtz and Robert Johnston, "Singapore Airlines: What It Takes to Sustain Service Excellence—A Senior Management Perspective," *Managing Service Quarterly* 13/1 (2003): 10–19; and Loizos Heracleous, Jochen Wirtz, and Nitin Pangarkar, *Flying High in a Competitive Industry: Cost-Effective Service Excellence at Singapore Airlines,* Singapore: McGraw-Hill (2006): 155.

12. Meredith A. Vey, "Avoiding the Dark Side of 'Service with a Smile,'" *Research Note,* Accenture Institute for High Performance Business, April 2005; available online at www.accenture.com/Global/Research_and_Insights/Institute_For_High_Performance_Business/By_Publication_Type/Research_Notes/AvoidingASmile.htm, accessed September 15, 2006.

13. "The Bangalore Paradox," *The Economist* (April 23, 2005): 67–69.

14. NBI/Michael Sone & Associates, *Canadian ACD/Contact Centre Market Report,* 2000 Edition.

15. Dan Moshavi and James R. Terbord, "The Job Satisfaction and Performance of Contingent and Regular Customer Service Representatives: A Human Capital Perspective," *International Journal of Service Industry Management* 13/4 (2002): 333–47.

16. See also Vaikalathur Shankar Mahesh and Anand Kasturi, "Improving Call Centre Agent Performance," *International Journal of Service Industry Management* 17/2 (2006): 136–157.

17. The terms "cycle of failure" and "cycle of success" were coined by Leonard L. Schlesinger and James L. Heskett, "Breaking the Cycle of Failure in Services," *MIT Sloan Management Review* 31 (Spring 1991): 17–28. The term "cycle of mediocrity" comes from Christopher H. Lovelock, "Managing Services: The Human Factor," in W.J. Glynn and J.G. Barnes, (eds.), *Understanding Services Management*, Chichester, UK: John Wiley (1995): 228.

18. Lloyd C. Harris and Emmanuel Ogbonna, "Exploring Service Sabotage: The Antecedents, Types, and Consequences of Frontline, Deviant, Antiservice Behaviors," *Journal of Service Research* 4/3 (2002): 163–83. See also Lorna Douget, "Service Provider Hostility and Service Quality," *Academy of Management Journal* 47/5 (2004): 761–71.

19. Schlesinger and Heskett (1991), op. cit.

20. Reg Price and Roderick J. Brodie, "Transforming a Public Service Organization from Inside Out to Outside In," *Journal of Service Research* 4/1 (2001): 50–59.

21. www.iccs-isac.org/eng/about.htm, accessed September 15, 2006.

22. Mahn Hee Yoon, "The Effect of Work Climate on Critical Employee and Customer Outcomes," *International Journal of Service Industry Management* 12/5 (2001): 500–21.

23. Leonard L. Berry and A. Parasuraman, *Marketing Services: Competing Through Quality,* New York: Free Press (1991): 151–52.

24. Charles A. O'Reilly III and Jeffrey Pfeffer, *Hidden Value: How Great Companies Achieve Extraordinary Results with Ordinary People,* Boston: Harvard Business School Press (2000): 1.

25. Michael Palmer, "The Branding Effect: Why a Strong Employer Brand Will Help You Win the Talent War," Ceridian Canada Whitepaper, www.ceridian.ca/en/media/whitepapers.html#branding, accessed September 15, 2006.

26. Bill Fromm and Len Schlesinger, *The Real Heroes of Business and Not a CEO Among Them*, New York: Currency Doubleday (1994): 315–16.

27. Jim Collins, "Turning Goals into Results: The Power of Catalytic Mechanisms," *Harvard Business Review* 77/4 (July–August 1999): 77.

28. This section was adapted from Benjamin Schneider and David E. Bowen, *Winning the Service Game*, Boston: Harvard Business School Press, 1995: 115–26.

29. John Wooden, *A Lifetime of Observations and Reflections On and Off the Court*, Chicago: Lincolnwood, 1997: 66.

30. Serene Goh, "All the Right Staff," and Arlina Arshad, "Putting Your Personality to the Test," *The Straits Times* (September 5, 2001): H1.

31. For a review of this literature see Benjamin Schneider, "Service Quality and Profits: Can You Have Your Cake and Eat It, Too?" *Human Resource Planning* 14/2 (1991): 151–57.

32. This section was adapted from Leonard L. Berry, *On Great Service: A Framework for Action*, New York: Free Press, 1995: 181–82.

33. Schlesinger and Heskett (1991), op. cit.: 26.

34. Schneider and Bowen (1995), op. cit.: 131.

35. Leonard L. Berry, *Discovering the Soul of Service: The Nine Drivers of Sustainable Business Success*, New York: Free Press, 1999: 161.

36. Schneider and Bowen (1995), op. cit.: 138–39.

37. Graham Lowe, "A Proper Welcome," *Canadian Business* 79/14–15 (July 17–August 3, 2006): 67–69.

38. David A. Tansik, "Managing Human Resource Issues for High Contact Service Personnel," in D.E. Bowen, R. B. Chase, T.G. Cummings et al., (eds.), *Service Management Effectiveness*, San Francisco: Jossey-Bass, 1990: 152–76.

39. Parts of this section are based on David E. Bowen, and Edward E. Lawler, III, "The Empowerment of Service Workers: What, Why, How and When," *Sloan Management Review* (Spring 1992): 32–39.

40. Dana Yagil, "The Relationship of Customer Satisfaction and Service Workers' Perceived Control: Examination of Three Models," *International Journal of Service Industry Management* 13/4 (2002): 382–98.

41. Graham L. Bradley and Beverley A. Sparks, "Customer Reactions to Staff Empowerment: Mediators and Moderators," *Journal of Applied Social Psychology* 30/5 (2000): 991–1012.

42. Bowen and Lawler (1992), op. cit.: 32–39.

43. Schneider and Bowen (1995), op. cit.: 250.

44. These two paragraphs are based on Michelle Magnan, "People Power," *Canadian Business* 78/20 (October 10–23, 2005): 125–26.

45. Andrew Sergeant and Stephen Frenkel, "When Do Customer Contact Employees Satisfy Customers?" *Journal of Service Research* 3/1 (August 2000): 18–34.

46. For a recent study on self-managed team performance see Ad de Jong, Ko de Ruyter, and Jos Lemmink, "Antecedents and Consequences of the Service Climate in Boundary-Spanning Self-Managing Service Teams," *Journal of Marketing* 68 (April 2004): 18–35.

47. Jon R. Katzenbach and Douglas K. Smith, "The Discipline of Teams," *Harvard Business Review* 71/2 (March–April, 1993): 112.

48. Berry (1995), op. cit.: 131.

49. O'Reilly and Pfeffer (2000) op. cit.: 9.

50. Berry (1999), op. cit.: 189.

51. Schneider and Bowen (1995), op. cit.: 141; Berry (1995), op. cit.: 225.

52. Ron Zemke, "Experience Shows Intuition Isn't the Best Guide to Teamwork," *The Service Edge* 7/1 (January 1994): 5.

53. This section is based on Schneider and Bowen (1995), op. cit.: 145–73.

54. A good summary of goal setting and motivation at work can be found in Edwin A. Locke and Gary Latham, *A Theory of Goal Setting and Task Performance*, Englewood Cliffs, NJ: Prentice Hall, 1990.

55. Schneider and Bowen (1995), op. cit.: 165.

56. O'Reilly and Pfeffer (2000), op. cit.: 232.

57. David Brown, "Soft Side of Rewards Has Hard Impact," *Canadian HR Reporter* 17/7 (April 5, 2004): 5–6.

58. Jeffrey Pfeffer, *Competitive Advantage Through People*, Boston: Harvard Business School Press, 1994: 160–63.

59. Jody Hoffer Gittell, Andrew von Nordenflycht, and Thomas A. Kochan, "Mutual Gains for Zero Sum? Labor Relations and Firm Performance in the Airline Industry," *Industrial and Labor Relations Review* 57/2 (2004): 163–80.

60. The authors of the following paper emphasize the role of alignment between tradition, culture, and strategy, which together form the basis for the firm's HR practices: Benjamin Schneider, Seth C. Hayes, Beng-Chong Lim, et al., "The Human Side of Strategy: Employee Experiences of a Strategic Alignment in a Service Organization," *Organizational Dynamics* 32/2 (2003): 122–41.

61. Scott B. MacKenzie, Philip M. Podsakoff, and Gregory A. Rich, "Transformational and Transactional Leadership and Salesperson Performance," *Journal of the Academy of Marketing Science* 29/2 (2001): 115–34.

62. Berry (1995), op. cit.: 236–37. The following study emphasized the importance of the perceived ethical climate in driving service commitment of employees: Charles H. Schwepker Jr. and Michael D. Hartline, "Managing the Ethical Climate of Customer-Contact Service Employees," *Journal of Service Research* 7/4 (2005): 377–97.

63. Schneider and Bowen (1995), op. cit.: 240.

64. Catherine DeVrye, *Good Service is Good Business*, Upper Saddle River, NJ: Prentice Hall, 2000: 11.

65. Hemp (2002), op. cit.: 8–11.

66. Tony Simons, "The High Cost of Lost Trust," *Harvard Business Review* 80/9 (September 2002): 2–3.

Kung-Fu Service Development at Singapore Airlines

LOIZOS HERACLEOUS, JOCHEN WIRTZ, AND
ROBERT JOHNSTON

How should firms approach the task of new service development? The lesson from Singapore Airlines (SIA) is that, to succeed as a serial innovator, a company requires both a "hard," formalized approach employing a centralized department and a "soft," flexible process in which service delivery teams surface and implement new ideas. SIA's product development department conceives new ideas from many sources and takes selected ones through to commercial application. Meantime, the airline's culture encourages a stream of ideas for service enhancement and implementation from its various functions, including both in-flight and ground services and also loyalty marketing.

The highest state of attainment in the martial art of kung-fu is the ability to seamlessly combine the hard and the soft. Speed and flexibility derive from being soft and fluid while penetrating attacks derive from applying hard energy at the right time to specific, targeted points. This winning combination of soft and hard does not come naturally; it needs to be ceaselessly practised.

In competitive, threatening situations, people—and organisations—unwittingly tend to tense and seize up. In so doing, they reduce their adaptive ability and diminish their chances of responding effectively. The only way to enter the realm of the kung-fu master is to drill this soft/hard orientation into one's sub-conscious through continuous practice, so that it becomes second nature.

This martial arts metaphor sheds light on how Singapore Airlines (SIA) has become the recognised master of innovation in the airline industry and has consistently outperformed the industry for decades. SIA has never incurred a loss on an annual basis and has shown healthy returns since its founding in 1972 (see Tables 1 and 2 for SIA's relative performance dur-

ing 1992–2004). In contrast, the airline industry as a whole has suffered from a cyclical pattern of bubble, crash, stabilisation and recovery, with nearly half the years in the last two and a half decades marked by heavy losses.

BOOKING THE COOKS

SIA's success is built on its ability to be a serial innovator, introducing many firsts in the airline industry, and sustaining this over the decades in the face of intense cost pressures, industry crises, and trends towards commoditisation. SIA is known worldwide as a paragon of in-flight service and continuous innovation, and is continuously rewarded with prestigious industry awards that confirm its status as the airline that others seek to emulate. In addition to regularly introducing discontinuous, substantial innovations (such as the launch of the first on-demand in-flight entertainment system in all classes, the first non-stop flight to the US which only has two classes of travel, business class and "executive economy," or its current uses of biometric technology), SIA seems to have the ability to churn out a large quantity of incremental, cost-effective innovations across all its operating units (such as internet check-in, SMS check in or the "Book the Cook" service for passengers who like to order specific dishes in advance).

SIA's approach to innovation appears to deviate from the standard, linear, normative models of new service development (NSD) as propagated in many text books. It involves the seamless combination of both hard, structured, rigorous, centralised innovation, with soft, emergent, distributed, but equally significant, innovation.

Table 1 SIA vs Top 20 Airlines Net Profit Margin Performance 1992–2004

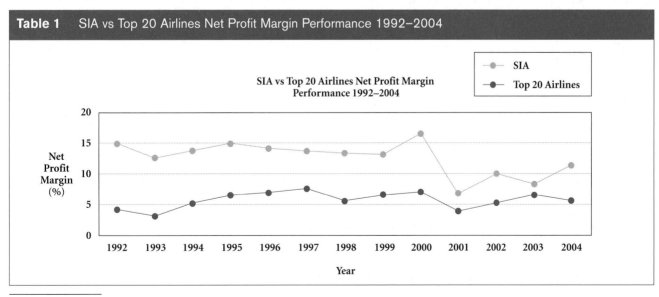

Business Strategy Review (Winter 2005): 26, 28–31.

Table 2 SIA vs Top 20 Airlines ROA Performance 1992–2004

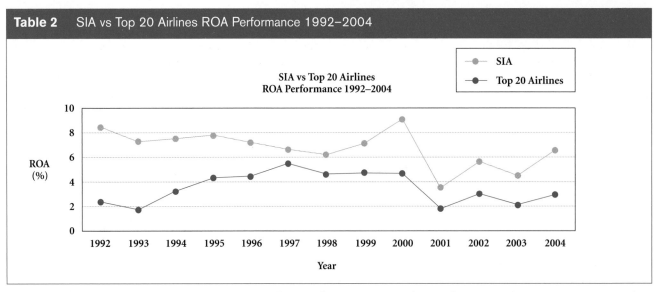

Note: The performance comparisons compare Singapore Airlines' performance in terms of net profit margin and return on assets against the weighted average for the top 20 airlines by market capitalisation (as at 15 May 2004), for the period 1992–2004. The 20 airlines are Southwest Airlines, Singapore Airlines, Cathay Pacific, Japan Airlines, Lufthansa, British Airways, All Nippon Airways, Qantas, Air France, Ryanair, JetBlue Airways, China Southern Airlines (A shares), China Eastern Airlines (A shares), Thai Airways, American Airlines, Malaysian Airlines, SAS AB, China Airlines, WestJet Airlines, and Alitalia.

The hard aspect is enshrined in a centralised product innovation department that tends to undertake major, discontinuous innovations, such as "LeaderShip", the first non-stop service between Singapore and Los Angeles with upgraded business and executive economy classes. SIA will be the first airline to fly the A380 super-jumbo plane and is currently working on designing the new services to be offered on it. The potential of biometrics is also currently being considered by SIA. The company has already identified 113 potential uses of biometrics and is looking at which ones would add value to the customer and to the company, and provide strategic differentiation while simultaneously improving efficiency. Its breakthrough pilot project where passengers use their biometrically coded cards at a separate gateway to clear immigration and police checks and check in within around one minute has been ongoing since November 2004. This is expected not only to provide higher security and reduce costs, but also to significantly improve the customer experience, reinforcing SIA's image as a serial innovator and a paragon of service excellence.

There is a well-defined innovation framework guiding activities in the airline's product innovation department. This involves a sequential process of having inspirations or making discoveries; capturing them on the e-log, an electronic storage space of innovative ideas; having "war cabinet" meetings to explore feasibility and flesh out the details; preliminary endorsement of the idea by senior vice presidents; the holding of a user conference where SIA frequent flyers are invited to debate the idea and give their inputs; development of a robust business case with detailed cost and revenue projections; approval by senior management; and further refinement and implementation. Yap Kim Wah, SIA's senior vice president responsible for product and service explained: "SIA is a profit-

Figure 1 The Hard and Soft Approach

NSD PROCESS	NSD ORGANISATIONAL ACTIVITY	
	CENTRALISED PD DEPARTMENT	DISTRIBUTED FUNCTIONAL DEPARTMENTS
Hard highly structured NSD process	Well-defined and structured innovation framework, with a number of fixed points, focusing on major and usually high cost innovations.	Major NSD permitted within their areas of control; but subject to the same key fixed points. Structured assessment of customer feedback and rewards for innovation.
Soft flexible, unstructured, emerging process	Flexible process allowing individuals to pursue less orthodox ideas before being fed into the formal NSD process, or being handed over for development to the operational units.	Primarily an unstructured, emergent process that focuses on continuous improvements. Often, budget is absorbed in operating expenses.

generating organisation. We are not an institute of technology and whatever we do must make business sense and that is the guiding principle. To support the guiding principle we have to make a profit and customers must want to return."

The Product Development (PD) department in SIA is made up of a small number of people who eat, drink, sleep and breathe innovation. Their sole task is to conceive of innovative ideas and take selected ones through the development cycle to commercial introduction. There are several sources of ideas, including customer feedback, ideas from service staff, or competitor benchmarking. The most interesting ideas, however, are stumbled upon while panning for gold. The product development team surf the internet and read magazines in search of good ideas or existing technologies that can be adapted for airline use, such as biometrics.

SIA's strategic partners are always companies with a robust brand image. Its in-flight Dolby sound for example was initially developed by a company called Lake. While SIA was interested in the technology, it wanted Lake to find a partner with a robust brand before it became involved. Lake invited Dolby to enter the alliance, which paved the way for SIA's support of further development and a two-year exclusivity agreement.

FLUID ONLY

SIA's service research and development involves a soft and flexible process. Although there are a few key fixed points, such as senior vice president endorsement, costing and approval, the other stages are quite fluid. For example, some innovations are developed in great detail, even tested, before seeking senior vice president endorsement; others are simply at the idea stage. There is also flexibility to allow individuals in the product development department to pursue less orthodox ideas and let them simmer and potentially feed at a later point into the formal NSD process, or hand them over to operational units for development.

In SIA there is a breed of softer emergent new service development which can best be described as distributed innovation. Dr Yeoh Teng Kwong, SIA's former senior manager of product innovation, explained: "I would not consider my department as the central product development unit as this would give the impression that we drive all new developments in SIA. Far from it, the culture of innovation is so pervasive in the company that most functional departments have the innovation objective as part of their mission. SIA strives to excel in a multitude of areas so that our competitors find it a near insurmountable task to try to rival us."

SIA's culture encourages a stream of new ideas from its various functions, such as in-flight services, ground services and loyalty marketing. These ideas are developed and implemented by people in those functions in a decentralised, distributed manner, using department budgets at least for the initial stages of development. One example is the recently developed internet check-in, building on customer acceptance and high utilisation of telephone and SMS check-in, which

was conceptualised, developed and implemented by the ground services department. This fluid process enables and encourages "live", continuously fine-tuned, innovations that are owned by specific departments which continuously monitor and develop them further, based on staff and customer feedback. Continuous enhancements to the SMS check-in process, for example, were made to improve functionality without sacrificing ease of use. Other improvements which have resulted from distributed innovation include the now commonly available ability to choose one's seat online or through SMS, or the unique service where business and first class passengers can order their favourite dish beforehand, and it is delivered to them on their flight.

This distributed innovation capability also guards against the company blindly following technological fads, because it engages the people who are close to the actual processes involved and can see hype for what it is. For example, the ground services department made a conscious decision, at the height of the hype about WAP, that it did not want to follow this technology, and that it would instead focus on SMS check-in because it was more user-friendly and the infrastructure was more widely available.

In addition, the influence and direct involvement of operations on the innovation process means that the ability to consistently and seamlessly deliver, a cornerstone of SIA's success, is not compromised by the introduction of innovations that sound good but cannot be delivered reliably. One example was the proposed idea of passengers ordering in-flight drinks through SIA's in-flight entertainment system, Krisflyer. It was decided not to pursue this, since the ability to deliver the drinks to passengers within a reasonable time frame and with the necessary level of customisation would be compromised. This operational ownership of innovations is crucial for SIA, reinforcing its key competency of the operational ability to deliver consistent and reliable service every time, in every customer transaction.

THE HARD SIDE

This soft distributed innovation process also has a hard edge. While minor adjustments can be made by almost anyone at any time, the more expensive and significant changes are subject to the key fixed points process also adhered to by the PD department: senior vice president endorsement, costing and approval. These developments are carried out totally independently of the PD department, but are still overseen by the senior vice president responsible for product and service innovation.

Other harder, structural and process-related aspects of SIA's organisational context support the development of this capability for distributed innovation. For example, the high importance given to customer feedback, means that any inputs by customers to boundary, front-line workers, such as the famous Singapore Girl, are duly recorded and swiftly transferred to the relevant departments for deliberation. Flexible rewards based on company performance give every incentive to employees to think innovatively, even though they are not part of the centralised PD department. SIA's team concept, where the in-flight teams composed of the same individuals remain the same for years, further reinforces the feeling that personal fortunes are tied with company fortunes, and introduce peer pressure to perform. Job rotation of everyone from junior manager level upwards further enables company-wide rather than myopic, department-based thinking. Cultural values encouraging continuous improvement, change and innovation also support un-learning, the removal of legacy processes that may inhibit further innovations. For example, developing internet check-in meant having to challenge and reconstitute long-standing airport security and check-in procedures, which was duly implemented.

This hard/soft kung-fu approach to innovation is drilled into SIA's sub-conscious through conscious design, ceaseless practice and cultural reinforcement. As a result SIA is capable of deploying kung-fu tactics effortlessly even when the odds are stacked against it. During 2002–2003 when the global airline industry felt the devastating effects of the 9/11 terrorist attacks and then SARS, some airlines tensed up so much their business collapsed. SIA also had to cut costs, but it did so without compromising service levels and innovation, the cornerstones of its success. Costs were cut, for example, by imposing substantial salary cuts on senior management, encouraging employees to take unpaid leave, and temporarily suspending recruitment. At the same time, however, SIA continued its soft, fluid but penetrating attacks by continuously developing its people's innovative skills, investing in brand new planes, upgrading its facilities (such as by introducing the lie-flat "space-bed" seat in business class), and ultimately sustaining its competitive success and exceptional performance.

Resources

Costa, P.R., R.S. Harnet, and J.T. Lunquist, (2002), "Rethinking the Aviation Industry," *McKinsey Quarterly* (Special edition: *Risk and Resilience*).

Heracleous, L., and J. Wirtz, (2005), "Biometrics Meets Services," *Harvard Business Review*, "Breakthrough Ideas for 2005," February: 48.

Heracleous, L., J. Wirtz, and R. Johnston, (2004), "Effective Service Excellence: Lessons from Singapore Airlines," *Business Strategy Review*, 15, 1.

Heracleous, L., J. Wirtz, and N. Pangarkar, (2006), *Flying High in a Competitive Industry: Cost Effective Service Excellence at Singapore Airlines*, McGraw-Hill.

Staw, B., L. Sanderlands, and J. Dutton, (1981), "Threat-rigidity Effects in Organisational Behaviour: A Multi-level Analysis," *Administrative Science Quarterly*, 21.

Wirtz, J., and R. Johnston, (2003), "Singapore Airlines: What it Takes to Sustain Service Excellence," *Managing Service Quality*, 13, 1.

Reading 3-2

How to Lead the Customer Experience

STEPHAN H. HAECKEL, LEWIS P. CARBONE, AND LEONARD L. BERRY

Customers always have an experience when they interact with a firm. The question for managers is whether the firm is prepared to systematically manage the customers' experience or simply hope for the best. The customers' overall experience—influenced by sensory and emotional clues—evokes a value perception that determines brand preference. Through experience management principles, a firm can design a composite of clues that resonate with customers and earn their loyalty.

Business strategies centered on the holistic design and delivery of total customer experiences consistently create superior customer value. Holistic experiences begin and end long before and after actual transactions. They incorporate functional and affective attributes. They are orchestrated to deliver both intrinsic and extrinsic values. And they result in stronger, more sustainable customer preference than do independently managed communication, process, and service-centric strategies.

By "total experience" we mean the feelings customers take away from their interaction with a firm's goods, services, and "atmospheric" stimuli. Companies that interact with customers can't avoid giving them a total experience. They can, however, avoid managing it in a systematic way, and almost all do. Organizations that simply tweak design elements or focus on the customer experience in isolated pockets of their business will be disappointed in the results.

A number of organizations are starting to systematically apply customer experience management principles to strengthen customer preference and improve business outcomes. Unlike many goods or service enhancements, the holistic nature of these experiential designs makes it very difficult for competitors to copy them. Customer value creation is moving into a new arena—one that encompasses goods and service quality, but is a broader concept.

The customer's total experience directly affects perceptions of value, word-of-mouth endorsement, and repatronage

"How to Lead the Customer Experience" by Stephan H. Haeckel, Lewis P. Carbone and Leonard L. Berry, *Marketing Management* (January/February 2003). Authors' note: The authors acknowledge the contribution of Suzie Goan, experience director of Experience Engineering Inc. in Minneapolis.

intentions. A well-prepared, well-served meal consumed in a noisy restaurant with uncomfortable chairs is one experience for customers. The same food served the same way in a comfortable and relaxing environment is a completely different experience. The meal and the atmosphere are inextricably linked; both are part of the customer's overall restaurant experience. The facility design; servers' skills, attitudes, body language, choice of words, tone, inflection, and dress; pace of service; presentation and taste of the food; noise level; smell; texture of tableware; spacing, height, and shape of tables; and a multitude of other stimuli all coalesce into a positive, neutral, or negative experience.

The problem-solving properties of goods and services provide functional benefits. Managers must recognize two realities, however. First, competing goods and services often are quite similar in functionality. Second, customers desire more than functionality. They are emotional beings who also want intangible values such as a sense of control, fun, aesthetic pleasure, and enhanced self-esteem.

Companies compete best when they combine functional and emotional benefits in their market offer. Firms that make customers feel good are formidable competitors because customers like to feel good and few companies make them feel that way. Emotional bonds between firms and customers are difficult for competitors to penetrate.

CREATING CLUES

Customers always have an experience when they interact with an organization. They consciously and unconsciously filter a barrage of "clues" and organize them into a set of impressions, both rational and emotional. Anything perceived or sensed (or recognized by its absence) is an experience clue. If you can see, smell, taste, or hear it, it's a clue. Goods and services emit clues, as does the physical environment in which they're offered. The employees are another source of experience clues. Each clue carries a message; the composite of clues creates the total experience.

Effectively managing the customers' experience involves presenting an integrated series of clues that collectively meet or exceed customers' expectations. One category of clues concerns the actual functioning of the good or service. Did the key issued at the front desk open the hotel room door? Did the room's television set work? Was the wake-up call made as promised? These goods and service clues strictly concern functionality and are interpreted primarily by the conscious and logical circuitry of the brain.

A second category of clues stimulates the brain's emotional circuitry and evokes affective responses. The smell and feel of leather upholstery, the sound and smell of a steak on the grill, and the laugh, phrasing, and tone of voice of the person answering the customer service call line are clues that envelop the functionality of a good or service. Two types of clues affect customers' emotional perceptions: mechanics (clues emitted by things) and humanics (clues emitted by people).

The distinction between functional service clues and humanics clues is subtle. A retail salesperson who answers a customer's question about what other stores might carry an out-of-stock item is producing a functional service clue. The salesperson's choice of words, tone, and body language produce humanics clues. One salesperson may offer the information grudgingly or disinterestedly. Another may offer the information enthusiastically. The information is accurate in both cases, but the customer's emotional response to the two salespeople is quite different.

In the August 2000 issue of *Travel & Leisure*, Peter John Lindberg reported on Singapore Airlines, which is consistently rated by travelers as one of the world's best airlines. It invests heavily to orchestrate in-flight service mechanics and humanics clues, including fresh orchids in first- and business-class bathrooms, galley carts scrubbed before every flight, and female flight attendants who wear designer dresses and receive intensive training in body posture, grooming, and voice tone. One veteran flight attendant believes the dresses reduce air-rage incidents: "It's hard to be nasty to a girl in a sarong kebaya. Put them in pants, and passengers think they can take more abuse."

Functional, mechanics, and humanics clues are synergistic rather than additive; they must be melded from creation to execution. To fully leverage experience as a customer value proposition, organizations must understand and manage the emotional component of experiences with the same rigor they bring to managing manufactured product and service functionality.

THE CUSTOMER EXPERIENCE

Customer experience management focuses different parts of an organization on the common goal of creating an integrated, aligned customer feeling. It provides a means for breaking down organizational barriers. We have identified three fundamental principles that provide a foundation for creating distinctive customer value through experiences. Each requires a cross-functional organizational perspective.

Principle 1: Fuse Experiential Breadth and Depth

Experiential breadth refers to the sequence of experience customers have in interacting with an organization. These experiences may begin well before customers pass through the firm's doors. For example, hotel guests' experiences begin before they walk into the lobby. Was the reservations agent competent and courteous? Was the hotel easy to find and access? And, even further back in the experience journey, was the promotional packet the hotel sent about its loyalty program well-designed and informative? Imagine the opportunity for a hotel company in defining the full breadth of the customers' experience, becoming attuned to the hundreds of clues along the way and seeking to manage these clues to evoke positive perceptions.

Whereas breadth refers to identifiable stages customers undergo in the experience, depth refers to the number and diversity of sensory clues at each stage. The more layers of multi-sensory clues that reinforce the targeted impression, the more successful an organization will be in anchoring and sustaining that impression in the customer's perception. Consider the depth of reinforcing clues embedded in the room experience at a Ritz-Carlton hotel. They typically include plush carpet, distinctive furniture and rich fabrics; the smell of fresh flowers; a complimentary refreshment stocked in the room; a welcome call from the concierge offering assistance; an iron and ironing board; a robe, thick towels, and distinctively scented "Ritz-Carlton" shampoos; a leather-bound television viewing guide with a bookmark on the current day; room service 24 hours a day; turn-down service; and *The New York Times* and *Wall Street Journal* delivered outside one's door in the morning.

Congruence or fusion of clues within and among experience stages is critical. Incongruent clues convey an incongruent message with customers likely to recall facets of the experience most salient to their needs. This is why a spacious, well-furnished hotel lobby can't make up for a cramped, poorly furnished hotel room. Guests don't live in the lobby. However, if lobby clues fuse with guest room clues, then one part of the experience reinforces another.

Principle 2: Use Mechanics and Humanics to Improve Function

In some cases, humanics and mechanics clues can be introduced to enhance goods or service functionality. Customers process these different types of clues holistically, so firms should manage them as such. Stimuli that envelop goods or services can affect customers' perceptions of functional quality. Mechanics and humanics must be simultaneously addressed and blended with the functional clues of the offering into reciprocally supported experience clues.

Roger Ulrich, a landscape architect with Texas A&M University, has done considerable research documenting how environmental factors in a hospital can affect patients' medical outcomes. For example, Ulrich has found that surgery patients with a bedside window overlooking trees had more favorable recovery courses than patients overlooking a brick wall. Based on accumulating research in environmental psychophysiology, Ulrich recommends designing hospital environments that foster patient control (including their privacy), encourage social support from family and friends, and provide access to nature and other positive distractions. The field of environmental psychophysiology has developed from the fundamental idea that environment affects function.

Principle 3: Connect Emotionally

Organizations with effective experience management systems understand and respond to the emotional needs of their customers. They orchestrate a series of clues designed to provoke positive emotional reactions, such as joy, awe, interest, affection, and trust. They integrate emotional value into the total experience because consumers are not Spock-like Vulcans who make purchases on the basis of cold logic.

Managing customers' experiences requires awareness of all of their senses throughout the experience. Sight, motion, sound, smell, taste, and touch are direct pathways to customers' emotions. Connecting with customers in a sensory way is crucial to managing positive emotional elements of the experience.

The sensory-loaded experience of buying and consuming Krispy Kreme doughnuts illustrates the power of emotional connections with customers. At a time when consumers are inundated with information on healthy eating, Krispy Kreme's fried doughnut oozing with glaze enticed more than 3000 people to wait in a Denver line extending for three city blocks on opening day. Even the name connects on a sensory level. Everything conspires to evoke a feeling of "delicious decadence."

No logical reason compels a person to stand in a long line for hours to buy a doughnut. But an experience so effectively choreographed and integrated with the product is hard to resist. The performance includes the counter person going into the production area, which is in full view, to box up the customer's dozen "original glazed" doughnuts hot off the line. A neon sign in the window lights up only when "HOT Donuts" are actually coming off the line, further heightening the anticipation. The light almost creates a Pavlovian response that, combined with the tempting smell that's pumped outside, brings customers in off the street like cartoon characters hypnotized by a pleasurable wafting scent. The customer walks out with a warm box, still another sensory clue. With its multi-sensory managed experience, Krispy Kreme makes customers feel good about indulging and forgetting their diets. And yes, the doughnuts taste very good.

MANAGEMENT TOOLS

More than anything else, customer experience management requires customer empathy—seeing what the customer sees, feeling what the customer feels. Organizations don't develop experience management competency overnight. They need to apply specialized tools in the context of a systematic methodology.

An experience audit is used to thoroughly analyze the current customer experience and to illuminate customers' emotional responses to specific clues. Videotape and digital photographs document actual customer experiences and provide the raw data for comprehensive study and categorization of clues. Hours of video are generated—some (with appropriate notification and approval) from pinhole cameras embedded in wrist-watches, handbags, coats, or hats. Additionally, in-depth interviews with customers and employees reveal their feelings about different aspects of an experience and the emotional associations it generates. Emotional strands are defined during an experience audit. An emotional strand is a charting of the emotional highs and lows customers commonly experience in a specific setting or situation. For example, female apparel customers commonly move from an emotional high when spotting a great-looking dress in a store to an emotional low if the dress doesn't fit. A goal of experience management is anticipating customers' emotional highs and lows and designing clues to support customers in their emotional strand.

An experience motif is developed based on findings from the experience audit and the organization's core values and branding strategy. Captured in a few words, the motif becomes the North Star—the foundation and filter for integrating and reconciling all elements of the experience. The motif is the unifying element for every clue in the experience design. One financial institution wanted its customers to feel "recognized, reassured, and engaged," terminology formalized into a motif. Subsequently, only clues that reinforced these three motif watchwords were incorporated into the experience design.

Based on the experience motif and other experience design criteria, clues are developed and translated into a blueprint. Mechanics clues are represented graphically in drawings on the blueprint, and humanics clues are described in employee role performance narratives. These narratives, which capture the tone and texture of desired performance, augment existing job descriptions that typically concern job functions rather than performance of a role. The blueprint and narratives become a critical part of an organization's roadmap for communicating, implementing, monitoring, and measuring the outcomes of an experience management system.

CASE STUDY

The Health and Wellness Center by Doylestown Hospital (Doylestown, Penn.) is a one-of-a-kind healthcare model: a combination clinic, health club, and spa with interactive health design services. Patrons just as frequently visit the center for their daily workout or to browse the bookstore as they do for outpatient surgery, a diabetes check, or their annual mammogram.

Construction of the Health and Wellness Center was completed in spring 2001 and expanded the hospital's market into a nearby, rapidly growing community. Beyond the business motivation was management's deepseated determination to make a positive difference in serving the community's modern healthcare needs. This legacy of community service dates from the turn of the century when an inspired women's group, the Village Improvement Association (VIA), founded Doylestown Hospital, which it still owns and oversees. It remains the only women's club in the United States to own and operate a community hospital.

The mandate for the new Center was to create a distinctive healthcare experience integrating traditional medical services with specialized retail, wellness, and fitness services. This means incorporating medical specialties like cardiology, orthopedics, dentistry, day surgery, and women's diagnostics with a full spa and fitness center, an interactive learning center, a restaurant, and a bookstore.

During the construction phase, senior hospital staff began applying experience management techniques. The resulting experience design became central to the planning and development of the facility. The services provided are related through a distinctive architectural and landscape design.

Connecting Emotionally

An experience audit provided deep insights into the basic emotions that surface in patients while on their health and wellness experience journey. Patients shared their feeling that medical process generally predominates over staff empathy for their personal situation. The experience audit, along with internal strategy sessions, produced an experience motif centered on patrons feeling understood, strengthened, and renewed through every interaction with the Health and Wellness Center.

The Center included only clues that reinforce understanding, strengthening, and renewal in the experience design. For example, in addition to standard amenities, the spa and fitness center are capable of downloading patient profiles sent from physicians and health design services—a clue that signals a unique understanding of that person's needs. Spa personnel will have information that an MS patient's whirlpool cannot exceed a certain temperature. In the fitness center, they will be aware of certain parameters for someone just coming out of cardiac rehab. In women's diagnostics, completion of a mammogram is rewarded with a coupon for the restaurant or bookstore—a strengthening and renewing clue. The meticulous building design adheres to the principles of Feng Shui that focus on energy and revitalization.

Integrating Clues

The center's experience management design specified more than 200 clues derived from the experience motif:

- Seasonal healing gardens surrounding the building, complete with meditation benches, music, and a labyrinth walk
- A 25-foot interior waterfall and pond
- A unique stone and wood atrium surrounding the waterfall that serves as a central and communal gathering point
- Internet hookups, overstuffed chairs, and library-style newspaper and magazine racks throughout the atrium
- A fitness center and spa that provide support to cardiac and orthopedic rehab patients as well as the public
- Health design nurses whose sole role is to help consumers create a customized health plan and then mentor and monitor their journey
- Numerous seminars and community events built around health and wellness
- Mammograms and blood pressure checks available without an appointment
- Beepers allowing clients to wait for appointments or test results in any area of the facility
- A bookstore and lending library centered on wellness and linked to the leading recommended Web sites on disease management and wellness strategies
- Distinguishing staff behaviors ranging from voice inflection to gestures to reinforce the motif

Customizing Healthcare

A key element of the differentiated experience is the Health Design Center, which provides customized, coordinated health and wellness plans. Studies show people place great value in coordinated healthcare and the perceived benefit expands dramatically when a person must deal with multiple conditions. The Health Design Center, available to anyone who desires the experience, provides an effective way of delivering a sense of unity and completeness.

The Health Design Center opened with one nurse and has expanded to three in a year's time. While most of the health design services are on a fee basis and not covered by insurance, customized health designs have become a popular service, with more than 200 generated per month.

No single clue at the Health and Wellness Center provides the magic for a distinctive, preferred experience. The benefit comes in the integrated design and layering of clues that support the Center's experience motif. It's the cumulative effect of the customer's take-away feeling from the experience.

The Center is making a difference. Benchmarked against other high-performing health facilities in the nation, it ranked third out of 357 facilities in its first participation in the national Press Ganey patient satisfaction survey. The Center scored in the 98th percentile in overall satisfaction and in the 99th percentile for "sensitivity to patient needs" and "explanations given by staff."

DELIVERING THE BRAND

An increasing number of experience-oriented executives will soon be changing their understanding of what their brand should be in the future. In fact, they will be changing their very understanding of what "brand" means. Rather than creating a set of messages and images that associate a company and its products with emotional values, experience pioneers will be focused on creating a business that delivers the brand as an experience incorporating these values. And this, we assert, is the real transformation, the real meaning, and the real potential of becoming a customer-centric business.

Reading 3-3

Can a Parallel Private System Reduce Waiting Times in the Public Healthcare System?

CANADIAN HEALTH SERVICES RESEARCH FOUNDATION

In Canada and around the world, public healthcare systems continue to struggle with the problem of long waiting times for some treatments. For those needing these healthcare services, long waiting times can cause patients already sick and in pain to fear they won't receive the care they need. Furthermore, when the media report on long waiting times, Canadians begin to doubt the quality of their healthcare systems.

 Taking the pulse of the public, provincial and federal leaders have vowed to do something about long waiting times, but they face many conflicting suggestions on how to fix the problem. One frequent suggestion is to create a parallel private healthcare system—specifically, allowing private facilities to operate alongside public ones, so that patients who can afford to pay privately do so. Proponents argue that private spending will both increase total funding available for healthcare and free up places in the queue for public services, so that everyone can get faster treatment.

According to these critics, Canada is one of the last countries to resist the logical evolution to a mixed-payer system. It's only a matter of time, they argue, before Canada gets it and joins the rest of the crowd.

THE PROBLEM OF WAITING TIMES

Canada has a long way to go in addressing waiting times, beginning with our understanding of the problem. In order to shorten waiting times, we need to know how many people are waiting for treatment, for how long they're waiting, and which procedures have the longest waits. Most facilities and providers maintain their own lists, but governments to date have failed to provide sufficiently centralized or co-ordinated information, so no one can say how many people in the country—or even in one province—are waiting for a given procedure. Nor is there any way to move people onto a shorter list in another area,[1] although several jurisdictions are trying to fix this.[2, 3, 4]

There is also no agreement on when a wait for treatment starts. Some people say it's when patients get referrals from

---

Mythbusters—Myth: A parallel private system would reduce waiting times in the public system. Myth Busted March 2001. Busted Again! March 2005. *Mythbusters* are prepared by Knowledge Transfer staff at the Canadian Health Services Research Foundation and published only after review by researcher experts on the topic. © CHSRF 2005. The title "Can a Parallel Private System Reduce Waiting Times in the Public Healthcare System?" was created by Harvir S. Bansal for use in this textbook. Reprinted with permission of the Canadian Health Services Research Foundation, February 2007.

their GPs. Some say it's when the specialists decide to treat. Still others say it's when patients are put on hospital waiting lists.5 Without a consensus, people use varying methods to define waiting times. For example, the Fraser Institute uses physicians' opinions of how long they think their patients have to wait to determine waiting times between referral from a general practitioner and treatment.[6] On the other hand, provincial analyses of data on waiting times show that waits are not nearly as long as physicians might think they are.[7]

MORE EVIDENCE AGAINST PARALLEL PRIVATE HEALTHCARE

All of the administrative headaches mask a larger truth—parallel private systems don't cut public waiting lists. In fact, research evidence shows they appear to lengthen waits for healthcare in public systems.

A detailed recent study of how private financing affects public healthcare systems found that countries with parallel public and private healthcare systems have the longest waiting times. For example, England and New Zealand, which have parallel private hospital systems, appear to have larger waiting lists and longer waiting times in the public system than countries with a single-payer system, such as Canada.[8]

Waiting times in England and New Zealand are also longer than in countries such as the Netherlands, where a separate private hospital system exists for the wealthiest citizens, who are not able to use the public system.[8]

Researchers have also looked at the variation in waiting times within countries, based on the co-existence of public and private care. Studies in both Australia and England have found the more care provided in the private sector in a given region, the longer the waiting times for public hospital patients.[9, 10]

This backs up Canadian evidence from the province of Manitoba where, until 1999, patients paid an additional facility fee or "tray fee" if they chose to have cataract surgery in a private facility (the surgery itself was still paid for by the provincial health plan). At the time the fee was in place, the Manitoba researchers found that patients whose surgeons worked only in public facilities could expect a median wait of 10 weeks in 1998/99; however, patients whose surgeons worked in both public and private facilities could expect a median wait of 26 weeks.[7]

One final issue is that parallel private systems may tend to leave expensive cases to the public systems and "cherry pick" patients who are healthier and younger or who have conditions that are easier and cheaper to treat.[11, 12] In Australia, despite rules designed to prevent older patients from automatically paying more, younger people still pay significantly less for their private insurance.[13] Private insurance is also used primarily for non-emergency care; in 2001/02, only eight percent of private hospital admissions in Australia were for emergency care, compared to 42 percent of admissions to public hospitals.[13]

THE PROBLEM OF SCARCE RESOURCES

The mountain of evidence against parallel private healthcare underscores some logical flaws in arguments for it. First, since healthcare practitioners can't be in more than one place at the same time, creating a parallel private system simply takes badly needed doctors and nurses out of our public hospitals. Given that most people believe we already have a shortage of both, it's hard to see how removing them from the public system will help alleviate public waits.[1] Second, since doctors earn more in the private sector, they have what economists call a "perverse incentive" to keep public waiting lists long, to encourage patients to pay for private care.[9]

A parallel private system can provide faster care—to those with deeper pockets. However, it seriously compromises access for those waiting for care in the public system, and contradicts one of the features of public healthcare of which Canadians are most proud: that citizens should receive care based on their need, not on their ability to pay.[14]

References

1. Sanmartin C et al. 2000. "Waiting for medical services in Canada: lots of heat, but little light." Canadian Medical Association Journal; 162(9): 1305–1310.
2. Cardiac Care Network of Ontario. 2005. "About CCN." http://www.ccn.on.ca/mission.html.
3. Saskatchewan Surgical Care Network. 2005. "About SSCN." http://www.sasksurgery.ca/about-sscn.html.
4. Western Canada Waiting List Project. 2005. "About WCWL." http://www.wcwl.ca/about/synopsis/.
5. Sanmartin C. 2003. "Toward Standard Definitions for Waiting Times." Healthcare Management Forum; Summer: 49–53.
6. Esmail N and M Walker. 2004. "Waiting your turn: Hospital waiting lists in Canada (14th edition)." http://www.fraserinstitute.ca/shared/readmore.asp?sNav=pb&id=705.
7. DeCoster C et al. 2000. "Waiting Times for Surgery: 1997/98 and 1998/99 Update." Manitoba Centre for Health Policy and Evaluation. http://www.umanitoba.ca/centres/mchp/reports/pdfs/waits2.pdf.
8. Hughes Tuohy C et al. 2004. "How does private financing affect public health care systems? Marshaling the evidence from OECD nations." Journal of Health Politics, Policy and Law; 29(3): 359–396.
9. Duckett SJ. 2005. "Private care and public waiting." Australian Health Review; 29(1): 87–93.

10. Besley T et al. 1998. "Public and private health insurance in the UK." European Economic Review; 42(3-5): 491–497.

11. Schokkaert E and C Van de Voorde. 2003. "Belgium: risk adjustment and financial responsibility in a centralised system." Health Policy; 65(1): 5–19.

12. Gonzalez P. 2004. "On a policy of transferring public patients to private practice." Health Economics; online pre-publication October 20.

13. Vaithianathan R. 2004. "A critique of the private health insurance regulations." Australian Economic Review; 37(3): 257–70.

14. Abelson J et al. 2004. "Canadians confront health care reform." Health Affairs; 23(3): 186–193.

PART 4

Implementing Profitable Service Strategies

Part 4 focuses on four key issues in implementation. First, we recognize that achieving profitability requires creating relationships with customers from the right segments and then finding ways to build and reinforce their loyalty. Second, developing a strategy for effective complaint handling and service recovery often determines whether a firm can build a loyal customer base or has to watch its customers take their business elsewhere.

Third, productivity and quality are both necessary and related ingredients for financial success in services. Productivity is concerned with bringing down costs, and quality increases revenues as a result of greater customer satisfaction.

The final chapter addresses the challenge of how organizations can remain competitive and forward-looking. A firm must be prepared to make ongoing, proactive changes not only in its marketing but also in its operations and human resources stategies. The calibre of managerial leadership determines whether a firm can be a service leader in its industry.

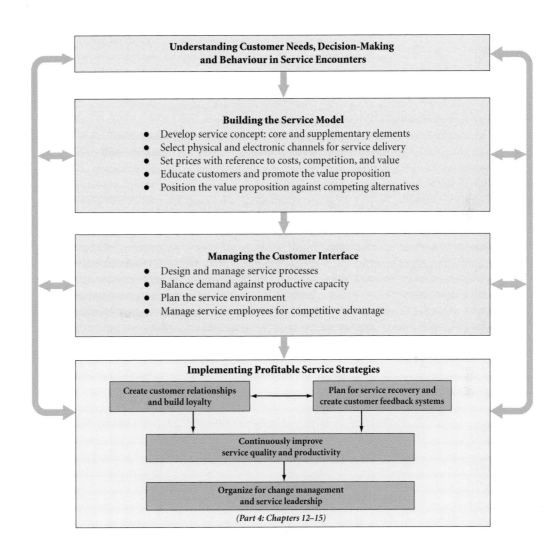

Understanding Customer Needs, Decision-Making and Behaviour in Service Encounters

Building the Service Model
- Develop service concept: core and supplementary elements
- Select physical and electronic channels for service delivery
- Set prices with reference to costs, competition, and value
- Educate customers and promote the value proposition
- Position the value proposition against competing alternatives

Managing the Customer Interface
- Design and manage service processes
- Balance demand against productive capacity
- Plan the service environment
- Manage service employees for competitive advantage

Implementing Profitable Service Strategies

Create customer relationships and build loyalty

Plan for service recovery and create customer feedback systems

Continuously improve service quality and productivity

Organize for change management and service leadership

(Part 4: Chapters 12–15)

CHAPTER **12**

Managing Relationships and Building Loyalty

The first step in managing a loyalty-based business system is finding and acquiring the right customers.

—Frederick F. Reichheld

Strategy first, then CRM.

—Steven S. Ramsey

Targeting, acquiring, and retaining the "right" customers is at the core of many successful service firms. In Chapter 7 we discussed segmentation and positioning. In this chapter, we emphasize the importance of carefully focusing on desirable, loyal customers within the chosen segments, and then taking pains to build and maintain their loyalty through well-conceived relationship-marketing strategies. The objective is to build relationships and to develop loyal customers who will do a growing volume of business with the firm in the future.

Building relationships is a challenge, especially when a firm has many, often millions of customers, who interact with the firm in many different ways (from email and websites to call centres and face-to-face interactions). When implemented well, customer relationship management (CRM) systems provide managers with the tools to understand their customers and to tailor their service, cross-selling, and retention efforts, often on a one-on-one basis.

In this chapter, we explore the following questions:

1. Why is customer loyalty an important driver of profitability for service firms?
2. Why is it so important for service firms to target the "right" customers?
3. How can a firm calculate the life-time value of its customers?
4. What strategies are associated with the concept of relationship marketing and the Wheel of Loyalty?
5. How can tiering of service, loyalty bonds, and membership programs help in building customer loyalty?
6. What is the role of CRM systems in delivering customized services and building loyalty?

THE SEARCH FOR CUSTOMER LOYALTY

Loyalty is an old-fashioned word that has traditionally been used to describe fidelity and enthusiastic devotion to a country, cause, or individual. More recently, in a business context, it has been used to describe a customer's willingness to continue patronizing a firm over the long term (preferably on an exclusive basis), and to recommend the firm's products to friends and associates. Customer loyalty extends beyond behaviour, and includes preference, liking, and future intentions.

"Few companies think of customers as annuities," says Frederick Reichheld, author of *The Loyalty Effect*, and a major researcher in this field.[1] And yet that is precisely what a loyal customer can mean to a firm—a consistent source of revenue over a period of many years. The active management of the customer base and the cultivation of customer loyalty are also referred to collectively as customer asset management.[2]

"Defector" was a nasty word during the Cold War. It described disloyal people who sold out their own side and went over to the enemy. Even when they defected toward "our" side, they were still suspect. Today, in a marketing context, the term defection is used to describe customers who drop off a company's radar screen and transfer their brand loyalty to another supplier. Reichheld and Sasser popularized the term "zero defections," which they describe as keeping every customer the company can profitably serve.[3] Not only does a rising defection rate indicate that something is wrong with quality (or that competitors offer better value), it may also be a leading indicator and signal a coming fall in profits. Large customers don't necessarily disappear overnight. They may signal their mounting dissatisfaction by steadily reducing their purchases and shifting part of their business elsewhere.

Why Is Customer Loyalty Important to a Firm's Profitability?

How much is a loyal customer worth in terms of profits? In a classic study, Reichheld and Sasser analyzed the profit per customer in different service businesses, categorized by the number of years that a customer had been with the firm.[4] They found that the longer customers remained with a firm in each of these industries, the more profitable they became. Annual profits per customer, which have been indexed over a five-year period for easier comparison, are summarized in Figure 12.1. The industries studied (with average profits from a first-year customer shown in parentheses) were credit cards (US$30), industrial laundry (US$144), industrial distribution (US$45), and automobile servicing (US$25). Similar loyalty effects were also uncovered in the internet context, where it typically took more than a year to recoup acquisition costs, and profits increased as customers stayed longer with the firm.[5]

Underlying this profit growth, say Reichheld and Sasser, are four factors working to the supplier's advantage to create incremental profits. In order of magnitude at the end of seven years, these factors are

1. *Profit derived from increased purchases* (or, in a credit card or banking environment, higher account balances). Over time, business customers often grow larger and so need to purchase in greater quantities. Individuals may also purchase more as their

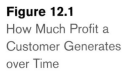

Figure 12.1
How Much Profit a Customer Generates over Time

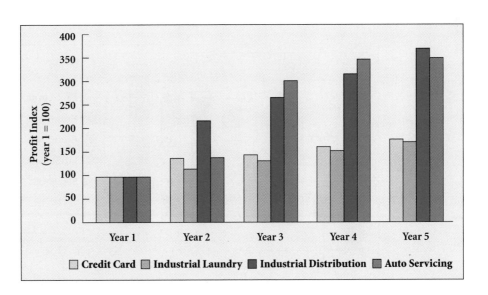

Source: Based on reanalysis of data from Frederick R. Reichheld and W. Earl Sasser, Jr., "Zero Defections: Quality Comes to Services," *Harvard Business Review* 68/5 (September–October 1990): 105–11.

families grow or as they become more affluent. Both types of customers may decide to consolidate their purchases with a single supplier who provides high-quality service.

2. *Profit from reduced operating costs.* As customers become more experienced, they make fewer demands on the supplier (for instance, less need for information and assistance). They may also make fewer mistakes when involved in operational processes, thus contributing to greater productivity.

3. *Profit from referrals to other customers.* Positive word-of-mouth recommendations are like free sales and advertising, saving the firm from having to invest as much money in these activities.

4. *Profit from price premium.* New customers often benefit from introductory promotional discounts, whereas long-term customers are more likely to pay regular prices, and when highly satisfied are even willing to pay a price premium.[6] Moreover, when customers trust a supplier they may be more willing to pay higher prices at peak periods or for express work.

Figure 12.2 shows the relative contribution of each of these different factors over a seven-year period, based on an analysis of 19 different product categories (both goods and services). Reichheld argues that the economic benefits of customer loyalty noted above often explain why one firm is more profitable than a competitor. Furthermore, the upfront costs of attracting these buyers can be amortized over many years.

Assessing the Value of a Loyal Customer

It would be a mistake to assume that loyal customers are always more profitable than those making one-time transactions.[7] On the cost side, not all types of services incur heavy promotional expenditures to attract a new customer. Sometimes, it is more important to invest in a good retail location that will attract walk-in traffic. Unlike banks, insurance companies, and other "membership" organizations that incur costs for review of applications and account setup, many service firms face no such costs when a new customer first seeks to make a purchase. On the revenue side, loyal customers may not necessarily spend more than one-time buyers, and in some instances they may even expect price discounts.

Finally, revenue does not necessarily increase with time for all types of customers.[8] In most mass-market B2C services like banking, cellphone services, or hospitality, customers can't negotiate prices. However, in many B2B contexts, large customers have significant bargaining power and therefore will nearly always try to negotiate lower prices when contracts come up for renewal, which forces suppliers to share the cost savings resulting from doing business with a large, loyal customer. DHL has found that although its major

Figure 12.2

Why Customers Become More Profitable Over Time

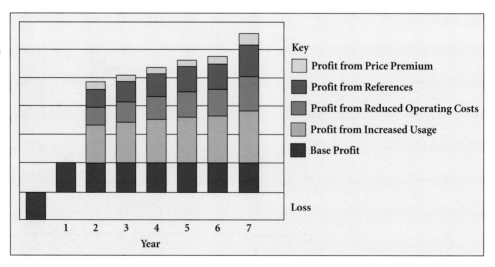

Source: Why Customers Are More Profitable Over Time from Freferick J. Reichheld and W. Earl Sasser Jr. "Zero Defections: Quality Comes to Services," *Harvard Business Review* 73 (Sep.–Oct. 1990): p. 108. Reprinted by permission of Harvard Business School.

WORKSHEET
CALCULATING CUSTOMER LIFETIME VALUE

Calculating customer value is an inexact science that is subject to a variety of assumptions. You may want to try varying these assumptions to see how it affects the final figures. Generally speaking, revenues per customer are easier to track on an individualized basis than are the associated costs of serving a customer, unless (1) no individual records are kept and/or (2) the accounts served are very large and all account-related costs are individually documented and assigned.

Acquisition Revenues Less Costs

If individual account records are kept, the initial application fee paid and initial purchase (if relevant) should be found in these records. Costs, by contrast, may have to be based on average data. For instance, the marketing cost of acquiring a new client can be calculated by dividing the total marketing costs (advertising, promotions, selling, etc.) devoted toward acquiring new customers by the total number of new customers acquired during the same period. If each acquisition takes place over an extended period of time, you may want to build in a lagged effect between when marketing expenditures are incurred and when new customers come on board. The cost of credit checks—where relevant—must be divided by the number of new customers, not the total number of applicants, because some applicants will probably fail this hurdle. Account set-up costs will also be an average figure in most organizations.

Annual Revenues and Costs

If annual sales, account fees, and service fees are documented on an individual-account basis, account revenue streams (except referrals) can be easily identified. The first priority is to segment your customer base by the length of its relationship with your firm. Depending on the sophistication and precision of your firm's records, annual costs in each category may be directly assigned to an individual account holder or averaged for all account holders in that age category.

Value of Referrals

Computing the value of referrals requires a variety of assumptions. To get started, you may need to conduct surveys to determine (1) what percentage of new customers claim that they were influenced by a recommendation from another customer and (2) what other marketing activities also drew the firm to that individual's attention. From these two items, estimates can be made of what percentage of the credit for all new customers should be assigned to referrals. Additional research may be needed to clarify whether long-standing customers are more likely to be effective recommenders than more recent ones.

Net Present Value

Calculating net present value (NPV) from a future profit stream will require choice of an appropriate annual discount figure. (This could reflect estimates of future inflation rates.) It also requires assessment of how long the average relationship lasts. The NPV of a customer, then, is the sum of the anticipated annual profit on each customer for the projected relationship lifetime, suitably discounted each year into the future.

ACQUISITION			YEAR 1	YEAR 2	YEAR 3	YEAR n
Initial Revenue		*Annual Revenues*				
Application fee[a]	____	Annual account fee[a]	____	____	____	____
Initial purchase[a]	____	Sales	____	____	____	____
		Service fees[a]	____	____	____	____
		Value of referrals[b]	____	____	____	____
Total Revenues	____		____	____	____	____
Initial Costs	____	*Annual Costs*				
Marketing	____	Account management	____	____	____	____
Credit check[a]	____	Cost of sales	____	____	____	____
Account setup[a]	____	Write-offs (e.g., bad debts)	____	____	____	____
Less total costs	____		____	____	____	____
Net Profit (Loss)	____		____	____	____	____

[a]If applicable.

[b]Anticipated profits from each new customer referred (could be limited to the first year or expressed as the net present value of the estimated future stream of profits through year n); this value could be negative if an unhappy customer starts to spread negative word of mouth that causes existing customers to defect.

accounts generate significant amounts of business, they yield below-average margins. In contrast, DHL's smaller, less powerful accounts show significantly higher profitability.[9]

Research published in 2003 has also shown that the profit impact of a customer can vary dramatically depending on the stage of the product life cycle the service is in. For instance, referrals of satisfied customers and negative word of mouth of defected customers have a much higher profit impact in the early stages of the product life cycle than in later stages.[10]

One of the challenges that you will probably face in your work is to determine the costs and revenues associated with serving customers from different market segments at different points in their customer life cycles, and to predict future profitability. For insights on how to calculate customer value, see the worksheet for calculating customer lifetime value.[11]

The Gap between Actual and Potential Customer Value

For profit-seeking firms, the potential profitability of a customer should be a key driver in marketing strategy. As Alan Grant and Leonard Schlesinger declare: "Achieving the full profit potential of each customer relationship should be the fundamental goal of every business . . . Even using conservative estimates, the gap between most companies' current and full potential performance is enormous."[12] They suggest analysis of the following gaps between the actual and potential value of customers:

- What is the current purchasing behaviour of customers in each target segment? What would be the impact on sales and profits if they exhibited the ideal behaviour profile of (1) buying all services offered by the firm, (2) using these to the exclusion of any purchases from competitors, and (3) paying full price?

- How long, on average, do customers remain with the firm? What impact would it have if they remained customers for life?

As we showed earlier, the profitability of a customer often increases over time. Management's task is to design and implement marketing programs that increase loyalty—including share of wallet, upselling, and cross-selling—and identify the reasons why customers defect and then take corrective action.

UNDERSTANDING THE CUSTOMER–FIRM RELATIONSHIP

A fundamental distinction exists between strategies intended to bring about a single transaction and those designed to create extended relationships with customers. Repeated transactions form the necessary basis for a relationship between customer and supplier, although we should not assume that every customer who uses a service with some frequency wishes to engage in an active relationship.

Relationship Marketing

The term *relationship marketing* has been widely used to describe marketing in the context of an active, ongoing relationship with a customer (rather than the one-off relationship with a customer who only needs to use the service once, or very occasionally), but until recently it was only loosely defined. Research by Nicole Coviello, Rod Brodie, and Hugh Munro suggest that there are, in fact, four distinct types of marketing involved: transactional marketing and three categories of what they call relational marketing: database marketing, interaction marketing, and network marketing.[13]

Transactional Marketing A transaction is an event during which an exchange of value takes place between two parties. One transaction, or even a series of transactions, don't necessarily constitute a relationship, which requires mutual recognition and knowledge between the parties. When each transaction between a customer and a supplier is essentially discrete and anonymous, with no long-term record kept of a customer's purchasing history, and little or no mutual recognition between customer and employees, then no meaningful marketing relationship can be said to exist. This is true for many services, which can range from passenger transport to food service or visits to a cinema, where each purchase and use is a discrete event.

Database Marketing   In database marketing, the focus is still on the market transaction but now includes information exchange. Marketers rely on information technology, usually in the form of a database, to form a relationship with targeted customers and retain their patronage over time. However, the nature of these relationships is often not a close one, with communication being driven and managed by the seller. Technology is used to (1) identify and build a database of current and potential customers, (2) deliver differentiated messages based on consumers' characteristics and preferences, and (3) track each relationship to monitor the cost of acquiring the consumer and the lifetime value of the resulting purchases.[14] Although technology can be used to personalize the relationship, relations remain somewhat distant. Utility services such as electricity, gas, and cable TV are good examples.

Interaction Marketing   A closer relationship often exists in situations where there is face-to-face interaction between customers and representatives of the supplier (or "ear-to-ear" interaction by phone). Although the service itself remains important, value is added by people and social processes. Interactions may include negotiations and sharing of insights in both directions. This type of relationship has long existed in many local environments ranging from community banks to dentistry, where buyer and seller know and trust each other. It is also commonly found in many business-to-business services. Both the firm and the customer are prepared to invest resources to develop a mutually beneficial relationship. This investment may include time spent sharing and recording information.

As service companies grow larger and make increasing use of technologies such as interactive websites and self-service equipment, maintaining meaningful relationships with customers becomes a significant marketing challenge. Firms with large customer bases find it increasingly difficult to build and maintain meaningful relationships through call centres, websites, and other mass-delivery channels (Figure 12.3).

Network Marketing   We often say that someone is a "good networker" because he or she is able to put individuals in touch with others who have a mutual interest. This type of marketing occurs primarily in a B2B context, where firms commit resources to

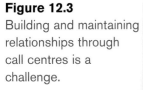

Figure 12.3
Building and maintaining relationships through call centres is a challenge.

developing positions in a network of relationships with customers, distributors, suppliers, the media, consultants, trade associations, government agencies, competitors, and even the customers of their customers. There's often a team of individuals within the supplier's firm who must collaborate to provide effective service to a parallel team within the customer's organization.

The four types of marketing described above are not necessarily mutually exclusive. A firm may have transactions with some customers who have neither the desire nor the need to make future purchases, while working hard to move others up the loyalty ladder.[15] Evert Gummesson identifies no fewer than 30 types of relationships. He advocates *total relationship marketing*, describing it as

> ... marketing based on relationships, networks, and interaction, recognizing that marketing is embedded in the total management of the networks of the selling organization, the market, and society. It is directed to long-term, win–win relationships with individual customers, and value is jointly created between the parties involved.[16]

Creating "Membership" Relationships

Ideally we would like to create ongoing relationships with our customers. This is easier where customers receive service on a continuing basis. However, even where the transactions are themselves discrete, there may still be an opportunity to create an ongoing relationship, as we will discuss later in the chapter in the context of loyalty reward programs.

The nature of the current relationship can be analyzed by asking first: does the supplier enter into a formal "membership" relationship with customers, as with telephone subscriptions, banking, and the family doctor? Or is there no defined relationship? And second: is the service delivered on a continuous basis, as in insurance, broadcasting, and police protection? Or is each transaction recorded and charged separately? Table 12.1 shows the matrix resulting from this categorization, with examples in each category.

A *membership relationship* is a formalized relationship between the firm and an identifiable customer, which may offer special benefits to both parties. Services involving discrete transactions can be transformed into membership relationships either by selling the service in bulk (for instance, a theatre series subscription or a commuter ticket on public transportation) or by offering extra benefits to customers who choose to register with the firm (loyalty programs for hotels, airlines, and credit cards issued by banks fall into this category). The advantage to the service organization of having membership relationships is that it knows who its current customers are and, usually, what use they make of the services offered. This can be valuable information for segmentation purposes if good records are kept and the data are readily accessible for analysis. Knowing the identities and addresses of current customers enables the organization to make effective use of direct

---

Table 12.1 Relationships with Customers

| | TYPE OF RELATIONSHIP BETWEEN THE SERVICE ORGANIZATION AND ITS CUSTOMERS | |
NATURE OF SERVICE DELIVERY	MEMBERSHIP RELATIONSHIP	NO FORMAL RELATIONSHIP
Continuous delivery of service	Insurance Cable TV subscription College enrolment Banking	Radio station Police protection Lighthouse Public highway
Discrete transactions	Long-distance calls from subscriber phone Theatre series subscription Travel on commuter ticket Repair under warranty Health treatment for HMO member	Car rental Mail service Toll highway Pay phone Movie theatre Public transportation Restaurant

mail (including email), telephone selling, and personal sales calls—all highly targeted methods of marketing communication. In turn, members can be given access to special numbers or even designated account managers to facilitate their communications with the firm.

THE WHEEL OF LOYALTY

Building customer loyalty is difficult. Just try and think of all the service firms you yourself are loyal to. Most people cannot think of more than perhaps a handful of firms they truly like (i.e., to which they give a high share of "heart") and to which they are committed to going back (i.e., they give a high share of wallet). This shows that although firms spend enormous amounts of money and effort on loyalty initiatives, they are often not successful in building true customer loyalty.

We use the "Wheel of Loyalty" shown in Figure 12.4 as an organizing framework for thinking about how to build customer loyalty. It comprises three sequential strategies.

First, you need a solid foundation for creating customer loyalty, which includes having the right portfolio of customer segments, attracting the right customers, tiering the service, and delivering high levels of satisfaction.

Second, to truly build loyalty, a firm needs to develop close bonds with its customers, which either deepen the relationship through cross-selling and bundling, or add value to the customer through loyalty rewards and higher-level bonds.

Third, service marketers should be working to identify and eliminate the factors that result in "churn"—the loss of existing customers and the need to replace them with new ones. We discuss each of the components of the Wheel of Loyalty in the following sections.

Figure 12.4
The Wheel of Loyalty

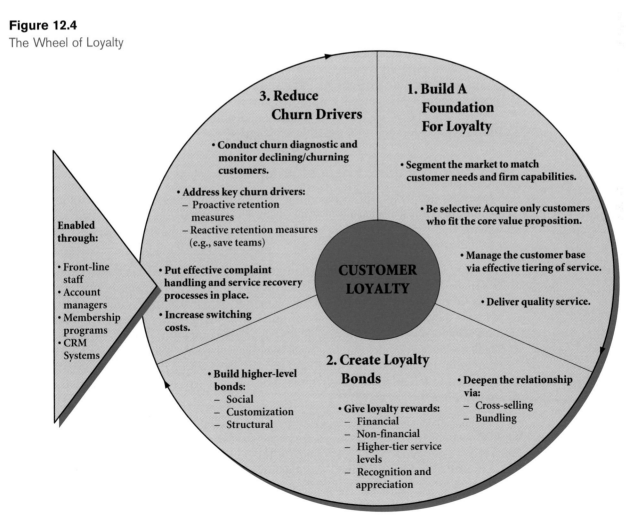

Many elements are involved in creating long-term customer relationships and loyalty. In Chapter 7, we discussed segmentation and positioning. In this section, we emphasize the importance of carefully focusing on desirable customers, and then taking pains to build their loyalty through well-conceived relationship-marketing strategies, including delivery of quality service.

Good Relationships Start with a Good Fit between Customer Needs and Company Capabilities

The process starts with identifying and targeting the right customers. "Who should we be serving?" is a question that every service business needs to raise periodically. Customers often differ widely in terms of needs. They also differ in terms of the value they can contribute to a company. Not all customers offer a good fit with the organization's capabilities, delivery technologies, and strategic direction.

Companies need to be selective about the segments they target if they want to build successful customer relationships. In this section, we emphasize the importance of serving a portfolio of several carefully chosen target segments, and of taking pains to build and maintain their loyalty.

Matching customers to the firm's capabilities is vital. Managers must think carefully about how customer needs relate to such operational elements as speed and quality, the times when service is available, the firm's capacity to serve many customers simultaneously, and the physical features and appearance of service facilities. They also need to consider how well their service personnel can meet the expectations of specific types of customers, in terms of both personal style and technical competence.[17] Finally, they need to ask themselves whether their company can match or exceed competing services that are directed at the same types of customers.

The result of carefully targeting customers by matching the company's capabilities and strengths with customers' needs should be a superior service offering—at least in the eyes of those customers who value what the firm has to offer. As Frederick Reichheld said, " . . . the result should be a win–win situation, where profits are earned through the success and satisfaction of customers, and not at their expense."[18]

Searching for Value, Not Just Volume

Too many service firms still focus on the *number* of customers they serve without giving sufficient attention to the *value* of each customer. Generally speaking, heavy users who buy more frequently and in larger volumes are more profitable than occasional users. Roger Hallowell makes this point nicely in a discussion of banking:

> A bank's population of customers undoubtedly contains individuals who either cannot be satisfied, given the service levels and pricing the bank is capable of offering, or will never be profitable, given their banking activity (their use of resources relative to the revenue they supply). Any bank would be wise to target and serve only those customers whose needs it can meet better than its competitors in a profitable manner. These are the customers who are most likely to remain with that bank for long periods, who will purchase multiple products and services, who will recommend that bank to their friends and relations, and who may be the source of superior returns to the bank's shareholders.[19]

Relationship customers are, by definition, not buying services simply as a commodity. Service customers whose purchases are based strictly on lowest price (a minority in most markets) are not good target customers for relationship marketing in the first place. They are deal-prone, and continuously seek the lowest price on offer.

Loyalty leaders are picky about acquiring only the right customers, which are those for whom their firms have been designed to deliver the best value. Acquiring the right customers can bring in long-term revenues, continued growth from referrals, and enhanced satisfaction from employees whose daily jobs are improved when they can deal with appreciative customers. Attracting the wrong customers typically results in costly churn, a diminished company reputation, and disillusioned employees. Ironically, it is often the firms that are highly focused and selective in their acquisition, rather than those that focus on unbridled acquisition, that grow fastest over long periods.[20] Best Practice in Action 12.1 shows how several Canadian mutual fund companies are designing their products to attract and retain the right customers for their businesses.

Managers shouldn't assume that the "right customers" are always high spenders. Depending on the service business model, the right customers can come from a large group of people that no other supplier is doing a good job of serving. Many firms have built successful strategies serving customer segments that were neglected by established players who didn't perceive them as sufficiently "valuable." Examples of such firms include Enterprise Rent-A-Car, which targeted customers who need a temporary replacement car and avoided the more traditional segment of business travellers pursued by its principal competitors; Charles Schwab, which focused on retail stock buyers; and Paychex, which provides small businesses with payroll and HR services.[21] Success has also come to Canadian firms that have adopted this strategy, in B2C as well as B2B settings. Examples include Meritas Mutual Funds (www.meritas.ca), which focuses on retail investors and helps them "join beliefs with deeds using the tools of socially responsible investing"; and High Road Communications (www.highroad.com), a public relations agency that focuses exclusively on serving "technology and digital lifestyle companies."

Different segments offer different value for a service firm. Like investments, some types of customers may be more profitable than others in the short term, but others may have greater potential for long-term growth. Similarly, the spending patterns of some customers may be stable over time, while others may be more cyclical, spending heavily in boom times but cutting back sharply in recessions. A wise marketer seeks a mix of segments in order to reduce the risks associated with volatility.[22]

In many cases, David Maister emphasizes, marketing is about getting *better* business, not just *more* business.[23] For instance, the calibre of a professional firm is measured by the type of clients it serves and the nature of the tasks on which it works. Volume alone is no measure of excellence, sustainability, or profitability. In professional services, such as consulting firms or legal partnerships, the mix of business attracted may play an important role in both defining the firm and providing a suitable mix of assignments for staff members at different levels in the organization.

Managing the Customer Base through Effective Tiering of Service

Marketers should adopt a strategic approach to retaining, upgrading, and even terminating customers. Customer retention involves developing long-term, cost-effective links with customers for the mutual benefit of both parties, but these efforts need not necessarily target all the customers in a firm with the same level of intensity. Recent research has confirmed that most firms have different tiers of customers in terms of profitability, and that these tiers often have quite different service expectations and needs. According to Valarie Zeithaml, Roland Rust, and Katharine Lemon, it's critical that service firms should understand the needs of customers within different profitability tiers and adjust their service levels accordingly.[24]

Just as service product categories can be tiered to reflect the level of value included (see Chapter 7, p. 195), so can groups of customers. In the latter instance, customer tiers can be developed around different levels of profit contribution, needs (including sensitivities to variables such as price, comfort, and speed), and identifiable personal profiles such as demographics. Zeithaml, Rust, and Lemon illustrate this principle through a four-level pyramid (Figure 12.5).

- *Platinum.* These customers constitute a very small percentage of a firm's customer base. They are heavy users and contribute a large share of the profits generated. Typically, this segment is less price-sensitive, but expects the highest service levels in return, and is likely to be willing to invest in and try new services.

Best Practice in Action 12.1

Targeting the Socially Responsible Investors with Ethical Funds

Gabriella Catolino has long been a passionate advocate of socially responsible investing (SRI), which fits seamlessly with her outlook on the world. "I was brought up to have a strong and healthy respect for people . . . and social justice issues," says the London, Ontario-based executive director of the St. Peter's Seminary Foundation. "I believe using investment screens that promote human rights, good employee working environments, and environmental care, and that guard against the support and growth of negative things like pornography, nuclear war, and weapons creation can only help get us closer to that idyllic world I envision." That's a key reason why Catolino, who deals with Meritas Mutual Funds, a company that focuses exclusively on SRI, has all her RRSP investments tied up in SRI-related funds. The other fact that pleases her is the return of close to 20 percent she earned on that portfolio over the past year. "I think I've probably done better this past year than at any other time in my RRSP," she says.

Catolino has discovered what a growing number of other SRI investors have found: that investing with a conscience and investing to earn a decent return for retirement need not be mutually exclusive. "The fog is beginning to clear on the myth you can't invest in a way that takes into account environmental considerations, human rights or [other issues] and still make money. That myth is dissipating—not as quickly as I'd like—but it is dissipating," says Michael Jantzi, president and founder of Toronto-based Michael Jantzi Research Inc., an independent investment research firm.

SRI-related funds are also growing in popularity in the corporate world, as companies respond to the public demand for investments that reflect the promotion of a healthier society. For several years, there has been a growing belief that true profitability encompasses a "triple bottom line"—namely environmental, social, and financial performance. Some companies, such as the Ethical Funds Co. and Real Assets Investment Management Inc., both subsidiaries of Vancouver City Savings Credit Union, as well as Meritas Mutual Funds based in Cambridge, Ontario, offer investments that are exclusively SRI- related. Real Assets manages its global equity-based Social Leaders Fund and Social Impact Balanced Fund. Meritas offers the Balanced Portfolio Fund, Canadian Bond Fund, International Equity Fund, and Money Market Fund, among others. Other firms, such as Toronto-based Acuity Funds Ltd. and Philips, Hager & North Investment Management Ltd. (PH&N) of Vancouver, offer specific SRI funds and other investments, in addition to non-SRI vehicles. Acuity offers three Clean Environment and two Social Values mutual funds. PH&N

has a family of four funds within its Community Values Funds Family. Its component investments are selected based on a range of social and environmental factors.

According to the Social Investment Organization's Social Investment Review, there were just over $65 billion in assets managed according to social responsibility guidelines in June 2004, up 27 percent from two years earlier. They represented 3.6 percent of the retail mutual fund market and the institutional investment market. "Consumers are becoming more conscious of the social and environmental consequences of their decisions," says Eugene Ellmen, executive director of the organization, a Canadian network that promotes the integration of social responsibility and environmental sustainability with financial investment. This affects both RRSP and registered retirement income fund (RRIF) investments, since many mutual funds wind up in registered retirement plans. Of the approximately $100 million in assets that Meritas has accumulated since it began operations in 2001, for example, two-thirds is invested in client RRSPs.

What issues do SRI investors deem to be the most important? Experts say social and environmental issues, as well as worker rights, have always been major concerns. But over the past five years—particularly since highly publicized business failures of giant corporations like Enron and WorldCom—corporate governance matters, such as audit committee independence and separation of duties between the board of directors and senior management, have also faced greater scrutiny. Screens around alcohol and tobacco, military involvement and gambling are also a concern for many clients, says Gary Hawton, chief executive officer of Meritas Mutual Funds.

A national survey conducted in November 2005 by GlobeScan Inc., a Toronto-based public opinion and stakeholder research company, revealed that 69 percent of Canadians would be very likely (46 percent) or somewhat likely (23 percent) to deliberately avoid investing in a company or specific fund they knew was not socially or environmentally responsible.

But it would be hard for all of them to act on their convictions because many Canadians don't have enough knowledge about what constitutes responsible or irresponsible corporate behaviour, says GlobeScan vice-president Chris Coulter. "In terms of ethical consumerism, overall these are still early days," he says.

Source: Jeff Buckstein, "Ethical funds earn decent returns," *Edmonton Journal* (February 15, 2006): H.6. Material reprinted with the express permission of CanWest News Service, a CanWest Partnership

- *Gold.* The gold tier includes a larger percentage of customers than the platinum, but individual customers contribute less profit than platinum customers. They tend to be slightly more price sensitive and less committed to the firm.

- *Iron.* These customers provide the bulk of the customer base. Their numbers give the firm economies of scale. Hence, they are often important because they allow a firm to build and maintain the capacity level and infrastructure needed for serving gold and platinum customers. However, each individual iron customer is often only marginally profitable. Their level of business is not sufficiently substantial for special treatment.

- *Lead.* Customers in this tier tend to generate low revenues for a firm, but often still require the same level of service as iron customers, which turns them into a loss-making segment from a firm's perspective.

The precise characteristics of customer tiers vary, of course, from one type of business to another, and even between firms. Service Perspectives 12.1 provides an illustration from the marketing research industry.

Customer tiers are typically based on profitability and service needs. Instead of providing the same level of service to all customers, each segment receives a service level that is customized to its requirements, and to its value to the firm providing the service. For example, the platinum tier will be provided some exclusive benefits, which are not available to other segments. The benefit levels for platinum and gold customers are often designed with retention in mind, because these customers are the ones competitors would like to entice to switch.

Marketing efforts can be used to encourage an increased volume of purchases, upgrading the type of service used, or cross-selling additional services to any of the four tiers. However, these efforts have different thrusts for the different tiers, as their needs, usage behaviour, and spending patterns are usually very different. Among segments where the firm already has a high share of wallet, the focus should be on nurturing, defending, and retaining these customers, potentially via loyalty programs.[25]

For lead-tier customers, the options are to either migrate them to the iron segment or to terminate them. Migration can be achieved via a combination of strategies, including base fees and price increases. Imposing a minimum fee that is waived when a certain level of revenue is generated may encourage customers who use several suppliers to consolidate their transactions with a single provider.

Figure 12.5

The Customer Pyramid

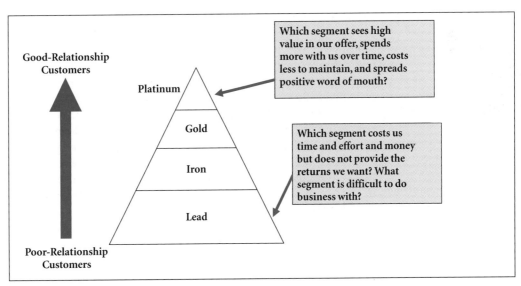

Service Perspectives 12.1

Tiering the Customers of a Market Research Agency

Tiering its clients helped a leading market research agency to better understand its customers (though note that, in this case, the names given to each tier were for internal use only, not an advertised part of the agency's public offering). The agency defined *platinum clients* as large accounts that were not only willing to plan a certain amount of research work during the year, but also able to commit to the timing, scope, and nature of their projects, which made capacity management and project planning much easier for the research firm. The acquisition costs for projects sold to these clients were only 2 percent to 5 percent of project values (as compared to as much as 25 percent for clients who required extensive proposal work and project-by-project bidding). Platinum accounts were also more willing to try new services, and to buy a wider range of services from their preferred provider. These customers were generally very satisfied with the research agency's work and were willing to act as references to potential new clients.

Gold accounts had a similar profile to platinum clients, except that they were more price sensitive, and were more inclined to spread their budgets across several firms. Although these accounts had been clients for many years, they were not willing to commit their research work for a year in advance even though the research firm would have been able to offer them better quality and priority in capacity allocation.

Iron accounts spent moderate amounts on research, and commissioned work on a project basis. Selling costs were high, as these firms tended to send out requests-for-proposals (RFPs) to a number of firms for all their projects. They sought the lowest price, and often did not allow for sufficient time for the research firm to perform a good-quality job.

Lead accounts conducted only isolated, low-cost projects that tended to be "quick and dirty" in nature, with little opportunity for the research firm to add value or to apply its skill sets appropriately. Sales costs were high as the client typically invited several firms to quote. Furthermore, because these firms were inexperienced in conducting research and in working with research agencies, selling a project often took several meetings and required multiple revisions to the proposal. Lead accounts also tended to be high maintenance, as they did not understand research work well; they often changed project parameters, scope, and deliverables midstream, and then expected the research agency to absorb the cost of any rework, thus further reducing the profitability of the engagement.

Source: Adapted from Valarie A. Zeithaml, Roland T. Rust, and Katharine N. Lemon, "The Customer Pyramid: Creating and Serving Profitable Customers," *California Management Review* 43/4 (Summer 2001): 127–28.

There may be opportunities to cut service costs to those customers. Customer behaviour can be shaped in ways that reduces the cost of serving them; for instance, transaction charges for electronic channels may be priced lower than for people-intensive channels. Another option is to create an attractively priced, low-cost platform. In the cellphone industry, for example, low-use subscribers are directed to pre-paid packages that do not require the firm to send out bills and collect payments, which also eliminates the risk of bad debts on such accounts.

Terminating customers comes as a logical consequence of the realization that not all existing customer relationships are worth keeping. Many relationships are no longer profitable for the firm, since they may cost more to maintain than the revenues they generate. Some customers no longer fit the firm's strategy, either because that strategy has changed or because the customers' behaviour and needs have changed. Just as investors need to dispose of poor investments and banks may have to write off bad loans, each service firm needs to regularly evaluate its customer portfolio and consider terminating unsuccessful relationships. Legal and ethical considerations, of course, will determine whether it is proper to take such actions.

Occasionally customers are fired outright (although concern for due process is still important). ING Direct is the "fast-food" model of consumer banking—it is about as "no-frills" as it gets. It only has a handful of basic products, and lures low-maintenance customers with high interest rates. (Its Orange savings account paid 3.8 percent in January 2006, which was a few times the industry averages!) To offset that generosity, its business model pushes its customers to online transactions, and the bank routinely fires customers who don't fit its business model. When a customer calls too often (the average customer phone call costs the bank $5.25 to handle), or wants too many exceptions to the rule, the sales associates respond with something like the following: "Look, this doesn't fit you. You need to go back to your community bank and get the kind of contact you're comfortable with." As a result, ING Direct's cost per account is only one-third of the industry average.[26]

When the Toronto-based Quartet Service Inc., a provider of outsourced IT and telecom services, was acquired by Robert Bracey in 2002, the firm was losing substantial amounts of money despite phenomenal revenue growth. The reason turned out to be unprofitable customers, such as a client who paid $42 000 in annual fees but cost Quartet $65 000 annually to service. A cost–benefit analysis on each of Quartet's customers was done, and a decision was made to let go of the ten least profitable customers—about seven percent of Quartet's clients. The result was an almost instant turnaround in profitability. According to Bracey, "We went from losing a huge amount of money to making money almost instantly."[27]

Other examples where customers get fired for non-financial reasons include students who are caught cheating in examinations and country club members who consistently abuse the facilities or other people. In some instances, termination may be somewhat less confrontational. Banks wishing to divest themselves of certain types of accounts, when they no longer fit with corporate priorities, have been known to sell them to other banks; a related example is credit card holders who receive a letter telling them that their account has been transferred to another card issuer.

Customer Satisfaction and Service Quality Are Prerequisites for Loyalty

The foundation for true loyalty lies in customer satisfaction, for which service quality is a key input. Highly satisfied or even delighted customers are more likely to become loyal apostles of a firm,[28] consolidate their buying with one supplier, and spread positive word of mouth. In contrast, dissatisfaction drives customers away and is a key factor in switching behaviour. Recent research has even demonstrated that increases in customer satisfaction lead to increases in stock prices—see Research Insights 12.1.

The satisfaction/loyalty relationship can be divided into three main zones: defection, indifference, and affection (Figure 12.6). The *zone of defection* occurs at low satisfaction levels. Customers will switch unless switching costs are high or there are no viable or convenient alternatives. Extremely dissatisfied customers can turn into "terrorists,"

Figure 12.6

The Customer Satisfaction/Loyalty Relationship

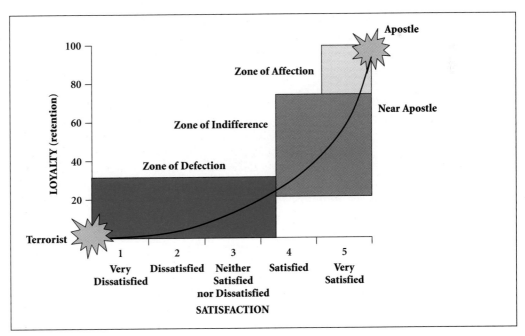

Source: The Customer Satisfaction-Loyalty Relationship from Thomas O. Jones and W. Earl Sasser, Jr., "Why Satisfied Customers Defect," *Harvard Business Review*, Nov.–Dec. 1995, p. 91. Reprinted by permission of Harvard Business School.

Research Insights 12.1

Customer Satisfaction and Wall Street: High Returns and Low Risk!

Do a firm's customer-satisfaction levels have anything to do with its stock price? This was the intriguing research question Claes Fornell and his colleagues worked on to answer. More specifically, they examined whether investments in customer satisfaction lead to excess stock returns (see Figure 12.7), and if yes, whether these returns were associated with higher risks, as would be predicted by financial theory. The researchers built two stock portfolios, and measured the return and risks of the firms in those portfolios compared to the firm's American Customer Satisfaction Index (ACSI) scores.

Their findings are striking for managers and investors alike! Fornell and his colleagues discovered that the American Customer Satisfaction Index (ACSI) was significantly related to stock prices of the individual firms. However, simply publishing the latest data on the ACSI index did not immediately move share prices, as efficient market theory would have predicted. Rather, share prices seemed to adjust slowly over time as firms published other results (perhaps earnings data or other "hard" facts that may lag customer satisfaction), and excess stock returns

were generated as a result. It represents a stock market imperfection, but it is consistent with research in marketing, which holds that satisfied customers improve the level and the stability of cash flow.

For marketing managers, this study's findings confirm that investments (or "expenses" if you talk to accountants) into managing customer relationships and the cash flows they produce are fundamental to the firm's, and therefore the shareholders', value creation.

Although the results are convincing, be careful should you want to exploit this apparent market inefficiency and invest in firms that show high increases in customer satisfaction in future ACSI releases—your finance friends will tell you that efficient markets learn fast! You know this has happened when you see stock prices move as a response to future ACSI releases. You can learn more about the ACSI at www.theacsi.org.

Source: Claes Fornell, Sunil Mithas, Forrest V. Morgeson III, and M.S. Krishnan, "Customer Satisfaction and Stock Prices: High Returns, Low Risk," *Journal of Marketing* 70 (January 2006): 3–14.

Figure 12.7 Can customer satisfaction data help to outperform the market?

providing an abundance of negative word of mouth for the service provider.[29] The *zone of indifference* is found at intermediate satisfaction levels. Here, customers are willing to switch if they find a better alternative. Finally, the *zone of affection* is located at very high satisfaction levels, where customers may have such high attitudinal loyalty that they do not look for alternative service providers. Customers who praise the firm in public and refer others to the firm are described as "apostles."

What makes customers loyal to a firm, and how can marketers increase their loyalty? In this section, we first review the common loyalty drivers for customers, and then explore how firms can build or enhance such loyalty drivers further.

How Do Customers See Relational Benefits?

Relationships create value for individual consumers through such factors as inspiring greater confidence, offering social benefits, and providing special treatment (see Research Insights 12.2). In a B2B service context, relationships are largely dependent on the quality of the interactions between individuals at each of the partnering firms, and service firms need to take care to communicate the relevant benefits to the right people in the client organization, since purchasing decisions are often made jointly.[30] As relationships strengthen over time, the service provider's employees often take on the role of an outsourced department and make critical decisions on behalf of their client.[31]

Strategies for Developing Loyalty Bonds with Customers

Having the right portfolio of customer segments, attracting the right customers, tiering the service, and delivering high levels of satisfaction are a solid foundation for creating customer loyalty as shown in the wheel of loyalty diagram in Figure 12.4 on page 355. However, there is more that firms can do to "bond" more closely with their customers, and specific strategies for developing loyalty bonds include deepening the relationship through cross-selling and bundling, and creating loyalty rewards and higher-level bonds such as social, customization, and structural bonds.[32]

Deepening the Relationship

To tie customers closer to the firm, bundling and/or cross-selling services is an effective strategy for deepening the relationship. For example, banks like to sell as many financial products into an account or household as possible. Once a family has its current account, credit card, savings account, safe deposit box, car loan, and mortgage with the same bank, the relationship is so deep that switching becomes a major exercise, making it unlikely, unless the customer has a reason to become extremely dissatisfied with the bank.

Customers can benefit from consolidating their purchasing of various services from the same provider through the added convenience of one-stop-shopping and potentially higher service levels and/or higher service tiers because of the higher volume of business they bring to the firm.

Reward-Based Bonds

Within any competitive product category, managers recognize that few customers consistently buy only one brand, especially in situations where service delivery involves discrete transactions (such as a car rental) rather than being continuous in nature (as with insurance coverage). In many instances, consumers are loyal to several brands while spurning others (sometimes described as "polygamous loyalty"). In such instances, the marketing goal becomes one of strengthening the customer's preference for one brand over the others, and well-designed loyalty programs can achieve increased loyalty and share of wallet.[33]

Incentives that offer rewards based on the frequency of purchase, value of purchase, or a combination of both represent a basic level of customer bonds. Reward-based bonds can be financial or non-financial in nature. Financial bonds are built when loyal customers are rewarded with incentives that have a financial value, such as discounts on purchases, loyalty program rewards such as frequent flier miles, or the cash-back programs provided by some credit card issuers.

Non-financial rewards provide customers with benefits or value that cannot be translated directly into monetary terms. Examples include giving priority to loyalty program members for wait lists and queues in call centres, and access to special services. Some airlines provide benefits such as heavier baggage allowances, priority upgrading, and access

Research Insights 12.2

What benefits do customers see themselves receiving from an extended relationship with a service firm? Researchers seeking answers to this question conducted two studies. The first consisted of in-depth interviews with 21 respondents from a broad cross-section of backgrounds. Respondents were asked to identify service providers that they used on a regular basis, and invited to identify and discuss any benefits they received as a result of being a regular customer. Among some of the verbatim comments were

- "I like him [hair stylist] . . . He's really funny and always has lots of good jokes. He's kind of like a friend now."
- "I know what I'm getting—I know that if I go to a restaurant that I regularly go to, rather than taking a chance on all of the new restaurants, the food will be good."
- "I often get price breaks. The little bakery that I go to in the morning, every once in a while, they'll give me a free muffin and say, 'You're a good customer, it's on us today.'"
- "You can get better service than drop-in customers. . . . We continue to go to the same automobile repair shop because we have gotten to know the owner on a kind of personal basis, and he . . . can always work us in."
- "Once people feel comfortable, they don't want to switch to another dentist. They don't want to train or break a new dentist in."

After evaluating and categorizing the comments, the researchers designed a second study in which they collected 299 survey questionnaires. The respondents were told to select a specific service provider with whom they had a strong, established relationship. Then the questionnaire asked them to assess the extent to which they received each of 21 benefits (derived from analysis of the first study) as a result of their relationship with the specific provider they had identified. Finally, they were asked to assess the importance of these benefits for them.

A factor analysis of the results showed that most of the benefits that customers derived from relationships could be grouped into three clusters. The first, and most important, group concerned what the researchers labelled confidence benefits, followed by social benefits and special treatment.

Confidence benefits included feelings by customers that in an established relationship there was less risk of something going wrong, and there was confidence in correct performance, ability to trust the provider, lowered anxiety when purchasing, a knowledge of what to expect, and receipt of the firm's highest level of service.

Social benefits embraced mutual recognition between customers and employees, being known by name, friendship with the service provider, and enjoyment of certain social aspects of the relationship.

Special treatment benefits included better prices, discounts on special deals that were unavailable to most customers, extra services, higher priority when there was a wait, and faster service than most customers.

Source: Kevin P. Gwinner, Dwayne D. Gremler, and Mary Jo Bitner, "Relational Benefits in Services Industries: The Customer's Perspective," *Journal of the Academy of Marketing Science* 26/2 (1998): 101–14.

---

to airport lounges to their frequent flyers, even when they are only flying in economy class. Informal loyalty rewards, sometimes found in small businesses, may take the form of periodically giving regular customers a small treat as a way of thanking them for their custom.

Important intangible rewards include special recognition and appreciation. Customers tend to value the extra attention given to their needs. They also appreciate the implicit service guarantee offered by high-tier memberships, including efforts to meet special requests. One objective of reward-based bonds is to motivate customers to consolidate their purchases with one provider, or at least make it their most preferred provider. Tiered loyalty programs often provide direct incentives for customers to achieve the next higher level of membership. However, reward-based loyalty programs are relatively easy for other suppliers to copy, and rarely provide a sustained competitive advantage. By contrast, the higher-level bonds that we discuss next tend to be more sustainable.

Social Bonds Have you ever noticed how your favourite hairdresser addresses you by name when you go for a haircut, or how she asks why she hasn't seen you for a long time, and hopes everything went well when you were away on a long business trip? Social bonds are typically based on personal relationships between providers and customers.

Alternatively, they may reflect pride or satisfaction in holding membership in an organization. Although social bonds are more difficult to build than financial bonds, and may require considerable time to achieve, for the same reason they are also harder for other suppliers to replicate for that same customer. A firm that has created social bonds with its customers has a better chance of retaining them for the long term. When social bonds extend to shared relationships or experiences between customers, such as in country clubs or educational settings, they can be a major loyalty driver for the organization.[34]

Customization Bonds   These bonds are built when the service provider succeeds in providing customized service to its loyal customers. For example, Starbucks' employees are encouraged to learn their regular customers' preferences and customize their service accordingly (Figure 12.8). One-to-one marketing is a more specialized form of customization, in which each individual is treated as a segment in itself.[35] Many large hotel chains capture the preferences of their customers through their loyalty program databases, so that when customers arrive at their hotel, they find that their individual needs have already been anticipated, from preferred drinks and snacks in the mini-bar to the kind of pillow they like and the newspaper they want to receive in the morning. When a customer becomes used to this special service, he or she may find it difficult to adjust to another provider who is not able to customize the service (at least immediately, since it takes time for the new provider to learn about someone's needs).

Structural Bonds   Structural bonds are mostly seen in B2B settings and aim to stimulate loyalty through structural relationships between the provider and the customer. Examples include joint investments in projects and sharing of information, processes, and equipment. Structural bonds can be created in a B2C environment, too. For instance, some airlines have introduced SMS alerts for flight arrival and departure times—such as the Flight Reminder service from WestJet—so that travellers do not have to waste time waiting at the airport in the event of delay. Some car rental companies offer travellers the opportunity to create customized pages on the firm's website where they can retrieve details of past trips including the types of cars, insurance coverage, and so forth. This simplifies and speeds the task of making new bookings. Once customers have integrated their way of doing things with the firm's processes, structural bonds are created that link the customer to the firm and make it more difficult for competition to draw them away.

Figure 12.8
Starbucks' employees are encouraged to learn their customers' preferences.

Notice that while all these bonds tie a customer closer to the firm, when combined they also deliver the confidence, social, and special-treatment benefits that customers desire (see Research Insights 12.1 above). In general, bonds will not work well unless they also generate value for the customer.

Creation of Customer Bonds through Membership Relationships and Loyalty Programs

Discrete transactions, when each usage involves a payment to the service supplier by an essentially "anonymous" consumer, are typical of services like transport, restaurants, cinemas, and shoe repairs. The problem for marketers of such services is that they tend to be less informed about who their customers are, and what use each customer makes of the service, than their counterparts in membership-type organizations. Managers in businesses that sell discrete transactions have to work a little harder to establish relationships. In small businesses such as hairdressers, frequent customers are (or should be) welcomed as "regulars" whose needs and preferences are remembered. Keeping formal records of customers' needs, preferences, and purchasing behaviour is useful even in small firms, since it helps employees avoid having to ask repetitive questions on each service occasion, allows them to personalize the service given to each customer, and also enables the firm to anticipate future needs.

Transforming Discrete Transactions into Membership Relationships   In large companies with substantial customer bases, transactions can still be transformed into relationships by implementing loyalty reward programs, which require customers to apply for membership cards with which transactions can be captured and customers' preferences communicated to the front line. For transaction-type businesses, loyalty reward programs become a necessary enabler for implementing the strategies discussed in the wheel of loyalty.

Besides airlines and hotels, more and more service firms—ranging from retailers (such as department stores, supermarkets, bookshops, and petrol stations), telecommunications providers, and café chains to courier services and cinema chains, have, or are launching, similar reward programs in response to the increasing competitiveness of their markets. Although some provide their own rewards—such as free merchandise, class of vehicle upgrades, or free hotel rooms in vacation resorts—many firms denominate their awards in miles that can be credited to a selected frequent-flyer program. In short, air miles have become a form of promotional currency in the service sector. Best Practice in Action 12.2 describes how British Airways has designed its Executive Club.

Customers may even get frustrated with a reward program, and rather than creating loyalty and goodwill, it then breeds dissatisfaction! Examples include when customers feel they are excluded from the program by low balances or volume of business, if they cannot redeem their loyalty points because of black-out dates during high-demand periods, if the rewards are seen as having little or no value, or if redemption processes are cumbersome and time consuming.[36]

Of course, even if well designed, rewards programs alone will not suffice to retain a firm's most desirable customers. If customers are dissatisfied with the quality of service they receive, or believe that they can obtain better value from a less expensive service, they may quickly become disloyal. No service business that has instituted an awards program for frequent users can ever afford to lose sight of its broader goals of offering high-quality service and good value relative to the price and other costs incurred by customers.[37]

One of the risks associated with a focus on strengthening relationships with high-value customers is that a firm may allow service to other customers to deteriorate. In Reading 4.1, "Why Service Stinks" (p. 457), Diane Brady explores the negative aspects of customer stratification.

The assignment of points also varies according to the class of service. BA seeks to recognize higher ticket expenditures with proportionately higher awards. Longer trips earn more points than shorter ones (a domestic or short haul European trip in economy class generates 15 points, a transatlantic trip 60 points, and a trip from the UK to Australia,

Best Practice in Action 12.2

Rewarding Value of Use, Not Just Frequency, at British Airways

Unlike some frequent flyer programs, in which customer usage is measured simply in miles, British Airways' (BA's) Executive Club members receive both *air miles,* toward redemption of air travel awards, and *points,* toward silver- or gold-tier status for travel on BA. With the creation of the "OneWorld" airline alliance with American Airlines, Qantas, Cathay Pacific, and other carriers, Executive Club members have been able to earn miles (and sometimes points) by flying these partner airlines, too.

As shown in Table 12.A, silver and gold cardholders are entitled to special benefits such as priority reservations and a superior level of on-the-ground service. For instance, even if a gold cardholder is only travelling in economy class, he or she will be entitled to first-class standards of treatment at check-in and in the airport lounges. However, while miles can be accumulated for up to three years (after which they expire), tier status is only valid for twelve months beyond the membership year in which it was earned. In short, the right to special privileges must be re-earned each year. The objective of awarding tier status (which is not unique to BA) is to encourage passengers who have a choice of airlines to concentrate their travel on British Airways, rather than to join several frequent flyer programs and collect mileage awards from all of them. Few passengers travel with such frequency that they will be able to obtain the benefits of gold tier status (or its equivalent) on more than one airline. However, one of the rewards of that status may be the ability to use lounges and other amenities in other airlines that belong to the same international alliance (such as OneWorld).

Table 12.A Benefits Offered by British Airways to Its Most Valued Passengers

BENEFIT	SILVER-TIER MEMBERS	GOLD-TIER MEMBERS
Reservations Reservation assurance	Dedicated silver phone line If flight is full, guaranteed seat in Economy when booking full fare ticket at least 24 hours in advance	Dedicated gold phone line If flight is full, guaranteed seat in Economy when booking full fare ticket at least 24 hours in advance
Priority waitlist and standby Advance notification of delays over 4 hours from U.S. or Canada Check-in desk	Higher priority Yes Club (when travelling economy class)	Highest priority Yes First (when travelling Club or economy class)
Lounge access	Club departure lounges for passenger and one guest regardless of class of travel	First class departure lounge for passenger and one guest regardless of travel class; use of arrivals lounges if travelling economy; lounge access anytime, allowing use of lounges even when not flying BA intercontinental flights
Preferred boarding Special services assistance	Board aircraft at leisure	Board aircraft at leisure Problem solving beyond that accorded to other BA travellers
Bonus air miles Upgrade for two	+25%	+50% Free upgrade to next cabin for member and companion after earning 2500 tier points in one year; another upgrade for two after 3500 points in same year. Award someone else with a Silver Partner card on reaching 4500 points within membership year

Source: British Airways Executive Club, www.britishairways.com/travel/ecbenftgold/public/en_us, accessed January 2006.

100 points). However, tickets at deeply discounted prices may earn fewer miles and no points at all. To reward purchase of higher-priced tickets, passengers earn points at double the economy rate if they travel in Club (business class), and at triple the rate in First.

To encourage gold and silver card holders to remain loyal, BA offers incentives for Executive Club members to retain their current tier status (or to move up from silver to gold). Silver cardholders receive a 25 percent bonus on all air miles, regardless of class of service, while gold cardholders receive a 50 percent bonus. In other words, it doesn't pay spread the miles among several frequent-flyer programs!

Although the airline makes no promises on complimentary upgrades, members of BA's Executive Club are more likely to receive such invitations than other passengers, with tier status being an important consideration. Unlike many airlines, BA tends to limit upgrades to situations in which a lower class of cabin is overbooked, rather than letting frequent travellers believe that they can plan on buying a less expensive ticket and then automatically receive an upgraded seat.

How Customers Perceive Loyalty Reward Programs   Recent research in the credit card industry suggests that loyalty programs strengthen the customers' perception of the value proposition, and lead to increased revenues due to fewer defections and higher usage levels.[38] To assess the potential of a loyalty program to alter normal patterns of behaviour, Grahame Dowling and Mark Uncles argue that marketers need to examine three psychological effects.[39]

Brand loyalty versus deal loyalty. To what extent are customers loyal to the core service (or brand) rather than to the loyalty program itself? Marketers should focus on loyalty programs that directly support the value proposition and the positioning of the product in question.

How buyers value rewards. Several elements determine a loyalty program's value to customers: (1) the cash value of the redemption rewards (if customers had to purchase them); (2) the range of choice among rewards—for instance a selection of gifts rather than just a single gift; (3) the aspirational value of the rewards—something exotic that the consumer would not normally purchase may have greater appeal than a cash-back offer; (4) whether the amount of usage required to obtain an award places it within the realm of possibility for any given consumer; (5) the ease of using the program and making claims for redemption; and (6) the psychological benefits of belonging to the program and accumulating points.

Timing. How soon can benefits from participating in the rewards program be obtained by customers? Deferred gratification tends to weaken the appeal of a loyalty program. One solution is to send customers periodic statements of their account status, indicating progress toward reaching a particular milestone and promoting the rewards that might be forthcoming when that point is reached.

STRATEGIES FOR REDUCING CUSTOMER DEFECTIONS

So far, we have discussed drivers of loyalty and strategies to tie customers closer to the firm. A complementary approach is to understand the drivers for customer defection, also called customer churn, and work on eliminating or reducing those drivers.

Analyze Customer Defections and Monitor Declining Accounts   The first step is to understand the reasons for customer switching. Susan Keaveney conducted a large-scale study across a range of services and found several key reasons why customers switch to another provider.[40] (Figure 12.9). Core service failures were mentioned by 44 percent of respondents as a reason for switching; dissatisfactory service encounters by 34 percent; high, deceptive, or unfair pricing by 30 percent; inconvenience in terms of time, location, or delays by 21 percent, and poor response to service failure by 17 percent. Many respondents described a decision to switch as resulting from interrelated incidents, such as a service failure followed by an unsatisfactory service recovery.

Figure 12.9

What drives customers to switch away from a service firm?

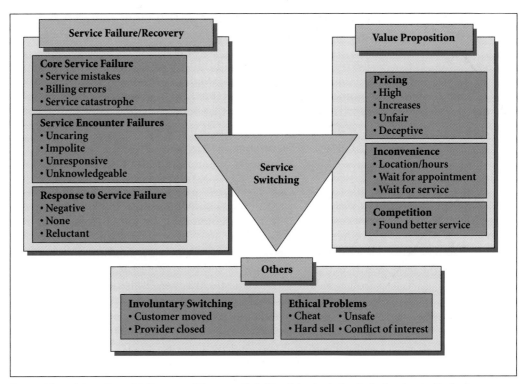

Source: Adapted from Susan M. Keaveney, "Customer Switching Behavior in Service Industries: An Exploratory Study," *Journal of Marketing* 59 (April 1995): 71–82.

In the cellphone industry, players regularly conduct what is called churn diagnostics. It includes the analysis of data warehouse information on churned and declining customers, exit interviews (call-centre staff often have a short set of questions they ask when a customer cancels an account to gain a better understanding of why customers defect), and in-depth interviews of former customers by a third party research agency, which typically yield a more detailed understanding of churn drivers.[41]

Many cellphone service operations use so-called churn alert systems, which monitor the activity in individual customer accounts with the objective of predicting impending customer switching. Accounts at risk are flagged and trigger proactive retention efforts such as sending a voucher and/or having a customer service representative call the customer to check on the health of the customer relationship and initiate corrective action if needed.

Address Key Churn Drivers

Keaveney's findings underscore the importance of addressing some generic churn drivers by delivering quality service (see Chapter 14), minimizing inconvenience and other non-monetary costs, and fair and transparent pricing (Chapter 5). In addition to these generic drivers, there are often industry-specific drivers as well. For example, handset replacement is a common reason for cellphone service subscribers to discontinue an existing relationship, as new subscription plans typically come with heavily subsidized new handsets. To prevent handset-related churn, many providers now offer proactive handset replacement programs, where their current subscribers are offered the chance to buy heavily discounted new-model handsets at regular intervals. Some providers even give high-value customers handsets for free, or set them off against redemption of loyalty points.

In addition to such proactive retention measures, many firms have implemented reactive measures as well. They include specially trained call-centre staff, the so-called "save teams," who deal with customers who intend to cancel their accounts. The main job of save-team employees is to listen to customer needs and issues, and try to address these with the key focus of retaining the customer.

Implement Effective Complaint-Handling and Service-Recovery Procedures

Effective complaint handling and excellent service recovery are crucial in persuading unhappy customers not to switch providers. That includes making it easy for customers to voice their problems with the firm, and then responding with a strong service recovery. We will discuss how to do that effectively in Chapter 13.

Increase Switching Costs

Another way to reduce churn is to increase switching barriers.[42] Many services have natural switching costs (e.g., it is a lot of work for customers to change their primary banking account, especially when many direct debits, credits, and other related banking services are tied to that account; also, many customers are reluctant to learn about the products and processes of a new provider).[43]

Switching costs can also be created by instituting contractual penalties for switching, such as the transfer fees levied by some brokerage firms for moving shares and bonds to another financial institution. However, firms need to be cautious so that they are not perceived as holding their customers hostage. A firm with high switching barriers and poor service quality is likely to generate negative attitudes and bad word-of-mouth. "At some point, the last straw is reached and a previously inert customer will have had enough," and will switch to another provider.[44]

CRM: CUSTOMER RELATIONSHIP MANAGEMENT

Service marketers have understood for some time the power of relationship management, and certain industries have applied it for decades. Examples include the corner grocery store, the neighbourhood car repair shop, and providers of banking services to high net-worth clients.

Mention CRM, and costly and complex IT systems and infrastructure, and CRM vendors such as SAP, Siebel Systems, and Oracle come immediately to mind. However, CRM actually signifies the whole process by which relations with customers are built and maintained.[45] It should be seen as an enabler of the successful implementation of the wheel of loyalty. Let us first look at CRM systems before we move to a more strategic perspective.

Common Objectives of CRM Systems

Many firms have large numbers of customers (often millions), many different touch points (for instance, tellers, call-centre staff, self-service machines, and websites), at multiple geographic locations. At a single large facility, it's unlikely that a customer will be served by the same front-line staff on two consecutive visits. In such situations, managers historically lacked the tools to practise relationship marketing. But today CRM systems act as an enabler, capturing customer information and delivering it to the various touch points.

From a customer perspective, well-implemented CRM systems can offer a "unified customer interface" that delivers customization and personalization. This means that at each transaction, the relevant account details, knowledge of customer preferences and past transactions, or history of a service problem are at the fingertips of the person serving the customer. This can result in a vast service improvement and increased customer value.

From a company perspective, CRM systems allow the company to better understand, segment, and tier its customer base, better target promotions and cross-selling, and even implement churn-alert systems that signal if a customer is in danger of defecting.[46] Service Perspectives 12.2 highlights some common CRM applications.

What Does a Comprehensive CRM Strategy Encompass?[47]

Rather than viewing CRM as a technology, we subscribe to a more strategic view of CRM that focuses on the profitable development and management of customer relationships.

Common CRM Applications

- **Data collection:** the system captures customer data such as contact details, demographics, purchasing history, and service preferences.

- **Data analysis:** the data captured is analyzed and categorized by the system according to criteria set by firm. This is used to tier the customer base and tailor service delivery accordingly.

- **Sales force automation:** sales leads, along with cross-selling and up-selling opportunities, can be effectively identified and processed, and the entire sales cycle from lead generation to close of sales and after-sales service can be tracked and facilitated through the CRM system.

- **Marketing automation:** mining of customer data enables the firm to target its market. A good CRM system enables the firm to achieve one-to-one marketing and cost savings, often in the context of loyalty and retention programs. This results in increasing the ROI on its marketing expenditure. CRM systems also enable the assessment of the effectiveness of marketing campaigns through the analysis of responses.

- **Call-centre automation:** call-centre staff have customer information at their fingertips and can improve their service levels to all customers. Furthermore, caller ID and account numbers allow call centres to identify the customer tier the caller belongs to, and to tailor the service accordingly. For example, platinum callers get priority in waiting loops.

Figure 12.10 provides an integrated framework of five key processes involved in a CRM strategy:

1. *Strategy development* involves the assessment of business strategy (including articulation of the company's vision, industry trends, and competition). The business strategy is typically the responsibility of top management. Once determined, the business strategy should be guiding the development of customer strategy, including the choice of target segments, customer-base tiering, the design of loyalty bonds, and churn management (as discussed in the wheel of loyalty, Figure 12.4).

2. *Value creation* translates the business and customer strategies into specific value propositions for customers and the firm. The value created for customers includes all the benefits that are delivered through priority tiered services, loyalty rewards, and customization and personalization. The value created for the firm needs to include reduced customer acquisition and retention costs, and increased share of wallet. The core of CRM is the concept of dual creation of value—customers need to participate in CRM (e.g., through volunteering information) so that they can reap value from the firm's CRM initiatives. For instance, only if my driver's licence, billing address, credit card details, and car and insurance preferences are stored in a car rental's CRM system can I benefit from the increased convenience of not having to provide those data for each reservation. Firms can even create value through information drawn from one customer for others (e.g., Amazon's analysis of which other books customers with a profile similar to yours have bought, and customer ratings of books). CRM seems most successful when there is a win–win situation for the firm and its customers.[48]

3. *Multichannel integration.* Most service firms interact with their customers through a multitude of channels, and it has become a challenge to serve customers well across these many potential interfaces while offering a "unified customer interface" that delivers customization and personalization. CRM's channel integration addresses this challenge.

4. *Information management.* Service delivery across many channels relies on the firm's ability to collect customer information from all channels, to integrate it with other relevant information, and to make the relevant information available to the front line (or to the customer in a self-service context) at the various touch points. The information management process encompasses the data repository (which contains all the customer data), IT systems (which encompasses the IT hardware and software), analytical tools (which include data-mining packages and more specific application

Figure 12.10 An Integrated Framework for CRM Strategy

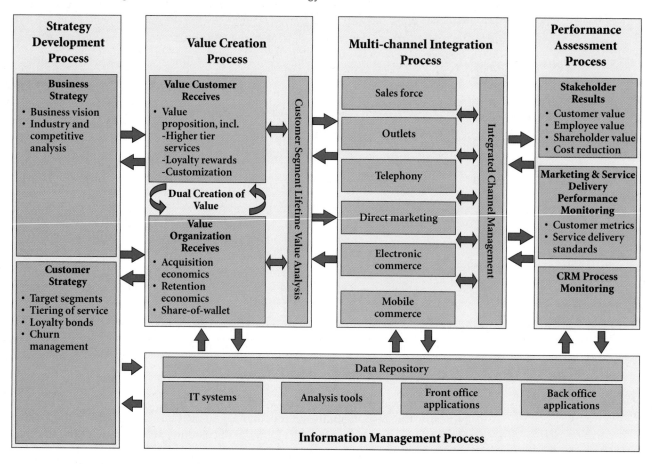

Source: adapted from Adrian Payne and Pennie Frow, "A Strategic Framework for Customer Relationship Management," *Journal of Marketing* 69 (October 2005): 167–76.

packages such as campaign management analysis, credit assessment, customer profiling, and churn alert systems), front-office applications (which support activities that involve direct customer contact, including sales-force automation and call-centre management applications), and back-office applications (which support internal customer-related processes, including logistics, procurement, and financial processing).

5. *Performance assessment* must address three critical questions. First, is the CRM strategy creating value for its key stakeholders (i.e., customers, employees, and shareholders)? Second, are the marketing objectives (ranging from customer acquisition and share of wallet to retention and customer satisfaction) and service-delivery performance objectives (e.g., call-centre service standards such as call waiting, call abortion, and first-time resolution rates) being achieved? Third, is the CRM process itself performing up to expectations (e.g., relevant strategies being set, customer and firm value being created, information management process working effectively, and integration across customer-service channels being achieved effectively)? The performance-assessment process should drive the continuous improvement of the CRM strategy itself.

Common Failures in CRM Implementation

Unfortunately, the majority of CRM implementations tend to fail. According to the Gartner Group, the implementation failure rate is 55 percent, while Accenture claims it to be around 60 percent. A key reason for this high failure rate is that firms often equate installing CRM systems with having a customer relationship strategy. One analyst, speaking to a group of Canadian technology executives, labelled this approach the "airplane magazine syndrome." He remarked: "The CEO's on a plane, he picks up the airline magazine and reads in a page-and-a-half everything you have to do to put CRM in your company. Then he goes back to the organization and says, 'We have to get on this' without really thinking through it."[49] Managers forget that the system is just a tool to enhance the firm's customer-servicing capabilities; it is not the strategy itself.

Furthermore, CRM cuts across many departments and functions (e.g., from customer-contact centres, online services and distributions to branch operations, employee training, and IT departments), programs (ranging from sales and loyalty programs to launching of new services and cross-selling/upselling initiatives), and processes (e.g., from credit-line authorization all the way to complaint handling and service recovery). The wide-ranging scope of CRM implementation, and the unfortunate reality that it is often the weakest link that determines the success of an implementation, shows the challenge of getting it right. Common reasons for CRM failures include[50]

- *Viewing CRM as a technology initiative.* It's easy to let the focus shift toward technology and its features, with the result that the IT department rather than top management or marketing takes the lead in devising CRM strategy. This often results in a lack of strategic direction, and a misunderstanding of customers and markets during implementation.

- *Lack of customer focus.* Many firms implement CRM without the ultimate goal of enabling consistent service delivery for valued customers across all customer service processes and delivery channels.

- *Insufficient appreciation of customer lifetime value (LTV).* The marketing of many firms is not sufficiently structured around the vastly different profitability of different customers. Furthermore, servicing costs of different customers are often not well captured (e.g., as they could be by using activity-based costing, as discussed in Chapter 5).

- *Inadequate support from top management.* Without ownership and active involvement of top management, the CRM strategic intent will not survive the implementation intact.

- *Failing to re-engineer business processes.* It is virtually impossible to implement CRM successfully without redesigning customer service and back-office processes. Many implementations fail because CRM is being fitted into existing processes rather than redesigning the processes to fit a customer-centric CRM implementation. Redesigning also requires effective change management and employee engagement and support, which are often lacking.

- *Underestimating the challenges in data integration.* Firms frequently fail to integrate customer data that usually are scattered all over the organization. However, a key to unlocking the full potential of CRM is to make customer knowledge available in real time to all employees who need it.

In the long run, firms can put their CRM strategies at substantial risk if customers believe that CRM is being used in a way detrimental to them.[51] Examples include perceptions of not being treated fairly (including not being offered attractive pricing or promotions that are offered, for example, to new accounts, but not to existing customers), and potential privacy concerns (see Service Perspectives 12.3). Being aware and actively avoiding these pitfalls is a first step toward a successful CRM implementation.

How to Get CRM Implementation Right

In spite of the many horror stories of millions of dollars sunk into unsuccessful CRM projects, more and more firms are getting it right. "No longer a black hole, CRM is becoming a basic building block of corporate success," argue Darrell Rigby and Dianne Ledingham.[52] Seasoned McKinsey consultants believe that even CRM systems that have been implemented and have not yet been showing results can be well positioned for future success. They recommend taking a step back and focusing on how to build customer loyalty, rather than focusing on the technology itself.[53] Common to many successful CRM implementations is a highly focused approach that is narrow in scope. Rather than using CRM to transform entire businesses through the wholesale implementation of the CRM model advanced in Figure 12.10, successful implementations focus on clearly defined

Service Perspectives 12.3

CRM Extreme: A Glimpse into Ordering Pizza in 2012?

Operator: "Thank you for calling Pizza Delight. Linda speaking, how may I help you?"

Customer: "Good evening, can I order ... "

Operator: "Sir, before taking your order, could I please have the number of your multipurpose smart card?"

Customer: "Hold on ... it's ... um ... 4555 1000 9831 3213."

Operator: "Thank you! Can I please confirm you're Mr Thompson calling from 10940 Wilford Boulevard? You are calling from your home number 4321-3876, your cellphone number is 9923-4566, and your office number is 4322-9377."

Customer: "How in the world did you get my address and all my numbers?"

Operator: "Sir, we are connected to the Integrated Customer Intimacy System."

Customer: "I would like to order a large seafood pizza ... "

Operator: "Sir, that's not a good idea."

Customer: "Why?!?"

Operator: "According to your medical records, you have very high blood pressure and a far too high cholesterol level, Sir."

Customer: "What? ... What do you recommend then?"

Operator: "Try our Low Fat Soybean Yoghurt Pizza. You'll like it."

Customer: "How do you know?"

Operator: "You borrowed the book *Popular Soybean Dishes* from the City Library last week, Sir."

Customer: "OK, I give up ... Get me three large ones then. How much will that be?

Operator: "That should be enough for your family of eight, Sir. The total is $47.97."

Customer: "Can I pay by credit card?"

Operator: "I'm afraid you'll have to pay us cash, Sir. Your credit card is over the limit and your chequing account has an overdue balance of $2435.54. That's excluding the late payment charges on your home equity loan, Sir."

Customer: "I guess I'll have to run to the ATM and withdraw some cash before your guy arrives."

Operator: "You can't do that, Sir. Based on the records, you've reached your daily machine withdrawals limit for today."

Customer: "Never mind. Just send the pizzas, I'll have the cash ready. How long is it gonna take?"

Operator: "About 45 minutes, Sir, but if you don't want to wait you can always come and collect it on your Harley, registration number L.A.6468 ... "

Customer: "#@$#@%^%%@"

Operator: "Sir, please watch your language. Remember, on April 28, 2011 you were convicted of using abusive language at a traffic warden ... "

Customer: (Speechless)

Operator: "Is there anything else, Sir?"

Source: This story was adapted from various sources, including www.lawdebt.com/gazette/nov2004/nov2004.pdf (accessed January 2006) and a video created by the American Civil Liberties Union (ACLU) available at www.aclu.org/pizza. This video aims to communicate the privacy threats that CRM poses to consumers. ACLU is a non-profit organization that campaigns against government's and corporations' aggressive collection of information on people's personal lives and habits.

problems within their customer relationship cycle. These narrow CRM strategies often reveal additional opportunities for further improvements that, taken together, can over time evolve into broad CRM implementation extending across the entire company.[54]

Rigby, Reichheld, and Schefter recommend focusing on the customer strategy and not the technology, posing the question:

> If your best customers knew that you planned to invest $130 million to increase their loyalty ... how would they tell you to spend it? Would they want you to create a loyalty card or would they ask you to open more cash registers and keep enough milk in stock. The answer depends on the kind of company you are and the kinds of relationships you and your customers want to have with one another.[55]

Among the key questions that managers should debate when defining their customer relationship strategy for a potential CRM system implementation are

1. How does our value proposition need to change to increase customer loyalty?

2. How much customization or one-to-one marketing and service delivery is appropriate and profitable?

3. What is the incremental profit potential of increasing the share of wallet with our current customers? How much does this vary by customer tier and/or segment?

4. How much time and resources can we allocate to CRM right now?

5. If we believe in customer relationship management, why haven't we taken more steps in that direction in the past? What can we do today to develop customer relationships without spending on technology?[56]

Answering these questions may lead to the conclusion that a CRM system may currently not be the best investment or highest priority for a given firm, or that a scaled-down version may suffice to deliver the intended customer strategy. In any case, we emphasize that the system is merely a tool to drive the strategy, and must thus be tailored to deliver that strategy.

Conclusion

Many elements are involved in gaining market share, increasing share of wallet, cross-selling other products and services to existing customers, and creating long-term loyalty. We used the wheel of loyalty as an organizing framework, which starts with identifying and targeting the right customers, then learning about their needs (including their preferences for various forms of service delivery). Translating this knowledge into service delivery, tiered service levels, and customer-relationship strategies are the key steps toward achieving customer loyalty.

Marketers need to pay special attention to those customers who offer the firm the greatest value, as they purchase its products with the greatest frequency and spend the most on premium services. Programs to reward frequent users—of which the most highly developed are the frequent flyer clubs created by airlines—identify and provide rewards for high-value customers and facilitate tiered service delivery. These programs also enable marketers to track the behaviour of high-value customers in terms of where and when they use the service, what service classes or types of product they buy, and how much they spend.

CRM is a key enabler for the strategies discussed in the wheel of loyalty, and is often integrated with loyalty programs. From a customer perspective, CRM can result in a vast service improvement and increased customer value (e.g., through mass customization and increased convenience).

Review Questions

1. Why is targeting the "right customers" so important for successful customer relationship management?

2. How can you estimate a customer's lifetime value (LTV)?

3. Explain what is meant by a customer portfolio. How should a firm decide what is the most appropriate mix of customers to have?

4. What is tiering of services? Explain the rationale and strategic implications.

5. Identify some key measures that can be used to create customer bonds and encourage long-term relationships with customers?

6. What are the arguments for spending money to keep existing customers loyal?

7. How do the various strategies described in the wheel of loyalty relate to one another?

8. What is the role of CRM in delivering a customer relationship strategy?

9. Review the reading "Why Service Stinks" (p. 457). Do you agree with the author's view that loyalty programs result in poor service for less valuable customers? If so, what do you recommend should be done about this?

Application Exercises

1. Identify three service businesses that you patronize on a regular basis. For each business, complete the following sentence: "I am loyal to this business because . . . "

2. What conclusions do you draw about (a) yourself as a consumer, and (b) the performance of each of the businesses? Assess whether any of these businesses managed to develop a sustainable competitive advantage through the way it won your loyalty?

3. Identify two service businesses that you used several times but have now ceased to patronize (or plan to stop patronizing soon) because you were dissatisfied. Complete the sentence: "I stopped using (or will soon stop using) this organization as a customer because . . . "

4. Again, what conclusions do you draw about yourself and the firms in question? How could each of these firms potentially avoid your defection? What could each of these firms do to avoid defections in the future of customers with a similar profile to yours?

5. Identify the major players in the field of socially responsible investing (SRI; see Best Practice in Action 12.1 for some of the names) in Canada and evaluate how they design and position their service offerings to appeal to SRI investors. Pay special attention to the screens applied by different companies in designing their offerings. Are these screens consistent across the key players? Can a consumer easily discern differences across these offerings?

6. Design a questionnaire and conduct a survey asking about two loyalty programs. The first is about a membership/loyalty program your classmates or their families like best and that makes them loyal to that firm. The second is about a loyalty program that is not well perceived and does not seem to add value to the customer. Use open-ended questions, such as "What motivated you to sign up in the first place?" "Why are you using this program?" "Has participating in the program changed your purchasing/usage behaviour in any way?" "Has it made you less likely to use competing suppliers?" "What do you think of the rewards available?" "Did membership in the program lead to any immediate benefits in the use of the service?" "What role does the loyalty program play in making you loyal?" "What are the three things you like best/least about this loyalty/membership program?" And "What improvements would you suggest?" Analyze which features make loyalty/membership programs successful, and which features do not achieve the desired results. Use frameworks such as the wheel of loyalty to guide your analysis and presentation.

7. Approach service employees in two or three firms with implemented CRM systems. Ask the employees about their experience interfacing with these systems, whether the systems help them in understanding their customers better, and whether this understanding leads to improved service experiences for their customers. Also ask them about any concerns they may have about their organization's CRM systems, and suggestions for improvement.

Endnotes

1. Frederick F. Reichheld and Thomas Teal, *The Loyalty Effect,* Boston: Harvard Business School Press, 1996.
2. Ruth Bolton, Katherine N. Lemon, and Peter C. Verhoef, "The Theoretical Underpinnings of Customer Asset Management: A Framework and Propositions for Future Research," *Journal of the Academy of Marketing Science* 32/3 (2004): 271–92.
3. Frederick F. Reichheld and W. Earl Sasser, Jr., "Zero Defections: Quality Comes to Services," *Harvard Business Review* 68/5 (September–October 1990): 105–11.
4. Ibid.
5. Frederick F. Reichheld and Phil Schefter, "E-Loyalty: Your Secret Weapon on the Web," *Harvard Business Review* 78/4 (July–August, 2000): 105–13.
6. Christian Homburg, Nicole Koschate, and Wayne D. Hoyer, "Do Satisfied Customers Really Pay More? A Study of the Relationship between Customer Satisfaction and Willingness to Pay," *Journal of Marketing* 69 (April 2005): 84–96.
7. Grahame R. Dowling and Mark Uncles, "Do Customer Loyalty Programs Really Work?' *Sloan Management Review* (Summer 1997): 71–81; Werner Reinartz and V. Kumar, "The Mismanagement of Customer Loyalty," *Harvard Business Review* 80/7 (July 2002): 86–94.
8. Werner J. Reinartz and V. Kumar, "On the Profitability of Long-Life Customers in a Noncontractual Setting: An Empirical Investigation and Implications for Marketing," *Journal of Marketing* 64 (October 2000): 17–35.
9. Jochen Wirtz, Indranil Sen, and Sanjay Singh, "Customer Asset Management at DHL in Asia," in Jochen Wirtz and Christopher Lovelock, (eds.), *Services Marketing in Asia: A Case Book,* Singapore: Prentice Hall, 2005: 379–96.
10. John E. Hogan, Katherine N. Lemon, and Barak Libai, "What is the True Cost of a Lost Customer?" *Journal of Services Research* 5/3 (2003): 196–208.
11. For a discussion on how to evaluate the customer base of a firm, see Sunil Gupta, Donald R. Lehmann, and Jennifer Ames Stuart, "Valuing Customers," *Journal of Marketing Research* 41/1 (2004): 7–18.

12. Alan W.H. Grant and Leonard H. Schlesinger, "Realize Your Customer's Full Profit Potential," *Harvard Business Review* 73/5 (September–October 1995): 59–75.

13. Nicole E. Coviello, Roderick J. Brodie, and Hugh J. Munro, "Understanding Contemporary Marketing: Development of a Classification Scheme," *Journal of Marketing Management* 13/6 (1995): 501–22.

14. J.R. Copulsky and M.J. Wolf, "Relationship Marketing: Positioning for the Future," *Journal of Business Strategy* 11/4 (1990): 16–20.

15. Johnson and Selnes proposed a typology of exchange relationships that included "strangers," "acquaintances," "friends," and "partners," and derived implications for customer portfolio management. For details see Michael D. Johnson and Fred Selnes, "Customer Portfolio Management: Towards a Dynamic Theory of Exchange Relationships," *Journal of Marketing* 68/2 (2004): 1–17.

16. Evert Gummesson, *Total Relationship Marketing*, Oxford: Butterworth-Heinemann, 1999: 24.

17. It has even been suggested that the best option for dealing with chronically dissatisfied customers is to let them go "to allow front-line staff [to] focus on satisfying the 'right' customers"; see Ka-shing Woo and Henry K.Y. Fock, "Retaining and Divesting Customers: An Exploratory Study of Right Customers, 'At-Risk' Right Customers, and Wrong Customers," *Journal of Services Marketing* 18/3 (2004): 187–97.

18. Frederick F. Reichheld, *Loyalty Rules: How Today's Leaders Build Lasting Relationships*, Boston: Harvard Business School Press, 2001: 45.

19. Roger Hallowell, "The Relationships of Customer Satisfaction, Customer Loyalty, and Profitability: An Empirical Study," *International Journal of Service Industry Management* 74 (1996): 27–42.

20. Reichheld, 2001, op. cit.: 43, 84–85.

21. David Rosenblum, Doug Tomlinson, and Larry Scott, "Bottom-Feeding for Blockbuster Business," *Harvard Business Review* 81/3 (March 2003): 52–59.

22. Ravi Dhar and Rashi Glazer, "Hedging Customers," *Harvard Business Review* 81/5 (May 2003): 86–92.

23. David H. Maister, *True Professionalism*, New York: Free Press, 1997 (see especially Chapter 20).

24. Valarie A. Zeithaml, Roland T. Rust, and Katharine N. Lemon, "The Customer Pyramid: Creating and Serving Profitable Customers," *California Management Review* 43/4 (Summer 2001): 118–42.

25. Werner J. Reinartz and V. Kumar, "The Impact of Customer Relationship Characteristics on Profitable Lifetime Duration," *Journal of Marketing* 67/1 (2003): 77–99.

26. Elizabeth Esfahani, "How to Get Tough with Bad Customers," *ING Direct* (October 2004); http://home.ingdirect.com, accessed January 19, 2006.

27. Susanne Baillie, "How to Fire Your Customers," *Profit* 22/5 (November 2003): 72.

28. Not only is there a positive relationship between satisfaction and share of wallet, but the greatest positive impact is seen at the upper extreme levels of satisfaction. For details, refer to Timothy L. Keiningham, Tiffany Perkins-Munn, and Heather Evans, "The Impact of Customer Satisfaction on Share of Wallet in a Business-to-Business Environment," *Journal of Service Research* 6/1 (2003): 37–50.

29. Florian V. Wangenheim, "Postswitching Negative Word of Mouth," *Journal of Service Research* 8/1 (2005): 67–78.

30. Das Narayandas, "Building Loyalty in Business Markets," *Harvard Business Review* 83/9 (September 2005): 131–39.

31. Piyush Kumar, "The Impact of Long-Term Client Relationships on the Performance of Business Service Firms," *Journal of Service Research* 2 (August 1999): 4–18.

32. Leonard L. Berry and A. Parasuraman, "Three Levels of Relationship Marketing," in *Marketing Services: Competing through Quality*, New York: Free Press, 1991: 136–42; and Valarie A. Zeithaml, Mary Jo Bitner, and Dwayne D. Gremler, *Services Marketing: Integrating Customer Focus Across the Firm*, 4th ed., Boston: McGraw-Hill, 2006: 196–201.

33. Michael Lewis, "The Influence of Loyalty Programs and Short-Term Promotions on Customer Retention," *Journal of Marketing Research* 41 (August 2004): 281–92.

34. Mark S. Rosenbaum, Amy L. Ostrom, and Ronald Kuntze, "Loyalty Programs and a Sense of Community," *Journal of Services Marketing* 19/4 (2005): 222–33; Isabelle Szmigin, Louise Canning, and Alexander E. Reppel, "Online Community: Enhancing the Relationship Marketing Concept Through Customer Bonding," *International Journal of Service Industry Management* 16/5 (2005): 480–96; and Inger Roos, Anders Gustafsson, and Bo Edvardsson, "The Role of Customer Clubs in Recent Telecom Relationships," *International Journal of Service Industry Management* 16/5 (2005): 436–54.

35. Don Peppers and Martha Rogers, *The One-to-One Manager*, New York: Currency/Doubleday, 1999.

36. Bernd Stauss, Maxie Schmidt, and Adreas Schoeler, "Customer Frustration in Loyalty Programs," *International Journal of Service Industry Management* 16/3 (2005): 229–52.

37. See, for example, Iselin Skogland and Judy Siguaw, "Are Your Satisfied Customers Loyal?" *Cornell Hotel and Restaurant Administration Quarterly* 45/3 (2004): 221–34.

38. Ruth N. Bolton, P.K. Kannan and Matthew D. Bramlett, "Implications of Loyalty Program Membership and Service Experience for Customer Retention and Value," *Journal of the Academy of Marketing Science* 28/1 (2000): 95–108; and Michael Lewis (2004), op. cit.: 281–92.

39. Dowling and Uncles (1997), op. cit.

40. Susan M. Keaveney, "Customer Switching Behavior in Service Industries: An Exploratory Study," *Journal of Marketing* 59 (April 1995): 71–82.

41. For a more detailed discussion of situation-specific switching behaviour, refer to Inger Roos, Bo Edvardsson, and Anders Gustafsson, "Customer Switching Patterns in Competitive and Noncompetitive Service Industries," *Journal of Service Research* 6/3 (2004): 256–71.

42. Jonathan Lee, Janghyuk Lee, and Lawrence Feick, "The Impact of Switching Costs on the Consumer Satisfaction–Loyalty Link: Mobile Phone Service in France," *Journal of Services Marketing* 15/1 (2001): 35–48; and Shun Yin Lam, Venkatesh Shankar, M. Krishna Erramilli, and Bvsan Murthy, "Customer Value, Satisfaction, Loyalty, and Switching Costs: An Illustration from a Business-to-Business Service Context," *Journal of the Academy of Marketing Science* 32/3 (2004): 293–311.

43. Moonkyu Lee and Lawrence F. Cunningham, "A Cost/Benefit Approach to Understanding Loyalty," *Journal of Services Marketing* 15/2 (2001): 113–30; and Simon J. Bell, Seigyoung Auh, and Karen Smalley, "Customer Relationship Dynamics: Service Quality and Customer Loyalty in the Context of Varying Levels of Customer Expertise and Switching Costs," *Journal of the Academy of Marketing Science* 33/2 (2005): 169–83.

44. Lesley White and Venkat Yanamandram, "Why Customers Stay: Reasons and Consequences of Inertia in Financial Services," *International Journal of Service Industry Management* 14/3 (2004): 183–94.

45. For an excellent book on CRM see: V. Kumar and Werner J. Reinartz, *Customer Relationship Management: A Database Approach.* Hoboken, NJ: John Wiley, 2006.

46. Kevin N. Quiring and Nancy K. Mullen, "More Than Data Warehousing: An Integrated View of the Customer," in John G. Freeland, (ed.), *The Ultimate CRM Handbook: Strategies and Concepts for Building Enduring Customer Loyalty and Profitability*, New York: McGraw-Hill, 2002: 102–08.

47. This section is adapted from Adrian Payne and Pennie Frow, "A Strategic Framework for Customer Relationship Management," *Journal of Marketing* 69 (October 2005): 167–76.

48. William Boulding, Richard Staelin, Michael Ehret, and Wesley J. Johnston, "A Customer Relationship Management Roadmap: What is Known, Potential Pitfalls, and Where to Go," *Journal of Marketing* 69/4 (2005): 155–66.

49. Shane Schick, "Ad-hoc CRM Initiatives a Bust," *Computer Dealer News* 17/19 (2001): 10.

50. This section is largely based on Sudhir H. Kale, "CRM Failure and the Seven Deadly Sins," *Marketing Management* (September/October 2004): 42–46.

51. William Boulding, Richard Staelin, Michael Ehret, and Wesley J. Johnston, "A Customer Relationship Management Roadmap: What is Known, Potential Pitfalls, and Where to Go," *Journal of Marketing* 69/4 (2005): 155–66.

52. Darrell K. Rigby and Dianne Ledingham, "CRM Done Right," *Harvard Business Review* 82/11 (November 2004): 118–29.

53. Manuel Ebner, Arthur Hu, Daniel Levitt, and Jim McCrory, "How to Rescue CRM?" *McKinsey Quarterly* 4 (2002).

54. Rigby and Ledingham (2004), op. cit.

55. Darrell K. Rigby, Frederick F. Reichheld, and Phil Schefter, "Avoid the Four Perils of CRM," *Harvard Business Review* 80/2 (February 2002): 108.

56. Ibid.

CHAPTER 13

Achieving Service Recovery and Obtaining Customer Feedback

One of the surest signs of a bad or declining relationship is the absence of complaints from the customer. Nobody is ever that satisfied, especially not over an extended period of time.

—Theodore Levitt

Customer complaints are the schoolbooks from which we learn.

—Unknown

To err is human; to recover, divine.

—Christopher Hart, James Hart, James Heskett, and Earl Sasser
(paraphrasing eighteenth-century poet Alexander Pope)

The first law of service productivity and quality might be: do it right the first time. But we cannot ignore the fact that failures continue to occur, sometimes for reasons outside the organization's control. Many "moments of truth" in service encounters are vulnerable to breakdowns. Such distinctive service characteristics as real-time performance, customer involvement, and people as part of the product greatly increase the chance of service failures. How well a firm handles complaints and resolves problems may determine whether it builds customer loyalty or watches former customers take their business elsewhere.

In this chapter, we explore the following questions:

1. Why do customers complain, and what do they expect from the firm?

2. How should an effective service recovery strategy be designed?

3. Under what circumstances should firms offer service guarantees, and is it wise to make them unconditional?

4. How should firms and their frontline staff respond to abusive and/or opportunistic customers?

5. How can organizations institutionalize systematic and continuous learning from customer feedback?

CUSTOMER COMPLAINING BEHAVIOUR

Chances are that you will not be satisfied with at least some of the services you receive. How do you respond to your dissatisfaction with this service? Do you complain informally to an employee, ask to speak to the manager, or file a complaint? If not, perhaps you just mutter darkly to yourself, grumble to your friends and family, and the next time you need a similar type of service choose an alternative supplier.

If you are among those who do not complain about poor service, you are not alone. Research around the globe has shown that most people will not complain, especially if they think it will do no good.

Customer Response Options to Service Failures

Figure 13.1 depicts the courses of action a customer may take in response to a service failure. This model suggests at least three major courses of action:

- Take some form of public action (including complaining to the firm, or to a third party, such as a customer advocacy group, customer affairs or regulatory agency, or even civil or criminal courts).
- Take some form of private action (including abandoning the supplier)
- Take no action

It's important to remember that any one or a combination of alternatives can be pursued by the customer. Managers need to be aware that the impact of a defection can go far beyond the loss of that person's future revenue stream. Angry customers often tell many other people about their problems.[1] The internet allows unhappy customers to reach thousands, or perhaps millions, of people by posting complaints on bulletin boards or setting up websites to publicize their bad experiences with specific organizations.[2] A popular strategy when naming the domains of such sites has been to add a derogatory suffix (such as "sucks") to the name of the offending company.

Understanding Customer Responses to Service Failures

To be able to deal effectively with dissatisfied and complaining customers, managers need to understand key aspects of complaining behaviour, starting with the questions posed below.

Why Do Customers Complain?   In general, studies of consumer complaining behaviour have identified four main purposes for complaining.

- *Obtain restitution or compensation.* Often, consumers complain to recover some economic loss by seeking a refund, compensation, and/or having the service performed again.[3]

Figure 13.1

Customer Response Categories to Service Failures

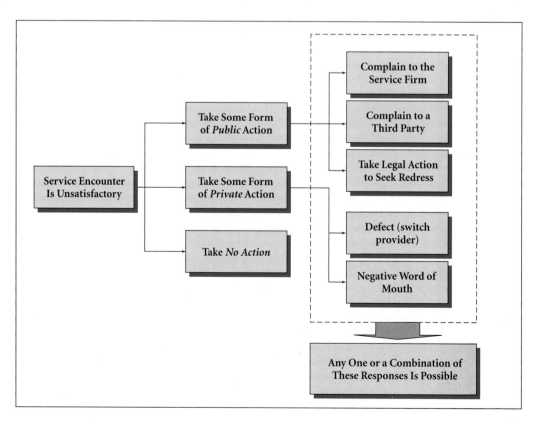

- *Vent their anger.* Some customers complain to rebuild self-esteem and/or to vent their anger and frustration. When service processes are bureaucratic and unreasonable, or when employees are rude, deliberately intimidating, or apparently uncaring, the customers' self-esteem, self-worth, or sense of fairness can be negatively affected. They may become angry and emotional as a result.

- *Help to improve the service.* When customers are highly involved with a service (e.g., at a college, an alumni association, or their main banking connection), they give feedback to try to contribute toward service improvements.

- *For altruistic reasons.* Finally, some customers are motivated by altruistic reasons. They want to spare other customers from experiencing the same problems, and they might feel bad if a problem is not highlighted.

What Proportion of Unhappy Customers Complain?   Research shows that on average only five to ten percent of customers who have been unhappy with a service actually complain.[4] Sometimes the percentage is far lower. One of the present authors analyzed the complaints a public bus company received, which occurred at the rate of about three complaints for every million passenger trips. Assuming two trips a day, each individual would need 1370 years (roughly 27 lifetimes) to make a million trips. In other words, the rate of complaints was incredibly low, given that public bus companies are usually not known for service excellence. However, although generally only a minority of dissatisfied customers complain, there is evidence that consumers across the world are becoming better informed, more self-confident, and more assertive about seeking satisfactory outcomes for their complaints.

Why Don't Unhappy Customers Complain?   TARP, a customer satisfaction and measurement firm, has identified a number of reasons why customers don't complain.[5] They don't wish to take the time to write a letter, send an email, fill out a form, or make a phone call, not least if they don't see the service as sufficiently important to them to merit the effort. Many customers see the payoff as uncertain, and believe that no one would be concerned about their problem or willing to resolve it. In some situations, people simply do not know where to go or what to do. Additionally, many people feel that complaining is unpleasant (Figure 13.2). They may be afraid of confrontation, especially if the complaint involves someone whom the customer knows and may have to deal with again.

Figure 13.2
Customers often view complaining as difficult and unpleasant.

Courtesy of Images.com.

Chapter 13   Achieving Service Recovery and Obtaining Customer Feedback   **381**

Complaining behaviour can be influenced by role perceptions and social norms. Customers are less likely to voice complaints in service situations where they perceive they have low "power" (ability to influence or control the transaction).[6] This is particularly true when the problem involves professional service providers, such as doctors, lawyers, or architects. Social norms tend to discourage customer criticism of such individuals, because of their perceived expertise. In other situations, though, social norms can encourage complaining. Toronto's Mojo Radio, the AM640 "Talk Radio For Guys" launched in 2001, faced complaints for its perceived "offensive" programming (albeit only sometimes) right from its inception. Listener complaints and the resultant censuring of its programming led to its demise, and in 2004 AM640 was relaunched as a "serious" radio talk station.[7]

Who Is Most Likely to Complain?   Research findings consistently show that people in higher socioeconomic levels are more likely to complain than those in lower levels. Their better education, higher income, and greater social involvement give them the confidence, knowledge, and motivation to speak up when they encounter problems.[8] Further, those who complain also tend to be more knowledgeable about the products in question.

Service Perspectives 13.1

Complaint Courier: Making Consumer Complaints Simpler, Faster, Better Connected

Complaint Courier is an online tool offered by Industry Canada's Office of Consumer Affairs that helps Canadian consumers manage the process of complaining in an effective, easy manner. According to the website (http://consumerinformation.ca), "The Complaint Courier is a powerful online tool that transforms the process of filing consumer complaints. The Courier empowers consumers and levels the playing field so that all can be effective, regardless of limitations in their knowledge and time. For example, the Complaint Courier educates consumers on their rights and responsibilities, then provides them guidance on how to contact the business and effectively voice a complaint. Its innovative Letter Wizard helps consumers prepare complete and effective letters of complaint simply by filling in a customized template. Its Dialogue Coach can help you communicate with the business by offering guidance and suggestions for pertinent questions, appropriate language, and possible rebuttal strategies, and can allow you to capture important details of your interaction(s) with the company. Its powerful database automatically channels complaints to the appropriate agency. Thanks to this leading-edge technology, consumers save time, construct well-documented complaints, and no longer need to know which agency to deal with. When all else fails the Courier also provides consumers with information on available alternative dispute resolution."

The hope is that the tool would encourage Canadian consumers to be more forthcoming with their complaints, thereby helping them on the way toward effective complaint resolution.

Figure 13.A Complaint Courier helps consumers manage the complaints process.

Source: http://consumerinformation.ca/app/oca/complaintcourier/index.do?lang=e, accessed December 2006. Reproduced with the permission of Industry Canada and the Minister of Public Works and Government Services, 2006.

Where Do Customers Complain?   Studies show that the majority of complaints are made at the place where the service was received. One of the present authors recently completed a consulting project developing and implementing a customer feedback system, and found that, astoundingly, more than 99 percent of customer feedback was given face-to-face or over the phone to customer service representatives. Less than one percent of all complaints were submitted via email, letters, faxes, or customer feedback cards. A survey of airline passengers found that only three percent of respondents who were unhappy with their meal actually complained about it, and they all complained to the flight attendant! None complained to the company's headquarters or to a consumer affairs office.[9] Also, customers tend to use non-interactive channels to complain (e.g., email or letters) when they mainly want to vent their anger and frustration, but resort to interactive channels, such as face to face or the telephone, when they want a problem to be fixed, or they want redress.[10] In practice, even when customers do complain, managers often do not hear about the complaints made to front-line staff. Less than five percent of complaints made to front-line staff reach corporate headquarters.[11] Sometimes the government can play a significant role in facilitating the complaint process for consumers, helping them overcome the constraints such as knowledge and time that might stand in the way of the complaint process (see Service Perspectives 13.1).

What Do Customers Expect Once They Have Made a Complaint?

Whenever a service failure occurs, people expect to be adequately compensated in a fair manner. However, recent studies have shown that many customers feel they were not treated fairly and did not receive adequate justice. When this happens, customer reactions tend to be immediate, emotional, and enduring.[12]

Stephen Tax and Stephen Brown found that as much as 85 percent of the variation in the satisfaction with a service recovery was determined by three dimensions of fairness.[13] These are shown in Figure 13.3.

- *Procedural justice* concerns the policies and rules that any customer will have to go through in order to seek fairness. Here, customers expect the firm to assume responsibility, which is the key to the start of a fair procedure, followed by a convenient and

Figure 13.3

Three Dimensions of Perceived Fairness in Service Recovery Processes

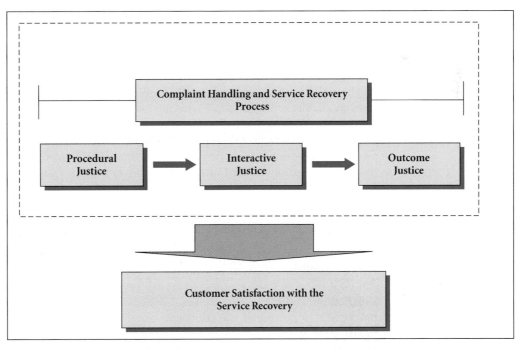

Source: Reprinted from Three Dimensions of Perceived Fairness in Service Recovery Processes by Stephen S. Tax and Stephen W. Brown, "Recovering and Learning from Service Failure," *Sloan Management Review* 49, no. 1 (Fall 1998), pp. 75–88, by permission of publisher. Copyright © 2003 by Massachusetts Institute of Technology. All rights reserved.

responsive recovery process. That includes flexibility of the system and consideration of customer inputs into the recovery process.

- *Interactional justice* involves the employees of the firm who provide the service recovery, and their behaviour toward the customer. Giving an explanation for the failure and making an effort to resolve the problem are very important. However, the recovery effort must be perceived as genuine, honest, and polite.
- *Outcome justice* concerns the compensation that a customer receives as a result of the losses and inconveniences incurred because of a service failure. This includes compensation not only for the failure, but also for the time, effort, and energy spent during the process of service recovery.[14]

CUSTOMER RESPONSES TO EFFECTIVE SERVICE RECOVERY

"Thank Heavens for Complainers" was the provocative title of an article about customer complaining behaviour that also featured a successful manager exclaiming "Thank goodness I've got a dissatisfied customer on the phone! The ones I worry about are the ones I never hear from."[15] Customers who do complain give a firm the chance to correct problems (including some the firm may not even know it has), restore relationships with the complainer, and, potentially, improve future satisfaction for all.

"Service recovery" is an umbrella term for systematic efforts by a firm to correct a problem following a service failure, and to retain a customer's goodwill. Service recovery efforts play a crucial role in achieving (or restoring) customer satisfaction.[16] In every organization, things may occur that have a negative impact on its relationships with customers. The true test of a firm's commitment to satisfaction and service quality isn't in the advertising promises it makes, but in the way it responds when things go wrong for the customer.

Effective service recovery requires thoughtful procedures for resolving problems and handling disgruntled customers. It is critical for firms to have effective recovery strategies, because even a single service problem can destroy a customer's confidence in a firm under the following conditions.

- The failure is totally outrageous (for instance, blatant dishonesty on the part of the supplier).
- The problem fits a pattern of failure rather than being an isolated incident.
- The recovery efforts are weak, serving to compound the original problem rather than correct it.[17]

The risk of defection is especially high when there are a variety of competing alternatives available. One study of customer switching behaviour in service industries found that close to 60 percent of all respondents who reported changing suppliers did so because of a service failure: 25 percent cited failures in the core service, 19 percent reported an unsatisfactory encounter with an employee, 10 percent reported an unsatisfactory response to a prior service failure, and 4 percent described unethical behaviour on the part of the provider.[18]

Impact of Effective Service Recovery on Customer Loyalty

When complaints are satisfactorily resolved, there is a much higher chance that the customers involved will remain loyal. TARP research found that intentions to repurchase for different types of products ranged from 9 percent to 37 percent when customers were dissatisfied but did not complain. For a major complaint, the retention rate increased from 9 percent to 19 percent if the company offered a sympathetic ear to the customer's complaint, even if it was unable to resolve the complaint to the satisfaction of the customer. If the complaint *could* be resolved to the satisfaction of the customer, retention rate jumped to 54 percent. The highest retention rate of 82 percent was achieved when problems were fixed quickly, typically on the spot![19]

In another empirical benchmarking study done with data collected from customer service managers in 40 UK organizations, it was found that effective complaint management processes resulted not only in improved customer satisfaction but also in operational improvements and enhanced employee attitudes and retention. All these factors result in an improved financial performance for the organization.[20]

The conclusion to be drawn is that complaint handling should be seen as a profit centre and not a cost centre. When a dissatisfied customer defects, the firm loses more than just the value of the next transaction. It may also lose a long-term stream of profits from that customer, and from anyone else who switches suppliers or is deterred from doing business with that firm because of negative comments from an unhappy friend. However, as can be seen in Service Perspectives 13.2, many organizations have not yet bought into the concept that it pays to invest in the service recovery that's designed to protect those long-term profits.

The Service Recovery Paradox

The service recovery paradox refers to the sometimes observed effect that customers who experience a service failure and then have it resolved to their full satisfaction are more likely to make future purchases than are customers who experience no problem in the first place.[21] A study of repeated service failures in a retail banking context showed that the service recovery paradox held for the first service failure that was recovered to customers' full satisfaction.[22] However, when a second service failure occurred, the paradox disappeared. It seems that customers may forgive a firm once, but get disillusioned if failures recur. Furthermore, the study also showed that customers' expectations were raised after they experienced a very good recovery; thus, excellent recovery becomes the standard they expect for dealing with future failures.

Some recent studies have challenged the existence of the service recovery paradox. For example, Tor Andreassen conducted a major study with some 8600 telephone interviews across a wide range of consumer services. The findings showed that after a service recovery, customers' intention to repurchase, and their perceptions of and attitudes towards the company, never surpassed the ratings of satisfied customers who did not experience a service problem in the first place. This was true even when the service recovery had gone very well and the customer expressed full satisfaction with the recovery.[23]

Service Perspectives 13.2

Common Service Recovery Mistakes

Here are some typical service recovery mistakes made by many organizations:

- *Managers disregard evidence showing that service recovery provides a significant financial return.* In recent years, many organizations have focused on cost cutting, and only paid lip service to retaining their most profitable customers. On top of that, they also lost sight of the need to respect all their customers.

- *Companies do not invest enough in actions that would prevent service issues.* Ideally, service planners address potential problems before they become customer problems. Although preventive measures do not eliminate the need for good service recovery systems, they greatly reduce the burden on front-line staff and on the recovery systems they operate.

- *Customer service employees fail to display good attitudes.* The three most important things in service recovery are attitude, attitude, and attitude. No matter how well designed and well planned the service recovery system is, it will not work without the friendly and proverbial smile-in-the-voice attitude from front-line staff.

- *Organizations fail to make it easy for customers to complain or give feedback.* Although some improvement can be seen, such as hotels and restaurants offering comment cards, little is done to communicate their simplicity and value to customers. Research shows that a large proportion of customers complain that they are unaware of the existence of a proper feedback system that could help them get their problems solved.

Source: Adapted from Rod Stiefbold, "Dissatisfied Customers Require Service Recovery Plans," *Marketing News* 37/22 (October 27, 2003): 44–45.

Whether a customer comes out delighted from a service recovery probably also depends on the severity and "recoverability" of the failure—no one can replace spoilt wedding photos or a ruined holiday, or entirely make up for an injury caused by service equipment. In such situations, it's hard to imagine anyone being truly delighted even when a most professional service recovery is conducted. Contrast these examples with a lost hotel reservation, for which the recovery is an upgrade to a suite. When the service is recovered in a way that allows the delivery of a superior product, the customer is, of course, delighted, and probably hopes for another lost reservation in the future.

The best strategy is to do it right the first time. As Michael Hargrove puts it: "Service recovery is turning a service failure into an opportunity you wish you never had."[24] It is critical that service recovery is well executed, but failures cannot be tolerated. Unfortunately, empirical evidence shows that a large proportion of customers are dissatisfied with the outcome of their complaints. In recent studies, some 40 to 60 percent of customers reported dissatisfaction with the service recovery process.[25]

PRINCIPLES OF EFFECTIVE SERVICE RECOVERY SYSTEMS

Recognizing that current customers are a valuable asset base, managers need to develop effective procedures for service recovery following unsatisfactory experiences. We discuss three guiding principles for how to do this well: make it easy for customers to give feedback, enable effective service recovery, and establish appropriate compensation levels. The components of an effective service recovery system are shown in Figure 13.4.[26]

Make It Easy for Customers to Give Feedback

How can managers overcome unhappy customers' reluctance to complain about service failures? The best way is to address the reasons for their reluctance directly. Table 13.1 gives an overview of potential measures that can be taken to overcome those reasons we had identified earlier in this chapter. Many companies have improved their complaint-collection procedures by adding special toll-free phone lines, links on their websites,

Figure 13.4

Components of an Effective Service Recovery System

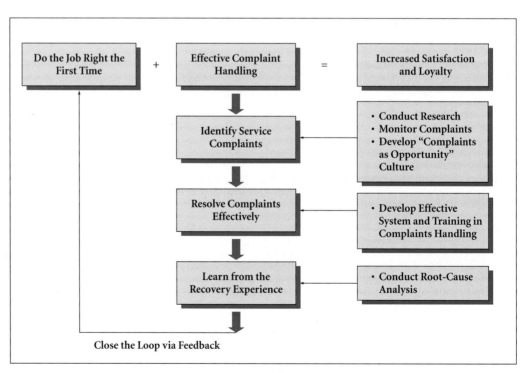

Source: Adapted from Christopher H. Lovelock, Paul G. Patterson, and Rhett Walker, *Services Marketing: An Asia-Pacific and Australian Perspective,* 3rd ed., Melbourne: Prentice Hall Australia, 2004: 135.

Table 13.1 Strategies to Reduce Customer Complaint Barriers

COMPLAINT BARRIERS FOR DISSATISFIED CUSTOMERS	STRATEGIES TO REDUCE THESE BARRIERS
Inconvenience • Difficult to find the right complaint procedure • Effort, e.g., writing and mailing a letter	Make feedback easy and convenient: • Print customer service hotline numbers and email and postal addresses on all customer communications materials (letters, faxes, bills, brochures, phone book listing, yellow pages, etc.)
Doubtful payoff • Uncertain what, if any, action will be taken by the firm to address the issue the customer is unhappy with	Reassure customers that their feedback will be taken seriously and will pay off: • Have service recovery procedures in place and communicate this to customers, e.g., in customer newsletter and website. • Feature service improvements that resulted from customer feedback.
Unpleasantness • Fear of being treated rudely • Fear of being hassled • Feeling embarrassed	Make providing feedback a positive experience: • Thank customers for their feedback (can be done publicly and in general by addressing the entire customer base). • Train the front line not to hassle and to make customers feel comfortable. • Allow for anonymous feedback.

prominently displayed customer comment cards in their branches, or even providing video terminals for recording complaints. In their customer newsletters, some companies feature service improvements that were the direct result of customer feedback under such mottoes as "you told us, and we responded."

Enable Effective Service Recovery

Recovering from service failures takes more than just pious expressions of determination to resolve any problems that may occur. It requires commitment, planning, and clear guidelines. Specifically, effective service recovery procedures should be: (1) proactive, (2) planned, (3) trained, and (4) empowered.

Service Recovery Should Be Proactive   Service recovery needs to be initiated on the spot, ideally before customers have a chance to complain (see Best Practice in Action 13.1). Service personnel should be sensitized to signs of dissatisfaction and ask whether customers might be experiencing a problem. For example, the waiter may ask a guest who has only eaten half of his dinner, "Is everything all right, sir?" The guest may say, "Yes, thank you, I am not very hungry," or "The steak is well done but I had asked for medium-rare, plus it is very salty." The latter response then gives the waiter a chance to recover the service, rather than have an unhappy diner leave the restaurant and potentially not return.

Recovery Procedures Need to Be Planned   Contingency plans have to be developed for service failures, especially for those that can occur regularly and cannot be designed out of the system.[27] Revenue management practices in the travel and hospitality industries often result in overbooking, and travellers are denied boarding or hotel guests are "walked" even though they had a confirmed seat or reservation. To simplify the task of front-line staff, firms should identify the most common service problems, such as overbooking, and develop predetermined solution sets for employees to follow. For example, Air Canada has set guidelines that are followed in case of overbooked flights. If customers are denied boarding due to overbooking in Canada, they are compensated by being given travel vouchers or cash. Further, they are booked on the next Air Canada flight that has available seats.

In the case of overnight delays, Air Canada provides out-of-town customers with meal vouchers, hotel accommodation, and transportation to and from the airport.[28]

Recovery Skills Must Be Taught   Customers easily feel insecure at the point of service failure because things are not turning out as anticipated. Effective training arms front-line staff with the confidence and competence to turn distress into delight.[29]

Recovery Requires Empowered Employees   Service recovery efforts should be flexible and employees should be empowered to use their judgment and communication skills to develop solutions that will satisfy complaining customers.[30] This is especially true for out-of-the-ordinary failures for which a firm may not have developed, or given training in, potential solution sets. Employees need to have the authority to make decisions and spend money in order to resolve service problems promptly and recover customer goodwill.

How Generous Should Compensation Be?

Clearly, vastly different costs are associated with possible recovery strategies. How much compensation should a firm offer when there has been a service failure? Or would an apology be sufficient instead? The following rules of thumb can help to answer these questions:

- *What is the positioning of your firm?* If a firm is known for service excellence, and charges a high premium for quality, then customers will expect service failures to be rare, so the firm should make a demonstrable effort to recover the few failures that do occur and be prepared to offer something of significant value. But in a more down-scale, mass-market business, customers are likely to consider something quite modest, such as a free coffee or dessert as fair compensation.

Best Practice in Action 13.1

Effective Service Recovery in Action

The lobby is deserted. It is not hard to overhear the conversation between the night manager at the Marriott Long Wharf Hotel in Boston and the late-arriving guest.

"Yes, Dr. Jones, we've been expecting you. I know you are scheduled to be here three nights. I'm sorry to tell you, sir, but we are booked solid tonight. A large number of guests we assumed were checking out did not. Where is your meeting tomorrow, sir?"

The doctor told the clerk where it was.

"That's near the Omni Parker House! That's not very far from here. Let me call them and get you a room for the evening. I'll be right back."

A few minutes later the desk clerk returned with the good news.

"They're holding a room for you at the Omni Parker House, sir. And, of course, we'll pick up the tab. I'll forward any phone calls that come here for you. Here's a letter that will explain the situation and expedite your check-in, along with my business card so you can call me directly here at the front desk if you have any problems."

The doctor's mood was moving from exasperation towards calm. But the desk clerk was not finished with the encounter. He reached into the cash drawer. "Here are two $5 bills. That should more than cover your cab fare from here to the Parker House and back again in the morning. We don't have a problem tomorrow night, just tonight. And here's a coupon that will get you complimentary continental breakfast on our concierge level on the fifth floor tomorrow morning . . . and again, I am so sorry this happened."

As the doctor walks away, the night manager turns to the desk clerk, "Give him about 15 minutes and then call to make sure everything went okay."

A week later, when it is still a peak period for hotels in that city, the same guest who had overheard the exchange is in a taxi, en route to the same hotel. Along the way, he tells about the great service recovery episode he had witnessed the week before. The pair arrived at the hotel and made their way to the front desk—ready to check in.

They are greeted with unexpected news: "I am so sorry gentlemen. I know you were scheduled here for two nights. But we are booked solid tonight. Where is your meeting scheduled tomorrow?"

The would-be guests exchange a rueful glance as they give the desk clerk their future plans. "That's near the Meridian. Let me call over there and see if I can get you a room. It won't but take a minute." As the clerk walks away, the tale teller says, "I'll bet he comes back with a letter and a business card."

Sure enough, the desk clerk returns to deliver the solution; not a robotic script but all the elements from the previous week's show were on display. What the tale teller thought he witnessed the previous week as pure desk-clerk initiative, he now realized was planned, a spontaneous-feeling yet predetermined response to a specific category of customer problem.

Source: Ron Zemke and Chip R. Bell, *Knock Your Socks Off Service Recovery.* New York: AMACOM, 2000, 59–60.

- *How severe was the service failure?* The general guideline is "let the punishment fit the crime." Customers expect less for minor inconveniences, and a much more significant compensation if major damage in terms of time, effort, annoyance, anxiety, etc., was caused on the customer's side.

- *Who is the affected customer?* Long-term customers, and those who spend heavily, expect more, and it is worth making an effort to save their business. One-off customers tend to be less demanding, and have less economic importance to the firm. Hence, compensation can be less, but should still be fair—there is always the possibility that a first-time user will become a repeat customer if treated fairly. The overall rule of thumb for compensation of service failures should be "well-dosed generosity." Being perceived as stingy adds insult to injury, and the firm would probably be better off apologizing rather than offering minimal compensation.

In an empirical study done with guests of a Canadian hotel, it was found that consumers' reactions to service-failure recovery strategies varied depending upon the nature and extent of the failure. For instance, in high-severity failures, offering assistance or compensation was more effective than just offering an apology. The most effective strategy in this case was offering an apology, assistance, *and* compensation. In the case of low-severity situations, diminishing returns to service recovery efforts were found. Offering customers assistance or compensation along with an apology was as effective as offering both assistance and compensation along with the apology.[31]

One also needs to be careful in calibrating the amount of compensation, if that is part of the service-recovery effort. Overly generous compensation is not only expensive but may even be negatively interpreted by customers.[32] It may raise questions about the soundness of the business and lead customers to become suspicious about the underlying motives. Customers may worry about the implications for the employee as well as for the business. Also, overgenerosity does not seem to result in higher repeat purchase rates than simply offering fair compensation.[33] There is also the risk that a reputation for overgenerosity might encourage dishonest customers to "seek" service failures.

Dealing with Complaining Customers

Both managers and front-line employees must be prepared to deal with angry customers who are confrontational and sometimes behave in insulting ways toward service personnel who aren't personally at fault in any way. Service Perspectives 13.3 provides specific guidelines for effective problem resolution, designed to help calm upset customers and to deliver a resolution that they will see as fair and satisfying.

SERVICE GUARANTEES

A growing number of companies offer customers a service guarantee, promising that if service delivery fails to meet pre-defined standards, the customer is entitled to one or more forms of compensation, such as an easy-to-claim replacement, refund, or credit. Some firms place conditions on these guarantees, others offer them unconditionally.

The Power of Service Guarantees

Christopher Hart declares that service guarantees are powerful tools for both promoting and achieving service quality, for the following reasons:[34]

1. Guarantees force firms to focus on what their customers want and expect in each element of the service.

2. Guarantees set clear standards, telling customers and employees alike what the company stands for. Payouts to compensate customers for poor service cause managers to take guarantees seriously, because they highlight the financial costs of quality failures.

Guidelines for the Front Line: How to Handle Customer Complaints

1. Act fast. If the complaint is made during service delivery, then time is of the essence to achieve a full recovery. When complaints are made after the fact, many companies have established policies of responding within 24 hours or less. Even when full resolution is likely to take longer, fast acknowledgment remains very important.

2. Acknowledge the customer's feelings, either tacitly or explicitly (for example, "I can understand why you're upset"). This action helps to build rapport, the first step in rebuilding a bruised relationship.

3. Don't argue with customers. The goal should be to gather facts to reach a mutually acceptable solution, not to win a debate or prove that the customer is an idiot. Arguing gets in the way of listening and seldom diffuses anger.

4. Show that you understand the problem from each customer's point of view. Seeing situations through the customers' eyes is the only way to understand what they think has gone wrong and why they're upset. Service personnel should avoid jumping to conclusions with their own interpretations.

5. Clarify the truth and sort out the cause. A failure may result from inefficiency of service, misunderstanding by customers, or the misbehaviour of a third party. If the company has done something wrong, apologize immediately in order to win the understanding and trust of the customer. The more the customer can forgive you, the less he or she expects to be compensated. Don't be defensive. Acting defensively may suggest that the organization has something to hide or is reluctant to fully explore the situation.

6. Give customers the benefit of the doubt. Not all customers are truthful, and not all complaints are justified. However, customers should be treated as though they have a valid complaint until clear evidence to the contrary emerges. If a lot of money is at stake (as in insurance claims or potential lawsuits), careful investigation is warranted. If the amount involved is small, it may not be worth haggling over a refund or other compensation. However, it's still a good idea to check records to see if there is a past history of dubious complaints by the same customer.

7. Propose the steps needed to solve the problem. When instant solutions aren't possible, telling customers how the organization plans to proceed shows that corrective action is being taken. It also sets expectations about the time involved. (So firms should be careful not to over-promise!)

8. Keep customers informed of progress. Nobody likes being left in the dark. Uncertainty breeds anxiety and stress. People tend to be more accepting of disruptions if they know what's going on and receive periodic progress reports.

9. Consider compensation. When customers do not receive the service outcomes that they have paid for, or have suffered serious inconvenience and/or loss of time and money because the service failed, either a monetary payment or an offer of equivalent service in kind is appropriate. This type of recovery strategy may also reduce the risk of legal action by an angry customer. Service guarantees often lay out in advance what such compensation will be, and the firm should ensure that all guarantees are met.

10. Persevere to regain customer goodwill. When customers have been disappointed, one of the biggest challenges is to restore their confidence and preserve the relationship for the future. Perseverance may be required to defuse customers' anger and to convince them that actions are being taken to avoid a recurrence of the problem. Truly exceptional recovery efforts can be extremely effective in building loyalty and referrals.

11. Self-check the system and pursue evidence. After the customer has left, you should check to determine whether the service failure was caused by accidental mistakes or system defects. Take advantage of every complaint to perfect the whole service system. Even if the complaint is disclosed to be a misunderstanding by customers, it implies the ineffectiveness of a certain part of your communication system.

3. Guarantees require the development of systems for generating meaningful customer feedback and acting on it.

4. Guarantees force service organizations to understand why they fail, and encourage them to identify and overcome potential fail points.

5. Guarantees build "marketing muscle" by reducing the risk of the purchase decision and building long-term loyalty.

From the customer's perspective, the primary function of service guarantees is to lower the perceived risks associated with purchase.[35] The presence of a guarantee may also make it easier for customers to complain and more likely that they will do so, since they will anticipate that front-line employees will be prepared to resolve the problem and provide appropriate compensation. Sara Björlin Lidén and Per Skålén found that even when dissatisfied customers were unaware that a service guarantee existed before making their complaints, they were positively impressed to learn that the company had a pre-planned procedure for handling failures, and to find that their complaints were taken seriously.[36]

The benefits of service guarantees can be seen clearly in the case of Hampton Inn's 100 percent Satisfaction Guarantee ("If you're not 100% satisfied, you don't pay"—see Figure 13.5), which has now been extended to the Embassy Suites and Homewood Suites chains of the Hilton group of hotels.[37] As a business-building program, Hampton's strategy of offering to refund the cost of the room to a guest who expresses dissatisfaction has attracted new customers and also served as a powerful retention device. People choose to stay at a Hampton Inn because they are confident they will be satisfied. At least as important, the guarantee has become a vital tool to help managers identify new opportunities for quality improvement.

Discussing the impact on staff and managers, the vice president of marketing for Hampton Inn stated, "Designing the guarantee made us understand what made guests

Figure 13.5
Hampton Inn includes its "100% Hampton Guarantee" in its advertising.

Courtesy of Hilton

satisfied, rather than what *we thought* made them satisfied." It became imperative that everyone, from reservation takers and front-line employees to general managers and personnel at corporate headquarters, listen carefully to guests, anticipate their needs to the greatest extent possible, and remedy problems quickly so that guests were satisfied with the solution. Viewing a hotel's function in this customer-centric way had a profound impact on the way the firm conducted business.

The guarantee "turned up the pressure in the hose," as one manager put it, showing where "leaks" existed, and providing the financial incentive to plug them. As a result, the guarantee has had an important impact on product consistency and service delivery across the Hampton Inn chain. Finally, studies have shown the dramatic positive effect of the "100 % Satisfaction Guarantee" on financial performance. However, it is worth noting that such policies also have the potential to be abused by certain customers. (See Service Perspectives 13.5, p. 395.)

How to Design Service Guarantees

Some guarantees are simple and unconditional. Others appear to have been written by lawyers and contain many restrictions. Compare the examples in Service Perspectives 13.4 and ask yourself which guarantees instil trust and confidence in you, and would make you like to do business with that supplier.

Both the MFA Group and L.L. Bean guarantees are powerful, unconditional, and instil trust. The others are weakened by the many conditions. Hart argues that service guarantees should be designed to have the following qualities:[38]

1. *Unconditional:* whatever is promised in the guarantee must be totally unconditional, and there should not be any element of surprise for the customer.

2. *Easy to understand and communicate* to the customer so that he is clearly aware of the benefits that can be gained from the guarantee.

3. *Meaningful to the customer*, in that the guarantee is on something important to the customer and the compensation should be more than adequate to cover the service failure.[39]

4. *Easy to invoke:* less of the guarantee should be dependent on the customers, and more on the service provider.

5. *Easy to collect:* if a service failure occurs, the customer should be able to collect on the guarantee easily and without any problems.

6. *Credible:* the guarantee should be believable.

Is Full Satisfaction the Best You Can Guarantee?

Full satisfaction guarantees have generally been considered the best possible design. However, it has been suggested that the unquantifiable nature of "satisfaction" can lead to a discounting of their perceived value. Customers may raise questions such as "What does full satisfaction mean?" or "Can I invoke a guarantee when I am dissatisfied, even if the fault does not lie with the service firm?"[40] A new type of guarantee, called the "combined guarantee," addresses this issue.[41] This combines the wide scope of a full-satisfaction guarantee with the low uncertainty of specific performance standards. The combined guarantee was shown to be superior to the pure full-satisfaction or attribute-specific guarantee designs. Specific performance standards are guaranteed (e.g., on-time delivery), but should the consumer be dissatisfied with any other element of the service, the full satisfaction coverage of the combined guarantee applies. Table 13.2 shows examples of the various types of guarantees.

Service Perspectives 13.4

Examples of Service Guarantees

Excerpt from the "Quality Standard Guarantees" from an Office Services Company

"We guarantee 6-hour turnaround on documents of two pages or less . . . (does not include client subsequent changes or equipment failures).

We guarantee that there will be a receptionist to greet you and your visitors during normal business hours . . . (short breaks of less than five minutes are not subject to this guarantee).

You will not be obligated to pay rent for any day on which there is not a manager on site to assist you (lunch and reasonable breaks are expected and not subject to this guarantee)."

Source: Reproduced in Eileen C. Shapiro, *Fad Surfing in the Boardroom.* Reading, MA: Addison-Wesley, 1995: 18.

MFA Group Inc. (Oakville, Ontario-based professional staff search and selection firm)

"An Unconditional Guarantee: We 'put our money where our mouth is,' in two ways, not just one:

1. Money back

We offer an unconditional money back guarantee—if at any point during the search process you are unhappy with progress, simply address the fact with us and if you are still not 100% satisfied after that discussion, we will cheerfully and unconditionally refund every cent you have paid as a retainer. No quibbles, no hassle, guaranteed, period.

2. Twelve month candidate guarantee

All candidates placed by us are guaranteed for a full 12 months. If, during this period they leave your firm, for any reason whatsoever, we will conduct an additional search, completely free of charge, until a suitable replacement has been found. We focus on doing the job right in the first place and have never been called upon to do either of the above actions, but we would not hesitate to do so if asked."

Source: www.mfagroup.com/recruiting.htm, accessed October 2006. Reprinted with permission of MFA Group Inc.

L.L. Bean's Guarantee (Maine-based outdoor apparel and equipment retailer)

"Our Guarantee. Our products are guaranteed to give 100 percent satisfaction in every way. Return anything purchased from us at any time if it proves otherwise. We do not want you to have anything from L.L. Bean that is not completely satisfactory."

Source: All L.L. Bean catalogues and at www.llbean.com/customer Service/aboutLLBean/guarantee.html, accessed June 4, 2006.

The Bugs Burger Bug Killer (a Pest Control Company) Guarantee

- You don't owe us a penny until all the pests on your premises have been eradicated.
- If you're ever dissatisfied with the BBBK's service, you will receive a refund for as much as 12 months of service—plus fees for another exterminator of your choice for the next year.
- If a guest spots a pest on your premises, the exterminator will pay for the guest's meal or room, send a letter of apology, and pay for a future meal or stay.
- If your premises are closed down because of the presence of roaches or rodents, BBBK will pay any fines, as well as all lost profit, plus $5,000.

Source: Reproduced in Christopher W. Hart, "The Power of Unconditional Service Guarantees." *Harvard Business Review* (July–August 1990).

Is It Always Appropriate to Introduce a Service Guarantee?

Managers should think carefully about their firm's strengths and weaknesses when deciding whether or not to introduce a service guarantee. In many instances, it may be inappropriate to do so.[42] Companies that already have a strong reputation for service excellence may not need a guarantee. In fact, it might even be incongruent with their image to offer one, as there is a risk of it confusing the market.[43] By contrast, a firm whose service is currently poor must first work to improve quality to a level above that at which the guarantee might be invoked on a regular basis by most of its customers.

Service firms whose quality is truly uncontrollable because of external forces would be foolish to consider a guarantee. For example, the Markham, Ontario-based tele-

Table 13.2 Types of Service Guarantees

TERM	GUARANTEE SCOPE	EXAMPLE
Single attribute-specific guarantee	One key attribute of the service is covered by the guarantee.	"Any of three specified popular pizzas is guaranteed to be served within 10 minutes of ordering on working days between 12 A.M. and 2 P.M. If the pizza is late, the customer's next order is free."
Multi-attribute-specific guarantee	A few important attributes of the service are covered by the guarantee.	Minneapolis Marriott's guarantee: "Our quality commitment to you is to provide • A friendly, efficient check-in • A clean, comfortable room, where everything works • A friendly, efficient check-out If we, in your opinion, do not deliver on this commitment, we will give you $20 in cash. No questions asked. It is your interpretation."
Full-satisfaction guarantee	All aspects of the service are covered by the guarantee. There are no exceptions.	Lands' End's guarantee: "If you are not completely satisfied with any item you buy from us, at any time during your use of it, return it and we will refund your full purchase price. We mean every word of it. Whatever. Whenever. Always. But to make sure this is perfectly clear, we've decided to simplify it further. GUARANTEED. Period."
Combined guarantee	All aspects of the service are covered by the full-satisfaction promise of the guarantee. Explicit minimum performance standards on important attributes are included in the guarantee to reduce uncertainty.	Datapro Information Services guarantees "to deliver the report on time, to high quality standards, and to the contents outlined in this proposal. Should we fail to deliver according to this guarantee, *or should you be dissatisfied with any aspect of our work,* you can deduct any amount from the final payment which is deemed as fair."

Source: Adapted from Jochen Wirtz and Doreen Kum, "Designing Service Guarantees: Is Full Satisfaction the Best You Can Guarantee?" *Journal of Services Marketing* 15/4 (2001): 282–99.

communication firm FCI Broadband explicitly states under its general terms of service that "FCI Broadband does not represent, warrant, covenant or guarantee that transmissions initiated by the Customer in the course of using the Services cannot or will not be received or intercepted by any other person(s)."[44] It would be impossible for FCI or any other telecommunication firm to uphold any such guarantee on the security of transmissions initiated by the customer.

In a market where consumers see little financial, personal, or physiological risk associated with purchasing and using a service, a guarantee adds little value but still costs money to design, implement, and manage. Where little perceived difference in service quality among competing firms exists, the first company to institute a guarantee may be able to obtain a first-mover advantage and create a valued differentiation for its services. If more than one competitor already has a guarantee in place, offering a guarantee may become a qualifier for the industry, meaning the only real way for a firm to make an impact would be to launch a highly distinctive guarantee beyond that already offered by competitors.[45]

DISCOURAGING ABUSE AND OPPORTUNISTIC BEHAVIOUR

Throughout this chapter, we advocate that firms should welcome complaints and invocations of service guarantees, and even encourage them. But how can this be done without inviting potential abuse by that undesirable group of people termed jaycustomers? (see Chapter 8).

Dealing with Consumer Fraud

Dishonest customers can take advantage of generous service recovery strategies, service guarantees, or simply a strong customer orientation in a number of ways. For example, they may steal from the firm, refuse to pay for the service, fake dissatisfaction, purposely cause service failures to occur, or overstate losses at the time of genuine service failures. What steps can a firm take to protect itself against opportunistic customer behaviour?

Treating customers with suspicion is likely to alienate them, especially in situations of service failure. The president of TARP notes:

> Our research has found that premeditated rip-offs represent 1 to 2 percent of the customer base in most organizations. However, most organizations defend themselves against unscrupulous customers by ... treating the 98 percent of honest customers like crooks to catch the 2 percent who *are* crooks.[46]

Using the knowledge that this approach is likely to be counterproductive, the working assumption should instead be "if in doubt, believe the customer." However, as Service Perspectives 13.5 shows, it's crucial to monitor the invocations of service guarantees and of payments compensating for service failure by maintaining databases of all such cases and monitoring repeated service payouts to the same customer. For example, one Asian airline found that the same customer lost his suitcase on three consecutive flights. The chances of this happening are very low, so front-line staff were told to look out for this individual. The next time he checked in his suitcase, the check-in staff video-taped the suitcase almost continuously from check-in to pickup in the baggage claim at the destination. It turned out that an accomplice collected the suitcase and took it through customs while the traveller again made his way to the lost-baggage counter to report his suitcase missing. This time, the police were waiting for him and his friend.

Recent research shows that the amount of a guarantee payout (e.g., whether it is a 10 percent or 100 percent money-back guarantee) had no effect on consumer cheating. However, repeat purchase intention significantly reduced cheating intent. These findings suggest important managerial implications: 1) managers can implement and thus reap the bigger marketing benefits of 100 percent money-back guarantees without worrying that the large payouts would increase cheating; and 2) guarantees can be offered to regular customers or as part of a membership program, since repeat customers are unlikely to cheat on service guarantees. A further finding was that customers were also more reluctant to

Service Perspectives 13.5

Tracking Down Guests Who Cheat

As part of its guarantee tracking system, Hampton Inn has developed ways to identify guests who appeared to be cheating—using aliases or various dissatisfaction problems to invoke the guarantee repeatedly in order to get the cost of their room refunded. Guests showing high invocation trends receive personalized attention and follow-up from the company's Guest Assistance Team. Wherever possible, senior managers telephone these guests to ask about their recent stays. The conversation might go as follows: "Hello, Mr. Jones. I'm the director of guest assistance at Hampton Inn, and I see that you've had some difficulty with the last four properties you've visited. Since we take our guarantee very seriously, I thought I'd give you a call and find out what the problems were."

The typical response is dead silence! Sometimes the silence is followed with questions of how headquarters could possibly know about their problems. These calls have their humorous moments as well. One individual, who had invoked the guarantee seventeen times in what appeared to be a long road trip, was asked, innocuously, "Where do you like to stay when you travel?" "Hampton Inn," came the enthusiastic response. "But," said the executive making the call, "our records show that the last seventeen times you have stayed at a Hampton Inn, you have invoked the 100 percent Satisfaction Guarantee." "That's why I like them!" proclaimed the guest (who turned out to be a long-distance truck driver).

Source: Christopher W. Hart and Elizabeth Long, *Extraordinary Guarantees*, New York: AMACOM, 1997).

cheat if the service quality provided was truly high than when it was just satisfactory. This implied that truly excellent services firms have less cause to worry than the average provider, and that even open-ended guarantees whose interpretation is at the discretion of the customer, such as Hampton Inn's, had a positive impact that significantly outweighed losses from the frivolous claims to which such a guarantee is vulnerable.[47]

LEARNING FROM CUSTOMER FEEDBACK[48]

There are two ways of looking at complaints: first, as individual customer problems, each of which requires a resolution, and second, as a stream of information that can be used to measure quality and suggest improvements. So far in this chapter, we have taken the former perspective of the individual customer. In this section we discuss how customer feedback can be systematically collected, analyzed, and disseminated via an institutionalized customer feedback system (CFS) to achieve customer-driven learning.[49]

Key Objectives of Effective Customer Feedback Systems

"It is not the strongest species that survive, nor the most intelligent, but the ones most responsive to change" wrote Charles Darwin. Similarly, many strategists have concluded that in increasingly competitive markets, the ultimate competitive advantage for a firm is to learn and change faster than the competition.[50] Specific objectives of effective customer feedback systems typically fall into three main categories:

Assessment and Benchmarking of Service Quality and Performance The objective is to answer the question, "How satisfied are our customers?" This objective includes learning about how well a firm performed in comparison to its main competitor(s), how it performed in comparison to the previous year (or quarter or month), whether investments in certain service aspects have paid off in terms of customer satisfaction, and where the firm wants to be the following year. Often, a key objective of comparison against other units (branches, teams, service products, competitors) is to motivate managers and service staff to improve performance, especially when the results are linked to pay.

Customer-driven Learning and Improvements Here, the objective is to answer the questions, "What makes our customers happy or unhappy?" and "What are the strengths we need to maintain, and where and how do we need to improve?" For this, more specific or detailed information on processes and products is required to guide a firm's service improvement efforts, and to pinpoint areas with potentially high returns for quality investment. It is also about gaining an understanding of the things that other suppliers do well, and those that make customers happy.

Creating a Customer-Oriented Service Culture This objective is concerned with focusing the organization on customer needs and customer satisfaction, and rallying the entire organization toward a service-quality culture.

Of the three objectives just discussed, firms seem to be doing well on the first, but to be missing great opportunities in the other two. Neil Morgan, Eugene Anderson, and Vikas Mittal, in their research on customer satisfaction information usage (CSIU), concluded the following:

> Many of the firms in our sample do not appear to gain significant customer-focused learning benefits from their CS [customer satisfaction] systems, because they are designed to act primarily as a control mechanism [i.e., our assessment or benchmarking]. . . . [Firms] may be well served to re-evaluate how they deploy their existing CSIU resources. The majority of CSIU resources . . . are consumed in CS data collection. This often leads to too few resources being allocated to the analysis, dissemination, and utilization of this information to realize fully the potential payback from the investment in data collection.[51]

Use a Mix of Customer Feedback Collection Tools

Ernest Hemingway once said: "I like to listen. I have learned a great deal from listening carefully. Most people never listen." Likewise, firms need to listen to the voice of the customer. Table 13.3 gives an overview of typically used feedback tools and their ability to meet various requirements. Recognizing that different tools have different strengths and weaknesses, service marketers should select a mix of customer feedback collection tools that jointly deliver the needed information. As Leonard Berry and "Parsu" Parasuraman observe, "Combining approaches enables a firm to tap the strengths of each and compensate for weaknesses."[52]

Total Market Surveys, Annual Surveys, and Transactional Surveys

Total market surveys and *annual surveys* typically measure satisfaction with all major customer service processes and products.[53] Measurement is usually made at a high level, with the objective of obtaining a global index or indicator of overall service satisfaction for the entire firm. This could be based on indexed (e.g., using various attribute ratings) and/or weighted data (e.g., weighted by core segments and/or products).

Overall indices such as these tell how satisfied customers are, but not why they are happy or unhappy. There are limits to the number of questions that can be asked about each individual process or product. For example, a typical retail bank has some 30 to 50 key customer service processes (from car loan applications to cash deposits at the teller). Because of the sheer number of processes, many surveys have room for only one or two questions per process (e.g., how satisfied are you with our ATM services?) and cannot address issues in greater detail.

In contrast, *transactional surveys* are typically conducted after customers have completed a specific transaction (Figure 13.6). At that point, if time permits, they may be queried about the process in some depth. In the case of the bank, all key attributes and aspects of ATM

Table 13.3 Strengths and Weaknesses of Key Customer Feedback Collection Tools

Collection Tools	Firm	Process	Transaction Specific	Actionable	Representative, Reliable	Potential for Service Recovery	First-Hand Learning	Cost-Effectiveness
Total market survey (including competitors)	●	○	○	○	●	○	○	○
Annual survey on overall satisfaction	●	◑	○	○	●	○	○	○
Transactional survey	●	●	◑	◑	●	○	○	○
Service feedback cards	◑	●	●	◑	◑	●	◑	●
Mystery shopping	○	◑	●	●	○	○	◑	○
Unsolicited feedback (e.g., complaints)	○	◑	●	●	○	●	◑	●
Focus group discussions	○	◑	●	●	○	◑	●	◑
Service reviews	○	◑	●	●	○	●	●	◑

(meets requirements fully, ●; moderately, ◑; hardly/not at all, ○)

Source: Adapted from Jochen Wirtz and Monica Tomlin, "Institutionalizing Customer-driven Learning through Fully Integrated Customer Feedback Systems," *Managing Service Quality* 10/4 (2000): 210.

services could be included in the survey, including some open-ended questions, such as which aspects customers "liked best" or "liked least," and "suggested improvements." Such feedback is more actionable, can tell the firm why customers are happy or unhappy with the process, and usually yields specific insights about how to improve customer satisfaction.

All three survey types are representative and reliable when designed properly. Representativeness and reliability are required for: (1) accurate assessments of where the company, a process, branch, or individual stands relative to quality goals (having a representative and reliable sample means that observed changes in quality scores are not the result of sample biases and/or random errors); and (2) evaluations of individuals, staff, teams, branches, and/or processes, especially when incentive schemes are linked to such measures. The methodology has to be water-tight if staff are to trust and buy into the results, especially when surveys deliver bad news.

The potential for service recovery is important and should, if possible, be designed into feedback collection tools. However, many surveys promise anonymity, making it impossible to identify and respond to dissatisfied respondents. In personal encounters or telephone surveys, interviewers can be instructed to ask customers whether they would like the firm to report back to them on dissatisfaction issues.

Service Feedback Cards   This powerful and inexpensive tool involves giving customers a feedback card following completion of each major service process and inviting them to return it by mail or other means to a central customer feedback unit. For example, a feedback card can be attached to each housing mortgage approval letter, or to each car service invoice. Although these cards are a good indicator of process quality, and yield specific feedback on what works well and what doesn't, the respondents are self-selecting and thus tend not to be representative, being biased toward customers who are either very satisfied or very dissatisfied.

Mystery Shopping   Service businesses often use this method to determine whether front-line staff are displaying desired behaviours. Banks, retailers, car rental firms, and hotels are among the industries making active use of mystery shoppers. For example, the central reservation offices of a global hotel chain contracts for a large-scale monthly mystery caller survey to assess the skills of individual associates related to the phone sales process. Such actions as correctly positioning the various products, upselling and cross-selling, and closing the deal are measured. On top of that, the survey also assesses the quality of the phone conversation on such dimensions as "a warm and friendly greeting" and "establishing rapport with the caller." Mystery shopping gives highly actionable and in-depth insights for coaching, training, and performance evaluation.

Because the number of mystery calls or visits is typically small, no individual survey is reliable or representative. However, if a particular staff member performs well (or poorly) month after month, managers can infer with reasonable confidence that this person's performance is good (or poor).

Mystery shopping is a growing business, worth over $50 million in Canada and $500 million in North America as a whole. At the turn of the century there were no more than ten companies providing mystery shopping services in Canada. Currently, there are more than forty, including key players such as the Toronto-based Sensors Quality Management Inc. (SQM; see www.sqm.ca) and the Georgia, U.S.-based Service Intelligence (www.serviceintelligence.com), which has its Canadian headquarters in Calgary. The focus is on conducting "objective customer service evaluations" so that companies can find ways to improve customer service for increased differentiation and competitive advantage. As Craig Henry, one of the founders of SQM, asks, "What's the only thing that sets you apart from your competitor? It's service . . . It's the final frontier," he adds.[54] Not surprisingly, companies such as Tim Hortons, Canadian Tire, Hudson's Bay, and Shoppers Drug Mart undertake mystery shopping research on a regular basis to objectively evaluate various aspects of customer service.

Unsolicited Customer Feedback   Customer complaints, compliments, and suggestions can be transformed into a stream of information that can be used to help monitor quality and highlight needed improvements to the service design and delivery. Complaints and compliments are rich sources of detailed feedback on what drives customers nuts and what delights them.

Similar to feedback cards, unsolicited feedback is not a reliable measure of overall customer satisfaction, but it is a good source of improvement ideas. If the objective of collecting feedback is mainly to get feedback on what to improve (rather than for benchmarking and/or assessing staff), reliability and representativeness are not needed, and more qualitative tools, such as complaints/compliments or focus groups, generally suffice.

Detailed customer complaint and compliment letters, recorded telephone conversations, and direct feedback from employees can serve as an excellent tool for communicating internally what customers want, and enable employees and managers at all levels to "listen" to customers at first hand. This first-hand learning is much more powerful in shaping the thinking and customer-orientation of service staff than using "clinical" statistics and reports.

For example, Singapore Airlines prints complaint and compliment letters in its monthly employee magazine *Outlook*. Southwest Airlines shows staff videotapes containing footage of customers providing feedback. Seeing actual customers giving comments about their service leaves a much deeper and more lasting impression on staff, and motivates them to improve further.

Focus Group Discussions and Service Reviews   Both tools give great specific insights into potential service improvements and ideas. Typically, focus groups are organized by key customer segments or user groups to drill down on the needs of these users.

Service reviews are in-depth, one-on-one interviews, usually conducted once a year with a firm's most valuable customers. Usually, a senior executive of the firm visits the customer and discusses issues such as how well the firm performed the previous year, and what should be maintained or changed. That senior person then goes back to the organization and discusses the feedback with his/her account managers, and then both write a letter to the client detailing how the firm will respond to that customer's service needs, and how the account will be managed the following year.

Apart from providing an excellent learning opportunity (especially when the reviews across all customers are compiled and analyzed), service reviews focus on retention of the most valuable customers, and get high marks for service-recovery potential.

As we noted earlier, there are advantages to using a mix of feedback tools. Best Practice in Action 13.2 features FedEx's excellent customer feedback system, which combines various customer feedback collection tools with a detailed process performance measurement system.

FedEx's Approach to Listening to the Voice of the Customer

"We believe that service quality must be mathematically measured" declares Frederick W. Smith, chairman, president, and CEO of Federal Express Corporation. The company has a commitment to clear, frequently repeated quality goals, followed up with continuous measurement of progress against those goals. This practice forms the foundation for its approach to quality.

FedEx initially set two ambitious quality goals: 100 percent customer satisfaction for every interaction and transaction, and 100 percent service performance on every package handled. Customer satisfaction was measured by the percentage of on-time deliveries, which referred to the number of packages delivered on time as a percentage of total package volume. However, as things turned out, percentage of on-time delivery was an internal standard that was not synonymous with customer satisfaction.

Since FedEx had systematically catalogued customer complaints, it was able to develop what CEO Smith calls the "Hierarchy of Horrors," which referred to the eight most common complaints by customers: (1) wrong day delivery, (2) right day, late delivery, (3) pickup not made (4) lost package, (5) customer misinformed by FedEx, (6) billing and paperwork mistakes, (7) employee performance failures, and (8) damaged packages. This list was the foundation on which FedEx built its customer feedback system.

FedEx refined the list of "horrors" and developed the Service Quality Indicator (SQI), a 12-item measure of satisfaction and service quality from the customers' viewpoint. Weights have been assigned to each item based on its relative importance in determining overall customer satisfaction. All items are tracked daily, so that a continuous index can be computed.

In addition to the SQI, which has been modified over time to reflect changes in procedures, services, and customer priorities, FedEx uses a variety of other ways to capture feedback.

Customer Satisfaction Survey: this telephone survey is conducted on a quarterly basis with several thousand randomly selected customers, stratified by its key segments. The results are relayed to senior management on a quarterly basis.

Targeted Customer Satisfaction Survey: this covers specific customer service processes and is conducted on a semiannual basis with clients who have experienced one of the specific FedEx processes within the last three months.

FedEx Center Comment Cards: Comment cards are collected from each FedEx store-front business centre. The results are tabulated twice a year and relayed to managers in charge of the centres.

On-line Customer Feedback Surveys: FedEx has commissioned regular studies to get feedback for its online services (e.g., package tracking), as well as ad hoc studies on new products.

The information from these various customer feedback measures has helped FedEx to maintain a leadership role in its industry, and has played an important role in enabling it to receive the prestigious Malcolm Baldridge National Quality Award from the U.S.-based National Institute of Standards and Technology.

Sources: "Blueprints for Service Quality: The Federal Express Approach," *AMA Management Briefing*, New York: American Management Association, 1991: 51–64; Linda Rosencrance, "BetaSphere Delivers FedEx Some Customer Feedback," *Computerworld* 14/14 (2000): 36.

Capturing Unsolicited Customer Feedback

For complaints, suggestions, and inquiries to be useful as research input, they have to be funnelled into a central collection point, logged, categorized, and analyzed.[55] That requires a system for capturing customer feedback where it is made, and then reporting it to a central unit. Some firms use a simple intranet site to record all feedback received by any staff member. Co-ordinating such activities is not a simple matter, because of the many entry points, including the following:

- The firm's own front-line employees, who may be in contact with customers face to face, by telephone, or via mail or email.
- Intermediary organizations acting on behalf of the original supplier.
- Managers who normally work backstage, but who are contacted by a customer seeking higher authority.
- Suggestion or complaint cards mailed, emailed, posted on the firm's website, or placed in a special box.

- Complaints to third parties, such as consumer advocate groups, legislative agencies, trade organizations, and other customers.

Analysis, Reporting, and Dissemination of Customer Feedback

Choosing the relevant feedback tools and collecting customer feedback is meaningless if the company is unable to disseminate the information to the relevant parties to take action. Hence, to drive continuous improvement and learning, a reporting system needs to deliver feedback and its analysis to front-line staff, process owners, branch or department managers, and top management.

The feedback loop to the front line should be immediate for complaints and compliments, as is practised in a number of service businesses where complaints, compliments, and suggestions are discussed with staff during a daily morning briefing. In addition, we recommend three types of service performance reports to provide the information necessary for service management and team learning.

A monthly Service Performance Update provides process owners with timely feedback on customer comments and operational process performance. Here, the verbatim feedback is provided to the process manager, who can in turn discuss it with his or her service staff.

A quarterly Service Performance Review provides process owners and branch or department managers with trends in process performance and service quality.

An annual Service Performance Report gives top management a representative assessment of the status and long-term trends relating to customer satisfaction with the firm's services.

The reports should be short and reader-friendly, focusing on key indicators and providing an easily understood commentary.

Conclusion

Collecting customer feedback via complaints, suggestions, and compliments provides a means of increasing customer satisfaction. It is an opportunity to get into the hearts and minds of the customer. In all but the worst instances, complaining customers are indicating that they want to continue their relationship with the firm, but they are also indicating that all is not well and that they expect the company to make things right.

Service firms need to develop effective strategies to recover from service failures so that they can maintain customer goodwill. That is vital for the long-term success of the company. Even the best recovery strategy is not as good as being treated right the first time. Well-designed unconditional service guar-

antees have proved to be a powerful vehicle for identifying and justifying needed improvements, as well as creating a culture in which employees take proactive steps to ensure that customers will be satisfied.

Finally, a service firm and its staff must also learn from their mistakes, and try to ensure that problems, once exposed, are being eliminated. Customer feedback systems should ensure that information originating from complaints, compliments, and other feedback tools is systematically collected, analyzed, and disseminated to drive service improvements. The ultimate objective of an effective customer feedback system is to institutionalize systematic and continuous customer-driven learning.

Review Questions

1. Why don't unhappy customers always complain? What do customers expect the firm to do once they have filed a complaint?

2. Why would a firm prefer its unhappy customers to come forward and complain?

3. What is the service-recovery paradox? Under what conditions is this paradox most likely to hold? Why is it best to

deliver the service as planned, even if the paradox holds in a specific context?

4. What could a firm do to make it easy for dissatisfied customers to complain?

5. Why should a service recovery strategy be proactive, planned, trained for, and empowering to employees?

6. How generous should compensation related to service recovery be? What are the economic costs to the firm of the typical types of compensation firms offer?

7. How should service guarantees be designed? What are the benefits of service guarantees over and above a good complaint-handling and service-recovery system?

8. What are some of the steps that managers take to discourage customers from abusing service guarantees?

9. What are the main objectives of customer feedback systems?

10. What customer feedback collection tools do you know, and what are the strengths and weaknesses of each of these tools?

Application Exercises

1. Think about the last time you experienced a less-than-satisfactory service experience. Did you complain? Why? If you did not complain, explain why not.

2. As suggested in the chapter, sometimes the government can play a significant role in facilitating the complaint process for consumers. (See Service Perspectives 13.1.) Identify similar efforts being made by some trade associations within Canada, and compare and contrast the efforts of one such body to Industry Canada's Complaint Courier. As a consumer, which appears more helpful in managing the complaint process? Why?

3. Design a highly effective service guarantee for a service with high perceived risk. Explain why and how your guarantee would reduce perceived risk of potential customers, and why current customers would appreciate being offered this guarantee even though they are already a customer of that firm, and therefore likely to perceive lower levels of risk.

4. Find instances among Canadian companies where service recovery strategies had to be altered because of customer abuse of their service guarantees. What was the action most commonly taken by the service companies? Do you agree with their approach or would you have taken a different course of action? Explain.

5. Collect a few customer feedback forms and tools (e.g., customer feedback cards, questionnaires, and online forms) and assess how the information gathered in those tools could be used to achieve the three main objectives of effective customer feedback systems.

6. How generous should compensation be? Review the following incident and comment. Then evaluate the available options, comment on each, select the one you recommend, and defend your decision.

"The shrimp cocktail was half frozen. The waitress apologized and didn't charge me for any of my dinner," was the response of a very satisfied customer about the service recovery he received. Consider the following range of service recovery policies a restaurant chain could set:

Option 1: Smile and apologize, defrost the prawn cocktail, return it, smile and apologize again.
Option 2: Smile and apologize, replace the prawn cocktail with a new one, smile and apologize again.
Option 3: Smile, apologize, replace the prawn cocktail, and offer a free coffee or dessert.
Option 4: Smile, apologize, replace the prawn cocktail, and waive the bill of $80 for the entire meal.
Option 5: Smile, apologize, replace the prawn cocktail, waive the bill for the entire dinner, and offer a free bottle of champagne.
Option 6: Smile, apologize, replace the prawn cocktail, waive the bill for the entire dinner, offer a free bottle of champagne, and give a voucher valid for another dinner, to be redeemed within three months.

Try to establish the costs for each policy. Some data are provided in the endnotes,[56] but before peeking at these data, think about the costs yourself.

Endnotes

1. Roger Bougie, Rik Pieters, and Marcel Zeelenberg, "Angry Customers Don't Come Back, They Get Back: The Experience and Behavioral Implications of Anger and Dissatisfaction in Service," *Journal of the Academy of Marketing Science* 31/4 (2003): 377–93; and Florian V. Wangenheim, "Postswitching Negative Word of Mouth," *Journal of Service Research* 8/1 (2005): 67–78.

2. Bernd Stauss, "Global Word of Mouth," *Marketing Management* (Fall 1997): 28–30.

3. For research on cognitive and affective drivers of complaining behaviour see Jean-Charles Chebat, Moshe Davidow, and Isabelle Codjovi, "Silent Voices: Why Some Dissatisfied Consumers Fail to Complain," *Journal of Service Research* 7/4 (2005): 328–42.

4. Stephen S. Tax and Stephen W. Brown, "Recovering and Learning from Service Failure," *Sloan Management Review* 49/1 (Fall 1998): 75–88.

5. Technical Assistance Research Programs Institute (TARP), *Consumer Complaint Handling in America: An Update Study*, Part 2, Washington D.C.: TARP and U.S. Office of Consumer Affairs, April 1986; Nancy Stephens and Kevin P. Gwinner, "Why Don't Some People Complain? A

Cognitive-Emotive Process Model of Consumer Complaining Behavior," *Journal of the Academy of Marketing Science* 26/3 (1998): 172–89.

6. Cathy Goodwin and B.J. Verhage, "Role Perceptions of Services: A Cross-Cultural Comparison with Behavioral Implications," *Journal of Economic Psychology* 10 (1990): 543–58.

7. David Menzies, "His Favourite Things," *Marketing* 111/10 (March 13, 2006): 13.

8. Nancy Stephens, "Complaining," in Teresa A. Swartz and Dawn Iacobucci, (eds.), *Handbook of Services Marketing and Management*, Thousand Oaks, CA: Sage, 2000: 291.

9. John Goodman, "Basic Facts on Customer Complaint Behavior and the Impact of Service on the Bottom Line," *Competitive Advantage* (June 1999): 1–5.

10. Anna Mattila and Jochen Wirtz, "Consumer Complaining to Firms: The Determinants of Channel Choice," *Journal of Services Marketing* 18/2 (2004): 147–55; and Kaisa Snellman and Tiina Vihtkari, "Customer Complaining Behavior in Technology-based Service Encounters," *International Journal of Service Industry Management* 14/2 (2003): 217–31.

11. Technical Assistance Research Programs Institute (TARP), *Consumer Complaint Handling in America; An Update Study, Part II*.

12. Kathleen Seiders and Leonard L. Berry, "Service Fairness: What It Is and Why It Matters," *Academy of Management Executive* 12/2 (1990): 8–20.

13. Tax and Brown (1998), op. cit.

14. Stephen S. Tax and Stephen W. Brown, "Service Recovery: Research, Insight and Practice," in Swartz and Iacobucci, 2000, op. cit.: 277; Tor Wallin Andreassen, "Antecedents of Service Recovery," *European Journal of Marketing* 34/1 and 2 (2000): 156–75; Ko de Ruyter and Martin Wetzel, "Customer Equity Considerations in Service Recovery," *International Journal of Service Industry Management* 13/1 (2002): 91–108; Janet R. McColl-Kennedy and Beverley A. Sparks, "Application of Fairness Theory to Service Failures and Service Recovery," *Journal of Service Research* 5/3 (2003): 251–66; and Jochen Wirtz and Anna Mattila, "Consumer Responses to Compensation, Speed of Recovery and Apology After a Service Failure," *International Journal of Service Industry Management* 15/2 (2004): 150–66.

15. Oren Harari, "Thank Heavens for Complainers," *Management Review* (March 1997): 25–29.

16. Clyde A. Warden, Tsung-Chi Liu, Chi-Tsun Huang, and Chi-Hsun Lee, "Service Failures Away from Home: Benefits in Intercultural Service Encounters," *International Journal of Service Industry Management* 14/4 (2003): 436–57; Anna S. Mattila and Paul G. Patterson, "Service Recovery and Fairness Perceptions in Collectivist and Individualist Contexts," *Journal of Service Research* 6/4 (2004): 336–46.

17. Leonard L. Berry, *On Great Service: A Framework for Action*, New York: Free Press, 1995: 94.

18. Susan M. Keaveney, "Customer Switching Behavior in Service Industries: An Exploratory Study," *Journal of Marketing* 59 (April 1995): 71–82.

19. TARP, *Consumer Complaint Handling*.

20. Robert Johnston, "Linking Complaint Management to Profit," *International Journal of Service Industry Management* 12/1 (2001): 60–69.

21. Stefan Michel, "Analyzing Service Failures and Recoveries: A Process Approach," *International Journal of Service Industry Management* 12/1 (2001): 20–33.

22. James G. Maxham III and Richard G. Netemeyer, "A Longitudinal Study of Complaining Customers' Evaluations of Multiple Service Failures and Recovery Efforts," *Journal of Marketing* 66/4 (2002): 57–72.

23. Tor Wallin Andreassen "From Disgust to Delight: Do Customers Hold a Grudge?" *Journal of Service Research* 4/1 (2001): 39–49. Other studies also confirmed that the service recovery paradox does not hold universally; e.g., Michael A. McCollough, Leonard L. Berry, and Manjit S. Yadav, "An Empirical Investigation of Customer Satisfaction after Service Failure and Recovery," *Journal of Service Research* 3/2 (2000): 121–37; and James G. Maxham III, "Service Recovery's Influence on Consumer Satisfaction, Positive Word-of-Mouth, and Purchase Intentions," *Journal of Business Research* 54 (2001): 11–24.

24. Michael Hargrove, cited in Ron Kaufman, *Up Your Service!*, Singapore: Ron Kaufman, 2005: 225.

25. Tax and Brown (1998): op. cit.; Stephen S. Tax, Stephen W. Brown, and Murali Chandrashekaran, "Customer Evaluation of Service Complaint Experiences: Implications for Relationship Marketing," *Journal of Marketing* 62/2 (Spring 1998): 60–76; for a study in the online environment see Betsy B. Holloway and Sharon E. Beatty, "Service Failure in Online Retailing: A Recovery Opportunity," *Journal of Service Research* 6/1 (2003): 92–105.

26. For a discussion on how to quantify complaint management profitability see Bernd Stauss and Andreas Schoeler, "Complaint Management Profitability: What do Complaint Managers Know?" *Managing Service Quality* 14/2–3 (2004): 147–56; for a comprehensive treatment of all aspects of effective complaint management, see Bernd Stauss and Wolfgang Seidel, *Complaint Management: The Heart of CRM*, Mason, OH: Thomson, 2004.

27. Christian Homburg and Andreas Fürst, "How Organizational Complaint Handling Drives Customer Loyalty: An Analysis of the Mechanistic and the Organic Approach," *Journal of Marketing* 69 (July 2005): 95–114.

28. www.aircanada.com/en/about/customer/#overbooking, accessed November 25, 2006.

29. Ron Zemke and Chip R. Bell, *Knock Your Socks Off Service Recovery*, New York: AMACOM, 2000: 60.

30. Barbara R. Lewis, "Customer Care in Services," in W.J. Glynn and J.G. Barnes, (eds.), *Understanding Services Management*, Chichester, UK: Wiley, 1995: 57–89. Prior rapport between employees and customers has also been shown to improve service recovery satisfaction; see Tom DeWitt and Michael K. Brady, "Rethinking Service Recovery Strategies: The Effect of Rapport on Customer Responses to Service Failure," *Journal of Service Research* 6/2 (2003): 193–207.

31. Terrence J. Levesque and Gordon H.. McDougall, "Service Problems and Recovery Strategies: An Experiment," *Canadian Journal of Administrative Sciences* 17/01): 20–7.

32. Hooman Estelami and Peter De Maeyer, "Customer Reactions to Service Provider Overgenerosity," *Journal of Service Research* 4/3 (2002): 205–17.

33. Rhonda Mack, Rene Mueller, John Crotts, and Amanda Broderick, "Perceptions, Corrections and Defections: Implications for Service Recovery in the Restaurant Industry," *Managing Service Quality* 10/6 (2000): 339–46.

34. Christopher W.L. Hart, "The Power of Unconditional Service Guarantees," *Harvard Business Review* 68/4 (July–August 1990), 54–62.

35. L.A. Tucci and J. Talaga, "Service Guarantees and Consumers' Evaluation of Services," *Journal of Services Marketing* 11/1 (1997): 10–18; Amy Ostrom and Dawn Iacobucci, "The Effect of Guarantees on Consumers' Evaluation of Services," *Journal of Services Marketing* 12/5 (1998): 362–78.

36. Sara Björlin Lidén and Per Skålén, "The Effect of Service Guarantees on Service Recovery," *International Journal of Service Industry Management* 14/1 (2003): 36–58.

37. Christopher W. Hart and Elizabeth Long, *Extraordinary Guarantees*, New York: AMACOM, 1997.

38. Hart (1990), op. cit.

39. For a scientific discussion on the optimal guarantee payout amount see: Tim Baker and David A. Collier, "The Economic Payout Model for Service Guarantees," *Decision Sciences* 36, no. 2 (2005): 197-220).

40. Gordon H. McDougall, Terence Levesque, and Peter VanderPlaat, "Designing the Service Guarantee: Unconditional or Specific?" *Journal of Services Marketing* 12/4 (1998): 278–93; Jochen Wirtz, "Development of a Service Guarantee Model," *Asia Pacific Journal of Management* 15/1 (1998): 51–75.

41. Jochen Wirtz and Doreen Kum, "Designing Service Guarantees: Is Full Satisfaction the Best You can Guarantee?" *Journal of Services Marketing* 15/4 (2001): 282–99.

42. Amy L. Ostrom and Christopher Hart, "Service Guarantee: Research and Practice," in Schwartz and Iacobucci, 2000, op. cit.: 299–316.

43. Jochen Wirtz, Doreen Kum, and Khai Sheang Lee, "Should a Firm with a Reputation for Outstanding Service Quality Offer a Service Guarantee?" *Journal of Services Marketing* 14/6 (2000): 502–12.

44. www.futureway.ca/about-legal-general-terms.php, accessed October 16, 2006.

45. For a decision-support model on the question of whether to have a service guarantee—and if yes, on how to design and implement it—see Louis Fabien, "Design and Implementation of a Service Guarantee," *Journal of Services Marketing* 19/1 (2005): 33–38.

46. John Goodman, quoted in "Improving Service Doesn't Always Require Big Investment," *Service Edge* (July–August, 1990): 3

47. Jochen Wirtz and Doreen Kum, "Consumer Cheating on Service Guarantees," *Journal of the Academy of Marketing Science* 32/2 (2004): 159–75.

48. This section is based partially on Jochen Wirtz and Monica Tomlin, "Institutionalizing Customer-driven Learning Through Fully Integrated Customer Feedback Systems," *Managing Service Quality* 10/4 (2000): 205–15.

49. Customer listening practices have been shown to affect service performance, growth, and profitability: see William J. Glynn, Sean de Búrca, Teresa Brannick, et al., "Listening Practices and Performance in Service Organizations," *International Journal of Service Industry Management* 14/3 (2003): 310–30.

50. W.E. Baker and Sinkula J.M., "The Synergistic Effect of Market Orientation and Learning Orientation on Organizational Performance," *Journal of the Academy of Marketing Science* 27/4 (1999): 411–27.

51. Neil A. Morgan, Eugene W. Anderson, and Vikas Mittal, "Understanding Firms' Customer Satisfaction information Usage," *Journal of Marketing* 69 (July 2005): 131–51.

52. Leonard L. Berry and A. Parasuraman provide an excellent overview of all key research approaches discussed in this section, plus a number of other tools, in their paper, "Listening to the Customer: The Concept of a Service Quality Information System," *Sloan Management Review* (Spring 1997): 65–76.

53. For a discussion on suitable satisfaction measures, see Jochen Wirtz and Lee Meng Chung, "An Examination of the Quality and Context-Specific Applicability of Commonly Used Customer Satisfaction Measures," *Journal of Service Research* 5 (May 2003): 345–55.

54. Mitch Moxley, "Spies for Hire Wage War on Tipsy Tables, Filthy Toilets," *Financial Post* (004).

55. Robert Johnston and Sandy Mehra, "Best-Practice Complaint Management," *Academy of Management Executive* 16/4 (2002): 145–54.

56. Data for calculation of recovery costs in Application Exercise #6. Option 1 has no direct costs, merely extra time for one or more employees. Option 2: add the material costs of the shrimp cocktail, typically about one third of the $8–$10 cost charged in a good restaurant. Option 3: add the extra costs of the free coffee or dessert—material costs only if the diner would not otherwise have ordered these items, but full costs (say $6 and $3) if the diner would otherwise have ordered and paid for these items. What probability would you assign to these alternatives? Option 4: Costs are for option 1 plus $80, since that is the revenue actually foregone. Option 5, as for Option 4, plus the costs of the bottle of champagne, which needs to be computed using the probabilities of incremental and substitutional consumption and their respective costs. Option 6, as for Option 5 plus the cost of the voucher. The latter cost depends on the probability of its actually being used and whether the customer is using the voucher to pay for a meal he would otherwise have had at this restaurant and paid for himself, or whether this is an incremental meal.

CHAPTER 14

Improving Service Quality and Productivity

Not everything that counts can be counted, and not everything that can be counted, counts.

—Albert Einstein

Our mission remains inviolable: offer the customer the best service we can provide; cut our costs to the bone; and generate a surplus to continue the unending process of renewal.

—Joseph Pillay former chairman, Singapore Airlines

Productivity has been a managerial imperative since the 1970s. During the 1980s and early 1990s, improving quality became a priority. In a service context, this strategy entails creating better service processes and outcomes to improve customer satisfaction. At the beginning of the twenty-first century, we're seeing growing emphasis on linking these two strategies in order to create better value for both customers and the firm.

Both quality and productivity have historically been seen as issues for operations managers. When improvements in these areas required better employee selection, training, and supervision—or renegotiation of labour agreements relating to job assignments and work rules—then human resource managers were expected to get involved too. It was not until service quality was explicitly linked to customer satisfaction that marketers, too, were seen as having an important role to play.

Broadly defined, the task of value enhancement requires quality improvement programs to deliver and continuously enhance the benefits desired by customers. At the same time, productivity improvement efforts must seek to reduce the associated costs. The challenge is to ensure that these two programs are mutually reinforcing in achieving common goals, rather than operating at loggerheads with each other in pursuit of conflicting goals.

In this chapter, we review the challenges involved in improving both productivity and quality in service organizations, and explore the following questions:

1. What is meant by quality and productivity in a service context, and why should the two be linked when formulating marketing strategy?

2. How can the gaps model be used to diagnose and address service quality problems?

3. What are the key tools for measuring and improving service productivity?

4. How do concepts like TQM, ISO 9000, the National Quality Institute's (NQI) Business Excellence Framework, and Six Sigma relate to managing and improving productivity and service quality?

INTEGRATING SERVICE QUALITY AND PRODUCTIVITY STRATEGIES

A key theme of this book is that, where services are concerned, marketing cannot operate in isolation from other functional areas. Tasks that might be considered the sole preserve of operations in a manufacturing environment must involve marketers, because customers are often exposed to—even actively involved in—service processes. Making service processes more efficient does not necessarily result in a better-quality experience for customers, nor does it always lead to improved benefits for them. Likewise, getting service employees to work faster may sometimes be welcomed by customers, but at other times it may make them feel rushed and unwanted. Thus, marketing, operations, and human resource managers should work together to ensure that they can deliver quality experiences more efficiently.

Similarly, implementing marketing strategies that are designed to improve customer satisfaction can prove costly and disruptive if the implications for operations and human resources have not been carefully thought through. The bottom line: quality and productivity improvement strategies must be considered jointly rather than in isolation.

Service Quality, Productivity, and Marketing

Marketing's interest in service quality is obvious: poor quality places a firm at a competitive disadvantage, potentially driving away dissatisfied customers. Recent years have witnessed a veritable explosion of discontent with service quality, at a time when the quality of many manufactured goods has been improving. Improving productivity is important to marketers for several reasons. First, it helps to keep costs down. Lower costs either mean higher profits or the ability to hold down prices. The company with the lowest costs in an industry has the option to position itself as the low-price leader—usually a significant advantage among price-sensitive market segments. Second, firms with lower costs also have the option of generating higher margins, giving them the option of spending more than the competition in marketing activities, improved customer service, and supplementary services. Such firms may also be able to offer higher margins to attract and reward the best distributors and intermediaries. Third is the opportunity to secure the firm's long-term future through investments in new service technologies and in research to create superior new services, improved features, and innovative delivery systems. Finally, efforts to improve productivity often have an impact on customers. Marketers are responsible for ensuring that negative impacts are avoided or minimized, and that new procedures are carefully presented to customers. Positive impacts can be promoted as a new advantage.

Quality and productivity are twin paths to creating value for both customers and companies. In broad terms, quality focuses on the benefits created for the customer's side of the equation and productivity addresses the financial costs incurred by the firm. Carefully integrating quality and productivity improvement programs will improve the long-term profitability of the firm.

WHAT IS SERVICE QUALITY?

What do we mean when we speak of "service quality"? Company personnel need an agreed understanding of the term in order to be able to address issues such as the measurement of service quality, the identification of causes of shortfalls in service quality, and the design and implementation of corrective actions.

Different Perspectives of Service Quality

The word *quality* means different things to people, according to the context. David Garvin identifies five perspectives on quality.[1]

Figure 14.1

Service quality is difficult to manage.

1. *The transcendent view* of quality is synonymous with innate excellence: a mark of uncompromising standards and high achievement. This viewpoint is often applied to the performing and visual arts. It argues that people learn to recognize quality only through the experience gained from repeated exposure. From a practical standpoint, however, suggesting that managers or customers will know quality when they see it is not very helpful.

2. *The product-based approach* sees quality as a precise and measurable variable. Differences in quality, it argues, reflect differences in the amount of an ingredient or attribute possessed by the product. Because this view is totally objective, it fails to account for differences in the tastes, needs, and preferences of individual customers (or even entire market segments).

3. *User-based definitions* start with the premise that quality lies in the eye of the beholder. These definitions equate quality with maximum satisfaction. This subjective, demand-oriented perspective recognizes that different customers have different wants and needs.

4. *The manufacturing-based approach* is supply based, and is concerned primarily with engineering and manufacturing practices. (In services, we would say that quality was *operations driven.*) It focuses on conformance to internally developed specifications, which are often driven by productivity and cost-containment goals.

5. *Value-based definitions* define quality in terms of value and price. By considering the trade-off between performance (or conformance) and price, quality comes to be defined as "affordable excellence."

Garvin suggests that these alternative views of quality help to explain the conflicts that sometimes arise between managers in different functional departments.

Manufacturing-Based Components of Quality   To incorporate the different perspectives, Garvin developed the following components of quality that could be useful as a framework for analysis and strategic planning. These are: (1) performance (primary operating characteristics), (2) features (bells and whistles), (3) reliability (probability of malfunction or failure), (4) conformance (ability to meet specifications), (5) durability (how long the product continues to provide value to the customer), (6) serviceability (speed, courtesy, competence, and ease of having problems fixed), (7) aesthetics (how the product appeals to any or all of the user's five senses), and (8) perceived quality (associations such as the reputation of the company or brand name). Note that these categories were developed from a manufacturing perspective, but they do address the notion of the "serviceability" of a physical good.

Service-Based Components of Quality   Researchers argue that the nature of services requires a distinctive approach to defining and measuring service quality. Because of the intangible, multifaceted nature of many services, it may be harder to evaluate the quality of a service compared to a good. Because customers are often involved in service production, a distinction needs to be drawn between the *process* of service delivery (what Christian Grönroos calls functional quality) and the actual *output* of the service (what he calls technical quality).[2] Grönroos and others also suggest that the perceived quality of a service is the result of an evaluation process in which customers compare their perceptions of service delivery and its outcome against what they expect.

The most extensive research into service quality is strongly user-oriented. From focus group research, Valarie Zeithaml, Leonard Berry, and A. Parasuraman identified ten criteria used by consumers in evaluating service quality (Table 14.1). In subsequent research they found a high degree of correlation between several of these variables, and thus consolidated them into five broad dimensions:

- *Tangibles* (appearance of physical elements)
- *Reliability* (dependable, accurate performance)
- *Responsiveness* (promptness and helpfulness)
- *Assurance* (competence, courtesy, credibility, and security)
- *Empathy* (easy access, good communications, and customer understanding)[3]

Only one of these five dimensions, *reliability,* has a direct parallel to findings from Garvin's research on manufacturing quality.

Capturing the Customer's Perspective of Service Quality

To measure customer satisfaction with various aspects of service quality, Valarie Zeithaml and her colleagues developed a survey research instrument called SERVQUAL.[4] It's based on the premise that customers can evaluate a firm's service quality by comparing their perceptions of its service with their own expectations. SERVQUAL is seen as a generic measurement tool that can be applied across a broad spectrum of service industries. In its basic form, the scale contains 22 perception items and a series of expectation items, reflecting the five dimensions of service quality described in Table 14.2. Respondents complete a series of scales that measure their expectations of companies in a particular industry over a wide array of specific service characteristics. Subsequently, they are asked to record their perceptions of a specific company whose services they have used. When perceived performance ratings are lower than expectations, this is a sign of poor quality. The reverse indicates good quality.

Limitations of SERVQUAL

Although SERVQUAL has been widely used by service companies, doubts have been expressed about both its conceptual foundation and its methodological limitations.[5] For example, Anne Smith notes that the majority of researchers using SERVQUAL have omitted from, added to, or altered the list of statements purporting to measure service quality.[6] To evaluate the stability of the five underlying dimensions when applied to a variety of different service industries, Gerhard Mels, Christo Boshoff, and Denon Nel analyzed data sets from banks, insurance brokers, vehicle repair firms, electrical repair firms, and life insurance companies.[7] Their findings suggest that, in reality, SERVQUAL scores only measure two factors: intrinsic service quality (resembling what Grönroos termed "functional quality") and extrinsic service quality (which refers to the tangible aspects of service delivery and *"resembles to some extent* what Grönroos refers to as technical quality").

Table 14.1 Generic Dimensions Used by Customers to Evaluate Service Quality

DIMENSION	DEFINITION	EXAMPLES OF CUSTOMERS' QUESTIONS
Credibility	Trustworthiness, believability, honesty of the service provider	Does the hospital have a good reputation? Does my stockbroker refrain from pressuring me to buy? Does the repair firm guarantee its work?
Security	Freedom from danger, risk, or doubt	Is it safe for me to use the bank's ATMs at night? Is my credit card protected against unauthorized use? Can I be sure that my insurance policy provides complete coverage?
Access	Approachability and ease of contact	How easy is it for me to talk to a supervisor when I have a problem? Does the airline have a 24-hour toll-free phone number? Is the hotel conveniently located?
Communication	Listening to customers and keeping them informed in language they can understand	When I have a complaint, is the manager willing to listen to me? Does my doctor avoid using technical jargon? Does the electrician call when he or she is unable to keep a scheduled appointment?
Understanding the customer	Making the effort to know customers and their needs	Does someone in the hotel recognize me as a regular customer? Does my stockbroker try to determine my specific financial objectives? Is the moving company willing to accommodate my schedule?
Tangibles	Appearance of physical facilities, equipment, personnel, and communication materials	Are the hotel's facilities attractive? Is my accountant dressed appropriately? Is my bank statement easy to understand?
Reliability	Ability to perform the promised service dependably and accurately	Does my lawyer call me back when promised? Is my telephone bill free of errors? Is my TV repaired right the first time?
Responsiveness	Willingness to help customers and provide prompt service	When there's a problem, does the firm resolve it quickly? Is my stockbroker willing to answer my questions? Is the cable TV company willing to give me a specific time when the installer will show up?
Competence	Possession of the skills and knowledge required to perform the service	Can the bank teller process my transaction without fumbling around? Is my travel agent able to obtain the information I need when I call? Does the dentist appear to be competent?
Courtesy	Politeness, respect, consideration, and friendliness of contact personnel	Does the flight attendant have a pleasant demeanour? Are the telephone operators consistently polite when answering my calls? Does the plumber take off muddy shoes before stepping on my carpet?

Source: Adapted from Valarie A. Zeithaml, A. Parasuraman, and Leonard L. Berry, *Delivering Quality Service: Balancing Customer Perceptions and Expectations,* New York: Free Press, 1990.

These findings don't undermine the value of Zeithaml, Berry, and Parasuraman's achievement in identifying some of the key underlying constructs in service quality, but they do highlight the difficulty of measuring customer perceptions of quality, and the need to customize dimensions and measures to the research context.

Table 14.2 *The SERVQUAL Scale*

The SERVQUAL scale includes five dimensions: tangibles, reliability, responsiveness, assurance, and empathy. Within each dimension, several items are measured on a 7-point scale, from *strongly agree* to *strongly disagree*, for a total of 21 items.

SERVQUAL Questions

Note: For actual survey respondents, instructions are also included, and each statement is accompanied by a seven-point scale ranging from "strongly agree = 7" to "strongly disagree = 1." Only the end points of the scale are labeled; there are no words above the numbers 2 through 6.

Tangibles
- Excellent banks (refer to cable TV companies, hospitals, or the appropriate service business throughout the questionnaire) will have modern-looking equipment.
- The physical facilities at excellent banks will be visually appealing.
- Employees at excellent banks will be neat in appearance.
- Materials (e.g., brochures or statements) associated with the service will be visually appealing in an excellent bank.

Reliability
- When excellent banks promise to do something by a certain time, they will do so.
- When customers have a problem, excellent banks will show a sincere interest in solving it.
- Excellent banks will perform the service right the first time.
- Excellent banks will provide their services at the time they promise to do so.
- Excellent banks will insist on error-free records.

Responsiveness
- Employees of excellent banks will tell customers exactly when service will be performed.
- Employees of excellent banks will give prompt service to customers.
- Employees of excellent banks will always be willing to help customers.
- Employees of excellent banks will never be too busy to respond to customer requests.

Assurance
- The behaviour of employees of excellent banks will instill confidence in customers.
- Customers of excellent banks will feel safe in their transactions.
- Employees of excellent banks will be consistently courteous with customers.
- Employees of excellent banks will have the knowledge to answer customer questions.

Empathy
- Excellent banks will give customers individual attention.
- Excellent banks will have operating hours convenient to all their customers.
- Excellent banks will have employees who give customers personal attention.
- The employees of excellent banks will understand the specific needs of their customers.

Source: Adapted from A. Parasuraman, Valarie A. Zeithaml, and Leonard L. Berry, "SERVQUAL: A Multiple Item Scale for Measuring Consumer Perceptions of Service Quality," *Journal of Retailing* 64 (1988): 12–40.

Measuring Service Quality in Online Environments

SERVQUAL was developed to measure service quality mostly in the context of a face-to-face service encounter. In the online environment, different dimensions of service quality with new measurement items were shown to be relevant. Parasuraman, Zeithaml, and Malhotra identified the four key dimensions of *efficiency* (e.g., is navigation easy, can transactions be completed quickly, and does the website load fast?), *system availability* (e.g., is the site always available, does it launch right away, and is it stable and does not crash?), fulfillment (e.g., are orders delivered as promised, and are offerings truthfully described?), and privacy (e.g., information privacy is protected, personal information is not shared with other sites).[8] Research Insights 14.1, "New Thinking on Defining and Measuring E-Service Quality," offers the latest perspectives on this topic and addresses the challenge of integrating measures of service quality across both virtual and physical channels.

Research Insights 14.1

New Thinking on Defining and Measuring E-Service Quality

"To managers of companies with a Web presence," say Joel Collier and Carol Bienstock, "an awareness of how customers perceive service quality is essential to understanding what [they] value in an online-service transaction." E-service quality involves more than just interactions with a website, described as process quality, and extends to outcome quality and recovery quality. And each must be measured. The separation of customers from providers during online transactions highlights the importance of evaluating how well a firm handles customers' questions, concerns, and frustrations when problems arise.

- *Process Quality.* Customers initially evaluate their experiences with an etailing website against five process-quality dimensions: privacy, design, information, ease of use, and functionality. This last construct refers to quick page loads, links that don't dead-end, payment options, accurate execution of customer commands, and ability to appeal to a universal audience (including the disabled and those who speak other languages).
- *Outcome Quality.* Customers' evaluations of process quality have a significant effect on their evaluation of outcome quality, made up of order timeliness, order accuracy, and order condition.
- *Recovery Quality.* In the event of a problem, customers evaluate the recovery process against interactive fairness (ability to locate and interact with technology support for a website, including telephone-based assistance), procedural fairness (policies, procedures, and responsiveness in the complaint process), and outcome fairness. How the company responds has a significant effect on the customer's satisfaction level and future intentions.

Multi-channel Issues

Going one step further, Rui Sousa and Christopher Voss note that many services offer customers a choice of both virtual and physical delivery channels. Customers' evaluations of service quality are formed across all points of contact they have with the firm. In a multi-channel setting, researchers must measure physical quality, virtual quality, and integration quality—the ability to provide customers with a seamless service experience across multiple channels. Achieving consistency across such interactions is particularly relevant when a firm adds new virtual channels, accompanied by specialist support systems that are often poorly integrated with existing systems. To avoid such fragmentation and achieve consistent service quality, Sousa and Voss call for explicit links between the firm's marketing and operations functions.

Source: Joel E. Collier and Carol C. Bienstock, "Measuring Service Quality in E-Retailing," *Journal of Service Research* 8 (February 2006): 260–75; Rui Sousa and Christopher A. Voss, "Service Quality in Multichannel Services Employing Virtual Channels," *Journal of Service Research* 8 (May 2006): 356–71.

Other Considerations in Service Quality Measurement

Comparing performance to expectations works well in reasonably competitive markets where customers have sufficient knowledge to purposefully choose a service that meets their needs and wants. However, in uncompetitive markets, or in situations where customers do not have a free choice (e.g., because switching costs would be prohibitive, or because of time or location constraints), there are risks to defining service quality primarily in terms of customers' satisfaction with outcomes relative to their prior expectations. If customers' expectations are low and actual service delivery proves only to be marginally better than the dismal level that had been expected, we can hardly claim that customers are receiving good-quality service! In such situations, it is better to use needs or wants as comparison standards, and define good service quality as meeting or exceeding customer wants and needs rather than expectations.[9]

Satisfaction-based research into quality assumes that customers are dealing with services high in search or experience characteristics (see Chapter 2). But a problem arises when they're asked to evaluate the quality of services that are high in *credence* characteristics, such as complex legal cases or medical treatments, which they may find difficult to evaluate even after delivery is completed. In short, customers may be unsure what to expect in advance and may not know for years—if ever—how good a job the professional actually did. A natural tendency in such situations is for clients or patients to use process factors and tangible cues as proxies for evaluating quality.

Process factors include customers' feelings about the personal style of individual providers, and satisfaction levels with those supplementary elements they feel competent to evaluate (for example, the tastiness of hospital meals or the clarity of bills for legal services). As a result, customers' perceptions of core service quality may be strongly influenced by their evaluation of process attributes and tangible elements of the service—a process of inference known as a halo effect.[10] In order to obtain credible measures of professional performance quality, it may be necessary to include peer reviews of both processes and outcomes, as these relate to service execution on the core product.

THE GAPS MODEL: A CONCEPTUAL TOOL TO IDENTIFY AND CORRECT SERVICE-QUALITY PROBLEMS

If one accepts the view that quality entails consistently meeting or exceeding customers' expectations, the manager's task is to balance customer expectations and perceptions, and to close any gaps between the two.

Gaps in Service Design and Delivery

Zeithaml, Berry, and Parasuraman identify four potential gaps within the service organization that may lead to a fifth and most serious final gap: the difference between what customers expected and what they perceived was delivered.[11] Figure 14.2 extends and refines their framework to identify a total of seven types of gaps that can occur at different points during the design and delivery of a service performance. Let's look at each in turn.

1. *The knowledge gap* is the difference between what service providers believe customers expect and customers' actual needs and expectations.
2. *The standards gap* is the difference between management's perceptions of customer expectations and the quality standards established for service delivery.
3. *The delivery gap* is the difference between specified delivery standards and the service provider's actual performance on these standards.
4. *The internal communications gap* is the difference between what the company's advertising and sales personnel think are the product's features, performance, and service quality level, and what the company is actually able to deliver.
5. *The perceptions gap* is the difference between what is, in fact, delivered and what customers perceive they have received (because they are unable to accurately evaluate service quality).
6. *The interpretation gap* is the difference between what a service provider's communication efforts (in advance of service delivery) actually promise and what a customer thinks was promised by these communications.
7. *The service gap* is the difference between what customers expect to receive and their perceptions of the service that is actually delivered.

Gaps 1, 5, 6, and 7 represent external gaps between the customer and the organization. Gaps 2, 3, and 4 are internal gaps between various functions and departments within the organization.

Gaps at any point in service design and delivery can damage relationships with customers. The Service Gap (no. 7) is the most critical; hence the ultimate goal in improving service quality is to close or narrow this gap as much as possible. However, to achieve this, service organizations usually need to work on closing the other six gaps depicted in Figure 14.2. Improving service quality requires identifying the specific causes of each gap and then developing strategies to close them.

Figure 14.2

Seven Service Quality Gaps

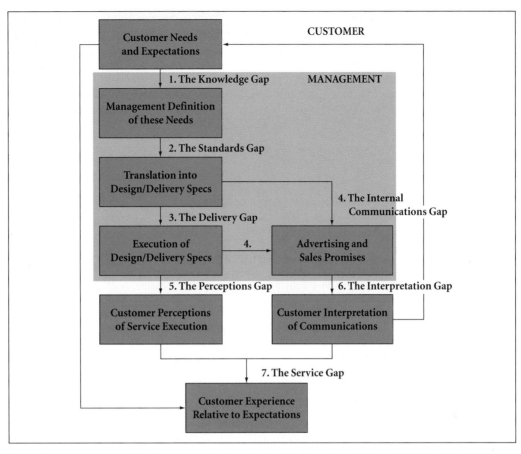

Source: The seven-gaps model, in Christopher Lovelock, *Product Plus*, New York: McGraw-Hill, 1994: 112, with further refinement by Lauren Wright, adapts and expands the original five-gaps model created by A. Parasuraman, Valarie A. Zeithaml, and Leonard L. Berry, "A Conceptual Model of Service Quality and Its Implications for Future Research," *Journal of Marketing* 49 (Fall 1985): 41–50.

Core Strategies to Address Service Quality Gaps

The strength of the gap model is that it offers generic insights and solutions that can be applied across industries. We summarized a series of generic prescriptions for closing the seven quality gaps in Table 14.3. These prescriptions are a good starting point to think about how to close specific gaps in an organization. But of course, each firm must develop its own customized approach to ensure that service quality becomes and remains a key objective.

MEASURING AND IMPROVING SERVICE QUALITY

It is commonly said that "what is not measured is not managed." Without measurement, managers can't be sure whether service quality gaps exist, let alone what types of gaps, or where they exist, or what potential corrective action should be taken. And, of course, measurement is needed to determine whether goals for improvement are being met after changes have been implemented.

Soft and Hard Service-Quality Measures

Customer-defined standards and measures of service quality can be grouped into two broad categories: "soft" and "hard." Soft measures are those that cannot easily be

Table 14.3 Prescriptions for Closing the Seven Service Quality Gaps

Gap 1—The Knowledge Gap

Prescription: Learn What Customers Expect

- Sharpen market research procedures, including questionnaire and interview design, sampling, and field implementation, and repeat research studies periodically.
- Implement an effective customer feedback system that includes satisfaction research, complaint content analysis, and customer panels.
- Increase interactions between managers (middle and top management) and customers.
- Facilitate and encourage communication between front-line employees and management.

Gap 2—The Standards Gap

Prescription: Establish the Right Service Processes and Specify Standards

- Get the customer service processes right:
  - Use a rigorous, systematic, and customer-centric process for designing and redesigning customer service processes.
  - Standardize repetitive work tasks to ensure consistency and reliability by substituting hard technology for human contact and improving work methods (soft technology).
- Set, communicate, and reinforce measurable customer-oriented service standards for all work units:
  - Establish for each step in service delivery a set of clear service quality goals that are challenging, realistic, and explicitly designed to meet customer expectations.
  - Ensure that employees understand and accept goals, standards, and priorities.

Gap 3—The Delivery Gap

Prescription: Ensure That Performance Meets Standards

- Ensure that customer service teams are motivated and able to meet service standards:
  - Improve recruitment with a focus on employee–job fit; select employees for the abilities and skills needed to perform their job well.
  - Train employees on the technical and soft skills needed to perform their assigned tasks effectively, including interpersonal skills, especially for dealing with customers under stressful conditions.
  - Clarify employee roles and ensure that employees understand how their jobs contribute to customer satisfaction; teach them about customer expectations, perceptions, and problems.
  - Build cross-functional service teams that can offer customer-centric service delivery and problem resolution.
  - Empower managers and employees in the field by pushing decision-making power down the organization.
  - Measure performance, provide regular feedback, and reward customer service team performance as well as individual employees and managers for attaining quality goals.
- Install the right technology, equipment, support processes, and capacity:
  - Select the most appropriate technology and equipment for enhanced performance.
  - Ensure that employees working on internal support jobs provide good service to their own internal customers, the front-line personnel.
  - Balance demand against productive capacity.
- Manage customers for service quality:
  - Educate customers so that they can perform their roles and responsibilities in service delivery effectively.

---

observed and must be collected by talking to customers, employees, or others. As noted by Valarie Zeithaml, Mary Jo Bitner, and Dwayne D. Gremler, "Soft standards provide direction, guidance and feedback to employees on ways to achieve customer satisfaction, and can be quantified by measuring customer perceptions and beliefs."[12] SERVQUAL is an example of a sophisticated soft-measurement system.

By contrast, hard standards and measures relate to those characteristics and activities that can be counted, timed, or measured through audits. Such measures may include how many telephone calls were abandoned while the customer was on hold, how many minutes customers had to wait in line at a particular stage in the service delivery, the time required to complete a specific task, the temperature of a particular food item, how many trains arrived late, how many bags were lost, how many patients made a complete recovery following a specific type of operation, and how many orders were filled correctly. Standards are often set with reference to the percentage of occasions on which a particular measure is achieved. The challenge for service marketers is to ensure that operational measures of service quality reflect customer input.

- Educate, control, or terminate jaycustomers who negatively affect other customers, employees, service processes, or facilities.

Gap 4—The Internal Communications Gap

Prescription: Ensure That Communications Promises Are Realistic

- Educate managers responsible for sales and marketing communications about operational capabilities:
  - Seek inputs from front-line employees and operations personnel when new communications programs are being developed.
  - Let service providers preview advertisements and other communications before customers are exposed to them.
  - Get sales staff to involve operations staff in face-to-face meetings with customers.
  - Develop internal educational and motivational advertising campaigns to strengthen understanding and integration among the marketing, operations, and human resource functions, and to standardize service delivery across different locations.
- Ensure that communications content sets realistic customer expectations.

Gap 5—The Perceptions Gap

Prescription: Tangibilize and Communicate the Service Quality Delivered

- Develop service environments and physical evidence cues that are consistent with the level of service provided.
- For complex and credence services, keep customers informed during service delivery of what is being done, and give debriefings after the delivery so that customers can appreciate the quality of service they received.
- Provide physical evidence (e.g., for repairs, show customers the damaged components that were removed).

Gap 6—The Interpretation Gap

Prescription: Be Specific with Promises and Manage Customers' Understanding of Communication Content

- Pre-test all advertising, brochures, telephone scripts, and website content prior to external release, to determine if the target audience interprets them as the firm intends (if not, revise and re-test):
  - Ensure that advertising content accurately reflects those service characteristics that are most important to customers.
  - Let customers know what is and is not possible—and the reasons why.
- Offer customers different levels of service at different prices, explaining the distinctions.
- Identify and explain in real time the reasons for shortcomings in service performance, highlighting those that cannot be controlled by the firm.
- Document precisely:
  - Upfront, what tasks and performance guarantees are included in an agreement or contract.
  - Afterward, what work was performed in relation to a specific billing statement.

Gap 7—The Service Gap

Prescription: Close Gaps 1 to 6 to Meet Customer Expectations Consistently

- Gap 7 is the accumulated outcome of all preceding open gaps. It will be closed when Gaps 1 through 6 have been addressed.

Sources: Prescriptions for Gaps 1 through 4 were distilled from Valarie A. Zeithaml, A. Parasuraman, and Leonard L. Berry, *Delivering Service Quality: Balancing Customer Perceptions and Expectations,* New York: Free Press, 1990: chapters 4–7; and Valarie A. Zeithaml, Mary Jo Bitner, and Dwayne Gremler, *Services Marketing: Integrating Customer Focus Across the Firm,* 4th ed., New York: McGraw-Hill, 2006: chapter 2. The remaining prescriptions were developed by the authors.

Organizations that are known for excellent service make use of both soft and hard measures. These organizations are good at listening to both their customers and their customer-contact employees. The larger the organization, the more important it is to create formalized feedback programs using a variety of professionally designed and implemented research procedures.

Soft Measures of Service Quality

How can companies measure their performance against soft standards of service quality? According to Leonard Berry and A. Parasuraman:

[C]ompanies need to establish ongoing listening systems using multiple methods among different customer groups. A single service quality study is a snapshot taken at a point in time and from a particular angle. Deeper insight and more informed decision making come from a continuing series of snapshots taken from various angles and through different lenses, which form the essence of systematic listening.[13]

They recommend that ongoing research be conducted through a portfolio of research approaches. Key customer-centric service quality measures include total market surveys, annual surveys, transactional surveys, service feedback cards, mystery shopping, analysis of unsolicited feedback, focus group discussions, and service reviews (which we discussed in Chapter 13). Other soft measures include *customer advisory panels* to offer feedback and advice on service performance, and *employee surveys and panels* to determine perceptions of the quality of service delivered to customers on specific dimensions, barriers to better service, and suggestions for improvement.

Designing and implementing a large-scale customer survey to measure service across a wide array of attributes is no simple task. Line managers sometimes view the findings as threatening when direct comparisons are made of the performance of different departments or branches.

Hard Measures of Service Quality

Hard measures typically refer to operational processes or outcomes and include such data as uptime, service response times, failure rates, and delivery costs. In a complex service operation, multiple measures of service quality will be recorded at many different points. In low-contact services, in which customers are not deeply involved in the service delivery process, many operational measures apply to backstage activities that have only a second-order effect on customers.

FedEx was one of the first service companies to understand the need for a firm-wide index of service quality that embraced all the key activities that had an impact on customers. By publishing a single, composite index on a frequent basis, senior managers hoped that all FedEx employees would work toward improving quality. The firm recognized the danger of using percentages as targets, because they might lead to complacency. In an organization as large as FedEx, which ships millions of packages a day, even delivering 99 percent of packages on time or having 99.9 percent of flights arrive safely would lead to horrendous problems. Instead, the company decided to approach quality measurement from the baseline of zero failures. As noted by one senior executive:

> It's only when you examine the types of failures, the number that occur of each type, and the reasons why, that you begin to improve the quality of your service. For us the trick was to express quality failures in absolute numbers. That led us to develop the Service Quality Index or SQI [pronounced "sky"], which takes each of 12 different events that occur every day, takes the numbers of those events and multiplies them by a weight . . . based on the amount of aggravation caused to customers—as evidenced by their tendency to write to Federal Express and complain about them.[14]

This design of this "hard" index reflected the findings of extensive "soft" customer research (and has been periodically modified in the light of new research insights). Looking at service failures from the customer's perspective, the Service Quality Index (SQI) measures daily the occurrence of 12 different activities that are likely to lead to customer dissatisfaction. The index is composed by taking the raw number of each event and multiplying it by a weighting factor—which highlights the seriousness of that event for customers—to give a point score for each item. The points are then totalled to generate that day's index (Table 14.4). Like a golf score, the lower the index, the better the performance. However, unlike golf, the SQI involves substantial numbers—typically six figures—reflecting the huge number of packages shipped daily. An annual goal is set for the average daily SQI, based on reducing the occurrence of failures over the previous year's total.

To ensure a continuing focus on each separate component of the SQI, FedEx established 12 Quality Action Teams, one for each component. The teams were charged with understanding and correcting the root causes underlying the observed problems.

Table 14.4 Composition of FedEx's Service Quality Index (SQI)

FAILURE TYPE	WEIGHTING FACTOR × NO. OF INCIDENTS = DAILY POINTS
Late delivery—right day	1
Late delivery—wrong day	5
Tracing requests unanswered	1
Complaints reopened	5
Missing proofs of delivery	1
Invoice adjustments	1
Missed pickups	10
Lost packages	10
Damaged packages	10
Aircraft delays (minutes)	5
Overgoods (packages missing labels)	5
Abandoned calls	1
Total failure points (SQI)	XXX,XXX

Source: Christopher Lovelock, *Product Plus: How Product + Service = Competitive Advantage,* New York: McGraw-Hill, 1994: 131.

Control charts offer a simple method of displaying performance on hard measures over time against specific quality standards. The charts can be used to monitor and communicate individual variables or an overall index. Since they present the information visually, trends are easily identified. Figure 14.3 shows an airline's performance on the important hard standard of on-time departures. The trends displayed suggest that this issue needs to be addressed by management, as performance is erratic and not very satisfactory. Of course, control charts are only as good as the data on which they are based.

Tools to Analyze and Address Service-Quality Problems

When a problem is caused by controllable, internal forces, there's no excuse for allowing it to recur. In fact, maintaining customers' goodwill after a service failure depends on keeping promises made to the effect that "we're taking steps to ensure that it doesn't happen again!" With prevention in mind, let's look briefly at some tools for determining the root causes of specific service quality problems.

Figure 14.3

Control Chart for Departure Delays, Showing Percentage of Flights Departing within 15 Minutes of Schedule

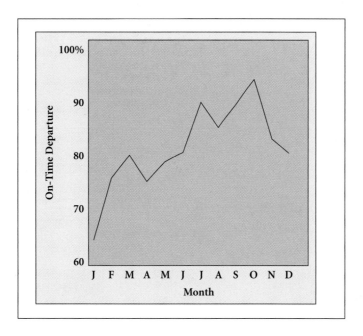

Root Cause Analysis: The Fishbone Diagram Cause-and-effect analysis employs a technique first developed by the Japanese quality expert Kaoru Ishikawa. Groups of managers and staff brainstorm all the possible reasons that might cause a specific problem. The resulting factors are then categorized into one of five groupings—Equipment, Manpower (or People), Material, Procedures, and Other—on a cause-and-effect chart, popularly known as a fishbone diagram because of its shape. This technique has been used for many years in manufacturing and, more recently, also in services.

To sharpen the value of the analysis for use in service organizations, we show an extended framework that comprises eight rather than five groupings.[15] "People" has been broken into Front-Stage Personnel and Backstage Personnel, to highlight the fact that front-stage service problems are often experienced directly by customers, whereas backstage failures tend to show up more obliquely through a ripple effect. "Information" has been split out from "Procedures," recognizing that many service problems result from information failures—often failures by front-stage personnel to tell customers what to do and when. In manufacturing, customers have little impact on day-to-day operational processes, but in a high-contact service, they are involved in front-stage operations. If they don't play their own roles correctly, they may reduce service productivity and cause quality problems for themselves and other customers. For instance, an aircraft can be delayed if a passenger tries to board at the last minute with an oversized suitcase that then has to be loaded into the cargo hold. An example of the extended fishbone is shown in Figure 14.4, displaying 27 possible reasons for late departures of passenger aircraft.[16]

Once all the main potential causes for flight delays have been identified, it's necessary to assess how much impact each cause has on actual delays.

Pareto analysis (named for the Italian economist who first developed it) seeks to identify the principal causes of observed outcomes. This type of analysis underlies the so-called 80/20 rule, because it often reveals that around 80 percent of the value of one variable (in this instance, the number of service failures) is accounted for by only 20 percent of the causal variables (i.e., the number of possible causes).

Figure 14.4 Cause-and-Effect Chart for Flight Departure Delays

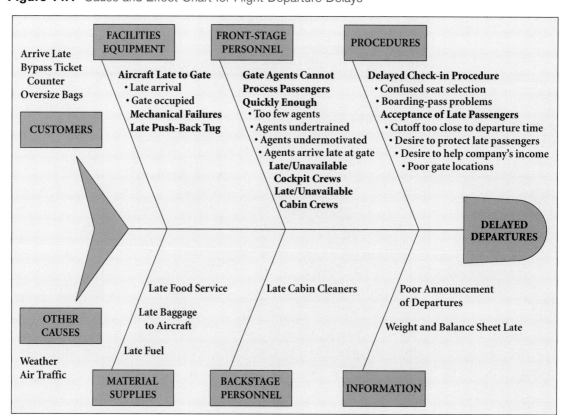

In the airline example, findings showed that 88 percent of the company's late departures from the airports it served were caused by only four (15 percent) of all the possible factors. In fact, more than half the delays were caused by a single factor: acceptance of late passengers (situations when the staff held a flight for one more passenger who was checking in after the official cut-off time).

On such occasions, the airline made a friend of that late passenger—possibly encouraging a repeat of this undesirable on a future occasion—but risked alienating all the other passengers who were already onboard, waiting for the aircraft to depart. Other major delays included waiting for pushback (a vehicle must arrive to pull the aircraft away from the gate), waiting for fuelling, and delays in signing the weight and balance sheet (a safety requirement, relating to the distribution of the aircraft's load, that the captain must observe on each flight). Further analysis, however, showed some significant variations in reasons between one airport and another (see Figure 14.5).

Combining the Fishbone diagram and Pareto analysis serves to highlight the main causes of service failure.

Blueprinting: A Powerful Tool for Identifying Fail Points

As described in Chapter 8, a well-constructed blueprint enables us to visualize the process of service delivery by depicting the sequence of front-stage interactions that customers experience as they encounter service providers, facilities, and equipment, together with supporting backstage activities, which are hidden from the customers and thus are not part of their service experience.

Blueprints can be used to identify potential *fail points* where failures are most likely to occur. Blueprints help us to understand how failures at one point (such as incorrect entry of an appointment date) may have a ripple effect later in the process (the customer arrives at the doctor's office and is told the doctor is unavailable). Using frequency counts,

Figure 14.5

Analysis of Causes of
Flight Departure Delays

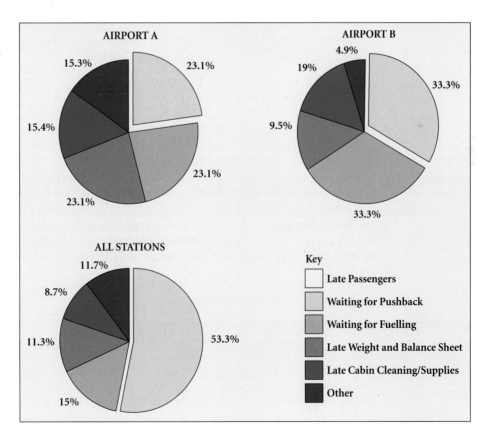

Source: Based on D. Daryl Wyckoff, "New Tools for Achieving Service Quality," *Cornell Hotel and Restaurant Administration Quarterly* 42 (August–September 2001): 25–38.

managers can identify the specific types of failures that occur most frequently and thus need urgent attention. One desirable solution is to design fail points out of the system (see Chapter 8, p. 238, for a discussion of Poka Yokes technique for approaching this). In the case of failures that cannot easily be designed out of a process, or are not easily prevented (such as problems related to weather or the public infrastructure), solutions may revolve around development of contingency plans and service recovery guidelines. Knowing what can go wrong, and where, is an important first step in preventing service-quality problems.

Return on Quality

Despite the attention paid to improving service quality, there are companies that been disappointed by the results. Even firms recognized for service-quality efforts have sometimes run into financial difficulties, in part because they spent too lavishly on quality improvements. In other instances, such outcomes reflect poor or incomplete execution of the quality program itself.

Assess Costs and Benefits of Quality Initiatives   Roland Rust, Anthony Zahonik, and Timothy Keiningham argue for a "Return on Quality" (ROQ) approach, based on the assumptions that (1) quality is an investment, (2) quality efforts must be financially accountable, (3) it is possible to spend too much on quality, and (4) not all quality expenditures are equally valid.[17] Hence expenditures on quality improvement must be related to anticipated increases in profitability. An important implication of the ROQ perspective is that quality improvement efforts may benefit from being co-ordinated with productivity improvement programs.

To determine the feasibility of new quality-improvement efforts, they must be carefully costed in advance and then related to anticipated customer response. Will the program enable the firm to attract more customers (e.g., through word of mouth by current customers), increase share of wallet, and/or reduce defections, and if so, how much additional net income will be generated?

With good documentation, it is sometimes possible for a firm that operates in multiple locations to examine past experience and determine whether a relationship exists between service quality and revenues. (See Research Insights 14.2.)

Determine the Optimal Level of Reliability   A company with poor service quality can often achieve big jumps in reliability with relatively modest investments in improvements. As illustrated in Figure 14.6, initial investments in reducing service failure often bring dramatic results, but at some point diminishing returns set in as further improvements require increasing levels of investment, even becoming prohibitively expensive. What level of reliability should we target?

Typically, the cost of service recovery is lower than the cost of an unhappy customer. This suggests a strategy of increasing reliability up to the point that the incremental improvement equals the cost of service recovery or the cost of failure. Although this strategy results in a service that is less than 100 percent failure-free, the firm can still aim to satisfy 100 percent of its target customers by ensuring that either they receive the service as planned or, if a failure occurs, they obtain a satisfying service recovery (see Chapter 13).

DEFINING AND MEASURING PRODUCTIVITY

Simply defined, productivity measures the output produced relative to the input used. Hence, improvements in productivity require an increase in the ratio of outputs to inputs. An improvement in this ratio might be achieved by cutting the resources required to create a given volume of output, or by increasing the output obtained from a given level of inputs.

Quality of Facilities and Room Revenues at Holiday Inn

To determine the relationship between product quality and financial performance in a hotel context, Sheryl Kimes analyzed three years of quality and operational performance data from 1135 franchised Holiday Inn hotels in Canada and the United States.

Indicators of product quality came from the franchisor's quality assurance reports. These reports were based on unannounced, semi-annual inspections by trained quality auditors who were rotated among different regions and who spent most of a day inspecting and rating 19 different areas of each hotel. Twelve of these areas were included in the study: two relating to the guest rooms (bedroom and bathroom) and ten relating to so-called commercial areas (e.g., exterior, lobby, public restrooms, dining facilities, lounge facilities, corridors, meeting area, recreation area, kitchen, back of house). Each area typically included 10–12 individual items that could be passed or failed. The inspector noted the number of defects for each area and the total number for the entire hotel.

Holiday Inn Worldwide also provided data on revenue per available room (RevPAR) at each hotel. To adjust for differences in local conditions, Kimes analyzed sales and revenue statistics obtained from thousands of Canadian and U.S. hotels, which are reported in the monthly Smith Travel Accommodation Reports (a widely used service in the travel industry). This data enabled Kimes to calculate the RevPAR for the immediate mid-scale competitors of each Holiday Inn hotel. The resulting information was then used to normalize the RevPARs for all Holiday Inns in the sample so that they were now truly comparable. The average daily room rate at the time was about $50.

The analysis was conducted using six-month intervals over a three-year period (1990–92). For the purposes of the research, if a hotel had failed at least one item in an area, it was considered "defective" in that area. A comparison was then made, on an area-by-area basis, of the average normalized RevPAR for hotels that were defective in an area against those that were "non-defective."

The findings showed that as the number of defects in a hotel increased, the RevPAR decreased. Hotel areas that showed a particularly strong impact on RevPAR were the exterior, the guest bedroom, and the guest bathroom. Even a single deficiency resulted in a statistically significant reduction in RevPAR, but the combination of deficiencies in all three areas showed an even larger effect on RevPAR over time. Kimes calculated that the average annual revenue impact on a defective hotel was $204 400.

Using a Return on Quality perspective, the implication was that the primary focus of increased expenditures on housekeeping and preventive maintenance should be the hotel exterior, the guest bedrooms, and guest bathrooms.

Source: Adapted from Sheryl E. Kimes, "The Relationship between Product Quality and Revenue per Available Room at Holiday Inn," *Journal of Service Research* 2 (November 1999): 138–44.

Defining Productivity in a Service Context

What do we mean by "input" in a service context? Input varies according to the nature of the business, but may include labour (both physical and intellectual), materials, energy, and capital (consisting of land, buildings, equipment, information systems, and financial assets). The intangible nature of service performances makes it more difficult to measure the productivity of service industries than of manufacturing. The problem is especially acute for information-based services.

Measuring productivity is difficult in services when the output is difficult to define. In a people-processing service, such as a hospital, we can look at the number of patients treated in the course of a year and at the hospital's "census," or average bed occupancy. But how do we account for the various types of interventions performed, such as removal of cancerous tumours, treatment of diabetes, or setting of broken bones? What about differences between patients? How do we evaluate the inevitable difference in outcomes? Some patients get better, some develop complications, and sadly, some even die. Relatively few standardized medical procedures offer highly predictable outcomes.

The measurement task is perhaps simpler in possession-processing services, since many are quasi-manufacturing organizations performing routine tasks with easily measurable inputs and outputs. Examples include garages that change a car's oil and rotate its tires, or fast food restaurants that offer limited and simple menus. However, the task gets

Figure 14.6

When does improving service reliability become uneconomical?

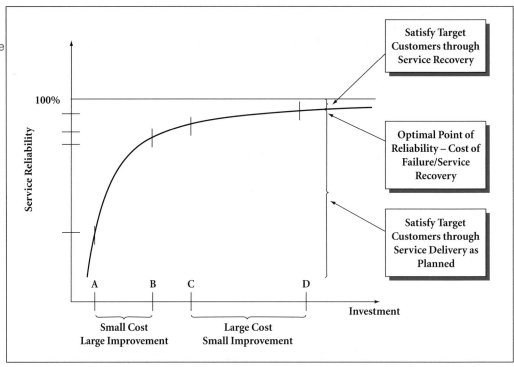

more complicated when the garage mechanic has to find and repair a water leak, or when we are dealing with a French restaurant known for its varied and exceptional cuisine. What about information-based services? How should we define the output of a bank or a consulting firm? And how does the latter's output compare to a law firm's?

Service Efficiency, Productivity, and Effectiveness

We need to distinguish among efficiency, productivity, and effectiveness.[18] Efficiency involves comparison to a standard, which is usually time-based—such as how long it takes for an employee to perform a particular task relative to a pre-defined standard. Productivity, however, involves financial valuation of outputs to inputs. Effectiveness, by contrast, can be defined as the degree to which an organization is meeting its goals.

A major problem in measuring service productivity concerns variability. As James Heskett points out, traditional measures of service output tend to ignore variations in the quality or value of service. In freight transport, for instance, a ton-mile of output for freight that is delivered late is treated the same for productivity purposes as a similar shipment delivered on time.[19]

Another approach—counting the number of customers served per unit of time—suffers from the same shortcoming. What happens when an increase in customer throughput is achieved at the expense of perceived service quality? Suppose a hairdresser serves a customer every 20 minutes, but finds that she can increase her output to one every 15 minutes by using a faster but noisier hairdryer, by reducing conversation with the customer, and by rushing her customers. Even if the haircut itself is just as good, the delivery process may be perceived as functionally inferior, leading customers to rate the overall service experience less positively.

Classical techniques of productivity measurement focus on outputs rather than outcomes, stressing efficiency but neglecting effectiveness. In the long run, organizations that are more effective in consistently delivering outcomes desired by customers should be able to command higher prices for their output. The need to emphasize effectiveness and outcomes suggests that issues of productivity cannot be divorced from those of quality and value. Loyal customers who remain with a firm tend to become more profitable over time, an indication of the payback to be obtained from providing quality service.

Intensive competition in many service sectors pushes firms to continually seek ways to improve their productivity.[20] This section discusses various potential approaches to, and sources of, productivity gains.

Generic Productivity Improvement Strategies

The task of improving service productivity has traditionally been assigned to operations managers, whose approach has typically centred on such actions as

- Careful control of costs at every step in the process
- Efforts to reduce wasteful use of materials or labour
- Matching productive capacity to average levels of demand rather than peak levels, so that workers and equipment are not underemployed for extended periods
- Replacement of workers by automated machines
- Providing employees with equipment and databases that enable them to work faster and/or to a higher level of quality
- Teaching employees how to work more productively (faster is not necessarily better if it leads to mistakes or unsatisfactory work that has to be redone)
- Broadening the array of tasks that a service worker can perform (which may require revised labour agreements) so as to eliminate bottlenecks and wasteful downtime by allowing managers to deploy workers wherever they are most needed
- Installing expert systems that allow para-professionals to take on work previously performed by more experienced individuals earning higher salaries

Although improving productivity can be approached in an incremental way, major gains often require redesigning customer service processes. For example, it is time for service process redesign when poor processes and low productivity result in unbearably long waiting time for customers (e.g., Figure 14.7). We discussed the redesign of service processes in depth in Chapter 8.

Figure 14.7

Long waiting times often indicate a need for redesign of the service process.

Customer-Driven Approaches to Improve Productivity

In situations where customers are deeply involved in the service production process (typically, people-processing services), operations managers should be examining how customer inputs can be made more productive. Marketing managers should be thinking about what marketing strategies should be used to influence customers to behave in more productive ways. We review three strategies: changing the timing of customer demand, involving customers more actively in the production process, and asking customers to use third parties.

Changing the Timing of Customer Demand   Managing demand in capacity-constrained service businesses has been a recurring theme in this book. (See especially Chapters 6 and 9.) Customers often complain that the services they use are crowded and congested, reflecting time-of-day, seasonal, or other cyclical peaks in demand. During the off-peak periods of those same cycles, managers often worry that there are too few customers and that their facilities and staff are not fully productive. By shifting demand away from peaks, managers can make better use of their productive assets, and provide better service. For example, Canada Post uses its website to publicize suggested mailing dates to the United States and various overseas destinations in the run-up to Christmas, in order to help its customers plan ahead, rather than leaving it until a few days before the holiday to send their cards and packages. Offering access through alternative channels, such as the internet and voice or text telephone, can facilitate demand management by reducing the pressure on employees and certain types of physical facilities at peak hours.

Involve Customers More in Production   Customers who assume a more active role in the service production and delivery process can take over some labour tasks from the service organization. Benefits for both parties may result when customers perform self-service.

Many technological innovations are designed to get customers to perform tasks previously undertaken by service employees (e.g., see Figure 14.8). The internet has become a vital tool in productivity improvement. Increasing numbers of customers are using the web (instead of telephoning or visiting a firm in person) to perform an array of self-service tasks that might previously have required employee assistance. Text messaging, too, is now substituting for some personal interactions.

Figure 14.8

Self-service pumps with credit card readers have increased gas station productivity.

Even five-star hotels with traditionally high levels of personal service have been asking their guests to do more of the work. For example, in-room safe deposit boxes and voice-mail attached to telephones have been implemented in most hotel rooms. In the past, these services were provided by a service counter or concierge. However, despite the reduction in personal service, this innovation has been positioned as a benefit that is actually more convenient for guests. They can have fast and easy access to their in-room safe deposit boxes, and can easily see from a blinking light on the phone whether there is a voicemail waiting for them, rather than having to contact the concierge.

Some customers may be more willing than others to serve themselves. In fact, research suggests that this may be a useful segmentation variable. A large-scale study presented respondents with the choice of a do-it-yourself option versus traditional delivery systems at gas stations, banks, restaurants, hotels, airports, and travel services.[21] For each service, a particular scenario was outlined, since earlier interviews had determined that decisions to choose self-service options were very situation-specific. Analysis showed some overlap of preference for self-service (or for being served) across different service settings. If respondents didn't pump their own gas, for instance, they were also less likely to carry their luggage to their room in a hotel.

Quality and productivity improvements often depend on customers' willingness to learn new procedures, follow instructions, and interact co-operatively with employees and other people. Customers who arrive at the service encounter with a set of pre-existing norms, values, and role definitions may resist change. Cathy Goodwin suggests that insights from research on socialization can help service marketers redesign the nature of the service encounter in ways that increase the chances of gaining customer co-operation.[22] In particular, she argues that customers will need help to learn new skills, form a new self-image ("I can do it myself"), develop new relationships with providers and fellow customers, and acquire new values.

Ask Customers to Use Third Parties
In some instances, managers may be able to improve service productivity by delegating one or more marketing support functions to third parties. The purchase process often breaks down into four components: information, reservation, payment, and consumption. When consumption of the core product takes place at a location not easily accessible from customers' homes or workplaces (for instance, an airport, theatre, stadium, or a hotel in a distant city), it makes sense to delegate delivery of supplementary service elements to intermediary organizations.

Specialist intermediaries may enjoy economies of scale, enabling them to perform the task more cheaply than the core service provider, allowing the latter to focus on quality and productivity in its own area of expertise. Some intermediaries are identifiable local organizations, like travel agencies, which customers can visit in person. Others, such as hotel reservations centres, often subjugate their own identity to that of the client service company.

How Productivity Improvements Affect Quality and Value

Managers would do well to examine productivity from the broader perspective of the business processes used to transform resource inputs into the outcomes desired by customers—processes that not only cross departmental and sometimes geographic boundaries, but also link the backstage and front-stage areas of the service operation.

How Backstage Changes May Affect Customers
The marketing implications of backstage changes depend on whether they affect or are noticed by customers. If airline mechanics develop a procedure for servicing jet engines more quickly, without incurring increased wage rates or material costs, the airline has obtained a productivity improvement that has no impact on the customer's service experience.

Other backstage changes, however, may have a ripple effect that extends front stage and affects customers. Marketers should keep abreast of proposed backstage changes, not only to identify such ripples but also to prepare customers for them. At a bank, for instance, the decision to install new computers and printer peripherals may be driven by plans to improve internal quality controls and reduce the cost of preparing monthly statements. However, this new equipment may change the appearance of bank statements, and the time of the month when they are posted. If customers are likely to notice such changes, an explanation may be warranted. If the new statements are easier to read and understand, the change may be worth promoting as a service enhancement.

Front-Stage Efforts to Improve Productivity   In high-contact services, many productivity enhancements are quite visible. Some changes simply require passive acceptance by customers, while others require customers to adopt new patterns of behaviour in their dealings with the organization. If substantial changes are proposed, then it makes sense to conduct market research first to determine how customers may respond. Failure to think through impacts on customers may result in a loss of business and cancel out anticipated productivity gains. Service Perspectives 14.1 identifies ways of addressing customer resistance to change, particularly when the innovation is a radical one. Once the

Service Perspectives 14.1

Managing Customers' Reluctance to Change

Customer resistance to changes in familiar environments and long-established behaviour patterns can thwart attempts to improve productivity and even quality. Failure to examine proposed changes from the customer's perspective may spur resistance. The following six steps can help smooth the path of change.

1. **Develop customer trust.** It's more difficult to introduce productivity-related changes when people are basically distrustful of the initiator, as they often are in the case of large, seemingly impersonal institutions. Customers' willingness to accept change may be closely related to the degree of goodwill they bear towards the organization.

2. **Understand customers' habits and expectations.** People often get into a routine around the use of a particular service, with certain steps being taken in a specific sequence. In effect, they have their own individual flow chart in mind. Innovations that disrupt ingrained routines are likely to face resistance unless consumers are carefully briefed as to what changes to expect.

3. **Pre-test new procedures and equipment.** To determine probable customer response to new procedures and equipment, marketing researchers can employ concept and laboratory testing, and/or field testing. If service personnel are going to be replaced by automatic equipment, it's essential to create designs that customers of almost all types and backgrounds will find easy to use. Even the phrasing of instructions needs careful thought. Ambiguous, complex, or authoritarian instructions may discourage customers with poor reading skills, as well as those used to personal courtesies from the service personnel whom the machine replaces.

4. **Publicize the benefits.** Introduction of self-service equipment or procedures requires consumers to perform part of the task themselves. Although this additional "work" may be associated with such benefits as extended service hours, time savings, and (in some instances) monetary savings, these benefits are not necessarily obvious—they have to be promoted. Useful strategies may include use of mass media advertising, on-site posters and signage, and personal communications to inform people of the innovation, arouse their interest in it, and clarify the specific benefits to customers of changing their behaviour to use the new delivery systems.

5. **Teach customers to use innovations and promote trial.** Assigning service personnel to demonstrate new equipment and answer questions—providing reassurance as well as educational assistance—is a key element in gaining acceptance of new procedures and technology. The costs of such demonstration programs can be spread across multiple outlets by moving staff members from one site to another if the innovation is rolled out sequentially across the various locations. For web-based innovations, it's important to provide access to email, chat, or even telephone-based assistance. Promotional incentives and price discounts may also serve to stimulate initial trial. Once customers have tried a self-service option (particularly an electronically based one) and found that it works well, they will be more likely to use it regularly in the future.

6. **Monitor performance and continue to seek improvements.** Introducing quality and productivity improvements is an ongoing process. The competitive edge provided by productivity improvements may quickly be erased as other firms adopt similar or better procedures. Service managers have to work hard to keep up the momentum so that programs achieve their full potential and are not allowed to flag. If customers are displeased by new procedures, they may revert to their previous behaviour, so it's important to continue monitoring utilization over time.

nature of the changes has been decided, marketing communication can help prepare customers for the change, explaining the rationale, the benefits, and what customers will need to do differently in the future.

A Cautionary Note on Cost-Reduction Strategies   In the absence of new technology, most attempts to improve service productivity tend to centre on efforts to eliminate waste and reduce labour costs. Cutbacks in front-stage staffing mean either that remaining employees have to work harder and faster, or that there are insufficient personnel to serve customers promptly at busy times. Although employees may be able to work faster for a brief period of time, few can maintain a rapid pace for extended periods: they become exhausted, make mistakes, and treat customers in a cursory manner. Workers who are trying to do two or three things at once—serving a customer face to face while simultaneously answering the telephone and sorting papers, for example—may do a poor job of each task. Excessive pressure breeds discontent and frustration, especially among customer contact personnel who are caught between trying to meet customer needs and attempting to achieve management's productivity goals. A better way is to search for opportunities to redesign service processes that lead to drastic improvements in productivity while at the same time increasing service quality. Biometrics is set to become a new technology that may allow both. (See Service Perspectives 14.2.)

Service Perspectives 14.2

Biometrics: The Next Frontier in Driving Productivity and Service Quality?

Intense competitive pressures and razor-thin margins in service industries do not allow firms the luxury of increasing costs to improve quality. Rather, the trick is to constantly seek ways to achieve leaps in service quality simultaneously with ones in efficiency, something Heracleous, Wirtz, and co-authors termed *cost-effective service excellence*. The internet has in the past allowed many firms to do just that, and has redefined industries, including financial services, book and music retailing, and travel agencies. Biometrics may be the next major technology driving further service and productivity enhancements.

Biometrics is the authentication of an individual's identity by a measurement of some physical characteristic or trait. Physical characteristics include fingerprints, facial recognition, hand geometry, or iris configuration, and traits include signature formation, keystroke patterns, or voice recognition. Biometrics, since it measures something you are, is both more convenient and more secure than something you know (passwords or pieces of personal information) or something you have (card keys, smart cards or tokens). There is no risk of forgetting, losing, copying, loaning, or having your biometrics stolen. (See Figure 14.9.)

Applications of biometrics range from controlling access to service facilities (used by Disneyworld to provide access to season pass holders), voice recognition (such as the one used by Bell Canada, called MAYA, for over 5000 employees to reduce hold time and operator costs and to enhance productivity of off-site employees), passports (such as the ones issued by Passport Canada since 2005 that use digitized

photos), access to safe deposit vaults at banks (used by the Bank of Hawaii), secure access to company portals (used by the Credit Union Central of British Columbia to allow secure access to it's Central Security Portal by staff of credit unions and corporate clients across Canada), and cashing cheques in supermarkets (used by U.S. chains such as Kroger and BI-LO).

Singapore Airlines (SIA) and the Civil Aviation Authority of Singapore, which operates Changi Airport, arguably one of the best airports in the world, are planning to use biometric technologies to offer every traveller's dream when it comes to airport procedures: the ability to breeze through airline check-in, security checks, and immigration checks in less than a minute, all within a context of enhanced travel security. A pilot test of Fully Automated Seamless Travel, as the process is called, integrated three processes: airline check-in, pre-immigration security checks, and immigration clearance, whereas most other biometrics-based trials elsewhere primarily focus on improving security. This initiative at Changi Airport is a world's first in integrating these processes with the clear objective of driving service excellence at airport operations and SIA's ground services, while at the same time driving efficiency and improving security.

The pilot phase involved 9000 of SIA's frequent flyers who are Singapore citizens, and was implemented at terminal 2 at Changi Airport. Participants signed up first at an enrolment station of the Immigration and Checkpoints Authority, where their biometric information (fingerprints and facial features) were captured on a smart card called

SVIP (Smart Visa for Identification with Passport). When travelling, these registered users can simply walk through a separate gateway at immigration, where they can do a self-service check-in at a computerized service station. Here, they tap their card onto a reader, have their fingerprint scanned, and use a touch screen to check in while their face is being scanned by a camera. The system identifies the card holder, clears security checks and immigration, recommends a seat based on the known preferences of the traveller, and upon acceptance by the traveller, prints a boarding pass. If the traveller is happy with the suggested seat, the entire process takes less than 60 seconds (or some three minutes if a passenger wished to change his or her seat up to three times). The pilot test does not handle passengers with check-in baggage, but a separate process, the "baggage drop-off" concept, is being considered for that. Hand luggage is taken on board as usual.

SIA believes that in the not too distant future most international travellers will be carrying a passport, visa, or smartcard, which will contain selected biometric information of its owner. In response to this opportunity, a task force in SIA identified an astounding 113 potential biometrics applications in a recent retreat, and is currently exploring which ones would provide simultaneous strategic differentiation through service excellence, while improving productivity, as well as security.

Sources: Loizos Heracleous, Jochen Wirtz, and Nitin Pangarkar, *Flying High in a Competitive Industry: Cost Effective Service Excellence at Singapore Airlines*, Singapore: McGraw Hill, 2006: 104–12; Loizos T. Heracleous, Jochen Wirtz, and Robert Johnston, "Cost-effective Service Excellence: Lessons from Singapore Airlines," *Business Strategy Review* 15/1 (2004): 33–38; Jochen Wirtz and Loizos Heracleous, "Biometrics Meets Services," *Harvard Business Review* 83/2 (February 2005): 48–49; Loizos Heracleous and Jochen Wirtz, "Biometrics: The Next Frontier in Service Excellence, Productivity and Security in the Service Sector," *Managing Service Quality* 16/1 (2006): 12–22.

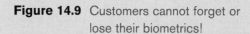

Figure 14.9 Customers cannot forget or lose their biometrics!

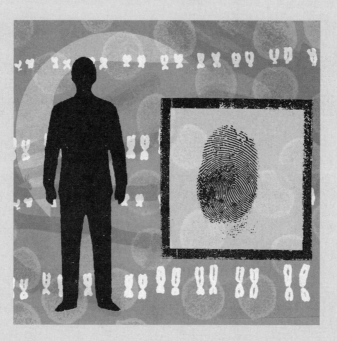

Conclusion

Enhancing service quality and improving service productivity are often two sides of the same coin, offering powerful potential to improve value for both customers and the firm. A key challenge for any service business is to deliver satisfactory outcomes to its customers in ways that are cost effective for the company. If customers are dissatisfied with the quality of a service, they won't be willing to pay very much for it, or even to buy it at all if competitors offer better quality. Low sales volumes and/or low prices mean less-productive assets.

It is a widely accepted notion that customers are the best judges of the quality of a service process and its outcome. When the customer is seen as the final arbiter of quality, then marketing managers come to play a key role in defining customer expectations and in measuring their satisfaction. However, service marketers need to work closely with other management functions in service design and implementation.

This chapter presented a number of frameworks and tools for defining, measuring, managing, and improving service quality, including research programs to identify quality gaps, and various analytical tools to identify and improve fail points.

Service process redesign is an important tool to increase service productivity. Marketing managers should be included in productivity improvement programs whenever these efforts are likely to have an impact on customers. Because customers are often involved in the service production process, marketers should keep their eyes open for opportunities to reshape customer behaviour in ways that may help the service firm to become more productive. Possibilities for co-operative behaviour include adopting self-service options, changing the timing of customer demand to less busy periods, and making use of third-party suppliers of supplementary services.

In summary, value, quality, and productivity are all of great concern to senior management, as they relate directly to an organization's profitability and survival in the competitive marketplace. Strategies designed to enhance value are dependent in large measure on continuous improvement in service quality (as defined by customers) and productivity that reinforce rather than counteract customer satisfaction. The marketing function has much to offer in reshaping our thinking about these issues, as well as in helping to achieve significant improvements in all of them.

Review Questions

1. Explain the relationship between service quality, productivity, and marketing.

2. Identify the gaps that can occur in service quality, and the steps that service marketers can take to prevent them.

3. Why are both "soft" and "hard" measures of service quality needed?

4. What are the main tools service firms can use to analyze and address service quality problems?

5. Why is productivity a more difficult issue for service firms than for manufacturers?

6. What are the key tools for improving service productivity?

7. How do productivity improvements affect the quality and value of a service offering?

8. How do concepts such as TQM, ISO 9000, National Quality Institute's (NQI) Business Excellence Framework, and Six Sigma (see Appendix below) relate to managing and improving productivity and service quality?

Application Exercises

1. Review the five dimensions of service quality. What do they mean in the context of (a) an industrial repair shop, (b) a retail bank, (c) a Big 4 accounting firm?

2. Consider your own recent experiences as a service consumer. On which dimensions of service quality have you most often experienced a large gap between your expectations and your perceptions of the service performance? What do you think the underlying causes might be? What steps should management take to improve quality?

3. In what ways can you, as a consumer, help to improve productivity for at least three service organizations that you patronize? What distinctive characteristics of each service make some of these actions possible?

4. What key measures could be used for monitoring service quality, productivity, and profitability for a large pizza restaurant chain? Specifically, what measures would you recommend such a firm to use, taking administration costs into consideration? Who should receive what type of feedback on the results, and why? On which measures would you base a part of the salary of branch-level staff, and why?

5. The use of Biometrics as a tool to improve productivity as well as service quality is set to grow enormously in the

coming years. (See Service Perspectives 14.2.) Identify some key commercial uses of biometrics in Canada and assess whether the application was put in place to improve: 1) service quality; 2) productivity; or 3) both? What concerns, if any, are likely to be voiced by consumers in the applications mentioned above in which biometrics has been used primarily for productivity enhancements?

6. *(Refers to Appendix)* Undertake a literature search and identify the critical factors for a successful implementation of ISO 9000, the National Quality Institute's Business Excellence Framework, and Six Sigma in service firms. Contrast the success factors suggested in the literature.

Appendix: Systematic Approaches to Productivity and Quality Improvement, and to Process Standardization

Many of the thinking, tools, and concepts introduced in this chapter originate from the Total Quality Management (TQM), ISO 9000, NQI's Business Excellence Framework, and Six Sigma models. This appendix provides a brief overview of each approach.

Total Quality Management

Total Quality Management (TQM) concepts, originally developed in Japan, are widely used in manufacturing, and more recently also in service firms. Some concepts and tools of TQM can be directly applied to services. TQM tools such as control charts, flow charts, and fishbone diagrams are being used by service firms with great results for monitoring service quality and determining the root causes of specific problems. Sureshchandar et al. identified twelve critical dimensions for the successful implementation of TQM in a service context: (1) top management commitment and visionary leadership, (2) human resource management, (3) technical system, including service process design and process management, (4) information and analysis system, (5) benchmarking, (6) continuous improvement, (7) customer focus, (8) employee satisfaction, (9) union intervention and employee relations, (10) social responsibility, (11) servicescapes, and (12) service culture.[23]

ISO 9000 Certification

More than 90 countries are members of the ISO (the International Organization for Standardization based in Geneva, Switzerland), which promotes standardization and quality to facilitate international trade. ISO 9000 comprises a set of requirements, definitions, guidelines, and related standards to provide an independent assessment and certification of a firm's quality management system. The official ISO 9000 definition of quality is: "The totality of features and characteristics of a product or service that bear on its ability to satisfy a stated or implied need. Simply stated, quality is about meeting or exceeding your customer's needs and requirements."

To ensure quality, ISO 9000 uses many TQM tools and routinizes their use in participating firms.

As in other quality initiatives, such as TQM and Six Sigma, service firms were late in adopting the ISO 9000 standards, and the majority (around two-thirds) of the total of 510 616 organizations that had been certified ISO 9000-compliant by the end of 2001 were in manufacturing industries.[24] Major service sectors that have adopted ISO 9000 certification include wholesale and retail firms, IT service providers, health care providers, consultancy firms, and educational institutions.

By adopting ISO 9000 standards, service firms, especially small ones, can not only ensure that their services conform to customer expectations, but also achieve improvements in internal productivity.

National Quality Institute's Business Excellence Framework

The National Quality Institute (NQI) is an independent, not-for-profit organization that focuses on promoting and recognizing workplace excellence based on quality systems and healthy workplace criteria in Canada. NQI acts as a national partner with many organizations to advance the excellence "movement" in Canadian business. It provides member organizations with business frameworks, services, and tools that help them on their path toward business excellence via NQI's "Roadmap to Excellence." This "Roadmap" also serves to guide members through four levels of NQI's Progressive Excellence Program (NQI PEP) certification, which in turn makes them eligible to compete for the coveted Canada Awards for Excellence. Canadian services firms that have won the award include Purolator Courier Ltd, Telus Mobility, Delta Hotels, and AMEX Canada Inc.

NQI's Business Excellence Framework assesses firms on seven areas: (1) leadership commitment to creating culture, values, and overall direction for long-term success; (2) business planning, the linkage of planning to strategic direction/intent, the implementation of planning, and the measurement of performance to assess progress; (3) organizational focus on the customer and marketplace, and achievement of customer satisfaction and loyalty; (4) human resources management practices focusing on how people are encouraged, enabled, and involved to achieve organizational goals, while reaching their full potential; (5) process management that focuses on process development, process control, and continuous improvement; (6) supplier/partner relationships that allow the firm to reach its strategic objectives; and (7) overall business performance.[25]

Six Sigma Applied to Service Organizations

The six sigma approach was originally developed by Motorola engineers in the mid-1980s to address the issue of increasing numbers of complaints from its field sales force regarding warranty claims; it was soon adopted by other manufacturing firms to reduce defects in a variety of areas.

Subsequently, service firms embraced various six sigma strategies to reduce defects, reduce cycle times, and improve productivity.[26] As early as 1990, GE Capital applied six sigma methodology to reduce the backroom costs of selling consumer loans, credit card insurance, and payment protection. Its president and CEO Denis Nayden said,

Although Six Sigma was originally designed for manufacturing, it can be applied to transactional services. One obvious example is in making sure the

millions of credit card and other bills GE sends to customers are correct, which drives down our costs of making adjustments. One of our biggest costs in the financial business is winning new customers. If we treat them well, they will stay with us, reducing our customer-origination costs.[27]

Statistically, six sigma means achieving a quality level of only 3.4 defects per million opportunities (DPMO). To understand how stringent this target is, consider mail deliveries. If a mail service delivers with 99 percent accuracy, it misses 10 000 items out of 1 million deliveries. But if it achieved a six-sigma performance level, only three or four items out of this total would go astray!

Over time, six sigma has evolved from a defect reduction approach to an overall business improvement approach. As defined by Pande et al.:

Six sigma is a comprehensive and flexible system for achieving, sustaining and maximizing business success. Six sigma is uniquely driven by close understanding of customer needs, disciplined use of facts, data and statistical analysis, and diligent attention to managing, improving, and reinventing business processes.[28]

Two strategies—namely process improvement and process design/redesign—form the cornerstone of the six sigma approach. Process improvement strategies aim at identifying and eliminating the root causes of the

---

Table 14.5 Applying the DMAIC Model to Process Improvement and Redesign

	SIX SIGMA METHODOLOGY TO IMPROVE AND REDESIGN PROCESSES	
	PROCESS IMPROVEMENT	PROCESS DESIGN/REDESIGN
Define	Identify the problem Define requirements Set goals	Identify specific or broad problems Define goal/change vision Clarify scope and customer requirements
Measure	Validate problem/process Refine problem/goal Measure key steps/inputs	Measure performance to requirements Gather process efficiency data
Analyze	Develop causal hypothesis Identify "vital few" root causes Validate hypothesis	Identify best practices Assess process design • Value/non–value-adding • Bottlenecks/disconnects • Alternative paths Refine requirements
Improve	Develop ideas to remove root causes Test solutions Standardize solution/measure results	Design new process • Challenge assumptions • Apply creativity • Workflow principles Implement new process, structures, systems
Control	Establish standard measures to maintain performance Correct problems as needed	Establish measures and reviews to maintain performance Correct problems as needed

Source: Reproduced from Peter Pande, Robert P. Neuman, and Ronald R. Cavanagh, *The Six Sigma Way.* New York: McGraw-Hill, 2000.

service delivery problems, and thereby improving service quality. Process design/redesign strategies act as supplements to improvement strategies. If a root cause can't be identified or effectively eliminated within the existing processes, either new processes are *designed* to do so, or existing process are *redesigned* to fully or partially address the problem.

The most popular six sigma improvement model used for analyzing and improving business processes is the DMAIC model, shown in Table 14.5. DMAIC stands for **D**efine the opportunities, **M**easure key steps/inputs, **A**nalyze to identify root causes, **I**mprove performance, and **C**ontrol to maintain performance.

Which Methodology Should We Adopt?

As there are various approaches to systematically improving a service firm's service quality and productivity, the question arises which approach should be adopted—TQM, ISO 9000, NQI's Business Excellence Framework, or Six Sigma? Some firms have implemented more than one program. In terms of complexity, it seems that TQM can be applied at differing levels of sophistication, and basic tools such as flowcharts, frequency charts, and fishbone diagrams should probably be adopted by any type of service firm. ISO 9000 seems

the next level of commitment and complexity, followed by the NQI's Business Excellence Framework and finally Six Sigma.

By reviewing the various approaches, it becomes clear that in fact any one of them can be a useful framework for understanding customer needs, analyzing processes, and improving service quality and productivity. Firms can choose a particular program, depending on their own needs and desired level of sophistication. Each program has its own merits, and firms can adopt more than one program to supplement another. For example, the ISO 9000 program can be used for standardizing the procedures and process documentation, which can lead to reduction in variability. Six sigma and NQI's Business Excellence Framework can be used to improve processes and to focus on performance improvement across the organization.

A key success factor of any of these programs depends on how well the particular quality improvement program is integrated with the overall business strategy. Firms who adapt one of these programs due to peer pressure, or just as a marketing tool, will be less likely to succeed than firms who view these programs as useful development tools.[29] Service champions make best practices in service-quality management a core part of their organizational culture.[30]

Endnotes

1. David A. Garvin, *Managing Quality,* New York: Free Press, 1988, especially Chapter 3.
2. Christian Grönroos, *Service Management and Marketing*, 2nd ed., Chichester, UK: John Wiley, 2001.
3. Valarie A. Zeithaml, A. Parasuraman, and Leonard L. Berry, *Delivering Quality Service: Balancing Customer Perceptions and Expectations,* New York: Free Press, 1990.
4. A. Parasuraman, Valarie A. Zeithaml, and Leonard Berry, "SERVQUAL: A Multiple Item Scale for Measuring Consumer Perceptions of Service Quality," *Journal of Retailing* 64 (1988): 12–40.
5. See, for instance, Francis Buttle, "SERVQUAL: Review, Critique, Research Agenda," *European Journal of Marketing* 30/1, (1996): 8–32; Simon S.K. Lam and Ka Shing Woo, "Measuring Service Quality: A Test–Retest Reliability Investigation of SERVQUAL," *Journal of the Market Research Society* 39 (April 1997): 381–93; Terrence H. Witkowski and Mary F. Wolfinbarger, "Comparative Service Quality: German and American Ratings Across Service Settings," *Journal of Business Research* 55 (2002): 875–81; Lisa J. Morrison Coulthard, "Measuring Service Quality: A Review and Critique of Research Using SERVQUAL," *International Journal of Market Research* 46 (Quarter 4, 2004): 479–97.
6. Anne M. Smith, "Measuring Service Quality: Is

SERVQUAL Now Redundant?" *Journal of Marketing Management* 11 (Jan/Feb/April 1995): 257–76.
7. Gerhard Mels, Christo Boshoff, and Denon Nel, "The Dimensions of Service Quality: The Original European Perspective Revisited," *Service Industries Journal* 17 (January 1997): 173–89.
8. A. Parasuraman, Valarie A. Zeithaml, and Arvind Malhotra, "E-S-QUAL: A Multiple-Item Scale for Assessing Electronic Service Quality," *Journal of Service Research* 7/3 (2005): 213–33.
9. Jochen Wirtz and Anna S. Mattila, "Exploring the Role of Alternative Perceived Performance Measures and Needs-Congruency in the Consumer Satisfaction Process," *Journal of Consumer Psychology* 11/3 (2001): 181–92.
10. Jochen Wirtz, "Halo in Customer Satisfaction Measures: The Role of Purpose of Rating, Number of Attributes, and Customer Involvement," *International Journal of Service Industry Management* 14/1 (2003): 96–119.
11. A. Parasuraman, Valarie A. Zeithaml, and Leonard L. Berry, "A Conceptual Model of Service Quality and Its Implications for Future Research," *Journal of Marketing* 49 (Fall 1985): 41–50; and Valarie A. Zeithaml, Leonard L. Berry, and A. Parasuraman, "Communication and Control Processes in the Delivery of Services," *Journal of Marketing* 52 (April 1988), 36–58.

12. Valarie A. Zeithaml, Mary Jo Bitner, and Dwayne D. Gremler, *Services Marketing: Integrating Customer Focus Across the Firm*, 4th ed., Boston: McGraw-Hill/Irwin, 2006: 292.

13. Leonard L. Berry and A. Parasuraman, "Listening to the Customer: The Concept of a Service Quality Information System," *Sloan Management Review* (Spring 1997): 65–76.

14. Comments by Thomas R. Oliver, then senior vice president of sales and customer service, Federal Express; reported in Christopher H. Lovelock, *Federal Express: Quality Improvement Program*, Lausanne: International Institute for Management Development, 1990.

15. Christopher Lovelock, *Product Plus: How Product + Service = Competitive Advantage*, New York: McGraw-Hill, 1994: 218.

16. These categories and the research data that follow have been adapted from information in D. Daryl Wyckoff, "New Tools for Achieving Service Quality," *Cornell Hotel and Restaurant Administration Quarterly* (August–September 2001): 25–38.

17. Roland T. Rust, Anthony J. Zahonik, and Timothy L. Keiningham, "Return on Quality (ROQ): Making Service Quality Financially Accountable," *Journal of Marketing* 59 (April 1995): 58–70; and Roland T. Rust, Christine Moorman, and Peter R. Dickson, "Getting Return on Quality: Revenue Expansion, Cost Reduction, or Both?" *Journal of Marketing* 66 (October 2002), 7–24.

18. Kenneth J. Klassen, Randolph M. Russell, and James J. Chrisman, "Efficiency and Productivity Measures for High Contact Services," *Service Industries Journal* 18 (October 1998): 1–18.

19. James L. Heskett, *Managing in the Service Economy*, Boston: Harvard Business School Press, 1986.

20. For a more in-depth discussion on service productivity, see Cynthia Karen Swank, "The Lean Service Machine," *Harvard Business Review* 81/10 (October 2003): 123–29.

21. Eric Langeard, John E.G. Bateson, Christopher H. Lovelock, and Pierre Eiglier, *Services Marketing: New Insights from Consumers and Managers*, Cambridge, MA: Marketing Science Institute, 1981, especially Chapter 2. A good summary of this research is provided in J.E.G. Bateson, "Self-Service Consumer: An Exploratory Study," *Journal of Retailing* 51 (Fall 1985): 49–76.

22. Cathy Goodwin, "I Can Do It Myself: Training the Service Consumer to Contribute to Service Productivity," *Journal of Services Marketing* 2 (Fall 1988): 71–78.

23. G.S. Sureshchandar, Chandrasekharan Rajendran, and R.N. Anantharaman, "A Holistic Model for Total Service Quality," *International Journal of Service Industry Management* 12/4 (2001): 378–412.

24. ISO, *The ISO Survey of ISO 9000 and ISO 14000 Certificates (Eleventh Cycle)*, Geneva: International Organization for Standardization, 2001.

25. "Canadian Framework For Business Excellence: Overview Document," www.nqi.ca/nqistore/product_details.aspx?ID=61, accessed October 29, 2006.

26. Jim Biolos, "Six Sigma Meets the Service Economy," *Harvard Business Review* 80/11 (November 2002): 3–5.

27. Mikel Harry and Richard Schroeder, *Six Sigma: The Breakthrough Management Strategy Revolutionizing the World's Top Corporations*, New York: Currency, 2000: 232.

28. Peter S. Pande, Robert P. Neuman, and Ronald R. Cavanagh, *The Six Sigma Way: How GE, Motorola, and Other Top Companies Are Honing their Performance*, New York: McGraw-Hill, 2000.

29. Gavin Dick, Kevin Gallimore, and Jane C. Brown, "ISO 9000 and Quality Emphasis: An Empirical study of Front-room and Back-room Dominant Service Industries," *International Journal of Service Industry Management* 12/2 (2001): 114–36; and Adrian Hughes and David N. Halsall, "Comparison of the 14 Deadly Diseases and the Business Excellence Model," *Total Quality Management* 13/2 (2002): 255–63.

30. Cathy A. Enz and Judy A. Siguaw, "Best Practices in Service Quality," *Cornell Hotel and Restaurant Administration Quarterly* (October 2000): 20–29.

CHAPTER 15

Organizing for Change Management and Service Leadership

Marketing is so basic that it cannot be considered a separate function. . . . It is the whole business seen from the point of view of its final result, that is, from the customer's point of view. Concern and responsibility for marketing must, therefore, permeate all areas of the enterprise.

—Peter Drucker

[T]he more short-term a company's focus becomes, the more likely the firm will be to engage in behavior that actually destroys value.

—Don Peppers and Martha Rogers

Throughout this book, we've examined how to manage service businesses to achieve customer satisfaction and profitable performance. Our focus has been on marketing, the only function that actually generates operating revenues for a business. However, we've consistently emphasized that the array of marketing activities in service organizations, embracing each element of the 8Ps, extends beyond the responsibilities assigned to a traditional marketing department.

Hence both planning and implementation of service marketing strategies require active collaboration with operations and human resources management. We've shown that marketing itself can be viewed in several ways: as a strategic and competitive thrust pursued by senior management, as a set of functional activities performed by line managers, or as a customer-driven orientation for the entire organization. In fact, all three perspectives are necessary to develop strategies for service success.

Service organizations that are already successful cannot afford to rest on their laurels. They must continuously evolve to take advantage of new or developing markets, meet new customer needs, counter competitors, and exploit new technologies. By contrast, underperforming or dysfunctional organizations require a turnaround strategy if they are to survive and prosper. As we'll see in this chapter, both situations involve change management. However, it's very difficult for a firm to achieve and maintain leadership in a service industry if it lacks human leaders who can articulate the necessary vision and help bring it to fruition. The emphasis could include defining the terms on which the company seeks to compete, creating an outstanding work environment, ensuring that customers receive good value, initiating important innovations, implementing new technologies for competitive advantage, setting the standards for service quality, or a combination of any of these strategic elements.

We now draw together themes and insights from earlier chapters, particularly those on managing employees, building customer loyalty, and improving service quality, as we examine the challenging task of leading a service business that seeks to be both customer-focused and market-oriented. In particular, this chapter explores the following questions:

1. What are the implications of the service-profit chain for service management?

2. What actions are required to move a service firm from a reactive position—merely being available for service—toward the status of world-class service delivery? How should management set priorities?

3. Why do the marketing, operations, and human resource management functions need to be closely co-ordinated and integrated in service businesses? What are the means to achieving this?

4. When seeking to transform a service business, what is the distinction between evolutionary change and turnaround? For each case, what role should the CEO play?

5. What role do service leaders play in fostering success within their organizations?

EFFECTIVE MARKETING LIES AT THE HEART OF VALUE CREATION

"Businesses succeed by getting, keeping, and growing customers," state respected consultants and authors Don Peppers and Martha Rogers.[1] Arguing that Wall Street's ongoing obsession with current-period revenue and earnings can actually destroy value, they declare:

> Investors today want executives to demonstrate that their companies can make money and grow, the old-fashioned way—by earning it from the value proposition they offer customers. They want a firm's customers to buy more, to buy more often, and to stay loyal longer. They want a firm to show that it can go out and get more customers. . . .
>
> Growth fuels innovation and creativity, generating new ideas and initiatives, and stimulating managers in all areas to "think outside the box." Growth keeps a company vibrant and alive, making it a good place to work—a place that provides employees with economic benefits and opportunities for advancement.[2]

The Service–Profit Chain

James Heskett and his colleagues at Harvard argue that when service companies put employees and customers first, a radical shift occurs in the way they manage and measure success. They relate profitability, customer loyalty, and customer satisfaction to the value created by satisfied, loyal and productive employees.

> Top-level executives of outstanding service organizations spend little time setting profit goals or focusing on market share. . . . Instead they understand that in the new economics of service, frontline workers and customers need to be the center of management concern. Successful service managers pay attention to the factors that drive profitability . . . investment in people, technology that supports frontline workers, revamped recruiting and training practices, and compensation linked to performance for employees at every level. . . .
>
> The service–profit chain, developed from analyses of successful service organizations, puts "hard" values on "soft" measures. It helps managers target new investments to develop service and satisfaction levels for maximum competitive impact, widening the gap between service leaders and their merely good competitors.[3]

The service–profit chain portrayed in Figure 15.1 displays a series of hypothesized links in a managerial process that can lead to success in service businesses.

Table 15.1 provides a useful summary, highlighting the behaviours required of service leaders in order to manage their organizations effectively. Working backwards from the desired end results of revenue growth and profitability, links 1 and 2 focus on customers and include an emphasis on identifying and understanding customer needs, investments

Figure 15.1 The Service–Profit Chain

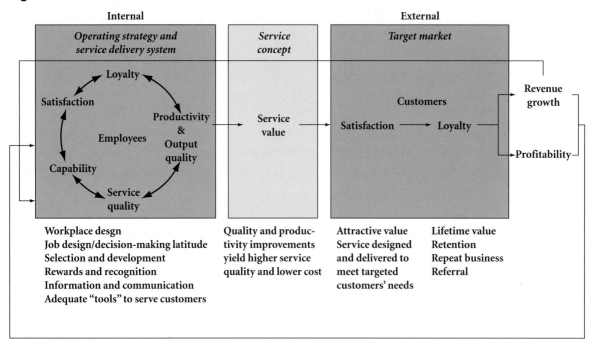

Source: James L. Heskett, Thomas O. Jones, Gary W. Loveman, et al., "Putting the Service–Profit Chain to Work," *Harvard Business Review* 72/3 (March–April 1994): 166. Reprinted by permission of the Harvard Business School.

to ensure customer retention, and a commitment to adopting new performance measures that track such variables as satisfaction and loyalty among both customers and employees.[4] Link 3 focuses on the value for customers created by the service concept, and highlights the need for investments to create both higher service quality and productivity improvements that will reduce costs.

Another set of service leadership behaviours (links 4–7) relate to employees, and include spending time on the front line, investing in the development of promising managers, and supporting the design of jobs that offer greater latitude for employees. Also included in this category is the concept that paying higher wages actually decreases labour costs after reduced turnover, higher productivity, and higher quality are taken into account. Underlying the chain's success (link 8) is top management leadership.

What Qualities Are Associated with Service Leaders?

The themes and relationships underlying this chain illustrate compellingly the mutual dependence among marketing, operations, and human resources. An organization that is recognized as a service leader offers its customers superior value and quality. It has marketing strategies that beat the competition, yet is viewed as a trustworthy organization that does business in ethical ways. It is seen as a leader in operations, too—respected for its superior operational processes and innovative use of technology. Finally, it is recognized as an outstanding place to work, leading its industry in human resource management practices and staffed by loyal, productive, and customer-oriented employees. Although managers within each function may have specific responsibilities, effective co-ordination is the name of the game. All must participate in strategic planning, and the execution of specific tasks must be well co-ordinated. Clearly, implementation of the service–profit chain requires a thorough understanding of how marketing, operations, and human resources each relate to a company's broader strategic concerns and jointly contribute to creation of value.

Table 15.1 Links in the Service–Profit Chain
1. Customer loyalty drives profitability and growth.
2. Customer satisfaction drives customer loyalty.
3. Value drives customer satisfaction.
4. Quality and productivity drive value.
5. Employee loyalty drives service quality and productivity.
6. Employee satisfaction drives employee loyalty.
7. Internal quality drives employee satisfaction.
8. Top management leadership underlies the chain's success.

Source: Heskett, James, Loveman, et al., "Putting the Service–Profit Chain to Work," *Harvard Business Review* (March–April 1994): 164–74; James L. Heskett, W. Earl Sasser, and Leonard L. Schlesinger, *The Service–Profit Chain*, Boston: Harvard Business School Press, 1997.

Attaining service leadership requires a coherent vision of what it takes to succeed, with the resulting strategy defined and driven by a strong, effective leadership team. Implementation of that strategy involves careful co-ordination between marketing (which, broadly defined, includes all aspects of customer service), operations (which includes management of technology), and human resources. As emphasized throughout this book, the marketing function in service businesses cannot easily be separated from other management activities, and is typically much broader than the work performed by the marketing department.

Ideally, service firms should be organized in ways that enable the three functions of marketing, operations, and human resources to work closely together so that the organization can be responsive to its various stakeholders and achieve success in its chosen markets. For firms that do it right, that success is ultimately rewarded by an increase in the value attached to the organization itself, expressed in public companies by their stock price. In a National Quality Institute (NQI) study tracking publicly traded companies (many of them service organizations) that had won the Canada Award for Excellence (CAE) during a 15-year period (1990–2005), it was found that these winners outperformed the TSX Composite Index, the S&P 500 Index, and the Dow Jones Industrial Average by a ratio of as much as 2.17:1.[5] An important distinction between service leaders and firms in other categories is how they approach value creation. The former seek to create value creation through customer satisfaction and its antecedents, whereas the others often aim to boost shareholder value through tactical measures to boost sales, short-term cost cutting, unlocking asset value through selected sell-offs, and taking advantage of financial market dynamics.

INTEGRATING MARKETING, OPERATIONS, AND HUMAN RESOURCES

Although there's a long tradition of functional specialization in business, narrow perspectives get in the way of effective service management. One of the challenges facing senior managers in any type of organization is to avoid creating what are sometimes referred to as "functional silos," in which each function exists in isolation from the others, jealously guarding its independence.

Why is it so important in service firms to integrate the activities performed by the marketing, operations, and human resource functions? As we've seen, many service enterprises—especially those involving people-processing services—are literally "factories in the field," which customers enter whenever they need the service in question. When customers are actively involved in production, and the service output is consumed as it is produced, active engagement between production (operations) and consumers should be mandatory. Despite the rise of self-service technologies, contact between operations personnel and customers remains the rule rather than the exception in many industries—although its extent varies according to the nature of the service. The net result is that the function of marketing in a service business can't avoid being entwined with—and dependent on—the procedures, personnel, and facilities managed by operations. In a high-contact service, competitive outcomes may live or die on the basis of the calibre of service personnel recruited and trained by HR. Nowadays, companies can't afford to have HR specialists who don't understand customers.

In many service businesses, in fact, the calibre and commitment of the labour force have become a major source of competitive advantage.[6] Think WestJet, Delta Hotels, VanCity, and Deloitte & Touche LLP (Canada). As a consumer, you can and do differentiate among competing firms on the basis of their employees. A strong commitment by top management to human resources is a feature of many successful service firms.[7] For Human Resources Management (HRM) to succeed, argues Terri Kabachnick, "it must be a business-driven function with a thorough understanding of the organization's big picture. It must be viewed as a strategic consulting partner, providing innovative solutions and influencing key decisions and policies."[8] To the extent that employees understand and support the goals of their organization, have the skills and training needed to succeed in their jobs, and recognize the importance of creating and maintaining customer satisfaction, both marketing and operations activities should be easier to manage.

Reducing Interfunctional Conflict

As service firms place more emphasis on developing a strong market orientation and serving customers well, there's increased potential for conflict among the three functions, especially between marketing and operations. How comfortably can the three functions coexist in a service business, and how are their relative roles perceived? Sandra Vandermerwe makes the point that high-value creating enterprises should be thinking in term of *activities*, not functions.[9] Yet in many firms, we still find individuals from marketing and operations backgrounds at odds with each other. Marketers may see their role as one of continually adding value to the product offering, enhancing its appeal to customers and stimulating sales. Operations managers, by contrast, may see their job as paring back "extras" to reflect the reality of service constraints—such as staff and equipment—and the need for cost containment. After all, they may argue, no value will be created if we operate at a loss. Conflicts may also occur between human resources and the other two functions, especially where employees are in boundary spanning roles that require them to balance customer satisfaction against operational efficiency.

Changing traditional organizational perspectives doesn't come readily to managers who have been comfortable with established approaches. However, as long as a service business continues to be organized along functional lines (and many are), achieving the necessary co-ordination and strategic synergy requires that top management establish clear imperatives for each function. Each imperative should relate to customers and define how a specific function contributes to the overall mission. Part of the challenge of service management is to ensure that each of these three functional imperatives is compatible with the others, and that all are mutually reinforcing. Although a firm will need to phrase each imperative in ways that are specific to its own business, we can express them generically as follows:

- *The marketing imperative.* To target specific types of customers whom the firm is well equipped to serve, and create ongoing relationships with them by delivering a carefully defined service-product package in return for a price that offers value to customers and the potential for profits to the firm. Customers will recognize this package as being one of consistent quality that delivers solutions to their needs and is superior to competing alternatives.

- *The operations imperative.* To create and deliver the specified service package to targeted customers by selecting those operational techniques that allow the firm to meet customer-driven cost, schedule, and quality goals consistently, and also to enable the business to reduce its costs through continuing improvements in productivity. The chosen operational methods will match skills that employees and intermediaries or contractors currently possess or can be trained to develop. The firm will have the resources to support these operations with the necessary facilities, equipment, and technology, while avoiding negative impacts on employees and the broader community.

- *The human resources imperative.* To recruit, train, and motivate managers, supervisors, and employees who can work well together for a realistic compensation package to balance the twin goals of customer satisfaction and operational effectiveness. Employees will want to stay with the firm and to enhance their own skills because they value the working environment, appreciate the opportunities that it presents, and take pride in the services they help to create and deliver.

CREATING A LEADING SERVICE ORGANIZATION

In your own life as a consumer, you've probably encountered an assortment of service organizations, ranging from those you can always trust to deliver excellent service, at one extreme, and those that consistently deliver bad service and mistreat their customers, on the other. But why are some service organizations so much better than others? What separates the sheep from the goats?

From Losers to Leaders: Four Levels of Service Performance

Service leadership is not based on outstanding performance within a single dimension. Rather, it reflects excellence across multiple dimensions. In an effort to capture this performance spectrum, we need to evaluate the organization within each of the three functional areas described earlier—marketing, operations, and human resources. Table 15.2 modifies and extends an operations-oriented framework proposed by Richard Chase and Robert Hayes.[10] It categorizes service performers into four levels: loser, nonentity, professional, and leader. At each level, there is a brief description of a typical organization across 12 dimensions.

Under the marketing function, we look at the role of marketing, competitive appeal, customer profile, and service quality. Under the operations function, we consider the role of operations, service delivery (front stage), backstage operations, productivity, and introduction of new technology. Finally, under the human resources function, we consider the role of HRM, the workforce, and front-line management. Obviously, there are overlaps between these dimensions and across functions. Additionally, there may be variations in the relative importance of some dimensions between industries. For instance, human resource management tends to play a more prominent strategic role in high-contact services. The goal of this overall service performance framework is to generate insights into how service leaders perform so well and what needs to be changed in organizations that are not performing as well as they might.

If you want to do an in-depth appraisal of a company in a specific industry, you may find it useful to view Table 15.2 as a point of departure, modifying some of the elements to create a customized framework for analysis.

Service Losers   These organizations are at the bottom of the barrel from both customer and managerial perspectives, getting failing grades in marketing, operations, and human resource management alike. Customers patronize them for reasons other than performance; typically, because there is no viable alternative—which is one reason why service losers continue to survive. Managers of such organizations may even see service delivery as a necessary evil. New technology is only introduced under duress, and the

Table 15.2 Four Levels of Service Performance

LEVEL	1. LOSER	2. NONENTITY
Marketing Function		
Role of marketing	Tactical role only; advertising and promotions lack focus; no involvement in product or pricing decision	Uses mix of selling and mass communication, using simple segmentation strategy; makes selective use of price discounts and promotions; conducts and tabulates basic satisfaction surveys
Competitive appeal	Customers patronize firm for reasons other than performance	Customers neither seek out nor avoid the firm
Customer profile	Unspecified; a mass market to be served at a minimum cost	One or more segments whose basic needs are understood
Service quality	Highly variable, usually unsatisfactory. Subservient to operations priorities	Meets some customer expectations; consistent on one or two key dimensions, but not all
Operations Function		
Role of operations	Reactive; cost oriented	The principal line management function: creates and delivers product, focuses on standardization as key to productivity, defines quality from internal perspective
Service delivery (front-stage)	A necessary evil. Locations and schedules are unrelated to preferences of customers, who are routinely ignored	Sticklers for tradition; "If it ain't broke, don't fix it"; tight rules for customers; each step in delivery run independently
Backstage operations	Divorced from front-stage; cogs in a machine	Contributes to individual front-stage delivery steps but organized separately; unfamiliar with customers
Productivity	Undefined; managers are punished for failing to stick within budget	Based on standardization; rewarded for keeping costs below budget
Introduction of new technology	Late adopter, under duress, when necessary for survival	Follows the crowd when justified by cost savings
Human Resources Function		
Role of human resources	Supplies low-cost employees who meet minimum skill requirements for the job	Recruits and trains employees who can perform competently
Workforce	Negative constraint: poor performers, don't care, disloyal	Adequate resource, follows procedures but uninspired; turnover often high
Front-line management	Controls workers	Controls the process

Note: This framework was inspired by—and expands upon—work in service operations management by Richard Chase and Robert Hayes.

Table 15.2 Four Levels of Service Performance *(continued)*

3. PROFESSIONAL	4. LEADER

Marketing Function

Has clear positioning strategy against competition; uses focused communications with distinctive appeals to clarify promises and educate customers; pricing is based on value; monitors customer usage and operates loyalty programs; uses a variety of research techniques to measure customer satisfaction and obtain ideas for service enhancements; works with operations to introduce new delivery systems	Innovative leader in chosen segments, known for marketing skills; brands at product/process level; conducts sophisticated analysis of relational databases as inputs to one-to-one marketing and proactive account management; uses state-of-the-art research techniques; uses concept testing, observation, and use of lead customers as inputs to new-product development; close to operations/HR
Customers seek out the firm, based on its sustained reputation for meeting customer expectations	Company name is synonymous with service excellence; its ability to delight customers raises expectations to levels that competitors can't meet
Groups of individuals whose variation in needs and value to the firm are clearly understood	Individuals are selected and retained based on their future value to the firm, including their potential for new service opportunities and their ability to stimulate innovation.
Consistently meets or exceeds customer expectations across multiple dimensions	Raises customer expectations to new levels; improves continuously

Operations Function

Plays a strategic role in competitive strategy; recognizes trade-off between productivity and customer-defined quality; willing to outsource; monitors competing operations for ideas, threats	Recognized for innovation, focus, and excellence; an equal partner with marketing and HR management; has in-house research capability and academic contacts; continually experimenting
Driven by customer satisfaction, not tradition; willing to customize, embrace new approaches; emphasis on speed, convenience, and comfort	Delivery is a seamless process organized around the customer; employees know whom they are serving; focuses on continuous improvement
Process is explicitly linked to front-stage activities; sees role as serving "internal customers," who in turn serve external customers	Closely integrated with front-stage delivery, even when geographically far apart; understands how own role relates to overall process of serving external customers; continuing dialogue
Focuses on re-engineering backstage processes; avoids productivity improvements that will degrade customers' service experience; continually refining processes for efficiency	Understands concept of return on quality; actively seeks customer involvement in productivity improvement; ongoing testing of new processes and technologies
An early adopter when IT promises to enhance service for customers and provide a competitive edge	Works with technology leaders to develop new applications that create first-mover advantage; seeks to perform at levels competitors can't match

Human Resources Function

Invests in selective recruiting, ongoing training; keeps close to employees, promotes upward mobility; strives to enhance quality of working life	Sees quality of employees as strategic advantage; firm is recognized as outstanding place to work; HR helps top management to nurture culture
Motivated, hard working, allowed some discretion in choice of procedures, offers suggestions	Innovative and empowered; very loyal, committed to firm's values and goals; creates procedures
Listens to customers; coaches and facilitates workers	Source of new ideas for top management; mentors workers to enhance career growth, value to firm

Figure 15.2

Dilbert's boss loses focus—and his audience.

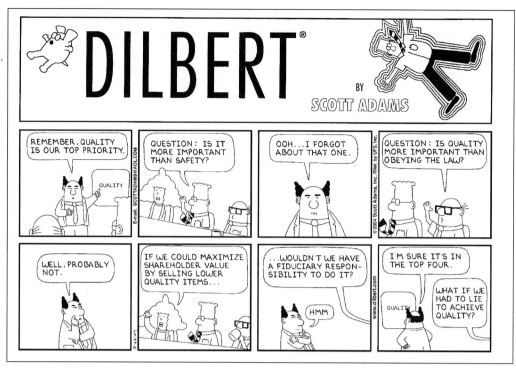

DILBERT: © Scott Adams/Dist. by permission of United Syndicates, Inc.

uncaring workforce is a negative constraint on performance. The cycle of failure presented earlier in Chapter 11 (see Figure 11.4, p. 312) describes how such organizations behave in relation to employees, and what the consequences are for customers.

Service Nonentities   Although their performance still leaves much to be desired, nonentities have eliminated the worst features of losers. As shown in Table 15.2, nonentities are dominated by a traditional operations mindset, typically based on achieving cost savings through standardization. Their marketing strategies are unsophisticated, and the roles of human resources and operations might be summed up, respectively, by the philosophies "adequate is good enough" and "if it ain't broke, don't fix it." Consumers neither seek out nor avoid such organizations. Managers may spout platitudes about improving quality and other goals, but are unable to set clear priorities, chart a clear course, or command the respect and commitment of their subordinates (Figure 15.2). Several such firms can often be found competing in lacklustre fashion within a given marketplace, and you might have difficulty distinguishing one from the others. Periodic price discounts tend to be the primary means of trying to attract new customers. The cycle of mediocrity (see Figure 11.5, p. 314) portrays the human resources environment of many such organizations and its consequences for customers.

Service Professionals   These organizations are in a different league from nonentities, and have a clear market-positioning strategy. Customers within the target segments seek out these firms based on their sustained reputation for meeting expectations. Marketing is more sophisticated, using targeted communications and pricing based on value to the customer. Research is used to measure customer satisfaction and obtain ideas for service enhancement. Operations and marketing work together to introduce new delivery systems and recognize the trade-off between productivity and customer-defined quality. There are explicit links between backstage and front-stage activities and a much more proactive, investment-oriented approach to human-resource management than is found among nonentities. The Cycle of Success (see Figure 11.6, p. 315) highlights the HR strategies that lead to a high level of performance by most employees of organizations in the service professionals category (and by all who work for service leaders), together with its positive impact on customer satisfaction and loyalty.

Service Leaders   These organizations are the *crème de la crème* of their respective industries. Whereas service professionals are good, service leaders are outstanding. Their company names are synonymous with service excellence and an ability to delight customers. Service leaders are recognized for their innovation in each functional area of management as well as for their excellent internal communications and co-ordination among these three functions—often the result of a relatively flat organizational structure and extensive use of teams. As a result, service delivery is a seamless process organized around the customer.

Marketing efforts by service leaders make extensive use of relational databases that offer strategic insights about customers, who are often addressed on a one-to-one basis. Concept testing, observation, and contacts with lead customers are employed in the development of new, breakthrough services that respond to previously unrecognized needs. Operations specialists work with technology leaders around the world to develop new applications that will create a first-mover advantage and enable the firm to perform at levels that competitors cannot hope to reach for a long period of time. Senior executives see quality of employees as a strategic advantage. HRM works with them to develop and maintain a service-oriented culture and to create an outstanding working environment that simplifies the task of attracting and retaining the best people.[11] The employees themselves are committed to the firm's values and goals. Because they are engaged, empowered, and quick to embrace change, they are an ongoing source of new ideas.

Moving to a Higher Level of Performance

Firms can move either up or down the performance ladder. Once-stellar performers can become complacent and sluggish. Organizations that are devoted to satisfying their current customers may miss important shifts in the marketplace and find themselves turning into has-beens. These businesses may continue to serve a loyal but dwindling band of conservative customers, but are unable to attract demanding new consumers with different expectations. Companies whose original success was based on mastery of a specific technological process may find that, in defending their control of that process, they have encouraged competitors to find higher-performing alternatives. And organizations whose management has worked for years to build up a loyal workforce with a strong service ethic may find that such a culture can be quickly destroyed as a result of a merger or acquisition that brings in new leaders who emphasize short-term profits. Unfortunately, senior managers sometimes delude themselves into thinking that their company has achieved a superior level of performance when, in fact, the foundations of that success are crumbling.

In most markets, we can also find companies that are moving up the performance ladder through conscious efforts to co-ordinate their marketing, operations, and human resource management functions in order to establish more favourable competitive positions and to better satisfy their customers. Best Practice in Action 15.1 describes how Stena Lines, a Swedish ferry company, successfully enhanced the performance level of a newly acquired subsidiary that had earlier been state owned.

IN SEARCH OF HUMAN LEADERSHIP

Service leader organizations are those that stand out in their respective markets and industries. But it still requires human leaders to take them in the right direction, set the right strategic priorities, and ensure that the relevant strategies are implemented throughout the organization. Much of the literature on leadership is concerned with turnarounds and transformation. It is easy to see why poorly performing organizations may require a major transformation of their culture and operating procedures in order to make them more competitive. But in times of rapid change, even high-performing firms need to evolve on a continuing basis, transforming themselves in evolutionary fashion.

Leading a Service Organization

John Kotter, perhaps the best-known authority on leadership, argues that in most successful processes of change management, those in leadership roles must navigate through eight complicated and often time-consuming stages:[12]

Best Practice in Action 15.1

Building Marketing Competence in a Ferry Company

When Stena Line purchased Sealink British Ferries (whose routes linked Britain to Ireland and several European countries), the Swedish company more than doubled in size to become one of the world's largest car-ferry operators. Stena boasted a whole department dedicated to monitoring quality improvements. By contrast, this philosophy was described as "alien" to Sealink's culture, which reflected a top-down, military-style structure that focused on the operational aspects of ship movements. The quality of customers' experiences received only secondary consideration.

Managerial weaknesses included lack of attention to growing competition from other companies, whose new, high-speed ferries offered customers a faster and more comfortable ride. Sealink's top management exercised tight control, issuing directives and applying company-wide standards across all divisions, rather than customizing policies to the needs of individual routes. All decisions were subject to head-office review. Divisional managers were separated by two management levels from the functional teams engaged in the actual operation. This organizational structure led to conflicts, slow decision-making, and inability to respond quickly to market changes.

Stena's philosophy was very different. It operated a decentralized structure, believing that each management function should be responsible for its own activities and accountable for the results. Stena wanted management decisions in the British subsidiary to be taken by people who were close to the market, and who understood local competition and demand. Some central functions were moved out to the divisions, including much responsibility for marketing activities. New skills and perspectives came from retraining, transfers, and outside hiring.

Prior to the merger, no priority had been given to punctual or reliable operations. Ferries were often late, but standard excuses were used in reports, customer complaints were ignored, and there was little pressure from customer service managers to improve the situation. After the takeover, things started to change. The challenge of late departures and arrivals was resolved through concentration on individual problem areas. On one route, for instance, the port manager involved all operational staff and gave each person "ownership" of a specific aspect of the improvement process. They kept detailed records of each sailing, together with reasons for late departures, as well as monitoring competitor's performance. This participative approach created close liaison between staff members in different job positions, and also helped customer service staff to learn from experience. Within two years, the Stena ferries on this route were operating at close to 100 percent punctuality.

On-board service was another area singled out for improvement. Historically, customer service managers did what was convenient for staff rather than customers, including meal breaks at times when customer demand for service was greatest. As one observer noted, "customers were ignored during the first and last half hour on board, when facilities were closed. . . . Customers were left to find their own way around [the ship]. . . . Staff only responded to customers when [they] initiated a direct request and made some effort to attract their attention." So personnel from each on-board functional area had to choose a specific area for improvement and work in small groups to achieve this. Initially, some teams were more successful than others, resulting in inconsistent levels of service and customer orientation from one ship to another. Subsequently, managers shared ideas, reviewed experiences, and made adaptations for individual ships. Key changes during the first two years (Table 15.A) contributed to eventual success in achieving consistent service levels on all sailings and all ferries.

By 2006, Stena Line had 34 ships sailing on 18 routes (of which 7 routes served UK ports), carrying some 17 million passengers and 3 million vehicles annually. They included three of the world's largest fast ferries. A leader in all its markets, Stena emphasizes constant service and product improvement. Says the company's website:

> The phrase Making Good Time summarises the core of the Stena Line business in three words: fast, enjoyable and efficient sea travel. . . . Today's customers are looking for more. Basic factors such as punctuality, safety, clean and well-equipped ferries with good service are now taken for granted, so at Stena Line we're trying even harder to give guests that little extra so they'll want to travel with us again. A way of meeting these new demands is to develop new products and services, and to further customise our offers to suit different requirements. Our ambition is that everyone should find a travel offer in our selection that they like.

continues

Table 15.A Changing Contexts, Competencies and Performance Following the Takeover

	INHERITED SITUATION	SITUATION AFTER TWO YEARS
External Context	Inactive competition—"share" market with one competitor	Aggressive competitive activity (two competitors, one operating new, high-speed ferries)
	Static market demand	Growing market
Internal Context	Centralized organization	Decentralized organization
	Centralized decision-making	Delegation to specialized decision-making units
	Top management directives	Key manager responsible for each unit team
Managerial Competencies		
Knowledge	General to industry rather than specific to local markets	Understand both industry and local market
Experience	Operational and tactical	Operational and decision-making
	General, industry-based	Functional management responsibility
	Non-competitive environment	Exposed to competitive environment
Expertise	Vague approach to judging situations	Diagnostic judgmental capabilities
	Short-term focus	Longer-term focus
	Generalist competencies	Specific skills for functional tasks
Marketing Decision-making		
Planning	React to internal circumstances and external threats	Proactive identification of problems
	Minimal information search or evaluation of alternatives	Collect information, consider options
	Focus on tactical issues	Choose among several options
	Inconsistent with other marketing activities	Consistent with other marketing activities
Actions	Follow top management directives	Delegation of responsibility
	Look to next in line for responsibility	Responsibility and ownership for activity
	Minimal or intermittent communication between functions	Liaison between functions
Marketing Efforts		
Pre-purchase	Mostly media advertising	Advertising plus promotions and informational materials
Service delivery	Slow manual booking system	New computerized reservation system
	Focus on tangible aspects of on-board customer service (e.g., seating, cabins, food, bar)	Better tangibles, sharply improved staff/customer interactions
	Little pressure on operations to improve poor punctuality	Highly reliable, punctual service
	Poor communications at ports and on board ships	Much improved signage, printed guides, electronic message boards, public announcements
	Reactive approach to problem-solving	Proactive approach to welcoming customers and solving their problems

Sources: Adapted from Audrey Gilmore, "Services Marketing Management Competencies: A Ferry Company Example," *International Journal of Service Industry Management* 9/1 (1998): 74–92; and website: www.stenaline.com, accessed June 2006.

- Creating a sense of urgency to develop the impetus for change
- Putting together a strong enough team to direct the process
- Creating an appropriate vision of where the organization needs to go
- Communicating that new vision broadly
- Empowering employees to act on that vision
- Producing sufficient short-term results to create credibility and counter cynicism
- Building momentum and using that to tackle the tougher change problems
- Anchoring the new behaviours in the organizational culture

Leadership versus Management   The primary force behind successful change is *leadership*, which is concerned with the development of vision and strategies, and the empowerment of people to overcome obstacles and make the vision happen. *Management*, by contrast, involves keeping the current situation operating through planning, budgeting, organizing, staffing, controlling, and problem-solving. Warren Bennis and Bert Nanus distinguish between leaders who emphasize the emotional and even spiritual resources of an organization and managers who stress its physical resources, such as raw materials, technology, and capital.[13] Says Kotter:

> Leadership works through people and culture. It's soft and hot. Management works through hierarchy and systems. Its harder and cooler. . . . The fundamental purpose of management is to keep the current system functioning. The fundamental purpose of leadership is to produce useful change, especially nonincremental change. It's possible to have too much or too little of either. Strong leadership with no management risks chaos; the organization might walk right off a cliff. Strong management with no leadership tends to entrench an organization in deadly bureaucracy.[14]

Leadership is an essential and growing aspect of managerial work because the rate of change has been increasing. Reflecting both competition and technological advances, new services or service features are being introduced at a faster rate, and tend to have shorter life cycles. Meantime, the competitive environment shifts continually as a result of international firms entering new geographic markets, mergers, and acquisitions, and the exit of former competitors. The process of service delivery itself has speeded up, with customers demanding faster service and faster responses when things go wrong. As a result, declares Kotter, effective top executives may now spend up to 80 percent of their time leading; double the figure required not that long ago. Even those at the bottom of the management hierarchy may spend at least 20 percent of their time on leadership.

Setting Direction Is Different from Planning   People often confuse these two activities. Planning, according to Kotter, is a management process, designed to produce orderly results, not change. Setting a direction, by contrast, is more inductive than deductive. Leaders look for patterns, relationships, and linkages that help to explain things and suggest future trends. Direction setting creates visions and strategies that describe a business, technology, or corporate culture in terms of what it should become over the long term, and that articulate a feasible way of achieving this goal. Effective leaders have a talent for simplicity in communicating with others who may not share their background or knowledge; they know their audiences and are able to distill their messages, conveying even complicated concepts in just a few phrases.[15]

Many of the best visions and strategies are not brilliantly innovative; rather, they combine some basic insights and translate them into a realistic competitive strategy that serves the interests of customers, employees, and stockholders. Some visions, however, fall into the category that Gary Hamel and C.K. Pralahad describe as "stretch"—a challenge to attain new levels of performance and competitive advantage that might, at first sight, seem to be beyond the organization's reach.[16] Stretching to achieve such bold goals requires creative reappraisal of traditional ways of doing business, and leverage of existing resources through partnerships. (See Service Perspectives 15.1.) It also requires creating the energy and the will among managers and employees alike to perform at higher levels than they believe themselves able to do. Planning follows and complements direction setting, serving as a useful reality check and a road map for strategic execution. A good plan provides an action agenda for accomplishing the mission, using existing resources, or identifying potential new sources.

Leonard Berry and his colleagues emphasize that executives who seek to develop strategies based on service innovation must concentrate on the tasks that determine success or failure, and recognize that innovation starts with culture and requires a champion.[17] Their research (reprinted in Reading 4.2, "Creating New Markets Through Service Innovation" (p. 464), identifies nine success drivers, including comprehensive customer-experience management, investment in employee performance, brand differentiation, and a superior customer benefit. Planning follows and complements direction setting, serving as a useful reality check and a road map for strategic execution. A good plan provides an action agenda for accomplishing the mission, using existing resources or identifying potential new sources.

Individual Leadership Qualities

Many commentators have written on the topic of leadership. It has even been described as a service in its own right.[18] The late Sam Walton, founder of the Wal-Mart retail chain, highlighted the role of managers as "servant leaders."[19]

Leonard Berry argues that service leadership requires a special perspective. "Regardless of the target markets, the specific services, or the pricing strategy, service leaders visualize quality of service as the foundation for competing."[20] Recognizing the key role of employees in delivering service, he emphasizes that service leaders need to believe in the people who work for them and make communicating with employees a priority. Love of the business is another service leadership characteristic he highlights, to the extent that it combines natural enthusiasm with the right setting in which to express it. Such enthusiasm motivates individuals to teach the business to others and to pass on to them the nuances, secrets, and craft of operating it. Berry also stresses the importance for leaders of being driven by a set of core values that they infuse into the organization, arguing that "A critical role of values-driven leaders is cultivating the leadership qualities of others in the organization." And he notes that "values-driven leaders rely on their values to navigate their companies through difficult periods."[21]

Rakesh Karma warns against excessive emphasis on charisma in selecting CEOs, arguing that it leads to unrealistic expectations.[22] He also highlights the unethical behaviour that may occur when charismatic but unprincipled leaders induce blind obedience in their followers, citing the illegal activities stimulated by the leadership of Enron, which eventually led to the company's collapse. Jim Collins also concluded that a leader does not require a larger-than-life personality. Rather, for a leader to be able to take a company to greatness, he considers it important to have personal humility blended with intensive professional will, ferocious resolve, and the tendency to give credit to others while taking the blame to themselves.[23]

In hierarchical organizations, structured on a military model, it's often assumed that leadership at the top is sufficient. However, as Sandra Vandermerwe points out, forward-looking service businesses need to be more flexible. Today's greater emphasis on using teams within service businesses means that

> [L]eaders are everywhere, disseminated throughout the teams. They are found especially in the customer facing and interfacing jobs in order that decision-making will lead to long-lasting relationships with customers. . . . [L]eaders are customer and project champions who energize the group by virtue of their enthusiasm, interest, and know-how.[24]

CHANGE MANAGEMENT: EVOLUTION AND TRANSFORMATION

There are important distinctions between leading a successful organization that is functioning well, redirecting a firm into new areas of activity, and trying to turn around a dysfunctional organization. Clive Beddoe, a private pilot and a successful entrepreneur prior to becoming one of the founders of WestJet Airlines, used his entrepreneurial acumen and

Can Cirque du Soleil Stretch Further?

Who would have believed in the mid-1980s that Le Club des Talons Hauts (The High Heels Club), a small band of street performers living in a youth hostel not far from Quebec City, would one day become the world-famous Cirque du Soleil (Circus of the Sun)? With its unique mix of music, dance, and acrobatics—but no animals—the Cirque du Soleil has created a new category of live entertainment, packaged in a variety of distinctive shows, that has been attended around the world by millions of people (Figure 15.3). "People said we reinvented the circus—we didn't reinvent the circus," declares president Guy Laliberté:

> We repackaged a way of presenting the circus show in a much more modern way. . . . We took an art form that was known, that had a lot of dust on it, where people had forgotten it could be something other than what they knew, and we organized for ourselves a new creative platform.

To achieve its present eminence, featuring six touring shows, a live music concert, and six permanent shows in conjunction with partnering resorts in the United States—five with Las Vegas casino complexes and one at Walt Disney Resort in Florida—the Cirque has had to face and resolve financial, managerial, and artistic challenges. For the well-paid performers, who include many former Olympic athletes, the notion of stretch (both physically and metaphorically!) is central to their professional lives. "Creative people always need new challenges," says CEO Daniel Lamarre. Organizations, by contrast, sometimes find it easier to rest on their laurels. However, such an approach could contain the seeds of failure for the Cirque.

Cirque du Soleil faces new competitors today, including two that have emerged from its home turf, Cirque Éloize and Cirque Éos, both spawned by the growing supply of graduates from two recently formed circus schools in Quebec. Cirque copycats have also sprung up in France and Argentina. An even greater challenge comes from the U.S. company, Feld Enterprises, which owns the famous Ringling Bros. and Barnum & Bailey Circus. Feld has created a new production, Barnum's Kaleidoscope, that replaces the traditional circus performers with a mix of acrobatic performers and live music at much higher admission prices.

Cirque du Soleil has grown in recent years by adding new shows with new partner resorts. In 2006 it launched *Love*, a show based on the music of the Beatles, making the Mirage casino its fifth partner in Las Vegas. However, a key question for Cirque is where future growth will come from as its core market becomes more crowded. Not only is new competition driving up the cost of finding and retaining top performers, it is unclear how much longer the privately held Canadian company can continue filling 1000-seat theatres at high admission prices with what some critics view as essentially variations on the same product. Continued evolution will be required.

Source: Robert J. David and Amir Motamedi, "Cirque du Soleil: Can It Burn Brighter?" *Journal of Strategic Management Education* 1/2 (2004): 369–82; www.cirquedusoleil.com, accessed June 2006.

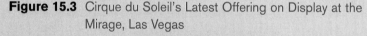

Figure 15.3 Cirque du Soleil's Latest Offering on Display at the Mirage, Las Vegas

a "Do as I do" approach to shape and reinforce the company's distinctive culture as it evolved into one of the most successful air operations in Canada. The challenge for Mr. Beddoe now is to find a successor who will maintain an appropriate culture as the company continues to grow and he seeks to relinquish control over the day-to-day operations of the company. Wayne Sales, vice president of retail sales, who had little profile with analysts and investors, was recruited as CEO of Canadian Tire in 2000 after an extensive international search, when it became clear that fundamental change in strategic direction and management was required after a major share-price crash resulting from a writedown of $58 million for the fourth quarter of 1999. Under his guidance, the company has gone through a tremendous growth phase with the stock price of its non-voting shares trading in late 2006 at almost $72, from the low of around $15 when he took over in 2000.[25] At the end of his contract in 2007, Mr. Sales is to be succeeded by Tom Gauld, a ten-year veteran of Canadian Tire. Meg Whitman, who had both consulting and managerial experience, was recruited as CEO of eBay when it became clear to the founders that the fledgling internet start-up needed leadership from someone possessing the insights and discipline of an experienced marketer.

Evolution Versus Turnaround

Transformation of an organization can take place in two different ways: evolution or turnaround. *Evolution* in a business context involves continual mutations designed to ensure the survival of the fittest. Top management must proactively evolve the focus and strategy of the firm to take advantage of changing conditions and the advent of new technologies. Without a continuing series of mutations, it's unlikely that a firm can remain successful in a dynamic marketplace.

A different type of transformation occurs in *turnaround* situations, in which leaders (usually new ones) seek to bring distressed organizations back from the brink of failure and set them on a healthier course. Such an approach is exemplified by the experience of American Express, which has undergone several transformations during its more than 150-year history. (See Service Perspectives 15.2.)

According to noted author Rosabeth Moss Kanter, it can be advantageous in turnaround situations to bring in a new CEO from outside the organization.[26] Such individuals, she argues, are better able to disentangle system dynamics because they were not previously caught up in them, and to voice problems and change habits. New CEOs may also have more credibility in representing and respecting customers. Exemplary turnaround leaders, she says, understand the powerful, unifying effect of focusing on customers. This focus can facilitate the difficult task of obtaining collaboration across departments and divisions. In addition to breaking down barriers between marketing, operations, and human resources, or between various product or geographic divisions, turnaround CEOs may also need to reorient financial priorities to enable collaborative groups to tackle new business opportunities.

Chan Kim and Renée Mauborgne, both professors at INSEAD, have identified four hurdles that leaders face in reorienting and formulating strategy.[27]

- *Cognitive hurdles* are present when people cannot agree on the causes of current problems and the need for change.
- *Resource hurdles* exist when the organization is constrained by limited funds.
- *Motivational hurdles* prevent a strategy's rapid execution when employees are reluctant to make needed changes.
- *Political hurdles* take the form of organized resistance from powerful vested interests seeking to protect their positions.

Turning around an organization that has limited resources requires concentrating those resources where the need and the likely payoffs are greatest. Michael Hirsh, co-founder of the kid's entertainment production company Nelvana Ltd., which held such hit titles as *Babar* and *Franklin*, came out of retirement in 2003 to take over the scandal-hit children's show production company Cinar Corp. At the time of his leading a consortium to take

Service Perspectives 15.2

Reinvention and Leadership at American Express

"Frankly, you can't be a jerk in the service business and be successful for a long period of time," says Kenneth Chenault, CEO of American Express. "When you're in the service business, reputation is everything." However, he also cautions: "Sometimes when you are very successful, you become arrogant, and what I've tried to instill [here] is a very strong sense of customer needs [and] respect for your colleagues." American Express, best known today as an icon in travel and financial services, has evolved through what it describes as "150 years of reinvention and customer service." Established in 1850 in New York, it was among the first and most successful express delivery firms created during the westward expansion of the United States. Intrepid expressmen, typically on horseback or driving stagecoaches, transported letters, parcels, freight, gold, and currency from Eastern cities to the Western Frontier. The largest and most consistent clients were banks. Delivering their small but very high-value parcels—stock certificates, notes, currency, and other financial instruments—was much more profitable than transporting larger freight. As the railways grew, the company scaled down its delivery business in favour of creating and selling its own financial products, launching money orders in 1882 and the world's first traveller's cheques in 1891. American Express began its operations in Canada in 1853, with two offices based in Toronto and Hamilton. As the American Express name became increasingly visible overseas, offices were opened in Europe.

From the 1920s on, the company focused on travel services, supported by selling traveller's cheques and money orders (and profits from investing the substantial float on these products). The first American Express charge card was issued in 1958. This business grew rapidly and included both individual and corporate cardholders. Gold and platinum cards followed, offering extra features and privileges in return for a higher annual fee. In an effort to diversify, American Express sought to create a "financial supermarket" through acquisition of other financial service firms. However, the anticipated synergies were never realized and the company stumbled in the early 1990s. Meantime, its card

business faced intense competition from Visa and MasterCard, on which merchants paid lower fees. In 1991, a group of Boston restaurateurs, upset about high rates, staged a revolt nicknamed the Boston Fee Party, and refused to accept American Express cards. Other merchants joined them, both at home and abroad. Chenault, then a rising young executive, headed the successful effort to achieve reconciliation and to reduce rates. Promoted to president and CEO, he broadened the cards' appeal by offering new features and loyalty programs, creating new types of cards, such as the American Express Aeroplan and AeroplanPlus credit cards for the Canadian market, and signing up mass-market retailers, including Wal-Mart. Spending through American Express cards, once dominated by travel and entertainment, is today led by retail and everyday purchases, including office expenditures by small-business cardholders. Soon after being named CEO in 2001, Chenault faced the daunting challenge of helping the company recover from both the human trauma of seeing the World Trade Center destroyed across the street from the firm's headquarters and the sharp decline in travel that followed 9/11. Widely praised for his leadership, Chenault offered a road map designed to make the company leaner and able to respond faster to business opportunities as the economy recovered. By 2005 he had completed the dismantling of the "financial supermarket" and refocused the business on its core activities of card services and travel, with operations in 130 countries. Chenault looks back at 2001 as "critical and fundamental to our company's success. It tested our management in incredible ways." Asked by a reporter to describe his leadership philosophy, he responded: "The role of a leader is to define reality and give hope."

Sources: Nelson D. Schwartz, "What's in the Cards for Amex?" *Fortune* (January 22, 2001): 58–70; Greg Farrell, "A CEO and a Gentleman," *USA Today* (April 25, 2005): 1B, 3B; "Our History: Becoming American Express—150+ Years of Reinvention and Customer Service." http://home3.americanexpress.com/corp/os/history.asp, accessed June 2006; www.americanexpress.com/canada/en/homepage/default.shtml, accessed June 2006.

over the company, the two Montreal-based founders of Cinar Corp. were embroiled in charges of fraud and a hedge-fund fiasco. Asked at one point whether there was any aspect of Cinar that wasn't "broken," his curt response was a "no." Taking the company private after buying and renaming it the Cookie Jar Group, Hirsh has spent the next two years revitalizing some of the established brands, while introducing some new ones.

His plan is to make his brands "pervasive," a plan that seems to be on track. For example, the live-action show *Doodlebops*, only two years in the making, is already being broadcast in three countries, and an 80-city live tour based on the show started in the fall of 2006. It doesn't end there: available online are interactive games, and in stores there are *Doodlebops* backpacks, books, and DVDs, all aimed at making Hirsch's brands "pervasive." His plans for the Cookie Jar Group include refloating the company on the stock exchange in 2007, and using the proceeds to launch an education channel, *@cademy*, approval for which has already been obtained from CRTC and is due to be launched in 2007. His ultimate aim is to "build an empire of kids' brands spanning the media spectrum, from TV to the internet to books, CDs, DVDs, toys, and live concerts."[28]

In many organizations, the search for growth involves expansion—even diversification—into new lines of business. Many manufacturing businesses have transformed themselves by expanding into services. However, if they are marketed under the company's corporate brand, the challenge of transformation extends to shifting the market's perception of that company's capabilities. The further removed the new services are from the original physical product, the greater the challenge. Consider IBM. It's one thing to persuade existing users of its computers that it can offer them value with new or expanded services relating to equipment installation, maintenance, upgrades, networking, or security. But how to build awareness and credibility for an international management consulting subsidiary called IBM Business Consulting? The company developed an advertising campaign headlined "The Other IBM" several years ago, raising a series of strategic questions to which it promises to "find the answers with an altogether different kind of thinking." The home page of IBM Business Consulting mirrors the theme in the advertisement campaign (Figure 15.4). To succeed, it must, of course, deliver on that promise.

Role Modelling Desired Behaviour

One of the traits of successful leaders is their ability to act as role models for the behaviour they expect of managers and other employees. Often, this requires the approach known as "management by wandering [or walking] around," popularized by Thomas Peters and Robert Waterman in their book *In Search of Excellence*.[29] Wandering around involves regular visits, sometimes unannounced, to various areas of the company's operation. This approach provides insights into both backstage and front-stage operations, the ability to observe and meet both employees and customers, and an opportunity to see how corporate strategy is implemented on the front line. During the early part of his tenure as CEO of WestJet Airlines, people would not have been surprised to find Clive Beddoe help clean up after the flight on one of his airplanes, getting rid of the trash or scraping some chewing gum stuck to a seat.

Periodically, this approach may lead to recognition that changes are needed in the company's strategy. Encountering the CEO on such a visit can be motivating for service personnel. It also provides an opportunity for role-modelling. Best Practice in Action 15.2

Figure 15.4
The Other IBM

A Hospital President Learns the Power of Role-Modelling

During his 30-year tenure as president of Boston's Beth Israel Hospital (now Beth Israel-Deaconess Medical Center), Mitchell T. Rabkin, MD, was known for regularly spending time making informal visits to all parts of the hospital. "You learn a lot from 'management by walking around,'" he said. "And you're also seen. When I visit another hospital and am given a tour by its CEO, I watch how that CEO interacts with other people, and what the body language is in each instance. It's very revealing. Even more, it's very important for role modeling." To reinforce that point, Dr Rabkin liked to tell the following story against himself.

> People learn to *do* as a result of the way they see you and others *behave*. An example from the Beth Israel that's now almost apocryphal—but *is* true—is the story of the bits of litter on the floor.
>
> One of our trustees, the late Max Feldberg, head of the Zayre Corporation, asked me one time to take a walk around the hospital with him and inquired, "Why do you think there are so many pieces of paper scattered on the floor of this patient care unit?"

"Well, it's because people don't pick them up," I replied.

He said, "Look, you're a scientist. We'll do an experiment. We'll walk down this floor and we'll pick up every other piece of paper. And then we'll go upstairs, there's another unit, same geography, statistically the same amount of paper, but we won't pick up anything."

So this 72-year-old man and I went picking up alternate bits of the litter on one floor and nothing on the other. When we came back 10 minutes later, virtually all the rest of the litter on the first floor had been removed and nothing, of course, had changed on the second.

And "Mr. Max" said to me, "You see, it's not because *people* don't pick them up, it's because *you* don't pick them up. If you're so fancy that you can't bend down and pick up a piece of paper, why should anybody else?"

Source: Christopher Lovelock, *Product Plus: How Product + Service = Competitive Advantage*, New York: McGraw-Hill, 1994.

describes how the CEO of a major hospital in the United States learned the power of role-modelling early in his tenure.

There is a risk, of course, that prominent leaders may become too externally focused at the risk of their internal effectiveness. A CEO who enjoys an enormous income (often through the exercise of huge stock options), maintains a princely lifestyle, and basks in widespread publicity, may even turn off low-paid service workers at the bottom of the organization.

Leadership Development

The need for leadership is not confined to chief executives or other top managers. Leadership traits are needed of everyone in a supervisory or managerial position, including those heading teams. Increasingly, companies are paying attention and spending considerable amounts on leadership development programs. Richard Peddie, president and CEO of Maple Leaf Sports and Entertainment (MLSE), believes in the concept so strongly that leadership development has been a major focus of his company in the last few years.[30]

Every six months, MLSE undergoes an exercise in "corporate engineering"—a term it uses to describe succession planning. Prior to the session, every vice president is required to submit an organizational chart to show whether a "replacement is in place at the moment, if there will be one in a year's time, and three to four years down the road. Then strengths and development needs are identified and a plan created." Peddie takes a keen personal interest and provides leadership in this endeavour—he has taught a course in strategic leadership at the University of Windsor. The course is used as a foundation for intensive in-house training for people who have been identified as having "great leadership potential." "Fit" with company values, "energy" and the ability to energize people, and having an "edge"—the ability to make tough decisions in a timely fashion—are some of the traits on which people are evaluated for their leadership potential. Leadership development also takes place within the organization through cross-functional moves and stretch assignments. While this comprehensive succession planning through extensive training and development enables MLSE to produce leaders in-house, Peddie acknowledges that some of these highly trained individuals would be hired away by other companies: "Not all [leadership hopefuls] will get to my job. That is impossible. But they are going to really benefit from being here, they are going to contribute terrifically while they are here."

Unfortunately, not every company is equally thorough in addressing the role of leadership development in their organization. In many firms, promotional decisions often appear haphazard, or based on such criteria as duration of tenure in a previous position.

Leadership, Culture, and Climate

To close this chapter, we take a brief look at a theme that has run through the chapter and, indeed, the book: the leader's role in nurturing an effective culture within the firm.[31] *Organizational culture* can be defined as including

- Shared perceptions or themes regarding what is important in the organization
- Shared values about what is right and wrong
- Shared understanding about what works and what doesn't work
- Shared beliefs and assumptions about *why* these things are important
- Shared styles of working and relating to others

Transforming an organization to develop and nurture a new culture along each of these five dimensions is no easy task for even the most gifted leader. It's doubly difficult when the organization is part of an industry that prides itself on deeply rooted traditions, including many different departments run by independent-minded professionals in disparate fields who are very attuned to how they are perceived by fellow professionals in the same field at other institutions.

Organizational climate represents the tangible surface layer of the organization's underlying culture. Among six key factors that influence an organization's working environment are its *flexibility* (how free employees feel to innovate); their sense of *responsibility* to the organization; the level of *standards* that people set; the perceived aptness of *rewards*; the *clarity* people have about mission and values; and the level of *commitment* to a common purpose.[32] From an employee perspective, this climate is directly related to managerial policies and procedures, especially those associated with human resource management. In short, climate represents the shared perceptions of employees about the practices, procedures, and types of behaviours that get rewarded and supported in a particular setting.

Because multiple climates often exist simultaneously within a single organization, a climate must relate to something specific—for instance, service, support, innovation, or safety. A climate for service refers to employee perceptions of those practices, procedures, and behaviours that are expected with regard to customer service and service quality, and that get rewarded when performed well. Essential features of a service-oriented culture include clear marketing goals and a strong drive to be the best in delivering superior value or service quality.[33]

Leaders are responsible for creating cultures and the service climates that go along with them. Transformational leadership may require changing a culture that has become dysfunctional in the context of what it takes to be successful. Why are some leaders more effective than others in bringing about a desired change in climate? As presented in Research Insights 15.1, research suggests that it may be a matter of style.

Creating a new climate for service, based upon an understanding of what is needed for market success, may require a radical rethink of human resource management activities, operational procedures, and the firm's reward and recognition policies. Newcomers to an organization must quickly familiarize themselves with the existing culture, otherwise they will find themselves being led by it, rather than leading through it and, if necessary, changing it.

Research Insights 15.1

The Impact of Leadership Styles on Climate

Daniel Goleman, an applied psychologist, is known for his work on emotional intelligence—the ability to manage ourselves and our relationships effectively. Having earlier identified six styles of leadership, he investigated how successful each style has proved to be in affecting climate or working atmosphere, based on a major study of the behaviour and impact on their organizations of thousands of executives.

Coercive leaders demand immediate compliance ("Do what I tell you") and were found to have a negative impact on climate. Goleman comments that this controlling style, often highly confrontational, has value only in a crisis or in dealing with problem employees. *Pacesetting leaders* set high standards for performance and exemplify these through their own energetic behaviour; this style can be summarized as "Do as I do, now." Somewhat surprisingly, this style was also found to have a negative impact on climate. In practice, the pacesetting leader may destroy morale by assuming too much, too soon, of subordinates—expecting them to know already what to do and how to do it. Finding others to be less capable than expected, the leader may lapse into obsessing over details and micromanaging. This style is likely to work only when seeking to get quick results from a highly motivated and competent team.

The research found that the most effective style for achieving a positive change in climate came from *authoritative leaders*, who have the skills and personality to mobilize people towards a vision, building confidence and using a "Come with me" approach. The research also found that three other styles had quite positive impacts on climate: *affiliative leaders*, who believe that "People come first," seeking to create harmony and build emotional bonds; *democratic leaders*, who forge consensus through participation ("What do you think?"); and *coaching leaders*, who work to develop people for the future and whose style might be summarized as "Try this."

Source: Daniel Goleman, "Leadership that Gets Results," *Harvard Business Review* 78 (March–April 2000): 78–93.

Conclusion

As illustrated by the service–profit chain, service leadership in an industry requires high performance across a number of dimensions, including managing and motivating employees, continuously improving service quality and productivity, creating and delivering a value proposition that target customers will perceive as superior to competing offerings, managing customer relationships effectively, and developing strategies for building and sustaining customer loyalty. These tasks cross traditional functional boundaries. Ultimately, a company's ability to achieve and maintain profitability will hinge on top management's skills in integrating the activities of marketing, operations, and human resources. Failure to do so may doom the organization to the status of a service nonentity or even service loser.

No organization can hope to achieve enduring success without change. The primary force behind effective change management is human leadership, which is concerned with the development of vision and strategies, the empowerment of people to overcome obstacles, and the ability to make the vision happen. One of the challenges for top management is to create a culture for innovation that gives employees the confidence to take risks, share ideas, and be willing to try new approaches.

Transformation of an organization can take place in two different ways: evolution or turnaround. Evolution in a business context involves continual changes and enhancements designed to ensure the survival of the fittest in often fiercely competitive markets. Top management must proactively evolve the firm's focus and strategy to take advantage of such factors as changing customer needs, the growth and decline of different markets, and the advent of new technologies. New and evolving strategies should anticipate the entry of new competitors and the repositioning of existing ones. A different type of transformation occurs in turnaround situations, in which leaders (often new to the firm) seek to bring distressed organizations back from the brink of failure and set them on a healthier course.

Exemplary leaders understand the powerful, unifying effect of focusing on customers and creating a culture for service. In turnaround situations, especially, this focus can facilitate the difficult task of obtaining collaboration across departments and divisions. Among the traits of successful leaders is their ability to act as role models of the behaviour they expect of others. Turning around an organization that has limited resources requires concentrating those resources where the need and the likely payoffs are greatest. However, the need for leadership in service organizations is not confined to chief executives and other top managers. Leadership skills are required of everyone in a supervisory or managerial position, particularly those who head teams charged with key elements of the change management process. In summary, transforming an organization to develop and nurture a new culture and its accompanying service climate is no easy task for even the most gifted leader. It's doubly difficult when the organization is part of an industry that prides itself on maintaining deeply rooted traditions.

Review Questions

1. Supporters of the service–profit chain concept argue that there are links connecting employee satisfaction and loyalty; service quality and productivity; value; and customer satisfaction and loyalty. Do you think these same relationships would prevail in a low-contact environment in which customers use self-service technology? Why (or why not)?

2. What are the causes of tension among the marketing, operations, and human resource functions? Provide specific examples of how these tensions might vary from one service industry to another.

3. How are the four levels of service performance defined? Based on your own service experiences, provide an example of a company for each category.

4. What is meant by transformational leadership? Explain how the challenges differ between an organization that is undergoing evolutionary change and one that requires a turnaround.

5. "Exemplary turnaround leaders understand the powerful, unifying effect of focusing on customers." Comment on this statement. Is focusing on customers more likely to have a unifying effect within a company under turnaround conditions than at other times?

6. What is the relationship among leadership, climate, and culture?

Application Exercises

1. Contrast the roles of marketing, operations, and human resources in (1) a gas station chain, (2) a web-based brokerage firm, and (3) an insurance company.

2. Select a company that you know well and obtain additional information from a literature review, website, company publications, and so on. Evaluate the company on as many dimensions of service performance as you can, identifying where you believe it fits on the service performance spectrum shown in Table 15.2 (p. 440–441).

3. It has been argued that transforming an organization's culture and service climate is a difficult task, and more so for organizations that have deep-rooted traditions such as not-for-profits. Profile an individual whose leadership skills played a significant role in the successful transformation of a not-for-profit Canadian service organization, identifying personal characteristics and leadership style that you consider were key to bringing about such a change.

Endnotes

1. Don Peppers and Martha Rogers, *Return on Customer*, New York: Currency Doubleday, 2005: 1.
2. Ibid.: 7–8.
3. James L. Heskett, Thomas O. Jones, Gary W. Loveman, et al., "Putting the Service–Profit Chain to Work," *Harvard Business Review* 72/3 (March–April 1994):164–74; and James L. Heskett, W. Earl Sasser, Jr., and Leonard A. Schlesinger, *The Service–Profit Chain*, New York: Free Press, 1997.
4. Note that a relationship between employee satisfaction and customer satisfaction may be more likely in high-contact situations where employee behaviour is an important aspect of the customers' experience. See Rhian Silvestro and Stuart Cross, "Applying the Service–Profit Chain in a Retail Environment: Challenging the 'Satisfaction Mirror,'" *International Journal of Service Industry Management* 11/3 (2000): 244–68.
5. Adam J. Stoehr, "Impressive Stock Performance of CAE winners from 1990–2005," *Excellence Magazine*(November 1, 2005); available online at www.nqi.com/articles/article_details.aspx?ID=547, accessed November 1, 2006.
6. See, for example, Jeffrey Pfeffer, *Competitive Advantage through People*, Boston: Harvard Business School Press, 1994.
7. See, for example, Benjamin Schneider and David E. Bowen *Winning the Service Game*, Boston: Harvard

Business School Press, 1995; and Leonard L. Berry, *On Great Service: A Framework for Action,* New York: Free Press, 1995, Chapters 8–10.

8. Terri Kabachnick, "The Strategic Role of Human Resources," *Arthur Andersen Retailing Issues Letter* 11/1 (January 1999): 3.

9. Sandra Vandermerwe, *From Tin Soldiers to Russian Dolls,* Oxford: Butterworth-Heinemann, 1993: 82.

10. Richard B. Chase and Robert H. Hayes, "Beefing Up Operations in Service Firms," *Sloan Management Review* (Fall 1991): 15–26.

11. Claudia H. Deutsch, "Management: Companies Scramble to Fill Shoes at the Top," *New York Times* (November 1, 2000).

12. John P. Kotter, *What Leaders Really Do,* Boston: Harvard Business School Press, 1999: 10–11.

13. Warren Bennis and Burt Nanus, *Leaders: The Strategies for Taking Charge,* New York: Harper and Row, 1985: 92.

14. Kotter, 1999, op. cit.

15. Deborah Blagg and Susan Young, "What Makes a Leader?" *Harvard Business School Bulletin* (February 2001): 31–36.

16. Gary Hamel and C.K. Prahlahad, *Competing for the Future,* Boston: Harvard Business School Press, 1994.

17. Leonard L. Berry, Venkatesh Shankar, Janet Turner Parish, et al., "Creating New Markets Through Service Innovation," *MIT Sloan Management Review* 47 (Winter 2006): 56–63.

18. See, for instance, the special issue on Celeste Wilderom (guest ed.) "Leadership as a Service" (special edition), *International Journal of Service Industry Management* 3/2 (1992).

19. Heskett, Sasser, and Schlesinger, 1997, op. cit.: 236.

20. Berry, 1995, op. cit.: 9.

21. Leonard L. Berry, *Discovering the Soul of Service: The Nine Drivers of Sustainable Business Success,* New York: Free Press, 1999: 44, 47. See also D. Michael Abrashoff, "Retention Through Redemption," *Harvard Business Review* 79/2 (February 2001): 136–41, which provides a fascinating example of successful leadership in the U.S. Navy.

22. Rakesh Karma, "The Curse of the Superstar CEO," *Harvard Business Review* 80/9 (September 2002): 60–66.

23. Jim Collins, "Level 5 Leadership: The Triumph of Humility and Fierce Resolve," *Harvard Business Review* 79/1 (January 2001): 66–76.

24. Vandermerwe, 1993, op. cit.: 129.

25. Zena Olijnyk, "Top CEO 2005," *Canadian Business* (April 25–May 8, 2005); available online at www.canadian business.com/managing/strategy/article.jsp?content= 20060118_183311_5192, accessed November 2, 2006.

26. Rosabeth Moss Kanter, "Leadership and the Psychology of Turnaround," *Harvard Business Review* 81/6 (June 2003): 58–67.

27. W. Chan Kim and Renée Mauborgne, "Tipping Point Leadership," *Harvard Business Review* 81/4 (April 2003): 61–69.

28. Mark Brown, "Serious Kid's Play," *Financial Post Business* (September 2006): 11.

29. Thomas J. Peters and Robert H. Waterman, *In Search of Excellence,* New York: Harper and Row, 1982: 122.

30. "Leadership Development," *Canadian HR Reporter* 16/21 (December 1, 2003): 9–13.

31. This section is based, in part, on Benjamin Schneider, and David E. Bowen, *Winning the Service Game,* Boston: Harvard Business School Press, 1995; and David E. Bowen, Benjamin Schneider, and Sandra S. Kim, "Shaping Service Cultures through Strategic Human Resource Management," in T. Schwartz and D. Iacobucci, (eds.), *Handbook of Services Marketing and Management,* Thousand Oaks, CA: Sage, 2000: 439–54.

32. Daniel Goleman, "Leadership that Gets Results," *Harvard Business Review* 78 (March–April 2000): 78–93.

33. Hans Kasper, "Culture and Leadership in Market-oriented Service Organisations," *European Journal of Marketing* 36/9–10 (2002): 1047–57.

Why Service Stinks

DIANE BRADY

The essence of relationship management is that the best customers get the most attention and are encouraged to remain loyal through rewards and special treatment. However, there's a downside to loyalty strategies that group customers into tiers based on their profitability for the firm. The evidence from industries as diverse as financial services, utilities, telecommunications, airlines, and hotels is that top-tier customers are getting unprecedented attention while those who spend less and use a service infrequently are being treated poorly and forced into self-service options if they want customer service. Tiering may seem logical, but it poses some drawbacks for marketers. Most programs tend to measure only the current value of a customer, based on past transactions, not his or her potential value. Another concern is that the segmentation of service, based on a wealth of personal information, raises troubling questions about privacy and what constitutes appropriate use of customer data drawn from many different sources.

Companies know just how good a customer you are—and unless you are a high roller, they would rather lose you than take the time to fix your problem.

When Tom Unger of New Haven started banking at First Union Corp. several years ago, he knew he wasn't top of the heap. But Unger didn't realize just how dispensable he was until mysterious service charges started showing up on his account. He called the bank's toll-free number, only to reach a bored service representative who brushed him off. Then he wrote two letters, neither of which received a response. A First Union spokeswoman, Mary Eshet, says the bank doesn't discuss individual accounts but notes that customer service has been steadily improving. Not for Unger. He left. "They wouldn't even give me the courtesy of listening to my complaint," he says.

And Unger ought to know bad service when he sees it. He works as a customer-service representative at an electric utility where the top 350 business clients are served by six people. The next tier of 700 are handled by six more, and 30 000 others get Unger and one other rep to serve their needs. Meanwhile, the 300 000 residential customers at the lowest end are left with an 800 number. As Unger explains: "We don't ignore anyone, but our biggest customers certainly get more attention than the rest."

As time goes on, that service gap is only growing wider. Studies by groups ranging from the Council of Better Business Bureaus Inc. to the University of Michigan vividly detail what consumers already know: Good service is increasingly rare (see Figures A and B). From passengers languishing in airport queues to bank clients caught in voice-mail hell, most consumers feel they're getting squeezed by Corporate America's push for profits and productivity. The result is more efficiencies for companies—and more frustration for their less valuable customers. "Time saved for them is not time saved for us," says Claes Fornell, a University of Michigan professor who created the [American Customer] Satisfaction Index, which shows broad declines across an array of industries. Fornell points to slight improvements in areas like autos and computers.

Figure A

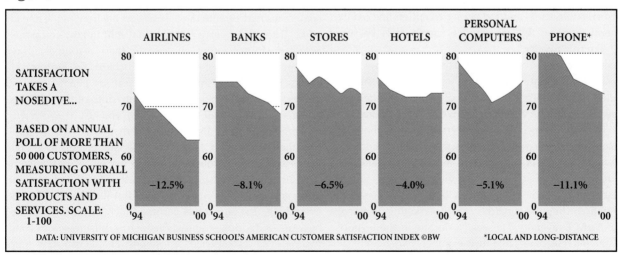

SATISFACTION TAKES A NOSEDIVE...

BASED ON ANNUAL POLL OF MORE THAN 50 000 CUSTOMERS, MEASURING OVERALL SATISFACTION WITH PRODUCTS AND SERVICES. SCALE: 1-100

AIRLINES −12.5% BANKS −8.1% STORES −6.5% HOTELS −4.0% PERSONAL COMPUTERS −5.1% PHONE* −11.1%

DATA: UNIVERSITY OF MICHIGAN BUSINESS SCHOOL'S AMERICAN CUSTOMER SATISFACTION INDEX ©BW   *LOCAL AND LONG-DISTANCE

Diane Brady, "Why Service Stinks," *Business Week* (October 23, 2000). Reprinted by permission.

Figure B

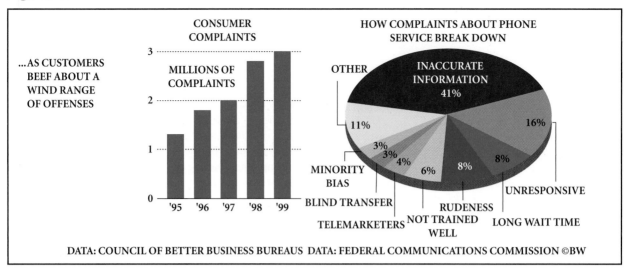

...AS CUSTOMERS BEEF ABOUT A WIND RANGE OF OFFENSES

CONSUMER COMPLAINTS

MILLIONS OF COMPLAINTS

HOW COMPLAINTS ABOUT PHONE SERVICE BREAK DOWN

INACCURATE INFORMATION 41%

OTHER 11%

MINORITY BIAS 3%

BLIND TRANSFER 3%

TELEMARKETERS 4%

NOT TRAINED WELL 6%

RUDENESS 8%

LONG WAIT TIME 8%

UNRESPONSIVE 16%

DATA: COUNCIL OF BETTER BUSINESS BUREAUS DATA: FEDERAL COMMUNICATIONS COMMISSION ©BW

Andrew Chan's experience with Ikea is typical. The Manhattan artist recently hauled a table home from an Ikea store in New Jersey only to discover that all the screws and brackets were missing. When he called to complain, the giant furniture retailer refused to send out the missing items and insisted he come back to pick them up himself, even though he doesn't own a car. Maybe he just reached the wrong guy, says Tom Cox, customer-service manager for Ikea North America, noting that the usual procedure is to mail small items out within a couple of days.

NO ELEPHANT?

Life isn't so tough for everyone, though. Roy Sharda, a Chicago Internet executive and road warrior is a "platinum" customer of Starwood Hotels & Resorts Worldwide. When he wanted to propose to his girlfriend, Starwood's Sheraton Agra in India arranged entry to the Taj Mahal after hours so he could pop the question in private. Starwood also threw in a horse-drawn carriage, flowers, a personalized meal, upgrades to the presidential suite, and a cheering reception line led by the general manager. It's no wonder Sharda feels he was "treated like true royalty."

Welcome to the new consumer apartheid. Those long lines and frustrating telephone trees aren't always the result of companies simply not caring about pleasing the customer anymore. Increasingly, companies have made a deliberate decision to give some people skimpy service because that's all their business is worth. Call it the dark side of the technology boom, where marketers can amass a mountain of data that gives them an almost Orwellian view of each buyer. Consumers have become commodities to pamper, squeeze, or toss away, according to Leonard L. Berry, marketing professor at Texas A&M University. He sees "a decline in the level of respect given to customers and their experiences."

More importantly, technology is creating a radical new business model that alters the whole dynamic of customer service. For the first time, companies can truly measure exactly what such service costs on an individual level and assess the return on each dollar. They can know exactly how much business someone generates, what he is likely to buy, and how much it costs to answer the phone. That allows them to deliver a level of service based on each person's potential to produce a profit—and not a single phone call more.

The result could be a whole new stratification of consumer society. The top tier may enjoy an unprecedented level of personal attention. But those who fall below a certain level of profitability for too long may find themselves bounced from the customer rolls altogether or facing fees that all but usher them out the door. A few years ago, GE Capital decided to charge $25 a year to GE Rewards MasterCard holders who didn't rack up at least that much in annual interest charges. The message was clear: Those who pay their bills in full each month don't boost the bottom line. GE has since sold its credit-card business to First USA. Others are charging extra for things like deliveries and repairs or reducing service staff in stores and call centers.

Instead of providing premium service across the board, companies may offer to move people to the front of the line for a fee. "There has been a fundamental shift in how companies assess customer value and apply their resources," says Cincinnati marketing consultant Richard G. Barlow. He argues that managers increasingly treat top clients with kid gloves and cast the masses "into a labyrinth of low-cost customer service where, if they complain, you just live with it."

Companies have always known that some people don't pay their way. Ravi Dhar, an associate professor at Yale University, cites the old rule that 80 percent of profits come from 20 percent of customers. "The rest nag you, call you, and don't add much revenue," he says. But technology changed everything. To start, it has become much easier to track and measure individual transactions across businesses. Second, the Web has also opened up options. People can now serve themselves at their convenience at a negligible cost, but they have to accept little or no human contact in return. Such huge savings in service costs have proven irresistible to marketers, who are doing everything possible to push their customers—especially low-margin ones—toward self-service.

FRONT-LOADING ELITE

That's a far cry from the days when the customer was king. In the data-rich new millennium, sales staff no longer let you return goods without question while rushing to shake your hand. And they don't particularly want to hear from you again unless you're worth the effort. How they define that top tier can vary a lot by industry. Airlines and hotels love those who buy premier offerings again and again. Financial institutions, on the other hand, salivate over day traders and the plastic-addicted who pay heavy interest charges because they cover only the minimum on their monthly credit-card bills.

Almost everyone is doing it (see Table A). Charles Schwab Corp.'s top-rated Signature clients—who start with at least $100 000 in assets or trade 12 times a year—never wait longer than 15 seconds to get a call answered, while other customers can wait 10 minutes or more. At Sears, Roebuck & Co., big spenders on the company's credit card get to choose a preferred two-hour time slot for repair calls while regular patrons are given a four-hour slot. Maytag Corp. provides premium service to people who buy pricey products such as its front-loading Neptune washing machines, which sell for about $1000, twice the cost of a top-loading washer. This group gets a dedicated staff of "product experts," an exclusive toll-free number, and speedy service on repairs. When people are paying this much, "they not only want more service; they deserve it," says Dale Reeder, Maytag's general manager of customer service.

Of course, while some companies gloat about the growing attention to their top tier, most hate to admit that the bottom rungs are getting less. GE Capital would not talk. Sprint Corp. and WorldCom Inc. declined repeated requests to speak about service divisions. Off the record, one company official explains that customers don't like to know they're being treated differently.

Obviously, taking service away from the low spenders doesn't generate much positive press for companies. Look at AT&T, which recently agreed to remove its minimum usage charges on the 28 million residential customers in its lowest-level basic plan, many of whom don't make enough calls to turn a profit. "To a lot of people, it's not important that a company make money," says AT&T Senior Vice-President Howard E. McNally, who argues that AT&T is still treated by regulators and the public as a carrier of last resort. Now, it's trying to push up profits by giving top callers everything from better rates to free premium cable channels.

SERIAL CALLERS

Is this service divide fair? That depends on your perspective. In an era when labor costs are rising while prices have come under pressure, U.S. companies insist they simply can't afford to spend big bucks giving every customer the hands-on service of yesteryear (see Table B). Adrian J. Slywotzky, a partner with Mercer Management Consulting Inc., estimates that gross margins in many industries have shrunk an average of 5 to 10 percentage points over the past decade because of competition. "Customers used to be more profitable 10 years ago, and they're becoming more different than similar" in how they want to be served, he says.

The new ability to segment customers into ever finer categories doesn't have to be bad news for consumers. In many cases, the trade-off in service means lower prices. Susanne D. Lyons, chief marketing officer at Charles Schwab, points out that the commission charged on Schwab stock trades has dropped by two-thirds over the past five years. Costs to Schwab, meanwhile, vary from a few cents for Web deals to several dollars per live interaction. And companies note that they're delivering a much wider range of products and

---

Table A How You Can Get Stiffed

Flying
Canceled flight? No problem. With top status, you're whisked past the queue, handed a ticket for the next flight, and driven to the first-class lounge.

Billing
Big spenders can expect special discounts, promotional offers, and other goodies when they open their bills. The rest might get higher fees, stripped-down service, and a machine to answer their questions.

Banking
There's nothing like a big bank account to get those complaints answered and service charges waived every time. Get pegged as a money-loser, and your negotiating clout vanishes.

Lodging
Another day, another upgrade for frequent guests. Sip champagne before the chef prepares your meal. First-time guest? So sorry. Your room is up three flights and to the left.

Retailing
Welcome to an after-hours preview for key customers, where great sales abound and staff await your every need. Out in the aisles, it's back to self-service.

services than ever before—as well as more ways to handle transactions. Thanks to the Internet, for example, consumers have far better tools to conveniently serve themselves.

Look at a company like Fidelity Investments, which not only has a mind-boggling menu of fund options but now lets people do research and manipulate their accounts without an intermediary. Ten years ago, the company got 97 000 calls a day, of which half were automated. It now gets about 550 000 Web site visits a day and more than 700 000 daily calls, about three-quarters of which go to automated systems that cost the company less than a buck each, including development and research costs. The rest are handled by human beings, which costs about $13 per call. No wonder Fidelity last year contacted 25 000 high-cost "serial" callers and told them they must use the Web or automated calls for simple account and price information. Each name was flagged and routed to a special representative who would direct callers back to automated services—and tell them how to use it. "If all our customers chose to go through live reps, it would be cost-prohibitive," says a Fidelity spokeswoman.

ENTITLED?

Segmenting is one way to manage those costs efficiently. Bass Hotels & Resorts, owners of such brands as Holiday Inn and Inter-Continental Hotels, knows so much about individual response rates to its promotions that it no longer bothers sending deals to those who did not bite in the past. The result: 50 percent slashed off mailing costs but a 20 percent jump in response rates. "As information becomes more sophisticated, the whole area of customer service is becoming much more complex," says Chief Marketing Officer Ravi Saligram.

Consumers themselves have cast a vote against high-quality service by increasingly choosing price, choice, and convenience over all else. Not that convenience always takes the sting out of rotten service—witness Priceline.com Inc., the ultimate self-service site that lets customers name their own price for plane tickets, hotels, and other goods. Many consumers didn't fully understand the trade-offs, such as being forced to stop over on flights, take whatever brand was handed to them, and forgo the right to any refund. And when things went wrong, critics say, no one was around to help. The result: a slew of complaints that has prompted at least one state investigation. Priceline.com responds that it's revamping the Web site and intensifying efforts to improve customer service. While many consumers refuse to pay more for service, they're clearly dismayed when service is taken away. "People have higher expectations now than two or three years ago because we have all this information at our fingertips," says Jupiter Communications Inc. analyst David Daniels.

Indeed, marketers point to what they call a growing culture of entitlement, where consumers are much more demanding about getting what they want. One reason is the explosion of choices, with everything from hundreds of cable channels to new players emerging from deregulated industries like airlines and telecom companies. Meanwhile, years of rewards programs such as frequent-flier miles have contributed to the new mind-set. Those who know their worth expect special privileges that reflect it. Says Bonnie S. Reitz, senior vice-president for marketing, sales, and distribution at Continental Airlines Inc.: "We've got a hugely educated, informed, and more experienced consumer out there now."

For top-dollar clients, all this technology allows corporations to feign an almost small-town intimacy. Marketers can know your name, your spending habits, and even details of your personal life. Centura Banks Inc. of Raleigh, N.C., now rates its 2 million customers on a profitability scale from 1 to 5. The real moneymakers get calls from service reps several times a year for what Controller Terry Earley calls "a friendly chat" and even an annual call from the CEO to wish them happy holidays. No wonder attrition in this group is down by 50 percent since 1996, while the percentage of unprofitable customers has slipped to 21 percent from 27 percent. Even for the lower tier, companies insist that this intense focus on data

Table B   "We're Sorry, All of Our Agents Are Busy with More Valuable Customers"

Companies have become sophisticated about figuring out if you're worth pampering—or whether to just let the phone keep ringing. Here are some of their techniques:

Coding
Some companies grade customers based on how profitable their business is. They give each account a code with instructions to service staff on how to handle each category.

Routing
Based on the customer's code, call centers route customers to different queues. Big spenders are whisked to high-level problem solvers. Others may never speak to a live person at all.

Targeting
Choice customers have fees waived and get other hidden discounts based on the value of their business. Less valuable customers may never even know the promotions exist.

Sharing
Companies sell data about your transaction history to outsiders. You can be slotted before you even walk in the door, since your buying potential has already been measured.

Table C   Making the Grade: How to Get Better Service

Consolidate Your Activities
Few things elevate status and trim costs like spending big in one place. Be on the lookout for packages or programs that reward loyal behavior.

Protect Your Privacy
Avoid surveys and be frugal with releasing credit-card or Social Security information. The less companies know, the less they can slot you.

Jump the Phone Queue
If you want to reach a live human, don't admit to having a touch-tone phone at the prompt. Or listen for options that are less likely to be handled automatically.

Fight Back
If you feel badly treated, complain. Make sure management knows just how much business you represent and that you're willing to take it elsewhere.

---

is leading to service that's better than ever. To start with, it's more customized. And while executives admit to pushing self-help instead of staff, they contend that such service is often preferable. After all, many banking customers prefer using automated teller machines to standing in line at their local branch. American Airlines Inc., the pioneer of customer segmentation with its two-decade-old loyalty program, says it's not ignoring those in the cheap seats, pointing to the airline's recent move to add more legroom in economy class. Says Elizabeth S. Crandall, managing director of personalized marketing: "We're just putting more of our energies into rewarding our best customers."

MARKED MAN

This segmentation of sales, marketing, and service, based on a wealth of personal information, raises some troubling questions about privacy. It threatens to become an intensely personal form of "redlining"—the controversial practice of identifying and avoiding unprofitable neighborhoods or types of people. Unlike traditional loyalty programs, the new tiers are not only highly individualized but they are often invisible. You don't know when you're being directed to a different telephone queue or sales promotion. You don't hear about the benefits you're missing. You don't realize your power to negotiate with everyone from gate agents to bank employees is predetermined by the code that pops up next to your name on a computer screen.

When the curtain is pulled back on such sophisticated tiering, it can reveal some uses of customer information that are downright disturbing. Steve Reed, a West Coast sales executive, was shocked when a United Airlines Inc. ticketing agent told him: "Wow, somebody doesn't like you." Not only did she have access to his Premier Executive account information but there was a nasty note about an argument he had had with a gate agent in San Francisco several months earlier. In retrospect, he feels that explained why staff seemed less accommodating following the incident. Now, Reed refuses to give more than his name for fear "of being coded and marked for reper-

cussions." United spokesman Joe Hopkins says such notes give agents a more complete picture of passengers. "It's not always negative information," says Hopkins, adding that the practice is common throughout the industry.

Those who don't make the top tier have no idea how good things can be for the free-spending few. American Express Co. has a new Centurion concierge service that promises to get members almost anything from anywhere in the world. The program, with an annual fee of $1000, is open by invitation only. "We're seeing a lot of people who value service more than price," says Alfred F. Kelly Jr., AmEx group president for consumer and small-business services. Dean Burri, a Rock Hill (S.C.) insurance executive, found out how the other half lives when he joined their ranks. Once he became a platinum customer of Starwood Hotels, it seemed there was nothing the hotel operator wouldn't do for him. When the Four Points Hotel in Lubbock, Tex., was completely booked for Texas Tech freshman orientation in August, it bumped a lower-status guest to get Burri a last-minute room. Starwood says that's part of the platinum policy, noting that ejected customers are put elsewhere and compensated for inconvenience. With the right status, says Burri, "you get completely different treatment."

The distinctions in customer status are getting sliced ever finer. Continental Airlines Inc. has started rolling out a Customer Information System where every one of its 43 000 gate, reservation, and service agents will immediately know the history and value of each customer. A so-called intelligent engine not only mines data on status but also suggests remedies and perks, from automatic coupons for service delays to priority for upgrades, giving the carrier more consistency in staff behavior and service delivery. The technology will even allow Continental staff to note details about the preferences of top customers so the airline can offer them extra services. As Vice-President Reitz puts it: "We even know if they put their eyeshades on and go to sleep." Such tiering pays off. Thanks to its heavy emphasis on top-tier clients, about 47 percent of Continental's customers now pay higher-cost, unrestricted fares, up from 38 percent in 1995.

Elsewhere, the selectivity is more subtle. At All First Bank in Baltimore, only those slotted as top customers get the option to click on a Web icon that directs them to a live service agent for a phone conversation. The rest never see it. First Union meanwhile, codes its credit-card customers with tiny colored squares that flash when service reps call up an account on their computer screens. Green means the person is a profitable customer and should be granted waivers or otherwise given white-glove treatment. Reds are the money losers who have almost no negotiating power, and yellow is a more discretionary category in between. "The information helps our people make decisions on fees and rates," explains First Union spokeswoman Mary Eshet.

Banks are especially motivated to take such steps because they have one of the widest gaps in profitability. Market Line Associates, an Atlanta financial consultancy, estimates that the top 20 percent of customers at a typical commercial bank generate up to six times as much revenue as they cost, while the bottom fifth cost three to four times more than they make for the company. Gartner Group Inc. recently found that, among banks with deposits of more than $4 billion, 68 percent are segmenting customers into profitability tranches while many more have plans to do so.

Tiering, however, poses some drawbacks for marketers. For one thing, most programs fail to measure the potential value of a customer. Most companies can still measure only past transactions—and some find it tough to combine information from different business units. The problem, of course, is that what someone spends today is not always a good predictor of what they'll spend tomorrow. Life situations and spending habits can change. In some cases, low activity may be a direct result of the consumer's dissatisfaction with current offerings. "We have to be careful not to make judgments based on a person's interaction with us," cautions Steven P. Young, vice-president for worldwide customer care at Compaq Computer Corp.'s consumer-products group. "It may not reflect their intentions or future behavior."

PAY NOT TO WAIT?

Already, innovative players are striving to use their treasure trove of information to move customers up the value chain instead of letting them walk out the door. Capital One Financial Corp. of Falls Church, Va., is an acknowledged master of tiering, offering more than 6000 credit cards and up to 20 000 permutations of other products, from phone cards to insurance. That range lets the company match clients with someone who has appropriate expertise. "We look at every single customer contact as an opportunity to make an unprofitable customer profitable or make a profitable customer more profitable," says Marge Connelly, senior vice-president for domestic card operations.

In the future, therefore, the service divide may become much more transparent. The trade-off between price and service could be explicit, and customers will be able to choose where they want to fall on that continuum. In essence, customer service will become just another product for sale. Walker Digital, the research lab run by Priceline.com founder Jay S. Walker, has patented a "value-based queuing" of phone calls that allows companies to prioritize calls according to what each person will pay. As Walker Digital CEO Vikas Kapoor argues, customers can say: "I don't want to wait in line—I'll pay to reduce my wait time."

For consumers, though, the reality is that service as we've known it has changed forever. As Roger S. Siboni, chief executive of customer-service software provider E. piphany Inc., points out, not all customers are the same. "Some you want to absolutely retain and throw rose petals at their feet," Siboni says. "Others will never be profitable." Armed with detailed data on who's who, companies are learning that it makes financial sense to serve people based on what they're worth. The rest can serve themselves or simply go away.

HOW TO IMPROVE YOUR PROFILE

Even if you're not a big spender, there are ways to improve your standing with companies in order to command better service. The key is to recognize that your spending habits, payment history, and any information you volunteer can be used for or against you. What's more, if you do think you're being pegged at a low tier, there are ways to get the recognition you feel you deserve.

The first step in fighting segmentation is to be stingy with the information you give out—especially if it's unlikely to help your status. Don't fill out surveys, sweepstakes forms, or applications if you're not comfortable with how the information might be used. Be wary when a company asks if it can alert you to other products and services. A yes may permit them to sell data that you don't want distributed.

Pigeonholing

The Consumers Union (CU) points out that it's unnecessary to fill out surveys with warranty cards. Just send in a proof of purchase with your name and address. "Protecting your privacy is a significant tool to prevent yourself from being pigeonholed as undesirable," says Gene Kimmelman, Washington co-director for the CU. It's equally important to recognize what kind of information companies are looking for. If you don't live in an upmarket Zip Code, consider using your work address for correspondence. Be optimistic when estimating your income or spending: The better the numbers look, the better you'll be treated.

Still, it's tough to keep personal information to yourself, especially when companies are compiling data on the business they do with you. A critical concern for all consumers is their actual payment record. Donna Fluss, a vice-president at the technology consultants Gartner Group Inc., advises pulling your credit history at least once a year to check if there are any liens or mistakes. "You may discover that you're listed as having missed a payment that you thought you made on time," she says. The three main reporting bureaus—Experian, Trans Union, and Equifax—charge a small fee for a copy of your credit history. If, however you have recently been denied credit, employment, or insurance, such a report is free from all three companies. The largest bureau is Equifax, which has data on 190 million Americans, but all three may have slightly different records based on who reports to them.

Multiple credit cards can be a mistake, especially if they're the no-frills variety that are frequently offered to less desirable candidates. Not only can they drain the credit you might need for other activities, but they're also unlikely to propel you into a higher category. Using a spouse's card or account is also to be avoided, because it robs you of a chance to build your own credit history. If a mistake is made on your account, fight it.

Pros disagree on tactics for bypassing the service maze. One customer representative argues that when calling a service center it's better to punch in no account number if you're a low-value customer. The reason? Without proper identification, he says, a live person has to get on the line. "Pretend you're calling from a rotary phone," he advises. But another tactic may be to punch zero or choose an option that's likely to get immediate attention.

In the end, resistance may be futile, and the best strategy for beating the system may be to join it. Shop around for the best company, and try to consolidate your business there. These days, the best way to ensure good service is to make yourself look like a high-value, free-spending customer.

Creating New Markets Through Service Innovation

LEONARD L. BERRY, VENKATESH SHANKAR, JANET TURNER
PARISH, SUSAN CADWALLADER, AND THOMAS DOTZEL

Many companies make incremental improvements to their service offerings, but few succeed in creating service innovations that generate new markets or reshape existing ones. To move in that direction, executives must understand the different types of market-creating service innovations as well as the nine factors that enable these innovations.

For decades, the importance of services to the global economy has grown steadily while the importance of goods has declined. In fact, services now dominate, making up about 70% of the aggregate production and employment in the Organization for Economic Cooperation and Development (OECD) nations and contributing about 75% of the GDP in the United States.[1] It's only natural, then, that companies are constantly seeking to provide better services, regardless of whether they are in a "pure" service business or in a manufacturing industry that must increasingly rely on its service operations for continued profitability.

However, most improvements to service activities are incremental. Stores stay open longer; product makers establish Web sites with e-commerce functions; airlines, casinos and supermarket chains enhance loyalty card programs. These improvements are useful and indeed necessary, but they are limited in the kind of returns they can produce. Only rarely does a company develop a service that creates an entirely new market or so reshapes a market that the company enjoys unforeseen profits for a considerable length of time.

One such organization is Enterprise Rent-A-Car Company. Enterprise has been strikingly successful: In an industry long led by The Hertz Corp. and Avis Rent-A-Car System Inc., it exploited a new idea to overtake them both. Founded by Jack Taylor in St. Louis in 1957 as a car leasing business, Enterprise added a rental division in 1962 when Taylor's customers began telling him that they often needed a car when theirs was in the shop for repair. While other rental car companies targeted travelers at airports, Enterprise focused on local customers who needed a replacement vehicle temporarily. This strategy required Enterprise to locate its offices close to where people live and work, and encouraged the company to develop such innovations as its "We'll pick you up" service. Today, Enterprise's revenues exceed $8 billion, and the company boasts the largest fleet size and the most rental locations in the United States.[2] Ninety percent of the U.S. population lives within a 15-mile drive of one of Enterprise's offices.[3]

In effect, Enterprise's innovative view created a new market for car rentals in the same way that FedEx Corp. redefined the package delivery market. Both companies exemplify "market-creating service innovation," which we define as an idea for a performance enhancement that customers perceive as offering a new benefit of sufficient appeal that it dramatically influences their behavior, as well as the behavior of competing companies.

Market-creating service innovation promises far greater upside potential than imitative or incrementally improved service offerings. Consider, for example, that market creators Google (incorporated in 1998) and eBay Inc. (started in 1996) have market capitalizations of approximately $110 billion and $60 billion respectively, placing them in the top ranks of U.S. companies.

Service innovation differs from product innovation in important ways. First, for labor-intensive, interactive services, the actual providers—the service delivery staff—are part of the customer experience and thus part of the innovation. Second, services requiring the physical presence of the customer necessitate "local" decentralized production capacity. (Customers will drive only so far to eat at a restaurant, no matter how innovative it may be.) Third, service innovators usually do not have a tangible product to carry a brand name.

Over the past year, we have conducted research on service innovation and have developed a matrix that offers a different way of thinking strategically about service innovations that can create new markets. Our research has helped us to better understand how service innovation differs from product innovation, and to envision the central drivers of success in a service innovation effort. Executives who develop an understanding of these issues will be better prepared to lead effective initiatives in service innovation. (See "About the Research.")

ARRIVING AT A TAXONOMY OF SERVICE INNOVATIONS

Service innovations that create new markets differ from each other along two primary dimensions: the type of benefit offered and the degree of service "separability." On the first dimension, businesses can innovate by offering an important new core benefit or a new delivery benefit that revolutionizes customers' access to the core benefit. For example, Cirque du

ABOUT THE RESEARCH

Our research involved several steps spanning one year. First, we developed and refined a working definition of market-creating service innovations. Then, based on reviews of published materials, we developed a list of services that created entirely new markets. Building on the service management literature, we developed a matrix to classify market-creating service innovations. Next, we analyzed each innovation to answer such questions as: What need did it address? What factors contributed to its performance? Our sources included books, articles, annual reports, Web sites and interviews with company executives. We also identified several market-creating product innovations and collected information on these innovations in a similar manner. Then we compared our analyses of both types of market-creating innovations and developed a list of success drivers for each. Finally, we presented our analysis, results and insights to several academicians and executives involved in service management and innovation management and made refinements as a result of their feedback.

Soleil created a new market for live entertainment—a core benefit—by offering a show that is neither a circus nor a dance performance but a hybrid of the two.[4] The unique shows are a phenomenal success, selling 97% of available seats.[5] The delivery of the service, however, is standard: Customers buy tickets in advance and see the performance in a theater. Conversely, the University of Phoenix Inc. enables students to receive an established core benefit—a college degree—by a new delivery system: the Internet. The University of Phoenix has become America's largest institution of higher education in just a few years.

The second dimension concerns whether the service must be produced and consumed simultaneously. Health care has traditionally been an "inseparable" service: The doctor must be in the room with the patient. Although patients, for the most part, continue to go to a clinic or hospital when they need health care, the delivery of "separable" care is growing. Doctors and nurses can advise patients via privacy-protected e-mail or voice mail and can monitor patients' health through telemedicine.[6] Technology has transformed many formerly inseparable services into services that can be consumed at any time or place. Customers who want to plan a trip no longer have to check their watches to see if the local travel agency is open.

Combining the dimensions of separability and type of benefit creates a two-by-two matrix that can help managers see where their companies fit and how they may seek to innovate. (See "The Four Types of Market-Creating Service Innovations.") For instance, executives from IBM Corp.—which has identified service science as the next frontier discipline after computer and information sciences—believe they can use this type of matrix to facilitate strategic thinking about market-creating service innovation. Like many large companies today, IBM is betting on new services for its future growth.

Each cell in the matrix offers a way to imagine a particular approach to market-creating service innovation. It is useful for managers to identify the cell in which they are targeting innovation and to understand the cell's dynamics and leverage points. A failure to do so may lead to lost growth opportunities. Consider Amazon.com Inc.'s creation of the online market for book retailing—a highly innovative separable service. An analysis of the matrix in 1999 might have tempted

The Four Types of Market-Creating Service Innovations

These innovations can be characterized on two dimensions: (1) whether they offer a new core benefit or new way of delivering a core benefit, and (2) whether the service must be consumed where and when it is produced or can be consumed separately from its production.

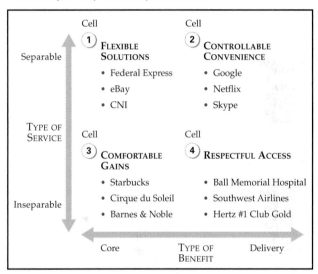

Amazon's management, flush with capital, to try to acquire the Borders Group Inc.'s Borders bookstore chain, which, at the time, had a minimal online presence. By combining "clicks with bricks," Amazon could have extended its reach into a second (inseparable) cell and created synergies between the two. But the company chose not to do so. Notwithstanding Amazon's bookselling prowess today, this was a lost opportunity for an even larger market impact. What follows is a breakdown of the characteristics of each cell.

Cell 1: Flexible Solutions

This cell describes service innovations that offer a new core benefit and that can be consumed apart from where and when they are produced. These innovations allow their users to break free of the constraints of time and place.

An early pioneer of this type of innovation was FedEx. The idea for the business was born in 1965, when Frederick W. Smith wrote a college term paper about shortcomings of air-freight shippers using passenger route systems for moving deadline-critical items.[7] At first glance, it might seem that FedEx was simply offering a new delivery benefit. But FedEx didn't invent the idea of delivering documents and packages by air. The company created a new market for the core benefit: the rapid, reliable delivery of time-sensitive materials. Combining speed and reliability has made FedEx a trusted deadline-beater and productivity booster for many businesses. In fact, executives from Merrill Lynch & Co. Inc. once learned that their employees were using FedEx to deliver documents between floors of its Manhattan headquarters building. FedEx's service was faster and more reliable than interoffice mail![8] FedEx has become synonymous with dependable just-in-time delivery. Its results justify its status: A share of FedEx stock purchased in 1978 for $31.36 was worth more than $2600 by July 2005.

Other examples in this cell include Time Warner Inc.'s CNN, the television network that for the first time allowed viewers around the world to watch updated news 24 hours a day, and eBay, the online marketplace that allows buyers and sellers to transact business day or night, weekday or weekend. CNN's business model brought a new core benefit for viewers who couldn't tune in at 6:00 p.m. or 11:00 p.m.; eBay created the first never-closed worldwide garage sale.

FedEx, CNN, and eBay offer a valuable lesson to managers. By focusing on a fundamental service benefit that can be experienced separately from the service provider, executives can turn unsolved customer problems into service innovation opportunities that spawn new markets.

Cell 2: Controllable Convenience

Innovations that create markets on the basis of new delivery benefits offer controllable convenience. As with flexible solutions, customers can enjoy the service benefits in this cell at any time and place.

Consider the changes in information delivery created by Google. Of course, Google didn't invent the core benefit of providing information, but its market-creating service innovation is the availability of relevant and rapid Web searches for information on virtually any subject. Paid for by advertising revenue, Google offers free access to an index comprising more than 8 billion URLs. In effect, Google is an information department store available where and whenever it is needed.

Founders Larry Page and Sergey Brin led two crucial innovations that positioned the company for dominance. First, they developed search algorithms that interpret hypertext links to Web pages as votes of importance; the more links, the higher the site rises to the top of the list that searchers see. This approach proved superior to that of competitors, whose search engines operated primarily by looking for keywords and tallying their frequency. Second, Google developed its own serving infrastructure—rejecting conventional, larger server configurations that slow under peak loads—by

employing linked computers to quickly find each query's answer. These innovations reshaped the world of Internet searching, and Google now averages more than 80 million users per month. The company's share price more than tripled within a year of its 2004 initial public offering.

Other companies offering controllable convenience include Netflix Inc. and Skype Technologies SA. Netflix offers a familiar core benefit—movie rentals—through a delivery system that combines the Internet and regular mail. Its customers don't have to race back to the store at 10:59 p.m. to return their rentals and avoid late fees. Skype, the peer-to-peer telephone company, offers free calling between Skype members over the Internet (for a small fee, members can connect to any traditional phone worldwide). The company thus uses a delivery innovation to offer the benefit of global telecommunications. Launched in August 2003, Skype had more than 60 million registered customers by late 2005.[9] In October 2005, eBay acquired the company for $2.6 billion, promising additional payments if performance targets are met.[10]

Companies should look for innovative ways to put customers in control of how they access a desired service. Creative service system design and technology application can enable customers to reach and use a service more easily—and can open up untapped markets.

Cell 3: Comfortable Gains

This cell refers to service innovations that offer a new core benefit consumed at the time and place of production. These innovations provide comfortable gains—substantially new experiences with direct benefits to customers' emotional or physical comfort.

The Starbucks sign has become ubiquitous—so much so that it may be hard to remember life before the coffee retailer became a feature of urban street corners. Coffee shops existed in abundance before Starbucks Corp. came along, to be sure, but the quality of both the coffee and the customer experience were inconsistent. Since 1987, when Howard Schultz bought the original Starbucks and began its transformation, the company has worked to offer an improved experience for coffee lovers. First, it has brewed coffee of uniform quality and pioneered the development of premium-priced drinks. Second, it has emphasized a relaxing atmosphere. Tables are purposely spaced apart so private conversations can take place or customers can be alone with their thoughts (or their laptops). Even the decision to use round tables is deliberate, since research indicates that a customer can be alone at a round table without feeling isolated or uncomfortable.[11] In Starbucks' first 12 years as a public company, its stock value increased by more than 3000%.

Cirque du Soleil also fits into this cell, as does Barnes & Noble Inc. The United States was populated with bookstores before Barnes & Noble developed its superstores. Barnes & Noble, however, created a new market nationwide based on the idea that Americans of all stripes would respond positively to a radically enhanced core benefit. Thus, its bookstores came to be known for their large stocks of books on an array of topics, easy chairs for reading, and co-located Starbucks coffee bars.

Managers of services that are produced and experienced in the same location need to look for creative ways by which the service experience can be made more comfortable, distinctive, enjoyable or memorable. Service innovations in this cell allow customers to benefit from a distinctive experience.

Cell 4: Respectful Access

In this cell, service innovators offer a new delivery benefit, and the production and consumption of the service are inseparable. Companies that create new markets in this space are granting their customers respectful access: They're demonstrating respect for their customers' time and physical presence in using the service. (See "Lowering Stress in the ER.")

Walgreen Co.'s Walgreens, America's largest and fastest-growing drugstore chain, with 2005 sales of $42 billion, opened its 5000th store in October 2005. It is the only Fortune 500 company other than Wal-Mart Stores Inc. to achieve sales and earnings gains for 30 years in a row.[12] Walgreens makes its stores easy to get to and easy to get through. Its market-creating innovation is in fact an array of innovations geared to shoppers who place a premium on saving time and effort. Walgreens'

strategy is to blanket its markets with freestanding stores that are easily accessible—stores on the corner of "Main and Main." Ample parking, drive-through pharmacy windows, 24-hour stores, wide aisles, low shelves, excellent in-store signage, one-hour photo departments, telephone prescription refills and automated queuing of prescriptions to reduce customer waiting time are all part of Walgreens' strategy of superior access.

Other companies that have created new markets through respectful access include Southwest Airlines Co. and The Hertz Corp. Southwest successfully created a market for affordable, reliable short-haul air transportation, in part by abandoning the hub-and-spoke strategy of its larger competitors. The company flies passengers directly to their destination rather than first taking them to a hub airport. Hertz was the first to create a membership program, Hertz #1 Club Gold, which gave frequent users faster and easier access to the company's core benefit—the temporary use of a car.

By fundamentally enhancing the ease with which customers can experience a service, companies can attract new customers and even create new markets. In the case of inseparable services, a company's greatest opportunity to win is at the service location. The key is to respect the customer's presence and time.

LOWERING STRESS IN THE ER

Few experiences are dreaded more than a trip to a hospital emergency room. Such trips are usually notable for the anxiety and pain associated with the illness or injury, for the impersonal and crowded waiting area and for long waits for treatment. But one hospital now offers far superior service, reshaping the market for emergency health care in its region and potentially influencing emergency departments throughout the country. The hospital found an innovative way to demonstrate respect for patients in their access to emergency medical services.

Ball Memorial Hospital Inc., in Muncie, Indiana, had been offering a typical ER experience when growth forced construction of a larger facility. The CEO of the hospital's parent, Cardinal Health System Inc., challenged the staff and the architects of the new facility "to think differently about the patient and family experience—to look at [the] service in terms of the patient and not what was most convenient for the staff."[1]

The result was the nation's first hospital emergency department with no waiting room. The walk-in area is similar to a small hotel lobby. An arriving patient gives basic information at a triage desk, receives an account number and is escorted (with any accompanying family members) to a private room that has a TV and telephone. A nurse records the patient's vital signs and gathers other health information; a physician arrives within 30 minutes. Patient registration is completed electronically at the bedside.

Ball Memorial's delivery-benefit innovation was the conversion of a soulless, stressful public space into a calm and comforting private space for patients and family. The service process was re-engineered to remove bottlenecks. An electronic board keeps track of all patients. The staff communicates with one another via wireless phones. The department has its own radiology and CT scanner services, which minimize delays in receiving test results. Every patient room has a locked, electronically controlled medical supply cabinet with automated inventory control and billing.

The results, to date, are encouraging. Previously, Ball Memorial received patient satisfaction scores below the 50th percentile in a national database; in the year after the new facility opened, the scores topped the 80th percentile, while a patient's length of stay dropped by 30 minutes. Local residents are more willing to consider Ball Memorial first when they need immediate medical attention. Although the area's population is shrinking. Ball Memorial's new emergency department saw 17% growth in patient volume from start-up in 2003 to the middle of 2005—a crucial metric given that 47% of the hospital's admissions come through its emergency department.[2]

1. "Want to Keep Patients Flowing Out of the Waiting Room? Don't Have Chairs," *ED Management* (January 2005): 2.
2. K. Kirby, administrative director of emergency services, Ball Memorial Hospital, interviews with authors, July 7 and Nov. 7, 2005.

SUCCESS DRIVERS OF MARKET-CREATING SERVICE INNOVATIONS

Executives who attempt to create a new market through service innovation must concentrate on the tasks that determine success or failure. Our research identified nine success drivers behind such innovations, some of which will be familiar to readers. But the key insight is that the cases studied featured all these drivers, with slight variations in emphasis depending on the specific cell in question. (See "The Nine Drivers of Successful Service Innovations.") In other words, the best service innovators take a holistic approach to market leadership. Close examination of the nine drivers reveals how each contributes to successful innovation.

1. A Scalable Business Model

The path to scalability for a product innovation is relatively straightforward. When The Gillette Company comes out with a new razor, for example, it can achieve scale through production economies and distribution benefits. However, many service innovations are people-intensive and thus harder to scale. This is especially true in the cells where service usage is inseparable from production. In these businesses, employees are both the primary cost center and customer-value creator, so their productivity is critical to long-term profitability.[13]

Service providers can consider a variety of strategies to strengthen their business models. One option is to become more capital-intensive. For example, eBay invests in its auction trading platform's features and security technologies, minimizing the need to add large numbers of new employees to serve an expanding market. Another option is to encourage customers to perform more of the service themselves. Hertz #1 Club Gold members can go directly to their rental cars, bypassing the customer service counter. A variable compensation plan that rewards employee productivity is another way to encourage profit growth in labor-intensive businesses. Enterprise Rent-A-Car emphasizes variable pay for its office managers; the more profitable a rental office, the more the manager earns.

Yet another alternative is to create a separable version of the service to extend the market while reducing labor intensity. For most of its history, tax preparation company H&R Block Inc. expanded primarily by opening new retail offices with its own dedicated staff. But it has recently been able to scale the business substantially by creating TaxCut, online and software tax preparation versions of its services.

2. Comprehensive Customer-experience Management

Services generally involve many more customer "touchpoints," or discrete experiences, than do manufactured goods. These experiences hinge upon "experience clues" in three forms: functional clues, those that point to the technical quality of the offering; mechanical clues, relating to nonhuman elements such as the design of the facility; and human clues, coming from the behavior and appearance of employees.[14] The clues converge to create a total experience that directly influences the customer's assessment of quality and value.

Customer experience management is relevant to some degree for all market-creating innovations, but it is critical to the success of inseparable services because customers visit the service "factory" and directly experience what occurs there. Starbucks' success, for example, depends on an excellent product (functional), a pleasing physical environment (mechanical), and service-minded employees (the human component). To implement its core strategy, Starbucks must excel in managing all the categories of customer experience clues.

3. Investment in Employee Performance

The more important, personal, and enduring the service, the more pronounced the human effects of the customer-provider interaction. Customers' perceptions of employee effort in delivering service have an especially strong impact on customer satisfaction and switching behavior.[15]

Successful service innovators invest in their employees' willingness and capability to perform at consistently high levels. These investments commonly include careful hiring, initial and ongoing training and education, information sharing, performance-based compensation and internal branding (that is, teaching, selling and reinforcing the desired brand image to employees). Cirque du Soleil has more than 30 individuals in its casting department who travel the world looking for talent. About three-fourths of Cirque du Soleil's onstage performers are former athletes; some have competed in the Olympics. Prospective cast members complete a rigorous 16-week training program in Montreal, receiving instruction in acting, movement, voice and makeup application, in addition to acrobatic and athletic skills. They are paid and housed during the training phase.[16]

The Nine Drivers of Successful Service Innovations

There are nine success drivers behind market-creating service innovations. Some are more important for service innovations; others apply to all innovations. The most innovative companies exploit all these drivers.

MARKET-CREATING INNOVATIONS

1. A scalable business model
2. Comprehensive customer experience management
3. Investment in employee performance
4. Continuous operational innovation
5. Brand differentiation

MARKET-CREATING SERVICE INNOVATIONS

6. An innovation champion
7. A superior customer benefit
8. Affordability
9. Continuous strategic innovation

The importance of investing in employee performance is not limited to companies offering inseparable services. Services are performances, and well-managed companies invest in their performers regardless of whether they are "onstage" or "offstage." A good example is Google, which depends on cutting-edge technology to stay ahead and vies aggressively for technical talent, sometimes even raiding its competitors.

4. Continuous Operational Innovation

Service businesses are operations-intensive regardless of whether their offerings are separable or inseparable, or whether they provide a core or delivery benefit. It is difficult for imitators to catch up with service innovators that are continually improving operations.

FedEx has been particularly innovative in this area. When it was established in 1973, customers had to call the company to initiate service. FedEx's introduction of drop boxes in 1975 led the company to consider the need to allow customers to track their shipments. As Frederick W. Smith put it, "It was not acceptable . . . that customers should be willing to take goods that were very valuable to them into this big anonymous transportation system and hope they came out the other end."[17] In 1984, FedEx began providing free computers and proprietary software to key customers, enabling them to monitor their shipments. In 1994, the company launched fedex.com, the first transportation Web site that offered online shipment tracking.

Starbucks, in addition to serving sit-down coffee drinkers, serves another big market segment: takeout customers who want fast service. In 2005, a Starbucks customer spent about three minutes on average from getting in line to receiving an order, a wait time reduced by about 30 seconds from that of five years earlier. Among the company's timesaving innovations are eliminating credit card signatures for purchases under $25, inventing a more efficient ice scoop for cold beverages, and creating a new position in which an employee "floats" to where he or she is needed most to shorten overall service time.[18]

5. Brand Differentiation

This success driver is important for market-creating product innovators, but may be even more so for service innovators. Because services are performances, there are no "tires to kick" prior to purchasing. A trusted brand reduces perceived risk. Distinctively communicating a consistent message, performing core services reliably and finding ways to connect emotionally with customers—these factors help build strong, trusted brands.

A strong brand is vital for service innovations in Cell 1: Flexible Solutions. Customers face increased risk with innovations in this cell because they have to evaluate an unfamiliar core benefit and cannot control or observe when or how the benefit is produced. FedEx has invested heavily in keeping its brand positioning promise of on-time delivery by solving problems before they reach customers. Each night, some of the company's aircraft start out empty or partially full so they can be diverted to airports where they are needed because of over-load, mechanical or other problems. Also, on-call aircraft and crews (called "hot spares") are on standby each night.[19]

6. An Innovation Champion

Market-creating innovations of all kinds require a champion—a mobilizer of resources, a master persuader and doer, someone who can imagine the possibilities embedded in an idea and lead the transformation of the idea into a market reality. The stories of successful major innovations typically begin with the story of a person: Edwin Land at Polaroid Corp., Ted Turner at CNN, or Ray Kroc at McDonald's Corp.

7. A Superior Customer Benefit

Innovations can create new markets only if they offer a clear and better solution to a problem of sufficient importance to stimulate customers to try the product or service—and then to repeat the action and give the product or service favorable word of mouth. Saving customers time and effort is a common benefit of market-creating innovations. In product categories, consider the microwave oven, the videocassette recorder and the cellular telephone; for services, the bank ATM, the online bookstore and the Internet search engine.

8. Affordability

Creating a market requires that customers not only are willing to change their behavior (for a superior benefit), but also have the means to do so. Cost-structure innovation is a common path to customer affordability. Southwest Airlines was designed to compete on price with automobile and bus travel. The entire operating model—including the use of a single type of aircraft to minimize training and servicing costs, fast airport turnarounds so planes spend more time in the air, and no seat assignments—emphasizes cost efficiency.

9. Continuous Strategic Innovation

Neither service businesses nor their manufacturing counterparts can neglect strategic innovation. Google maintains its strategic edge by allowing technical staff to devote one day a week to work on new business ideas called "Googlettes," and by sponsoring an online "Ideas List," open office hours with managers and periodic brainstorming sessions for employees to pitch ideas on new technologies and businesses.[20] Netflix is teaming with TiVo Inc. to develop a video-on-demand service that will make movies available over the Internet.

SERVICE INNOVATION STARTS WITH CULTURE

The success drivers discussed above require an organizational culture that supports human performance and innovation. For companies operating in the inseparable cells, the quality of employees' interactions with customers is critical. Competitors can more easily imitate the infrastructure and technology of an innovator like Netflix than they can re-create the employee culture of Starbucks or Southwest Airlines. These companies have invested considerable time, effort and money to build work cultures that amount to a form of competitive advantage. For companies operating in the separable cells, it's especially important to use continuous innovation to stay ahead of the competition, because these businesses place greater reliance on factors that can easily be replicated.

In addition to fostering a corporate culture that builds human capital, companies seeking to create new markets with services must create a culture for innovation—a "style of corporate behavior that is comfortable with, even aggressive about, new ideas, change, risk and failure."[21] Employees must

have the confidence to take risks and to freely share thoughts and suggestions with anyone in the organization. They must care enough and trust enough to try to create something new.

Companies that successfully create cultures that value human capital and innovation will see a steady stream of incremental improvements that help the bottom line. But when leaders understand the types of innovations that lead to new markets and work to implement the drivers of success, they also can build new businesses that position their companies for sustained growth and profitability. By thinking about a service in terms of its core benefits and the separability of its use from its production, managers can more easily determine how to out-innovate their competitors.

Endnotes

1. A. Wölfl, "The Service Economy in OECD Countries," working paper 2005/3, OECD—Directorate for Science, Technology and Industry, Feb. 11, 2005; and Office of the U.S. Trade Representative, "U.S. Submits Revised Services Offer to the WTO," press release (Washington, D.C.: Executive Office of the President, May 31, 2005).

2. "Enterprise Rent-A-Car Revenue Exceeds $8 Billion: Records Set in Revenues, Fleet Size and Locations," September 21, 2005, www.enterprise.com; and "Car Rental in the United States—Industry Profile," October 2004, www.datamonitor.com.

3. "Rental Car Industry Expansion into Neighborhoods Fuels and Fills Americans' Appetites," Enterprise Rent-A-Car press release, May 18, 2005.

4. W.C. Kim and R. Mauborgne, "Blue Ocean Strategy," Harvard Business Review 82 (October 2004): 76–84.

5. G. Keighley, "The Phantasmagoria Factory," Business 2.0 (February 2004): 103–107.

6. L.L. Berry, K. Seiders, and S.S. Wilder, "Innovations in Access to Care: A Patient-Centered Approach," Annals of Internal Medicine 139, no. 7 (2003): 568–574.

7. "FedEx Corporate History," accessed October 30, 2005, www.fedex.com.

8. D. Foust, "Frederick W. Smith: No Overnight Success," Business Week, Sept. 20, 2004, 18.

9. "Skype Gives Small Businesses Market Advantage," Skype press release, Oct. 25, 2005.

10. "Change in Assets: Item 2.01 Completion of Acquisition or Disposition of Assets," SEC Filings for eBay, Form 8-K for eBay Inc., Oct. 18, 2005.

11. M. Krauss, "Starbucks 'architect' explains brand design," Marketing News 39, no. 8 (May 1, 2005): 19-20.

12. M. Boyle, "Drug Wars," Fortune, June 13, 2005, 79.

13. F. F. Barber and R. Strack, "The Surprising Economics of 'People Business'," Harvard Business Review (June 2005): 80–90.

14. L.L. Berry, L.P. Carbone, and S.H. Haeckel, "Managing the Total Customer Experience," MIT Sloan Management Review 43, no. 3 (Spring 2002): 85-89.

15. S.M. Keaveney, "Customer Switching Behavior in Service Industries: An Exploratory Study," Journal of Marketing 59 (April 1995): 71–82; and L.A. Mohr and M.J. Bitner, "The Role of Employee Effort in Satisfaction with Service Transactions," Journal of Business Research 32, no. 3 (March 1995): 239–252.

16. B. DeSimone, "Cirque's Siren Call to Athletes," USA Today, July 7, 2005, sec. C, p. 1.

17. D. Joachim, "FedEx Delivers on CEO's IT Vision," Oct. 25, 1999, www.internetweek.com.

18. S. Gray, "Coffee on the Double," Wall Street Journal, Apr. 12, 2005, B1.

19. S. Munoz, media relations manager, FedEx, interview with authors, July 8, 2005.

20. B. Elgin, "Managing Google's Idea Factory," Business Week, Oct. 3, 2005, 88–90.

21. B. O'Reilly, "The Secrets of America's Most Admired Corporations: New Ideas, New Products," Fortune, March 3, 1997, 60–64.

How to Grow Great Leaders

DOUGLAS A. READY

The biggest test that rising leaders face is aggressively championing a business unit while looking out for the enterprise as a whole. Helping them meet that challenge demands a new approach to leadership development.

While it may be true that "all politics is local," as the late Speaker of the U.S. House of Representatives Tip O'Neill famously said, leadership is another story. Ground-level execution and networking are essential leadership skills, but so are framing and communicating broad, sweeping issues of national importance. Chris Matthews, the host of the television talk show *Hardball*, has dubbed these two sets of skills "retail" and "wholesale," respectively. Very few political leaders—only the most effective, like Franklin D. Roosevelt and Lee Kuan Yew—excel at both.

The same can be said of business leaders. But the structure of modern corporations and the nature of modern markets have begun to call for leaders of the Rooseveltian sort, men and women who can run business units, functions, or regions (in other words, are retail savvy) *and* have the vision to work well at the enterprise (or wholesale) level. Many companies have a sufficient pipeline of strong retail leaders yet lack wholesale leaders. The challenge is not to teach the former to focus on the enterprise agenda alone; it's to develop leaders who can manage the inherent tensions between unit and enterprise priorities.

In some ways, this problem is as old as the modern corporation. It has confounded the likes of DuPont, GM, Philips Electronics, and Unilever over the past century. As soon as a company becomes large enough to offer multiple lines of business in various regions, it begins to face tensions regarding how to go to market, who has primary accountability for which customers, and how to factor revenue and profitability into performance measurement. What has changed in the past few years is that companies must synchronize the actions of business units and the goals of the enterprise as a whole more tightly than ever. This is because customers increasingly demand integrated or global solutions, which require the collaboration of multiple business units or locations.

Look at what happened when PriceWaterhouse merged with Coopers & Lybrand in the late 1990s to create PricewaterhouseCoopers. The merger made PwC the largest professional services firm in the world. Then-CEO Jim Schiro pressed the idea of PwC's becoming the first truly globally integrated services firm; he envisioned PwC drawing on expertise from its six lines of service to provide complete solutions. He believed that joining forces from within could allow the firm to quickly gain a powerful competitive advantage due to its sheer size and reach. So Schiro was stunned when the partners heading the service lines staunchly resisted executing his strategy.

This resistance was grounded in institutional history. Both PriceWaterhouse and Coopers & Lybrand had deep-rooted cultures that rewarded excellence within each line of client service. The partners and their subordinates had little experience crossing boundaries and no role models to emulate. So it was natural for them to continue striving to provide the best possible service within unit boundaries. Furthermore, both pricing authority and profit-and-loss (P&L) accountability were vested in the individual lines' practice—tax, audit, and so on. There was no organizational mechanism to maximize revenue at the firm level, especially if it meant sacrificing revenue at the line-of-business level. What's more, the new strategy affected client relationships. Before the merger, the companies consisted of 150 small to midsize independent businesses brought together by brand and a shared infrastructure. The leaders of these businesses had deep relationships with their client firms' CEOs. Rolf Windemöller, the former head of Coopers's German firm, was a close friend of Lufthansa CEO Jurgen Weber. After the merger, Windemöller was expected to become an enabler for cross selling into Lufthansa, a position that threatened to put a strain on his relationship with both Weber and his new colleagues at PwC.

For a more detailed example of the tensions between retail and wholesale thinking, consider the challenges facing RBC Financial Group, one of the largest and most profitable companies in Canada. Founded 140 years ago as a small trading bank, RBC now serves more than 12 million customers throughout the world; its assets of $446 billion make it the seventh-largest bank in North America. The group comprises five main divisions (internally called "platforms"): RBC Banking, RBC Investments, RBC Insurance, RBC Capital Markets, and RBC Global Services.

For most of its history, RBC followed a straightforward strategy: Offer high-quality products at a fair price in every line of business. The company's approach to executing that strategy was equally simple: Get the best people, make them accountable for building successful business franchises, and

Douglas A. Ready is the founder and president of the International Consortium for Executive Development Research and contributes to executive education programs at London Business School. He provided consulting services to RBC Financial Group as part of the work described in this article.

pay them very well. It worked until about the mid-1990s, when two forces collided to change RBC's competitive dynamics. First, in an effort to preclude monopolies, the government announced that the Big Six banks in Canada (which dominate the country's domestic-banking business) could neither merge with nor acquire one another. This led to a major change in RBC's strategy—the decision to grow through cross-border acquisitions, primarily in the United States. Second, there was a shift in customer preferences. Quality was no longer enough in financial services. Customers wanted to simplify their decisions, so they wanted to be able to purchase bundled products and services. This sparked another big change in RBC's competitive strategy. The company would reach across its traditional stand-alone businesses to offer integrated solutions, an initiative that RBC leaders referred to as achieving cross-enterprise leverage.

Gordon Nixon, RBC's chief executive, knew that to make the new strategy work he would need to get the support of many different constituencies throughout the organization. He worked with his top executive team, the group management committee (GMC), to craft a clear statement of the company's new strategic priorities, and he sent it to the entire organization.

The statement didn't immediately elicit support. Employees reacted instinctively against what would amount to a delicate balancing act: They would have to lift their focus out of their silos while continuing to deliver on plan. Despite the best of intentions, Nixon's effort to articulate the new strategy initially raised more questions than it answered. Regional heads in Canada wondered whether their roles had dimin-

ished in importance and whether they should go after the new jobs opening up in the United States. The heads of RBC's businesses and platforms understood the importance of the strategic initiative, but they knew they could make the strongest contributions to RBC's growth in the short term by continuing to run their stand-alone businesses effectively. They understood how to manage growth, boost profitability, and earn bonuses within their businesses; it was less clear how they could produce cross-platform revenues, even it they wanted to. In short, managers of regions and business units had well-developed retail skills but lacked the wholesale ability to lead across boundaries.

This is a familiar story. Obstacles like those RBC faced are difficult to clear because the retail–wholesale tensions are very real, with three common conditions serving to reinforce them. First, most organizational structures lack mechanisms to air and resolve the natural conflicts that may arise between business-unit and enterprise priorities. Second, most foster silo thinking and unimaginative career paths. And third, many have well-intentioned but misguided reward systems that pit unit performance against enterprise considerations in a zero-sum game. Fortunately, people and companies can be trained to think and act differently, as you'll see in the case of RBC.

AIR THE TENSIONS

RBC's directive to fuel growth and develop markets across boundaries clearly made sense from an enterprise point of view, but it sparked zero-sum thinking among platform lead-

---

Are You Growing Great Leaders?
A checklist for senior executive teams

1. Have you crafted a clear policy that encourages employees to develop expertise and vision outside their current business units, functions, and regions?	yes ☐	no ☐
2. Do you seek candidates from other units when trying to fill key openings?	yes ☐	no ☐
3. Have you created formal mechanisms (such as leadership groups or task forces) that bring together high-potentials from across your company so managers can discuss the natural tensions and conflicts inherent in leaderships?	yes ☐	no ☐
4. Are leaders rewarded for sending talented employees outside their domains and for accepting individuals from other areas for developmental purposes?	yes ☐	no ☐
5. Will strong individual contributors and successful business builders who fail to pay attention to broad enterprise priorities continue to make it to the senior executive team in your company?	yes ☐	no ☐

ers: *If I share a client with another business unit, I'll lose power and control, as well as the revenue and profitability associated with that client.* Managers anticipated that they would need to make trade-offs on a daily basis and that customers might be confused if they were approached by (or heard conflicting messages from) different parts of RBC. In the absence of a forum for addressing these tensions, frustrations began to build and collaboration became a casualty of conflict.

So RBC's management team designed a series of leader-facilitated discussions, an initiative called the RBC Leadership Dialogues. Each session was run by Nixon and two rotating members of the GMC, and approximately 30 senior leaders were invited to attend at a time. Committee members who led the sessions told stories of their experiences trying to reconcile dilemmas similar to those that RBC's next generation of leaders would face. The objective was not to portray the GMC and Nixon as having all the answers; rather, it was to have the committee acknowledge that the dilemmas did exist, to open them up for discussion among the RBC's managerial ranks, and to help prepare rising leaders for the tough choices they would inevitably face.

The first dialogues were led by two of RBC's most powerful vice chairs—Jim Rager, head of personal and commercial banking (now known as RBC Banking), and Suzanne Labarge, head of group risk management. Rager's unit is by far the largest division in the company and is considered by employees and analysts to be the firm's most powerful growth engine. That expectation requires RBC Banking to be "suitably entrepreneurial," as Rager once put it. Labarge's role is to protect RBC from inappropriate risk that might threaten the bank's long-term health. Not surprisingly, Rager and Labarge often disagree on what constitutes appropriate risk. Before the dialogues took place, the party line was "It's not personal; we're both just doing our jobs." Employees knew better, but the mistrust between units was understood to be one of many "undiscussables."

To their credit, both Rager and Labarge acknowledged during the dialogues that, in addition to being vice chairs, they were both human and that the competing priorities hardwired into their respective roles sometimes placed a strain on their personal relationship. They emphasized their respect for each other and openly discussed the steps they were taking to resolve their concerns—meeting more frequently so tensions wouldn't build, for example, and bringing their staffs together more often so those relationships would improve as well. And both vice chairs stated emphatically that if the participants in the dialogues aspired to lead at the enterprise level, they should be prepared to face similar tensions in their future roles. Virtually all of RBC's top 150 executives participated in the dialogues.

These meetings had a genuine impact on the leaders who attended. One such leader was Ann Louise Vehovec, who had spent her entire career before the dialogues in RBC Capital Markets. In her 20 years at the company, she had developed a passion for that platform and hadn't worried much about the enterprise as a whole. The dialogues helped her see that she could remain a passionate advocate for her business unit while leading with an enterprise perspective. Taking note, Nixon offered her a new job that would require cross-platform thinking: RBC's first senior vice president for brand management and advertising. Leaders of the various platforms were reluctant to take part in enterprisewide marketing and advertising efforts because in the past they'd seen little direct benefit to their individual units. But Vehovec drew on the networks she'd developed through the dialogues to organize an operating committee for marketing. At committee meetings, she invited people to voice their concerns; ultimately, she won them over because she paid attention to their requests for a better link between broad-based advertising—image advertising, you might say—and product advertising. But at the same time, she stayed focused on doing what was best for RBC as a whole. "Three years ago, meetings of this nature simply wouldn't have taken place," Vehovec told me. "We'd all be worrying about protecting our platforms or holding on to the power we had built up in our functions."

The next step was to create ways to bring managers who were further down in the organization into the conversation. After all, plans for cross-platform collaboration often get undone not at the executive level but below, where individual incentives and career goals are tied to unit results. To change that at RBC, Nixon and his team created another series of leader-facilitated discussions closely patterned after the dialogues; these were called Leaders' Exchanges. Participants in the dialogues became the coaches for the exchanges, to ensure that the message cascading throughout RBC would be consistent. The coaches shared their own stories of conflicting priorities at these meetings, just as GMC members had done at the dialogues.

Nixon and his top team also instituted a quarterly conference call with thousands of employees to deliver the same core messages to every employee in every platform and region where RBC did business. And finally, Nixon and the GMC set up task forces to deal with the many tensions that were surfacing daily as the company executed its new strategy. One task force was called E^2, which stood for *efficiency* and *effectiveness*. In trying to manage business and enterprise priorities simultaneously, managers continuously struggled to decide what held a higher priority: the efficiencies of implementing enterprisewide actions or the targeted effectiveness of focusing on what was best for a particular business or region. E^2 took on the job of resolving this dilemma when it arose.

For instance, like many committees, RBC has "global" functions—HR, IT, finance, and so forth—but those functions are embedded in each of the company's business units as well. RBC Banking has its own HR, IT, and finance departments. This duplication often results in redundancies, bureaucratic decision making, and excessive costs, with little value added to customers. Each function had the opportunity to present its best business case to the E^2 group by describing the value it added both to its individual platform and to the enterprise. This was just one of 35 E^2 projects focused on reducing costs while improving service.

The dialogues and exchanges went well beyond assessing the contributions of various functions; they opened the lines of communication across platforms, generated free-flowing conversations, and allowed as many people as possible to put their thumbprints on the company's strategy. It's this kind of open environment that can dispel confusion, anger, and cynicism, and engender straight talk, collaboration, and shared accountability. Two years into the process of airing tensions, employees reported that they had a much better understanding of the company's enterprise strategy and perceived a significant improvement in the quality of communication between the GMC and the next several layers of management.

ESCAPE THE SILOS

RBC had invested heavily in leadership development. In the 1980s and 1990s, the company was, in the words of one executive, "a consultant's dream come true." It made avid use of university-based executive programs, funded an array of academic research initiatives, and bought the services of dozens of brand-name consultants in every facet of management and leadership development. It had the latest competencies package, the most up-to-date performance management system, the most sophisticated assessment instruments, and a turbo-charged e-learning platform.

But despite the hundreds of millions of dollars invested, the leadership development programs weren't producing leaders with the capacity to manage the inherent tensions between unit and enterprise considerations. That's because, as with most companies, RBC's leadership development efforts were piecemeal, focused on particular skills and challenges, and therefore didn't prepare employees to take on broader roles. Development was confined to within the organization's various silos. Every time a key position became available in one of the company's platforms or functions, the only candidates offered up were managers who had already worked in that area. So rising executives never had a reason to venture outside their silos.

Organizations have been managed in this way for years, and managers have had little reason to question the approach until recently. Why? As former New York Yankees great Yogi Berra might have put it, the problem with this problem is that most of the time there is no problem. In many cases, it makes great sense to have clear lines of authority and strong unit boundaries, and to give ultimate power to those who manage P&Ls. However, silos become pathological when they deprive customers of better products and services or, in pursuit of conflicting priorities, hinder a company's overall growth. The dialogues and exchanges at RBC stimulated open discussion of tensions that go along with leading across boundaries. But if managers returned from these discussions to develop their careers exclusively in their silos, their progress would be short-lived.

To build leaders who don't see the world in zero-sum terms but who appreciate the unique contributions of businesses, divisions, functions, and regions, companies must take people out of their career comfort zones and offer them challenging assignments in different roles. Ann Louise Vehovec's transition from line management to an enterprise job wasn't easy, but Vehovec saw the new job as key to her professional develop-

ment. In her words:

This has been the most challenging time for me at RBC. I came to realize how narrow my networks were, having worked only in Capital Markets for my entire career. It soon dawned on me that in order to succeed in the new role, I needed to build relationships across all of RBC's businesses, functions, and regions—and I didn't have them. For the first time in my career, I was worried about failing. When I was in investment banking, I thought if you weren't directly wired into a profit center, you were pure overhead and had little to no value. Now I understand the importance of platform performance, but with an enterprise perspective. We need to run our businesses and functions and do whatever is possible to contribute to RBC's overall success. That learning wouldn't have happened without this assignment.

Many others made a similar shift as part of the company's effort to bring people out of their silos. The head of North American markets for RBC Banking was asked to serve as chief operating office for RBC Investments in Canada, for example, and the chief strategy office for RBC Investments in Canada was recruited to serve as chief risk officer for RBC Centura in North Carolina. Nixon himself had grown up in a silo (Capital Markets), and he needed to learn more about RBC's other businesses—banking, wealth, management, insurance, custody, and so forth.

To ensure that these assignments would be made strategically and that high-potentials wouldn't slip through the cracks, Nixon took accountability for executive development out of the business units and built it into the individual goals of GMC members. The committee members are now assessed in terms of their participation in the dialogues, the quality and diversity of the succession pools for their own jobs, and the extent to which their employees feel they are receiving the coaching to grow as leaders.

RIGHT THE REWARDS

Companies are used to paying for performance—but most of the time, rewards are tied to unit performance, regardless of overall strategy. This was the case at a very large, profitable company whose strategy for ten years had been based exclusively on acquiring distressed companies. The firm slashed costs in its acquired companies and installed managers who would follow scripted, standardized operating practices. These leaders were chosen for their capacity to aggressively manage P&Ls; those who did this successfully could easily meet the metrics of the company's incentive system and double their base pay.

The company changed its strategy when market research indicated that its customers were looking for integrated solutions rather than the stand-alone products offered by its fiercely independent lines of businesses. Yet while the new strategy was clear and the company's managers intellectually understood the nature of the challenge, managers continued to operate independently. Why? The company's rewards and incentives were still geared toward strong unit performance. Most senior managers had company stock or options, which would theoretically reward cross-boundary cooperation, but the chain of results to rewards with equity-based compensation is indirect and long, especially in a large company. There's little incentive for people to change their behavior if they're giving up an immediate, certain payoff for stocks or options that may or may not eventually increase in price.

Rewards can also be noneconomic, with equally fruitful or damaging consequences. Some years ago, the CEO of a financial services institution in New England was interested in launching a leadership program to transform the bank's culture. His concern was that his managers were too risk averse and that the bank would miss out on important growth opportunities. Thus, the CEO named the new course "The Entrepreneurial Leadership Program." His opening remarks to participants went something like this:

> Welcome. This is an exciting day, as we set out to transform our culture to one of searching for new opportunities and embracing a spirit of entrepreneurship. As members of our first class, you are our crown jewels . . . and let me tell you why. The industry benchmark data are just in, and I am delighted to inform you that we have won the coveted spot of having the lowest loan-loss ratio in the industry nationally!

Although the goal was to develop scores of innovative and enterprising leaders, the CEO was unintentionally praising people for being the most conservative managers in the country.

At RBC, Nixon and his team learned during the quarterly conference calls that employees saw little personal benefit in complying with the company's new strategy; they saw RBC's performance management system as rewarding unit rather than enterprise results. So the company made changes to its reward system, creating both economic and noneconomic incentives to manage the tensions between platform and enterprise priorities.

Economic Rewards

RBC now combines salary with both short- and long-term incentives. It approaches salary and long-term incentives as it always has: paying slightly more than its competitors to recruit employees and using shares and options to motivate people to strive for sustained success. The short-term incentives, however, have changed; they encourage employees to pay attention to business growth and enterprise performance simultaneously. Short-term incentives are divided into two categories: personal performance and the bonus pool.

The personal performance incentives are rewards offered for growing one's business unit and contributing to RBC's enterprise strategy. An individual may earn incentives for meeting or surpassing specific objectives within his or her platform and also for making clear, measurable contributions to the company as a whole. The bonus pool is calculated in terms of how close RBC comes to achieving its return-on-equity goal

and how its earnings-per-share growth fares against that of its competition. So a functional leader can be granted short-term incentives for contributing to his or her function and to RBC, but that person's bonus is based 100% on what he or she does for the company. Enterprise contributions might include participating on the E^2 task force or collaborating across platforms to create new products or services. RBC Banking and RBC Investments, for example, worked together to create a new advisory service for people with high net worth.

Similarly, GMC members who run platforms might receive certain short-term incentives for building their business units, but their bonuses are based entirely on RBC's overall performance. The bonus pool percentages change for people at other levels of the organization to reflect their relative contributions to either business or enterprise priorities. For example, a senior platform leader would receive 50% of his or her bonus on the basis of enterprise results linked to cross-border initiatives, such as RBC Banking managers collaborating with RBC Investments to deliver on the financial advisory service created for high-net-worth individuals. Meanwhile, the bonus for a leader the next level down would be 30% for the company's results as a whole. In the past, the bonus for a lower-level business manager or functional professional would have been based solely on unit performance.

Noneconomic Rewards

Participation in special sessions like the dialogues and exchanges is by invitation only, and participants are told from the outset that they have been selected because the are critical players in helping the company achieve its objectives. This is an unusual move for the typically egalitarian RBC. Although the company still provides extensive training and development for everyone, it has decided to cultivate its next generation of senior leaders without worrying too much about discouraging the rest.

Even within this select group, further incentives are used to motivate behavior. The participants who contributed most valuably to the dialogues demonstrated the courage to discuss the undiscussables—for instance, by pointing to specific GMC members who have served as poor role models for cross-border collaboration—and were later asked to serve as coaches in the exchanges. Being anointed as a role model is a powerful motivator. So is placement on an enterprisewide task force such as E^2 or Vehovec's operating committee for marketing.

When Nixon revamped RBC's reward system, he recognized that employees took great pride in working for one of the largest, most profitable financial services firms in Canada, not to mention the most admired. He drew on this pride, which was deeply entrenched in the culture, and shared stories that he hoped would promote leadership behavior. For example, in one dialogue session, he told participants about a highly successful business builder who had been asked to leave the company because of his inability to pay attention to larger enterprise priorities. Nixon had attempted to help the executive shift his focus, but time after time, the employee made it clear that he was interested in serving his own clients and not helping RBC as a whole. In other words, he was a great moneymaker for the company but didn't demonstrate the organization's values. Such stories have sent the unambiguous signal that RBC is interested in growing leaders who are committed to managing both retail and wholesale priorities.

RBC doesn't try to formally assess the impact of the dialogues and exchanges. When asked, Nixon has said:

> Look, you either believe that developing leaders is important or you don't. There are so many variables that could be used to either make or break your argument for leadership development. We're not going to play that game. We firmly believe it's important to grow leaders who can run their businesses, their functions, and their regions, yet who can lead with an enterprisewide perspective. People make this business happen, and we will let our performance speak for the importance of developing leaders.

But even without a formal analysis, the picture looks promising: 154 of RBC's senior executives have participated in the dialogues (virtually all of its top 150, with the normal employee churn), and 477 managers have participated in the exchanges. All of the GMC members have acted as coaches for the dialogues multiple times.

What's more, 20% of RBC's high-potential senior executives are currently working on cross-platform/enterprise assignments; almost no one did this before the implementation of the dialogues. People are still allowed to grow in their silos, but then they are not considered to be high-potential enterprise leaders. And new products and services have emerged directly from the dialogues. RBC's Snowbird Package is one example. Roughly four million Canadians spend four months of the year in Florida and other parts of the southeastern coast of the United States to get away from the harsh Canadian winters. Participants in the dialogues created a seamless extension of services that could be offered through RBC's acquisition of Centura Banks in North Carolina, with branches that extend deep into Florida—services that cut across platforms to include retail banking, mortgages, insurance, and wealth management.

For many companies, implementing the sorts of remedies outlined in this article will be much harder than they expected, because the silo focus is so ingrained in their cultures. RBC certainly struggled at times and made some missteps. Nixon initially announced the cross-enterprise leverage strategy without communicating it broadly to the GMC. Then he faced the challenge of building ownership for a strategy he had already announced, rather than the opportunity of helping executives discover its value for themselves. He also, at first, didn't define what the cross-enterprise approach would mean to customers but instead essentially offered up pure "strategy as slogan." But he was able to get past these mistakes by engaging and communicating extensively with employees, cross-fertilizing talent across RBC's platform boundaries, and targeting rewards to shape behavior.

Competition has changed, as have customers' expectations. Leadership development has not kept pace. Many companies have created new organizational structures to accompany the need for a broader perspective on the business, but the vast majority of leadership development initiatives still take place in the very silos the organizations are trying to transform. When people are trapped in business units, functions, or regions, they're at risk of becoming prisoners of zero-sum thinking.

The responsibility for solving the problem rests primarily with a company's senior executives. Only they have their hands on all of the necessary levers of change. Top managers must work tirelessly to break down their silos and forge imaginative career paths. They must create robust venues for managers to openly discuss the tensions that are a natural by-product of managing complexity. They must realign reward systems and motivate managers to lead according to the realities of today's competitive environment. And they must acknowledge that there will be no easy answers and take decisive action instead of running from the ambiguity surrounding the challenge.

CASES

Case 1 Susan Munro, Service Consumer

CHRISTOPHER LOVELOCK

In the course of a single day, a busy young woman makes use of a wide array of services.

Susan Munro, a final-year business student, had worked late the night before on a big paper and overslept the following morning in the apartment she shared with three other students. Her roommates, who had early classes, had already left when she got up. After showering, she dressed hurriedly, then made a quick cup of coffee. But she skipped her usual bowl of cereal, figuring she could pick up a bagel at school.

Noticing that the weather outside looked ominous, she clicked onto the Internet to check the local weather forecast. It predicted rain, so she grabbed an umbrella before leaving the apartment and walking to the bus stop for her daily ride to the university. On the way, she dropped a letter in a mailbox. The bus arrived on schedule. It was the usual driver, who recognized her and gave a cheerful greeting as she showed her monthly pass. The bus was quite full, carrying a mix of students and office workers, so she had to stand.

Arriving at her destination, Susan left the bus and walked to the School of Business. Feeling hungry, she entered the main lobby and headed to the small, cheerfully decorated food stand in the far corner. "Sorry," said the attendant in answer to her question. "We just sold the last of the bagels and are waiting for more French Roast. Would you like decaf?" Susan sighed. It wasn't the first time this had happened. But the class was about to start and she couldn't wait.

Joining a crowd of other students, she took a seat in the large classroom where her finance class was held. The professor lectured in a near monotone for 75 minutes, occasionally projecting charts on a large screen to illustrate certain calculations. It didn't help that she was still feeling sleepy. Susan reflected that it would be just as effective—and far more convenient—if the course were transmitted over the Web or recorded on DVDs that students could watch at their leisure. She much preferred the marketing course that followed because this professor was a very dynamic individual who believed in having an active dialogue with the students. Susan made several contributions to the discussion and felt that she learned a lot from listening to others' analyses and opinions.

She and three friends ate lunch at the recently modernized Student Union. The old cafeteria, a gloomy place that served unappetizing food at high prices, had been replaced by a well-lit and colorfully painted new food court, featuring a variety of options. These included both local suppliers and brand-name fast-food chains, which offered choices of sandwiches, as well as ethnic foods, salads, and a variety of desserts. Although she had wanted a sandwich, the line of waiting customers at the sandwich shop was rather long, so Susan joined her friends at Burger King and then splurged on a caffe latte from the adjacent Hav-a-Java coffee stand. The food court was unusually crowded today, perhaps because of the rain now pouring down outside. When they finally found a table, they had to clear off the dirty trays. "Lazy slobs!" commented her friend Mark, referring to the previous customers.

After lunch, Susan stopped at an ATM, inserted her card, and withdrew some money. Remembering that she had a job interview at the end of the week, she telephoned her hairdresser and counted herself lucky to be able to make an appointment for later in the day because of a cancellation by another client. Leaving the Student Union, she ran across the rain-soaked plaza to the Language Department. In preparation for her next class, Business Spanish, she spent an hour in the language lab, watching an engaging video of customers making purchases at different types of stores, then repeating key phrases and listening to her own recorded voice. "My accent's definitely getting better!" she said to herself.

With her last class over and Spanish phrases filling her head, Susan headed off to visit the hairdresser. She liked the store, which had a bright, trendy decor and well-groomed, friendly staff. Unfortunately, the cutter was running late and Susan had to wait 20 minutes, which she used to review a chapter for tomorrow's human resources course. Some of the other waiting customers were reading magazines provided by the store. Eventually, it was time for a shampoo, after which the cutter proposed a slightly different cut. Susan agreed, although she drew the line at the suggestion to lighten her hair color. She sat very still, watching the process in the mirror and turning her head when requested. She was pleased with the result and complimented the cutter on her work.

Including the shampoo, the process had lasted about 40 minutes. She tipped the cutter and paid at the reception desk.

The rain had stopped and the sun was shining as Susan left the store, so she walked home, stopping to pick up clothes from the cleaners. This store was rather gloomy, smelled of cleaning solvents, and badly needed repainting. She was annoyed to find that although her silk blouse was ready as promised, the suit she would need for her interview was not. The assistant, who had dirty fingernails, mumbled an apology in an insincere tone without making eye contact. Although the store was convenient and the quality of work quite good, Susan considered the employees unfriendly and not very helpful.

Back at her apartment building, she opened the mailbox in the lobby and collected the mail for herself and her roommates. Her own mail, which was rather dull, included a quar-terly bill from her insurance company, which required no action since she had signed an agreement to deduct the funds automatically from her bank account. There was also a post-card from her optometrist, reminding her that it was time to schedule a new eye exam. Susan made a mental note to call for an appointment, anticipating that she might need a revised prescription for her contact lenses. She was about to discard the junk mail when she noticed a flyer promoting a new dry-cleaning store and including a coupon for a discount. She decided to try the new firm and pocketed the coupon.

Since it was her turn to cook dinner, she wandered into the kitchen, turned on the light, and started looking in the refrig-erator and then the cupboards to see what was available. Susan sighed—there wasn't much in there. Maybe she would make a salad and call for home delivery of a large pizza.

Study Questions

1. *Identify each of the services that Susan Munro has used or is planning to use. Categorize them according to the nature of the underlying process.*

2. *What needs is she attempting to satisfy in each instance?*

3. *What proportion of these services (a) involve self-service, (b) some degree of customer involvement with the production process, (c) dependence on the service provider? Where do you see more potential for self-service, and what would be the implications for customer and supplier?*

4. *What similarities and differences are there between the dry-cleaning store and the hair salon? What could each learn from studying the other?*

Case 2   Four Customers in Search of Solutions

CHRISTOPHER LOVELOCK

Four telephone subscribers from suburban Toronto call their telephone company to complain about a variety of problems. How should the company respond in each instance?

Among the many customers of Bell Canada in Toronto, Ontario, are four individuals living on Willow Street in a middle-class suburb of the city. Each of them has a telephone-related problem and decides to call the company about it.

WINSTON CHEN

Winston Chen grumbles constantly about the amount of his home telephone bill (which is, in fact, in the top 2% of all household phone bills in Ontario). There are many calls to countries in Southeast Asia on weekday evenings, almost daily calls to Kingston (a smaller city not far from Toronto) around mid-day, and calls to Vancouver, British Columbia, most weekends. One day, Mr. Chen receives a telephone bill which is even larger than usual. On reviewing the bill, he is convinced that he has been overcharged, so he calls the phone company to complain and request an adjustment.

MARIE PORTILLO

Marie Portillo has missed several important calls recently because the caller received a busy signal. She phones the customer service department to determine possible solutions to this problem. Ms. Portillo's telephone bill is at the median level for a household subscriber. (The median is the point at which 50% of all bills are higher and 50% are lower.) Most of the calls from her house are local, but there are occasional international calls to Mexico or to countries in South America. She does not subscribe to any value-added services.

ELEANOR VANDERBILT

During the past several weeks, Mrs. Vanderbilt has been distressed to receive a series of obscene telephone calls. It sounds like the same person each time. She calls the telephone company to see if they can put a stop to this harassment. Her phone bill is in the bottom 10% of all household subscriber bills and almost all calls are local.

RICHARD ROBBINS

For more than a week, the phone line at Rich Robbins' house has been making strange humming and crackling noises, making it difficult to hear what the other person is saying. After two of his friends comment on these distracting noises, Mr. Robbins calls to report the problem. His guess is that it is being caused by the answering machine, which is getting old and sometimes loses messages. Mr. Robbins' phone bill is at the 75th percentile for a household subscriber. Most calls are made to locations within Canada, usually at evenings and weekends, although there are a few calls to the U.S., too.

Study Questions

1. *Based strictly on the information in the case, how many possibilities do you see to segment the telecommunications market?*

2. *As a customer service rep, how would you address each of the problems and complaints reported?*

3. *As a marketing manager, do you see any marketing opportunities for the telephone company in these complaints?*

Case 3   Starbucks: Delivering Customer Service

YOUNGME MOON AND JOHN QUELCH

Starbucks, the dominant specialty-coffee brand in North America, must respond to recent market research indicating that the company is not meeting customer expectations in terms of service. To increase customer satisfaction, the company is debating a plan that would increase the amount of labor in its stores and theoretically increase speed-of-service. However, the impact of the plan (which would cost US$40 million annually) on the company's bottom line is unclear.

In mid-2002, Christine Day, Starbucks' senior vice president of administration in North America, sat in the seventh-floor conference room of Starbucks' Seattle headquarters and reached for her second cup of toffee nut latte. The handcrafted beverage—a buttery, toffee-nut flavored espresso concoction topped with whipped cream and toffee sprinkles—had become a regular afternoon indulgence for Day ever since its introduction earlier that year.

As she waited for her colleagues to join her, Day reflected on the company's recent performance. While other retailers were still reeling from the post-9/11 recession, Starbucks was enjoying its 11th consecutive year of 5% or higher comparable store sales growth, prompting its founder and chairman, Howard Schultz, to declare: "I think we've demonstrated that we are close to a recession-proof product."[1]

Day, however, was not feeling nearly as sanguine, in part because Starbucks' most recent market research had revealed some unexpected findings. "We've always taken great pride in our retail service," said Day, "but according to the data, we're not always meeting our customers' expectations in the area of customer satisfaction."

As a result of these concerns, Day and her associates had come up with a plan to invest an additional US$40 million annually in the company's 4,500 stores, which would allow each store to add the equivalent of 20 hours of labor a week. "The idea is to improve speed-of-service and thereby increase customer satisfaction," said Day.

In two days, Day was due to make a final recommendation to both Schultz and Orin Smith, Starbucks' CEO, about whether the company should move forward with the plan. "The investment is the EPS [earnings per share] equivalent of almost seven cents a share," said Day. In preparation for her meeting with Schultz and Smith, Day had asked one of her associates to help her think through the implications of the plan. Day noted, "The real question is, do we believe what our customers are telling us about what constitutes 'excellent' customer service? And if we deliver it, what will the impact be on our sales and profitability?"

COMPANY BACKGROUND

The story of how Howard Schultz managed to transform a commodity into an upscale cultural phenomenon had become the stuff of legends. In 1971, three coffee fanatics—Gerald Baldwin, Gordon Bowker, and Ziev Siegl—opened a small coffee shop in Seattle's Pike Place Market. The shop specialized in selling whole arabica beans to a niche market of coffee purists.

In 1982, Schultz joined the Starbucks marketing team; shortly thereafter, he traveled to Italy, where he became fascinated with Milan's coffee culture, in particular, the role the neighborhood espresso bars played in Italians' everyday social lives. Upon his return, the inspired Schultz convinced the company to set up an espresso bar in the corner of its only downtown Seattle shop. As Schultz explained, the bar became the prototype for his long-term vision:

> The idea was to create a chain of coffeehouses that would become America's "third place." At the time, most Americans had two places in their lives—home and work. But I believed that people needed another place, a place where they could go to relax and enjoy others, or just be by themselves. I envisioned a place that would be separate from home or work, a place that would mean different things to different people.

A few years later, Schultz got his chance when Starbucks' founders agreed to sell him the company. As soon as Schultz took over, he immediately began opening new stores. The stores sold whole beans and premium-priced coffee beverages by the cup and catered primarily to affluent, well-educated, white-collar patrons (skewed female) between the ages of 25 and 44. By 1992, the company had 140 such stores in the Northwest and Chicago and was successfully competing against other small-scale coffee chains such as Gloria Jean's Coffee Bean and Barnie's Coffee & Tea.

That same year, Schultz decided to take the company public. As he recalled, many Wall Street types were dubious about the idea: "They'd say, 'You mean, you're going to sell

---

Professors Youngme Moon and John Quelch prepared this case. HBS cases are developed solely as the basis for class discussion. Cases are not intended to serve as endorsements, sources of primary data, or illustrations of effective or ineffective management.

coffee for a dollar in a paper cup, with Italian names that no one in America can say? At a time in America when no one's drinking coffee? And I can get coffee at the local coffee shop or doughnut shop for 50 cents? Are you kidding me?'"[2]

Ignoring the skeptics, Schultz forged ahead with the public offering, raising US$25 million in the process. The proceeds allowed Starbucks to open more stores across the nation.

By mid-2002, Schultz had unequivocally established Starbucks as the dominant specialty-coffee brand in North America. Sales had climbed at a compound annual growth rate (CAGR) of 40% since the company had gone public, and net earnings had risen at a CAGR of 50%. The company was now serving 20 million unique customers in well over 5,000 stores around the globe and was opening on average three new stores a day. (**See Exhibits 1–3** for company financials and store growth over time.)

What made Starbucks' success even more impressive was that the company had spent almost nothing on advertising to achieve it. North American marketing primarily consisted of point-of-sale materials and local-store marketing and was far less than the industry average. (Most fast-food chains had marketing budgets in the 3%–6% range.)

For his part, Schultz remained as chairman and chief global strategist in control of the company, handing over day-to-day operations in 2002 to CEO Orin Smith, a Harvard MBA (1967) who had joined the company in 1990.

THE STARBUCKS VALUE PROPOSITION

Starbucks' brand strategy was best captured by its "live coffee" mantra, a phrase that reflected the importance the company attached to keeping the national coffee culture alive. From a retail perspective, this meant creating an "experience" around the consumption of coffee, an experience that people could weave into the fabric of their everyday lives.

There were three components to this experiential branding strategy. The first component was the coffee itself. Starbucks prided itself on offering what it believed to be the highest-quality coffee in the world, sourced from the Africa, Central and South America, and Asia-Pacific regions. To enforce its exacting coffee standards, Starbucks controlled as much of the supply chain as possible—it worked directly with growers in various countries of origin to purchase green coffee beans, it oversaw the custom-roasting process for the company's various blends and single-origin coffees, and it controlled distribution to retail stores around the world.

The second brand component was service, or what the company sometimes referred to as "customer intimacy." "Our goal is to create an uplifting experience every time you walk through our door," explained Jim Alling, Starbucks' senior vice president of North American retail. "Our most loyal customers visit us as often as 18 times a month, so it

Exhibit 1 Starbucks' Financials, FY 1998 to FY 2002 (US$ in millions)

	FY 1998	FY 1999	FY 2000	FY 2001	FY 2002
Revenue					
Co-Owned North American	1,076.8	1,375.0	1,734.9	2,086.4	2,583.8
Co-Owned Int'l (UK, Thailand, Australia)	25.8	48.4	88.7	143.2	209.1
Total Company-Operated Retail	1,102.6	1,423.4	1,823.6	2,229.6	2,792.9
Specialty Operations	206.1	263.4	354.0	419.4	496.0
Net Revenues	**1,308.7**	**1,686.8**	**2,177.6**	**2,649.0**	**3,288.9**
Cost of Goods Sold	578.5	747.6	961.9	1,112.8	1,350.0
Gross Profit	**730.2**	**939.2**	**1,215.7**	**1,536.2**	**1,938.9**
Joint-Venture Income[a]	1.0	3.2	20.3	28.6	35.8
Expenses					
Store Operating Expense	418.5	543.6	704.9	875.5	1,121.1
Other Operating Expense	44.5	54.6	78.4	93.3	127.2
Depreciation & Amortization Expense	72.5	97.8	130.2	163.5	205.6
General & Admin Expense	77.6	89.7	110.2	151.4	202.1
Operating Expenses	**613.1**	**785.7**	**1,023.8**	**1,283.7**	**1,656.0**
Operating Profit	**109.2**	**156.7**	**212.3**	**281.1**	**310.0**
Net Income	**68.4**	**101.7**	**94.5**	**181.2**	**215.1**
% Change in Monthly Comparable Store Sales[b]					
North America	5%	6%	9%	5%	7%
Consolidated	5%	6%	9%	5%	6%

Source: Adapted from company reports and Lehman Brothers, November 5, 2002.

[a]Includes income from various joint ventures, including Starbucks' partnership with the Pepsi-Cola Company to develop and distribute Frappuccino and with Dreyer's Grand Ice Cream to develop and distribute premium ice creams.

[b]Includes only company-operated stores open 13 months or longer.

Exhibit 2 Starbucks' Store Growth

	FY 1998	FY 1999	FY 2000	FY 2001	FY 2002
Total North America	**1,755**	**2,217**	**2,976**	**3,780**	**4,574**
Company-Operated	1,622	2,038	2,446	2,971	3,496
Licensed Stores[a]	133	179	530	809	1,078
Total International	**131**	**281**	**525**	**929**	**1,312**
Company-Operated	66	97	173	295	384
Licensed Stores	65	184	352	634	928
Total Stores	**1,886**	**2,498**	**3,501**	**4,709**	**5,886**

Source: Company reports.

[a]Includes kiosks located in grocery stores, bookstores, hotels, airports, and so on.

could be something as simple as recognizing you and knowing your drink or customizing your drink just the way you like it."

The third brand component was atmosphere. "People come for the coffee," explained Day, "but the ambience is what makes them want to stay." For that reason, most Starbucks had seating areas to encourage lounging and layouts that were designed to provide an upscale yet inviting environment for those who wanted to linger. "What we have built has universal appeal," remarked Schultz. "It's based on the human spirit, it's based on a sense of community, the need for people to come together."[3]

Channels of Distribution

Almost all of Starbucks' locations in North America were company-operated stores located in high-traffic, high-visibility settings such as retail centers, office buildings, and university campuses.[4] In addition to selling whole-bean coffees, these stores sold rich-brewed coffees, Italian-style espresso drinks, cold-blended beverages, and premium teas. Product mixes tended to vary depending on a store's size and location, but most stores offered a variety of pastries, sodas, and juices, along with coffee-related accessories and equipment, music CDs, games, and seasonal novelty items. (About 500 stores even carried a selection of sandwiches and salads.)

Beverages accounted for the largest percentage of sales in these stores (77%); this represented a change from 10 years earlier, when about half of store revenues had come from sales of whole-bean coffees. (**See Exhibit 4** for retail sales mix by product type; **see Exhibit 5** for a typical menu board and price list.)

Starbucks also sold coffee products through non-company-operated retail channels; these so-called "Specialty Operations" accounted for 15% of net revenues. About 27% of these revenues came from North American food-service accounts, that is, sales of whole-bean and ground coffees to hotels, airlines, restaurants, and the like. Another 18% came from domestic retail store licenses that, in North America, were only granted when there was no other way to achieve access to desirable retail space (e.g., in airports).

The remaining 55% of specialty revenues came from a variety of sources, including international licensed stores, grocery stores and warehouse clubs (Kraft Foods handled marketing and distribution for Starbucks in this channel), and online and mail-order sales. Starbucks also had a joint venture with Pepsi-Cola to distribute bottled Frappuccino beverages in North America, as well as a partnership with Dreyer's Grand Ice Cream to develop and distribute a line of premium ice creams.

Day explained the company's broad distribution strategy:

Our philosophy is pretty straightforward—we want to reach customers where they work, travel, shop, and dine. In order to do this, we sometimes have to establish relationships with third parties that share our values and commitment to quality. This is a particularly effective way to reach newcomers with our brand. It's a lot less intimidating to buy Starbucks at a grocery store than it is to walk into one of our coffeehouses for the first time. In fact, about 40% of our new coffeehouse customers have already tried the Starbucks brand before they walk through our doors. Even something like ice cream has become an important trial vehicle for us.

Exhibit 3 Additional Data, North American Company-Operated Stores (FY2002)

	AVERAGE
Average hourly rate with shift supervisors and hourly partners US	US$ 9.00
Total labor hours per week, average store	360
Average weekly store volume US	US$15,400
Average ticket	US$3.85
Average daily customer count, per store	570

Source: Company reports.

Exhibit 4 Product Mix, North American Company-Operated Stores (FY2002)

	PERCENT OF SALES
Retail Product Mix	
Coffee Beverages	77%
Food Items	13%
Whole-Bean Coffees	6%
Equipment & Accessories	4%

Source: Company reports.

Espresso Traditions	Tall	Grande	Venti
Classic Favorites			
Toffee Nut Latte	2.95	3.50	3.80
Vanilla Latte	2.85	3.40	3.70
Caffe Latte	2.55	3.10	3.40
Cappuccino	2.55	3.10	3.40
Caramel Macchiato	2.80	3.40	3.65
White Chocolate Mocha	3.20	3.75	4.00
Caffe Mocha	2.75	3.30	3.55
Caffe Americano	1.75	2.05	2.40

Espresso	Solo		Doppio
Espresso	1.45		1.75

Extras			
Additional Espresso Shot			.55
Add flavored syrup			.30
Organic milk & soy available upon request			

Frappuccino	Tall	Grande	Venti
Ice Blended Beverages			
Coffee	2.65	3.15	3.65
Mocha	2.90	3.40	3.90
Caramel Frappuccino	3.15	3.65	4.15
Mocha Coconut (limited offering)	3.15	3.65	4.15

Crème Frappuccino	Tall	Grande	Venti
Ice Blended Crème			
Toffee Nut Crème	3.15	3.65	4.15
Vanilla Crème	2.65	3.15	3.65
Coconut Crème	3.15	3.65	4.15

Tazo Tea Frappuccino	Tall	Grande	Venti
Ice Blended Teas			
Tazo Citrus	2.90	3.40	3.90
Tazoberry	2.90	3.40	3.90
Tazo Chai Crème	3.15	3.65	4.15

Brewed Coffee	Tall	Grande	Venti
Coffee of the Day	1.40	1.60	1.70
Decaf of the Day	1.40	1.60	1.70

Cold Beverages	Tall	Grande	Venti
Iced Caffe Latte	2.55	3.10	3.50
Iced Caramel Macchiato	2.80	3.40	3.80
Iced Caffe Americano	1.75	2.05	3.40

Coffee Alternatives	Tall	Grande	Venti
Toffee Nut Crème	2.45	2.70	2.95
Vanilla Crème	2.20	2.45	2.70
Caramel Apple Cider	2.45	2.70	2.95
Hot Chocolate	2.20	2.45	2.70
Tazo Hot Tea	1.15	1.65	1.65
Tazo Chai	2.70	3.10	3.35

Whole Beans: Bold	1/2 lb	1 lb
Our most intriguing and exotic coffees		
Gold Coast Blend	5.70	10.95
French Roast	5.20	9.95
Sumatra	5.30	10.15
Decaf Sumatra	5.60	10.65
Ethiopia Sidame	5.20	9.95
Arabian Mocha Sanani	8.30	15.95
Kenya	5.30	10.15
Italian Roast	5.20	9.95
Sulawesi	6.10	11.65

Whole Beans: Smooth	1/2 lb	1 lb
Richer, more flavorful coffees		
Espresso Roast	5.20	9.95
Decaf Espresso Roast	5.60	10.65
Yukon Blend	5.20	9.95
Café Verona	5.20	9.95
Guatemala Antigua	5.30	10.15
Arabian Mocha Java	6.30	11.95
Decaf Mocha Java/SWP	6.50	12.45

Whole Beans: Mild	1/2 lb	1 lb
The perfect introduction to Starbucks coffees		
Breakfast Blend	5.20	9.95
Lightnote Blend	5.20	9.95
Decaf Lightnote Blend	5.60	10.65
Colombia Narino	5.50	10.45
House Blend	5.20	9.95
Decaf House Blend	5.60	10.65
Fair Trade Coffee	5.95	11.45

Source: Starbucks location: Harvard Square, Cambridge, Massachusetts, February 2003.

Starbucks Partners

All Starbucks employees were called "partners." The company employed 60,000 partners worldwide, about 50,000 in North America. Most were hourly-wage employees (called baristas) who worked in Starbucks retail stores. Alling remarked, "From day one, Howard has made clear his belief that partner satis-

faction leads to customer satisfaction. This belief is part of Howard's DNA, and because it's been pounded into each and every one of us, it's become part of our DNA too."

The company had a generous policy of giving health insurance and stock options to even the most entry-level partners, most of whom were between the ages of 17 and 23. Partly as a result of this, Starbucks' partner satisfaction rate consistently hovered in the 80% to 90% range, well above the industry norm,[5] and the company had recently been ranked 47th in the Fortune magazine list of best places to work, quite an accomplishment for a company with so many hourly-wage workers.

In addition, Starbucks had one of the lowest employee turnover rates in the industry—just 70%, compared with fast-food industry averages as high as 300%. The rate was even lower for managers, and as Alling noted, the company was always looking for ways to bring turnover down further: "Whenever we have a problem store, we almost always find either an inexperienced store manager or inexperienced baristas. Manager stability is key—it not only decreases partner turnover, but it also enables the store to do a much better job of recognizing regular customers and providing personalized service. So our goal is to make the position a lifetime job."

To this end, the company encouraged promotion from within its own ranks. About 70% of the company's store managers were ex-baristas, and about 60% of its district managers were ex-store managers. In fact, upon being hired, all senior executives had to train and succeed as baristas before being allowed to assume their positions in corporate headquarters.

DELIVERING ON SERVICE

When a partner was hired to work in one of Starbucks' North American retail stores, he or she had to undergo two types of training. The first type focused on "hard skills" such as learning how to use the cash register and learning how to mix drinks. Most Starbucks beverages were handcrafted, and to ensure product quality, there was a prespecified process associated with each drink. Making an espresso beverage, for example, required seven specific steps.

The other type of training focused on "soft skills." Alling explained:

> In our training manual, we explicitly teach partners to connect with customers—to enthusiastically welcome them to the store, to establish eye contact, to smile, and to try to remember their names and orders if they're regulars. We also encourage partners to create conversations with customers using questions that require more than a yes or no answer. So for example, "I noticed you were looking at the menu board—what types of beverages do you typically enjoy?" is a good question for a partner to ask.

Starbucks' "Just Say Yes" policy empowered partners to provide the best service possible, even if it required going beyond company rules. "This means that if a customer spills a drink and asks for a refill, we'll give it to him," said Day. "Or if a customer doesn't have cash and wants to pay with a check (which we aren't supposed to accept), then we'll give her a sample drink for free. The last thing we want to do is win the argument and lose the customer."

Most barista turnover occurred within the first 90 days of employment; if a barista lasted beyond that, there was a high probability that he or she would stay for three years or more. "Our training ends up being a self-selection process," Alling said. Indeed, the ability to balance hard and soft skills required a particular type of person, and Alling believed the challenges had only grown over time:

> Back in the days when we sold mostly beans, every customer who walked in the door was a coffee connoisseur, and it was easy for baristas to engage in chitchat while ringing up a bag. Those days are long gone. Today, almost every customer orders a handcrafted beverage. If the line is stretching out the door and everyone's clamoring for their coffee fix, it's not that easy to strike up a conversation with a customer.

The complexity of the barista's job had also increased over time; making a *venti tazoberry and crème*, for instance, required 10 different steps. "It used to be that a barista could make every variation of drink we offered in half a day," Day observed. "Nowadays, given our product proliferation, it would take 16 days of eight-hour shifts. There are literally hundreds of combinations of drinks in our portfolio."

This job complexity was compounded by the fact that almost half of Starbucks' customers customized their drinks. According to Day, this created a tension between product quality and customer focus for Starbucks:

> On the one hand, we train baristas to make beverages to our preestablished quality standards—this means enforcing a consistent process that baristas can master. On the other hand, if a customer comes in and wants it their way—extra vanilla, for instance—what should we do? Our heaviest users are always the most demanding. Of course, every time we customize, we slow down the service for everyone else. We also put a lot of strain on our baristas, who are already dealing with an extraordinary number of sophisticated drinks.

One obvious solution to the problem was to hire more baristas to share the workload; however, the company had been extremely reluctant to do this in recent years, particularly given the economic downturn. Labor was already the company's largest expense item in North America (see **Exhibit 3**), and Starbucks stores tended to be located in urban areas with high wage rates. Instead, the company had focused on increasing barista efficiency by removing all non-value-added tasks, simplifying the beverage production process, and tinkering with the facility design to eliminate bottlenecks.

In addition, the company had recently begun installing automated espresso machines in its North American cafés. The verismo machines, which decreased the number of steps required to make an espresso beverage, reduced waste, improved consistency, and had generated an overwhelmingly positive customer and barista response.

Measuring Service Performance

Starbucks tracked service performance using a variety of metrics, including monthly status reports and self-reported checklists. The company's most prominent measurement tool was a mystery shopper program called the "Customer Snapshot." Under this program, every store was visited by an anonymous mystery shopper three times a quarter. Upon completing the visit, the shopper would rate the store on four "Basic Service" criteria:

- Service—Did the register partner verbally greet the customer? Did the barista and register partner make eye contact with the customer? Say thank you?
- Cleanliness—Was the store clean? The counters? The tables? The restrooms?
- Product quality—Was the order filled accurately? Was the temperature of the drink within range? Was the beverage properly presented?
- Speed of service—How long did the customer have to wait? The company's goal was to serve a customer within three minutes, from back-of-the-line to drink-in-hand. This benchmark was based on market research which indicated that the three-minute standard was a key component in how current Starbucks customers defined "excellent service."

In addition to Basic Service, stores were also rated on "Legendary Service," which was defined as "behavior that created a memorable experience for a customer, that inspired a customer to return often and tell a friend." Legendary Service scores were based on secret shopper observations of service attributes such as partners initiating conversations with customers, partners recognizing customers by name or drink order, and partners being responsive to service problems.

During 2002, the company's Customer Snapshot scores had increased across all stores (**see Exhibit 7**), leading Day to comment, "The Snapshot is not a perfect measurement tool, but we believe it does a good job of measuring trends over the course of a quarter. In order for a store to do well on the Snapshot, it needs to have sustainable processes in place that create a well-established pattern of doing things right so that it gets 'caught' doing things right."

COMPETITION

In the United States, Starbucks competed against a variety of small-scale specialty coffee chains, most of which were regionally concentrated. Each tried to differentiate itself from Starbucks in a different way. For example, Minneapolis-based Caribou Coffee, which operated more than 200 stores in nine states, differentiated itself on store environment. Rather than offer an upscale, pseudo-European atmosphere, its strategy was to simulate the look and feel of an Alaskan lodge, with knotty-pine cabinetry, fireplaces, and soft seating. Another example was California-based Peet's Coffee & Tea, which operated about 70 stores in five states. More than 60% of Peet's revenues came from the sale of whole beans. Peet's strategy was to build a super-premium brand by offering the freshest coffee on the market. One of the ways it delivered on this promise was by "roasting to order," that is, by hand roasting small batches of coffee at its California plant and making sure that all of its coffee shipped within 24 hours of roasting.

Starbucks also competed against thousands of independent specialty coffee shops. Some of these independent coffee shops offered a wide range of food and beverages, including beer, wine, and liquor; others offered satellite televisions or Internet-connected computers. Still others differentiated themselves by delivering highly personalized service to an eclectic clientele.

Finally, Starbucks competed against donut and bagel chains such as Dunkin Donuts, which operated over 3,700 stores in 38 states. Dunkin Donuts attributed half of its sales to coffee and in recent years had begun offering flavored coffee and noncoffee alternatives, such as Dunkaccino (a coffee and chocolate combination available with various toppings) and Vanilla Chai (a combination of tea, vanilla, honey, and spices).

CAFFEINATING THE WORLD

The company's overall objective was to establish Starbucks as the "most recognized and respected brand in the world."[6] This ambitious goal required an aggressive growth strategy, and in 2002, the two biggest drivers of company growth were retail expansion and product innovation.

Retail Expansion

Starbucks already owned close to one-third of America's coffee bars, more than its next five biggest competitors combined. (By comparison, the U.S.'s second-largest player, Diedrich Coffee, operated fewer than 400 stores.) However, the company had plans to open 525 company-operated and 225 licensed North American stores in 2003, and Schultz believed that there was no reason North America could not eventually expand to at least 10,000 stores. As he put it, "These are still the early days of the company's growth."[7]

The company's optimistic growth plans were based on a number of considerations:

- First, coffee consumption was on the rise in the United States, following years of decline. More than 109 million people (about half of the U.S. population) now drank coffee every day, and an additional 52 million drank it on occasion. The market's biggest growth appeared to be among drinkers of specialty coffee,[8] and it was estimated that about one-third of all U.S. coffee consumption took place outside of the home, in places such as offices, restaurants, and coffee shops. (**See Exhibit 6.**)
- Second, there were still eight states in the United States without a single company-operated Starbucks; in fact, the company was only in 150 of the roughly 300 metropolitan statistical areas in the nation.
- Third, the company believed it was far from reaching saturation levels in many existing markets. In the Southeast, for example, there was only one store for every 110,000 people (compared with one store for every 20,000 people in the Pacific Northwest). More generally, only seven states had more than 100 Starbucks locations.

Starbucks' strategy for expanding its retail business was to open stores in new markets while geographically clustering stores in existing markets. Although the latter often resulted in significant cannibalization, the company believed that this was more than offset by the total incremental sales associated with the increased store concentration. As Schultz readily conceded, "We self-cannibalize at least a third of our stores every day."[9]

When it came to selecting new retail sites, the company considered a number of criteria, including the extent to which the demographics of the area matched the profile of the typical Starbucks drinker, the level of coffee consumption in the area, the nature and intensity of competition in the local market, and the availability of attractive real estate. Once a decision was made to move forward with a site, the company was capable of designing, permitting, constructing, and opening a new store within 16 weeks. A new store typically averaged about US$610,000 in sales during its first year; same-store sales (comps) were strongest in the first three years and then continued to comp positively, consistent with the company average.

Starbucks' international expansion plans were equally ambitious. Starbucks already operated over 300 company-owned stores in the United Kingdom, Australia, and Thailand, in addition to about 900 licensed stores in various countries in Asia, Europe, the Middle East, Africa, and Latin America. (Its largest international market was Japan, with close to 400 stores.) The company's goal was to ultimately have 15,000 international stores.

Product Innovation

The second big driver of company growth was product innovation. Internally, this was considered one of the most significant factors in comparable store sales growth, particularly since Starbucks' prices had remained relatively stable in recent years. New products were launched on a regular basis; for example, Starbucks introduced at least one new hot beverage every holiday season.

The new product development process generally operated on a 12- to 18-month cycle, during which the internal research and development (R&D) team tinkered with product formulations, ran focus groups, and conducted in-store

Exhibit 6 Total U.S. Retail Coffee Market (includes both in-home and out-of-home consumption)

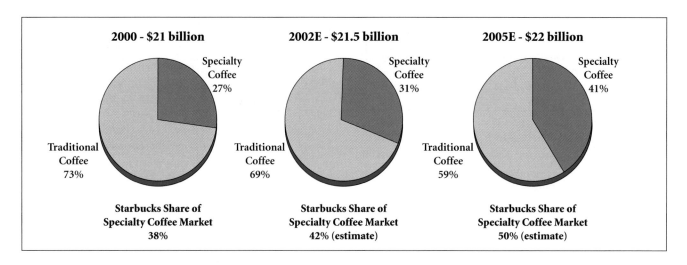

Other estimates[a] for the U.S. retail coffee market in 2002:

- In the home, specialty coffee[b] was estimated to be a US$3.2 billion business, of which Starbucks was estimated to have a 4% share.
- In the food-service channel, specialty coffee was estimated to be a US$5 billion business, of which Starbucks was estimated to have a 5% share.
- In grocery stores, Starbucks was estimated to have a 7.3% share in the ground-coffee category and a 21.7% share in the whole-beans category.
- It was estimated that over the next several years, the overall retail market would grow less than 1% per annum, but growth in the specialty-coffee category would be strong, with compound annual growth rate (CAGR) of 9% to 10%.
- Starbucks' U.S. business was projected to grow at a CAGR of approximately 20% top-line revenue growth.

Source: Adapted from company reports and Lehman Brothers, November 5, 2002.

[a]The value of the retail coffee market was difficult to estimate given the highly fragmented and loosely monitored nature of the market (i.e., specialty coffeehouses, restaurants, delis, kiosks, street carts, grocery and convenience stores, vending machines, etc.).

[b]Specialty coffee includes espresso, cappuccino, latte, café mocha, iced/ice-blended coffee, gourmet coffee (premium whole bean or ground), and blended coffee.

Exhibit 7   Customer Snapshot Scores (North American stores)

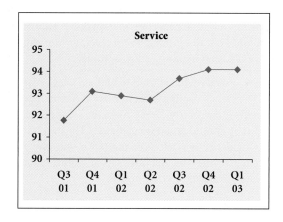

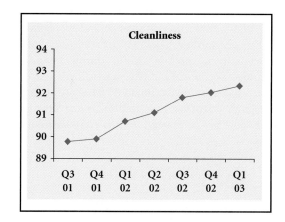

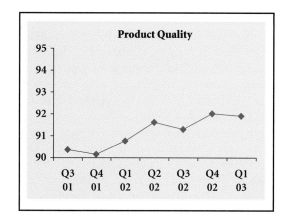

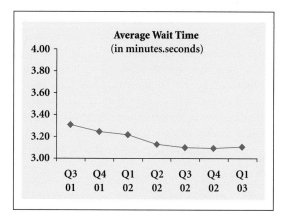

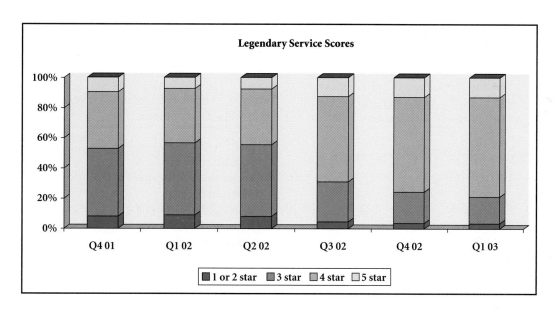

Source: Company information.

experiments and market tests. Aside from consumer acceptance, whether a product made it to market depended on a number of factors, including the extent to which the drink fit into the "ergonomic flow" of operations and the speed with which the beverage could be handcrafted. Most importantly, the success of a new beverage depended on partner acceptance.

"We've learned that no matter how great a drink it is, if our partners aren't excited about it, it won't sell," said Alling.

In recent years, the company's most successful innovation had been the 1995 introduction of a coffee and non-coffee-based line of Frappuccino beverages, which had driven same-store sales primarily by boosting traffic during nonpeak hours. The bottled version of the beverage (distributed by PepsiCo) had become a US$400 million[10] franchise; it had managed to capture 90% of the ready-to-drink coffee category, in large part due to its appeal to non-coffee-drinking 20-somethings.

SERVICE INNOVATION

In terms of nonproduct innovation, Starbucks' stored-value card (SVC) had been launched in November 2001. This prepaid, swipeable smart card—which Schultz referred to as "the most significant product introduction since Frappuccino"[11]—could be used to pay for transactions in any company-operated store in North America. Early indications of the SVC's appeal were very positive: After less than one year on the market, about 6 million cards had been issued, and initial activations and reloads had already reached US$160 million in sales. In surveys, the company had learned that cardholders tended to visit Starbucks twice as often as cash customers and tended to experience reduced transaction times.

Day remarked, "We've found that a lot of the cards are being given away as gifts, and many of those gift recipients are being introduced to our brand for the first time. Not to mention the fact that the cards allow us to collect all kinds of customer-transaction data, data that we haven't even begun to do anything with yet."

The company's latest service innovation was its T-Mobile HotSpot wireless Internet service, which it planned to introduce in August 2002. The service would offer high-speed access to the Internet in 2,000 Starbucks stores in the United States and Europe, starting at US$49.99 a month.

STARBUCKS' MARKET RESEARCH: TROUBLE BREWING?

Interestingly, although Starbucks was considered one of the world's most effective marketing organizations, it lacked a strategic marketing group. In fact, the company had no chief marketing officer, and its marketing department functioned as three separate groups—a market research group that gathered and analyzed market data requested by the various business units, a category group that developed new products and managed the menu and margins, and a marketing group that developed the quarterly promotional plans.

This organizational structure forced all of Starbucks' senior executives to assume marketing-related responsibilities. As Day pointed out, "Marketing is everywhere at Starbucks—it just doesn't necessarily show up in a line item called 'marketing.' Everyone has to get involved in a collaborative marketing effort." However, the organizational structure also meant that market- and customer-related trends could sometimes be overlooked. "We tend to be great at measuring things, at collecting market data," Day noted, "but we are not very disciplined when it comes to using this data to drive decision making." She continued:

This is exactly what started to happen a few years ago. We had evidence coming in from market research that contradicted some of the fundamental assumptions we had about our brand and our customers. The problem was that this evidence was all over the place—no one was really looking at the "big picture." As a result, it took awhile before we started to take notice.

Starbucks' Brand Meaning

Once the team did take notice, it discovered several things. First, despite Starbucks' overwhelming presence and convenience, there was very little image or product differentiation between Starbucks and the smaller coffee chains (other than Starbucks' ubiquity) in the minds of specialty coffeehouse customers. There was significant differentiation, however, between Starbucks and the independent specialty coffeehouses (see Table A below).

More generally, the market research team discovered that Starbucks' brand image had some rough edges. The number of respondents who strongly agreed with the statement "Starbucks cares primarily about making money" was up from 53% in 2000 to 61% in 2001, while the number of respondents who strongly agreed with the statement "Starbucks cares primarily about building more stores" was up from 48% to 55%. Day noted, "It's become apparent that we need to ask ourselves, 'Are we focusing on the right things? Are we clearly communicating our value to our customers, instead of just our growth plans?'" (see Table B on the next page).

Table A Qualitative Brand Meaning: Independents vs. Starbucks

Independents:
- Social and inclusive
- Diverse and intellectual
- Artsy and funky
- Liberal and free-spirited
- Lingering encouraged
- Particularly appealing to younger coffeehouse customers
- Somewhat intimidating to older, more mainstream coffeehouse customers

Starbucks:
- Everywhere—the trend
- Good coffee on the run
- Place to meet and move on
- Convenience oriented; on the way to work
- Accessible and consistent

Source: Starbucks, based on qualitative interviews with specialty-coffeehouse customers.

Table B The Top Five Attributes Consumers Associate with the Starbucks Brand

- Known for specialty/gourmet coffee (54% strongly agree)
- Widely available (43% strongly agree)
- Corporate (42% strongly agree)
- Trendy (41% strongly agree)
- Always feel welcome at Starbucks (39% strongly agree)

Source: Starbucks, based on 2002 survey.

The Changing Customer

The market research team also discovered that Starbucks' customer base was evolving. Starbucks' newer customers tended to be younger, less well-educated, and in a lower income bracket than Starbucks' more established customers. In addition, they visited the stores less frequently and had very different perceptions of the Starbucks brand compared to more established customers (**see Exhibit 8**).

Furthermore, the team learned that Starbucks' historical customer profile—the affluent, well-educated, white-collar female between the ages of 24 and 44—had expanded. For example, about half of the stores in southern California had large numbers of Hispanic customers. In Florida, the company had stores that catered primarily to Cuban-Americans.

Customer Behavior

With respect to customer behavior, the market research team discovered that, regardless of the market—urban versus rural, new versus established—customers tended to use the stores the same way. The team also learned that, although the company's most frequent customers averaged 18 visits a month, the typical customer visited just five times a month (**see Figure A**).

Exhibit 8 Starbucks' Customer Retention Information

% of Starbucks' customers who first started visiting Starbucks . . .	
In the past year	27%
1–2 years ago	20%
2–5 years ago	30%
5 or more years ago	23%

Source: Starbucks, 2002. Based on a sample of Starbucks' 2002 customer base.

	New Customers (First Visited in past year)	Estimated Customers (First Visited 5 + years ago)
Percent female	45%	49%
Average Age	36	40
Percent with College Degree +	37%	63%
Average income	US$65,000	US$81,000
Average # cups of coffee/week (includes at home and away from home)	15	19
Attitudes toward Starbucks:		
High-quality brand	34%	51%
Brand I trust	30%	50%
For someone like me	15%	40%
Worth paying more for	8%	32%
Known for specialty coffee	44%	60%
Known as the coffee expert	31%	45%
Best-tasting coffee	20%	31%
Highest-quality coffee	26%	41%
Overall opinion of Starbucks	**25%**	**44%**

Source: Starbucks, 2002. "Attitudes toward Starbucks" measured according to the percent of customers who agreed with the above statements.

Figure A Customer Visit Frequency

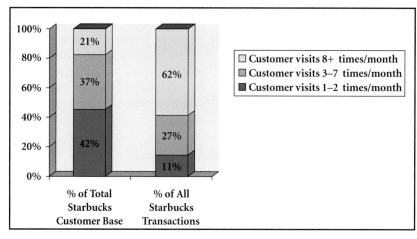

Source: Starbucks, 2002.

Measuring and Driving Customer Satisfaction

Finally, the team discovered that, despite its high Customer Snapshot scores, Starbucks was not meeting expectations in terms of customer satisfaction. The satisfaction scores were considered critical because the team also had evidence of a direct link between satisfaction level and customer loyalty (**see Exhibit 9** for customer satisfaction data).

While customer satisfaction was driven by a number of different factors (**see Exhibit 10**), Day believed that the customer satisfaction gap could primarily be attributed to a service gap between Starbucks scores on key attributes and customer expectations. When Starbucks had polled its customers to determine what it could do to make them feel more like valued customers, "improvements to service"—in particular, speed-of-service—had been mentioned most frequently (**see Exhibit 11** for more information).

REDISCOVERING THE STARBUCKS CUSTOMER

Responding to the market research findings posed a difficult management challenge. The most controversial proposal was the one on the table before Day—it involved relaxing the labor-hour controls in the stores to add an additional 20 hours of labor, per week, per store, at a cost of an extra US$40 million per year. Not surprisingly, the plan was being met with significant internal resistance. "Our CFO is understandably concerned about the potential impact on our bottom line," said Day. "Each [US]$6 million in profit contribution translates into a penny a share. But my argument is that if we move away from seeing labor as an expense to seeing it as a customer-oriented investment, we'll see a positive return." She continued:

> We need to bring service time down to the three-minute level in all of our stores, regardless of the time of day. If we do this, we'll not only increase customer satisfaction and build stronger long-term relationships with our customers, we'll also improve our customer throughput. The goal is to move each store closer to the [US]$20,000 level in terms of weekly sales, and I think that this plan will help us get there.

In two days, Day was scheduled to make a final recommendation to Howard Schultz and Orin Smith about whether the company should roll out the US$40 million plan in October 2002. In preparation for this meeting, Day had asked Alling to help her think through the implications of the plan one final time. She mused:

Exhibit 9 Starbucks' Customer Behavior, by Satisfaction Level

	Unsatisfied Customer	Satisfied Customer	Highly Satisfied Customer
Number of Starbucks Visits/Month	3.9	4.3	7.2
Average Ticket Size/Visit	US$3.88	US$4.06	US$4.42
Average Customer Life (Years)	1.1	4.4	8.3

Source: Self-reported customer activity from Starbucks survey, 2002.

To be read: *83% of Starbucks' customers rate a clean store as being highly important (90+ on a 100-point scale) in creating customer satisfaction.*

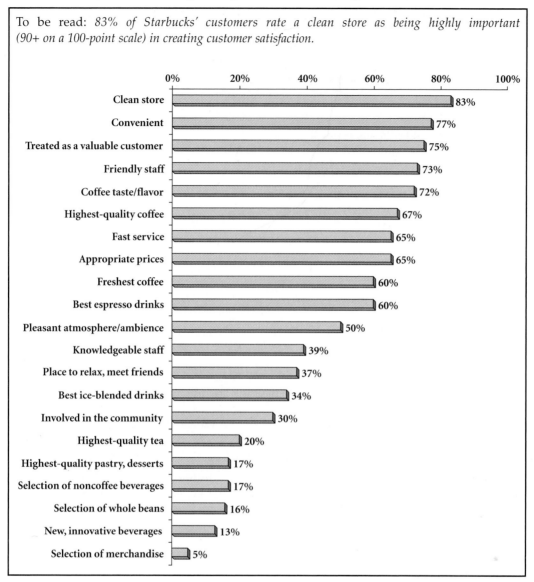

Source: Self-reported customer activity from Starbucks survey, 2002.

We've been operating with the assumption that we do customer service well. But the reality is, we've started to lose sight of the consumer. It's amazing that this could happen to a company like us—after all, we've become one of the most prominent consumer brands in the world. For all of our focus on building the brand and introducing new products, we've simply stopped talking about the customer. We've lost the connection between satisfying our customers and growing the business.

Alling's response was simple: "We know that both Howard and Orin are totally committed to satisfying our retail customers. Our challenge is to tie customer satisfaction to the bottom line. What evidence do we have?"

Exhibit 11   Factors Driving "Valued Customer" Perceptions

How could Starbucks Make you feel more like a valued customer?`	% Response
Friendlier, more attentive staff	19%
Faster, more efficient service	10%
Personal treatment (remember my name, remember my order)	4%
More knowledgeable staff	4%
Better service	2%
Offer Better Prices/Incentive Programs (total)	**31%**
Free cup after X number of visits	19%
Reduce prices	11%
Offer promotions, specials	3%
Other (total)	**21%**
Better quality/Variety of products	9%
Improve atmosphere	8%
Community outreach/Charity	2%
More stores/More convenient locations	2%
Don't Know/Already Satisfied	**28%**

Source: Starbucks, 2002. Based on a survey of Starbucks' 2002 customer base, including highly satisfied, satisfied, and unsatisfied customers.

Endnotes

1. Jake Batsell, "A Grande Decade for Starbucks," *The Seattle Times*, June 26, 2002.
2. Batsell.
3. Batsell.
4. Starbucks had recently begun experimenting with drive-throughs. Less than 10% of its stores had drive-throughs, but in these stores, the drive-throughs accounted for 50% of all business.
5. Industrywide, employee satisfaction rates tended to be in the 50% to 60% range. *Source:* Starbucks, 2000.
6. Starbucks 2002 Annual Report.
7. Dina ElBoghdady, "Pouring It On: The Starbucks Strategy? Locations, Locations, Locations," *The Washington Post*, August 25, 2002.
8. National Coffee Association.
9. ElBoghdady.
10. Refers to sales at retail. Actual revenue contribution was much lower due to the joint-venture structure.
11. Stanley Holmes, "Starbucks' Card Smarts," *BusinessWeek*, March 18, 2002.

Study Questions

1. *What factors accounted for Starbucks' success in the early 1990s and what was so compelling about its value proposition? What brand image did Starbucks develop during this period?*

2. *Why have Starbucks' customer satisfaction scores declined? Has the company's service declined or is it simply measuring satisfaction the wrong way?*

3. *How has Starbucks changed since its early days?*

4. *Describe the ideal Starbucks customer from a profitability standpoint. What would it take to ensure that this customer is highly satisfied? How valuable to Starbucks is a highly satisfied customer?*

5. *Should Starbucks make the US$40 million investment in labor in the stores? What's the goal of this investment? Is it possible for a mega-brand to deliver customer intimacy?*

Case 4   Giordano: Positioning for International Expansion

JOCHEN WIRTZ

To make people "feel good" and "look great."—Giordano's Corporate Mission

---

As it looks to the future, a successful Asian retailer of casual apparel must decide whether to maintain its existing positioning strategy. Management wonders what factors will be critical to success and whether the firm's competitive strengths in merchandise selection and service are readily transferable to new international markets.

In early 2006, Giordano, a Hong Kong-based retailer of casual clothes targeted at men, women and children through its four company brands, Giordano, Giordano Ladies, Giordano Junior and Blue Star Exchange, was operating over 1,600 retail stores and counters in some 31 markets in the Asia-Pacific and Middle-East region. Its main markets were Mainland China, Hong Kong, Japan, Korea, Singapore, and Taiwan. Other countries in which it had a presence were Australia, Indonesia, Malaysia and the Middle East. In its main markets there were 1478 Giordano and Giordano Junior stores, 27 Giordano Ladies stores, and 132 Blue Star Exchange stores. Sales had grown to HK$4,003 million (US$517 million) by 2004 (see **Exhibit 1**). Giordano stores were located in retail shopping districts with good foot traffic. Views of a typical storefront and store interior are shown in **Exhibit 2**. In most geographic markets serviced by Giordano, the retail clothing business was deemed to be extremely competitive.

Exhibit 1   Giordano Financial Highlights

	2004	2003	2002	2001	2000	1999	1998	1997	1996	1995	1994
Turnover (million HK$)	4,003	3,389	3,588	3,479	3,431	3,092	2,609	3,014	3,522	3,482	2,864
Turnover increase (percent)	18.1	(5.5)	3.1	1.4	11.0	18.5	(13.4)	(14.4)	1.1	21.5	22.7
Profit after tax and minority interests (million HK$)	393	266	328	377	416	360	76	68	261	250	195
Profit after tax and minority interests increase over previous year (percent)	47.7	(18.9)	(13.0)	(9.4)	15.3	373.7	11.8	(73.9)	4.4	28.2	41.9
Shareholders' fund (million HK$)	1,954	1,799	1,794	1,695	1,558	1,449	1,135	1,069	1,220	976	593
Working capital (million HK$)	1,004	961	861	798	1,014	960	725	655	752	560	410
Total debt to equity ratio	0.35	0.4	0.3	0.4	0.3	0.3	0.3	0.3	0.4	0.7	0.9
Inventory turnover on sales (days)	30	24	26	30	32	28	44	48	58	55	53
Return on total assets (percent)	14.9	10.7	13.7	16.8	20.7	21.5	5.3	4.5	16.8	19.5	20.9
Return on average equity (percent)	20.9	14.8	18.8	23.2	27.7	27.9	6.9	5.9	23.8	31.8	35.8
Return on sales (percent)	9.8	7.8	9.1	10.8	12.1	11.6	2.9	2.3	7.4	7.2	6.8
Earning per share (cents)	27.20	18.50	22.80	26.30	29.30	25.65	5.40	4.80	18.45	19.40	15.45
Cash dividend per share (cents)	23.00	21.00	19.00	14.00	15.25	17.25	2.25	2.50	8.00	6.75	5.50

Source: Annual Report 2004, Giordano International.

This case is based on published information and quotes from a wide array of sources. The generous help and feedback provided by Alison Law, former Assistant to Chairman, Giordano International Ltd, to earlier versions of this case are gratefully acknowledged. The author thanks Zhaohui Chen for his excellent research assistance.

Exhibit 2   Typical Giordano Storefront

The board and top management team were eager to maintain Giordano's success in existing markets and to enter new markets in Asia and beyond. Several issues were under discussion. First, in what ways, if at all, should Giordano change its current positioning in the marketplace? Second, would the factors that had contributed to Giordano's success in the past remain equally critical over the coming years or were new key success factors emerging? Finally, as Giordano sought to enter new markets around the world, were its competitive strengths readily transferable to other markets?

COMPANY BACKGROUND

Giordano was founded in Hong Kong in 1980 by Jimmy Lai. In 1981, it opened its first retail store in Hong Kong and also began to expand its market by distributing Giordano merchandise in Taiwan through a joint venture. In 1985, it opened its first retail outlet in Singapore.

Responding to slow sales, Giordano changed its positioning strategy in 1987. Until 1987, it had sold exclusively men's casual apparel. When Lai and his colleagues realized that an increasing number of female customers were attracted to its stores, he repositioned the chain as a retailer of value-for-money merchandise, selling discounted casual unisex apparel, with the goal of maximizing unit sales instead of margins. This shift in strategy was successful, leading to a substantial increase in turnover. In 1994, Peter Lau Kwok Kuen succeeded Lai and became Chairman.

Management Values and Style

A willingness to try new and unconventional ways of doing business and to learn from past errors was part of Lai's management philosophy and soon became an integral part of Giordano's culture. Lai saw the occasional failure as a current limitation that indirectly pointed management to the right decision in the future. To demonstrate his commitment to this philosophy, Lai took the lead by being a role model for his employees, adding, " . . . Like in a meeting, I say, look, I have made this mistake. I'm sorry for that. I hope everybody learns from this. If I can make mistakes, who . . . do you think you are that you can't make mistakes?" He also believed strongly that empowerment would minimize mistakes—that if everyone was allowed to contribute and participate, mistakes could be minimized.

Another factor that contributed to the firm's success was its dedicated, ever-smiling sales staff of over 8000. Giordano considered front-line workers to be its customer-service heroes. Charles Fung, executive director and chief operations officer (Southeast Asia), remarked:

> Even the most sophisticated training program won't guarantee the best customer service. People are the key. They make exceptional service possible. Training is merely a skeleton of a customer service program. It's the people who deliver that give it form and meaning.

Giordano had instituted stringent selection procedures to make sure that the candidates selected matched the desired employee profile. Selection continued into its training workshops, which tested the service orientation and character of a new employee.

Giordano's philosophy of quality service could be observed not only in Hong Kong but also in its overseas outlets. The company had been honored by numerous service awards over the years (see **Exhibit 3**). Fung described its obsession with providing excellent customer service in the following terms:

> The only way to keep abreast with stiff competition in the retail market is to know the customers' needs and serve them well. Customers pay our pay checks; they are our bosses.... Giordano considers service to be a very important element [in trying to draw customers];... service is in the blood of every member of our staff.

Giordano believed and invested heavily in employee training and had been recognized for its commitment to training and developing its staff by such awards as the Hong Kong Management Association Certificate of Merit for Excellence in Training and the People Developer Award from Singapore, among others.

Training is important. However, what is more important is the transfer of learning to the store. When there is a transfer of learning, each dollar invested in training yields a high return. We try to encourage this [transfer of learning] by cultivating a culture and by providing positive reinforcement, rewarding those who practice what they learned.

Giordano offered what Fung claimed was "an attractive package in an industry where employee turnover is high." Giordano motivated its people through a base salary that probably was below market average, but added attractive performance-related bonuses. These initiatives and Giordano's emphasis on training had resulted in a lower staff turnover rate.

Managing its vital human resources (HR) became a challenge to Giordano when it decided to expand into global markets. To replicate its high-service-quality positioning, Giordano needed to consider the HR issues involved in setting up retail outlets in unfamiliar territory. For example, the recruitment, selection and training of local employees could require modifications to its formula for success in its current

Exhibit 3 Selected Awards Giordano Received over the Years

AWARD	AWARDING ORGANIZATION	CATEGORY	YEAR(S)
American Service Excellence Award	American Express	Fashion/Apparel	1995
Ear Award	Radio Corporation of Singapore	Listeners' Choice & Creative Merits	1996
Excellent Service Award	Singapore Productivity and Standards Board	—	1996, 1997, 1998
People Developer Award	Singapore Productivity and Standards Board	—	1998
HKRMA Customer Service Award	Hong Kong Retail Management Association	—	1999
The Fourth Hong Kong Awards for Services	Hong Kong Trade Development Council	Export Marketing & Customer Service	2000
Grand Award (Giordano International)	Hong Kong Trade Development Council	Export Marketing	2002
Grand Award (Giordano Ladies)	Hong Kong Retail Management Association	—	2002
Business-to-Consumer Service Supplier Award	Middle East Economic Digest (MEED)	—	2002
Dubai Services Excellence Scheme Award	Dubai Department of Economic Development Customer Service	Customer Service	2003
Hong Kong Superbrands(TM) Award	Hong Kong Superbrands Council	—	2004
Top Service Award	Next Magazine	Chain Stores of Fashion & Accessories	2004

markets, owing to differences in the culture, education and technology of the new countries. Labor regulations could also affect such HR policies as compensation and welfare benefits. Finally, management needed to consider expatriate policies for staff members who had been seconded to help run Giordano outside their home countries, as well as the management practices themselves in those countries.

Focusing Giordano's Organizational Structure on Simplicity and Speed

Giordano maintained a flat organizational structure. The company's decentralized management style empowered line managers, and at the same time encouraged fast and close communication and coordination. For example, top management and staff had desks located next to each other, separated only by shoulder panels. This closeness allowed easy communication, efficient project management and speedy decision making, which were all seen as critical ingredients to success amid fast-changing consumer tastes and fashion trends. This kept Giordano's product development cycle short. The firm made similar demands on its suppliers.

Service

Giordano's commitment to service began with its major Customer Service Campaign in 1989. In that campaign, yellow badges bearing the words "Giordano Means Service" were worn by every Giordano employee, and its service philosophy had three tenets: "We welcome unlimited try-ons; we exchange—no questions asked; and we serve with a smile." As a result, the firm started receiving its numerous service-related awards over the years. It had also been ranked number one for eight consecutive years by the *Far Eastern Economic Review* for being innovative in responding to customers' needs.

Management had launched several creative, customer-focused campaigns and promotions to extend its service orientation. For instance, in Singapore, Giordano asked its customers what they thought would be the fairest price to charge for a pair of jeans and charged each customer the price that they were willing to pay. This one-month campaign was immensely successful, with some 3,000 pairs of jeans sold every day during the promotion. In another service-related campaign, over 10,000 free T-shirts were given to customers for giving feedback and criticizing Giordano's services.

To ensure customer service excellence, performance evaluations were conducted frequently at the store level, as well as for individual employees. Internal competitions were designed to motivate employees and store teams to do their best in serving customers. Every month, Giordano awarded the "Service Star" to individual employees, based on nominations provided by shoppers. In addition, every Giordano store was evaluated every month by mystery shoppers. Based on the combined results of these evaluations, the "Best Service Shop" award was given to the top store. Customer feedback cards were available at all stores, and were collected and posted at the office for further action. Increasingly, customers were providing feedback via the firm's corporate Web site.

Value for Money

Lai explained the rationale for Giordano's value-for-money policy.

> Consumers are learning a lot better about what value is. So we always ask ourselves how can we sell it cheaper, make it more convenient for the consumer to buy and deliver faster today than [we did] yesterday. That is all value, because convenience is value for the consumer. Time is value for the customer.

Giordano was able to sell value-for-money merchandise consistently through careful selection of suppliers, strict cost control and by resisting the temptation to increase retail prices unnecessarily. For instance, to provide greater - shopping convenience to customers, Giordano started to open kiosks in subway and train stations in 2003 aimed at providing their customers with a "grab and go" service.

Inventory Control

In order to maximize use of store space for sales opportunities, a central distribution center replaced the function of a back storeroom in its outlets. Information technology (IT) was used to facilitate inventory management and demand forecasting. When an item was sold, the barcode information—identifying size, color, style and price—was recorded by the point-of-sale cash register and transmitted to the company's main computer. At the end of each day, the information was compiled at the store level and sent to the sales department and the distribution center. The compiled sales information became the store's order for the following day. Orders were filled during the night and were ready for delivery by early morning, ensuring that before a Giordano store opened for business, new inventory was already on the shelves.

Another advantage of its IT system was that information was disseminated to production facilities in real time. Such information allowed customers' purchase patterns to be understood, and this provided valuable input to its manufacturing operations, resulting in less problems and costs related to slow-moving inventory. The use of IT also afforded more efficient inventory holding. Giordano's inventory turnover on sales was reduced from 58 days in 1996 to merely 30 days in 2004. Its excellent inventory management reduced costs and allowed reasonable margins, while still allowing Giordano to reinforce its value-for-money philosophy. All in all, despite the relatively lower margins as compared to its peers, Giordano was still able to post healthy profits. Such efficiency became a crucial factor when periodic price wars were encountered.

PRODUCT POSITIONING

Fung recognized the importance of limiting the firm's expansion and focusing on one specific area. Simplicity and focus were reflected in the way Giordano merchandised its goods. Its stores featured no more than 100 variants of 17 core items, whereas competing retailers might feature 200 to 300 items. He believed that merchandising a wide range of products made it difficult to react quickly to market changes.

Giordano's willingness to experiment with new ideas and its perseverance despite past failures could also be seen in its introduction of new product lines. It ventured into mid-priced women's fashion with the label "Gio Ladies"—featuring a line of smart blouses, dress pants and skirts—targeted at executive women. Reflecting retailer practices for such clothing, Giordano enjoyed higher margins on upscale women's clothing—typically 50 to 60 percent of selling price as compared to 40 percent for casual wear.

Here, however, Giordano ran into some difficulties as it found itself competing with more than a dozen seasoned players in the retail clothing business, including Theme and Esprit. Initially, the firm failed to differentiate its new Giordano Ladies line from its mainstream product line, and even sold both through the same outlets. In 1999, however, Giordano took advantage of the financial troubles facing rivals such as Theme, as well as the boom that followed the Asian currency crisis in many parts of Asia, to aggressively re-launch its "Giordano Ladies" line, which subsequently met with great success. As of January 2006, the reinforced "Giordano Ladies" focused on a select segment, with 27 "Giordano Ladies" shops in Hong Kong, Taiwan, Singapore and China, offering personalized service. Among other things, the staff were trained to memorize names of regular customers and recall their past purchases.

Differentiation and Repositioning

During the late 1990s, Giordano had begun to reposition its brand, by emphasizing differentiated, functionally value-added products clothes and broadening its appeal by improving on visual merchandising and apparel. A typical storefront and store layout are shown in **Exhibit 2** and **Exhibit 4**. Giordano's relatively mid-priced positioning worked well—inexpensive, yet contemporary-looking outfits appealed to Asia's frugal customers, especially during a period of economic slowdown. However, over time, this positioning became inconsistent with the brand image that Giordano had tried hard to build over the years. As one senior executive remarked, "The feeling went from 'this is nice and good value' to 'this is cheap.'"

Giordano gradually remarketed its core brand in ways that sought to create the image of a trendier label. To continue meeting the needs of customers who favored its value-for-money positioning, Giordano launched several promotions.

Exhibit 4   A Typical Store Layout

Among its successes was the "Simply Khakis" promotion, launched in April 1999, which emphasized basic, street-culture style that "mixed and matched," and thus fitted all occasions. Within days of its launch in Singapore, the new line sold out and had to be re-launched two weeks later. By October 1999, over a million pairs of khaki trousers and shorts had been sold. The firm's skills in executing innovative and effective promotional strategies helped the retailer to reduce the impact of the Asian crisis on its sales and to take advantage of the slight recovery seen in early 1999.

In 1999, the firm launched a new brand of casual clothing, Blue Star Exchange (BSE), following successful prototyping in Hong Kong and Taiwan. In 2002, the first Blue Star Exchange store was set up in Southern China. The strong market response to this new brand led the company to expand the number of stores branded as Blue Star Exchange to 132 by 2005. The Group was also evaluating the possibility of launching the Blue Star chain in its other markets.

In June 2003, right after the SARS (severe acute respiratory syndrome) health crisis, which discouraged shopping and consumer spending, Giordano launched the "Yoga Collection" which used a moisture-managed fabric, Dry-Tech™. It was an instant big hit, allowing Giordano to recover nicely from the SARS crisis in Hong Kong and enabling its new brand to stand out from competing offerings.

Giordano's Competitors

To beat the intense competition prevalent in Asia—especially in Hong Kong—founder Jimmy Lai believed that Giordano had to develop a distinctive competitive advantage. So he benchmarked Giordano against best-practice organizations in four key areas: (1) computerization (from The Limited), (2) a tightly controlled menu (from McDonald's), (3) frugality (from Wal-Mart), and (4) value pricing (as implemented at the British retail chain Marks & Spencer). The emphasis on service and the value-for-money concept had proven to be successful.

Giordano's main competitors in the value-for-money segment had been Hang Ten, Bossini, and Baleno, and at the higher end, Esprit. **Exhibit 5** shows the relative positioning of Giordano and its competitors: The Gap, Bossini, Hang Ten, Baleno, and Esprit.

Hang Ten and Bossini were generally positioned as low-price retailers offering reasonable quality and service. The clothes emphasized versatility and simplicity. But while Hang Ten and Baleno were more popular among teenagers and young adults, Bossini had a more general appeal. Their distribution strategies were somewhat similar, but they focused on different markets. For instance, while Hang Ten was mainly strong in Taiwan, Baleno increasingly penetrated Mainland China and Taiwan. On the other hand, Bossini was very strong in Hong Kong and relatively strong in China. The company planned to make its business in China into the group's largest turnover and profit contributor. The geographic areas in which Giordano, The Gap, Espirit, Bossini, Baleno, and Hang Ten operate are shown in **Exhibit 6**.

Esprit was an international fashion lifestyle brand. Esprit promoted a "lifestyle" image and its products were strategically positioned as good quality and value for money—a position that Giordano was occupying. By 2005, Esprit had a distribution network of over 10,000 stores and outlets in 40 countries in Europe, Asia, America, Middle East and Australia. The main markets were in Europe, which accounted for approximately 65 percent sales. The Esprit brand products were principally sold via directly managed retail outlets, wholesale customers (including department stores, specialty stores and franchisees), and by licensees for products manufactured under license, principally through the licensees' own distribution networks.

Theme International Holdings Limited was founded in Hong Kong in 1986 by Chairman and CEO Kenneth Lai. He identified a niche in the local market, for high-quality, fashionable ladies' businesswear, although the firm subsequently expanded into casual wear. The Theme label and chain were

Exhibit 5 Market Positioning of Giordano and Principal Competitors

FIRMS	POSITIONING	TARGET MARKET
Giordano (www.giordano.com.hk)	Value for money Mid-priced but trendy fashion	Unisex casual wear for all ages (under different brands)
The Gap (www.gap.com)	Value for money Mid-priced but trendy fashion	Unisex casual wear for all ages (under different brands)
Esprit (www.esprit-intl.com)	More up-market than Giordano Stylish, trendy	Ladies' casual, but also other specialized lines for children and men
Bossini (www.bossini.com)	Value for money (comparable to Giordano)	Unisex, casual wear, both young and old (above 30s)
Baleno (www.baleno.com.hk)	Value for money Trendy, young age casual wear	Unisex appeal, young adults
Hang Ten (www.hangten.com)	Value for money Sporty lifestyle	Casual wear and sports wear, teens and young adults

Exhibit 6 Geographic Presence of Giordano and Its Principal Competitors

COUNTRY	GIORDANO	THE GAP	ESPRIT	BOSSINI	BALENO	HANG TEN
Asia						
Hong Kong/Macau	X	—	X	X	X	X
Singapore	X	—	X	X	X	X
South Korea	X	—	X	—	—	X
Taiwan	X	—	X	X	X	X
China	X	—	X	X	X	X
Malaysia	X	—	X	—	X	—
Indonesia	X	—	X	X	—	—
Philippines	X	—	X	X	—	X
Thailand	X	—	X	X	—	—
World						
U.S. and Canada	—	X	X	X	—	X
Europe	—	X	X	—	—	X
Japan	X	X	—	—	—	X
Australia	X	—	X	—	—	X
Total	1,585	3,117	9,751	827	1,160	NA

Note: "X" indicates presence in the country/region; "—" indicates no presence.

Sources: Annual Report 2004, Giordano International; Gap Inc., retrieved June 23, 2004, from http://www.gapinc.com/about/realestate/storecount.htm; Annual Report 2004/5, Esprit; Financial Report 2004/5, Bossini International Holdings Limited; Baleno, retrieved December 12, 2005, from http://www.baleno.com.hk/EN/stores_list.asp?area=cn; Hang Ten, retrieved December 12, 2005, from http://www.hangten.com.

in direct competition with "Giordano Ladies." From the first store in 1986 to a chain comprising over 130 outlets in Hong Kong, Mainland China, Macau, Taiwan, Singapore, Malaysia, Indonesia, the Philippines, the phenomenal growth of Theme was built on a vertically integrated corporate structure and advanced management system. However, its ambitious expansion proved to be costly. In 1999, the company announced a HK$106.1 million net loss for the six months up to September 30, 1998, and was subsequently acquired by High Fashion International, a Hong Kong-based fashion retailer specializing in up-market, trendy apparel. Theme was then focusing on expansion in China, after having fortified its image as a sophisticated and high-end smart-casual fashion for career women.

Although each of these firms had slightly different positioning strategies, they competed in a number of areas. For example, all firms heavily emphasized advertising and sales promotion—selling fashionable clothes at attractive prices. Almost all stores were also located primarily in good ground-floor areas, drawing high-volume traffic and facilitating shopping, browsing and impulse buying. However, none had been able to match the great customer value offered by Giordano.

A threat from U.S.-based The Gap was also looming. The Gap had already entered Japan. After 2005, when garment quotas were largely abolished, imports into the region had become more cost effective for this U.S. competitor.

Financial data for Giordano, Esprit, The Gap, Bossini, and Theme are shown in **Exhibit 7**.

Exhibit 7 Competitive Financial Data for Giordano, The Gap, Esprit, Bossini and Theme

	GIORDANO	THE GAP	ESPRIT	BOSSINI	THEME
Turnover (US$ million)	517	16,267	2,662	260	26
Profit after tax and minority interests (US$ million)	51	1,150	431	23	(1)
Return on total assets (percent)	14.9	11.1	36.2	24.9	(7.3)
Return on average equity (percent)	20.9	24	53.6	36.2	NA
Return on sales (percent)	9.8	7.1	20.6	13.5	(3.2)
Number of employees	9,000	152,000	7,720	3,963	2,500
Sales per employee (US$ '000)	57.44	107.02	344.82	65.61	10.4

Note: The Gap reports its earnings in US$. All reported figures have been converted into US$ at the following exchange rate (as of January 2006): US$1 = HK$7.75.

Sources: Annual Report 2004, Giordano International; Annual Report 2004, The Gap; Financial Highlights 2004/5, Esprit International; Financial Report 2004/5, Bossini International Holdings Limited; Annual Report 2004, Theme Holdings; Reuters, Retrieved December 12, 2005, from www.knowledge.reuters.com.

GIORDANO'S GROWTH STRATEGY

Early in its existence, Giordano's management had realized that regional expansion was required to achieve substantial growth and economies of scale. By 2006, Giordano had over 1,600 stores in 31 markets. **Exhibit 8** shows the growth achieved across a number of dimensions from 1994 to 2004.

Driven in part by its desire for growth and in part by the need to reduce its dependence on Asia in the wake of the 1998 economic meltdown, Giordano set its sights on markets outside Asia. Australia was an early target and the number of retail outlets increased from four in 1999 to 46 in 2006. In Japan, Giordano opened 21 outlets from 2001 to 2006. Although the Asian financial crisis had caused Giordano to rethink its regional strategy, it was still determined to enter and further penetrate new Asian markets. This determination led to successful expansion in Mainland China (see **Exhibit 9**), where the number of retail outlets grew from 253 in 1999 to 644 by 2006. Giordano's management foresaw both challenges and opportunities arising from the People's Republic of China's accession to the World Trade Organization.

Giordano opened more stores in Indonesia, bringing its total in that country to 39 stores. In Malaysia, Giordano planned to refurnish its outlets and intensify its local promotional campaigns to consolidate its leadership position in the Malaysian market. To improve store profitability, Giordano had already converted some of its franchised Malaysian stores into company-owned stores.

The senior management team knew that Giordano's future success in such markets would depend on a detailed understanding of consumer tastes and preferences for fabrics, colors and advertising. In the past, the firm had relied on maintaining a consistent strategy across different countries, including such elements as positioning, service levels, information systems, logistics, and human resource policies. However, implementation of such tactical elements as promotional campaigns was usually left mostly to local managers. A country's overall performance in terms of sales, contribution, service levels and customer feedback was monitored by regional headquarters (for instance, Singapore for Southeast Asia) and the head office in Hong Kong. Weekly performance reports were distributed to all managers.

As the organization expanded beyond Asia, it was becoming clear that different strategies had to be developed for different regions or countries. For instance, to enhance profitability in Mainland China, the company recognized that better sourcing was needed to enhance price competitiveness. Turning around the Taiwan operation required refocusing on basic designs, streamlining product portfolio, and implementing their micromarketing strategy more aggressively. The company was continuing to explore the market in Japan and planned to open a few more stores in the second half of 2006. In Europe, it was investigating a variety of distribution channels, including a wholesale-based business model.

Decisions Facing the Senior Management Team

Although Giordano had been extremely successful, it faced a number of challenges. A key issue was how the Giordano

Exhibit 8 Operational Highlights for Giordano's Retail and Distribution Division

	2004	2003	2002	2001	2000	1999	1998	1997	1996	1995	1994
Number of retail outlets											
—Managed directly by the group	811	550	473	456	367	317	308	324	294	280	283
—Franchised	774	813	783	703	553	423	370	316	221	171	77
Total number of retail outlets	1,585	1,363	1,256	1,159	920	740	678	640	515	451	360
Retail floor area managed directly by the group (in '000 sq. ft.)	846	650	599	597	465	301	358	313	295	286	282
Sales per square foot (HK$)	4,300	4,200	4,500	5,100	7,400	8,400	6,800	8,000	9,900	10,500	10,600
Number of employees	9,000	7,900	8,000	8,287	7,166	6,237	6,319	8,175	10,004	10,348	6,863
Comparable store sales: increase/(decrease) (percent)	7	(9)	(2)	(4)	4	21	(13)	(11)	(6)	8	(9)
Number of sales associates	NA	3,200	2,900	2,603	2,417	2,026	1,681	1,929	1,958	2,069	1,928

Source: Annual Report 2004, Giordano International.

Exhibit 9   Giordano's Flagship Store in Shanghai

brand should be positioned against the competition in both new and existing markets. Was a repositioning required in existing markets and would it be necessary to follow different positioning strategies for different markets (e.g., Hong Kong versus Southeast Asia)?

A second issue was the sustainability of Giordano's key success factors. Giordano had to carefully explore how its core competencies and the pillars of its success were likely to develop over the coming years. Which of its competitive advantages were likely to be sustainable and which ones were likely to be eroded?

A third issue was Giordano's growth strategy in Asia as well as across continents. Would Giordano's competitive strengths be readily transferable to other markets? Would strategic adaptations to its strategy and marketing mix be required, or would tactical moves suffice?

Study Questions

1. *Describe and evaluate Giordano's product, business and corporate strategies.*

2. *Describe and evaluate Giordano's current positioning strategy. Should Giordano reposition itself against its competitors in its current and new markets, and should it have different positioning strategies for different geographic markets?*

3. *What are Giordano's key success factors and sources of competitive advantage? Are its competitive advantages sustainable, and how would they develop in the future?*

4. *Could Giordano transfer its key success factors to new markets as it expands both in Asia and in other parts of the world?*

5. *How do you think Giordano had/would have to adapt its marketing and operations strategies and tactics when entering and penetrating your country?*

6. *What general lessons can major clothing retailers in your country learn from Giordano?*

Case 5   Aussie Pooch Mobile

CHRISTOPHER LOVELOCK AND LORELLE FRAZER

After creating a mobile service that washes dogs outside their own-ers' homes, a young entrepreneur has successfully franchised the concept. Her firm now has more than 100 franchises in many parts of Australia, as well as a few in other countries. She and her man-agement team are debating how best to plan future expansion.

Elaine and Paul Beal drew up in their 4 × 4 outside 22 Ferndale Avenue, towing a bright blue trailer with red and white lettering. As Aussie Pooch Mobile franchisees whose territory covered four suburbs of Brisbane, Australia, they were having a busy day. It was only 1:00 p.m. and they had already washed and groomed 16 dogs at 12 different houses. Now they were at their last appointment—a "pooch party" of ten dogs at number 22, where five other residents of the street had arranged to have their dogs washed on a fortnightly basis.

Prior to their arrival outside the house, there had been fero-cious growling and snarling from a fierce-looking Rottweiler. But when the animal caught sight of the brightly-colored trailer, he and two other dogs in the yard bounded forward eagerly to the chain link fence, in a flurry of barking and wagging tails.

Throughout residential areas of Brisbane and in a number of other Australian cities, dogs of all shapes and sizes were being washed and groomed by Aussie Pooch Mobile fran-chisees. By early 2002, the company had grown to over 100 franchisees and claimed to be "Australia's largest mobile dog wash and care company." A key issue facing its managing director, Christine Taylor, and members of the management team was how to plan and shape future expansion.

COMPANY BACKGROUND

Located in Burpengary, Queensland, just north of Brisbane, Aussie Pooch Mobile Pty. Ltd. (APM) was founded in 1991 by Christine Taylor, then aged 22. Taylor had learned customer service early, working in her parents' bait and tackle shop from the age of 8. Growing up in an environment with dogs and horses as pets, she knew she wanted to work with animals and learned dog grooming skills from working in a local salon. At 16, Chris left school and began her own grooming business on a part-time basis, using a bathtub in the family garage. Since she was still too young to drive, her parents would take her to pick up the dogs from their owners. She washed and groomed the animals at home and then returned them.

Once Taylor had learned to drive and bought her own car, she decided to take her service to the customers. So she went mobile, creating a trailer in which the dogs could be washed outside their owners' homes and naming the fledgling ven-ture The Aussie Pooch Mobile. Soon, it became a full-time job.

Eventually, she found she had more business than she could handle alone, so hired assistants. The next step was to add a second trailer. Newly married, she and her husband, David McNamara, ploughed their profits into the purchase of addi-tional trailers and gradually expanded until they had six mobile units.

The idea of franchising came to Taylor when she found her-self physically constrained by a difficult pregnancy:

> David would go bike riding or head to the coast and have fun with the jet ski and I was stuck at home and felt like I was going nuts, because I'm a really active person. I was hungry for information on how to expand the business, so I started researching other companies and reading heaps of books and came up with franchising as the best way to go, since it would provide capital and also allow a dedicated group of small business people to help expand the business further.

As existing units were converted from employees to fran-chisee operations, Taylor noticed that they quickly became about 20% more profitable. Initially, APM focused on Brisbane and the surrounding region of southeast Queensland. Subsequently, it expanded into New South Wales and South Australia in 1995, into Canberra, Australian Capital Territory (ACT), in 1999, and into Victoria in 2000 (**Exhibit 1**). Expansion into Western Australia was expected in mid 2002. In 1996, a New Zealand division of the firm was launched in Tauranga, a small city some 200 km southeast of Auckland, under the name Kiwi Pooch Mobile. In 2001 Aussie Pooch Mobile launched into the United Kingdom, beginning with a town in northern England. Soon, there were four operators under a master franchisee. The following year saw the official launch of The Pooch Mobile Malaysia, also under a master franchisee.

By early 2002, the company had 125 mobile units in Australia, of which 55 were located in Queensland, 42 in New South Wales, 8 in ACT, 12 in South Australia and 8 in Victoria. In addition, representatives operated another six company-owned units. The company bathed more than 20,000 dogs each month and had an annual turnover of some $3 million. (Financial data are in Australian dollars. Exchange rates at this time were A$1.00 = US$0.57 = 10.58.) APM was a member of the Franchise Council of Australia and complied with the Franchising Code of Conduct. The management team consisted of Chris Taylor as managing director and David McNamara as director responsible for overseeing trailer design and systems support. Each state had its own manager and training team. The central support office also housed staff who provided further assistance to managers and franchisees.

Exhibit 1 Map of Australia

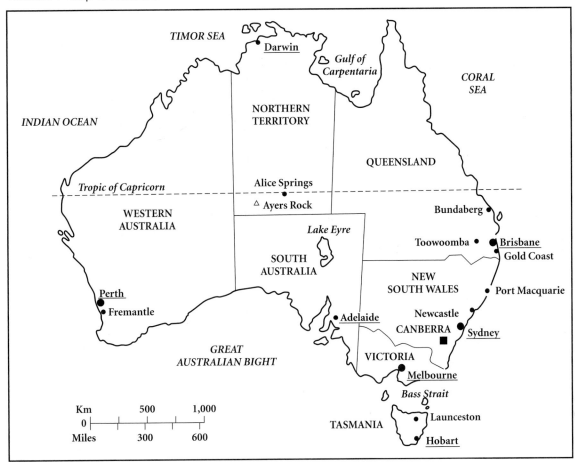

Expansion had benefitted from the leverage provided by several master franchisees, who had obtained the rights to work a large territory and sell franchises within it. Said Taylor:

I look at the business as if it's my first child. I see it now starting to get into those early teens where it wants to go alone, but it still needs me to hold its hand a little bit, whereas initially it needed me there the whole time. With the support staff we have in place, the business is now gaining the support structure it needs to work without me; this is what I am aiming towards. I appreciate that a team of people can achieve much more than one person alone.

The Service Concept

Aussie Pooch Mobile specialized in bringing its dog washing services to customers' homes. Dogs were washed in a hydrobath installed in a specially-designed trailer, which was parked in the street. The trailer had partly open sides and a roof to provide protection from sun and rain (**Exhibit 2**). Apart from flea control products and a few grooming aids, APM did not attempt to sell dog food and other pet supplies. The company had resisted the temptation to diversify into other fields. "Our niche is in the dog bathing industry," declared Chris Taylor:

I don't want us to be a jack of all trades because you'll never be good at anything. We now have an exclusive range of products that customer demand has driven us to providing, but we still work closely with vets and pet shops and are by no means a pet shop on wheels.

In contrast to retail pet service stores, where customers brought their animals to the store or kennel, APM brought the service to customers' homes, with the trailer being parked outside on the street. The use of hydrobath equipment, in which warm, pressurized water was pumped through a shower head, enabled operators to clean dogs more thoroughly than would be possible with a garden hose. The bath was designed to rid the dog of fleas and ticks and improve its skin condition as well as to clean its coat and eliminate smells. Customers supplied water and electrical power.

The fee paid by customers varied from $15–$30 per dog, depending on breed and size, condition of coat and skin, behavior, and geographic location, with discounts for multiple animals at the same address. On average, regular customers paid a fee of $25 for one dog, $47 for two, and $66 for three. At "pooch parties," a concept developed at APM, the homeowner acting as host typically received one complimentary dogwash at the discretion of the operator. Additional services, for which an extra fee was charged, included the recently

Exhibit 2   The Aussie Pooch Mobile Trailer

The rear door of the trailer has been swung open and the franchisee is washing a dog inside.

introduced aromatherapy bath ($2.50) and blow drying of the animal's coat for $5–10 (on average, $8). Blow drying was especially recommended in cool weather to prevent the animal from getting cold.

Operators also offered free advice to customers about their dogs' diet and health care, including such issues as ticks and skin problems. They encouraged customers to have their dogs bathed on a regular basis. The most commonly scheduled frequencies were once every two or four weeks.

A Satisfied User

The process of bathing a dog involved a sequence of carefully coordinated actions, as exemplified by Elaine Beal's treatment of Zak, the Rottweiler. "Hello my darling, who's a good boy?" crooned Elaine as she patted the enthusiastic dog, placed him on a leash and led him out through the gate to the footpath on this warm, sunny day. Paul busied himself connecting hoses and electrical cords to the house, while Elaine began back-combing Zak's coat in order to set it up for the water to get underneath. She then led the now placid dog to the hydrobath inside the trailer, where he sat patiently while she removed his leash and clipped him to a special collar in the bath for security. Meanwhile the water had been heating to the desired temperature.

Over the next few minutes Elaine bathed the dog, applied a medicated herbal shampoo to his coat and rinsed him thoroughly with the pressure driven hose (**Exhibit 3**). After releasing Zak from the special collar and reattaching his leash, she led him out of the hydrobath and onto the footpath, where she

wrapped him in a chamois cloth and dried him. Next, she cleaned the dog's ears and eyes with disposable baby wipes, all the time continuing to talk soothingly to him. She checked his coat and skin to ensure that there were no ticks or skin problems, gave his nails a quick clip, and sprayed a herbal conditioner and deodoriser onto Zak's now gleaming coat and brushed it in. Returning Zak to the yard and removing the leash, Elaine patted him and gave him a large biscuit, specially formulated to protect the animal's teeth.

THE AUSTRALIAN MARKET

Australia's population of 19.3 million in 2001 was small in relation to the country's vast land area of 7.7 million km^2 (almost three million square miles). By contrast, the United States had a population 15 times that of Australia on a land area, including Alaska and Hawaii, of 9.2 million km^2. A federal nation, Australia was divided into six states—New South Wales (NSW), Victoria, Queensland, South Australia, Western Australia, and the island of Tasmania—plus two territories: the large but thinly populated Northern Territory and the small Australian Capital Territory (ACT) which contained the federal capital, Canberra, and its suburbs and was an enclave within NSW. The average annual earnings for employed persons were $35,000.

With much of the interior of the continent uninhabitable and many other areas inhospitable to permanent settlement, most of the Australian population was concentrated in a narrow coastal band running clockwise from Brisbane on the

Exhibit 3   Elaine Beal bathes Zak the rottweiler in an Aussie Pooch Mobile hydrobath.

southeast coast through Sydney and Melbourne to Adelaide, the capital of South Australia. Some 2700 km (1600 miles) to the west lay Perth, known as the most isolated city in the world. A breakdown of the population by state and territory is shown in **Exhibit 4**. The northern half of the country was in the tropics, Brisbane and Perth enjoyed a subtropical climate, and the remaining major cities had a temperate climate (**Exhibit 5**). Melbourne was known for its sharp fluctuations in temperature.

Exhibit 4   Population of Australia by State and Territory, June 2001

STATE/TERRITORY	POPULATION (000)
New South Wales	6,533
Victoria	4,829
Queensland	3,628
South Australia	1,502
Western Australia	1,910
Tasmania	470
Australian Capital Territory	314
Northern Territory	198
Australia Total	*19,387*

Source: Australian Bureau of Statistics 2001.

There were about four million domestic dogs in the country and approximately 42% of the nation's 7.4 million households owned at least one. Ownership rates were slightly above average in Tasmania, the Northern Territory and Queensland, and somewhat below average in Victoria and the ACT. In 1995, it was estimated that Australians spent an estimated $1.3 billion on dog-related goods and services, of which 46% went to dog food, 22% to veterinary services, 12% to dog products and equipment, and 11% to other services, including washing and grooming (**Exhibit 6**).

Franchising in Australia

By the beginning of the 21st Century, the Australian franchising sector had reached a stage of early maturity. McDonald's, KFC and Pizza Hut opened their first outlets in Australia in the 1970s. These imported systems were followed by many home-grown business format franchises such as Just Cuts (hairdressing), Snap Printing, Eagle Boys Pizza, and VIP Home Services, all of which grew into large domestic systems and then expanded internationally, principally to New Zealand and Southeast Asia.

In 2002, Australia boasted approximately 700 business format franchise systems holding over 50,000 outlets. Although the United States had many more systems and outlets,

Exhibit 5 Average Temperatures for Principal Australian Cities (in degrees Celsius)

	JULY (WINTER)		JANUARY (SUMMER)	
	HIGH	LOW	HIGH	LOW
Adelaide, SA	14.9	6.9	27.9	15.7
Brisbane, Qld	20.6	9.5	29.1	20.9
Canberra, ACT	11.5	0.0	28.5	13.6
Darwin, NT	30.7	19.7	32.4	25.2
Hobart, Tas	12.3	4.0	22.3	11.9
Melbourne, Vic	12.9	5.2	26.0	13.5
Perth, WA	17.7	8.1	31.5	16.9
Sydney, NSW	16.9	6.9	26.3	18.6

Source: Australian Bureau of Meteorology, http://www.bom.gov.au.

Australia had more franchisors per capita, reflecting the relative ease of entry into franchising in this country. Most of the growth in franchising had occurred in business format franchising as opposed to product franchising.

Exhibit 6 Distribution of Consumer Expenditures on Dog-Related Goods and Services, 1995

PRODUCT/SERVICE	ALLOCATION
Dog food	46%
Vet charges	21%
Dog products	10%
Dog equipment	2%
Dog services	11%
Pet purchases	5%
Other expenses	4%
Total dog-related expenditures	$1.3 billion

Source: BIS Shrapnell Survey 1995.

Business format franchises provided franchisees with a full business system and the rights to operate under the franchisor's brand name, whereas product franchises merely allowed independent operators to supply a manufacturer's product, such as car dealerships or soft-drink bottlers. Typically, franchisees were required to pay an upfront franchise fee (averaging $30,000 in service industries and $40,000 in retailing) for the right to operate under the franchise system within a defined geographic area. This initial fee was included in the total start-up cost of the business (ranging from around $60,000 in the service sector to more than $200,000 in the retail industry). In addition, franchisees paid a royalty on all sales and an ongoing contribution towards advertising and promotional activities that were designed to build brand awareness and preference. Would-be franchisees who lacked sufficient capital might be able to obtain bank financing against personal assets such as property or an acceptable guarantor.

Franchising Trends

The rapid growth of franchising in Australia had been stimulated in part by demographic trends, including the increase in dual-income families, which had led to greater demand for outsourcing of household services such as lawn mowing, house cleaning and pet grooming. Some franchise systems offered multiple concepts under a single corporate brand name. For instance, VIP Home Services had separate franchises available in lawn mowing, cleaning, car washing and rubbish removal. Additional growth came from conversion of existing individual businesses to a franchise format. For instance, Eagle Boys Pizza had often approached local pizza operators and offered them the opportunity to join this franchise.

Almost half the franchise systems in Australia were in retail trade (32% non-food and 14% food). Another large and growing industry was the property and business services sector (20%), as shown in **Exhibit 7**. Most franchisees were ex-white collar workers or blue collar supervisors who craved independence and a lifestyle change.

Exhibit 7 Distribution of Franchise Systems in Australia by Industry, 1999

INDUSTRY	PERCENTAGE
Retail trade—non-food	31
Property and business services	20
Retail trade—food	14
Personal and other services	7
Construction and trade services	6
Accommodation, cafes and restaurants	4
Education	4
Cultural and recreation services	4
Unclassified	3
Manufacturing and printing	3
Finance and insurance	2
Transport and storage	1
Communication services	1
Total—all industries	100%

Source: Lorelle Frazer and Colin McCosker, Franchising Australia 1999, *Franchise Council of Australia/University of Southern Queensland, Toowoomba, 1999, p. 39.*

Over the years, Australia's franchising sector had experienced a myriad of regulatory regimes. Finally in 1998, in response to perceived problems in many franchising systems, the federal government introduced a mandatory Franchising Code of Conduct, administered under the Trade Practices Act. Among other things, the Code required that potential franchisees be given full disclosure about the franchisor's background and operations prior to signing a franchise agreement. In contrast, the franchising sector in the United States faced a patchwork of regulations that varied from one state to another. Yet in the United Kingdom, there were no specific franchising regulations beyond those applying to all corporations operating in designated industries.

Master franchising arrangements had become common in Australian franchise systems. Under master franchising, a local entrepreneur was awarded the rights to sub-franchise the system within a specific geographic area, such as an entire state. Because of Australia's vast geographic size it was difficult for a franchisor to monitor franchisees who were located far from the head office. The solution was to delegate to master franchisees many of the tasks normally handled by the franchisor itself, making them responsible for recruiting, selecting, training and monitoring franchisees in their territories, as well as overseeing marketing and operations.

Not all franchisees proved successful and individual outlets periodically failed. The main reasons for failure appeared to be poor choice of location or territory and a franchisee's own shortcomings. In addition to the obvious technical skills required in a given field, success often hinged on possession of sales and communication abilities. Disputes in franchising were not uncommon, but could usually be resolved internally without recourse to legal action. The causes of conflict most frequently cited by franchisees related to franchise fees and alleged misrepresentations made by the franchisor. By contrast, franchisors cited conflicts based on lack of adherence to the system by franchisees.

Australia was home to a number of internationally known franchise operators, including Hertz Rent-a-Car, Avis, McDonald's, KFC, Pizza Hut, Subway, Kwik Kopy and Snap-on Tools. By contrast, most Burger King outlets operated under the name Hungry Jack's, an acquired Australian chain with significant brand equity.

Jim's Group

Among Australia's best-known, locally developed franchisors was Melbourne-based Jim's Group, which described itself as one of the world's largest home service franchise organizations. The company had originated with a mowing service started by Jim Penman in Melbourne in 1982 when he abandoned ideas of an academic career after his PhD thesis was rejected. In 1989, Penman began franchising the service, now known as Jim's Mowing, as a way to facilitate expansion. The business grew rapidly, using master franchisees in different regions to recruit and manage individual franchisees. The company's dark green trucks, displaying a larger-than-life logo of Penman himself, bearded and wearing a hat, soon became a familiar sight on suburban streets around

Melbourne. Before long, the franchise expanded to other parts of Victoria and then to other states.

Over the following years, an array of other home-related services was launched under the Jim's brand, including Jim's Trees, Jim's Paving, Jim's Cleaning, Jim's Appliance Repair, and Jim's Floors. Each service featured the well-recognized logo of Jim Penman's face on a different colored background. Jim's Dogwash made its debut in 1996, employing a bright red, fully enclosed trailer, emblazoned by a logo that had been amended to show Jim with a dog. By early 2002, Jim's Group comprised more than two dozen different service divisions, over ninety master franchisees, and some 1,900 individual franchisees. In many instances, master franchisees were responsible for two or more different service divisions within their regions. Jim's Group's philosophy was to price franchises according to local market conditions. If work in a prospective territory were easy to find but franchisees hard to attract, the price might be lowered somewhat, but not too much, otherwise the company felt there would be insufficient commitment.

In recent years, Jim's Group had expanded overseas. In New Zealand, it had six master franchisees and 232 franchisees and offered mowing, tree work, cleaning, and dogwashing services. It had also established a significant presence for Jim's Mowing in the Canadian province of British Columbia. But attempts to launch Jim's Mowing in the United States had failed due to difficulty in finding good operators.

Jim's Dogwash had over 60 franchises operating in Australia (primarily in Victoria) and New Zealand. This firm's experience had shown that growth was hampered by the shortage of suitable franchisees, since operators needed to be dog lovers with a background in dog care.

FRANCHISING STRATEGY AT AUSSIE POOCH MOBILE

New APM franchisees were recruited through newspaper advertisements and "advertorials" (**Exhibit 8**) as well as by word of mouth. The concept appealed to individuals who sought to become self-employed but wanted the security of a proven business system rather than striking out entirely on their own. Interested individuals were invited to meet with a representative of the company to learn more. If they wished to proceed further, they had to complete an application form and submit a deposit of $250 to hold a particular area for a maximum of four weeks, during which the applicant could further investigate the characteristics and prospects of the designated territory. This fee was credited to the purchase cost of the franchise if the applicant decided to proceed or returned if the applicant withdrew. A new franchise cost $24,000 (up from $19,500 in 1999). An additional 10% had to be added to this fee to pay the recently introduced federal goods and services tax (GST). **Exhibit 9** identifies how APM costed out the different elements.

Selection Requirements for Prospective Franchisees

The company had set a minimum educational requirement of passing Year 10 of high school (or equivalent). Taylor noted that successful applicants tended to be outdoor people who shared four characteristics:

> They are self motivated and outgoing. They love dogs and they want to work for themselves. Obviously, being great with dogs is one part of the business—our franchisees understand that the dog's even an extended member of the customer's family—but it's really important that they can handle the bookwork side of the business as well, because that's basically where your bread and butter is made.

Other desirable characteristics included people skills and patience, plus a good telephone manner. Would-be franchisees also had to have a valid driver's license, access to a vehicle that was capable of towing a trailer, and the ability to do this type of driving in an urban setting. Originally, Taylor had expected that most franchisees would be relatively young, with parents being willing to buy their children a

franchise and set them up with a job, but in fact only about half of all franchisees were aged 21–30; 40% were aged 31–40 and 10% were in their forties or fifties. About 60% were female.

Potential franchisees were offered a trial work period with an operator to see if they liked the job and were suited to the business, including not only skills with both animals and people but also sufficient physical fitness.

In return for the franchise fee, successful applicants received the rights to a geographically defined franchise, typically comprising about 12,000 homes. Franchisees also obtained an APM trailer with all necessary products and solutions to service the first one hundred dogs, plus red uniform shirts and cap, advertising material, and stationery. The trailer was built to industrial grade standards and its design included many refinements developed by APM in consultation with franchisees to simplify the process of dog washing and enhance the experience for the animal. Operators were required to travel with a mobile phone, which they had to pay for themselves.

In addition to franchised territories, APM had six company-owned outlets. These were operated by representatives, who

Exhibit 9 Aussie Pooch Mobile: Breakdown of Franchise Purchase Cost, 2002 vs. 1999

ITEM	1999		2002	
	$	$	$	$
Initial training		2,200.00		2,200.00
Initial franchise fee		4,021.50		6,173.00
Guaranteed income		5,000.00		N/A
Exclusive territory plus trailer registration		N/A		6,600.00
Fixtures, fittings, stock, insurance etc:				
Aussie Pooch Mobile trailer and hydrobath	4,860.00		5,340.00	
Consumables (shampoo, conditioner, etc.)	160.00		230.00	
Trade equipment and uniforms	920.00		881.65	
Insurance	338.50	6,278.50	575.35	7,027.00
Initial advertising		2,000.00		2,000.00
*Total franchise cost**		$19,500.00		$24,000.00

*Total franchise costs excludes 10% GST, introduced in July 2000.

leased the territory and equipment and in return paid APM 25% of the gross weekly revenues (including GST). Taylor had no plans to increase the number of representatives. The reps were generally individuals who either could not currently afford the start-up cost or who were being evaluated by the company for their suitability as franchisees. Typically, reps either became franchisees within about six months or left the company.

Assisting New Franchisees

The franchisor provided two weeks' pre-opening training for all new franchisees and representatives also spent about 10 hours with each one to help them open their new territories. Training topics included operational and business procedures, effective use of the telephone, hydrobathing techniques, dog grooming techniques, and information on dog health and behavior. Franchisees were given a detailed operations manual containing 104 pages of instructions on running the business in accordance with company standards.

To help new franchisees get started, APM placed advertisements in local newspapers for a period of 20 weeks. It also prepared human interest stories for distribution to these newspapers. Other promotional activities at the time of launch included distributing pamphlets in the territory and writing to local vets and pet shops to inform them of the business. APM guaranteed new franchisees a weekly income of $600 for the first ten weeks and paid for a package of insurance policies for six months, after which the franchisee became responsible for the coverage.

Fees and Services

Ongoing support by the franchisor included marketing efforts, monthly newsletters, a telephone hotline service for advice, an insurance package, regular (but brief) field visits, and additional training. If a franchisee fell sick or wished to take a vacation, APM would offer advice on how to best deal with this situation, in many cases being able to organise a trained person to help out. It also organized periodic meetings for franchisees in the major metropolitan areas at which guest presenters spoke on topics relating to franchise operations. Previous guest speakers had included veterinarians, natural therapists, pharmacists, and accountants. More recently, APM had offered one-day seminars, providing more team support and generating greater motivation than the traditional meeting style.

Exhibit 10 Average Annual Operating Expenses for an Aussie Pooch Mobile Franchisee, 1999 vs. 2002

EXPENSE	1999 $	2002 $
Consumable products	3,552	2,880
Car registration	430	430
Car insurance	500	500
Fuel	2,400	3,360
Insurances	642	1,151
Repairs and maintenance	1,104	1,104
Phones, stationery, etc.	1,440	1,920
Communication levy	624	624
Franchise royalties	4,416	5,583
Advertising levy	1,104	1,395
Total	*$16,212*	*$18,947*

In return for these services, franchisees paid a royalty fee of 10% of their gross weekly income, plus an advertising levy of an additional 2.5%. Income was reported on a weekly basis and fees had to be paid weekly. In addition to these fees, operating costs for a franchisee included car-related expenses, purchase of consumable products such as shampoo, insurance, telephone, and stationery. **Exhibit 10** shows the average weekly costs that a typical franchisee might expect to incur.

Franchisees included several couples, like the Beals, but Taylor believed that having two operators work together was not really efficient, although it could be companionable. Paul

Beal, a retired advertising executive, had other interests and did not always accompany Elaine. Some couples split the work, with one operating three days a week and the other three or even four days. All franchisees were required to be substantially involved in the hands-on running of the business; some had more than one territory and employed additional operators to help them.

To further support individual franchisees, APM had formed a Franchise Advisory Council, composed of a group of experienced franchisees who had volunteered their time to help other franchisees and the system as a whole. Each franchisee was assigned to a team leader, who was a member of the FAC. The Council facilitated communications between franchisees and the support office, meeting with the managers every three months to discuss different issues within the company.

MARKETING AND COMPETITION

The company advertised Aussie Pooch Mobile service in the Yellow Pages as well as paying for listings in the White Pages of local phone directories. It promoted a single telephone number nationwide in Australia, staffed by an answering service 24 hours a day, seven days a week. Customers paid only a local call charge of 25 cents to access this number. They could leave their name and telephone number, which would then be electronically sorted and forwarded via alphanumeric pagers to the appropriate franchisee, who would then return the call to arrange a convenient appointment time. APM also offered expert advice on local advertising and promotions, and made promotional products and advertising templates available to franchisees. Other corporate communications activities included maintaining the web site (www.hydrobath.com), distributing public relations releases to the media, and controlling all aspects of corporate identity such as trailer design, business cards, and uniforms.

"I try to hold the reins pretty tightly on advertising matters," said Taylor, noting that the franchise agreement required individual franchisees to submit their plans for promotional activities for corporate approval. She shook her head as she remembered an early disaster, involving an unauthorized campaign by a franchisee who had placed an offer of a free dog wash in a widely distributed coupon book. Unfortunately, this promotion had set no expiration date or geographic restriction, with the result that customers were still presenting the coupon more than a year later across several different franchise territories.

With APM's approval, some franchisees had developed additional promotional ideas. For example, Elaine and Paul Beal wrote informative articles and human interest stories about dogs for their local newspaper. When a client's dog died, Elaine sent a sympathy card and presented the owner with a small tree to plant in memory of the pet.

Developing a Territory

Obtaining new customers and retaining existing ones was an important aspect of each franchisee's work. The brightly colored trailer often attracted questions from passers-by and presented a useful opportunity to promote the service. Operators could ask satisfied customers to recommend the service to their friends and neighbors. Encouraging owners to increase the frequency of washing their dogs was another way to build business. Knowing that a dog might become lonely when its owner was absent and was liable to develop behavior problems, Elaine Beal sometimes recommended the acquisition of a "companion pet." As Paul remarked, "Having two dogs is not twice the trouble, it halves the problem!"

However, to maximize profitability, franchisees also had to operate as efficiently as possible, minimizing time spent in non-revenue producing activities such as travel, set up, and socializing. As business grew, some franchisees employed additional operators to handle the excess workload, so that the trailer might be in service extended hours, seven days a week. Eventually, a busy territory might be split, with a portion being sold off to a new franchisee.

APM encouraged this practice. The company had found that franchisees reached a comfort zone at about 80 dogs a week and then their business stopped growing because they could not physically wash any more dogs. Franchisees could set their own price when selling all or part of a territory and APM helped them to coordinate the sale. When a territory was split, a franchisee was usually motivated to rebuild the remaining half to its maximum potential.

Competition

Although many dog owners had traditionally washed their animals themselves (or had not even bothered), there was a growing trend towards paying a third party to handle this task. Dog washing services fell into two broad groups. One consisted of fixed-site operations to which dog owners brought their animals for bathing. The location of these businesses included retail sites in suburban shopping areas, kennels, and service providers' own homes or garages. The second type of competition, which had grown in popularity in recent years, consisted of mobile operations that traveled to customers' homes.

With few barriers to entry, there were numerous dog washing services in most major metropolitan areas; many of these services included the word "hydrobath" in their names. In Brisbane, for example, the Yellow Pages listed 19 mobile suppliers in addition to APM and 26 fixed-site suppliers, a few of which also washed other types of animals (**Exhibit 11**). The majority of dog washing services in Australia were believed to be stand-alone operations, but there were other franchisors in addition to Aussie Pooch Mobile. Of these, the most significant appeared to be Jim's Dogwash and Hydrodog.

Jim's Dogwash (part of Melbourne-based Jim's Group) had nine master franchisees and 52 franchises in Australia and four masters and nine franchisees in New Zealand (**Exhibit 12**). Jim's expansion strategy had been achieved in part by creating smaller territories than APM and pricing them relatively inexpensively, in order to stimulate recruitment of new franchisees. A territory, typically encompassing

Exhibit 11 Competing Dog Washing Services in the Greater Brisbane Area, 2002

(A) Services including the word "mobile" in their names

A & Jane's Mobile Dog Wash
A Spotless Dog Mobile Hydrobath
Akleena K9 Mobile Hydrobath
Alan's Mobile Dog and Cat Wash
Fancy Tails Mobile Hydrobath
Fido's Mobile Dog Wash and Clipping
Go-Go's Mobile Pet Parlour
Happy Pets Mobile Hydrobath
Itch-Eeze Mobile Dog Grooming and Hydrobath Service
James' Mobile Pet Grooming and Hydrobath
My Pets Mobile Hydrobath
Paw Prints Mobile Dog Grooming
Preen A Pooch-Mobile
Rainbow Mobile Dog Wash
Redlands Mobile Pet Grooming and Hydrobath
Sallie's Mobile Dogwash
Scrappy Doo's Mobile Hydrobath
Superdog Mobile Hydrobath
Western Suburbs Mobile Dog Bath

(B) Other listings containing the words "bath," "wash," "hydro," or similar allusions

Aussie Dog Hydrobath
Budget K9 Baths
Conmurra Hydrobaths
Dandy Dog Hydrobath
Dial A Dogwash
Doggy Dunk
Flush-Puppy
Heavenly Hydropet
Helen's Hydrobath
Herbal Dog Wash
Home Hydrobath Service
Hydro-Hound
Jo's Hydrowash
K9 Aquatics
K9 Kleeners
Keep Em Kleen
Maggie's Shampooch
Nome's Turbo Pet Wash
P.R. Turbo Pet Wash
Paws n More Hydrobath and Pet Care Services
Puppy Paws Dog Wash
Splish Splash Hydrobath
Scrubba Dub Dog
Soapy Dog
Super Clean Professional Dog Wash
Tidy Tim's Hydrobath

Source: Yellow Pages Online, March 2002 under "Dog & Cat Clipping & Grooming" (excludes services delivered only to cats).

about 2,000 homes, currently sold for $10,000 (comprising an initial franchise fee of $6,000, $3000 for the trailer, and $1000 for other equipment) plus 10% GST. Jim's fee for washing a dog, including blow drying, ranged from $28 to $38. However, the firm did not offer aromatherapy or anything similar.

Another franchised dogwashing operation was Hydrodog, based on the Gold Coast in Queensland with 49 units in Queensland, 9 in New South Wales, 8 in Western Australia and one each in Victoria, South Australia, and the Northern Territory. Hydrodog began franchising in 1994. By 2002, a new franchise unit cost $24,950 (including GST), of which $10,800 was accounted for by the initial franchise fee for a 10,000-home territory. In addition to their dog grooming services, which included blowdrying and ranged in price from $15 to $40, Hydrodog franchisees sold dog food products, including dry biscuits and cooked or raw meats (chicken, beef or kangaroo). They did not offer aromatherapy.

DEVELOPING A STRATEGY FOR THE FUTURE

Managing continued expansion presented an ongoing challenge to the directors of Aussie Pooch Mobile. However, as Chris Taylor pointed out, "You can be the largest but you may not be the best. Our focus is on doing a good job and making our franchisees successful."

To facilitate expansion outside its original base of southeast Queensland, APM had appointed a franchise sales manager in Sydney for the New South Wales market and another in Melbourne for both Victoria and South Australia. One question was whether to adopt a formal strategy of appointing master franchisees. Currently, there were master franchises on the Gold Coast (a fast-growing resort and residential area southeast of Brisbane), in the ACT, and in the regional cities of Toowoomba and Bundaberg in Queensland, and in Newcastle and Port Macquarie in New South Wales.

For some years, Taylor had been attracted by the idea of expanding internationally. In 1996, the company had licensed a franchisee in New Zealand to operate a subsidiary named Kiwi Pooch Mobile. However, there was only one unit operating by early 2002 and she wondered how best to increase this number. Another subsidiary had been established as a master franchise in the French province of New Caledonia, a large island northeast of Australia. Launched in late 2000 under the name of La Pooch Mobile, it had one unit. Another master franchise territory had been established in Malaysia in late 2001 and there were two units operating in 2002.

In 2001, APM had granted exclusive rights for operation in the United Kingdom to a British entrepreneur, who operated under the name The Pooch Mobile. Thus far, four units were operating in the English county of Lincolnshire, some 200 km (125 miles) north of London. This individual noted that English people traditionally washed their dogs very infrequently, often as little as once every two to three years, but once they had tried The Pooch Mobile, they quickly converted to becoming monthly clients, primarily for the hygiene benefits.

As the company grew, the directors knew it was likely to face increased competition from other providers of dogwashing services. But as one successful franchisee remarked: "Competition keeps us on our toes. It's hard being in the lead and maintaining the lead if you haven't got anybody on your tail."

Exhibit 12   Profile of Jim's Group Franchisees

LOCATION	ALL MASTER FRANCHISEES	MASTER DOGWASH FRANCHISEES	INDIVIDUAL DOGWASH FRANCHISEES
Victoria	41	6	36
New South Wales 1 ACT	8	1	7
Queensland	13	—	—
South Australia	6	1	4
Western Australia	13	—	3
Tasmania	1	—	—
Northern Territory	1	1	2
Australia	83	9	52
New Zealand	6	4	9
Canada	1	—	—
Grand Total	90	13	61

Source: Jim's Group website, www.jims.net, January 2002.

Study Questions

1. *How did Christine Taylor succeed in evolving the local dogwashing service she developed as a teenager into an international franchise business?*

2. *Compare and contrast the tasks involved in recruiting new customers and recruiting new franchisees.*

3. *From a franchisee's perspective, what are the key benefits of belonging to the APM franchise in (a) the first year and (b) the third and subsequent years?*

4. *In planning for future expansion, what strategy should Taylor adopt for APM and why?*

Case 6 Pacific Cataract and Laser Institute: Competing in the LASIK Eye Surgery Market

JOHN J. LAWRENCE AND LINDA J. MORRIS

An eye surgery clinic providing services throughout the Pacific Northwest is facing increasingly stiff competition from lower-priced eye surgery centers in Canada. Changes are required to help the organization succeed in meeting the price competition in this market.

Dr. Mark Everett, clinic coordinator and optometric physician (OP) of the Pacific Cataract and Laser Institute (PCLI) office in Spokane, Washington, looked at the ad that Vancouver, Canada-based Lexington Laser Vision (LLV) had been running in the Spokane papers and shook his head. This was not the first ad nor the only clinic advertising low-priced LASIK eye surgeries. Dr. Everett just could not believe that doctors would advertise and sell laser eye surgery based on low price as if it were a stereo or a used car. The fact that they were advertising based on price was bad enough, but the price they were promoting—$900 for both eyes—was ridiculous. PCLI and its cooperating optometric physicians would not even cover their variable cost if they performed the surgery at that price. A typical PCLI customer paid between $1,750 and $2,000 per eye for corrective laser surgery. Although Dr. Everett knew that firms in Canada had several inherent cost advantages, including a favorable exchange rate and regulatory environment, he could not understand how they could undercut PCLI's price so much without compromising service quality.

PCLI was a privately held company that operated a total of 11 clinics throughout the northwestern United States and provided a range of medical and surgical eye treatments including laser vision correction. Responding to the challenge of the Canadian competitors was one of the points that would be discussed when Dr. Everett and the other clinic coordinators and surgeons who ran PCLI met next month to discuss policies and strategy. Dr. Everett strongly believed that the organization's success was based on surgical excellence and compassioned concern for its patients and the doctors who referred them. PCLI strived to provide the ultimate in patient care and consideration. Dr. Everett had joined PCLI in 1993 in large part because of how impressed he had been at how PCLI treated its patients, and he remained committed to this patient-focused value.

He was concerned, however, about his organization's ability to attract laser vision correction patients. He knew that many prospective PCLI customers would be swayed by the low prices and would travel to Canada to have the procedure performed, especially because most medical insurance programs covered only a small portion of the cost of this procedure. Dr. Everett believed strongly that PCLI achieved better results and provided a higher quality service experience than the clinics in Canada offering low-priced LASIK procedures. He also felt PCLI did a much better job of helping potential customers determine which of several procedures, if any, best met the customer's long-term vision needs. Dr. Everett wondered what PCLI should do to win over these potential customers—both for the good of the customers and for the good of PCLI.

PACIFIC CATARACT AND LASER INSTITUTE

Pacific Cataract and Laser Institute (PCLI) was founded in 1985 by Dr. Robert Ford and specialized in medical and surgical eye treatment. The company was headquartered in Chehalis, Washington, and operated clinics in Washington, Oregon, Idaho, and Alaska. (**Exhibit 1** shows a map of PCLI locations.) In addition to laser vision correction, PCLI provided cataract surgery, glaucoma consultation and surgery, corneal transplants, retinal care and surgery, and eyelid surgery. Dr. Ford founded PCLI on the principle that doctors must go beyond science and technology to practice the art of healing through the Christian principles of love, kindness, and compassion. The organization had defined eight core values that were based on these principles. These core values, shown in **Exhibit 2**, guided PCLI's decision making as it attempted to fulfill its stated mission of providing the best possible "comanaged" services in the profession of optometry.

Comanagement involved PCLI working closely with a patient's optometrists, or OD (for doctor of optometry). In comanaged eye care, family ODs were the primary care eye doctors who diagnosed, treated, and managed certain diseases of the eye that did not require surgery. When surgery was needed, the family OD referred patients to ophthalmologists (e.g., PCLI's eye surgeons) for specialized treatment and surgery. Successful comanagement, according to PCLI, depended upon a relationship of mutual trust and respect built through shared learning, constant communication and commitment to providing quality patient care. PCLI's comanagement arrangements did not restrict ODs to working with just PCLI, although PCLI sought out ODs who would use PCLI as their primary surgery partner and who shared PCLI's values. Many ODs did work exclusively with PCLI unless a specific patient

Reprinted by permission from the *Case Research Journal*. Copyright 2002 by John J. Lawrence and Linda J. Morris and the North American Case Research Association. All rights reserved.

This case was prepared by the authors for the sole purpose of providing material for class discussion. It is not intended to illustrate either effective or ineffective handling of a managerial situation. The authors thank Dr. Mark Everett for his cooperation and assistance with this project. The authors also thank the anonymous *Case Research Journal* reviewers and the anonymous North American Case Research Association 2000 annual meeting reviewers for their valuable input and suggestions.

Exhibit 1 Map Showing PCLI Clinic Locations
(Clinics designed by a ◆; Anchorage, Alaska, clinic not shown)

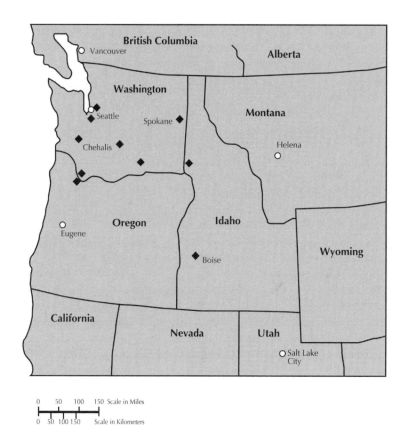

requested otherwise. PCLI–Spokane had developed a network of 150 family ODs in its region.

PCLI operated its eleven clinics in a very coordinated manner. It had seven surgeons that specialized in the various forms of eye surgery. These surgeons, each accompanied by several surgical assistants, traveled from center to center to perform specific surgeries. The company owned two aircraft that were used to fly the surgical teams between the centers. Each clinic had a resident optometric physician who served as that's clinic's coordinator and essentially managed the day-to-day operations of the clinic. Each clinic also employed its own office support staff. PCLI's main office in Chehalis, Washington, also employed patient counselors who worked with the referring family ODs for scheduling the patient's

Exhibit 2 Pacific Cataract and Laser Institute's Core Values

- We believe patients' families and friends provide important support, and we encourage them to be as involved as possible in our care of their loved ones.
- We believe patients and their families have a right to honest and forthright medical information presented in a manner they can understand.
- We believe that a calm, caring, and cheerful environment minimizes patient stress and the need for artificial sedation.
- We believe that all our actions should be guided by integrity, honesty, and courage.
- We believe that true success comes from doing the right things for the right reasons.
- We believe that efficient, quality eye care is provided best by professionals practicing at the highest level of their expertise.
- We believe that communicating openly and sharing knowledge with our optometric colleagues is crucial to providing outstanding patient care.
- We believe that the ultimate measure of our success is the complete satisfaction of the doctors who entrust us with the care of their patients.

surgery and a finance team to help patients with medical insurance claims and any financing arrangements (which were made through third-party sources). Dr. Everett was the Spokane clinic's resident optometric physician and managed the day-to-day activities to that clinic. Actual surgeries were performed in the Spokane clinic only one or two days a week, depending upon demand and the surgeons' availability.

LASER EYE SURGERY AND LASIK

Laser eye surgery was performed on the eye to create better focus and lessen the patient's dependence on glasses and contact lenses. Excimer lasers were the main means of performing this type of surgery. Although research on the excimer laser began in 1973, it was not until 1985 that excimer lasers were introduced to the ophthalmology community in the United States. The FDA approved the use of excimer lasers for photorefractive keratectomy (PRK) in October 1995 for the purpose of correcting nearsightedness. PRK entailed using computer-controlled beams of laser light to permanently resculpt the curvature of the eye by selectively removing a small portion on the outer top surface of the cornea (called *epithelium*). The epithelium naturally regenerated itself, although eye medication was required for 3 to 4 months after the procedure.

In the late 1990s, laser in-situ keratomileusis, or LASIK, replaced PRK as the preferred method to correct or reduce moderate to high levels of nearsightedness (i.e., myopia). The procedure required the surgeon to create a flap in the cornea using a surgical instrument called a *microkeratome*. This instrument used vacuum suction to hold and position the cornea and a motorized cutting blade to make the necessary incision. The surgeon then used an excimer laser to remove a microthin layer of tissue from the exposed, interior corneal surface (as opposed to removing a thin layer of tissue on the outer surface of the cornea as was the case with PRK). The excimer laser released a precisely focused beam of low temperature, invisible light. Each laser pulse removed less than one hundred-thousandth of an inch. After the cornea had been reshaped, the flap was replaced. The actual surgical procedure took only about 5 minutes per eye. LASIK surgery allowed a patient to eliminate the regular use of glasses or contact lenses although many patients still required reading glasses.

Although LASIK used the same excimer laser that had been approved for other eye surgeries in the United States by the Ophthalmic Devices Panel of the FDA, it was not an approved procedure in the United States, but was considered an "off-label" use of the laser. "Off label" was a phrase given to medical services and supplies that had not been thoroughly tested by the FDA, but which the FDA permitted to be performed and provided by a licensed medical professional. Prescribing aspirin as a blood thinner to reduce the risk of stroke was another example of an off-label use of a medical product—the prescribing of aspirin for this purpose did not have formal FDA approval but was permitted by the FDA.

The LASIK procedure was not without some risks. Complications arose in about 5 percent of all cases, although experienced surgeons had complication rates of less than 2 percent. According to the American Academy of Ophthalmology, complications and side effects included irregular astigmatism, resulting in a decrease in best corrected vision; glare; corneal haze; overcorrection; undercorrection; inability to wear contact lenses; loss of the corneal cap, requiring a corneal graft; corneal scarring and infection; and in an extremely rare number of cases, loss of vision. If lasering were not perfect, a patient might develop haze in the cornea. This could make it impossible to achieve 20/20 vision, even with glasses. The flap could also heal improperly, causing fuzzy vision. Infections were also occasionally an issue.

Although PRK and LASIK were the main types of eye surgery currently performed to reduce a patient's dependence on contact lenses, there were new surgical procedures and technologies that were in the test stage that could receive approval in the United States within the next 3 to 10 years. These included intraocular lenses that were implanted behind a patient's cornea, laser thermokeratoplasty (LTK) and conductive keratoplasty (CK) that used heat to reshape the cornea, and "custom" LASIK technologies that could better measure and correct the total optics of the eye. These newer methods had the potential to improve vision even more than LASIK, and some of these new processes also might allow additional corrections to be made to the eye as the patient aged. Intraocular lenses were already widely available in Europe.

LASIK MARKET POTENTIAL

The market potential for LASIK procedures was very significant, and the market was just beginning to take off. According to officials of the American Academy of Ophthalmology, over 150 million people wore glasses or contact lenses in the United States. About 12 million of these people were candidates for current forms of refractive surgery. As procedures were refined to cover a wider range of vision conditions, and as the FDA approved new procedures, the number of people who could have their vision improved surgically was expected to grow to over 60 million. As many as 1.7 million people in the United States were expected to have some form of laser eye surgery during 2000, compared to 500,000 in 1999 and 250,000 in 1998. Laser eye repair was the most frequently performed surgery in all of medicine.

Referrals were increasingly playing a key role in the industry's growth. Surgeons estimated that the typical patient referred five friends and that as many as 75 percent of new patients had been referred by a friend. A few employers were also beginning to offer laser eye surgery benefits through managed care vision plans. These plans offered discounts from list prices of participating surgeons and clinics to employees. Vision Service Plan's (VSP) partners, for example, gave such discounts and guaranteed a maximum price of $1,800 per eye for VSP members. The number of people eligible for such benefits was expected to grow significantly in the coming years. PCLI did not participate in these plans and did not offer such discounts.

LASIK AT PCLI

The process of providing LASIK surgery to patients at PCLI began with the partnering OD. The OD provided the patient with information about LASIK and PCLI, reviewed the treatment options available, and answered any questions the patient might have concerning LASIK or PCLI. If a patient was interested in having the surgery performed, the OD performed a pre-exam to make sure the patient was a suitable candidate for the surgery. Assuming the patient was able to have the surgery, the OD made an appointment for the patient with PCLI and forwarded the results of the pre-exam to Dr. Everett. PCLI had a standard surgical fee of $1,400 per eye for LASIK. Each family OD added an additional fee for pre- and postoperative exams depending on the number of visits per patient and the OD's costs. Most of the ODs charged $700 to $1,200, making the total price of laser surgery to the patient between $3,500 and $4,000. This total price rather than two separate service fees was presented to the patient.

Once a patient arrived at PCLI, an ophthalmic assistant measured the patient's range of vision and took a topographical reading of the eyes. Dr. Everett would then explain the entire process to the patient, discuss the possible risks, and have the patient read and sign an informed consent form. The patient would then meet the surgeon and have any final questions answered. The meeting with the surgeon was also intended to reduce any anxiety that the patient might have regarding the procedure. The surgical procedure itself took less than 15 minutes to perform. After the surgery was completed, the patient was told to rest his/her eyes for a few hours and was given dark glasses and eyedrops. The patient was required to either return to PCLI or to his or her family OD 24 hours after their surgery for a follow-up exam. Additional follow-up exams were required at 1 week, 1 month, 3 months, 6 months, and 1 year to make sure the eyes healed properly and to insure that any problems were caught quickly. The patient's family OD performed all of these follow-up exams.

Three of PCLI's seven surgeons specialized in LASIK and related procedures. The company's founder, Dr. Robert Ford, had performed over 16,000 LASIK procedures during his career, more than any other surgeon in the Northwest. His early training was as a physicist, and he was very interested in and knowledgeable about the laser technology used to perform LASIK procedures. Because of this interest and understanding, Dr. Ford was an industry innovator and had developed a number of procedural enhancements that were unique to PCLI. Dr. Ford had developed an enhanced software calibration system for PCLI's lasers that was better than the system provided by the laser manufacturers.

More significantly, Dr. Ford had also developed a system to track eye movements. Using superimposed live and saved

Exhibit 3 Eye Consultant's Advertisement

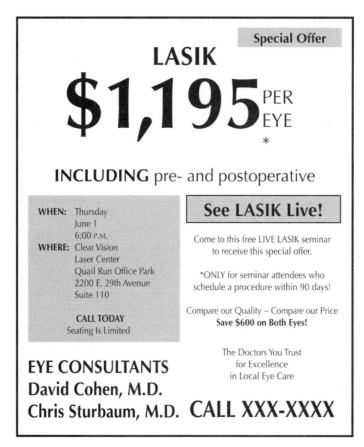

computer images of the eye, PCLI surgeons could achieve improved eye alignment to provide more accurate laser resculpting of the eye. Dr. Ford was working with Laser Sight, a laser equipment manufacturer developing what PCLI and many others viewed as the next big technological step in corrective eye surgery—custom LASIK. Custom LASIK involved developing more detailed corneal maps and then using special software to convert these maps into a program that would run a spot laser to achieve theoretically perfect corrections of the cornea. This technology was currently in clinical trials in an effort to gain FDA approval of the technology, and Dr. Ford and PCLI were participating in these trials. Although Dr. Ford was on the leading edge of technology and had vast LASIK surgical experience, very few of PCLI's patients were aware of his achievements.

COMPETITION

PCLI in Spokane faces stiff competition from clinics in both the United States and Canada. There were basically three types of competitors. There were general ophthalmology practices that also provided LASIK surgeries, surgery centers like PCLI that provided a range of eye surgeries, and specialized LASIK clinics that focused solely on LASIK surgeries.

General ophthalmology practices provided a range of services covering a patient's basic eye care needs. They performed general eye exams, monitored the health of patients' eyes, and wrote prescriptions for glasses and contact lenses. Most general ophthalmology practices did not perform LASIK surgeries (or any other types of surgeries) because of the high cost of the equipment and the special training needed to perform the surgery, but a few did. These clinics were able to offer patients a continuity of care that surgery centers and centers specializing solely in LASIK surgeries could not. Customers could have all pre- and postoperative exams performed at the same location by the same doctor. In the Spokane market, a clinic called Eye Consultants was the most aggressive competitor of this type. This organization advertised heavily in the local newspaper, promoting an $1,195 per eye price (**Exhibit 3**). The current newspaper promotion invited potential customers to a free LASIK seminar put on by the clinic's staff, and seminar attendees who chose to have the procedure qualified for the $1,195 per eye price, which was a $300 per eye discount from the clinic's regular price.

Surgery centers did not provide for patients' basic eye care needs, but rather specialized in performing eye surgeries. These centers provided a variety of eye surgeries, including such procedures as cataract surgeries and LASIK surgeries in addition to other specialty eye surgeries. PCLI was this type of clinic. The other surgery center of this type in the Spokane area was Empire Eye. PCLI viewed Empire Eye as its most formidable competitor in the immediate geographical area. Empire Eye operated in a similar way as PCLI. It relied heavily on referrals from independent optometric physicians, did not advertise aggressively, and did not attempt to win customers with low prices. It did employ a locally based surgeon

who performed its LASIK procedures, although this surgeon was not nearly as experienced as Dr. Ford at PCLI.

LASIK clinics provided only LASIK or LASIK and PRK procedures. They did not provide for general eye care needs nor did they provide a range of eye surgeries like surgery centers. These clinics generally had much higher volumes of LASIK patients than general ophthalmology or surgery centers, allowing them to achieve much higher utilization of the expensive capital equipment required to perform the surgeries. The capital cost of the equipment to perform the LASIK procedure was about US$500,000.

The largest of these firms specializing in LASIK surgeries was the TLC Laser Eye Centers, Inc. TLC was based in Mississauga, Ontario, and had 56 clinics in the United States and 7 in Canada. During the first quarter of 2000, TLC generated revenues of US$49.3 million by performing 33,000 surgeries. This compared with first quarter of 1999 when the company had revenues of US$41.4 million on 25,600 procedures. TLC was the largest LASIK eye surgery company in North America and performed more LASIK surgeries in the United States than any other company. The closest TLC centers to Spokane were in Seattle, Washington, and Vancouver, British Columbia. The second largest provider of LASIK surgeries in the United States was Laser Vision Centers (LVC), based in St. Louis, Missouri. Its closest center to Spokane was also in Seattle.

Almost all of the Canadian competitors that had been successful at attracting U.S. customers were clinics that specialized solely in LASIK surgeries. The largest Canadian competitor was Lasik Vision Corporation (LVC), based in Vancouver, British Columbia. LVC operated 15 clinics in Canada and 14 in the United States, and was growing rapidly. LVC had plans to add another 21 clinics at the end of 2000. During the first quarter of 2000, LVC generated revenues of US$20.1 million by performing 26,673 procedures. This compared to first quarter of 1999, when the company had revenues of only US$4.3 million on 6,300 procedures.

In total, there were 13 companies specializing in providing LASIK surgeries in British Columbia, mostly in the Vancouver area. One of the British Columbia firms that advertised most aggressively in the Spokane area was Lexington Laser Vision (LLV). LLV operated a single clinic staffed by nine surgeons and equipped with four lasers. The clinic scheduled surgeries 6 days a week and typically had a 2-month wait for an appointment.

The service design process at LLV was designed to accommodate many patients and differed significantly from PCLI's service process. To begin the process, a patient simply called a toll-free number for LLV to schedule a time to have the surgery performed. Once the patient arrived at the LLV clinic, he or she received a preoperative examination to assess the patient's current vision and to scan the topography of the patient's eyes. The next day, the patient returned to the clinic for the scheduled surgery. The typical sequence was to first meet with a patient counselor who reviewed with the patient all pages of a LASIK information booklet that had been sent to the patient following the scheduled surgery date. The patient counselor answered any questions the patient had regarding the information in the booklet and ensured that the patient had signed all necessary surgical consent forms. Following this step, a medical assistant surgically prepped the patient and explained the postcare treatment of the eyes. After this preparation, the surgeon greeted the patient, reviewed the topographical eye charts with the patient, explained the recommended eye adjustments for the patient, and reiterated the surgical procedure once again. The patient would then be transferred to the surgery room, where two surgical assistants were available to help the doctor with the 5- to 10-minute operation. Once the surgery was completed, a surgical assistant led the patient to a dark unlit room so that the patient's eyes could adjust. After a 15-minute waiting period, the surgical assistant checked the patient for any discomfort and repeated the instructions for postcare treatment. Barring no problems or discomfort, the surgical assistant would hand the patient a pair of dark, wraparound sunglasses with instructions to avoid bright lights for the next 24 hours. At the scheduled postoperative exam the next day, a medical technician measured the patient's corrected vision and scheduled any additional postoperative exams. If desired, the patient could return to the clinic for the 1-week, 1-month, and 3-month postoperative exams at either the LLV clinic or one of the U.S.-based partner clinics of LLV. In some cases, the patient might opt to have these postoperative exams performed by his or her family OD.

U.S. patients traveling to LLV or the other clinics in British Columbia to have the surgery performed needed to allow for 3 days and 2 nights for the surgery. A pre-exam to insure the patient was a suitable candidate for the surgery was performed the first day, the surgery itself was performed the second day, and the 24-hour postexam was performed on the third day. Two nights in a hotel near LLV cost approximately US$100, and airfare to Vancouver, British Columbia, Canada cost approximately US$150 from Spokane, Washington. Lexington Laser Vision had a sister clinic in the Seattle area where patients could go for postoperative exams. LLV requested patients to undergo follow-up exams at 1 week, 1 month, and 3 months. These exams were included in the price as long as the patient came to either the Seattle or Vancouver clinics. Some patients outside of the Seattle/Vancouver area arranged with their family ODs to perform these follow-ups at their own expense to avoid the time and cost of traveling to Seattle or Vancouver, British Columbia.

A breakdown of the estimated cost structure for each of these different competitors is shown in **Exhibit 4**. Dr. Everett believed that both Eye Consultants and LLV were probably incurring losses. Both were believed to be offering below-cost pricing in response to the significant price competition going on in the industry. Eye Consultants was also believed to be

Exhibit 4 LASIK-Related Revenue and Cost Estimates for PCLI's Competitors (all figures are in US$)[a]

Competitor	Eye Consultants	Empire Eye	TLC Clinic	Lexington Laser Vision[b]
Type of Operation	General Ophthalmology Practice	Eye Surgery Center	Specialized LASIK Clinic	Specialized LASIK Clinic
Location of Operation	Spokane, WA	Spokane, WA	Seattle, WA	Vancouver, B.C.
Number of Procedures/Year	600	1,000	4,000	10,000
Price to Customer, per Eye	$1,195	$1,900	$1,600	$500
Estimated Revenues	$717,000	$1,900,000	$6,400,000	$5,000,000
Estimated Expenses				
Payment for Pre- and Postoperative Care[c]	120,000	450,000	1,400,000	1,500,000
Royalties	150,000	250,000	1,000,000	0
Surgeon's Fees/Salary	120,000	300,000	1,200,000	1,500,000
Medical Supplies	30,000	50,000	200,000	500,000
Laser Service	100,000	100,000	200,000	400,000
Depreciation	125,000	125,000	250,000	500,000
Marketing	75,000	75,000	400,000	500,000
Overhead	200,000	350,000	500,000	600,000
Total Annual Expenses	$925,000	$1,700,000	$5,150,000	$5,500,000

[a]This table was developed based on a variety of public sources on both the LASIK industry in general and on individual competitors. In a number of cases, the figures represent aggregated "estimates" of data from several sources. Estimated expenses are based largely, but not entirely, on discussion of the LASIK industry cost structure provided in "Eyeing the Bottom Line: Just Who Profits from Your Laser Eye Surgery May Surprise You," by James Pethokoukis, *U.S. News & World Report*, March 30, 1998, pp. 80–82.

[b]This cost structure was thought to be typical of all of the specialized LASIK clinics located in British Columbia, Canada, that competed with PCLI.

[c]In some cases, these costs are paid directly by the patient to the postoperative care provider; they have been included here because they represent a part of the total price paid by the customer.

offering below-cost pricing in order to build volume and gain surgeon experience. PCLI's own cost structure was fairly similar to Empire Eye's cost structure, as both operated in a similar fashion.

THE CANADIAN ADVANTAGE

LASIK clinics operating in Canada had a number of advantages that allowed them to charge significantly less than competitors in the United States. First, the Canadian dollar had been relatively weak compared to the U.S. dollar for some time, fluctuating between C$1.45 per U.S. dollar and C$1.50 per U.S. dollar. This exchange rate compared to rates in the early 1990s that fluctuated between C$1.15 per U.S. dollar and C$1.20 per U.S. dollar. On top of this, the inflation rate in Canada averaged only 1.5 percent during the 1990s compared to 2.5 percent in the United States. This dual effect of a weakened Canadian dollar combined with somewhat higher inflation in the United States meant that Canadian providers had, over time, acquired a significant exchange rate cost average.

Second, laser surgery equipment manufacturers charged a $250 patent royalty fee for each surgery (i.e., each eye) performed in the United States. The legal system in Canada prevented equipment manufacturers from charging such a royalty every time a surgery was performed, amounting to a $500 cost savings per patient for Canadian clinics. Competitive pressure among surgery equipment manufacturers had caused this fee to drop in recent months to as low as $100 for certain procedures performed on some older equipment in the United States, giving U.S. clinics some hope that this cost disadvantage might decrease over time.

Third, clinics in the United States generally paid higher salaries or fees to surgeons and support staff than did their Canadian rivals. The nationalized health system in Canada tended to limit what doctors in Canada could earn compared to their peers in the United States. LASIK clinics themselves were not part of the Canadian national health system because they represented elective surgeries. However, Canadian LASIK clinics could pay their surgeons a large premium over what they could make in the nationalized system, but this was still significantly less than a comparable surgeon's earnings in the United States. This cost differential extended to the referring optometrists who provided pre- and postoperative exams and whose fees were typically included in the price quoted to customers. Many Canadian clinics relied more heavily on advertising and word-of-mouth customer referral rather than referrals from optometrists and de-emphasized pre- and postoperative exams.

Fourth, there was some speculation among U.S. clinics that some low-priced Canadian clinics were making a variety of care-compromising quality trade-offs, such as not performing equipment calibration and maintenance as frequently as recommended by the equipment manufacturers and reusing the microkeratome blades used to make the initial incision in the cornea. Canadian clinics denied that the choices that they made compromised the quality of care received by the patient. Finally, it seemed clear to Dr. Everett that Canadian providers were in the midst of a price war and that at least some of the clinics were not generating any profit at the prices they were charging.

Canadian providers also had significant noncost advantages. Because of differences in the approval process of medical equipment and procedures, laser eye surgery technologies were often available in Canada before they became readily available in the United States. Approval of new medical technologies in Canada was often based on evidence from other countries that the technology was safe, whereas approval of new medical technologies in the United States required equipment manufacturers to start from scratch with a series of studies. As a result of this, and combined with the volume that the Canadian clinics' low price generated, many Canadian clinics had more experience with laser eye surgery than comparable clinics in the United States. Experience was a critical factor in a clinic or specific surgeon having low rates of complications. Further, the differences in the approval processes between the countries allowed Canadian providers the ability to offer advanced equipment not yet available in the United States. For example, the FDA approved the first generation of excimer laser for use in the United States in October 1995. No centers in Canada, however, had purchased this particular laser since 1995 because more advanced versions of the technology had become available for use in Canada. Although some of these equipment advances have had minimal impact on the results for the average patient, they have, at the very least, provided Canadian clinics a marketing advantage.

U.S. COMPETITORS' RESPONSES TO THE CANADIAN CHALLENGE

The surgeons and staff at PCLI knew from reading a variety of sources and from following changes in the industry that most U.S.-based clinics were experiencing some loss of customers to Canadian competitors. These companies were responding in a variety of ways in an attempt to keep more patients in the United States. One company in the industry, LCA, had created a low-priced subsidiary, LasikPlus, as a way to compete with lower priced competitors in Canada. LasikPlus had facilities in Maryland and California and charged $2,995 compared to the $5,000 price charged by the parent company's LCA Vision Centers. One way that the LasikPlus subsidiary had cut cost was by employing its own surgeons. Regular LCA Vision Centers provided only the facilities and equipment, and contracted out with independent surgeons to perform the procedures.

Another strategy that U.S. firms were using to compete was to partner with managed care vision benefits firms, HMOs, and large businesses. TLC Laser Eye Centers had been the most aggressive at using this strategy. It had partnered with Vision Service Plan (VSP) to provide the surgery to VSP members at a $600 discount and had partnered with

HMO Kaiser Permanente to provide Kaiser members a $200 discount. TLC was also attempting to get employers to cover part of the cost for their employees and was letting participating companies offer a $200 discount on the procedure to their employees. Over 40 businesses had signed up by late 1999, including Southern California Edison, Ernst & Young, and Office Depot. TLC was not the only provider pursuing this strategy. LCA Vision centers had partnered with Cole Managed Vision to provide the surgery to Cole members at a 15 percent discount.

One of the significant advantages that U.S. providers had over their Canadian competitors was convenience, because patients did not have to travel to Canada to have the procedure performed. Most facilities providing the surgery in the United States, however, were located in major metropolitan areas, which may not be seen as being all that much more convenient for potential patients living in smaller communities and rural areas. One competitor had taken this convenience a step further. Laser Vision Centers was using mobile lasers to bring greater convenience to patients living in these

smaller communities. It used a patented cart to transport the laser to ophthalmologists' offices, where it could be used for a day or two by local surgeons. LVC could also provide a surgery team in locations where no surgeons were qualified to perform the procedure. The company was serving patients in over 1000 locations in this manner and was expanding its efforts.

Technological or procedural advances offered clinics another basis upon which to compete. For example, during the summer of 1999, Dr. Barrie Soloway's clinic was the first in the United States to get an Autonomous laser. This laser was designed to overcome a major problem in eye surgery, the tendency for the eye to move while the procedure was being performed. In an interview with *Fortune* magazine, Autonomous's founder, Randy Frey, described the advantages of this new technology.

> At present, doctors stabilize the eye merely by asking the patient to stare at a blinking red light. But, says Frey, aiming a laser at the eye is "a very precise thing. I couldn't imagine that you could make optics for the human eye while the eye

Exhibit 5 Pacific Cataract and Laser Institute Advertisement

was moving." The eye, he explains, makes barely perceptible, involuntary movements about five times a second. This "saccadic" motion can make it difficult to get a perfectly smooth correction. "The doctor can compensate for the big, noticeable movements," Frey says, "but not the little ones."

Frey's machine uses radar to check the position of the eye 4,000 times a second. He's coupled this with an excimer laser whose beam is less that 1 millimeter in diameter versus 6 millimeters for the standard beam. Guided by the tracker, this laser ablates the cornea in a pattern of small overlapping dots. (Murray, 1999)

There were a number of technological advances under development like the Autonomous laser system that could have a significant impact on this industry. With approvals for new procedures generally coming more quickly in Canada than the United States, however, it was unclear whether technological advances could help U.S. providers differentiate themselves from their Canadian competitors.

THE UPCOMING STRATEGY AND POLICY MEETING

Every time Dr. Everett saw an exuberant patient after surgery, or read a letter of gratitude from a patient, he knew in his heart that they were doing something special. He was energized by the fact that the laser vision corrections they were performing were changing peoples' lives. He was also proud of the fact that they continued to treat all of their customers as special guests. However, he knew that for every LASIK patient they saw at PCLI, there was another potential PCLI patient who went to Canada to have the surgery performed. PCLI had the capacity to do more laser vision correction surgeries in Spokane than they were currently doing, and he wanted to make use of that capacity. He felt both PCLI and prospective patients from Spokane and the surrounding communities would be better off if more of these patients chose PCLI for laser vision correction surgeries.

However, Dr. Everett was not sure what, if anything, should change at PCLI to attract these potential customers. PCLI had already begun to advertise. Advertising, in general, was not a commonly used practice in the U.S. medical community, and some in the medical profession considered much of the existing advertising in the industry to be ethically questionable. Although Dr. Everett was comfortable with the advertisements they had started running three months ago (**Exhibit 5**), he was still unsure whether PCLI should be advertising at all. More importantly, he felt that advertising represented only a partial solution, at best. What was needed was a clear strategic focus for the organization that would help it respond to the Canadian challenge.

One obvious answer was to also compete on price; however, he simply could not conceive of PCLI treating eye surgery like a commodity and competing solely on price. Such a strategy seemed inconsistent with PCLI's core values, unwise from a business standpoint because PCLI's operating costs were much higher than its Canadian competitors, and simply wrong from an ethical standpoint. The problem was, he was not sure what strategic focus PCLI should pursue in order to retain its strong position in the Pacific Northwest LASIK market. What he did know was that whatever this strategy was to be, it needed to emerge from next month's meeting, and he wanted to be prepared to help make that happen. He wanted to have a clear plan to bring to the table at this meeting to share with his colleagues, even if it was simply a reaffirmation to continue doing what they were currently doing.

Study Questions

1. *What are some of the most important aspects of the external environment that PCLI should take into account when formulating and implementing strategies?*

2. *Describe the major sources of LLV's cost advantage over PCLI? Which source provides LLV with the most significant cost advantage? Do these sources of cost advantage have any impact on quality?*

3. *Given the price competition strategies used by Canadian clinics and some U.S. clinics, what can PCLI do to more effectively compete for customers in the LASIK surgery market?*

Specifically, how should PCLI position itself relative to these low-cost competitors?

4. *Advertising and marketing are new to the U.S. optometric services industry. Compare the two newspaper advertisements in Exhibits 3 and 5. Discuss whether you think the push communication strategy works better than the pull communication strategy. Should PCLI also follow a price discount advertising theme? In consideration of the U.S. medical community's ethical concerns with advertising medical services, what other promotional mix elements might be used?*

Case 7   The Accra Beach Hotel
Block Booking of Capacity During a Peak Period

SHERYL KIMES, JOCHEN WIRTZ, AND CHRISTOPHER LOVELOCK

The sales manager for a Caribbean hotel wonders whether to accept a large block booking at a discount rate from a group participating in an international sporting event. Do the promised publicity benefits justify the risk of turning away guests from higher-paying segments?

Cherita Howard, sales manager for the Accra Beach Hotel, a 141-room hotel on the Caribbean island of Barbados, was debating what to do about a request from the West Indies Cricket Board. The Board wanted to book a large block of rooms more than six months ahead during several of the hotel's busiest times and was asking for a discount. In return, it promised to promote the Accra Beach in all advertising materials and television broadcasts as the host hotel for the upcoming West Indies Cricket Series, an important international sporting event.

THE HOTEL

The Accra Beach Hotel and Resort had a prime beach-front location on the south coast of Barbados, just a short distance from the airport and the capital city of Bridgetown. Located on $3\frac{1}{2}$ acres (1.4 ha) of tropical landscape and fronting one of the best beaches on Barbados, the hotel featured rooms offering panoramic views of the ocean, pool or island.

The centerpiece of its lush gardens was the large swimming pool, which had a shallow bank for lounging plus a swim-up bar. In addition, there was a squash court and a fully equipped gym. Golf was also available only 15 minutes away at the Barbados Golf Club, with which the hotel was affiliated.

The Accra Beach had two restaurants and two bars, as well as extensive banquet and conference facilities. It offered state-of-the-art conference facilities to local, regional and international corporate clientele and had hosted a number of summits in recent years. Three conference rooms, which could be configured in a number of ways, served as the setting for large corporate meetings, training seminars, product displays, dinners, and wedding receptions. A business center provided guests with Internet access, faxing capabilities, and photocopying services.

The hotel's 122 standard rooms were categorized into three groups—Island View, Pool View, and Ocean View—and there were also 13 Island View Junior Suites, and 6 Penthouse

Suites, each decorated in tropical pastel prints and handcrafted furniture. All rooms were equipped with cable/satellite TV, air-conditioning, ceiling fans, hair-dryer, coffee percolator, direct-dial telephone, bathtub/shower and a balcony.

Standard rooms were configured with either a king-size bed or two twin beds in the Island and Ocean View categories, while the Pool Views had two double beds. The six Penthouse Suites, which all offered ocean views, contained all the features listed for the standard rooms plus added comforts. They were built on two levels, featuring a living room with a bar area on the third floor of the hotel and a bedroom accessed by an internal stairway on the fourth floor. These suites also had a bathroom containing a Jacuzzi, shower stall, double vanity basin and a skylight.

The thirteen Junior Suites were fitted with either a double bed or two twin beds, plus a living room area with a sofa that converted to another bed.

HOTEL PERFORMANCE

The Accra Beach enjoyed a relatively high occupancy rate, with the highest occupancy achieved from January through March and the lowest generally during the summer (**Exhibit 1**). The hotel's average room rates followed a similar pattern, with the highest rates (US$150–$170) being achieved from December through March but relatively low rates (US $120) during the summer months (**Exhibit 2**). The hotel's RevPAR (revenue per available room—a product of the occupancy rate times the average room rate) showed even more variation,

with RevPARs exceeding $140 from January through March but falling to less than $100 from June through October (**Exhibit 3**). The rates on the Penthouse suites ranged from $310 to $395, while those on the junior suites ranged from $195 to $235. Guests had to pay Barbados value-added tax (VAT) of 7.5 percent on room charges and 15 percent on meals.

The Accra Beach had traditionally promoted itself as a resort destination, but in the last few years, it had been promoting its convenient location and had attracted many business customers. Cherita worked extensively with tour operators and corporate travel managers. The majority of hotel guests were corporate clients from companies such as Barbados Cable & Wireless, and the Caribbean International Banking Corporation (**Exhibit 4**). The composition of hotel guests had changed drastically over the past few years. Traditionally, the hotel's clientele had been dominated by tourists from the UK and Canada, but during the past few years, the percentage of corporate customers had increased dramatically. The majority of corporate customers come for business meetings with local companies.

Sometimes, guests who were on vacation (particularly during the winter months) felt uncomfortable finding themselves surrounded by business people. As one vacationer put it, "There's just something weird about being on vacation and going to the beach and then seeing suit-clad business people chatting on their cell phones." However, the hotel achieved a higher average room rate from business guests than vacationers and management had found the volume of corporate business to be much more stable than that from tour operators and individual guests.

Exhibit 1 Accra Beach Hotel: Monthly Occupancy Rate

YEAR	MONTH	OCCUPANCY
2 Years Ago	January	87.7%
2 Years Ago	February	94.1%
2 Years Ago	March	91.9%
2 Years Ago	April	78.7%
2 Years Ago	May	76.7%
2 Years Ago	June	70.7%
2 Years Ago	July	82.0%
2 Years Ago	August	84.9%
2 Years Ago	September	64.7%
2 Years Ago	October	82.0%
2 Years Ago	November	83.8%
2 Years Ago	December	66.1%
Last Year	January	87.6%
Last Year	February	88.8%
Last Year	March	90.3%
Last Year	April	82.0%
Last Year	May	74.7%
Last Year	June	69.1%
Last Year	July	76.7%
Last Year	August	70.5%
Last Year	September	64.7%
Last Year	October	71.3%
Last Year	November	81.7%
Last Year	December	72.1%

Exhibit 2 Accra Beach Hotel: Average Daily Room Rate (ADR)

YEAR	MONTH	AVERAGE DAILY ROOM RATE (ADR) (IN US$)
2 Years Ago	January	$159.05
2 Years Ago	February	$153.73
2 Years Ago	March	$157.00
2 Years Ago	April	$153.70
2 Years Ago	May	$144.00
2 Years Ago	June	$136.69
2 Years Ago	July	$122.13
2 Years Ago	August	$121.03
2 Years Ago	September	$123.45
2 Years Ago	October	$129.03
2 Years Ago	November	$141.03
2 Years Ago	December	$152.87
Last Year	January	$162.04
Last Year	February	$167.50
Last Year	March	$158.44
Last Year	April	$150.15
Last Year	May	$141.79
Last Year	June	$136.46
Last Year	July	$128.49
Last Year	August	$128.49
Last Year	September	$127.11
Last Year	October	$132.76
Last Year	November	$141.86
Last Year	December	$151.59

Note: Average daily room rate (ADR) is inclusive of VAT.

Exhibit 3 Accra Beach Hotel: Revenue per Available Room (RevPAR)

YEAR	MONTH	REVENUE PER AVAILABLE ROOM (IN US$)
2 Years Ago	January	$139.49
2 Years Ago	February	$144.66
2 Years Ago	March	$144.28
2 Years Ago	April	$120.96
2 Years Ago	May	$110.45
2 Years Ago	June	$96.64
2 Years Ago	July	$100.15
2 Years Ago	August	$102.75
2 Years Ago	September	$79.87
2 Years Ago	October	$105.80
2 Years Ago	November	$118.18
2 Years Ago	December	$101.05
Last Year	January	$141.90
Last Year	February	$148.67
Last Year	March	$143.02
Last Year	April	$123.12
Last Year	May	$105.87
Last Year	June	$94.23
Last Year	July	$98.55
Last Year	August	$90.59
Last Year	September	$82.24
Last Year	October	$94.62
Last Year	November	$115.89
Last Year	December	$109.24

Note: RevPAR refers to revenue per available room and is computed by multiplying the room occupancy rate (see **Exhibit 1**) with the average room rate (**Exhibit 2**). Revenue per available room is inclusive of VAT.

THE WEST INDIES CRICKET BOARD

Cherita Howard, the hotel's sales manager, had been approached by the West Indies Cricket Board (WICB) about the possibility of the Accra Beach Hotel serving as the host hotel for the following spring's West Indies Cricket Home Series, an important international sporting event among cricket-loving nations. The location of this event rotated among several different Caribbean nations and Barbados would be hosting the next one, which would feature visiting teams from India and New Zealand.

Cherita and Jon Martineau, general manager of the hotel, both thought that the marketing exposure associated with hosting the teams would be very beneficial for the hotel but were concerned about accepting the business because they knew from past experience that many of the desired dates were usually very busy days for the hotel. They were sure that the rate that the WICB was willing to pay would be lower than the average rate of US$140–$150 (including VAT) they normally achieved during these times. In contrast to regular guests, who could usually be counted upon to have a

Exhibit 4 Accra Beach Hotel: Market Segments 2002

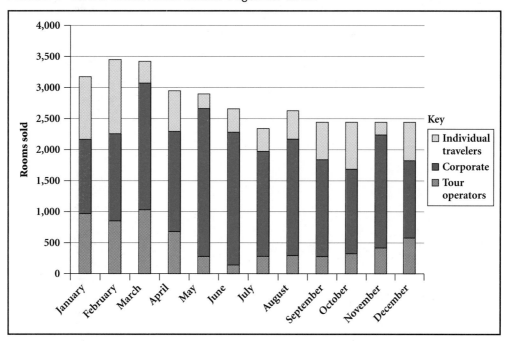

number of meals at the hotel, team members and officials would probably be less likely to dine at the hotel because they would be on a per diem budget. On average, both corporate customers and vacationers spent $8 per person for breakfast and $25 per person for dinner (per person, including VAT). The margin on food and beverage was approximately 30%. About 80% of all guests had breakfast at the hotel and approximately 30% of all guests dined at the hotel (there were many other attractive restaurant options nearby). Jon Martineau thought that only about 25% of the cricket group would have breakfast at the hotel and maybe only about 10% would dine at the hotel. Also, they worried about how the hotel's other guests might react to the presence of the cricket teams. Still, the marketing potential for the hotel was substantial. The WICB had promised to list the Accra Beach as the host hotel in all promotional materials and during the televised matches.

The West Indies Home Series was divided into three parts, and each would require bookings at the Accra Beach Hotel. The first part pitted the West Indies team against the Indian team and would run from April 24 to May 7. The second part featured the same two teams and would run from May 27 to May 30. The final part showcased the West Indies against New Zealand and would run from June 17 to June 26.

The WICB wanted 50 rooms (including two suites at no additional cost) for the duration of each part and was willing

to pay US$130 per night per room. Both breakfast and VAT (value-added tax) were included in this price and each team had to be housed on a single floor of the hotel. In addition, the WICB insisted that laundry service for team uniforms (cricket teams typically wear all-white clothing) and practice gear be provided at no additional charge for all team members. Cherita estimated that it would cost the hotel about $20 per day if they could do the laundry in-house, but about $200 per day if they had to send it to an outside source.

Cherita called Ferne Armstrong, the Reservations Manager of the hotel, and asked her what she thought. Like Cherita, Ferne was concerned about the possible displacement of higher-paying customers, but offered to do further investigation into the expected room sales and associated room rates for the desired dates. Since the dates were over six months in the future, Ferne had not yet developed forecasts. But she was able to provide data on room sales and average room rates from the same days of the previous year (**Exhibit 5**).

Soon after Cherita returned to her office to analyze the data, she was interrupted by a phone call from the head of the WICB wanting to know the status of his request. She promised to have an answer for him before the end of the day. As soon as she hung up, Jon Martineau called and chatted about the huge marketing potential of being the host hotel.

Cherita shook her head and wondered, "What should I do?"

Exhibit 5 Room Sales and Average Daily Room Rates for Same Periods in Previous Year

DATE OF WICB HOME SERIES	ROOMS SOLD IN LAST YEAR DURING THE SAME PERIOD	AVERAGE DAILY ROOM RATE (ADR) IN US$
Part I		
4/24	141	$138.68
4/25	138	$129.00
4/26	135	$137.60
4/27	134	$145.13
4/28	123	$142.98
4/29	128	$133.30
4/30	141	$127.93
5/1	141	$133.30
5/2	141	$103.08
5/3	139	$131.15
5/4	112	$126.85
5/5	78	$135.45
5/6	95	$139.75
5/7	113	$148.35
Part II		
5/27	99	$140.83
5/28	114	$141.90
5/29	114	$146.20
5/30	125	$146.20
Part III		
6/17	124	$134.38
6/18	119	$131.15
6/19	112	$135.45
6/20	119	$119.33
6/21	125	$118.25
6/22	116	$112.88
6/23	130	$113.95
6/24	141	$108.58
6/25	141	$118.25
6/26	125	$123.63

Note: ADR includes VAT of 7.5 percent.

Study Questions

1. *What factors lead to variations in demand for rooms at a hotel such as the Accra Beach?*

2. *Identify the various market segments currently served by the hotel. What are the pros and cons of seeking to serve customers from several segments?*

3. *What are the key considerations facing the hotel as it reviews the booking requests from the West Indies Cricket Board?*

4. *What action should Cherita Howard take and why?*

Case 8   J.M.'s Signature Restaurant

LISA CALLAGHAN AND GORDON H.G. MCDOUGALL

A successful entrepreneur is planning to open a new restaurant but his accountant has serious doubts about the likelihood of its success.

Joshua Mathew had just finished reviewing his accountant's evaluation of his plan to open a new high-class restaurant, J.M.'s Signature Restaurant, in the entertainment district in Toronto. He was troubled to see that his accountant considered his goals to be overly optimistic. Mathew, an experienced restaurant owner, had the idea for the new restaurant when he learned that a restaurant had recently failed in a location directly across from the Cedarcroft Centre, one of Toronto's largest and best known theatres. He liked the downtown location, and the landlord was offering a very attractive lease. While the area was heavily populated with restaurants, Mathew felt the opportunity was too good to pass up—a great location with a low lease rate. He knew he would have to move quickly to obtain the space.

Based on his previous success in the restaurant business, Mathew had set a goal of $4 million in revenue in J.M.'s Signature Restaurant's first year of operations. However, he knew he should carefully review his plan in light of his accountant's comments to determine if he should move forward as well as determine the most appropriate marketing plan to ensure J.M.'s Signature Restaurant success.

RESTAURANT INDUSTRY

The total Canadian restaurant industry was estimated at $38 billion in annual sales with growth in the 2–4 percent range in recent years. The growth could be attributed, in part, to a shift in consumption patterns with more of the household food dollar being spent in the fast food segment. It was estimated that 15 percent of all personal expenditures were spent on food and 34.6 percent of every dollar spent on food was spent in restaurants. The industry was highly competitive with over 63,000 restaurants offering consumers everything from fast food to fine dining where the bill could exceed $100 per person. The majority, 65 percent, of restaurants were independently owned and operated. Of these, approximately 5 percent failed in 2000. Industry data revealed an interesting phenomena. New independent restaurants had a higher failure rate, 18 percent, in their first year of operation.

Overall, the restaurant industry catered to virtually every taste and consumer; from ethnic to fast food; from chains to independents; from low to high price; and from middle of the road to trendy. As well, the industry could be broadly delineated into two different markets; full service and partial service, and was often further categorized by bill size per person. Selected financial information on full service restaurants in Canada is provided in **Exhibit 1**.

J.M.'s Signature Restaurant would be competing in the full-service segment, with a higher average bill size per person. In this highly competitive segment, traditional areas of competitive advantage, including food quality and service, were rapidly becoming a strategic necessity. Today, high class restaurants often sought a competitive advantage through alternative means, such as decor. It was not unusual for restaurants with an average bill over $50 per person to spend over $4500 on decor per seat. Reputation was another key factor; a strong positive reputation was an intangible asset that could translate into real value, especially in an industry that was heavily influenced by hot trends and fickle customers. As well, 70 percent of annual restaurant sales were from repeat customers.

TORONTO AND THE ENTERTAINMENT DISTRICT

Toronto, with a city population of approximately one million residents, was Canada's largest urban centre. Approximately 5.2 million people resided within a one hour drive of the downtown core, and 22 million tourists visited Toronto each year. Selected demographic and income-based statistics for Toronto are provided in **Exhibit 2**.

Toronto's entertainment district was located in downtown Toronto, bordered by Queen Street to the North, Lakeshore Boulevard to the south, Spadina Avenue to the west and Jarvis

Exhibit 1   Selected Financial Information–Full Service Restaurants

Average Annual Revenue	$610,000
Average Pretax Net Income	6.4%
Average Sales per square foot	$498
Average Annual Sales per seat	$14,000
Average square feet per seat	28.1
Seat Turnover*	0.9

*i.e., on average, on a per daily basis, there are 0.9 customers per seat.

Source: Various sources

Canadian Marketing Cases, Gordon H.G. McDougall and Charles B. Weinberg. © 2003, pp. 232–243, Pearson Education Canada. Reprinted with permission by Pearson Education Canada.

Exhibit 2   Toronto Selected Statistics

City of Toronto (excludes East York, North York, Etobicoke, Scarborough and York).

Population: 993,700
Income: 45% above the national average
Working population: 612,238
Spend 10.7% of household expenditures on food.
Business Mosaic: 10.8% of all businesses are "eat, drink and be merry" compared to 3.2% commerce and 2% large investment and service companies. Mid-sized business services = 11%

Financial Mosaic:		
	Platinum card elite:	4% of households
	Gold card boomers:	3%
	Prosperous planners:	4%
	Middle class and mature:	10%
	Still getting established:	30%

Metro Toronto

Population: 5,016,400
Income: 17% above national average (3rd highest per capita income for cities in Canada with populations greater than 100,000)
Working population: 2,444,025

Source: Statistics Canada.

Street to the east. This district partially overlapped with, and extended slightly south of, the Toronto downtown business district. Major entertainment centres in the theatre district included: the Cedarcroft Centre, a 3,200 seat house for ballet, opera, concerts and musicals; the Sky Dome, home of Toronto's baseball and football teams; the Air Canada Centre, home of Toronto's hockey and basketball teams, the historic Elgin & Winter theatre centre; the Pantages theatre, best known as the home of Andrew Lloyd Webber's *Phantom of the Opera*; Roy Thomson Hall, home of the Toronto Symphony Orchestra, and the Royal Alexandra Theatre. This downtown area, which included the financial district, supported the largest business workforce in Canada, with thousands of individuals commuting from surrounding communities to work in the downtown core. It was well populated with hotels and amenities. Approximately 12,000 first class hotel rooms were within walking distance of the theatre district.

Within this district there were over one hundred restaurants, each offering a different dining experience. One critic commented about the district that there were "so many restaurants, bars and shops that on some streets they are stacked on top of each other." The recent economic prosperity of the late 1990s and early 2000s was causing new restaurants to "spring up like mushrooms after rain." There were approximately 71 prominently advertised restaurants in downtown Toronto that fell within a similar price range to J.M.'s Signature Restaurant. Of these restaurants, 12 showcased a European or French atmosphere. Specifically in the theatre district, 29 restaurants with average bills per person

greater than $41, were being advertised over the internet on Toronto restaurant guide websites. Over 55 percent of these restaurants had average bills per person greater than $50.

One key to being successful in this segment was "style." A popular food critic for a Toronto paper commented that a restaurant with great food and no style (or the wrong style for the moment) will flunk out faster than you can say, "Pass the crème brûlée." It could be perilous to ignore the latest fashion and trend. One of J.M.'s Signature Restaurant main competitors would be Reds—a bistro located in the First Canadian Place in the heart of Toronto's financial district. Its ultra-cool bistro brand had become the darling of the young downtown business crowd since it opened in October 2000. Even though some critics found the food itself to be unappealing, the restaurant was always packed, except on Saturday nights when the financial district became deserted.

JOSHUA MATHEW

As a child, Joshua loved food and its preparation. At high school, he had even written a restaurant column for a local paper. After completing a degree in commerce, Joshua Mathew went on to pursue a career in hotel management. However, when the opportunity arose, he opened his own European-influenced restaurant in 1987. Unfortunately, the critics were not kind, and the restaurant lost money before ultimately closing in 1990. However, in 1997, Joshua went on to open a second restaurant, Karma, located in the heart of the Toronto downtown business community. Unlike its predecessor, Karma was an instant success and acclaimed as a trendy restaurant in the business market. Mathew's reputation as a restaurateur grew dramatically with Karma, and not only his restaurant, but also his name were well known in the business sector. Despite its short hours (Monday to Friday, 11:30–2:30 and 5–10), the low building lease rate, convenient location, and check size ranging from $27 to $70 per person translated into $7 million annual revenue in its most recent year of operation and a net income rate between 12 and 20 percent over the recent past. Mathew had since opened another successful restaurant, Lynx (see **Appendix A** for descriptions of the two restaurants, both of which had won critical awards). Mathew was confident that he could repeat his success with J.M.'s Signature Restaurant, and make it the trendy place to dine in the theatre district.

THE PLAN FOR J.M.'S SIGNATURE

A key strategy in Mathew's business plan included taking over the lease of the failed Cape Cod Club, located across from the Cedarcroft Centre. The Cape Cod Club was run by a previously successful restaurateur and well known chef, but the Toronto crowd never warmed to its wood-panelled New England atmosphere. In hindsight, many critics blamed both the atmosphere and the location for its dismal performance. One such critic commented "the theatre district is a terrible location, where dining is only an afterthought and never the main event." Mathew was negotiating to take over the lease and pay the base rent at $22 a square foot per year. Given the forecasted revenue, Mathew viewed this lease rate as a bargain.

Mathew envisioned renovating the interior to portray a decor that was "French bistro with London cool." Mathew felt that a spacious decor was necessary to generate the right feel and was considering incorporating more open space (the plan was for 96 seats plus a 40 seat bar) and using a well-trained staff of 71 to cultivate a feeling of preppy informality. He envisioned the maitre d' sporting a James Bond style tuxedo to let people know that J.M.'s Signature Restaurant was about show business. Mathew was focused on attracting business clientele who would see J.M.'s Signature Restaurant as a place where "love affairs, business deals and friendships begin." Every two weeks, the chef would create a special signature dish meant to demonstrate the quality of the dining experience and a reason for coming back. As a special, customers could choose to have the recipes emailed to them—to remind them of the meal or, for the adventurous, to allow them to try this at home (see **Appendix B**). The award winning chef Mathew had hired was enthusiastic about this concept, and they agreed to a restaurant with a traditional European selection (**Exhibit 3**). Diners, they felt, wanted fantastic yet predictable food in a great atmosphere. The chef suggested they should strive to be the "corporate cafeteria to the six figure lunching crowd."

Lunch was anticipated to be a busy time, but the signature menu should attract evening business as well. Mathew also envisioned Sunday brunch as a highlight of the seven days a week of operation. The average check per person during the dinner hours was forecasted to be $55 per person.

MARKETING

To reach his goal of making J.M.'s Signature Restaurant a hot and trendy place fast, Mathew considered various marketing tools, including mailing 2000 postcards to a client base that had frequented his other restaurants and inviting newspapers and magazines to view the development of the restaurant. In Mathew's mind, any media coverage would be good coverage, as long as it was free. Additionally, the use of the internet as a marketing tool for restaurants was growing in popularity, and Mathew wondered about its applicability for J.M.'s Signature Restaurant.

Mathew knew that the average full service restaurant spent approximately 5 percent of revenue on advertising and promotion. Of this, 70 percent was directed toward advertising while the remaining budget was generally allocated to promotions. Given the average full service restaurant revenue of $610,000 (**Exhibit 1**), a reasonable marketing budget for an average restaurant would be estimated at approximately $30,000. J.M.'s Signature would probably be considerably higher. Mathew had researched the costs of advertising across different media in Toronto (**Exhibit 4**). Knowing that his reputation would draw an initial crowd, Mathew wondered how much his advertising budget should be?

THE ACCOUNTANT'S COMMENTS

Mathew had asked his accountant, Sheila Bruyn, to review his concept. Sheila focused on industry averages and the plan that Mathew had proposed. First, she based her revenue projections on an average of one turn for lunch and for dinner ("turns" in the restaurant business are defined as the number of customers per seat per meal period—breakfast, lunch or dinner—or per day). She recognized that the bar would also contribute to the total revenue figures and accounted for it in her revenue calculations (**Exhibit 5**). Second, cost of goods sold (the food costs), averaged 35 percent. Third, the restaurant industry was very labour intensive. Generally, salaries consumed 30 percent of revenue and the average annual sales per full-time employee was around $50,000. She noted that Mathew planned to have a staff of 71, and based her estimate of salary expenses on those numbers. Mismanagement of this key area could spell disaster for a restaurant. After estimating the remaining expenses, she calculated a net profit of $28,400.

Sheila was very concerned that the 5,800 square foot restaurant would only have 96 seats (excluding the 40-seat bar), or more than 60 square feet per seat, which would require a high seat turnover at an average of $20 per meal at

Exhibit 3   Sample menu from J.M.'s Signature Restaurant

Appetizers

2 dozen steamed mussels	$9.25
(with frites)	$16.25
Grilled sea scallops	$14.75
Fish Soup	$9.00
Vegetable Pistou soup	$7.00

Main Course

Rare entrecote steak	$26.00
With wild mushrooms and escargot butter	
Loin of Provimi veal	$26.00
With prune stuffing, gratin dauphinoise of melted goat cheese with thyme coated potatoes	

Dessert

Plateau de fromage du chariot	$12.00
(cheese platter)	
Assiette du citron	$10.25
Lemon pot de crème, lemon tart and lemon sour ice	
Lemon grass infused Concord grape soup	$9.00
Earl Grey Tea	$3.00

lunch and $55 per meal at dinner to generate $4 million in annual sales. She noted that the average square feet per seat for full service restaurants was 28.1 (**Exhibit 1**). In summary, using the industry figures (**Exhibit 5**), Mathew would need to outperform the industry by a considerable margin to achieve the target revenue of $4 million. Mathew had estimated start-up costs at $750,000, which covered redecorating, some salaries, initial rent, insurance and permits.

THE DECISION

The comments and estimates made by the accountant troubled Mathew. Sheila was concerned that the proposed business plan would be insufficient to generate targeted revenues, even if capacity was met. Had his previous success made him overly optimistic? Was he overstaffed? How much advertising did he really need? Should he decide to move forward and if so, what marketing plan would ensure him the required instant success?

Exhibit 4 Various Advertising Costs in Toronto

Newspapers

Toronto Star

Saturday delivery,	
Circulation in Ontario	693,038
General advertising, $\frac{1}{6}$ th of a page	$5830

Globe and Mail

Saturday delivery	
Circulation in Ontario	299,329
Travel, Special Interest and Technology section, $\frac{1}{6}$ th of a page	$4670
News and Report on Business section, $\frac{1}{6}$ th of a page	$7450

Exhibit 4 Various Advertising Costs in Toronto   *(continued)*

Magazines

Toronto Life
   12 issues per year
   Circulation in Ontario   100,000

Advertisements per year	1	3	6	9	12
½ page colour*	$ 7,710	$ 7,520	$ 7,325	$ 7,135	$ 6,940
Full page colour	$11,185	$10,905	$10,625	$10,345	$10,065

Food & Drink
   6 issues per year
   Circulation in Ontario 520,800

# of ads per year	1	2	3	4	5	6
½ page colour*	$ 8,311	$ 7,896	$ 7,502	$ 7,130	$ 6,773	$ 6,437
Full page colour	$13,309	$12,642	$12,012	$11,414	$10,841	$10,301

Radio**
   CHFI

Breakfast	5 am–10 am
Midday	10 am–3 pm
Drive	3 pm–8 pm
Evening	8 pm–1 am
Overnight	1 am–5 am

	1	2	3	4	5
Breakfast					
60 sec***	$1,270	$890	$740	$660	$600
30 sec	$ 635	$530	$460	$410	$375
Midday					
60 sec	$1,250	$865	$720	$645	$585
30 sec	$ 325	$520	$450	$400	$365
Drive					
60 sec	$1,010	$690	$575	$515	$470
30 sec	$ 505	$420	$365	$325	$295
Evening					
60 sec	$290	$205	$170	$150	$135
30 sec	$145	$120	$105	$ 95	$ 85
Overnight					
60 sec	$400	$80	$70	$60	$55
30 sec	$ 70	$60	$40	$35	$30

*costs per advertisement
**Reaches 22% of population weekly. On average people are tuned in for 11.4 hours/week, which is the most of any Toronto radio station surveyed.
***Costs are per advertisement. Discount given for higher repetitions.

Internet

Banner Ad: $30 per thousand impressions (monthly rate). An impression is the number of times an advertisement is located on a comprehensive website. The ad will appear in locations appropriate for the target market.
Minimum number of impressions: 400/month
Maximum number of impressions: 200,000/month

Average *Toronto Life* impressions (equivalent to circulation) are 3 million a month.

Exhibit 4 Various Advertising Costs in Toronto *(continued)*

Brochures

Corporate program $5,100
           100 corporate locations in Toronto.
           35,000 brochures, colour, 4"x 9"

Hotel program $8,430
           185 Toronto hotels
           70,000 brochures, colour, 4" x 9"

Exhibit 5 Accountant's Assessment

Revenue[1]	$2,772,000
Cost of goods sold[2]	970,200
Gross margin	1,801,800
Expenses	
Salaries and benefits[3]	1,170,000
Occupancy costs[4]	207,000
Direct operating expenses[5]	155,200
General and administrative[6]	102,600
Marketing[7]	138,600
Total expenses	$1,773,400
Net profit[8]	28,400

[1]Assume average lunch bill of $20; 96 seats, 350 days open, 1 turn (each seat generates one customer at lunch). Total lunch sales equals $672,000. Dinner same at bill of $55 ($55 × 96 × 350 × 1). Total dinner sales equals $1,848,000. Assume bar generates $18/seat/day × 350 days equals $18 × 40 seats × 350 days equals $252,000. Total equals $2,772,000.

[2]Industry average is 35% of sales.

[3]71 total staff. Assume 60 staff @ $8.00 per hour × 34 hours/week × 50 weeks. Total equals $840,000. Assume 11 staff × $30,000/year equals $330,000. Total equals $1,170,000.

[4]$22/square foot × 5,500 square feet equals $127,000. Property taxes and insurance equals $80,000. Total equals $207,000.

[5]Direct operating expenses include paper supplies, cleaning supplies, linens, tableware and kitchen utensils. Industry average is 5.6% of sales equals $155,200.

[6]General and administrative includes office supplies, postage and telephone, data processing, commissions on credit card charge collection fees, and other related expenses. Industry average is 3.7% of sales equals $102,600.

[7]Marketing expenses include advertising and promotions. Industry average is 5% of sales equals $138,600.

[8]Net profit before taxes. Total startup costs are $750,000.

Appendix A

JOSHUA MATHEW RESTAURANTS

Karma

Karma still seems to be everyone's favourite. Many of our critics simply want more diners to discover the superlative job the chef is doing at creating memorable dishes. One dish cited among many was "an artistic course of scallops, perfectly cooked, with a spinach wrap in a light polenta with tomato coulis and parsley oil." Others saluted the "astounding fish soup" and the "truly remarkable rack of lamb." The silky service of the wait staff is a true delight. Great food, superb staff, and views from a top floor building help explain the restaurant's success with busy lunch time patrons and more leisurely eating diners.

Lynx

Lynx neatly merged two recent Toronto dining trends: the born-again embrace of all things French, and the shift to a more evolved style of bistro dining. The kitchen is anchored by Andre Miller, a cook of enormous discipline. "Order the soup—Miller's are always delicious, especially his new stringing lobster bisque," said one.

One veteran observer called it a "lovely big open space with the kitchen as view. Great food, and a menu that surprised several of our critics. One of whom announced that Miller "has made a clear shift from the modern Italian cooking that made his name," to a "broader card that is more French than Italian."

Appendix B

J.M.'S SIGNATURE DISHES

J.M.'s Duck

1 duck, giblets removed
1 onion, peeled and cut in half
4 sprigs parsley
4 sprigs fresh thyme
2 stalks celery, cut into 3-inch-long pieces
2 teaspoons ground ginger
½ cup of sugar
½ cup soy sauce
1 teaspoon salt
½ cup sherry or Madeira
1 small bunch of watercress, trimmed and washed

The day before, stuff the duck with onion, celery, parsley and thyme. Place the duck, breast side up, in a large soup pot with enough water to half cover it. Add the ginger and bring to a boil. Cover and reduce the heat so that it simmers gently for an hour.

After one hour, turn the duck over. Add the sugar, soy sauce and salt. Continue simmering for another hour. Turn duck once again and simmer until tender and almost falling apart, about another hour. Turn off the heat and when cool enough, remove duck from pot and place in a roasting pan. Cover and refrigerate until the next day.

Pour the broth into a container and use for soup or sauces.

Before serving, bring duck to room temperature in roasting pan. Preheat oven to 350 degrees. Add the sherry or Madeira and 1 cup of the duck broth to the roasting pan and place in the oven. Roast uncovered for 30 to 45 minutes, basting occasionally with the juices from the pan. The duck is done when it is heated through and the skin is crisp and chestnut brown.

Transfer the duck to a serving platter and garnish with watercress.

Result: Dinner for 4

Paella Supreme

6 chicken thighs or half breasts of chicken
3 ounces prosciutto, cut into ¼ inch dice
2 tablespoons extra-virgin olive oil
1 ounce chorizo, cut into ¼-inch dice
1 medium Spanish onion, finely chopped
1 clove garlic, lightly crushed
1 bay leaf
1 tablespoon chopped fresh thyme
1 tablespoon saffron threads soaked overnight in 2 cups chicken stock
1 cup uncooked long-grain rice, rinsed until water runs clear and drained
1 jalapeno pepper, seeded and minced
1 medium red bell pepper, finely chopped
1 medium beefsteak tomato, blanched, peeled, seeded and coarsely chopped
3 ounces fresh shelled English peas, blanched in salted water and rinsed until cold
24 mussels steamed until shells open
2 cups diced cooked lobster or peeled cooked prawns
8 oz scallops lightly cooked in a little butter
1 or 2 pinches cayenne pepper
Salt and freshly ground white pepper to taste

Preheat the oven to 350 degrees. Saute the chicken and prosciutto in oil in a casserole over medium heat for 5 minutes, until lightly brown. Add the chorizo and saute 3 minutes more.

Add the onions and garlic, cover and cook until the onions are soft. Stir in the rice and jalapeno and cook for 3 minutes.

Add the broth with saffron and tomato and bring to a boil. Stir in the saffron. Cover and bake for 15 minutes, until the rice is al dente.

Stir in the peas and seafood.

Bake for 15 minutes, basting with oil every 5 minutes.

Result: Dinner for 6

Study Questions

1. *Recommend whether or not Mr. Mathew should proceed with this new venture.*

2. *Who is the real target market for this service and why?*

3. *Assuming Mr. Mathew were to proceed, prepare a marketing plan for J.M.'s.*

Case 9   Fletcher Ford Motors Ltd.

CHRISTOPHER LOVELOCK

A young health care manager unexpectedly finds herself running a family-owned car dealership that is in financial trouble. She is very concerned about the poor performance of the service department and wonders whether a turnaround is possible.

Viewed from Queen's Avenue, the Fletcher Ford Motors dealership presented a festive sight. Flags waved and strings of triangular pennants in red and white fluttered gaily in the late afternoon breeze. Rows of new-model cars and trucks gleamed and winked in the sunlight. Geraniums graced the flowerbeds outside the showroom entrance. A huge rotating sign at the corner of Queen's Avenue and Highway 23 sported the Ford logo and identified the business as Fletcher Ford Motors Ltd. Banners below urged "Let's Make a Deal!"

Inside the handsome, high-ceilinged showroom, four of the new-model Fords were on display—a silver Escape hybrid SUV, a blue Mustang convertible, a black Five Hundred sedan, and a red Ranger pickup truck. Each vehicle was polished to a high sheen. Two groups of customers were chatting with salespeople, and a middle-aged man sat in the driver's seat of the Mustang, studying the controls.

Upstairs in the comfortably furnished general manager's office, Gail Fletcher finished running another spreadsheet analysis on her laptop. She felt tired and depressed. Her father, David Fletcher, had died four weeks earlier at the age of 56 of a sudden heart attack. As executor of his estate, the bank had asked her to temporarily assume the position of general manager of the dealership. The only visible change that she had made to her father's office was installing an all-in-one laser printer, scanner, copier, and fax, but she had been very busy analyzing the current position of the business.

Fletcher did not like the look of the numbers on the printout. Fletcher Ford Motor's financial situation had been deteriorating for 18 months, and it had been running in the red for the first half of the current year. New-car sales had declined, dampened in part by rising interest rates. Margins had been squeezed by promotions and other efforts to move new cars off the lot. Reflecting rising fuel prices, industry forecasts of future sales were discouraging, and so were her own financial projections for Fletcher Ford Motor's sales department. Service revenues, which were below average for a dealership of this size, had also declined, although the service department still made a small surplus.

Had she had made a mistake last week, Gail wondered, in turning down George Playter's offer to buy the business? Admittedly, the amount was substantially below the offer from Playter that her father had rejected two years earlier, but the business had been more profitable then.

THE FLETCHER FAMILY

David Fletcher had purchased a small Ford dealership in 1983, renaming it Fletcher Motors Ltd., and had built it up to become one of the best known in the metropolitan area. In 1999, he had borrowed heavily to purchase the current site at a major suburban highway intersection, in an area of the city with many new housing developments.

There had already been a dealership on the site, but its buildings were by then 30 years old. Fletcher had retained the service and repair bays, but torn down the showroom in front of them and replaced it by an attractive modern facility. On moving to the new location, which was substantially larger than the older one, he had renamed his business Fletcher Ford Motors Ltd.

Everybody had seemed to know David Fletcher. He had been a consummate showman and entrepreneur, appearing in his own radio and television commercials and active in community affairs. His approach to car sales had emphasized promotions, discounts, and deals in order to maintain volume. He was never happier than when making a sale.

Gail Fletcher, aged 28, was the eldest of David and Judith Fletcher's three daughters. After obtaining a bachelor's degree in economics, she had gone on to take an MBA degree and had then embarked on a career in health care management. She was married to Dr. Francisco Forlippa, a surgeon at St. Michael's Hospital. Her 20-year old twin sisters, Angela and Marilyn, who were second year students at university, lived with their mother.

In her own student days, Gail Fletcher had worked part-time in her father's business on secretarial and bookkeeping tasks, and also as a service writer in the service department; so she was quite familiar with the operations of the dealership. At business school, she had decided on a career in health care management. After graduation, she had worked as an executive assistant to the president of St. Michael's, a large teaching hospital. Two years later, she joined Heritage Hospitals, a large multi-hospital facility that also provided long term care, as assistant director of marketing—a position she had now held for almost three years. Her responsibilities included designing new services, complaint handling, market research, and introducing an innovative day care program for hospital employees and neighbourhood residents.

Gail's employer had given her a six-week leave of absence to put her father's affairs in order. She doubted that she could extend that leave much beyond the two weeks still remaining. Neither she nor other family members were interested in making a career of running the dealership. However, she was prepared to take time out from her health care career to work on a turnaround if that seemed a viable proposition. She had been successful in her present job and believed it would not be difficult to find another health management position in the future.

THE DEALERSHIP

Like other car dealerships, Fletcher Ford Motors Ltd. operated both sales and service departments, often referred to in the trade as "front end" and "back end," respectively. Both new and used vehicles were sold, since a high proportion of new car and van purchases involved trading in the purchaser's existing vehicle. The business would also buy well-maintained used cars at auction for resale. Purchasers who decided that they could not afford a new car would often buy a "preowned" vehicle instead, while shoppers who came in looking for a used car could sometimes be persuaded to buy a new one. Before being put on sale, used vehicles were carefully serviced, with parts being replaced as needed. They were then thoroughly cleaned by a detailer whose services were hired as required. Dents and other blemishes were removed at a nearby body shop and occasionally the vehicle's paintwork was resprayed, too.

The front end of the dealership employed a sales manager, seven salespeople, an office manager, and a secretary. One of the salespeople had given notice and would be leaving at the end of the following week. The service department, when fully staffed, consisted of a service manager, a parts supervisor, nine mechanics, and two service writers. The Fletcher twins often worked part-time as service writers, filling in at busy periods, when one of the other writers was sick or on vacation, or when—as currently—there was an unfilled vacancy. The job entailed scheduling appointments for repairs and maintenance, writing up each work order, calling customers with repair estimates, and assisting customers when they returned to pick up the cars and pay for the work that had been done.

Fletcher knew from her own experience as a service writer that it could be a stressful job. Few people liked to be without their car, even for a day. When a car broke down or was having problems, the owner was often nervous about how long it would take to get it fixed and, if the warranty had expired, how much the labour and parts would cost. Customers were quite unforgiving when a problem was not resolved completely on the first attempt and they had to return their vehicle for further work.

Major mechanical failures were not usually difficult to repair, although the parts replacement costs might be expensive. It was often the "little" things like water leaks and wiring problems that were the hardest to diagnose and correct, and it might be necessary for the customer to return two or three times before such a problem was resolved. In these situations, parts and materials costs were relatively low, but labour costs mounted up quickly, being charged out at $75 an hour. Customers could sometimes be quite abusive, yelling at service writers over the phone or arguing with service writers, mechanics, and the service manager in person.

Turnover in the service writer job was high, which was one reason why Gail—and more recently her sisters—had often been pressed into service by their father to "hold the fort" as he described it. More than once, she had seen an exas-perated service writer respond sharply to a complaining customer or hang up on one who was being abusive over the telephone. Angela and Marilyn were currently taking turns to cover the vacant position, but there were times when both of them had classes and the dealership had only one service writer on duty.

By national standards, Fletcher Ford Motors Ltd. stood toward the lower end of medium-sized dealerships, selling around 1,100 cars a year, equally divided between new and used vehicles. In the most recent year, its revenues totalled $26.6 million from new and used car sales and $2.9 million from service and parts—down from $30.5 million and $3.6 million, respectively, in the previous year. Although the unit value of car sales was high, the margins were quite low, with margins for new cars being substantially lower than for used ones. Industry guidelines suggested that the contribution margin (known as the departmental selling gross) from car sales should be about 5.5 percent of sales revenues, and from service, around 25 percent of revenues. In a typical dealership, 60 percent of the selling gross had traditionally come from sales and 40 percent from service, but the balance was shifting from sales to service. The selling gross was then applied to fixed expenses, such as administrative salaries, rent or mortgage payments, and utilities.

For the most recent 12 months at Fletcher Ford Motors Ltd., Gail had determined that the selling gross figures were 4.6 percent and 24 percent, respectively, both of them lower than in the previous year and insufficient to cover the dealership's fixed expenses. Her father had made no mention of financial difficulties and she had been shocked to learn from the bank after his death that the dealership had been two months behind in mortgage payments on the property. Further analysis showed that accounts payable had risen sharply in the previous six months. Fortunately, the dealership held a large insurance policy on David's life, and the proceeds from this had been more than sufficient to bring mortgage payments up to date, pay down all overdue accounts, and leave some funds for future contingencies.

OUTLOOK

The opportunities for expanding new car sales did not appear promising, given declining consumer confidence and recent layoffs at several local plants that were expected to hurt the local economy. However, promotional incentives had reduced the inventory to manageable levels. From discussions with James Gable, Fletcher Ford Motors' sales manager, Fletcher had concluded that costs could be cut by not replacing the departing sales rep, maintaining inventory at its current reduced level, and trying to make more efficient use of advertising and promotion. Although Gable did not have David's exuberant personality, he had been the firm's leading sales rep before being promoted, and had shown strong managerial capabilities in his current position.

As she reviewed the figures for the service department, Fletcher wondered what potential might exist for improving its sales volume and selling gross. Her father had never been very interested in the parts and service business, seeing it simply as a necessary adjunct of the dealership. "Customers always seem to be miserable back there," he had once remarked to her. "But here in the front end, everybody's happy when someone buys a new car." The service facility was not easily visible from the main highway, being hidden behind the showroom.

Although the building looked old and greasy, the equipment itself was modern and well maintained. There was sufficient capacity to handle more repair work, but a higher volume would require hiring one or more new mechanics.

Customers were required to bring cars in for servicing before 8:30 a.m. After parking their cars, customers entered the service building by a side door and waited their turn to see the service writers, who occupied a cramped room with peeling paint and an interior window overlooking the service bays. Customers stood while work orders for their cars were prepared. Ringing telephones frequently interrupted the process. Filing cabinets containing customer records and other documents lined the far wall of the room.

If the work were of a routine nature, such as an oil change or tune up, the customer was given an estimate immediately. For more complex jobs, they would be called with an estimate later in the morning once the car had been examined. Customers were required to pick up their cars by 6:00 p.m. on the day the work was completed. On several occasions, Gail had urged her father to computerize the service work order process, but he had never acted on her suggestions, so all orders continued to be handwritten on large yellow sheets, with carbon copies below.

The service manager, Marshall Heyer, who was in his late forties, had held the position since Fletcher Ford Motors opened at its current location. The Fletcher family considered him to be technically skilled, and he managed the mechanics effectively. However, his manner with customers could be gruff and argumentative.

CUSTOMER SURVEY RESULTS

Another set of data that Fletcher had studied carefully were the results of the customer satisfaction surveys that were mailed to the dealership monthly by a research firm retained by Ford Canada.

Purchasers of all new Ford cars were sent a questionnaire by mail within 30 days of making the purchase and asked to use a five-point scale to rate their satisfaction with the dealership sales department, vehicle preparation, and the characteristics of the vehicle itself.

The questionnaire asked how likely the purchaser would be to recommend the dealership, the salesperson, and the manufacturer to someone else. Other questions asked if the customers had been introduced to the dealer's service department and been given explanations on what to do if their cars needed service. Finally, there were some classification questions relating to customer demographics.

A second survey was sent to new car purchasers nine months after they had bought their cars. This questionnaire began by asking about satisfaction with the vehicle and then asked customers if they had taken their vehicles to the selling dealer for service of any kind. If so, respondents were then asked to rate the service department on 14 different attributes—ranging from the attitudes of service personnel to the quality of the work performed—and then to rate their overall satisfaction with service from the dealer.

Customers were also asked about where they would go in the future for maintenance service, minor mechanical and electrical repairs, major repairs in those same categories, and bodywork. The options listed for service were selling dealer, another Ford dealer, "some other place," or "do-it-yourself." Finally, there were questions about overall satisfaction with the dealer sales department and the dealership in general, as well as the likelihood of their purchasing another Ford product and buying it from the same dealership.

Dealers received monthly reports summarizing customer ratings of their dealership for the most recent month and for several previous months. To provide a comparison with how other Ford dealerships performed, the reports also included regional and national rating averages. After analysis, completed questionnaires were returned to the dealership; since these included each customer's name, a dealer could see which customers were satisfied and which were not.

In the 30-day survey of new purchasers, Fletcher Ford Motors achieved better than average ratings on most dimensions. One finding which puzzled Gail was that almost 90 percent of respondents answered "yes" when asked if someone from Fletcher Ford Motors had explained what to do if they needed service, but less than a third said that they had been introduced to someone in the service department. She resolved to ask James Gable about this discrepancy.

The nine-month survey findings disturbed her. Although vehicle ratings were in line with national averages, the overall level of satisfaction with service at Fletcher Motors was consistently low, placing it in the bottom 25 percent of all Ford dealerships. The worst ratings for service concerned promptness of writing up orders, convenience of scheduling the work, convenience of service hours, and appearance of the service department. On length of time to complete the work, availability of needed parts, and quality of work done ("was it fixed right?"), their rating was close to the average. For interpersonal variables such as attitude of service department personnel, politeness, understanding of customer problems, and explanation of work performed, its ratings were relatively poor.

When Fletcher reviewed the individual questionnaires, she found that there was a wide degree of variation between customers' responses on these interpersonal variables, ranging all the way across a 5-point scale from "completely satisfied" to "very dissatisfied." Curious, she had gone to the service files and examined the records for several dozen customers who had recently completed the nine-month surveys. At least part of the ratings could be explained by which service writers the customer had dealt with. Those who had been served two or more times by her sisters, for instance, gave much better ratings than those who had dealt primarily with Peter Ries, the service writer who had recently quit.

Perhaps the most worrying responses were those relating to customers' likely use of Fletcher Ford Motors' service department in the future. More than half indicated that they would use another Ford dealer or "some other place" for maintenance service (such as oil change, lubrication, or tune-up) or for minor mechanical and electrical repairs. About 30 percent would use another source for major repairs. The rating for overall satisfaction with the selling dealer after nine months was below average and the customer's likelihood of purchasing from the same dealership again was a full point below that of buying another Ford product.

OPTIONS

Fletcher pushed aside the spreadsheets she had printed out and shut down her laptop. It was time to go home for dinner. She saw the options for the dealership as basically twofold: either prepare the business for an early sale at what would amount to a distress price, or take a year or two to try to turn it around financially. In the latter instance, if the turnaround succeeded, the business could subsequently be sold at a higher price than it presently commanded, or the family could install a general manager to run the dealership for them.

George Playter, owner of another nearby dealership plus three more in nearby cities, had offered to buy Fletcher Ford Motors for a price that represented a fair valuation of the net assets, according to Fletcher's own accountants, plus $250,000 in goodwill. However, the rule of thumb when the auto industry was enjoying good times was that goodwill should be valued at $1,200 per vehicle sold each year. Gail knew that Playter was eager to develop a network of dealerships in order to achieve economies of scale. His prices on new cars were very competitive and his nearest dealership clustered several franchises—Ford, Lincoln-Mercury, Volvo, and Jaguar—on a single large property.

AN UNWELCOME DISTURBANCE

As Gail left her office, she spotted the sales manager coming up the stairs leading from the showroom floor. "James," she said, "I've got a question for you."

"Fire away!" replied the sales manager.

"I've been looking at the customer satisfaction surveys. Why aren't our sales reps introducing new customers to the folks in the Service Department? It's supposedly part of our sales protocol, but it only seems to be happening about one-third of the time!"

James Gable shuffled his feet. "Well, Gail, basically I leave it to their discretion. We tell them about service, of course, but some of the folks on the floor feel a bit uncomfortable taking people over to the service bays after they've been in here. It's quite a contrast, if you know what I mean."

Suddenly, the sound of shouting arose from the floor below. A man of about 40, wearing a windbreaker and jeans, was standing in the doorway yelling at one of the salespeople. The two managers could catch snatches of what he was saying, in between various obscenities:

" . . . three visits . . . still not fixed right . . . service stinks . . . who's in charge here?" Everybody else in the showroom had stopped what they were doing and had turned to look at the newcomer.

Gable looked at his young employer and rolled his eyes. "If there was something your dad couldn't stand, it was guys like that, yelling and screaming in the showroom and asking for the boss. Dave would go hide out in his office! Don't worry, Roy'll take care of that fellow and get him out of here. What a jerk!"

"No," said Fletcher, firmly. "I'll deal with him! One thing I learned when I worked at St. Michael's was that you don't let people yell about their problems in front of everybody else. You take them off somewhere, calm them down, and find out what's bugging them."

She stepped quickly down the stairs, wondering to herself, "What else have I learned in health care that I can apply to this business?"

Study Questions

1. *How does marketing cars differ from marketing service for those same vehicles?*

2. *Compare and contrast the sales and service departments at Fletcher Ford Motors.*

3. *From a consumer perspective, what useful parallels do you see between operating a car sales and service dealership and operating health services?*

4. *What advice would you give to Gail Fletcher?*

Case 10   Praeda Management Systems Inc.

KENNETH G. HARDY

In April 2004, Paul Paolatto had to decide what to do with the project he had taken on a year earlier. In April 2003, a venture fund had asked if he would meet with the employee-owners of Praeda Management Systems Inc. to discuss helping them sell the company and failing that, to dig the company out of its operating mess. At the time, Paolatto was chief executive officer (CEO) of Keigan Systems, another local software company, but he agreed to take a small retainer plus options (subject to performance) to help the Praeda entrepreneurs and the venture fund that had been supporting them for several years. It was agreed relatively quickly that he would need to take on the CEO role at Praeda to accomplish what needed to be done.

Prior to his CEO roles at Keigan and Praeda, Paolatto had been a senior executive in a $150-million, 2,500-employee energy services business. He had spent most of his career in business development, acquisitions and operations so he felt quite comfortable helping these smaller companies with deal-making and growth. As of 2003, Praeda had sold licenses to Ottawa, Kingston and Windsor in addition to London, the total sales thus represented 15 per cent of the province's sworn officer complement. Paolatto commented:

> In attempting to shop the company, I found very little interest in Praeda across the industry. The company had accumulated a significant amount of debt ($2.5 million) against average annual revenues of $350,000, derived mostly through project work. The company had limited market prospects and the IP (Intellectual Property) was deemed too Ontario-specific with very little transferability prospects. We did receive one offer but the amount was so small, the venture fund would only have recovered a one-third of their investment and the employee-owners would have received nothing. Software companies increasingly recognized that the huge number of diverse yet highly vested interests and operating silos in the justice sector made it almost impossible to bring about a consolidated and effective business solution. The reason was there were few if any consequences to the various justice players if they simply maintained the status quo. Ontario's Integrated Justice (IJ) projects across North America were failing so most leading companies moved on to more promising opportunities.

COMPANY HISTORY

Praeda Management Systems had begun as a custom software company in 1978. All four founding partners had backgrounds in computer science, and they agreed to take equal pay irrespective of their particular responsibilities. A 1993 software application with the London (Ontario) Police had evolved into a specialized product called *inCharge* that Praeda executives believed could save millions of dollars for justice systems across Canada and the United States. The London Police had partnered in the development of the system but Praeda had retained the rights to it. However, the partners quickly found it difficult to lease or sell the *inCharge* system. With a monthly "burn rate" of Cdn$40,000, their venture capital backers had wanted Praeda to achieve significant sales and self-sufficiency as quickly as possible.

THE CHARGE PROCESS

Before a charge was laid, a police officer first responded to an occurrence. To lay a charge in small police departments, the arresting officer selected and typed the charge forms. In larger forces with court services divisions, a clerk typed the forms from hand written or dictated officer statements. Much of the information on the initial charge forms needed to be copied to many other more specific forms, even for a single charge. More often than not, multiple charges were filed.

The manual preparation of these forms was tedious and led to errors about 30 per cent of the time. If not corrected, charges were dismissed without penalty. Police officers detested this part of the job. A study conducted at Waterloo Regional Police concluded that preparing court forms caused more stress for police officers than violent confrontations. An arresting officer was required to attend court, and court officials and attorneys who found errors in charges had been known to chastise and berate the officer responsible.

In Ontario, a Justice of the Peace reviewed incoming charges and accepted or rejected the sworn police statements depending on content and accuracy. Sworn charges were forwarded to court administration for resource scheduling, and charge folders were directed to the Crown Attorney where they were screened and vetted for prosecution and disclosure.

Richard Ivey School of Business
The University of Western Ontario

Professor Kenneth G. Hardy prepared this case solely to provide material for class discussion. The author does not intend to illustrate either effective or ineffective handling of a managerial situation. The author may have disguised certain names and other identifying information to protect confidentiality.

If a Justice of the Peace rejected a charge, the documents were sent back to the police for correction. In such cases, the charge information was recreated on a new set of forms. In a manual environment, this process was time-consuming and error-prone.

Many courts were so overburdened that there were lengthy delays in cases being tried. In Ontario's Askov versus Crown case, the court had ruled that the defendant's right to a timely trial had been violated because the case had taken too long to come to trial. As a consequence of that ruling, 50,000 charges were withdrawn in Ontario. For example, as of mid-year 2001, there were 70,000 additional criminal charges eligible for dismissal on the same grounds. In some jurisdictions, the court backlog had become so acute that minor charges, such as shoplifting, were routinely withdrawn or plea-bargained by the Crown, and police had stopped investigating and laying those charges.

Laying charges could be tricky and time-consuming. For example, an assault charge could have 36 wording variations. A charge could also spawn multiple forms and require several copies of each form. Police officers quickly became familiar with charges for driving infractions, assaults and thefts that made up 80 per cent of all charges and were based on only 20 per cent of the criminal statutes. However, they were much less familiar with the charge wordings based on the other 80 per cent of less-used statutes.

Municipal and regional police forces in Canada enforced a combination of federal, provincial and municipal laws. The administration of the laws in the Province of Ontario was supervised by the Ministry of the Attorney General that oversaw the judiciary, including judges, crown attorneys and court facilities. The Ministry of the Solicitor General and Correctional Services was in charge of policing and corrections. This division of powers between law making and law enforcement posed challenges in providing a coordinated system of justice.

An accused person needed to be charged using the legislation in force at the time of the alleged offence. The age of the accused on the date of the offense were also needed to be considered in order to prepare the appropriate forms. Laws were constantly changing; some would say that the legal system had become a patchwork quilt of laws and amendments. There were no statues of limitations with many criminal charges, such as murder and sexual assault, and such charges needed to be laid with the correct wording for an act that may have been in force years earlier.

THE PRODUCT

Most large police services had some form of 1) Computer Aided Dispatch (CAD), 2) Record Management Systems (RMS) and 3) a radio communications system. An RMS in larger police services could initially cost several million (Canadian) dollars to license. Annual maintenance and support fees could be several hundred thousand dollars. *inCharge* was an automated data management system for police departments that interfaced between the RMS and the courts. Without technology such as *inCharge*, all charge documents were created and transferred on paper rather than electronically. Users selected an appropriate charge and entered basic information on the accused. *inCharge* then generated the appropriate forms, repeated the originally provided name and address and stored the particular charge information with consideration to pertinent acts, date of the offense, regulations in force at the time of the offense, and the age of the accused. The system provided complete functionality from the initiation of a charge and creation of related forms through to witness subpoena production.

The *inCharge* interface between the RMS and the court services environment was based on proprietary technology and a comprehensive understanding of the law and court systems. The product had evolved as a collaborative effort between Praeda, the police, the crown's office and others; it had taken Praeda programmers several years to develop. To cope with changing laws, Praeda created in excess of 1,300 charge templates that dynamically created more than 5,500 interpreted long form charge wordings for prosecution, to cover, at least minimally, the more pertinent acts and their variations. Periodic revisions to the wordings database were made as required by legislated changes. The last update had involved 90 additions and changes; the authors of the interpreted long-form wordings used for real-time charge production by *inCharge* were a Crown Attorney and a police court liaison officer. Praeda and its development partners had invested 20 person-years to define all the workflow functionality, and several hundred thousand lines of code had been written to create the *inCharge* applications. Others had attempted to develop similar systems but, to Praeda executives' knowledge, none had so far been successful. *inCharge* had been sold since 1994, and copyright protection applied. Patent protection for software did not exist in Canada.

inCharge operated on a dedicated server. Praeda would install it as a turnkey (complete) application, or work with the customer's Information Technology (IT) personnel and other suppliers. Praeda maintained *inCharge* under annual support contracts. A typical installation license cost for a larger centre such as Ottawa-Carleton was Cdn$170,000 with an annual maintenance and support contract of Cdn$110,000.

The cost savings from reduced time and improved accuracy for police officers had been demonstrated in practice. With a manual system, the average time for a police officer to complete a set of charges was three hours and 30 minutes. Using *inCharge*, the average time to complete the identical set of charges was 20 minutes (a saving of more than three hours). In 1999, a total of 600,000 charges were laid in the Province of Ontario. At an assigned average cost of Cdn$99.00 per hour of police work, Praeda founders calculated the immediate efficiency savings alone from using *inCharge* province-wide would have exceeded Cdn$180 million annually.

In larger forces where court services clerks were employed, *inCharge* could dramatically reduce the number of clerks required. They could be deployed into other departments or released. For example, London Police had five clerks in court services before using *inCharge* and faced a substantial backlog of unprocessed charges. After implementing *inCharge*, one clerk processed all charges, and the backlog was completely eliminated.

In practice, police officers liked using *inCharge* because it saved them time and tedium. Near the end of a shift, officers were sometimes reluctant to lay a charge if it meant they would spend the next several hours filling out paperwork. With multiple forms required for most charges, many required identical data, such that there was a high risk of error and ultimate dismissal of charges. The use of *inCharge* improved cross-form accuracy to 100 per cent.

THE BUYING PROCESS

Police chiefs were the final decision-makers in the adoption of new technology such as *inCharge*. However, they were seldom strong technically, and it was possible for IT or court services personnel to object to new products such as *inCharge* on technical grounds to the testing or incorporation of the product. Savings were often a low priority. Typically, chiefs wanted purchases that could be incorporated into operating budgets each year. There also appeared to be resistance to programs that were new and different.

Some difficulties arose in demonstrating the hard savings that accrued from *inCharge*. For example, staff that was deployed to other departments did not appear as hard savings in police accounting systems because their reassignment precluded the need to hire new people. Moreover, overtime costs in police forces were frequently buried because the forces offered time off in lieu of overtime hours, usually at time-and-a-half or double-time rates. This arrangement allowed the force to hire more officers, the ongoing cost of which was quickly buried in annual operating budgets that once approved, were seldom ever questioned again. If a police chief was approached with, "We'll help you with your overtime problem," he or she might question that there was no overtime problem.

IT departments were gatekeepers, and many of them preferred to write their own programs. Toronto Police Service has several hundred IT employees and had attempted on several occasions to create a charge management system.

Crown attorneys, the prosecuting officials, generally liked *inCharge* because it improved accuracy leading to better use of court time and higher conviction rates. Unfortunately, they were not members of the buying group. Judges also embraced *inCharge*. However, like crown attorneys, judges did not have input to the purchasing decision for police services.

THE SELLING APPROACHES

Praeda had participated in pertinent trade shows and had tried a variety of selling approaches. The company has tried to sell directly to the Royal Canadian Mounted Police (RCMP) and to provincial forces such as the Ontario Provincial Police (OPP). The front-line OPP officers in the southwestern Ontario region where London is located had seen *inCharge* in use at London Police and expressed enthusiastic interest.

Existing *inCharge* users were enthusiastic about its performance and the resulting savings. In 2000, London Police won an ITX award for its technology, vision and leadership, and Praeda was mentioned in the award. Despite the positive feedback, Praeda owners had a difficult time selling the product to other sites. Two of the first users dropped *inCharge* through no fault of the system. The town of Aylmer encountered a Y2K problem in its infrastructure and, as a small community with a limited budget, it was not prepared to spend the money to resolve the issue. In 1999, policing for the region of Haldimand-Norfolk was taken over by the Ontario Provincial Police (OPP) who earlier had looked at *inCharge* but had not yet adopted it. Support for *inCharge* was dropped in Haldimand-Norfolk when the OPP took over.

ONTARIO'S INTEGRATED JUSTICE PROJECT

Ontario's Integrated Justice (IJ) project was designed to provide an infrastructure for integrating electronic data exchange among all justice ministries including police, crown prosecutor's office, courts, corrections (penal system), probation, parole and peripheral agencies such as the Children's Aid Society. In 1997, the Ontario government assembled a prime vendor consortium consisting of SHL, DMR, KPMG, and TeraNet. (Originally, there were six vendors but IMB and Bell Canada had opted out.) The consortium came under the direction of representatives from Ontario's Ministry of the Attorney General and Ministry of the Solicitor General and Correctional Services. All bids or responses to requests for proposals (RFPs) were to be submitted as a complete response from a single source. Specialized products, such as *inCharge*, were not allowed to have separate standing and could not be identified as a separate part of a prime vendor's proposal.

The prime vendors were to be paid through a government-purchasing plan called Common Purpose Procurement and were to bear the initial investment in IJ software, systems, equipment, management and personnel. They would receive payment in the form of a specified proportion of the savings stemming from the project, only as the savings to the government materialized over time. It had taken 18 months just to write the contract describing the way in which the savings were to be measured, counted and assigned. The Province of Ontario had forecast the total project cost to be Cdn$190 million. However, before the agreement was signed, IBM and Bell had withdrawn from the project. SHL, Systemhouse (now EDS Systemhouse) assumed leadership of the consortium.

From the outset, technicians working for the prime vendors assumed that police-to-courts integration aspects of the IJ project would be easily achieved. Praeda executives, supporting the London Police, agreed that these people did not appreciate the complexity of integrating the various justice agencies. Indeed, there appeared to have been no consideration given to integration with police. After expenditures of many millions of dollars and three years of working with Ontario ministry officials, the four remaining prime contractors had made little progress. There were rumors of great frustration, mistakes and concerns regarding the lack of project progress and the Ontario government replaced several senior government appointments on the project.

Praeda attempted to become a subcontractor to DMR, an integrator and administrator organization focused on government clients, but DMR was worried about a potential conflict of interest because DMR had retained the right to participate directly in the project and bid on portions of it. DMR worried that internal 'Chinese walls' would be insufficient to handle the dual role.

Some RMS vendors had been reluctant to include *inCharge* in their bids because *inCharge* was not a specified component, and they might end up competing against a bid that did not include the cost of *inCharge*. IJ senior project members did not acknowledge the need for the *inCharge* functionality and, as of June 2001, they still did not publicly acknowledge the necessary functionality. When pushed by Praeda to incorporate the *inCharge* functions, the IJ senior members had been non-committal — as though the charge system was a peripheral program rather than a central building block for the system.

In 1997, Bill C-105 was introduced into the Ontario Provincial parliament. This bill transferred responsibility for policing costs from the Province of Ontario to the municipalities. Praeda had been trying to sell to these ministries on the basis of cost savings and accuracy. After Bill C-105, Praeda was told that savings would accrue to the municipalities, and the ministries would not pay for this system.

Praeda was told to sell to the municipalities. When they approached the municipalities, they were told that IJ project approval was needed before they would buy the system.

Praeda tried to sell the big cities in Ontario with the thought that the smaller cities would fall in line. When that did not work, Praeda tried to sell the smaller cities. If initial price was an objection, Praeda reconfigured the initial installation so that some costs were covered in the monthly lease. None of these approaches was effective. Praeda had also retained a lobbyist, a 'rainmaker,' who was supposed to connect the company with the right people in the Ontario government. However, neither this person nor anyone within the IJ project had so far been willing to take the issue "upstairs" to the Management Board of the Ontario government.

Praeda's employee-owners, who paid themselves equal draws of $75,000 per year, were technicians with very little experience in business development and customer service. The venture fund managers recognized that this partnership approach had made it difficult to assign and determine specific accountabilities and responsibilities in executing the business plan. As a result, in 2000, the venture fund had attempted to use its majority share position and introduce a new CEO into the mix. However, its first CEO selection had proved to be a failure, drawing thousands of dollars in salary with little or no results, which created considerable ill will and resentment between the employee-owners and the venture capital fund.

As of 2001, Praeda's founders believed that they had developed, tested and sold a charge management system that would save taxpayers hundreds of millions of dollars every year. They said that any knowledgeable buyers who looked at *inCharge* said it was a great system, and after testing it, they were pleased with the results. However, the founders said that for some potential buyers, Praeda was deemed to be too small, and for other buyers it was deemed to be too cost-savings oriented. They had been informed by an American justice analyst that *inCharge*, as it existed, was about an 85 per cent fit for the U.S. market. However, Praeda lacked the resources to modify the product and market it abroad. Praeda founders wanted to make a go of the company as it stood, but they were prepared to partner with a company with an existing stake in this market sector that would allow it to leverage the capabilities of *inCharge*, or even to sell the company. Another two years went by before the venture fund introduced Paul Paolatto to the founders in April of 2003 and they agreed that he should become the CEO of the company.

APRIL 2004

After a year of attempting to sell the company and/or the intellectual property (IP), Paolatto had found very little interest and only one tepid offer. He then decided to focus on growing the business. In speaking with customers and reviewing the operation, he discovered what he described as "a frightening number of operating and market weaknesses." He commented:

1. The product and maintenance contracts were too expensive for municipal police services. The policy simply could not justify to their respective boards the outlay when compared to the derived benefit. Moreover, the police often did not want to reveal this savings because they feared the board would seek to recover those savings from future budget deliberations. Worse still, Praeda asked customers to engage in an 18-page contract that often took a year to process through civic reviews.

2. The savings from *inCharge* were overstated. A revised estimate of the aggregate value of the automated charge process was approximately $25 million across the province.

3. Praeda had failed to engage in any form of marketing or brand-building within the justice community. Despite considerable endorsement from its current client group, the company did little to leverage up those relationships to expand its market. Praeda's sales technique often focused on the technology and not the value proposition for its customers. Leads were lost or became stale and prospective clients simply did

not have the energy to endure the long sales cycle associated with 18-page contracts and significant upfront costs across the range of municipal approvals often needed to purchase such products.

4. Prior to the development of the *inCharge* system, Praeda developed a number of administrative customer-specific applications (e.g. Toronto Blue Jays payroll system, ETR Rail's accounting system), which they continued to support for years. Despite only earning a few thousand dollars from these old maintenance contracts, the systems often required days of support time from a very small team.

5. There was no succession plan or knowledge transfer amongst the employee-owners. If they left, a considerable portion of the company's IP went with them.

6. The system was designed primarily in London. While helpful in mitigating the cost of external sources of subject matter and design expertise, the London system proved very London-centric, making it difficult to adapt to other jurisdictions.

7. The charge management application was designed as a middleware system, making it very difficult for the company to ascertain which side of the exchange (police vs. the courts) benefited most from its implementation and thus which client would be willing to pay for the product.

8. Finally, the Ontario government was badly stung by the IJ failure. Over $363 million had been expended by three different provincial governments in this space without success. Paolatto believed that IJ had become a "dirty little secret" in the minds of Ontario bureaucrats that rendered any *inCharge*'s successes outside of IJ to be irrelevant.

OPTIONS

As of April 2004, Paul Paolatto was considering a wide variety of possibilities in targeting, positioning, pricing, branding, selling and organizational structure for Praeda. He had to decide whether or not to target the police side or the justice side within municipalities. Then he needed to decide whether or not to continue efforts to get the province as a whole to endorse Praeda's charge system, and again should he be approaching policing authorities or justice department authorities? Finally, there were sales leads in New Brunswick, Saskatchewan and Nova Scotia that needed to be either followed up or abandoned. Were these provinces worthy targets?

He really needed to decide the main benefit or value proposition. Should he focus it on savings, accuracy, or convenient tool for police officers or another value? Furthermore, should he retain the Praeda and *inCharge* names that had been developed and used for many years in the justice market? If there were an argument to develop a new brand name for *inCharge*, what would it be, and what would be the rationale for it?

In his other software businesses, Paolatto was accustomed to selling subscriptions or "seats" on some annual fee basis. This approach might fit the budgeting processes of municipalities but he worried about the amount to charge and the basis, for example, an amount per police officer or and amount per IT employee? There were approximately 25,000 sworn officers in the Province of Ontario. How much would they pay and how could he determine this amount? He did not want to leave money on the table, but he thought that a range of $75 to $125 per police officer per year could be justified and would fly under the radar screens of most municipal budgeting systems. And would he still need an 18-page contract if he were selling a continuous service rather than a major capital project?

The company still lacked enough professional selling talent. He wondered how many people would be needed to sell the product and how they should be organized — by region, by customers or by another factor? In fact, he thought several changes needed to be undertaken in terms of defining roles, responsibilities, accountabilities and even succession plans. With a forecast of only $150,000 in recurring or known revenues for 2005, Paul Paolatto knew that he needed to take some fairly quick action.

Study Questions

1. *Why was* inCharge *failing to sell?*

2. *What marketing strategy should now be developed? What financial results might you project over the next three years if your strategy were to be adopted?*

3. *Would you pursue markets outside of Ontario right away? If so, which ones? What changes in the product and marketing strategy may be involved in selling to those markets?*

Case 11   Dr. Mahalee Goes to London

CHRISTOPHER LOVELOCK

A senior account officer at an international bank is about to meet a wealthy Asian businessman who seeks funding for a buyout of his company. The prospective client has already visited a competing bank.

It was a Friday in mid-February and Dr. Kadir Mahalee, a wealthy businessman from the southeast Asian nation of Tailesia, was visiting London on a trip that combined business and pleasure. Mahalee, who held a doctorate from the London School of Economics and had earlier been a professor of international trade and government trade negotiator, was the founder of Eximsa, a major export company in Tailesia. Business brought him to London every two to three months. These trips provided him with the opportunity to visit his daughter, Leona, the eldest of his four children, who lived in London. Several of his ten grandchildren were attending college in Britain and he was especially proud of his grandson, Anson, who was a student at the Royal Academy of Music. In fact, he had scheduled this trip to coincide with a violin recital by Anson at 2:00 P.M. on this day.

The primary purpose of Mahalee's visit was to resolve a delicate matter regarding his company. He had decided to retire and wished to make arrangements for the company's future. His son, Victor, was involved in the business and ran Eximsa's trading office in Europe. However, Victor was in poor health and unable to take over the firm. Mahalee believed that a group of loyal employees were interested in buying his company if the necessary credit could be arranged.

Before leaving Tailesia, Mahalee had discussed the possibility of a buyout with his trusted financial adviser, Li Sieuw Meng, who recommended that he talk to several banks in London because of the potential complexity of the business deal:

> The London banks are experienced in buyouts. Also, you need a bank that can handle the credit for the interested buyers in New York and London, as well as Asia. Once the buyout takes place, you'll have significant cash to invest. This would be a good time to review your estate plans as well.

Referring Mahalee to two competitors, The Trust Company and Global Private Bank, Li added:

> I've met an account officer from Global who called on me several times. Here's his business card; his name is Miguel Kim. I've never done any business with him, but he did

seem quite competent. Unfortunately, I don't know anyone at the Trust Company, but here's their address in London.

After checking into the Savoy Hotel in London the following Wednesday, Mahalee telephoned Kim's office. Since Kim was out, Mahalee spoke to the account officer's secretary, described himself briefly, and arranged to stop by Global's Lombard Street office around mid-morning on Friday.

On Thursday, Mahalee visited The Trust Company. The two people he met were extremely pleasant and had spent some time in Tailesia. They seemed very knowledgeable about managing estates and gave him some good recommendations about handling his complex family affairs. However, they were clearly less experienced in handling business credit, his most urgent need.

The next morning, Mahalee had breakfast with Leona. As they parted, she said, "I'll meet you at 1:30 P.M. in the lobby of the Savoy, and we'll go to the recital together. We mustn't be late if we want to get front-row seats."

On his way to Global Private Bank, Mahalee stopped at Mappin & Webb's jewelry store to buy his wife a present for their anniversary. His shopping was pleasant and leisurely; he purchased a beautiful emerald necklace that he knew his wife would like. When he emerged from the jewelry store, he was caught in an unexpected snow flurry. He had difficulty finding a taxi and his arthritis started acting up, making walking to the nearest Tube station out of the question. At last he caught a taxi and arrived at the Lombard Street location of Global Bancorp about noon. After going into the street-level branch of Global Retail Bank, he was redirected by a security guard to the Private Bank offices on the second floor.

He arrived at the Private Bank's nicely appointed reception area at 12:15 P.M. The receptionist greeted him and contacted Miguel Kim's secretary, who came out promptly to see Mahalee, and declared:

> Mr. Kim was disappointed that he couldn't be here to welcome you, Dr. Mahalee, but he had a lunch appointment with one of his clients that was scheduled over a month ago. He expects to return at about 1:30. In the meantime, he has asked another senior account officer, Sophia Costa, to assist you.

Sophia Costa, 41, was a vice president of the bank and had worked for Global Bancorp for 14 years (two years longer than Miguel Kim). She had visited Tailesia once, but had not met Mahalee's financial adviser nor any member of the Mahalee family. An experienced relationship manager, Costa was knowledgeable about offshore investment management and fiduciary services. Miguel Kim had looked into her office at 11:45 A.M. and asked her if she would cover for him in case a prospective client, a Dr. Mahalee, whom he had expected to see earlier, should happen to arrive. He told Costa that Mahalee was a successful Tailesian businessman planning for his retirement, but that he had never met the prospect personally, then rushed off to lunch.

The phone rang in Costa's office and she reached across the desk to pick it up. It was Kim's secretary. "Dr. Mahalee is in reception, Ms. Costa."

Study Questions

1. *Prepare a flowchart of Dr. Mahalee's service encounters.*

2. *Putting yourself in Mahalee's shoes, how do you feel (both physically and mentally) after speaking with the receptionist at Global? What are your priorities right now?*

3. *As Sophia Costa, what action would you take in your first five minutes with Mahalee?*

4. *What would constitute a good outcome of the meeting for both the client and the bank? How should Costa try to bring about such an outcome?*

Case 12   Maritime Bank

CHRISTOPHER LOVELOCK

Problems arise when a large bank, attempting to develop a stronger customer service orientation, enlarges the tellers' responsibilities to include selling activities.

"I'm concerned about Karen," said Margaret Costanzo to David Reeves. The two bank officers were seated in the former's office at Maritime Bank. Costanzo was a vice president of the bank and manager of the Scotia Square branch, the third largest in Maritime's large branch network. She and Reeves, the branch's customer service director, were having an employee appraisal meeting. Reeves was responsible for the customer service department, which co-ordinated the activities of the customer service representatives (CSRs, formerly known as tellers) and the customer assistance representatives (CARs, formerly known as new accounts assistants).

Costanzo and Reeves were discussing Karen Mitchell, a 24-year-old customer service rep, who had applied for the soon-to-be-vacant position of head CSR. Mitchell had been with the bank for three and a half years. She had applied for the position of what had then been called head teller a year earlier, but the job had gone to a candidate with more seniority. Now that individual was leaving—his wife had been transferred to a new job in another city—and the position was once again open. Two other candidates had also applied for the job.

Both Costanzo and Reeves were agreed that, against all criteria used in the past, Karen Mitchell would have been the obvious choice for head teller. She was both fast and accurate in her work, presented a smart and professional appearance, and was well liked by customers and her fellow CSRs. However, the nature of the teller's job had been significantly revised nine months earlier to add a stronger marketing component. CSRs were now expected to offer polite suggestions that customers use automated teller machines (ATMs) for simple transactions. They were also required to stimulate customer interest in the broadening array of financial services offered by the bank. "The problem with Karen," as Reeves put it, "is that she simply refuses to sell."

THE NEW FOCUS ON CUSTOMER SERVICE AT MARITIME BANK

Although it was one of the larger banks in Canada, Maritime had historically focused on corporate business and its share of the retail consumer banking business had declined in the face of aggressive competition from other financial institutions. Three years earlier, the Board of Directors had appointed a new chief executive officer (CEO) and given him the mandate of developing a stronger consumer orientation at the retail level.

The goal was to seize the initiative in marketing the ever-increasing array of financial services now available to retail customers. The CEO's strategy, after putting in a new management team, was to begin by ordering an expansion and speed-up of Maritime's investment in electronic delivery systems, which had fallen behind the competition. To achieve this strategy, a new banking technology team had been created.

During the past eighteen months, the bank had tripled the number of automated teller machines (ATMs) located inside its branches, replacing older ATMs by the latest models featuring colour touch screens and capable of a broader array of transactions in multiple languages. Maritime was already a member of several ATM networks, giving its customers access to freestanding 24-hour booths in shopping centres, airports, and other high-traffic locations. The installation of new ATMs was coupled with a branch renovation program, designed to improve the physical appearance of the branches. A pilot program to test the impact of these "new look" branches was already underway. Longer term, top management intended to redesign the interior of each branch. As more customers switched to electronic banking from remote locations, the bank planned to close a number of its smaller branches.

Another important move had been to introduce automated telephone banking, which allowed customers to check account balances and to move funds from one account to another by touching specific keys on their phone in response to the instructions of a computerized voice. This service was available 24/7 and utilization was rising steadily. Customers could also call a central customer service office to speak with a bank representative concerning service questions or problems with their accounts, as well as to request new account applications or new chequebooks, which would be sent by mail. This office currently operated on weekdays from 8:00 a.m. to 8:00 p.m. and on Saturdays from 8:00 a.m. to 2:00 p.m., but Maritime was evaluating the possibility of expanding the operation to include a broad array of retail bank services, offered on a 24-hour basis.

The technology team had completely redesigned the bank's website to make it possible to offer what were described as the region's most "user-friendly" internet banking services. Customers had online access to their accounts and could also obtain information about bank services, branch locations and service hours, location of ATMs, as well as answers to commonly asked questions. Maritime was also testing the use of web-enabled services for customers who had digital cell phones with internet access.

Finally, the bank had recently started issuing new credit cards containing chips with embedded radio-frequency identification (RFID), which speeded transactions by allowing customers to wave their cards close to a special reader rather than having to swipe them in the traditional way. All these actions seemed to be bearing fruit. In the most recent six months, Maritime had seen a significant increase in the number of new accounts opened, compared to the same period of the previous year. And quarterly data released by the Bank of Canada showed that Maritime Bank was steadily increasing its share of new deposits in the region.

CUSTOMER SERVICE ISSUES

New financial products had been introduced at a rapid rate. But the bank found that many existing "platform" staff—known as new accounts assistants—were ill equipped to sell these services because of lack of product knowledge and inadequate training in selling skills. As Costanzo recalled:

> The problem was that they were so used to sitting at their desks waiting for a customer to approach them with a specific request, such as a mortgage or car loan, that it was hard to get them to take a more positive approach that involved actively probing for customer needs. Their whole job seemed to revolve around filling out forms or responding to prompts on their computer screens. We were way behind most other banks in this respect.

As the automation program proceeded, the mix of activities performed by the tellers started to change. A growing number of customers were using the ATMs, the website, and automated telephone banking for a broad array of transactions, including cash withdrawals and deposits (from the ATMs), transfers of funds between accounts, and requesting account balances. The ATMs at the Scotia Square branch had the highest utilization of any of Maritime's branches, reflecting the large number of students and young professionals served at that location. Costanzo noted that customers who were older or less well-educated seemed to prefer being served by "a real person, rather than a machine." They were particularly reluctant to make deposits via an ATM.

A year earlier, the head office had selected three branches, including Scotia Square, as test sites for a new customer service program, which included a radical redesign of the branch interior. The Scotia Square branch was in a busy urban location, about one mile from the central business district and less than 10-minutes' walk from the campus of a large university. The branch was surrounded by retail stores and close to commercial and professional offices. The other test branches were among the bank's larger suburban offices in two different metropolitan areas and were located in a shopping mall and next to a big hospital, respectively.

As part of the branch renovation program, each of these three branches had previously been remodelled to include no fewer than four ATMs (Scotia Square had six), which could be closed off from the rest of the branch so that they would remain accessible to customers 24 hours a day. Further remodelling was then undertaken to locate a customer service desk near the entrance; close to each desk were two electronic information terminals, featuring colour touch screens that customers could activate to obtain information on a variety of bank services. The teller stations were redesigned to provide two levels of service: an express station for simple deposits and for cashing of approved cheques, and regular stations for the full array of services provided by tellers. The number of stations open at a given time was varied to reflect the volume of anticipated business, and staffing arrangements were changed to ensure that more tellers were on hand to serve customers during the busiest periods. Finally, the platform area in each branch was reconstructed to create what the architect described as "a friendly, yet professional appearance."

HUMAN RESOURCES

With the new environment came new training programs for the staff of these three branches and new job descriptions and job titles: customer assistance representatives (for the platform staff), customer service representatives (for the tellers), and customer service director (instead of assistant branch manager). The head teller position was renamed head CSR. Details of the new job descriptions are shown in the **Appendix**. The training programs for each group included sessions designed to develop improved knowledge of both new and existing retail products. (CARs received more extensive training in this area than did CSRs.) The CARs also attended a 15-hour course, offered in three separate sessions, on basic selling skills. This program covered key steps in the sales process, including building a relationship, exploring customer needs, determining a solution, and overcoming objections.

The sales training program for CSRs, by contrast, consisted of just two 2-hour sessions designed to develop skills in recognizing and probing customer needs, presenting product features and benefits, overcoming objections, and referring customers to CARs. All staff members in customer service positions participated in sessions designed to improve their communication skills and professional image: clothing and personal grooming and interactions with customers were all discussed. Said the trainer, "Remember, people's money is too important to entrust to someone who doesn't look and act the part!"

CARs were instructed to rise from their seats and shake hands with customers. Both CARs and CSRs were given exercises designed to improve their listening skills and their powers of observation. All employees working where they could be seen by customers were ordered to refrain from drinking soda and chewing gum on the job. (Smoking by both employees and customers had been banned some years earlier under the bank's smoke-free office policy.)

Although Maritime Bank's management anticipated that most of the increased emphasis on selling would fall to the CARs, they also foresaw a limited selling role for the customer service reps, who would be expected to mention various products and facilities offered by the bank as they served customers at the teller windows. For instance, if a customer happened to say something about an upcoming vacation, the CSR was supposed to mention traveller's cheques; if the customer complained about bounced cheques, the CSR should suggest speaking to a CAR about opening a personal line of credit that would provide an automatic overdraft protection; if the customer mentioned investments, the CSR was expected to refer him or her to a CAR who could provide information on money market accounts, certificates of deposit, or Maritime's discount brokerage service. All CSRs were supplied with their own business cards. When making a referral, they were expected to write the customer's name and the product of interest on the back of a card, give it to the customer and send that individual to the customer assistance desks.

In an effort to motivate CSRs at the three branches to sell specific financial products, the bank experimented with various incentive programs. The first involved cash bonuses for referrals to CARs that resulted in sale of specific products. During a one-month period, CSRs were offered a $50 bonus for each referral leading to a customer's opening a personal line of credit account; the CARs received a $20 bonus for each account they opened, regardless of whether or not it came as a referral or simply a walk-in. Eight such bonuses were paid to CSRs at Scotia Square, with three each going to just two of the full-time CSRs, Jean Warshawski and Bruce Greenfield. Karen Mitchell was not among the recipients. However, this program was not renewed, since it was felt that there were other, more cost-effective means of marketing this product. In addition, Reeves, the customer service director, had reason to believe that Greenfield had colluded with one of the CARs, his girlfriend, to claim referrals which he had not, in fact, made. Another test branch reported similar suspicions of two of its CSRs.

A second promotion followed and was based on allocating credits to the CSRs for successful referrals. The value of the credit varied according to the nature of the product—for instance, a debit card was worth 500 credits—and accumulated credits could be exchanged for merchandise gifts. This program was deemed ineffective and discontinued after three months. The basic problem seemed to be that the value of the gifts was seen as too low in relation to the amount of effort required. Other problems with these promotional schemes included lack of product knowledge on the part of the CSRs and time pressures when many customers were waiting in line to be served.

The bank had next turned to an approach which, in David Reeves' words, "used the stick rather than the carrot." All CSRs had traditionally been evaluated half-yearly on a variety of criteria, including accuracy, speed, quality of interactions with customers, punctuality of arrival for work, job attitudes, co-operation with other employees, and professional image. The evaluation process assigned a number of points to each criterion, with accuracy and speed being the most heavily weighted. In addition to appraisals by the customer service director and the branch manager, with input from the head CSR, Maritime had recently instituted a program of anonymous visits by what was popularly known as the "mystery client." Each CSR was visited at least once a quarter by a professional evaluator posing as a customer. This individual's appraisal of the CSR's appearance, performance, and attitude was included in the overall evaluation. The number of points scored by each CSR had a direct impact on merit pay raises and on selection for promotion to the head CSR position or to platform jobs.

To encourage improved product knowledge and "consultative selling" by CSRs, the evaluation process was revised to include points assigned for each individual's success in sales referrals. Under the new evaluation scheme, the maximum number of points assignable for effectiveness in making sales—directly or through referrals to CARs—amounted to 30 percent of the potential total score. Although CSR-initiated sales had risen significantly in the most recent half-year, Reeves sensed that morale had dropped among this group, in contrast to the CARs, whose enthusiasm and commitment had risen significantly. He had also noticed an increase in CSR errors. One CSR had quit, complaining of too much pressure.

Karen Mitchell

Under the old scoring system, Karen Mitchell had been the highest-scoring teller/CSR for four consecutive half-years. But after two half-years under the new system, her ranking had dropped to fourth out of the seven full-time tellers. The top-ranking CSR, Mary Bell, had been with Maritime Bank for sixteen years, but had declined repeated invitations to apply for a head teller position, saying that she was happy where she was, earning at the top of the CSR scale, and did not want "the extra worry and responsibility." Mitchell ranked first on all but one of the operationally related criteria (interactions with customers, where she ranked second), but sixth on selling effectiveness (**Exhibit 1**).

Costanzo and Reeves had spoken to Mitchell about her performance and expressed disappointment. Mitchell had informed them, respectfully but firmly, that she saw the most important aspect of her job as giving customers fast, accurate, and courteous service, telling the two bank officers:

> I did try this selling thing but it just seemed to annoy people. Some said they were in a hurry and couldn't talk now; others looked at me as if I were slightly crazy to bring up the subject of a different bank service than the one they were currently transacting. And then, when you got the odd person who seemed interested, you could hear the other customers in the line grumbling about the slow service.
>
> Really, the last straw was when I noticed on the computer screen that this woman had several thousand in her savings account so I suggested to her, just as the trainer had told us, that she could earn more interest if she opened a money market account. Well, she told me it was none of my business what she did with her money, and stomped off. Don't get me wrong, I love being able to help customers, and if they ask for my advice, I'll gladly tell them about what the bank has to offer.

Exhibit 1   Maritime Bank: Summary of Performance Evaluation Scores for Customer Service Representatives at Scotia Square Branch During Latest Two Half-Year Periods

CSR Name[3]	Length of Full-Time Bank Service	Operational Criteria[1] (max.: 70 points)		Selling Effectiveness[2] (max.: 30 points)		Total Score	
		1st Half	2nd Half	1st Half	2nd Half	1st Half	2nd Half
Mary Bell	16 years, 10 months	65	64	16	20	81	84
Scott Dubois	2 years, 3 months	63	61	15	19	78	80
Bruce Greenfield	12 months	48	42	20	26	68	68
Karen Mitchell	3 years, 7 months	67	67	13	12	80	79
Sharon Rubin	1 year, 4 months	53	55	8	9	61	64
Swee Hoon Chen	7 months	—	50	—	22	—	72
Jean Warshawski	2 years, 1 month	57	55	21	28	79	83

[1]Totals based on sum of ratings points against various criteria, including accuracy, work production, attendance and punctuality, personal appearance, organization of work, initiative, cooperation with others, problem-solving ability, and quality of interaction with customers.

[2]Points awarded for both direct sales by CSR (e.g., traveller's cheques) and referral selling by CSR to CAR (e.g., debit card, certificates of deposit, personal line of credit).

[3]Full-time CSRs only (part-time CSRs were evaluated separately).

Selecting a New Head CSR

Two weeks after this meeting, it was announced that the head CSR was leaving. The job entailed some supervision of the work of the other CSRs (including allocation of work assignments and scheduling part-time CSRs at busy periods or during employee vacations), consultation on—and, where possible, resolution of—any problems occurring at the teller stations, and handling of large cash deposits and withdrawals by local retailers (see position description in the **Appendix**). When not engaged on such tasks, the head CSR was expected to operate a regular teller window.

The pay scale for a head CSR ranged from $10.00 to $15.00 per hour, depending on qualifications, seniority, and branch size, as compared to a range $8.40 to $12.00 per hour for CSRs. The pay scale for CARs ranged from $9.20 to $13.50. Full-time employees (who were not unionized) worked a 40-hour week, including some evenings until 6:00 p.m. and certain Saturday mornings. Costanzo indicated that the pay scales were typical for banks in the region, although the average CSR at Maritime was better qualified than those at smaller banks and therefore higher on the scale. Karen Mitchell was currently earning $10.80 per hour, reflecting her education, which included an associate's degree in business administration from the local community college, three-and-a-half years' experience, and significant past merit increases. If promoted to head CSR, she would qualify for an initial rate of $12.50 an hour. When applications for the positions closed, Mitchell was one of three candidates. The other two candidates were Jean Warshawski, 42, another CSR at the Scotia Square branch; and Curtis Richter, 24, the head CSR at one of Maritime Bank's small suburban branches, who was seeking more responsibility.

Warshawski was married with two sons in school. She had started working as a part-time teller at Scotia Square some three years previously, switching to full-time work a year later in order, as she said, to put away some money for her boys' college education. Warshawski was a cheerful woman with a jolly laugh. She had a wonderful memory for people's names and Reeves had often seen her greeting customers on the street or in a restaurant during her lunch hour. Reviewing her evaluations over the previous three years, Reeves noted that she had initially performed poorly on accuracy and at one point, when she was still a part-timer, had been put on probation because of frequent inaccuracies in the balance in her cash drawer at the end of the day. Although Reeves considered her much improved on this score, he still saw room for improvement. The customer service director had also had occasion to reprimand her for tardiness during the past year. Warshawski attributed this to health problems with her elder son who, she said, was now responding to treatment.

Both Reeves and Costanzo had observed Warshawski at work and agreed that her interactions with customers were exceptionally good, although she tended to be overly chatty and was not as fast as Karen Mitchell. She seemed to have a natural ability to size up customers and to decide which ones were good prospects for a quick sales pitch on a specific financial product. Although slightly untidy in her personal appearance, she was very well organized in her work and was quick to help her fellow CSRs, especially new hires. She was currently earning $10.20 per hour as a CSR and would qualify for a rate of $12.10 as head CSR. In the most recent six months, Warshawski had ranked ahead of Mitchell as a result of being very successful in consultative selling (**Exhibit 1**).

Richter, the third candidate, was not working in one of the three test branches, so had not been exposed to the consultative selling program and its corresponding evaluation scheme. However, he had received excellent evaluations for his work in Maritime's small Longmeadow branch, where he had been employed for three years. A move to Scotia Square would increase his earnings from $11.20 to $12.10 per hour. Reeves and Costanzo had interviewed Richter and considered him intelligent and personable. He had joined the bank after dropping out of college midway through his third year, but had recently started taking evening courses in order to complete his degree. The Longmeadow branch was located in an older part of town, where commercial and retail activity were rather stagnant. This branch (which was rumoured to be under consideration for closure) had not yet been renovated and had no ATMs, although there was an ATM accessible to Maritime customers one block away. Richter supervised three CSRs and reported directly to the branch manager, who spoke very highly of him. Since there were no CARs in this branch, Richter and another experienced CSR took turns to handle new accounts and loan or mortgage applications.

Costanzo and Reeves were troubled by the decision that faced them. Prior to the bank's shift in focus, Mitchell would have been the natural choice for the head CSR job which, in turn, could be a stepping stone to further promotions, including customer assistance representative, customer service director, and, eventually, manager of a small branch or a management position in the head office. Mitchell had told her superiors that she was interested in making a career in banking and that she was eager to take on further responsibilities.

Compounding the problem was the fact that the three branches testing the improved branch design and new customer service program had just completed a full year of the test. Costanzo knew that sales and profits were up significantly at all three branches, relative to the bank's performance as a whole. She anticipated that top management would want to extend the program system-wide after making any modifications that seemed desirable.

Appendix

MARITIME BANK: JOB DESCRIPTIONS FOR CUSTOMER SERVICE STAFF IN BRANCHES

Previous Job Description for Teller

FUNCTION: Provides customer services by receiving, paying out, and keeping accurate records of all moneys involved in paying and receiving transactions. Promotes the bank's services.

RESPONSIBILITIES
1. Serves customers:
   * Accepts deposits, verifies cash and endorsements, and gives customers their receipts.
   * Cashes cheques within the limits assigned or refers customers to supervisor for authorization.
   * Accepts savings deposits and withdrawals, verifies signatures, and posts interest and balances as necessary.
   * Accepts loan, credit card, utility, and other payments.
   * Issues money orders, cashier's cheques, traveller's cheques, and foreign currency, and issues or redeems Canada savings bonds.
   * Reconciles customer statements and confers with bookkeeping personnel regarding discrepancies in balances or other problems.
   * Issues credit card advances.
2. Prepares individual daily settlement of teller cash and proof transactions.

3. Prepares branch daily journal and general ledger.
4. Promotes the bank's services:
   * Cross-sells other bank services appropriate to customer's needs.
   * Answers inquiries regarding bank matters.
   * Directs customers to other departments for specialized services.
5. Assists with other branch duties:
   * Receipts night and mail deposits.
   * Reconciles ATM transactions.
   * Provides safe deposit services.
   * Performs secretarial duties.

New Job Description for Customer Service Representative

FUNCTION: Provides customers with the highest-quality services, with special emphasis on recognizing customer need and cross-selling appropriate bank services. Plays an active role in developing and maintaining good relations.

RESPONSIBILITIES
1. Presents and communicates the best possible customer service:
   * Greets all customers with a courteous, friendly attitude.

- Provides fast, accurate, friendly service.
- Uses customer's name whenever possible.

2. Sells bank services and maintains customer relations:
   - Cross-sells retail services by identifying and referring valid prospects to a customer assistance representative or customer service director. When time permits (no other customers waiting in line), should actively cross-sell retail services.
   - Develops new business by acquainting non-customers with bank services and existing customers with additional services that they are not currently using.

3. Provides a prompt and efficient operation on a professional level:
   - Receives cash and/or cheques for chequing accounts, savings accounts, taxes withheld, loan payments, MasterCard and Visa, mortgage payments, money orders, traveller's cheques, cashier's cheques.
   - Verifies amount of cash and/or cheques received, being alert to counterfeit or fraudulent items.
   - Cashes cheques in accordance with bank policy. Watches for stop payments and holds funds per bank policy.
   - Receives payment of collection items, safe deposit rentals, and other miscellaneous items.
   - Confers with head CSR or customer service director on non-routine situations.
   - Sells traveller's cheques, money orders, monthly transit passes, and cashier's cheques, Canada savings bonds, and may redeem coupons and sell or redeem foreign currency.
   - Prepares coin and currency orders as necessary.
   - Services, maintains, and settles ATMs as required.
   - Ensures only minimum cash exposure necessary for efficient operation is kept in cash drawer; removes excess cash immediately to secured location.
   - Prepares accurate and timely daily settlement of work.
   - Performs bookkeeping and operational functions as assigned by customer service director.

New Job Description for Head Customer Service Representative

FUNCTION: Supervises all customer service representatives in the designated branch office, ensuring efficient operation and the highest-quality service to customers. Plays an active role in developing and maintaining good customer relations. Assists other branch personnel on request.

RESPONSIBILITIES

1. Supervises the CSRs in the branch:
   - Allocates work, co-ordinates work flow, reviews and revises work procedures.
   - Ensures teller area is adequately and efficiently staffed with well-trained, qualified personnel. Assists CSRs with more complex transactions.
   - Resolves routine personnel problems, referring more complex situations to customer service director.
   - Participates in decisions concerning performance appraisal, promotions, wage changes, transfers, and termination of subordinate CSR staff.

2. Assumes responsibility for CSRs' money:
   - Buys and sells money in the vault, ensuring adequacy of branch currency and coin supply.
   - Ensures that CSRs and cash sheets are in balance.
   - Maintains necessary records, including daily branch journal and general ledger.

3. Accepts deposits and withdrawals by business customers at the commercial window.

4. Operates teller window to provide services to retail customers (see Responsibilities for CSRs).

New Job Description for Customer Assistance Representative

FUNCTION: Provides services and guidance to customers/prospects seeking banking relationships or related information. Promotes and sells needed products and responds to special requests by existing customers.

RESPONSIBILITIES

1. Provides prompt, efficient, and friendly service to all customers and prospective customers:
   - Describes and sells bank services to customers/prospects who approach them directly or via referral from customer service reps or other bank personnel.
   - Answers customers' questions regarding bank services, hours, etc.

2. Identifies and responds to customers' needs:
   - Promotes and sells retail services and identifies any existing cross-sell opportunities.
   - Opens new accounts for individuals, businesses, and private organizations.
   - Prepares temporary cheques and deposit slips for new chequing/NOW accounts.
   - Sells cheques and deposit slips.

- Interviews and takes applications for and pays out on instalment/charge card accounts and other credit-related products.
- Certifies cheques.
- Handles stop payment requests.
- Responds to telephone mail inquiries from customers or bank personnel.
- Receives notification of name or address changes and takes necessary action.
- Takes action on notification of lost passbooks, credit cards, ATM cards, collateral, and other lost or stolen items.
- Demonstrates ATMs to customers and assists with problems.
- Co-ordinates closing of accounts and ascertains reasons.

3. Sells and services all retail products:
- Advises customers and processes applications for all products covered in CAR training programs (and updates).
- Initiates referrals to the appropriate department when a trust or corporate business need is identified.

New Job Description for Customer Service Director

FUNCTION: Supervises customer service representatives, customer assistance representatives, and other staff as assigned to provide the most effective and profitable retail banking delivery system in the local marketplace. Supervises sales efforts and provides feedback to management concerning response to products and services by current and prospective banking customers. Communicates goals and results to those supervised and ensures operational standards are met in order to achieve outstanding customer service.

RESPONSIBILITIES

1. Supervises effective delivery of retail products:
- Selects, trains, and manages CSRs and CARs.
- Assigns duties and work schedules.
- Completes performance reviews.
2. Personally, and through those supervised, renders the highest level of professional and efficient customer service available in the local marketplace:

- Provides high level of service while implementing most efficient and customer-sensitive staffing schedules.
- Supervises all on-the-job programs within office.
- Ensures that outstanding customer service standards are achieved.
- Directs remedial programs for CSRs and CARs as necessary.

3. Develops retail sales effectiveness to the degree necessary to achieve market share objectives: Ensures that all CSRs and CARs possess comprehensive product knowledge.
- Directs co-ordinated cross-sell program within office at all times.
- Reports staff training needs to branch manager and/or regional training director.

4. Ensures adherence to operational standards: Oversees preparation of daily and monthly operational and sales reports.
- Estimates, approves, and co-ordinates branch cash needs in advance.
- Oversees ATM processing function.
- Handles or consults with CSRs/CARs on more complex transactions.
- Ensures clean and businesslike appearance of the branch facility.

5. Informs branch manager of customer response to products:
- Reports customer complaints and types of sales resistance encountered
- Describes and summarizes reasons for account closings

6. Communicates effectively the goals and results of the bank to those under supervision:
- Reduces office goals into format which translates to goals for each CSR or CAR.
- Reports sales and cross-sell results to all CSRs and CARs.
- Conducts sales- and service-oriented staff meetings with CSRs/CARs on a regular basis.
- Attends all scheduled customer service management meetings organized by regional office.

Study Questions

1. *Identify the steps taken by Maritime Bank to develop a customer orientation in its retail branches.*

2. *Compare and contrast the jobs of CAR and CSR. How important is each (a) to bank operations and (b) to customer satisfaction?*

3. *Evaluate the strengths and weaknesses of Karen Mitchell and other candidates for head CSR.*

4. *What action do you recommend for filling the head CSR position?*

Case 13   Hilton HHonors Worldwide: Loyalty Wars

JOHN DEIGHTON AND STOWE SHOEMAKER

Hilton Hotels regards frequent guest programs as the lodging industry's most important marketing tool, serving to direct promotional and customer service efforts at the heavy user. How should management of Hilton's international guest rewards program respond when Starwood, a competing hotel group operating several brands, ups the ante in the loyalty stakes?

Jeff Diskin, head of Hilton HHonors® (Hilton's guest reward program), opened *The Wall Street Journal* on February 2, 1999, and read the headline, "Hotels Raise the Ante in Business-Travel Game." The story read, "Starwood Hotels and Resorts Worldwide Inc. is expected to unveil tomorrow an aggressive frequent-guest program that it hopes will help lure more business travelers to its Sheraton, Westin and other hotels. Accompanied by a $50 million ad campaign, the program ratchets up the stakes in the loyalty-program game that big corporate hotel companies, including Starwood and its rivals at Marriott, Hilton and Hyatt are playing."[1]

Diskin did not hide his concern: "These guys are raising their costs, and they're probably raising mine too. They are reducing the cost-effectiveness of the industry's most important marketing tool by deficit spending against their program. Loyalty programs have been at the core of how we attract and retain our best customers for over a decade. But they are only as cost-effective as our competitors let them be."

LOYALTY MARKETING PROGRAMS

The idea of rewarding loyalty had its origins in coupons and trading stamps. First in the 1900s and again in the 1950s, America experienced episodes of trading-stamp frenzy that became so intense that congressional investigations were mounted. Retailers would give customers small adhesive stamps in proportion to the amount of their purchases, to be pasted into books and eventually redeemed for merchandise. The best-known operator had been the S&H Green Stamp Company. Both episodes had lasted about 20 years, declining as the consumer passion for collecting abated and vendors came to the conclusion that any advantage they might once have held had been competed away by emulators.

Loyalty marketing in its modern form was born in 1981 when American Airlines introduced the AAdvantage frequent-flyer program, giving "miles" in proportion to the miles traveled, redeemable for free travel. It did so in response to the competitive pressure that followed airline deregulation. The American Airlines program had no need of stamps, because it took advantage of the data-warehousing capabilities of computers. Soon program administrators realized that they had a tool that did not merely reward loyalty but identified by name and address the people who accounted for most of aviation's revenues and made a one-to-one relationship possible.

Competing airlines launched their own programs, but, unlike stamp programs, frequent-flyer programs seemed to survive emulation. By 1990, almost all airlines offered them. In the late 1990s, Delta Air Lines and United Airlines linked their programs together, as did American and US Airways in the United States. Internationally, United Airlines and Lufthansa combined with 11 other airlines to form Star Alliance, and American, British Airways, and four others formed an alliance called Oneworld. In these alliances, qualifying flights on any of the member airlines could be credited to the frequent-flyer club of the flyer's choice.

As the decade ended, computer-based frequency programs were common in many service industries, including car rentals, department stores, video and book retailing, credit cards, movie theaters, and the hotel industry.

THE HOTEL INDUSTRY

Chain brands were a major factor in the global hotel market of 13.6 million rooms.[2] The chains supplied reservation services, field sales operations, loyalty program administration, and the management of hotel properties under well-recognized names such as Hilton and Marriott. (See **Exhibit 1** for details of the seven largest U.S. hotel chains competing in the business-class hotel segment.)

While the brands stood for quality, there was less standardization of operations in hotel chains than in many other services. The reason was that behind a consumer's experience of a hotel brand might lie any of many methods of control. A branded hotel might be owned and managed by the chain, but it might be owned by a third party and managed by the chain, or owned by the chain and managed by a franchisee, or, in

Professor John Deighton of Harvard Business School and Professor Stowe Shoemaker of the William F. Harrah College of Hotel Administration, University of Nevada, Las Vegas, prepared this case. HBS cases are developed solely as the basis for class discussion. Cases are not intended to serve as endorsements, sources of primary data, or illustrations of effective or ineffective management. The case reflects the status of Hilton Hotels Corporation and Hilton HHonors Worldwide as of January 1999. Hilton has made numerous changes since that time, including Hilton Hotels Corporation's acquisition of Promus Hotel Corporation.

some cases, owned and managed by the franchisee. Occasionally chains managed one another's brands, because one chain could be another's franchisee. Starwood, for example, ran hotels under the Hilton brand as Hilton's franchisee. Information about competitors' operating procedures therefore circulated quite freely in the industry.

Consumers

For most Americans, a stay in a hotel was a relatively rare event. Of the 74% of Americans who traveled overnight in a year, only 41% used a hotel, motel, or resort. The market in which Hilton competed was smaller still, defined by price point and trip purpose and divided among business, convention, and leisure segments.

The **business** segment accounted for one-third of all room nights in the market that Hilton served. About two-thirds of these stays were at rates negotiated between the guest's employer and the chain, but since most corporations negotiated rates with two and sometimes three hotel chains, business travelers had some discretion to choose where they would stay. About one-third of business travelers did not have access to negotiated corporate rates and had full discretion to choose their hotel.

The **convention** segment, comprising convention, conference, and other meeting-related travel, accounted for another third of room nights in Hilton's competitive set. The choice of hotel in this instance was in the hands of a small number of professional conference organizers, typically employees of professional associations and major corporations.

The **leisure** segment accounted for the final third. Leisure guests were price sensitive, often making their selections from among packages of airlines, cars, tours, and hotels assembled by a small group of wholesalers and tour organizers at rates discounted below business rates.

Exhibit 1 The U.S. Lodging Industry

	COUNTRIES	PROPERTIES	ROOMS	OWNED PROPERTIES	FRANCHISED PROPERTIES	MANAGEMENT CONTRACTS
Marriott International[a]	53	1,764	339,200	49	936	776
Bass Hotels and Resorts[b]	90	2,700	447,967	76	2,439	185
Hilton Hotels Corp.[c]	11	272	91,060	39	207	16
Starwood Hotels and Resorts Worldwide, Inc.[d]	72	695	212,950	171	291	233
Hyatt[e]	45	246	93,729	NA	NA	NA
Carlson[f]	50	581	112,089	1	542	38
Hilton International[g]	50	224	62,941	154	0	70
Promus[h]	11	1,398	198,526	160	1,059	179

[a]Includes Marriott Hotels, Resorts and Suites; Courtyard, Residence Inn, TownePlace Suites, Fairfield Inn, SpringHill Suites, Marriott Vacation Club International; Conference Centers, Marriott Executive Residences, Ritz-Carlton, Renaissance, Ramada International.

[b]Includes Inter-Continental, Forum, Crowne Plaza, Holiday Inn, Holiday Inn Express, Staybridge.

[c]Includes Hilton Hotels, Hilton Garden Inns, Hilton Suites, Hilton Grand Vacation Clubs, and Conrad International.

[d]Includes St. Regis, Westin Hotels and Resorts, Sheraton Hotels and Resorts, Four Points, Sheraton Inns, The W Hotels. Does not include other Starwood-owned hotels, flagged under other brands (93 properties for 29,322 rooms).

[e]Includes Hyatt Hotels, Hyatt International, and Southern Pacific Hotel Corporation (SPHC). Because it is a privately held corporation, it will not divulge the breakdown of rooms between ownership, franchise, and management contract.

[f]Includes Radisson Hotels Worldwide, Regent International Hotels, Country Inns and Suites.

[g]A wholly owned subsidiary of what was once known as the Ladbroke Group. In spring 1999, Ladbroke changed their name to Hilton Group PLC to reflect the emphasis on hotels.

[h]Includes such brands as Doubletree, Red Lion, Hampton Inn, Hampton Inn & Suites, Embassy Suites, and Homewood Suites.

Source: World Trade Organization and company information.

Although the chains as a whole experienced demand from all segments, individual properties tended to draw disproportionately from one segment or another. Resort hotels served leisure travelers and some conventioneers; convention hotels depended on group and business travel; and hotels near airports were patronized by guests on business, for example. These segmentation schemes, however, obscured the fact that the individuals in segments differentiated by trip purpose and price point were often the same people. Frequent travelers patronized hotels of various kinds and price segments, depending, for example, on whether a stay was a reimbursable business expense, a vacation, or a personal expense.

Competition

Four large global brands dominated the business-class hotel market (**Table A**). Each competed at more than one price point. (**Exhibit 2** shows the price points in the industry, and **Exhibit 3** shows the distribution of brands across price points.)

Starwood

Beginning in 1991, Barry Sternlicht built Starwood Hotels and Resorts Worldwide from a base in a real estate investment trust. In January 1998, Starwood bought Westin Hotels and Resorts, and a month later it bought ITT Corporation, which included Sheraton Hotels and Resorts, after a well-publicized battle with Hilton Hotels Corporation. By year-end, Starwood had under unified management the Westin, Sheraton, St. Regis, Four Points, and Caesar's Palace brands. Starwood had recently announced plans to create a new brand, W, aimed at younger professionals.

Table A

Marriott International	339,200 rooms
Starwood Hotels and Resorts	212,900 rooms
Hyatt Hotels	93,700 rooms
Hilton Hotels	91,100 rooms
Hilton International	62,900 rooms

Source: Company records.

Exhibit 2 Price Segments in the Lodging Industry

- Luxury: Average rack rate over US$125, full-service hotels with deluxe amenities for leisure travelers and special amenities for business and meeting markets. Chains in this segment include Four Seasons, Hilton, Hyatt, Inter-Continental (a Bass Hotels and Resorts brand), Marriott Hotels and Resorts, Renaissance (a Marriott International brand), Ritz-Carlton (also a Marriott International brand), Sheraton (a Starwood Hotels and Resorts brand), and Westin (also a Starwood Hotels and Resorts brand).
- Upscale: Average rack rate between US$100 and $125, full-service hotels with standard amenities. Includes most all-suite, non-extended-stay brands. Crowne Plaza (a Bass Hotels and Resorts brand), Doubletree Guest Suites (a Promus Hotel Corp. brand), Embassy Suites (also a Promus Hotel Corp. brand), Radisson (a Carlson Worldwide Hospitality brand), Hilton Inn, and Clarion (a Choice Hotels brand) are all examples of chains in this segment.
- Midmarket with food and beverage (F&B): Average rack rate between US$60 and $90, full-service hotels with lower service levels and amenities than the upscale segment. Examples include Best Western, Courtyard (a Marriott International brand), Garden Inn (a Hilton brand), Holiday Inn (a Bass Hotels and Resorts brand), and Howard Johnson (a Cendant brand).
- Midmarket without F&B: Average rack rate between US$45 and $70, with limited-service and comparable amenities to the midmarket with F&B segment. Examples of chains in this segment include Hampton Inns (a Promus brand), Holiday Inn Express (a Bass Hotels and Resorts brand), and Comfort Inn (a Choice Hotels brand).
- Economy: Average rack rate between US$40 and $65, with limited service and few amenities. Fairfield Inn (a Marriott International brand), Red Roof Inn, Travelodge, and Days Inn of America (a Cendant brand) are examples of economy chains.
- Budget: Average rack rate between US$30 and $60, with limited service and basic amenities. Motel 6, Super 8, and Econo Lodge are the best-known chains in this segment.
- Extended stay: Average rack rate between US$60 and $90, targeted to extended-stay market and designed for extended length of stay. Marriott International has the following two brands in this market: Residence Inn by Marriott and TownePlace Suites. Other chains include Homewood Suites (a Bass Hotels and Resorts brand), Summerfield Suites, and Extended Stay America.

Source: U.S. lodging chains segmented by RealTime Hotel Reports Inc., authors of the 1998 Lodging Survey.

Exhibit 3 Segments Served by the Major Chains

	LUXURY	UPSCALE	MID-MARKET WITH FOOD AND BEVERAGE	MID-MARKET WITHOUT FOOD AND BEVERAGE	ECONOMY	BUDGET	EXTENDED STAY
Hilton	X	X	X	X			
Hyatt	X						
Marriott	X	X	X		X		X
Starwood	X	X	X				X

Source: Company records.

Marriott

Marriott International operated and franchised hotels under the Marriott, Ritz-Carlton, Renaissance, Residence Inn, Courtyard, TownePlace Suites, Fairfield Inn, SpringHill Suites, and Ramada International brands. It also operated conference centers and provided furnished corporate housing. A real estate investment trust, Host Marriott, owned some of the properties operated by Marriott International, as well as some Hyatt, Four Season, and Swissotel properties.

Hyatt

The Pritzker family of Chicago owned Hyatt Corporation, the only privately owned major hotel chain. Hyatt comprised Hyatt Hotels, operating hotels and resorts in the United States, Canada, and the Caribbean; and Hyatt International, operating overseas. Hyatt also owned Southern Pacific Hotel Group, a three- and four-star hotel chain based primarily in Australia. Although the companies operated independently, they ran joint marketing programs.

The 1990s had been a time of consolidation and rationalization in the lodging industry, partly due to application of information technologies to reservation systems and control of operations. Diskin reflected on the trend: "Historically, bigger has been better because it has led to economies of scale and bigger and better brands to leverage. Historically, big players could win even if they did not do a particularly good job on service, performance, or programs. Now [after the Starwood deal] there's another big player. It would have been nice if it had been Hilton that was the largest hotel chain in the world, but biggest is not the only way to be best."

MARKETING THE HILTON BRAND

The Hilton brand was controlled by two entirely unrelated corporations, Hilton Hotels Corporation (HHC), based in Beverley Hills, California, and Hilton International (HIC), headquartered near London, England. In 1997, however, HHC and HIC agreed to reunify the Hilton brand worldwide. They agreed to cooperate on sales and marketing, standardize operations, and run the Hilton HHonors loyalty program across all HHC and HIC hotels. At the end of 1998, HHC divested itself of casino interests and announced "a new era as a dedicated hotel company."

The exit from gaming, the reunification of Hilton's worldwide marketing, and the extension of the brand into the middle market under the Hilton Garden Inns name were initiatives that followed the appointment in 1997 of Stephen F. Bollenbach as president and chief executive officer of Hilton. Bollenbach had served as chief financial officer of Marriott and most recently as chief financial officer of Disney, and he brought to Hilton a passion for branding. To some members of the Hilton management team, the focus on brand development was a welcome one. "Hilton's advantage has been a well-recognized name, but a potentially limiting factor has been a widely varying product and the challenge of managing customer expectation with such a variety of product offerings. Since Hilton includes everything from world-renowned properties like The Waldorf-Astoria and Hilton Hawaiian Village to the smaller middle-market Hilton Garden Inns, it's important to give consumers a clear sense of what to expect from the various types of hotels," observed one manager.

In mid-1999, the properties branded as Hilton hotels comprised:

1. 39 owned or partly owned by HHC in the United States
2. 207 franchised by HHC to third-party managers in the United States
3. 16 managed by HHC in the United States on behalf of third-party owners
4. 10 managed internationally under HHC's Conrad International brand
5. 220 managed by HIC in over 50 countries excluding the U.S.

The executives at Hilton HHonors worked for these 492 hotels and their 154,000 rooms. The previous year had been successful. Revenues had been in the region of $158 per night per guest, and occupancy had exceeded break-even. Hotels like Hilton's tended to cover fixed costs at about 68% occupancy, and 80% of all revenue at higher occupancy levels flowed to the bottom line. Advertising, selling, and other

Exhibit 4 Hilton HHonors Worldwide: 1998 Income Statement

(While these data are broadly reflective of the economic situation, certain competitively sensitive information has been masked.)

	US$ (THOUSANDS)	
Revenue		
Contributions from hotels		
Domestic	$39,755	
International	$10,100	
Strategic partner contributions	$18,841	
Membership fees[a]	$1,141	
Total		**$69,837**
Expense		
Redemptions		
Cash payments to hotels	$12,654	
Deferred liability[b]	$9,436	
Airline miles purchases	$17,851	
Member acquisition expenses	$7,273	
Member communication expenses	4,236	
Program administration expenses	$17,988	
Total		**$69,438**
Net Income		**$399**

[a]From members of the Hilton Senior HHonors program only. The Senior HHonors program invited people over 60 to receive discounted stays in exchange for a membership fee. Regular HHonors members do not pay a membership fee.

[b]More points were issued than redeemed. From the outstanding balance a deferred liability was charged to HHW's income statement, based on estimating the proportion of points that would ultimately be redeemed.

Source: Company records (masked). For purposes of consistency in calculation among class members, assume an average nightly revenue of $158 per room. Assume that airline miles are purchased from the airline by Hilton at 1 cent per mile.

marketing costs (a component of fixed costs) for this group of hotels were not published, but industry norms ran at about $750 per room per year.[3]

Hilton HHonors Program

Hilton HHonors was the name Hilton gave to its program designed to build loyalty to the Hilton brand worldwide. Hilton HHonors Worldwide (HHW) operated the program, not as a profit center but as a service to its two parents, HHC and HIC. It was required to break even each year and to measure its effectiveness through a complex set of program-metrics. Diskin ran the limited liability corporation with a staff of 30, with one vice president overseeing the program's marketing efforts and one with operational and customer service oversight. (**Exhibit 4** shows the income statement for HHW.)

Membership in the Hilton HHonors program was open to anyone who applied, at no charge. Members earned points toward their Hilton HHonors account whenever they stayed at HHC or HIC hotels. When Hilton HHonors members accumulated enough points in the program, they could redeem them for stays at HHonors hotels, use them to buy products and services from partner companies, or convert them to miles in airline frequent-flyer programs. (**Exhibit 5** shows how

points in the program flowed among participants in the program, as detailed in the text that follows.)

There were four tiers of membership—Blue, Silver, Gold, and Diamond. The program worked as follows at the **Blue** level in 1998.

- When a member stayed at a Hilton hotel and paid a so-called business rate,[4] the hotel typically paid HHW 4.5 cents per dollar of the guest's folio (folio is the total charge by the guest before taxes). HHW credited the guest's Hilton HHonors account with 10 points per eligible dollar of folio.
- Hilton guests could earn mileage in partner airline frequent-flyer programs for the same stay that earned them HHonors points, a practice known as Double Dipping. (Hilton was the only hotel chain to offer double dipping; other chains with frequency programs required guests to choose between points in the hotel program or miles in the airline program.) If the member chose to double-dip, HHW bought miles from the relevant airline and credited the guest's airline frequent-flyer account at 500 miles per stay.
- If the guest used points to pay for a stay, HHW reimbursed the hosting hotel at more than the costs incremental to the cost of leaving the room empty but less than

Exhibit 5 How the Hilton HHonors Program Works

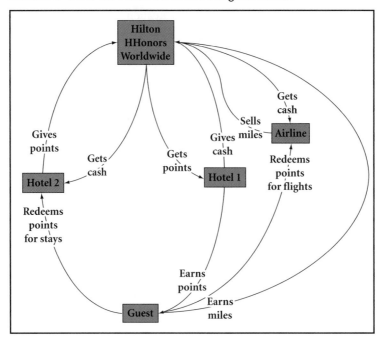

Source: Company.

the revenue from a paying guest. The points needed to earn a stay depended on the class of hotel and fell when occupancy was low. As illustration, redemption rates ranged from 5,000 points to get 50% off the $128 cost of a weekend at the Hilton Albuquerque, to 25,000 points for a free weekend night at the $239 per night Hilton Boston Back Bay. A number of exotic rewards were offered, such as a two-person, seven-night diving adventure in the Red Sea for 350,000 points, including hotel and airfare.

- Members earned points by renting a car, flying with a partner airline, using the Hilton Credit Card from American Express, or buying products promoted in mailings by partners such as FTD Florists and Mrs. Field's Cookies. Members could buy points at $10 per thousand for up to 20% of the points needed for a reward.

- Members had other benefits besides free stays. They had a priority-reservation telephone number. Check-in went faster because information on preferences was on file. Members were favored over nonmembers when they asked for late checkout. If members were dissatisfied, they were guaranteed a room upgrade certificate in exchange for a letter explaining their dissatisfaction. Points could be exchanged for airline miles and vice versa and to buy partner products such as airline tickets, flowers, Mrs. Field's Cookies products, Cannondale bicycles, AAA membership, Princess Cruises trips, and car rentals.

Members were awarded **Silver VIP** status if they stayed at HHonors hotels four times in a year. They earned a 15% bonus on base points, received a 5,000-point bonus after seven stays in a quarter, and received a 10,000-point discount

when they claimed a reward costing 100,000 points. They were given a certificate for an upgrade to the best room in the hotel after every fifth stay.

Members were awarded **Gold VIP** status if they stayed at HHonors hotels 16 times or for 36 nights in a year. They earned a 25% bonus on base points, received a 5,000-point bonus after seven stays in a quarter, and received a 20,000-point discount when they claimed a reward costing 100,000 points. They were given a certificate for an upgrade to the best room in the hotel after every fifth stay and were upgraded to best available room at time of check-in.

The top 1% of members were given **Diamond VIP** status. This level was not mentioned in promotional material, and no benefits were promised. Diskin explained, "Our goal at the time was to underpromise and overdeliver. If you stay a lot, we say thank you, and as a reward we want to give you Diamond VIP status. We get a lot more bang, more affinity, more vesting from the customer if we do something unexpected. As an industry, we should never overpromise. It leads the public to decide that this is all smoke and mirrors, and it makes it harder for us to deliver genuine value." **Table B** shows HHW's member activity in 1998.

A further 712,000 stays averaging 2.4 nights were recorded in 1998 for which no Hilton HHonors membership card was presented but instead airline miles were claimed and airline membership numbers were captured, so that the guest could be given a unique identifier in the Hilton database. Spending on these stays totaled $327 million.

Guests identified by their HHonors or airline membership numbers occupied 22.5% of all the rooms occupied in the Hilton Hotels and Hilton International network in a year. They were a much smaller proportion of all the guests who

Table B Members' Paid Activity in 1998

	Members (000)	Members Active in 1998 (000)	Stays for Which Members Paid (000)	Nights for Which They Paid (000)	Spending on Which They Earned Points ($000)	Stays per Active Member in 1998	Nights per Active Member in 1998	Reward Claimed by Member
Diamond	24	20	310	521	$62,000	15.5	26.1	27,000
Gold	220	84	1,110	1,916	$266,000	13.2	22.8	34,200
Silver	694	324	1,023	1,999	$341,000	3.2	6.2	70,200
Blue	1,712	992	1,121	2,579	$439,000	1.1	2.6	48,600
Total	2,650	1,420	3,564	7,015	$1,108,000	2.5	4.9	180,000

Source: Company records (certain competitively sensitive information has been masked).

stayed with Hilton in a year because they tended to be frequent travelers. Hilton's research found that Hilton HHonors members spent about $4.6 billion on accommodation per year, not all of which was with Hilton. The industry estimated that members of the frequent-stayer programs of all the major hotel chains represented a market worth $11.1 billion and that the average member belonged to 3.5 programs.

Rationales for the Program

1. Revenue and Yield Management

Hotel profitability was acutely sensitive to revenue. A trend in the industry was to appoint a "revenue manager" to each property to oversee the day-to-day decisions that affected hotel revenue. Yield management models were probabilistic algorithms that helped this manager set reservations policy. He or she used past history and other statistical data to make continuously updated recommendations regarding hotel booking patterns and what price to offer a particular guest. Simulation studies had shown that when booking was guided by a good yield management model, a company's revenue increased by 20% over a simple "first come, first served, fixed price" policy.

In the hotel industry, effectively managing yield meant utilizing a model to predict that a room was highly likely to come available due to cancellation or no-show, as well as driving business to higher-paying or longer-staying guests. Variable pricing meant that the rate charged for a room depended not only on its size and fittings but also on the day of booking, the day of occupation, the length of stay, and customer characteristics. Of these factors, customer characteristics were the most problematic.

Customer characteristics were needed by the model to estimate "walking cost," the cost of turning a customer away. That cost in turn depended on the customer's future lifetime value to the chain, a function of their willingness to pay, and past loyalty to the chain. These were considered "soft" variables, notoriously difficult to estimate. The better the historical information on a customer, however, the better the estimate. As Adam Burke, HHonors' senior director of marketing for North America, put it, "Who gets the room—the person paying $20 more that you may never see again, or the guy spending thousands of dollars in the system? If we have the right data, the model can be smart enough to know the difference." Some in the hotel industry argued that a benefit of a frequent-guest program was to let the reservations system make those distinctions.

2. Collaborating with Partners

HHW partnered with 25 airlines, three car rental firms, and a number of other firms. Burke explained, "Why is Mrs. Field's Cookies in the program? We have several objectives—regional relevance to consumers, access to partners' customers, making it easier for members to attain rewards. A franchisee may say, 'Why are we doing something with FTD Florists?' We point out that their investment keeps costs down and gives a broader range of rewards to our members."

Burke explained why Hilton offered double dipping: "We have 2.5 million members. The airline frequent-flyer programs have 20, 30, 40 million members who aren't HHonors members and do travel a lot. Airlines don't mind us talking to their members because—through double dipping—we don't compete with their programs. In fact, we complement them by allowing our joint customers to earn both currencies."

3. Working with Franchisees

The Hilton HHonors program was a strong factor in persuading hotel owners to become Hilton franchisees or give Hilton a management contract to run their property. Franchisees tended to be smaller hotels, more dependent on "road warrior" business than many of Hilton's convention hotels, resort hotels, and flagship properties. They saw value in a frequent-guest program to attract business, and HHW's program cost was comparable with or lower than its competitors'. The program's ability to drive business, however, remained its biggest selling point. Diskin elaborated, "Seven or eight years ago some operators were concerned about the cost of the program. We took a bunch of the most vocal, critical guys and we put them in a room for two days with us to discuss the importance of building long-term customer loyalty, and they came out saying, 'We need to spend more money on the program!'"

4. Relations with Guests

The program let the most valuable guests be recognized on-property. Diskin explained:

> In a sense, the loyalty program is a safe haven for the guest. If there is a problem and it is not taken care of at the property level, the guest can contact our customer service team. It's a mechanism to make sure we hear about those problems. We also do outbound after-visit calling, and we call HHonors members because they're the best database and the most critical guests we have. They have the most experience and the highest expectations. We do feedback groups with members in addition to focus groups and quantitative research. We invite a bunch of members in the hotel down for dinner, and we say we want to talk about a subject. I get calls from people that are lifelong loyalists, not because of any changes we've made, but because once we invited them and asked them their opinion. People care about organizations that care about them.

Hilton customized a guest's hotel experience. Diskin explained, "We build guest profiles that keep track of preferences, enabling the hotel to provide customized services. For instance, consider the guest that always wants a room that is for nonsmokers and has a double bed. This information can be stored as part of the member's record so that when she or he makes a reservation, the guest will receive this type of room without having to ask, no matter where the guest is staying."

HHW used direct mail to cultivate the relationship between members and the Hilton brand. Diskin explained, "Certainly you want to focus much of your effort on your highest-revenue guests, but there are also opportunities to reach out and try to target other customer segments. For example, we worked with a nontravel partner to overlay data from their customer files onto our total membership base and identified segments that might like vacation ownership, others who would be great for the casinos, and some that might like the business and teleconferencing services we offer."

Diskin was concerned that some travelers spread their hotel patronage among several chains and did not receive the service to which their total expenditure entitled them. He noted, "Our research suggests that a quarter of the frequent travelers are members of loyalty programs but don't have true loyalty to any one brand. They never get to enjoy the benefits of elite-program status because they don't consolidate their business with one chain. They typically don't see the value in any of the loyalty schemes because they haven't changed their stay behavior to see the benefits."

5. Helping Travel Managers Gain Compliance

A significant proportion of Hilton's business came from contracts with large corporate clients. Hilton offered discounted rates if the corporation delivered enough stays. Burke explained:

> If you are a corporate travel manager, you want employees to comply with the corporate travel policy. You negotiated a rate by promising a volume of stays. While some travel managers can tell employees that they have to follow the company policy if they want to get reimbursed, many others can only recommend. What if someone is a very loyal Marriott customer, yet Marriott is not one of that company's preferred vendors? A travel office is going to have a real hard time getting that guy to stay at Hilton if they can't mandate it.

> We respond with a roster of offerings to give that Marriott traveler a personal incentive to use us, the preferred vendor. Our overall objective is to use the program as a tool that can help the travel manager with compliance to their overall travel policy.

Member Attitudes

HHW made extensive use of conjoint analysis to measure what members wanted from the Hilton HHonors program. Burke explained:

> Members come in for an hour-and-a-half interview. They're asked to trade off program elements, including services and amenities in the hotel, based on the value they place on those attributes relative to their cost. The results help us determine the appropriate priorities for modifying the program. We find that different people have different needs. Some people are service oriented. No amount of miles or points is ever going to replace a warm welcome and being recognized by the hotel as a loyal customer. Other people are games players. They go after free stays, and they know the rules as well as we do. We've been in feedback groups where these people will educate us on how our program works! And, of course, many people are a combination of both.

Using a sample that was broadly representative of the program's upper-tier membership categories, program research found that Hilton HHonors members had an average of over 30 stays in all hotel chains per year, staying 4.2 nights per stay. Between 1997 and 1998, Hilton experienced a 17.5% increase in member utilization of HHonors hotels globally. Despite this improvement, more than half of HHonors member stays went to competing chains annually—this was primarily attributable to Hilton's relatively limited network size and distribution. The conjoint analysis suggested that roughly one in five HHonors member stays were solely attributable to their membership in the program—making these stays purely incremental.

The study found that the most important features of a hotel program were room upgrades and airline miles, followed by free hotel stays and a variety of on-property benefits and services. Members wanted a streamlined reward-redemption process and points that did not expire. These findings led to refinements in the terms of membership for 1999, but Diskin was exploring more innovative approaches to the rewards program.

Diskin recognized that in their market research studies, consumers tended to describe an ideal program that was simply a version of the programs with which they were familiar. He was looking for more radical innovation:

Hilton and Marriott tend to attract "games players." We want to compete effectively on the reward elements but also introduce them to the more high-touch, high-feel kind of guest experience as well. The customer base that we have accumulated comprises games players primarily. So we've got to deliver that benefit but still go further.

We've been on a mission to dramatically improve the stay experience for members of the upper-tier ranks of the program. That is the key to competitive distinctiveness. That's not something that anybody can imitate. We want our best customers to feel that when they go to Hilton, they know Hilton knows they're the best customer and they're treated special. We want them to think, "I'm going to have the kind of room I want, I'm going to have the kind of stay I like, and if I have a problem, they're going to take care of it." We want the staff to know who's coming in each day and make sure that these guests get a personal welcome. Our new customer reservation system will get more information down to the hotel. We'll know a lot more about our incoming guests. We will have a guest manager in the hotel whose job it is to make you feel special and to address any concerns you may have.

THE STARWOOD ANNOUNCEMENT

The Wall Street Journal of February 2, 1999, announced the birth of the Starwood Preferred Guest Program, covering Westin Hotels Resorts, Sheraton Hotels Resorts, The Luxury Collection, Four Points, Caesar's, and Starwood's new W brand hotels, representing more than 550 participating properties worldwide. It became clear that Starwood was adding program features that might be expensive to match. Four features in particular were of concern.

No blackout dates   All frequent guest and airline programs until now had ruled that members could not claim free travel during the very height of seasonal demand and when local events guaranteed a hotel full occupancy. Starwood was saying that if there was a room to rent, points were as good as money.

No capacity control   Programs until now had let hotel properties limit the number of rooms for free stays. Starwood was telling hotels that all unreserved rooms should be available to guests paying with points.

Paperless rewards   Guests had had previously to exchange points for a certificate and then use the certificate to pay for an authorized stay. Under Starwood's system, individual properties would be able to accept points to pay for a stay.

Hotel reimbursement   Now that blackout dates were abolished, a property, particularly an attractive vacation destination, might have to contend with many more points-paying guests than before. Starwood therefore raised the rate at which it reimbursed hotels for these stays. To meet the cost, it charged participating hotels 20%–100% more than its competitors on paid stays.

Starwood was pledging to invest $50 million in advertising to publicize the program—significantly more than HHW had historically spent on program communications. **(Exhibit 6 compares the loyalty programs of the four major business-class hotel chains after the Starwood announcement.)**

Diskin's Dilemma

Without any doubt, Starwood had raised the ante in the competition for customer loyalty. Diskin had to decide whether to match or pass. He mused:

Do we have to compete point for point? Or do we want to take a different positioning and hold on to our loyal members and differentiate HHonors from Starwood and other competitors? We're in a cycle where for 10 years the cost to our hotels of our frequent-guest program as a percent of the folio has been cycling down. Yet activation, retention, and member spend per visit all have improved. If we can deliver the same amount of business to the Hilton brand and it costs less, Hilton makes more margin. That attracts investors, franchise ownership, new builders. That's another reason why they buy the Hilton flag.

As Diskin saw it, Starwood's Preferred Guest announcement was a solution to a problem Hilton did not have, arising from its recent purchases of the Sheraton and Westin chains:

They are trying to develop the Starwood brand with the Starwood Preferred Guest Program. They are targeting the most lucrative part of the business, the individual business traveler, where Sheraton and Westin independently have never been as effective as Marriott, Hyatt, and Hilton. Sheraton's frequent-guest program wasn't very effective. They changed it every few years; they used to have members pay for it. Westin never had enough critical mass of properties for it to be important for enough people. So now, together they can address Westin's critical-mass problem and Sheraton's relevance.

But if frequent-guest programs were a good idea, perhaps bigger programs were an even better idea. Diskin reflected: "Hotel properties routinely pay 10% commission to a travel agent to bring them a guest. Yet they continually scrutinize

Exhibit 6   Membership Offerings of the Four Major Business-Class Hotel Chains in 1998

CHAIN	MEMBERSHIP RESTRICTIONS[a]	POINT VALUE (US$)	ELIGIBLE CHARGES	NEW MEMBER BONUS	AIRLINE MILEAGE ACCRUAL
Starwood	One stay per year to remain active—basic; 10 stays or 25 room nights per year— medium; 25 stays or 50 room nights—premium	2 Starpoints = $1 basic; 3 Starpoints = $1 medium or premium	Room rate, F&B, laundry/valet, phone, in-room movies	Periodically	Starpoints earned can be converted to miles 1:1; cannot earn both points and miles for the same stay
Hilton	One stay per year to remain active— Blue; 4 stays per year or 10 nights—medium; 16 stays per year or 36 nights—premium; 28 stays or 60 nights—top	10 pts. = $1—Blue; 115% bonus on points earned—medium; 125% bonus on points earned—premium; 150% bonus on points earned—top	Room rate, F&B, laundry, phone	Periodically	500 miles per qualifying stay in addition to point earnings
Hyatt	One stay per year to remain active—basic; 5 stays or 15 nights per year—medium; 25 stays or 50 nights per year—premium	5 pts. = $1; 115% bonus on points earned—medium; 130% bonus on points earned— premium	Room rate, F&B, laundry, phone	Periodically	500 miles per stay; not available if earning points
Marriott	No requirements for basic; 15 nights per year—medium; 50 nights per year—premium	10 pts. = $1; 120% bonus on points earned—medium; 125% bonus on points earned—premium	Room rate, F&B, laundry, phone	Double points first 120 days	3 miles per dollar spent at full-service hotels; 1 mile per dollar spent at other hotels; not available if earning points

[a]Most programs run three tiers. For ease of comparison, the three levels are named basic, medium, and premium. HHonors has four tiers.

the cost of these programs. Of course, they're justified in doing so, but the return on investment clearly justifies the expenditure. And our competitors certainly seem to see a value in increasing their investment in their programs."

Diskin tried to predict Hyatt's and Marriott's response to the Starwood announcement. The industry was quite competitive enough. He thought back to his early years at United Airlines and recalled the damage that price wars had done to that industry.

Exhibit 6 *(Continued)*

CHAIN	AFFINITY CREDIT CARD POINT ACCRUAL[a]	POINT PURCHASE (US$)	BONUS THRESHOLD REWARD	EXHANGE HOTEL POINTS FOR AIRLINE MILES	HOTEL REWARDS
Starwood	1,000 hotel pts. first card use; 1 hotel pt. = $1 spent; 4 hotel points = $1 spent at Starwood hotels	NA	NA	1:1 conversion except JAL, KLM, Ansett, Qantas, Air New Zealand; 5,000 bonus miles when you convert 20,000 hotel points; minimum 2,000 Starpoints—basic; minimum 15,000—medium; no minimum for premium	5 categories; 1 free night category 1 is 3,000 Starpoints; 1 free night category 5 is 12,000 Starpoints
Hilton	5,000 hotel pts. for application; 2,500 hotel points first card use; 2 hotel pts. = $1 spent; 3 hotel pts. = $1 spent at HHonors Hotels	$10 = 1,000 pts. up to 20% of the total points of the reward	2,000 pts. = 4 stays per quarter	10,000 pts. = 1,500 miles; 20,000 pts. = 3,500 miles; 50,000 pts. = 10,000 miles; minimum 10,000 hotel points exchange, can also exchange airline miles for hotel points	5 categories: free weekend night 10,000 lowest; 35,000 highest
Hyatt	None	$10 = 500 pts. up to 10% of the total points of the reward	None basic	3 pts. = 1 mile; minimum 9,000-point exchange	Weekend night no category: 8,000 pts.; if premium time there is an additional 5,000 pts.; partner awards
Marriott	5,000 hotel pts. first card use; 1 hotel pt. = $1 spent; 3 hotel points = $1 spent at Marriott Rewards hotels	$10 = 1,000 pts. up to 10% of the total points of the reward	None basic	10,000 pts. = 2,000 miles; 20,000 pts. = 5,000 miles; 30,000 pts. = 10,000 miles; minimum = 10,000 hotel point exchanges	2 categories: 20,000 free weekend low category, and 30,000 high category

Source: Assembled by the casewriters from the promotional materials of each hotel chain in 1999.

Endnotes

1. *The Wall Street Journal*, February 2, 1999, p. B1.
2. World Trade Organization.
3. For the purpose of consistency in calculation among class members, assume an occupancy of 70%. The information in this paragraph has been masked. No data of this kind are publicly available, and these data are not to be interpreted as indicative of information private to either HHC or HIC.
4. Hilton distinguished three kinds of rate. "Business rates" were higher than "leisure rates," which in turn were higher than "ineligible rates," which referred to group tour wholesale rates, airline crew rates, and other deeply discounted rates.

Study Questions

1. What are the strengths and weaknesses of the Hilton HHonors program from the standpoints of:
   a. Hilton Hotels Corp and Hilton International
   b. member properties (franchised hotels)
   c. guests
   d. corporate travel departments

2. How does the value generated to Hilton by the program compare to its cost?

3. What is Starwood attempting to do and how should Jeff Diskin respond?

Case 14 The Complaint Letter

T.F. CAWSEY AND GORDON H.G. MCDOUGALL

The general manager of a U.K. hotel needs to decide how to respond to a complaint letter received from a Canadian visitor. He also needs to decide on what actions to take internally to ensure the problem does not recur, and what implications this might have for the hotel staff.

As Andres Metz, general manager of the Heathrow ATMI Hotel, finished a second reading of the complaint letter (**Appendix**), he was very concerned. The series of events described in the letter indicated that the hotel employees had failed to perform the basic services for this guest. As well, there were potential systems problems that needed examination. While Andres knew it was only one letter, it suggested significant issues that needed attention.

The Heathrow ATMI Hotel, a 578 guest-room hotel, targeted the business traveller. Extensive renovations had been completed recently and a marketing campaign announcing the new improvements had been launched. The hotel itself was billed as a "contemporary upscale hotel" offering two restaurants, three lounges or bars and a conference and training centre. The hotel staff spoke Afrikaans, Arabic, Chinese, Dutch, English, French, German, Greek, Hindi, Italian, Japanese, Maltese, Portuguese, Punjabi, Russian, Spanish and Swahili and were well trained to serve the needs of international travellers.

ATMI Hotels was a subsidiary of a global hotel company which owned or leased over 2,500 hotels worldwide. The ATMI Division, headed by Christopher Britton, was operated as an independent business unit. Recently, the operating profit for the unit was up over 50% driven by market share gains in the United Kingdom. ATMI took third place in an industry rating of business hotel chains in the U.K.

The strategy of ATMI's parent was to:

- Strengthen our portfolio of strongly differentiated brands through increased room night delivery to franchisees, enhanced hotel management skills and brand innovation.
- Grow our management and franchised fee income by exploiting significant potential in the *upscale* segment worldwide and building large-scale, strong *midscale* positions in major world markets.
- Focus the organization by containing or reducing operating costs through simplification, reduction of asset ownership, infrastructure improvements and investing in the skills of our people.
- Continue to reduce capital by selling the real estate assets of the majority of our hotel portfolio while retaining management or franchise agreements in most cases. Ownership of assets will continue only if assets present strategic brand value for the group.
- Return excess funds to shareholders or reinvest in growth opportunities, while maintaining appropriate efficient debt levels.

As Andres reviewed the letter, he remembered the "hospitality promise" — If any part of your stay is not satisfactory, we promise to make it right or you won't pay for that part of your stay. He wondered how to respond and what action he should take with hotel staff.

APPENDIX: THE COMPLAINT LETTER

Mr. Christopher Britton   September 8, 2004
Chief Operating Officer
ATMI Hotels
368 Bridgeport Avenue
Rummidge, England

Dear Sir,

As a customer of yours, I want to provide you with our experiences at ATMI Hotels Heathrow on 24 August of this year. Initially, I had not planned to do anything but since then I have reflected on my experience and finally decided I needed to provide you with feedback—particularly given the "hospitality promise" on your web site.

My wife and I arrived at the hotel around 10 p.m. after a flight from Canada and the usual tiring immigration procedures, baggage check and struggle to find your hotel. On arrival, we hoped to check in and proceed to our room quickly as we had been up since 5 a.m., our time.

As I entered the hotel, I was somewhat apprehensive because a busload of tourists had arrived just ahead of us. However, they gathered to one side of the hotel lobby and I was able to line up at one of the three open check-in lines. The initial greeting was courteous and appropriate. We were checked in and the desk person asked if we wanted a room upgrade. After I clarified that this would cost money, I declined the offer.

While it is not permitted to copy this case, copies or permission to reproduce are available from The School of Business & Economics, Wilfrid Laurier University, Waterloo, Ontario. Please contact The School of Business & Economics at 519-884-0710 ext. 6999. This material is not covered under authorization from CanCopy or any other reproduction rights organization

We then went to our room on the third floor, I believe, and discovered the room was a disaster, totally not made up. I phoned the switchboard and was put through to reception immediately. There were profuse apologies and we were told that someone would be up immediately with another key. Within 5 minutes, someone did meet us with a key to a room on the fifth floor, a quick, fast response.

However, when we got to the new room, it was not made up! If anything it was worse. Frankly, I did not want to touch anything in that room but did go to the phone.

I phoned the switchboard. The operator said, "This shouldn't have happened. I will put you through to the night manager." I said that was not necessary. I just wanted a room.

However, the operator insisted that I was put through to the night manager. Again, there were profuse apologies and the manager said, "This shouldn't have happened. I will fix this and get right back to you." I indicated that I just wanted a room—I didn't want the organization fixed, just a room. The manager repeated, "I will get right back to you."

We waited 5, 10, 15 minutes. Inexplicably, the manager did not return the call even though he said he would.

Finally around 20 minutes later, I phoned switchboard again. I said we were waiting for a room and that the night manager had promised to call me back. The operator said, "This is probably my fault as I was doing work for the assistant manager." I did not and do not understand this part of the conversation but again, I was told that they would call right back. Again, I repeated that "I just need a room."

I waited another 5 minutes—it was now 11 p.m. at night and we were quite tired—there was no return phone call. My wife and I went down to reception and again lined up. After a brief time, we were motioned forward by the person who initially registered us. I explained that we needed a room. He said "You were taken care of. You got a room." I replied: "No, I did not have a room, I just had two rooms that were not made up and we needed a clean one for the night."

Again there were profuse apologies. The reception person then said, "Excuse me, just for a moment so I can fix this." I said "Really, I just would like a room." The person at the reception desk went around the corner and began to yell at someone working there. This went on for several minutes. He then returned to his station, called me forward again, apologized again and located a third room for us. As well, he gave us coupons for a complimentary breakfast.

The third room was made up. We had hoped for an upgrade but this was clearly not the case. The room looked clean but was "more tired" than the previous rooms. The car-

pets were a bit worn and the wallpaper was faded. However, it was clean and we were delighted to find a place to sleep.

In the middle of the night, I woke up and went to the washroom. I noticed that the invoice for the room had been delivered to our room. To my absolute shock, a £72 "room change" charge was added to the price of our room.

I woke early the next morning (because we had to catch an early plane to Paris) to discuss this charge with someone at reception. One person was serving a hotel guest and I waited for a few minutes until the same reception person from the previous night came to the desk. He motioned me forward and then immediately left to open up the five or six other computer stations in the reception area. He had a tendency to not make eye contact. This may have been a cultural phenomenon or it may have been his dismay at having to deal with me again. I cannot say.

I showed him the invoice. He said, "Oh, there will be no charge for that room." I said that I was concerned as the invoice did show the charge. He said, "It is taken care of." I said "Regardless, I would like something to prove that there would not be another charge to my credit card." After one further exchange and insistence on my part, he removed the charge from my invoice.

My wife and I had breakfast and appreciated it being complimentary. We were able to get to the airport in time for our flight.

We thought that you would want to know of our experience. Customer service is a critical part of the hospitality industry and I am certain that ATMI Hotels would wish feedback on experiences such as these.

I look forward to your reply.

Yours truly,

Dr. Mark Hankins
666 Newberry Dr.
Kitchener, Ontario
Canada

cc.   General Manager
       ATMI Hotel
       London Heathrow
       22 Uphill Road
       Heathrow, England

       Guest Relations Department
       ATMI Hotels
       17 Cedar Road
       Birmingham, England

Study Questions

1. *What are the issues that Mr. Metz should note and be concerned with?*

2. *How credible is the evidence provided by the letter? That is, does it form the basis for action or is it part of the background noise of running a complex service operation such as the hotel in this case?*

3. *What services marketing concepts can help us to understand the situation faced by the Hotel Manager?*

Case 15   Shouldice Hospital Limited (Abridged)

JAMES HESKETT AND ROGER HALLOWELL

A Canadian hospital specializing in hernia operations is considering whether and how to expand the reach of its services, including expansion into other specialty areas. Various proposals have been advanced to increase the capacity of the hospital without demotivating the staff or losing control over service quality, which, in addition to achieving excellent medical outcomes, has created a very devoted base of patient "alumni." Options include adding Saturday surgical operations, building an extension, and constructing a new hospital in another location, perhaps in the United States.

Two shadowy figures, enrobed and in slippers, walked slowly down the semi-darkened hall of the Shouldice Hospital. They didn't notice Alan O'Dell, the hospital's managing director, and his guest. Once they were out of earshot, O'Dell remarked good naturedly, "By the way they act, you'd think our patients own this place. And while they're here, in a way they do." Following a visit to the five operating rooms, O'Dell and his visitor once again encountered the same pair of patients still engrossed in discussing their hernia operations, which had been performed the previous morning.

HISTORY

An attractive brochure that was recently printed, although neither dated nor distributed to prospective patients, described Dr. Earle Shouldice, the founder of the hospital:

> Dr. Shouldice's interest in early ambulation stemmed, in part, from an operation he performed in 1932 to remove the appendix from a seven-year-old girl and the girl's subsequent refusal to stay quietly in bed. In spite of her activity, no harm was done, and the experience recalled to the doctor the postoperative actions of animals upon which he had performed surgery. They had all moved about freely with no ill effects.

By 1940, Shouldice had given extensive thought to several factors that contributed to early ambulation following surgery. Among them were the use of a local anesthetic, the nature of the surgical procedure itself, the design of a facility to encourage movement without unnecessarily causing discomfort, and the postoperative regimen. With these things in mind, he began to develop a surgical technique for repairing hernias[1] that was superior to others; word of his early success generated demand.

Dr. Shouldice's medical license permitted him to operate anywhere, even on a kitchen table. However, as more and more patients requested operations, Dr. Shouldice created new facilities by buying a rambling 130-acre estate with a 17,000-square foot main house in the Toronto suburb of Thornhill. After some years of planning, a large wing was added to provide a total capacity of 89 beds.

Dr. Shouldice died in 1965. At that time, Shouldice Hospital Limited was formed to operate both the hospital and clinical facilities under the surgical direction of Dr. Nicholas Obney. In 1999, Dr. Casim Degani, an internationally recognized authority, became surgeon-in-chief. By 2004, 7,600 operations were performed per year.

THE SHOULDICE METHOD

Only external (vs. internal) abdominal hernias were repaired at Shouldice Hospital. Thus most first-time repairs, "primaries," were straightforward operations requiring about 45 minutes. The remaining procedures involved patients suffering recurrences of hernias previously repaired elsewhere.[2] Many of the recurrences and very difficult hernia repairs required 90 minutes or more.

In the Shouldice method, the muscles of the abdominal wall were arranged in three distinct layers, and the opening was repaired—each layer in turn—by overlapping its margins as the edges of a coat might be overlapped when buttoned. The end result reinforced the muscular wall of the abdomen with six rows of sutures (stitches) under the skin cover, which was then closed with clamps that were later removed. (Other methods might not separate muscle layers, often involved fewer rows of sutures, and sometimes involved the insertion of screens or meshes under the skin.)

A typical first-time repair could be completed with the use of preoperative sedation (sleeping pill) and analgesic (pain killer) plus a local anesthetic, an injection of Novocain in the region of the incision. This allowed immediate post-operative patient ambulation and facilitated rapid recovery.

Professor James Heskett prepared the original version of this case, "Shouldice Hospital Limited," HBS No. 683-068. This version was prepared jointly by Professor James Heskett and Roger Hallowell (MBA 1989, DBA 1997). HBS cases are developed solely as the basis for class discussion. Cases are not intended to serve as endorsements, sources of primary data, or illustrations of effective or ineffective management.

THE PATIENTS' EXPERIENCE

Most potential Shouldice patients learned about the hospital from previous Shouldice patients. Although thousands of doctors had referred patients, doctors were less likely to recommend Shouldice because of the generally regarded simplicity of the surgery, often considered a "bread and butter" operation. Typically, many patients had their problem diagnosed by a personal physician and then contacted Shouldice directly. Many more made this diagnosis themselves.

The process experienced by Shouldice patients depended on whether or not they lived close enough to the hospital to visit the facility to obtain a diagnosis. Approximately 10% of Shouldice patients came from outside the province of Ontario, most of these from the United States. Another 60% of patients lived beyond the Toronto area. These out-of-own patients often were diagnosed by mail using the Medical Information Questionnaire shown in **Exhibit 1**. Based on information in the questionnaire, a Shouldice surgeon would determine the type of hernia the respondent had and whether there were signs that some risk might be associated with surgery (for example, an overweight or heart condition, or a patient who had suffered a heart attack or a stroke in the past six months to a year, or whether a general or local anesthetic was required). At this point, a patient was given an operating date and sent a brochure describing the hospital and the Shouldice method. If necessary, a sheet outlining a weight-loss program prior to surgery was also sent. A small proportion was refused treatment, either because they were overweight, represented an undue medical risk, or because it was determined that they did not have a hernia.

Arriving at the clinic between 1:00 P.M. and 3:00 P.M. the day before the operation, a patient joined other patients in the waiting room. He or she was soon examined in one of six examination rooms staffed by surgeons who had completed their operating schedules for the day. This examination required no more than 20 minutes, unless the patient needed reassurance. (Patients typically exhibited a moderate level of anxiety until their operation was completed.) At this point it occasionally was discovered that a patient had not corrected his or her weight problem; others might be found not to have a hernia at all. In either case, the patient was sent home.

After checking administrative details, about an hour after arriving at the hospital, a patient was directed to the room number shown on his or her wrist band. Throughout the process, patients were asked to keep their luggage (usually light) with them.

All patient rooms at the hospital were semiprivate, containing two beds. Patients with similar jobs, backgrounds, or interests were assigned to the same room to the extent possible. Upon reaching their rooms, patients busied themselves unpacking, getting acquainted with roommates, shaving themselves in the area of the operation, and changing into pajamas.

At 4:30 P.M., a nurse's orientation provided the group of incoming patients with information about what to expect, including the need for exercise after the operation and the daily routine. According to Alan O'Dell, "Half are so nervous they don't remember much." Dinner was then served, followed by further recreation, and tea and cookies at 9:00 P.M. Nurses emphasized the importance of attendance at that time because it provided an opportunity for preoperative patients to talk with those whose operations had been completed earlier that same day.

Patients to be operated on early were awakened at 5:30 A.M. to be given preop sedation. An attempt was made to schedule operations for roommates at approximately the same time. Patients were taken to the preoperating room where the circulating nurse administered Demerol, an analgesic, 45 minutes before surgery. A few minutes prior to the first operation at 7:30 A.M., the surgeon assigned to each patient administered Novocain, a local anesthetic, in the operating room. This was in contrast to the typical hospital procedure in which patients were sedated in their rooms prior to being taken to the operating rooms.

Upon the completion of their operation, during which a few patients were "chatty" and fully aware of what was going on, patients were invited to get off the operating table and walk to the post-operating room with the help of their surgeons. According to the director of nursing:

> Ninety-nine percent accept the surgeon's invitation. While we use wheelchairs to return them to their rooms, the walk from the operating table is for psychological as well as physiological [blood pressure, respiratory] reasons. Patients prove to themselves that they can do it, and they start their all-important exercise immediately.

Throughout the day after their operation, patients were encouraged to exercise by nurses and housekeepers alike. By 9:00 P.M. on the day of their operations, all patients were ready and able to walk down to the dining room for tea and cookies, even if it meant climbing stairs, to help indoctrinate the new "class" admitted that day. On the fourth morning, patients were ready for discharge.

During their stay, patients were encouraged to take advantage of the opportunity to explore the premises and make new friends. Some members of the staff felt that the patients and their attitudes were the most important element of the Shouldice program. According to Dr. Byrnes Shouldice, son of the founder, a surgeon on the staff, and a 50% owner of the hospital:

> Patients sometimes ask to stay an extra day. Why? Well, think about it. They are basically well to begin with. But they arrive with a problem and a certain amount of nervousness, tension, and anxiety about their surgery. Their first morning here they're operated on and experience a sense of relief from something that's been bothering them for a long time. They are immediately able to get around, and they've got a three-day holiday ahead of them with a perfectly good reason to be away from work with no sense of guilt. They share experiences with other patients, make friends easily, and have the run of the hospital. In summer, the most common after-effect from the surgery is sunburn.

Exhibit 1 Medical Information Questionnaire

SHOULDICE HOSPITAL

7750 Bayview Avenue
Box 379, Thornhill, Ontario L3T 4A3 Canada
Phone (418) 889-1125

(Thornhill - One Mile North Metro Toronto)

MEDICAL

INFORMATION

Patients who live at a distance often prefer their examination, admission and operation to be arranged all on a single visit — to save making two lengthy journeys. The whole purpose of this questionnaire is to make such arrangements possible, although, of course, it cannot replace the examination in any way. Its completion and return will not put you under any obligation.

Please be sure to fill in both sides.

This information will be treated as confidential.

(continued on next page)

FAMILY NAME (Last Name)	FIRST NAME	MIDDLE NAME

STREET & NUMBER (or Rural Route or P.O. Box)   Town/City   Province/State

County	Township	Zip or Postal Code	Birthdate: Month	Day	Year

Married or Single   Religion

Telephone
Home _____   if none, give
Work _____   neighbour's number

NEXT OF KIN: Name   Address   Telephone #

Date form completed

INSURANCE INFORMATION: Please give name of Insurance Company and Numbers.

HOSPITAL INSURANCE: (Please bring hospital certificates)   OTHER HOSPITAL INSURANCE

O.H.I.P.   BLUE CROSS   Company Name
Number   Number   Policy Number

SURGICAL INSURANCE: (Please bring insurance certificates)   OTHER SURGICAL INSURANCE

O.H.I.P.   BLUE SHIELD   Company Name
Number   Number   Policy Number

WORKMEN'S COMPENSATION BOARD   Approved   Social Insurance (Security) Number

Claim No.   Yes   No

Occupation   Name of Business   Are you the owner? If Retired – Former Occupation

Yes   No

How did you hear about Shouldice Hospital? (If referred by a doctor, give name & address)

Are you a former patient of Shouldice Hospital?   Yes   No   Do you smoke?   Yes   No

Have you ever written to Shouldice Hospital in the past?   Yes   No

What is your preferred admission date? (Please give as much advance notice as possible)

No admissions Friday, Saturday or Sunday.

FOR OFFICE USE ONLY

Date Received   Type of Hernia   Weight Loss   lbs.

Consent to Operate ☐   Special Instructions   Approved
Heart Report ☐

Referring Doctor Notified   Operation Date

Exhibit 1 (Continued)

THIS CHART IS FOR EXPLANATION ONLY

Ordinary hernias are mostly either
at the navel ("belly-button") - or just above it

or down in the groin area on either side

An "incisional hernia" is one that bulges through the scar of any other surgical operation that has failed to hold - wherever it may be.

THIS IS YOUR CHART – PLEASE MARK IT!

(MARK THE POSITION OF EACH HERNIA YOU WANT REPAIRED WITH AN "X")

Left Groin

Right Groin

APPROXIMATE SIZE...
Walnut (or less) ☐ ☐
Hen's Egg or Lemon ☐ ☐
Grapefruit (or more) ☐ ☐

ESSENTIAL EXTRA INFORMATION

Use only the sections that apply to your hernias and put a ✓ in each box that seems appropriate.

NAVEL AREA (AND JUST ABOVE NAVEL) ONLY

Is this navel (bellybutton) hernia your FIRST one?

Yes ☐   No ☐

If it's NOT your first, how many repair attempts so far? ☐

GROIN HERNIAS ONLY

	RIGHT GROIN		LEFT GROIN	
	Yes	No	Yes	No
Is this your FIRST GROIN HERNIA ON THIS SIDE?	☐	☐	☐	☐

How many hernia operations in this groin already?   Right ☐   Left ☐

DATE OF LAST OPERATION _____

INCISIONAL HERNIAS ONLY (the ones bulging through previous operation scars)

Was the original operation for your Appendix? ☐ , or Gallbladder? ☐ , or Hysterectomy? ☐
or Stomach? ☐ , or Prostate? ☐

How many attempts to repair the hernias have been made so far? ☐

PLEASE BE ACCURATE!: Misleading figures, when checked on a admission day, could mean postponement of your operation till your weight is suitable.

HEIGHT.........ft.........ins.   WEIGHT.........lbs. Nude   Recent gain?.........lbs.
or just pyjamas   Recent loss?.........lbs.

Waist (muscles relaxed).........ins.   Chest (not expanded).........ins.

GENERAL HEALTH

Age.........years   is your health now GOOD ☐ , FAIR ☐ , or POOR ☐

Please mention briefly any severe past illness – such as a "heart attack" or a "stroke", for example, from which you have now recovered (and its approximate date).........

We need to know about other present conditions, even though your admission is NOT likely to be refused because of them.

Please tick ✓ any condition for which you are having regular treatment:

Blood Pressure ☐
Excess body fluids ☐
Chest pain ("angina") ☐
Irregular Heartbeat ☐
Diabetes ☐
Asthma & Bronchitis ☐
Ulcers ☐
Anticoagulants
(to delay blood-clotting
or to "thin the blood") ☐
Other......... ☐

Name of any prescribed pills, tablets or capsules you take regularly -

, or Other?.........Did you remember to MARK AN "X" on your body chart to show us where each of your hernias is located?

THE NURSES' EXPERIENCE

Thirty-four full-time-equivalent nurses staffed Shouldice each 24 hour period. However, during non-operating hours, only six full-time-equivalent nurses were on the premises at any given time. While the Canadian acute-care hospital average ratio of nurses to patients was 1:4, at Shouldice the ratio was 1:15. Shouldice nurses spent an unusually large proportion of their time in counseling activities. As one supervisor commented, "We don't use bedpans." According to a manager, "Shouldice has a waiting list of nurses wanting to be hired, while other hospitals in Toronto are short-staffed and perpetually recruiting."

THE DOCTORS' EXPERIENCE

The hospital employed 10 full-time surgeons and 8 part-time assistant surgeons. Two anesthetists were also on site. The anesthetists floated among cases except when general anesthesia was in use. Each operating team required a surgeon, an assistant surgeon, a scrub nurse, and a circulating nurse. The operating load varied from 30 to 36 operations per day. As a result, each surgeon typically performed three or four operations each day.

A typical surgeon's day started with a *scrubbing* shortly before the first scheduled operation at 7:30 A.M. If the first operation was routine, it usually was completed by 8:15 A.M. At its conclusion, the surgical team helped the patient walk from the room and summoned the next patient. After scrubbing, the surgeon could be ready to operate again at 8:30 A.M. Surgeons were advised to take a coffee break after their second or third operation. Even so, a surgeon could complete three routine operations and a fourth involving a recurrence and still be finished in time for a 12:30 P.M. lunch in the staff dining room.

Upon finishing lunch, surgeons not scheduled to operate in the afternoon examined incoming patients. A surgeon's day ended by 4:00 P.M. In addition, a surgeon could expect to be on call one weekday night in ten and one weekend in ten. Alan O'Dell commented that the position appealed to doctors who "want to watch their children grow up. A doctor on call is rarely called to the hospital and has regular hours." According to Dr. Obney:

When I interview prospective surgeons, I look for experience and a good education. I try to gain some insight into their domestic situation and personal interests and habits. I also try to find out why a surgeon wants to switch positions. And I try to determine if he's willing to perform the repair exactly as he's told. This is no place for prima donnas.

Dr. Shouldice added:

Traditionally a hernia is often the first operation that a junior resident in surgery performs. Hernia repair is regarded as a relatively simple operation compared to other major operations. This is quite wrong, as is borne out by the resulting high recurrence rate. It is a tricky anatomical area and occasionally very complicated, especially to the novice

or those doing very few hernia repairs each year. But at Shouldice Hospital a surgeon learns the Shouldice technique over a period of several months. He learns when he can go fast and when he must go slow. He develops a pace and a touch. If he encounters something unusual, he is encouraged to consult immediately with other surgeons. We teach each other and try to encourage a group effort. And he learns not to take risks to achieve absolute perfection. Excellence is the enemy of good.

Chief Surgeon Degani assigned surgeons to an operating room on a daily basis by noon of the preceding day. This allowed surgeons to examine the specific patients that they were to operate on. Surgeons and assistants were rotated every few days. Cases were assigned to give doctors a non-routine operation (often involving a recurrence) several times a week. More complex procedures were assigned to more senior and experienced members of the staff. Dr. Obney commented:

If something goes wrong, we want to make sure that we have an experienced surgeon in charge. Experience is most important. The typical general surgeon may perform 25 to 50 hernia operations per year. Ours perform 750 or more.

The 10 full-time surgeons were paid a straight salary, typically $144,000.[3] In addition, bonuses to doctors were distributed monthly. These depended on profit, individual productivity, and performance. The total bonus pool paid to the surgeons in a recent year was approximately $400,000. Total surgeon compensation (including benefits) was approximately 15% more than the average income for a surgeon in Ontario.

Training in the Shouldice technique was important because the procedure could not be varied. It was accomplished through direct supervision by one or more of the senior surgeons. The rotation of teams and frequent consultations allowed for an ongoing opportunity to appraise performance and take corrective action. Where possible, former Shouldice patients suffering recurrences were assigned to the doctor who performed the first operation "to allow the doctor to learn from his mistake." Dr. Obney commented on being a Shouldice surgeon:

A doctor must decide after several years whether he wants to do this for the rest of his life because, just as in other specialties—for example, radiology—he loses touch with other medical disciplines. If he stays for five years, he doesn't leave. Even among younger doctors, few elect to leave.

THE FACILITY

The Shouldice Hospital contained two facilities in one building—the hospital and the clinic. On its first-level, the hospital contained the kitchen and dining rooms. The second level contained a large, open lounge area, the admissions offices, patient rooms, and a spacious glass-covered Florida room. The third level had additional patient rooms and recreational areas. Patients could be seen visiting in each others' rooms, walking up and down hallways, lounging in the sunroom, and making use of light recreational facilities ranging from a pool table to an exercycle. Alan O'Dell pointed out some of the features of the hospital:

> The rooms contain no telephone or television sets. If a patient needs to make a call or wants to watch television, he or she has to take a walk. The steps are designed specially with a small rise to allow patients recently operated on to negotiate the stairs without undue discomfort. Every square foot of the hospital is carpeted to reduce the hospital feeling and the possibility of a fall. Carpeting also gives the place a smell other than that of disinfectant.

> This facility was designed by an architect with input from Dr. Byrnes Shouldice and Mrs. W. H. Urquhart (the daughter of the founder). The facility was discussed for years and many changes in the plans were made before the first concrete was poured. A number of unique policies were also instituted. For example, parents accompanying children here for an operation stay free. You may wonder why we can do it, but we learned that we save more in nursing costs than we spend for the parent's room and board.

Patients and staff were served food prepared in the same kitchen, and staff members picked up food from a cafeteria line placed in the very center of the kitchen. This provided an opportunity for everyone to chat with the kitchen staff several times a day, and the hospital staff to eat together. According to O'Dell, "We use all fresh ingredients and prepare the food from scratch in the kitchen."

The director of housekeeping pointed out:

> I have only three on my housekeeping staff for the entire facility. One of the reasons for so few housekeepers is that we don't need to change linens during a patient's four-day stay. Also, the medical staff doesn't want the patients in bed all day. They want the nurses to encourage the patients to be up socializing, comparing notes [for confidence], encouraging each other, and walking around, getting exercise. Of course, we're in the rooms straightening up throughout the day. This gives the housekeepers a chance to josh with the patients and to encourage them to exercise.

The clinic housed five operating rooms, a laboratory, and the patient-recovery room. In total, the estimated cost to furnish an operating room was $30,000. This was considerably less than for other hospitals requiring a bank of equipment with which to administer anesthetics for each room. At Shouldice, two mobile units were used by the anesthetists when needed. In addition, the complex had one "crash cart" per floor for use if a patient should suffer a heart attack or stroke.

ADMINISTRATION

Alan O'Dell described his job:

> We try to meet people's needs and make this as good a place to work as possible. There is a strong concern for

employees here. Nobody is fired. [This was later reinforced by Dr. Shouldice, who described a situation involving two employees who confessed to theft in the hospital. They agreed to seek psychiatric help and were allowed to remain on the job.] As a result, turnover is low.

> Our administrative and support staff are non-union, but we try to maintain a pay scale higher than the union scale for comparable jobs in the area. We have a profit-sharing plan that is separate from the doctors'. Last year the administrative and support staff divided up $60,000.

> If work needs to be done, people pitch in to help each other. A unique aspect of our administration is that I insist that each secretary is trained to do another's work and in an emergency is able to switch to another function immediately. We don't have an organization chart. A chart tends to make people think they're boxed in jobs.[4] I try to stay one night a week, having dinner and listening to the patients, to find out how things are really going around here.

Operating Costs

The 2004 budgets for the hospital and clinic were close to $8.5 million[5] and $3.5 million, respectively.[6]

THE MARKET

Hernia operations were among the most common performed on males. In 2000 an estimated 1,000,000 such operations were performed in the United States alone. According to Dr. Shouldice:

> When our backlog of scheduled operations gets too large, we wonder how many people decide instead to have their local doctor perform the operation. Every time we've expanded our capacity, the backlog has declined briefly, only to climb once again. Right now, at 2,400, it is larger than it has ever been and is growing by 100 every six months.

The hospital relied entirely on word-of-mouth advertising, the importance of which was suggested by the results of a poll carried out by students of DePaul University as part of a project (**Exhibit 3** shows a portion of these results). Although little systematic data about patients had been collected, Alan O'Dell remarked that "if we had to rely on wealthy patients only, our practice would be much smaller."

Patients were attracted to the hospital, in part, by its reasonable rates. Charges for a typical operation were four days of hospital stay at $320 per day, and a $650 surgical fee for a primary inguinal (the most common hernia). An additional fee of $300 was assessed if general anesthesia was required (in about 20% of cases). These charges compared to an average charge of $5,240 for operations performed elsewhere.

Round-trip fares for travel to Toronto from various major cities on the North American continent ranged from roughly $200 to $600.

Exhibit 2 Organization Chart

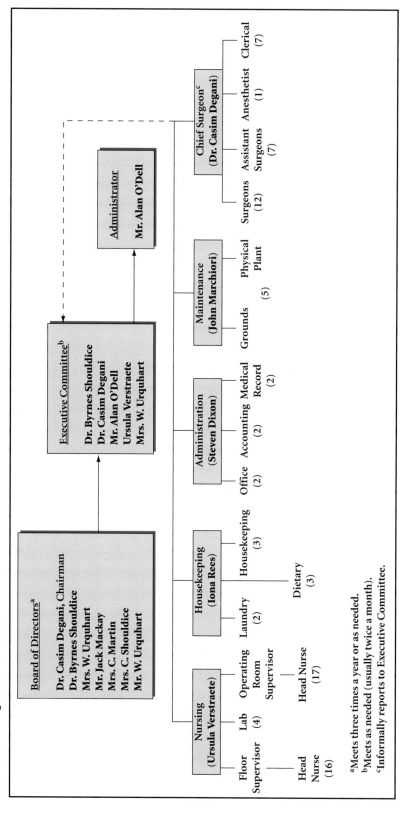

Board of Directors[a]

Dr. Casim Degani, Chairman
Dr. Byrnes Shouldice
Mrs. W. Urquhart
Mr. Jack Mackay
Mrs. C. Martin
Mrs. C. Shouldice
Mr. W. Urquhart

Executive Committee[b]

Dr. Byrnes Shouldice
Dr. Casim Degani
Mr. Alan O'Dell
Ursula Verstraete
Mrs. W. Urquhart

Administrator
Mr. Alan O'Dell

Nursing
(Ursula Verstraete)

Floor
Supervisor

Head
Nurse
(16)

Lab
(4)

Operating
Room
Supervisor

Head Nurse
(17)

Housekeeping
(Iona Rees)

Laundry
(2)

Dietary
(3)

Housekeeping
(3)

Administration
(Steven Dixon)

Office
(2)

Accounting
(2)

Medical
Record
(2)

Maintenance
(John Marchiori)

Grounds

Physical
Plant
(5)

Chief Surgeon[c]
(Dr. Casim Degani)

Surgeons
(12)

Assistant
Surgeons
(7)

Anesthetist
(1)

Clerical
(7)

[a]Meets three times a year or as needed.
[b]Meets as needed (usually twice a month).
[c]Informally reports to Executive Committee.

The hospital also provided annual checkups to alumni, free of charge. Many occurred at the time of the patient reunion. The most recent reunion, featuring dinner and a floor show, was held at a first-class hotel in downtown Toronto and was attended by 1,000 former patients, many from outside Canada.

PROBLEMS AND PLANS

When asked about major questions confronting the management of the hospital, Dr. Shouldice cited a desire to seek ways of increasing the hospital's capacity while at the same time maintaining control over the quality of service delivered, the future role of government in the operations of the hospital, and the use of the Shouldice name by potential competitors. As Dr. Shouldice put it:

> I'm a doctor first and an entrepreneur second. For example, we could refuse permission to other doctors who want to visit the hospital. They may copy our technique and misapply it or misinform their patients about the use of it. This results in failure, and we are concerned that the technique will be blamed. But we're doctors, and it is our obligation to help other surgeons learn. On the other hand, it's quite clear that others are trying to emulate us. Look at this ad. [The advertisement is shown in **Exhibit 4**.]
>
> This makes me believe that we should add to our capacity, either here or elsewhere. Here, we could go to

Saturday operations and increase our capacity by 20%. Throughout the year, no operations are scheduled for Saturdays or Sundays, although patients whose operations are scheduled late in the week remain in the hospital over the weekend. Or, with an investment of perhaps $4 million in new space, we could expand our number of beds by 50%, and schedule the operating rooms more heavily.

> On the other hand, given government regulation, do we want to invest more in Toronto? Or should we establish another hospital with similar design, perhaps in the United States? There is also the possibility that we could diversify into other specialties offering similar opportunities such as eye surgery, varicose veins, or diagnostic services (e.g., colonoscopies).
>
> For now, we're also beginning the process of grooming someone to succeed Dr. Degani when he retires. He's in his early 60s, but at some point we'll have to address this issue. And for good reason, he's resisted changing certain successful procedures that I think we could improve on. We had quite a time changing the schedule for the administration of Demerol to patients to increase their comfort level during the operation. Dr. Degani has opposed a Saturday operating program on the premise that he won't be here and won't be able to maintain proper control.

Alan O'Dell added his own concerns:

> How should we be marketing our services? Right now, we don't advertise directly to patients. We're even

Exhibit 3 Shouldice Hospital Annual Patient Reunion Data

```
Direction:  For each question, please place a check mark as it applies to
you.

1.  Sex   Male    41    95.34%      2.  Age    20 or less
          Female   2     4.65%                 21–40        4      9.30%
                                                41–60       17     39.54%
                                                61 or more  22     51.16%

3.  Nationality                     4.  Education level

    Directions:   Please place a
    check mark in nation you            Elementary      5      11.63%
    represent and please write in       High School    18      41.86%
    your province, state or             College       1980     30.23%
    country where it applies.           Graduate work   7      16.28%

    Canada   38   Province   88.37%
    America   5   State      11.63%    5.  Occupation _____
    Europe        Country
    Other

6.  Have you been overnight in a hospital other than      Yes   31
    Shouldice before your operation?                      No    12

7.  What brought Shouldice Hospital to your attention?

    Friend   23   Doctor   9   Relative   7   Article    Other    4
             53.49%        20.93%         16.28%        (Please explain) 9.30%

8.  Did you have a single   25   or double   18   hernia operation?
                            58.14%            41.86%

9.  Is this your first Annual Reunion?  Yes   20    No   23     2–5 reunions–11   47.63%
                                              46.51%     53.49%  6–10 reunions  –5 21.73%
    If no, how many reunions have you attended? ____      11–20 reunions –4 12.39%
                                                          21–36 reunions –3 13.05%
10. Do you feel that Shouldice Hospital cared for you as a person?

    Most definitely   37    Definitely  6   Very little      Not at all  _____
                      86.05%              13.95%
```

Exhibit 3 *continued*

11. What impressed you the most about your stay at Shouldice? Please check one answer for each of the following.

A. Fees charged for operation and hospital stay

Very Important		Important		Somewhat Important		Not Important	
	10		3		6		24

B. Operation Procedure

Very Important		Important		Somewhat Important		Not Important	
	33		9		1		
	76.74%		20.93%		2.33%		

C. Physician's Care

Very Important		Important		Somewhat Important		Not Important	
	31		12		-		-
	72.10%		27.90%				

D. Nursing Care

Very Important		Important		Somewhat Important		Not Important	
	28		14		1		
	65.12%		32.56%		2.32%		

E. Food Service

Very Important		Important		Somewhat Important		Not Important	
	23		11		7		2
	53.48%		25.59%		16.28%		4.65%

F. Shortness of Hospital Stay

Very Important		Important		Somewhat Important		Not Important	
	17		15		8		3
	39.53%		34.88%		18.60%		6.98%

G. Exercise; Recreational Activities

Very Important		Important		Somewhat Important		Not Important	
	17		14		12		-
	39.53%		32.56%		27.91%		

H. Friendships with Patients

Very Important		Important		Somewhat Important		Not Important	
	25		10		5		3
	58.15%		23.25%		11.63%		6.98%

I. "Shouldice Hospital hardly seemed like a hospital at all."

Very Important		Important		Somewhat Important		Not Important	
	25		13		5		
	58.14%		30.23%		11.63%		

12. In a few words, give the MAIN REASON why you returned for this annual reunion.

afraid to send out this new brochure we've put together, unless a potential patient specifically requests it, for fear it will generate too much demand. Our records show that just under 1% of our patients are medical doctors, a significantly high percentage. How should we capitalize on that? I'm also concerned about this talk of Saturday operations. We are already getting good utilization of this facility. And if we expand further, it will be very difficult to maintain the same kind of working relationships and attitudes. Already there are rumors floating around among the staff about it. And the staff is not pleased.

The matter of Saturday operations had been a topic of conversation among the doctors as well. Four of the older doctors were opposed to it. While most of the younger doctors were indifferent or supportive, at least two who had been at the hospital for some time were particularly concerned about the possibility that the issue would drive a wedge between the two groups. As one put it, "I'd hate to see the practice split over the issue."

Exhibit 4 Advertisement by a Shouldice Competitor Alan O'Dell added his own concerns:

Endnotes

1. Most hernias, knows as external abdominal hernias, are protrusions of some part of the abdominal contents through a hole or slit in the muscular layers of the abdominal wall which is supposed to contain them. Well over 90% of these hernias occur in the groin area. Of these, by far the most common are inguinal hernias, many of which are caused by a slight weakness in the muscle layers brought about by the passage of the testicles in male babies through the groin area shortly before birth. Aging also contributes to the development of inguinal hernias. Because of the cause of the affliction, 85% of all hernias occur in males.

2. Based on tracking of patients over more than 30 years, the gross recurrence rate for all operations performed at Shouldice was 0.8%. Recurrence rates reported in the literature for these types of hernia varied greatly. However, one text stated, "In the United States the gross rate of recurrence for groin hernias approaches 10%."

3. All monetary references in the case are to Canadian dollars. $1 US equaled $1.33 Canadian on February 23, 2004.

4. The chart in Exhibit 2 was prepared by the casewriter, based on conversations with hospital personnel.

5. This figure included a provincially mandated return on investment.

6. The latter figure included the bonus pool for doctors.

Study Questions

1. *What is the market for this service? How successful is Shouldice Hospital?*

2. *Define the service model for Shouldice. How does each of its elements contribute to the hospital's success?*

3. *As Dr. Shouldice, what actions, if any, would you take to expand the hospital's capacity and how would you implement such changes?*

Case 16 Capital One: Launching a Mass Media Campaign

ROBERT J. FISHER AND KEN MARK

INTRODUCTION

At the end of March 2005, Clinton Braganza, senior brand manager, was preparing to present his recommendations to his Canadian senior management team at Capital One's Toronto office. Braganza had been tasked with determining Capital One's strategy for its first mass media advertising campaign in Canada. He had spent the last few months conducting and analysing consumer research, and had started to adapt several U.S. and U.K. television ads for use in Canada.

Capital One's intent was to maintain its competition with Canadian banks, which defined the objective of this mass media advertising campaign: *To raise Capital One's awareness and communicate a position in the marketplace in order to achieve growth and change the market's perception of its financial products.*

With a limited budget, Braganza knew he couldn't invest in all the options in front of him. To design his strategy, Braganza revisited the consumer research findings he had compiled. Braganza faced three major challenges:

1. Choosing the appropriate target segments;
2. Selecting different advertisements for a nationwide launch;
3. Drafting an advertising plan that best delivered the message to Capital One's target audience groups.

THE CANADIAN BANKING INDUSTRY

In 2005, the Canadian banking industry was made up of 13 domestic banks, 34 foreign bank subsidiaries and 11 foreign bank branches. The six major domestic banks—Royal Bank, Bank of Montreal, TD Canada Trust, Imperial Bank of Commerce, Scotiabank and National Bank—accounted for more than 90 per cent of the assets held by the banking industry. In Canada, these six banks operated a total of 8,000 branches and nearly 17,000 automated banking machines. The other seven domestic banks were significantly smaller and, as a group, accounted for less than two per cent of the total assets held by the Canadian banking industry. With a combined seven per cent share, foreign banks that operated in Canada accounted for the remaining assets of the Canadian banking industry.

Ninety-three per cent of Canadians had banking relationships, and it was common for customers to consolidate their mortgage, car loan, personal loan, line of credit, investments and credit card at the same retail bank.

In contrast, the U.S. retail banking industry was less consolidated, owing to the legacy of interstate banking regulations and the preference of U.S. consumers to use different financial institutions for their various financial needs.

Credit Cards

Credit cards provided consumers a means of payment, a source of consumer loans and were used as marketing tools by companies. By 2005, credit cards were accepted at more than 1.1 million merchant outlets in Canada. Issued through banks and financial services firms, credit cards belonged to one of the following payment solution organizations: Visa, MasterCard (the two most dominant players), American Express or Diners Club. Merchants remit between one and two per cent of the total transaction charged to Visa or MasterCard. The exact fee charged varies depending on the size of the merchant, with larger firms paying close to one per cent and smaller firms paying close to two per cent. In Canada, the 23 principal issuers of Visa or MasterCard branded credit cards were banks, credit unions, caisses populaires and retailers. For an overview of Visa and MasterCard statistics, see **Exhibit 1**. For the market share of Visa and MasterCard, see **Exhibit 2**.

The Canadian credit card industry had been traditionally controlled by the six major banks, but, in recent years, had experienced higher levels of competition because of several U.S.-based players, such as Capital One and MBNA, who had entered the market. From 1996 to 2004, as the number of Visa and MasterCard issuers grew from 15 to 23, the circulation of cards in Canada grew from 30.2 million to 53.4 million. In

Credit Card Statistics—Visa and MasterCard

Fiscal Year Ended Oct. 31	Number of Cards in Circulation[1a] (Millions)	*No. of Accts with balances (Millions), including those that are paid off every month[1b]	Net Retail Volume[2] (Billions)	Average Sale	% Delinquency 90 days & over[3][7]	Number of Cards Fraudulently used	$ Amount of Fraudulent Accounts written off[6] (Millions)	Merchant Outlets[5]	VISA/MCI Principal Issuers
1977	8.2		$3.61	$30.46	1.3%	–	–	271,150	–
1978	9.0		$4.90	$32.50	1.3%	–	–	290,692	–
1979	9.9		$6.64	$35.72	1.2%	–	–	322,115	–
1980	10.8		$8.82	$39.47	1.3%	–	–	347,845	–
1981	12.0		$10.59	$42.43	1.0%	–	–	371,831	–
1982	11.6		$13.83	$50.30	1.7%	–	$15.88	382,206	–
1983	12.1		$14.84	$49.88	0.9%	19,200	$17.39	419,610	10
1984	13.1		$16.92	$52.05	0.7%	21,332	$16.79	442,928	10
1985	14.0	7.3	$19.35	$51.90	0.7%	21,026	$17.54	527,042	10
1986	15.5	7.9	$23.01	$55.15	0.8%	22,326	$18.61	571,771	10
1987	17.6	8.8	$26.37	$58.52	0.7%	28,913	$15.78	642,429	12
1988	19.4	9.5	$30.33	$61.90	0.7%	25,773	$15.63	646,844	13
1989	20.4	10.3	$36.10	$66.00	0.9%	30,919	$19.20	709,674	14
1990	23.2	11.1	$38.60	$67.22	1.8%	32,851	$28.90	786,288	14
1991	24.3	11.8	$40.45	$67.40	1.3%	53,968	$44.60	857,159	14
1992	24.4	12.2	$43.10	$69.30	1.0%	61,234	$63.50	896,365	14
1993	25.0	12.4	$47.90	$70.50	0.7%	63,442	$75.20	904,689	13
1994	27.5	13.2	$55.10	$72.40	0.9%	63,635	$70.60	955,993	13
1995	28.8	13.6	$61.26	$74.51	0.9%	66,109	$72.64	981,851	13
1996	30.2	14.1	$67.70	$77.80	1.0%	77,740	$83.60	1,076,694	15
1997	31.9	15.0	$76.00	$82.50	0.9%	89,982	$88.08	1,106,141	17
1998	35.3	16.0	$84.10	$89.96	0.9%	126,384	$104.80	1,143,110	19
1999	37.7	17.3	$94.30	$90.35	0.9%	132,836	$134.10	1,139,228	18
2000	40.1	18.5	$109.87	$95.57	0.7%	112,070	$156.38	1,187,745	19
2001	44.1	19.6	$121.82	$99.16	0.8%	116,139	$142.27	1,206,779	19
2002	49.4	20.8	$135.69	$99.16	0.7%	136,598	$128.42	1,265,157	23
2003	50.4	22.2	$150.49	$102.00	0.8%	146,310	$138.60	1,187,384	23
2004	53.4	23.2	$168.78	$104.00	0.8%	177,081	$163.18	1,128,410	23

(1a) As at last day of the fiscal year-end.
(1b) As at last day of the fiscal year-end, including accounts with balances paid off every month.
(2) Reported total for the fiscal year.
(3) Percentage of outstandings as at fiscal year-end.
(4) Total of Net Retail Volume ($ sales) and cash advance volume ($).
(5) Merchants accepting VISA and/or MASTERCARD. Note that merchants accepting both cards have been reported by each plan.
      To estimate # of merchant outlets accepting VISA or MASTERCARD, divide Merchants Outlets by 2 and multiply by 1.1.
(6) Includes total cardholder and merchant fraud for the fiscal year.
(7) Effective October 31, 1991, a new interpretation of "90 days & over" was adopted. This resulted in a one-time reduction in the delinquency ratio of approx. 0.2%.

PRINCIPAL VISA AND MASTERCARD ISSUERS:

VISA Bank of America, Bank of Nova Scotia, Caisses Populaires Desjardins, CIBC, Citizens Bank of Canada, Home Trust, Laurentian Bank, Royal Bank, TD Bank, US Bank, Vancouver City Savings Credit Union.
MCI Alberta Treasury Branches, Bank of Montreal, Canadian Tire Acceptance Ltd, Capital One, Citibank Canada, Credit Union Electronic Transaction Services Inc., G.E. Capital Corp., MBNA Canada, National Bank of Canada, President's Choice Financial, Wells Fargo/Trans Canada, Sears Canada
(Data from Affiliated Issuers reported through Principal Issuers)

Source: Canadian Bankers Association, Table includes data from all VISA & MASTERCARD issuers.

Exhibit 2 Card Ownership–Canada

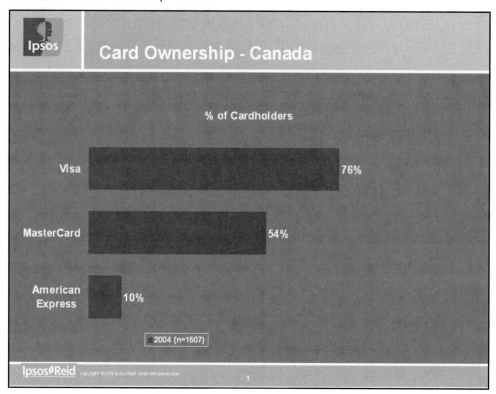

Source: Ipsos-Reid.

2004, about 23.2 million of these credit card accounts were considered "active," which meant they held balances, including those that were paid off every month.

A common trait shared by U.S. and Canadian retail banks was their tendency to run their credit card business as part of an integrated operation. Managers at North American retail banks relied on a combination of these four objectives to run their line of business and optimize profits:

1. Improving marketing to new accounts
2. Retaining existing accounts
3. Minimizing credit losses
4. Minimizing costs

Retail banks in both countries primarily tended to market their credit cards to their own customers through their extensive branch networks. In addition to their trusted brand names, retail banks had lower costs of capital—up to 75 basis points lower—than the U.S. issuers, such as Capital One and MBNA. It was not surprising to see that retail banks garnered the greatest share of new acquisitions in 2004. More than half of the 2004 card applications were received through store and bank branch channels (see **Exhibit 3**).

Credit Card Customers

Consumers were typically divided into three categories depending on their default risk:

- Super prime
- Prime
- Sub prime

At one extreme, super prime customers were considered a low risk for default; at the other end, sub prime customers were considered high risk for default. As a result, Canadian

Table 1

Risk Segment	Risk Score	% of Cdn Adults	Average Credit Card Debt	Average Credit Available on Credit Cards	Average Number of Credit Cards
Sub prime	<600	17%	$4,500	$6,600	1.8
Prime	660–719	17%	$5,300	$12,500	2.2
Super prime	>720	66%	$2,000	$13,700	1.8

Source: Equifax elB Tool, June 2005

Exhibit 3 Distribution Channel for Card Applications

Distribution Channel for Card Applications

Channel used:	2002 (n=289)	2003 (n=256)	2004 (n=322)
	%	%	%
In store	26	26	32
At bank branch	20	17	26
Kiosk/shopping centre	-	-	3
Through the mail	33	26	18
Inbound telephone	9	6	10
Outbound telephone	4	7	4
Over the Internet	3	6	7

Ipsos◆Reid   Privileged and confidential © 2004 Ipsos-Reid   3   Q.23

Source: Ipsos-Reid.

Exhibit 4 Reported Value of Card Balance

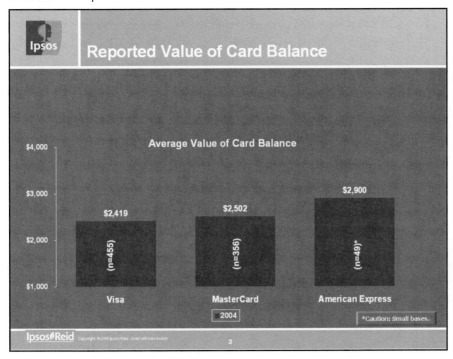

Source: Ipsos-Reid.

retail banks typically offered credit cards only to prime or super prime customers. For a look at selected statistics available on the three segments, see **Table 1**.

Within each segment, customers could be further divided into "transactors" and "revolvers." *Transactors* typically paid off their entire credit balance every month and tended to avoid interest charges. *Revolvers* generally carried a balance from month to month and would pay their minimum monthly payments (which was two or three per cent of the total amount owed) but not their full amount. Because customers paid interest on the balances they carried forward, as a group, *revolvers* were a significant source of revenue for credit companies. An Ipsos Reid survey estimated the average customer carried a balance between $2,400 and $2,900 (see **Exhibit 4**).

Exhibit 5   Reported Monthly Personal Spend On All Cards

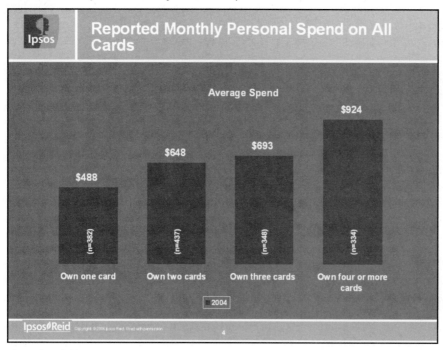

Source: Ipsos-Reid.

Exhibit 6   Reasons For Using/Switching Primary Card

Reasons for Using/Switching Primary Card

% of Primary Cardholders:	Reason for Using (n=1477) %	Reason for Switching (n=283) %
REWARD PROGRAMS	23	27
COST	11	19
BANK RELATIONSHIP	16	13
CONVENIENCE	14	13
USAGE	8	1
CREDIT/LIMIT	3	4
ONLY CARD I HAVE	15	-

Source: Ipsos-Reid.

Customers who had more credit cards were likely to have higher monthly spends (see **Exhibit 5**). Regardless of how many credit cards customers possessed, however, they typically relied on one primary card. While customers had key reasons for using their primary cards, some were willing to replace their primary card with another if they were offered the right value proposition (see **Exhibit 6**).

CAPITAL ONE

In 2005, Capital One had a global customer base of 49 million and managed loans of $105 billion. In addition to issuing credit cards, Capital One offered other financial products and services, such as auto loans, home equity loans, small business loans, installment loans, consumer financing for elective medical and dental procedures and savings products.

Established in 1995, Capital One had developed into a global diversified financial services provider with operations in the United States, Canada and the United Kingdom. The firm was founded by Richard Fairbank on his belief that the power of information, technology, testing and great people could be combined to deliver highly customized financial products directly to customers. Capital One was known for its proprietary Information-Based Strategy (IBS), which referred to its practice of relying heavily on data to make management decisions. Using scientific testing on a large scale, Capital One gathered huge amounts of information to help tailor products and services to the individual consumer, rather than simply offering one product to broad socio-economic groups. Capital One attributed its financial services success to its focus on information technology, customer acquisition and customer retention. Less than one decade after it had been established, Capital One joined the Fortune 500.

In 1996, Capital One entered Canada but, unlike its U.S. parent, the focus was issuing credit cards. With a foothold in Canada, Capital One leveraged its IBS to take advantage of the opportunity to offer all Canadians—in all risk segments—low-interest rates and access to credit. Capital One's initial strategy was to present a unique credit card offer to Canadians. When it began operations, Capital One relied on an initial 9.9 per cent introductory offer to rapidly gain market share. As a comparison, its competitors were offering fixed-rate credit cards with interest rates of 16 per cent and higher. In subsequent years, Capital One's low-price offerings became attractive to prime customers who "revolved." For the sub prime segment—a segment the major banks tended to ignore—Capital One offered product not previously available, giving sub prime customers an opportunity to build their credit history.

Canadians responded to Capital One's unique products and, by 2004, they had US$2.4 billion in outstanding balances. To manage its growth, Capital One increased its staff to 100 employees in its Toronto office. Capital One's main focus in 2005 was to establish a clear positioning in the marketplace and to expand its credit card product offerings and channels to acquire new customers.

The Capital One Customer

Capital One customers used credit cards for several reasons:

- For convenience
- To avoid carrying cash
- To keep track of expenses
- For collecting loyalty reward points

If customers chose not to use credit cards, they either wanted to avoid interest and debt, or had a preference for cash or debit payment methods. Of note, Capital One customers were as equally likely to use credit cards for special occasion purchases as they were for business-related purchases; whereas, the general populace was more likely to use credit cards for the latter purpose. For a list of Capital One credit cards available to Canadian consumers, see **Exhibit 7**.

Customer Acquisition and Retention Using IBS

Capital One relied heavily on its IBS for growth. An entrepreneurial structure supported the culture of testing and learning, which was at the heart of the IBS. The responsibilities for the two core activities of customer acquisition and retention

Exhibit 7 Capital One's Credit Cards Available to Canadians

Credit Card	Capital One® Low-Rate Platinum MasterCard®	Capital One® 1% Cash Rebate Platinum MasterCard®	Capital One® MasterCard®	Capital One® Secured MasterCard®
This card is right for you if	You have excellent credit and have had Canadian cards for at least 3 years	You have excellent credit and have had Canadian cards for at least 3 years	You would like to strengthen your credit and have had Canadian cards for at least 3 years	You want to establish credit
Annual Purchase Rates	6.99%	17.90%	9.9% until May 2006; 19.8% variable thereafter (a variable annual interest rate of Canadian Prime plus15.55%, currently equal to 19.8% as of July 2005)	19.8% variable (a variable annual interest rate of Canadian Prime plus 15.55%, currently equal to 19.8% as of July 2005)
Annual Fee	None	None	$59	$59
Security Funds Required	None	None	None	Either $75 or $200

Source: *www.capitalone.ca, accessed January 27, 2006.*

resided with the Acquisitions division and the Account Management division, respectively. Capital One built consumer tests, analysed and applied results from large quantities of data to reduce credit risk, provided customized products for consumers and improved operational efficiency.

In the United States, Capital One combined public bureau data with its private data. In contrast, the Canadian branch only had access to bureau data in Canada after a consumer had completed an application for a credit card. Thus, from a consumer targeting perspective, Capital One felt the management of direct mail was its largest tactical challenge across all segments. As a result, to better target consumers with appropriate direct mail, Capital One had to rely on other means to segment consumers. By actively testing a wide variety of products and service features, marketing channels (in Canada, Capital One utilized both direct mail and the Internet to solicit applications) and other aspects of offerings, Capital One enhanced the response levels and maximized returns on investment within its underwriting parameters.

Credit evaluation began during the application process. Generally credit card issuers used a combination of credit bureau information, statistical models and decision rules to approve or decline applicants. These procedures were constantly changing in response to dynamic market conditions and new insights.

Driving innovation was always a key concern at Capital One, because it was the foundation of the company's success. Communicating Capital One's innovation was equally important, as Sartaj Alag, president of the Canadian branch of Capital One, pointed out:

> How do we come up with an advertising strategy that 1) speaks directly to our target segment, 2) is distinctive from our competitors and 3) is a position we can immediately deliver on?

Youssef Lahrech, Capital One's head of Marketing and Analysis in Canada added:

> How can Capital One change Canadian consumers' negative attitude towards credit cards through our advertising campaign? Can Capital One build one campaign for all consumer segments or do we need to differentiate our ads?

To determine whether their programs were on the right track, Capital One relied on quantitative measures, such as net present value per marketing dollar. After a customer was acquired, the Account Management Division ran tests to determine which marketing programs would either increase revenues or decrease default. Some of these programs included building balances, credit line increases and cross-selling products.

DAY-TO-DAY CHALLENGES
Competitive Responses by Retail Banks

In 2004, major banks continued to issue the majority of new credit cards. With their infrastructure of branches and relationships with banking customers, acquisition costs for banks were lower than similar costs for U.S. credit card issuers. To respond to products offered by U.S. issuers, retail banks didn't need to innovate, advocate or educate. All they had to do was watch and follow. For example, while balance transfers had been a market niche for Capital One, retail banks had since entered the market.

Although Capital One was constantly inventing new products to keep ahead of its competitors, one advantage it maintained over retail banks was its ability to target offers to select consumers. A second advantage that favored Capital One was its expertise in credit cards, among other financial services offered. Because retail banks ran their credit card operations as part of a diversified portfolio of products, they seemed disinclined to grow their credit card operations if it meant cannibalizing other products in their portfolio.

A Focused Operation That Had Not Partnered with a Rewards Program

For other card issuers, a strong rewards program, such as Air Canada's Aeroplan (to which 21 per cent of all Canadian card holders belonged in 2004, up from 12 per cent in 2002), provided quantified incentives to customers to increase their spending in the hunt for reward miles. Such programs also allowed partners to exchange mailing lists. There were several rewards programs in Canada other than Aeroplan, including Air Miles (by Loyalty Management Group), Hudson's Bay Company's HBC Rewards and Club Z program, Shoppers Drug Mart's Optimum program and Canadian Tire money. Twenty-three per cent of respondents cited the availability of a rewards program as a reason for using their primary credit card. By 2005, Capital One had built a strong business without having to rely on a rewards program or partner in Canada.

Working without Physical Branches

Capital One's lack of physical branches in Canada posed a unique challenge. Without face-to-face contact, several Capital One associates reasoned, it could be difficult to build a relationship with customers that appreciated and fulfilled their needs.

Substitutes for Credit Cards

For customers who used credit cards purely as transaction vehicles, cash, cheques, debit cards and direct deposits were used as substitutes. Although they didn't demonstrate a cardholder's creditworthiness, debit cards allowed consumers to withdraw cash from the point of sale, giving them "cash back," while making purchases. For customers who carried balances on their credit cards, product substitutes included bank lines of credit, bank installment loans, home equity loans (with lower interest rates), retail layaway plans, retail store credit (such as Leon's and The Brick), cash advances against pay cheques from companies such as Money Mart, and vehicle loans from automobile manufacturers or leasing organizations, such as GE Capital.

THE MARKETING AND PROMOTIONS CHOICES

Capital One's global value proposition had been centered on the tagline "What's in Your Wallet?" positioning Capital One as offering "great value without the hassle." This proposition had been conveyed to customers through a series of long-running television ads in the United States and, more recently, in the United Kingdom. In both the United States and the United Kingdom, Capital One's locally made advertisements had proven extremely successful, with awareness levels of 98 per cent in the United States and 95 per cent in the United Kingdom. Up until now, Canadians primarily knew Capital One as a price player, with some Canadians aware of "great value without the hassle" because of U.S. advertising spillover.

Braganza wondered about the implications of using the U.S. positioning in Canada, and asked himself several questions:

- Could "great value" refer to price or should it refer to rewards?
- How important were rewards to Canadians and what were the implications for Capital One?
- What were the "hassles" that Canadian consumers wanted to avoid and how could Capital One show that it was providing "great value without the hassle" to Canadians?

To sum it up, was "great value" the right positioning for Capital One in Canada?

Aside from determining the right positioning, Braganza also had to decide if he would adapt U.S. and or U.K. advertisements, or develop advertisements unique to Canada. He recalled that consumer packaged goods companies (Procter & Gamble, for example) developed a significant portion of their advertising in the United States, and then adapted the same advertisement for various countries. In contrast, MasterCard's "priceless" campaign gave flexibility to individual countries' organizations to develop their own unique advertisements based on a common global theme (tagline: "There are some things money can't buy; for everything else, there's MasterCard").

Braganza projected a minimum of four months to develop new advertising. He would need to find and hire an advertising agency, organize customer research and obtain internal approvals at various stages. These tasks would require Capital One to shift precious marketing management resources from other programs designed to enhance customer acquisition and retention. And, according to Millward Brown's research, there was a greater than 50 per cent probability that a new advertisement in the financial services industry would score below the Canadian average. But the opportunity to develop an advertisement that truly "cut through the clutter" of average advertising had a strong appeal. Adapting a U.S. or U.K. advertisement would include paying licensing fees and could be accomplished in four weeks or less. However, it wasn't clear that the portfolio of available advertisements would enable Capital One to meet its objectives in the Canadian market.

But which segment should Capital One focus on? According to the Canadian test results, the various executions appealed to different target segments. Although competitors had largely ignored the sub prime customer (who seemed more responsive to offers), Capital One could also target prime and super prime customers (who were less responsive to offers, and were targeted by retail banks). Also should Capital One aim to book additional accounts or target existing customers? Put another way, should the television advertisements boost Capital One's direct mail response rate, or should they encourage current customers to use their cards more often?

Exhibit 8 Capital One Financial Corporation: Contribution by Geographic Region (US$)

	December 31			
	2004		2005	
	Loans	Percentage of Total	Loans	Percentage of Total
Geographic Region:				
Domestic				
South	$25,034,582	31.34%	$23,262,643	32.65%
West	15,873,159	19.88	14,662,193	20.58
Midwest	15,220,162	19.06	13,643,202	19.15
Northeast	13,198,619	16.53	12,029,894	16.89
Total Domestic	69,326,522	86.81%	63,597,932	89.27%
International				
U.K.	8,163,109	10.22%	5,546,644	7.78%
Canada	2,360,297	2.96	1,935,396	2.72
Other	11,371	.01	164,824	0.23
Total International	10,534,777	13.19%	7,646,864	10.73%
Less securitization adjustments	(41,645,708)		(38,394,527)	
Total	$38,215,591		$32,850,269	

Source: Capital One Annual Report.

Exhibit 9   2004 Competitive Median Spend (Nielsen)

Class	Company	Total Media ($ MT)	Shr%	Daily Paper ($)	Magazine ($)	Out of Home ($)	Radio ($)	Total TV ($)	Network TV ($)	Selective TV ($)
Cards: Credit; Debit	(Jetsgo Corporation)	25,000	0.0	0	0	25,000	0	0	0	0
Cards: Credit; Debit	Alaska Air Group, Inc.	592,699	0.8	222,202	0	0	10,650	359,847	0	359,847
Cards: Credit; Debit	American Express Company	13,477,478	17.2	4,433,944	2,049,491	519,502	215,011	6,259,530	5,373,450	886,080
Cards: Credit; Debit	Bank of America	56,792	0.1	0	0	0	56,792	0	0	0
Cards: Credit; Debit	Bank of Nova Scotia	330,160	0.4	29,524	15,316	0	0	285,320	193,616	91,704
Cards: Credit; Debit	Bayview Credit Union	3,303	0.0	3,303	0	0	0	0	0	0
Cards: Credit; Debit	BENQ America Corp	4,757	0.0	0	4,757	0	0	0	0	0
Cards: Credit; Debit	BMO Financial Group	3,221,715	4.1	2,355,300	191,540	0	372,866	302,009	294,529	7,480
Cards: Credit; Debit	Canadian Automobile Association	43,069	0.1	0	26,673	0	0	16,396	0	16,396
Cards: Credit; Debit	Canadian Cooperative Agricultural Finance	30,179	0.0	0	0	30,179	0	0	0	0
Cards: Credit; Debit	Canadian Imperial Bank of Commerce	7,068,982	9.0	2,122,847	1,910,396	293,255	758,920	1,983,564	1,349,306	634,258
Cards: Credit; Debit	Canadian Tire Corporation Limited	41,304	0.1	41,304	0	0	0	0	0	0
Cards: Credit; Debit	Choice Rewards	42,783	0.1	39,079	3,704	0	0	0	0	0
Cards: Credit; Debit	Citigroup Inc	373,472	0.5	56,234	11,520	305,718	0	0	0	0
Cards: Credit; Debit	Corp-Rate	2,998	0.0	0	2,998	0	0	0	0	0
Cards: Credit; Debit	Credit Union Electronic Transaction Serv	14,578	0.0	14,578	0	0	0	0	0	0
Cards: Credit; Debit	Dexit Inc	563,220	0.7	0	0	357,452	205,768	0	0	0
Cards: Credit; Debit	GM Corp	1,945,383	2.5	873,921	1,043,734	23,960	3,768	0	0	0
Cards: Credit; Debit	Groupe Marie Claire, Le	20,552	0.0	0	20,552	0	0	0	0	0
Cards: Credit; Debit	Island Savings Credit Union	7,834	0.0	7,834	0	0	0	0	0	0
Cards: Credit; Debit	Kootenay Savings Credit Union	3,055	0.0	3,055	0	0	0	0	0	0
Cards: Credit; Debit	MasterCard International Inc	10,717,720	13.7	787,066	111,522	127,325	187,701	9,504,106	5,692,158	3,811,948
Cards: Credit; Debit	MBNA Canada Bank	576,959	0.7	246,342	0	0	0	330,617	68,981	261,636
Cards: Credit; Debit	Morgan Stanley & Co Ltd	116	0.0	0	0	0	0	116	0	116
Cards: Credit; Debit	Mouvement de Caisses Desjardins	534,326	0.7	249,425	17,264	267,637	0	0	0	0
Cards: Credit; Debit	National Bank of Canada	284,991	0.4	138,877	146,114	0	0	0	0	0
Cards: Credit; Debit	Pattison Group, Jim	40,223	0.1	40,223	0	0	0	0	0	0
Cards: Credit; Debit	Petro Canada Ltd	4,065,060	5.2	1,642,395	0	0	695,976	1,726,689	667,088	1,059,601
Cards: Credit; Debit	RBC Financial Group	9,670,473	12.3	3,920,508	1,017,955	296,857	540,463	3,894,690	2,904,384	990,306
Cards: Credit; Debit	Rona Inc	4,037	0.0	4,037	0	0	0	0	0	0
Cards: Credit; Debit	Sears Canada Inc	77,305	0.1	77,305	0	0	0	0	0	0
Cards: Credit; Debit	Solstice Publishing Inc	4,320	0.0	0	4,320	0	0	0	0	0
Cards: Credit; Debit	TD Bank Financial Group	4,020,993	5.1	1,988,483	1,018,804	287,718	276,230	449,758	449,758	0
Cards: Credit; Debit	Valero Energy Corporation	33,396	0.0	0	0	0	33,396	0	0	0
Cards: Credit; Debit	Visa International	20,448,857	26.1	1,461,989	1,286,796	135,213	354,561	17,210,298	12,548,090	4,662,208
Cards: Credit; Debit	Weston Limited, George	3,334	0.0	3,334	0	0	0	0	0	0
Total*		78,351,423	100.0	20,763,109	8,883,456	2,669,816	3,712,102	42,322,940	29,541,360	12,781,580

Source: Nielsen Media Research Canada.

Exhibit 10   Competitive Credit Cards–Five Major Banks

Credit Cards*	Interest Rate	Annual Fee	Insurance Programs	Reward Programs	Guaranteed Hotel Reservations	Emergency Card Replacement	Discounts
BMO Bank of Montreal							
Mosaik MasterCard (customizable)							
12 different combinations possible	Variable	Yes	√	√			
CIBC							
Visa Cards							
Aventura Gold	19.5%	120	√	√	√	√	
Aerogold	19.5%	120	√	√	√	√	
Aero Classic	19.5%	29		√			
Classic	18.5%	Free	√		√		√
Select	10.5%	29	√		√	√	
Dividend	19.5%	Free	√		√	√	√
Dividend Platinum	19.5%	79	√		√	√	√
Gold	18.5%	99	√	√	√	√	
Shoppers Optimum	19.5%	Free	√	√	√	√	
Classic for Students	18.5%	Free	√		√	√	
US Dollar	18.5%	35	√			√	√
Royal Bank							
RBC Rewards Cards							
Visa Platinum Avion	19.5%	120	√	√	√	√	√
Visa Platinum Preferred	18.5%	110	√	√	√	√	√
Visa Gold Preferred	18.5%	110	√	√	√	√	√
Visa Classic II	18.5%	35	√	√	√	√	√
Visa Classic II Student	18.5%	35	√	√	√	√	√
RBC Rewards Visa Classic	18.5%	Free	√	√	√	√	√
US Dollar Visa Gold (US$)	18.5%	65	√	√	√	√	√
RBC Mike Weir Visa Card	19.5%	35	√	√	√	√	√
Partner Rewards Cards							
Aadvantage Visa Gold	20.5%	70	√	√	√	√	√
British Airways Visa Platinum	20.5%	75	√	√	√	√	√
Cathay Pacific Visa Platinum	20.5%	75	√	√	√	√	√
Esso Visa	18.5%	Free	√	√	√	√	√
Starbucks Duetto Visa Card	19.5%	Free	√	√	√	√	√
Everyday Convenience Cards							
Visa Platinum	18.5%	Free	√		√	√	√
Visa Gold	18.5%	Free	√		√	√	√
Visa Classic Low Rate	11.5%	20	√		√	√	√
Visa Classic	18.5%	Free	√		√	√	√
Visa Classic Student	18.5%	Free	√		√	√	√
Scotiabank							
Visa Cards							
ScotiaGold Preferred Visa	17.9%	95	√	√	√	√	√
No-Fee ScotiaGold Visa	18.5%	Free	√		√	√	√
Scotia Moneyback Visa	17.9%	8 or Free		√	√	√	√
ScotiaLine Visa	Variable	Free	√		√	√	√
Scotia Value Visa	10.4%–12.9%	29			√	√	√
TD Canada Trust							
Reward Cards							
TD Gold Travel Visa	19.5%	120	√	√	√	√	√
TD Gold Elite Visa	19.5%	99	√	√	√	√	√
The GM Card	19.5%	Free	√	√	√	√	
Low Rate Cards							
TD Emerald Visa**	7.15%–12.15%	25	√		√	√	√
Other Cards							
TD Green Visa Card	19.8%	Free	√		√	√	√
TD Gold Select Visa	19.8%	Free	√		√	√	√
TD U.S. Dollar Advantage Visa (US$)	18.5%	25	√		√	√	√
Small Business Credit Cards							
TD Business Visa Card	19.8%	50	√		√	√	√
TD Venture Line of Credit Visa	9.3%	Free	√		√	√	√

**Based on TD Prime of 5.25%

Source: This list was created from information gathered from the various bank websites on 20th Feb 2006. Some features may differ from card to card, and between banks. In addition, more features may be available than are depicted in this list.

Exhibit 11   Canadian Test Scores for Capital One Ads

The Link™ Copy Test was designed to provide a complete understanding of how an ad is likely to perform in-market. It provides both evaluative and diagnostic measures and uses a standard questionnaire targeted at a custom sample. Respondents are screened against appropriate criteria; exposed to a reel of four ads with the Test Ad in the second position; re-exposed to the first ad and asked warm-up questions; re-exposed to the Test Ad and asked a full set of questions; and then re-exposed to the Test Ad again for Interest Trace. Link quantifies branded impact through the Awareness Index (AI). AI is the awareness generated per 100 GRPs (gross rating points). The AI indicates how efficient the ad is at generating awareness. The components of the AI are as follows:

- Branding: Is the brand integral to the storyline? Does the brand play the 'hero'? Is the brand character a fit with the brand? Are there brand cues such as colors, icons, memories, music/jingles, slogans, executional branding (e.g., Gap), package shots?
- Enjoyment: Do the aspects of the creative lead to the ad's enjoyment? Some include: music, talent, animals, kids, scenery/visuals, storyline, humor, surprise
- Active Involvement: Determine the ad's ability to engage the viewer; its "stopping power"; its style or message of ad; the level of emotional involvement. The ad can also be negatively involving. For many brands, this is likely not desirable.

Millward Brown relied on its large database of ads tested: 11,000 tests had been conducted worldwide and, of those, over 600 tests had been in Canada, with two-thirds being English ads.

Source: Millward Brown.

Below are the Canadian tests scores for Capital One's U.S. and U.K. commercials.

Prime + Super Prime Segments (Percent of respondents agreeing)	Bee	Catapault	Cinderella	Crab	Envelope	Poppers	Troll	Visigoths	Canada* Ever Aired Norms
Branded Impact									
Branding (Most important)	44	42	38	40	37	30	45	42	**38**
Enjoyment (2ndary Importance)	42	45	50	44	35	30	45	37	**39**
Involving/Unique/Interesting	56	56	58	55	50	38	55	60	**55**
Irritating/Unpleasant/Disturbing	2	10	12	2	5	2	25	13	**7**
Communication									
Unaided recall	36	38	45	35	35	30	50	40	**37**
Aided recall	57	44	65	68	49	35	70	55	**49**

*Average for all industry ads tested by Millward Brown

Underserved Segment (Percent of respondents agreeing)	Bee	Catapault	Cinderella	Crab	Envelope	Poppers	Troll	Visigoths	Canada* Ever Aired Norms
Branded Impact									
Branding (Most important)	45	42	38	40	37	30	43	38	**38**
Enjoyment (2ndary Importance)	45	50	50	55	39	30	55	45	**39**
Involving/Unique/Interesting	57	56	58	55	57	35	55	60	**55**
Irritating/Unpleasant/Disturbing	2	10	15	2	5	2	20	13	**7**
Communication									
Unaided recall	34	34	40	32	37	25	55	50	**37**
Aided recall	55	47	70	48	49	32	75	69	**49**

Source: Casewriter.

Note: Results have been disguised, including Canada Ever Aired Norms.

Generally, different advertisement executions were needed to achieve either target. For example, focusing on an introductory interest rate could be enticing to new customers but not to existing ones. However, there were some advertisements—such as those focusing on fraud protection—that could be used for either segment. But would focusing on fraud protection be too general? Also, could any of the U.K. and U.S. advertisements be relevant to a Canadian audience? Capital One was a relatively small player in Canada, as could be seen by Canada's contribution to the firm's overall loan portfolio (see **Exhibit 8**).

With regard to executing the strategy, John McNain, head of Brand and New Ventures at Capital One, wondered:

How do we build a sustainable brand in Canada yet recognize our current limitations such as resources, infrastructure and product offerings? Also, how do we balance the growth of general awareness versus quickly demonstrating the returns from a more direct advertising campaign? We have to consider three dimensions. First, geography: Should we target just Toronto or the entire country? Second, how do we target our customer segments—Do we offer something general or consider a rewards or price play? Third, to what extent should our advertisements target new accounts or existing customers?

CONCLUSION

Braganza knew that a presentation to Capital's One's senior management team would be more convincing if he could back up his recommendations with numbers and logic. While other firms could choose to invest in brand development over a longer time frame, Capital One's senior management team would want to see how the company's investment would pay out in the short to medium term. Braganza knew that advertising in the United States and United Kingdom would continue—clear evidence that their campaigns were paying out. But Braganza didn't want to focus solely on payout because it could compromise Capital One's brand-building efforts. His challenge was to balance the needs of driving new customer signups with the longer term goals of influencing customer behavior, increasing satisfaction rates and reducing attrition.

Braganza outlined the decisions he faced:

- On which customer segments should Capital One focus?
- What value proposition should Capital One be signaling to these segments?
- What advertisements should be used to deliver these messages, and what customization efforts were needed?

Braganza took a look at the competitive media spend for Canadian credit cards, as compiled by Nielsen, a media research firm (see **Exhibit 9**). Next, he looked at a list of competitive cards and their features, as can be seen in **Exhibit 10**. He also reviewed results from Capital One's U.K. and U.S. advertising copy tests in Canada for both the prime and sub prime segments (see **Exhibit 11**).

This was the first time that Capital One would be investing in mass media advertising. Braganza wanted to recommend the best set of options to his senior management team.

Study Question

1. *Given the objectives of the mass media advertising campaign, how can each of the three challenges faced by Clinton Braganza be addressed?*

Case 17 GoodLife Fitness Clubs

GORDON H.G. MCDOUGALL

A manager is faced with the challenge of preparing a plan to increase member retention rates for a fitness club. Her strategy will serve as a model for more than 40 branches of the club in Ontario and Quebec.

"These retention rates are poor. I need to do a better job of keeping members," thought Krista Swain, manager of the GoodLife Fitness Club in Kitchener, Ontario, as she reviewed her retention rates for the 1999–2000 fiscal year.

As she was analyzing the report, Jane Riddell, chief operating officer, entered her office. Krista looked up and said, "Hi Jane. I've just been looking over the retention rates for the clubs. I'm not happy with my numbers."

"Neither is the head office," Jane replied, "and that's why I'm here today. You run one of our best clubs, and yet your retention rates are around 60 percent, the average for the 40 GoodLife Clubs. We lose 40 percent of our members each year. By improving your club's retention rates from 60 percent to 65 percent, based on last year's figures, gross revenues would increase by over $35,000. You are one of our top performers, and you should be leading the way."

"I agree," said Krista. "We have to figure out how to keep the members enthused and show that the club offers them value." "That's what I wanted to hear," replied Jane. "As a first step, let's both think about this and meet again next week with some ideas. Then I'd like you to prepare a retention plan that will be the model for all the clubs."

THE FITNESS MARKET

In a national study, the Canadian Fitness and Research Institute found that most Canadians believed that physical activity was beneficial in preventing heart disease or other chronic conditions, in reducing stress, and in maintaining the ability to perform everyday tasks with aging. However, physical inactivity remained pervasive in Canada, with 63 percent of adults age 18 and older still considered insufficiently active for optimal health benefits in 1998.[1]

The study also revealed that for a variety of reasons most Canadians tended to "talk" positively about the importance of physical activity but didn't "walk the talk." The most popular physical activities were walking (86 percent of Canadians had participated at least once in this activity within the past 12 months), gardening (75 percent), swimming (57 percent), bicycling (55 percent), and home exercise (50 percent). Exercise class/aerobics was ranked thirteenth (21 percent) with significantly more women (33 percent) than men (9 percent) participating.

Although the overall physical activity of Canadians was relatively low, the fitness market was growing at approximately 6 percent a year. The growth was due to demographic changes (baby boomers were increasingly interested in maintaining a good level of physical fitness), marketing (increasing numbers of health/fitness clubs extolling the benefits of fitness through their programs), and individuals selecting fitness clubs over other physical activities as their choice for exercise.

Industry estimates were that about 10 percent of the Canadian population belonged to a health club. However, there was considerable "churning" (the percentage of members lost in a month or year); many Canadians had good intentions and joined a club, only to leave at the end of their membership for a variety of reasons. Industry research revealed the following major reasons for leaving; decline in interest, took too much time, too hard and didn't like the club. It was estimated that on an annual basis the average health/fitness club in Canada lost between 36 percent to 45 percent of its members.

Another reason for the high average churn rates was that many clubs, referred to as "factories," did not take a professional approach in managing their operations. Typically, a sports personality (e.g., a retired hockey player) would own these "factories" and offer low initial memberships to get people into the club. These clubs had few trained instructors, frequent equipment breakdowns, and poor facilities maintenance. These clubs often failed within a year or two, leaving customers with a valid membership and no facility.

GOODLIFE

The Philosophy and Goals

In March 1979, David Patchell-Evans established GoodLife as a sole proprietorship. "Patch," as he was called, saw an opportunity. Canadian fitness clubs were largely cash and sales oriented with little emphasis on scientific fitness or member retention. By May 2000, Patch had built this privately owned fitness company to over 40 clubs (10 were franchises, the rest were company owned) in Ontario and Quebec. GoodLife had the largest group of fitness clubs in Canada with over 70,000 members. (**Appendix 1** provides more details on the philosophy and growth of the GoodLife Clubs.)

From the beginning, the company's goal was to provide the best in equipment, facilities, and service with a well-trained staff. The goal was based on high-quality service with education and training, superior cleanliness, and programs that made the individual a member for life based on their "needs and goals." The GoodLife motto, "Measurable Constant Improvement," underlaid its plan to grow to 100 clubs by 2004.

Head Office

The head office was located at the Galleria Mall Fitness Club in London, Ontario. Head office personnel numbered approximately 40, led by "Patch," Jane Riddell, chief operating officer, and Maureen Hagen, national director of fitness. Head office's main role was to provide leadership and support for the franchisees and company-owned clubs. Among the group's major activities were determining the advertising strategy, designing new fitness programs, ensuring that all clubs maintained quality standards, providing training programs for staff, and keeping all club managers abreast of the latest trends and issues in the fitness industry.

One of Jane Riddell's responsibilities was the design and management of GoodLife University, where each month 50 to 60 new associates went through a 1-week program. The training included an orientation to GoodLife (basic knowledge of GoodLife and its philosophy), personal training (skills required to assist members as a personal trainer), and computer program training. When club managers hired the associates, they typically spent their first few weeks "learning the ropes" at the club and then attended the university program. Jane led some of the training sessions and evaluated the participants, some of whom failed and left GoodLife.

Jane was generally pleased with the caliber of the participants. She rated about 70 percent of them as good to great and 30 percent as poor. In the past, the GoodLife clubs had focused on hiring physical education and kinesiology graduates. However, as the economy improved in the late 1990s, these graduates chose other job opportunities, requiring GoodLife to broaden its hiring criteria. Now GoodLife hired individuals with the "right" attitude (i.e., customer focused). However, the attitude of some new employees was that this was not a "real" job or a career. Rather it was a fun place to be for awhile, a "cool," easy job until they got a "real" job. Jane felt that this was part of the issue of employee retention at GoodLife. In the past 2 years, employee turnover had increased, and last year 600 employees (out of a total of 1,400) had left GoodLife. Jane estimated that most of the employee retention problem was GoodLife's "fault"—they either hired the wrong people, or didn't do enough to keep them.

Advertising spending, at 6 percent of revenue, used a "call to action" versus a "branding" approach. The call to action used variations on "$99 for 99 days," "one month free," "no initiation fee," or "save now."

The company allocated advertising expenditures by season (winter, 40 percent; summer, 25 percent; and October to December, 35 percent), which reflected the general interest level of people in joining a fitness club. Each month headquarters evaluated each club on sales targets—the new members obtained through internal marketing (e.g., referrals or *Yellow Pages*), external marketing (e.g., newspaper, flyers, radio, or television), and walk-ins (e.g., potential member walks into the club and asks about memberships). This information, along with conference calls with the regions, set the regional advertising allocation.

GoodLife's commitment to club members, staff, and community resulted in numerous awards and achievements. GoodLife was the first to bring many innovations to the fitness industry, including the Fit Fix training concept and the PUNCH program. GoodLife raised over $500,000 annually for various charities and supported a wide range of community activities.

The GoodLife Staff

GoodLife's size (over 1,400 associates) and rapid growth provided many opportunities for advancement. The career path of GoodLife could take an associate to any number of areas: group exercise classes, personal training, sales, administration, management, accounting, and even to owning one of the clubs.

Compensation consisted of a base salary plus club sales commissions and bonuses. The club sales commissions were based on the number of memberships sold per week against a target. Depending on the type of membership sold and/or specialty programs sold, the associate could receive a commission on sales ranging from 5 percent to 15 percent. Bonuses were based on weekly targets set for the individual club. Depending on the hours and shifts worked by the staff, if the goals were met, the staff member could earn a bonus of $15 to $25 per week. As well, there was an employee referral bonus: Any current staff member who referred an individual for employment with GoodLife could receive a bonus of $100, or $200 for individuals hired on a part-time or full-time basis. Finally, there were incentive programs for good ideas. The rewards, called "Patch Bucks," could be redeemed for fitness conferences.

GoodLife offered company awards on a monthly and yearly basis. On a monthly basis, awards were given to (1) group exercise coordinator (gift and plaque), (2) manager of the month ($200 and plaque), (3) associate ($100 and plaque), (4) sales manager ($200 and plaque), (5) sales associate ($100 and plaque), (6) personal training associate ($100 and plaque), and (7) customer service representative ($100 plus plaque). On a yearly basis, awards were given to (1) manager (free fitness conference, valued at $2,500), (2) group exercise instructor, and (3) group exercise coordinator.

GOODLIFE KITCHENER

The New Location

In September 1998, the GoodLife Kitchener Club reopened on the second floor of an indoor mall in downtown Kitchener, Ontario. Prior to that, it was located two blocks away in a relatively small (12,000 square feet) and poorly designed facility. The new facility was larger (30,000 square feet), had an open concept design, and an extensive range of equipment and programs. Over the next 18 months, membership increased dramatically under Krista Swain's guidance. As of May 2000, the club had 3,500 members, an increase of 2,300 over the original 1,200 members who moved from the old club.

Krista, a 1995 graduate in kinesiology and physical education from Wilfrid Laurier University in Waterloo, Ontario, worked for GoodLife as a fitness instructor while she was attending the university. After graduation, she joined the GoodLife Waterloo Club as a service trainer. In addition, she handled corporate sales for the GoodLife Women Only Club in Kitchener. Within 10 months, she was appointed manager of the GoodLife Kitchener Club and was actively involved in the transition from the old to the new location. When asked how she had rapidly advanced to club manager, she said:

I have a passion for fitness and I'm committed to the company. I'm convinced that the GoodLife values, mission, and philosophy are right; I truly feel that we are helping people at GoodLife. I like working with people. My role is

to be a coach and mentor, and I lead by example. I think the staff understand my goals and respect me because I respect them. Sometimes I can't believe what the staff are willing to do to help the club and the members. But I'll also say, if you are not a top performer, you won't fit in at GoodLife.

In early 2000, the Kitchener club was signing up over 230 new members per month (**Exhibit 1**). At the same time, the club was losing about 100 members per month for a net gain of about 130 members. On an annual basis, the club was losing 40 percent of its members. Overall, the rapid growth in membership had a very positive impact on revenues, which increased by over 60 percent between June 1999 and March 2000 (**Exhibit 2**).

The Associates

The Kitchener club's 40 associates (10 full-time, 30 part-time) worked in four groups: sales, customer service, personal training, and service.

- The four sales associates (all full-time) were responsible for getting new members.
- Customer service employees, who were primarily part-time, worked the front desk.
- Personal trainers worked with individual club members on fitness programs.
- Service employees introduced new members to the club and its philosophy through a series of programs on fitness and equipment use.

Exhibit 1 GoodLife Kitchener Club–Members by Month

Month	Members Lost During Month	Members Gained During Month	Net Members Gained During Month	Members (at end of month)	Retention Rate per Year (%)	Loss Rate per Month (%)
March '99	–	–	–	1900	–	–
April '99	58[a]	163	105	2005	63.5[b]	3.0
May '99	61	158	97	2102	64.0	3.0
June '99	73	156	83	2185	59.4	3.4
July '99	75	155	80	2263	60.9	3.3
August '99	68	150	82	2341	65.2	2.9
September '99	70	168	98	2423	64.8	2.9
October '99	108	196	88	2521	48.5	4.3
November '99	91	220	129	2609	57.9	3.5
December '99	90	223	133	2738	60.1	3.3
January '00	103	244	141	2871	56.4	3.6
February '00	99	238	139	3012	60.1	3.3
March '00	113	234	121	3151	56.4	3.6
Annual Average	59.8[c]	3.4				

[a]At the beginning of April, the club had 1,900 members. The monthly loss rate for April is 3.0% (based on a yearly retention rate for April of 63.5%, which is a yearly loss rate of 36.5%). The club lost 1,900 x.03 = 58 members in April.

[b]63.5% of the members as of April '98 were still members as of April '99; 36.5% were no longer members.

[c]The average retention rate for the year shown is 59.8%; average loss per month is 3.4% (1–.598 =.402/12).

Source: GoodLife Fitness Clubs.

Exhibit 2   GoodLife Kitchener Club—Selected Revenues and Expenses

	June 30 '99 Month	June 30 '99 YTD (12 months)	March 31 '00 Month	March 31, '00 YTD (9 months)
Revenues	(%)	(%)	(%)	(%)
Membership	88.9	88.2	86.9	83.3
Services[a]	9.3	10.2	11.9	15.5
Other	1.8	1.6	1.2	1.2
Total Revenue	100.0	100.0	100.0	100.0
Expenses				
Sales Wages and Commissions[b]	10.5	12.1	8.3	8.9
Service Wages and Commissions[c]	9.0	7.1	5.3	12.3
Service and Other[d]	19.4	28.6	20.4	17.1
Total Direct Expenses	38.9	47.8	34.0	38.3
Manager Controlled[e]	9.2	15.6	4.8	10.4
Administrative[f]	31.8	31.1	26.3	32.6
Total Expenses[g]	79.9	94.5	65.1	81.3
Members	2,200		3,200	
Total Revenue ($)	120,000	1,004,000	195,000	1,177,000

[a]Includes personal training, specialty programs, tanning, and pro shop
[b]Related to new membership sales
[c]Includes personal training and member services
[d]Includes service staff wages and expenses
[e]Includes utilities, supplies and services
[f]Includes advertising, administrative management, rent, realty taxes, equipment leasing
[g]Not included are depreciation, amortization, interest, and taxes

Source: GoodLife Fitness Clubs.

All employees were involved in selling. Although the sales associates were dedicated to selling new memberships, the personal trainers spent time encouraging members to sign up for personal training. The customer service employees would sell tanning programs and other services to members. Typically, each group or individual had sales targets and earned bonuses and commissions based on meeting those targets.

Most of the employees earned a base salary of $8 per hour plus bonuses if they achieved the weekly targets. As an example, a sales associate might have a target of eight new members per week. If the target was achieved or exceeded, the associate could earn $1,250 or more every 2 weeks. Customer service staff could earn up to $25 per week if they met targets that included phoning members to remind them of upcoming events, encouraging them to use the club, and selling various club products and services such as tanning. Personal trainers could make up to $27 per hour for personal training in addition to their base pay of $8 per hour. The more members the trainer signed up, the more hours he/she spent in personal training.

Through these incentive programs GoodLife encouraged its staff, particularly the sales associates, to be entrepreneur-

ial. As Krista often said, "The staff have to make things happen; they can't wait for them to happen. Both GoodLife and the staff do better when they make things happen."

As noted, GoodLife had formal training programs for new employees. In addition, Krista spent time with the new employees teaching them the technical side of the job and establishing the norms and culture of the club. By emphasizing what was important to her, Krista hoped they would understand the importance of excellent customer service. "If I can show the new employees what's important to me, and get them to trust me, they come on board and are part of the team. For example, we hold weekly staff meetings where we discuss a number of issues, including how to improve the club. People don't miss the meetings. Every once in a while, a new associate decides not to come to the meetings. The team lets him or her know that's not acceptable. Those people either become part of the team or decide to leave GoodLife."

Employee turnover at the Kitchener GoodLife Club was slightly better than the average across all the GoodLife clubs. In the past year, Krista had a turnover of about 35 percent, with the rate of full-time slightly lower than for part-time. Part-time turnover was higher, in part, because many of the part-time employees were students who left to go to university or left after completing their degree programs.

Like Jane Riddell, Krista was concerned about employee turnover, but she wasn't sure what actions could improve the situation. She had noticed that some new employees were surprised at the amount of selling involved in their positions. She also felt that some employees were not satisfied with the base salary of $8 per hour.

Typically, when an employee left, Krista needed to hire a new associate relatively quickly. She would place an ad in the local paper, *The Record*; get some applications; conduct interviews; and hire the individual she felt was most suited for the position. With full-time employees, Krista was not always happy with the pool of applicants she interviewed, but there was always the pressure of filling the job, which had to be balanced against the quality of the applicants. With the economy improving and a low local unemployment rate, it was sometimes difficult to attract high-quality applicants.

The Members

Most new members joined the club through referrals. When an individual asked about joining the club, a sales associate would show them the club and discuss the benefits of membership and the GoodLife philosophy. Assuming the individual decided to join, the sales associate would ask if he or she had any friends who might be interested in joining the club and, if so, they would receive a free membership for 1 week. Typically, the associate tried to give five referrals. The associate would then contact these people, offer the free 1-week membership, and set up a meeting with them if they accepted. The cycle was repeated with each new member. On average, the sales associates converted between one or two of the five contacts to new members. Referrals generated between 60 percent and 80 percent of all new members.

The price for a new membership varied depending on the promotion option. The two main options were (1) a $199 initiation fee, the first 6 months free, and $40 per 4 weeks after that or (2) the initiation fee was waived and the member paid $40 per 4 weeks. Payments were on a biweekly basis through an automatic payment plan that the member signed. The new member also paid a total of $54 for the membership card ($15) and a processing fee ($39). A new member could also decide to join for a 3-month period for $180. Members could also decide to pay once a year and not use the automatic payment plan.

When an individual joined the club, an associate from the service group would take the new member through three programs as an introduction to the club and the GoodLife approach to a healthy lifestyle. The three programs were (1) Fit Fix 1—an introduction to strength training, (2) Cardio—basic information about cardiovascular training principles, and (3) Fit Fix 2—adding exercise to your program. Any new member could also have a fitness assessment (including resting heart rate and body fat measurements). After 6 weeks, the new member could also have a second fitness assessment to track his/her progress.

The club offered a wide range of cardio equipment, weights, and personal training programs. Members could participate in over 20 aerobics programs each week, from Steps 'n Abs to Circuit Training to Newbody to PUNCH. On average, 12 members were participating in each program. Typically, members had been going to these programs for years, and few new members joined any program. The club attempted to address this issue with new members by having a "new members only" aerobic class. On average, the club would get 50 new members to sign up for the program, 15 would show up for the first class, and it would be down to six people when the class ended in 12 weeks.

This issue reflected a broader problem common to most of the GoodLife Clubs, often referred to as the "20-20-60 phenomenon." Twenty percent of the club members were hardcore fitness and health people. These members came three or more times a week, were serious about their training, and would tolerate a lot (such as uneven service) as long as it didn't interfere with their training. The second 20 percent were the new members. They were enthusiastic, wanted to get fit, and over time they either became committed or not. The largest group, the remaining 60 percent, were those members who came on an irregular basis. The club staff didn't know their names; these members often were not sure how the equipment worked or what they should be doing; and they often wouldn't ask for help. Even when they stopped coming, this group kept their membership for a period until they decided to cancel. When one came to cancel, an associate tried to get her or him to stay, usually with little success.

Krista and other associates at GoodLife believed that getting members to feel that they were part of the GoodLife Club was important in retaining them. Krista believed that many of the 60 percent probably never felt they were part of the club because they didn't know many or any of the other members or the staff. Krista remembered that although many of the 1,200 members from the old club liked the new facility, they felt that the club was more impersonal. In particular, as the membership grew, the "original" members felt less at home. Krista estimated that, within a year, about 50 percent of these members had left the club.

The advertising for GoodLife consisted of an ad in the *Yellow Pages* and ads in a local free weekly newspaper, *The Pennysaver*. Local businesses were targeted with brochures offering specials. Krista felt that most of the new members came from the referral program and *Pennysaver* ads (**Exhibit 2**). As she said, "*The Pennysaver* ads get the phones ringing."

Although Krista believed that overall the members were satisfied with the club, she felt there was always room for improvement. For example, members sent her about 14 written complaints or concerns every week through the suggestion box. Each week, the front office staff received about a dozen verbal complaints. Most complaints or concerns dealt with equipment problems (e.g., equipment not working properly) and a few dealt with staff (e.g., a particular staff member was not friendly). Krista dealt with the complaints as they arose.

COMPETITION

In the Kitchener/Waterloo (K/W) area (Kitchener and Waterloo are twin cities), there were about 15 fitness/exercise clubs serving a population base of 450,000 people. The Kitchener GoodLife Club had four major competitors:

- The two YMCAs in K/W offered aerobic programs and had workout areas. The "Ys" had a good reputation as being friendly, family-oriented clubs. The annual membership fee ranged from $400 to $650 depending on the type of membership and the services required.

- The International Family Fitness Centre was also located in downtown Kitchener within three blocks of the GoodLife Club. It offered equivalent facilities to the GoodLife Club, was of a similar size, and had over 40 programs a week. Its membership rates were very similar to those of GoodLife.

- Popeye's Gym previously had a reputation as a male-oriented facility where bodybuilders worked out. However, the image was slowly changing to a men's and women's fitness club that offered aerobic programs and a variety of weight and training machines. It was located approximately 3 kilometres from downtown Kitchener and was open 24 hours a day. The membership fees were approximately $350 per year.

CUSTOMER RETENTION

As Krista prepared for the meeting with Jane, she knew that improved customer retention rates were possible but was uncertain as to what actions would be most effective. She identified three major areas that she could address: employee turnover, a new bonus system, and swipe card technology.

Employee turnover, at over 40 percent, created a lack of stability at the club. Every time a new employee started, he or she did not know any members. Over time, the new employee would hear the members' names (often those who visited frequently). If the employee left, so did the knowledge. Krista had always felt that members would have a greater sense of "belonging" to the club if the front desk staff could greet them by name. Although many of the front desk staff knew some of the members by name (most of these members were the hard-core regulars who came frequently), most of the front desk staff were part-time associates or had recently joined GoodLife; therefore, they knew relatively few members by name. Further, because most of the "60 percent" group came infrequently, few staff knew their names.

Krista had two ideas for reducing employee turnover, both based on increasing wages. Increasing the hourly base rate from $8 to $9 for most employees (excluding managers and sales associates) would add about $4,000 per month to wage costs. The problem was that, although she knew that employee turnover would decline, she did not know by how much, nor did she know the effect on retention rates. A second opinion was to focus only on the front desk employees who greeted members. Increasing their rate to $9 would increase monthly costs by about $1,000. She preferred this option because the front desk associates greeted all members as they entered and swiped their card. With the increase in their wages, Krista would ensure that the front desk staff knew that an important part of their job was to greet members by name.

Next, Krista considered introducing a bonus plan for increasing customer retention. Virtually all the targets and bonuses at GoodLife focused on increasing sales, reflecting, in part, Patch's aggressive growth targets. Although she did not have a specific plan in mind, Krista felt that an allocation of at least $1,000 to bonuses for increased retention was feasible. Her initial idea was that for every percent increase in retention rates per month (e.g., from 60 percent to 61 percent), staff would receive $200 in bonuses. Krista was uncertain how the target should be set—on an individual or group basis. The front desk staff had the most contact with members, but potentially all the employees could be involved. What was important to Krista was that the associates have a goal and a bonus attached to customer retention. She knew that this plan would get the associates to focus more of their efforts on customer retention.

Krista felt that better use of the swipe card information could improve retention. Members swiped their membership card when they visited the club. A valid card allowed a member to go through a turnstile; a nonvalid card (because it had expired) did not release the turnstile. Krista knew that other information (e.g., number of member visits) was available, but no one at the club or head office had developed a software program to track member visits. Krista contacted two software companies, one of which offered a membership management program that would provide interface with swipe scanners and provide reports on members' frequency of visits, along with a host of other member information. The cost ranged from $3,500 for a license for five sites up to $8,500 for unlimited site use.

One of the targets for the front desk associates was to make "motivation" calls to members each week. Associates would call a specific number of members to reach their target. The associates would begin anywhere on the member list (a binder at the front desk) and begin calling members to encourage them to use the facilities or inform them of special events. After the call, the associate would record the date called and his or her name next to the member's name. Ideally, all members were called once every 6 weeks, but this didn't always happen.

With the new software system, reports could identify members who had not visited the club for a particular period. Staff could then contact members who had not visited for a specific time period, such as 3 weeks or 4 weeks. Krista felt that this would substantially improve the existing approach and would improve member retention rates.

Krista knew that there were other available approaches or tactics to improve retention rates. In particular, any activities that build a greater sense of "community" would increase interaction between members and a sense of "belonging." But it was difficult to find the time to figure it out. Managing a club with 3,500 members kept her very busy making sure everything was running smoothly, and she spent most of her time "doing" not "planning."

A week later, Jane met Krista in her office. Jane started the conversation. "Let me review the situation. As I mentioned last week, if we could improve your club's retention rates from 60 percent to 65 percent, based on last year's numbers, gross revenues would increase by more than $35,000. In this business, most of the costs tend to be fixed, probably about 60 percent of revenues, so most of the revenue would be profits. If we could do that for all the clubs, it would be great for business, and I think we would have more satisfied members. Just to put this in perspective, on average, we have about 2,000 members per club."

Jane continued, "In the past year, the story has been about the same for most of our clubs. For every 100 new members signed up each month, we have about 40 people who don't renew or cancel their membership. We spend a lot on marketing to get them in the door. Then we spend time with them setting up an exercise or training program. They are enthusiastic to begin with; then they stop coming to classes or exercise. They cancel or don't renew when their membership comes up. When they cancel, we ask them why they are leaving. The most common reasons are that they don't have enough time or they can't fit it into their schedule. I think that about 30 percent of the time, they have a good reason for leaving, such as they are moving out of town. I think that 70 percent of the time, we could have done something to keep them with the club.

"From the head office point of view, we have had a number of debates about the amount of advertising we do, which is about 6 percent of revenues. That's a lot of money and sometimes we think that we should be spending more of that in staff training. Another question is—what type of training would be most effective?

"Let me mention one other issue we are concerned about," Jane continued. "We don't use the swipe card to collect data. We need to do more with that."

"That was one of my thoughts," Krista replied. She then told Jane about the software program's capabilities and costs.

"Very interesting," replied Jane. "That's certainly something to consider." Krista then presented her other ideas to Jane. As she finished, Krista said, "I think my cost estimates wouldn't be too far out of line for our average club."

Then Krista added, "Sometimes I think that maybe we should focus more on service than sales. As an example, my front desk staff have sales targets and other assignments as well as greeting members. Also, there are few opportunities for the staff to walk around and just talk to our members and see how they are doing. That's why I suggested a bonus plan based on increasing retention rates. We have very aggressive growth targets for each club and plan to add a lot more clubs. As an organization, we are really getting stretched. Most of our time is spent on growth, not service."

"Yes, but the strategy has worked well so far," Jane replied. "I'm not sure if we could justify adding more staff to focus on service; we would need to see a payback. But it's another interesting idea."

Krista and Jane continued the discussion and then decided that Krista would prepare a customer retention plan for the Kitchener GoodLife Club with the goal of increasing retention rates by 5 percentage points or more within 6 months. "I want to at least get the average retention up to 65 percent," Jane said. "As I mentioned last week, we'll use this plan as a model for all the clubs."

As Jane left, she said, "Krista, I have every confidence in you. I'm going to send an assistant manager from the other Kitchener club down here to help you run the club while you work on the plan. I look forward to positive results."

After Jane left, Krista sat down and began thinking about the approaches she could take to increase retention rates. She had always liked a challenge, and she knew that she would do her best to meet this one.

APPENDIX 1: MUSCLE MANIA

David Patchell-Evans may not be a natural athlete, but he's a confirmed fitness fanatic. He works and dreams physical fitness. Even his vacations are spent pursuing extreme sports such as mountain climbing or skiing. But that wasn't always the case. In his first year at university, a motorcycle accident paralyzed the right side of his body. Following extensive rehabilitation, Patchell-Evans was determined to return to full physical fitness. He took up rowing and eventually became a five-time Canadian rowing champion and a member of the 1980 Canadian Olympic team.

Those experiences taught Patchell-Evans the role health and fitness play in creating a satisfying life and fostered a life-long commitment to sell the idea to others. In 1979 he bought a workout club in London, Ontario, and began implementing his vision: to provide customers with an affordable club offering state-of-the-art equipment and, more importantly, knowledgeable staff eager to teach them how to get the most from it. "The opportunity in the marketplace," he says, "was to provide service."

In an industry notorious for dubious claims and fly-by-night operators, GoodLife Fitness Clubs has built its business on highly trained staff, innovative programming, and reinvesting in its facilities. In 20 years, it has become Canada's largest health club chain, with 42 clubs, 100,000 members, and 1998 sales of $40 million. In an industry that's adding new clubs and members at 9% a year, GoodLife is growing at almost three times that rate. By 2004 Patchell-Evans goal is to have 100 facilities.

To reach the goal Patchell-Evans will rely on the same philosophies on which the chain was founded: providing health, fitness, and self-esteem so that people feel better about themselves. It's part of the strategy to raise the bar of service excellence and bring a new professionalism to an industry where clubs were traditionally run by sports jocks with little business training. The GoodLife philosophy of ensuring consistently high standards in every club goes a long way to building brand loyalty among the members. "When people work out, they want to know that the shower will be clean, the equipment is going to work, and the staff know what they are talking about."

That philosophy has served GoodLife well as the chain expanded, opening new clubs and buying others that were doing poorly in strong locations. "One of the ways we grew in the early days was to take over clubs that really nobody else wanted to touch," says Jane Riddell, GoodLife's vice president and director of franchising. "A classic example is our club at the corner of Queen and Yonge Street in downtown Toronto. When we took over the club, the membership was languishing around 100, and the facility was losing $60,000 a month. The club needed refurbishment and new equipment, but it had huge potential, with its high-profile location in a dense work population." GoodLife invested $400,000 and the facility is one of the firm's most financially successful clubs with a membership of 3,000.

One fitness expert says, "GoodLife developed a niche underneath the well-established clubs. Patchell-Evans runs a professional organization and he has a well-honed management style that includes business and financial acumen. The old-style clubs were run by squash players or golfers." One example was the innovative client billing system. While most fitness clubs demanded on up-front annual fee. Patchell-Evans debited monthly membership fees ranging from $30 to $50. Members like the system because it eliminates the needs for large up-front payments, and it stabilizes cash flow for GoodLife, which is attractive to lenders and investors.

The key to any fitness club's success is attracting and keeping members. At GoodLife it starts with the staff. Some 75% of its 1,200 employees hold kinesiology or physical education degrees. In addition to competitive salaries, staff benefits from ongoing training—GoodLife's annual education and

training budget exceeds $2.4 million—and recognition for individual achievement, such as a weekly top performer's list. "Good staff retention leads to good membership retention," says Jane Riddell. "Members don't have a relationship with a treadmill or a whirlpool. They have a relationship with the staff." That commitment to human resources gives GoodLife an edge, says the industry expert. "GoodLife has good equipment, but they also have a very proactive staff with an attitude that says they want to help you out. The club's employee training program is probably more extensive than any other in the industry. It's difficult for an independent operator to compete with this."

In 1998 GoodLife was recognized for its mandate to provide leading edge programs. The U.S.-based International Dance Exercise Association named the club's fitness director, Maureen Hagen, program director of the year for her creative programming and leadership abilities. Hagan's innovations include Newbody, a low-impact, cardiovascular conditioning class designed for both fit and "underactive" participants.

Programming and services are also tailored to fit the demographics of each club. Some 70% of members are women, reflecting the club's focus on aerobics programs, to which women tend to gravitate. To ensure that women enjoy a high comfort level, GoodLife designated more than a dozen clubs for women only, where they are provided with such services as daycare, tanning facilities, and individual change rooms. GoodLife was one of the first clubs to develop the trend to women-only sections and clubs. As an example, GoodLife recently spent $500,000 upgrading the facility and equipment of a women's club in Cambridge, Ontario.

This formula to exceed customers' expectations is the foundation for GoodLife's aggressive growth plans for the future. Two trends will help the growth: industry consolidation, where GoodLife has achieved a critical mass, and an expanding market, where the number of people who will work out in clubs will increase substantially because the baby boomers want to stay in shape.

A challenge for Patchell-Evans is finding staff to keep pace with growth. "There was a time," he says, "when we had a bigger pool of people waiting for the next manager's job." To that end he says GoodLife will focus on giving staff the skills and knowledge they need to get to a higher level within the firm. "Staying on the cutting edge of the industry is a challenge, but it's also a passion for me," says Patchell-Evans. "Running a business is like a sport. You're driven to go fast, go hard, and find the ways you can do it better."

Source: Excerpts from Louise Dearden, "Muscle Mania," *Profit*, May, 1999, 46–49.

Endnotes

1. Canadian Fitness and Research Institute, *Canadian Physical Activity Monitor*, 1998.

Study Questions

1. *Why do people join and leave a fitness club? What are the major challenges facing fitness clubs in general?*

2. *What are the major challenges facing GoodLife? Why has GoodLife been successful so far?*

3. *Evaluate the strengths and weaknesses of GoodLife's customer acquisition and retention strategies.*

4. *Calculate the revenues and net profits at GoodLife Kitchener if retention rates were 65% and 70% versus 60% in the past year.*

5. *What is the average long-term value of a member at GoodLife in terms of total revenues at 60%, 70% and 80% retention rates?*

Case 18   Williams Coffee Pub

KENNETH G. HARDY

In March 2004, George and William (Bill) Giannakopoulos looked over their latest financial results with some pride. The brothers had grown up in Stratford, Ontario, where Bill had owned an ice cream business and a bar. His brother George, an engineering graduate, joined Bill to buy a franchised muffin business in Stratford that they eventually turned into their first Williams Coffee Pub (WCP) in 1992. Bill, 46, and George, 49, always knew they would work together. While searching for a good business, they had to choose between developing one big restaurant or creating a franchisable concept. Their research suggested that any high-volume food concept had to offer quick service in a non-rushed atmosphere. Furthermore, the coffee market in Canada had reached $1 billion[1] and was still growing rapidly. They thought about combining coffee with quick casual food and calling their new restaurant concept a bistro, coffee-shop or café. However, they felt those names were all overworked so they settled on "pub," which suggested a public meeting place.

WCP offered "quick casual" dining positioned in the middle of, and drawing business from, coffee shops, specialty coffee shops, special bakery and dessert shops, family casual dining and general quick service restaurants (see **Exhibit 1**). After testing the WCP concept in Stratford, they sold their first franchise. Now, 44 units later, the Giannakopoulos brothers could sit back with some satisfaction. They had created free-standing, full-size units and mid-size units and kiosks. Most offered either sit-down or takeout service. There were units with drive-throughs, and one outlet per city offered catering. The kiosks were located at universities and colleges. Almost all the units had turned a profit for the franchisees within 18 months. The brothers had reluctantly taken back five of the earliest units. In two cases, the franchises had become profitable, and the remaining three were still owned by Williams Coffee Pub.

In December of 2003, the Giannakopoulos brothers had been honored for their business achievements, as Entrepreneurs of the Year by *Food Service and Hospitality* magazine. In February 2004, the Giannakopoulos brothers restructured their finances, raising $1.5 million and converting $650,000 of debt to equity. The proceeds were being used to pay off debt and provide funds for growth. They also added a full-time chief executive officer and created a new board of directors that included two experienced investors and a business professor.

Despite this steady success, the Giannakopoulos brothers foresaw several issues in gearing up for rapid growth. Although they liked the broad positioning of their franchise concept, they wondered if it could be improved. Now that they had 44 units clustered in Southwestern Ontario (see **Exhibit 2**), they could begin to use broadcast advertising and additional promotions to build traffic and sales. However, they had been told by experienced franchisors that the usual progression in marketing communications for a new franchise chain would be to focus first on in-store promotions, then supplement this with billboard advertising, then add radio to the mix and finally, television advertising. To date, WCP had used only in-store promotions and local media but the brothers were still reviewing the marketing communications plan. They also were trying to feel out whether or not they were better off making a priority of opening new in-store and in-mall kiosks rather than the original free-standing, full-service sites. The Giannakopoulos brothers could grow WCP quickly by adding new outlets at a faster rate, or they could focus on driving more sales through existing stores. They could also expand their product line. As they saw it, the greatest obstacles were to find good sites, funds for sites and good operators. They sensed that they had a huge opportunity in front of them. What they needed most was to decide how fast to grow and how aggressively to spend on marketing communications.

THE SERVICE CONCEPT

The brothers' original units were free-standing restaurants with ample parking, located in mid-size Ontario cities. The exterior and interior décor had been professionally designed to yield a warm distinctive look (see **Exhibit 3**). Inside, there was booth seating for about 140 in a 3,900-square-foot store. The service counter typically was fairly close to the main entrance doors so that customers could walk in, take in the pictorial menu boards above the counter and place their order at one of three available cash register stations (see **Exhibit 4**). The counter staff was trained to be helpful, especially with new customers who were sometimes a bit overawed with the available choices among breakfasts, desserts, salads, soups, wraps, ciabattas, baguettes and specialty coffees (see **Exhibit 5**). The brothers had purchased a special rich coffee that was served fresh and hot in a WCP mug in regular specialty forms. The coffee was handed to the customer instantly to take to a table. For food items, customers were given a small plastic numbered tent card that they took to their table. Within four minutes, a server brought the food to the table.

The food menu was featured in the front area above the order counter. There was a broad variety of desserts, drinks, soups, salads, wraps and sandwiches. All food was assembled on-site behind the counter using only a warmer or microwave as needed. The brothers had designed the operations so that food was fresh, healthy, good value and could be served quickly. In 2002, the average purchase was about $3.90, and business was reasonably steady through the major parts of the day. **Table 1** shows the key benchmark performance indicators.

Table 1 WCP Early Performance Indicators, 2002

Number of stores in 2002: 27
Stores under development: 10
Sales mix: food 55 per cent, beverage 45 per cent
Target sales mix: food 45 per cent, beverage 55 per cent
Sales mix: on-premise 55 per cent, drive-through
    24 per cent, kiosk 21 per cent

Average cheques compared to competitor's

Tim Hortons (coffee shops)	$1.88
WCP 1 (small units, mid-level income areas)	$2.20
Second Cup (specialty coffee)	$2.53
Starbucks (specialty coffee)	$2.99
WCP 2 (large units, higher income areas)	$3.90

Source: Williams Coffee Pub brochure for franchisees.

The broad positioning of WCP had prompted several business specialists to advise the brothers to tighten the focus of the restaurants. However, Bill said, "George and I, we really shy away from being really good at just one thing." George quickly added: "It scares the dickens out of us."

Bill went on:

It isn't just one thing. Our customers like different parts of WCP, which combines into a nice feeling. They know the coffee is good, the atmosphere is relaxing, and there is no pressure and no waitress coming to your table trying to rush you out so they can turn it over for the next customer.

THE MARKET

The quick casual market, also known as fast casual, was perceived to offer higher quality food than typical fast-food restaurants.[2] Quick casual restaurants attempted to offer a casual dining experience with the convenience of a quick service concept. By 2004, the average eater check was US$6.50 for restaurants such as Pita Pizzazz, Quiznos Sub, Williams Coffee Pub and various upscale deli sandwich concepts. By contrast, quick service restaurant (QSR) concepts offered a limited, usually specialized menu with a significant portion of takeout and drive-through and no table service. The average check for McDonald's, Wendy's, Burger King, Pizza Pizza and Kentucky Fried Chicken was about US$4.50. Casual dining was a step up from quick casual with a diverse menu, higher food quality and table service. It also had a focus on alcohol and bar service. The average check at Kelsey's, East Side Mario's and Casey's was about US$14. Family dining restaurants attracted more of a mid-range segment of customers with two-thirds of value consumed on premise. The average check for Swiss Chalet, St. Hubert, Denny's and Perkins was about US$9.

The brothers believed that the quick casual segment was growing rapidly because it was taking advantage of its fundamental low-priced, high-value fast-food and the trend toward eating healthier foods. As further validation, they saw Subway scoring real gains with low fat sandwiches, and Panera Bread in the United States had grown to 2,000 locations with average annual sales per restaurant of US$2.3 million. By contrast, Wendy's U.S. restaurants had annual sales of only about US$1.3 million.

Peter Schwartz believed the market for quick casual was booming:

Coffee and fast food segments are losing to quick casual. On the fast-food side, McDonald's is playing catch up because they are not as tuned in to the healthy aspect of quick casual while Wendy's started out ahead because of their fresh reputation. On the coffee side, Coffee Time is getting hit while Tim Hortons is doing well because of the successful introduction of sandwiches and soups to alter their mix away from unhealthy doughnuts.

Another industry expert said that quick casual dining was growing fast because of other reasons:

Baby boomers and their kids, both of whom don't do much cooking, who have grown somewhat tired of fast food, and who want a more healthy, fresher alternative.[3]

The same industry expert continued that the sub-segments poised for the largest growth were the bakery and the Mexican niches because they were unlimited from a product innovation standpoint, and new menu items would keep customers interested. He concluded that quick casual was a legitimate trend because people wanted good food served quickly.

Williams Coffee Pub was listed as one of the Eat Smart restaurants by various health departments in Ontario. An Eat Smart restaurant offered healthy food choices, exceptional standards in food safety and more non-smoking seating than was required by law. In the quick casual segment, Club Sub, Subway and Tai Sattay shared this Eat Smart rating.

From a quick Web survey of restaurant concepts, the most similar concept in Ontario seemed to be Symposium Café that was operating throughout the province. The Web search also turned up 11 coffee house franchises.

Early reaction to Williams Coffee Pub from restaurant critics was mixed. One restaurant critic listed it as "menu sounds better than it tastes" and gave the restaurant two out of five stars. Another critic gave it great ratings for food, taste and price, and said the only problem with Williams was that there were not enough of them. The review rated Williams Coffee Pub five stars for coffee, four for price, four for atmosphere, four for food and four for convenience. Yet another critic stated that its coffee prices were comparable to other chains but the quality was slightly off in comparison. He mentioned that, although pricing was reasonable for "liquids," they got quite ridiculous when purchasing "solids." However, the critic commended the restaurant for its atmosphere.

WCP was about to collect systematic information on customer satisfaction with the restaurants. A manager for one of the investors wrote:

> I have tried to visit the local Williams at all different times of day and different days of the week. I have yet to walk into an empty Williams. The clientele ranges greatly depending on time of day. For example, this morning I arrived at 6:30 a.m., and there were already two men in their late 40s to early 50s sitting reading the paper, and having breakfast at two separate tables. Two more men, mid-40s stood at the counter placing their order. By 6:45 there were a couple more tables of men in the restaurant and one other woman. A couple more women came in, but only for take-out, as well as a couple of businessmen (men in suits anyway). By 7:00, there were even a couple of teenage boys sitting at a table, having coffee, and a few more people came in. I found this time of day, there were a lot of men!

- Early evening, tend to be a lot of women ranging from early 30s to mid-50s.
- Lunch—variety of business people having lunch meetings, women of all ages and some couples or friends out for lunch with kids.
- Saturday afternoon—again, broad range but a lot more women with children.
- Sunday—a lot of seniors.
- Late evenings—late-teens to late-20s.

GROWTH HISTORY

In 1994, WCP sales through three outlets were $770,000, and by 2003, WCP sales through 44 outlets were $28 million as shown in **Table 2**. However the growth had not been without incident. In 1998, despite sales of almost $8.2 million, WCP began to develop a cash bind. The cash bind resulted from two main factors: the rapid growth in the number of franchisees and the brothers' use of WCP money to bridge new franchises between the approval of the site and the bank's financing for the site. To add to the problem, some of the early franchisees were slow paying their accounts payable to WCP, and the brothers took a very soft line with them. The brothers turned to a friend, Peter Schwartz, whom they had known for several years. Schwartz lived in the area, was a business school graduate, a leader in a successful high-tech company, and he had some money to lend.

Although WCP was profitable every year, by 2001, the cumulative difference between income and cash flow was almost $1 million. Furthermore, WCP had been capitalized with the brothers' savings supplemented by loans from friends and family. The fast growth had strained their resources and created some strain with the bank manager who advised them that WCP needed more equity. By 2002, Schwartz had loaned the brothers almost $500,000 with the understanding that they would convert the loan into equity when they could reach an agreed valuation of the company and develop a mutually agreed business plan. Schwartz and the brothers stopped the growth for one year in order to let cash flow catch up to earnings. Schwartz also began to advise the brothers on matters of finance, senior personnel and organizational structure. The plan was that as soon as they got everything in order and built an executive team, WCP could resume its growth. Together they hired a part-time chief financial officer, Doug Pagnutti, who also had experience in fast growth entrepreneurial companies.

In 2002, WCP had 36 locations delivering a total gross sales of $26 million, a 20 per cent growth over sales in 2001. In 2003, WCP added eight new locations with many of the new outlets on university campuses, such as the kiosks (100 to 800 square feet) at The University of Western Ontario in London, Guelph University in Guelph, McMaster University College in Hamilton and Redeemer College in Ancaster. There were 3,300-square-foot stores with seating for 110 at The University of Windsor and Humber College in Toronto. At the smaller WCP "liquid concept" locations, menus were restricted to beverages and baked goods (see **Exhibit 6**). By 2004, 22 of the 44 locations were free-standing, full-size stores offering the complete menu.

In 2004, another major investor and friend of Schwartz's, joined the group and invested both loan and equity money into WCP. He had operated approximately 15 franchises for

Table 2 WCP Number of Locations and Total Systems Sales by Year

	1994	1995	1996	1997	1998	1999	2000	2001	2002	2003
Locations	3	3	7	10	14	19	23	29	36	44
Sales ($000s)	0.8	1.4	3.7	6.1	8.2	11.5	16.7	21.6	26.0	27.7

Source: Company files.

Table 3 Sales Projections 2004–2013

Williams Coffee Pubs, Inc. ($000s)

	2004	2005	2006	2007	2008	2009	2010	2011	2012	2013
Franchise outlets*	39	57	69	80	92	104	116	128	140	152
Franchisees' annual growth (%)	4%	12%	9%	8%	5%	5%	5%	4%	4%	4%
Total system revenue, all sources	$32	$39	$53	$70	$88	$107	$128	$150	$173	$198
WCP Inc. revenue (all sources)	$2.2	$2.8	$3.8	$5.0	$6.2	$7.5	$9.0	$10.5	$12.1	$13.9
Marketing communications spending assumed (approx 3% of sales)	.5	1.2	1.6	2.1	2.4	3.2	3.8	4.5	5.2	5.9

Plus five corporate stores.

Source: Williams Coffee Pub records.

one of the world's largest fast-food chains and was looking to invest in a new concept. He liked the fast casual market and knew of WCP before Schwartz made the connection. He would also join the board of the new company. The final piece of the puzzle was put in place in March of 2004 when WCP finished its financial restructuring and hired Mark White as the new chief executive officer. White had been the chief financial officer of Wendy's (Canada) Limited and had then become the president of the second investor's diversified company, including the fast-food franchises.

WCP had also grown by refreshing the menu each year. Every time a new product was added, a slower mover was removed so that the menu did not become too large. In addition, there were seasonal promotional items, such as the 2003 summer promotion featuring three new salads and a cappuccino shake.

THE WCP FRANCHISE MODEL, 2004

Of the 44 WCP outlets, 39 were franchised and five were owned corporately. Each franchisee paid a franchise fee of $35,000, about $250,000 for leasehold improvements for a full-size store and about $250,000 for the site, which was owned by WCP and mortgaged through the Business Development Bank of Canada for almost its full amount. Thus, WCP franchisees were able to secure about 50 per cent financing for a new outlet. By contrast, Tim Hortons' franchisees could secure 80 per cent financing for a new outlet. WCP franchisees paid a royalty of six per cent and a marketing fee ranging from zero per cent to 1.5 per cent to Williams Coffee Pub, Inc., the franchising company. The marketing fee was spent on behalf of franchisees by Williams Coffee Pub, Inc., mainly on in-store promotions.

The brothers spent a large amount of time interviewing potential franchisees and helping them to find suitable locations. Their corporate trainer worked with the franchisee operators and their staff. Quite frequently, the brothers held extensive accounts receivable for the two or three WCP outlets that were having a difficult time financially. They worked for extended periods of time with any franchisee facing any kind of difficulty. "The Giannakopoulos brothers were too nice," said Schwartz.

WCP Inc., worked with realtors and other agents in each city to identify suitable sites. Many of these sites had already been developed for other retail concepts that had not met expectations. For example, the WCP on Richmond Street, London, Ontario, was in the heart of the university nightlife district. It had formerly been a wine store and a record store. It was located in a high-traffic peninsula property that could not be configured for a drive-through and offered limited parking. The Wellington Street location in London had been a Kenny Rogers outlet, and it featured a drive-through lane and ample parking.

The brothers were looking for potential franchisees who would be customer-friendly and work hard. Although they periodically placed advertisements for franchisee applications in a particular city's newspaper, many of their best franchisees sought out the brothers by word of mouth from existing franchisees. An advisory council consisting of eight members, four of whom were franchisees, oversaw new ideas regarding marketing and menu items. In addition to the corporate advertising and promotion fund, WCP assisted each franchisee to develop its own marketing program through the use of various local media.

The brothers wanted franchisees to be successful. To this end, they developed a financial model for outlets achieving various sales levels. **Exhibit 7** shows the results projected to franchisees delivering annual sales from $341,000 to $1 million. New outlets reaching annual sales of $400,000 were supposed to deliver an annual operating profit of $31,000 to the franchisee. Operating profit tended to rise disproportionately with increases in revenue, such that sales of $625,000 was expected to yield $137,000 in operating profit, and $1 million in sales was expected to yield $294,000 in operating profit.

MARCH 2004

The 2004 financial projections for the franchise holding company, Williams Coffee Pub, Inc., looked very promising, with total revenue of $2.2 million and operating expenses of $1.4 million forecasted, thus leaving a projected income from operations of about $800,000 (see **Exhibit 8**). However, after this projection was made, WCP added some increased marketing expenditures and the salaries of the new chief executive officer and the new chief financial officer. The combined effect was to reduce the projected income from operations for 2004 to about $450,000. This projection assumed 39 franchised and five corporate outlets with spending of $500,000 on advertising and promotion. The projections that the Giannakopoulos brothers and the investors used to value the company assumed annual sales growth of almost 10 per cent in the next three years and then levelling out to about five per cent (**Table 3**). Both the Giannakopoulos brothers and the investors agreed that these assumed growth rates were very conservative.

The Giannakopoulos brothers wondered whether they should try to grow sales more aggressively. WCP had never undertaken any kind of attitude and usage surveys that might track general consumer awareness, interest, trial or adoption of WCP. White observed:

> Most stores are contributing 1.5 per cent of sales (to the advertising and promotion fund) and the agreements allow this to be increased to three per cent. With the system sales forecast in 2004 of somewhere around $32 million, the associated advertising and promotion

fund is about $500,000. The sales growth in the 10-year projections [Table 3] assumes that we increase the advertising and promotion contributions to three per cent. This should happen next year; 1.5 per cent is just too light. I have looked at very similar cases in the past. The investment spending has typically been targeted at increasing the budget to get more media, targeted mostly to television. We are a little spread out in Ontario so any media buy would not be very efficient right now if we had to cover all the stores.

Another idea was for WCP to match the advertising and promotion funds contributed by the franchisees even though it could lead to more debt for WCP or more dilution for the investors. The Giannakopoulos brothers and the investors would clearly want to see the kind of sales and profit response that might come from a doubling of advertising and promotion expenditures. Over the next three years, they would also want to see proposed advertising and promotion mixes of in-store, billboard, radio and television spending. Any marketing communications plan would be expected to contain overall objectives, media objectives, spending, media vehicles, messages and measurements.

Exhibit 1   The WCP Coffee Pot Unique Positioning Platform

The Next Generation Quick Casual Coffee Restaurant

A) Williams Coffee Pub has the ability to participate in and "bridge" the five major restaurant industry segments, most notably coffee.

B) Williams Coffee Pub menu mix and unique service delivery system will allow the brand to extend and compete in all day parts.

C) Rapid unit growth and market penetration will also be driven by:

- Williams superior value proposition to many mainstream coffee brands and specialty coffee brands including Tim Hortons, Starbucks and Second Cup.
- Williams more comfortable restaurant design and décor than main stream coffee/donut chains.
- Williams unique quick order and table service delivery process that provides guests with a convenient "quick service" meal occasion with the added benefit of "casual dining" service.
- Williams menu philosophy that brings great creative food to the general population.
- Williams ability to diversify its menu offering to attract different markets including individuals, couples, business people and families.
- Williams flexibility with its kitchen/production delivery service to change menu offering to match changing consumer, lifestyle and culinary trends.
- Williams near perfect brand fit with its menu diversity, quick service format, multiple day part menu and design flexibility to dominate the growing and high profile non-traditional market.

Better value proposition.

Better coffee experience.

Ability to compete in five distinct restaurant markets.

Ability to compete in almost every day part.

Great food without the attitude, price or wait.

The Williams brand possesses the fundamental dynamics to grow fast and dominate the quick casual coffee market!

Source: Williams Coffee Pub brochure for potential franchisees.

Exhibit 1 *(continued)*

Segment Penetration

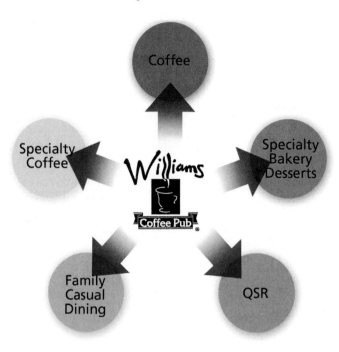

* QSR = quick service restaurants.

Source: Williams Coffee Pub brochure for franchisees.

Exhibit 1 *(continued)*

Competitive Benchmark by Day Parts

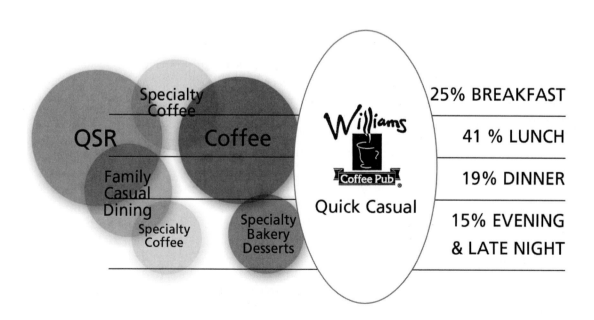

25% BREAKFAST

41 % LUNCH

19% DINNER

15% EVENING
& LATE NIGHT

Source: Williams Coffee Pub brochure for franchisees.

Exhibit 2 Williams Coffee Pubs Locations in Southwestern Ontario, 2004

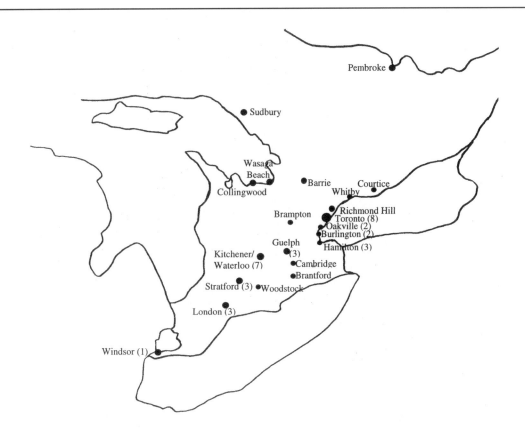

Williams Coffee Pub Locations in Southwestern Ontario

Location	Opening Date
Barrie	March 1999
Beaches, Toronto	June 2003
Brampton	August 2000
Brantford	January 2002
Burlington East	July 1999
Burlington West	October 1998
Cambridge	November 1997
Collingwood	September 2001
Courtice	December 1998
Durham College University	December 2002
Etobicoke—Dixon Road (Toronto)	November 1995
Etobicoke—Sherway (Toronto)	October 1999
Guelph	December 1996
University of Guelph—#1	September 2000
University of Guelph—#2	September 2003
Hamilton	August 1995
Humber Lakeshore (Toronto)	August 2002
Humber—Finch (Toronto)	September 2003
IBM (Toronto)	July 2003
Kitchener Auditorium Kiosk	May 2002
Kitchener City Hall	May 1994
Kitchener—Fairway Road	November 2000
Kitchener—Tulane	February 2001
Kitchener—Richmond Street	February 2000
Kitchener—Wellington Road	January 2001
London—Richmond Street	February 2000

Exhibit 2 *(continued)*

London—Wellington Road	January 2001
McMaster University, Hamilton	September 2003
Oakville	February 2002
Oakville—Upper Middle	July 2002
Pembroke	September 1993
Redeemer College, Ancaster (Hamilton)	October 2003
Richmond Hill	April 1998
RIM Park, Waterloo	January 2002
Stratford 1	1992
Stratford 2	January 1997
Sudbury	June 1999
Terminal 3 Pearson Airport, Toronto	May 2000
University of Toronto	December 2003
Wasaga Beach	May 2001
Waterloo East	September 1998
Waterloo West	March 1996
University of Windsor, Windsor	November 2003
University of Western Ontario, London	November 2003
Whitby	September 1997
Woodstock	October 1996

Exhibit 3 Full Store Modules

Source: Company files.

Exhibit 4 Interiors

Source: Company files.

Exhibit 5   Menus

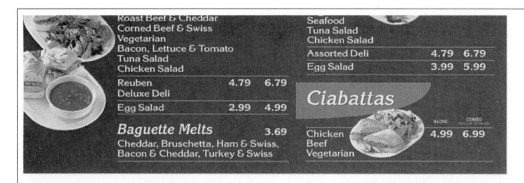

Roast Beef & Cheddar
Corned Beef & Swiss
Vegetarian
Bacon, Lettuce & Tomato
Tuna Salad
Chicken Salad

Reuben	4.79	6.79
Deluxe Deli		
Egg Salad	2.99	4.99

Baguette Melts   3.69
Cheddar, Bruschetta, Ham & Swiss,
Bacon & Cheddar, Turkey & Swiss

Seafood
Tuna Salad
Chicken Salad

| Assorted Deli | 4.79 | 6.79 |
| Egg Salad | 3.99 | 5.99 |

Ciabattas

	ALONE	COMBO WITH SOUP OR SALAD
Chicken	4.99	6.99
Beef		
Vegetarian		

Entrees

		ALONE	COMBO WITH SOUP OR SALAD
Meat Lasagna		4.99	6.99
Vegetarian Lasagna			
Chicken Pot Pie			
Chicken on a Bagel		4.79	6.79
add Bruschetta for			1.20

Quiche

	ALONE	COMBO WITH SOUP OR SALAD
Ham & Cheese	4.49	6.49
Broccoli & Cheese		
Daily Feature		
add Bruschetta or a Melt for		1.20

Salads

Greek Salad	4.79
Caesar Salad	4.79
California Salad	4.79
House Salad	4.79
Spinach Salad	4.79
Seafood Caesar Salad	5.79
Grilled Chicken Caesar Salad	6.78
add Bruschetta or a Melt for	1.20

Soups

Prepared daily with the freshest ingredients.

| Soup & Salad Combo | 4.79 |
| add Bruschetta or a Melt for | 1.20 |

Daily Featured Soups

Coffee

	SMALL	REGULAR	LARGE	XLARGE
Williams House Blend	.93	1.03	1.26	1.40
Bodums (Assorted Flavours)	1.99			
Bodum au Lait	2.99			
Hot Chocolate	1.25			
Tea – Red Rose	1.15			
Tea – Flavoured	1.25			
Steamers (Assorted Flavours)	1.59			
Add a Flavoured Shot	.55			

AUTHENTIC EUROPEAN Coffees

Espresso	1.25	1.55
Cappuccino	1.95	2.75
Café Latte	2.49	3.29
Mocha Cappuccino	2.79	3.69
Flavoured Cappuccino	2.79	
add a Flavoured Shot	.55	

Authentic ICED COFFEES

Iced Mocha Cappuccino	2.99
Iced Latte Royale	2.79
Iced Cappuccino	2.49
Iced Americano	1.79

| WILLIAMS ORIGINAL *Iced Cappuccino* | REGULAR 2.49 | LARGE 2.99 |

WILLIAMS ORIGINAL *Frappe*   16 OZ   2.99

Deluxe Frappes   16 OZ   3.59
Mint Chocolate
Strawberry Banana
Mocha Chocolate
Chocolate Banana
Caramel Mocha

CHILLY *Willys*   16 OZ   2.59
Peach Banana
Raspberry Banana
Very Berry Banana

Desserts/Pastries

Muffins	.99
Assorted Cookies	.80
Cinnamon Buns	1.60

Cold Beverages

	REGULAR	LARGE
Assorted Soft Drinks (Cans)	1.25	
Milk	1.35	1.60
Milk (Chocolate)	1.55	1.95
Assorted Juices	from 1.29 to 2.25	

Source: Company files.

Exhibit 6 Fast Food/Kiosk

Source: Company files.

Exhibit 7 Prototypical Income Statements For Varying Levels of Annual Sales per Unit (financial models as at January, 2003)

	$$	$$	$$	$$	$$
Average store sales	341,490	400,000	625,000	750,000	1,000,000
Average checks	3	3	3	3	3
Drive through mix	–	–	–	–	–
Sales					
Coffee	136,596	160,000	250,000	300,000	400,000
Other beverages	68,298	80,000	125,000	150,000	200,000
Baked goods	68,298	80,000	125,000	150,000	200,000
Sandwiches/soups/salads/entrées	68,298	80,000	125,000	150,000	200,000
Desserts	–	–	–	–	–
Retail	–	–	–	–	–
Total sales	341,490	400,000	625,000	750,000	1,000,000
Cost of sales					
Coffee	24,587	28,800	45,000	54,000	72,000
Other beverages	17,075	20,000	31,250	37,500	50,000
Baked goods	30,734	36,000	56,250	67,500	90,000
Sandwiches/soups/salads/entrées	25,612	30,000	46,875	56,250	75,000
Desserts	–	–	–	–	–
Retail	–	–	–	–	–
Total cost of sales	98,008	114,800	179,375	215,250	287,000
Gross profit	243,482	285,200	445,625	534,750	713,000
Paper cost	17,075	20,000	31,250	37,500	50,000
Direct labor	137,149	137,149	150,864	164,579	189,814
Benefits	20,572	20,572	22,630	24,687	28,472
Total labor cost	157,721	157,721	173,494	189,266	218,286
Advertising	8,537	10,000	15,625	18,750	25,000
Royalties	20,489	24,000	37,500	45,000	60,000
Total variable costs	186,747	191,721	226,619	253,016	303,286
Contribution margin	39,660	73,479	187,756	244,234	359,714
Occupancy cost	–	–	–	–	–
Other operating costs	39,661	42,001	51,001	56,001	66,001
Operating profit	**(1)**	**31,478**	**136,755**	**188,233**	**293,713**
Average unit capital cost	170,000	170,000	170,000	170,000	170,000
Hours of operation	18	18	18	18	18
Average body count	2.5	2.5	2.8	3.0	3.5
Hourly rate without benefits	8.35	8.35	8.35	8.35	8.35
Days open	365	365	365	365	365
Transactions per hour	16	19	29	35	47

Source: Company files.

Exhibit 8   Projected Income Statement for the Holding Company—Williams Coffee Pub, Inc.
(for 12 months ending December 2003) (in $000s)

Revenue		
Royalties		$1,574
Royalties—expansion		137
Rebates		460
Franchise fees		—
Increase in sales (3%)		47
Total revenue		2,218
Expenses		
Wages and benefits	$705	
Advertising	12	
Bank charges interest	10	
Consulting fees	158	
Equipment lease	—	
Franchise costs	33	
Insurance	7	
Interest on long-term debt	89	
Occupancy	36	
Office and general	34	
Professional fees	60	
Repairs, maintenance	1	
Telecommunications	25	
Travel	113	
Amortization	52	
Management expenses	120	
Total operating expenses		1,455
Income from operations		763
Add back:		
Interest expense	89	
Amortization	52	
EBITDA		$904

Source: Company files.

Endnotes

1. All monies in Cdn$ unless otherwise specified.

2. Corinne Lynds, "The Brew Brothers," *Food Service and Hospitality*, January 2004, pp. 26–30.

3. Gina LaVecchia, "Fast Casual Enters the Fast Lane: A Host of Old and New Fast Casual Restaurants are Proving that Good Food Can Happen in an Instant," *Restaurant Hospitality*, February 2003, pp. 12–17.

Study Questions

1. *How well have the Giannakopoulos brothers done to date with the Williams Coffee Pub enterprise?*

2. *How attractive is the "quick casual" restaurant market?*

3. *How well have the Giannakopoulos brothers positioned Williams Coffee Pub?*

4. *Given their growth objectives, how should Williams Coffee Pub grow in terms of the rate of adding franchisees, spending on marketing communications and mix of marketing communication vehicles?*

Glossary of Service Marketing and Management Terms

This glossary defines key terms used in this book and more generally in service marketing and management. For a broader coverage of marketing terms, see the glossaries in marketing management texts such as Philip Kotler and Kevin Lane Keller, *Marketing Management*, 12/e (Upper Saddle River, NJ: Prentice Hall, 2006) or consult the American Marketing Association's online *Dictionary of Marketing Terms* (www.marketingpower.com/mg-dictionary.php).

You should be aware that not everyone attaches precisely the same meaning to the same term. That's why it's important that you know and can clarify your own understanding when using a particular word or phrase. As often happens in an evolving field, the same terms are sometimes defined and used in different ways by academics and practitioners and among managers in different industries. Even individual companies may attach distinctive meanings to specific terms.

Words and phrases may also mean entirely different things when applied in nonmanagerial contexts. This situation, is of course, typical of language in general. For example, the 3 750-page, two-volume *Shorter Oxford English Dictionary*, 5/e (Oxford, UK, and New York: Oxford University Press, 2003) contains no less than 31 definitions of the word "service," embracing applications from domestic work, waiting in restaurants, and military duty to tennis, legal procedures, and the breeding of farm animals!

A

activity-based costing (ABC): an approach to costing based on identifying the activities being performed and then determining the resources that each consumes.

adequate service: minimum level of service that a customer will accept without being dissatisfied.

advertising: any paid form of nonpersonal communication by a marketer to inform, educate, or persuade members of target audiences.

arm's-length transactions: interactions between customers and service suppliers in which mail or telecommunications minimize the need to meet face to face.

attitude: a person's consistently favourable or unfavourable evaluations, feelings, and action tendencies toward an object or idea.

auction: a selling procedure managed by a specialist intermediary in which the price is set by allowing prospective purchasers to bid against each other for a product offered by a seller.

augmented product: a core product (a good or a service) plus supplementary elements that add value for customers (*see also* **flower of service**).

B

backstage (or technical core): those aspects of service operations that are hidden from customers.

balking: a decision by a customer not to join a queue because the wait appears too long.

banner ads: small, rectangular boxes on websites that contain text and perhaps a picture to support a brand.

benchmarking: comparing an organization's products and processes to those of competitors or leading firms in the same or other industries to find ways to improve performance, quality, and cost effectiveness.

benefit: an advantage or gain that customers obtain from performance of a service or use of a physical good.

benefit-driven pricing: strategy of relating price to that aspect of the service that directly creates benefits for customers.

blog: a publicly accessible "web log" containing frequently updated pages in the form of journals, diaries, news listings, etc.; authors—known as bloggers—typically focus on specific topics.

blueprint: a visual map of the sequence of activities required for service delivery that specifies front-stage and backstage elements and the linkages between them.

boundary-spanning positions: jobs that straddle the boundary between the external environment, where customers are encountered, and the internal operations of the organization.

brand: a name, phrase, design, symbol, or some combination of these elements that identifies a company's services and differentiates it from competitors.

business model: means by which an organization generates income from sales and other sources through choice of pricing mechanisms and payors (e.g, user, advertiser or sponsor, other third parties), ideally sufficient to cover costs and create value for its owners. (*Note:* For nonprofits and public agencies, donations and designated tax revenues may be an integral part of the model.)

C

chain stores: two or more outlets under common ownership and control, and selling similar goods and services.

chase demand strategy: adjusting the level of capacity to meet the level of demand at any given time.

churn: loss of existing customer accounts and the need to replace them with new ones.

clicks and mortar: a strategy of offering service through both physical stores and virtual storefronts via websites on the Internet.

competition-based pricing: setting prices relative to those charged by competitors.

competitive advantage: a firm's ability to perform in ways that competitors cannot or will not match.

complaint: a formal expression of dissatisfaction with any aspect of a service experience.

complaint log: a detailed record of all customer complaints received by a service provider.

conjoint analysis: a research method for determining the utility values that consumers attach to varying levels of a product's attributes.

consumption: purchase and use of a service or good.

control chart: a chart that graphs quantitative changes in service performance on a specific variable relative to a predefined standard.

control model of management: an approach based on clearly defined roles, top-down control systems, a hierarchical organizational structure, and the assumption that management knows best.

core competency: a capability that is a source of competitive advantage.

corporate culture: shared beliefs, norms, experiences, and stories that characterize an organization.

corporate design: consistent application of distinctive colours, symbols, and lettering to give a firm an easily recognizable identity.

cost leader: a firm that bases its pricing strategy on achieving the lowest costs in its industry.

cost-based pricing: relating the price to be charged for a product to the costs associated with producing, delivering, and marketing it.

credence attributes: product characteristics that customers may not be able to evaluate even after purchase and consumption.

critical incident: a specific encounter between customer and service provider in which the outcome has proved especially satisfying or dissatisfying for one or both parties.

critical incident technique (CIT): a methodology for collecting, categorizing, and analyzing critical incidents that have occurred between customers and service providers.

CRM system: information technology (IT) systems and infrastructure that support the implementation and delivery of a customer-relationship management strategy.

customer contact personnel: service employees who interact directly with individual customers, either in person or through mail and telecommunications.

customer equity: total combined customer lifetime value (*see definition*) of the company's entire customer base.

customer interface: all points at which customers interact with a service organization.

customer lifetime value (CLV): net present value of the stream of future contributions or profits expected over each customer's purchases during his or her anticipated lifetime as a customer of a specific organization.

customer relationship management (CRM): overall process of building and maintaining profitable customer relationships by delivering superior customer value and satisfaction.

customer satisfaction: a short-term emotional reaction to a specific service performance.

customer training: training programs offered by service firms to teach customers about complex service products.

customization: tailoring service characteristics to meet each customer's specific needs and preferences.

cyberspace: a virtual reality without physical existence, in which electronic transactions or communications occur.

D

data mining: extracting useful information about individuals, trends, and segments from often massive amounts of customer data.

data warehouse: a comprehensive database containing customer information and transaction data.

database marketing: building, maintaining, and using customer databases and other databases for contacting, selling, cross-selling, up-selling, and building customer relationships.

defection: a customer's decision to transfer brand loyalty from a current service provider to a competitor.

delivery channels: physical and electronic means by which a service firm (sometimes assisted by intermediaries) delivers one or more product elements to its customers.

demand curve: A curve that shows the number of units the market will buy at different prices.

demand cycle: a period of time during which the level of demand for a service will increase and decrease in a somewhat predictable way before repeating itself.

demographic segmentation: dividing the market into groups based on demographic variables such as age, gender, family life cycle, family size, income, occupation, education, religion, or ethnic group.

desired service: the "wished for" level of service quality that a customer believes can and should be delivered.

discounting: a strategy of reducing the price of an item below the normal level.

dynamic pricing: a technique, employed primarily by e-tailers, to charge different customers different prices for the same products, based on information collected about their purchase history, preferences, and price sensitivity.

E

e-commerce: buying, selling, and other marketing processes supported by the Internet (*see also* **e-tailing**).

eight (8) Ps: eight strategic elements, each beginning with P, in the services marketing mix, representing the key ingredients required to create viable strategies for meeting customer needs profitably in a competitive marketplace.

emotional labour: expressing socially appropriate (but sometimes false) emotions toward customers during service transactions.

empowerment: authorizing employees to find solutions to service problems and make appropriate decisions about responding to customer concerns without having to obtain a supervisor's approval.

enablement: providing employees with the skills, tools, and resources they need to use their own discretion confidently and effectively.

enhancing supplementary services: supplementary services that may add extra value for customers.

e-tailing: retailing through the Internet instead of through physical stores.

excess capacity: an organization's capacity to create service output that is not fully utilized.

excess demand: demand for a service at a given time that exceeds the organization's ability to meet customer needs.

expectations: internal standards that customers use to judge the quality of a service experience.

experience attributes: product performance features that customers can evaluate only during service delivery.

expert systems: interactive computer programs that mimic a human expert's reasoning to draw conclusions from data, solve problems, and give customized advice.

F

facilitating supplementary services: supplementary services that aid in the use of the core product or are required for service delivery.

fail point: a point in a process at which there is a significant risk of problems that can damage service quality (sometimes referred to humorously as an OTSU, short for "opportunity to screw up").

financial outlays: all monetary expenditures incurred by customers in purchasing and consuming a service.

fishbone diagram: a chart-based technique that relates specific service problems to different categories of underlying causes (also known as a cause-and-effect chart).

fixed costs: costs that do not vary with production or sales revenue.

flat-rate pricing: quoting a fixed price for a service in advance of delivery.

flowchart: a visual representation of the steps involved in delivering service to customers (*see also* **blueprint**).

flower of service: a visual framework for understanding the supplementary service elements that surround and add value to the product core (*see also* **augmented product**).

focus group: a group, typically consisting of six to eight people and carefully preselected on certain characteristics (e.g., demographics, psychographics, or product ownership), who are convened by researchers for in-depth, moderator-led discussion of specific topics.

franchise: A contractual association between a franchiser (typically a manufacturer, wholesaler, or service organization) and independent businesspeople (franchisees), who buy the right to own and operate one or more units in the franchise system.

frequency program (FPs): a program designed to reward customers who buy frequently and in substantial amounts.

front stage: those aspects of service operations and delivery that are visible or otherwise apparent to customers.

G

geographic segmentation: dividing a market into geographic units such as countries, regions, or cities.

goods: physical objects or devices that provide benefits for customers through ownership or use.

H

halo effect: tendency for consumer ratings of one prominent product characteristic to influence ratings for many other attributes of that same product.

high-contact services: services that involve significant interaction among customers, service personnel, and equipment and facilities.

human resource management (HRM): coordination of tasks related to job design, employee recruitment, selection, training, and motivation; also includes planning and administering other employee-related activities.

I

image: a set of beliefs, ideas, and impressions held regarding an object.

impersonal communications: one-way communications directed at target audiences who are not in personal contact with the message source (including advertising, promotions, and public relations).

information processing: intangible actions directed at customers' assets.

information-based services: all services in which the principal value comes from the transmission of data to customers; also includes mental stimulus processing and information processing (*see definitions*).

in-process wait: a wait that occurs during service delivery.

inputs: all resources (labour, materials, energy, and capital) required to create service offerings.

intangibility: (*see* **mental intangibility** *and* **physical intangibility**).

intangible: something that is experienced and that cannot be touched or preserved.

integrated marketing communications (IMC): a concept under which an organization carefully integrates and coordinates its many communications channels to deliver a clear, consistent, and compelling message about the organization and its products

internal communications: all forms of communication from management to employees within an organization.

internal customers: employees who receive services from an internal supplier (another employee or department) as a necessary input to performing their own jobs.

internal marketing: marketing activities directed internally to employees to train and motivate them and instill a customer focus.

internal services: service elements within any type of business that facilitate creation of, or add value to, its final output.

internet: a large public web of computer networks that connects users from around the world to each other and to a vast information repository.

inventory: for *manufacturing,* physical output stockpiled after production for sale at a later date; for *services,* future output that has not yet been reserved in advance, such as the number of hotel rooms still available for sale on a given day.

involvement model of management: an approach based on the assumption that employees are capable of self-direction and, if properly trained, motivated, and informed, can make good decisions concerning service operations and delivery.

iTV: (interactive television) procedures that allow viewers to alter the viewing experience by controlling TV program delivery (e.g., TiVo, video on demand) and/or content.

J

jaycustomer: a customer who acts in a thoughtless or abusive way, causing problems for the firm, its employees, and other customers.

L

levels of customer contact: extent to which customers interact physically with the service organization.

low-contact services: services that require minimal or no direct contact between customers and the service organization.

loyalty: a customer's commitment to continue patronizing a specific firm over an extended period of time.

M

market focus: extent to which a firm serves few or many markets.

market segmentation: process of dividing a market into distinct groups within each of which all customers share relevant characteristics that distinguish them from customers in other segments, and respond in similar ways to a given set of marketing efforts.

marketing communications mix: full set of communication tools (both paid and unpaid) available to marketers, including advertising, sales promotion, events, public relations and publicity, direct marketing, and personal selling.

marketing implementation: process that turns marketing plans into projects and ensures that such projects are executed in a way that accomplishes the plan's stated objectives.

marketing research: systematic design, collection, analysis, and reporting of customer and competitor data and findings relevant to a specific marketing situation facing an organization.

marketplace: a location in physical space or cyberspace (*see definition*) where suppliers and customers meet to do business.

mass customization: offering a service with some individualized product elements to a large number of customers at a relatively low price.

maximum capacity: upper limit to a firm's ability to meet customer demand at a particular time.

medium-contact services: services that involve only a limited amount of contact between customers and elements of the service organization.

membership relationship: a formalized relationship between the firm and a specified customer that may offer special benefits to both parties.

mental intangibility: difficulty for customers in visualizing an experience in advance of purchase and understanding the process and even the nature of the outcome (*see also* **physical intangibility**).

mental stimulus processing: intangible actions directed at people's minds.

mission statement: succinct description of what the organization does, its standards and values, whom it serves, and what it intends to accomplish.

molecular model: a framework that uses a chemical analogy to describe the structure of service offerings.

moment of truth: a point in service delivery at which customers interact with service employees or self-service equipment and the outcome may affect perceptions of service quality.

mystery shopping: a research technique that employs individuals posing as ordinary customers to obtain feedback on the service environment and customer–employee interactions.

N

needs: subconscious, deeply felt desires that often concern long-term existence and identity issues.

net value: the sum of all perceived benefits (gross value) minus the sum of all perceived outlays.

nonfinancial outlays: time expenditures, physical and mental effort, and unwanted sensory experiences associated with searching for, buying, and using a service.

nonmonetary costs: (*see* **nonfinancial outlays**).

O

opportunity cost: potential value of income or other benefits foregone as a result of choosing one course of action instead of other alternatives.

optimum capacity: point beyond which a firm's efforts to serve additional customers will lead to a perceived decline in service quality.

organizational climate: employees' shared perceptions of the practices, procedures, and types of behaviours that are rewarded and supported in a particular setting.

organizational culture: shared values, beliefs, and work styles that are based on an understanding of what is important to the organization and why.

OTSU ("opportunity to screw up"): (*see* **fail point**).

outputs: final outcome of the service delivery process as perceived and valued by customers.

P

Pareto analysis: an analytical procedure to identify what proportion of problem events is caused by each of several different factors.

people: customers and employees who are involved in service production.

people processing: services that involve tangible actions to people's bodies.

perception: process by which individuals select, organize, and interpret information to form a meaningful picture of the world.

perceptual map: a visual illustration of how customers perceive competing services.

permission marketing: a marketing communication strategy that encourages customers to volunteer permission to a company to communicate with them through specified channels so they may learn more about its products and continue to receive useful information or something else of value to them.

personal communications: direct communications between marketers and individual customers that involve two-way dialogue (including face-to-face conversations, phone calls, and email).

personal selling: two-way communications between service employees and customers designed to influence the purchase process directly.

physical effort: undesired consequences to a customer's body resulting from involvement in the service delivery process.

physical evidence: visual or other tangible clues that provide evidence of service quality.

physical intangibility: service elements that are not accessible to examination by any of the five senses; (*more narrowly*) elements that cannot be touched or preserved by customers.

place and time: management decisions about when, where, and how to deliver services to customers.

positioning: establishing a distinctive place in the minds of customers relative to the attributes possessed by or absent from competing products.

possession processing: tangible actions to goods and other physical possessions belonging to customers.

postprocess wait: a wait that occurs after service delivery has been completed.

post-encounter stage: final stage in the service purchase process, in which customers evaluate the service experienced, form their satisfaction/dissatisfaction judgment with the service outcome, and establish future intentions.

post-transaction survey: a technique to measure customer satisfaction and perceptions of service quality while a specific service experience is still fresh in the customer's mind.

predicted service: level of service quality a customer believes a firm will actually deliver.

preprocess wait: a wait before service delivery begins.

prepurchase stage: first stage in the service purchase process, in which customers identify alternatives, weigh benefits and risks, and make a purchase decision.

price and other user outlays: expenditures of money, time, and effort that customers incur in purchasing and consuming services.

price bucket: an allocation of service capacity (e.g., seats) for sale at a particular price.

price bundling: charging a base price for a core service plus additional fees for optional supplementary elements.

price elasticity: extent to which a change in price leads to a corresponding change in demand in the opposite direction. (Demand is described as *price inelastic* when changes in price have little or no effect on demand.)

price leader: a firm that takes the initiative on price changes in its market area and is copied by others.

process: a particular method of operations or series of actions, typically involving steps that need to occur in a defined sequence.

product: the core output (either a service or a manufactured good) produced by a firm.

product attributes: all features (both tangible and intangible) of a good or service that can be evaluated by customers.

product elements: all components of the service performance that create value for customers.

productive capacity: amount of facilities, equipment, labour, infrastructure, and other assets available to a firm to create output for its customers.

productivity: how efficiently service inputs are transformed into outputs that add value for customers.

promotion and education: all communication activities and incentives designed to build customer preference for a specific service or service provider.

psychographic segmentation: dividing a market into different groups based on personality characteristics, social class, or lifestyle.

psychological burdens: undesired mental or emotional states experienced by customers as a result of the service delivery process.

public relations: efforts to stimulate positive interest in a company and its products by sending out news releases, holding press conferences, staging special events, and sponsoring newsworthy activities put on by third parties.

purchase process: the stages a customer goes through in choosing, consuming, and evaluating a service.

Q

quality: the degree to which a service satisfies customers by consistently meeting their needs, wants, and expectations.

queue: a line of people, vehicles, other physical objects, or intangible items waiting their turn to be served or processed.

queue configuration: the way in which a waiting line is organized.

R

rate fences: techniques for separating customers so that segments for whom the service offers high value are unable to take advantage of lower-priced offers.

reciprocal marketing: a marketing communication tactic in which an online retailer allows paying customers to receive promotions for another online retailer and vice versa, at no upfront cost to either party.

re-engineering: analysis and redesign of business processes to create dramatic performance improvements in such areas as cost, quality, speed, and customers' service experiences.

relationship marketing: activities aimed at developing long-term, cost-effective links between an organization and its customers for the mutual benefit of both parties.

reneging: a decision by a customer to leave a queue before reaching its end because the wait is longer or more burdensome than originally anticipated.

repositioning: changing the position a firm holds in a consumer's mind relative to competing services.

retail displays: presentations in store windows and other locations of merchandise, service experiences, and benefits.

retail gravity model: a mathematical approach to retail site selection that involves calculating the geographic centre of gravity for the target population and then locating a facility to optimize customers' ease of access.

return on quality: financial return obtained from investing in service quality improvements.

revenue management: a pricing and product-design strategy based on charging different prices to different segments at different times to maximize the revenue that can be derived from a firm's available capacity during a specific time frame (also known as *yield management*).

role: a combination of social cues that guides behaviour in a specific setting or context.

role congruence: extent to which both customers and employees act out their prescribed roles during a service encounter.

S

sales promotion: a short-term incentive offered to customers and intermediaries to stimulate faster or larger purchase.

satisfaction: a person's feelings of pleasure or disappointment resulting from a consumption experience when comparing a product's perceived performance or outcome in relation to his or her expectations.

script: a learned sequence of behaviours obtained through personal experience or communication with others.

search attributes: product characteristics that consumers can readily evaluate prior to purchase.

segment: a group of current or prospective customers who share common characteristics, needs, purchasing behaviour, or consumption patterns.

sensory burdens: negative sensations experienced through a customer's five senses during the service delivery process.

service: an economic activity offered by one party to another, typically without transfer of ownership, creating value from rental of, or access to, goods, labour, professional skills, facilities, networks, or systems, singly or in combination.

service blueprint: (*see* **blueprint, flowchart**).

service concept: what the firm offers, to whom, and through what processes.

service delivery system: that part of the total service system during which final "assembly" of the elements takes place and the product is delivered to the customer; it includes the visible elements of the service operation.

service encounter: a period of time during which customers interact directly with a service.

service encounter stage: the second stage in the service purchase process, in which the required service is delivered through interactions between customers and the service provider.

service factory: a physical site where service operations take place.

service failure: a perception by customers that one or more specific aspects of service delivery have not met their expectations.

service focus: extent to which a firm offers few or many services.

service guarantee: a promise that if service delivery fails to meet predefined standards, the customer is entitled to one or more forms of compensation.

service marketing system: that part of the total service system in which the firm has any form of contact with its customers, from advertising to billing; it includes contacts made at the point of delivery.

service model: an integrative statement that specifies the nature of the service concept (what the firm offers, to whom, and through what processes), the service blueprint (how the concept is delivered to target customers), and the accompanying business model (how revenues will be generated sufficient to cover costs and ensure financial viability).

service operations system: that part of the total service system in which inputs are processed and the elements of the service product are created.

service preview: a demonstration of how a service works, to educate customers about the roles they are expected to perform in service delivery.

service quality: customers' long term, cognitive evaluations of a firm's service delivery.

service quality information system: an ongoing service research process that provides timely, useful data to managers about customer satisfaction, expectations, and perceptions of quality.

service recovery: systematic efforts by a firm after a service failure to correct a problem and retain a customer's goodwill.

service sector: the portion of a nation's economy represented by services of all kinds, including those offered by public and nonprofit organizations.

service–profit chain: a strategic framework that links employee satisfaction to performance on service attributes to customer satisfaction, then to customer retention, and finally to profits.

services marketing mix (*see* **eight (8) Ps**).

servicescape: the design of any physical location where customers come to place orders and obtain service delivery.

SERVQUAL: a pair of standardized 22-item scales that measure customers' expectations and perceptions concerning five dimensions of service quality.

standardization: reducing variation in service operations and delivery.

stickiness: a website's ability to encourage repeat visits and purchases by providing users with easy navigation, problem-free execution of tasks, and keeping its audience engaged with interactive communication presented in an appealing fashion.

sustainable competitive advantage: a position in the marketplace that can't be taken away or minimized by competitors in the short run.

T

tangible: capable of being touched, held, or preserved in physical form over time.

target market: a part of the qualified available market with common needs or characteristics that a company decides to serve.

target segments: segments selected because their needs and other characteristics fit well with a specific firm's goals and capabilities.

third-party payments: payments to cover all or part of the cost of a service or good made by a party other than the user (who may or may not have made the actual purchase decision).

three-stage model of service consumption: a framework depicting how consumers move from a prepurchase stage (in which they recognize their needs, search for and evaluate alternative solutions, and make a decision), to a service encounter search (in which they obtain service delivery), and thence a post-encounter stage (in which they evaluate service performance against expectations).

time expenditures: time spent by customers during all aspects of the service delivery process.

total costs: the sum of the fixed and variable costs for any given level of production.

transaction: an event during which an exchange of value takes place between two parties.

U

undesirable demand: requests for service that conflict with the organization's mission, priorities, or capabilities.

V

value chain: the series of departments within a firm or external partners and subcontractors that carry out value-creating activities to design, produce, market, deliver, and support a product or service offering.

value exchange: transfer of the benefits and solutions offered by a seller in return for financial and other value offered by a purchaser.

value net (*or* value network): a system of partnerships and alliances that a firm creates to source, augment, and deliver its service offering.

value proposition: a specified package of benefits and solutions that a company intends to offer and how it proposes to deliver them to customers, emphasizing key points of difference relative to competing alternatives.

value-based pricing: the practice of setting prices based on what customers are willing to pay for the value they believe they will receive.

variability: a lack of consistency in inputs and outputs during the service production process.

variable costs: costs that depend directly on the volume of production or service transactions.

viral marketing: using the internet to create word-of-mouth effects to support marketing efforts.

W

wheel of loyalty: a systematic and integrated approach to targeting, acquiring, developing, and retaining a valuable customer base.

word of mouth: positive or negative comments about a service made by one individual (usually a current or former customer) to another.

Y

yield: the average revenue received per unit of capacity offered for sale.

yield management: (*see* **revenue management**).

Z

zone of tolerance: the range within which customers are willing to accept variations in service delivery.

Name Index

Subject Index

implications for service design and management, 251
jaycustomers, challenge of, 246
rule-breaker, 247–248
types of jaycustomers, 246–251
undesirable customers, 252
vindictive customers, 252

E

e-commerce, 114–116
economic activities, 13
economic costs, 134
economies of scale, 110, 124
editorial coverage, 180
education, 24, 268
effect-creating medium, 283
effectiveness, 422
efficiency, 422
8Ps of services marketing, 22–25, 23f
electronic recommendation agents, 173
email marketing, 176, 180
emergency services, 264
emerging-market economies, 193
emotional connection, 340
emotional labour, 309–310
empathy, 408
employee cycle of failure, 311–313, 312f
employee empowerment, 322–324, 387–388
employee involvement, 323–324
employee training, 320–321
employees
see also front-line employees
competitive advantage, source of, 307
confrontations with customers, 248–249, 248f
cross-training employees, 260
customer loyalty, source of, 307
customers as partial employees, 245–246
cycle of failure, 311–313, 312f
cycle of mediocrity, 314–315, 314f
cycle of success, 315–317, 315f
energizing, 327–329
importance of, 306–308
involvement of, 323–324
motivation, 327–329
rewards, 327
as secondary audience, 168
temporary employees, 260
employment, 9–10, 9f
empowerment, 322–324, 387–388
enhancing supplementary services, 82
environmental psychology, 286
ephemeral, 16
ethics, 147–152, 180–181
European Commission, 122
European Union, 122
evaluation of services, 41–42, 167
evidence management, 45
evoked set, 40
evolution, 449–451
evolutionary positioning, 203
exceptions, 90–91, 90t

expectations. See customer expectations
experience attributes, 44
experience properties, 18
experiential breadth, 339–340
experiential depth, 339–340
expertise rentals, 12
explicit signals, 296
exporting the service concept, 120
extended operating hours, 113

F

face-to-face interaction, 353
facilitating supplementary services, 82
fail points, 230, 236, 419–420
failure cycle, 311–314, 312f
failure proofing, 237
fairness, 150–152
family feuders, 249
feedback
analysis of, 401
customer-driven learning and improvement, 396
customer-oriented service culture, 396
dissemination of, 401
ease of, 386
learning from, 396–401
as motivation, 327
objectives of effective feedback systems, 396
performance, assessment and benchmarking of, 396
reporting of, 401
during service delivery, 58–59
service quality, assessment and benchmarking of, 396
for servicescape design, 301
unsolicited customer feedback, 399, 400–401
feedback collection tools
annual surveys, 397–398
focus group discussions, 399
key tools, 397t
mystery shopping, 398–399
service feedback cards, 398
service reviews, 399
total market surveys, 397–398
transactional surveys, 397–398, 398f
unsolicited customer feedback, 399, 400–401
fees, increasing, 149–150
fences, 146, 147t, 150, 221
field experiments, 301–302
fines, 149–151
fishbone diagram, 418–419, 418f
fixed costs, 134
flat-rate pricing, 139
flexible capacity, 260–261
flowcharting, 79–82, 229
Flower of Service
billing, 86, 86t
consultation, 87–88, 87t
described, 82–83, 83f
exceptions, 90–91, 90t
hospitality, 88–89, 88t
information, 83–84, 84t

managerial implications, 91–92
order-taking, 85–86, 85t
payment, 86–88, 87t
safekeeping, 89–90, 89t
fluctuations in demand, 256–258
focus group discussions, 399
focus strategy, 190–191, 258
for-profit businesses, goals of, 5–6
forecasts, 279
formalized queuing systems, 265
framework for strategy development, 26–28, 27f
franchising, 117–118, 502–512
fraud, 395
front-line employees
see also employees
boundary spanning, 308–309
complaints handling, 390
conflict, sources of, 309
customer service from, 170–171
cycle of success, 316, 317
difficulty of front-line work, 308–311
emotional labour, 309–310
empowerment of, 322–324
high-performance service-delivery teams, 324–326
inter-client conflict, 309
key role of, 307
and lack of interdepartmental support, 325
in low-contact services, 307–308
multiplicity of roles, 309
organization/client conflict, 309
person/role conflict, 309
quality of, 308
service sabotage, 313
service sweat shops, 310–311
stress of front-line work, 308–311
full satisfaction guarantees, 392
fully focused organization, 190
functionality, 295–296
future scenarios, 207–208

G

gaps model, 412–415
generality, 162
generic productivity improvement strategies, 423
geographical factors, 110
global trade. See international trade in services
globalization. See international trade in services
globalization drivers, 122–124
goal accomplishment, 327
goals, 5–6
gold tier, 359
golf courses, 222
goods, 16t, 17, 17f
government drivers, 124
government regulations, 247–248
gross domestic product (GDP), 5, 5f, 7–9, 8f
gross value, 138
guarantees. See service guarantees

Credits

Chapter 1, p. 7: Cunard Line Limited; p. 19: © Ben Sharifian; p. 20: Copyright © 2007 Athabasca University, www.athabascau.ca. Reproduced with permission; p. 21: Copyright Hudson's Bay Company, used with their permission.

Chapter 2, p. 36: © Cylla von Tiedemann; p. 40 © Queen's Printer for Ontario, 2006. Reproduced with permission.; p. 41: © Randy Lincks, www.randylincks.com; p. 42: Courtesy of Lasik MD; p. 44: AOL Canada; p. 45: Equitable Life Canada; p. 56: Courtesy Fairmont Hotels and Resorts.

Chapter 3, p. 81: Reproduced with the permission of Environment Canada and the Minister of Public Works and Government Services 2007, weatheroffice.ec.gc.ca; p. 84: Courtesy of Your Credit Card Companies; p. 85 Canada Post Corporation; p. 90: Wilfrid Laurier University; p. 98: Bombardier.

Chapter 4, p. 111: SKI Dubai; p. 114: Courtesy of Swissôtel; p. 117: Photo by Jen Handel; p. 123: DHL Systems, Inc. Reprinted with permission of DHL International Ltd.

Chapter 5, p. 132: Just Ladies Fitness; p. 135: Ad was created for Tom's Place by their advertising agency MVP Marketing. MVP's team included Mike Phillips, Account Director, Catharine Barker, Graphic Design and Joanne Macrae, Writer; p. 156: This photo has been reprinted with the permission of Visa Canada ("Visa"). Any other use of this material is expressly prohibited without permission from Visa. Visa® is a registered trademark of Visa International; Visa Canada is a licensed user.

Chapter 6, p. 161: Used with permission of AIC Limited; p. 164 (top): Courtesy of Accenture; p. 164 (bottom): Cisco Systems; p. 166: Courtesy of DHL Express Singapore; p. 167: WestJet; p. 174: TELUS Advertisement at page 174 used with permission. © TELUS. All rights reserved; p. 175: Royal Bank of Canada; p. 177: Gold's Gym, Regina.

Chapter 7, p. 199: Courtesy Grant Thornton, LLP; p. 200: Valeurs Mobilières Desjardins.

Chapter 8, p. 242: Kelowna International Airport/Photo by Henry Castorf; p. 243: Courtesy of HSBC; p. 248: Richard Hutchings, PhotoEdit Inc.

Chapter 9, p. 261: WestJet; p. 267: Intrawest Corporation. Courtesy of Intrawest Corporation. Photo by Randy Links; p. 270: TELUS Advertisement at page 270 used with permission. © TELUS. All rights reserved; p. 277: © Andrew Rubtsov/Alamy.

Chapter 10, p. 284 (top): © Ed Malitsky/CORBIS; p. 284 (bottom): photo by www.TaxiMike.com; p. 288 (top and bottom): Photo appears courtesy of Marineland, Niagara Falls, Canada; p. 293: Getty Images/Digital Vision; p. 296: Vancouver International Airport; p. 297: Iean-Leo Dugast, Panos Pictures; p. 299 (top): Gordon, Larry Dale, Getty Images, Inc.–Image Bank; p. 299 (bottom): Angus Oborn, Rough Guides; Dorling Kindersley; Angus Oborn © Rough Guides.

Chapter 11, p. 308: liquidlibrary/Jupiter Images Unlimited; p. 311: Jagadeesh, Corbis/Reuters America. LLC. © Jagadeesh/Reuters/CORBIS. All rights reserved; p. 321: Spencer Grant, PhotoEdit Inc.; p. 325: © Zuma Press/ZUMA/CORBIS; p. 328: Copyright © Hewitt Associates LLC.

Chapter 12, p. 353: Corbis RF; p. 362: AP Wide World Photos; p. 365: AP Wide World Photos.

Chapter 13, p. 382: Reproduced with the permission of Industry Canada and the Minister of Public Works and Government Services, 2006; p. 391: "Hampton Inn 100% Satisfaction Guarantee, Research Justifying the Guarantee." Used with permission of the Hilton Family. All rights reserved; p. 398: Bob Daemmrich, The Image Works.

Chapter 14, p. 407: Betsie Van der Meer, Getty Images, Inc.–Stone Allstock; p. 423: Picture Contact/Alamy; p. 424: CHUCK STOODY/Canadian Press; p. 428: Randy Matusow.

Chapter 15, p. 448: REUTERS/Las Vegas Sun/Steve Marcus/Landov; p. 451: Reprint Courtesy of International Business Machines Corporation copyright 2007 © International Business Machines Corporation.

Cases, p. 494, 497, and 501: Giordano International Limited.